D1234960

AMERICAN HISTORY

THIRTEENTH EDITION

A Survey
Volume II

Alan Brinkley

Columbia University

 Higher Education

Boston   Burr Ridge, IL   Dubuque, IA   New York   San Francisco   St. Louis
Bangkok   Bogotá   Caracas   Kuala Lumpur   Lisbon   London   Madrid   Mexico City
Milan   Montreal   New Delhi   Santiago   Seoul   Singapore   Sydney   Taipei   Toronto

Higher Education

Published by McGraw-Hill, an imprint of The McGraw-Hill Companies, Inc., 1221 Avenue of the Americas, New York, NY 10020. Copyright © 2009, 2007, 2003, 1999 by The McGraw-Hill Companies. All rights reserved. Previous editions © 1995, 1991 by McGraw-Hill, Inc. All rights reserved. © 1987, 1983 by Richard N. Current, T. H. W. Inc., Frank Freidel, and Alan Brinkley. All rights reserved. © 1979, 1971, 1966, 1964, 1961, 1959 by Richard N. Current, T. Harry Williams, and Frank Freidel. All rights reserved. No part of this publication may be reproduced or distributed in any form or by any means, or stored in a database or retrieval system, without the prior written consent of The McGraw-Hill Companies, Inc., including, but not limited to, in any network or other electronic storage or transmission, or broadcast for distance learning.

This book is printed on acid-free paper.

3 4 5 6 7 8 9 0 DOW/DOW 0

ISBN: 978-0-07-723854-4
MHID: 0-07-723854-0

Editor in Chief: *Michael Ryan*
Publisher: *Frank Mortimer*
Marketing Manager: *Pam Cooper*
Director of Development: *Lisa Pinto*
Development Editor: *Nicole Bridge*
Production Editor: *David Blatty*
Manuscript Editor: *Margaret Moore*
Interior Designer: *Glenda King*
Design Manager and Cover Designer: *Ashley Bedell*
Art Editor: *Robin Mouat*
Illustrators: *Mapping Specialists, Parrot Graphics, LineWorks*
Senior Photo Research Coordinator: *Nora Agbayani*
Photo Research: *Photosearch, Inc.*
Production Supervisor: *Rich DeVitto*
Composition: *10/12 ITC Garamond Book by Aptara®, Inc.*
Printing: *45# Pub Matte Plus, R. R. Donnelley & Sons*

Cover: The Granger Collection, New York

Library of Congress Cataloging-in-Publication Data

Brinkley, Alan.
    American history: a survey / Alan Brinkley.—Thirteenth ed.
      p. cm.
    Includes index.
    ISBN-13: 978-0-07-338549-5 (alk. paper)
    ISBN-10: 0-07-338549-2 (alk. paper)
    ISBN-13: 978-0-07-723855-1 (alk. paper)
    ISBN-10: 0-07-723855-9 (alk. paper) [etc.]
    1. United States—History—Textbooks. I. Title.
E178.1.B826 2009
973—dc22
                                                                2008045185

The Internet addresses listed in the text were accurate at the time of publication. The inclusion of a Web site does not indicate an endorsement by the authors or McGraw-Hill, and McGraw-Hill does not guarantee the accuracy of the information presented at these sites.

www.mhhe.com

About the Author

ALAN BRINKLEY is the Allan Nevins Professor of History and Provost at Columbia University. He is the author of *Voices of Protest: Huey Long, Father Coughlin, and the Great Depression,* which won the 1983 National Book Award; *The Unfinished Nation: A Concise History of the American People; The End of Reform: New Deal Liberalism in Recession and War;* and *Liberalism and its Discontents.* He was educated at Harvard, Princeton, the City University of New York Graduate School, and Oxford University, where he was the Harmsworth Professor of American History. He won the Joseph R. Levenson Memorial Teaching Award at Harvard in 1987 and the Great Teacher Award at Columbia in 2003. He is a member of the American Academy of Arts and Sciences, a member of the board of trustees of the National Humanities Center, and chairman of the board of trustees of the Century Foundation.

BRIEF CONTENTS

CONTENTS

Chapter 15
RECONSTRUCTION AND THE NEW SOUTH 404

THE SHACKLE BROKEN — BY THE GENIUS OF FREEDOM.

DISCARD

Chapter 16
THE CONQUEST OF THE FAR WEST 438

Chapter 17
INDUSTRIAL SUPREMACY 470

Chapter 18
THE AGE OF THE CITY 496

Chapter 19
FROM CRISIS TO EMPIRE 528

Chapter 20
THE PROGRESSIVES 566

Chapter 21
AMERICA AND THE GREAT WAR   600

I WANT YOU FOR U.S. ARMY
NEAREST RECRUITING STATION

Chapter 22
THE "NEW ERA" 632

Chapter 23
THE GREAT DEPRESSION 658

Chapter 24
THE NEW DEAL   682

Chapter 25
THE GLOBAL CRISIS, 1921–1941   708

Chapter 26
AMERICA IN A WORLD AT WAR   728

Chapter 27
THE COLD WAR 756

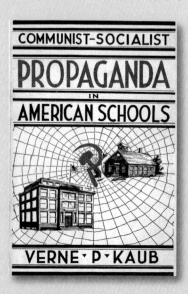

Chapter 28
THE AFFLUENT SOCIETY 778

Chapter 29
CIVIL RIGHTS, VIETNAM,
AND THE ORDEAL OF
LIBERALISM 810

Chapter 30
THE CRISIS OF AUTHORITY 840

Chapter 31
FROM THE "AGE OF LIMITS" TO THE AGE OF REAGAN 870

Chapter 32
THE AGE OF GLOBALIZATION 892

T IS A DAUNTING TASK to attempt to convey the remarkable history of the United States in a single book, but that is what this volume attempts to do. Like any history, it is a product of its time and reflects the views of the past that historians of recent generations have developed. A comparable book published decades from now will likely seem as different from this one as this book appears different from histories written a generation or more ago. The writing of history changes constantly—not, of course, because the past changes, but because of shifts in the way historians, and the publics they serve, ask and answer questions about the past.

There are now, as there have always been, critics of changes in historical understanding. Many people argue that history is a collection of facts and should not be subject to "interpretation" or "revision." But historians insist that history is not and cannot be simply a collection of facts. They are only the beginning of historical understanding. It is up to the writers and readers of history to try to interpret the evidence before them; and in doing so, they will inevitably bring to the task their own questions, concerns, and experiences.

This book, now in its thirteenth edition, has itself been an example of the changing character of historical understanding. Published first in the late 1950s by three distinguished historians—Richard Current, Frank Freidel, and T. Harry Williams—it began as a traditional political and diplomatic narrative with relatively little attention given to the people and the cultures that lay outside the public world. Over the last several decades, I have attempted to broaden the focus of this book to incorporate the many kinds of history that scholars have more recently created; to combine the traditional histories of politics, diplomacy, and great public events with the newer histories of society and culture, to present the American past in all its great diversity and complexity. Our history requires us to examine the experience of the many different peoples and ideas that have shaped American society. But it also requires us to understand that the United States is a nation, whose people share many things: a common political system, a connection to an integrated national (and now international) economy, and a familiarity with a shared and enormously powerful mass culture. To understand the American past, it is necessary to understand both the forces that divide Americans and the forces that draw them together.

Among the changes in the thirteenth edition of *American History: A Survey* is an effort to broaden still further our understanding of our national past. That includes expanding the chronological boundaries of our history. In this edition, there is both an expanded treatment of the history of the Americas before Columbus and a presentation of the history of the several years since the publication of the last edition. This edition also continues the effort of recent years to place American history more clearly in the context of the history of the rest of the world—as exemplified by the essays in the "America in the World" series. This edition also continues to expand the treatment of science, technology, and the environment. And it represents as well a significant reorganization of some parts of the book—particularly Chapters 19–22, which have been combined and revised to become two chapters. Throughout the book, I have worked to reduce the length of the narrative. Textbooks tend to grow longer as the span of time they cover grows. But the time students and teachers have to devote to American history stays the same. So I have attempted to keep the size of this book relatively constant even as we add new material.

I am grateful to many people for their help on this book. I was particularly fortunate to have the help once again of Kevin Murphy as I worked on this most recent edition. I also appreciate the many suggestions and corrections I have received from students over the last several years, as well as the reviews provided by a group of talented scholars and teachers.

Alan Brinkley
Columbia University
New York, NY

ORGANIZATION AND COVERAGE

NEW! The thirteenth edition of *American History: A Survey* has been streamlined and condensed into 32 chapters to make it easier for instructors to fit each volume into a semester. To provide even more flexibility, the book is divided into two volumes with an overlapping Chapter Fifteen that covers "The Reconstruction and the New South." The chapters follow the history of the United States chronologically, and the subheadings allow instructors to select portions of chapters to suit their syllabi.

NARRATIVE

One Voice. *American History's* most distinctive feature is that it is the work of one single author. Consistently praised for its unparalleled cohesive narrative, students will benefit from the consistent organizing concept and writing style. The unity and coherence to the story, in itself, provides an excellent example of historical writing.

The Story. *American History* has always been characterized by its straightforward account of the past and the connections it draws among historical themes. In each new edition, it has expanded its scope while maintaining the clear prose and structure that have made it so accessible and versatile for both students and instructors.

The Themes. Today, the traditional political narrative is woven together with more contemporary themes in American history: the history of women and gender, race and ethnicity, economic growth and the changing character of labor, region and religion, popular culture and intellectual life, the environment, and the economy. *American History: A Survey* is at the cutting edge of the effort to put politics into social history and society and culture into political history.

FEATURES

Globalization

Today, historians constantly consider how the American experience fits into a global context. To study the history of our country in isolation from the rest of the world is to neglect an essential part of the story. This edition continues to present American history in a more international context, while preserving the distinctiveness of the nation's past. This coverage can be found within both the narrative of the text and the "America in the World" essays.

The Nature of Historical Scholarship

American History is clear and accessible, but does not condescend students by shying away from complex issues and complicated debates. The "Where Historians Disagree" essays encourage readers to think for themselves about the debates surrounding historical evidence and consider how the story of our past is constantly evolving.

Culture and Society

Students will enjoy the "Patterns of Popular Culture" feature, which demonstrates the impact of the times upon society. Topics like "Colonial Almanacs," "Horse Racing," "The Slaves' Music," and "The Golden Age of Comic Books" add texture and context to American history.

CONTENT

Scholarship

NEW! The author has updated Chapter 1 to focus more heavily on our continent prior to Columbian contact. This chapter examines North America's environmental history and earliest societies.

NEW! Chapters 31 and 32 bring the text up to date on new developments in 21st century America, including George W. Bush's second term, the 2008 election, Hurricane Katrina, weblogs, and the war in Iraq.

Art Program

NEW! The art program has been enhanced with redesigned maps and enlarged images. These features complement the narrative and enhance clarity, visual appeal, and make the book more accessible to students.

PRIMARY SOURCE INVESTIGATOR ONLINE

NEW! McGraw-Hill's Primary Source Investigator (PSI), now available online at www.mhhe.com/psi, is designed to support and enrich the text discussion in *American History: A Survey,* 13/e. PSI gives instructors and students access to hundreds of primary and secondary sources including documents, images, maps, and videos, keyed to each chapter of *American History: A Survey,* 13/e. Students can use these resources to formulate and defend their arguments and as a study tool to further their understanding of the topics discussed in each chapter. All assets are also indexed by type, subject, place, and time period, allowing students and instructors to locate resources in all chapters quickly and easily.

Student Resources in PSI:

Primary Source Documents: This database, which has been updated for the thirteenth edition, includes items from a wide range of contemporary accounts. Each document is accompanied by a series of critical thinking questions that draws students into the content and engages them in thoughtful analysis.

Images: This extensive collective includes photographs of artifacts and buildings as well as contemporary paintings, engravings, and drawings. Each image is also accompanied by critical thinking questions.

Interactive Maps: Each map's legend is interactive, allowing students to see historical change over time and to compare various factors in the order in which they choose.

Sites: Organized by chapter, this feature lists reliable Internet sites which provide further information on particular topics. These can be particularly useful to students who are searching for dependable research sources.

Books: This list includes both standard texts as well as the most recent scholarship on topics within each chapter, another valuable resource for student researchers.

Movies: This list includes both educational and commercial films.

Events: More than simply a timeline, this feature includes annotated entries of important events in chronological order.

Online Reader: The Online Reader provides students an opportunity to try their hand at historical analysis. Based upon sources found in PSI, the reader's modules ask students to evaluate sources and create their own interpretation of an historical event, providing valuable skills for their own research.

Writing Guide: The online Writing Guide offers both general assistance for writing college papers, as well as specific tips for history papers. Topics include research,

paragraph and argument creation, a comparison of style guides, information on plagiarism and source citation, and much more.

Instructor Resources in PSI:

Faculty Guide: The Faculty Guide provides easy reference to all learning assets, both in the text and on PSI, available to teachers and students. Resources are organized within chapters by a-heads to streamline lecture and assignments preparation. Icons quickly identify text and PSI sources. Each asset is listed by title and includes a brief annotation.

In addition to assets, the Faculty Guide also includes chapter overviews, themes, lecture strategies, discussion suggestions, suggestions for further reading, and chapter-specific film recommendations. These, too, are organized by chapter and a-head to make classroom implementation simple.

ONLINE LEARNING CENTER

Instructor Resources on the OLC:

The Online Learning Center located at http://www .mhhe.com/brinkley13e Includes a link to PSI and the Faculty Guide, computerized test bank, and power point presentations.

The Classroom Performance System (CPS) brings ultimate interactivity to *American History: A Survey*. CPS is a wireless response system that gives you immediate feedback from every student in the class. With CPS you can ask subjective and objective questions during your lecture, prompting every student to respond with their individual, wireless response pad, and providing you with instant results. A complete CPS Tutorial is available at www.einstruction.com.

Student Resources on the OLC:

The Student Online Learning Center, also located at http://www.mhhe.com/brinkley13e, provides students with a wide range of tools that will help them test their understanding of the book. It includes chapter overviews, interactive maps, quizzes, and primary source indexes.

This textbook includes a number of features and study aids to augment and enhance the study of American history. The following "Guided Tour" gives examples of these features and suggestions for making good use of them.

CHAPTER 30

THE CRISIS OF AUTHORITY

"TODAY'S TEENAGERS" The coming of age of the "baby-boom" generation, and the rise of youthful activism, led *Time* magazine to devote a 1965 cover story to "Today's Teen-Agers." As notable as the choice of subject was the choice of artist for the cover image: Andy Warhol, the great pop artist whose serial portraits of both famous and unknown people helped define his era. Warhol's work was instrumental in breaking down barriers between serious art and popular culture, both in its subject matter (celebrities, commercial products) and in its techniques, which drew heavily from commercial art. This series of silk-screened photographs made use of one of his trademark media. *(Time Life Pictures/Getty Images)*

RICHARD NIXON'S ELECTION IN 1968 was the result of more than the unpopularity of Lyndon Johnson and the war. It was the result, too, of a strong popular reaction against what many Americans considered a frontal assault on the foundations of their culture.

Throughout the late 1960s and early 1970s, new movements and interest groups were mobilizing to demand protections and benefits. New values and assumptions were emerging to challenge traditional patterns of thought and behavior. The United States was in the throes, it sometimes seemed, of a cultural revolution.

Some Americans welcomed the changes. But the 1968 election returns suggested that more people feared them. There was growing resentment against the attention directed toward minorities and the poor, against the federal social programs that were funneling billions of dollars into the inner cities to help the poor and unemployed, against the increasing tax burden on the middle class, against the "hippies" and radicals who were dominating public discourse with their bitter critiques of values that many middle-class Americans revered. It was time, their critics believed, for a restoration of stability and a relegitimation of traditional centers of authority.

In Richard Nixon they found a man who seemed to match their mood. Himself a product of a hardworking, middle-class family, he had risen to prominence on the basis of his own unrelenting efforts. He projected an image of stern dedication to traditional values. Yet the presidency of Richard Nixon, far from returning calm and stability to American politics, coincided with, and in many ways helped to produce, more years of crisis.

Several crises were not wholly of Nixon's making. He inherited an unpopular war in Vietnam. Nixon attempted to reduce opposition to the war by withdrawing some American troops and replacing them with Vietnamese soldiers. But in other ways he escalated the war, through higher levels of bombing and through an incursion into Cambodia in the spring of 1970. Nixon also inherited an economy that was beginning to weaken and which, by the beginning of his second term, was reeling under rapidly rising energy prices and growing inflation.

One crisis, at least, was attributable to Nixon and the people in his administration. An obscure break-in at the Democratic National Committee headquarters in Washington, D.C., in June 1972, hardly noticed at the time, gradually expanded to create one of the most serious crises in the history of the presidency—and the first such crisis to drive a president from office. Having won election by railing against crises of authority that threatened social stability, Nixon left office having created a major crisis of authority himself.

SIGNIFICANT EVENTS

1961 ▶ Representatives of sixty-seven tribes draft Declaration of Indian Purpose
1962 ▶ Students for a Democratic Society formed at Port Huron, Michigan
▶ Supreme Court decides *Baker v. Carr*
1963 ▶ Betty Friedan publishes *The Feminine Mystique*
1964 ▶ Free Speech Movement begins at UC Berkeley
▶ Beatles come to America
1965 ▶ United Farm Workers strike
1966 ▶ National Organization for Women (NOW) formed
▶ *Miranda v. Arizona* expands rights of criminal suspects
1967 ▶ Antiwar protesters march on Pentagon
▶ Israel and Arabs clash in Six-Day War
1968 ▶ Campus riots break out at Columbia University and elsewhere
▶ American Indian Movement (AIM) launched
1969 ▶ Antiwar movement stages Vietnam "moratorium"
▶ Theodore Roszak publishes *The Making of a Counter Culture*
▶ People's Park uprising at Berkeley
▶ Nixon orders secret bombing of Cambodia
▶ Nixon begins withdrawing American troops from Vietnam
▶ "Stonewall Riot" in New York City launches gay liberation movement
▶ 400,000 people attend rock concert in Woodstock, N.Y.
1970 ▶ American troops enter Cambodia
▶ Antiwar protests increase
▶ Students killed at Kent State and Jackson State universities
▶ Charles Reich publishes *The Greening of America*
▶ Pentagon Papers published
1971 ▶ Supreme Court decides *Swann v. Charlotte-Mecklenburg Board of Education*
▶ Nixon imposes wage-price freeze and controls
1972 ▶ Congress approves Equal Rights Amendment
▶ Nixon visits China
▶ SALT I signed
▶ United States mines Haiphong harbor in North Vietnam
▶ Nixon orders "Christmas bombing" of North Vietnam
▶ Supreme Court decides *Furman v. Georgia*
▶ Burglary interrupted in Watergate office building
▶ Nixon reelected president
1973 ▶ Indians demonstrate at Wounded Knee
▶ Supreme Court decides *Roe v. Wade*
▶ Paris accords produce cease-fire; America withdraws from Vietnam
▶ Israel and Arabs clash in Yom Kippur War
▶ Arab oil embargo produces first American energy crisis
▶ Watergate scandal expands
1974 ▶ Impeachment proceedings begin against Nixon
▶ Vice President Spiro Agnew resigns; Gerald Ford appointed to replace him
▶ Nixon resigns; Ford becomes president
1975 ▶ South Vietnam falls
▶ Khmer Rouge seize control of Cambodia
1977 ▶ President Carter pardons Vietnam draft resisters
1978 ▶ Supreme Court hands down *Bakke* decision
1980 ▶ Large Cuban migration to Florida
1982 ▶ Equal Rights Amendment fails to be ratified

841

CHAPTER INTRODUCTION
The chapter openers have been enhanced.

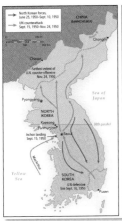

THE KOREAN WAR, 1950–1953 These two maps illustrate the changing fortunes of UN forces (which were mostly American) during the 1950–1953 Korean War. The map at the left shows the extent of the North Korean invasion of the South in 1950; communist forces for a time controlled all of Korea except a small area around Pusan in the southeast. On September 15, 1950, UN troops under Douglas MacArthur landed in force at Inchon and soon drove the North Koreans back across the border. MacArthur then pursued the North Koreans well into their own territory. The map at right shows the very different circumstances once the Chinese entered the war in November 1950. Chinese forces drove the UN army back below the 38th parallel and, briefly, deep into South Korea, below Seoul. The UN fought troops back to the prewar border between North and South Korea late in 1951, but the war then bogged down into a stalemate that continued for a year and a half. *What impact did the Korean War have on American politics in the early 1950s?*

Truman-MacArthur Controversy

than once, the president had warned the general to keep his objections to himself. The release of the Martin letter, therefore, struck the president as intolerable insubordination. On April 11, 1951, he relieved MacArthur of his command.

There was a storm of public outrage. Sixty-nine percent of the American people supported MacArthur, a Gallup poll reported. When the general returned to the United States later in 1951, he was greeted with wild enthusiasm. His televised farewell appearance before a joint session of Congress—which he concluded by saying, "Old soldiers never die, they just fade away"—attracted

an audience of millions. Public criticism of Truman finally abated somewhat when a number of prominent military figures, including General Omar Bradley, publicly supported the president's decision. But substantial hostility toward Truman remained. In the meantime, the Korean stalemate continued. Negotiations between the opposing forces began at Panmunjom in July 1951, but the talks—and the war—dragged on until 1953.

Limited Mobilization

Just as the war in Korea produced only a limited American military commitment abroad, so it created only a limited

MAPS

American History includes a wealth of maps, all of which have been enhanced and redesigned for this edition. Captions make specific reference to map content and include critical thinking questions about each.

POPULISM

American history offers few examples of successful popular movements operating outside the two major parties. Perhaps that is why Populism, which in its brief, meteoric life became one of the few such phenomena to gain real national influence, has attracted particular attention from historians. It has also produced deep disagreements among them. Scholars have differed in many ways in their interpretations of Populism, but at the heart of most such disagreements have been disparate views of the value of popular, insurgent politics. Some historians have harbored a basic mistrust of such mass uprisings and have therefore viewed the Populists with suspicion and hostility. Others have viewed such

insurgency approvingly, as evidence of a healthy resistance to oppression and exploitation; and to them, the Populists have appeared as essentially admirable, democratic activists.

This latter view was the basis of the first, and for many years the only, general history of Populism: John D. Hicks's *The Populist Revolt* (1931). Rejecting the then-prevailing view of the Populists as misguided and unruly radicals, Hicks described them as people reacting rationally and progressively to economic misfortune. Hicks was writing in an era in which the ideas of Frederick Jackson Turner were dominating historical studies, and he brought to his analysis of Populism a strong emphasis on regionalism. Populists, he argued, were part of the democratic West, resisting pressures from the more aristocratic East. (He explained southern Populism by describing the South as an "economic frontier" region—not newly settled like the West, but prey to many of the same pressures and misfortunes.) The Populists, Hicks suggested, were aware of the harsh, even brutal, impact of eastern industrial growth on rural society. They were proposing reforms that would limit the oppressive power of the new financial titans and restore a measure of control to the farmers. Populism was, he wrote, "the last phase of a long and perhaps a losing struggle—the struggle to save

agricultural America from the devouring jaws of industrial America." A losing struggle, perhaps, but not a vain one; for many of the reforms the Populists advocated, Hicks implied, became the basis of later progressive legislation.

This generally approving view of Populism prevailed among historians for more than two decades, amplified in particular by C. Vann Woodward, whose *Origins of the New South* (1951) and *The Strange Career of Jim Crow* (1955) portrayed southern Populism as a challenge to the stifling power of old elites and even, at times, to at least some elements of white supremacy. But Woodward was not typical of most scholars viewing Populism in the early 1950s. For others, the memory of European fascism and uneasiness about contemporary communism combined to create a general hostility toward mass popular politics; and a harsh new view of the Populist movement appeared in a work by one of the nation's leading historians. Richard Hofstadter, in *The Age of Reform* (1955), admitted that Populism embraced some progressive ideas and advocated some sensible reforms. But the bulk of his effort was devoted to exposing both the "soft" and the "dark" sides of the movement. Populism was "soft," Hofstadter claimed, because it rested on a nostalgic and unrealistic myth, because it romanticized the nation's agrarian

(Kansas State Historical Society)

creating currency (the "mint ratio") was 16 to 1: sixteen ounces of silver equaled one ounce of gold. But the actual commercial value of silver (the "market ratio") was much higher than that. Owners of silver could get more by selling it for manufacture into jewelry and other objects than they could by taking it to the mint for conversion to coins. So they stopped taking it to the mint, and the mint stopped coining silver.

In 1873, Congress passed a law that seemed simply to recognize the existing situation by officially discontinuing silver coinage. Few people objected at the time. But in the course of the 1870s, the market value of silver fell well below the official mint ratio of 16 to 1. (Sixteen ounces of silver, in other words, were now worth less, not more, than one ounce of gold.) Silver was available for coinage again. Congress had thus foreclosed a potential method of

expanding the currency and had eliminated a potential market for silver miners. Before long, many Americans concluded that a conspiracy of big bankers had been responsible for the "demonetization" of silver and referred to the law as the "Crime of '73."

Two groups of Americans were especially determined to undo the "Crime of '73." One consisted of the silver-mine owners, now understand-ably eager to have the government

"Crime of '73"

take their surplus silver and pay them much more than the market price. The other group consisted of discontented farmers, who wanted an increase in the quantity of money—an inflation of the currency—as a means of raising the prices of farm products and easing payment of the farmers' debts. The inflationists demanded that the government return at once to "free silver"—that is, to the

542

WHERE HISTORIANS DISAGREE

This popular feature demonstrates for students that history is not simply a collection of facts but rather many complex stories that are open to interpretation. These essays illustrate the contested quality of much of the American past and encourage students to analyze and think critically about evidence presented in history.

THE GLOBAL DEPRESSION

The Great Depression began in the United States. But it did not end there. The American economy was the largest in the world, and its collapse sent shock waves around the globe. By 1931, the American depression had become a world Depression, with important implications for the course of global history.

The origins of the worldwide depression lay in the pattern of debts that had emerged during and after World War I, when the United States loaned billions of dollars to European nations. In 1931, with American banks staggering and in many cases collapsing, large banks in New York began desperately calling in their loans from Germany and Austria. That precipitated the failure of one of Austria's largest banks, which in turn created panic through much of central Europe. The economic collapse in Germany and Austria meant that those nations could not continue paying reparations to Britain and France (required by the Treaty of Versailles of 1919), which meant in turn that Britain and France could not continue paying off their loans to the United States.

This spreading financial crisis was accompanied by a dramatic contraction of international trade, precipitated in part by the Smoot-Hawley Tariff in the United States, which established the highest import duties in history and stifled much global commerce. Depressed agricultural prices—a result of worldwide overproduction—also contributed to the downturn. By 1932, worldwide industrial production had declined by more than a third, and world trade had plummeted by nearly two-thirds. By 1933, thirty million people in industrial nations were unemployed, five times the number four years before.

But the Depression was not confined to industrial nations. Imperialism and industrialization had drawn almost all regions of the world into the international industrial economy. Colonies in Africa, Asia, and South America—critically dependent on exporting raw materials and agricultural goods to industrial countries—experienced a decline in demand for their products, which led to rising

LOOKING FOR WORK IN LONDON, 1935 An unemployed London man wears a sign that seems designed to convince passersby that he is an educated, respectable person despite his present circumstances. *(Getty Images)*

levels of poverty and unemployment. Some nations—among them the Soviet Union and China—remained relatively unconnected to the global economy and suffered relatively little from the Great Depression. But in most parts of the world, the Depression caused tremendous social and economic hardship.

It also created political turmoil. Among the countries hardest hit by the Depression was Germany, where industrial production declined by 50 percent and unemployment reached 35 percent in the early 1930s. The desperate economic conditions there contributed greatly to the rise of the Nazi Party and its leader Adolf Hitler, who became chancellor in 1932. Japan suffered greatly as well, dependent as it was on world trade to sustain its growing industrial economy and purchase essential commodities for its needs at home. And in Japan, as in Germany, economic troubles produced political turmoil and aided the rise of a new militaristic regime. In Italy, the fascist government of Benito Mussolini, which had first taken power in the 1920s, also saw militarization and territorial expansion as a way out of economic difficulties.

In other nations, governments sought solutions to the Depression through reform of their domestic economies. The most prominent example of that was the New Deal in the United States. But there were important experiments in other nations as well. Among the most common responses to the Depression around the world was substantial government investment in public works. In the United States, Britain, France, Germany, Italy, the Soviet Union, and other countries, there was substantial investment in roads, bridges, dams, public buildings, and other large projects. An other response was the expansion of government-funded relief for the unemployed. All the industrial countries of the world experienced with some form of relief, often borrowing ideas from one another in the process.

In addition, the Depression helped create new approaches to economics, in the face of the apparent failure of classical models of economic behavior to explain, or provide solutions to, the crisis. The great British economist John Maynard Keynes revolutionized economic thought in much of the world. His 1936 book *The General Theory of Employment, Interest, and Money*, despite its bland title, created a sensation by arguing that the Depression was a result not of declining production, but of inadequate consumer demand. Governments, he said, could stimulate their economies by increasing the money supply and creating investment—through a combination of lowering interest rates and public spending. Keynesianism, as Keynes's theories became known, began to have an impact in the United States in 1938, and in much of the rest of the world in subsequent years.

The Great Depression was an important turning point not only in American history, but in the history of the twentieth-century world as well. It transformed ideas of public policy and economics in many nations. It toppled old regimes and created new ones. And perhaps above all, it was a major factor—maybe the single most important factor—in the coming of World War II.

665

AMERICA IN THE WORLD

The "America in the World" features place America in a more global context. America has never existed in isolation from the rest of the world, and these essays demonstrate the importance of the many global influences on the American story.

PATTERNS OF POPULAR CULTURE

"Patterns of Popular Culture" essays spotlight the ways popular culture has affected the lives of Americans at different times and places in history.

TAVERNS IN REVOLUTIONARY MASSACHUSETTS

In colonial Massachusetts, as in many other American colonies in the 1760s and 1770s, taverns (or "public houses," as they were often known) were crucial to the development of popular resistance to British rule. The Puritan culture of New England created some resistance to taverns, and there were continuing efforts by reformers to regulate or close them to reduce the problems caused by "public drunkenness," "lewd behavior," and anarchy. But as the commercial life of the colonies expanded, and as increasing numbers of people began living in towns and cities, taverns became a central institution in American social life—and eventually in its political life as well.

Taverns were appealing, of course, because they provided alcoholic drinks in a culture where the craving

THE SCALES OF JUSTICE This sign for a Hartford tavern promises hospitality (from "the charming Patroness") and "entertainment" as well as food and drink. *(The Connecticut Historical Society, Hartford)*

for alcohol—and the extent of drunkenness—was very high. But taverns had other attractions as well. There were few other places where people could meet and talk openly in public, and to many colonists the life of the tavern came to seem the only vaguely democratic experience available to them. Gradually, many came to see the attacks on the public houses as efforts to increase the power of existing elites and suppress the freedoms of ordinary people. The tavern was a mostly male institution, just as politics was considered a mostly male concern. And so the fusion of male camaraderie and political discourse emerged naturally out of the tavern culture.

As the revolutionary crisis deepened, taverns and pubs became the central meeting places for discussions of the ideas that fueled resistance to British policies. Educated and uneducated men alike joined in animated discussions of events. Those who could not read—and there were many—could learn about the contents of revolutionary pamphlets from listening to tavern discussions. They could join in the discussion of the new republican ideas emerging in the Americas by participating in tavern celebrations of, for example, the anniversaries of resistance to the Stamp Act. Those anniversaries inspired elaborate toasts in public houses throughout the colonies. Such toasts were the equivalents of political speeches, and illiterate men could learn much from them about the political concepts that were circulating through the colonies.

Taverns were important sources of information in an age before any wide distribution of newspapers. Tavernkeepers were often trusted informants and confidants to the Sons of Liberty and other activists, and they

TAVERN BILLIARDS Gentlemen in Hanover Town, Virginia, gather for a game of billiards in a local tavern in this 1797 drawing by Benjamin Henry Latrobe. *(Maryland Historical Society, Baltimore)*

were fountains of information about the political and social turmoil of the time. Taverns were also the settings for political events. In 1770, for example, a report circulated through the taverns of Danvers, Massachusetts, about a local man who was continuing to sell tea despite the colonial boycott. The Sons of Liberty brought the seller to the Bell Tavern and persuaded him to sign a confession and apology before a crowd of defiant men in the public room.

Almost all politicians found it necessary to visit taverns in colonial Massachusetts if they wanted any real contact with the public. Samuel Adams spent considerable time in the public houses of Boston, where he sought to encourage resistance to British rule while taking care to drink moderately so as not to erode his stature as a leader. His cousin John Adams was somewhat more skeptical of taverns, more sensitive to the vices they encouraged. But he, too, recognized their political value. In taverns, he once said, "bastards, and legislators are frequently begotten."

The boycott was an important event in the history of colonial resistance. Unlike earlier protests, most of which had involved relatively small numbers of people, the boycott mobilized large segments of the population. It also helped link the colonies in a common experience of mass popular protest. Particularly important to the movement

124

were the activities of colonial women, who were among the principal consumers of tea and now became leaders of the effort to boycott it.

Women had played a significant role in resistance activities from the beginning. Several women (most prominently Mercy Otis Warren) had been important in writing

MARGINAL NOTES

One of the most popular features of this book, the marginal notes highlight key terms, events, and concepts as they appear within the narrative. These notes are useful place holders when reading and are especially helpful to students when reviewing and preparing for tests.

RECONSTRUCTION AND THE NEW SOUTH 419

The Soldier President

Grant could have had the nomination of either party in 1868. But believing that Republican Reconstruction policies were more popular in the North, he accepted the Republican nomination. The Democrats nominated former governor Horatio Seymour of New York. The campaign was a bitter one, and Grant's triumph was surprisingly narrow. Without the 500,000 new black Republican voters in the South, he would have had a minority of the popular vote.

U.S. Grant

Grant entered the White House with no political experience, and his performance was clumsy and ineffectual from the start. Except for Hamilton Fish, whom Grant appointed secretary of state and who served for eight years with great distinction, most members of the cabinet were ill equipped for their tasks. Grant relied chiefly, and increasingly, on established party leaders—the group most ardently devoted to patronage—and his administration used the spoils system even more blatantly than most of its predecessors, embittering reform-minded members of his party. Grant also alienated the many Northerners who were growing disillusioned with Radical Reconstruction policies, which the president continued to support. Some Republicans suspected, correctly, that there was also corruption in the Grant administration itself.

By the end of Grant's first term, therefore, members of a substantial faction of the party—who referred to themselves as Liberal Republicans—had come to oppose what they called "Grantism." In 1872, hoping to prevent Grant's reelection, they bolted the party and nominated their own presidential candidate: Horace Greeley, veteran editor and publisher of the *New York Tribune*. The Democrats, somewhat reluctantly, named Greeley their candidate as well, hoping that the alliance with the Liberals would enable them to defeat Grant. But the effort was in vain. Grant won a substantial victory, polling 286 electoral votes to Greeley's 66, and nearly 56 percent of the popular total.

Liberal Republicans

The Grant Scandals

During the 1872 campaign, the first of a series of political scandals came to light that would plague Grant and the Republicans for years. It involved the Crédit Mobilier construction company, which had helped build the Union Pacific Railroad. The heads of Crédit Mobilier had used their positions as Union Pacific stockholders to steer large fraudulent contracts to their construction company, thus bilking the Union Pacific (and the federal government, which provided large subsidies to the railroad) of millions. To prevent investigations, the directors had given Crédit Mobilier stock to key members of Congress. But in 1872, Congress did conduct an investigation, which revealed that some highly placed Republicans—including Schuyler Colfax, now Grant's vice president—had accepted stock.

Crédit Mobilier

GRANT THE TRAPEZE ARTISTS This cartoon by the eminent cartoonist Joseph Keppler shows President Ulysses S. Grant swinging on a trapeze holding on to the "whiskey ring" and the "navy ring" (references to two of the many scandals that plagued his presidency). Using a strap labeled "corruption," he holds aloft some of the most notorious figures in those scandals. The cartoon was published in 1880, when Grant was attempting to win the Republican nomination to run for another term as president. *(Library of Congress)*

One dreary episode followed another in Grant's second term. Benjamin H. Bristow, Grant's third Treasury secretary, discovered that some of his officials and a group of distillers operating as a "whiskey ring" were cheating the government out of taxes by filing false reports. Then a House investigation revealed that William W. Belknap, secretary of war, had accepted bribes to retain an Indian-post trader in office (the so-called Indian ring). Other, lesser scandals added to the growing impression that "Grantism" had brought rampant corruption to government.

The Greenback Question

Compounding Grant's, and the nation's, problems was a financial crisis, known as the Panic of 1873. It began with

---

CIVIL RIGHTS, VIETNAM, AND THE ORDEAL OF LIBERALISM 839

and grievances that had no easy solutions. The civil rights movement ended legalized segregation and disfranchisement, but it also awakened expectations of social and economic equality that laws alone could not provide and that remained in many respects unfulfilled. The peaceful, interracial crusade of the early 1960s gradually turned into a much more militant, confrontational, and increasingly separatist movement toward the decade's end. The idealism among white youths that began the 1960s, and played an important role in the political success of John Kennedy, evolved into an angry rebellion against many aspects of American culture and politics and produced a large upsurge of student protest that rocked the nation at the decade's end. Perhaps most of all, a small and largely unnoticed Cold War commitment to defend South Vietnam against communist aggression from the north led to a large and disastrous American military commitment that destroyed the presidency of Lyndon Johnson, shook the faith of millions in their leaders and their political system, sent thousands of young American men to their deaths, and showed no signs of producing a victory. A decade that began with high hopes and soaring ideals ended with ugly and at times violent division, and deep disillusionment.

INTERACTIVE LEARNING

The *Primary Source Investigator CD-ROM* offers the following materials related to this chapter:
- Interactive maps: **U.S. Elections** (M7); **The Vietnam War** (M29); and **Patterns of Protest** (M30).
- Documents, images, and maps related to the turbulent decade of the 1960s, including the Kennedy and Johnson presidencies and the escalation of the Vietnam War. Highlights include the text of the Gulf of Tonkin Resolution authorizing massive force in Vietnam, images of missile sites in Cuba, and images of soldiers in Vietnam.

Online Learning Center (www.mhhe.com/brinkley13)

For quizzes, Internet resources, references to additional books and films, and more, consult this book's Online Learning Center.

FOR FURTHER REFERENCE

Allen J. Matusow, *The Unraveling of America: A History of Liberalism in the 1960s* (1984) is a provocative history of this turbulent decade. David Farber, *The Age of Great Dreams: America in the 1960s* (1994) is an intelligent and lively general history. Arthur M. Robert Dallek, *Lone Star Rising: Lyndon Johnson and His Times, 1908–1960* (1991), *Flawed Giant: Lyndon B. Johnson, 1960–1973* (1998), and *An Unfinished Life: John F. Kennedy, 1917–1963* (2003) are important biographies. Raymond Arsenault, *Freedom Rides, 1961 and the Struggle for Justice* (2006) is an important study. John Dittmer, *Local People: The Struggle for Civil Rights in Mississippi* (1994) is an study of the grassroots origins of the movement. William Chafe, *Civilities and Civil Rights: Greensboro, North Carolina, and the Black Struggle for Freedom* (1980) examines the southern civil rights movement and the white reaction to it. Taylor Branch, *Parting the Waters: America in the King Years, 1959–1963* (1988), *Pillar of Fire: America in the King Years, 1963–1965*, and *At Canaan's Edge: America in the King Years, 1965–68* (2006) are good narrative histories of the movement (1998). Nicholas Lemann, *The Promised Land: The Great Black Migration and How It Changed America* (1991) is a challenging study of the postwar African-American migration to northern cities and of the Great Society's response to it. Graham T. Allison, *The Essence of Decision: Explaining the Cuban Missile Crisis* (1971) is an important interpretation of the greatest crisis of the Cold War. Ernest R. May and Philip D. Zelikow, *The Kennedy Tapes: Inside the White House During the Cuban Missile Crisis* (1997) provides the annotated transcripts of the taped meetings of Kennedy's inner circle during the crisis. Robert D. Schulzinger, *A Time for War: The United States and Vietnam, 1945–1975* (1997) is a good general history of the war. Neil Sheehan, *A Bright Shining Lie: John Paul Vann and America in Vietnam* (1988) is a compelling picture of the war as experienced by a significant military figure of the 1960s. Christian J. Appy, *Working-Class War: American Combat Soldiers and Vietnam* (1993) examines the class basis of the army that fought in Vietnam. Larry Berman, *Planning a Tragedy* (1982) and *Lyndon Johnson's War* (1989); Leslie Gelb and Richard Betts, *The Irony of Vietnam: The System Worked* (1979); and David Halberstam, *The Best and the Brightest* (1972) are important interpretations of the American decision to intervene and stay in Vietnam. Dan T. Carter, *The Politics of Rage: George Wallace, The Origins of the New Conservatism, and the Transformation of American Politics* (1995) is a good study of the career of George Wallace. David Farber, *Chicago '68* (1988) examines the turbulent Democratic Convention and, through it, the passions that shaped a traumatic year in American history. Mark Kurlansky, *1968: The Year That Rocked the World* (2003) is a broader history of that turbulent year.

FOR FURTHER REFERENCE

For Further Reference lists at the end of every chapter highlight the most significant books available about topics covered in the chapter, allowing readers to do further research or follow up on a topic of particular interest.

LIST OF ILLUSTRATIONS, MAPS, AND CHARTS

ILLUSTRATIONS

MAPS

CHARTS

CHAPTER 15

RECONSTRUCTION AND THE NEW SOUTH

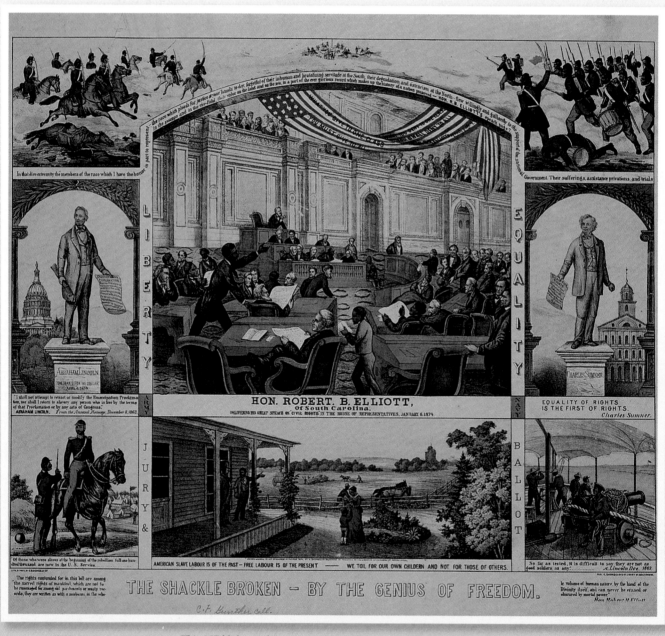

THE GENIUS OF FREEDOM This 1874 lithograph portrays a series of important moments in the history of African Americans in the South during Reconstruction—among them the participation of black soldiers in the Civil War, a speech by a black representative in the North Carolina legislature, and the movement of African-American workers from slavery into a system of free labor. It also portrays some of the white leaders (among them Lincoln and Charles Sumner) who had promoted the cause of the freedmen. *(Chicago Historical Society)*

F EW PERIODS IN THE HISTORY of the United States have produced as much bitterness or created such enduring controversy as the era of Reconstruction—the years following the Civil War, when Americans attempted to reunite their shattered nation. Those who lived through Reconstruction viewed it in sharply different ways. To many white Southerners, it was a vicious and destructive experience—a time when vindictive Northerners inflicted humiliation and revenge on the prostrate South and unnecessarily delayed a genuine reunion of the sections. Northern defenders of Reconstruction, in contrast, argued that their policies were the only way to keep unrepentant Confederates from restoring Southern society as it had been before the war. Without forceful federal intervention, it would be impossible to stop the reemergence of a backward aristocracy and the continued subjugation of former slaves. There would be no way, in other words, to prevent the same sectional problems that had produced the Civil War in the first place.

To most African Americans at the time, and to many people of all races since, Reconstruction was notable for other reasons. Neither a vicious tyranny, as white Southerners charged, nor a thoroughgoing reform, as many Northerners claimed, it was, rather, a small but important first step in the effort by former slaves to secure civil rights and economic power. Reconstruction did not provide African Americans with either the legal protections or the material resources to assure them anything like real equality. And when it came to an end, finally, in the late 1870s—as a result of an economic crisis, a lack of political will in the North, and organized, at times violent, resistance by white Southerners—the freed slaves found themselves abandoned by the federal government to face alone a system of economic peonage and legal subordination. For the remainder of the nineteenth century, those African Americans who continued to live in what came to be known as the New South were unable effectively to resist oppression. And yet for all its shortcomings, Reconstruction did help African Americans create institutions and legal precedents that they carried with them into the twentieth century, which became the basis for later efforts to win freedom and equality.

SIGNIFICANT EVENTS

1863 ▶ Lincoln announces preliminary Reconstruction plan

1864 ▶ Louisiana, Arkansas, and Tennessee readmitted to Union under Lincoln plan
   ▶ Wade-Davis Bill passed

1865 ▶ Lincoln assassinated (April 14); Andrew Johnson becomes president
   ▶ Johnson tries to readmit rest of Confederate states to Union
   ▶ Black Codes enacted in South
   ▶ Freedmen's Bureau established
   ▶ Congress reconvenes (December) and refuses to admit Southern representatives; creates Joint Committee on Reconstruction

1866 ▶ Freedmen's Bureau Act renewed
   ▶ Congress approves Fourteenth Amendment; most Southern states reject it
   ▶ Republicans gain in congressional elections
   ▶ *Ex parte Milligan* challenges Radicals' Reconstruction plans
   ▶ Ku Klux Klan formed in South

1867 ▶ Military Reconstruction Act (and two supplementary acts) outlines congressional plan of Reconstruction
   ▶ Tenure of Office Act and Command of the Army Act restrict presidential power
   ▶ Southern states establish Reconstruction governments under congressional plan
   ▶ United States purchases Alaska

1868 ▶ Most Southern states readmitted to Union under congressional plan
   ▶ Andrew Johnson impeached but not convicted
   ▶ Fourteenth Amendment ratified
   ▶ Ulysses S. Grant elected president

1869 ▶ Congress passes Fifteenth Amendment
   ▶ First "redeemer" governments elected in South

1870 ▶ Last Southern states readmitted to Union
   ▶ "Enforcement Acts" passed

1871 ▶ *Alabama* claims settled

1872 ▶ Liberal Republicans defect
   ▶ Grant reelected president

1873 ▶ Commercial and financial panic disrupts economy

1875 ▶ Specie Resumption Act passed
   ▶ "Whiskey ring" scandal discredits Grant administration

1877 ▶ Rutherford B. Hayes elected president after disputed election
   ▶ Last federal troops withdrawn from South after Compromise of 1877
   ▶ Last Southern states "redeemed"

1879 ▶ Readjusters win control of Virginia legislature

1880 ▶ Joel Chandler Harris publishes *Uncle Remus*

1883 ▶ Supreme Court upholds segregation in private institutions

1890s ▶ "Jim Crow" laws passed throughout South
   ▶ Lynchings increase in South

1895 ▶ Booker T. Washington outlines Atlanta Compromise

1896 ▶ *Plessy* v. *Ferguson* upholds "separate but equal" racial facilities

1898 ▶ *Williams* v. *Mississippi* validates literacy tests for voting

THE PROBLEMS OF PEACEMAKING

In 1865, as it became clear that the war was almost over, no one in Washington knew what to do. Abraham Lincoln could not negotiate a treaty with the defeated government; he continued to insist that the Confederate government had no legal right to exist. Yet neither could he simply readmit the Southern states into the Union as if nothing had happened.

The Aftermath of War and Emancipation

What happened to the South in the Civil War was a catastrophe with no parallel in America's experience as a nation. Towns had been gutted, plantations burned, fields neglected, bridges and railroads destroyed. Many white Southerners, stripped of their slaves through emancipation and stripped of the capital they had invested in now-worthless Confederate bonds and currency, had almost no personal property. Many families had to rebuild their fortunes without the help of adult males. Some white Southerners faced starvation and homelessness.

The Devastated South

More than 258,000 Confederate soldiers had died in the war—more than 20 percent of the adult white male population of the region; thousands more returned home wounded or sick. Almost all surviving white Southerners had lost people close to them in the fighting. A cult of ritualized mourning developed throughout the region in the late 1860s, particularly among white women—many of whom wore mourning clothes (and jewelry) for two years or longer. At the same time, white Southerners began to romanticize the "Lost Cause" and its leaders, and to look back nostalgically at the South as it had existed before the terrible disruptions of war. Such Confederate heroes as Robert E. Lee, Stonewall Jackson, and (later) Jefferson Davis were treated with extraordinary reverence, almost as religious figures. Communities throughout the South built elaborate monuments to their war dead in town squares. The tremendous sense of loss that pervaded the white South reinforced the determination of many whites to protect what remained of their now-vanished world.

Myth of the "Lost Cause"

RICHMOND, 1865   By the time Union forces captured Richmond in early 1865, the Confederate capital had been under siege for months and much of the city lay in ruins, as this photograph reveals. On April 4, President Lincoln, accompanied by his son Tad, visited Richmond. As he walked through the streets of the shattered city, hundreds of former slaves emerged from the rubble to watch him pass. "No triumphal march of a conqueror could have equalled in moral sublimity the humble manner in which he entered Richmond," a black soldier serving with the Union army wrote. "It was a great deliverer among the delivered. No wonder tears came to his eyes." *(Library of Congress)*

A MONUMENT TO THE LOST CAUSE This monument in the town square of Monroe, Georgia, was typical of many such memorials erected all across the South after the Civil War. They served both to commemorate the Confederate dead and to remind white Southerners of what was by the 1870s already widely known and romanticized as the "Lost Cause." (©Lee Snider/Corbis)

If conditions were bad for many Southern whites, they were far worse for most Southern blacks—the 4 million men and women emerging from bondage. Some of them had also seen service during the war—as servants to Confederate officers or as teamsters and laborers for the Southern armies. Nearly 200,000 had fought for the Union, and 38,000 had died. Others had worked as spies or scouts for Union forces in the South. Many more had flocked to the Union lines to escape slavery. Even before Emancipation, thousands of slaves in many parts of the South had taken advantage of wartime disruptions to leave their owners and move off in search of freedom. As soon as the war ended, hundreds of thousands more former slaves—young and old, healthy and sick—left their plantations. But most had nowhere to go. Many of them trudged to the nearest town or city, roamed the countryside camping at night on the bare ground, or gathered around Union occupation forces, hoping for assistance. Others spent months, even years, searching for relatives from whom they had been separated. Virtually none, of course, owned any land or property. Most had no possessions except the clothes they wore.

In 1865, in short, Southern society was in disarray. Blacks and whites, men and women faced a future of great uncertainty. Yet all Southerners faced this future with some very clear aspirations. For both blacks and whites, Reconstruction became a struggle to define the meaning of freedom. But the former slaves and the defeated whites had very different conceptions of what freedom meant.

Competing Notions of Freedom

For African Americans, freedom meant above all an end to slavery and to all the injustices and humiliation they associated with it. But it also meant the acquisition of rights and protections that would allow them to live as free men and women in the same way white people did. "If I cannot do like a white man," one African-American man told his former master, "I am not free."

African Americans differed with one another on how to achieve that freedom. Some demanded a redistribution of economic resources, especially land, because, as a convention of Alabama freedmen put it in a formal resolution, "The property which they hold was nearly all earned by the sweat of our brows." Others asked simply for legal equality, confident that given the same opportunities as white citizens they could advance successfully in American society. But whatever their particular demands, virtually all former slaves were united in their desire for independence from white control. Freed from slavery, blacks throughout the South began almost immediately to create autonomous African-American communities. They pulled out of white-controlled churches and established their own. They created fraternal, benevolent, and mutual-aid societies. When they could, they began their own schools.

For most white Southerners, freedom meant something very different. It meant the ability to control their own destinies without interference from the North or the federal government. And in the immediate aftermath of the war, they attempted to exercise this version of freedom by trying to restore their society to its antebellum form. Slavery had been abolished in the former Confederacy by the Emancipation Proclamation, and everywhere else (as of December 1865) by the Thirteenth Amendment. But many white planters wanted to continue slavery in an altered form by keeping black workers legally tied to the plantations. When these white Southerners fought for what they considered freedom, they were fighting above all to preserve local and regional autonomy and white supremacy.

> Freedom for the Ex-slaves

A FREEDMEN'S BUREAU SCHOOL African-American students and teachers stand outside a school for former slaves, one of many run by the Freedmen's Bureau throughout the defeated Confederacy in the first years after the war. *(U.S. Army Military History Institute, Carlisle, Pennsylvania. Photo by Jim Enos)*

The federal government kept troops in the South after the war to preserve order and protect the freedmen. In March 1865, Congress established the Freedmen's Bureau, an agency of the army directed by General Oliver O. Howard. The Freedmen's Bureau distributed food to millions of former slaves. It established schools staffed by missionaries and teachers who had been sent to the South by Freedmen's Aid Societies and other private and church groups in the North. It made modest efforts to settle blacks on lands of their own. (The bureau also offered considerable assistance to poor whites, many of whom were similarly destitute and homeless after the war.) But the Freedmen's Bureau was not a permanent solution. It had authority to operate for only one year; and in any case it was far too small to deal effectively with the enormous problems facing Southern society. By the time the war ended, other proposals for reconstructing the defeated South were emerging.

> The Freedmen's Bureau

Issues of Reconstruction

The terms by which the Southern states rejoined the Union had important implications for both major political parties. The Republican victories in 1860 and 1864 had been a result in large part of the division of the Democratic Party and, later, the removal of the South from the electorate. Readmitting the South, leaders of both parties believed, would reunite the Democrats and weaken the Republicans. In addition, the Republican Party had taken advantage of the South's absence from Congress to pass a program of nationalistic economic legislation—railroad subsidies, protective tariffs, banking and currency reforms, and other measures to benefit Northern business leaders and industrialists. Should the Democratic Party regain power with heavy Southern support, these programs would be in jeopardy. Complicating these practical questions were emotional concerns. Many Northerners believed the South should be punished in some way for the suffering and sacrifice its rebellion had caused. Many Northerners believed, too, that the South should be transformed, made over in the North's urbanized image—its supposedly backward, feudal, undemocratic society civilized and modernized.

Even among the Republicans in Congress, there was considerable disagreement about the proper approach to Reconstruction—disagreement that reflected the same factional divisions that had created disputes over emancipation during the war. Conservatives insisted that the South accept the abolition of slavery, but proposed few other conditions for the readmission of the seceded states. The Radicals, led by Representative Thaddeus Stevens of Pennsylvania and Senator Charles Sumner of Massachusetts, urged that the civil and military leaders of the Confederacy be punished, that large numbers of Southern whites be disenfranchised, that the legal rights of former slaves be protected, and that the property of wealthy white Southerners who had aided the Confederacy be confiscated and distributed among the freedmen. Some Radicals favored granting suffrage to the former slaves. Others hesitated, since few Northern states permitted blacks to vote. Between the Radicals and the Conservatives stood a faction of uncommitted Republicans, the Moderates, who rejected the punitive goals of the Radicals but supported extracting at least some concessions from the South on African-American rights.

> Conservative and Radical Republicans

Plans for Reconstruction

President Lincoln's sympathies lay with the Moderates and Conservatives of his party. He believed that a lenient Reconstruction policy would encourage Southern unionists and other former Whigs to join the Republican Party and would thus prevent the readmission of the South from strengthening the Democrats. More immediately, the Southern unionists could become the nucleus of new, loyal state governments in the South. Lincoln was not uninterested in the fate of the freedmen, but he was willing to defer questions about their future for the sake of rapid reunification.

Lincoln's Reconstruction plan, which he announced in December 1863, offered a general amnesty to white Southerners—other than high officials of the Confederacy—who

> Lincoln's 10% Plan

would pledge loyalty to the government and accept the elimination of slavery. Whenever 10 percent of the number of voters in 1860 took the oath in any state, those loyal voters could set up a state government. Lincoln also hoped to extend suffrage to those blacks who were educated, owned property, and had served in the Union army. Three Southern states—Louisiana, Arkansas, and Tennessee, all under Union occupation—reestablished loyal governments under the Lincoln formula in 1864.

The Radical Republicans were astonished at the mildness of Lincoln's program. They persuaded Congress to deny seats to representatives from the three "reconstructed" states and refused to count the electoral vote of those states in the election of 1864. But for the moment, the Radicals were uncertain about what form their own Reconstruction plan should take. Their first effort to resolve that question was the Wade-Davis Bill, passed by Congress in July 1864. It authorized the president to appoint a provisional governor for each conquered state. When a majority (not Lincoln's 10 percent) of the white males of the state pledged their allegiance to the Union, the governor could summon a state constitutional convention, whose delegates were to be elected by those who would swear (through the so-called Ironclad Oath) that they had never borne arms against the United States—another departure from Lincoln's plan. The new state constitutions would have to abolish slavery, disfranchise Confederate civil and military leaders, and repudiate debts accumulated by the state governments during the war. After a state had met these conditions, Congress would readmit it to the Union. Like the president's proposal, the Wade-Davis Bill left up to the states the question of political rights for blacks. Congress passed the bill a few days before it adjourned in 1864, and Lincoln disposed of it with a pocket veto. His action enraged the Radical leaders, and the pragmatic Lincoln became convinced he would have to accept at least some of the Radical demands. He began to move toward a new approach to Reconstruction.

`Wade-Davis Bill`

The Death of Lincoln

What plan he might have produced no one can say. On the night of April 14, 1865, Lincoln and his wife attended a play at Ford's Theater in Washington. As they sat in the presidential box, John Wilkes Booth, a member of a distinguished family of actors and a zealous advocate of the Southern cause, entered the box from the rear and shot Lincoln in the head. The president was carried unconscious to a house across the street, where early the next morning, surrounded by family, friends, and political associates (among them a tearful Charles Sumner), he died.

The circumstances of Lincoln's death earned him immediate martyrdom. It also produced something close to hysteria throughout the North. There were accusations

ABRAHAM LINCOLN This haunting photograph of Abraham Lincoln, showing clearly the weariness and aging that four years as a war president had created, was taken in Washington only four days before his assassination in 1865. *(Library of Congress)*

that Booth had acted as part of a great conspiracy—accusations that contained some truth. Booth did indeed have associates, one of whom shot and wounded Secretary of State Seward the night of the assassination, another of whom abandoned at the last moment a plan to murder Vice President Johnson. Booth himself escaped on horseback into the Virginia countryside, where, on April 26, he was cornered by Union troops and shot to death in a blazing barn. A military tribunal convicted eight other people of participating in the conspiracy (at least two of them on the basis of virtually no evidence). Four were hanged.

To many Northerners, however, the murder of the president seemed evidence of an even greater conspiracy—one masterminded and directed by the unrepentant leaders of the defeated South. Militant Republicans exploited such suspicions relentlessly for months, ensuring that Lincoln's death would help doom his plans for a relatively easy peace.

Johnson and "Restoration"

Leadership of the Moderates and Conservatives fell to Lincoln's successor, Andrew Johnson, who was not well suited, by either circumstance or personality, for the task. A Democrat until he had joined the Union ticket with Lincoln in 1864, he became a Republican president at a moment when partisan passions were growing. Johnson

Andrew Johnson's Personality

himself was an intemperate and tactless man, filled with resentments and insecurities. He was also openly hostile to the freed slaves and unwilling to support any plans that guaranteed them civil equality or enfranchisement. He once declared, "White men alone must manage the South."

Johnson revealed his plan for Reconstruction—or "Restoration," as he preferred to call it—soon after he took office, and he implemented it during the summer of 1865, when Congress was in recess. Like Lincoln, he offered amnesty to those Southerners who would take an oath of allegiance. (High-ranking Confederate officials and any white Southerner with land worth $20,000 or more would have to apply to the president for individual pardons. Johnson, a self-made man, apparently liked the thought of the great planter aristocrats humbling themselves before him.) In most other respects, however, his plan resembled that of the Wade-Davis Bill. For each state, the president appointed a provisional governor, who was to invite qualified voters to elect delegates to a constitutional convention. Johnson did not specify how many qualified voters were necessary, but he implied that he would require a majority (as had the Wade-Davis Bill). In order to win readmission to Congress, a state had to revoke its ordinance of secession, abolish slavery, ratify the Thirteenth Amendment, and repudiate the Confederate and state war debts. The final procedure before restoration was for a state to elect a state government and send representatives to Congress.

By the end of 1865, all the seceded states had formed new governments—some under Lincoln's plan, some under Johnson's—and were prepared to rejoin the Union as soon as Congress recognized them. But Radical Republicans vowed not to recognize the Johnson governments, just as they had previously refused to recognize the Lincoln regimes; for by now, Northern

Northern Attitudes Harden

opinion had become more hostile toward the South than it had been a year earlier when Congress passed the Wade-Davis Bill. Many Northerners were disturbed by the apparent reluctance of some delegates to the Southern conventions to abolish slavery, and by the refusal of all the conventions to grant suffrage to any blacks. They were astounded that states claiming to be "loyal" should elect prominent leaders of the recent Confederacy as state officials and representatives to Congress. Particularly hard to accept was Georgia's choice of Alexander H. Stephens, former Confederate vice president, as a United States senator.

RADICAL RECONSTRUCTION

Reconstruction under Johnson's plan—often known as "presidential Reconstruction"—continued only until Congress reconvened in December 1865. At that point,

Congress refused to seat the representatives of the "restored" states and created a new Joint Committee on Reconstruction to frame a Reconstruction policy of its own. The period of "congressional," or "Radical," Reconstruction had begun.

The Black Codes

Meanwhile, events in the South were driving Northern opinion in more radical directions. Throughout the South in 1865 and early 1866, state legislatures were enacting sets of laws known as the Black Codes, designed to give whites substantial control over former slaves. The codes authorized local officials to apprehend unemployed African Americans, fine them for vagrancy, and hire them out to private employers to satisfy the fine. Some of the codes forbade blacks to own or lease farms or to take any jobs other than as plantation workers or domestic servants.

Congress first responded to the Black Codes by passing an act extending the life of the Freedmen's Bureau and widening its powers so that it could nullify work agreements

Johnson's Vetoes

forced on freedmen under the Black Codes. Then, in April 1866, Congress passed the first Civil Rights Act, which declared African Americans to be citizens of the United States and gave the federal government power to intervene in state affairs to protect the rights of citizens. Johnson vetoed both bills, but Congress overrode him on each of them.

The Fourteenth Amendment

In April 1866, the Joint Committee on Reconstruction proposed a new amendment to the Constitution, which Congress approved in early summer and sent to the states for ratification. Eventually, it became one of the most important of all the provisions in the Constitution.

The Fourteenth Amendment offered the first constitutional definition of American citizenship. Everyone born in the United States, and everyone naturalized, was automatically a citizen and entitled to all the "privileges and immunities" guaranteed by the Constitution, including equal

Citizenship for Blacks

protection of the laws by both the state and national governments. There could be no other requirements for citizenship. The amendment also imposed penalties—reduction of representation in Congress and in the electoral college—on states that denied suffrage to any adult male inhabitants. (The wording reflected the prevailing view in Congress and elsewhere that the franchise was properly restricted to men.) Finally, it prohibited former members of Congress or other former federal officials who had aided the Confederacy from holding any state or federal office unless two-thirds of Congress voted to pardon them.

Congressional Radicals offered to readmit to the Union any state whose legislature ratified the Fourteenth

THE MEMPHIS RACE RIOT, 1866 Angry whites (shown here shooting down African Americans) rampaged through the black neighborhoods of Memphis, Tennessee, during the first three days of May 1866, burning homes, schools, and churches and leaving forty-six people dead. Some contemporaries claimed the riot was a response to strict new regulations protecting blacks that had been imposed on Tennessee by General George Stoneman, the military commander of the district; others argued that it was an attempt by whites to intimidate and control an African-American population that was trying to exercise its new freedom. Such riots were among the events that persuaded Radical Republicans in Congress to press for a harsher policy of Reconstruction. *(The Granger Collection)*

Amendment. Only Tennessee did so. All the other former Confederate states, along with Delaware and Kentucky, refused, leaving the amendment temporarily without the necessary approval of three-fourths of the states.

But by now, the Radicals were growing more confident and determined. Bloody race riots in New Orleans and other Southern cities—riots in which African Americans were the principal victims—were among the events that strengthened their hand. In the 1866 congressional elections, Johnson actively campaigned for Conservative candidates, but he did his own cause more harm than good with his intemperate speeches. The voters returned an overwhelming majority of Republicans, most of them Radicals, to Congress. In the Senate, there were now 42 Republicans to 11 Democrats; in the House, 143 Republicans to 49 Democrats. (The South remained largely unrepresented in both chambers.) Congressional Republicans were now strong enough to enact a plan of their own even over the president's objections.

The Congressional Plan

The Radicals passed three Reconstruction bills early in 1867 and overrode Johnson's vetoes of all of them. These bills finally established, nearly two years after the end of the war, a coherent plan for Reconstruction.

Three Reconstruction Bills

Under the congressional plan, Tennessee, which had ratified the Fourteenth Amendment, was promptly readmitted. But Congress rejected the Lincoln-Johnson governments of the other ten Confederate states and, instead, combined those states into five military districts. A military commander governed each district and had orders to register qualified voters (defined as all adult black males

AMERICAN CITIZENS (TO THE POLLS) The artist T. W. Wood painted this watercolor of voters standing in line at the polls during the 1866 elections. A prosperous Yankee, a working-class Irishman, and a Dutch coach driver stand next to the newest addition to the American electorate: an African American, whose expression conveys his excitement at being able to join the community of voters. Wood meant this painting to celebrate the democratic character of American life after the Civil War. *(T. W. Wood Art Gallery, Vermont College, Montpelier)*

RECONSTRUCTION, 1866–1877 This map shows the former Confederate states and provides the date when each was readmitted to the Union as well as a subsequent date when each state managed to return political power to traditional white, conservative elites—a process white Southerners liked to call "redemption." ◆ *What had to happen for a state to be readmitted to the Union? What had to happen before a state could experience "redemption"?*

and those white males who had not participated in the rebellion). Once registered, voters would elect conventions to prepare new state constitutions, which had to include provisions for black suffrage. Once voters ratified the new constitutions, they could elect state governments. Congress had to approve a state's constitution, and the state legislature had to ratify the Fourteenth Amendment. Once that happened, and once enough states ratified the amendment to make it part of the Constitution, then the former Confederate states could be restored to the Union.

By 1868, seven of the ten former Confederate states (Arkansas, North Carolina, South Carolina, Louisiana, Alabama, Georgia, and Florida) had fulfilled these conditions (including ratification of the Fourteenth Amendment, which now became part of the Constitution) and were readmitted to the Union. Conservative whites held up the return of Virginia and Texas until 1869 and Mississippi until 1870. By then, Congress had added an additional requirement for readmission—ratification of another constitutional amendment, the Fifteenth,

Fifteenth Amendment

which forbade the states and the federal government to deny suffrage to any citizen on account of "race, color, or previous condition of servitude."

To stop the president from interfering with their plans, the congressional Radicals passed two remarkable laws of dubious constitutionality in 1867. One, the Tenure of Office Act, forbade the president to remove civil officials, including members of his own cabinet, without the consent of the Senate. The principal purpose of the law was to protect the job of Secretary of War Edwin M. Stanton, who was cooperating with the Radicals. The other law, the Command of the Army Act, prohibited the president from issuing military orders except through the commanding general of the army (General Grant), who could not be relieved or assigned elsewhere without the consent of the Senate.

The congressional Radicals also took action to stop the Supreme Court from interfering with their plans. In 1866, the Court had declared in the case of *Ex parte Milligan* that military tribunals were unconstitutional in places where civil courts were functioning, a decision that seemed to threaten the system of military government the Radicals were planning for the South. Radicals in Congress immediately proposed several bills that would require two-thirds of the justices to support any decision overruling a law of Congress, would deny the

Court jurisdiction in Reconstruction cases, would reduce its membership to three, and would even abolish it. The justices apparently took notice. Over the next two years, the Court refused to accept jurisdiction in any cases involving Reconstruction (and the congressional bills concerning the Court never passed).

The Impeachment of the President

President Johnson had long since ceased to be a serious obstacle to the passage of Radical legislation, but he was still the official charged with administering the Reconstruction programs. As such, the Radicals believed, he remained a serious impediment to their plans. Early in 1867, they began looking for a way to impeach him and remove him from office. Republicans found grounds for impeachment, they believed, when Johnson dismissed Secretary of War Stanton despite Congress's refusal to

Tenure of Office Act

agree, thus deliberately violating the Tenure of Office Act in hopes of testing the law before the courts. Elated Radicals in the House quickly impeached the president and sent the case to the Senate for trial.

The trial before the Senate lasted throughout April and May 1868. The Radicals put heavy pressure on all the Republican senators, but the Moderates (who were losing

Johnson Acquitted

faith in the Radical program) vacillated. On the first three charges to come to a vote, seven Republicans joined the Democrats and independents to support acquittal. The vote was 35 to 19, one short of the constitutionally required two-thirds majority. After that, the Radicals dropped the impeachment effort.

THE SOUTH IN RECONSTRUCTION

When white Southerners spoke bitterly in later years of the effects of Reconstruction, they referred most frequently to the governments Congress helped impose on them—governments they claimed were both incompetent and corrupt, that saddled the region with enormous debts, and that trampled on the rights of citizens. When black Southerners and their defenders condemned Reconstruction, in contrast, they spoke of the failure of the national and state governments to go far enough to guarantee freedmen even the most elemental rights of citizenship—a failure that resulted in a harsh new system of economic subordination. (See "Where Historians Disagree," pp. 422–423.)

The Reconstruction Governments

In the ten states of the South that were reorganized under the congressional plan, approximately one-fourth of the white males were at first excluded from voting or holding office. That produced black majorities among

voters in South Carolina, Mississippi, and Louisiana (states where blacks were also a majority of the population), and in Alabama and Florida (where they were not). But the government soon lifted most suffrage restrictions so that nearly all white males could vote. After that, Republicans maintained control only with the support of many Southern whites.

Critics called these Southern white Republicans "scalawags." Many were former Whigs who had never felt comfortable in the Democratic Party—some of them wealthy

"Scalawags"

(or once wealthy) planters or businessmen interested in the economic development of the region. Others were farmers who lived in remote areas where there had been little or no slavery and who hoped the Republican program of internal improvements would help end their economic isolation. Despite their diverse social positions, scalawags shared a belief that the Republican Party would serve their economic interests better than the Democrats.

THE BURDENED SOUTH This Reconstruction-era cartoon expresses the South's sense of its oppression at the hands of Northern Republicans. President Grant (whose hat bears Abraham Lincoln's initials) rides in comfort in a giant carpetbag, guarded by bayonet-wielding soldiers, as the South staggers under the burden in chains. More evidence of destruction and military occupation is visible in the background. *(Culver Pictures, Inc.)*

THE LOUISIANA CONSTITUTIONAL CONVENTION, 1868 This lithograph commemorates the brief moment during which black voters actually dominated the politics of Louisiana. When the state held a constitutional convention in 1868, a majority of the delegates were African Americans (many of them freeborn blacks who had moved to Louisiana from the North). The constitution they passed guaranteed political and civil rights to black citizens. When white conservatives regained control of the state several years later, they passed a new constitution of their own, repealing most of those guarantees. *(Library of Congress)*

White men from the North also served as Republican leaders in the South. Critics of Reconstruction referred to them pejoratively as "carpetbaggers," which conveyed an image of penniless adventurers who arrived with all their possessions in a carpetbag (a common kind of cheap suitcase covered with carpeting material). In fact, most of the so-called carpetbaggers were well-educated people of middle-class origin, many of them doctors, lawyers, and teachers. Most were veterans of the Union army who looked on the South as a new frontier, more promising than the West. They had

"Carpetbaggers"

settled there at war's end as hopeful planters, or as business and professional people.

But the most numerous Republicans in the South were the black freedmen, most of whom had no previous experience in politics and who tried, therefore, to build institutions through which they could learn to exercise their power. In several states, African-American voters held their own conventions to chart their future course. One such "colored convention," as Southern whites called them, assembled in Alabama in 1867 and announced: "We claim exactly the same rights, privileges and immunities as are enjoyed by white men—we ask nothing more and will be content with nothing less." The black churches that freedmen created after emancipation also helped give unity and political self-confidence to the former slaves. African Americans played a significant role in the politics of the Reconstruction South. They served as delegates to the constitutional conventions. They held public offices of practically every kind. Between 1869 and 1901, twenty African Americans served in the U.S. House of Representatives, two in the Senate (Hiram Revels of Mississippi and Blanche K. Bruce of Mississippi). African Americans served, too, in state legislatures and in various other state offices. Southern whites complained loudly (both at the time and for generations to come) about "Negro rule" during Reconstruction, but no such thing ever actually existed in any of the states. No black man was ever elected governor of a Southern state (although Lieutenant Governor P. B. S. Pinchback briefly performed gubernatorial duties in Louisiana). Blacks never controlled any of the state legislatures, although they held a majority in the lower house in South Carolina for a short time. In the South as a whole, the percentage of black officeholders was always far lower than the percentage of blacks in the population.

Freedmen

The record of the Reconstruction governments is mixed. Critics at the time and since denounced them for corruption and financial extravagance, and there is some truth to both charges. Officeholders in many states enriched themselves through graft and other illicit activities. State budgets expanded to hitherto unknown totals, and state debts soared to previously undreamed-of heights. In South Carolina, for example, the public debt increased from $7 million to $29 million in eight years.

But the corruption in the South, real as it was, was hardly unique to the Reconstruction governments. Corruption was at least as rampant in the Northern states. And in both North and South, it was a result of the same thing:

a rapid economic expansion of government services (and revenues) that put new strains on (and new temptations before) elected officials everywhere. The end of Reconstruction did not end corruption in Southern state governments. In many states, in fact, corruption increased.

And the state expenditures of the Reconstruction years were huge only in comparison with the meager budgets of the antebellum era. They represented an effort to provide the South with desperately needed services that antebellum governments had never offered: public education, public works programs, poor relief, and other costly new commitments. There were, to be sure, graft and extravagance in Reconstruction governments; there were also positive and permanent accomplishments.

Education

Perhaps the most important of those accomplishments was a dramatic improvement in Southern education. In the first years of Reconstruction, much of the impetus for educational reform in the South came from outside groups—from the Freedmen's Bureau, from Northern private philanthropic organizations, from many Northern women, black and white, who traveled to the South to teach in freedmen's schools—and from black Southerners themselves. Over the opposition of many Southern whites, who feared that education would give African Americans "false notions of equality," these reformers established a large network of schools for former slaves—4,000 schools by 1870, staffed by 9,000 teachers (half of them black), teaching 200,000 students (about 12 percent of the total school-age population of the freedmen). In the 1870s, Reconstruction governments also began to build a comprehensive public school system in the South. By 1876, more than half of all white children and about 40 percent of all black children were attending schools in the South. Several black "academies," offering more advanced education, also began operating. Gradually, these academies grew into an important network of black colleges and universities, which included such distinguished schools as Fisk and Atlanta Universities and Morehouse College.

Already, however, Southern education was becoming divided into two separate systems, one black and one white. Early efforts to integrate the schools of the region were a dismal failure. The Freedmen's Bureau schools, for example, were open to students of all races, but almost no whites attended them. New Orleans set up an integrated school system under the Reconstruction government; again, whites almost universally stayed away. The one federal effort to mandate school integration—the Civil Rights Act of 1875—had its provisions for educational desegregation removed before it was passed. As soon as the Republican governments of Reconstruction were

Segregated Schools

replaced, the new Southern Democratic regimes quickly abandoned all efforts to promote integration.

Landownership and Tenancy

The most ambitious goal of the Freedmen's Bureau, and of some Republican Radicals in Congress, was to make Reconstruction the vehicle for a fundamental reform of landownership in the South. The effort failed. In the last years of the war and the first years of Reconstruction, the Freedmen's Bureau did oversee the redistribution of substantial amounts of land to freedmen in a few areas—notably the Sea Islands of South Carolina and Georgia, and areas of Mississippi that had once belonged to the family of Jefferson Davis. By June 1865, the bureau had settled nearly 10,000 black families on their own land—most of it drawn from abandoned plantations—arousing dreams among former slaves throughout the South of "forty acres and a mule." By the end of that year, however, the experiment was already collapsing. Southern plantation owners were returning and demanding the restoration of their property, and President Johnson was supporting their demands. Despite the resistance of the Freedmen's Bureau, the government eventually returned most of the confiscated land to the original white owners. Congress, moreover, never had much stomach for the idea of land redistribution.

Failure of Land Redistribution

Very few Northern Republicans believed that the federal government had the right to confiscate property. Even so, distribution of landownership in the South changed considerably in the postwar years. Among whites, there was a striking decline in landownership, from 80 percent before the war to 67 percent by the end of Reconstruction. Some whites lost their land because of unpaid debt or increased taxes; some left the marginal lands they had owned to move to more fertile areas, where they rented.

Among African Americans, during the same period, the proportion who owned land rose from virtually none to more than 20 percent. Many black landowners acquired their property through hard work or luck or both. But some relied on assistance from white-dominated financial or philanthropic institutions. One of them was the Freedman's Bank, established in 1865 by antislavery whites in an effort to promote landownership among African Americans. They persuaded thousands of freedmen to deposit their modest savings in the bank, but then invested heavily in unsuccessful enterprises. It was ill prepared, therefore, for the national depression of the 1870s and it failed in 1874.

Still, most blacks, and a growing minority of whites, did not own their own land during Reconstruction; and some who acquired land in the 1860s had lost it by the 1890s. These people worked for others in one form or another. Many African-American agricultural laborers—perhaps

Sharecropping

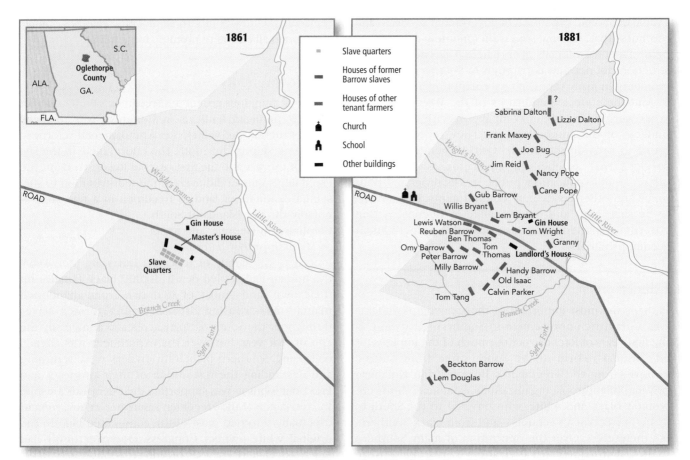

THE SOUTHERN PLANTATION BEFORE AND AFTER EMANCIPATION This map shows the distribution of lands and dwellings on the Barrow Plantation in Oglethorpe County, Georgia, before and after the emancipation of slaves at the close of the Civil War. The map on the left shows the plantation in 1861, as the war began. Like the Hopeton Plantation shown on p. 303, the Barrow plantation was highly centralized before the war, with slaves living all together in a complex of dwellings near the master's house. Twenty years later, as the map on the right shows, the same landscape was very differently divided. Housing was now widely dispersed, as former slaves became tenants or sharecroppers and began working their own small pieces of land and living more independently. Churches had sprung up away from the landowner's house as well. ◆ *Why did former slaves move so quickly to relocate their homes and churches away from their former masters?*

For an interactive version of this map, go to www.mhhe.com/brinkley13ech15maps

25 percent of the total—simply worked for wages. Most, however, became tenants of white landowners—working their own plots of land and paying their landlords either a fixed rent or a share of their crop (see pp. 428–430).

The new system represented a repudiation by former slaves of the gang-labor system of the antebellum plantation, in which slaves had lived and worked together under the direction of a master. As tenants and sharecroppers, African Americans enjoyed at least a physical independence from their landlords and had the sense of working their own land, even if in most cases they could never hope to buy it. But tenantry also benefited landlords in some ways, relieving them of any responsibility for the physical well-being of their workers.

The Crop-Lien System

In some respects, the postwar years were a period of remarkable economic progress for African Americans. If the material benefits they had received under slavery are

calculated as income, then prewar blacks had earned about a 22 percent share of the profits of the plantation system. By the end of Reconstruction, they were earning 56 percent. Measured another way, the per capita income of Southern blacks rose 46 percent between 1857 and 1879, while the per capita income of Southern whites declined 35 percent. This represented one of the most significant redistributions of income in American history.

But these figures are somewhat misleading. For one thing, while the black share of profits was increasing, the total profits of Southern agriculture were declining—a result of the dislocations of the war and a reduction in the world market for cotton. In addition, while African Americans were earning a greater return on each hour of labor than they had under slavery, they were working fewer hours. Women and children were less likely to labor in the fields than in the past. Adult men tended to work shorter days. In all, the black labor force worked about one-third fewer hours during Reconstruction than slaves had been compelled to work under slavery—a reduction that brought the working schedule of blacks roughly into line with that of white farm laborers. Nor did the income redistribution of the postwar years lift many African Americans out of poverty. Black per capita income rose from about one-quarter of white per capita income to about one-half in the first few years after the war. And after this initial increase, it rose hardly at all.

For blacks and poor whites alike, whatever gains there might have been as a result of land and income redistribution were often overshadowed by the ravages of the crop-lien system. Few of the traditional institutions of credit in the South—the "factors" and banks—returned after the war. In their stead emerged a new system of credit, centered in large part on local country stores, some of them owned by planters, others by independent merchants. Blacks and whites, landowners and tenants—all depended on these stores for such necessities as food, clothing, seed, and farm implements. And since farmers did not have the same steady cash flow as other workers, customers usually had to rely on credit from these merchants in order to purchase what they needed. Most local stores had no competition (and went to great lengths to ensure that things stayed that way). As a result, they were able to set interest rates as high as 50 or 60 percent. Farmers had to give the merchants a lien (or claim) on their crops as collateral for the loans (thus the term "crop-lien system"). Farmers who suffered a few bad years in a row, as often happened, could become trapped in a cycle of debt from which they could never escape.

New System of Credit

This burdensome credit system had a number of effects on the region, almost all of them unhealthy. One effect was that some blacks who had acquired land during the early years of Reconstruction gradually lost it as they fell into debt. So, to a lesser extent, did white small landowners. Another effect was that Southern farmers became almost wholly dependent on cash crops—and most of all on cotton—because only such marketable commodities seemed to offer any possibility of escape from debt. Thus Southern agriculture, never sufficiently diversified even in the best of times, became more one-dimensional than ever. The relentless planting of cotton, moreover, was contributing to an exhaustion of the soil. The crop-lien system, in other words, was not only helping to impoverish small farmers; it was also contributing to a general decline in the Southern agricultural economy.

The African-American Family in Freedom

One of the most striking features of the black response to Reconstruction was the effort to build or rebuild family structures and to protect them from the interference they had experienced under slavery. A major reason for the rapid departure of so many emancipated slaves from plantations was the desire to find lost relatives and reunite families. Thousands of African Americans wandered through the South—often over vast distances—looking for husbands, wives, children, or other relatives from whom they had been separated. In the few black newspapers that circulated in the South, there were many advertisements by people searching for information about their relatives. Former slaves rushed to have marriages, previously without legal standing, sanctified by church and law. Black families resisted living in the former slave quarters and moved instead to small cabins scattered widely across the countryside, where they could enjoy at least some privacy. Within the black family, the definition of male and female roles quickly came to resemble that within white

A VISIT FROM THE OLD MISTRESS Winslow Homer's 1876 painting of an imagined visit by a Southern white woman to a group of her former slaves was an effort to convey something of the tension in relations between the races in the South during Reconstruction. The women, once intimately involved in one another's lives, look at each other guardedly, carefully maintaining the space between them. White Southerners attacked the painting for portraying white and black women on a relatively equal footing. Some black Southerners criticized it for depicting poor rural African Americans instead of the more prosperous professional blacks who were emerging in Southern cities. "There were plenty of well-dressed negroes if he would but look for them," one wrote. *(National Museum of American Art, Smithsonian Institution. Gift of William T. Evans/Art Resource, NY)*

WASH DAY ON THE PLANTATION One of the most common occupations of women recently emancipated from slavery was taking in laundry from white families who no longer had slaves as household servants. This photograph of a group of African-American women illustrates how arduous a task laundry was. *(Library of Congress)*

families. Many women and children ceased working in the fields. Such work, they believed, was a badge of slavery. Instead, many women restricted themselves largely to domestic tasks—cooking, cleaning, gardening, raising children, attending to the needs of their husbands. Some black husbands refused to allow their wives to work as servants in white homes. "When I married my wife I married her to wait on me," one freedman told a former master who was attempting to hire his wife as a servant. "She got all she can do right here for me and the children."

Still, middle-class notions of domesticity were often difficult to sustain in the impoverished circumstances of most former slaves. Economic

Changing Gender Roles

necessity required many black women to engage in income-producing activities, including activities that they and their husbands resisted because

they reminded them of slavery: working as domestic servants, taking in laundry, or helping in the field. By the end of Reconstruction, half of all black women over the age of sixteen were working for wages. And unlike white working women, most black female income-earners were married.

THE GRANT ADMINISTRATION

Exhausted by the political turmoil of the Johnson administration, American voters in 1868 yearned for a strong, stable figure to guide them through the troubled years of Reconstruction. They turned trustingly to General Ulysses S. Grant, the hero of the war and, by 1868, a revered national idol.

The Soldier President

Grant could have had the nomination of either party in 1868. But believing that Republican Reconstruction poli-

U. S. Grant

cies were more popular in the North, he accepted the Republican nomination. The Democrats nominated former governor Horatio Seymour of New York. The campaign was a bitter one, and Grant's triumph was surprisingly narrow. Without the 500,000 new black Republican voters in the South, he would have had a minority of the popular vote.

Grant entered the White House with no political experience, and his performance was clumsy and ineffectual from the start. Except for Hamilton Fish, whom Grant appointed secretary of state and who served for eight years with great distinction, most members of the cabinet were ill equipped for their tasks. Grant relied chiefly, and increasingly, on established party leaders—the group most ardently devoted to patronage—and his administration used the spoils system even more blatantly than most of its predecessors, embittering reform-minded members of his party. Grant also alienated the many Northerners who were growing disillusioned with Radical Reconstruction policies, which the president continued to support. Some Republicans suspected, correctly, that there was also corruption in the Grant administration itself.

By the end of Grant's first term, therefore, members of a substantial faction of the party—who referred to them-

Liberal Republicans

selves as Liberal Republicans— had come to oppose what they called "Grantism." In 1872, hoping to prevent Grant's reelection, they bolted the party and nominated their own presidential candidate: Horace Greeley, veteran editor and publisher of the *New York Tribune*. The Democrats, somewhat reluctantly, named Greeley their candidate as well, hoping that the alliance with the Liberals would enable them to defeat Grant. But the effort was in vain. Grant won a substantial victory, polling 286 electoral votes to Greeley's 66, and nearly 56 percent of the popular total.

The Grant Scandals

During the 1872 campaign, the first of a series of political scandals came to light that would plague Grant and the

Crédit Mobilier

Republicans for years. It involved the Crédit Mobilier construction company, which had helped build the Union Pacific Railroad. The heads of Crédit Mobilier had used their positions as Union Pacific stockholders to steer large fraudulent contracts to their construction company, thus bilking the Union Pacific (and the federal government, which provided large subsidies to the railroad) of millions. To prevent investigations, the directors had given Crédit Mobilier stock to key members of Congress. But in 1872, Congress did conduct an investigation, which revealed that some highly placed Republicans—including Schuyler Colfax, now Grant's vice president—had accepted stock.

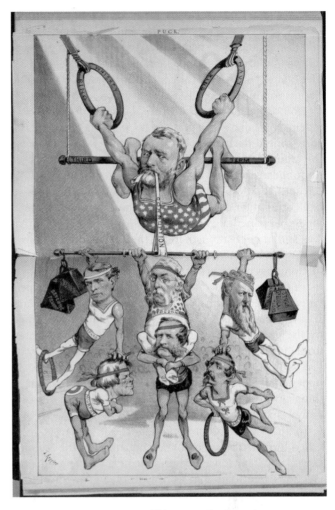

GRANT THE TRAPEZE ARTISTS This cartoon by the eminent cartoonist Joseph Keppler shows President Ulysses S. Grant swinging on a trapeze holding on to the "whiskey ring" and the "navy ring" (references to two of the many scandals that plagued his presidency). Using a strap labeled "corruption," he holds aloft some of the most notorious figures in those scandals. The cartoon was published in 1880, when Grant was attempting to win the Republican nomination to run for another term as president. *(Library of Congress)*

One dreary episode followed another in Grant's second term. Benjamin H. Bristow, Grant's third Treasury secretary, discovered that some of his officials and a group of distillers operating as a "whiskey ring" were cheating the government out of taxes by filing false reports. Then a House investigation revealed that William W. Belknap, secretary of war, had accepted bribes to retain an Indian-post trader in office (the so-called Indian ring). Other, lesser scandals added to the growing impression that "Grantism" had brought rampant corruption to government.

The Greenback Question

Compounding Grant's, and the nation's, problems was a financial crisis, known as the Panic of 1873. It began with

Panic of 1873

the failure of a leading investment banking firm, Jay Cooke and Company, which had invested too heavily in postwar railroad building. There had been panics before—in 1819, 1837, and 1857—but this was the worst one yet. The depression it produced lasted four years.

Debtors now pressured the government to redeem federal war bonds with greenbacks, paper currency of the sort printed during the Civil War, which would increase the amount of money in circulation. But Grant and most Republicans wanted a "sound" currency—based solidly on gold reserves—which would favor the interests of banks and other creditors. There was approximately $356 million in paper currency issued during the Civil War that was still in circulation. In 1873, the Treasury issued more in response to the panic. But in 1875, Republican leaders in Congress, in an effort to crush the greenback movement for good, passed the Specie Resumption Act. It provided that after January 1, 1879, the greenback dollars, whose value constantly fluctuated, would be redeemed by the government and replaced with new certificates, firmly pegged to the price of gold. The law satisfied creditors, who had worried that debts would be repaid in paper currency of uncertain value. But "resumption" made things more difficult for debtors, because the gold-based money supply could not easily expand.

In 1875, the "greenbackers," as the inflationists were called, formed their own political organization: the National Greenback Party. It was active in the next three presidential elections, but it failed to gain widespread support. It did,

National Greenback Party

however, keep the money issue alive. The question of the proper composition of the currency was to remain one of the most controversial and enduring issues in late-nineteenth-century American politics.

Republican Diplomacy

The Johnson and Grant administrations achieved their greatest successes in foreign affairs. The accomplishments were the work not of the presidents themselves, who displayed little aptitude for diplomacy, but of two outstanding secretaries of state: William H. Seward, who had served Lincoln and who remained in office until 1869; and Hamilton Fish, who served throughout the two terms of the Grant administration.

An ardent expansionist, Seward acted with as much daring as the demands of Reconstruction politics and

"Seward's Folly"

the Republican hatred of President Johnson would permit. Seward accepted a Russian offer to sell Alaska to the United States for $7.2 million, despite criticism from many who considered Alaska a frozen wasteland and derided it as "Seward's Folly." In 1867, Seward also engineered the American annexation of the tiny Midway Islands, west of Hawaii.

Alabama Claims

Hamilton Fish's first major challenge was resolving the longstanding controversy with England over the American claims that the British government had violated neutrality laws during the Civil War by permitting English shipyards to build ships (among them the *Alabama*) for the Confederacy. American demands that England pay for the damage these vessels had caused became known as the "*Alabama* claims." In 1871, after a number of failed efforts, Fish forged an agreement, the Treaty of Washington, which provided for international arbitration and in which Britain expressed regret for the "escape" of the *Alabama* from England.

THE ABANDONMENT OF RECONSTRUCTION

As the North grew increasingly preoccupied with its own political and economic problems, interest in Reconstruction began to wane. The Grant administration continued to protect Republican governments in the South, but less because of any interest in ensuring the position of freedmen than because of a desire to prevent the reemergence of a strong Democratic Party in the region. But even the presence of federal troops was not enough to prevent white Southerners from overturning the Reconstruction regimes. By the time Grant left office, Democrats had taken back (or, as white Southerners liked to put it, "redeemed") the governments of seven of the eleven former Confederate states. For three other states—South Carolina, Louisiana, and Florida—the end of Reconstruction had to wait for the withdrawal of the last federal troops in 1876, a withdrawal that was the result of a long process of political bargaining and compromise at the national level. (One former Confederate state, Tennessee, had never been part of the Reconstruction process because it had ratified the Fourteenth Amendment and rejoined the Union in 1866.)

The Southern States "Redeemed"

In the states where whites constituted a majority—the states of the upper South—overthrowing Republican control was relatively simple. By 1872, all but a handful of Southern whites had regained suffrage. Now a clear majority of the electorate, they needed only to organize and vote for their candidates.

In other states, where African Americans were a majority or the black and white populations were almost equal, whites used intimidation and violence to undermine the Reconstruction regimes. Secret societies—the Ku Klux Klan, the Knights of the White Camellia, and others—used terrorism to frighten or physically bar blacks from voting or otherwise exercising citizenship. Paramilitary organizations—the Red Shirts and White Leagues—armed themselves to "police" elections and worked to force all white males to join the Democratic Party and to exclude all African Americans from meaningful political activity.

The Ku Klux Klan was the largest and most effective of these organizations. Formed in 1866 and led by former Confederate general Nathan Bed-

Ku Klux Klan

ford Forrest, it gradually absorbed many of the smaller terrorist organizations. Its leaders devised rituals, costumes, secret languages, and other airs of mystery to create a bond among its members and make it seem even more terrifying to those it was attempting to intimidate. The Klan's "midnight rides"—bands of men clad in white sheets and masks, their horses covered with white robes and with hooves muffled—created terror in black communities throughout the South.

Many white Southerners considered the Klan and the other secret societies and paramilitary groups proud, patriotic societies. Together such groups served, in effect, as a military force (even if a decentralized and poorly organized one) continuing the battle against Northern rule. They worked in particular to advance the interests of those with the most to gain from a restoration of white supremacy—above all the planter class and the Southern Democratic Party. Even stronger than the Klan in discouraging black political power, however, was the simple weapon of economic pressure. Some planters refused to rent land to Republican blacks; storekeepers refused to extend them credit; employers refused to give them work.

The Ku Klux Klan Acts

The Republican Congress tried for a time to turn back this new wave of white repression. In 1870 and 1871, it

Enforcement Acts

passed two Enforcement Acts, also known as the Ku Klux Klan Acts, which were in many ways the most radical measures of the era. The Enforcement Acts prohibited the states from discriminating against voters on the basis of race and gave the federal government power to supersede the state courts and prosecute violations of the law. It was the first time the federal government had ever claimed the power to prosecute crimes by individuals under federal law. Federal district attorneys were now empowered to take action against conspiracies to deny African Americans such rights as voting, holding office, and serving on juries. The new laws also authorized the president to use the military to protect civil rights and to suspend the right of habeas corpus when violations of the rights seemed particularly egregious. In October 1871, President Grant used this provision of the law when he declared a "state of lawlessness" in nine counties in South Carolina and sent in federal troops to occupy the area. Hundreds of suspected Klan members were arrested; some were held for long periods without trial; some were eventually convicted under the law and sent to jail.

The Enforcement Acts were seldom used as severely as they were in South Carolina, but they were effective in

Decline of the Klan

the effort by blacks and Northern whites to weaken the Klan. By 1872, Klan violence against blacks was in decline throughout the region.

Waning Northern Commitment

The Ku Klux Klan Acts marked the peak of Republican commitment to enforce the new rights Reconstruction was extending to black citizens. But that commitment did not last for very long. Southern blacks were gradually losing the support of many of their former backers in the North. As early as 1870, after the adoption of the Fifteenth Amendment, some reformers convinced themselves that their long campaign on behalf of black people was now over—that with the vote, African Americans ought to be able to take care of themselves. Over the next several years, former Radical leaders such as Charles Sumner and Horace Greeley now began calling themselves Liberals, cooperating with Democrats, and at times outdoing even the Democrats in denouncing what they viewed as black and carpetbag misgovernment. Within the South itself, many white Republicans joined the Liberals and eventually moved into the Democratic Party.

The Panic of 1873 further undermined support for Reconstruction. This economic crisis spurred Northern industrialists and their allies to find an explanation for the poverty and instability around them.

Impact of Social Darwinism

They found it in a new idea known as "Social Darwinism" (see p. 451–452), a harsh theory that argued that individuals who failed did so because of their own weakness and "unfitness." Those influenced by Social Darwinism came to view the large number of unemployed vagrants in the North—and poor African Americans in the South—as irredeemable misfits. Social Darwinism also encouraged a broad critique of government intervention in social and economic life, which further weakened commitment to the Reconstruction program. Support for land redistribution, never great, and willingness to spend money from the depleted federal treasury to aid the freedmen, waned quickly after 1873. State and local governments also found themselves short of funds, and rushed to cut back on social services—which in the South meant the end of almost all services to the former slaves.

In the congressional elections of 1874, the Democrats won control of the House of Representatives for the first time since 1861. Grant took note of the changing temper of the North and made use of military force to prop up the Republican regimes that were still standing in the South. By the end of 1876, only three states were left in the hands of the Republicans—South Carolina, Louisiana, and Florida. In state elections that year, Democrats (after using terrorist tactics) claimed victory in all three. But the Republicans challenged the results and claimed victory as well, and they were able to remain in office because of the presence of federal troops. Without federal troops, it was now clear, the last of the Republican regimes would quickly fall.

RECONSTRUCTION

Debate over the nature of Reconstruction—not only among historians, but among the public at large—has created so much controversy over the decades that one scholar, writing in 1959, described the issue as a "dark and bloody ground." Among historians, the passions of the debate have to some extent subsided since then; but in the popular mind, Reconstruction continues to raise "dark and bloody" images.

For many years, a relatively uniform and highly critical view of Reconstruction prevailed among historians, a reflection of broad currents in popular thought. By the late nineteenth century, most white Americans in both the North and the South had come to believe that few real differences any longer divided the sections, that the nation should strive for a genuine reconciliation. And most white Americans believed as well in the superiority of their race, in the inherent unfitness of African Americans for political or social equality. Out of this mentality was born the first major historical interpretation of Reconstruction, through the work of William A. Dunning. In *Reconstruction, Political and Economic* (1907), Dunning portrayed Reconstruction as a corrupt outrage perpetrated on the prostrate South by a vicious and vindictive cabal of Northern Republican Radicals. Reconstruction governments were based on "bayonet rule." Unscrupulous and self-aggrandizing carpetbaggers flooded the South to profit from the misery of the defeated region. Ignorant, illiterate blacks were thrust into positions of power for which they were entirely unfit. The Reconstruction experiment, a moral abomination from its first moments, survived only because of the determination of the Republican Party to keep itself in power. (Some later writers, notably Howard K. Beale, added an economic motive—to protect Northern business interests.) Dunning and his many students (who together formed what became known as the "Dunning school") compiled state-by-state evidence to show that the legacy of Reconstruction was corruption, ruinous taxation, and astronomical increases in the public debt.

The Dunning school not only shaped the views of several generations of historians. It also reflected and helped to shape the views of much of the public. Popular depictions of Reconstruction for years to come (as first the 1915 film *The Birth of a Nation* and then the 1936 book and 1939 movie *Gone with the Wind* illustrated) portrayed the era as one of tragic exploitation of the South by the North. Even today, many white southerners and others continue to accept the basic premises of the Dunning interpretation. Among historians, however, the old view of Reconstruction has gradually lost credibility.

The great African-American scholar W. E. B. Du Bois was among the first to challenge the Dunning view in a 1910 article and, later, in a 1935 book, *Black Reconstruction*. To him, Reconstruction politics in the Southern states had been an effort on the part of the masses, black and white, to create a more democratic society. The misdeeds of the Reconstruction governments, he claimed, had been greatly exaggerated, and their achievements overlooked. The governments had been expensive,

(U.S. Army Military History Institute, Carlisle, Pennsylvania. Photo by Jim Enos)

he insisted, because they had tried to provide public education and other public services on a scale never before attempted in the South. But Du Bois' use of Marxist theory in his work caused many historians to dismiss his argument; and it remained for a group of less radical, white historians to shatter the Dunning image of Reconstruction.

In the 1940s, historians such as C. Vann Woodward, David Herbert Donald, Thomas B. Alexander, and others began to reexamine the Reconstruction governments in the South and to suggest that their records were not nearly as bad as most historians had previously assumed. They also looked at the Radical Republicans in Congress and suggested that they had not

The Compromise of 1877

Grant had hoped to run for another term in 1876, but most Republican leaders—shaken by recent Democrat successes, afraid of the scandals with which Grant was associated, and concerned about the president's failing health—resisted. Instead, they sought a candidate not associated with the problems of the Grant years, one who might entice Liberals back and unite the party again. They settled

Hayes Versus Tilden

on Rutherford B. Hayes of Ohio, a former Union army officer, governor, and congressman, champion of civil service reform. The Democrats united behind Samuel J. Tilden, the reform governor of New York who had been instrumental in challenging the corrupt Tweed Ring of New York City's Tammany Hall.

Although the campaign was a bitter one, there were few differences of principle between the candidates, both of whom were conservatives committed to moderate been motivated by vindictiveness and partisanship alone.

By the early 1960s, a new view of Reconstruction was emerging from these efforts, a view whose appeal to historians grew stronger with the emergence of the "Second Reconstruction," the civil rights movement. The revisionist approach was summarized by John Hope Franklin in *Reconstruction After the Civil War* (1961) and Kenneth Stampp in *The Era of Reconstruction* (1965), who claimed that the postwar Republicans had been engaged in a genuine, if flawed, effort to solve the problem of race in the South by providing much-needed protection to the freedmen. The Reconstruction governments, for all their faults, had been bold experiments in interracial politics. The congressional Radicals were not saints, but they had displayed a genuine concern for the rights of slaves. Andrew Johnson was not a martyred defender of the Constitution, but an inept, racist politician who resisted reasonable compromise and brought the government to a crisis. There had been no such thing as "bayonet rule" or "Negro rule" in the South. African Americans had played only a small part in Reconstruction governments and had generally acquitted themselves well. The Reconstruction regimes had, in fact, brought important progress to the South, establishing the region's first public school system and other important social changes. Corruption in the South had been no worse than corruption in the North at that time. What was tragic about Reconstruction, the revisionist view claimed, was not what it did to Southern whites but what it did not do for Southern blacks. By stopping short of the reforms necessary to ensure blacks genuine equality, Reconstruction had consigned them

(Library of Congress)

to more than a century of injustice and discrimination.

In later years, scholars began to question the revisionist view—not in an effort to revive the old Dunning interpretation but, rather, in an attempt to draw attention to those things Reconstruction in fact achieved. Eric Foner, in *Nothing but Freedom* (1983) and *Reconstruction: America's Unfinished Revolution* (1988), concluded that what is striking about the American experience in this period is not how little was accomplished, but how far the former slaves moved toward freedom and independence in a short time, and how large a role African Americans themselves played in shaping Reconstruction. During Reconstruction, blacks won a certain amount of legal and political power in the South; and even though they held that power only temporarily, they used it for a time to strengthen

their economic and social positions and to win a position of limited but genuine independence. Through Reconstruction they won, if not equality, a measure of individual and community autonomy, building blocks of the freedom that emancipation alone had not guaranteed.

Historians writing from the perspective of African-American and women's history have made related arguments. Leon Litwack's *Been in the Storm So Long* (1979) maintained that former slaves used the relative latitude they enjoyed under Reconstruction to build a certain independence for themselves within Southern society. They strengthened their churches; they reunited their families; they refused to work in the "gang-labor" system of the plantations and forced the creation of a new labor system in which they had more control over their own lives. Amy Dru Stanley and Jacqueline Jones have both argued that the freed slaves displayed considerable independence in constructing their households on their own terms and asserting their control over family life, reproduction, and work. Women in particular sought the opportunity, according to Jacqueline Jones in *Labor of Love, Labor of Sorrow* (1985), "to labor on behalf of their own families and kin within the protected spheres of household and community."

But Reconstruction, some historians have begun to argue, was not restricted to the South alone. Heather Richardson, in *West from Appomattox* (2007) and *The Death of Reconstruction* (2001), shows how the entire nation changed during and as a result of the Civil War and Reconstruction—with the South, perhaps, changing least of all. The age of Reconstruction was also the age of western expansion and industrialization.

reform. The November election produced an apparent Democratic victory. Tilden carried the South and several large Northern states, and his popular margin over Hayes was nearly 300,000 votes. But disputed returns from Louisiana, South Carolina, Florida, and Oregon, whose total electoral vote was 20, threw the election in doubt. Tilden had undisputed claim to 184 electoral votes, only one short of a majority. But Hayes could still win if he managed to receive all 20 disputed votes.

The Constitution had established no method to determine the validity of disputed returns. It was clear that the decision lay with Congress, but it was not clear with which house or through what method. (The Senate was Republican, the House, Democratic.) Members of each party naturally supported a solution that would yield them the victory.

Finally, late in January 1877, Congress tried to break the deadlock by creating a special electoral commission to

Special Electoral Commission

judge the disputed votes. The commission was to be composed of five senators, five representatives, and five justices of the Supreme Court. The congressional delegation would consist of five Republicans and five Democrats. The Court delegation would include two Republicans, two Democrats, and an independent. But the independent seat ultimately went to a justice whose real sympathies were with the Republicans. The commission voted along straight party lines, 8 to 7, awarding every disputed vote to Hayes. Congress accepted their verdict on March 2. Two days later, Hayes was inaugurated.

Behind the resolution of the deadlock, however, lay a series of elaborate compromises among leaders of both parties. When a Democratic filibuster threatened to derail the commission's report, Republican Senate leaders met secretly with Southern Democratic leaders to work out terms by which the Democrats would allow the election of Hayes. According to traditional accounts, Republicans and Southern Democrats met at Washington's Wormley Hotel. In return for a Republican pledge that Hayes would withdraw the last federal troops from the South, thus permitting the overthrow of the last Republican governments there, the Southerners agreed to abandon the filibuster.

Actually, the story behind the "Compromise of 1877" is somewhat more complex. Hayes was already on record

Compromise of 1877

favoring withdrawal of the troops, so Republicans needed to offer more than that if they hoped for Democratic support. The

real agreement, the one that won over the Southern Democrats, was reached well before the Wormley meeting. As the price of their cooperation, the Southern Democrats (among them some former Whigs) exacted several pledges from the Republicans in addition to withdrawal of the troops: the appointment of at least one Southerner to the Hayes cabinet, control of federal patronage in their areas, generous internal improvements, and federal aid for the Texas and Pacific Railroad. Many powerful Southern Democrats supported industrializing their region. They believed Republican programs of federal support for business would aid the South more than the states' rights policies of the Democrats.

In his inaugural address, Hayes announced that the South's most pressing need was the restoration of "wise, honest, and peaceful local self-government"—a signal that he planned to withdraw federal troops and let white Democrats take over the state governments. That statement, and Hayes's subsequent actions, supported the widespread charges that he was paying off the South for acquiescing in his election and strengthened those who referred to him as "his Fraudulency." Hayes tried to counter such charges by projecting an image of stern public (and private) rectitude. But the election had already created such bitterness that even Hayes's promise to serve only one term could not mollify his critics.

The president and his party had hoped to build up a "new Republican" organization in the South drawn from Whiggish conservative white groups and committed to some modest acceptance of African-American rights. But all such efforts failed. Although many white Southern leaders sympathized with Republican

Republican Failure in the South

economic policies, popular resentment of Reconstruction was so deep that supporting the party was politically impossible. At the same time, the withdrawal of federal troops signaled that the national government was giving up its attempts to control Southern politics and to improve the lot of African Americans in Southern society.

The Legacies of Reconstruction

Reconstruction made some important contributions to the efforts of former slaves to achieve dignity and equality in American life. And it was not as disastrous an experience for Southern whites as most believed at the time. But Reconstruction was in the end largely a failure, for in those years the United States abandoned its first serious effort to resolve its oldest and deepest social problem— the problem of race. Moreover, the experience so disappointed, disillusioned, and embittered white Americans that it would be nearly a century before they would try again in any serious way.

Why did this great assault on racial injustice not achieve more? In part, it was because of the weaknesses and errors of the people who directed it. But in greater part, it was because

Ideological Limits

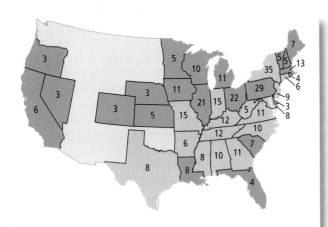

Candidate (Party)	Electoral Vote	Popular Vote (%)
Rutherford B. Hayes (Republican)	185	4,036,298 (48)
Samuel J. Tilden (Democratic)	184	4,300,590 (51)

81.8% of electorate voting

THE ELECTION OF 1876 The election of 1876 was one of the most controversial in American history. As in the elections of 1824, 1888, and 2000, the winner of the popular vote—Samuel J. Tilden—was not the winner of the electoral college, which he lost by one vote. The final decision as to who would be president was not made until the day before the official inauguration in March. ◆ *How did the Republicans turn this apparent defeat into a victory?*

For an interactive version of this map, go to www.mhhe.com/brinkley13ech15maps

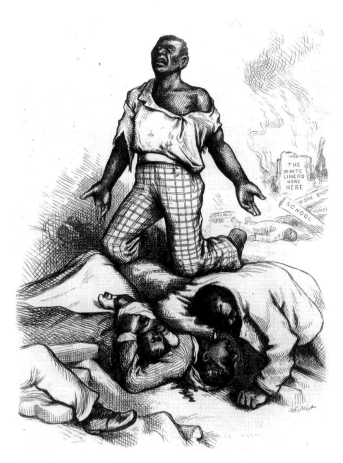

"IS *THIS* A REPUBLICAN FORM OF GOVERNMENT?" The New York artist and cartoonist Thomas Nast marked the end of Reconstruction in 1876 with this biting cartoon in *Harper's Weekly,* expressing his dismay at what he considered the nation's betrayal of the former slaves, who still had not received adequate guarantees of their rights. The caption of the cartoon continued: "Is *this* protecting life, liberty, or property? Is *this* equal protection of the laws?" *(Courtesy of The Newberry Library, Chicago)*

attempts to produce solutions ran up against conservative obstacles so deeply embedded in the nation's life that they could not be dislodged. Veneration of the Constitution sharply limited the willingness of national leaders to infringe on the rights of states and individuals. A profound respect for private property and free enterprise prevented any real assault on economic privilege in the South. Above all, perhaps, a pervasive belief among many of even the most liberal whites that African Americans were inherently inferior served as an obstacle to equality. Given the context within which Americans of the 1860s and 1870s were working, what is surprising, perhaps, is not that Reconstruction did so little, but that it did even as much as it did.

Considering the odds confronting them, therefore, African Americans had reason for pride in the gains they were able to make during Reconstruction. And future generations had reason for gratitude for two great charters of freedom—the Fourteenth and Fifteenth Amendments to the Constitution—which, although largely ignored at the time, would one day serve as the basis for a "Second

Reconstruction" that would renew the drive to bring freedom and equality to all Americans.

THE NEW SOUTH

The agreement between southern Democrats and northern Republicans that helped settle the disputed election of 1876 was supposed to be the first step toward developing a stable, permanent Republican Party in the South. In that respect, at least, it failed. In the years following the end of Reconstruction, white southerners established the Democratic Party as the only viable political organization for the region's whites. Even so, the South did change in the years after Reconstruction in some of the ways the framers of the Compromise of 1877 had hoped.

The "Redeemers"

By the end of 1877—after the last withdrawal of federal troops—every southern state government had been "redeemed" by white Democrats. Many white southerners rejoiced   Bourbon Rule
at the restoration of what they liked to call "home rule." But in reality, political power in the region was soon more restricted than at any time since the Civil War. Once again, the South fell under the control of a powerful, conservative oligarchy, whose members were known variously as the "Redeemers" (to themselves and their supporters) or the "Bourbons" (a term for aristocrats used by some of their critics).

In a few places, this post-Reconstruction ruling class was much the same as the ruling class of the antebellum period. In Alabama, for example, the old planter elite—despite challenges from new merchant and industrial forces—retained much of its former power and continued largely to dominate the state for decades. In most areas, however, the Redeemers constituted a genuinely new ruling class. They were merchants, industrialists, railroad developers, and financiers. Some of them were former planters, some of them northern immigrants who had become absorbed into the region's life, some of them ambitious, upwardly mobile white southerners from the region's lower social tiers. They combined a commitment to "home rule" and social conservatism with a commitment to economic development.

The various Bourbon governments of the New South behaved in many respects quite similarly to one another. Conservatives had complained that the Reconstruction governments fostered widespread corruption, but the Redeemer regimes were, if anything, even more awash in waste and fraud. (In this, they were little different from governments in every region of the country.) At the same time, virtually all the new Democratic regimes lowered taxes, reduced spending, and drastically diminished state services—including many of the most important accomplishments of Reconstruction. In one state after another, for example, state support for public school systems was

THE MINSTREL SHOW

The minstrel show was one of the most popular forms of entertainment in America in the second half of the nineteenth century. It was also a testament to the high awareness of race (and the high level of racism) in American society both before and after the Civil War. At the same time, however, African-American performers themselves formed their own minstrel shows and transformed them, at least to a degree, into vehicles for training black entertainers and developing important new forms of music and dance.

Before and during the Civil War, minstrel shows consisted almost entirely of white performers who blackened their faces with cork and presented grotesque stereotypes of the slave culture of the American South. Among the most popular of the stumbling, ridiculously ignorant characters invented for these shows were such figures as "Zip Coon" and "Jim Crow" (whose name later resurfaced as a label for late-nineteenth-century segregation laws). A typical minstrel show presented a group of seventeen or more men seated in a semicircle facing the audience. The man in the center ran the show, played the straight man for the jokes of others, and led the music—lively dances and sentimental ballads played on banjos, castanets, and other instruments and sung by soloists or the entire group.

The shows were popular in the South, but they were particularly popular in the North, where black life was less familiar and more exotic and where white audiences (who, whatever their views of slavery, generally held a low opinion of African Americans) reveled in the demeaning portrayals of slaves. White minstrel performers were so invested in portraying the stupidity and inferiority of blacks that they lashed out savagely at abolitionists and antislavery activists and, during the Civil War, portrayed black soldiers as incompetents and cowards—creating a military stereotype as insulting and inaccurate as the stereotypes they had used to portray slaves.

After the Civil War, white minstrels began to expand their repertoire. Drawing from the famous and successful freak shows of P.T. Barnum and other entertainment entrepreneurs, some began to include Siamese twins, bearded ladies, and even a supposedly 8-foot 2-inch "Chinese giant" in their shows. They also incorporated sex, both by including women in some shows and, even more popularly, by recruiting female impersonators. One

MINSTRELSY AT HIGH TIDE The Primrose & West minstrel troupe—a lavish and expensive entertainment that drew large crowds in the 1800s—was one of many companies to offer this brand of entertainment to eager audiences all over the country. Although minstrelsy began with white musicians performing in blackface, the popularity of real African-American minstrels encouraged the impresarios of the troupe to include groups of white and black performers alike. (*©Collection of the New-York Historical Society*)

---

reduced or eliminated. "Schools are not a necessity," an economy-conscious governor of Virginia commented.

By the late 1870s, significant dissenting groups were challenging the Bourbons: protesting the cuts in services and denouncing the commitment of the Redeemer governments to paying off the prewar and Reconstruction debts in full, at the original (usually high) rates of interest. In Virginia, for example, a vigorous "Readjuster" movement emerged, demanding that the state revise its debt payment procedures so as to make more money available for state services. In 1879, the Readjusters won control of the legislature, and in the next few years they captured the governorship and a U.S. Senate seat. Other states produced similar movements, some of them adding demands as well for greenbacks, debt relief, and other economic reforms. (A few such independent movements included significant numbers of African Americans in their ranks, but all consisted primarily of lower-income whites.) By the mid-1880s, however, conservative southerners—largely by exploiting racial prejudice—had effectively destroyed most of the dissenting movements.

The Readjuster Challenge

THE ELECTRIC 3 MINSTRELS For every large troupe such as Primrose & West there were dozens of smaller traveling minstrel bands such as Callan, Haley, and Callan's shown here on the road in the 1880s. In concert, these men performed in exaggerated blackface. Posing for photographs, they tried to exhibit sober, middle-class respectability. *(Brown Brothers)*

While the black minstrel shows had few openly political aims, they did help develop some important forms of African-American entertainment and transform them into a part of the national culture. Black minstrels introduced new forms of dance, derived from the informal traditions of slavery and black community life: the "buck and wing," the "stop time," and the "Virginia essence," which established the foundations for the tap and jazz dancing of the early twentieth century. They also improvised musically and began experimenting with forms that over time contributed to the growth of ragtime, jazz, and rhythm and blues.

Eventually, black minstrelsy—like its white counterpart—evolved into other forms of theater, including the beginnings of serious black drama. At Ambrose Park in Brooklyn in the 1890s, for example, the celebrated black comedian Sam Lucas (a veteran of the minstrel circuit) starred in the play *Darkest America,* which one black newspaper later described as a "delineation of Negro life, carrying the race through all their historical phases from the plantation, into reconstruction days and finally painting our people as they are today, cultured and accomplished in the social graces, [holding] the mirror faithfully up to nature."

But interest in the minstrel show did not die altogether. In 1927, Hollywood released *The Jazz Singer,* the first feature film with sound. It was about the career of a white minstrel performer, and its star was one of the most popular singers of the twentieth century: Al Jolson, whose career had begun on the blackface minstrel circuit years before.

of the most successful minstrel performers of the 1870s was Francis Leon, who delighted crowds with his portrayal of a flamboyant "prima donna."

One reason white minstrels began to move in these new directions was that they were now facing competition from black performers, who could provide more authentic versions of black music, dance, and humor, and usually bring more talent to the task. The Georgia Minstrels, organized in 1865, was one of the first all-black minstrel troupes, and it had great success in attracting white audiences in the Northeast for several years. By the 1870s, touring African-American minstrel groups were numerous. The black minstrels used many of the conventions of the white shows. There were dances, music, comic routines, and sentimental recitations. Some black performers even chalked their faces to make themselves look as dark as the white blackface performers with whom they were competing. Black minstrels sometimes denounced slavery (at least indirectly) and did not often speak demeaningly of the capacities of their race. But they could not entirely escape caricaturing African-American life as they struggled to meet the expectations of their white audiences.

Industrialization and the "New South"

Some white southern leaders in the post-Reconstruction era hoped to see their region become the home of a vigorous industrial economy. The South had lost the war, such leaders argued, because its economy had been unable to compete with the modernized manufacturing capacity of the North. Now the region must "out-Yankee the Yankees" and build a "New South." Henry Grady, editor of the *Atlanta Constitution,* and other prominent spokesmen for a New South seldom challenged white supremacy, but

Henry Grady

they did advocate other important changes in southern values. Above all, they promoted the virtues of thrift, industry, and progress—qualities that prewar southerners had often denounced in northern society. "We have sown towns and cities in the place of theories," Grady boasted to a New England audience in the 1880s, "and put business above politics. . . . We have fallen in love with work." But even the most fervent advocates of the New South creed were generally unwilling to break entirely with the southern past. That was evident in, among other things, the popular literature of the region. At the same time that white southern writers were extolling the virtues of industrialization in newspaper editorials and speeches, they were painting nostalgic portraits of the Old South in their literature. Few southerners advocated a literal return to the old ways, but most whites eagerly embraced romantic talk of the "Lost Cause." And they responded warmly to the local-color fiction of such writers as Joel Chandler Harris, whose folk tales—the most famous being *Uncle Remus* (1880)—portrayed the slave society of the antebellum years as a harmonious world marked by engaging dialect and close emotional bonds between the races. The writer Thomas Nelson Page similarly extolled the old Virginia aristocracy. The growing popularity of minstrel shows also reflected the romanticization of the Old South (see "Patterns of Popular Culture"). The white leaders of the New South, in short, faced their future with one foot still in the past.

Even so, New South enthusiasts did help southern industry expand dramatically in the years after Reconstruction and become a more important part of the region's economy than ever before. Most visible was the growth in textile manufacturing, which increased ninefold in the last twenty years of the century. In the past, southern planters had usually shipped their cotton out of the region to manufacturers in the North or in Europe. Now textile factories appeared in the South itself—many of them drawn to the region from New England by the abundance of water power, the ready supply of cheap labor, the low taxes, and the accommodating conservative governments. The tobacco-processing industry, similarly, established an important foothold in the region, largely through the work of James B. Duke of North Carolina, whose American Tobacco Company established for a time a virtual monopoly over the processing of raw tobacco into marketable materials. In the lower South, and particularly in Birmingham, Alabama, the iron (and, later, steel) industry grew rapidly. By 1890, the southern iron and steel industry represented nearly a fifth of the nation's total capacity.

Railroad development increased substantially in the post-Reconstruction years—at a rate far greater than that of the nation at large. Between 1880 and 1890, trackage in the South more than doubled. And the South took a major step toward integrating its transportation system with that of the rest of the country when, in 1886, it changed the gauge (width) of its trackage to correspond with the standards of the North. Yet southern industry developed within strict limits, and its effects on the region were never even remotely comparable to the effects of industrialization on the North. The southern share of national manufacturing doubled in the last twenty years of the century, to 10 percent of the total. But that percentage was the same the South had claimed in 1860; the region, in other words, had done no more than regain what it

Railroad Development

had lost during the war and its aftermath. The region's per capita income increased 21 percent in the same period. But at the end of the century, average income in the South was only 40 percent of that in the North; in 1860 it had been more than 60 percent. And even in those areas where development had been most rapid—textiles, iron, railroads—much of the capital had come from the North. In effect, the South was developing a colonial economy.

The growth of industry in the South required the region to recruit a substantial industrial work force for the first time. From the beginning, a high percentage of the factory workers (and an especially high percentage of textile workers) were women. Heavy male casualties in the Civil War had helped create a large population of unmarried women who desperately needed employment. Factories also hired entire families, many of whom were moving into towns from failed farms. Hours were long (often as much as twelve hours a day) and wages were far below the northern equivalent; indeed, one of the greatest attractions of the South to industrialists was that employers were able to pay workers there as little as one-half what northern workers received.

Life in most mill towns was rigidly controlled by the owners and managers of the factories, who rigorously suppressed attempts at protest or union organization. Company stores sold goods to workers at inflated prices and issued credit at exorbitant rates (much like country stores in agrarian areas), and mill owners ensured that no competitors were able to establish themselves in the community. At the same time, however, the conditions of the mill town helped create a strong sense of community and solidarity among workers (even if they seldom translated such feelings into militancy).

Some industries, textiles for example, offered virtually no opportunities to African-American workers. Others—tobacco, iron, and lumber, among others—did provide some employment for blacks, usually the most menial and lowest-paid positions. Some mill towns, therefore, were places where black and white culture came into close contact. That proximity contributed less to the growth of racial harmony than to the determination of white leaders to take additional measures to protect white supremacy.

At times, industrialization proceeded on the basis of no wage-paying employment at all. Through the "convict-lease" system, southern states leased gangs of convicted criminals to private interests as a cheap labor supply. The system exposed the convicts to brutal and at times fatal mistreatment. It paid them nothing (the leasing fees went to the states, not the workers). And it denied employment in railroad construction and other projects to the free labor force.

"Convict-Lease" System

FAMILY PORTRAIT An African-American family poses for a portrait in a cotton field in South Carolina in the 1880s. The images shown here are part of a stereograph, a relatively new and highly popular photographic technique that creates the illusion of a three-dimensional image when viewed through a special device. *(Robert N. Dennis Collection of Stereoscopic Views, New York Public Library Picture Collection)*

Tenants and Sharecroppers

Despite significant growth in southern industry, the region remained primarily agrarian. The most important economic reality in the post-Reconstruction South, therefore, was the impoverished state of agriculture. The 1870s and 1880s saw an acceleration of the trends that had begun in the immediate postwar years: the imposition of systems of tenantry and debt peonage on much of the region; the reliance on a few cash crops rather than on a diversified agricultural system; and increasing absentee ownership of valuable farmlands (many of them purchased by merchants and industrialists who paid little attention to whether the land was being properly used). During Reconstruction, perhaps a third or more of the farmers in the South were tenants; by 1900, the figure had increased to 70 percent. That was in large part the result of the crop-lien system, the system by which farmers borrowed money against their future crops and often fell deeper and deeper into debt.

Tenantry took several forms. Farmers who owned tools, equipment, and farm animals—or who had the money to buy them—usually paid an annual cash rent for their land. But many farmers (including most black ones) had no money or equipment. Landlords would supply them with land, a crude house, a few tools, seed, and sometimes a mule. In return, farmers would promise the landlord a large share of the annual crop—hence the

term "sharecropping." After paying their landlords and their local furnishing merchants (who were often the same people), sharecroppers seldom had anything left to sell on their own.

The crop-lien system was one of several factors contributing to a particularly harsh social and economic transformation of the southern backcountry, the piney woods and mountain regions where cotton and slavery had always been rare and where farmers lived ruggedly independent lives. Subsistence agriculture had long been the norm in these areas; but as indebtedness grew, many farmers now had to grow cash crops such as cotton instead of the food crops they had traditionally cultivated in order to make enough money to pay off their loans.

Transformation of the Backcountry

But the transformation of the backcountry was a result of other factors as well. Many backcountry residents had traditionally subsisted by raising livestock, which had roamed freely across the landscape. In the 1870s, as commercial agriculture began to intrude into these regions, many communities began to pass "fence laws," which required farmers to fence in their animals (as opposed to fencing off their crops, as had once been the custom). There were widespread protests against the new laws and, at times, violent efforts to resist them. But the existence of the open range (which had once been as much a

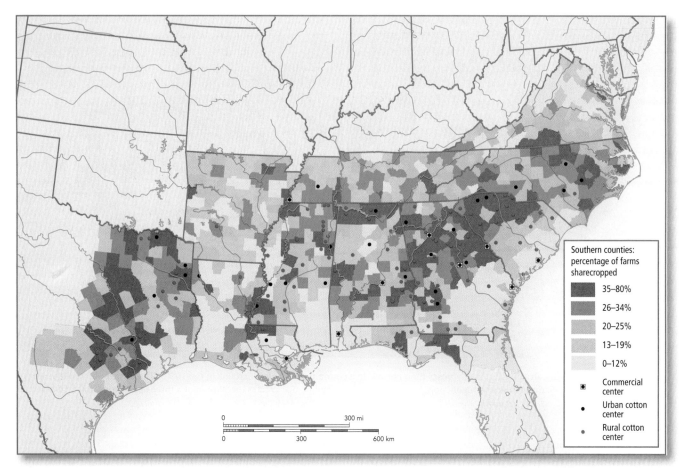

THE CROP-LIEN SYSTEM IN 1880 In the years after the Civil War, more and more southern farmers—white and black—became tenants or sharecroppers on land owned by others. This map shows the percentage of farms that were within the so-called crop-lien system, the system by which people worked their lands for someone else, who had a claim (or "lien") on a part of the farmers' crops. Note the high density of sharecropping and tenant farming in the most fertile areas of the Deep South, the same areas where slaveholding had been most dominant before the Civil War. ◆ *How did the crop-lien system contribute to the shift in southern agriculture toward one-crop farming?*

For an interactive version of this map, go to www.mhhe.com/brinkley13ech15maps

part of life in the backcountry South as it was in the American West) could not survive the spread of commercial agriculture. Increasingly, therefore, opportunities for families to live largely self-sufficiently were declining. At the same time, opportunities for profiting within the market remained slim. The people of the backcountry would be among the most important constituents for the populist protests of the 1880s and 1890s.

African Americans and the New South

The "New South creed" was not the property of whites alone. Many African Americans were attracted to the vision of progress and self-improvement as well. Some blacks succeeded in elevating themselves into a distinct middle class—economically inferior to the white middle class, but nevertheless significant. These were former

Black Middle Class

slaves (and, as the decades passed, their offspring) who managed to acquire property, establish small businesses, or enter professions. A few African Americans accumulated substantial fortunes by establishing banks and insurance companies to serve the black community. One of those was Maggie Lena, a black woman who became the first female bank president in the United States when she founded the St. Luke Penny Savings Bank in Richmond in 1903. Most middle-class blacks experienced more modest gains by becoming doctors, lawyers, nurses, or teachers.

A cardinal tenet of this rising group of African Americans was that education was vital to the future of their race. With the support of northern missionary societies and, to a far lesser extent, a few southern state governments, they expanded the network of black colleges and institutes that had taken root during Reconstruction into an important educational system.

The chief spokesman for this commitment to education, and for a time the major spokesman for African Americans in the South (and beyond), was Booker T. Washington, founder and president of the Tuskegee Institute in Alabama. Born into slavery, Washington had worked his way out of poverty after acquiring an education (at Virginia's famous Hampton Institute). He urged other blacks to follow the same road to self-improvement.

Booker T. Washington

Washington's message was both cautious and hopeful. African Americans should attend school, learn skills, and establish a solid footing in agriculture and the trades. Industrial, not classical, education should be their goal. They should, moreover, refine their speech, improve their dress, and adopt habits of thrift and personal cleanliness; they should, in short, adopt the standards of the white middle class. Only thus, he claimed, could they win the respect of the white population, the prerequisite for any larger social gains. African Americans should forgo agitating for political rights, he said, and concentrate on self-improvement and preparation for equality. In a famous speech in Georgia in 1895, Washington outlined a philosophy of race relations that became widely known as the Atlanta Compromise. "The wisest among my race understand," he said, "that the agitation of questions of social equality is the extremest folly." Rather, blacks should engage in "severe and constant struggle" for economic gains; for, as he explained, "no race that has anything to contribute to the markets of the world is long in any degree ostracized." If African Americans were ever to win the rights and privileges of citizenship, they must first show that they were "prepared for the exercise of these privileges." Washington offered a powerful challenge to those whites who wanted to discourage African Americans from acquiring an education or winning any economic gains. He helped awaken the

The Atlanta Compromise

TUSKEGEE INSTITUTE, 1881 From these modest beginnings, Booker T. Washington's Tuskegee Institute in Alabama became the preeminent academy offering technical and industrial training to black men. It deliberately de-emphasized the traditional liberal arts curricula of most colleges. Washington considered such training an unnecessary frill and encouraged his students to work on developing practical skills. *(Bettmann/Corbis)*

THE ORIGINS OF SEGREGATION

Not until after World War II, when the emergence of the civil rights movement forced white Americans to confront the issue of racial segregation, did historians pay much attention to the origins of the institution. Most had assumed that the separation of the races had emerged naturally and even inevitably out of the abolition of slavery. It had been a response to the failure of Reconstruction, the weakness and poverty of the African-American community, and the pervasiveness of white racism. It was (as W. J. Cash argued in his classic and controversial 1941 study, *The Mind of the South*) the way things had always been.

The first major challenge to these assumptions, indeed the first serious scholarly effort to explain the origins of segregation, was C. Vann Woodward's *The Strange Career of Jim Crow*, published in 1956. Not only was it important in reshaping scholarship. It had a significant political impact as well. As a southern liberal, Woodward was eager to refute assumptions that segregation was part of an unchanging and unchangeable southern tradition. He wanted to convince scholars that the history of the South had been one of sharp discontinuities; and he wanted to convince a larger public that the racial institutions they considered part of a long, unbroken tradition were in fact the product of a particular set of historical circumstances.

In the aftermath of emancipation, and indeed for two decades after Reconstruction, Woodward argued, race relations in the South had remained relatively fluid. Blacks and whites did not often interact as equals, certainly, but black southerners enjoyed a degree of latitude in social and even political affairs that they would subsequently lose. Blacks and whites often rode together in the same railroad cars, ate in the same restaurants, used the same public facilities. African Americans voted in significant numbers. Blacks and whites considered a number of different visions of how the races should live together, and as late as 1890 it was not at all clear which of those visions would prevail.

By the end of the nineteenth century, however, a great wave of racist legislation—the Jim Crow laws, which established the basis of segregation—had hardened race relations and destroyed the gentler alternatives that many whites and blacks had considered viable only a few years before. The principal reason, Woodward argued, was the Populist political insurgency of the 1890s, which mobilized blacks and whites alike and which frightened many white southerners into thinking that African Americans might soon be a major political power in the region. Southern conservatives, in particular, used the issue of white supremacy to attack the Populists and to prevent African Americans from forming an alliance with them. The result was segregation and the disfranchisement of African Americans (along with many poor whites).

Woodward's argument suggested that laws are important in shaping social behavior—that laws had made segregation and, by implication, other laws could unmake it. Not all historians agreed. A more pessimistic picture of segregation emerged in 1965 from Joel Williamson's study of South Carolina, *After Slavery*. Williamson argued that the laws of the 1890s did not mean very much, that they simply ratified a set of conditions that had been firmly established by the end of Reconstruction. As early as the mid-1870s, Williamson claimed, the races had already begun to live in two separate societies. African Americans had constructed their own churches, schools, businesses, and neighborhoods; whites had begun to exclude blacks from white institutions. The separation was partly a result of pressure and coercion from whites, partly a result of the desire of blacks to develop their own, independent culture. Whatever the reasons, however, segregation was largely in place by the end of the 1870s, continuing in a different form a pattern of racial separation established under slavery. The laws of the 1890s did little more than codify an already established system.

In the same year that Williamson published his argument, Leon Litwack joined the debate, even if somewhat indirectly, with the publication of *North of Slavery*. Litwack revealed the existence of widespread segregation, supported by an early version of Jim Crow laws, in the North before the Civil War. In almost every northern state, he revealed, free blacks experienced a kind of segregation not very different from what freed slaves would experience in the South after the Civil War. A few years later, Ira Berlin argued in *Slaves Without Masters* (1974) that

interest of a new generation to the possibilities for self-advancement through self-improvement. But his message was also an implicit promise that African Americans would not challenge the system of segregation that whites were then in the process of erecting.

The Birth of Jim Crow

Few white southerners had ever accepted the idea of racial equality. That the former slaves acquired any legal and political rights at all after emancipation was in large part the result of federal support. That support all but vanished after 1877. Federal troops withdrew. Congress lost interest. And the Supreme Court effectively stripped the Fourteenth and Fifteenth Amendments of much of their significance. In the so-called civil rights cases of 1883, the Court ruled that the Fourteenth Amendment prohibited state governments from discriminating against people because of race but did not restrict private organizations or individuals from doing so. Thus railroads, in the antebellum South, too, white people had created a wide range of discriminatory laws aimed at free blacks and ensuring segregation. The postbellum regime of Jim Crow, such works suggested, emerged naturally out of well-established precedents from before the Civil War, in both the North and the South.

Other scholars have challenged all these interpretations by attempting to link the rise of legal segregation to changing social and economic circumstances in the South. Howard Rabinowitz's *Race Relations in the Urban South* (1978) linked the rise of segregation to the new challenge of devising a form of race relations suitable to life in the growing southern cities, into which rural blacks were moving in substantial numbers. The creation of separate public facilities— schools, parks, waiting rooms, etc.— was not so much an effort to drive blacks out of white facilities; they had never had access to those facilities, and few whites had ever been willing to consider granting them access. It was, rather, an attempt to create for a black community that virtually all whites agreed must remain essentially separate a set of facilities where none had previously existed. Without segregation, in other words, urban blacks would have had no schools or parks at all. The alternative to segregation, Rabinowitz suggested, was not integration, but exclusion.

In the early 1980s, a number of scholars began examining segregation anew in light of the rising American interest in South Africa, whose system of apartheid seemed to them to be similar in many ways to the by-then largely dismantled Jim Crow system

THE NEGRO GALLERY.

(Collection of the Louisiana Museum)

in the South. John Cell's *The Highest Stage of White Supremacy* (1982) used the comparison to construct a revised explanation of how segregation emerged in the American South. Like Rabinowitz, he considered the increasing urbanization of the region the principal factor. But he ascribed different motives to those whites who promoted the rise of Jim Crow. The segregation laws, Cell argued, were a continuation of an unchanging determination by southern whites to retain control over the African-American population. What had shifted was not their commitment to white supremacy but the things necessary to preserve it.

The emergence of large black communities in urban areas and of a significant black labor force in factories presented a new challenge to white southerners. In the city, blacks and whites were in more direct competition than they had been in the countryside. There was more danger of social mixing. The city therefore required different, and more rigidly institutionalized, systems of control. The Jim Crow laws were a response not just to an enduring commitment to white supremacy, but also to a new reality that required white supremacy to move to its "highest stage," where it would have a rigid legal and institutional basis.

hotels, theaters, and workplaces could legally practice segregation.

Eventually, the Court also validated state legislation that institutionalized the separation of the races. In *Plessy v. Ferguson* (1896), a case involving a Louisiana law that required separate seating arrangements for the races on railroads, the Court held that separate accommodations *Plessy* v. *Ferguson* did not deprive blacks of equal rights if the accommodations were equal, a decision that survived for years as part of the legal basis for segregated schools. In *Cumming* v. *County Board of Education* (1899), the Court ruled that laws establishing separate schools for whites were valid even if there were no comparable schools for African Americans.

Even before these decisions, white southerners were working to strengthen white supremacy and to separate the races to the greatest extent possible. One illustration of this movement from subordination to segregation was black voting rights. In some states, disfranchisement had begun almost as soon as Reconstruction ended. But in other areas, black voting continued for some time after Reconstruction—largely because conservative whites believed they could control the black electorate and use it to beat back the attempts of poor white farmers to take control of the Democratic Party. In the 1890s, however, franchise restrictions became much more rigid. During those years, some small white farmers began to demand complete black disfranchisement—both because of racial prejudice and because they objected to the black vote being used against them by the Bourbons. At the same time, many members of the conservative elite began to fear that poor whites might unite politically with poor African Americans to challenge them. They too began to support further franchise restrictions.

In devising laws to disfranchise black males, the southern states had to find ways to evade the Fifteenth Amendment, which prohibited states from denying anyone the

Restricting the Franchise

right to vote because of race. Two devices emerged before 1900 to accomplish this goal. One was the poll tax or some form of property qualification; few African Americans were prosperous enough to meet such requirements. Another was the "literacy" or "understanding" test, which required voters to demonstrate an ability to read and to interpret the Constitution. Even those African Americans who could read had trouble passing the difficult test white officials gave them. Such restrictions were often applied unequally. Literacy tests for whites, for example, were sometimes much easier than those for blacks. Even so, the laws affected poor white voters as well as African Americans. By the late 1890s, the black vote had decreased by 62 percent, the white vote by 26 percent. One result was that some states passed so-called grandfather laws, permitting men who could not meet the literacy and property qualifications to be enfranchised if their ancestors had voted before Reconstruction began, thus barring the descendants of slaves from the polls while allowing poor whites access to them. In many areas, however, ruling elites were quite content to see poor whites, a potential source of opposition to their power, barred from voting.

The Supreme Court proved as compliant in ruling on the disfranchising laws as it was in dealing with the civil rights cases. The Court eventually voided the grandfather laws, but it validated the literacy test (in the 1898 case of *Williams* v. *Mississippi*) and displayed a general willingness to let the southern states define their own suffrage standards as long as evasions of the Fifteenth Amendment were not too glaring.

Laws restricting the franchise and segregating schools were only part of a network of state statutes—known as the Jim Crow laws—that by the first years of the twentieth century had institutionalized an elaborate system of segregation reaching into almost every area of southern life. Blacks and whites could not ride together in the same railroad cars, sit in the same waiting

White Control Perpetuated

rooms, use the same washrooms, eat in the same restaurants, or sit in the same theaters. Blacks had no access to many public parks, beaches, and picnic areas; they could not be patients in many hospitals. Much of the new legal structure did no more than confirm what had already been widespread social practice in the South since well before the end of Reconstruction. But the Jim Crow laws also stripped African Americans of many of the modest social, economic, and political gains they had made in the more fluid atmosphere of the late nineteenth century. They served, too, as a means for whites to retain control of social relations between the races in the newly growing cities and towns of the South, where traditional patterns of deference and subjugation were more difficult to preserve than in the countryside. What had been maintained by custom in the rural South was to be maintained by law in the urbanizing South.

More than legal efforts were involved in this process. The 1890s witnessed a dramatic increase in white violence against blacks, which, along with the Jim Crow laws, served to inhibit black agitation for equal rights. The worst such violence—lynching of blacks by white mobs, either because the victims were accused of crimes or because they had seemed somehow to violate their expected station—

Lynchings

reached appalling levels. In the nation as a whole in the 1890s, there was an average of 187 lynchings each year, more than 80 percent of them in the South. The vast majority of victims were black.

The most celebrated lynchings occurred in cities and towns, where large, well-organized mobs—occasionally with the tacit cooperation of local authorities—seized black prisoners from the jails and hanged them in great public rituals. Such public lynchings were often planned well in advance and elaborately organized. They attracted large audiences from surrounding regions. Entire families traveled many miles to witness the spectacles. But such great public lynchings were relatively rare. Much more frequent, and more dangerous to African Americans because less visible or predictable, were lynchings performed by small vigilante mobs, often composed of friends or relatives of the victim (or supposed victim) of a crime. Those involved in lynchings often saw their actions as a legitimate form of law enforcement; and indeed, some victims of lynchings had in fact committed crimes. But lynchings were also a means by which whites controlled the black population through terror and intimidation. Thus, some lynch mobs killed African Americans whose only "crime" had been presumptuousness. Others chose as victims outsiders in the community, whose presence threatened to disturb the normal pattern of race relations.

A LYNCH MOB, 1893 A large, almost festive crowd gathers to watch the lynching of a black man accused of the murder of a three-year-old white girl. Lynchings remained frequent in the South until as late as the 1930s, but they reached their peak in the 1890s and the first years of the twentieth century. Lynchings such as this one—published well in advance and attracting whole families who traveled great distances to see them—were relatively infrequent. Most lynchings were the work of smaller groups, operating with less visibility. *(Library of Congress)*

Black men who had made any sexual advances toward white women (or who white men thought had done so) were particularly vulnerable to lynchings; the fear of black sexuality, and the unspoken fear among many men that white women might be attracted to that sexuality, was always an important part of the belief system that supported segregation. Whatever the reasons or circumstances, the victims of lynch mobs were denied the protection of the laws and the opportunity to prove their innocence.

The rise of lynchings shocked the conscience of many white Americans in a way that other forms of racial injustice did not. Almost from the start there was a substantial anti-lynching movement. In 1892 Ida B. Wells, a committed black journalist, launched what became an international anti-lynching movement with a series of impassioned articles after the lynching of three of her friends in Memphis, Tennessee, her home. The movement gradually gathered strength in the first years of the twentieth century, attracting substantial support from whites (particularly white women) in both the North and South. Its goal was a federal anti-lynching law, which would allow the national government to do what state and local governments in the South were generally unwilling to do: punish those responsible for lynchings.

But the substantial white opposition to lynchings stood as an exception to the general white support for suppression of African Americans. Indeed, just as in the antebellum period, the shared commitment to white supremacy helped dilute class animosities between poorer whites and the Bourbon oligarchies. Economic issues tended to play a secondary role to race in southern politics, distracting people from the glaring social inequalities that afflicted blacks and whites alike. The commitment to white supremacy, in short, was a burden for poor whites as well as for blacks.

White Unity

CONCLUSION

Reconstruction, long remembered by many white Americans as a vindictive outrage or a tragic failure, was in fact a profoundly important moment in American history. Despite the bitter political battles in Washington and throughout the South, culminating in the unsuccessful effort to impeach President Andrew Johnson, the most important result of the effort to reunite the nation after its long and bloody war was a reshaping of the lives of ordinary people in all regions of the nation.

In the North, Reconstruction solidified the power of the Republican Party and ensured that public policy would support the continued growth of an advanced industrial economy. The rapid growth of the northern economy continued and accelerated, drawing more and more of its residents into an expanding commercial world.

In the South, Reconstruction did more than simply bring slavery to an end. It fundamentally rearranged the relationship between the region's white and black citizens. Only for a while did Reconstruction permit African Americans to participate actively and effectively in southern politics. After a few years of widespread black voting and significant black officeholding, the forces of white supremacy forced most African Americans to the margins of the southern political world, where they would mostly remain until the 1960s.

But in other ways, the lives of southern blacks changed dramatically. Overwhelmingly, they left the plantations. Some sought work in towns and cities. Some left the region altogether. But the great majority began farming on small farms of their own—not as landowners, except in rare cases, but as tenants and sharecroppers on land owned mostly by whites. The result was a form of economic bondage, driven by debt, only scarcely less oppressive than the legal bondage of slavery. But within this system, African Americans managed to carve out a much larger sphere of social and cultural autonomy than they had ever been able to create under slavery. Black churches organized in great numbers. African-American schools emerged in some communities, and black colleges began to appear in the region. Some former slaves owned businesses and flourished. In southern cities and towns, a fledgling black middle class began to emerge.

The system of tenantry, which emerged in the course of Reconstruction, continued after its end to dominate the southern economy. Strenuous efforts by "New South" advocates to advance industry and commerce in the region produced significant results in a few areas. But the South on the whole remained what it had always been, an overwhelmingly rural society with a sharply defined class structure. It was also a region with a deep commitment among its white citizens to the subordination of African Americans—a commitment solidified in the 1890s and the early twentieth century when white southerners erected an elaborate legal system of segregation (the "Jim Crow" laws). The promise of the great Reconstruction amendments to the Constitution—the Fourteenth and Fifteenth—remained largely unfulfilled in the South as the century drew to its close.

INTERACTIVE LEARNING

The *Primary Source Investigator CD-ROM* offers the following materials related to this chapter:

- Interactive maps: **U.S. Elections** (M7); **Barrow Plantation** (M18); and **African Americans and Crop Lien** (M19).

- Documents, images, and maps related to the Reconstruction era following the Civil War, including examples of Black Codes passed by southern states and communities early in the aftermath of the Civil War, several firsthand accounts from former slaves, the Fourteenth and Fifteenth Amendments to the U.S. Constitution, and an image of the Tuskegee Institute.

Online Learning Center (www.mhhe.com/brinkley13e)

For quizzes, Internet resources, references to additional books and films, and more, consult this book's Online Learning Center.

FOR FURTHER REFERENCE

Eric Foner, *Reconstruction: America's Unfinished Revolution, 1863-1877* (1988), the most important modern synthesis of Reconstruction scholarship, emphasizes the radicalism of Reconstruction and the role of freed people in the process of political and economic renovation. Thomas Holt, *Black over White: Negro Political Leadership in South Carolina*

During Reconstruction (1977) examines Reconstruction in the state where black political power reached its apex. C. Vann Woodward, *Origins of the New South* (1951) is a classic work on the history of the South after Reconstruction and argues that a rising middle class defined the economic and political transformation of the New South. Nicholas Lemann, *Redemption: The Last Battle of the Civil War* (2006) reveals the determination of white southerners to regain control of their society. Edward Ayers, *The Promise of the New South* (1992) offers a rich portrait of social and cultural life in the New South. Jacqueline Jones, *Labor of Love, Labor of Sorrow* (1985) examines the lives of African-American women after Emancipation. Leon Litwack, *Been in the Storm So Long: The*

Aftermath of Slavery (1979) is a major study of the experiences of freed slaves. Steven Hahn, *A Nation Under Our Feet: Black Political Struggles in the Rural South from Slavery to the Great Migration* (2003) is an excellent, wide-ranging history. C. Vann Woodward, *The Strange Career of Jim Crow* (rev. 1974) claims that segregation emerged only gradually across the South after Reconstruction. The "Woodward Thesis" has been challenged by, among others, Joel Williamson, *After Slavery: The Negro in South Carolina During Reconstruction* (1965); John W. Cell, *The Highest Stage of White Supremacy: The Origins of Segregation in South Africa and the American South* (1982); and Howard N. Rabinowitz, *Race Relations in the Urban South, 1865–1890* (1978).

CHAPTER 16

THE CONQUEST OF THE FAR WEST

TOURISTS IN YOSEMITE By the end of the nineteenth century, the great "wild west" had become a popular tourist attraction for men and women from all over the United States, and beyond. Yosemite Falls, the site of this picture, is one of the most celebrated sights in Yosemite National Park, established in 1900. *(Library of Congress)*

THROUGH MUCH OF THE FIRST HALF of the nineteenth century, relatively few English-speaking Americans considered moving into the vast lands west of the Mississippi River. For some the obstacle was distance; for others it was lack of money; for many more it was the image of much of the Far West, popularized by some early travelers, as the "Great American Desert," unfit for civilization.

By the mid-1840s, however, enough migrants from the eastern regions of the nation had settled in the West to begin to challenge that image. Some were farmers, who had found fertile land in areas once considered too arid for agriculture. Others were ranchers, who had discovered great open grasslands on which they could raise large herds of cattle or sheep for the market. Many were miners, including some of the hundreds of thousands of people who had flocked to California during the 1848–1849 gold rush. By the end of the Civil War, the West had already become legendary in the eastern states. No longer the Great American Desert, it was now the "frontier": an empty land awaiting settlement and civilization; a place of wealth, adventure, opportunity, and untrammeled individualism; a place of fresh beginnings and bold undertakings.

In fact, the real West of the mid-nineteenth century bore little resemblance to either of these images. It was a diverse land, with many different regions, many different climates, many different stores of natural resources. And it was extensively populated, with a number of well-developed societies and cultures. The

Myth and Reality

English-speaking migrants of the late nineteenth century did not find an empty, desolate land. They found Indians, Mexicans, French and British Canadians, Asians, and others, some of whose families had been living in the West for generations. The Anglo-American settlers helped create new civilizations in this vast and complicated land, but they did not do so by themselves. Although they tried, with considerable success, to conquer and disperse many of the peoples already living in the region, they were never able to make the West theirs alone. They interacted in countless ways with the existing population. Almost everything the Anglo-Americans did and built reflected the influence of these other cultures.

Most of all, however, English-speaking Americans transformed the West by connecting it with, and making it part of, the growing capitalist economy of the East. And despite their self-image as rugged individualists, they relied heavily on assistance from the federal government—land grants, subsidies, and military protection—as they developed the region.

THE SOCIETIES OF THE FAR WEST

The Far West (or what many nineteenth-century Americans called the "Great West")—the region beyond the Mississippi River into which millions of Anglo-Americans moved in the years after the Civil War—was in fact many lands. It contained some of the most arid territory in the United States, and some of the wettest and lushest. It contained the flattest plains and the highest mountains. It contained vast treeless prairies and deserts and great forests. And it contained many peoples.

The Western Tribes

The largest and most important western population group before the great Anglo-American migration was the Indian tribes. Some were members of eastern tribes—Cherokee, Creek, and others—who had been forcibly resettled west of the Mississippi to "Indian Territory" (later Oklahoma) and elsewhere before the Civil War. But most were members of tribes that had always lived in the West.

The western tribes had developed several forms of civilization. More than 300,000 Indians (among them the Serrano, Chumash, Pomo, Maidu, Yurok, and Chinook) had lived on the Pacific coast before the arrival of Spanish settlers. Disease and dislocation decimated the tribes, but in the mid-nineteenth century 150,000 remained—some living within the Hispanic society the Spanish and Mexican settlers had created, many still living within their own tribal communities. The Pueblos of the Southwest had long lived largely as farmers and had established permanent settlements there even before the Spanish arrived in the seventeenth century. The Pueblos grew corn; they built towns and cities of adobe houses; they practiced elaborate forms of irrigation; and they participated in trade and commerce. In the eighteenth and nineteenth centuries, their intimate relationship with the Spanish (later Mexicans) produced, in effect, an alliance against the Apaches, Navajos, and Comanches of the region.

The complex interaction between the Pueblos and the Spanish, and between both of them and other tribes, produced an elaborate caste system in the Southwest. At the top were the Spanish or Mexicans, who owned the largest estates and controlled the trading centers at Santa Fe and elsewhere. The Pueblos, subordinate but still largely free, were below them. Apaches, Navajos, and others—some captured in war and enslaved for a fixed time, others men and women who had voluntarily left their own tribes—were at the bottom. They were known as *genizaros,* Indians without tribes, and they had become in many ways part of Spanish society. This caste system reflected the preoccupation of the Spanish Empire in America with racial ancestry; almost every group in the Southwest—not just Spanish and Indians, but several categories of mulattoes and mestizos (people of mixed race) had a clear place in an elaborate social hierarchy.

| Caste System |

The most widespread Indian presence in the West was the Plains Indians, a diverse group of tribes and language groups. Some formed alliances with one another; others were in constant conflict. Some lived more or less sedentary lives as farmers; others were highly nomadic hunters. Despite their differences, however, the tribes shared some traits. Their cultures were based on close and extended family networks and on an intimate relationship with nature. Tribes (which sometimes numbered several thousand) were generally subdivided into "bands" of up to 500 men and women. Each band had its own governing council, but the community had a decision-making process in which most members participated. Within each band, tasks were divided by gender. Women's roles were largely domestic and artistic: raising children, cooking, gathering roots and berries, preparing hides, and creating many of the impressive artworks of tribal culture. They also tended fields and gardens in those places where bands remained settled long enough to raise crops. Men worked as hunters and traders and supervised the religious and military life of the band. Most of the Plains Indians practiced a religion centered on a belief in the spiritual power of the natural world—of plants and animals and the rhythms of the days and the seasons.

| Plains Indians |

Many of the Plains tribes—including some of the most powerful tribes in the Sioux Nation—subsisted largely through hunting buffalo. Riding small but powerful horses, descendants of Spanish stock, the tribes moved through the grasslands following the herds. Permanent settlements were rare. When a band halted, it constructed tepees as temporary dwellings; when it departed, it left the landscape almost completely undisturbed, a reflection of the deep reverence for nature that was central to Indian culture and religion.

The buffalo, or bison, provided the economic basis for the Plains Indians' way of life. Its flesh was their principal source of food, and its skin supplied materials for clothing, shoes, tepees, blankets, robes, and utensils. "Buffalo chips"—dried manure—provided fuel; buffalo bones became knives and arrow tips; buffalo tendons formed the strings of bows.

| Economic Importance of the Buffalo |

The Plains Indians were proud and aggressive warriors, schooled in warfare from their frequent (and usually brief) skirmishes with rival tribes. The male members of each tribe were, in effect, a warrior class. They competed with one another to develop reputations for fierceness and bravery both as hunters and as soldiers. By the early nineteenth century, the Sioux had become the most powerful tribe in the Missouri River valley and had begun expanding west and south until they dominated much of the plains.

The Plains warriors proved to be the most formidable foes white settlers encountered. But they also suffered from several serious weaknesses that in the end made it impossible for them to prevail. One weakness was the

BUFFALO CHASE The painter George Catlin captured this scene of Plains Indians in the 1830s hunting among the great herds of buffalo, which provided the food and materials on which many tribes relied. *(Smithsonian American Art Museum, Washington, DC/ Art Resource, NY)*

inability of the various tribes (and often even of the bands within tribes) to unite against white aggression. Not only were they seldom able to draw together a coalition large enough to counter white power; they were also frequently distracted from their battles with whites by conflicts among the tribes themselves. At times, tribal warriors faced white forces who were being assisted by guides and even fighters from other, usually rival, tribes.

Even so, some tribes were able to overcome their divisions and unite effectively for a time. By the mid-nineteenth century, for example, the Sioux, Arapaho, and Cheyenne had forged a powerful alliance that dominated the northern plains. But there remained other impor-

Indian Weaknesses

tant ecological and economic weaknesses of the western tribes in their contest with white society. Indians were tragically vulnerable to eastern infectious diseases. Smallpox epidemics, for example, decimated the Pawnees in Nebraska in the 1840s and many of the California tribes in the early 1850s. And the tribes were, of course, at a considerable disadvantage in any long-term battle with an economically and industrially advanced people. They were, in the end, outmanned and outgunned.

Hispanic New Mexico

For centuries, much of the Far West had been part of, first, the Spanish Empire and, later, the Mexican Republic. Although the lands the United States acquired in the 1840s did not include any of Mexico's most populous regions, considerable numbers of Mexicans did live in them and suddenly became residents of American territory. Most of them stayed.

Spanish-speaking communities were scattered throughout the Southwest, from Texas to California. All of them were transformed in varying degrees by the arrival of Anglo-American migrants and, equally important, by the expansion of the American capitalist economy into the region. For some, the changes created opportunities for greater wealth. But for most it meant an end to the communal societies and economies they had built over many generations.

In New Mexico, the centers of Spanish-speaking society were the farming and trading communities the Spanish had established in the seventeenth century (see p. 20). Descendants of the original Spanish settlers (and more recent migrants from Mexico) lived alongside the Pueblo Indians and some American traders and engaged primarily in cattle and sheep ranching. There was a small aristocracy of great landowners, whose estates radiated out from the major trading center at Santa Fe. And there was a large population of Spanish (later Mexican) peasants, who worked on the great estates, farmed small plots of their own, or otherwise scraped out a subsistence. There were also large groups of Indian laborers, some enslaved or indentured.

When the United States acquired title to New Mexico in the aftermath of the Mexican War, General Stephen Kearny—who had commanded the American troops in the region during the conflict—tried to establish a territorial government that excluded the established Mexican ruling class (the landed aristo-crats from around Santa Fe and

Taos Indian Rebellion

the most influential priests). He drew most of the officials from among the approximately 1,000 Anglo-Americans in the region, ignoring the over 50,000 Hispanics. There were widespread fears among Hispanics and Indians alike that the new American rulers of the region would confiscate their lands and otherwise threaten their societies. In 1847, Taos Indians rebelled; they killed the new governor and other Anglo-American officials before being subdued by United States Army forces. New Mexico remained under military rule for three years, until the United States finally organized a territorial government there in 1850.

By the 1870s, the government of New Mexico was dominated by one of the most notorious of the many "territorial rings" that sprang up in the West in the years before statehood. These were circles of local businesspeople and ambitious politicians with access to federal money who worked together to make the territorial government mutually profitable. In Santa Fe, the ring used its influence to gain control of over 2 million acres of land, much of which had long been in the possession of the original Mexican residents of the territory. The old Hispanic elite in New Mexico had lost much of its political and economic authority.

Even without its former power and despite the expansion of Anglo-American settlement, Hispanic society in New Mexico survived and grew. The U.S. Army finally did what the Hispanic residents had been unable to accomplish for 200 years: it broke the power of the Navajo, Apache, and other tribes that had so often harassed the residents of New Mexico and had prevented them from expanding their society and commerce. The defeat of the tribes led to substantial Hispanic migration into other areas of the Southwest and as far north as Colorado. Most of the expansion involved peasants and small tradespeople who were looking for land or new opportunities for commerce.

Hispanic societies survived in the Southwest in part because they were so far from the centers of English-speaking society that Anglo-American migrants (and the railroads that carried them) were slow to get there. But

Hispanic Resistance

Mexican Americans in the region also fought at times to preserve control of their societies. In the late 1880s, for example, Mexican peasants in an area of what is now Nevada successfully fended off the encroachment of English-speaking cattle ranchers.

But by then, such successes were already the exception. The Anglo-American presence in the Southwest grew rapidly once the railroads established lines into the region in the 1880s and early 1890s. With the railroads came extensive new ranching, farming, and mining. The expansion of economic activity in the region attracted a new wave of Mexican immigrants—perhaps as many as 100,000 by 1900—who moved across the border (which was unregulated until World War I) in search of work. But the new immigrants, unlike the earlier Hispanic residents of the Southwest, were coming to a society in which they were from the beginning subordinate to Anglo-Americans. The English-speaking proprietors of the new enterprises restricted most Mexicans to the lowest-paying and least stable jobs.

Hispanic California and Texas

In California, Spanish settlement began in the eighteenth century with a string of Christian missions along the Pacific coast. The missionaries and the soldiers who accompanied them gathered most of the coastal Indians into their communities, some forcibly and some by persuasion. The Indians were targets of the evangelizing efforts of the missionaries, who baptized over 50,000 of them. But they were also a labor force for the flourishing and largely self-sufficient economies the missionaries created; the Spanish forced most of these laborers into a state of servitude little different from slavery. The missions had enormous herds of cattle, horses, sheep, and goats, most

A CALIFORNIAN MAGNATE IN HIS HOME General Don Andres Pico, a wealthy rancher in Mexican California, is shown here in his home—a former mission—in the San Fernando Valley in southern California. It portrays some of the characteristic features of Mexican life in California—a busy and crowded household filled with servants and relatives; an orchard in the distance; *vaqueros* (cowboys) lassoing cattle in the background. *(Courtesy of the Bancroft Library, University of California, Berkeley, 19xx.039:33—ALB)*

of them tended by Indian workers; they had brickmakers, blacksmiths, weavers, and farmers, most of them Indians as well. Few of the profits of the mission economy flowed to the workers.

In the 1830s, after the new Mexican government began reducing the power of the church, the mission society largely collapsed, despite strenuous resistance from the missionaries themselves. In its place emerged a secular Mexican aristocracy, which controlled a chain of large estates (some of them former missions) in the fertile lands west of the Sierra Nevada. For them, the arrival of Anglo-Americans before and after the Civil War was disastrous. So vast were the numbers of English-speaking immigrants that the *californios* (as the Hispanic residents of the state were known) had little power to resist the onslaught. In the central and northern parts of the state, where the Anglo population growth was greatest, the *californios* experienced a series of defeats. English-speaking prospectors organized to exclude them, sometimes violently, from the mines during the gold rush. Many *californios* also lost their lands—either through corrupt business deals or through outright seizure (sometimes with the help of the courts and often through simple occupation by squatters). Years of litigation by the displaced Hispanics had very little effect on the changing distribution of landownership.

Decline of Mission Society

In the southern areas of California, where there were at first fewer migrants than in other parts of the state, some Mexican landowners managed to hang on for a time. The booming Anglo communities in the north of the state created a large market for the cattle that southern *rancheros* were raising. But a combination of reckless expansion, growing indebtedness, and a severe drought in the 1860s devastated the Mexican ranching culture. By the 1880s, the Hispanic aristocracy in California had largely ceased to exist. Increasingly, Mexicans and Mexican Americans became part of the lower end of the state's working class, clustered in barrios in Los Angeles or elsewhere, or becoming migrant farmworkers. Even small landowners who managed to hang on to their farms found themselves unable to raise livestock, as the once communal grazing lands fell under the control of powerful Anglo ranchers. The absence of herding destroyed many family economies and, by forcing farmers into migrant work, displaced much of the peasantry.

A similar pattern of dispossession occurred in Texas, where many Mexican landowners lost their land after the territory joined the United States (see pp. 346–347). This occurred as a result of fraud, coercion, and the inability of even the most substantial Mexican ranchers to compete with the enormous emerging Anglo-American ranching kingdoms. In 1859, Mexican resentments erupted in an armed challenge to American power: a raid on a jail in Brownsville, led by the rancher Juan

Declining Status of Hispanics

Cortina, who freed all the Mexican prisoners inside. But such resistance had little long-term effect. Cortina continued to harass Anglo communities in Texas until 1875, but the Mexican government finally captured and imprisoned him. As in California, Mexicans in southern Texas (who constituted nearly three-quarters of the population there) became an increasingly impoverished working class relegated largely to unskilled farm or industrial labor.

On the whole, the great Anglo-American migration was less catastrophic for the Hispanic population of the West than it was for the Indian tribes. Indeed, for some Hispanics, it created new opportunities for wealth and station. For the most part, however, the late nineteenth century saw the destruction of Mexican Americans' authority in a region they had long considered their own; and it saw the movement of large numbers of Hispanics—both longtime residents of the West and more recent immigrants—into an impoverished working class serving the expanding capitalist economy of the United States.

The Chinese Migration

At the same time that ambitious or impoverished Europeans were crossing the Atlantic in search of opportunities in the New World, many Chinese crossed the Pacific in hopes of better lives than they could expect in their own poverty-stricken land. Not all came to the United States. Many Chinese moved to Hawaii, Australia, South and Central America, South Africa, and even the Caribbean—some as "coolies" (indentured servants whose condition was close to slavery).

A few Chinese had come to California even before the gold rush (see pp. 356–357), but after 1848 the flow increased dramatically. By 1880, more than 200,000 Chinese had settled in the United States, mostly in California, where they constituted nearly a tenth of the population. Almost all came as free laborers. For a time, white Americans welcomed the Chinese as a conscientious, hard-working people. In 1852, the governor of California called them "one of the most worthy classes of our newly adopted citizens" and called for more Chinese immigration to swell the territory's inadequate labor force. Very quickly, however, white opinion turned hostile—in part because the Chinese were so industrious and successful that some white Americans began considering them rivals, even threats. The experience of Chinese immigrants in the West became, therefore, a struggle to advance economically in the face of racism and discrimination.

Racism

In the early 1850s, large numbers of Chinese immigrants worked in the gold mines, and for a time some of them enjoyed considerable success. But opportunities for Chinese to prosper in the mines were fleeting. In 1852, the California legislature began trying to exclude the Chinese from gold mining by enacting a "foreign miners" tax (which also helped exclude Mexicans).

A series of other laws in the 1850s were designed to discourage Chinese immigration into the territory. Gradually, the effect of the discriminatory laws, the hostility of white miners, and the declining profitability of the surface mines drove most Chinese out of prospecting. Those who remained in the mountains became primarily hired workers in the mines built by corporations with financing from the East. These newer mines—which extended much deeper into the mountains than individual prospectors or small, self-financed groups had been able to go—replaced the early, smaller operations.

As mining declined as a source of wealth and jobs for the Chinese, railroad employment grew. Beginning in 1865, over 12,000 Chinese found work building the transcontinental railroad. In fact, Chinese workers formed 90 percent of the labor force of the Central Pacific and were mainly responsible for construction of the western part of the new road. The company preferred them to white workers because they had no experience of labor organization. They worked hard, made few demands, and accepted relatively low wages. Many railroad workers were recruited in China by agents for the Central Pacific. Once employed, they were organized into work gangs under Chinese supervisors.

Building the Transcontinental Railroad

Work on the Central Pacific was arduous and often dangerous. As the railroad moved through the mountains, the company made few concessions to the difficult conditions and provided their workers with little protection from the elements. Work continued through the winter, and many Chinese tunneled into snowbanks at night to create warm sleeping areas for themselves. The tunnels frequently collapsed, suffocating those inside; but the company allowed nothing to disrupt construction.

Chinese laborers, however, were not always as docile as their employers imagined them to be. In the spring of 1866, 5,000 Chinese railroad workers went on strike, demanding higher wages and a shorter workday. The company isolated them, surrounded them with strikebreakers, and starved them. The strike failed, and most of the workers returned to their jobs.

In 1869 the transcontinental railroad was completed. Thousands of Chinese were now out of work. Some hired themselves out on the vast new drainage and irrigation projects in the agricultural valleys of central California. Some became common agricultural laborers, picking fruit for low wages. Some became tenant farmers, often on marginal lands that white owners saw no profit in working themselves. Some managed to acquire land of their own and establish themselves as modestly successful truck farmers.

Increasingly, however, Chinese immigrants flocked to cities. By 1900, nearly half the Chinese population of California lived in urban areas. By far the largest single Chinese community was in San Francisco.

Establishment of "Chinatowns"

THE TRANSCONTINENTAL RAILROAD This complicated trestle under construction by the Union Pacific was one of many large spans necessary for the completion of the transcontinental railroad. It gives some indication of the enormous engineering challenges the railroad builders had to overcome. (*Union Pacific Railroad Museum Collection*)

A CHINESE FAMILY IN SAN FRANCISCO Like many other Americans, Chinese families liked to pose for photograph portraits in the late nineteenth century. And like many other immigrants, they often sent them back to relatives in China. This portrait of Chun Duck Chin and his seven-year-old son, Chun Jan Yut, was taken in a studio in San Francisco in the 1870s. Both father and son appear to have dressed up for the occasion, in traditional Chinese garb, and the studio—which likely took many such portraits of Chinese families—provided a formal Chinese backdrop. The son is holding what appears to be a chicken, perhaps to impress relatives in China with the family's prosperity. (*National Archives and Records Administration*)

Much of community life there, and in other "Chinatowns" throughout the West, revolved around powerful organizations—usually formed by people from the same clan or community in China—that functioned as something like benevolent societies and filled many of the roles that political machines often served in immigrant communities in eastern cities. They were often led by prominent merchants. (In San Francisco, the leading merchants—known as the "Six Companies"—often worked together to advance their interests in the city and state.) These organizations became, in effect, employment brokers, unions, arbitrators of disputes, defenders of the community against outside persecution, and dispensers of social services. They also organized the elaborate festivals and celebrations that were such a conspicuous and important part of life in Chinatowns.

Other Chinese organizations were secret societies, known as "tongs." Some of the tongs were violent criminal organizations, involved in the opium trade and prostitution. Few people outside the Chinese communities were aware of their existence, except when rival tongs engaged in violent conflict (or "tong wars"), as occurred frequently in San Francisco in the 1880s.

Life was hard for most urban Chinese, in San Francisco and elsewhere. The Chinese usually occupied the lower rungs of the employment ladder, working as common laborers, servants, and unskilled factory hands. Some established their own small businesses, especially laundries. They moved into this business not because of experience—there were few commercial laundries in China—but because they were excluded from so many other areas of employment. Laundries could be started with very little capital, and required only limited command of English. By the 1890s, Chinese constituted over two-thirds of all the laundry workers in California, many of them in shops they themselves owned and ran.

The relatively small number of Chinese women fared even worse. During the earliest Chinese migrations to California, virtually all the women who made the journey did so because they had been sold into prostitution. As late as 1880, nearly half the Chinese women in California were prostitutes. Both Anglo and Chinese reformers tried to stamp out the prostitution in Chinatowns in the 1890s, but more effective than their efforts was the growing number of Chinese women in America. Once the sex ratio became more balanced, Chinese men were more likely to seek companionship in families.

Anti-Chinese Sentiments

As Chinese communities grew larger and more conspicuous in western cities, anti-Chinese sentiment among white residents became increasingly strong. Anti-coolie clubs emerged | Anti-Coolie Clubs
in the 1860s and 1870s. They sought a ban on employing Chinese and organized boycotts of products made with Chinese labor. Some of these clubs attacked Chinese workers in the streets and were suspected of setting fire to factories in which Chinese worked. Such activities reflected the resentment of many white workers toward Chinese laborers for accepting low wages and thus undercutting union members.

As the political value of attacking the Chinese grew in California, the Democratic Party took up the call. So did the Workingmen's Party of California—created in 1878 by Denis Kearney, an Irish immigrant—which gained significant political power in the state in large part on the basis of its hostility to the Chinese. By the mid-1880s, anti-Chinese agitation and violence had spread up and down the Pacific coast and into other areas of the West.

But anti-Chinese sentiment did not rest on economic grounds alone. It rested on cultural and racial arguments

AN ANTI-CHINESE RIOT White citizens of Denver attacked the Chinese community of the city in 1880, beating many of its residents and vandalizing their homes and businesses. It was one of a number of anti-Chinese riots in the cities of the West. They were a result of a combination of racism and resentment by white workers of what they considered unfair competition from Chinese laborers who were willing to work for very low wages. *(Bettmann/Corbis)*

as well. For example, the reformer Henry George, a critic of capitalism and a champion of the rights of labor (see p. 484), described the Chinese as products of a civilization that had failed to progress, that remained mired in barbarism and savagery. They were, therefore, "unassimilable" and should be excluded.

In 1882, Congress responded to the political pressure and the growing violence by passing the Chinese Exclusion Act, which banned Chinese immigration into the United States for ten years and barred Chinese already in the country from becoming naturalized citizens. Support for the act came from representatives from all regions of the country. It reflected the growing fear of unemployment and labor unrest throughout the nation and the belief that excluding "an industrial army of Asiatic laborers" would protect "American" workers and help reduce class conflict. Congress renewed the law for another ten years in 1892 and made it permanent in 1902. It had a dramatic effect on the Chinese population, which declined by more than 40 percent in the forty years after its passage.

The Chinese in America did not accept the new laws quietly. They were shocked by the anti-Chinese rhetoric that lumped them together with African Americans and Indians.

Chinese Resistance

They were, they insisted, descendants of a great and enlightened civilization. How could they be compared to people who knew "nothing about the relations of society"? White Americans, they said, did not protest the great waves of immigration by Italians ("the most dangerous of men," one Chinese American said) or Irish or Jews. "They are all let in, while Chinese, who are sober, are duly law abiding, clean, educated and industrious, are shut out." The Six Companies in San Francisco organized strenuous letter-writing campaigns, petitioned the president, and even filed suit in federal court. Their efforts had little effect.

Migration from the East

The great wave of new settlers in the West after the Civil War came on the heels of important earlier migrations. California and Oregon were both already states of the Union by 1860. There were large and growing Anglo- and African-American communities in Texas, which had entered the Union in 1845 and had been part of the Confederacy during the war. And from Texas and elsewhere, traders, farmers, and ranchers had begun to establish Anglo-American outposts in parts of New Mexico, Arizona, and other areas of the Southwest.

But the scale of the postwar migration dwarfed everything that had preceded it. In previous decades, the settlers had come in thousands. Now they came in millions, spreading throughout the vast western territories—into empty and inhabited lands alike. Most of the new settlers were from the established Anglo-American societies of the eastern United States, but substantial numbers—over 2 million between 1870 and 1900—were foreign-born immigrants from Europe: Scandinavians, Germans, Irish, Russians, Czechs, and others. Settlers were attracted by gold and silver deposits, by the shortgrass pastures for cattle and sheep, and ultimately by the sod of the plains and the meadowlands of the mountains, which they discovered were suitable for farming or ranching. The completion of the great transcontinental railroad line in 1869, and the construction of the many subsidiary lines that spread out from it, also encouraged settlement.

The land policies of the federal government also encouraged settlement. The Homestead Act of 1862 permitted settlers to buy plots of 160 acres for a small fee if they occupied the land they purchased for five years and improved it. The Homestead Act was intended as a progressive measure. It would give a free farm to any American who needed one. It would be a form of government relief to people who otherwise might have no prospects. And it would help create new markets and new outposts of commercial agriculture for the nation's growing economy.

But the Homestead Act rested on a number of misperceptions. The framers of the law had assumed that mere possession of land would be enough to sustain a farm family. They had not recognized the effects of the increasing mechanization of agriculture and the rising costs of running a farm. Moreover, they had made many of their calculations on the basis of eastern agricultural experiences that were inappropriate for the region west of the Mississippi. A unit of 160 acres was too small for the grazing and grain farming of much of the Great Plains. Although over 400,000 homesteaders stayed on Homestead Act claims long enough to gain title to their land, a much larger number abandoned the region before the end of the necessary five years, unable to cope with the bleak life on the windswept plains and the economic realities that were making it difficult for families without considerable resources to thrive.

Not for the last time, beleaguered westerners looked to the federal government for solutions to their problems. In

Government Assistance response to their demands, Congress increased the homestead allotments. The Timber Culture Act (1873) permitted homesteaders to receive grants of 160 additional acres if they planted 40 acres of trees on them. The Desert Land Act (1877) provided that claimants could buy 640 acres at $1.25 an acre provided they irrigated part of their holdings within three years. The Timber and Stone Act (1878), which presumably applied to nonarable land, authorized sales at $2.50 an acre. These laws ultimately made it possible for individuals to acquire as much as 1,280 acres of land at little cost. Some enterprising settlers got much more. Fraud ran rampant in the administration of the acts. Lumber, mining, and cattle companies, by employing "dummy" registrants and using other illegal devices, seized millions of acres of the public domain.

Political organization followed on the heels of settlement. After the admission of Kansas as a state in 1861, the remaining territories of Washington, New Mexico, Utah, and Nebraska were divided into smaller units that would presumably be easier to organize. By the close of the 1860s, territorial governments were in operation in the new provinces of Nevada, Colorado, Dakota, Arizona, Idaho, Montana, and Wyoming. Statehood rapidly followed. Nevada became a state in 1864, Nebraska in 1867, and Colorado in 1876. In 1889, North and South Dakota, Montana, and Washington won admission; Wyoming and Idaho entered the next year. Congress denied Utah statehood until its Mormon leaders convinced the government in 1896 that polygamy (the practice of men taking several wives) had been abandoned. At the turn of the century, only three territories remained outside the Union. Arizona and New Mexico were excluded because their scanty white populations remained minorities in the territories, because their politics were predominantly Democratic in a Republican era, and because they were unwilling to accept admission as a single state. Oklahoma (formerly Indian Territory) was opened to white settlement and granted territorial status in 1889–1890.

SODBUSTERS As farmers moved onto the Great Plains in Nebraska and other states on the agrarian frontier, their first task was to cut through the sod that covered the land to get to soil in which they could plant crops. The sod itself was so thick and solid that some settlers (including the Summers family of West Custer County, Nebraska, pictured here in 1888) used it to build their houses. The removal of the sod made cultivation of the plains possible; it also removed the soil's protective covering and contributed to the great dust storms that plagued the region in times of drought. *(Nebraska State Historical Society)*

THE CHANGING WESTERN ECONOMY

Among the many effects of the new wave of Anglo-American settlement in the Far West was a transformation of the region's economy. The new American settlers tied the West firmly to the growing industrial economy of the East (and of much of the rest of the world). Mining, timbering, ranching, commercial farming, and many other economic activities relied on the East for markets and for capital. Some of the most powerful economic institutions in the West were great eastern corporations that controlled mines, ranches, and farms.

Labor in the West

As commercial activity increased, many farmers, ranchers, and miners found it necessary to recruit a paid labor force—not an easy task for those far away from major population centers and unable or unwilling to hire Indian workers. The labor shortage of the region led to higher wages for workers than were typical in most areas of the East. But working conditions were often arduous, and job security was almost nonexistent. Once a railroad was built, a crop harvested, a herd sent to market, a mine played out, hundreds and even thousands of workers could find themselves suddenly unemployed. Competition from Chinese immigrants, whom employers could usually hire for considerably lower wages than they had to pay whites, also forced some Anglo-Americans out of work. Communities of the jobless gathered in the region's few cities, in mining camps, and elsewhere; other unemployed people moved restlessly from place to place in search of work.

Those who owned no land were highly mobile, mostly male, and seldom married. Indeed, the West had the highest percentage of single adults (10 percent) of any region in the country—one reason why single women found working in dance halls and as prostitutes among the most readily available forms of employment.

Despite the enormous geographic mobility in western society, actual social mobility was limited. Many Americans thought of the West as a land of limitless opportunity, but, as in the rest of the country, advancement was easiest and most rapid for those who were economically advantaged to begin with. Studies of western communities suggest that social mobility in most of them was no greater than it was in the East. And the distribution of wealth in the region was little different from that in the older states as well.

Even more than in many parts of the East, the western working class was highly multiracial. English-speaking whites worked alongside African Americans and immigrants from southern and eastern Europe, as they did in the East. Even more, they worked with Chinese, Filipinos, Mexicans, and Indians. But the work force was highly stratified along racial lines. In almost every area of the western economy, white workers (whatever their ethnicity) occupied the upper tiers of employment: management and skilled labor. The lower tiers—people who did unskilled and often arduous work in the mines, on the railroads, or in agriculture—consisted overwhelmingly of nonwhites.

Reinforcing this dual labor system was a set of racial assumptions developed and sustained largely by white employers. Chinese, Mexicans, and Filipinos, they argued, were genetically or culturally suited to manual labor. Because they were small, those who promoted these racist stereotypes argued, they could work better in deep mines than whites. Because they were accustomed to heat, they could withstand arduous work in the fields better than whites. Because they were unambitious and unconcerned about material comfort, they would accept low wages and live in conditions that white people would not tolerate. These racial myths served the interests of employers above all, but white workers tended to embrace them too. That was in part because the myths supported a system that reserved whatever mobility there was largely for whites. An Irish common laborer might hope in the course of a lifetime to move several rungs up the occupational ladder. A Chinese or Mexican worker in the same job had no realistic prospects of doing the same.

The Arrival of the Miners

The first economic boom in the Far West came in mining, and the first part of the area to be extensively settled by migrants was the mineral-rich region of mountains and plateaus, where settlers hoped to make quick fortunes by finding precious metals. The life span of the mining boom was relatively brief. It began in earnest around 1860 (although there had, of course, been some earlier booms, most notably in California), and flourished until the 1890s. And then it abruptly declined.

News of a gold or silver strike in an area would start a stampede reminiscent of the California gold rush of 1849, followed by several stages of settlement. Individual prospectors would exploit the first shallow deposits of ore largely by hand, with pan and placer mining. After these surface deposits dwindled, corporations moved in to engage in lode or quartz mining, which dug deeper beneath the surface. Then, as those deposits dwindled, commercial mining either disappeared or continued on a restricted basis, and ranchers and farmers moved in and established a more permanent economy.

The first great mineral strikes (other than the California gold rush) occurred just before the Civil War. In 1858, gold was discovered in the Pike's Peak district of what would soon be the territory of Colorado; the following year, 50,000 prospectors stormed in from California, the

Limited Social Mobility

Racially Stratified Working Class

Life Cycle of a Mining Boom

Mississippi valley, and the East. Denver and other mining camps blossomed into "cities" overnight. Almost as rapidly as it had developed, the boom ended. After the mining frenzy died down, corporations, notably the Guggenheim interests, revived some of the profits of the gold boom, and the discovery of silver near Leadville supplied a new source of mineral wealth.

While the Colorado rush of 1859 was still in progress, news of another strike drew miners to Nevada. Gold had been found in the Washoe district, but the most valuable ore in the great Comstock Lode Comstock Lode (first discovered in 1858 by Henry Comstock) and other veins was silver. The first prospectors to reach the Washoe fields came from California; and from the beginning, Californians dominated the settlement and development of Nevada. In a remote desert without railroad transportation, the territory produced no supplies of its own, and everything—from food and machinery to whiskey and prostitutes—had to be shipped from California to Virginia City, Carson City, and other roaring camp towns. When the first placer (or surface) deposits ran out, California and eastern capitalists bought the claims of the pioneer prospectors and began to use the more difficult process of quartz mining, which enabled them to retrieve silver from deeper veins. For a few years these outside owners reaped tremendous profits; from 1860 to 1880, the Nevada lodes yielded bullion worth $306 million. After that, the mines quickly played out.

The next important mineral discoveries came in 1874, when gold was found in the Black Hills of southwestern Dakota Territory. Prospectors swarmed into the area, then (and for years to come) accessible only by stagecoach. Like the others, the boom flared for a time, until surface resources faded and corporations took over from the miners. One enormous company, the Homestake, came to dominate the fields. Population declined, and the Dakotas, like other boom areas of the mineral empire, ultimately developed a largely agricultural economy.

Although the gold and silver discoveries generated the most popular excitement, in the long run other, less glamorous natural resources proved more important to the development of the West. The great Anaconda copper mine launched by William Clark in 1881 marked the beginning of an industry that would remain important to Montana for many decades. In other areas, mining operations had significant success with lead, tin, quartz, and zinc. Such efforts generally proved more profitable in the long run than the usually short-lived gold and silver extraction.

Life in the boomtowns had a hectic tempo and a gaudy flavor unknown in any other part of the Far West. A speculative spirit, a mood of heady optimism, gripped almost everyone and dominated every phase of community activity. And while relatively few of the prospectors and miners who flocked to the bonanzas ever "struck it rich," there was at least some truth to the popular belief that mining provided opportunities for sudden wealth. The "bonanza kings"—the miners who did become enormously wealthy off a strike—were much more likely to have come from modest or impoverished backgrounds than the industrial tycoons of the East.

The conditions of mine life in the boom period—the presence of precious minerals, the vagueness of claim boundaries, the cargoes of gold being shipped out—attracted outlaws and "bad men," operating as individuals

COLORADO BOOMTOWN After a prospector discovered silver nearby in 1890, miners flocked to the town of Creede, Colorado. For a time in the early 1890s, 150 to 300 people arrived there daily. Although the town was located in a canyon so narrow that there was room for only one street, buildings sprouted rapidly to serve the growing community. As with other such boomtowns, however, Creede's prosperity was short-lived. In 1893 the price of silver collapsed, and by the end of the century, Creede was almost deserted. *(From the Collections of The Henry Ford)*

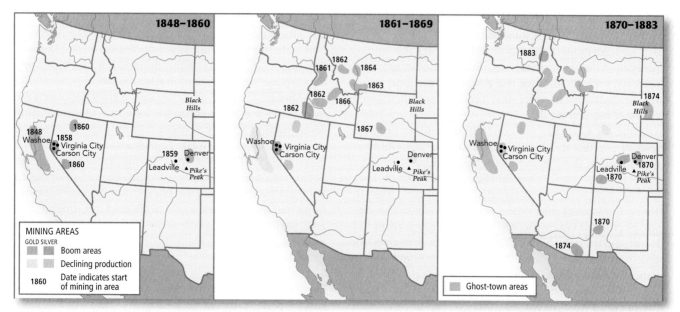

MINING TOWNS, 1848–1883   These three maps illustrate the rapid movement from boom to bust in the western mining industry in the mid-nineteenth century. Note how quickly the "boom" areas of gold and silver mining turn into places of "declining production," often in the space of less than a decade. Note, too, how mining for both metals moved from California and Nevada in the 1860s to areas farther east and north in the 1870s and beyond. The map also shows the areas in which "ghost towns"—mining communities abandoned by their residents once production ceased—proliferated.   ◆ *What impact did mining have on the population of the West?*

For an interactive version of this map, go to www.mhhe.com/brinkley13ech16maps

or gangs. When the situation became intolerable in a community, those members interested in order began enforcing their own laws through vigilante committees, an unofficial system of social control used earlier in California. Vigilantes were unconstrained by the legal system, and they often imposed their notion of justice arbitrarily and without regard for any form of due process. Sometimes criminals themselves secured control of the committees. Some vigilantes continued to operate as private "law" enforcers after the creation of regular governments.

Men greatly outnumbered women in the mining towns, and younger men in particular had difficulty finding female companions of comparable age. Those women who did gravitate to the new communities often came with their husbands, and their activities were generally (although not always) confined to the same kinds of domestic tasks that eastern women performed. Single women, or women whose husbands were earning no money, did choose (or find it necessary) to work for wages at times, as cooks, laundresses, and tavern keepers. And in the sexually imbalanced mining communities, there was always a ready market for prostitutes.

Gender Imbalance

The thousands of people who flocked to the mining towns in search of quick wealth and who failed to find it often remained as wage laborers in corporate mines after the boom period. Working conditions were almost uniformly terrible. The corporate mines were deep and extremely hot, with temperatures often exceeding 100 degrees Fahrenheit. Some workers died of heatstroke (or of pneumonia, a result of experiencing sudden changes of temperature when emerging from the mines). Poor ventilation meant large accumulations of poisonous carbon dioxide, which caused dizziness, nausea, and headaches. Lethal dusts stayed in the stagnant air to be inhaled over and over by the miners, many of whom developed silicosis (a disabling disease of the lungs) as a result. There were frequent explosions, cave-ins, and fires, and there were many accidents with the heavy machinery the workers used to bore into the earth. In the 1870s, before technological advances eliminated some of the dangers, one worker in every thirty was disabled in the mines, and one in every eighty was killed. That rate fell later in the nineteenth century, but mining remained one of the most dangerous and arduous working environments in the United States.

The Cattle Kingdom

A second important element of the changing economy of the Far West was cattle ranching. The open range—the vast grasslands of the public domain—provided a huge area on the Great Plains where cattle raisers could graze their herds free of charge and unrestricted by the boundaries of private farms. The railroads gave birth to the range-cattle industry by giving it access to markets. Eventually, the same railroads ended it by bringing farmers to the plains and thus destroying the open range.

The western cattle industry was Mexican and Texan by ancestry. Long before citizens of the United States invaded the

Mexican Origins

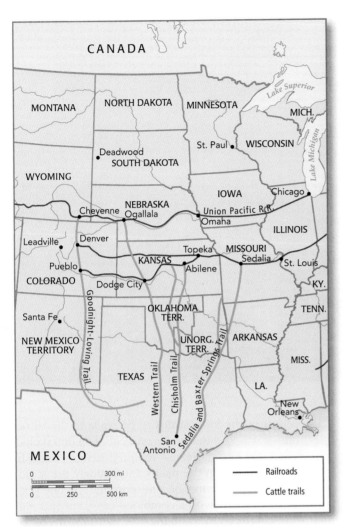

THE CATTLE KINGDOM, C. 1866–1887 Cattle ranching and cattle drives are among the most romanticized features of the nineteenth-century West. But they were also hardheaded businesses, made possible by the growing eastern market for beef and the availability of reasonably inexpensive transportation to take cattle to urban markets. ◆ *Why was that necessary for the great cattle drives, and what eventually ended it?* The other is the dense network of trails and railroads that together made possible the commerce in cattle.

For an interactive version of this map, go to www.mhhe.com/brinkley13ech16maps

Southwest, Mexican ranchers had developed the techniques and equipment that the cattlemen and cowboys of the Great Plains later employed: branding (a device known in all frontier areas where stock was common), roundups, roping, and the gear of the herders—their lariats, saddles, leather chaps, and spurs. Americans in Texas adopted these methods and carried them to the northernmost ranges of the cattle kingdom. Texas also had the largest herds of cattle in the country; the animals were descended from imported Spanish stock—wiry, hardy longhorns—and allowed to run wild or semiwild. From Texas, too, came the horses that enabled the caretakers of the herds, the cowboys, to control them—small, mus-

cular broncos or mustangs well suited to the requirements of cattle country.

At the end of the Civil War, an estimated 5 million cattle roamed the Texas ranges. Eastern markets were offering fat prices for steers in any condition, and the challenge facing the cattle industry was getting the animals from the range to the railroad centers. Early in 1866, some Texas cattle ranchers began driving their combined herds, as much as 260,000 head, north to Sedalia, Missouri, on the Missouri Pacific Railroad. Traveling over rough country and beset by outlaws, Indians, and property-conscious farmers, the caravan suffered heavy losses, and only a fraction of the animals arrived in Sedalia. But the drive was an important experiment. It proved that cattle could be driven to distant markets and pastured along the trail, and that they would even gain weight during the journey. This earliest of the "long drives," in other words, established the first, tentative link between the isolated cattle breeders of west Texas and the booming urban markets of the East. The drive laid the groundwork for the explosion of the industry—for the creation of the "cattle kingdom."

With the precedent of the long drive established, the next step was to find an easier route through more accessible country. Market facilities grew up at Abilene, Kansas, on the Kansas Pacific Railroad, and for years the town reigned as the railhead of the cattle kingdom. Between 1867 and 1871, cattlemen drove nearly 1.5 million head up the Chisholm Trail to Abilene—a town that, when filled with rampaging cowboys at the end of a drive, rivaled the mining towns in rowdiness. But by the mid-1870s, agricultural development in western Kansas was eating away at the open range land at the same time that the supply of animals was increasing. Cattlemen therefore had to develop other trails and other market outlets. As the railroads began to reach farther west, Dodge City and Wichita in Kansas, Ogallala and Sidney in Nebraska, Cheyenne and Laramie in Wyoming, and Miles City and Glendive in Montana all began to rival Abilene as major centers of stock herding.

A long drive was a spectacular sight, and it is perhaps unsurprising that it became the most romanticized and mythologized aspect of life in the West. It began with the spring, or calf, roundup. The cattlemen of a district met with their cowboys at a specified place to round up stock from the open range; these herds contained the stock of many different owners, with only their brands to distinguish them from one another. As the cattle were driven in, the calves were branded with the marks of their mothers. Stray calves with no identifying symbols, "mavericks," were divided on a pro-rata basis. Then the cows and calves were turned loose to pasture, while the yearling steers (year-old males) were readied for the drive to the north. The combined herds, usually numbering from 2,000 to 5,000 head, moved out. Cowboys representing each of the major ranchers accompanied them. Most of the cowboys in the early years were veterans of the Confederate army. The

COWBOYS ON A "LONG DRIVE" The "long drive" not only provided cattle for the eastern market, it also created communities of men who spent much of their lives on the trail, working for ranchers tending cattle. These cowboys were mostly young, unmarried men, mostly white but including many African Americans. Most of them later settled down, but many agreed with the former cowboy Charles Goodknight, who wrote years later, "All in all, my years on the trail were the happiest I ever lived. There were many hardships and dangers... but when all went well, there was no other life so pleasant. Most of the time we were solitary adventurers in a great land, ... and we were free and full of the zest of darers." This photograph of cowboys riding herd dates from the 1880s. *(Library of Congress)*

next largest group consisted of African Americans—over half a million of them. They were more numerous than white northerners or Mexicans and other foreigners. They were usually assigned such jobs as wrangler (herdsman) or cook.

Every cattleman had to have a permanent base from which to operate, and so the ranch emerged. A ranch consisted of the employer's dwelling, quarters for employees, and a tract of grazing land. In the early years of the cattle kingdom, most ranches were relatively small, since so much of the grazing occurred in the vast, open areas that cattlemen shared. But as farmers and sheep breeders began to compete for the open plains, ranches became larger and more clearly defined; cattlemen gradually had to learn to raise their stock on their own fenced land.

There was always an element of risk and speculation in the open-range cattle business. At any time, "Texas fever"—a disease transmitted to cattle by parasite-carrying ticks—might decimate a herd. Rustlers and Indians frequently seized large numbers of animals. But as settlement of the plains increased, new forms of competition joined these traditional risks. Sheep breeders from California and Oregon brought their flocks onto the range to compete for grass. Farmers ("nesters") from the East threw fences around their claims, blocking trails and breaking up the open range. A series of "range wars"—between sheepmen and cattlemen, between ranchers and farmers—erupted out of the tensions between these competing groups, resulting in significant loss of life and extensive property damage.

Competition with Farmers

Accounts of the lofty profits to be made in the cattle business—it was said that an investment of $5,000 would return $45,000 in four years—tempted eastern, English, and Scottish capital to the plains. Increasingly, the structure of the cattle economy became corporate; in one year, twenty corporations with a combined capital of $12 million were chartered in Wyoming. The inevitable result of this frenzied, speculative expansion was that the ranges, already severed and shrunk by the railroads and the farmers, became overstocked. There was not enough grass to support the crowding herds or sustain the long drives. Finally nature intervened with a destructive finishing blow. Two severe winters, in 1885–1886 and 1886–1887, with a searing summer between them, stung and scorched the plains. Hundreds of thousands of cattle died, streams and grass dried up, princely ranches and costly investments disappeared in a season.

The open-range industry never recovered; the long drive disappeared for good. Railroads displaced the trail as the route to market for livestock. But the established cattle ranches—with fenced-in grazing land and stocks of hay for winter feed—survived, grew, and prospered, eventually producing more beef than ever.

Although the cattle industry was overwhelmingly male in its early years, there were always a few women involved in ranching and driving. As ranching became more sedentary, the presence of women greatly increased. By 1890, more than 250,000 women owned ranches or farms in the western states (many of them as proxies for their husbands or fathers, but some in their own right). Indeed, the region provided women with many opportunities that were closed to them in the East—including the opportunity to participate in politics. Wyoming was the first state in the Union to guarantee woman suffrage; and throughout the West, women established themselves as an important political presence (and occasionally as significant officeholders).

Women won the vote earlier in the West than they did in the rest of the nation for different reasons in different

Political Gains for Women

places. In Utah, the Mormons granted women suffrage in an effort to stave off criticism of their practice of polygamy. In some places, women won suffrage before statehood to swell the electorate to the number required by Congress. In others, women won the vote by persuading men that they would help bring a "moral" voice into the politics of the region and strengthen the sense of community in the West. Because women were, most men (and many women) believed, more "generous and virtuous" than men, they might bring these special qualities to the raw societies of the region. (Many of the same arguments were ultimately used to justify suffrage in the East as well.)

THE ROMANCE OF THE WEST

The supposedly unsettled West had always occupied a special place in the Anglo-American imagination, beginning in the seventeenth century when the first white settlers along the Atlantic coast began to look to the interior for new opportunities and for refuge from the civilized world. The vast regions of this "last frontier" had a particularly strong romantic appeal to many whites.

The Western Landscape

The allure of the West was obvious. The Great Plains, the Rocky Mountains, the basin and plateau region beyond the Rockies, the Sierra Nevada, and the Cascade Range—all constituted a landscape of brilliant diversity and spectacular grandeur, different from anything white Americans had encountered before. It was

"Rocky Mountain School"

little wonder that newcomers looked on the West with reverence and wonder. Painters of the "Rocky Mountain School"—of whom the best known were Albert Bierstadt and Thomas Moran—celebrated the new West in grandiose canvases, some of which were taken on tours around eastern and midwestern states and attracted enormous crowds, eager for a vision of the Great West. Such paintings emphasized the ruggedness and dramatic variety of the region, and reflected the same awe toward the land that earlier regional painters had displayed toward the Hudson River valley and other areas.

The interest in paintings of the West helped inspire a growing wave of tourism. Increasingly in the 1880s and 1890s, as railroads extended farther into the region and as the Indian wars subsided, resort hotels began to spring up near some of the most spectacular landscapes in the region; and easterners began to come for visits of several weeks or more, combining residence in a comfortable hotel with hikes and excursions into the "wilderness."

The Cowboy Culture

Even more appealing than the landscape was the rugged, free-spirited lifestyle that many Americans associated with the West—a lifestyle that supposedly stood in sharp contrast to the increasingly stable and ordered world of the East. Many nineteenth-century Americans came to romanticize, especially, the figure of the cowboy and transformed him

Myth of the Cowboy

remarkably quickly from the low-paid worker he actually was into a powerful and enduring figure of myth.

Admiring Americans seldom thought about the many dismal aspects of the cowboy's life: the tedium, the loneliness, the physical discomforts, the low pay, the relatively few opportunities for advancement. Instead, in popular western novels such as Owen Wister's *The Virginian* (1902), they romanticized his freedom from traditional social constraints, his affinity with nature, even his supposed propensity for violence. Wister's character was a semi-educated man whose natural decency, courage, and compassion made him a powerful symbol of the supposed virtues of the frontier. But *The Virginian* was only the most famous example of a type of literature that soon swept throughout the United States: novels and stories about the West, and about the lives of cowboys in particular, that appeared in boys' magazines, pulp novels, theater, and even serious literature. The enormous popularity of traveling Wild West shows spread the cult of the cowboy still further. (See "Patterns of Popular Culture," pp. 454–455.)

The cowboy had become perhaps the most widely admired popular hero in America, and a powerful and enduring symbol of the important American ideal of the natural man (the same idea that had shaped James Fenimore Cooper's Natty Bumppo earlier). That symbol has survived into the twenty-first century—in popular literature, in song, in film, and on television.

The Idea of the Frontier

Yet it was not simply the particular character of the new West that made it so important to the nation's imagination. It was also that many Americans consid-

Romantic Image of the West

ered it the last frontier. Since the earliest moments of European settlement in America, the image of uncharted territory to the west had always comforted and inspired those who dreamed of starting life anew. Now, with the last of that unsettled land being slowly absorbed into the nation's civilization, that image exercised a stronger pull than ever.

THE WILD WEST SHOW

For many Americans, the "Old West" has always been a place of myth—a source of some of our culture's most romantic and exciting stories. Historians have offered a picture of the West sharply at odds with its popular image, but the image survives despite them. One reason the romantic depiction of the Old West has persisted is the astonishing popularity of the "Wild West show" in the late nineteenth and early twentieth centuries. This colorful entertainment may have had little connection with the reality of western life, but it stamped on its audiences an image of the West as a place of adventure and romance that has lasted for generations. The Wild West show emerged out of a number of earlier entertainment traditions. The great showman P. T. Barnum had begun popularizing the "Wild West" as early as the 1840s when he staged a "Grand Buffalo Hunt" for spectators in New York, and such shows continued into the 1870s, one of them featuring the famous "Wild Bill" Hickok. At about the same time, western cowboys began staging versions of the modern rodeo when their cattle drives passed near substantial towns. But the first real Wild West show opened in Omaha, Nebraska, in 1883. Its organizer was William F. Cody, better known as "Buffalo Bill."

Cody had ridden for the Pony Express, fought in the Civil War, and been a supplier of buffalo meat to workers on the transcontinental railroad (hence his celebrated nickname). But his real fame was a result of his work as a scout for the U.S. Cavalry during the Indian wars of the 1870s and as a guide for hunting parties of notable easterners. One of them, a dime-novel writer who published under the name Ned Buntline, wrote a series of books portraying (and greatly exaggerating) Buffalo Bill's exploits. The novels turned Cody into a national celebrity.

The Wild West show Cody began in 1883 inspired dozens of imitators, and almost all of them used some version of its format. Cody's shows included mock Indian attacks (by real Indians) on stagecoaches and wagon trains. There were portrayals of the Pony Express. There were shooting, riding,

PROMOTING THE WEST   Buffalo Bill's Wild West show was popular all over the United States and, indeed, through much of the world. He was so familiar a figure that many of his posters contained only his picture with the words "He is Coming." This more conventional poster announces a visit of the show to Brooklyn.   *(Culver Pictures, Inc.)*

Mark Twain, one of the great American writers of the nineteenth century, gave voice to this romantic vision of the frontier in a series of brilliant novels and memoirs. In some of his writings—notably *Roughing It* (1872)—he wrote of the Far West and of his own experience as a newspaper reporter in Nevada during the mining boom. His greatest works, however, dealt with life on an earlier frontier: the Mississippi Valley of his boyhood. In *The Adventures of Tom Sawyer* (1876) and *The Adventures of Huckleberry Finn* (1885), he produced characters who repudiated the constraints of organized society and attempted to escape into a natural world. For Huck Finn, the vehicle of escape might be a small raft on the Mississippi, but the yearning for freedom reflected a larger vision of the West as the last refuge from the constraints of civilization.

The painter and sculptor Frederic Remington also captured the romance of the West and its image as an alternative to the settled civilization of the East. He portrayed the cowboy as a natural aristocrat, much like Wister's Virginian, living in a natural world in which all the normal supporting structures of "civilization" were missing. The romantic quality of his work made Remington one of the most beloved and successful artists of the nineteenth century.

Frederic Remington

Theodore Roosevelt, who was, like both Wister and Remington, a man born and raised in the East, traveled to the Dakota Badlands in the mid-1880s to help himself recover from the sudden death of his young wife. He had long romanticized the West as a place of physical regeneration—a place where a man could gain strength through rugged activity (just as Roosevelt himself, a sickly,

ANNIE OAKLEY Annie Oakley had been a vaudeville and circus entertainer for years before joining Buffalo Bill's Wild West show in 1885. She was less than five feet tall and weighed less than a hundred pounds, but her exploits with pistols, rifles, and horses earned her a reputation as a woman of unusual strength and skill. *(Bettmann/Corbis)*

and roping exhibitions. And there was a grand finale—"A Grand Hunt on the Plains"—that included buffalo, elk, deer, mountain sheep, longhorn cattle, and wild horses. Later, Cody added a reenactment of Custer's last stand. And later still, he began to include stagings of such nonwestern heroics as Theodore Roosevelt's charge up Kettle Hill during the Spanish-American War.

But the effort to evoke the romance of the Old West always remained at the show's center.

Buffalo Bill was always the star performer in his own productions. But the show had other celebrities, too. A woman who used the stage name Annie Oakley became wildly popular for her shooting acts, during which she would throw into the air small cards with her picture on them, shoot a hole through their middle, and toss them into the audience as souvenirs.

Native Americans were important parts of the Wild West shows, and hundreds of them participated—showing off their martial skills and exotic costumes and customs. The great Sioux leader Sitting Bull toured with the show for four months in 1885, during which he discussed Indian affairs with President Cleveland, who was a member of one of his audiences. The famous Chiricahua Apache warrior Geronimo, who had fought against the United States until 1886, spent a season touring with one of Buffalo Bill's competitors—having previously been paraded around the country as a prisoner by the U.S. Army. He later appeared in a re-creation of an Apache village at the 1904 World's Fair in St. Louis.

Buffalo Bill's show was an immediate success and quickly began traveling across the nation and throughout Europe. Over 41,000 people saw it on one day in Chicago in 1884. In 1886, it played for six months on Staten Island in New York, where General William T.

Sherman, Mark Twain, P. T. Barnum, Thomas A. Edison, and the widow of General Custer all saw and praised it. Members of the royal family attended the show in England, and it drew large crowds as well in France, Germany, and Italy.

The Wild West shows died out not long after World War I, but many of their features survived in circuses and rodeos, and later in films, radio and television shows, and theme parks. Their popularity was evidence of the nostalgia with which late-nineteenth-century Americans looked at their own imagined past, and their eagerness to remember a "Wild West" that had never really been what they liked to believe. Buffalo Bill and his imitators confirmed the popular image of the West as a place of romance and glamour and helped keep that image alive for later generations.

FREE ADMISSION The managers of Buffalo Bill's company were eager to attract visits from the famous and influential and gave out many complimentary tickets (like this one for a show in Chicago in 1893) to local dignitaries in an effort to entice them to appear. *(Culver Pictures, Inc.)*

asthmatic boy, had hardened himself through adherence to the idea of a strenuous life). His long sojourn into the Badlands in the 1880s cemented his love of the region, which continued to the end of his life. And like Wister and Remington, he made his own fascination with the West a part of the nation's popular culture. In the 1890s, he published a four-volume history, *The Winning of the West,* with a romanticized account of the spread of white civilization into the frontier. These and other books on the West enhanced his own reputation. They also contributed to the public's fascination with the "frontier."

Frederick Jackson Turner

Perhaps the clearest and most influential statements of the romantic vision of the frontier came from the historian Frederick Jackson Turner, of the University of Wisconsin. In 1893, the thirty-three-year-old Turner delivered a memorable Turner's Frontier Thesis paper to a meeting of the American Historical Association in Chicago titled "The Significance of the Frontier in American History," in which he argued that the end of the "frontier" also marked the end of one of the most important democratizing forces in American life. (See "Where Historians Disagree," pp. 456–457.)

In fact, Turner's assessments were both inaccurate and premature. The West had never been a "frontier" in the sense he meant the term: an empty, uncivilized land awaiting settlement. White migrants into the region had joined (or displaced) already-established societies and cultures. At the same time, considerable unoccupied land remained in the West for many years to come. But Turner did express

THE "FRONTIER" AND THE WEST

The American West, and the process by which people of European descent settled there, has been central to the national imagination for at least two centuries. It has also, at times, been central to American historical scholarship.

Through most of the nineteenth century, the history of the West reflected the romantic and optimistic view of the region beloved by many Americans. The lands west of the Mississippi River were places of adventure and opportunity. The West was a region where life could start anew, where brave and enterprising people endured great hardships to begin building a new civilization. Francis Parkman's *The Oregon Trail* (1849), a classic of American literature, expressed many of these assumptions and in the process shaped the way in which later generations of Americans would view the West and its past. But the emergence of western history as an important field of scholarship can best be traced to the famous paper Frederick Jackson Turner delivered at a meeting of the American Historical Association in 1893. It was titled "The Significance of the Frontier in American History." The "Turner thesis" or "frontier thesis," as his argument quickly became known, shaped both popular and scholarly views of the West (and of much else) for two generations.

Turner stated his thesis simply. The settlement of the West by white people—"the existence of an area of free land, its continuous recession, and the advance of American settlement westward"—was the central story of American history. The process of westward expansion had transformed a desolate and savage land into a modern civilization. It had also continually renewed American ideas of democracy and individualism and had, therefore, shaped not just the West but the nation as a whole. "What the Mediterranean Sea was to the Greeks, breaking the bonds of custom, offering new experiences, calling out new institutions and activities, that, and more, the ever retreating frontier has been to the United States." The Turner thesis shaped the writing of American history for a generation, and it shaped the writing of western American history for even longer. In the first half of the twentieth century, virtually all the major figures in the field echoed and elaborated at least part of Turner's argument. Ray Allen Billington's *Westward Expansion* (1949) was for decades the standard textbook in the field; his skillful revision of the Turner thesis kept the idea of what he called the "westward course of empire" (the movement of Europeans into an unsettled land) at the center of scholarship. In *The Great Plains* (1931) and *The Great Frontier* (1952), Walter Prescott Webb similarly emphasized the bravery and ingenuity of white settlers in Texas and the Southwest in overcoming obstacles (most notably, in Webb's part of the West, aridity) to create a great new civilization.

The Turner thesis was never without its critics. But serious efforts to displace it as the explanation of western American history did not begin in earnest until after World War II. In *Virgin Land* (1950), Henry Nash Smith examined many of the same heroic images of the West that Turner and his disciples had presented; but he treated those images less as

READING THE WAR BULLETINS, SAN FRANCISCO Residents of San Francisco's Chinatown gather on a sidewalk to await a Chinese-language newspaper's posting of the reports from Asia of the progress of the Sino-Japanese War. The conflict between China and Japan in 1894–1895 left China so weakened that it could no longer effectively resist incursions from Western nations. *(Library of Congress)*

descriptions of reality than as myths, which many Americans had used to sustain an image of themselves that the actual character of the modern world contradicted. Earl Pomeroy, in an influential 1955 essay and in many other works, challenged Turner's notion of the West as a place of individualism, innovation, and democratic renewal. "Conservatism, inheritance, and continuity bulked at least as large," he claimed. "The westerner has been fundamentally imitator rather than innovator. . . . He was often the most ardent of conformists." Howard Lamar, in *Dakota Territory, 1861–1889* (1956) and *The Far Southwest* (1966), emphasized the highly diverse experiences of different areas of the West and thus challenged the emphasis of the Turnerians on a distinctive western environment as the crucial determinant of western experience.

The generation of western historians who began to emerge in the late 1970s launched an even more emphatic attack on the Turner thesis and the idea of the "frontier." Echoing the interest of historians in other fields in issues of race, gender, ethnicity, and culture, "new" western historians such as Richard White, Patricia Nelson Limerick, William Cronon, Donald Worster, Peggy Pascoe, and many others challenged the Turnerians on a number of points.

Turner saw the nineteenth-century West as "free land" awaiting the expansion of Anglo-American settlement and American democracy. Pioneers settled the region by conquering the "obstacles" in the way of civilization—the "vast forests," the "mountainous ramparts," the "desolate, grass-clad prairies, barren oceans of rolling plains, arid deserts, and a fierce race of savages." The "new western historians" rejected the concept of a "frontier" and emphasized, instead, the elaborate and highly developed civilizations (Native American, Hispanic, mixed-blood, and others) that already existed in the region. White, English-speaking Americans, they argued, did not so much settle the West as conquer it. And that conquest was never complete. Anglo-Americans in the West continue to share the region not only with the Indians and Hispanics

who preceded them there, but also with African Americans, Asians, Latino Americans, and others who flowed into the West at the same time they did. Western history, these scholars have claimed, is a process of cultural "convergence," a constant competition and interaction—economic, political, cultural, and linguistic—among diverse peoples.

The Turnerian West was a place of heroism, triumph, and, above all, progress, dominated by the feats of brave white men. The West the new historians describe is a less triumphant (and less masculine) place in which bravery and success coexist with oppression, greed, and failure; in which decaying ghost towns, bleak Indian reservations, impoverished barrios, and ecologically devastated landscapes are as characteristic of western development as great ranches, rich farms, and prosperous cities; and in which women are as important as men in shaping the societies that emerged. This aspect of the "new western history" has attracted particular criticism from those attached to traditional accounts. The novelist Larry McMurtry, for example, has denounced the new scholarship as "Failure Studies." He has insisted

that in rejecting the romantic image westerners had of themselves, the revisionists omit an important part of the western experience.

To Turner and his disciples, the nineteenth-century West was a place where rugged individualism flourished and replenished American democracy. To the new scholars, western individualism is a self-serving myth. The region was inextricably tied to a national and international capitalist economy; indeed, the only thing that sustained Anglo-American settlement of the West was the demand in other places for its natural resources. Western "pioneers" were never self-sufficient. They depended on government-subsidized railroads for access to markets, federal troops for protection from Indians, and (later) government-funded dams and canals for irrigating their fields and sustaining their towns.

And while Turner defined the West as a process—a process of settlement that came to an end with the "closing of the frontier" in the late nineteenth century—the new historians see the West as a region. Its distinctive history does not end in 1890. It continues into our own time.

(Montana Historical Society, Helena)

TWILIGHT ENCAMPMENT The western photographer Walter McClintock took this dramatic photograph of a Blackfoot Indian camp in the 1890s. By the time this picture was taken, the Indian tribes were already dwindling, and artists, photographers, and ethnographers flocked to the West to record aspects of Indian civilization that they feared would soon disappear. *(Beinecke Rare Book and Manuscript Library, Yale University)*

a growing and generally accurate sense that much of the best farming and grazing land was now taken, that in the future it would be more difficult for individuals to acquire valuable land for little or nothing.

The Loss of Utopia

In accepting the idea of the "passing of the frontier," many Americans were acknowledging the end of one of their most cherished myths. As long as it had been possible for them to consider the West an empty, open land, it was possible to believe that there were constantly revitalizing opportunities in American life. Now there was a vague and ominous sense of opportunities foreclosed, of individuals losing their ability to control their own destinies. The psychological loss was all the greater because of what historian Henry Nash Smith would later call, in *Virgin Land* (1950), the "myth of the garden": the once widely shared belief that the West had the potential to be a virtual Garden of Eden, where a person could begin life anew and where the ideals of democracy could be restored.

Psychological Loss

In late-nineteenth-century fiction, such as Helen Hunt Jackson's *Ramona,* the setting for utopia, once the New World as a whole, had shrunk to the West of the United States. And now even that West seemed to be vanishing.

THE DISPERSAL OF THE TRIBES

Having imagined the West as a "virgin land" awaiting civilization by white people, many Americans tried to force the region to match their image of it. That meant, above all, ensuring that the Indian tribes would not remain obstacles to the spread of white society.

White Tribal Policies

The traditional policy of the federal government was to regard the tribes simultaneously as independent nations and as wards of the president, and to negotiate treaties with them that were solemnly ratified by the Senate. This limited concept of Indian sovereignty had been responsible for the government's attempt before 1860 to erect a permanent frontier between whites and Indians, to reserve the region west of the bend of the Missouri River as permanent Indian country. However, treaties or agreements with the tribes seldom survived the pressure of white settlers eager for access to Indian lands. The history of relations between the United States and the Native Americans was, therefore, one of nearly endless broken promises.

By the early 1850s, the idea of establishing one great enclave in which many tribes could live gave way, in the face of white demands for access to lands in Indian Territory, to a new reservations policy, known as "concentration." In 1851, each tribe was assigned its own defined reservation, confirmed by separate treaties—treaties often illegitimately negotiated with unauthorized "representatives" chosen by whites, people known sarcastically as "treaty chiefs." The new arrangement had many benefits for whites and few for the Indians. It divided the tribes from one another and made them easier to control. It allowed the government to force tribes into scattered locations and to take over the most desirable lands for white settlement. But it did not survive as the basis of Indian policy for long.

"Concentration" Policy

In 1867, in the aftermath of a series of bloody conflicts, Congress established an Indian Peace Commission, composed of soldiers and civilians, to recommend a new and presumably permanent Indian policy. The commission recommended replacing the "concentration" policy with a plan to move all the Plains Indians into two large reservations—one in Indian Territory (Oklahoma), the other in the Dakotas. At a series of meetings with the tribes, government agents cajoled, bribed, and tricked representatives of the Arapaho, Cheyenne, Sioux, and other tribes into agreeing to treaties establishing the new reservations.

But this solution worked little better than previous ones. Part of the problem was the way in which the government administered the reservations it had es-

Poorly Administered Reservations

tablished. White management of Indian matters was entrusted to the Bureau of Indian Affairs, a branch of the Department of the Interior responsible for distributing land, making payments, and supervising the shipment of supplies. Its record was appalling. The bureau's agents in the West, products of political patronage, were often men of extraordinary incompetence and dishonesty. But even the most honest and diligent agents were generally ill prepared for their jobs, had no understanding of tribal ways, and had little chance of success.

Compounding the problem was what was, in effect, economic warfare by whites: the relentless slaughtering of the buffalo herds that supported the tribes' way of life. Even in the 1850s, whites had been killing buffalo at a rapid rate to provide food and supplies for the large bands of migrants traveling to the gold rush in California. After the Civil War the white demand for buffalo hides became a national phenomenon—partly for economic reasons and partly as a fad. (Everyone east of the Missouri seemed to want a buffalo robe from the romantic West, and there was a strong demand for buffalo leather, which was used to make machine belts in eastern factories.) Gangs of professional hunters swarmed over the plains to shoot the huge animals. Railroad companies hired riflemen (such as Buffalo Bill Cody) and arranged shooting expeditions to kill large numbers of buffalo, hoping to thin the herds, which were obstructions to railroad traffic. Some Indian tribes (notably the Blackfeet) also began killing large numbers of buffalo to sell in the booming new market.

It was not just the hunting that threatened the buffalo. The ecological changes accompanying white settlement—the reduction, and in some areas virtual disappearance, of the open plains—also decimated

Decimation of the Buffalo

CHIEF GARFIELD Edward Curtis, one of the most accomplished photographers of tribal life in the early twentieth century, made this portrait of a Jicarilla Apache chief in 1904. By then, the Jicarilla were living in a reservation in northern New Mexico, and white officials had assigned all members of the tribe Spanish or English names. The man depicted here, the head chief, had chosen the name Garfield himself. *(Chief Garfield-Jicarilla, 1904. Edward Curtis. Reproduced by permission of Christopher Cardozo, Inc.)*

the buffalo population. The southern herd was virtually exterminated by 1875, and within a few years the smaller northern herd had met the same fate. In 1865, there had been at least 15 million buffalo; a decade later, fewer than a thousand of the great beasts survived. The army and the agents of the Bureau of Indian Affairs condoned and even encouraged the killing. By destroying the buffalo herds, whites were destroying the Indians' source of food and supplies and their ability to resist the white advance. They were also contributing to a climate in which Indian warriors felt the need to fight to preserve their way of life.

The Indian Wars

There was almost incessant fighting between whites and Indians from the 1850s to the 1880s, as Indians struggled

HELD UP BY BUFFALO Once among the most numerous creatures in North America, the buffalo almost became extinct as a result of indiscriminate slaughter by white settlers and travelers, who often fired at herds from moving trains simply for the sport of it. This scene was painted around 1880 by N. H. Trotter. *(Smithsonian Institution)*

against the growing threats to their civilizations. Indian

Indian Resistance

warriors, usually traveling in raiding parties of thirty to forty men, attacked wagon trains, stagecoaches, and isolated ranches, often in retaliation for earlier attacks. As the United States Army became more deeply involved in the fighting, the tribes began to focus more of their attacks on white soldiers.

At times, this small-scale fighting escalated into something close to a war. During the Civil War, the eastern Sioux in Minnesota, cramped on an inadequate reservation and exploited by corrupt white agents, suddenly rebelled against the restrictions imposed on them by the government's policies. Led by Little Crow, they killed more than 700 whites before being subdued by a force of regulars and militiamen. Thirty-eight of the Indians were hanged, and the tribe was exiled to the Dakotas.

At the same time, fighting flared up in eastern Colorado, where the Arapaho and Cheyenne were coming into con-

Sand Creek Massacre

flict with white miners settling in the region. Bands of Indians attacked stagecoach lines and settlements in an effort to regain lost territory. In response to these incidents, whites called up a large territorial militia, and the army issued dire threats of retribution. The governor urged all friendly Indians to congregate at army posts for protection before the army began its campaign. One Arapaho and Cheyenne band under Black Kettle, apparently in response to the invitation, camped near Fort Lyon on Sand Creek in November 1864. Some members of the party were warriors, but Black Kettle believed he was under official protection and exhibited no hostile intention. Nevertheless, Colonel J. M. Chivington, apparently encouraged by the

army commander of the district, led a volunteer militia force—largely consisting of unemployed miners, many of whom were apparently drunk—to the unsuspecting camp and massacred 133 people, 105 of them women and children. Black Kettle himself escaped the Sand Creek massacre. Four years later, in 1868, he and his Cheyennes, some of whom were now at war with the whites, were caught on the Washita River, near the Texas border, by Colonel George A. Custer. White troops killed the chief and slaughtered his people.

At the end of the Civil War, white troops stepped up their wars against the western Indians on several fronts. The most serious and sustained conflict was in Montana, where the army was attempting to build a road, the Bozeman Trail, to connect Fort Laramie, Wyoming, to the new mining centers. The western Sioux resented this intrusion into the heart of their buffalo range. Led by one of their great chiefs, Red Cloud, they so harried the soldiers and the construction party—among other things, burning the forts that were supposed to guard the route—that the road could not be used.

But it was not only the United States Army that threatened the tribes. It was also unofficial violence by white vigilantes who engaged in what became known as "Indian hunt-

"Indian Hunting"

ing." In California, in particular, tracking down and killing Indians became for some whites a kind of sport. Some who did not engage in killing offered rewards (or bounties) to those who did; these bounty hunters brought back scalps and skulls as proof of their deeds. Sometimes the killing was in response to Indian raids on white communities. But often it was in service to a more basic and terrible purpose. Considerable numbers of whites were committed to the goal of literal "elimination" of the tribes, a goal that rested on the belief in the essential inhumanity of Indians and the impossibility of white society's coexisting with them. In Oregon in 1853, for example, whites who had hanged a seven-year-old Indian boy explained themselves by saying simply "nits breed lice." In California, civilians killed close to 5,000 Indians between 1850 and 1880—one of many factors (disease and poverty being the more important) that reduced the Indian population of the state from 150,000 before the Civil War to 30,000 in 1870.

The treaties negotiated in 1867 brought a temporary lull to many of the conflicts. But new forces soon shattered the peace again. In the early 1870s, more waves of white settlers, mostly miners, began to penetrate some of the lands in Dakota Territory supposedly guaranteed to the tribes in 1867.

Indian resistance flared anew, this time with even greater strength. In the northern plains, the Sioux rose up in 1875 and left their reservation. When white officials ordered them to return, bands of warriors gathered in Montana and united under two great leaders: Crazy Horse and Sitting Bull.

Three army columns set out to round them up and force them back onto the reservation. With the expedition, as colonel of the famous Seventh Cavalry, was the colorful

Little Bighorn

and controversial George A. Custer, golden-haired romantic and glory seeker. At the Battle of the Little Bighorn in southern Montana in 1876—perhaps the most famous of all conflicts between whites and Indians—the tribal warriors surprised Custer and 264 members of his regiment, surrounded them, and killed every man. Custer has been accused of rashness, but he seems to have encountered something that no white man would likely have predicted. The chiefs had gathered as many as 2,500 warriors, one of the largest Indian armies ever assembled at one time in the United States.

But the Indians did not have the political organization or the supplies to keep their troops united. Soon the warriors drifted off in bands to elude pursuit or search for food, and the army ran them down singly and returned them to Dakota. The power of the Sioux was soon broken. The proud leaders, Crazy Horse and Sitting Bull, accepted defeat and the monotony of life on reservations. Both were later killed by reservation police after being tricked or taunted into a last pathetic show of resistance.

One of the most dramatic episodes in Indian history occurred in Idaho in 1877. The Nez Percé were a small and relatively peaceful tribe, some of whose members had managed to live unmolested in Oregon into the 1870s without ever signing a treaty with the United States. But under pressure from white settlers, the government forced them to move into a reservation that another branch of the tribe had accepted by treaty in the 1850s. With no realistic prospect of resisting, the Indians began the journey to the reservation; but on the way, several younger Indians, drunk and angry, killed four white settlers.

The leader of the band, Chief Joseph, persuaded his followers to flee from the expected retribution. American troops pursued and attacked them, only to be driven off in a

Chief Joseph

battle at White Bird Canyon. After that, the Nez Percé scattered in several directions and became part of a remarkable chase. Joseph moved with 200 men and 350 women, children, and elders in an effort to reach Canada and take refuge with the Sioux there. Pursued by four columns of American soldiers smarting from their defeat at White Bird Canyon, the Indians covered 1,321 miles in seventy-five days, repelling or evading the army time and again. They were finally caught just short of the Canadian boundary. Some escaped and slipped across the border; but Joseph and most of his followers, weary and discouraged, finally gave up. "Hear me, my chiefs," Joseph said after meeting with the American general Nelson Miles. "I am tired. My heart is sick and sad. From where the sun now stands, I will fight no more forever." He surrendered to Miles in exchange for a promise that his band could return to the Nez Percé reservation in Idaho. But the government refused to honor Miles's promise, and the Nez Percé were shipped from one place to another for several years; in the process, many of them died of disease and malnutrition (although Joseph himself lived until 1908).

The last Indians to maintain organized resistance against the whites were the Chiricahua Apaches, who fought intermittently from the 1860s to the late 1880s. The two ablest chiefs of this fierce tribe were Mangas Colorados and Cochise. Mangas was murdered during the Civil War by white soldiers who tricked him into surrendering, and in 1872 Cochise agreed to peace in exchange for a reservation that included some of the tribe's traditional land. But Cochise died in 1874, and his successor, Geronimo—unwilling to bow to white pressures to assimilate—fought on for more than a decade longer, establishing bases in the mountains of Arizona and Mexico and leading warriors in intermittent raids against white outposts. With each raid, however, the number of warring Apaches dwindled, as some warriors died and others drifted away to the reservation. By 1886, Geronimo's plight was hopeless. His band consisted of only about thirty people, including women and children, while his white pursuers numbered perhaps ten thousand. Geronimo recognized the odds and surrendered, an event that marked the end of formal warfare between Indians and whites. The Apache wars were the most violent of all the Indian conflicts, perhaps because the tribes were now the most desperate. But it was the whites who committed the most flagrant and vicious atrocities. In 1871, for example, a mob of white miners invaded an Apache camp, slaughtered over a hundred Indians, and captured children, whom they sold as slaves to rival tribes. On other

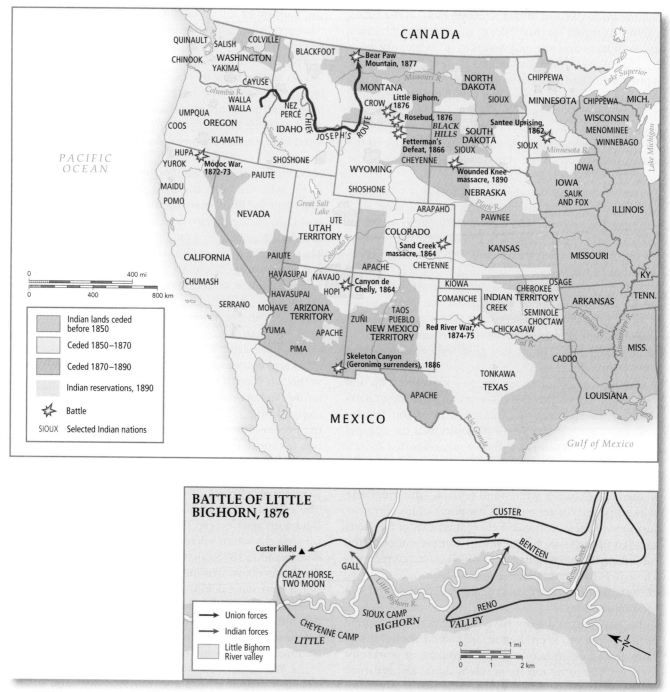

THE INDIAN FRONTIER   As conflict erupted between Indian and white cultures in the West, the government sought increasingly to concentrate tribes on reservations. Resistance to the reservation concept helped unite the Sioux and Cheyenne, traditionally enemies, in the Dakotas during the 1870s. Along the Little Bighorn River, the impetuous Custer underestimated the strength of his Indian opponents and attacked before the supporting troops of Reno and Benteen were in a position to aid him.

occasions, white troops murdered Indians who responded to invitations to peace conferences, once killing them with poisoned food.

Nor did the atrocities end with the conclusion of the Apache wars. Another tragic encounter occurred in 1890 as a result of a religious revival among the Sioux—a revival that itself symbolized the catastrophic effects of the white

assaults on Indian civilization. The Sioux were by now aware that their culture and their glories were irrevocably fading; some were also near starvation because corrupt government agents had reduced their food rations. As other tribes had done in trying times in the past, many of these Indians turned to a prophet who led them into a religious revival.

THE BATTLE OF THE LITTLE BIGHORN: AN INDIAN VIEW This 1898 watercolor by one of the Indian participants portrays the aftermath of the Battle of the Little Bighorn, June 25–26, 1876, in which an army unit under the command of General George Armstrong Custer was surrounded and wiped out by Sioux and Cheyenne warriors. This grisly painting shows Indians on horseback riding over the corpses of Custer and his men. Custer can be seen lying at left center, dressed in yellow buckskin with his hat beside him. The four standing men at center are Sitting Bull, Rain-in-the-Face, Crazy Horse, and Kicking Bear (the artist). At lower right, Indian women begin preparations for a ceremony to honor the returning warriors. *(Southwest Museum of the American Indian, Autry National Center; 1026.G.1)*

This time the prophet was Wovoka, a Paiute who inspired a spiritual awakening that began in Nevada and spread quickly to the plains. The new revival emphasized the coming of a messiah, but its most conspicuous feature was a mass, emotional "Ghost Dance," which inspired ecstatic visions that many participants believed were genuinely mystical. Among these visions were images of a retreat of white people from the plains and a restoration of the great buffalo herds. White agents on the Sioux reservation watched the dances in bewilderment and fear; some believed they might be the preliminary to hostilities.

"Ghost Dance"

On December 29, 1890, the Seventh Cavalry (which had once been Custer's regiment) tried to round up a group of about 350 cold and starving Sioux at Wounded Knee, South Dakota. Fighting broke out in which about 40 white soldiers and more than 300 of the Indians, including women and children, died. What precipitated the conflict is a matter of dispute. An Indian may well have fired the first shot, but the battle soon turned into a one-sided massacre, as the white soldiers turned their new machine guns on the Indians and mowed them down in the snow.

Wounded Knee

The Dawes Act

Even before the Ghost Dance and the Wounded Knee tragedy, the federal government had moved to destroy forever the tribal structure that had always been the cornerstone of Indian culture. Reversing its policy of nearly fifty years of creating reservations in which the tribes would be isolated from white society, Congress abolished the practice by which tribes owned reservation lands communally. Some supporters of the new policy believed they were acting for the good of the Indians, whom they considered a "vanishing race" in need of rescue by white society. But the action was frankly designed to force Indians to become landowners and farmers, to abandon their collective society and culture and become part of white civilization.

The Dawes Severalty Act of 1887 (usually known simply as the Dawes Act) provided for the gradual elimination of tribal ownership of land and the allotment of tracts to individual owners: 160 acres to the head of a family, 80 acres to a single adult or orphan, 40 acres to each dependent child. Adult owners were given United States citizenship, but unlike other citizens, they could not gain

Assimilation

full title to their property for twenty-five years (supposedly to prevent them from selling the land to speculators). The act applied to most of the western tribes. The Pueblo, who continued to occupy lands long ago guaranteed them, were excluded from its provisions. In applying the Dawes Act, the Bureau of Indian Affairs relentlessly promoted the idea of assimilation that lay behind it. Not only did they try to move Indian families onto their own plots of land; they also took Indian children away from their families and sent them to boarding schools run by whites, where they believed the young people could be educated to abandon tribal ways. They also moved to stop Indian religious rituals and encouraged the spread of Christianity and the creation of Christian churches on the reservations.

Few Indians were prepared for this wrenching change from their traditional collective society to capitalist individualism. In any case, white administration of the program was so corrupt and inept that ultimately the government simply abandoned it. Much of the reservation land, therefore, was never distributed to individual owners. Congress attempted to speed the transition with the Burke Act of 1906, but Indians continued to resist forced assimilation.

Neither then nor later did legislation provide a satisfactory solution to the problem of the Indians, largely because there was no entirely happy solution to be had. The interests of the Indians were not compatible with those of the expanding white civilization. Whites successfully settled the American West only at the expense of the region's indigenous peoples.

THE RISE AND DECLINE OF THE WESTERN FARMER

The arrival of the miners, the empire building of the cattle ranchers, the dispersal of the Indian tribes—all served as a prelude to the decisive phase of white settlement of the

WOUNDED KNEE This grim photograph shows Big Foot, chief of the Lakota Sioux, lying dead in the snow near Wounded Knee in South Dakota. He was one of many victims of an 1890 massacre of over 300 members of the tribe, killed by U.S. Army soldiers after the Indians had surrendered their weapons. Whether the massacre was planned and deliberate, or whether it was a result of confusion and fear, remains in dispute. *(Private Collection, Peter Newark American Pictures/The Bridgeman Art Library International)*

LE SABRE INDIAN SCHOOL, MONTANA Government authorities and private philanthropists tried in many ways to encourage Indians to assimilate into mainstream white American society after the end of the Indian wars of the late nineteenth century. One of the most ambitious, and controversial, was a series of boarding schools for Indian children, where white teachers worked to teach them the ways of the English-speaking world. Most such schools were for boys, but some—such as this school in Montana, run by Catholic nuns—were created for girls. *(Montana Historical Society)*

Far West. Even before the Civil War, farmers had begun moving into the plains region, challenging the dominance of the ranchers and the Indians and occasionally coming into conflict with both. By the 1870s, what was once a trickle had become a deluge. Farmers poured into the plains and beyond, enclosed land that had once been hunting territory for Indians and grazing territory for cattle, and established a new agricultural region.

For a time in the late 1870s and early 1880s, the new western farmers flourished, enjoying the fruits of an agricultural economic boom comparable in many ways to the booms that eastern industry periodically enjoyed. Beginning in the mid-1880s, however, the boom turned to bust. American agriculture—not only in the new West but in the older Midwest and the South as well—was producing more than it ever had, too much for the market to absorb. For that and other reasons, prices for agricultural goods declined. Both economically and psychologically, the agricultural economy began a long, steady decline.

Farming on the Plains

Many factors combined to produce this surge of western settlement, but the most important was the railroads. Before the Civil War, the Great Plains had been accessible only through a difficult journey by wagon. But beginning in the 1860s, a great new network of railroad lines developed, spearheaded by the transcontinental routes Congress had authorized and subsidized in 1862. They made huge new areas of settlement accessible.

The completion of the transcontinental line was a dramatic and monumental achievement. The two lines joined at Promontory Point in northern Utah in the spring of 1869.

But while this first transcontinental line captured the public imagination, the construction of subsidiary lines in the following years proved of greater importance to the West. State governments, imitating Washington, D.C., encouraged railroad development by offering direct financial aid, favorable loans, and more than 50 million acres of land (on top of the 130 million acres the federal government had already provided). Although operated by private corporations, the railroads were essentially public projects.

It was not only by making access to the Great Plains easier that the railroads helped spur agricultural settlement there. The railroad companies themselves actively

Key Role of the Railroad

promoted settlement, both to provide themselves with customers for their services and to increase the value of their vast landholdings. In addition, the companies set rates so low for settlers that almost anyone could afford the trip west. And they sold much of their land at very low prices and provided liberal credit to prospective settlers.

Contributing further to the great surge of white agricultural expansion was a temporary change in the climate of the Great Plains. For several years in succession, beginning in the 1870s, rainfall in the plains states was well above average. White Americans now rejected the old idea that the region was the Great American Desert. Some even claimed that cultivation of the plains actually encouraged rainfall.

Even under the most favorable conditions, farming on the plains presented special problems. First was the problem of fencing. Farmers had to enclose their land, if for no other reason than to protect it from the herds of the open-range cattlemen. But traditional wood or stone fences were too expensive and were ineffective as barriers to cattle. In 1873, however, two Illinois farmers, Joseph H. Glidden and I. L. Ellwood, solved this problem by develop-

Barbed Wire

ing and marketing barbed wire, which became standard equipment on the plains and revolutionized fencing practices all over the country.

The second problem was water. Much of the land west of the Mississippi was considerably more arid than the lands to the east. Some of it was literally desert. As a result, the growth of the West depended heavily on irrigation—providing water from sources other than rainfall. Water was diverted from rivers and streams and into farmlands throughout the West—in California and in the Southwest more than anywhere else. In other areas, farmers drilled wells or found other methods of channeling water onto their lands. The search for water—and the resulting battles over control of water (between different landowners and even between different states)—became a central and enduring characteristic of western life.

In the plains states, the problems of water created an epic disaster. After 1887, a series of dry seasons began, and lands that had been fertile now returned to semidesert. Some farmers dealt with the problem by using deep wells

Drought

pumped by steel windmills, by turning to what was called dry-land farming (a system of tillage designed to conserve moisture in the soil by covering it with a dust blanket), or by planting drought-resistant crops. In many areas of the plains, however, only large-scale irrigation could save the endangered farms. But irrigation projects of the necessary magnitude required government assistance, and neither the state nor federal governments were prepared to fund the projects.

Most of the people who moved into the region had previously been farmers in the Midwest, the East, or

Hard Times for Farmers

Europe. In the booming years of the early 1880s, with land values rising, the new farmers had no problem obtaining extensive and easy credit and had every reason to believe they would soon be able to retire their debts. But the arid years of the late 1880s—during which crop prices were falling while production was becoming more expensive—changed that prospect. Tens of thousands of farmers could not pay their debts and were forced to abandon their farms. There was, in effect, a reverse migration: white settlers moved back east, sometimes turning once flourishing communities into desolate ghost towns. Those who remained continued to suffer from falling prices (for example, wheat, which had sold for $1.60 a bushel at the end of the Civil War, dropped to 49 cents in the 1890s) and persistent indebtedness.

Commercial Agriculture

American farming by the late nineteenth century no longer bore very much relation to the comforting image many Americans continued to cherish. The sturdy, independent farmer of popular myth was being replaced by the commercial farmer—attempting to do in the agricultural economy what industrialists were doing in the manufacturing economy.

Commercial farmers were not self-sufficient and made no effort to become so. They specialized in cash crops, which they sold in national or world markets. They did not make their own household supplies or grow their own food but bought them instead at town or village stores. This kind of farming, when it was successful, raised the farmers' living standards. But it also made them dependent on bankers and interest rates, railroads and freight rates, national and European markets, world supply and demand. And unlike the capitalists of the industrial order, they could not regulate their production or influence the prices of what they sold.

Between 1865 and 1900, agriculture became an international business. Farm output increased dramatically, not only in the United States but also in Brazil, Argentina, Canada, Australia, New Zealand, Russia, and elsewhere. At the same time, modern forms of communication and transportation—the telephone, telegraph, steam navigation, railroads—were creating new markets around the world for agricultural goods. American commercial farmers, constantly opening new lands, produced much more than the domestic market could absorb; they relied on the world market to absorb their surplus, but in that market they faced major competition. Cotton farmers depended on export sales for 70 percent of their annual income, wheat farmers for 30 to 40 percent; but the volatility of the international market put them at great risk.

Beginning in the 1880s, worldwide overproduction led to a drop in prices for most agricultural goods and hence to great economic distress for many of the more than 6 million American farm families.

Consequences of Overproduction

By the 1890s, 27 percent of the farms in the country were mortgaged; by 1910, 33 percent. In 1880, 25 percent of all farms had been operated by tenants; by 1910, the proportion had grown to 37 percent. Commercial farming made some people fabulously wealthy. But the farm economy as a whole was suffering a significant decline relative to the rest of the nation.

The Farmers' Grievances

American farmers were painfully aware that something was wrong. But few yet understood the implications of national and world overproduction. Instead, they concentrated their attention and anger on immediate, comprehensible—and no less real—problems: inequitable freight rates, high interest charges, and an inadequate currency.

The farmers' first and most burning grievance was against the railroads. In many cases, the railroads charged higher freight rates for farm goods than for other goods, and higher rates in the South and West than in the Northeast. Railroads also controlled elevator and warehouse facilities in buying centers and charged arbitrary storage rates.

Farmers also resented the institutions controlling credit—banks, loan companies, insurance corporations. Since sources of credit in the West and South were few, farmers had to take loans on whatever terms they could get, often at interest rates ranging from 10 to 25 percent.

Farmers' Grievances

Many farmers had to pay these loans back in years when prices were dropping and currency was becoming scarce. Increasing the volume of currency eventually became an important agrarian demand.

A third grievance concerned prices—both the prices farmers received for their products and the prices they paid for goods. Farmers sold their products in a competitive world market over which they had no control and of which they had no advanced knowledge. A farmer could plant a large crop at a moment when prices were high and find that by harvesttime the price had declined. Farmers' fortunes rose and fell in response to unpredict-

able forces. But many farmers became convinced (often with valid reason) that "middlemen"—speculators, bankers, regional and local agents—were combining to fix prices so as to benefit themselves at the growers' expense. Many farmers also came to believe (again, not entirely without reason) that manufacturers in the East were conspiring to keep the prices of farm goods low and the prices of industrial goods high. Although farmers sold their crops in a competitive world market, they bought manufactured goods in a domestic market protected by tariffs and dominated by trusts and corporations.

The Agrarian Malaise

These economic difficulties produced a series of social and cultural resentments. Farm families in some parts of the

Isolation

country—particularly in the prairie and plains regions, where large farms were scattered over vast areas—were virtually cut off from the outside world and human companionship. During the winter months and spells of bad weather, the loneliness and boredom could become nearly unbearable. Many farmers lacked access to adequate education for their children, to proper medical facilities, to recreational or cultural activities, to virtually anything that might give them a sense of being members of a community. Older farmers felt the sting of watching their children leave the farm for the city. They felt the humiliation of being ridiculed as "hayseeds" by the new urban culture that was coming to dominate American life.

The result of this sense of isolation and obsolescence was a growing malaise among many farmers, a discontent that would help create a great national political movement in the 1890s. It found reflection, too, in the literature that emerged from rural America. Late-nineteenth-century writers often romanticized the rugged life of the cowboy and the western miner. For the farmer, however, the image was often different. Hamlin Garland, for example, reflected the growing disillusionment in a series of novels and short stories. In the past, Garland wrote in the introduction to his novel *Jason Edwards* (1891), the agrarian frontier had seemed to be "the Golden West, the land of wealth and freedom and happiness. All of the associations called up by the spoken word, the West, were fabulous, mythic, hopeful." Now, however, the bright promise had faded. The trials of rural life were crushing the human spirit. "So this is the reality of the dream!" a character in *Jason Edwards* exclaims. "A shanty on a barren plain, hot and lone as a desert. My God!" Once, sturdy yeoman farmers had viewed themselves as the backbone of American life. Now they were becoming painfully aware that their position was declining in relation to the rising urban-industrial society to the east.

CONCLUSION

To many Americans in the late nineteenth century, the West seemed a place utterly unlike the rest of the United States—an untamed "frontier" in which hardy pioneers were creating a new society, in which sturdy individuals still had a chance to be heroes. This image was a stark and deliberate contrast to the reality of the urbanizing, industrializing East, in which the role of the individual was being transformed by the rise of industrial life and its institutions.

The reality of the West in these years, however, was very different from the image. White Americans were moving into the vast regions west of the Mississippi at a remarkable rate in the years after the Civil War, and many of them, it is true, were settling in lands far from any civilization they had ever known. But the West was not an empty place in these years. It contained a large population of Indians, with whom the white settlers sometimes lived uneasily and sometimes battled, but almost always in the end pushed aside and (with help from the federal government) relocated onto lands whites did not want. There were significant numbers of Mexicans in some areas, small populations of Asians in others, and African Americans moving in from the South in search of land and freedom. The West was not a barren frontier, but a place of many cultures.

The West was also closely and increasingly tied to the emerging capitalist-industrial economy of the East. The miners who flooded into California, Colorado, Nevada, the Dakotas, and elsewhere were responding to the demand in the East for gold and silver, but even more for such utilitarian minerals as iron ore, copper, lead, zinc, and quartz, which had industrial uses. Cattle and sheep ranchers produced meat, wool, and leather for eastern consumers and manufacturers. Farmers grew crops for sale in national and international commodities markets. The West certainly looked different from the East, and its people lived their lives in surroundings very different from those of eastern cities. But the growth of the West was very much a part of the growth of the rest of the nation. And the culture of the West, despite the romantic images of pioneering individuals embraced by easterners and westerners alike, was at its heart as much a culture of economic growth and capitalist ambition as was the culture of the rest of the nation.

INTERACTIVE LEARNING

The *Primary Source Investigator CD-ROM* offers the following materials related to this chapter:

- A short documentary movie, **The Curtis Legacy**, about a well-known photographer who documented native peoples for years (D11).

- Interactive maps: **Indian Expulsion** (M9) and **Mining Towns** (M14).

- Documents, images, and maps related to the settlement of the American West following the Civil War, and the dispersal of the native peoples in the process.

Highlights include the text of the Dawes Act of 1887, the federal policy that broke up Indian tribal lands, images of Native Americans in the American West, and excerpts from Frederick Jackson Turner's *The Significance of the Frontier in American History*.

Online Learning Center (www.mhhe.com/brinkley13e)

For quizzes, Internet resources, references to additional books and films, and more, consult this book's Online Learning Center.

FOR FURTHER REFERENCE

Frederick Jackson Turner's *The Frontier in American History* (1920) is a classic argument on the centrality of the frontier experience to American democracy. His argument frames much of the later historical writing on the West, most of which rejects the "Turner thesis." Patricia Nelson Limerick's *The Legacy of Conquest: The Unbroken Past of the American West* (1987) argues that the West was not a frontier but rather an inhabited place conquered by Anglo-Americans. Richard White, *"It's Your Misfortune and None of My Own": A History of the American West* (1991) is an outstanding general history of the region that revises many myths about the West. Ronald Takaki, *Strangers from a Different Shore: A History of Asian Americans* (1989) surveys the experiences of Asian Americans as immigrants to America's western shore. Jean Pfaelzer, *Driven Out: The Forgotten War Against Chinese Americans* (2007) illustrates anti-Chinese sentiment. John Mack Faragher, *Women and Men on the Overland Trail* (1979) examines the social experience of westering migrants, and Peggy Pascoe, *Relations of Rescue: The Search for Female Authority in the American West, 1874-1939* (1990) describes the female communities of the West.

William Cronon, *Nature's Metropolis and the Great West* (1991) describes the relationships among economies and environments in the West. Jon Gjerde, *The Minds of the West: Ethnocultural Evolution in the Rural Middle West, 1830-1914* (1997) examines the impact of ethnicity on the shaping of the agrarian West. Robert Wooster, *The Military and United States Indian Policy, 1865-1902* (1988) and Sally Denton, *American Massacre: The Tragedy at Mountain Meadows, September 1857* (2003) examine the military campaigns against the Indians in the nineteenth century. Frederick E. Hoxie, *A Final Promise: The Campaign to Assimilate the Indians, 1880-1920* (1984) examines U.S. policies toward Native Americans in the years after the end of the Indian Wars. John Mack Faragher, *Daniel Boone* (1992) is a study of one of the West's most fabled figures. Richard Slotkin, *The Fatal Environment: The Myth of the Frontier in the Age of Industrialization* (1985) and *Gunfighter Nation* (1992) are provocative cultural studies of the idea of the West. Henry Nash Smith, *Virgin Land* (1950) is a classic study of the West in American culture. Rebecca Solnit, *River of Shadows: Edward Muybridge and the Technological Wild West* (2003) considers the impact of photography on images of the West. *The West* (1996), a documentary film by Stephen Ives and Ken Burns, offers a broad history of the region, along with a companion book of the same title by Geoffrey C. Ward.

CHAPTER 17

INDUSTRIAL SUPREMACY

CELEBRATING A TUNNEL The new industrial economy made possible many great feats that only decades before would have been unthinkable. In this striking photograph, the engineers and financiers who planned and paid for this underwater tunnel between Manhattan and New Jersey attend a banquet to celebrate its successful completion in 1907. *(Culver Pictures)*

WRITING SEVERAL DECADES LATER of the remarkable expansion of America's industrial economy in the late nineteenth and early twentieth centuries, the historians Charles and Mary Beard commented: "With a stride that astonished statisticians, the conquering hosts of business enterprise swept over the continent; twenty-five years after the death of Lincoln, America had become, in the quantity and value of her products, the first manufacturing nation of the world. What England had accomplished in a hundred years, the United States had achieved in half the time." Many Americans at the time experienced a similar amazement as they watched the changes around them.

In fact, America's rise to industrial supremacy was not as sudden as such observers suggested. The nation had been building a manufacturing economy since early in the nineteenth century, and industry was well established before the

| Transformation of the National Economy | Civil War. But Americans were clearly correct in observing that the developments of the last three decades of the nineteenth century overshadowed all |

that had come earlier. Those years witnessed nothing less than the transformation of the national economy.

Many factors contributed to this transformation. In these years, the economy of the United States (and of much of the rest of the industrial world) benefited enormously from important new technologies that were being developed in both America and Europe. Industrial growth also profited from new forms of corporate organization capable of amassing much larger amounts of capital than in the past and, eventually, of managing much vaster enterprises than earlier industrial leaders could have done. Great waves of immigration—from the countrysides of the Americas, Europe, and Asia into the great industrial centers of the United States—provided a large, cheap labor force for the ever-larger factory complexes the nation was creating.

Industrialization changed the physical landscape of the nation. It contributed to the rapid growth of cities. It helped stimulate the spread of railroads across the United States. It sent capitalists and workers into remote areas of the nation in search of natural resources that could be exploited for industrial production. Industrialization also changed America's relationship to the rest of the world, drawing the United States more and more into global trade and finance and into a search for overseas markets and foreign suppliers of needed materials.

And industrialization altered the nation's social landscape as well. The remarkable growth of the economy did much to increase the wealth and improve the lives of many Americans. But the benefits were far from universal. While industrial titans and a growing middle class were enjoying a prosperity without precedent in the nation's history, workers, farmers, and others were experiencing a disorienting and often painful transition that slowly edged the United States toward a great economic and political crisis.

SIGNIFICANT EVENTS

1851 ▶	I. M. Singer and Company, one of the first modern corporations, founded
1859 ▶	First oil well drilled in Pennsylvania
1866 ▶	William H. Sylvis founds National Labor Union
▶	First transatlantic cable laid
1868 ▶	Open-hearth steelmaking begins in America
1869 ▶	Knights of Labor founded
1870 ▶	John D. Rockefeller founds Standard Oil
1873 ▶	Carnegie Steel founded
▶	Commercial and financial panic disrupts economy
1876 ▶	Alexander Graham Bell invents telephone
1877 ▶	Railroad workers strike nationwide
1879 ▶	Thomas A. Edison invents electric lightbulb
▶	Henry George publishes *Progress and Poverty*
1881 ▶	American Federation of Labor founded
1882 ▶	Rockefeller creates first trust
1886 ▶	Haymarket bombing blamed on anarchists
1888 ▶	Edward Bellamy publishes *Looking Backward*
1892 ▶	Workers strike Homestead plant
1893 ▶	Depression begins
1894 ▶	Workers strike Pullman Company
1901 ▶	J. P. Morgan creates United States Steel Corporation
▶	American Socialist Party founded
▶	Spindletop oil field discovered in Texas
1903 ▶	Women's Trade Union League founded
▶	Wright brothers make first successful flight at Kitty Hawk, North Carolina
1906 ▶	Henry Ford produces his first automobiles
▶	William Graham Sumner publishes *Folkways*

SOURCES OF INDUSTRIAL GROWTH

Many factors contributed to the growth of American industry: abundant raw materials; a large and growing labor supply; a surge in technological innovation; the emergence of a talented, ambitious, and often ruthless group of entrepreneurs; a federal government eager to assist the growth of business; and a great and expanding domestic market for the products of manufacturing.

Industrial Technologies

Perhaps the most important technological development in a nation whose economy rested so heavily on railroads and urban construction was the revolutionizing of iron and steel production in the late nineteenth century. Iron production had developed slowly in the United States through most of the nineteenth century; steel production had developed hardly at all by the end of the Civil War. In the 1870s and 1880s, however, iron production soared as railroads added 40,000 new miles of track, and steel production made great strides toward what would soon be its dominance in the metals industry.

The story of the rise of steel is, like so many other stories of economic development, a story of technological discovery. An Englishman, Henry Bessemer, and an American, William Kelly, had developed, almost simultaneously, a process for converting iron into the much more durable and versatile steel. (The process, which took Bessemer's name, consisted of blowing air through molten iron to burn out the impurities.) The Bessemer process also relied on the discovery by the British metallurgist Robert Mushet that ingredients could be added to the iron during conversion to transform it into steel. In 1868, the New Jersey ironmaster Abram S. Hewitt introduced from Europe another method of making steel—the open-hearth process, which ultimately largely supplanted the Bessemer process. These techniques made possible the production of steel in great quantities and large dimensions, for use in the manufacture of locomotives, steel rails, and girders for the construction of tall buildings.

The steel industry emerged first in western Pennsylvania and eastern Ohio. That was partly because iron ore could be found there in abundance and because there was already a flourishing iron industry in the region. It was also because the new forms of steel production created a demand for new kinds of fuel—and particularly for the anthracite (or hard) coal that was plentiful in Pennsylvania. Later, new techniques made it possible to use soft bituminous coal (easily mined in western Pennsylvania), which could then be converted to coke to fuel steel furnaces. As a result, Pittsburgh quickly became the center of the steel world. But the industry was growing so fast that new sources of ore were soon necessary. The upper peninsula of Michigan, the Mesabi Range in Minnesota, and the area around Birmingham, Alabama, became important ore-producing centers by the end of the century, and new centers of steel production grew up near them: Cleveland, Detroit, Chicago, and Birmingham, among others.

Until the Civil War, iron and steel furnaces were mostly made of stone and usually built against the side of a hill to reduce construction demands. In the 1870s and after, however, furnaces were redesigned as cylindrical iron shells lined with brick. These massive new furnaces were 75 feet tall and higher and could produce over 500 tons a week.

As the steel industry spread, new transportation systems emerged to serve it. The steel production in the Great Lakes region was possible only because of the availability of steam freighters that could carry ore on the lakes. The demand for vessels capable of transporting oil and the development of new and more powerful steam engines encouraged, in turn, the design of larger and heavier freighters—such as the *R. J. Hackett,* launched in 1869, which could carry 1,200 tons of ore. Shippers also used new steam engines to speed the unloading of ore, a task that previously had been performed, slowly and laboriously, by men and horses.

There was even a closer relationship between the emerging steel companies and the railroads. Steel manufacturers provided rails and parts for cars to the railroads; railroads were both markets for and transporters of manufactured steel. The Pennsylvania Railroad, for example, literally created the Pennsylvania Steel Company, provided it with substantial initial capital, and ensured it a market for its products with an immediate contract for steel rails. That was only one of many cases in which railroad and steel companies effectively merged or formed intimate connections.

The steel industry's need for lubrication for its machines helped create another important new industry in the late nineteenth century— oil. (Not until later did oil become important primarily for its potential as a fuel.) The existence of petroleum reserves in western Pennsylvania had been common knowledge for some time. Not until the 1850s, however, after Pennsylvania businessman George Bissell showed that the substance could be burned in lamps and that it could also yield such products as paraffin, naphtha, and lubricating oil, was there any sense of its commercial value. Bissell raised money to begin drilling; and in 1859, Edwin L. Drake, one of Bissell's employees, established the first oil well, near Titusville, Pennsylvania, which was soon producing 500 barrels of oil a month. Demand for petroleum grew quickly, and promoters soon developed other fields in Pennsylvania, Ohio, and West Virginia. By the 1870s, oil had advanced to fourth place among the nation's exports.

New Steel Production Techniques

Pittsburgh

Rise of the Petroleum Industry

PIONEER OIL RUN, 1865 The American oil industry emerged first in western Pennsylvania, where speculators built makeshift facilities almost overnight. An oil field on the other side of the hill depicted here had been producing 600 barrels a day, and the wells quickly spilled over the hill and down the slope shown in this photograph. *(Library of Congress)*

The Airplane and the Automobile

Among the technological innovations that were to have the farthest-reaching impact on the United States was the invention of the automobile. Two technologies were critical to its development. One was the creation of gasoline (or petrol). It was the result of an extraction process developed in the late nineteenth century in the United States by which lubricating oil and fuel oil were removed separately from crude oil. As early as the 1870s, designers in France, Germany, and Austria—inspired by the success of railroad engines—had begun to develop an "internal combustion engine," which used the expanding power of burning gas to drive pistons. A German, Nicolaus August Otto, created a gas-powered "four-stroke" engine in the mid-1860s, which was a precursor to automobile engines. But he did not develop a way to untether it from gas lines to be used portably in machines. One of Otto's former employees, Gottfried Daimler, later perfected an engine that could be used in automobiles (including the famous early car that took Daimler's name).

The American automobile industry developed rapidly in the aftermath of these breakthroughs. Charles and Frank Duryea built the first gasoline-driven motor vehicle in America

Henry Ford

in 1893. Three years later, Henry Ford produced the first of the famous cars that would eventually bear his name. By 1910, the industry had become a major force in the economy, and the automobile was beginning to reshape American social and cultural life, as well as the nation's landscape. In 1895, there were only four automobiles on the American highways. By 1917, there were nearly 5 million.

The search for a means of human flight was as old as civilization, and had been almost entirely futile until the late nineteenth century, when engineers, scientists, and tinkerers in both the United States and Europe began to experiment with a wide range of aeronautic devices. Balloonists began to consider ways to make dirigibles useful vehicles of transportation. Others experimented with kites and gliders to see if they could somehow be used to propel humans through the air.

Among those testing gliders were two brothers in Ohio, Wilbur and Orville Wright, who owned a bicycle shop in which they began to construct a glider that could be propelled through the air by an internal combustion engine (the same kind of engine that was propelling automobiles). Four years after they began their experiments, Orville made a celebrated test flight near Kitty Hawk,

THE WRIGHT BROTHERS Orville and Wilbur Wright became closely watched celebrities after their famous flight at Kitty Hawk, North Carolina, in 1903. Although they made few additional contributions to the development of aviation technology, they were much in demand to demonstrate their "flying machine." Here they pose before a demonstration flight—Wilbur taking a reading of flight conditions and Orville watching, the struts of their plane visible in the background. *(Library of Congress)*

North Carolina, in which an airplane took off by itself and traveled 120 feet in 12 seconds under its own power before settling back to earth. By the fall of 1904, they had improved the plane to the point where they were able to fly over 23 miles, and in the following year they began to take a few passengers with them on their flights.

Although the first working airplane was built in the United States, aviation technology was slow to gain a foothold in America. Most of the early progress in airplane design occurred in France, where there was substantial government funding for research and development. The U.S. government created the National Advisory Committee on Aeronautics in 1915, twelve years after the Wright brothers' flight, and American airplanes became a significant presence in Europe during World War I. But the prospects for commercial flight seemed dim until the 1920s, when Charles Lindbergh's famous solo flight from New York to Paris electrified the nation and the world and helped make aviation a national obsession.

Research and Development

The rapid development of new industrial technologies, and the emergence of large integrated corporations taking advantage of those technologies, persuaded business leaders of the need to sponsor their own research to allow them to keep up with the rapid changes in industry. General Electric, fearful of technological competition, created one of the first corporate laboratories in 1900. By 1913, Bell Telephone, Du Pont, General Electric, Eastman Kodak, and about fifty other companies were budgeting hundreds of thousands of dollars each year for research by their own engineers and scientists. The emergence of corporate research and development laboratories

Corporate Research and Development

coincided with a decline in government support for research. That helped corporations to attract skilled researchers who had once worked for government agencies and were looking for new employment. It also decentralized the sources of research funding and ensured that inquiry would move in many different directions, and not just along paths determined by the government.

A rift began to emerge between scientists and engineers. Engineers—both inside and out of universities—became increasingly tied up with the research and development agendas of corporations and worked hard to be of practical use to the new economy. Many scientists scorned this "commercialization" of knowledge and preferred to stick to basic research that had no immediate practical applications. Even so, American scientists were more closely connected to practical challenges than were their European counterparts, and some joined engineers in corporate research and development laboratories, which over time began to sponsor not just practical but also basic research.

American universities transformed themselves in growing numbers in the late nineteenth and early twentieth centuries. And while there were many reasons for, and many results of, these transformations, one product of the change was a growing connection between university-based research and the needs of the industrial economy.

Transformation of Higher Education

University faculty and laboratories began to receive funding from corporations for research of interest to them, and a partnership began to develop between the academic world and the commercial world that has continued into the twenty-first century. No comparable partnership emerged in European universities in these years, and some scholars have argued that America's more rapid development in the twentieth century is in part a product of the market's success in harnessing knowledge—from the academic world and elsewhere—more effectively than the nation's competitors abroad.

The Science of Production

Central to the growth of the automobile and other industries were changes in the techniques of production. By the beginning of the twentieth century, many industrialists were turning to the new principles of "scientific management." Those principles were often known as "Taylorism," after their leading theoretician, Frederick Winslow Taylor. Taylor's ideas were controversial during his lifetime and have remained controversial since.

Taylor urged employers to reorganize the production process by subdividing tasks. This would speed up production; it would also make workers more interchangeable and thus diminish a manager's dependence on any particular employee.

"Taylorism"

And it would reduce the need for highly trained skilled workers. If properly managed by trained experts, Taylor

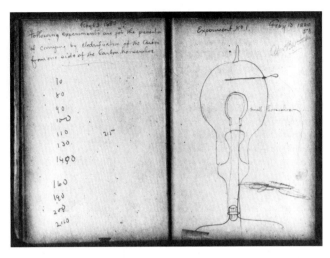

EDISON'S NOTEBOOK This page from one of Thomas Edison's notebooks shows sketches of and notes on some of his early experiments on an incandescent lamp—what we know as an electric lightbulb. Edison was not only the most celebrated inventor of his day, but by the early twentieth century one of the greatest popular heroes in American life in a time when scientific and technological progress was considered the defining feature of the age. *(U.S. Department of the Interior, National Park Service, Edison National Historic Site)*

claimed, workers using modern machines could perform simple tasks at much greater speed, significantly increasing productive efficiency. Taylor himself, and his many admirers, argued that scientific management was a way to manage human labor to make it compatible with the demands of the machine age. But scientific management was also a way to increase the employer's control of the workplace and to make working people less independent.

The most important change in production technology in the industrial era was the emergence of mass production and, above all, the moving assembly line, which Henry Ford introduced in his automobile plants in 1914. This revolutionary technique cut the time for assembling a chassis from 12½ hours to 1½ hours. It enabled Ford to raise the wages and reduce the hours of his workers while cutting the base price of his Model T from $950 in 1914 to $290 in 1929. Ford's assembly line became a standard for many other industries.

Moving Assembly Line

Railroad Expansion

Despite important advances in many other forms of technology and communication, the principal agent of industrial progress in the late nineteenth century remained the railroad. Railroads were the nation's principal form of transportation and gave industrialists access to distant markets and sources of raw materials. Railroads helped determine the path by which agricultural and industrial economies developed. When a railroad line ran through a sparsely populated region, new farms and other economic activity quickly sprang up along the route. When it reached

AUTOMOBILE PRODUCTION Workers labor to finish and paint automobile bodies in a Fisher Body plant in 1918, just after the end of World War I. By then, General Motors had emerged as the giant of the industry, and Fisher Body was one of many companies it had bought to consolidate its control over the entire production process. *(2002 General Motors Corporation. Used with permission of GM Media Archives.)*

forests, lumberers came quickly in its wake and began felling timber to send back to towns and cities for sale. When it moved through the great plains of the West, it brought buffalo hunters who nearly exterminated the great herds of bison and, later, helped transport cattle into the region and carry western meat back into the cities. Because Chicago was the principal railroad hub of the central United States, it also became the place where railroads brought livestock, making the city the slaughterhouse of the nation. Everywhere the railroad went, the economic, social, and physical landscape of the country changed as a result.

Railroads even altered concepts of time. Until the 1880s, there was no standard method of keeping time from one community to another. In most places, the position of the sun determined the time, which meant that clocks were set differently even between nearby towns. This created great difficulties for railroads, which were trying to set schedules for the entire nation. On November 18, 1883, the railroad companies, working together, agreed to create four time zones across the continent, each an hour apart from its closest neighbor. Although not until 1918 did the federal government make these time zones standard for all purposes, the action by the railroads very quickly solidified the idea of "standard time" through most of the United States.

Every decade in the late nineteenth century, total railroad trackage increased dramatically: from 30,000 miles in 1860 to 52,000 miles in 1870, to 93,000 in 1880, to 163,000 in 1890, and to 193,000 by 1900. Subsidies from federal, state, and local governments—as

Rapid Expansion of the Railroad

well as investments from abroad—were vital to these vast undertakings, which required far more capital than private entrepreneurs in America could raise by themselves. Equally important was the emergence of great railroad combinations that brought most of the nation's rails under the control of a very few men. Many railroad combinations continued to be dominated by individuals. The achievements (and excesses) of these tycoons—Cornelius Vanderbilt, James J. Hill, Collis P. Huntington, and others—became symbols to much of the nation of great economic power concentrated in individual hands. But railroad development was less significant for the individual barons it created than for its contribution to the growth of a new institution: the modern corporation.

The Corporation

There had been various forms of corporations in America since colonial times, but the modern corporation emerged as a major force only after the Civil War, when railroad magnates and other industrialists realized that no single person or group of limited partners, no matter how wealthy, could finance their great ventures.

Under the laws of incorporation passed in many states in the 1830s and 1840s, business organizations could raise money by selling stock to members of the public; after the Civil War, one industry after another began doing so. At the same time, affluent Americans began to consider the purchase of stock a good investment even if they were not themselves involved in the

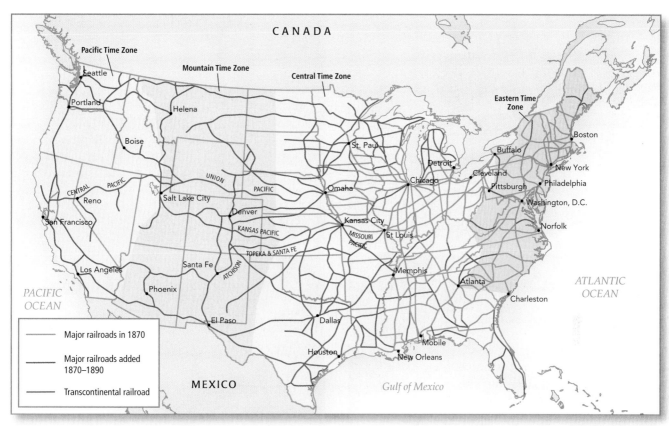

RAILROADS, 1870–1890 This map illustrates the rapid expansion of railroads in the late nineteenth century. In 1870, there was already a dense network of rail lines in the Northeast and Midwest, illustrated here by the green lines. The red lines show the further expansion of rail coverage between 1870 and 1890, much of it in the South and the areas west of the Mississippi River. ◆ *Why were railroads so essential to the nation's economic growth in these years?*

For an interactive version of this map, go to www.mhhe.com/brinkley13ech17maps

business whose stock they were purchasing. What made the practice appealing was that investors had only "lim-

Limited Liability

ited liability"—that is, they risked only the amount of their investments; they were not liable for any debts the corporation might accumulate beyond that. The ability to sell stock to a broad public made it possible for entrepreneurs to gather vast sums of capital and undertake great projects.

The Pennsylvania Railroad and others were among the first to adopt the new corporate form of organization. But it quickly spread beyond the railroad industry.

Andrew Carnegie

In steel, the central figure was Andrew Carnegie, a Scottish immigrant who had worked his way up from modest beginnings and in 1873 opened his own steelworks in Pittsburgh. Soon he dominated the industry. His methods were much like those of other industrial titans. He cut costs and prices by striking deals with the railroads and then bought out rivals who could not compete with him. With his associate Henry Clay Frick, he bought up coal mines and leased part of the Mesabi iron range in

Minnesota, operated a fleet of ore ships on the Great Lakes, and acquired railroads. Ultimately, Carnegie controlled the processing of his steel from mine to market. He financed his undertakings not only out of his own profits but out of the sale of stock. Then, in 1901, he sold out for $450 million to the banker J. Pierpont Morgan, who merged the Carnegie interests with others to create the giant United States Steel Corporation—a $1.4 billion enterprise that controlled almost two-thirds of the nation's steel production.

There were similar developments in other industries. Gustavus Swift developed a relatively small Chicago meatpacking company into a great national corporation, in part because of profits he earned selling to the military in the Civil War. Isaac Singer patented a sewing machine in 1851 and created I. M. Singer and Company, one of the first modern manufacturing corporations.

Many of the corporate organizations developed a new approach to management. Large, national business enterprises needed more systematic administrative structures than the limited, local ventures of the past. As a result, corporate leaders introduced a set of managerial

ANDREW CARNEGIE Carnegie was one of a relatively small number of great industrialists of the late nineteenth century who genuinely rose "from rags to riches." Born in Scotland, he came to the United States in 1848, at the age of thirteen, and soon found work as a messenger in a Pittsburgh telegraph office. His skill in learning to transcribe telegraphic messages (he became one of the first telegraphers in the country able to take messages by sound) brought him to the attention of a Pennsylvania Railroad official, and before he was twenty, he had begun his ascent to the highest ranks of industry. After the Civil War, he shifted his attention to the growing iron industry; in 1873 he invested all his assets in the development of the first American steel mills. Two decades later he was one of the wealthiest men in the world. In 1901 he abruptly resigned from his businesses and spent the remaining years of his life as a philanthropist. By the time of his death in 1919, he had given away more than $350 million. *(Culver Pictures, Inc.)*

JOHN D. ROCKEFELLER Rockefeller's Standard Oil Company became perhaps the largest and most powerful monopoly in America in the late nineteenth century, and Rockefeller himself became one of the nation's wealthiest and most controversial men. *(Culver Pictures, Inc.)*

breed of business executive: the "middle manager," who formed a layer of command between workers and owners. Beginning in the railroad corporations, these new management techniques moved quickly into virtually every area of large-scale industry. Efficient administrative capabilities helped make possible another major feature of the modern corporation: consolidation.

Consolidating Corporate America

Businessmen created large, consolidated organizations primarily through two methods. One was "horizontal integration"—the combining of a number of firms engaged in the same enterprise into a single corporation. The consolidation of many different railroad lines into one company was an example. Another method, which became popular in the 1890s, was "vertical integration"—the taking over of all the different businesses on which a company relied for its primary function (as in the case of Carnegie Steel).

Horizontal and Vertical Integration

New Managerial Techniques

techniques—the genesis of modern business administration—that relied on the division of responsibilities, a carefully designed hierarchy of control, modern cost-accounting procedures, and perhaps above all a new

The most celebrated corporate empire of the late nineteenth century was John D. Rockefeller's Standard Oil, a great combination created through both horizontal and vertical integration. Shortly after

Rockefeller's Standard Oil

the Civil War, Rockefeller launched a refining company in Cleveland and immediately began trying to eliminate his competition. Allying himself with other wealthy capitalists, he proceeded methodically to buy out competing refineries. In 1870, he formed the Standard Oil Company of Ohio; within a few years it had acquired twenty of the twenty-five refineries in Cleveland, as well as plants in Pittsburgh, Philadelphia, New York, and Baltimore. So far, Rockefeller had expanded only horizontally. But soon he began expanding vertically as well. He built his own barrel factories, terminal warehouses, and pipelines. Standard Oil owned its own freight cars and developed its own marketing organization. By the 1880s, Rockefeller had established such dominance within the petroleum industry that to much of the nation he served as the leading symbol of monopoly. He controlled access to 90 percent of the refined oil in the United States.

Rockefeller and other industrialists saw consolidation as a way to cope with what they believed was the greatest curse of the modern economy: "cutthroat competition." Most businessmen claimed to believe in free enterprise and a competitive marketplace, but in fact they feared the existence of too many competing firms, convinced that substantial competition could spell instability and ruin for all. A successful enterprise, many capitalists believed (but did not say publicly), was one that could eliminate or absorb its competitors.

As the movement toward combination accelerated, new vehicles emerged to facilitate it. The railroads began making so-called pool arrangements—informal agreements among various companies to stabilize rates and divide markets (arrangements that would in later years be known as cartels). But the pools did not work very well. If even a few firms in an industry were unwilling to cooperate (as was almost always the case), the pool arrangements collapsed.

The Trust and the Holding Company

The failure of the pools led to new techniques of consolidation, resting less on cooperation than on centralized control. At first, the most successful such technique was the creation of the "trust"—pioneered by Standard Oil in the early 1880s and perfected by the banker J. P. Morgan. Over time, "trust" became a term for any great economic combination. But the trust was in fact a particular kind of organization. Under a trust agreement, stockholders in individual corporations transferred their stocks to a small group of trustees in exchange for shares in the trust itself.

The Trust Agreement

Owners of trust certificates often had no direct control over the

J. PIERPONT MORGAN This arresting 1903 portrait by the great photographer Alfred Steichen captures something of the intimidating power of J. Pierpont Morgan, the most powerful financier in America. This photograph is sometimes known as the "dagger portrait," because Morgan appears to be holding a knife in his left hand. In fact, the shiny object is the arm of his chair. *(The Museum of Modern Art/Licensed by SCALA/Art Resource, NY)*

decisions of the trustees; they simply received a share of the profits of the combination. The trustees themselves, on the other hand, might literally own only a few companies but could exercise effective control over many.

In 1889, the State of New Jersey helped produce a third form of consolidation by changing its laws of incorporation to permit companies actually to buy up other companies. Other states soon followed. That made the trust unnecessary and permitted actual corporate mergers. Rockefeller, for example, quickly relocated Standard Oil to New Jersey and created there what became known as a "holding company"—a central corporate body that would buy up the stock of various members of the Standard Oil trust and establish direct, formal ownership of the corporations in the trust.

By the end of the nineteenth century, as a result of corporate consolidation, 1 percent of the corporations in America were able to control more than 33 percent of the manufacturing. A system of economic organization

Rapid Corporate Consolidation

was emerging that lodged enormous power in the hands of

a very few men: the great bankers of New York such as J. P. Morgan, industrial titans such as Rockefeller (who himself gained control of a major bank), and others.

Whether or not this relentless concentration of economic power was the only way or the best way to promote industrial expansion became a major source of debate in America. But it is clear that, whatever else they may have done, the industrial giants of the era were responsible for substantial economic growth. They were integrating operations, cutting costs, creating a great industrial infrastructure, stimulating new markets, creating jobs for a vast new pool of unskilled workers, and opening the way to large-scale mass production. They were also creating the basis for some of the greatest public controversies of their era.

CAPITALISM AND ITS CRITICS

The rise of big business produced many critics. Farmers and workers saw in the growth of the new corporate power centers a threat to notions of a republican society in which wealth and authority were widely distributed. Middle-class critics pointed to the corruption that the new industrial titans seemed to produce in their own enterprises and in local, state, and national politics. The growing criticisms challenged the captains of industry to defend the new corporate economy, to convince the public (and themselves) that it was compatible with the ideology of individualism and equal opportunity that had long been central to the American self-image.

The "Self-Made Man"

The most common rationale for modern capitalism rested squarely on the older ideology of individualism. The new industrial economy, its defenders argued, was not reducing opportunities for individual advancement, but expanding them. It was providing every individual with a chance to succeed and attain great wealth.

There was an element of truth in such claims, but only a small one. Before the Civil War there had been few millionaires in America; by 1892 there were more than 4,000. Some were in fact what almost all millionaires claimed to be: "self-made men." Andrew Carnegie had worked as a bobbin boy in a Pittsburgh cotton mill; John D. Rockefeller had begun as a clerk in a Cleveland commission house; E. H. Harriman, a great railroad tycoon, had begun as a broker's office boy. But most of

Myth of the Self-Made Man

the new business tycoons had begun their careers from positions of wealth and privilege.

Nor was their rise to power and prominence always a result simply of hard work and ingenuity, as they liked to claim. It was also a result of ruthlessness, arrogance, and, at times, rampant corruption. The railroad magnate Cornelius Vanderbilt expressed the attitude of many corporate tycoons with his belligerent question: "What do I care about the law? H'aint I got the power?" So did his son William, with his oft-quoted statement: "The public be damned." Industrialists made large financial contributions to politicians, political parties, and government officials in exchange

"MODERN COLOSSUS OF (RAIL) ROADS" Cornelius Vanderbilt, known as the "Commodore," accumulated one of America's great fortunes by consolidating several large railroad companies under his control in the 1860s. His name became a synonym not only for enormous wealth, but also (in the eyes of many Americans) for excessive corporate power—as suggested in this cartoon, showing him standing astride his empire and manipulating its parts. *(Culver Pictures, Inc.)*

for assistance and support. And more often than not, politicians responded as they hoped. Cynics said that Standard Oil did everything to the Ohio legislature except refine it. A member of the Pennsylvania legislature once reportedly said: "Mr. Speaker, I move we adjourn unless the Pennsylvania Railroad has more business for us to transact." During the notorious "Erie War" of 1868, in which Cornelius Vanderbilt battled Jay Gould and Jim Fisk for control of the Erie Railroad, both sides in the dispute offered lavish bribes to members of the New York State legislature. The market price of legislators during the fight was $15,000 a head. One enterprising politician collected $75,000 from Vanderbilt and $100,000 from Gould. Hardly innocent victims of this corruption, many politicians openly demanded bribes and in effect blackmailed businessmen.

The average industrialist of the late nineteenth century was not, however, a Rockefeller or a Vanderbilt. For every successful millionaire, there were dozens of aspiring businessmen whose efforts failed. Some industries fell under the monopolistic control of a single firm or a small group of large firms. But most industries remained fragmented, with many small companies struggling to carve out a stable position for themselves in an uncertain, highly competitive environment. The annals of business did indeed include real stories of individuals rising from rags to riches. They also included stories of people moving from riches back to rags.

Survival of the Fittest

Most tycoons liked to claim that they had attained their wealth and power through hard work, acquisitiveness, and thrift—the traditional virtues of Protestant America. Those who succeeded, they argued, deserved their success. "God gave me my money," explained John D. Rockefeller, expressing the assumption that riches were a reward for worthiness. Those who failed had earned their failure—through their own laziness, stupidity, or carelessness. "Let us remember," said a prominent Protestant minister, "that there is not a poor person in the United States who was not made poor by his own shortcomings."

Such assumptions helped strengthen a popular social theory of the late nineteenth century: Social Darwinism, the application of Charles Darwin's laws of evolution and natural selection among species to human society. Just as only the fittest survived in the process of evolution, so in human society only the fittest individuals survived and flourished in the marketplace.

Social Darwinism

The English philosopher Herbert Spencer was the first and most important proponent of this theory. Society, he argued, benefited from the elimination of the unfit and the survival of the strong and talented. Spencer's books were popular in America in the 1870s and 1880s. And his teachings found prominent supporters among American intellectuals, most notably William Graham Sumner of Yale, who promoted similar ideas in lectures, articles, and a famous 1906 book, *Folkways.* Sumner did not agree with everything Spencer wrote, but he did share Spencer's belief that individuals must have absolute freedom to struggle, to compete, to succeed, or to fail. Many industrialists seized on the theories of Spencer and Sumner to justify their own power. "The growth of a large business is merely the survival of the fittest," Rockefeller proclaimed. "This is not an evil tendency in business. It is merely the working out of the law of nature and a law of God."

Social Darwinism appealed to businessmen because it seemed to legitimize their success and confirm their virtues. It also appealed to them because it placed their activities within the context of traditional American ideas of freedom and individualism. Above all, it appealed to them because it justified their tactics.

Justifying the Status Quo

Social Darwinists insisted that all attempts by labor to raise wages by forming unions and all endeavors by government to regulate economic activities would fail, because economic life was controlled by a natural law, the law of competition. And Social Darwinism coincided with another "law" that seemed to justify business practices and business dominance: the law of supply and demand as defined by Adam Smith and the classical economists. The economic system, they argued, was like a great and delicate machine functioning by natural and automatic rules, by the "invisible hand" of market forces. The greatest among these rules, the law of supply and demand, determined all economic values—prices, wages, rents, interest rates at a level that was just to all concerned. Supply and demand worked because human beings were essentially economic creatures who understood and pursued their own interests, and because they operated in a free market regulated only by competition.

But Social Darwinism and the ideas of classical economics did not have very much to do with the realities of the corporate economy. At the same time that businessmen were celebrating the virtues of competition and the free market, they were actively seeking to protect themselves from competition and to replace the natural workings of the marketplace with control by great combinations. Rockefeller's great Standard Oil monopoly was the clearest example of the effort to free an enterprise from competition. Many other businessmen made similar attempts on a smaller scale. Vicious competitive battle—something Spencer and Sumner celebrated and called a source of healthy progress—was in fact the very thing that American businessmen most feared and tried to eliminate.

The Gospel of Wealth

Some businessmen attempted to temper the harsh philosophy of Social Darwinism with a more gentle, if in some ways equally self-serving, idea: the "gospel of wealth." People of great wealth, advocates of this idea argued, had not

THE NOVELS OF HORATIO ALGER

A young boy, perhaps an orphan, makes his perilous way through life on the rough streets of the city by selling newspapers or peddling matches. One day, his energy and determination catch the eye of a wealthy man, who gives him a chance to improve himself. Through honesty, charm, hard work, and aggressiveness, the boy rises in the world to become a successful man.

That, in a nutshell, is the story that Horatio Alger presented to his vast public in novel after novel—over 100 of them in all—for over forty years. During his lifetime, Americans bought many million copies of his novels. After his death in 1899, his books (and others written in his name) continued to sell at an astonishing rate. Even today, when the books themselves are largely forgotten, the name Horatio Alger has come to represent the idea of individual advancement through (in a phrase Alger coined) "pluck and luck."

Alger was born in 1832 into a middle-class New England family, attended Harvard, and spent a short time as a Unitarian minister. He himself never experienced the hardships he later chronicled. In the mid-1850s, he turned to writing stories and books, and he continued to do so for the rest of his life. His most famous novel, *Ragged Dick,* was published in 1868; but there were many others that were almost identical to it: *Tom, the Bootblack; Sink or Swim; Jed, the Poorhouse Boy; Phil, the Fiddler; Andy Grant's Pluck.* Most of his books were aimed at young people, and almost all of them were fables of a young man's rise "from rags to riches." The purpose of his writing, he claimed, was twofold. He wanted to "exert a salutary influence upon the class of whom [I] was writing, by setting before them inspiring examples of what energy, ambition, and an honest purpose may achieve." He also wanted to show his largely middle-class readers

A NEWSBOY'S STORY Alger's novels were even more popular after his death in 1899 than they had been in his lifetime. This reprint of one of his many "rags-to-riches" stories—about the rise of a New York newsboy to wealth and success—includes in the background a rendering of the "Met Life Building," an early skyscraper built in 1909.

"the life and experiences of the friendless and vagrant children to be found in all our cities."

But Alger's intentions probably had little to do with the success of his books. Most Americans of the late nineteenth and early twentieth centuries were attracted to Alger because his stories helped them to believe in one of the most cherished of all their national myths: that it is possible for individuals to rise in the world with willpower and hard work, that anyone can become a "self-made man." That belief was all the more important in the late nineteenth century, when the rise of large-scale corporate industrialization

was making it increasingly difficult for individuals to control their own fates.

Alger placed great emphasis on the moral qualities of his heroes; their success was a reward for their virtue. But many of his readers ignored the moral message and clung simply to the image of sudden and dramatic success. After the author's death, his publishers responded to that yearning by abridging many of Alger's works to eliminate the parts of his stories where the heroes do good deeds. Instead, they focused solely on the success of Alger's heroes in rising in the world.

Alger himself had very mixed feelings about the new industrial order he described. His books were meant to reveal not just the opportunities for advancement it sometimes created, but also its cruelty. That was one reason that in almost all his books, his heroes triumphed not just because of their own virtues or efforts, but because of some amazing stroke of luck. To Alger, at least, the modern age did not guarantee success through hard work alone; there had to be some providential assistance as well. Over time, however, Alger's admirers came to ignore his own misgivings about industrialism and to portray his books purely as celebrations of (and justifications for) laissez-faire capitalism and the accumulation of wealth.

An example of the transformation of Alger into a symbol of individual achievement is the Horatio Alger Award, established in 1947 by the American Schools and Colleges Association to honor "living individuals who by their own efforts had pulled themselves up by their bootstraps in the American tradition." Among its recipients have been Presidents Dwight D. Eisenhower and Ronald Reagan, evangelist Billy Graham, and Supreme Court justice Clarence Thomas.

only great power but great responsibilities as well. It was their duty to use their riches to advance social progress. Andrew Carnegie elaborated on the creed in his 1901 book, *The Gospel of Wealth,* in which he wrote that the wealthy should consider all revenues in excess of their own needs as "trust funds" to be used for the good of the community; the person of wealth, he said, was "the mere trustee and agent for his poorer brethren." Carnegie was only one of many great industrialists who devoted large parts of their fortunes to philanthropic works—much of

THE NOVELS OF LOUISA MAY ALCOTT

If Horatio Alger's rags-to-riches tales captured the aspirations of many men of the late nineteenth century, Louisa May Alcott's enormously popular novels helped give voice to the often unstated ambitions of many young women.

Alcott was born in 1832, the daughter of a prominent if generally impoverished reformer and educator, Bronson Alcott—a New England transcendentalist committed to abolishing slavery and advancing women's rights. Louisa May Alcott grew up wanting to write, one of the few serious vocations available to women. As a young adult, she wrote a series of popular adventure novels under the pen-name A. M. Barnard, populated by conventional male heroes. But after serving as a nurse in the Civil War (during which she contracted typhoid, from which she recovered, and mercury poisoning through her treatment, from which she suffered until her death in 1888), she chose a different path—writing realistic fiction and basing it on the lives and experiences of women. The publication of *Little Women* (1868, 1869) established Alcott as a major literary figure and as an enduring, if sometimes puzzling, inspiration for girls and, indeed, women of all ages.

Little Women—and its successors *Little Men* (1871) and *Jo's Boys* (1886)—were in many ways wholly unlike the formulaic Horatio Alger stories, in which young men inevitably rose from humble circumstances to great success. And yet they both echoed and altered the message of those books. The fictional March family in the novels was in fact modeled on Alcott's own impoverished if intellectually lively childhood, and much

(Bettmann/Corbis)

of *Little Women* is a chronicle of poverty, suffering, and even death. But it is also the story of a young girl—Jo March, modeled to some degree on Alcott herself—who struggles to build a life for herself that is not defined by conventional women's roles and ambitions. Jo March, like Louisa May Alcott herself, becomes a writer. She spurns a conventional marriage (to her attractive and wealthy neighbor Laurie). Unlike Alcott, who never married, Jo does find a husband—an older man, a German professor who does not support Jo's literary ambitions.

Many readers have found this marriage troubling—and false to the message of the rest of the book. It seems to contradict Alcott's belief that women can have intellectual independence and achievement. But to Alcott, this unconventional marriage was a symbol of her own repudiation of an ordinary domestic life. "Girls write to ask who

the little women marry, as if that was the only end and aim of a woman's life," Alcott wrote a friend after the publication of the first volume of the novel. "I won't marry Jo to Laurie to please any one." Jo's marriage to Professor Bhaer is in many ways a concession. "Jo should have remained a literary spinster [like Alcott herself]," she once wrote, "but so many enthusiastic ladies wrote to me clamorously demanding that she should marry Laurie, or somebody, that I didn't dare to refuse and out of perversity went and made a funny match for her."

It is tempting to see Louisa May Alcott's life—as an independent woman, a writer, and an active suffragist—as a better model to her readers than the characters in her fiction. But it was through *Little Women* and her other novels that Alcott mostly affected her time; and whatever their limitations, they present a group of young women who do challenge, even if indirectly, the expectations of their era. Jo March is willful, rebellious, stubborn, ambitious, and often selfish, not the poised, romantic, submissive woman of most sentimental novels of her time. She hates housekeeping and drudgery. She yearns at times to be a boy. She resists society's expectations—through her literary aspirations, her sharp temper, and ultimately her unconventional marriage. Through those qualities, she captured the imaginations of late-nineteenth-century female readers and continues to capture the imaginations of readers today. *Little Women* has survived far longer than the Horatio Alger stories did precisely because it presents a story of growing up that, unlike Alger's, is not predictable but complicated, conflicted, and surprising.

it to libraries and schools, institutions he believed would help the poor to help themselves.

The notion of private wealth as a public blessing existed alongside another popular concept: the notion of great wealth as something available to all. Russell H. Conwell, a Baptist minister, became the most prominent spokesman for the idea by delivering one lecture, "Acres of Diamonds," more than 6,000 times between 1880 and 1900. Conwell told a series of stories, which he claimed were true, of

Russell Conwell

individuals who had found opportunities for extraordinary wealth in their own backyards. (One such story involved a modest farmer who discovered a vast diamond mine in his own fields in the course of working his land.) "I say to you," he told his rapt audiences, "that you have 'acres of diamonds' beneath you right here . . . that the men and women sitting here have within their reach opportunities to get largely wealthy. . . . I say that you ought to get rich, and that it is your duty to get rich." Most of the millionaires in the country, Conwell claimed (inaccurately), had begun on the lowest rung of the economic ladder and had worked their way to success. Every industrious individual had the chance to do likewise.

Horatio Alger was the most famous promoter of the success story. (See "Patterns of Popular Culture," p. 482.) Alger

Horatio Alger

was originally a minister in a small town in Massachusetts but was driven from his pulpit as a result of a sexual scandal. He moved to New York, where he wrote his celebrated novels about poor boys who rise "from rags to riches"—more than 100 in all, which together sold more than 20 million copies. Alger's name became synonymous—both in his own time and in later years—with the powerful myth that anyone could advance to great wealth through hard work. Alger himself grew very wealthy from his writings, which were among the most popular of his time, and became something of a folk hero in American culture. Few of his many fans were aware of his homosexuality. Like most other gay men of his era, he kept his private life carefully hidden, fearful that publicity would destroy his reputation and his career.

Alternative Visions

Alongside the celebrations of competition, the justifications for great wealth, and the legitimization of the existing order stood a group of alternative philosophies, challenging the corporate ethos and at times capitalism itself.

One such philosophy emerged in the work of the sociologist Lester Frank Ward. Ward was a Darwinist, but he

Lester Frank Ward

rejected the application of Darwinian laws to human society. In *Dynamic Sociology* (1883) and other books, he argued that civilization was governed not by natural selection but by human intelligence, which was capable of shaping society as it wished. Unlike Sumner, who believed that state intervention to remodel the environment was futile, Ward thought that an active government engaged in positive planning was society's best hope. The people, through their government, could intervene in the economy and adjust it to serve their needs.

Other Americans skeptical of the laissez-faire ideas of the Social Darwinists adopted drastic approaches to reform. Some dissenters found a home in the Socialist Labor Party, founded in the 1870s and led for many years by Daniel De Leon, an immigrant from the West Indies. De Leon attracted a modest following in the industrial cities, but the party failed to become a major political force. It never polled more than 82,000 votes. De Leon's theoretical and dogmatic approach appealed to intellectuals more than to workers. A dissident faction of his party, eager to forge ties with organized labor, broke away and in 1901 formed the more enduring American Socialist Party.

Other radicals gained a wider following. One of the most influential was Henry George of California. His

Henry George

angrily eloquent *Progress and Poverty,* published in 1879,

became one of the best-selling nonfiction works in American publishing history. George tried to explain why poverty existed amidst the wealth created by modern industry. "This association of poverty with progress is the great enigma of our times," he wrote. "So long as all the increased wealth which modern progress brings goes but to build up great fortunes, to increase luxury and make sharper the contrast between the House of Have and the House of Want, progress is not real and cannot be permanent."

George blamed social problems on the ability of a few monopolists to grow wealthy as a result of rising land values. An increase in the value of land, he claimed, was a result not of any effort by the owner, but of the growth of society around the land. It was an "unearned increment," and it was rightfully the property of the community. And so George proposed a "single tax," to replace all other taxes, which would return the increment to the people. The tax, he argued, would destroy monopolies, distribute wealth more equally, and eliminate poverty. Single-tax societies sprang up in many cities. George himself moved east to New York; and in 1886, with the support of labor and the socialists, he narrowly missed being elected mayor.

Rivaling George in popularity was Edward Bellamy, whose utopian novel *Looking Backward,* published in 1888, sold more than 1 million copies. It described the experi-

Looking Backward

ences of a young Bostonian who went into a hypnotic sleep in 1887 and awoke in the year 2000 to find a new social order where want, politics, and vice were unknown. The new society had emerged from a peaceful, evolutionary process. The large trusts of the late nineteenth century had continued to grow in size and to combine with one another until ultimately they formed a single great trust, controlled by the government, which absorbed all the businesses of all the citizens and distributed the abundance of the industrial economy equally among all the people. Society had become a great machine, "so logical in its principles and direct and simple in its workings" that it almost ran itself. "Fraternal cooperation" had replaced competition. Class divisions had disappeared. Bellamy labeled the philosophy behind this vision "nationalism," and his work inspired the formation of more than 160 Nationalist Clubs to propagate his ideas.

The Problems of Monopoly

Relatively few Americans shared the views of those who questioned capitalism itself. But by the end of the century a growing number of people were becoming deeply concerned about a particular, glaring aspect of capitalism: the growth of monopoly (control of the market by large corporate combinations). Laborers, farmers, consumers, small manufacturers, conservative bankers and financiers, advocates of radical change—all began to assail monopoly and economic concentration.

CHILDREN OF WEALTH The children of the wealthy railroad executive George Jay Gould (son of the notorious financier Jay Gould) ride through a Paris park in *voiturettes,* miniature automobiles manufactured in France. *(Culver Pictures, Inc.)*

They blamed monopoly for creating artificially high prices and for producing a highly unstable economy. In the absence of competition, they argued, monopolistic industries could charge whatever prices they wished; railroads, in particular, charged very high rates along some routes because, in the absence of competition, they knew their customers had no choice but to pay them. Artificially high prices, moreover, contributed to the economy's instability, as production consistently outpaced demand. Beginning in 1873, the economy fluctuated erratically, with severe recessions creating havoc every five or six years, each recession worse than the previous one, until finally, in 1893, the system seemed on the verge of total collapse.

Hostility to monopoly was based on more than a concern about prices. Many Americans considered monopoly dangerous because the rise of large combinations seemed to threaten the ability of individuals to advance in the world. If a single person, or a small group, could control all economic activity in an industry, what opportunities would be left for others? To men, in particular, monopoly threatened the ideal of the wage-earning husband capable of supporting a family and prospering, because combinations seemed to reduce opportunities to succeed—to make less likely the idea of the "self-made man" memorialized in the novels of Horatio Alger. Monopoly, therefore, threatened not just competition, but certain notions of manhood as well.

Adding to the resentment of monopoly was the emergence of a new class of enormously and conspicuously wealthy people, whose lifestyles became an affront to those struggling to stay afloat. According to one estimate early in the century, 1 percent of the families in America controlled nearly 88 percent of the nation's assets. Some of the wealthy—Andrew Carnegie, for example—lived relatively unostentatiously and donated large sums to charities. Others, however, lived in almost grotesque luxury. Like a clan of feudal barons, the Vanderbilts maintained, in addition to many country estates, seven opulent mansions on seven blocks of New York City's Fifth Avenue. Other wealthy New Yorkers lavished vast sums on parties. The most notorious, a ball on which Mrs. Bradley Martin spent $368,000, created such a furor that she and her husband fled to England to escape public abuse.

Observing their flagrant displays of wealth were the four-fifths of the American people who lived modestly, and at least 10 million people who lived below the commonly accepted poverty line. The standard of living was rising for everyone, but the gap between rich and poor was increasing. To those in difficult economic circumstances, the sense of relative deprivation could be almost as frustrating and embittering as poverty itself.

Increasing Inequality

INDUSTRIAL WORKERS IN THE NEW ECONOMY

The American working class was both a beneficiary and a victim of the growth of industrial capitalism. Many workers in the late nineteenth century experienced a real rise in their standard of living. But they did so at the cost of arduous and often dangerous working conditions, diminishing control over their own work, and a growing sense of powerlessness.

The Immigrant Work Force

The industrial work force expanded dramatically in the late nineteenth century as demand for factory labor grew. The source of that expansion was a massive migration into industrial cities—migrations of two sorts. The first was the continuing flow of rural Americans into factory towns and cities—people disillusioned with or bankrupted by life on the farm and eager for new economic and social opportunities.

The second was the great wave of immigration from Mexico, Asia, Canada, and above all Europe in the decades following the Civil War—an influx greater than that of any previous era. The 25 million immigrants who arrived in the United States between 1865 and 1915 were more than four times the number who had arrived in the fifty years before.

In the 1870s and 1880s, most of the immigrants to eastern industrial cities came from the nation's traditional sources: England, Ireland, and northern Europe. By the end of the century, however, the major sources of immigration had shifted, with large numbers of southern and eastern Europeans (Italians, Poles, Russians, Greeks, Slavs, and others) moving to America and into the industrial work force. In the West, the major sources of immigration were Mexico and, until the Chinese Exclusion Act of 1882, Asia. No reliable figures are available for either group, but an estimated 1 million Mexicans entered the United States in the first three decades of the twentieth century, many of them swelling the industrial work force of western cities.

New Sources of Immigration

The new immigrants were coming to America in part to escape poverty and oppression in their homelands. But they were also lured to the United States by expectations of new opportunities. Sometimes such expectations were realistic, but often they were the result of false promises. Railroads tried to lure immigrants into their western landholdings by distributing misleading advertisements overseas. Industrial employers actively recruited immigrant workers under the Labor Contract Law, which—until its

APPROACHING SHORE This image of European immigrants aboard a ship approaching the American shore captures both the excitement and the tension of these newcomers to the United States. *(Library of Congress)*

repeal in 1885—permitted them to pay for the passage of workers in advance and deduct the amount later from their wages. Even after the repeal of the law, employers continued to encourage the immigration of unskilled laborers, often with the assistance of foreign-born labor brokers, such as the Greek and Italian padrones, who recruited work gangs of their fellow nationals.

The arrival of these new groups introduced heightened ethnic tensions into the dynamic of the working class. Low-paid Poles, Greeks, and French Canadians began to displace higher-paid British and Irish workers in the textile factories of New England. Italians, Slavs, and Poles emerged as a major source of labor for the mining industry in the East, traditionally dominated by native workers or northern European immigrants. Chinese and Mexicans competed with Anglo-Americans and African Americans in mining, farmwork, and factory labor in California, Colorado, and Texas. Even within industries, moreover, workers tended to cluster in particular occupations (and thus, often, at particular income levels) by ethnic group.

Heightened Ethnic Tensions

Wages and Working Conditions

The average standard of living for workers rose in the years after the Civil War, but for many laborers, the return for their labor remained very small. At the turn of the century, the average income of the American worker was $400 to $500 a year—below the $600 figure widely considered the minimum for a reasonable level of comfort. Nor did workers have much job security. All workers were vulnerable to the boom-and-bust cycle of the industrial economy, and some lost their jobs because of technological advances or because of the cyclical or seasonal nature of their work. Even those who kept their jobs could find their wages suddenly and substantially cut in hard times. Few workers, in other words, were ever far from poverty.

American laborers faced other hardships as well. For first-generation workers accustomed to the patterns of agrarian life, there was a difficult adjustment to the nature of modern industrial labor: the performance of routine, repetitive tasks, often requiring little skill, on a strict and monotonous schedule. To skilled artisans whose once valued tasks were now performed by machines, the new system was impersonal and demeaning. Factory laborers worked ten- to twelve-hour days, six days a week; in the steel industry they worked twelve hours a day. Many worked in appallingly unsafe or unhealthy factories. Industrial accidents were frequent and severe. Compensation to the victims, either from their employers or from the government, was often limited, until many states began passing workmen's compensation laws in the early twentieth century.

For many workers, the most disturbing aspect of factory labor in the new industrial system was their loss of control over the conditions of their labor. Even semiskilled workers and common laborers had managed to maintain some control over their labor in the relatively informal working conditions of the early and mid-nineteenth century. As the corporate form of organization spread, employers set out to make the factory more efficient (often in response to the principles of scientific management). That meant, they believed, centralizing control of the workplace in the hands of managers, ensuring that workers had no authority or control that might disrupt the flow of

Loss of Control

WEST LYNN MACHINE SHOP This machine tool shop in West Lynn, Massachusetts, photographed in the mid-1890s, suggests something of the growing scale of factory enterprise in the late nineteenth century—and also of the extraordinary dangers workers in these early manufacturing shops faced. *(Brown Brothers)*

production. This loss of control, as much as the low wages and long hours, lay behind the substantial working-class militancy in the late nineteenth century.

Women and Children at Work

The decreasing need for skilled work in factories induced many employers to increase the use of unskilled women and children, whom they could hire for lower wages than adult males. By 1900, women made up 17 percent of the industrial work force, a fourfold increase since 1870; and 20 percent of all women (well over 5 million) were wage earners. Some of these working women were single and took jobs to support themselves or their parents or siblings. Many others were married and had to work to supplement the inadequate earnings of their husbands; for many working-class families, two incomes were required to support even a minimal standard of living. In earlier periods of American history, women had regularly worked within the household economies that characterized most American families. But when women began working in factories in the mid-nineteenth century—outside the household, independently of husbands or fathers—many people began to consider their presence in the paid work force a social problem. Partly this was because many reformers, including many females, saw women as particularly vulnerable to exploitation and injury in the rough environment of the factory. It was also because many people considered it inappropriate for women to work independently. And so the "problem" of women in the work force became a significant public issue. In some communities the aversion to seeing married women work was so strong—among both men and women—that families struggled on inadequate wages rather than see a wife and mother take a job.

Women industrial workers were overwhelmingly white and mostly young, 75 percent of them under twenty-five. The vast majority were immigrants or the daughters of immigrants. There were some women in all areas of industry, even in some of the most arduous jobs. Most women, however, worked in a few industries where unskilled and semi-skilled machine labor (as opposed to heavy manual labor) prevailed. The textile industry remained the largest single industrial employer of women. (Domestic service remained the most common female occupation overall.) Women worked for wages as low as $6 to $8 a week, well below the minimum necessary for survival (and well below the wages paid to men working the same jobs). At the turn of the century, the average annual wage for a male industrial worker was $597; for a woman, it was $314. Even highly skilled women workers made about half what men doing the same job earned. Advocates of a minimum wage law for women created a sensation when they brought several women to a hearing in Chicago to testify that low wages and desperate poverty had driven them to prostitution. (The testimony was not, however, sensational enough for the Illinois legislature, which promptly defeated the bill.)

At least 1.7 million children under sixteen years of age were employed in factories and fields in 1900, more than twice the number of thirty years before. Ten percent of all girls aged ten to fifteen, and 20 percent of all boys, held jobs. This was partly because some families so desperately

SPINDLE BOYS Young boys, some of them barefoot, clamber among the great textile machines in a Georgia cotton mill adjusting spindles. Many of them were the children of women who worked in the plants. The photograph is by Lewis Hine. *(Bettmann/ Corbis)*

needed additional wages that parents and children alike were pressed into service. It was also because in some families the reluctance to permit wives to work led parents to send their children into the work force to avoid forcing mothers to go. This did not, however, prevent reformers from seeing children working in factories as a significant social problem. Under the pressure of outraged public opinion, thirty-eight state legislatures passed child-

Ineffective Child-Labor Laws

labor laws in the late nineteenth century; but these laws were of limited impact. Sixty percent of child workers were employed in agriculture, which was typically exempt from the laws; such children often worked twelve-hour days picking or hoeing in the fields. And even for children employed in factories, the laws merely set a minimum age of twelve years and a maximum workday of ten hours, standards that employers often ignored in any case. In the cotton mills of the South, children working at the looms all night were kept awake by having cold water thrown in their faces. In canneries, little girls cut fruits and vegetables sixteen hours a day. Exhausted children were particularly susceptible to injury while working at dangerous machines, and they were maimed and even killed in industrial accidents at an alarming rate.

As much as the appalling conditions of women and child workers troubled the national conscience, conditions for many men were at least equally dangerous. In mills and mines, and on the railroads, the American accident rate was higher than that of any industrial nation in the world. As late as 1907, an average of twelve railroad men a week died on the job. In factories, thousands of workers faced such occupational diseases as lead or phosphorus poisoning, against which few employers took precautions.

The Struggle to Unionize

Labor attempted to fight back against the poor conditions in the workplace by adopting some of the same tactics their employers had used so effectively: creating large combinations, or unions. But by the end of the century their efforts had met with little success.

There had been craft unions in America, representing small groups of skilled workers, since well before the Civil

National Labor Union

War. Alone, however, individual unions could not hope to exert significant power in the new corporate economy, and in the 1860s some labor leaders began to search for ways to combine the energies of the various labor organizations. The first attempt to federate separate unions into a single national organization came in 1866, when William H. Sylvis founded the National Labor Union—a polyglot association, claiming 640,000 members, that included a variety of reform groups having little direct relationship with labor. After the Panic of 1873, the National Labor Union disintegrated and disappeared.

The National Labor Union, like most of the individual unions that joined it, excluded women workers. Male workers argued (not entirely incorrectly) that women were used to drive down their wages; and they justified their hostility by invoking the ideal of domesticity. "Woman was created to be man's companion," a National Labor Union official said, "to be the presiding deity of the home circle." Most women workers agreed that "man should be the breadwinner," as one female union organizer said. But many argued that as long as conditions made it impossible for men to support their families, women should have full and equal opportunities in the workplace.

Unions faced special difficulties during the recession years of the 1870s. Not only was there widespread unemployment, which depression conditions created; there was also widespread middle-class hostility toward the unions. When labor disputes with employers turned bitter and violent, as they occasionally did, much of the public instinctively

Molly Maguires

blamed the workers (or the "radicals" and "anarchists" they believed were influencing the workers) for the trouble, rarely the employers. Particularly alarming to middle-class Americans was the emergence of the "Molly Maguires," a militant labor organization in the anthracite coal region of Pennsylvania. The Mollies operated within the Ancient Order of Hibernians, an Irish fraternal society, and sometimes used terrorist tactics. They attempted to intimidate the coal operators through violence and occasionally murder, and they added to the growing perception that labor

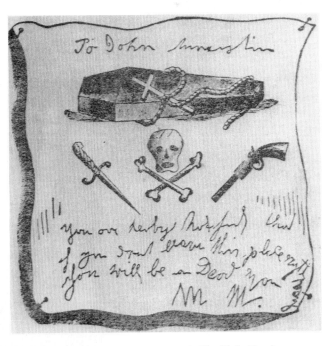

A WARNING FROM THE MOLLY MAGUIRES The Molly Maguires were known for their harsh, intimidating, and at times violent tactics against the owners and managers of anthracite coal mines. In this "coffin notice" sent to a mine foreman in the early 1870s, they inform him: "You are hereby notified that if you don't leave this place right away, you will be a dead man." *(The Historical Society of Schuylkill County)*

activism was motivated by dangerous radicals. Much of the violence attributed to the Molly Maguires, however, was instigated or performed by informers and agents employed by the mine owners, who wanted a pretext for ruthless measures to suppress unionization.

The Great Railroad Strike

Excitement over the Molly Maguires paled beside the near hysteria that gripped the country during the railroad strike of 1877, which began when the eastern railroads announced a 10 percent wage cut and which soon expanded into something approaching a class war. Strikers disrupted rail service from Baltimore to St. Louis, destroyed equipment, and rioted in the streets of Pittsburgh and other cities. State militias were called out, and in July President Hayes ordered federal troops to suppress the disorders in West Virginia. In Baltimore, eleven demonstrators died and forty were wounded in a conflict between workers and militiamen. In Philadelphia, state militia opened fire on thousands of workers and their families who were attempting to block the railroad crossings and killed twenty people. In all, over 100 people died before the strike finally collapsed several weeks after it had begun.

National Strike

The great railroad strike was America's first major, national labor conflict, and it illustrated how disputes between workers and employers could no longer be localized in the increasingly national economy. It illustrated as well the depth of resentment among many American workers toward their employers (and toward the governments allied with them) and the lengths to which they were prepared to go to express that resentment. And finally, it was an indication of the frailty of the labor movement. The failure of the strike seriously weakened the railroad unions and damaged the reputation of labor organizations in other industries as well.

The Knights of Labor

The first major effort to create a genuinely national labor organization was the founding in 1869 of the Noble Order of the Knights of Labor, under the leadership of Uriah S. Stephens. Membership was open to all who "toiled," a definition that included all workers and most business and professional people. The only excluded groups were lawyers, bankers, liquor dealers, and professional gamblers. Unlike most labor organizations of the time, the Knights welcomed women members—not just female factory workers, but domestic servants and women who worked in their own homes. Leonora Barry, an Irish immigrant who had worked in a New York hosiery factory, ran the Woman's Bureau of the Knights. Under her effective leadership, the Knights enlisted 50,000 women members (both black and white) and created over a hundred all-female locals.

The Knights were loosely organized, without much central direction. Members met in local "assemblies," which took many different forms. They were loosely affiliated with a national "general assembly." Their program was similarly vague. Although they championed an eight-hour day and the abolition of child labor, the leaders were more interested in long-range reform of the economy. Leaders of the Knights hoped to replace the "wage system" with a new "cooperative system," in which workers would themselves control a large part of the economy.

KNIGHTS OF LABOR DELEGATES, 1886
The Knights of Labor aspired to represent everyone in America who could be considered a producer, and it was the first, and for many years the only, labor organization to welcome women unreservedly, as this portrait of delegates to the Knights 1886 convention indicates. *(Brown Brothers)*

For several years, the Knights remained a secret fraternal organization. But in the late 1870s, under the leadership of Terence V. Powderly, the order moved into the open and entered a spectacular period of expansion. By 1886, it claimed a total membership of over 700,000, including some militant elements that the moderate leadership could not always control. Local unions or assemblies associated with the Knights launched a series of strikes in the 1880s in defiance of Powderly's wishes. In 1885, striking railway workers forced the Missouri Pacific, a link in the Gould system, to restore wage cuts and recognize their union. But the victory was temporary. In the following year, a strike on another Gould railroad, the Texas and Pacific, was crushed, and the power of the unions in the Gould system was broken. Their failure helped discredit the organization. By 1890, the membership of the Knights had shrunk to 100,000. A few years later, the organization disappeared.

Dissolution of the Knights of Labor

The AFL

Even before the Knights began to decline, a rival organization based on a very different organizational concept appeared. In 1881, representatives of a number of existing craft unions formed the Federation of Organized Trade and Labor Unions of the United States and Canada. Five years later, it changed its name to the American Federation of Labor (AFL), and it soon became the most important and enduring labor group in the country. Rejecting the Knights' idea of one big union for everybody, the Federation was an association of autonomous craft unions and represented mainly skilled workers. It was generally hostile to organizing unskilled workers, who did not fit comfortably within the craft-based structure of existing organizations.

Toward women, the AFL adopted an apparently contradictory policy. On the one hand, the male leaders of the AFL were hostile to the idea of women entering the paid work force. Because women were weak, they believed, employers could easily take advantage of them by paying them less than men. As a result, women workers drove down wages for everyone. "It is the so-called competition of the unorganized, defenseless woman worker, the girl and the wife, that often tends to reduce the wages of the father and husband," Samuel Gompers, the powerful leader of the AFL, once said. He talked often about the importance of women remaining in the home and argued (incorrectly) that "there is no necessity of the wife contributing to the support of the family by working." More than that, female labor was, the AFL newspaper wrote, "the knife of the assassin, aimed at the family circle." Gompers himself believed strongly that a test of a man's worth was his ability to support a family, and that women in the work force would undermine men's positions as heads of their families.

Opposition to Female Employment

Although hostile to the idea of women workers, the AFL nevertheless sought equal pay for those women who did work and even hired some female organizers to encourage unionization in industries dominated by women. These positions were, in fact, less contradictory than they seem. By raising the pay of women, the AFL could make them less attractive to employers and, in effect, drive them out of the work force.

Gompers accepted the basic premises of capitalism; his goal was simply to secure for the workers he represented a greater share of capitalism's material rewards. Gompers rejected the idea of fundamental economic reform; he opposed the creation of a worker's party; he was generally hostile to any government efforts to protect labor or improve working conditions, convinced that what government could give it could also take away. The AFL concentrated instead on the relationship between labor and management. It supported the immediate objectives of most workers: better wages and working conditions. And while the AFL hoped to attain its goals by collective bargaining, it was ready to use strikes if necessary.

The AFL's Agenda

As one of its first objectives, the AFL demanded a national eight-hour day and called for a general strike if workers did not achieve the goal by May 1, 1886. On that day, strikes and demonstrations calling for a shorter workday took place all over the country, most of them staged by AFL unions but a few by more radical groups.

In Chicago, a center of labor and radical strength, a strike was already in progress at the McCormick Harvester Company when the general strike began. City police had been harassing the strikers, and labor and radical leaders called a protest meeting at Haymarket Square. When the police ordered the crowd to disperse, someone threw a bomb that killed seven officers and injured sixty-seven other people. The police, who had killed four strikers the day before, fired into the crowd and killed four more people. Conservative, property-conscious Americans, frightened and outraged, demanded retribution, even though no one knew who had thrown the bomb. Chicago officials finally rounded up eight anarchists and charged them with murder, on the grounds that their statements had incited whoever had hurled the bomb. All eight scapegoats were found guilty after a remarkably injudicious trial. Seven were sentenced to death. One of the condemned committed suicide, four were executed, and two had their sentences commuted to life imprisonment.

Haymarket Square

To most middle-class Americans, the Haymarket bombing was an alarming symbol of social chaos and radicalism. "Anarchism" now became a code word in the public mind for terrorism and violence, even though most anarchists were relatively peaceful visionaries dreaming of a new social order. For the next thirty years, the specter of anarchism remained one of the most frightening concepts in the American middle-class imagination. It also became a constant obstacle to the goals of the AFL and other labor organizations, and it was particularly devastating to the Knights of Labor, which, as the most radical of the major labor organizations, never recovered from the post-Haymarket hysteria. However much they tried to distance themselves from radicals, unions were always vulnerable to accusations of anarchism, as the violent strikes of the 1890s occasionally illustrated.

The Homestead Strike

The Amalgamated Association of Iron and Steel Workers, which was affiliated with the American Federation of Labor, was the most powerful trade union in the country. Its members were skilled workers, in great demand by employers and thus able to exercise significant power in the workplace. Employers sometimes called such workers "little shopfloor autocrats," and they resented the substantial control over working conditions these skilled laborers often had. The union had a rulebook with fifty-six pages of what workers called "legislation" limiting the power of employers. In the emerging corporate world of the late nineteenth century, such challenges to management control were beginning to seem intolerable to many employers.

By the mid-1880s, the steel industry had introduced new production methods and new patterns of organization that were streamlining the steelmaking process and, at the same time, reducing the companies' dependence on skilled labor. In the Carnegie system, which was coming to dominate the steel industry, the union had a foothold in only one of the corporation's three major factories—the Homestead plant near Pittsburgh. By 1890, Carnegie and his chief lieu-

Henry Clay Frick

tenant, Henry Clay Frick, had decided that the Amalgamated "had to go," even at Homestead. Over the next two years, they repeatedly cut wages at Homestead. At first, the union acquiesced, aware that it was not strong enough to wage a successful strike.

In 1892, the company stopped even discussing its decisions with the Amalgamated, in effect denying the union's right to negotiate at all. Finally, when Frick announced another wage cut at Homestead and gave the union two days to accept it, the Amalgamated called for a strike. Frick abruptly shut down the plant and called in 300 guards from the Pinkerton Detective Agency to enable the company to hire nonunion workers. The hated Pinkertons were well-known strikebreakers, and their mere presence was often enough to incite workers to violence.

The Pinkertons approached the plant by river on barges on July 6, 1892. The strikers prepared for them by pouring oil on the water and setting it on fire, and they met the guards at the docks with guns and dynamite. After several hours of pitched battle, during which three guards and ten strikers were killed and many others injured, the Pinkertons surrendered and were escorted roughly out of town.

But the workers' victory was temporary. The governor of Pennsylvania, at the company's request, sent the state's entire National Guard contingent, some 8,000 troops, to Homestead.

The Union Defeated

Production resumed, with strikebreakers now protected by troops. And public opinion turned against the strikers when a radical made an attempt to assassinate Frick. Slowly workers drifted back to their jobs; and finally—four months after the strike began—the Amalgamated surrendered. By 1900, every major steel plant in the Northeast had broken with the Amalgamated, which now had no power to resist. Its membership shrank from a high of 24,000 in 1891 (two-thirds of all eligible steelworkers) to fewer than 7,000 a decade later. Its decline was symbolic of the general erosion of union strength in the late nineteenth century, as factory labor became increasingly unskilled and workers thus became easier to replace. The AFL unions were often powerless in the face of these changes.

The Pullman Strike

A dispute of greater magnitude and equal bitterness, if less violence, was the Pullman strike in 1894. The Pullman Palace Car Company manufactured sleeping and parlor cars for railroads, which it built and repaired at a plant near Chicago. There the company built the 600-acre town of Pullman and rented its trim, orderly houses to the employees. George M. Pullman, owner of the company, considered the town a model solution to the industrial problem; he referred to the workers as his "children." But many residents chafed at the regimentation and the high rents.

In the winter of 1893–1894, the Pullman Company slashed wages by about 25 percent, citing the declining revenues the depression was causing. At the same time, Pullman refused to reduce rents in its model town, which were 20 to 25 percent higher than rents for comparable accommodations in surrounding areas. Workers went on strike and persuaded the militant American Railway Union, led by Eugene V. Debs, to support them by refusing to han-

Eugene Debs

dle Pullman cars and equipment. Opposing the strikers was the General Managers' Association, a consortium of twenty-four Chicago railroads. It persuaded its member companies to discharge switchmen who refused to handle Pullman cars. Every time this happened, Debs's union instructed its members who worked for the offending companies to walk off their jobs. Within a few days thousands of railroad workers in twenty-seven states and territories were on strike, and transportation from Chicago to the Pacific coast was paralyzed.

Most state governors responded readily to appeals from strike-threatened businesses; but the governor of Illinois, John Peter Altgeld, was a man with demonstrated

THE PULLMAN STRIKE These two images portray two aspects of the great Pullman strike of 1894. The photograph above shows U.S. troops, ordered to Chicago to quell the strike, camping on the lakefront. The drawing below shows freight cars and an engine destroyed by striking workers. These images were published together in *Harper's Weekly* to illustrate the ferocity of the Pullman battle. *(Library of Congress)*

In July 1894, over Altgeld's objections, the president ordered 2,000 troops to the Chicago area. A federal court issued an injunction forbidding the union to continue the strike. When Debs and his associates defied it, they were arrested and imprisoned. With federal troops protecting the hiring of new workers and with the union leaders in a federal jail, the strike quickly collapsed.

Sources of Labor Weakness

The last decades of the nineteenth century were years in which labor, despite its organizing efforts, made few real gains and suffered many important losses. In a rapidly expanding industrial economy, wages for workers rose hardly at all, and not nearly enough to keep up with the rising cost of living. Labor leaders won a few legislative victories: the abolition by Congress in 1885 of the Contract Labor Law; the establishment by Congress in 1868 of an eight-hour day on public works projects and in 1892 of an eight-hour day for government employees; state laws governing hours of labor and safety standards; and gradually some guaranteed compensation for workers injured on the job. But many of these laws were not enforced, and neither strikes nor protests seemed to have much effect. The end of the century found most workers with less political power and considerably less control of the workplace than they had had forty years before.

Workers failed to make greater gains for many reasons. The principal labor organizations represented only a small percentage of the industrial work force. Four percent of all workers (fewer than 1 million people) belonged to unions in 1900. The AFL, the most important, excluded unskilled workers, who were emerging as the core of the industrial work force, and along with them most women, blacks, and recent immigrants. Women responded to this exclusion in 1903 by forming their own organization, the Women's Trade Union League. But after several frustrating years of attempting to unionize women, the WTUL turned the bulk of its attention to securing protective legislation for women workers, not general organization and mobilization of labor. Other divisions within the work force contributed further to union weakness. Tensions between different ethnic and racial groups kept laborers divided.

Another source of labor weakness was the shifting nature of the work force. Many immigrant workers came to America intending to remain only briefly, to earn some money and return home. The assumption that they had no long-range future in the country (even though it was often a mistaken one) eroded their willingness to organize. Other workers—natives and immigrants alike—were in constant motion, moving from one job to another, one town to another, seldom in one place long enough to establish any institutional ties or exert any real power. A study of Newburyport, Massachusetts, over a thirty-year period shows that 90 percent of the workers

Shifting Nature of the Work Force

sympathies for workers and their grievances. Altgeld had criticized the trials of the Haymarket anarchists and had pardoned the convicted men who were still in prison when he took office. He refused to call out the militia to protect employers now. Bypassing Altgeld, railroad operators asked the federal government to send regular army troops to Illinois, on the pretext that the strike was preventing the movement of mail on the trains. President Grover Cleveland and Attorney General Richard Olney, a former railroad lawyer and a bitter foe of unions, complied.

there vanished from the town records in those years, many of them because they moved elsewhere. Even workers who stayed put often did not remain in the same job for long.

Some real social mobility did exist. Workers might move from unskilled to semiskilled or skilled jobs during their lifetimes; their children might become foremen or managers. The gains were small, but they were enough to inspire considerable (and often unrealistic) hopes and to persuade some workers that they were not part of a permanent working class.

Above all, workers made few gains in the late nineteenth century because of the strength of the forces arrayed

Corporate Strength

against them. They faced corporate organizations of vast wealth and power, which were generally determined to crush any

efforts by workers to challenge their prerogatives—not just through brute force, but also through infiltration of unions, espionage within working-class communities, and sabotage of organizational efforts. And as the Homestead and Pullman strikes suggest, the corporations had the support of local, state, and federal authorities, who were willing to send in troops to "preserve order" and crush labor uprisings on demand.

Despite the creation of new labor unions, despite a wave of strikes and protests that in the 1880s and 1890s reached startling proportions, workers in the late nineteenth century failed to create successful organizations or to protect their interests in the way the large corporations managed to do. In the battle for power within the emerging industrial economy, almost all the advantages seemed to lie with capital.

CONCLUSION

In the four decades following the end of the Civil War, the United States propelled itself into the forefront of the industrializing nations of the world. Large areas of the nation remained overwhelmingly rural, to be sure, and the majority of the population was still engaged in activities closely tied to farming. Even so, America's economy, and along with it the nation's society and culture, were being profoundly transformed.

New technologies, new forms of corporate management, and new supplies of labor helped make possible the rapid growth of the nation's industries and the construction of its railroads. The factory system contributed to the growth of the nation's cities and at times created entirely new ones. Immigration provided a steady supply of new workers for the growing industrial economy. The result was a steady and substantial increase in national wealth, rising living standards for much of the population, and the creation of great new fortunes.

But industrialization did not spread its fruits evenly. Large areas of the country, most notably the South, and

large groups in the population, most notably minorities, women, and recent immigrants, profited relatively little from economic growth. Industrial workers experienced arduous conditions of labor and wages that rose much more slowly than the profits of the corporations for which they worked. Small merchants and manufacturers found themselves overmatched by great new combinations.

Industrialists strove to create a rationale for their power and to persuade the public that everyone had something to gain from it. But many Americans remained skeptical of modern capitalism, and some—workers struggling to form unions, reformers denouncing trusts, women fighting to win protections for female laborers, socialists envisioning a new world, and many others—created broad and powerful critiques of the new economic order. Industrialization brought both progress and pain to late-nineteenth-century America. Controversies over its effects defined the era and would continue to define the first decades of the twentieth century.

INTERACTIVE LEARNING

The *Primary Source Investigator CD-ROM* offers the following materials related to this chapter:

- Interactive map: **Transportation Revolution** (M12).
- Documents, images, and maps related to industrialization, economic growth, and labor strife in the late nineteenth century, including Thomas Edison's patent for the lightbulb, original railroad maps showing the

expansion of transportation networks, and panoramic photographs of the era's giant industrial plants.

Online Learning Center (www.mhhe.com/brinkley13e)

For quizzes, Internet resources, references to additional books and films, and more, consult this book's Online Learning Center.

FOR FURTHER REFERENCE

Robert Wiebe's *The Search for Order, 1877-1920* (1968) is a classic analysis of America's evolution from a society of what he calls island communities to a national urban society. David Nasaw, *Andrew Carnegie* (2006) is a biography of one of the first and most famous industrial tycoons, who also became a noted philanthropist. Alfred D. Chandler Jr. describes the new business practices that made industrialization possible in *The Visible Hand: The Managerial Revolution in American Business* (1977) and *Scale and Scope: The Dynamics of Industrial Capitalism* (1990). Olivier Zunz offers a provocative analysis of the social underpinnings of the new corporate order in *Making America Corporate, 1870-1920* (1990) and *Why the American Century?* (1998). David F. Noble, *America by Design: Science, Technology, and the Rise of Corporate Capitalism* (1977) and David Hounshell, *From the American System to Mass Production, 1800-1932* (1984) discuss the

explosion of science and technology in the era of rapid industrialization. Douglas Brinkley, *Wheels for the World* (2003) is a lively history of the Ford Motor Company. Daniel Rodgers, *The Work Ethic in Industrial America, 1850-1920* (1978) is an important intellectual history of the way Americans viewed industrial workers. David Montgomery, *The Fall of the House of Labor: The Workplace, the State, and American Labor Activism, 1865-1925* (1987) analyzes the way industrialization shaped (and was shaped by) the workers, their expertise, and the strong cultural traditions of the shop floor. Alice Kessler-Harris documents the tremendous movement of women into the work force in the period in *Out to Work: A History of Wage-Earning Women in the United States* (1982). John L. Thomas, *Alternative America: Henry George, Edward Bellamy, Henry Demarest Lloyd, and the Adversary Tradition* (1983) examines some important critics of corporate capitalism.

CHAPTER 18

THE AGE OF THE CITY

SEATTLE IN THE EARLY TWENTIETH CENTURY The late nineteenth and early twentieth centuries were times of tremendous urban growth in many areas of the United States. This postcard of downtown Seattle shows a dense and bustling city almost all of whose buildings are relatively new. *(© PoodlesRock/Corbis)*

THE INDUSTRIALIZATION AND COMMERCIALIZATION of America changed the face of society in countless ways. Nowhere were those changes more profound than in the growth of cities and the creation of an urban society and culture. Having begun its life as a primarily agrarian republic, the United States in the late nineteenth century was becoming an urban nation.

The change did not come easily. Cities grew so rapidly that their facilities and institutions could not keep pace. Housing, transportation, sewers, social services, governments—all lagged far behind the enormous demands the new urban population was placing on them. American sensibilities lagged behind as well. Many people rebelled at the new and intimidating pace of urban life and at the dazzling and at times uncomfortable diversity of the urban population. "Our cities," wrote the sociologist Charles Horton Cooley, "are full of the disintegrated materials of the old order looking for a place in the new."

But despite their many problems, cities continued to grow in both size and influence. People flocked to them because they were the sources of jobs—in factories, business offices, shops, and the countless other economic activities that cities created. People moved to urban areas as well to escape what many considered the boredom of rural life and to experience the new forms of entertainment that cities were helping to advance. Cities were also centers of educational and intellectual life, attracting writers and artists and becoming the homes of important schools and universities.

The enormous diversity of many urban populations required cities to assimilate different and sometimes hostile population groups—a challenge that has continued to face the nation into the present. For a time, urban areas dealt with diversity through separation. Individual racial and ethic groups formed their own communities and seldom moved out of them. Gradually, however, these ethnic divisions began to break down, creating significant tensions but also producing new forms of interaction among different groups.

As centers of wealth, cities also became the sites of great civic projects that have defined the identity of many urban centers ever since. Cities across the United States, and around much of the world, set out in these years to build public parks, museums, theaters, opera houses, monumental railroad stations, imposing libraries, and great boulevards. These dramatic urban projects served mostly the wealthiest citizens of cities, but the impact of many of them could be felt among all social classes.

The city of a century ago, like the city of today, symbolized many of the greatest achievements and desires of modern society and also many of its greatest fears.

SIGNIFICANT EVENTS

- 1836 ▶ Mount Holyoke College founded as seminary for women
- 1840s ▶ Modern baseball established
- 1850 ▶ First urban tenement built in New York City
- 1859 ▶ New York City's Central Park opened
- 1865 ▶ Vassar College founded
- 1869 ▶ Princeton and Rutgers play first intercollegiate football game
- 1870 ▶ New York City opens elevated railroads
  - ▶ Wellesley College founded
- 1871 ▶ Great fires destroy much of Chicago and Boston
  - ▶ Smith College founded
- 1872 ▶ Tammany's Boss Tweed convicted of corruption
  - ▶ Montgomery Ward distributes first catalog
- 1876 ▶ Baseball's National League founded
  - ▶ Johns Hopkins University creates first modern graduate school
- 1879 ▶ Carlisle Indian Industrial School founded in Pennsylvania
  - ▶ Salvation Army begins operations in America
  - ▶ First F. W. Woolworth store opens in Utica, New York
- 1882 ▶ Congress restricts Chinese immigration
- 1883 ▶ Brooklyn Bridge opened
- 1884 ▶ First steel girder "skyscraper" built in Chicago
  - ▶ William Dean Howells publishes *The Rise of Silas Lapham*
- 1887 ▶ American Protective Association founded
  - ▶ Sears Roebuck begins business in Chicago
- 1890 ▶ Jacob Riis publishes *How the Other Half Lives*
- 1891 ▶ James Naismith invents basketball
- 1893 ▶ Columbian Exposition opens in Chicago
- 1894 ▶ Immigration Restriction League founded
- 1895 ▶ Stephen Crane publishes *The Red Badge of Courage*
  - ▶ Boston opens first subway in America
  - ▶ First Coney Island amusement park opens
- 1899 ▶ Kate Chopin publishes *The Awakening*
- 1900 ▶ Theodore Dreiser publishes *Sister Carrie*
- 1901 ▶ Baseball's American League founded
- 1903 ▶ Boston Red Sox win first World Series
  - ▶ Henry James publishes *The Ambassadors*
- 1906 ▶ Earthquake and fire destroy much of San Francisco
  - ▶ Upton Sinclair publishes *The Jungle*
- 1910 ▶ National College Athletic Association founded to regulate college football
- 1913 ▶ Ashcan School artists stage Armory Show in New York City
- 1915 ▶ D. W. Griffith's *The Birth of a Nation* debuts

THE URBANIZATION OF AMERICA

The great migration from the countryside to the city was not unique to the United States. It was occurring simultaneously throughout much of the Western world in response to industrialization and the factory system. But America, a society with little experience of great cities, found urbanization both jarring and alluring.

The Lure of the City

"We cannot all live in cities," the journalist Horace Greeley wrote shortly after the Civil War, "yet nearly all seem deter-

Rapid Urban Growth — mined to do so." The urban population of America increased sevenfold in the half-century after the Civil War. And in 1920, the census revealed that for the first time, a majority of the American people lived in "urban" areas—defined as communities of 2,500 people or more. New York City and its environs grew from 1 million in 1860 to over 3 million in 1900. Chicago had 100,000 residents in 1860 and more

than a million in 1900. Cities were experiencing similar growth in all areas of the country.

Natural increase accounted for only a small part of the urban growth. In fact, urban families experienced a high rate of infant mortality, a declining fertility rate, and a high death rate from disease. Without immigration, cities would have grown slowly, if at all. The city attracted people from the countryside because it offered conveniences, entertainments, and cultural experiences unavailable in rural communities. Cities also offered people private social space to live their lives in ways that were far more difficult in small towns, where individuals had little privacy. Cities gave women the opportunity to act in ways that in smaller communities would have been seen to violate "propriety." They gave gay men and lesbian women space in which to build a culture (even if still a mostly hidden one) and experiment sexually at least partly insulated from the hostile gaze of others. But most of all, cities attracted people because they offered more and better-paying jobs than were available in rural America or in the foreign economies many immigrants were fleeing.

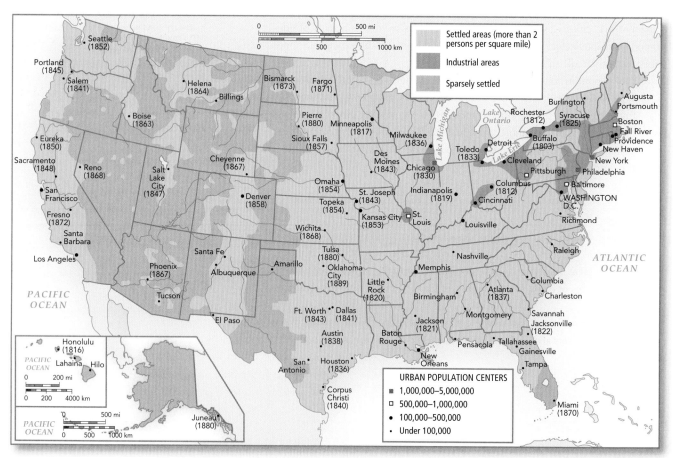

AMERICA IN 1900 This map helps illustrate the enormous increase in the nation's urban population in the nineteenth century. The map of America in 1800, on p. 197 in Chapter 7, reveals a nation with very few significant cities and with a population clustered largely along the eastern seaboard. By 1900, a much larger area of the United States had consistent areas of settlement, and many more of those areas consisted of towns and cities—including three cities (Chicago, New York, and Philadelphia) with populations of over a million and a considerable number of other cities with 100,000 or more people. Also striking, however, is the amount of land in the West with very light settlement or no settlement at all. ◆ *Do climate and geography help explain the variable patterns of settlement?*

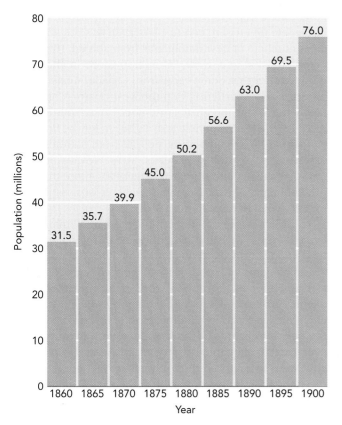

POPULATION GROWTH, 1860–1900 This chart illustrates the rapid increase in the nation's population in the last forty years of the nineteenth century. As you can see, the American population more than doubled in those years. ◆ *What were the principal factors behind this substantial population growth?*

People moved to cities, too, because new forms of transportation made it easier for them to get there. Railroads made simple, quick, and inexpensive what once might have seemed a daunting journey from parts of the American countryside to nearby cities. The development of large, steam-powered ocean liners created a highly competitive shipping industry, allowing Europeans and Asians to cross the oceans to America much more cheaply and quickly than they had in the past.

Migrations

As a result of urbanization, the late nineteenth century was an age of unprecedented geographic mobility, as Americans left the declining agricultural regions of the East at a Geographic Mobility dramatic rate. Some who left were moving to the newly developing farmlands of the West. But almost as many were moving to the cities of the East and the Midwest.

Among those leaving rural America for industrial cities in the late nineteenth century were young rural women, for whom opportunities in the farm economy were limited. As farms grew larger, more commercial, and more mechanized, they became increasingly male preserves; and since much of the work force on many farms consisted of unskilled and often transient workers, there were fewer family units than before. Farm women had once been essential for making clothes and other household goods, but those goods were now available in stores or through catalogs. Hundreds of thousands of women moved to the cities, therefore, in search of work and community.

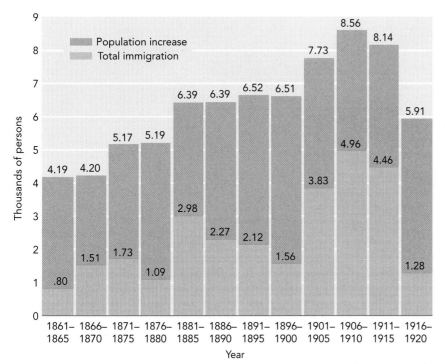

IMMIGRATION'S CONTRIBUTION TO POPULATION GROWTH, 1860–1920 Immigration, mostly from Europe, was responsible for a substantial share of the nation's population growth in the late nineteenth and early twentieth centuries—in some periods, as this chart shows, most of the population growth. ◆ *What factors drew so many immigrants to the United States in these years?*

Southern blacks were also beginning what would be a nearly century-long exodus from the countryside into the city. Their withdrawal was a testament to the poverty, debt, violence, and oppression African Americans encountered in the late-nineteenth-century rural South, because the opportunities they found in cities were limited. Factory jobs for blacks were rare, and professional opportunities almost nonexistent. Urban blacks tended to work as cooks, janitors, domestic servants, and in other low-paying service occupations. Since many such jobs were considered women's work, black women often outnumbered black men in the cities.

By the end of the nineteenth century, there were sub-stantial African-American communities (10,000 people or more) in over thirty cities—many of them in the South, but some (New York City, Chicago, Washington, D.C., Baltimore) in the North or in border states. Much more substantial African-American migration was to come during World War I and after; but the black communities established in the late nineteenth century paved the way for the great population movements of the future.

African-American Communities

The most important source of urban population growth in the late nineteenth century, however, was the arrival of great numbers of new immigrants from abroad: 10 million between 1860 and 1890, 18 million more in the three decades after that. Some came from Canada, Mexico, Latin America, and—particularly on the West Coast—China and Japan. But by far the greatest number came from Europe. After 1880, the flow of new arrivals began for the first time to include large numbers of people from southern and eastern Europe: Italians, Greeks, Slavs, Slovaks, Russian Jews, Armenians, and others. By the 1890s, more than half of all immigrants came from these new regions, as opposed to less than 2 percent in the 1860s.

In earlier stages of immigration, most new immigrants from Europe (with the exception of the Irish) were at least modestly prosperous and educated. Germans and Scandinavians in particular had headed west on their arrival, either to farm or to work as businessmen, merchants, professionals, or skilled laborers in midwestern cities such as St. Louis, Cincinnati, and Milwaukee. Most of the new immigrants of the late nineteenth century, however, lacked the capital to buy farmland and lacked the education to establish themselves in professions. So, like the poor Irish immigrants before the Civil War, they settled overwhelmingly in industrial cities, where most of them took unskilled jobs.

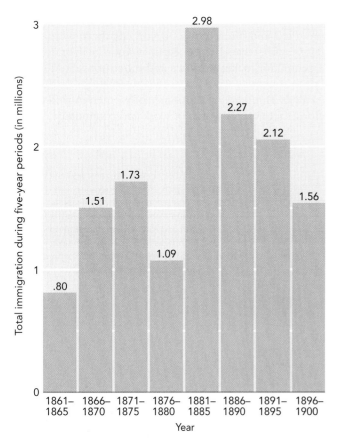

TOTAL IMMIGRATION, 1860–1900 Over 10 million immigrants from abroad entered the United States in the last forty years of the nineteenth century, with particularly high numbers arriving in the 1880s and 1890s. This chart shows the pattern of immigration in five-year intervals. ◆ *What external events might help explain some of the rises and falls in the rates of immigration in these years?*

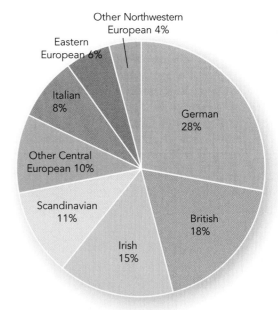

SOURCES OF IMMIGRATION FROM EUROPE, 1860–1900 This pie chart shows the sources of European immigration in the late nineteenth century. The largest number of immigrants continued to come from traditional sources (Britain, Ireland, Germany, Scandinavia), but the beginnings of what in the early twentieth century would become a major influx of immigrants from new sources—southern and eastern Europe in particular—are already visible here. Immigration from other sources—Mexico, South and Central America, and Asia—was also significant during this period. ◆ *Why would these newer sources of European and other kinds of immigration create controversy among older-stock Americans?*

GLOBAL MIGRATIONS

The large waves of immigration that transformed American society in the nineteenth and early twentieth centuries were not unique to the United States. They were part of a great, global movement of peoples—unprecedented in history—that affected every continent. These epic migrations were the product of two related forces: population growth and industrialization.

The population of Europe grew faster in the second half of the nineteenth century than it had ever grown before and than it has ever grown since—almost doubling between 1850 and the beginning of World War I. The population growth was a result of growing economies able to support more people and of more efficient and productive agriculture that helped end debilitating famines. But the rapid growth nevertheless strained the resources of many parts of Europe and affected, in particular, rural people, who were now too numerous to live off the available land. Many decided to move to other parts of the world, where land was more plentiful or jobs were available.

At the same time, industrialization drew millions of people out of the countryside and into cities—sometimes into cities in their own countries, but often into industrial cities in other, more economically advanced nations. Historians of migration speak of "push" factors (pressures on people to leave their homes) and "pull" factors (the lure of new lands) in explaining population movements. The "push" for many nineteenth-century migrants was poverty and inadequate land at home; for others it was political and religious oppression. The "pull" was the availability of land or industrial jobs in other regions or lands—and for some, the prospect of greater freedom abroad. Faster, cheaper, and easier transportation—railroads and steamships, in particular—also aided large-scale immigration.

From 1800 to the start of World War I, 50 million Europeans migrated to new lands overseas—people from almost all areas of Europe, but in the later years of the century (when migration reached its peak) mostly from poor rural areas in southern and eastern Europe. Italy, Russia, and Poland were among the biggest sources of late-nineteenth-century migrants. Almost two-thirds of these immigrants came to the United States. But nearly 20 million Europeans migrated to other lands. Migrants from England and Ireland (among others) moved in large numbers to those areas of the British Empire with vast, seemingly open lands: Canada, Australia, New Zealand, and South Africa. Large numbers of Italians moved to Argentina and other parts of South America. Many of these migrants moved to vast areas of open land in these countries; established themselves as farmers, using the new mechanical farming devices made possible by industrialization; and in many places—Australia, New Zealand, Argentina, South Africa, and the United States—evicted the original residents of their territories and created societies of their own. Many others settled in the industrial cities that were growing up in all these regions and formed distinctive ethnic and national communities within them.

But it was not only Europeans who were transplanting themselves in these years. Vast numbers of migrants—usually poor, desperate people—left Asia, Africa, and the Pacific Islands in search of better lives. Most of them could not afford the journey abroad on their own. They moved instead as indentured servants (in much the same way many English migrants moved to America in the seventeenth century), agreeing to a term of servitude in their new land in exchange for food, shelter, and transportation. Recruiters of indentured servants fanned out across China, Japan, areas of Africa and the Pacific Islands, and, above all, India. French and British recruiters brought hundreds of thousands of Indian migrants to work in planta-

(*Bodleian Library, University of Oxford*)

tions in their own Asian and African colonies. Chinese laborers were recruited to work on plantations in Cuba and Hawaii; mines in Malaya, Peru, South Africa, and Australia; and railroad projects in Canada, Peru, and the United States. African indentured servants moved in large numbers to the Caribbean, and Pacific Islanders tended to move to other islands or to Australia.

The migration of European peoples to new lands was largely voluntary and brought most migrants to the United States, where indentured servitude was illegal. But the migration of non-European peoples often involved an important element of coercion and brought relatively small numbers of people to the United States. This non-European migration was a function of the growth of European empires and it was made possible by the imperial system—by its labor recruiters, by its naval resources, by its laws, and by its economic needs. Together, these various forms of migration produced one of the greatest population movements in the history of the world and transformed not just the United States, but much of the globe.

The Ethnic City

By 1890, most of the population of some major urban areas consisted of foreign-born immigrants and their children: 87 percent of the population of Chicago, 80 percent in New York City, 84 percent in Milwaukee and Detroit. (London, the largest industrial city in Europe, by contrast, had a population that was 94 percent native.) New York had more Irish than Dublin and more Germans than Hamburg. Chicago eventually had more Poles than Warsaw.

Equally striking was the diversity of the new immigrant populations. In other countries experiencing heavy immigration in this period, most of the new arrivals were coming from one or two sources: Argentina, for example, was experiencing great migrations too, but almost everyone was coming from Italy and Spain. In the United States, however, no single national group dominated. In the last four decades of the nineteenth century, substantial groups arrived from Italy, Germany, Scandinavia, Austria, Hungary, Russia, Great Britain, Ireland, Poland, Greece, Canada, Japan, China, Holland, Mexico, and many other nations. In some towns, a dozen different ethnic groups might have found themselves living in close proximity.

The Diverse American City

Most of the new immigrants were rural people, and their adjustment to city life was often painful. To help ease the transition, many national groups formed close-knit ethnic communities within the cities: Italian, Polish, Jewish, Slavic, Chinese, French-Canadian, Mexican, and other neighborhoods (often called "immigrant ghettoes") that attempted to re-create in the New World many of the features of the Old.

Some ethnic neighborhoods consisted of people who had migrated to America from the same province, town, or village. Even when the population was more diverse, however, the community offered newcomers much that was familiar. They could find newspapers and theaters in their native languages, stores selling their native foods, churches or synagogues, and fraternal organizations that provided links with their national pasts. Many immigrants also maintained close ties with their native countries. They stayed in touch with relatives who had remained behind. Some (perhaps as many as a third in the early years) returned to Europe or Asia or Mexico after a short time; others helped bring the rest of their families to America.

Benefits of Ethnic Communities

The cultural cohesiveness of the ethnic communities clearly eased the pain of separation from the immigrants' native lands. What role it played in helping immigrants become absorbed into the economic life of America is a more difficult question to answer. It is clear that some ethnic groups (Jews and Germans in particular) advanced economically more rapidly than others (for example, the Irish). One explanation is that, by huddling together in ethnic neighborhoods, immigrant groups tended to reinforce the cultural values of their previous societies. When those values were particularly well suited to economic advancement in an industrial society—as was, for example, the high value Jews placed on education—ethnic identification may have helped members of a group to improve their lots. When other values predominated—maintaining community solidarity, sustaining family ties, preserving order—progress may have been less rapid.

But other factors were at least as important in determining how well immigrants fared in the New World. Immigrants who aroused strong racial prejudice among native-born whites—most notably African Americans, Asians, and Mexicans—found it very difficult to advance, whatever their talents. Among others, however, those who arrived with a valuable skill did better than those

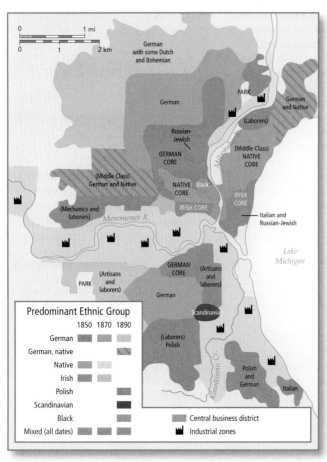

ETHNIC AND CLASS SEGREGATION IN MILWAUKEE, 1850–1890 This map illustrates the complex pattern of settlement in Milwaukee, a pattern that was in many ways typical of many industrial cities, in the late nineteenth century. Two related phenomena—industrialization and massive immigration from abroad—shaped the landscape of the city in these years. By 1890, first- and second-generation immigrants made up 84 percent of the city's population. Note the complicated distribution of ethnic groups in distinctive neighborhoods throughout the city, and note too the way in which middle-class people (especially "native-born" middle-class people, which included many people of German descent whose families had been in the United States for generations) isolated themselves from the areas in which the working class lived. ◆ *What were some of the advantages and disadvantages of this ethnic clustering to the immigrants who lived in these communities?*

who did not. Those who arrived with at least some capital had an enormous advantage over those who were penniless. And over time, those who lived in cities where people of their own nationality came to predominate—for example, the Irish in New York and Boston, or the Germans in Milwaukee—gained a tremendous advantage as they learned to exert their political power.

Assimilation

Despite the substantial differences among the various immigrant communities, virtually all groups of the foreign-born had certain things in common. Most immigrants, of course, shared the experience of living in cities (and of adapting from a rural past to an urban present). Most were young; the majority of newcomers were between fifteen and forty-five years old. And in virtually all communities of foreign-born immigrants, the strength of ethnic ties had to compete against another powerful force: the desire for assimilation.

Many of the new arrivals from abroad had come to America with romantic visions of the New World. And however disillusioning they might find their first contact with the United States, they usually retained the dream of becoming true "Americans." Even some first-generation immigrants worked hard to rid themselves of all vestiges of their old cultures, to become thoroughly Americanized. Second-generation immigrants were even more likely to attempt to break with the old ways, to try to assimilate

Americanization

completely into what they considered the real American culture. Some even looked with contempt on parents and grandparents who continued to preserve traditional ethnic habits and values.

The urge to assimilate put a particular strain on relations between men and women in immigrant communities. Many of the foreign-born came from cultures in which women were more subordinate to men, and more fully lodged within the family, than women in the United States. In some immigrant cultures, parents expected to arrange their children's marriages and to control almost every moment of their daughters' lives until marriage. But out of either choice or economic necessity, many immigrant women (and even more of the American-born daughters of immigrants) began working outside the home and developing friendships, interests, and attachments outside the family. The result was not the collapse of the family-centered cultures of immigrant communities; those cultures proved remarkably durable. But there were important adjustments to the new and more fluid life of the American city, and often considerable tension in the process.

Changing Gender Roles

Assimilation was not entirely a matter of choice. Native-born Americans encouraged it, both deliberately and inadvertently, in countless ways. Public schools taught children in English, and employers often insisted that workers speak English on the job. Although there were merchants in immigrant communities who sold ethnically distinctive foods and clothing, most stores by necessity sold mainly

PUSHCART VENDOR Many immigrants to American cities aspired to be merchants. But many people with such aspirations could not afford to rent or buy a shop. So they set up business instead in pushcarts, which they parked along sidewalks and from which they sold a variety of wares. This pushcart was photographed with its owner on the lower east side of Manhattan at around the end of the nineteenth century. (*New York Public Library, Astor, Lenox and Tilden Foundations*)

American products, forcing immigrants to adapt their diets, wardrobes, and lifestyles to American norms. Church leaders were often native-born Americans or assimilated immigrants who encouraged their parishioners to adopt American ways. Some even reformed their theology and liturgy to make it more compatible with the norms of the new country. Reform Judaism, imported from Germany to the United States in the mid-nineteenth century, was an effort by American Jewish leaders (as it had been among German leaders) to make their faith less "foreign" to the dominant culture of a largely Christian nation.

Exclusion

The arrival of so many new immigrants, and the way many of them clung to old ways and created culturally distinctive communities, provoked fear and resentment among

Nativism

some native-born Americans, just as earlier arrivals had done. Some people reacted against the immigrants out of generalized fears and prejudices, seeing in their "foreignness" the source of all the disorder and corruption of the urban world. "These people," a Chicago newspaper wrote shortly after the Haymarket bombing, referring to striking immigrant workers, "are not American, but the very scum and offal of Europe . . . Europe's human and inhuman rubbish." Native-born Americans on the West Coast had a similar cultural aversion to Mexican, Chinese, and Japanese immigrants. Other native laborers were often incensed by the willingness of the immigrants to accept lower wages and to take over the jobs of strikers.

The rising nativism provoked political responses. In 1887, Henry Bowers, a self-educated lawyer obsessed with a hatred of Catholics and foreigners, founded the American Protective Association, a group committed to stopping the immigrant tide. By 1894, membership in the organization had reportedly reached

Immigration Restriction League

500,000, with chapters throughout the Northeast and Midwest. That same year a more genteel organization, the Immigration Restriction League, was founded in Boston by five Harvard alumni. It was dedicated to the belief that immigrants should be screened, through literacy tests and other standards designed to separate the desirable from the undesirable. The league avoided the crude conspiracy theories and the rabid xenophobia of the American Protective Association, and its sophisticated nativism made it possible for many educated, middle-class people to support the restrictionist cause.

Even before the rise of these new organizations, politicians were struggling to find answers to the "immigration question." In 1882 Congress had responded to strong anti-Asian sentiment in California and elsewhere and restricted Chinese immigration, even though the Chinese made up only 1.2 percent of the population of the West Coast (see pp. 445–446). In the same year, Congress denied entry to "undesirables"—convicts, paupers, the mentally incompetent—and placed a tax of 50 cents on each person admitted. Later legislation of the 1890s enlarged the list of those barred from immigrating and increased the tax.

But these laws kept out only a small number of aliens, and more ambitious restriction proposals made little progress. Congress passed a literacy requirement for immigrants in 1897, but President Grover Cleveland vetoed it. The restrictions had limited success because many native-born Americans, far from fearing immigration,

Advantages of Cheap Labor

welcomed it and exerted strong political pressure against

IMMIGRATION UNDER ATTACK Louis Dalrymple, one of the most famous political cartoonists of the early twentieth century, published this harsh warning in 1903 about what he called "The High Tide of Immigration." He makes no secret here of his belief that the danger lay not only in the number of immigrants, but also in their origins and character as "riff raff." *(Special Collections, New York Public Library, Astor, Lenox and Tilden Foundations)*

the restrictionists. Immigration was providing a rapidly growing economy with a cheap and plentiful labor supply; many employers argued that America's industrial (and indeed agricultural) development would be impossible without it.

THE URBAN LANDSCAPE

The city was a place of remarkable contrasts. It had homes of almost unimaginable size and grandeur, and hovels of indescribable squalor. It had conveniences unknown to earlier generations, and problems that seemed beyond society's capacity to solve. Both the attractions and the problems were a result of the stunning pace at which cities were growing. The expansion of the urban population helped spur important new technological and industrial developments. But the rapid growth also produced misgovernment, poverty, congestion, filth, epidemics, and great fires. Planning and building simply could not match the pace of growth.

The Creation of Public Space

In the eighteenth and early nineteenth centuries, cities had generally grown up haphazardly, with little central planning. Public authorities basically responded to private decisions and did little to affect the shape of municipalities. By the mid-nineteenth century, however, reformers, planners, architects, and others began to call for a more ordered vision of the city. The result was the self-conscious creation of public spaces and public services.

Among the most important innovations of the mid-nineteenth century were great urban parks, which reflected the desire of a growing number of urban leaders to provide an antidote to the congestion of the city landscape. The most successful American promoters of this notion of the park as refuge were the landscape designers Frederick Law Olmsted and Calvert Vaux, who teamed up in the late 1850s to design New York's Central Park. They deliberately created a public space that would look as little like the city as possible. Instead of the ordered, formal spaces common in some European cities, they created a space that seemed to be entirely natural—even though almost every square inch of Central Park was carefully designed and constructed. Central Park was from the start one of the most popular and admired public spaces in the world, and as a result Olmsted and Vaux were recruited to design other great parks and public spaces in other cities: Brooklyn, Boston, Philadelphia, Chicago, and Washington, D.C.

Frederick Law Olmsted and Calvert Vaux

CENTRAL PARK BAND CONCERT By the late nineteenth century, New York City's Central Park was already considered one of the great urban landscapes of the world. To New Yorkers, it was an irresistible escape from the crowded, noisy life of the rest of the city. But the park itself sometimes became enormously crowded as well, as this well-dressed audience at a band concert makes clear. *(Brown Brothers)*

At the same time that cities were creating great parks, they were also creating great public buildings: libraries, art galleries, natural history museums, theaters, concert halls, and opera houses. New York's Metropolitan Museum of Art was only the largest and best known of many great museums taking shape in the late nineteenth century; others were created in such cities as Boston, Chicago, Philadelphia, and Washington, D.C. In one city after another, new and lavish public libraries appeared as if to confirm the city's role as a center of learning and knowledge.

Wealthy residents of cities were the principal force behind the creation of the great public buildings and at times even parks. As their own material and social aspirations grew, they wanted the public life of the city to provide them with amenities to match their expectations. Becoming an important patron of a major cultural institution was an especially effective route to social distinction.

But this philanthropy, whatever the motives behind it, also produced valuable assets for the city as a whole.

As both the size and the aspirations of the great cities increased, urban leaders launched monumental projects to remake the way their cities looked. Inspired by massive city rebuilding projects in Paris, London, Berlin, and other

"City Beautiful" Movement

European cities, some American cities began to clear away older neighborhoods and streets and create grand, monumental avenues lined with new and more impressive buildings. A particularly important event in inspiring this effort to remake the city was the 1893 Columbian Exposition in Chicago, a world's fair constructed to honor the 400th anniversary of Columbus's first voyage to America. At the center of the wildly popular exposition was a cluster of neoclassical buildings—the "Great White City"—constructed in the fashionable "beaux-arts" style of the time, arranged symmetrically around a formal lagoon. It became the inspiration for what became known as the "city beautiful" movement, led by the architect of the Great White City, Daniel Burnham. The movement aimed to impose a similar order and symmetry on the disordered life of cities around the country. "Make no little plans," Burnham liked to tell city planners. Those influenced by him strove to remake cities all across the country—from Washington, D.C., to Chicago and San Francisco. Only rarely, however, were planners, to overcome the obstacles of private landowners and complicated urban politics to realize more than a small portion of their dreams. There were no reconstructions of American cities to match the elaborate nineteenth-century reshaping of Paris and London.

The effort to remake the city did not just focus on redesigning the existing landscape. It occasionally led to the creation of entirely new ones. In Boston in the late 1850s, a large area of marshy tidal land was gradually filled in to create the neighborhood known as "Back Bay." The landfill project took more than forty years to complete and was one of the largest public works projects ever

The Back Bay

undertaken in America to that point. But Boston was not alone. Chicago reclaimed large areas from Lake Michigan as it expanded and at one point raised the street level for the entire city to help avoid the problems the marshy land created. In Washington, D.C., another marshy site, large areas were filled in and slated for development. In New York and other cities, the response to limited space was not so much creating new land as annexing adjacent territory. A great wave of annexations expanded the boundaries of many American cities in the 1890s and beyond.

Housing the Well-to-Do

One of the greatest problems of this precipitous growth was finding housing for the thousands of new residents who were pouring into the cities every day. For the prosperous, however, housing was seldom a worry. The availability of cheap labor and the increasing accessibility of tools and materials reduced the cost of building in the late nineteenth century and let anyone with even a moderate income afford a house.

Many of the richest urban residents lived in palatial mansions in the heart of the city and created lavish "fashionable districts"—Fifth Avenue in New York City, Back Bay and Beacon Hill in Boston, Society Hill in Philadelphia, Lake Shore Drive in Chicago, Nob Hill in San Francisco, and many others.

The moderately well-to-do (and as time went on, increasing numbers of wealthy people as well) took advantage of the less expensive land on the edges of the city and settled in new suburbs,

Growth of Suburbs

linked to the downtowns by trains or streetcars or improved roads. Chicago in the 1870s, for example, boasted nearly 100 residential suburbs connected with the city by railroad and offering the joys of "pure air, peacefulness, quietude, and natural scenery." Boston, too, saw the development of some of the earliest "streetcar suburbs"—Dorchester, Brookline, and others—which catered to both the wealthy and the middle class. New Yorkers of moderate means settled in new suburbs on the northern fringes of Manhattan and commuted downtown by trolley or riverboat. Real estate developers worked to create and promote suburban communities that would appeal to the nostalgia for the countryside that many city dwellers felt. Affluent suburbs, in particular, were notable for lawns, trees, and houses designed to look manorial. Even more modest communities strove to emphasize the opportunities suburbs provided for owning land.

Housing Workers and the Poor

Most urban residents, however, could not afford either to own a house in the city or to move to the suburbs. Instead, they stayed in the city centers and rented. Because demand was so high and space so scarce, they had little bargaining power in the process. Landlords tried to squeeze as many rent-paying residents as possible into the smallest available space. In Manhattan, for example, the average population density in 1894 was 143 people per acre—a higher rate than that of the most crowded cities of Europe (Paris had 127 per acre, Berlin 101) and far higher than in any other American city then or since. In some neighborhoods—the Lower East Side of New York City, for example—density was more than 700 people per acre, among the highest levels in the world.

Landlords were reluctant to invest much in immigrant housing, confident they could rent dwellings for a profit regardless of their conditions. In the cities of the South—Charleston, New Orleans, Richmond—poor African Americans lived in crumbling former slave quarters. In

A TENEMENT LAUNDRY Immigrant families living in tenements, in New York and in many other cities, earned their livelihoods as they could. This woman, shown here with some of her children, was typical of many working-class mothers who found income-producing activities they could pursue in the home (in this case, laundry). This room, dominated by large vats and piles of other people's laundry, is also the family's home, as the crib and religious pictures make clear. *(Bettmann/Corbis)*

Boston, they moved into cheap three-story wooden houses ("triple deckers"), many of them decaying fire hazards. In Baltimore and Philadelphia, they crowded into narrow brick row houses. And in New York, as in many other cities, more than a million people lived in tenements.

The word "tenement" had originally referred simply to a multiple-family rental building, but by the late nineteenth century it was being used to describe slum dwellings only. The first tenements, built in New York City in 1850, had been hailed as a great improvement in housing for the poor. "It is built with the design of supplying the laboring people with cheap lodgings," a local newspaper commented, "and will have many advantages over the cellars and other miserable abodes which too many are forced to inhabit." But tenements themselves soon became "miserable abodes," with many windowless

Tenements

rooms, little or no plumbing or central heating, and often a row of privies in the basement. A New York state law of 1870 required a window in every bedroom of tenements built after that date; developers complied by adding small, sunless air shafts to their buildings. Most of all, tenements were incredibly crowded, with three, four, and, sometimes many more people crammed into each small room.

Jacob Riis, a Danish immigrant and New York newspaper reporter and photographer, shocked many middle-class Americans with his sensational (and some would say sensationalized) descriptions and pictures of tenement life in his 1890 book, *How the Other Half Lives.* Slum dwellings, he said, were almost universally sunless, practically airless, and "poisoned" by "summer stenches." "The hall is dark and you might stumble over the children pitching pennies back there." But the solution many reformers (including Riis)

Jacob Riis

STREETCAR SUBURBS IN NINETEENTH-CENTURY NEW ORLEANS This map of streetcar lines in New Orleans reveals a pattern that repeated itself in many cities: changing residential patterns emerging in response to new forms of transportation. The map reveals the movement of population outward from the central city as streetcar lines emerged to make access to the downtown easier. Note the dramatic growth of residential suburbs in the last forty years of the nineteenth century in particular. ◆ *What other forms of mass transportation were emerging in American cities in these years?*

For an interactive version of this map, go to www .mhhe.com/brinkley13ech18maps

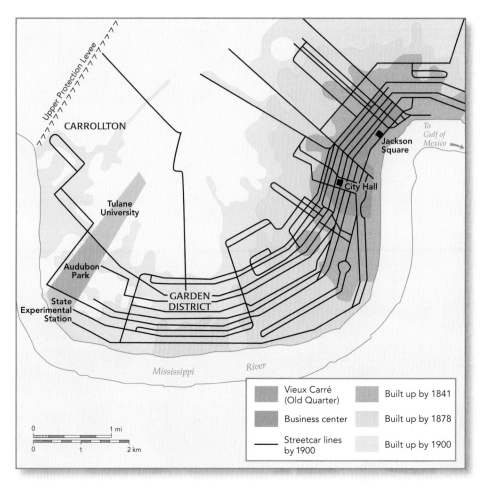

favored, and that governments sometimes adopted, was to raze slum dwellings without building any new housing to replace them.

Urban Transportation

Urban growth posed monumental transportation challenges. Old downtown streets were often too narrow for the heavy traffic that was beginning to move over them. Most were without a hard, paved surface and resembled either a sea of mud or a cloud of dust, depending on the weather. In the last decades of the century, more and more streets were paved, usually with wooden blocks, bricks, or asphalt; but paving could not keep up with the number of new thoroughfares the expanding cities were creating. By 1890, Chicago had paved only about 600 of its more than 2,000 miles of streets.

Transportation Problems

But it was not simply the conditions of the streets that impeded urban transportation. It was the numbers of people who needed to move every day from one part of the city to another, numbers that mandated the development of mass transportation. Streetcars drawn on tracks by horses had been introduced into some cities

even before the Civil War. But the horsecars were not fast enough, so many communities developed new forms of mass transit.

In 1870, New York opened its first elevated railway, whose noisy, filthy steam-powered trains moved rapidly above the city streets on massive iron structures. New York, Chicago, San Francisco, and other cities also experimented with cable cars, towed by continuously moving underground cables. Richmond, Virginia, introduced the first electric trolley line in 1888, and by 1895 such systems were operating in 850 towns and cities. In 1897, Boston opened the first American subway when it put some of its trolley lines underground. At the same time, cities were developing new techniques of road and bridge building. One of the great technological marvels of the 1880s was the completion of the Brooklyn Bridge in New York, a dramatic steel-cable suspension span designed by John A. Roebling.

Mass Transit

The "Skyscraper"

Cities were growing upward as well as outward. Until the mid-nineteenth century, almost no buildings more than four or five stories high could be constructed.

Construction techniques were such that it was difficult and expensive to build adequate structural supports for tall buildings. There was also a limit to the number of flights of stairs the users of buildings could be expected to climb. But by the 1850s, there had been successful experiments with machine-powered passenger elevators; and by the 1870s, new methods of construction using cast iron and steel beams made it easier to build tall buildings.

Not long after the Civil War, therefore, tall buildings began to appear in the major cities. The Equitable Building in New York, completed in 1870 and rising seven and a half floors above the street, was one of the first in the nation to be built with an elevator. A few years later, even taller buildings of ten and twelve stories were appearing elsewhere in New York, in Chicago, and in other growing cities around the country. With each passing decade, both the size and the number of tall buildings increased until, by the 1890s, the term "skyscraper" began to become a popular description of them.

The modern skyscraper was made possible above all by steel girder construction. The first tall building to use this technique appeared in Chicago in 1884. It was followed a few years later by several in New York—which soon became the site of more tall buildings than any other city in the world. That was in part because the location of New York's central business districts on the island of Manhattan made expansion outward difficult; instead, the city expanded upward.

Steel-Girder Construction

The greatest figure in the early development of the skyscraper was the Chicago architect Louis Sullivan, who introduced many modern, functional elements to the genre—large windows, sheer lines, limited ornamentation—in an attempt to emphasize the soaring height of the building as its most distinctive feature. Sullivan's students, among them Frank Lloyd Wright, expanded the influence of these innovations still further and applied them to low buildings as well as tall ones.

STRAINS OF URBAN LIFE

The increasing congestion of the cities and the absence of adequate public services produced serious hazards. Crime, fire, disease, indigence, and pollution all placed strains on the capacities of metropolitan institutions, and both governments and private institutions were for a time poorly equipped to respond to them.

Fire and Disease

One serious problem was fires. In one major city after another, fires destroyed large downtown areas, where many buildings were still constructed of wood. Chicago and Boston suffered "great fires" in 1871. Other cities—

among them Baltimore and San Francisco, where a tremendous earthquake produced a catastrophic fire in 1906—experienced similar disasters. The great fires were terrible and deadly experiences, but they encouraged the construction of fireproof buildings and the development of professional fire departments. They also forced cities to rebuild at a time when new technological and architectural innovations were available. Some of the modern, high-rise downtowns of American cities arose out of the rubble of great fires.

Development of Professional Fire Departments

Environmental Degradation

Modern notions of environmentalism were unknown to most Americans in the late nineteenth and early twentieth centuries. But the environmental degradation of many American cities was a visible and disturbing fact of life in those years. The frequency of great fires, the dangers of disease and plague, the extraordinary crowding of working-class neighborhoods were all examples of the environmental costs of industrialization and rapid urbanization.

Improper disposal of human and industrial waste was a common feature of almost all large cities in these years. Such practices contributed to the pollution of rivers and lakes, and also in many cases to the compromising of the city's drinking water. This was particularly true in poor neighborhoods with primitive plumbing (and sometimes no indoor plumbing at all), outdoor privies that leaked into the groundwater, and overcrowded tenements. The presence of domestic animals—horses, which were the principal means of transportation until the late nineteenth century, but in poor neighborhoods also cows, pigs, and other animals—contributed as well to the environmental problems.

Air quality in many cities was poor as well. Few Americans had the severe problems that London experienced in these years with its perpetual "fogs" created by the debris from the burning of soft coal. But air pollution from factories and from stoves and furnaces in offices, homes, and other buildings was constant and at times severe. The incidence of respiratory infection and related diseases was much higher in cities than it was in rural areas, and it accelerated rapidly in the late nineteenth century.

Air Pollution

By the early twentieth century, reformers were actively crusading to improve the environmental conditions of cities and were beginning to achieve some notable successes. New sewage and drainage systems were created to protect drinking water from sewage disposal. By 1910, most large American cities had constructed sewage disposal systems, often at great cost, to protect the drinking water of their inhabitants and to

THE GREAT FIRE IN CHICAGO This haunting photograph shows the intersection of State and Madison Streets, which Chicagoans liked to call "the world's busiest intersection," in the aftermath of the great fire of 1871, which destroyed much of the city's downtown. Horse-drawn streetcars are shown here traveling the ghostly, still smoke-filled streets. At left, posters advertise the new locations of displaced stores and offices—prompting the photographer to attach the optimistic title "Back in Business" to this image. *(Chicago Historical Society, ICHI-20811)*

prevent the great bacterial plagues that impure water had helped create in the past—such as the 1873 yellow fever epidemic in Memphis that killed more than 5,000 people.

Alice Hamilton, a physician who became an investigator for the United States Bureau of Labor, was a pioneer in the identification of pollution in the workplace. She documented ways in which improper disposal of such potentially dangerous substances as lead (she was one of the first physicians to identify lead poisoning), chemical waste, and ceramic dust was creating widespread sickness. And despite considerable resistance from many factory owners, she did bring such problems to public attention and, in some states at least, inspired legislation to require manufacturers to solve them. In 1912, the federal government created the Public Health Service, which was charged with preventing such occupational diseases as tuberculosis, anemia, and carbon dioxide poisoning, which were common in the garment industry and other trades. It attempted to create common health standards for all factories; but since the agency had few powers of enforcement, it had limited impact. It did, however, establish the protection of public health as a responsibility of

Public Health Service

the federal government and also helped bring to public attention the environmental forces that endangered health. The creation of the Occupational Health and Safety Administration in 1970, which gave government the authority to require employers to create safe and healthy workplaces, was a legacy of the Public Health Service's early work.

Urban Poverty

Above all, perhaps, the expansion of the cities spawned widespread and often desperate poverty. Despite the rapid growth of urban economies, the sheer number of new residents ensured that many people would be unable to earn enough for a decent subsistence.

Public agencies and private philanthropic organizations offered very limited relief. They were generally dominated by middle-class people, who tended to believe that too much assistance would breed dependency and that poverty was the fault of the poor themselves—a result of laziness or alcoholism or other kinds of irresponsibility. Most tried to restrict aid to the "deserving poor"—those who truly could not help themselves (at least according to the standards of the organizations themselves, which conducted elaborate "investigations" to separate the "deserving" from the "undeserving").

Other charitable societies—for example, the Salvation Army, which began operating in America in 1879, one year after it was founded in London—concentrated more on religious revivalism than on the relief of the homeless and hungry.

Salvation Army

Tensions often arose between native Protestant philanthropists and Catholic immigrants over religious doctrine and standards of morality.

Middle-class people grew particularly alarmed over the rising number of poor children in the cities, some of them orphans or runaways, living alone or in small groups scrounging for food. These "street arabs," as they were often called, attracted more attention from reformers than any other group—although that attention produced no lasting solutions to their problems.

Crime and Violence

Poverty and crowding naturally bred crime and violence. Much of it was relatively minor, the work of pickpockets, con artists, swindlers, and petty thieves. But some was more dangerous. The American murder rate rose rapidly in the late nineteenth century (even as such rates were declining in Europe), from 25 murders for every million people in 1880 to over 100 by the end of the century—a rate slightly higher than even the highest rates of the 1980s and 1990s. That reflected in part a very high level of violence in some nonurban areas: the American South, where rates of lynching and homicide were particularly

High Crime Rates

high; and the West, where the rootlessness and instability of new communities (cow towns, mining camps, and the like) created much violence. But the cities contributed their share to the increase in crime as well. Native-born Americans liked to believe that crime was a result of the violent proclivities of immigrant groups, and they cited the rise of gangs and criminal organizations in various ethnic communities. But even in the cities, native-born Americans were as likely to commit crimes as immigrants.

The rising crime rates encouraged many cities to develop larger and more professional police forces. In the early nineteenth century, police forces had often been private and informal organizations; urban governments had resisted professionalized law enforcement. By the end of the century, however, professionalized public police departments were a part of the life of virtually every city and town. They worked closely with district attorneys and other public prosecutors, who were also becoming more numerous and more important in city life. But police forces themselves could spawn corruption and brutality, particularly since jobs on them were often filled through political patronage. And complaints well known in recent years about police dealing differently with white and black suspects, or with rich and poor communities, were common in the late nineteenth century as well.

Some members of the middle class, fearful of urban insurrections, felt the need for even more substantial forms of protection. Urban national guard groups (many of them created and manned by middle-class elites) built imposing armories on the outskirts of affluent neighborhoods and stored large supplies of weapons and ammunition in preparation for uprisings that, in fact, never occurred.

The Machine and the Boss

Newly arrived immigrants, many of whom could not speak English, needed help in adjusting to American urban life: its laws, its customs, usually its language. Some ethnic communities created their own self-help organizations. But for many residents of the inner cities, the principal source of assistance was the political machine.

The urban machine was one of America's most distinctive political institutions. It owed its existence to the power vacuum that the chaotic growth of cities (and the very limited growth of city governments) had created. It was also a product of the potential voting power of large immigrant communities. Any politician who could

Boss Rule

"KEEPING TAMMANY'S BOOTS SHINED," C. 1887 This lithograph by cartoonist Joseph Keppler shows the heavy foot of New York City's Tammany Hall sitting atop City Hall, while Hugh Grant, a Tammany sheriff later elected mayor, applies the patronage polish that was the organization's lifeblood. The strap dangling from the boot bears the name of Richard Croker, who emerged as one of Tammany's principal leaders after the fall of Boss Tweed and who served as the undisputed chief of the organization from 1886 until 1901. *(Bettmann/Corbis)*

mobilize that power stood to gain enormous influence, if not public office. And so there emerged a group of urban "bosses," themselves often of foreign birth or parentage. Many were Irish, because they spoke English and because some had acquired previous political experience from the long Irish struggle against the English at home. Almost all were men (unsurprisingly, since in most states women could not yet vote). The principal function of the political boss was simple: to win votes for his organization. That meant winning the loyalty of his constituents. To do so, a boss might provide them with occasional relief—baskets of groceries, bags of coal. He might step in to save those arrested for petty crimes from jail. When he could, he found jobs for the unemployed. Above all, he rewarded many of his followers with patronage: with jobs in city government or in such city agencies as the police (which the machine's elected officials often controlled); with jobs building or operating the new transit systems; and with opportunities to rise in the political organization itself.

Machines were also vehicles for making money. Politicians enriched themselves and their allies through various forms of graft and corruption.

Graft and Corruption

Some of it might be fairly open—what George Washington Plunkitt of New York's Tammany Hall called "honest graft." For example, a politician might discover in advance where a new road or streetcar line was to be built, buy an interest in the land near it, and profit when the city had to buy the land from him or when property values rose as a result of the construction. But there was also covert graft: kickbacks from contractors in exchange for contracts to build streets, sewers, public buildings, and other projects; the sale of franchises for the operation of such public utilities as street railways, waterworks, and electric light and power systems. The most famously corrupt city boss was William M. Tweed, boss of New York City's Tammany Hall in the 1860s and 1870s, whose excesses finally landed him in jail in 1872.

Middle-class critics saw the corrupt machines as blights on the cities and obstacles to progress. In fact, political organizations were responsible not just for corruption, but also for modernizing city infrastructures, for expanding the role of government, and for creating stability in a political and social climate that otherwise would have lacked a center. The motives of the bosses may have been largely venal, but their achievements were often greater than those of the more scrupulous reformers who challenged them.

Several factors made boss rule possible. One was the power of immigrant voters, who were less concerned with middle-class ideas of political morality than with obtaining

Reasons for Boss Rule

the services that machines provided and reformers did not. Another was the link between the political organizations and wealthy, prominent citizens who profited from their dealings with bosses and resisted efforts to overthrow them. Still another was the structural weakness of city governments. Within the municipal government, no single official usually had decisive power or responsibility. Instead, authority was generally divided among many officeholders and was limited by the state legislature. The boss, by virtue of his control over his machine, formed an "invisible government" that provided an alternative to what was often the inadequacy of the regular government. Through his organization, the boss might control a majority of those who were in office even if (as was usually the case) he did not hold public office himself.

The urban machine was not without competition. Reform groups frequently mobilized public outrage at the corruption of the bosses and often succeeded in driving machine politicians from office. Tammany, for example, saw its candidates for mayor and other high city offices lose almost as often as they won in the last decades of the nineteenth century. But the reform organizations typically lacked the permanence of the machine, and more often than not, their power faded after a few years. Thus, many critics of machines began to argue for more basic reforms: for structural changes in the nature of city government.

THE RISE OF MASS CONSUMPTION

For urban middle-class Americans, the last decades of the nineteenth century were a time of dramatic advances. Indeed, it was in those years that a distinctive middle-class culture

Middle-Class Culture

began to exert a powerful influence over the whole of American life. Much of the rest of American society—the majority of the population, which was neither urban nor middle class—advanced less rapidly or not at all; but almost no one was unaffected by the rise of a new urban, consumer culture.

Patterns of Income and Consumption

American industry could not have grown as it did without the expansion of markets for the goods it produced. The growth of demand occurred at almost all levels of society, a result not just of the new techniques of production and mass distribution that were making consumer goods less expensive, but also of rising incomes.

Incomes in the industrial era were rising for almost everyone, although at highly uneven rates. While the most conspicuous result of the new economy was the creation of vast

Rising Income

fortunes, more important for society as a whole were the growth and increasing prosperity of the middle class. The salaries of clerks, accountants, middle managers, and other "white-collar" workers rose on average by a third between 1890 and 1910—and in some parts of the middle class salaries rose by much more. Doctors, lawyers, and other professionals, for example, experienced a particularly dramatic increase in both the prestige and the profitability of their professions.

Working-class incomes rose too in those years, although from a much lower base and considerably more slowly. Iron and steel workers, despite the setbacks their unions suffered, saw their hourly wages increase by a third between 1890 and 1910; but industries with large female, African-American, or Mexican work forces—shoes, textiles, paper, laundries, many areas of commercial agriculture—saw very small increases, as did almost all industries in the South. Still, some workers in these industries experienced a rise in family income because women and children often worked to supplement the husband's and father's earnings, or because families took in boarders or laundry or otherwise supplemented their incomes.

Also important to the new mass market were the development of affordable products and the creation of new

New Merchandising Techniques

merchandising techniques, which made many consumer goods available to a broad market for the first time. A good example of such changes was the emergence of ready-made clothing. In the early nineteenth century, most Americans had made their own clothing—usually from cloth they bought from merchants, at times from fabrics they spun and wove themselves. Affluent people contracted with private tailors to make their clothes. But the invention of the sewing machine and the spur that the Civil War (and its demand for uniforms) gave to the manufacture of clothing created an enormous industry devoted to producing ready-made garments. By the end of the century, virtually all Americans bought their clothing from stores.

Partly as a result, much larger numbers of people became concerned with personal style. Interest in women's fashion, for example, had once been a luxury reserved for the affluent. Now middle-class and even working-class women could strive to develop a distinctive style of dress. Substantial wardrobes, once a luxury reserved for the wealthy, began to become common at other levels of society as well. New homes, even modest ones, now included clothes closets. Even people in remote rural areas could develop more stylish wardrobes by ordering from the new mail-order houses.

Another example of the rise of the mass market was the way Americans bought and prepared food. The development and mass production of tin cans in the 1880s created a large new industry devoted to packaging and selling canned food and (as a result of the techniques Gail Borden discovered in the 1850s) condensed milk. Refrigerated railroad cars made it possible for perishables—meats, vegetables, dairy products, and other foodstuffs—to travel long distances without spoiling. The development of artificially frozen ice made it possible for many more households to afford iceboxes. Among other things, the changes meant improved diets and better health; life expectancy rose six years in the first two decades of the twentieth century.

Chain Stores and Mail-Order Houses

Changes in marketing also altered the way Americans bought goods. Small local stores faced competition from new "chain stores." The Great Atlantic & Pacific Tea Com-

Chain Stores

pany (the A & P) began creating a national network of grocery stores as early as the 1850s and expanded it rapidly after the Civil War.

F. W. Woolworth opened his first "Five and Ten Cent Store" in Utica, New York, in 1879 and went on to build a national chain of dry goods stores. Chain stores were able to sell manufactured goods at lower prices than the local, independent stores with which they competed. From the beginning, the chains faced opposition from the established merchants they threatened to displace, and from others who feared that they would jeopardize the character of their communities. (Similar controversies have continued into the twenty-first century over the spread of large chains such as Wal-Mart and Barnes & Noble.) But most customers, however loyal they might feel to a local merchant, found it difficult to resist the greater variety and lower prices the chains provided them.

Chain stores were slow to reach remote, rural areas, which remained dependent on poorly stocked and often very expensive country stores. But rural people gradually gained access to the new

Social Consequences of Mail-Order Catalogs

consumer world through the great mail-order houses. In 1872, Montgomery Ward—a Chicago-based traveling salesman—distributed a catalog of consumer goods in association with the farmers' organization, the Grange (see p. 535). By the 1880s, he was offering thousands of items at low prices to farmers throughout the Midwest and beyond. He soon faced stiff competition from Sears Roebuck, first established by Richard Sears in Chicago in 1887. Together, the bulky catalogs from Ward and Sears changed the lives of many isolated people—introducing them to (and explaining for them) new trends of fashion and home decor as well as making available new tools, machinery, and technologies for the home.

Department Stores

In larger cities, the emergence of great department stores (which had appeared earlier in Europe) helped transform buying habits and turn shopping into a more alluring and glamorous activity. Marshall Field in Chi-

Impact of the Department Store

cago created one of the first American department stores, and others soon followed: Macy's in New York, Abraham and Straus in Brooklyn, Jordan Marsh and Filene's in Boston, Wanamaker's in Philadelphia.

The department stores transformed the concept of shopping in several ways. First, they brought together under one roof an enormous array of products that had previously been sold in separate shops. Second, they strove to create an atmosphere of wonder and excitement, to make shopping a glamorous activity. The new stores were elaborately decorated to suggest great luxury and elegance. They included restaurants and tea rooms and comfortable lounges, to suggest that shopping could be a social event as well as a practical necessity. They were especially important as public spaces in which women could interact respectably as both customers and sales clerks. They hired well-dressed sales clerks, mostly women, to provide attentive service to customers. Third, department stores—like mail-order houses—took advantage of

THE MONTGOMERY WARD DEPARTMENT STORE   This advertising poster for the Montgomery Ward department store in downtown Chicago dates from about 1880. The designer has stripped away the outside walls to reveal the vast array of goods inside what the poster calls "the enormous establishment." *(Chicago Historical Society)*

economies of scale to sell merchandise at lower prices than many of the individual shops with which they competed.

Women as Consumers

The rise of mass consumption had particularly dramatic effects on American women, who were generally the primary consumers within families. Women's clothing styles changed much more rapidly and dramatically than men's, which encouraged more frequent purchases. Women generally bought and prepared food for their families, so the availability of new food products changed not only the way everyone ate, but also the way women shopped and cooked.

The consumer economy produced new employment opportunities for women as sales clerks in department stores and as waitresses in the rapidly proliferating restau-rants. And it spawned the creation of a new movement in which *National Consumer League* women were to play a vital role: the consumer protection movement. The National Consumers League, formed in the 1890s under the leadership of Florence Kelley, attempted to mobilize the power of women as consumers to force retailers and manufacturers to improve wages and working conditions for women workers. By defining themselves as consumers, many middle-class women were able to find a stance from which they could become active participants in public life. Indeed, the mobilization of women behind consumer causes—and eventually many other causes—was one of the most important political developments of the late nineteenth century.

LEISURE IN THE CONSUMER SOCIETY

Closely related to the growth of consumption was an increasing interest in leisure time, in part because time away from work was expanding rapidly for many people. Members of the urban middle and professional classes had large blocks of time in which they were not at work—evenings, weekends, even vacations (previously almost unknown among salaried workers). Working hours in many factories declined, from an average of nearly seventy hours a week in 1860 to under sixty in 1900. Industrial workers might still be on the job six days a week, but many of them had more time off in the evenings. Even farmers found that the mechanization of agriculture gave them more free time. The lives of many Americans were becoming compartmentalized, with clear distinctions between work and leisure that had not existed in the past. The change produced a search for new forms of recreation and entertainment.

Redefining Leisure

It also produced a redefinition of the idea of "leisure." In earlier eras, relatively few Americans had considered leisure a valuable thing. On the contrary, many equated it with *New Conceptions of Leisure* laziness or sloth. "Rest," as in the relative inactivity many Americans considered appropriate for the Sabbath, was valued because it offered time for spiritual reflection and because it prepared people for work. But leisure—time spent amusing oneself in nonproductive pursuits—was not only unavailable to most Americans, but faintly scorned.

But with the rapid expansion of the economy and the increasing number of hours workers had away from work, it became possible to imagine leisure time as a normal part of the lives of many people. Industrial workers, in pursuit of shorter hours, adopted the slogan "Eight hours for work, eight hours for rest, and eight hours for what we will." Others were equally adamant in claiming that leisure time was both a right and an important contribution to an individual's emotional and even spiritual health.

The economist Simon Patten was one of the first intellectuals to articulate this new view of leisure, which he tied closely to the rising interest in consumption. Patten,

Simon Patten

in *The Theory of Prosperity* (1902), *The New Basis of Civilization* (1910), and other works, challenged the centuries-old assumption that the normal condition of civilization was a scarcity of goods. In earlier times, Patten argued, fear of scarcity had caused people to place a high value on thrift, self-denial, and restraint. But in modern industrial societies, the problems of scarcity had been overcome. The new economies could create enough wealth to satisfy not just the needs, but also the desires, of all. "We are now in the transition stage," he wrote, "from this pain economy [the economy of scarcity] to a pleasure economy." The principal goal of such an economy, he claimed, "should be an abundance of goods and the pursuit of pleasure."

As Americans became more accustomed to leisure as a normal part of their lives, they not only made increased

Public Leisure

use of traditional forms of recreation and entertainment; they also began to look for new experiences with which to entertain themselves. In cities, in particular, the demand for popular entertainment produced a rich mix of spectacles, recreations, and other activities. One of the most distinctive characteristics of late-nineteenth- and early-twentieth-century urban leisure was its intensely public character. Entertainment usually meant "going out," spending their leisure time in public places where they would find not only entertainment, but also other people. Thousands of working-class New Yorkers flocked to the amusement park at Coney Island, for example, not just for the rides and shows, but for the excitement of the crowds, as did the thousands who spent evenings in dance halls, vaudeville houses, and concert halls. Affluent New Yorkers enjoyed afternoons in Central Park, where a principal attraction was seeing other people (and being seen by them). Moviegoers were attracted not just by the movies themselves, but by the energy of the audiences at the lavish "movie palaces" that began to appear in cities in the early twentieth century, just as sports fans were drawn by the crowds as well as by the games.

Mass entertainment did not always bridge differences of class, race, or gender. Saloons and some sporting events tended to be male preserves. Shopping (itself becoming a valued leisure-time activity) and going to tea rooms and luncheonettes were more characteristic of female leisure. Theaters, pubs, and clubs were often specific to particular ethnic communities or particular work groups. There were, in fact, relatively few places where people of widely diverse backgrounds gathered together.

When the classes did meet in public spaces—as they did, for example, in city parks—there was often considerable conflict over what constituted appropriate public behavior. Elites in New York City, for example, tried to prohibit anything but quiet, "genteel" activities in Central Park, while working-class people wanted to use the public spaces for sports and entertainments. But even divided by class, ethnicity, and gender, leisure and popular entertainment did help sustain a vigorous public culture.

Spectator Sports

The search for forms of public leisure hastened the rise of organized spectator sports, especially baseball, which by the end of the century was well on its way to becoming the national pastime. A game much like baseball, known as "rounders" and derived from cricket, had enjoyed limited popularity in Great Britain in the early nineteenth century. Versions of the game began to appear in America in the early 1830s, well before Abner Doubleday supposedly "invented" baseball. (Doubleday, in fact, had little to do with the creation of baseball and actually cared little for sports. Alexander Cartwright, a member of a New York City baseball club in the 1840s, defined many of the rules and features of the game as we know it today.)

By the end of the Civil War, interest in baseball had grown rapidly. More than 200 amateur or semiprofessional teams or clubs existed, many of which joined a national

Major League Baseball

association and agreed on standard rules. The first salaried team, the Cincinnati Red Stockings, was formed in 1869. Other cities soon fielded professional teams, and in 1876, at the urging of Albert Spalding, they banded together in the National League. A rival league, the American Association, soon appeared. It eventually collapsed, but in 1901 the American League emerged to replace it. In 1903, the first modern World Series was played, in which the American League Boston Red Sox beat the National League Pittsburgh Pirates. By then, baseball had become an important business and a great national preoccupation (at least among men), attracting paying crowds in the thousands.

The second most popular game, football, appealed at first to an elite segment of the male population, in part because it originated in colleges and universities. The first intercollegiate football game in America occurred between Princeton and Rutgers in 1869, and soon the game became entrenched as part of collegiate life. Early intercollegiate football bore only an indirect relation to

CONEY ISLAND

People who lived in the crowded cities of early-twentieth-century America yearned at times for ways to escape the noise and smells and heat and stress of the urban world. Wealthy families could travel to resorts or country houses. But most city dwellers could not afford to venture far, and for them ambitious entrepreneurs tried to provide dazzling escapes close to home. The most celebrated such escape was Coney Island in Brooklyn, New

POSTCARD FROM LUNA PARK Visitors to Coney Island sent postcards to friends and relatives by the millions, and those cards were among the most effective promotional devices for the amusement parks. This one shows the brightly lit entrance to Luna Park, Coney Island's most popular attraction for many years. *(Bettmann/Corbis)*

THE ELEPHANT HOTEL One of the early attractions of Coney Island as it became a popular resort was this hotel, built inside a large wooden elephant. This picture, taken in 1890, shows Coney Island at a point when development was still relatively modest. *(Photo Collection Alexander Alland, Sr./Corbis)*

York—which became for a time the most famous and popular urban resort in America.

Coney Island had been an attractive destination for visitors since the early nineteenth century, because it was near New York City and because it had a broad, sandy beach on the ocean. The first resort hotel was built there in 1824. In the 1870s and 1880s, investors built railroad lines from the city to the beach and began to create spectacular amusements to induce New Yorkers to visit: huge ballrooms and restaurants, a 300-foot-high iron tower, and a hotel shaped like an enormous elephant, with an observatory in its head. But the real success of Coney Island began in the 1890s, when the amusements and spectacles reached a new level. Sea Lion Park, which

opened in 1895, showcased trained sea lions and exotic water rides. Two years later, Steeplechase Park began operations, attracting visitors with a mechanical steeplechase ride in which visitors could pretend to be jockeys, and stunt rooms with moving floors and powerful blasts of compressed air.

By then, Coney Island was a popular site for real horse racing, for boxing matches, and for other sports. It was also attracting gambling casinos, saloons, and brothels. From the beginning, among affluent middle-class people at least, Coney Island had a reputation as a rough and unsavory place. "If the whole horrible aggregation of shanties, low resorts, shacks masquerading as hotels, and the rest were swept off the earth," one visitor wrote in 1915, "the thanksgivings of the community

the modern game; it was more similar to what is now known as rugby. By the late 1870s, however, the game was becoming standardized and was taking on the outlines of its modern form.

As college football grew in popularity, it spread to other sections of the country, notably to the midwestern state universities, which were destined soon to replace the eastern schools as the great powers of the game. It also began

to exhibit the taints of professionalism that have marked it ever since. Some schools used "ringers," tramp athletes who were not even registered as students. In an effort to eliminate such abuses, Amos Alonzo Stagg, athletic director and coach at the University of Chicago, led in forming the Western Conference, or Big Ten, in 1896, which established rules governing eligibility.

Growth of College Football

STEEPLECHASE PARK Steeplechase Park opened in 1897 and immediately began attracting crowds eager to ride the mechanical steeplechase shown here. *(Brown Brothers)*

would be in order." But to the working-class immigrants and lower-middle-class people who were always its most numerous visitors, it was a place of wonder, excitement, and escape.

The greatest of the Coney Island attractions, Luna Park, opened in 1903. It provided not just rides and stunts, but lavish reproductions of exotic places and spectacular adventures: Japanese gardens, Venetian canals with gondoliers, a Chinese theater, a simulated trip to the moon, and reenactments of such disasters as burning buildings, earthquakes, and even the volcanic eruption that destroyed Pompeii. A year later, a competing company opened Dreamland, which tried to outdo even Luna Park with a 375-foot tower (modeled after a famous building in Spanish Seville), a three-ring circus, chariot races, and a Lilliputian village inspired by *Gulliver's Travels*. It also tried to create a soothing alternative to the crowded city

around it, with neoclassical buildings, formal gardens, and, as the promoters promised, "avenues wide and imposing—no crowding." (A fire destroyed Dreamland in 1911.)

The popularity of Coney Island in these years was phenomenal. Thousands of people flocked to the large resort hotels that lined the beaches. Many thousands more made day trips out from the city by train and (after 1920) subway. In 1904, the average daily attendance at Luna Park alone was 90,000 people. On weekends, the Coney Island post office handled over 250,000 postcards, through which visitors helped spread the reputation of the resort throughout the region and the nation.

Coney Island's popularity reflected a number of powerful impulses among urban Americans at the turn of the century. At the simplest level, it provided visitors with an escape from the heat and crowding of the vast metropolis

around it. But it also offered many other things. It gave people who had few opportunities for travel a simulated glimpse of exotic places and events that they would never be able to experience in reality. For immigrants, many of whom lived in insular ethnic communities, Coney Island provided a way of experiencing American mass culture on an equal footing with people of backgrounds different from their own. And almost everyone who found Coney Island appealing did so in part because it provided an escape from the genteel standards of behavior that governed so much of American life at the time. In the amusement parks of Coney Island, decorum was often forgotten, and people delighted in finding themselves in situations that in any other setting would have seemed embarrassing or improper: women's skirts blown above their heads with hot air; people pummeled with water and rubber paddles by clowns; hints of sexual freedom as strangers were forced to come into physical contact with one another on rides and amusements and as men and women revealed themselves to each other wearing bathing suits on the beach.

Coney Island remained popular throughout the first half of the twentieth century, and it continues to attract visitors even today (although in much smaller numbers). But its heyday was in the years before World War I, when the exotic sights and thrilling adventures it was able to offer had almost no counterparts elsewhere in American culture. In the 1920s, when radio and movies began to offer their own kind of mass escapism—and their own entry into mainstream American culture for immigrants aspiring to assimilate—Coney Island ceased to be the dazzling, unmatchable marvel it had seemed to earlier generations.

Football also became known for a high level of violence on the field; eighteen college students died of football-related injuries and over a hundred were seriously hurt in 1905. The carnage prompted a White House conference on organized sports convened by President Theodore Roosevelt. As a result of its deliberations, a new intercollegiate association (which in 1910 became known as the National College Athletic Association,

the NCAA) revised the rules of the game in an effort to make it safer and more honest.

Other popular spectator sports were emerging at about the same time. Basketball was invented in 1891 at Springfield, Massachusetts, by Dr. James A. Naismith, a Canadian working as athletic director for a local college. Boxing, which had long been a disreputable activity concentrated primarily among the urban working classes, had

THE AMERICAN NATIONAL GAME Long before the modern major leagues began, local baseball clubs were active throughout much of the United States, establishing the game as the "national pastime." This print of a "grand match for the championship" depicts an 1866 game at Elysian Fields, a popular park just across the river from New York City in Hoboken, New Jersey. (*National Baseball Hall of Fame and Museum, Inc.*)

become by the 1880s a more popular and in some places more reputable sport, particularly after the adoption of the Marquis of Queensberry rules (by which fighters wore padded gloves and fought in three-minute rounds). The first modern boxing hero, John L. Sullivan, became heavyweight champion of the world in 1882. Even so, boxing remained illegal in some states until after World War I. Horse racing, popular since colonial times, became increasingly commercialized with the construction of large tracks and the establishment of large-purse races such as the Kentucky Derby.

Even in their infancy, spectator sports were closely associated with gambling. There was elaborate betting—some of it organized by underground gambling syndicates—on baseball and football almost from the start. One of the most famous incidents in the history of baseball was the alleged "throwing" of the 1919 World Series by the Chicago White Sox (an incident that became known as the "Black Sox Scandal"). That event resulted in the banning of some of the game's most notable figures from the sport for life and the establishment of the office of commissioner of baseball to "clean up" the game. Boxing was troubled throughout its history by the influence of gambling and the frequent efforts of managers to "fix" fights in the interests of bettors. Horse racing as it became commercialized was openly organized around betting, with the racetracks themselves establishing odds and taking bets.

The rise of spectator sports and gambling was largely a response to the desire of men to create a distinctively male culture in cities, where many of them had lost their economic independence and their connection with

Gambling and Sports

strenuous physical activity. But not all sports were the province of men. A number of sports were emerging in which women became important participants. Golf and tennis seldom attracted crowds in the late nineteenth century, but both experienced a rapid increase in participation among relatively wealthy men and women. Bicycling and croquet also enjoyed widespread popularity in the 1890s among women as well as men. Women's colleges were beginning to introduce their students to more strenuous sports as well—track, crew, swimming, and (beginning in the late 1890s) basketball—challenging the once prevalent notion that vigorous exercise was dangerous to women.

Music and Theater

Many ethnic communities maintained their own theaters, in which immigrants listened to the music of their homelands and heard comedians making light of their experiences in the New World. Italian theaters often drew on the traditions of Italian opera to create sentimental musical events. The Yiddish theater built on the experiences of American Jews—and was the training ground for a remarkable group of musicians and playwrights who later went on to play a major role in mainstream, English-speaking theater.

Ethnic Theater

Urban theaters also introduced one of the most distinctively American entertainment forms: the musical comedy, which evolved gradually from the comic operettas of European theater. George M. Cohan, an Irish vaudeville entertainer, became the first great creator of musical comedies in the early twentieth century; in the process

THE FLORADORA SEXTET The Floradora Sextet was a popular vocal group of the late nineteenth and early twentieth centuries and became fixtures on the vaudeville and burlesque stages of many cities and resorts. They are shown here in an elaborately costumed production number at the famous Weber and Fields Music Hall in New York, which opened in 1896. *(Bettmann/Corbis)*

of creating his many shows, he wrote a series of patriotic songs—"Yankee Doodle Dandy," "Over There," and "You're a Grand Old Flag"—that remained popular many decades later. Irving Berlin, a veteran of the Yiddish theater, wrote more than 1,000 songs for the musical theater during his long career, including such popular favorites as "Alexander's Ragtime Band" and "God Bless America."

Vaudeville, a form of theater adapted from French models, was the most popular urban entertainment in the first decades of the twentieth century. Even saloons and small community theaters could afford to offer their customers vaudeville, which consisted of a variety of acts (musicians, comedians, magicians, jugglers, and others) and was, at least in the beginning, inexpensive to produce. As the economic potential of vaudeville grew, some promoters—most prominently Florenz Ziegfeld of New York—staged much more elaborate spectacles. Vaudeville was also one of the few entertainment media open to black performers. They brought to it elements of the minstrel shows they had earlier developed for black audiences in the late nineteenth century. (See "Patterns of Popular Culture," pp. 426–427.)

Vaudeville

The Movies

The most important form of mass entertainment (until the invention of radio and television) was the movies.

Thomas Edison and others had created the technology of the motion picture in the 1880s. Not long after, short films became available to individual viewers through "peep shows" in pool halls, penny arcades, and amusement parks. Soon larger projectors made it possible to project the images onto big screens, which permitted substantial audiences to see films in theaters.

By 1900, Americans were becoming attracted in large numbers to these early movies—usually plotless films of trains or waterfalls or other spectacles designed mainly to show off the technology. D. W. Griffith carried the motion picture into a new era with his silent epics—*The Birth of a Nation* (1915), *Intolerance* (1916), and others—which introduced serious plots and elaborate productions to filmmaking. Some of these films—most notably *The Birth of a Nation*, with its celebration of the Ku Klux Klan and its demeaning portraits of African Americans—also contained notoriously racist messages, an indication, among other things, that the audiences for these early films were overwhelmingly white. Nevertheless, motion pictures were the first truly mass entertainment medium, reaching all areas of the country and almost all groups in the population.

The Birth of a Nation

Working-Class Leisure

Leisure had a particular importance to working-class men and women—in part because it was a relatively new part of their lives and in part because it stood in such sharp

A NICKELODEON, 1905 Before the rise of the great movie palaces, urban families flocked to "nickelodeons," smaller theaters that charged five cents for admission and showed many different films each day, including serials—dramas that drew audiences back into theaters day after day with new episodes of a running story. *(Brown Brothers)*

contrast to the grueling environments in which many industrial workers labored. More than most other groups in society, workers spent their leisure time on the streets—walking alone or in groups, watching street entertainers, meeting friends, talking and joking. For people with time but little money, the life of the street was an appealing source of camaraderie and energy.

Another important setting for the leisure time of working-class men was the neighborhood saloon, which

Importance of the Saloon

tended to be patronized by the same people over time and became a place where a worker could be sure of encountering a regular circle of friends. Saloons were often ethnically specific, in part because they served particular neighborhoods dominated by particular national groups. They also became political centers. Saloonkeepers were especially important figures in urban political machines, largely because they had regular contact with so many men in a neighborhood. When the Anti-Saloon League and other temperance organizations attacked the saloon, one of the reasons they cited was that eliminating saloons would weaken political machines.

Opponents also noted correctly that saloons were sometimes places of crime, violence, and prostitution—an entryway into the dark underworld of urban life.

Boxing was a particularly popular sport among working-class men. Many workers could not afford to attend the great public boxing matches pairing such popular heroes as John L. Sullivan and "Gentleman Jim" Corbett. But there were less glittering boxing matches in small rings and even in saloons—bare-knuckled fights organized by ethnic clubs and other groups that gave men an opportunity to demonstrate their strength and courage, something that the working world did not always provide them.

The Fourth of July

The Fourth of July played a large role in the lives of many working-class Americans. That was in part because in an age of six-day work-weeks and before regular vacations, it was for many decades one of the few full days of leisure—other than the Sabbath, during which activities were often restricted by law—that many workers had. Fourth of July celebrations were one of the highlights of the year in many ethnic, working-class communities. In Worcester, Massachusetts, for example, the Ancient Order of Hibernians (an Irish organization) sponsored boisterous picnics for the Irish working class of the city. Competing with them were Irish temperance organizations, which offered more sober and "respectable" entertainments to those relatively few workers who wished to avoid the heavy drinking at the Hibernian affairs. Other ethnic groups organized their own Fourth of July events—picnics, games, parades—making the day a celebration not just of the nation's independence, but of the cultures of immigrant communities. The city's affluent middle class, in the meantime, tended to stay away, remaining indoors or organizing family picnics at resort areas outside the city.

In southern cities such as Charleston, the Fourth of July was a more complicated affair, shaped in part by the memory of the Civil War and the continuing racial divisions within southern society. During Reconstruction, African-American workers in Charleston had exultantly celebrated the Fourth of July, seeing in it a symbol of the Union that had liberated them from slavery. Throughout the South, the Fourth was a day of celebration and self-congratulation for the Republican Party and its predominantly working-class or agrarian black constituency in the region. But white southerners slowly regained control of the Fourth, particularly once the drive toward sectional reconciliation had removed any pressure on them to change the racial culture of the region. Whites imposed ever tighter restrictions on how African Americans could celebrate the holiday. In the meantime, they themselves began once again to identify with the symbols of American patriotism.

Private Pursuits

Not all popular entertainment, however, involved public events. Many Americans amused themselves privately by reading novels and poetry. The so-called dime novels, cheaply bound and widely circulated, became popular after the Civil War, with tales of the Wild West, detective stories, sagas of scientific adventure (such as the Tom Swift stories), and novels of "moral uplift" (among them those of Horatio Alger). Publishers also continued to distribute sentimental novels of romance, which developed a large audience among women, as did books about animals and about young children growing up. Louisa May Alcott's *Little Women* (1869) proved to be enduringly popular; most of its readers were women, and it eventually sold more than 2 million copies.

Dime Novels

Music was also a popular form of private leisure. There were, of course, public performances of music that attracted large crowds. But equally popular, and much more readily accessible, were opportunities to perform music in the home. Middle-class families in particular placed a high value on learning to play an instrument. Middle-class girls often spent years studying the piano, the harp, or some other "parlor instrument" and giving performances for family and friends in the home. Sales of sheet music soared to provide material for these domestic musicales.

Many kinds of music were popular in the home. More affluent families emphasized classical music, and many middle-class families favored traditional and usually sentimental ballads. The great popularity of ragtime—a form of music that had originated in black music halls in the South and then spread into nightclubs in other parts of the country—extended into the home as well in the 1890s when the music of Scott Joplin and other ragtime composers was published for the first time.

Mass Communications

Urban industrial society created a vast market for new methods of transmitting news and information. Between 1870 and 1910, the circulation of daily newspapers increased nearly ninefold (from under 3 million to more than 24 million), a rate three times as great as the rate of population increase. And while standards varied widely from one paper to another, American journalism began to develop the beginnings of a professional identity. Salaries of reporters increased; many newspapers began separating the reporting of news from the expression of opinion; and newspapers themselves became important businesses.

One striking change was the emergence of national press services, which made use of the telegraph to supply news and features to papers throughout the country and which contributed as a result to the standardization of the product. By the turn of the century, important newspaper chains had emerged as well. The most powerful was William Randolph Hearst's, which by 1914 controlled nine newspapers and two magazines. Hearst and rival publisher Joseph Pulitzer helped popularize what became known as "yellow journalism"—a deliberately sensational, often lurid style of reporting presented in bold graphics, designed to reach a mass audience. (See "Patterns of Popular Culture," pp. 552–553.) Another major change occurred in the nature of American magazines. Beginning in the 1880s, new kinds of magazines appeared that were designed for a mass audience. One of the pioneers was Edward W. Bok, who took over the *Ladies' Home Journal* in 1899 and, by targeting a mass female audience, built its circulation to over 700,000.

Emergence of Newspaper Chains

HIGH CULTURE IN THE AGE OF THE CITY

In addition to the important changes in popular culture that accompanied the rise of cities and industry, there were profound changes in the realm of "high culture"—in the ideas and activities of intellectuals and elites. Even the notion of a distinction between "highbrow" and "lowbrow" culture was relatively new to the industrial era. In the early nineteenth century, most cultural activities attracted people of widely varying backgrounds and targeted people of all classes. By the late nineteenth century, however, elites were developing a cultural and intellectual life quite separate from the popular amusements of the urban masses.

The Literature of Urban America

Some writers and artists—the local-color writers of the South, for example, and Mark Twain, in such novels as *Huckleberry Finn* and *Tom Sawyer*—responded to the new industrial civilization by evoking an older, more natural world. But others grappled directly with the modern order.

One of the strongest impulses in late-nineteenth- and early-twentieth-century American literature was the effort to re-create urban social reality. This trend toward realism found an early voice in Stephen Crane, who—although best known for his novel of the Civil War, *The Red Badge of*

Social Realism

Courage (1895)—was the author of an earlier, powerful indictment of the plight of the working class. Crane created a sensation in 1893 when he published *Maggie: A Girl of the Streets,* a grim picture of urban poverty and slum life. Theodore Dreiser was even more influential in encouraging writers to abandon the genteel traditions of earlier times and turn to the social dislocations and injustices of the present. He did so both in *Sister Carrie* and in other, later novels (including *An American Tragedy,* published in 1925).

Many of Dreiser's contemporaries followed him in chronicling the oppression of America's poor. In 1901 Frank Norris published *The Octopus,* an account of a struggle between oppressed wheat farmers and powerful railroad interests in California. The socialist writer Upton Sinclair published *The Jungle* in 1906, a novel designed to reveal the depravity of capitalism. It exposed abuses in the American meatpacking industry; and while it did not inspire the kind of socialist response for which Sinclair had hoped, it did help produce legislative action to deal with the problem. Kate Chopin, a southern writer who explored the oppressive features of traditional marriage, encountered widespread public abuse after publication of her shocking novel *The Awakening* in 1899. It described a young wife and mother who abandons her family in search of personal fulfillment. It was formally banned in some communities. William Dean Howells, in *The Rise of Silas Lapham* (1884) and other works, described what he considered the shallowness and corruption in ordinary American lifestyles.

Other critics of American society responded to the new civilization not by attacking it but by withdrawing from it. The historian Henry Adams published a classic autobiography in 1906, *The Education of Henry Adams,* in which he portrayed himself as a man disillusioned with and unable to relate to his society, even though he continued to live in it. The novelist Henry James lived the major part of his adult life in England and Europe and produced a series of coldly realistic novels—*The American* (1877), *Portrait of a Lady* (1881), *The Ambassadors* (1903), and others—that showed his ambivalence about the character of modern, industrial civilization—and about American civilization in particular.

The growing popularity of literature helped spawn a remarkable network of clubs, mostly formed and populated by women, to bring readers together to talk about books. Reading clubs proliferated rapidly in cities and even small towns, among African-American as well as white women. They made literature a social experience for hundreds of thousands of women and created a tradition that has continued into the twenty-first century.

Art in the Age of the City

American art through most of the nineteenth century had been overshadowed by the art of Europe. Many American artists studied and even lived in Europe. But others broke from the Old World traditions and experimented with new styles. Winslow Homer was vigorously American in his paintings of New England maritime life and other native subjects. James McNeil Whistler was one of the first Western artists to appreciate the beauty of Japanese color prints and to introduce Oriental concepts into American and European art.

By the first years of the new century, some American artists were turning decisively away from the traditional academic style, a style perhaps best exemplified in America by the brilliant portraitist John Singer Sargent. Instead, many younger painters were exploring the same grim aspects of modern life that were becoming the subject of American literature. Members of the so-called Ashcan School produced work startling in its naturalism and stark in its portrayal of the social realities of the era. John Sloan portrayed the dreariness of American urban slums; George Bellows caught the vigor and violence of his time in paintings and drawings of prize fights; Edward Hopper explored the starkness and loneliness of the modern city. The Ashcan artists were also among the first Americans to appreciate expressionism and abstraction; and they showed their interest in new forms in 1913 when they helped stage the famous and controversial Armory Show in New York City, which displayed works of the French Postimpressionists and of some American moderns.

The work of these and other artists marked the beginning in America of an artistic movement known as modernism, a movement that had counterparts in many other areas of cultural and intellectual life as well. Rejecting the heavy reliance on established forms that characterized the "genteel tradition" of the nineteenth-century art world, modernists rejected the grip of the past and embraced new subjects and new forms. Where the genteel tradition emphasized the "dignified" and "elevated" aspects of civilization (and glorified the achievements of gifted elites), modernism gloried in the ordinary, even the coarse. Where the genteel tradition placed great importance on respect for the past and the maintenance of "standards," modernism looked to the future and gloried in the new. Eventually, modernism developed strict orthodoxies of its own. But in its early stages, it seemed to promise an escape from rigid, formal traditions and an unleashing of individual creativity.

The Impact of Darwinism

The single most profound intellectual development in the late nineteenth century was the widespread acceptance of the theory of evolution, associated most prominently with the English naturalist Charles Darwin. Darwinism argued that the human species had evolved from earlier forms of

Ashcan School

"Natural Selection"

HAIRDRESSER'S WINDOW This 1907 painting is by John Sloan, an American artist who belonged to the so-called Ashcan School. Sloan and others revolted against what they considered the sterile formalism of academic painting and chose instead to portray realistic scenes of ordinary life. In 1913 they stirred the art world with a startling exhibition in New York, known as the Armory Show. In it they displayed not only their own work (which was relatively conventional in technique, even if sometimes daring in its choice of subjects) but also the work of innovative European artists, who were already beginning to explore wholly new artistic forms. (*Wadsworth Atheneum Museum of Art, Hartford, CT. The Ella Gallup Sumner and Mary Catlin Sumner Collection Fund*)

DEMPSEY AND FIRPO The artist George Bellows began painting fight scenes in the first years of the twentieth century, when boxing appealed primarily to working-class urban communities. By 1924, when he painted this view of the Dempsey-Firpo fight, prizefighting had become one of the most popular sports in America. (*Whitney Museum of American Art, New York; Purchase, with funds from Gertrude Vanderbilt Whitney, 31.95*)

life (and most recently from simian creatures similar to apes) through a process of "natural selection." It challenged the biblical story of the Creation and almost every other tenet of traditional American religious faith. History, Darwinism suggested, was not the working out of a divine plan, as most Americans had always believed. It was a random process dominated by the fiercest or luckiest competitors.

The theory of evolution met widespread resistance at first from educators, theologians, and even many scientists. By the end of the century, however, the evolutionists had converted most members of the urban professional and educated classes. Even many middle-class Protestant religious leaders had accepted the doctrine, making significant alterations in theology to accommodate it. Evolution had become enshrined in schools and universities; virtually no serious scientist any longer questioned its basic validity.

Unseen by most urban Americans at the time, however, the rise of Darwinism was contributing to a deep schism between the new, cosmopolitan culture of the city—

CHARLES DARWIN Darwin's theories of natural selection, or evolution, revolutionized biological science. They also had a stunning impact on religious and even social thought. By challenging large parts of traditional religion and by suspecting that species were changeable, Darwinism opened the way for decades of theological controversy and for a series of spurious applications of his ideas to contemporary social problems. *(Bettmann/Corbis)*

which was receptive to new ideas such as evolution—and a more traditional, provincial culture located mainly (although not wholly) in rural areas—which remained wedded to more fundamentalist religious beliefs and older values. Thus the late nineteenth century saw not only the rise of a liberal Protestantism in tune with new scientific discoveries but also the beginning of an organized Protestant fundamentalism, which would make its presence felt politically in the 1920s and again in the 1980s and beyond.

Darwinism helped spawn other new intellectual currents. There was the Social Darwinism of William Graham Sumner and others, which industrialists used so enthusiastically to justify their favored position in American life. But there were also more sophisticated philosophies, among them a doctrine that became known as "pragmatism," which seemed peculiarly a product of America's changing material civilization. William James, a Harvard psychologist and brother of the novelist Henry James, was the most prominent publicist of the new theory, although earlier intellectuals such as Charles S. Peirce and later ones such as John Dewey were also important to its development and dissemination. According to the pragmatists, modern society should rely for guidance not on inherited ideals and moral principles but on the test of scientific inquiry. No idea or institution (not even religious faith) was valid, they claimed, unless it worked and unless it stood the test of experience. "The ultimate test for us of what a truth means," James wrote, "is the conduct it dictates or inspires."

"Pragmatism"

A similar concern for scientific inquiry was intruding into the social sciences and challenging traditional orthodoxies. Economists such as Richard T. Ely and Simon Patten argued for a more active and pragmatic use of scientific discipline. Sociologists such as Edward A. Ross and Lester Frank Ward urged applying the scientific method to the solution of social and political problems. Historians such as Frederick Jackson Turner and Charles Beard argued that economic factors more than spiritual ideals had been the governing force in historical development. John Dewey proposed a new approach to education that placed less emphasis on the rote learning of traditional knowledge and more on a flexible, democratic approach to schooling, one that enabled students to acquire knowledge that would help them deal with the realities of their society.

The relativistic implications of Darwinism also promoted the growth of anthropology and encouraged some scholars to begin examining other cultures—most

Growth of Anthropology

significantly, perhaps, the culture of American Indians—in new ways. A few white Americans began to look at Indian society as a coherent culture with its own norms and values that were worthy of respect and preservation, even though different from those of white society. But such ideas about Native Americans found very little support outside a few corners of the intellectual world until much later in the twentieth century.

Toward Universal Schooling

A society that was coming to depend increasingly on specialized skills and scientific knowledge was, of course, a society with a high demand for education. The late nineteenth century, therefore, was a time of rapid expansion and reform of American schools and universities.

One example was the spread of free public primary and secondary education. In 1860, there were only 100 public high schools in the entire United States. By 1900, the number had reached 6,000, and by 1914 over 12,000. By 1900, compulsory school attendance laws were in effect in thirty-one states and territories. But education was still far from universal. Rural areas lagged far behind urban-industrial ones in funding public education. And in the South, many blacks had access to no schools at all.

Spread of Public Education

Educational reformers, few of whom shared the more relativistic views of anthropologists, sought to provide educational opportunities for the Indian tribes as well, in an effort to "civilize" them and help them adapt to white society. In the 1870s, reformers recruited small groups of Indians to attend Hampton Institute, a primarily black college. In 1879, Richard Henry Pratt, a former army officer, organized the Carlisle Indian Industrial School in Pennsylvania. Like many black colleges, Carlisle emphasized the kind of practical "industrial" education that Booker T. Washington had urged. Equally important, it isolated Indians from their tribes and tried to force them to assimilate to white norms. The purpose, Pratt said, was to "kill the Indian and save the man." Carlisle spawned other, similar schools in the West. Ultimately, the reform efforts failed, both because of Indian resistance and because of inadequate funding, incompetent administration, and poor teaching.

Colleges and universities were also proliferating rapidly in the late nineteenth century. They benefited particularly from the Morrill Land Grant Act of the Civil War era, by which the federal government had donated land to states for the establishment of colleges. After 1865, states in the South and West took particular advantage of the law. In all, sixty-nine "land-grant" institutions were established in the last decades of the century—among them the state university systems of California, Illinois, Minnesota, and Wisconsin.

"Land-Grant" Institutions

Other universities benefited from millions of dollars contributed by business and financial tycoons. Rockefeller, Carnegie, and others gave generously to such schools as the University of Chicago, Columbia, Harvard, Northwestern, Princeton, Syracuse, and Yale. Other philanthropists founded new universities or reorganized and renamed older ones to perpetuate their family names—Vanderbilt, Johns Hopkins, Cornell, Duke, Tulane, and Stanford.

Education for Women

The post–Civil War era saw, too, an important expansion of educational opportunities for women, although such opportunities continued to lag far behind those available to men and were almost always denied to black women.

Most public high schools accepted women readily, but opportunities for higher education were few. At the end of the Civil War, only three American colleges were coeducational. In the years after the war, many of the land-grant colleges and universities in the Midwest and such private universities as Cornell and Wesleyan began to admit women along with men. But coeducation played a less crucial role in the education of women in this period than the creation of a network of women's colleges. Mount Holyoke, which had begun its life in 1836 as a "seminary" for women, became a full-fledged college in the 1880s. At about the same time, entirely new female institutions were emerging: Vassar, Wellesley, Smith, Bryn Mawr, Wells, and Goucher. A few of the larger private universities created separate colleges for women on their campuses (Barnard at Columbia and Radcliffe at Harvard, for example). Proponents of women's colleges saw the institutions as places where female students would not be treated as "second-class citizens" by predominantly male student bodies and faculties.

Women's Colleges

The female college was part of an important phenomenon in the history of modern American women: the emergence of a distinctive women's community. Most faculty members and many administrators were women (usually unmarried). And the life of the college produced a spirit of sorority and commitment among educated women that had important effects in later years, as women became the leaders of many reform activities. Most female college graduates ultimately married, but they married at a later age than their noncollege-educated counterparts and in some cases continued to pursue careers after marriage and motherhood. A significant minority, perhaps over 25 percent, did not marry at all, but devoted themselves exclusively to careers. A leader at Bryn Mawr remarked, "Our failures marry." That was surely rhetorical excess. But the growth of female higher education clearly became for some women a liberating experience, persuading them that they had roles to perform in society in addition to those of wives and mothers.

CONCLUSION

The extraordinary growth of American cities in the last decades of the nineteenth century led to both great achievements and enormous problems. Cities became centers of learning, art, and commerce. They produced great advances in technology, transportation, architecture, and communications. They provided their residents—and their many visitors—with varied and dazzling experiences, so much so that many rural people left the countryside to move to the city, and many more dreamed of doing so.

But cities were also places of congestion, filth, disease, and corruption. With populations expanding too rapidly for services to keep up, most American cities in this era struggled with makeshift governments and makeshift techniques to solve the basic problems of providing water, disposing of sewage, building roads, providing public transportation, fighting fire, stopping crime, and preventing or curing disease. City governments, many of them dominated by political machines and ruled by party bosses, were often models of inefficiency and corruption—although in their informal way they also provided substantial services to the working-class and immigrant constituencies who needed them most. They also managed, despite the administrative limitations of most municipal governments, to oversee great public projects: the building of parks, museums, opera houses, and theaters, usually in partnership with private developers.

The city brought together races, ethnic groups, and classes of extraordinary variety—from the families of great wealth that the new industrial age was creating to the vast working class, much of it consisting of immigrants, that crowded into densely packed neighborhoods sharply divided by ethnicity. The city also produced new forms of popular culture. It produced new opportunities (and risks) for women. It created temples of consumerism: shops, boutiques, and, above all, the great department stores. And it created forums for public recreation and entertainment: parks, theaters, athletic fields, amusement parks, and later movie palaces.

Urban life created such great anxiety among those who lived within the cities and among those who observed them from afar that in some cities middle-class people literally armed themselves to prepare for the insurrections they expected from the poor. But, in fact, American cities adapted reasonably successfully over time to the great demands their growth made of them and learned to govern themselves, if not entirely honestly and efficiently, at least adequately to allow them to survive and grow.

INTERACTIVE LEARNING

The *Primary Source Investigator CD-ROM* offers the following materials related to this chapter:

- A short documentary movie, **Age of Immigration**, is a study of the flood of immigration into the United States in the late nineteenth and early twentieth centuries (D14).

- Interactive map: **Streetcar Suburbs** (M17).

- Documents, images, and maps related to urbanization, immigration, and the rise of mass consumption in the late nineteenth century. Some highlights include the text of the Chinese Exclusion Act of 1882; images from the urban world, such as a tenement dwelling, Bohemian cigarmakers at work in their living quarters, and young children asleep in the street; an excerpt from the notebook of Alexander Graham Bell; and political cartoons showing the rise of nativism.

Online Learning Center (www.mhhe.com/brinkley13e)

For quizzes, Internet resources, references to additional books and films, and more, consult this book's Online Learning Center.

FOR FURTHER REFERENCE

Lewis Mumford, author of *The City in History* (1961), was America's foremost critic and chronicler of urbanization through the mid-twentieth century. John Bodnar provides a synthetic history of immigration in *The Transplanted: A History of Immigrants in America* (1985), which challenges an earlier classic study by Oscar Handlin, *The Uprooted: The Epic Story of the Great Migrations That Made the American People* (1973, 2nd ed.). The new urban mass culture of America's cities is the subject of William Leach, *Land of Desire: Merchants, Power, and the Rise of a New American Culture* (1993), and Kathy Peiss, *Cheap Amusements: Working Women and Leisure in Turn-of-the-Century New York* (1986). Stuart Blumin, *The Emergence of the Middle Class: Social Experience in the American City, 1760–1900* (1989) examines urban society and culture. T. J. Jackson Lears, *No Place of Grace: Antimodernism and the Transformation of American Culture, 1880-1920* (1981) chronicles patterns of resistance to the new culture. Debby Applegate, *The Most Famous Man in America: The Biography of Henry Ward Beecher* (2006) examines a renowned clergyman who was also a spokesman for modernity. Roy Rosenzweig and Elizabeth Blackmar, *The Park and the People: A History of Central Park* (1992) studies the creation of America's most famous public park. Edwin G. Burrows and Mike Wallace, *Gotham: A History of New York City to 1898* (1998) is a thorough history of New York's remarkable growth. John F. Kasson, *Amusing the Millions: Coney Island at the Turn of the Century* (1978) is an illustrated history and interpretation of the amusement park's place in American culture. *Coney Island* (1991), a film by Ric Burns, presents a colorful history of America's favorite seaside resort. The documentary film *Baseball* (1994), by Ken Burns and the companion book of the same name, by Geoffrey C. Ward provide sweeping narratives of the national pastime, its origins in the age of the city, and its wider social context of race relations, immigration, and popular culture. *New York* (1999-2001), a film by Ric Burns, is a sweeping documentary history of the city, accompanied by a companion book, Ric Burns et al., *New York: An Illustrated History* (1999).

CHAPTER 19

FROM CRISIS TO EMPIRE

BEARING THE CROSS OF GOLD   The cartoonist Grant Hamilton created this image of William Jennings Bryan shortly after he made his famous "Cross of Gold" speech at the Democratic National Convention, which subsequently nominated him for president. The cartoon highlights two of the most powerful images in Bryan's speech—a "crown of thorns" and a "cross of gold," both biblical references and both designed to represent the oppression that the gold standard imposed upon working people.   *(The Granger Collection, NY)*

THE UNITED STATES APPROACHED the end of the nineteenth century as a fundamentally different nation from what it had been at the beginning of the Civil War. With rapid change came cascading social and political problems—problems that the weak and conservative governments of the time showed little inclination or ability to address. And so it was perhaps not surprising that in the 1890s, the United States entered a period of national crisis.

The economic crisis of the 1890s was the most serious in the nation's history to that point. A catastrophic depression began in 1893, rapidly intensified, and created devastating hardship for millions of Americans. Farmers, particularly hard hit by the depression, responded by creating an agrarian political movement known as "populism," which briefly seemed to be gaining real political power. American workers, facing massive unemployment, staged large and occasionally violent strikes. Not since the Civil War had American politics been so polarized and impassioned. The election of 1896—which pitted the agrarian hero William Jennings Bryan against the solid, conservative William McKinley—was dramatic but anticlimactic. Bryan was a great orator and campaigner, but McKinley easily triumphed because of the support of the mighty Republican Party and of the many eastern groups who looked with suspicion and unease at the agricultural demands coming from the West.

McKinley did little in his first term in office to resolve the problems and grievances of his time, but the economy revived nevertheless. Having largely ignored the depression, however, McKinley took a great interest in another great national cause: the plight of Cuba in its war with Spain. In the spring of 1898, the United States declared war on Spain and entered the conflict in Cuba—a brief but bloody war that ended with an American victory four months later. The conflict had begun as a way to support Cuban independence from the Spanish. But a group of fervent and influential imperialists worked to convert the war into an occasion for acquiring overseas possessions: Puerto Rico and the Philippines. Despite a powerful anti-imperialist movement, the acquisition of the former Spanish colonies proceeded—only to draw Americans into yet another imperial war, this one in the Philippines, where the Americans, not the Spanish, were the targets of local enmity.

SIGNIFICANT EVENTS

1867 ▶	National Grange founded
1868–1878 ▶	Cubans revolt against Spanish rule in Ten Years' War
1873 ▶	Congress discontinues coinage of silver
1875 ▶	First Farmers' Alliances form in Texas
1880 ▶	James A. Garfield elected president
1881 ▶	Garfield assassinated; Chester A. Arthur succeeds him
1884 ▶	Grover Cleveland elected president
1886 ▶	Supreme Court in *Wabash* case restricts state regulation of commerce
1887 ▶	Interstate Commerce Act passed
1888 ▶	Benjamin Harrison elected president
1890 ▶	Alfred Thayer Mahan publishes *The Influence of Sea Power upon History*
▶	Sherman Antitrust Act passed
▶	Sherman Silver Purchase Act passed
▶	McKinley Tariff enacted
▶	Southern and Northwestern Alliances hold national convention at Ocala, Florida
1892 ▶	Cleveland elected president again
▶	People's Party formed in Omaha
1893 ▶	American planters in Hawaii stage revolution
▶	Commercial and financial panic launches severe and prolonged depression
▶	Congress repeals Sherman Silver Purchase Act
1894 ▶	Wilson-Gorman Tariff on sugar ravages Cuban economy
▶	Insurrection against Spanish begins in Cuba
▶	Wilson-Gorman Tariff enacted
▶	Coxey's Army marches on Washington
1895 ▶	*United States* v. *E. C. Knight Co.* weakens Sherman Antitrust Act
1896 ▶	William Jennings Bryan wins Democratic nomination after "Cross of Gold" speech
▶	Populists endorse Bryan for president
▶	William McKinley elected president
1898 ▶	U.S. battleship *Maine* explodes in Havana harbor
▶	Congress declares war on Spain (April 25)
▶	Dewey captures Philippines
▶	United States and Spain sign armistice (August 12)
▶	Treaty of Paris cedes Puerto Rico, Philippines, and other Spanish possessions to United States and recognizes Cuban independence
▶	United States formally annexes Hawaii
▶	Anti-Imperialist League formed
▶	Economy begins to revive
1898–1902 ▶	Philippines revolt against American rule
1899 ▶	Hay releases "Open Door notes"
1900 ▶	Foraker Act establishes civil government in Puerto Rico
▶	Hawaii granted territorial status
▶	Boxer Rebellion breaks out in China
▶	McKinley reelected president
▶	Gold Standard Act passed
1901 ▶	Congress passes Platt Amendment
1912 ▶	Alaska given territorial status
1917 ▶	Puerto Ricans granted U.S. citizenship

THE POLITICS OF EQUILIBRIUM

The most striking feature of late-nineteenth-century politics was the remarkable stability of the party system. From

Electoral Stability

the end of Reconstruction until the late 1890s, the electorate was divided almost precisely evenly between the Republicans and the Democrats. Sixteen states were solidly and consistently Republican, and fourteen states (most in the South) were solidly and consistently Democratic. Only five states (most importantly New York and Ohio) were usually in doubt, and their voters generally decided the results of national elections. The Republican Party captured the presidency in all but two of the elections of the era, but in the five presidential elections beginning in 1876, the average popular-vote margin separating the Democratic and Republican candidates was 1.5 percent. The congressional balance was similarly stable, with the Republicans generally controlling the Senate and the Democrats generally controlling the House.

As striking as the balance between the parties was the intensity of public loyalty to them. In most of the country, Americans viewed their party affiliations with a passion

High Turnout

and enthusiasm that is difficult for later generations to understand. Voter turnout in presidential elections between 1860 and 1900 averaged over 78 percent of all eligible voters (as compared with only about 50 percent in most recent elections). Even in nonpresidential years, from 60 to 80 percent of the voters turned out to cast ballots for congressional and local candidates. Large groups of potential voters were disfranchised in these years: women in most states; almost all blacks and many poor whites in the South. But for adult white males, there were few franchise restrictions.

What explains this extraordinary loyalty to the two political parties? It was not, certainly, that the parties took distinct positions on important public issues. They did so rarely. Party loyalties reflected other factors. Region was perhaps the most important. To white southerners, loyalty to the Democratic Party was a matter of unquestioned faith. It was the vehicle by which they had triumphed over Reconstruction and preserved white supremacy. To many northerners, white and black, Republican loyalties were equally intense. To them, the party of Lincoln remained a bulwark against slavery and treason.

Religious and ethnic differences also shaped party loyalties. The Democratic Party attracted most of the Catholic voters, recent immigrants, and poorer workers—groups that often overlapped. The Republican Party appealed to northern Protestants, citizens of old stock, and much of the middle class—groups that also had considerable overlap. Among the few substantive issues on which the parties took clearly different stands were matters connected with immigrants. Republicans tended to support measures restricting immigration and to favor temperance

legislation, which many believed would help discipline immigrant communities. Catholics and immigrants viewed such proposals as assaults on them and their cultures and opposed them; the Democratic Party followed their lead.

Party identification, then, was usually more a reflection of cultural inclinations than a calculation of economic interest. Individuals might affiliate with a party because their parents had done so, or because it

Cultural Basis of Party Identification

was the party of their region, their church, or their ethnic group.

The National Government

One reason the two parties managed to avoid substantive issues was that the federal government (and to some degree state and local governments as well) did relatively little. The government in Washington was responsible for delivering the mail, maintaining a military, conducting foreign policy, and collecting tariffs and taxes. It had few other responsibilities and few institutions with which it could have undertaken additional responsibilities even if it had chosen to do so.

There were significant exceptions. The federal government had been supporting the economic development of the nation for decades. In the late nineteenth century, that mostly meant giving tremendous subsidies to railroads, usually in the form of grants of federal land, to encourage them to extend their lines deeper into the nation. And as President Cleveland's intervention in the Pullman strike suggests, the government was also not averse to using its military and police power to protect capitalists from challenges from their workers.

In addition, the federal government administered a system of annual pensions for Union Civil War veterans who had retired from work and for their widows. At its peak, this pension system was making payments to a majority of the male citizens (black and white) of the North and to many women as well. Some reformers hoped to make the system permanent and universal. But

Civil War Pension System

their efforts failed, in part because the Civil War pension system was awash in party patronage and corruption. Other reformers—believers in "good government"—saw elimination of the pension system as a way to fight graft, corruption, and party rule. When the Civil War generation died out, the pension system died with it.

In most other respects, however, the United States in the late nineteenth century was a society without a modern, national government. The most powerful institutions were the two political parties (and the bosses and machines that dominated them) and the federal courts.

Presidents and Patronage

The power of party bosses had an important effect on the power of the presidency. The office had great symbolic importance, but its occupants were unable to do very much except distribute government appointments. A new president and his tiny staff had to make almost 100,000 appointments (most of them in the post office, the only really large government agency); and even in that function, presidents had limited latitude, since they had to avoid offending the various factions within their own parties.

Sometimes that proved impossible, as the presidency of Rutherford B. Hayes (1877–1881) demonstrated. By the

Stalwarts and Half-Breeds

end of his term, two groups—the Stalwarts, led by Roscoe Conkling of New York, and the Half-Breeds,

PRESIDENT AND MRS. RUTHERFORD B. HAYES Hayes was one of a series of generally undistinguished late-nineteenth-century presidents whose subordination to the fiercely competitive party system left them with little room for independent leadership. This photograph captures the dignity and sobriety that Hayes and his wife sought to convey to the public. His wife was a temperance advocate and refused to serve alcoholic beverages in the White House, thereby earning the nickname "Lemonade Lucy." Hayes attracted less whimsical labels. Because of the disputed 1876 election that had elevated him to the presidency, critics referred to him throughout his term as "His Fraudulency." *(Library of Congress)*

captained by James G. Blaine of Maine—were competing for control of the Republican Party. Rhetorically, the Stalwarts favored traditional, professional machine politics, while the Half-Breeds favored reform. In fact, both groups were mainly interested in a larger share of the patronage pie. Hayes tried to satisfy both and ended up satisfying neither.

The battle over patronage overshadowed all else during Hayes's unhappy presidency. His one important substantive initiative—an effort to create a civil service system—attracted no support from either party. And his early announcement that he would not seek reelection only weakened him further. (His popularity in Washington was not enhanced by the decision of his wife, a temperance advocate widely known as "Lemonade Lucy," to ban alcoholic beverages from the White House.) Hayes's presidency was a study in frustration.

The Republicans managed to retain the presidency in 1880 in part because they agreed on a ticket that included a Stalwart and a Half-Breed. They nominated James A. Garfield, a veteran congressman from Ohio and a Half-Breed, for president and Chester A. Arthur of New York, a Stalwart, for vice president. The Democrats nominated General Winfield Scott Hancock, a minor Civil War commander with no national following. Benefiting from the end of the recession of 1879, Garfield won a decisive electoral victory, although his popular-vote margin was very thin. The Republicans also captured both houses of Congress.

Garfield began his presidency by trying to defy the Stalwarts in his appointments and by showing support for civil service reform. He soon found himself embroiled in an

Garfield Assassinated

ugly public quarrel with Conkling and the Stalwarts. It was never resolved. On July 2, 1881, only four months after his inauguration, Garfield was shot twice while standing in the Washington railroad station by an apparently deranged gunman (and unsuccessful office seeker) who shouted, "I am a Stalwart and Arthur is president now!" Garfield lingered for nearly three months but finally died, a victim as much of inept medical treatment as of the wounds themselves.

Chester A. Arthur, who succeeded Garfield, had spent a political lifetime as a devoted, skilled, and open spoilsman and a close ally of Roscoe Conkling. But on becoming president, he tried—like Hayes and Garfield before him—to follow an independent course and even to promote reform,

Pendleton Act

aware that the Garfield assassination had discredited the traditional spoils system. To the dismay of the Stalwarts, Arthur kept most of Garfield's appointees in office and supported civil service reform. In 1883, Congress passed the first national civil service measure, the Pendleton Act, which required that some federal jobs be filled by competitive written examinations rather than by patronage. Relatively few offices fell under civil service at first, but its reach extended steadily.

Cleveland, Harrison, and the Tariff

In the unsavory election of 1884, the Republican candidate for president was Senator James G. Blaine of Maine—known to his admirers as the "Plumed Knight" but to many others as a symbol of seamy party politics. A group of disgruntled "liberal Republicans," known by their critics as the "mugwumps," announced they would bolt the party and support an honest Democrat. Rising to the bait, the Democrats nominated Grover Cleveland, the reform governor of New York. He differed from Blaine on no substantive issues but had acquired a reputation as an enemy of corruption.

In a campaign filled with personal invective, what may have decided the election was the last-minute introduction of a religious controversy. Shortly before the election, a delegation of Protestant ministers called on Blaine in New York City; their spokesman, Dr. Samuel Burchard, referred to the Democrats as the party of "rum, Romanism, and rebellion." Blaine was slow to repudiate Burchard's

indiscretion, and Democrats quickly spread the news that Blaine had tolerated a slander on the Catholic Church. Cleveland's narrow victory was probably a result of an unusually heavy Catholic vote for the Democrats in New York. Cleveland won 219 electoral votes to Blaine's 182; his popular margin was only 23,000.

Election of 1884

Grover Cleveland was respected, if not often liked, for his stern and righteous opposition to politicians, grafters, pressure groups, and Tammany Hall. He had become famous as the "veto governor," as an official who was not afraid to say no. He was the embodiment of an era in which few Americans believed the federal government could, or should, do very much. Cleveland had always doubted the wisdom of protective tariffs. The existing high rates, he believed, were responsible for the annual surplus in federal revenues, which was tempting Congress to pass "reckless" and "extravagant" legislation, which he frequently vetoed.

THE TOURNAMENT OF TO-DAY.—A SET-TO BETWEEN LABOR AND MONOPOLY.

LABOR AND MONOPOLY This 1883 cartoon appeared in *Puck,* a magazine popular for its satirical treatment of American politics. It expresses a common sentiment of the Populists and many others: that ordinary men and women (portrayed here by the pathetic figure of "labor" and by the grim members of the audience) were almost hopelessly overmatched by the power of corporate monopolies. The knight's shield, labeled "corruption of the legislature," and his spear, labeled "subsidized press," make clear that—in the view of the cartoonist at least—corporations had many allies in their effort to oppress workers. *(Culver Pictures, Inc.)*

In December 1887, therefore, he asked Congress to reduce the tariff rates. Democrats in the House approved a tariff reduction, but Senate Republicans defiantly passed a bill of their own actually raising the rates. The resulting deadlock made the tariff an issue in the election of 1888.

The Democrats renominated Cleveland and supported tariff reductions. The Republicans settled on former senator Benjamin Harrison of Indiana, who was obscure but respectable (the grandson of President William Henry Harrison); he endorsed protection. The campaign was the first since the Civil War to involve a clear question of economic difference between the parties. It was also one of the most corrupt (and closest) elections in American history. Harrison won an electoral majority of 233 to 168, but Cleveland's popular vote exceeded Harrison's by 100,000.

New Public Issues

Benjamin Harrison's record as president was little more substantial than that of his grandfather, who had died a month after taking office. Harrison had few visible convictions, and he made no effort to influence Congress. And yet during Harrison's passive administration, public opinion was beginning to force the government to confront some of the pressing social and economic issues of the day. Most notably, sentiment was rising in favor of legislation to curb the power of trusts.

By the mid-1880s, fifteen western and southern states had adopted laws prohibiting combinations that restrained competition. But corporations found it easy to escape limitations by incorporating in states, such as New Jersey and Delaware, that offered them special privileges. If antitrust legislation was to be effective, its supporters believed, it would have to come from the national government. Responding to growing popular demands, both houses of

Sherman Antitrust Act

Congress passed the Sherman Antitrust Act in July 1890, almost without dissent. Most members of Congress saw the act as a symbolic measure, one that would help deflect public criticism but was not likely to have any real effect on corporate power. For over a decade after its passage, the Sherman Act—indifferently enforced and steadily weakened by the courts—had no impact. As of 1901, the Justice Department had instituted many antitrust suits against unions, but only fourteen against business combinations; there had been few convictions.

The Republicans were more interested, however, in the issue they believed had won them the 1888 election: the tariff. Representative William McKinley of Ohio and Senator Nelson W. Aldrich of Rhode Island drafted the highest protective measure ever proposed to Congress. Known as the McKinley Tariff, it became law in October 1890. But Republican leaders apparently misinterpreted public sentiment.

McKinley Tariff

The party suffered a stunning reversal in the 1890 congressional election. The Republicans' substantial Senate majority was slashed to 8; in the House, the party retained only 88 of the 323 seats. McKinley himself was among those who went down in defeat. Nor were the Republicans able to recover in the course of the next two years. In the presidential election of 1892, Benjamin Harrison once again supported protection; Grover Cleveland, renominated by the Democrats, once again opposed it. A new third party, the People's Party, with James B. Weaver as its candidate, advocated substantial economic reform. Cleveland won 277 electoral votes to Harrison's 145 and had a popular margin of 380,000. Weaver ran far behind. For the first time since 1878, the Democrats won a majority of both houses of Congress.

The policies of Cleveland's second term were much like those of his first—devoted to minimal government and hostile to active efforts to deal with social or economic problems. Again, he supported a tariff reduction, which the House approved but the Senate weakened.

A SENATE FOR REVENUE ONLY.

SHACKLED BY THE TARIFF This 1894 cartoon by the political satirist Louis Dalrymple portrays an unhappy Uncle Sam bound hand and foot by the McKinley Tariff and by what tariff opponents considered a closely related evil—monopoly. Members of the Senate are portrayed as tools of the various industries and special interests protected by the tariff. The caption, "A Senate for Revenue Only," is a parody of the antitariff rallying cry, "A tariff for revenue only," meaning that duties should be designed only to raise money for the government, not to stop imports of particular goods to protect domestic industries. (*The Granger Collection*)

THE STATE, WAR, AND NAVY BUILDING This sprawling Victorian office building was one of the largest in Washington when it was constructed shortly after the Civil War. It housed the State, War, and Navy Departments until not long before World War II. It suggests both the degree to which the federal government was growing in the late nineteenth century and, more importantly, the degree to which it remained a tiny entity compared to what it would later become. This building, which stands directly next door to the White House, today houses a part (but only a part) of the president's staff. *(Library of Congress)*

Cleveland denounced the result but allowed it to become law as the Wilson-Gorman Tariff. It included only very modest reductions.

But public pressure was growing in the 1880s for other reforms, among them regulation of the railroads. Farm organizations in the Midwest (most notably the Grangers) had persuaded several state legislatures to pass regulatory legislation in the early 1870s. But in 1886, the Supreme Court—in *Wabash, St. Louis, and Pacific Railway Co.* v. *Illinois,* known as the *Wabash* case—ruled one of the Granger Laws in Illinois unconstitutional. According to the Court, the law was an attempt to control interstate commerce and thus infringed on the exclusive power of Congress. Later, the courts limited the powers of the states to regulate commerce even within their own boundaries.

Effective railroad regulation, it was now clear, could come only from the federal government. Congress responded to public pressure in 1887 with the Interstate Commerce Act, which banned discrimination in rates between long and short hauls, required that railroads publish their rate schedules and

Interstate Commerce Act

file them with the government, and declared that all interstate rail rates must be "reasonable and just"—although the act did not define what that meant. A five-person agency, the Interstate Commerce Commission (ICC), was to administer the act. But it had to rely on the courts to enforce its rulings. For almost twenty years after its passage, the Interstate Commerce Act—which was, like the Sherman Act, haphazardly enforced and narrowly interpreted by the courts—had little practical effect.

THE AGRARIAN REVOLT

No group watched the performance of the federal government in the 1880s with more dismay than American farmers. Suffering from a long economic decline, afflicted with a painful sense of obsolescence, rural Americans were keenly aware of the problems of the modern economy and particularly eager for government assistance in dealing with them. The result of their frustrations was the emergence of one of the most powerful movements of political protest in American history: what became known as populism.

"THE GRANGE AWAKENING THE SLEEPERS" This 1873 cartoon illustrates the way the Grange embraced many of the same concerns that the Farmers' Alliances and their People's Party later expressed. A farmer is attempting to arouse passive citizens (lying in place of the "sleepers," or cross ties on railroad tracks), who are about to be crushed by a train. The cars bear the names of the costs of the railroads' domination of the agrarian economy. *(Culver Pictures, Inc.)*

The Grangers

According to popular myth, American farmers were the most individualistic of citizens. In reality, however, farmers had been making efforts to organize for many decades. The first major farm organization appeared in the 1860s: the Grange.

The Grange had its origins shortly after the Civil War in a tour through the South by a minor Agriculture Department official, Oliver H. Kelley. Kelley was appalled by what he considered the isolation and drabness of rural life, and in 1867 he left the government and, with other department employees, founded the National Grange of the Patrons of Husbandry, to which he devoted years of labor as secretary and from which emerged a network of local organizations. At first, the Grangers defined their purposes modestly. They attempted to bring farmers together to learn new scientific agricultural techniques—to keep farming "in step with the music of the age." The Grangers also hoped to create a feeling of community, to relieve the loneliness of rural life.

Origins

The Grangers grew slowly for a time. But when the depression of 1873 caused a major decline in farm prices, membership rapidly increased. By 1875, the Grange

claimed over 800,000 members and 20,000 local lodges; it had chapters in almost every state but was strongest in the great staple-producing regions of the South and the Midwest.

As membership grew, the lodges in the Midwest began to focus less on the social benefits of organization and more on the economic possibilities. They attempted to organize marketing cooperatives to allow farmers to circumvent the hated middlemen. And they urged cooperative political action to curb monopolistic practices by railroads and warehouses.

Economic Grievances

The Grangers set up cooperative stores, creameries, elevators, warehouses, insurance companies, and factories that produced machines, stoves, and other items. More than 400 enterprises were in operation at the height of the movement, and some of them forged lucrative relationships with existing businesses. One corporation emerged specifically to meet the needs of the Grangers: the first mail-order business, Montgomery Ward and Company, founded in 1872. Eventually, however, most of the Grange enterprises failed, both because of the inexperience of their operators and because of the opposition of the middlemen they were challenging.

The Grangers also worked to elect state legislators pledged to their program. Usually they operated through the existing parties, although occasionally they ran candidates under such independent party labels as "Antimonopoly" and "Reform." At their peak, they managed to gain control of the legislatures in most of the midwestern states.

Political Program

Their purpose was to subject the railroads to government controls. The Granger laws of the early 1870s imposed strict regulations on railroad rates and practices.

But the new regulations were soon destroyed by the courts. That defeat, combined with the political inexperience of many Grange leaders and, above all, the temporary return of agricultural prosperity in the late 1870s, produced a dramatic decline in the power of the association. Some of the Granger cooperatives survived as effective economic vehicles for many years, but the movement as a whole dwindled rapidly. By 1880, its membership had shrunk to 100,000.

The Farmers' Alliances

The successor to the Grange as the leading vehicle of agrarian protest began to emerge even before the Granger movement had faded. As early as 1875, farmers in parts of the South (most notably in Texas) were banding together in so-called Farmers' Alliances. By 1880, the Southern Alliance had more than 4 million members; and a comparable Northwestern Alliance was taking root in the plains states and the Midwest and developing ties with its southern counterpart.

A POPULIST GATHERING Populism was a response to real economic and political grievances. But like most political movements of its time, it was also important as a cultural experience. For farmers in sparsely settled regions in particular, it provided an antidote to isolation and loneliness. This gathering of Populist farmers in Dickinson County, Kansas, shows how the political purposes of the movement were tightly bound up with its social purposes. *(Kansas State Historical Society)*

Like the Granges, the Alliances were principally concerned with local problems. They formed cooperatives and other marketing mechanisms. They established stores, banks, processing plants, and other facilities for their members—to free them from the hated "furnishing merchants" who kept so many farmers in debt. Some Alliance leaders, however, also saw the movement as an effort to build a society in which economic competition might give way to cooperation. They argued for a sense of mutual, neighborly responsibility that would enable farmers to resist oppressive outside forces. Alliance lecturers traveled throughout rural areas lambasting the concentration of power in great corporations and financial institutions and promoting cooperation as an alternative economic system.

From the beginning, women were full voting members in most local Alliances. Many held offices and served as lecturers. A few, most notably Mary E. Lease, went on to become fiery Populist orators. (Lease was famous for urging farmers to "raise less corn and more hell.") Most others emphasized issues of particular concern to women, especially temperance. Like their urban counterparts, agrarian women argued that sobriety was a key to stability in rural society. Alliances (and the populist party they eventually created) advocated extending the vote to women in many areas of the country.

Mary Lease

Although the Alliances quickly became far more widespread than the Granges had ever been, they suffered from similar problems. Their cooperatives did not always work well, partly because the market forces operating against them were sometimes too strong to be overcome, partly because the cooperatives themselves were often mismanaged. These economic frustrations helped push the movement into a new phase at the end of the 1880s: the creation of a national political organization.

In 1889, the Southern and Northwestern Alliances, despite continuing differences between them, agreed to a loose merger. The next year the Alliances held a national convention at Ocala, Florida, and issued the so-called Ocala Demands, which were, in effect, a party platform. In the 1890 off-year elections, candidates supported by the Alliances won partial or complete control of the legislatures in twelve states. They also won six governorships, three seats in the U.S. Senate, and approximately fifty in the U.S. House of Representatives. Many of the successful Alliance candidates were Democrats who had benefited—often passively—from Alliance endorsements. But dissident farmers drew enough encouragement from the results to contemplate further political action, including forming a party of their own.

MARY E. LEASE The fiery Populist orator Mary E. Lease was a fixture on the Alliance lecture circuit in the 1890s. She made some 160 speeches in 1890 alone. Her critics called her the "Kansas Pythoness," but she was popular among populist farmers with her denunciations of banks, railroads, and "middlemen," and her famous advice to "raise less corn and more hell." *(Brown Brothers)*

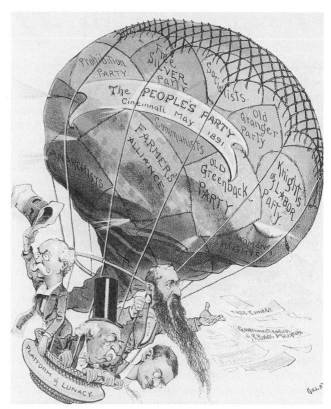

A PARTY OF PATCHES," *JUDGE* **MAGAZINE, JUNE 6, 1891** This political cartoon suggests the contempt and fear with which many easterners, in particular, viewed the emergence of the People's Party in 1891. *(Kansas State Historical Society)*

Sentiment for a third party was strongest among the members of the Northwestern Alliance. But several southern leaders supported the idea as well—among them Tom Watson of Georgia, the only southern congressman elected in 1890 openly to identify with the Alliance, and Leonidas L. Polk of North Carolina, perhaps the ablest mind in the movement. Alliance leaders discussed plans for a third party at meetings in Cincinnati in May 1891 and St. Louis in February 1892. Then, in July 1892, 1,300 exultant delegates poured into Omaha, Nebraska, to proclaim the creation of the new party, approve an official set of principles, and nominate candidates for the presidency and vice presidency. The new organization's official name was the People's Party, but its members were more commonly known as Populists.

Birth of the People's Party

The election of 1892 demonstrated the potential power of the new movement. The Populist presidential candidate was James B. Weaver of Iowa, a former Greenbacker who received the nomination after the death of Leonidas Polk, the early favorite. Weaver polled more than 1 million votes, 8.5 percent of the total, and carried six mountain and plains states for 22 electoral votes. Nearly 1,500 Populist candidates won election to seats in state legislatures. The party elected three governors, five senators, and ten congressmen. It could also claim the support of many Republicans and Democrats in Congress who had been elected by appealing to populist sentiment.

The Populist Constituency

The Populists dreamed of creating a broad political coalition. But populism always appealed principally to farmers, particularly to small farmers with little long-range economic security—people whose operations were minimally mechanized, if at all, who relied on one crop, and who had access only to limited credit. In the Midwest, the Populists were usually family farmers struggling to hold on to their land (or to get it back). In the South, there were many modest landowners too, but in addition there were significant numbers of sharecroppers and tenant farmers. Whatever their differences, however, most Populists had at least one thing in common: they were engaged in a type of farming that was becoming less viable in the face of new, mechanized, diversified, and consolidated commercial agriculture.

THE CHAUTAUQUAS

The Populist movement of the 1880s and 1890s revealed, in addition to a wide range of economic, political, and social grievances among American farmers, a tremendous thirst for knowledge. Men and women flocked by the hundreds, even the thousands, to hear speeches and discussions by the traveling lecturers of the Alliance movement. For many farmers, the Alliance lectures were among their only contacts with the wider world— their only access to information about events and ideas outside their own communities.

But it was not only Populist farmers who hungered for information and education in the late nineteenth and early twentieth centuries. Men and women throughout the United States were as eager for knowledge as were the people a generation earlier who had flocked to the Lyceum movement (see pp. 364–365). Out of that hunger emerged a wide range of systems for bringing lectures to otherwise isolated communities. The most famous of them were known as the Chautauquas.

The Chautauquas began in the summer of 1874, when two enterprising men in Chautauqua Lakes, New York, established a series of what they called "Assemblies" for the instruction of Sunday school teachers. A year later, the organizers persuaded President Ulysses S. Grant to attend an Assembly; his appearance brought them enormous publicity and helped ensure their success. Within a few years, the Chautauqua Assembly had expanded to include lectures on literary, scientific, theological, and practical subjects and was attracting ever larger audiences for one- or two-week "schools" throughout much of the year. In 1883, the New York State legislature granted the Assemblies a charter and gave them the name "The Chautauqua University."

So successful (and profitable) were the Chautauqua Assemblies that scores of towns and villages began establishing lecture series of their own—"Little Chautauquas"—throughout the Midwest. Finally, in 1904, a Chicago promoter began organizing traveling programs under tents and sending them on tours through rural areas across the United States—to over 8,000 different com-

THE HALL OF CHRIST, CHAUTAUQUA This ornate meeting hall, very different from the rustic structures of the early days of Chautauqua, was constructed after the organization became prosperous and nationally influential. Its name recalls the Christian origins of the organization and the religious character of many of its activities still. *(Brown Brothers)*

munities in the space of one year at the peak of their popularity.

From 1904 through the mid-1920s, these "traveling Chautauquas" attracted enormous crowds and generated great excitement almost everywhere they went. For rural men and women in particular, the Chautauquas were both sources of knowledge and great entertainments. A Chautauqua was often the

Populists tended to be not only economically but also culturally marginal. The movement appealed above all to geographically isolated farmers who felt cut off from the mainstream of national life and resented their isolation. Populism gave such people an outlet for their grievances; it also provided them with a social experience, a sense of belonging to a community that they had previously lacked.

The Populists were also notable for the groups they failed to attract. There were energetic efforts to include labor within the coalition. Representatives of the Knights of Labor attended early organizational meetings; the new party added a labor plank to its platform—calling for shorter hours for workers and restrictions on immigration, and denouncing the use of private detective agencies as strikebreakers in labor disputes. On the whole, however, Populism never attracted significant labor support, in part because the economic interests of labor and the interests of farmers were often at odds.

One exception was the Rocky Mountain states, where the Populists did have some significant success in attracting miners to their cause. They did so partly because local Populist leaders supported a broader platform than the national party embraced. In particular, they endorsed a demand "Free Silver" that the national party only later accepted: "free silver," the idea of permitting silver to become, along with gold, the basis of the currency so as to expand the money supply. In Colorado, Idaho, Nevada, and other areas of the Far West, silver mining was an important activity, and the People's Party enjoyed substantial, if temporary, success there.

In the South, white Populists struggled with the question of whether to accept African Americans into the party. Their numbers and poverty made black farmers possibly valuable allies. There was an important black component to the movement—a network of "Colored Alliances" that by 1890 had more than one and a quarter million members. But most white Populists were willing to accept the "Colored Alliances" assistance of African Americans only as long as it was clear that whites would remain indisputably in control. When southern conservatives began to attack the Populists for undermining white supremacy, the interracial character of the movement quickly faded.

BRYAN AT CHAUTAUQUA William Jennings Bryan, the most famous orator of the early twentieth century, was a fixture at Chautauqua meetings, not only at the original Chautauqua in New York, depicted here, but also in the traveling and tented Chautauquas that spread across the country. *(Brown Brothers)*

only large popular amusement to visit a community in the course of a year. On the day of a Chautauqua lecture, roads were sometimes clogged for miles in every direction with buggies and, later, automobiles transporting farm families dressed in their best clothes, carrying picnic baskets, straining excitedly to see the tents and the posters and the crowds in the distance.

Chautauqua speakers were drawn from many walks of life, but they included some of the greatest figures of the age: William Jennings Bryan, William McKinley, Theodore Roosevelt, Booker T. Washington, Eugene V. Debs, and many others. The Chautauquas themselves also made some speakers rich and famous. The Philadelphia minister Russell Conwell, for example, made a great name (and a great fortune) with his famous lecture "Acres of Diamonds," which he gave thousands of times over the course of several decades, preaching a simple and attractive message: "Get rich . . . for money is power and power ought to be in the hands of good people." Conwell's sermon was characteristic of one kind of popular Chautauqua event: lectures that stressed self-improvement. But equally popular were discussions of religion, health, current public issues, and politics. The Chautauqua circuit was one of the best ways for a speaker to reach large numbers of people and spread a message, which was one reason that so many progressive leaders and feminist reformers were eager to join it. It was, for a time, one of the nation's most powerful forms of national communication, and one of its most self-consciously serious. Its connections with the earnest lakefront "university" in New York pushed the Chautauqua circuit to keep its programs rooted in the original Assembly's desire for education and enlightenment, and not just entertainment. It reflected the hunger for knowledge and uplift that had resurfaced repeatedly throughout American history. Theodore Roosevelt once called the Chautauqua movement "the most American thing in America."

The traveling Chautauquas declined during the 1920s and vanished altogether in the 1930s—victims of radio, movies, and the automobile; of the spread of public education into rural areas; and of the reckless overexpansion of the enterprise by ambitious organizers. But the original Chautauqua Assembly in upstate New York survived, although in much-diminished form, and exists today as a resort—which continues to offer lectures and other educational events to its small but dedicated clientele.

Most of the Populist leaders were members of the rural middle class: professional people, editors and lawyers, or longtime politicians and agitators. Many active Populists were women. Some Populist leaders were somber, serious theoreticians; others were semihysterical rabble-rousers. In the South, in particular, Populism produced the first generation of what was to become a distinctive and enduring political breed—the "southern demagogue." Tom Watson in Georgia, Jeff Davis in Arkansas, and others attracted widespread popular support by arousing the resentment of poor southerners against the entrenched planter aristocracy.

Populist Ideas

The reform program of the Populists was spelled out first in the Ocala Demands of 1890 and then, even more clearly, in the Omaha platform of 1892. It proposed a system of "subtreasuries," which would replace and strengthen the cooperatives of Grangers and Alliances had been experimenting for years. The government would establish a network

Populist Platform

of warehouses, where farmers could deposit their crops. Using those crops as collateral, growers could then borrow money from the government at low rates of interest and wait for the price of their goods to go up before selling them. In addition, the Populists called for the abolition of national banks, the end of absentee ownership of land, the direct election of United States senators (which would weaken the power of conservative state legislatures), and other devices to improve the ability of the people to influence the political process. They called as well for regulation and (after 1892) government ownership of railroads, telephones, and telegraphs. And they demanded a system of government-operated postal savings banks, a graduated income tax, and the inflation of the currency. Eventually, the party as a whole embraced the demand of its western members for the remonetization of silver.

Some Populists were openly anti-Semitic, pointing to the Jews as leaders of the obscure financial forces attempting to enslave them. Others were anti-intellectual, anti-eastern, and anti-urban. A few of the leading Populists gave an impression of personal failure, brilliant instability, and brooding communion with mystic forces. Ignatius

THE CULT OF BRYAN After his famous "Cross of Gold" speech at the 1896 Democratic convention, Bryan became a figure of almost cultish importance to his many followers. This campaign poster presents icons of Bryan's sudden fame: the text of his convention speech, pictures of his young family, and "16 to 1," the slogan of the free-silver movement that Bryan now led. The slogan "16 to 1" represented Bryan's and the Populists' demand for making silver a basis for currency, with silver valued at one-sixteenth the value of gold.

Donnelly, for example, wrote one book locating the lost isle of Atlantis, another claiming that Bacon had written Shakespeare's plays, and still another—*Caesar's Column* (1891)—presenting a deranged vision of bloody revolution and the creation of a populist utopia. Tom Watson, once a champion of interracial harmony, ended his career baiting blacks and Jews.

Yet the occasional bigotry of some Populists should not dominate the image of Populism as a whole, which was a serious and usually responsible effort to find solutions to real problems. Populists emphatically rejected the laissez-faire orthodoxies of their time, including the idea that the rights of ownership are absolute. They raised one of the most overt and powerful chal-

Populism's Ideological Challenge

lenges of the era to the direction in which American industrial capitalism was moving.

THE CRISIS OF THE 1890s

The agrarian protest was only one of many indications of the national political crisis emerging in the 1890s. There was a severe depression, widespread labor unrest and violence, and the continuing failure of either major party to respond to the growing distress. The rigid conservatism of Grover Cleveland, who took office for the second time just at the moment that the economy collapsed, meant that the federal government did little to alleviate the crisis. Out of this growing sense of urgency came some of the most heated political battles in American history, culminating in the dramatic campaign of 1896, on which, many Americans came to believe, the future of the nation hung.

The Panic of 1893

The Panic of 1893 precipitated the most severe depression the nation had yet experienced. It began in March 1893, when the Philadelphia and Reading Railroad, unable to meet payments on loans, declared bankruptcy. Two months later, the National Cordage Company failed as well. Together, the two corporate failures triggered a collapse of the stock market. And since many of the major New York banks were heavy investors in the market, a wave of bank failures soon began. That caused a contraction of credit, which meant that many of the new, aggressive, and loan-dependent businesses soon went bankrupt.

There were other, longer-range causes of the financial collapse. Depressed prices in agriculture since 1887 had weakened the purchasing power of farmers, the largest group in the population.

Overexpansion and Weak Demand

Depression conditions in Europe caused a loss of American markets abroad and a withdrawal by foreign investors of gold invested in the United States. Railroads and other major industries had expanded too rapidly, well beyond market demand. The depression reflected the degree to which the American economy was now interconnected, the degree to which failures in one area affected all other areas. And the depression showed how dependent the economy was on the health of the railroads, which remained the nation's most powerful corporate and financial institutions. When the railroads suffered, as they did beginning in 1893, everything suffered.

Once the panic began, its effects spread with startling speed. Within six months, more than 8,000 businesses, 156 railroads, and 400 banks failed. Already low agricultural prices tumbled further. Up to 1 million workers,

TAKING ARMS AGAINST THE POPULISTS Kansas was a Populist stronghold in the 1890s, but the new party faced powerful challenges. In 1893, state Republicans disputed an election that the Populists believed had given them control of the legislature. When the Populists occupied the statehouse, Republicans armed themselves, drove out the Populists, and seized control of the state government. Republican members of the legislature pose here with their weapons in a photograph perhaps intended as a warning to any Populists inclined to challenge them. *(Kansas State Historical Society)*

20 percent of the labor force, lost their jobs—the highest level of unemployment in American history to that point. The depression was unprecedented not only in its severity but also in its persistence. Although there was slight improvement beginning in 1895, prosperity did not fully return until 1901.

The suffering the depression caused naturally produced social unrest, especially among the enormous numbers of unemployed workers. In 1894, Jacob S. Coxey, an Ohio businessman and Populist, began advocating a massive public works program to create jobs for the unemployed and an inflation of the currency. When it became clear that his proposals were making no progress in Congress, Coxey announced that he would "send a petition to Washington with boots on"—a march of the unemployed to the capital to present their demands to the government. "Coxey's Army," as it was known, numbered only about 500 when it reached Washington, after having marched on foot from Masillon, Ohio. Armed police barred them from the Capitol and arrested Coxey. He and his followers were herded into camps because their presence supposedly endangered public health. Congress took no action on their demands.

To many middle-class Americans, the labor turmoil of the time—the Homestead and Pullman strikes, for exam-

"Coxey's Army"

ple (see pp. 492-493)—was a sign of a dangerous instability, even perhaps a revolution. Labor radicalism—some of it real, more of it imagined by the frightened middle class, heightened the general sense of crisis among the public.

The Silver Question

The financial panic weakened the government's monetary system. President Cleveland believed that the instability of the currency was the primary cause of the depression. The "money question," therefore, became the basis for some of the most dramatic political conflicts of the era.

At the heart of the complicated debate was the question of what would form the basis of the dollar. Today, the value of the dollar rests on little more than public confidence in the government. But in the nineteenth century, many people believed that currency was worthless if there was not something concrete behind it—precious metal (specie), which holders of paper money could collect if they presented their currency to a bank or to the Treasury.

During most of its existence as a nation, the United States had recognized two metals—gold and silver—as a basis for the dollar, a situation known as "bimetallism." In the 1870s, however, that had changed. The official ratio of the value of silver to the value of gold for purposes of

POPULISM

American history offers few examples of successful popular movements operating outside the two major parties. Perhaps that is why Populism, which in its brief, meteoric life became one of the few such phenomena to gain real national influence, has attracted particular attention from historians. It has also produced deep disagreements among them. Scholars have differed in many ways in their interpretations of Populism, but at the heart of most such disagreements have been disparate views of the value of popular, insurgent politics. Some historians have harbored a basic mistrust of such mass uprisings and have therefore viewed the Populists with suspicion and hostility. Others have viewed such

(Kansas State Historical Society)

insurgency approvingly, as evidence of a healthy resistance to oppression and exploitation; and to them, the Populists have appeared as essentially admirable, democratic activists.

This latter view was the basis of the first, and for many years the only, general history of Populism: John D. Hicks's *The Populist Revolt* (1931). Rejecting the then-prevailing view of the Populists as misguided and unruly radicals, Hicks described them as people reacting rationally and progressively to economic misfortune. Hicks was writing in an era in which the ideas of Frederick Jackson Turner were dominating historical studies, and he brought to his analysis of Populism a strong emphasis on regionalism. Populists, he argued, were part of the democratic West, resisting pressures from the more aristocratic East. (He explained southern Populism by describing the South as an "economic frontier" region—not newly settled like the West, but prey to many of the same pressures and misfortunes.) The Populists, Hicks suggested, were aware of the harsh, even brutal, impact of eastern industrial growth on rural society. They were proposing reforms that would limit the oppressive power of the new financial titans and restore a measure of control to the farmers. Populism was, he wrote, "the last phase of a long and perhaps a losing struggle—the struggle to save

agricultural America from the devouring jaws of industrial America." A losing struggle, perhaps, but not a vain one; for many of the reforms the Populists advocated, Hicks implied, became the basis of later progressive legislation.

This generally approving view of Populism prevailed among historians for more than two decades, amplified in particular by C. Vann Woodward, whose *Origins of the New South* (1951) and *The Strange Career of Jim Crow* (1955) portrayed southern Populism as a challenge to the stifling power of old elites and even, at times, to at least some elements of white supremacy. But Woodward was not typical of most scholars viewing Populism in the early 1950s. For others, the memory of European fascism and uneasiness about contemporary communism combined to create a general hostility toward mass popular politics; and a harsh new view of the Populist movement appeared in a work by one of the nation's leading historians. Richard Hofstadter, in *The Age of Reform* (1955), admitted that Populism embraced some progressive ideas and advocated some sensible reforms. But the bulk of his effort was devoted to exposing both the "soft" and the "dark" sides of the movement.

Populism was "soft," Hofstadter claimed, because it rested on a nostalgic and unrealistic myth, because it romanticized the nation's agrarian

---

creating currency (the "mint ratio") was 16 to 1: sixteen ounces of silver equaled one ounce of gold. But the actual commercial value of silver (the "market ratio") was much higher than that. Owners of silver could get more by selling it for manufacture into jewelry and other objects than they could by taking it to the mint for conversion to coins. So they stopped taking it to the mint, and the mint stopped coining silver.

In 1873, Congress passed a law that seemed simply to recognize the existing situation by officially discontinuing silver coinage. Few people objected at the time. But in the course of the 1870s, the market value of silver fell well below the official mint ratio of 16 to 1. (Sixteen ounces of silver, in other words, were now worth less, not more, than one ounce of gold.) Silver was available for coinage again. Congress had thus foreclosed a potential method of

expanding the currency and had eliminated a potential market for silver miners. Before long, many Americans concluded that a conspiracy of big bankers had been responsible for the "demonetization" of silver and referred to the law as the "Crime of '73."

Two groups of Americans were especially determined to undo the "Crime of '73." One consisted of the silvermine owners, now understandably eager to have the government take their surplus silver and pay them much more than the market price. The other group consisted of discontented farmers, who wanted an increase in the quantity of money—an inflation of the currency—as a means of raising the prices of farm products and easing payment of the farmers' debts. The inflationists demanded that the government return at once to "free silver"—that is, to the

"Crime of '73"

past and refused to confront the realities of modern life. Farmers, he argued, were themselves fully committed to the values of the capitalist system they claimed to abhor. And Populism was "dark," he argued, because it was permeated with bigotry and ignorance. Populists, he claimed, revealed anti-Semitic tendencies, and they displayed animosity toward intellectuals, easterners, and urbanites as well.

Almost immediately, historians more favorably disposed toward mass politics in general, and Populism in particular, began to challenge what became known as the "Hofstadter thesis." Norman Pollack argued in a 1962 study, *The Populist Response to Industrial America,* and in a number of articles that the agrarian revolt had rested not on nostalgic, romantic concepts but on a sophisticated, far-sighted, and even radical vision of reform—one that recognized, and even welcomed, the realities of an industrial economy, but that sought to make that economy more equitable and democratic by challenging many of the premises of capitalism. Walter T. K. Nugent, in *Tolerant Populists* (1963), argued that the Populists in Kansas were far from bigoted, that they not only tolerated but welcomed Jews and other minorities into their party, and that they offered a practical, sensible program.

Lawrence Goodwyn, in *Democratic Promise* (1976), described the Populists as members of a "cooperative crusade," battling against the "coercive potential of the emerging corporate state." Populists were more than the nostalgic bigots Hofstadter described, more even than the progressive reformers portrayed by Hicks. They offered a vision of truly radical change, widely disseminated through what Goodwyn called a "movement culture." They advocated an intelligent, and above all a democratic, alternative to the inequities of modern capitalism.

At the same time that historians were debating the question of what Populism meant, they were also arguing over who the Populists were. Hicks, Hofstadter, and Goodwyn disagreed on many things, but they shared a general view of the Populists as victims of economic distress— usually one-crop farmers in economically marginal agricultural regions victimized by drought and debt. Other scholars, however, suggested that the problem of identifying the Populists is more complex. Sheldon Hackney, in *Populism to Progressivism in Alabama* (1969), argued that the Populists were not only economically troubled but also socially rootless, "only tenuously connected to society by economic function, by personal relationships, by stable community membership, by political participation, or by psychological identification with the South's distinctive myths."

Peter Argersinger, Stanley Parsons, James Turner, and others have similarly suggested that Populists were characterized by a form of social and even geographical isolation. Steven Hahn's 1983 study *The Roots of Southern Populism* identified poor white farmers in the "upcountry" as the core of Populist activity in Georgia; and he argued that they were reacting not simply to the psychic distress of being "left behind," but also to a real economic threat to their way of life—to the encroachments of a new commercial order of which they had never been and could never be a part.

Finally, there has been a continuing debate over the legacy of Populism. In *Roots of Reform* (1999), Elizabeth Sanders refutes the notion that Populism died as a movement after the 1896 election. On the contrary, she argues, the Populists succeeded in dominating much of the Democratic Party in the following decades and turning it into a vehicle for advancing the interests of farmers and the broader reform causes for which Populists had fought.

Michael Kazin, in *The Populist Persuasion* (1994), is one of a number of scholars who have argued that a Populist tradition has survived throughout much of American history, and into our own time, influencing movements as disparate as those led by Huey Long in the 1930s, both the New Left and George Wallace in the 1960s, and Ross Perot in the 1990s. Others have maintained that the term "populism" has been used (and misused) so widely as to have become virtually meaningless, that its only real value is in reference to the agrarian insurgents of the 1890s, who first gave meaning to the word in America.

"free and unlimited coinage of silver" at the old ratio of 16 to 1. But by the time the depression began in 1893, Congress had made no more than a token response to their demands.

At the same time, the nation's gold reserves were steadily dropping. President Cleveland believed that the chief cause of the weakening gold reserves was the Sherman Silver Purchase Act of 1890, which had required the government to purchase (but not to coin) silver and to pay for it in gold. Early in his second administration, therefore, a special session responded to his request and repealed the Sherman Act—although only after a bitter and divisive battle that helped create a permanent split in the Democratic Party. The president's gold policy had aligned the southern and western Democrats in a solid alliance against him and his eastern followers.

By now, both sides had invested the currency question with great symbolic and emotional importance. Indeed, the issue aroused passions rarely seen in American politics, culminating in the tumultuous presidential election of 1896. Supporters of the gold standard considered its survival essential to the honor and stability of the nation. Supporters of free silver considered the gold standard an instrument of tyranny. "Free silver" became to them a symbol of liberation. Silver would be a "people's money," as opposed to gold, the money of oppression and exploitation. It would eliminate the indebtedness of farmers and of whole regions of the country. A graphic illustration of the popularity of the silver issue was the enormous success of William H. Harvey's *Coin's Financial School,* published in 1894, which

> Symbolic Importance of the Currency Question

COXEY'S ARMY Jacob S. Coxey leads his "army" of unemployed men through the town of Allegheny, Pennsylvania, in 1894, en route to Washington, where he hoped to pressure Congress to approve his plans for a massive public works program to put people back to work. *(Culver Pictures, Inc.)*

became one of the great best-sellers of its age. The fictional Professor Coin ran an imaginary school specializing in finance, and the book consisted of his lectures and his dialogues with his students. The professor's brilliant discourses left even his most vehement opponents dazzled as he persuaded his listeners, with simple logic, of the almost miraculous restorative qualities of free silver: "It means the reopening of closed factories, the relighting of fires in darkened furnaces; it means hope instead of despair; comfort in place of suffering; life instead of death."

"A CROSS OF GOLD"

Most Populists did not pay much attention to the silver issue at first. But as the party developed strength, the money question became more important to its leaders. The Populists desperately needed funds to finance their campaigns. Silver-mine owners were willing to provide assistance but insisted on an elevation of the currency plank. The Populists also needed to form alliances with other political groups. The "money question" seemed a way to win the support of many people not engaged in farming but nevertheless starved for currency.

The Emergence of Bryan

As the election of 1896 approached, Republicans, watching the failure of the Democrats to deal effectively with the depression, were confident of success. Party leaders, led by the Ohio boss Marcus A. Hanna, settled on Governor William McKinley of Ohio, who had as a member of Congress authored the 1890 tariff act, as the party's presidential candidate. The Republican platform opposed the free coinage of silver except by agreement with the leading commercial nations (which everyone realized was unlikely). Thirty-four delegates from the mountain and plains states walked out of the convention in protest and joined the Democratic Party.

William McKinley

The Democratic convention of 1896 was the scene of unusual drama. Southern and western delegates, eager to neutralize the challenge of the People's Party, were determined to seize control of the party from conservative easterners and incorporate some Populist demands—among them free silver—into the Democratic platform. They wanted as well to nominate a pro-silver candidate.

Defenders of the gold standard seemed to dominate the debate, until the final speech. Then William Jennings Bryan, a handsome, thirty-six-year-old congressman from

BRYAN WHISTLE-STOPPING By long-established tradition, candidates for the presidency did not actively campaign after receiving their party's nomination. Nineteenth-century Americans considered public "stumping" to be undignified and inappropriate for a future president. But in 1896, William Jennings Bryan—a young candidate little known outside his own region, a man without broad support even among the leaders of his own party—decided that he had no choice but to go directly to the public for support. He traveled widely and incessantly in the months before the election, appearing before hundreds of crowds and hundreds of thousands of people. *(Library of Congress)*

"Cross of Gold" Speech   Nebraska already well known as an effective orator, mounted the podium to address the convention. His great voice echoed through the hall as he delivered what became one of the most famous political speeches in American history in support of free silver. The closing passage sent his audience into something close to a frenzy: "Having behind us the producing masses of this nation and the world, supported by the commercial interests, the laboring interests and the toilers everywhere, we will answer their demand for a gold standard by saying to them: 'You shall not press down upon the brow of labor this crown of thorns; you shall not crucify mankind upon a cross of gold.'" It became known as the "Cross of Gold" speech.

The convention voted to adopt a pro-silver platform. And the following day, Bryan (as he had eagerly and not entirely secretly hoped) was nominated for president on the fifth ballot. He was, and remains, the youngest person ever nominated for president by a major party. Republican and conservative Democrats attacked Bryan as a dangerous demagogue. But his many admirers hailed him as the Great Commoner. He was a potent symbol of rural, Protestant, middle-class America.

The choice of Bryan and the nature of the Democratic platform created a quandary for the Populists. They had expected both major parties to adopt conservative programs   "Fusion" and nominate conservative candidates, leaving the Populists to represent the growing forces of protest. But now the Democrats had stolen much of their thunder. The Populists faced the choice of naming their own candidate and splitting the protest vote or endorsing Bryan and losing their identity as a party. By now, the Populists had embraced the free-silver cause, but most Populists still believed that other issues were more important. Many argued that "fusion" with the Democrats—who had endorsed free silver but ignored most of the other Populist demands—would destroy their party. But the majority concluded that there was no viable alternative. Amid considerable acrimony, the convention voted to support Bryan.

Candidate (Party)	Electoral Vote	Popular Vote (%)
William McKinley (Republican)	271	7,104,779 (51.1)
William Jennings Bryan (Democratic)	176	6,502,925 (47.7)

ELECTION OF 1896 The results of the presidential election of 1896 are, as this map shows, striking for the regional differentiation they reveal. William McKinley won the election by a comfortable but not enormous margin, but his victory was not broad-based. He carried all the states of the Northeast and the industrial Midwest, along with California and Oregon, but virtually nothing else. Bryan carried the entire South and almost all of the agrarian West. ◆ *What campaign issues in 1896 help account for the regional character of the results?*

For an interactive version of this map, go to www.mhhe.com/brinkley13ech19maps

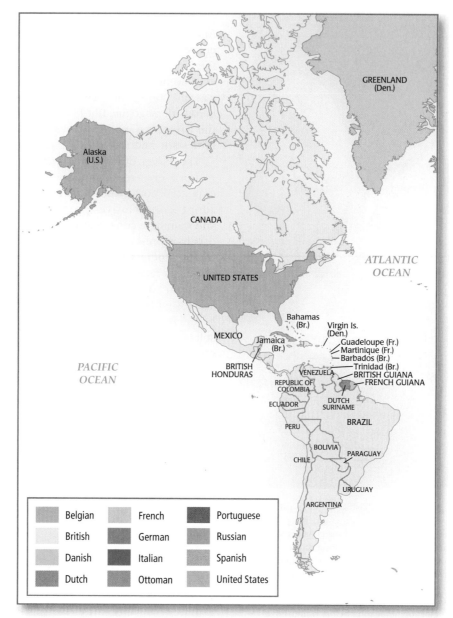

IMPERIALISM AT HIGH TIDE: 1900 The United States became a formal imperial power in 1898, when it acquired colonies in the aftermath of the Spanish-American War. But the U.S. was a decided latecomer to imperialism. During the nineteenth century, European nations dramatically expanded the reach of their empires, moving in particular into Africa and Asia. Although the British remained the world's largest imperial power by a significant margin, vast areas of the globe came under the control of other European colonizers, as this map shows. ◆ *How did the United States and the European imperial nations justify their acquisition of empire?*

The Conservative Victory

The campaign of 1896 produced desperation among conservatives. The business and financial community, frightened beyond reason at the prospect of a Bryan victory, contributed lavishly to the Republican campaign, which may have spent as much as $7 million, as compared to the Democrats' $300,000. From his home at Canton, Ohio, McKinley hewed to the tradition by which candidates for president did not actively campaign for the office. He conducted a dignified "front-porch" campaign by receiving pilgrimages of the Republican faithful, organized and paid for by Hanna.

Bryan showed no such restraint. He became the first presidential candidate in American history to stump every section of the country systematically, to appear in villages and hamlets, indeed the first to say frankly to the voters that he wanted to be president. He traveled 18,000 miles and addressed an estimated 5 million people. But Bryan may have done himself more harm than good. By violating a longstanding tradition of presidential candidates' remaining aloof from their own campaigns (the tradition by which they "stood" for office rather than "running" for it), Bryan helped establish the

> Birth of Modern Campaigning

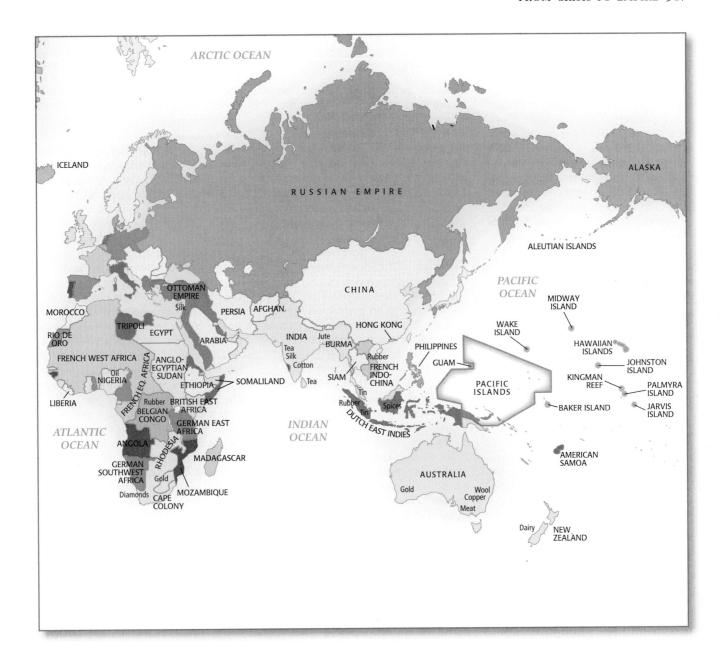

modern form of presidential politics. But he also antagonized many voters, who considered his campaign undignified.

On election day, McKinley polled 271 electoral votes to Bryan's 176 and received 51.1 percent of the popular vote to Bryan's 47.7. Bryan carried the areas of the South and West where miners or struggling staple farmers predominated. The Democratic program, like that of the Populists, had been too narrow to win a national election.

For the Populists and their allies, the election results were a disaster. They had gambled everything on their "fusion" with the Democratic Party and lost. Within months of the election, the People's Party began to dissolve. Never again would American farmers unite so militantly to demand economic reform.

End of the People's Party

McKinley and Recovery

The administration of William McKinley, which began in the aftermath of turmoil, saw a return to relative calm. One reason was the exhaustion of dissent. By 1897, when McKinley took office, the labor unrest that had so frightened many middle-class Americans and so excited working-class people had subsided. With the simultaneous decline of agrarian protest, the greatest destabilizing forces in the nation's politics were—temporarily at least—in retreat. Another reason was the shrewd character of the McKinley administration itself, committed as it was to reassuring stability. Most important, however, was the gradual easing of the economic crisis, a development that undercut many of those who were agitating for change.

IMPERIALISM

Empires were not, of course, new to the nineteenth century, when the United States acquired its first overseas colonies. They have existed since the early moments of recorded history—in Greece, Rome, China, and many other parts of the world—and continued into the sixteenth and seventeenth centuries with vast imperial projects undertaken by Spain, Portugal, France, the Netherlands, and Great Britain in the Americas.

But in the mid- and late nineteenth century, the construction of empires took on a new and different form from those of earlier eras, and the word "imperialism" emerged for the first time to describe it. In many places, European powers now created colonies not by sending large numbers of migrants to settle and populate new lands but, instead, by creating military, political, and business structures that allowed them to dominate and profit from the existing populations. This new imperialism changed the character of the imperial nations themselves, enriching them greatly and producing new classes of people whose lives were shaped by the demands of imperial business and administration. It changed the character of colonized societies even more, by drawing them into the vast nexus of global industrial capitalism and by introducing European customs, institutions, and technologies to the subject peoples.

As the popularity of empires grew in the West in the late nineteenth century, efforts to justify it grew as well. Champions of imperialism argued that the acquisition of colonies was essential for the health, even the survival, of their own industrializing nations. Colonies were sources of raw materials vital to industrial production, they were markets for manufactured goods, and they could be suppliers of cheap labor. But defenders of the idea of empire also argued that imperialism was good for the colonized people. Many saw colonization as an opportunity to export Christianity to "heathen" lands, and great new missionary movements emerged in Europe and America in response. Secular apologists argued that imperialism helped bring colonized people into the modern world. The British poet Rudyard Kipling was perhaps the most famous spokesman for empire. In his celebrated poem "The White Man's Burden," he spoke of the duty of the colonizers to lift up primitive peoples, to "fill full the mouth of famine and bid the sickness cease."

The growth of the idea of empire was not simply a result of need and desire. It was also a result of the new capacities of the imperial powers. The invention of steamships, railroads, telegraphs, and other modern vehicles of transportation and communication; the construction of canals (in particular the Suez Canal, completed in 1869, and the Panama Canal, completed in 1914); the birth of new military technologies (repeating rifles, machine guns, and modern artillery)—all contributed to the ability of Western nations to reach, conquer, and control distant lands.

The greatest imperial power of the nineteenth century, indeed one of the greatest imperial powers in all of human history, was Great Britain. By 1800, despite its recent loss of the colonies that became the United States, it already possessed vast territory in North America, the Caribbean, and the Pacific—most notably Canada and Australia. But in the second half of the nineteenth century, Britain greatly expanded its empire. Its most important acquisition was India, one of the largest and most populous countries in the world. Britain had carried on a substantial trade with India for many years and had gradually increased its economic and military power there. In 1857, when native Indians revolted against British authority, British forces brutally crushed the rebellion and established formal colonial control over the land. British officials, backed by substantial military power, now governed India through a large civil service staffed mostly by people from England and Scotland, but with some Indians serving in minor or symbolic

---

McKinley and his allies committed themselves fully to only one issue, one on which they knew virtually all Republicans agreed: the need for higher tariff rates. Within weeks of his inauguration, the administration won approval of the Dingley Tariff, raising duties to the highest point in American history. The administration dealt more gingerly with the explosive silver question (an issue that McKinley himself had never considered very important in any case). McKinley sent a commission to Europe to explore the possibility of a silver agreement with Great Britain and France. As he and everyone else anticipated, the effort produced no agreement. The Republicans then enacted the Currency, or Gold Standard, Act of 1900, which confirmed the nation's commitment to the gold standard by

Currency Act

assigning a specific gold value to the dollar and requiring all currency issued by the United States to hew to that value.

And so the "battle of the standards" ended in victory for the forces of conservatism. Economic developments at the time seemed to vindicate the Republicans. Prosperity began to return in 1898. Foreign crop failures sent farm prices surging upward, and American business entered another cycle of expansion. Prosperity and the gold standard, it seemed, were closely allied.

But while the free-silver movement had failed, it had raised an important question for the American economy. In the quarter-century before 1900, the countries of the Western world had experienced a spectacular growth in productive facilities and population. Yet the supply of money positions. The British invested heavily in railroads, telegraphs, canals, harbors, and agricultural improvements to enhance the economic opportunities available to them. They created schools for Indian children in an effort to draw them into British culture and make them supporters of the imperial system.

In those same years, the British extended their empire into Africa and other parts of Asia. The great imperial champion Cecil Rhodes expanded a small existing British colony at Cape Town into a substantial colony that included what is now South Africa. In 1895, he added new territories to the north, which he named Rhodesia (and which today are Zimbabwe and Zambia). Other imperialists spread British authority into Kenya, Uganda, Nigeria, and much of Egypt. British imperialists simultaneously extended the empire into east Asia, with the acquisition of Singapore, Hong Kong, Burma, and Malaya; and they built a substantial presence—although not formal colonial rule—in China.

Other European states, watching the vast expansion of the British empire, quickly jumped into the race for colonies. France created colonies in Indochina (Vietnam and Laos), Algeria, west Africa, and Madagascar. Belgium moved into the Congo in west Africa. Germany established colonies in the Cameroons, Tanganyika, and other parts of Africa, and in the Pacific islands north of Australia. Dutch, Italian, Portuguese, Spanish,

THE BRITISH RAJ The Drum Corps of the Royal Fusiliers in India poses here for a formal portrait, taken in 1877. Although the drummers are British, an Indian associate is included at top left. This blending of the dominant British with subordinate Indians was characteristic of the administration of the British Empire in India—a government known as the "raj," from the Indian word for "rule." *(Time Life Pictures/Getty Images)*

Russian, and Japanese imperialists created colonies as well in Africa, Asia, and the Pacific—driven both by a calculation of their own commercial interests and by the frenzied competition that had developed among rival imperial powers. And in 1898, the United States was drawn into the imperial race. Americans entered it in part inadvertently, as an unanticipated result of the Spanish-American War. But they also sought colonies as a result of the deliberate efforts of homegrown proponents of empire (among them Theodore Roosevelt), many of them heavily influenced by British friends and colleagues, who believed that in the modern industrial-imperial world a nation without colonies would have difficulty remaining, or becoming, a true great power.

had not kept pace with economic progress, because the supply was tied to gold and the amount of gold had remained practically constant. Had it not been for a dramatic increase in the gold supply in the late 1890s (a result of new techniques for extracting gold from low-content ores and the discovery of huge new gold deposits in Alaska, South Africa, and Australia), Populist predictions of financial disaster might in fact have proved correct. In 1898, two and a half times as much gold was produced as in 1890, and the currency supply was soon inflated far beyond anything Bryan and the free-silver forces had anticipated.

By then, however, Bryan—like many other Americans—was becoming engaged with another major issue: a growing United States presence in world affairs and the possibility of America becoming an imperialist nation.

STIRRINGS OF IMPERIALISM

For over two decades after the Civil War, the United States expanded hardly at all. By the 1890s, however, some Americans were ready—indeed, eager—to resume the course of Manifest Destiny that had inspired their ancestors to wrest an empire from Mexico in the expansionist 1840s.

The New Manifest Destiny

Several developments helped shift American attention to lands across the seas. The experience of subjugating the Indian tribes had established a precedent for exerting colonial control over dependent peoples. The concept of the "closing of the frontier," widely heralded by Frederick

Jackson Turner and many others in the 1890s, produced fears that natural resources would soon dwindle and that alternative sources must be found abroad. The depression of the 1890s encouraged some businessmen to look overseas for new markets. The bitter social protests of the time—the Populist movement, the free-silver crusade, the bloody labor disputes—led some politicians to urge a more aggressive foreign policy as an outlet for frustrations that would otherwise destabilize domestic life.

Foreign trade became increasingly important to the American economy in the late nineteenth century. The nation's exports had totaled about $392 million in 1870; by 1890, the figure was $857 million; and by 1900,
Increasing Importance of Trade
$1.4 billion. Many Americans began to consider the possibility of acquiring colonies that might expand such markets further.

Americans were well aware of the imperialist fever that was raging through Europe and leading the major powers to partition most of Africa among themselves and to turn eager eyes on the Far East and the feeble Chinese Empire. Some Americans feared that their nation would soon be left out, that no territory would remain to be acquired. Senator Henry Cabot Lodge of Massachusetts, a leading imperialist, warned that the United States "must not fall out of the line of march." The same distortion of Darwinism that industrialists and others had long been applying to domestic economic affairs in the form of Social Darwinism was now applied to world affairs. Many writers and public figures contended that nations or "races," like biological species, struggled constantly for existence and that only the fittest could survive. For strong nations to dominate weak ones was, therefore, in accordance with the laws of nature.

The popular writer John Fiske predicted in an 1885 article in *Harper's Magazine* that the English-speaking peoples would eventually control every land that was not already the seat of an "established civilization." The experience of white Americans in subjugating the native population of their own continent, Fiske argued, was "destined to go on" in other parts of the world.

John W. Burgess, founder of Columbia University's School of Political Science, gave a stamp of scholarly
Intellectual Justifications for Imperialism
approval to imperialism. In his 1890 study *Political Science and Comparative Law*, he flatly stated that the Anglo-Saxon and Teutonic nations possessed the highest political talents. It was their duty, therefore, to uplift less fortunate peoples, even to force superior institutions on them if necessary. "There is," he wrote, "no human right to the status of barbarism."

The ablest and most effective apostle of imperialism was Alfred Thayer Mahan, a captain and later admiral in the United States Navy. Mahan's thesis, presented in *The*
Alfred Thayer Mahan
Influence of Sea Power upon History (1890) and other works,

was simple: Countries with sea power were the great nations of history; the greatness of the United States, bounded by two oceans, would rest on its naval strength. The prerequisites for sea power were a productive domestic economy, foreign commerce, a strong merchant marine, a navy to defend trade routes—and colonies, which would provide raw materials and markets and could serve as naval bases. Mahan advocated that the United States construct a canal across the isthmus of Central America to join the oceans, acquire defensive bases on both sides of the canal in the Caribbean and the Pacific, and take possession of Hawaii and other Pacific islands.

Mahan feared the United States did not have a large enough navy to play the great role he envisioned. But during the 1870s and 1880s, the government launched a shipbuilding program that by 1898 had moved the United States to fifth place among the world's naval powers, and by 1900 to third.

Hemispheric Hegemony

James G. Blaine, who served as secretary of state in two Republican administrations in the 1880s, led early efforts to expand American influence into Latin America, where, he believed, the United States must look for markets for its surplus goods. In October 1889, Blaine helped organize the first Pan-American Congress, which attracted delegates from nineteen nations. The delegates agreed to create the Pan-American Union, a weak international organization located in Washington that served as a clearinghouse of information to the member nations. But they rejected Blaine's more substantive proposals: for an inter-American customs union and arbitration procedures for hemispheric disputes.

The Cleveland administration took a similarly active interest in Latin America. In 1895, it supported Venezuela in a dispute with Great Britain.
When the British ignored American demands that the matter be submitted to arbitration,
Venezuelan Dispute
Secretary of State Richard Olney charged that Britain was violating the Monroe Doctrine. Cleveland then created a special commission to settle the dispute: if Britain resisted the commission's decision, he insisted, the United States should be willing to go to war to enforce it. As war talk raged throughout the country, the British government prudently agreed to arbitration.

Hawaii and Samoa

The islands of Hawaii in the mid-Pacific had been an important way station for American ships in the China trade since the early nineteenth century. By the 1880s, officers of the expanding American navy were looking covetously at Pearl Harbor on the island of Oahu as a possible permanent base for United States ships. Pressure for an increased American presence in Hawaii was emerging from another source as well: the growing number of

Americans who had settled on the islands and who had gradually come to dominate their economic and political life.

In doing so, the Americans had been wresting authority away from the leaders of an ancient civilization. Settled by Polynesian people beginning in about 1500 B.C., Hawaii had developed an agricultural and fishing society in which different islands (and different communities on the same islands), each with its own chieftain, lived more or less self-sufficiently. When the first Americans arrived in Hawaii in the 1790s on merchant ships from New England, there were perhaps a half-million people living there. Battles among rival communities were frequent, as ambitious chieftains tried to consolidate power over their neighbors. In 1810, after a series of such battles, King Kamehameha I established his dominance, welcomed American traders, and helped them develop a thriving trade between Hawaii and China, from which the natives profited along with the merchants. But Americans soon wanted more than trade. Missionaries began settling there in the early nineteenth century; and in the 1830s, William Hooper, a Boston trader, became the first of many Americans to buy land and establish a sugar plantation on the islands.

The arrival of these merchants, missionaries, and planters was devastating to Hawaiian society. The newcomers inadvertently brought infectious diseases to which the Hawaiians, like the American Indians before them, were

Self-Sufficient Societies

tragically vulnerable. By the mid-nineteenth century, more than half the native population had died. By 1900, disease had more than halved the population again. But the Americans brought other incursions as well. Missionaries worked to undermine native religion. Other white settlers introduced liquor, firearms, and a commercial economy, all of which eroded the traditional character of Hawaiian society. By the 1840s, American planters had spread throughout the islands; and an American settler, G. P. Judd, had become prime minister of Hawaii under King Kamehameha III, who had agreed to establish a constitutional monarchy. Judd governed Hawaii for over a decade.

In 1887, the United States negotiated a treaty with Hawaii that permitted it to open a naval base at Pearl Harbor. By then, growing sugar for export to America had become the basis of the Hawaiian economy—as a result of an 1875 agreement allowing Hawaiian sugar to enter the United States duty-free. The American-dominated sugar plantation system not only displaced native Hawaiians from their lands but also sought to build a work force with Asian immigrants, whom the Americans considered more reliable and more docile than the natives. Indeed, finding adequate labor and keeping it under control were the principal concerns of many planters. Some planters deliberately sought to create a mixed-race work force (Chinese, Japanese, native Hawaiian, Filipinos, Portuguese, and others) as a way to keep the workers divided and unlikely to challenge them.

HAWAIIAN SUGARCANE PLANTATION The sugarcane plantations of nineteenth-century Hawaii (like the sugar plantations of Barbados in the seventeenth and eighteenth centuries) required a vast labor force that the island's native population could not provide. The mostly American owners of the plantations imported over 300,000 Asian workers from China, Japan, and Korea to work in the fields between 1850 and 1920. The work was arduous, as the words of a song by Japanese sugar workers suggests: "Hawaii, Hawaii, But when I came what I saw was Hell. The boss was Satan, The lunas [overseers] his helpers." *(Hawaii State Archives)*

YELLOW JOURNALISM

Joseph Pulitzer was a Hungarian immigrant, a Civil War veteran, and a successful newspaper publisher in St. Louis, Missouri, when he traveled to New York City in 1883 to buy a struggling paper, the *World*. "There is room in this great and growing city," he wrote in one of his first editorials, "for a journal that is not only cheap, but bright, not only bright but large, not only large but truly democratic . . . that will serve and battle for the people with earnest sincerity." Within a year, the *World*'s daily circulation had soared from 10,000 to over 60,000. By 1886, it had reached 250,000 and was making enormous profits.

The success of Pulitzer's *World* marked the birth of what came to be known as "yellow journalism," a phrase that reportedly derived from a character in one of the *World*'s comic strips: "the Yellow Kid." Color printing in newspapers was relatively new, and yellow was the most difficult color to print; so in the beginning, the term "yellow journalism" was probably a comment on the new technological possibilities that Pulitzer was so eagerly embracing. Eventually, however, it came to mean something else. It referred to a sensationalist style of reporting and writing, and a self-conscious effort to reach a mass market, that spread quickly through urban America and changed the character of newspapers forever.

Sensationalism was not new to journalism in the late nineteenth century, of course. Political scandal sheets had been publishing lurid stories since before the American Revolution, and the penny press that had emerged in the 1820s and 1830s (see pp. 258–259) incorporated scandal, crime, and intrigue into mainstream journals. But the yellow journalism of the 1880s and 1890s took the search for a mass audience to new levels. The *World* created one of the first Sunday editions, with lavishly colored special sections, comics, and illustrated features. It expanded coverage of sports, fashion, literature, and theater. It pioneered large, glaring, overheated headlines that captured the eyes of people who were passing newsstands. It published exposés of political corruption. It made considerable efforts to bring drama and energy to its coverage of crime. It tried to involve readers directly in its stories (as when a *World* campaign helped raise $300,000 to build a base for the Statue of Liberty, with much of the money coming in donations of five or ten cents from working-class readers). And it introduced a self-consciously populist style of writing that appealed to working-class readers. "The American people want something terse, forcible, picturesque, striking," Pulitzer said. His

THE YELLOW PRESS AND THE WRECK OF THE *MAINE* No evidence was ever found tying the Spanish to the explosion in Havana harbor that destroyed the American battleship *Maine* in February 1898. Indeed, most evidence indicated that the blast came from inside the ship, a fact that suggests an accident rather than sabotage. Nevertheless, the newspapers of Joseph Pulitzer and William Randolph Hearst ran sensational stories about the incident that were designed to arouse public sentiment in support of a war against the Spanish. This front page from Pulitzer's *New York World* is an example of the lurid coverage the event received. Circulation figures at the top of the page indicate, too, how successful the coverage was in selling newspapers. (*The Granger Collection*)

reporters wrote short, forceful sentences. They did not shy away from expressing sympathy or outrage. And they were not always constrained by the truth.

Pulitzer very quickly spawned imitators, the most important of them the California publisher William Randolph Hearst, who in 1895 bought the *New York Journal,* cut its price to one cent (Pulitzer quickly followed suit), copied many of the *World*'s techniques, and within a year raised its circulation to 400,000. Hearst used color even more lavishly than Pulitzer, recruited such notable writers as Stephen Crane, and committed the paper to an active role in civic affairs. The "new journalism," Hearst boasted in 1897, was not content simply to report news of crime, for example. It "strives to apprehend the criminal, to bring him to the bar of justice." He soon made the *Journal* the largest-circulation paper in the country—selling over a million copies a day. Pulitzer, whose own circulation was not far behind, accused him of "pandering to the worst tastes of the prurient and the horror-loving" and "dealing in bogus news." But the *World* wasted no time before imitating the *Journal.* The competition between these two great "yellow" journals soon drove both to new levels of sensationalism. Their success drove newspapers in other cities around the nation to copy their techniques.

The civil war in Cuba in the 1890s between native rebels and the Spanish colonial regime gave both papers their best opportunities yet for combining sensational reporting with shameless appeals to patriotism and moral outrage. They avidly published exaggerated reports of Spanish atrocities toward the Cuban rebels, fanning popular anger toward Spain. When the American battleship *Maine* mysteriously exploded in Havana harbor in 1898, both papers immediately blamed Spanish authorities (without any evidence). The *Journal* offered a $50,000 reward for information leading to the conviction of those responsible for the explosion, and

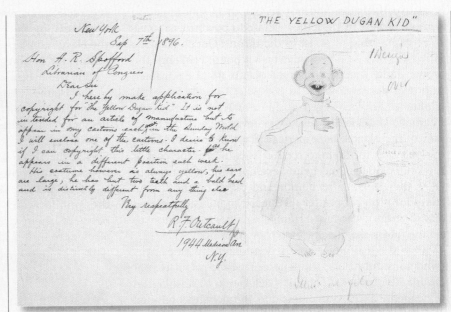

"THE YELLOW DUGAN KID" *Hogan's Alley*, one of the most popular cartoons of the late nineteenth and early twentieth centuries, debuted in the *New York World* in 1895. Perhaps its best-known character was Mickey Dugan, the goofy-looking creation of cartoonist Richard Outcault, known as "the Yellow Kid," whose nickname very likely was the source of the term "yellow journalism." *Hogan's Alley* was the forerunner of modern serial cartoons—not least because it was one of the first newspaper features to make elaborate use of color. (The drawing above accompanied Outcault's letter requesting copyright registration for the character of what he called "the yellow Dugan kid.") *(Library of Congress)*

it crowded all other stories off its front page ("There is no other news," Hearst told his editors) to make room for such screaming headlines as THE WHOLE COUNTRY THRILLS WITH WAR FEVER and HAVANA POPULACE INSULTS THE MEMORY OF THE *MAINE* VICTIMS. In the three days following the *Maine* explosion, the *Journal* sold over 3 million copies, a new world's record for newspaper circulation. The *World* exploited the destruction of the *Maine* less successfully (although not for lack of trying), but it made up for it in its highly sensationalized coverage of the Spanish-American War, which soon followed.

In the aftermath of the *Maine* episode, the more conservative press launched a spirited attack on yellow journalism. That was partly in response to Hearst's boast that the conflict in Cuba was "the *Journal*'s war" and to the publicity surrounding

a cable he sent to one of his reporters in Cuba saying: "You furnish the pictures, and I'll furnish the war." But it was also an effort to discourage a kind of journalism that more "respectable" editors both deplored and feared. Some schools, libraries, and clubs began to banish the papers from their premises. But the techniques the "yellow" press pioneered in the 1890s helped map the way for a tradition of colorful, popular journalism—later embodied in "tabloids," some elements of which eventually found their way into television news—that has endured into the present day.

Native Hawaiians did not accept their subordination without protest. In 1891, they elevated a powerful national-ist to the throne: Queen Liliuoka-lani, who set out to challenge the growing American control of the islands. But she remained in power only two years. In 1890, the United States had eliminated the privileged position of Hawaiian sugar in international trade. The result was devastating to the econ-omy of the islands, and American planters concluded that the only way for them to recover was to become part of the United States (and hence exempt from its tariffs). In 1893, they staged a revolution and called on the United States for protection. After the American minister ordered marines from a warship in Honolulu harbor to go ashore to aid the rebels, the queen yielded her authority.

A provisional government, dominated by Americans (who constituted less than 5 percent of the population of the islands), immediately sent a delegation to Washington to negotiate a treaty of annexation. But debate continued until 1898, when the Republicans returned to power and approved the agreement.

Three thousand miles south of Hawaii, the Samoan islands had also long served as a way station for American ships in the Pacific trade. As American commerce with Asia increased, business groups in the United States regarded Samoa with new interest, and the American navy began eyeing the Samoan harbor at Pago Pago. In 1878, the Hayes administration extracted a treaty from Samoan leaders for an American naval station at Pago Pago.

But Great Britain and Germany were also interested in the islands, and they too secured treaty rights from the native princes. For the next ten years the three pow-ers jockeyed for dominance in Samoa, occasionally com-ing dangerously close to war. Finally, the three nations agreed to share power over Samoa. The three-way arrangement failed to halt the rivalries of its members; and in 1899, the United States and Germany divided the islands between them, compensating Britain with territories elsewhere in the Pacific. The United States retained the harbor at Pago Pago.

WAR WITH SPAIN

Imperial ambitions had thus begun to stir within the United States well before the late 1890s. But a war with Spain in 1898 turned those stirrings into overt expansionism. The war transformed America's relationship to the rest of the world, and left the nation with a far-flung overseas empire.

THE DUTY OF THE HOUR:—TO SAVE HER NOT ONLY FROM SPAIN BUT FROM A WORSE FATE.

"THE DUTY OF THE HOUR" This 1892 lithograph was no doubt inspired by the saying "Out of the frying pan and into the fire." A despairing Cuba, struggling to escape from the frying pan of Spanish misrule, contemplates an even more dangerous alternative: "anarchy" (or home rule). Cartoonist Louis Dalrymple here suggests that the only real solution to Cuba's problems is control by the United States, whose "duty" to Cuba is "To Save Her Not Only from Spain but from a Worse Fate." *(The Granger Collection)*

Controversy over Cuba

The Spanish-American War emerged out of events in Cuba, which along with Puerto Rico represented all that remained of Spain's once extensive American empire. Cubans had been resisting Spanish rule since at least 1868. Many Americans had sympathized with the Cubans during that long struggle, but the United States did not intervene.

In 1895, the Cubans rose up again. This rebellion produced a ferocity on both sides that horrified Americans. The Cubans deliberately devastated the island to force the Spaniards to leave. The Spanish, commanded by General Valeriano Weyler, confined civilians in some areas to hastily prepared concentration camps, where they died by the thousands, victims of disease and malnutrition. The American press took to calling the general "Butcher Weyler." The Spanish had used some of these same savage methods during the earlier struggle in Cuba without shocking American sensibilities. But the revolt of 1895 was reported more fully and sensationally by the American press, which helped create the impression that the Spaniards were committing all the atrocities, when in fact there was considerable brutality on both sides.

Cuban Revolt

The conflict in Cuba came at a particularly opportune moment for the publishers of some American newspapers, Joseph Pulitzer with his *New York World* and William Randolph Hearst with his *New York Journal*. (See "Patterns of Popular Culture," pp. 552–553.) In the 1890s, Hearst and Pulitzer were engaged in a ruthless circulation war, and they both sent batteries of reporters and illustrators to the island with orders to provide accounts of Spanish atrocities. A growing population of Cuban émigrés in the United States—centered in Florida, New York, Philadelphia, and Trenton, New Jersey—gave extensive support to the Cuban Revolutionary Party (whose headquarters were in New York) and helped publicize its leader, Jose Marti, who was killed in Cuba in 1895. Later, Cuban Americans formed other clubs and associations to support the cause of *Cuba Libre*. In some areas of the country, their efforts were as important as those of the yellow journalists in generating American support for the revolution.

The mounting storm of indignation against Spain did not persuade President Cleveland to support intervention. He proclaimed American neutrality and urged authorities in New York City to try to stop the agitation by Cuban refugees there. But when McKinley became president in 1897, he formally protested Spain's "uncivilized and inhuman" conduct, causing the Spanish government (fearful of American intervention) to recall Weyler, modify the concentration policy, and grant the island a qualified autonomy.

But whatever chances there were for a peaceful settlement vanished as a result of two dramatic incidents in February 1898. The first occurred when a Cuban agent stole a private letter written by Dupuy de Lôme, the Spanish minister in Washington, and turned it over to the American press. The letter described McKinley as a weak man and "a bidder for the admiration of the crowd." This was no more than many Americans, including some Republicans, were saying about their president. (Theodore Roosevelt described McKinley as having "no more backbone than a chocolate eclair.") But coming from a foreigner, it created intense popular anger. Dupuy de Lôme promptly resigned.

While excitement over the de Lôme letter was still high, the American battleship *Maine* blew up in Havana harbor with a loss of more than 260 people. The ship had been ordered to Cuba in January to protect American lives and property. Many Americans assumed that the Spanish had sunk the ship, particularly when a naval court of inquiry hastily and inaccurately reported that an external explosion by a submarine mine had caused the disaster. (Later evidence suggested that the disaster was actually the result of an accidental explosion inside one of the engine rooms.) War hysteria swept the country, and Congress unanimously appropriated $50 million for military preparations. "Remember the *Maine*!" became a national chant for revenge.

The *Maine*

McKinley still hoped to avoid a conflict. But others in his administration (including Assistant Secretary of the Navy Theodore Roosevelt) were clamoring for war. In March 1898, the president asked Spain to agree to an armistice, negotiations for a permanent peace, and an end to the concentration camps. Spain agreed to stop the fighting and eliminate the concentration camps but refused to negotiate with the rebels and reserved the right to resume hostilities at its discretion. That satisfied neither public opinion nor the Congress; and a few days later McKinley asked for and, on April 25, received a congressional declaration of war.

"A Splendid Little War"

Secretary of State John Hay called the Spanish-American conflict "a splendid little war," an opinion that most Americans—with the exception of many of the enlisted men who fought in it—seemed to share. Declared in April, it was over in August. That was in part because Cuban rebels had already greatly weakened the Spanish resistance, which made the American intervention in many respects little more than a "mopping-up" exercise. Only 460 Americans were killed in battle or died of wounds, although some 5,200 others perished of disease: malaria, dysentery, and typhoid, among others. Casualties among Cuban insurgents, who continued to bear the brunt of the fighting, were much higher.

And yet the American war effort was not without difficulties. United States soldiers faced serious supply problems: a shortage of modern rifles and ammunition, uniforms too heavy for the warm Caribbean weather, inadequate medical services, and skimpy, almost indigestible food. The regular army numbered only 28,000 troops and officers, most of whom had experience in quelling Indian outbreaks but none in larger-scale warfare. That meant that, as in the Civil War, the United States had to rely heavily on National Guard units, organized by local communities and commanded for the most part by local leaders without military experience.

Supply and Mobilization Problems

There were also racial conflicts. A significant proportion of the American invasion force consisted of black soldiers. Some were volunteer troops put together by African-American communities (although some governors refused to allow the formation of such units). Others were members of the four black regiments in the regular army, who had been stationed on the frontier to defend white settlements against Indians and were now transferred east to fight in Cuba. As the black soldiers traveled through the South toward the training camps, they chafed at the rigid segregation to which they were subjected and occasionally resisted the restrictions openly. African-American soldiers in Georgia deliberately made use of a "whites only" park; in Florida, they beat a soda-fountain operator for refusing to serve them; in Tampa, white provocations and black retaliation led to a nightlong riot that left thirty wounded.

Racial tensions continued in Cuba itself, where African Americans played crucial roles in some of the important battles of the war (including the famous charge at San Juan Hill) and won many medals. Nearly half the Cuban insurgents fighting with the Americans were black, and unlike their American counterparts they were fully integrated into the rebel army. (Indeed, one of the leading insurgent generals, Antonio Maceo, was a black man.) The sight of black Cuban soldiers fighting alongside whites as equals gave African Americans a stronger sense of the injustice of their own position.

Seizing the Philippines

Assistant Secretary of the Navy Theodore Roosevelt was an ardent imperialist, an active proponent of war, and a man uninhibited by the knowledge that he was a relatively minor figure in the military hierarchy. Roosevelt strengthened the navy's Pacific squadron and instructed its commander, Commodore George Dewey, to attack Spanish naval forces in the Philippines, a colony of Spain, in the event of war.

Immediately after war was declared, Dewey sailed for Manila. On May 1, 1898, he steamed into Manila Bay and completely destroyed the aging Spanish fleet stationed there. Only one American sailor died in the battle (of heatstroke),

Dewey's Victory

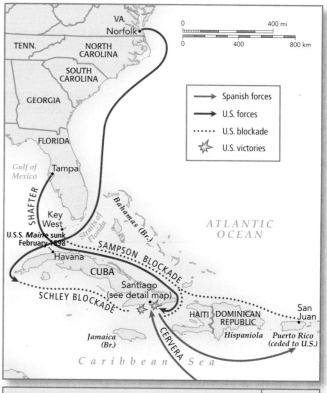

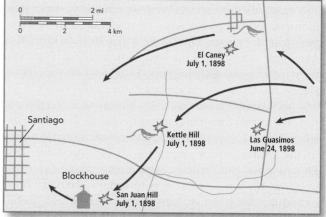

THE SPANISH-AMERICAN WAR IN CUBA, 1898 The military conflict between the United States and Spain in Cuba was a brief affair. The Cuban rebels and an American naval blockade had already brought the Spanish to the brink of defeat. The arrival of American troops was simply the final blow. In the space of about a week, U.S. troops won four decisive battles in the area around Santiago in southeast Cuba—one of them (the Battle of Kettle Hill) the scene of Theodore Roosevelt's famous charge up the adjacent San Juan Hill. This map shows the extent of the American naval blockade, the path of American troops from Florida to Cuba, and the location of the actual fighting. ◆ *What were the implications of the war in Cuba for Puerto Rico?*

For an interactive version of this map, go to www.mhhe.com/brinkley13ech19maps

and George Dewey, immediately promoted to admiral, became the first hero of the war. Several months later, after the arrival of an American expeditionary force, the Spanish surrendered the city of Manila itself. In the rejoicing over Dewey's victory, few Americans paused

Troop A, Ninth U. S. Cavalry.—Famous Indian Fighters.
Copyright 1898 by Strohmeyer & Wyman.

AFRICAN-AMERICAN CAVALRY Substantial numbers of African Americans fought in the United States Army during the Spanish-American War. Although confined to all-black units, they engaged in combat alongside white units and fought bravely and effectively. This photograph shows a troop of African-American cavalry in formation in Cuba. *(Corbis)*

to note that the character of the war was changing. What had begun as a war to free Cuba was becoming a war to strip Spain of its colonies. There had not yet been any decision about what the United States would do with the Spanish possessions it was suddenly acquiring.

The Battle for Cuba

Cuba remained the principal focus of American military efforts. At first, the American commanders planned a long period of training before actually sending troops into combat. But when a Spanish fleet under Admiral Pascual Cervera slipped past the American navy into Santiago harbor on the southern coast of Cuba, plans changed quickly. The American Atlantic fleet quickly bottled Cervera up in the harbor. And the U.S. Army's commanding general, Nelson A. Miles, hastily altered his strategy and left Tampa in June with a force of 17,000 to attack Santiago. Both the departure from Florida and the landing in Cuba were scenes of fantastic incompetence. It took five days for this relatively small army to be put ashore, and that with the enemy offering no opposition.

General William R. Shafter, the American commander, moved toward Santiago, which he planned to surround and capture. On the way he met and defeated Spanish forces at Las Guasimos and, a week later, in two simultaneous bat-

The Rough Riders

tles, El Caney and San Juan Hill. At the center of the fighting (and on the front pages of the newspapers) during many of these engagements was a cavalry unit known as the Rough Riders. Nominally commanded by General Leonard Wood, its real leader was Colonel Theodore Roosevelt, who had resigned from the Navy Department to get into the war and who had struggled with an almost desperate fury to ensure that his regiment made it to the front before the fighting ended. Roosevelt rapidly emerged as a hero of the conflict. His fame rested in large part on his role in leading a bold, if perhaps reckless, charge up Kettle Hill (a charge that was a minor part of the larger battle for the adjacent San Juan Hill) directly into the face of Spanish guns. Roosevelt himself emerged unscathed, but nearly a hundred of his soldiers were killed or wounded. He remembered the battle as "the great day of my life."

Although Shafter was now in position to assault Santiago, his army was so weakened by sickness that he feared he might have to abandon his position, particularly once the commander of the American naval force blockading Santiago refused to enter the harbor because of mines. But unknown to the Americans, the Spanish government had by now decided that Santiago was lost and had ordered Cervera to evacuate. On July 3, Cervera tried to escape the harbor. The waiting American squadron destroyed his entire fleet. On July 16, the commander of Spanish ground forces in Santiago surrendered. At about the same time, an American army landed in Puerto Rico and occupied it against virtually no opposition. On August 12, an armistice ended the war.

Under the terms of the armistice, Spain recognized the independence of Cuba. It ceded Puerto Rico (now occupied by American troops) and the Pacific island of Guam to the United States. And it accepted continued American occupation of Manila pending the final disposition of the Philippines.

Puerto Rico and the United States

The annexation of Puerto Rico produced relatively little controversy in the United States. The island of Puerto Rico had been a part of the Spanish Empire since Ponce de León arrived there in 1508, and it had

Annexation of Puerto Rico

contained Spanish settlements since the founding of San Juan in 1521. The native people of the island, the Arawaks, disappeared as a result of infectious diseases, Spanish brutality, and poverty. Puerto Rican society developed, therefore, with a Spanish ruling class and a large African work force for the coffee and sugar plantations that came to dominate its economy.

As Puerto Rican society became increasingly distinctive, resistance to Spanish rule began to emerge, just as it had in Cuba. Uprisings occurred intermittently beginning in the 1820s; the most important of them—the so-called Lares Rebellion—was, like the others, effectively crushed by the Spanish in 1868. But the growing resistance did prompt some reforms: the abolition of slavery in 1873, representation in the Spanish parliament, and other changes. Demands for independence continued

THE ROUGH RIDERS Theodore Roosevelt resigned as assistant secretary of the navy to lead a volunteer regiment in the Spanish-American War. They were known as the Rough Riders, and their bold charge during the battle of San Juan Hill made Roosevelt a national hero. Roosevelt is shown here (at center with glasses) posing with the other members of the regiment. *(Bettmann/Corbis)*

to grow, and in 1898, in response to political pressure organized by the popular politician Luis Muñoz Rivera, Spain granted the island a degree of independence. But before the changes had any chance to take effect, control of Puerto Rico shifted to the United States. American military forces occupied the island during the war. They remained in control until 1900, when the Foraker Act ended military rule and established a formal colonial government: an American governor and a two-chamber legislature (the members of the upper chamber appointed by the United States, the members of the lower elected by the Puerto Rican people). The United States could amend or veto any legislation the Puerto Ricans passed. Agitation for independence continued, and in 1917, under pressure to clarify the relationship between Puerto Rico and America, Congress passed the Jones Act, which declared Puerto Rico to be United States territory and made all Puerto Ricans American citizens.

The Puerto Rican sugar industry flourished as it took advantage of the American market that was now open to it without tariffs. As in Hawaii, Americans began establishing large sugar plantations on the island and hired natives to work them; many of the planters did not even live in Puerto Rico. The growing emphasis on sugar as a cash crop, and the transformation of many Puerto Rican farmers into paid laborers, led to a reduction in the growing of food for the island. Puerto Ricans became increasingly dependent on imported food and hence increasingly a part of the international commercial economy. When international sugar prices were high, Puerto Rico did well. When they dropped, the island's economy sagged, pushing the many plantation workers—already poor—into destitution. Unhappy with the instability, the poverty among natives, and the American threat to Hispanic culture, many Puerto Ricans continued to agitate for independence. Others, however, began to envision closer relations with the United States, even statehood.

Sugar Economy

The Debate over the Philippines

Although the annexation of Puerto Rico produced relatively little controversy, the annexation of the Philippines created a long and impassioned debate. Controlling a nearby Caribbean island fit reasonably comfortably into the United States's sense of itself as the dominant power in the Western Hemisphere. Controlling a large and densely populated territory thousands of miles away seemed different, and to many Americans more ominous.

McKinley claimed to be reluctant to support annexation. But, according to his own accounts, he came to believe there were no acceptable alternatives. Emerging from what he described as an "agoniz-

The Philippines Question

ing night of prayer," he claimed divine guidance for his decision to annex the islands. Returning them to Spain would be "cowardly and dishonorable," he claimed. Turning them over to another imperialist power (France, Germany, or Britain) would be "bad business and discreditable." Granting the islands independence would be irresponsible; the Filipinos were "unfit for self government." The only solution was "to take them all and to educate the Filipinos, and uplift and Christianize them, and by God's grace do the very best we could by them."

The Treaty of Paris, signed in December 1898, brought a formal end to the war. It confirmed the terms of the armistice concerning Cuba, Puerto Rico, and Guam. But American negotiators startled the Spanish by demanding that they cede the Philippines to the United States, something the original armistice had not included. The Spanish objected briefly, but an American offer of $20 million for the islands softened their resistance. They accepted all the American terms.

In the United States Senate, however, resistance was fierce. During debate over ratification of the treaty, a powerful anti-imperialist movement arose around the country to oppose acquisition of the Philippines. The anti-imperialists included some of the nation's wealthiest and most powerful figures: Andrew Carnegie, Mark Twain, Samuel Gompers, Senator John Sherman, and others. Their motives were various. Some believed simply that imperialism was immoral, a repudiation of America's commitment to human freedom. Some feared "polluting" the American population by introducing "inferior" Asian races into it. Industrial workers feared being undercut by a flood of cheap laborers from the new colonies. Conservatives worried about the large standing army and entangling foreign alliances that they believed imperialism would require and that they feared would threaten American liberties. Sugar growers and others feared unwelcome competition from the new territories. The Anti-Imperialist League, established late in 1898 by upper-class Bostonians, New Yorkers, and others to fight against annexation, attracted a widespread following in the Northeast and waged a vigorous campaign against ratification of the Paris treaty.

Anti-Imperialist League

Favoring ratification was an equally varied group. There were the exuberant imperialists such as Theodore Roosevelt, who saw the acquisition of empire as a way to reinvigorate the nation and keep alive what they considered the healthy, restorative influence of the war. Some businessmen saw opportunities to dominate the Asian trade. And most Republicans saw partisan advantages in acquiring valuable new territories through a war fought and won by a Republican administration. Perhaps the strongest argument in favor of annexation, however, was that the United States already possessed the islands.

When anti-imperialists warned of the danger of acquiring territories with large populations who might have to become citizens, the imperialists had a ready answer. The nation's longstanding policies toward Indians—treating them as dependents rather than as citizens—had created a precedent for annexing land without absorbing people. Supporters of annexation argued that the "uncivilized" Filipinos "would occupy the same status precisely as our Indians. . . . They are, in fact, 'Indians'—and the Fourteenth Amendment does not make citizens of Indians."

The fate of the treaty remained in doubt for weeks, until it received the unexpected support of William Jennings Bryan, a fervent anti-imperialist. He backed ratification not because he approved of annexation but because he hoped to move the issue out of the Senate and make it the subject of a national referendum in 1900, when he expected to be the Democratic presidential candidate again. Bryan persuaded a number of anti-imperialist Democrats to support the treaty so as to set up the 1900 debate. The Senate ratified it finally on February 6, 1899.

But Bryan miscalculated. If the election of 1900 was in fact a referendum on the Philippines, as Bryan expected, it proved beyond doubt that the nation had

Election of 1900

decided in favor of imperialism. Once again Bryan ran against McKinley; and once again McKinley won—even more decisively than in 1896. It was not only the issue of the colonies, however, that ensured McKinley's victory. The Republicans were the beneficiaries of growing prosperity—and also of the colorful personality of their vice presidential candidate, Theodore Roosevelt, the hero of San Juan Hill.

THE REPUBLIC AS EMPIRE

The new American empire was small by the standards of the great imperial powers of Europe. But it embroiled the United States in the politics of both Europe and the Far East in ways the nation had always tried to avoid in the past. It also drew Americans into a brutal war in the Philippines.

Governing the Colonies

Three of the American dependencies—Hawaii, Alaska (acquired from Russia in 1867), and Puerto Rico—presented relatively few problems. They received territorial status (and their residents American citizenship) relatively quickly: Hawaii in 1900, Alaska in 1912, and Puerto Rico in 1917. The navy took control of the Pacific islands of Guam and Tutuila. And some of the smallest, least populated Pacific islands now under American control the United States simply left alone. Cuba was a thornier problem. American military forces, commanded by

"MEASURING UNCLE SAM FOR A NEW SUIT," BY J. S. PUGHE, IN *PUCK* MAGAZINE, 1900 President William McKinley is favorably depicted here as a tailor, measuring his client for a suit large enough to accommodate the new possessions the United States obtained in the aftermath of the Spanish-American War. This detail from a larger cartoon tries to link this expansion with earlier, less controversial ones such as the Louisiana Purchase. *(Culver Pictures, Inc.)*

General Leonard Wood, remained there until 1902 to prepare the island for independence. They built roads, schools, and hospitals, reorganized the legal, financial, and administrative systems, and introduced medical and sanitation reforms. But the United States also laid the basis for years of American economic domination of the island.

When Cuba drew up a constitution that made no reference to the United States, Congress responded by passing the Platt Amendment in 1901 and pressuring Cuba into incorporating its terms into its constitution. The Platt Amendment

Platt Amendment

barred Cuba from making treaties with other nations (thus, in effect, giving the United States control of Cuban foreign policy); gave the United States the right to intervene in Cuba to preserve independence, life, and property; and required Cuba to permit American naval stations on its territory. The amendment left Cuba with only nominal political independence.

American capital, which quickly took over the island's economy, made the new nation an American economic appendage as well. American investors poured into Cuba, buying up plantations, factories, railroads, and refineries. Absentee American ownership of many of

American Economic Dominance

the island's most important resources was the source of resentment and agitation for decades. Resistance to "Yankee imperialism" produced intermittent revolts against the Cuban government—revolts that at times prompted U.S. military intervention. American troops occupied the island from 1906 to 1909 after one such rebellion; they returned again in 1912, to suppress a revolt by black plantation workers. As in Puerto Rico and Hawaii, sugar production—spurred by access to the American market—increasingly dominated the island's economy and subjected it to the same cycle of booms and busts that so plagued other sugar-producing appendages of the United States economy.

The Philippine War

Americans did not like to think of themselves as imperial rulers in the European mold. Yet, like other imperial powers, the United States soon discovered—as it had discovered at home in its relations with the Indians—that subjugating another people required more than ideals; it also required strength and brutality. That, at least, was the lesson of the American experience in the Philippines, where American forces soon became engaged in a long and bloody war with insurgent forces fighting for independence.

The conflict in the Philippines is the least remembered of all American wars. It was also one of the longest, lasting from 1898 to 1902, and one of the most vicious. It involved 200,000 American troops and resulted in 4,300 American deaths, nearly ten times the number who had died in combat in the Spanish-American War. The number of Filipinos killed in the conflict has long been a matter of dispute, but it seems likely that at least 50,000 natives (and perhaps many more) died. The American occupiers faced brutal guerrilla tactics in the Philippines, very similar to those the Spanish occupiers had faced prior to 1898 in Cuba. And they soon found themselves drawn into the same pattern of brutality that had outraged so many Americans when Weyler had used them in the Caribbean.

The Filipinos had been rebelling against Spanish rule even before 1898. And as soon as they realized the Americans had come to stay, they rebelled against them as well. Ably led by Emilio Aguinaldo, who claimed to head the legitimate government of the nation, Filipinos harried the American army of occupation from island to island

Emilio Aguinaldo

FILIPINO PRISONERS American troops guard captured Filipino guerrillas in Manila. The suppression of the Filipino insurrection was a much longer and costlier military undertaking than the Spanish-American War, by which the United States first gained possession of the islands. By mid-1900 there were 70,000 American troops in the Philippines, under the command of General Arthur MacArthur (whose son Douglas won fame in the Philippines during World War II). *(Library of Congress)*

for more than three years. At first, American commanders believed the rebels had only a small popular following. But by early 1900, General Arthur MacArthur, an American commander in the islands (and father of General Douglas MacArthur), was writing: "I have been reluctantly compelled to believe that the Filipino masses are loyal to Aguinaldo and the government which he heads."

To MacArthur and others, that realization was not a reason to moderate American tactics or conciliate the rebels. It was a reason to adopt much more severe measures. Gradually, the American military effort became more systematically vicious and brutal. Captured Filipino guerrillas were treated not as prisoners of war, but as murderers. Many were summarily executed. On some islands, entire communities were evacuated—the residents forced into concentration camps while American troops destroyed their villages, farms, crops, and livestock. A spirit of savagery grew among some American soldiers, who came to view the Filipinos as almost subhuman and at times seemed to take pleasure in killing arbitrarily. One American commander ordered his troops "to kill and burn, the more you kill and burn the better it will please me. . . . Shoot everyone over the age of 10." Over fifteen Filipinos were killed for every one wounded; in the American Civil War—the bloodiest conflict in U.S. history to that point—one person had died for every five wounded.

By 1902, reports of the brutality and of the American casualties had soured the American public on the war. But by then, the rebellion had largely exhausted itself and the occupiers had established control over most of the islands. The key to their victory *Growing Economic Dependence* was the March 1901 capture of Aguinaldo, who later signed a document urging his followers to stop fighting and declaring his own allegiance to the United States. (Aguinaldo then retired from public life and lived quietly

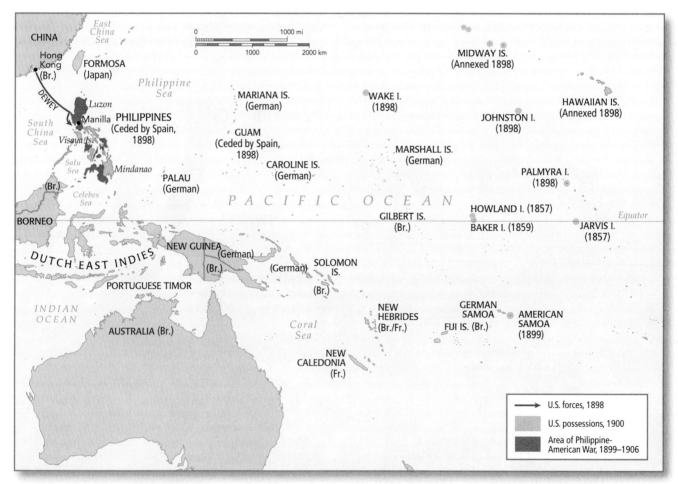

THE AMERICAN SOUTH PACIFIC EMPIRE, 1900 Except for Puerto Rico, all of the colonial acquisitions of the United States in the wake of the Spanish-American War occurred in the Pacific. The new attraction of imperialism persuaded the United States to annex Hawaii in 1898. The war itself gave America control of the Philippines, Guam, and other, smaller Spanish possessions in the Pacific. When added to the small, scattered islands that the United States had acquired as naval bases earlier in the nineteenth century, these new possessions gave the nation a far-flung Pacific empire, even if one whose total territory and population remained small by the standards of the other great empires of the age. ◆ *What was the reaction in the United States to the acquisition of this new empire?*

until 1964.) Fighting continued in some places for another year, and the war revived intermittently until as late as 1906; but American possession of the Philippines was now secure. In the summer of 1901, the military transferred authority over the islands to William Howard Taft, who became their first civilian governor. Taft announced that the American mission in the Philippines was to prepare the islands for independence, and he gave the Filipinos broad local autonomy. The Americans also built roads, schools, bridges, and sewers; instituted major administrative and financial reforms; and established a public health system. The Philippine economy—dominated by fishing, agriculture, timber, and mining—also became increasingly linked to the economy of the United States. Americans did not make many investments in the Philippines, and few Americans moved there. But trade with the United States grew to the point that the islands were almost completely dependent on American markets.

In the meantime, a succession of American governors gradually increased Filipino political autonomy. On July 4, 1946, the islands finally gained their independence.

The Open Door

The acquisition of the Philippines greatly increased the already strong American interest in Asia. Americans were particularly concerned about the future of China, with which the United States had an important trade and which was now so enfeebled that it provided a tempting target for exploitation by stronger countries. By 1900, England, France, Germany, Russia, and Japan were beginning to carve up China among themselves. They pressured the Chinese government for "concessions," which gave them effective control over various regions of China. In some cases, they simply seized Chinese territory and claimed it as their own. Many Americans feared that the process would soon cut them out of the China trade altogether.

Eager for a way to advance American interests in China without risking war, McKinley issued a statement in September 1898 saying the United States wanted access to China, but no special advantages there. "Asking only the open door for ourselves, we are ready to accord the open door to others." The next year, Secretary of State John Hay translated those words into policy when he addressed identical messages—which became known as the "Open Door notes"—to England, Germany, Russia, France, Japan, and Italy. He asked them to approve three principles: Each nation with a sphere

Hay's "Open Door Notes"

THE BOXER REBELLION, 1900 This photograph shows imprisoned Boxers in Beijing. Days earlier, they had been involved in the siege of the compound in which Western diplomats lived. An expeditionary force of numerous European powers in China, and of the United States, had broken the siege and captured the Boxers. *(Bettmann/Corbis)*

of influence in China was to respect the rights and privileges of other nations in its sphere; Chinese officials were to continue to collect tariff duties in all spheres (the existing tariff favored the United States); and nations were not to discriminate against other nations in levying port dues and railroad rates within their own spheres. Together, these principles would allow the United States to trade freely with the Chinese without fear of interference and without having to become militarily involved in the region. They would also retain the illusion of Chinese sovereignty and thus prevent formal colonial dismemberment of China, which might also create obstacles to American trade.

But Europe and Japan received the Open Door proposals coolly. Russia openly rejected them; the other powers claimed to accept them in principle but to be unable to act unless all the other powers agreed. Hay refused to consider this a rebuff. He boldly announced that all the powers had accepted the principles of the Open Door in "final and definitive" form and that the United States expected them to observe those principles.

No sooner had the diplomatic maneuvering over the Open Door ended than the Boxers, a secret Chinese martial-arts society with highly nationalist convictions, launched a bloody revolt against foreigners in China. The climax of the Boxer Rebellion was a siege of the entire foreign diplomatic corps, which took refuge in the British embassy in Peking. The imperial powers (including the United States) sent an international expeditionary force into China to rescue the diplomats. In August 1900, it fought its way into Peking and broke the siege.

Boxer Rebellion

McKinley and Hay had agreed to American participation in quelling the Boxer Rebellion so as to secure a voice in the settlement of the uprising and to prevent the partition of China by the European powers. Hay now won support for his Open Door approach from England and Germany and induced the other participating powers to accept compensation from the Chinese for the damages the Boxer Rebellion had caused. Chinese territorial integrity survived at least in name, and the United States retained access to its lucrative trade.

A Modern Military System

The war with Spain had revealed glaring deficiencies in the American military system. The army had exhibited the greatest weaknesses, but the entire military organization had demonstrated problems of supply, training, and coordination. Had the United States been fighting a more powerful foe, disaster might have resulted. After the war, McKinley appointed Elihu Root, an able corporate lawyer in New York, as secretary of war to supervise a major overhaul of the armed forces. (Root was one of the first of several generations of attorney-statesmen who moved easily between public and private roles and constituted much of what has often been called the American "foreign policy establishment.")

Between 1900 and 1903, the Root reforms enlarged the regular army from 25,000 to a maximum of 100,000. They established federal army standards for the National Guard, ensuring that never again would the nation fight a war with volunteer regiments trained and equipped differently than those in the regular army. They sparked the creation of a system of officer training schools, including the Army Staff College (later the Command and General Staff School) at Fort Leavenworth, Kansas, and the Army War College in Washington. And in 1903, a general staff (named the Joint Chiefs of Staff) was established to act as military advisers to the secretary of war. It was this last reform that Root considered most important: the creation of a central planning agency modeled on the example of European general staffs. The Joint Chiefs were charged with many functions. They were to "supervise" and "coordinate" the entire army establishment, and they were to establish an office that would plan for possible wars. An Army and Navy Board was to foster interservice cooperation. As a result of the new reforms, the United States entered the twentieth century with something resembling a modern military system.

Root's Military Reforms

CONCLUSION

For nearly three decades after the end of Reconstruction, American politics remained locked in a rigid stalemate. The electorate was almost evenly divided, and the two major parties differed on only a few issues. A series of dull, respectable presidents presided over this political system as unwitting symbols of its stability and passivity.

Beneath the calm surface of national politics, however, great social issues were creating deep divisions: battles between employers and workers, growing resentment among American farmers facing declining prosperity, outrage at what many voters considered corruption in government and excessive power in the hands of corporate titans. When a great depression, the worst in the nation's history to that point, began in 1893, these social tensions exploded.

The most visible sign of the challenge to the political stalemate was the Populist movement, a great uprising of American farmers demanding far-reaching changes in politics and the economy. In 1892, they created their own political party, the People's Party, which for a few years showed impressive strength. But in the climactic election of 1896, in which the Populist hero William Jennings Bryan became the presidential nominee of both the Democratic Party and the People's Party, the Republicans won a substantial victory—and in the process helped create a great electoral realignment that left the Republicans with a clear majority for the next three decades.

The crises of the 1890s coincided with, and helped to strengthen, a growing American engagement in the world. In 1898, the United States intervened in a colonial war between Spain and Cuba, won a quick and easy military victory, and signed a treaty with Spain that ceded significant territory to the Americans, including Puerto Rico and the Philippines. A vigorous anti-imperialist movement failed to stop the imperial drive. But taking the colonies proved easier than holding them. In the Philippines, American forces became bogged down in a brutal four-year war with Filipino rebels. The conflict soured much of the American public, and the annexation of colonies in 1898 proved to be both the beginning and the end of American territorial imperialism.

INTERACTIVE LEARNING

The *Primary Source Investigator CD-ROM* offers the following materials related to this chapter:

- Interactive maps: **U.S. Elections** (M7) and **The Spanish-American War** (M20).

- Documents, images, and maps related to the political and economic turmoil of the 1890s, including excerpts from the Interstate Commerce Act, the Sherman Antitrust Act, an image of James Garfield's inauguration, and the Gold Standard Act; the Spanish-American War of 1898 and the rise of American imperialism in this era, including a video clip of a scene from the Philippine War, the text of the Joint Resolution of Congress annexing Hawaii, and a video clip of Theodore Roosevelt and the Rough Riders.

Online Learning Center (www.mhhe.com/brinkley13e)

For quizzes, Internet resources, references to additional books and films, and more, consult this book's Online Learning Center.

FOR FURTHER REFERENCE

Morton Keller, *Affairs of State: Public Life in Late Nineteenth-Century America* (1977) is an important study of politics and government after Reconstruction. Nell Irvin Painter's *Standing at Armageddon: The United States, 1877-1919* (1987) explores the multicultural dimensions of industrialization, emphasizing the particularly cataclysmic effect of industrialization on minority populations and on race relations. Martin J. Sklar, *The Corporate Reconstruction of American Capitalism, 1890-1916* (1988) offers an interpretation of the evolution of American business practice and, by extension, American politics and society. Two significant books charting the growing capacities of the American state during this period are Theda Skocpol, *Protecting Soldiers and Mothers: The Political Origins of Social Policy in the United States* (1992); and Stephen Skowronek, *Building a New American State: The Expansion of National Administrative Capacities, 1877-1920* (1982). Richard Hofstadter's *The Age of Reform: From Bryan to FDR* (1955) and Lawrence Goodwyn's *The Populist Moment* (1978) offer sharply contrasting characterizations of the Populist and progressive reform movements of this time. Other important studies of Populism include John D. Hicks, *The Populist Revolt* (1931), a classic account, and Steven Hahn, *The Roots of Southern Populism: Yeoman Farmers and the Transformation of the Georgia Upcountry* (1983). Michael Kazin, *The Populist Persuasion: An American History* (1995) places Populist ideas in a broad historical context.

Walter LaFeber, *The New Empire: An Interpretation of American Expansion, 1860-1898* (1963) and Ernest May, *Imperial Democracy* (1961) are important introductions to the subject. David F. Healy, *U.S. Expansionism: Imperialist Urge in the 1890s* (1970) is a contrasting view. Walter LaFeber, *The Cambridge History of American Foreign Policy, Vol. 2: The Search for Opportunity, 1865-1913* (1993) is an important overview. William Appleman Williams, *The Tragedy of American Diplomacy*, rev. ed. (1972), is a classic revisionist work on the origins and tragic consequences of American imperialism, supplemented by his *Empire as a Way of Life: An Essay on the Causes and Character of America's Present Predicament* (1982). Anders Stephanson, *Manifest Destiny: American Expansionism and the Empire of Right* (1995) is a short and provocative history of Americans' ideology of expansionism. Warren Zimmermann, *First Great Triumph: How Five Americans Made Their Country a Great Power* (2002) describes a circle of powerful figures who together helped create an ideology of empire for the United States in the early twentieth century. Robert L. Beisner's *Twelve Against Empire* (1968) chronicles the careers of the leading opponents of imperial expansion. Emily S. Rosenberg, *Spreading the American Dream: American Economic and Cultural Expansion, 1890-1945* (1982) is a provocative cultural interpretation. Gerald F. Linderman, *The Mirror of War: American Society and the Spanish-American War* (1974) examines the social meaning of the war within the United States. Stuart Creighton Miller, *"Benevolent Assimilation": The American Conquest of the Philippines, 1899-1903* (1982) describes the American war in the Philippines. Michael Hunt, *The Making of a Special Relationship: The United States and China to 1914* (1983) is a good introduction to the subject.

CHAPTER 20

THE PROGRESSIVES

SUFFRAGE PAGEANT, 1913   On March 3, 1913—the day before Woodrow Wilson's Inauguration as President—more than 5,000 supporters of woman suffrage staged a parade in Washington that entirely overshadowed Wilson's own arrival in Washington. Crowds estimated at over half a million watched the parade, not all of them admirers of the woman suffrage movement, and some of the onlookers attacked the marchers. The police did nothing to stop them. This photograph depicts a suffragist, Florence Noyes, costumed as Liberty, posing in front of the U.S. Treasury Building, part of a pageant accompanying the parade. Suffrage was one of the most important and impassioned reform movements of the progressive era.   *(Library of Congress)*

WELL BEFORE THE END OF THE NINETEENTH CENTURY, many Americans had become convinced that the rapid changes in their society—industrialization, urbanization, immigration, and other jarring transformations—had created intolerable problems. Out of that concern there emerged a broad effort to impose order and justice on a society that seemed to be approaching chaos. By the early years of the twentieth century, this outlook had acquired a name: progressivism.

The progressive impulse took many forms—so many, in fact, that even today scholars do not agree on what progressivism meant. But despite, or perhaps because of, its great diversity, progressivism created a remarkable period of political and social innovation. From the late nineteenth century until at least the end of World War I, reformers were the most dynamic and influential force in American politics and culture. They brought into public debate such issues as the role of women in society, the ways to deal with racial difference, the question of how to govern cities, the fairest way to organize the economy, the role of political parties and political machines, the impact of immigration and cultural diversity, and the degree to which the state should impose moral norms on communities and individuals.

Progressivism began as a movement within communities, cities, and states—many different local efforts to improve the working of society. Slowly but steadily, these efforts began to become national efforts. Broad movements emerged around passionate issues: woman suffrage, racial equality, the rights of labor. And the federal government itself, beginning in the early twentieth century, became a crucible of progressive reform. Reformers attempted to make Washington more responsive to their demands. Some worked successfully for the direct popular election of United States senators—to replace what they considered the corrupt process by which state legislatures chose members of the Senate. But ultimately it was the presidency, not the Congress, that became the most important vehicle of national reform—first under the dynamic leadership of Theodore Roosevelt and then under the disciplined, moralistic leadership of Woodrow Wilson. By the time America entered World War I in 1917, the federal government—which had exercised very limited powers prior to the twentieth century—had greatly expanded its role in American life.

THE PROGRESSIVE IMPULSE

Progressivism was, first, an optimistic vision. Progressives believed, as their name implies, in the idea of progress.

Belief in Progress

They believed that society was capable of improvement and that continued growth and advancement were the nation's destiny.

But progressives believed, too, that growth and progress could not continue to occur recklessly, as they had in the late nineteenth century. The "natural laws" of the marketplace, and the doctrines of laissez faire and Social Darwinism that celebrated those laws, were not sufficient. Direct, purposeful human intervention in social and economic affairs was essential to ordering and bettering society.

Varieties of Progressivism

Progressives did not always agree on the form their intervention should take, and the result was a variety of reform impulses that sometimes seemed to have little in common. One powerful impulse was the spirit of "antimonop-

"Antimonopoly"

oly," the fear of concentrated power and the urge to limit and disperse authority and wealth. This vaguely populist impulse appealed not only to many workers and farmers but to some middle-class Americans as well. And it helped empower government to regulate or break up trusts at both the state and national level.

Another progressive impulse was a belief in the importance of social cohesion: the belief that individuals are part of a great web of social relationships, that each person's welfare is dependent on the welfare of society as a whole. That assumption produced a concern about the "victims" of industrialization.

Still another impulse was a deep faith in knowledge—in the possibilities of applying to society the principles of natural and social sciences. Many reformers believed that

Faith in Knowledge

knowledge was more important as a vehicle for making society more equitable and humane. Most progressives believed, too, that a modernized government could—and must—play an important role in the process of improving and stabilizing society. Modern life was too complex to be left in the hands of party bosses, untrained amateurs, and antiquated institutions.

The Muckrakers

Among the first people to articulate the new spirit of reform were crusading journalists who began to direct public attention toward social, economic, and political injustices. They became known as the "muckrakers," after Theodore Roosevelt accused one of them of raking up muck through his writings. They were committed to exposing scandal, corruption, and injustice to public view.

At first, their major targets were the trusts and particularly the railroads, which the muckrakers considered powerful and deeply corrupt. Exposés of the great corporate organizations began to appear as early as the 1860s, when Charles Francis Adams Jr. and others uncovered corruption among the railroad barons. One of the most notable of them was the journalist Ida Tarbell's enormous study of the Standard Oil trust (published first

Ida Tarbell and Lincoln Steffens

in magazines and then as a two-volume book in 1904). By the turn of the century, many muckrakers were turning their attention to government and particularly to the urban political machines. The most influential, perhaps, was Lincoln Steffens, a reporter for *McClure's* magazine and the author of a famous book based on his articles, *The Shame of the Cities*. His portraits of "machine government" and "boss rule"; his exposure of "boodlers" in cities as diverse as St. Louis, Minneapolis, Cleveland, Cincinnati, Chicago, Philadelphia, and New York; his tone of studied moral outrage—all helped arouse sentiment for urban political reform. The alternative to leaving government in the hands of corrupt party leaders, the muckrakers argued, was for the people themselves to take a greater interest in public life.

The muckrakers reached the peak of their influence in the first decade of the twentieth century. By presenting social problems to the public with indignation and moral fervor, they helped inspire other Americans to take action.

The Social Gospel

The growing outrage at social and economic injustice helped produce many reformers committed to the pursuit of social justice. That impulse helped create the rise of what became known as the "Social Gospel." By the early twentieth century, it had become a powerful movement within American Protestantism (and, to a lesser extent, within American Catholicism and Judaism). It was chiefly concerned with redeeming the nation's cities.

The Salvation Army, which began in England but soon spread to the United States, was one example of the fusion of religion with reform. A Christian social welfare organization with a vaguely military structure, by 1900 it had recruited 3,000 "officers" and 20,000 "privates" and was offering both material aid and spiritual service to the urban poor. In addition, many ministers, priests, and rabbis left traditional parish work to serve in the troubled cities. Charles Sheldon's *In His Steps* (1898), the story of a young minister who abandoned a comfortable post to work among the needy, sold more than 15 million copies and established itself as the most successful novel of the era.

Walter Rauschenbusch, a Protestant theologian from Rochester, New York, published a series of influential

"THE BOSSES OF THE SENATE" (1889), BY JOSEPH KEPPLER Keppler was a popular political cartoonist of the late nineteenth century who shared the growing concern about the power of the trusts—portrayed here as bloated, almost reptilian figures standing menacingly over the members of the U.S. Senate, to whose chamber the "people's entrance" is "closed." *(The Granger Collection)*

discourses on the possibilities for human salvation through Christian reform. To him, the message of Darwinism was not the survival of the fittest. He believed, rather, that all individuals should work to ensure a humanitarian evolution of the social fabric.

Father John Ryan

Some American Catholics seized on the 1893 publication of Pope Leo XIII's encyclical *Rerum Novarum* (New Things) as justification for their own crusade for social justice. Catholic liberals such as Father John A. Ryan took to heart the pope's warning that "a small number of very rich men have been able to lay upon the masses of the poor a yoke little better than slavery itself." For decades, he worked to expand the scope of Catholic social welfare organizations.

The Social Gospel was never the dominant element in the movement for urban reform. But the engagement of religion with reform helped bring to progressivism a powerful moral commitment to redeem the lives of even the least favored citizens.

The Settlement House Movement

An element of much progressive thought was the belief in the influence of the environment on individual devel-

opment. Social Darwinists such as William Graham Sumner had argued that people's fortunes reflected their inherent "fitness" for survival. Progressive theorists disagreed. Ignorance, poverty, even criminality, they argued, were not the result of inherent genetic failings or of the workings of providence; they were, rather, the effects of an unhealthy environment. To elevate the distressed, therefore, required an improvement of the conditions in which they lived.

Nothing produced more distress, many urban reformers believed, than crowded immigrant neighborhoods, which publicists such as Jacob Riis were exposing through vivid photographs and lurid descriptions. One response to the problems of such communities, borrowed from England, was the settlement house. The most famous, and one of the first, was Hull House, which opened in 1889 in Chicago as a result of the efforts of the

Jane Addams and Hull House

social worker Jane Addams. It became a model for more than 400 similar institutions throughout the nation. Staffed by members of the educated middle class, settlement houses sought to help immigrant families adapt to the language and customs of their new country. Settlement houses avoided the condescension and moral disapproval of earlier philanthropic efforts. But they generally embraced

PROGRESSIVE REFORM

Few issues in the history of twentieth-century America have inspired more disagreement, even confusion, than the nature of progressivism. Until about 1950, most historians were in general accord about the nature of the progressive "movement." It was, they generally agreed, just what it purported to be: a movement by the "people" to curb the power of the "special interests."

In the early 1950s, however, a new interpretation emerged to challenge the traditional view. It offered a new explanation of who the progressives were and what they were trying to do. George Mowry, in *The California Progressives* (1951), described the reform movement in the state not as a protest by the mass of the people, but as an effort by a small and privileged group of business and professional men to limit the overbearing power of large new corporations and labor unions. Richard Hofstadter expanded on this idea in *The Age of Reform* (1955), in which he described progressives throughout the country as people suffering from "status anxiety"—old, formerly influential, upper-middle-class families seeking to restore their fading prestige by challenging the powerful new institutions that had begun to displace them. Like the Populists, Hofstadter suggested, the progressives were suffering from psychological, not economic, discontent.

The Mowry-Hofstadter thesis was never without critics. In its wake, a bewildering array of new interpreta-

tions emerged. Perhaps the harshest challenge to earlier views came from Gabriel Kolko, whose influential 1963 study *The Triumph of Conservatism* dismissed the supposedly "democratic" features of progressivism as meaningless rhetoric. But he also rejected the Mowry-Hofstadter idea that it represented the efforts of a displaced elite. Progressivism, he argued, was an effort to regulate business. But it was not the "people" or "displaced elites" who were responsible for this regulation. It was corporate leaders themselves, who saw in government supervision a way to protect themselves from competition. Regulation, Kolko claimed, was "invariably controlled by the leaders of the regulated industry and directed towards ends they deemed acceptable or desirable." Martin Sklar's *The Corporate Reconstruction of American Capitalism* (1988) is a more sophisticated version of a similar argument.

A more moderate challenge to the "psychological" interpretation of progressivism came from historians embracing a new "organizational" view of history. Particularly influential was a 1967 study by Robert Wiebe, *The Search for Order, 1877–1920*. Wiebe presented progressivism as a response to dislocations in American life. There had been rapid changes in the nature of the economy, but there had been no corresponding changes in social and political institutions. Economic power had moved to large, national organizations, while social and politi-

(Library of Congress)

cal life remained centered primarily in local communities. The result was widespread disorder and unrest, culminating in the turbulent 1890s. Progressivism, Wiebe argued, was the effort of a "new middle class"—a class tied to the emerging national economy—to stabilize and enhance their position in society by creating national institutions suitable for the new national economy.

Despite the influences of these interpretations, some historians continued to argue that the reform phenomenon was indeed a movement of the people against the special interests,

a belief that middle-class Americans had a responsibility to impart their own values to immigrants and to teach them how to create middle-class lifestyles.

Central to the settlement houses were the efforts of college women. The settlement houses provided these women with an environment and a role that society considered "appropriate" for unmarried women: urban "homes" where settlement workers helped their immigrant neighbors to become better members of society. The settlement houses also helped spawn another important institution of reform, one in which women were also to play a vital role: the profession of social work. Workers

at Hull House, for example, maintained a close relationship with the University of Chicago's pioneering work in the field of sociology. A growing number of programs for the professional training of social workers began to appear in the nation's leading universities, partly in response to the activities of the settlements.

The Allure of Expertise

As the emergence of the social work profession suggests, progressives involved in humanitarian efforts placed a high value on knowledge and expertise. Even although some identified the "people" somewhat differently than earlier such interpretations. J. Joseph Huthmacher argued in 1962 that much of the force behind progressivism came from members of the working class, especially immigrants, who pressed for such reforms as workmen's compensation and wage and hour laws. John Buenker strengthened this argument in *Urban Liberalism and Progressive Reform* (1973), claiming that political machines and urban "bosses" were important sources of reform energy and helped create twentieth-century liberalism. David P. Thelen, in a 1972 study of progressivism in Wisconsin, *The New Citizenship,* pointed to a real clash between the "public interest" and "corporate privilege" in Wisconsin. The depression of the 1890s had mobilized a broad coalition of citizens of highly diverse backgrounds behind efforts to make both business and government responsible to the popular will. It marked the emergence of a new "consumer" consciousness that crossed boundaries of class and community, religion and ethnicity.

Other historians writing in the 1970s and 1980s attempted to link reform to some of the broad processes of political change that had created the public battles of the era. Richard L. McCormick's *From Realignment to Reform* (1981), for example, studied political change in New York State and argued that the crucial change in this era was the decline of the political parties as the vital players in public life and the rise of interest groups working for particular social and economic goals.

(Brown Brothers)

At the same time, many historians were focusing on the role of women (and the vast network of voluntary associations they created) in shaping and promoting progressive reform and were seeing in these efforts concerns rooted in gender. Some progressive battles, such historians as Kathryn Sklar, Linda Gordon, Ruth Rosen, Elaine Tyler May, and others argued, were part of an effort by women to protect their interests within the domestic sphere in the face of jarring challenges from the new industrial world. This protective urge drew women reformers to such issues as temperance, divorce, and prostitution. Many women mobilized behind protective legislation for women and children workers. Other women worked to expand their own roles in the public world. Progressivism cannot be understood, historians of women contend, without understanding the role of women and the importance of issues involving the family and the private world within it.

More recently, a number of historians have sought to revive a broader view of progressivism rather than breaking it down into its component parts. Daniel Rodgers's *Atlantic Crossings* (1998), a remarkable study of how European reforms influenced American progressives, suggests that the movement was not just an American phenomenon but had roots in a global process of change as well. Alan Dawley's *Struggles for Justice* (1993) characterized progressivism as the effort of liberal elites to manage the new pressures of the industrial era—and the problems of capitalism in particular—in ways that would modernize the state and undermine pressures from socialists. And Michael McGerr, in *A Fierce Discontent* (2003), portrayed progressivism as an essentially moral project through which reformers sought to remake not just government and politics, but also the ways Americans lived, thought, and interacted with each other.

Given the range of disagreement over the nature of the progressive movement, it is hardly surprising that some historians have despaired of finding any coherent definition for the term at all. Peter Filene, for one, suggested in 1970 that the concept of progressivism as a "movement" had outlived its usefulness. But Daniel Rodgers, in an important 1982 article, "In Search of Progressivism," disagreed. The very diversity of progressivism, he argued, accounted both for its enormous impact on its time and for its capacity to reveal to us today the "noise and tumult" of an age of rapid social change.

nonscientific problems, they believed, could be analyzed and solved scientifically. Many reformers came to believe that only enlightened experts and well-designed bureaucracies could create the stability and order America needed.

Some even spoke of the creation of a new civilization, in which the expertise of scientists and engineers could be brought to bear on the problems of the economy and society. The social scientist Thorstein Veblen, for example, proposed a new economic system in which power would reside in the hands of highly trained engineers. Only they, he argued, could fully understand the

"machine process" by which modern society must be governed.

The Professions

The late nineteenth century saw a dramatic expansion in the number of Americans engaged in administrative and professional tasks. Industries needed managers, technicians, and accountants as well as workers. Cities required commercial, medical, legal, and educational services. New technology required scientists and engineers, who, in turn, required institutions and instructors to

TENEMENT FAMILY, 1899 Jacob Riis, an indefatigable chronicler of the lives of tenant-dwelling immigrants, became one of the most influential photographers, and reformers, of his day. His book *How the Other Half Lives* became one of the classics of his era. In this photograph, he shows a girl in a grimy doorway cradling an infant—the kind of scene characteristic of his work. *(Bettmann/Corbis)*

train them. By the turn of the century, those performing these services had come to constitute a distinct social group—what some historians have called a new middle class.

The new middle class placed a high value on education and individual accomplishment. By the early twentieth century, its millions of members were building organizations and establishing standards to secure their position in society. The idea of professionalism had been a frail one in America even as late as 1880. When every patent-medicine salesman could claim to be a doctor, when every frustrated politician could set up shop as a lawyer, when anyone who could read and write could pose as a teacher, a professional label by itself carried little weight. There were, of course, skilled and responsible doctors, lawyers, teachers, and others; but they had no way of controlling or distinguishing themselves clearly from the amateurs, charlatans, and incompetents who presumed to practice their trades. As the demand for professional services increased, so did the pressures for reform.

Among the first to respond was the medical profession. In 1901, doctors who considered themselves trained professionals reorganized the American Medical Association into a national professional society. By

American Medical Association

TENEMENT CIGARMAKERS Among the social problems Jacob Riis attempted to illuminate were those of working conditions in immigrant communities. In this photograph from *How the Other Half Lives,* a cigarmaker works in his already crowded home surrounded by his children. Such home workers—many, perhaps most, of whom were women—were normally paid by the "piece," that is, by the amount of work they performed rather than the number of hours; the result was very long hours of labor (often with the help of the young children in the home) and very low pay. *(Museum of the City of New York)*

THE INFANT WELFARE SOCIETY, CHICAGO The Infant Welfare Society was one of many "helping" organizations in Chicago and other large cities—many of them closely tied to the settlement houses—that strove to help immigrants adapt to American life and create safe and healthy living conditions. Here, a volunteer helps an immigrant mother learn to bathe her baby sometime around 1910. *(Chicago Historical Society, ICHi-20216)*

tige and status to the professional level. Some professionals used their entrance requirements to exclude blacks, women, immigrants, and other "undesirables" from their ranks. Others used them simply to keep the numbers down, to ensure that demand would remain high.

Women and the Professions

Both by custom and by active barriers of law and prejudice, American women found themselves excluded from most of the emerging professions. But a substantial number of middle-class women—particularly those emerging from the new women's colleges and from the coeducational state universities—entered professional careers nevertheless.

A few women managed to establish themselves as physicians, lawyers, engineers, scientists, and corporate managers. Several leading medical schools admitted women, and in 1900 about 5 percent of all American physicians were female (a proportion that remained unchanged until the 1960s). Most, however, turned by necessity to those "helping" professions that society considered vaguely domestic and thus suitable for women: settlement houses, social work, and most important, teaching. Indeed, in the late nineteenth century, more than two-thirds of all grammar school teachers were women, and perhaps 90 percent of all professional women were teachers. For educated black women, in particular, the existence of segregated schools in the South created a substantial market for African-American teachers.

Female-Dominated Professions

Women also dominated other professional activities. Nursing had become primarily a women's field during and after the Civil War. By the early twentieth century, it was adopting professional standards. And many women entered academia—often receiving advanced degrees at such predominantly male institutions as the University of Chicago, MIT, or Columbia, and finding professional opportunities in the new and expanding women's colleges.

1920, nearly two-thirds of all American doctors were members. The AMA quickly called for strict, scientific standards for admission to the practice of medicine, with doctors themselves serving as protectors of the standards. State governments responded by passing new laws requiring the licensing of all physicians. By 1900, medical education at a few medical schools—notably Johns Hopkins in Baltimore (founded in 1893)—compared favorably with that in the leading institutions of Europe. Doctors such as William H. Welch at Hopkins revolutionized the teaching of medicine by moving students out of the classrooms and into laboratories and clinics.

There was similar movement in other professions. By 1916, lawyers in all forty-eight states had established professional bar associations. The nation's law schools accordingly expanded greatly. Businessmen supported the creation of schools of business administration and created their own national organizations: the National Association of Manufacturers in 1895 and the United States Chamber of Commerce in 1912. Even farmers, long the symbol of the romantic spirit of individualism, responded to the new order by forming, through the National Farm Bureau Federation, a network of agricultural organizations designed to spread scientific farming methods.

National Association of Manufacturers

While removing the untrained and incompetent, the admission requirements also protected those already in the professions from excessive competition and lent pres-

WOMEN AND REFORM

The prominence of women in reform movements is one of the most striking features of progressivism. In most states in the early twentieth century, women could not vote. They almost never held public office. They had footholds in only a few (and usually primarily

Key Role of Women in Reform Causes

female) professions and lived in a culture in which most people, male and female, believed that women were not suited for the public world. What, then, explains the prominent role so many women played in the reform activities of the period?

The "New Woman"

The phenomenon of the "new woman," widely remarked upon at the time, was a product of social and economic

Socioeconomic Origins of the New Woman

changes that affected the private world as much as the public one. By the end of the nineteenth century, almost all income-producing activity had moved out of the home and into the factory or the office. At the same time, children were beginning school at earlier ages and spending more time there. For wives and mothers who did not work for wages, the home was less of an all-consuming place. Technological innovations such as running water, electricity, and eventually household appliances made housework less onerous (even if higher standards of cleanliness counterbalanced many of these gains).

Declining family size also changed the lives of many women. Middle-class white women in the late nineteenth century had fewer children than their mothers and grandmothers had borne. They also lived longer. Many women thus now spent fewer years with young children in the home and lived more years after their children were grown.

Some educated women shunned marriage entirely, believing that only by remaining single could they play the roles they envisioned in the public world. Single women were among the most prominent female reformers of the time: Jane Addams and Lillian Wald in the settlement house movement, Frances Willard in the temperance movement, Anna Howard Shaw in the suffrage movement, and many others. Some of these women lived alone. Others lived with other women, often in long-term relationships—some of them secretly romantic—that were

"Boston Marriages"

known at the time as "Boston marriages." The divorce rate also rose rapidly in the late nineteenth century, from one divorce for every twenty-one marriages in 1880 to one in nine by 1916; women initiated the majority of them.

The Clubwomen

Among the most visible signs of the increasing public roles of women in the late nineteenth and early twentieth centuries were the women's clubs, which proliferated rapidly beginning in the 1880s and 1890s and became the vanguard of many important reforms.

The women's clubs began largely as cultural organizations to provide middle- and upper-class women with an outlet for their intellectual energies. In 1892, when women

GFWC

formed the General Federation of Women's Clubs to coordinate the activities of local organizations, there were more than 100,000 members in nearly 500 clubs. Eight years later, there were 160,000 members; and by 1917, over 1 million.

By the early twentieth century, the clubs were becoming less concerned with cultural activities and more concerned with contributing to social betterment. Because many club members were from wealthy families, some organizations had substantial funds at their disposal to make their influence felt. And ironically, because women could not vote, the clubs had a nonpartisan image that made them difficult for politicians to dismiss.

Black women occasionally joined clubs dominated by whites. But most such clubs excluded blacks, and so African Americans formed clubs of their own. Some of them affiliated with the General Federation, but most became part of the independent National Association of Colored Women. Some black clubs also took positions on issues of particular concern to African Americans, such as lynching and aspects of segregation.

The women's club movement seldom raised overt challenges to prevailing assumptions about the proper role of women in society. Few clubwomen were willing to accept the arguments of such committed feminists as Charlotte Perkins Gilman, who in her 1898 book *Women and Economics* argued that the tradi-

tional definition of gender roles was exploitative and obsolete. In-

A Public Space for Women

stead, club movement allowed women to define a space for themselves in the public world without openly challenging the existing, male-dominated order.

Much of what the clubs did was uncontroversial: planting trees; supporting schools, libraries, and settlement houses; building hospitals and parks. But clubwomen were also an important force in winning passage of state (and ultimately federal) laws that regulated the conditions of woman and child labor, established government inspection of workplaces, regulated the food and drug industries, reformed policies toward the Indian tribes, applied new standards to urban housing, and perhaps most notably outlawed the manufacture and sale of alcohol. They were instrumental in pressuring state legislatures in most states to provide "mother's pensions" to widowed or abandoned mothers with small children—a system that ultimately became absorbed into the Social Security system. In 1912, they pressured Congress into establishing the Children's Bureau in the Labor Department, an agency directed to develop policies to protect children.

In many of these efforts, the clubwomen formed alliances with other women's groups, such as the Women's Trade Union League, founded in 1903 by female union members

Women's Trade Union League

and upper-class reformers and committed to persuading women to join unions. In addition to working on behalf of protective legislation for

THE COLORED WOMEN'S LEAGUE OF WASHINGTON The women's club movement spread widely through American life and produced a number of organizations through which African-American women gathered to improve social and political conditions. The Colored Women's League of Washington, D.C., members of which appear in this 1894 photograph, was founded in 1892 by Sara Iredell Fleetwood, a registered nurse who married Christian Iredell, one of the first African-American soldiers to receive the Congressional Medal of Honor for his heroism in the Civil War. The league she founded was committed to "racial uplift," and it consisted mostly of teachers, who created nurseries for the infants of women who worked and evening schools for adults. They are shown here gathered on the steps of Frederick Douglass's home on Capitol Hill. Sara Fleetwood is in the second row on the far right. *(Manuscript Division, Library of Congress)*

women, WTUL members held public meetings on behalf of female workers, raised money to support strikes, marched on picket lines, and bailed striking women out of jail.

Woman Suffrage

Perhaps the largest single reform movement of the progressive era, indeed one of the largest in American history, was the fight for woman suffrage.

It is sometimes difficult for today's Americans to understand why the suffrage issue could have become the source of such enormous controversy. But at the time, suffrage seemed to many of its critics a very radical demand, in part because of the rationale some of its early supporters used to advance it. Throughout the late nineteenth century, many suffrage advocates presented their views in terms of "natural rights," arguing that

Radical Challenge of Women's Suffrage

women deserved the same rights as men—including, first and foremost, the right to vote. Elizabeth Cady Stanton, for example, wrote in 1892 of woman as "the arbiter of her own destiny . . . if we are to consider her as a citizen, as a member of a great nation, she must have the same rights as all other members." This was an argument that boldly challenged the views of the many men and women who believed that society required a distinctive female "sphere" in which women would serve first and foremost as wives and mothers. And so a powerful antisuffrage movement emerged, dominated by men but with the active support of many women. Opponents railed against the threat suffrage posed to the "natural order" of civilization. Antisuffragists, many of them women, associated suffrage with divorce (not without some reason, since many suffrage advocates also supported making it easier for women to obtain a divorce). They linked suffrage with promiscuity, looseness, and neglect of children.

SHIRTWAIST WORKERS ON STRIKE The Women's Trade Union League was notable for bringing educated, middle-class women together with workers in efforts to improve factory and labor conditions. These picketing women are workers in the "Ladies Tailors" garment factory in New York. *(Library of Congress)*

In the first years of the twentieth century, the suffrage movement began to overcome this opposition and win some substantial victories, in part because suffragists were becoming better organized and more politically sophisticated than their opponents. Under the leadership of Anna Howard Shaw, a Boston social worker, and Carrie Chapman Catt, a journalist from Iowa, membership in the National American Woman Suffrage Association grew from about 13,000 in 1893 to over 2 million in 1917. The movement gained strength because many of its most prominent leaders began to justify suffrage in "safer," less threatening ways. Suffrage, some supporters began to argue, would not challenge the "separate sphere" in which women resided. It was, they claimed, precisely because women occupied a distinct sphere—because as mothers and wives and homemakers they had special experiences and special sensitivities to bring to public life—that woman suffrage could make such an important contribution to politics.

NAWSA

In particular, many suffragists argued that enfranchising women would help the temperance movement, by giving its largest group of supporters a political voice. Some suffrage advocates claimed that once women had the vote, war would become a thing of the past, since women would—by their calming, maternal influence—help curb the belligerence of men. That was one reason why World War I gave a final, decisive push to the movement for suffrage.

Suffrage also attracted support for other, less optimistic reasons. Many middle-class people found persuasive the argument that if blacks, immigrants, and other "base" groups had access to the franchise, then it was a matter not only of justice but of common sense to allow educated, "well-born" women to vote.

Conservative Arguments for Suffrage

The principal triumphs of the suffrage movement began in 1910, when Washington became the first state in fourteen years to extend suffrage to women. California followed a year later, and four other western states in 1912. In 1913, Illinois became the first state east of the Mississippi to embrace woman suffrage. And in 1917 and 1918, New York and Michigan—two of the most populous states in the Union—gave women the vote. By 1919, thirty-nine states had granted women the right to vote in at least some elections; fifteen had allowed them full participation. In 1920, finally, suffragists won ratification of the Nineteenth Amendment, which guaranteed political rights to women throughout the nation.

Nineteenth Amendment

To some feminists, however, the victory seemed less than complete. Alice Paul, head of the militant National Woman's Party (founded in 1916), never accepted the relatively conservative "separate sphere" justification for suffrage. She argued that the Nineteenth Amendment alone would not be sufficient to protect women's rights. Women needed more: a constitutional amendment that would provide clear, legal protection for their rights and would prohibit all discrimination on the basis of sex. But Alice Paul's argument found limited favor even among many of the most important leaders of the recently triumphant suffrage crusade.

Equal Rights Amendment

"VOTES FOR WOMEN," BY B. M. BOYE This striking poster was the prize-winning entry in a 1911 contest sponsored by the College Equal Suffrage League of Northern California. *(Schlesinger Library, Radcliffe Institute, Harvard University)*

THE ASSAULT ON THE PARTIES

Sooner or later, most progressive goals required the involvement of government. Only government, reformers agreed, could effectively counter the many powerful private interests that threatened the nation. But American government at the dawn of the new century was, progressives believed, poorly adapted to perform their ambitious tasks. At every

Reforming Government

level political institutions were outmoded, inefficient, and corrupt. Before progressives could reform society effectively, they would have to reform government itself. Many reformers believed the first step must be an assault on the dominant role the political parties played in the life of the state.

Early Attacks

Attacks on party dominance had been frequent in the late nineteenth century. Greenbackism and Populism, for example, had been efforts to break the hammerlock with which the Republicans and Democrats controlled public life. The Independent Republicans (or mugwumps) had attempted to challenge the grip of partisanship.

The early assaults enjoyed some success. In the 1880s and 1890s, for example, most states adopted the secret ballot. Prior to that, the political parties themselves had printed ballots (or "tickets"), with the names of the party's candidates, and no others. They distributed the tickets to their supporters, who then simply went to the polls to deposit them in the ballot box. The old system had made it possible for bosses to monitor the voting behavior of their constituents; it had also made it difficult for voters to "split" their tickets—to vote for candidates of different parties for different offices. The new secret ballot—printed by the government and distributed at the polls to be filled out and deposited in secret—helped chip away at the power of the parties over the voters.

Municipal Reform

Many progressives, such as Lincoln Steffens, believed the impact of party rule was most damaging in the cities. Municipal government therefore became the first target of those working for political reform.

The muckrakers struck a responsive chord among a powerful group of urban, middle-class progressives. For several decades after the Civil War, "respectable" citizens of the nation's large cities had avoided participation in municipal government. Viewing politics as a debased and demeaning activity, they shrank from con-

Middle-Class Progressives

tact with the "vulgar" elements who were coming to dominate public life. By the end of the century, however, a new generation of activists—some of them members of old aristocratic families, others a part of the new middle class—were taking a growing interest in government.

They faced a formidable array of opponents. In addition to challenging the powerful city bosses and their entrenched political organizations, they were attacking a large group of special interests: saloon owners, brothel keepers, and, perhaps most significantly, those businessmen who had established lucrative relationships with the urban political machines and who viewed reform as a threat to their profits. Finally, there was the great constituency of urban working people, many of them recent immigrants, to whom the machines were a source of needed jobs and services. Gradually, however, the reformers gained in political strength.

New Forms of Governance

One of the first major successes came in Galveston, Texas, where the old city government proved completely unable to deal with the effects of a destructive tidal wave in 1900. Capitalizing on public dismay, reformers, many of them local businessmen, won approval of a new city charter.

SOCIAL DEMOCRACY

Enormous energy, enthusiasm, and organization drove the reform efforts in America in the late nineteenth and early twentieth centuries, much of it a result of social crises and political movements in the United States. But the "age of reform," as some scholars have called it, was not an American phenomenon alone. It was part of a wave of social experimentation that was occurring through much of the industrial world. "Progressivism" in other countries influenced the social movements in the United States. And American reform, in turn, had significant influence on other countries as well.

Several industrializing nations adopted the term "progressivism" for their efforts—not only the United States, but also England, Germany, and France. But the term that most broadly defined the new reform energies was "social democracy." Social democrats in many countries shared a belief in the betterment of society through the accumulation of knowledge—rather than through reliance on inherited ideology or faith. They favored improving the social condition of all people through reforms of the economy and government programs of social protection. And they believed that these changes could come through peaceful political change, rather than through radicalism or revolution. Political parties emerged in several countries committed to these goals: the Labour Party in Britain, Social Democratic parties in various European nations, and the short-lived Progressive Party in the United States. Intellectuals, academics, and government officials across the world shared the knowledge they were accumulating and observed one another's social programs.

American reformers at the turn of the century spent much time visiting Germany, France, Britain, Belgium, and the Netherlands, observing the reforms

(Archives Charmet/Bridgeman Art Library)

in progress there, and Europeans visited the United States in turn. Reformers from both America and Europe were also fascinated by the advanced social experiments in Australia and, especially, New Zealand—which the American reformer Henry Demarest Lloyd once called "the political brain of the modern world." But New Zealand's dramatic experiments in factory regulation, woman suffrage, old-age pensions, progressive taxation, and labor arbitration gradually found counterparts in many other nations as well. William Allen White, a progressive journalist from Kansas, said of this time: "We were parts of one another, in the United States and Europe. Something was welding us into one social and economic whole with local political variations . . . [all] fighting a common cause."

Social democracy—or, as it was sometimes called in the United States and elsewhere, social justice or the

Social Gospel—was responsible for many public programs. Germany began a system of social insurance for its citizens in the 1880s while undertaking a massive study of society that produced over 140 volumes of "social investigation" of almost every aspect of the nation's life. French reformers pressed in the 1890s for factory regulation, assistance to the elderly, and progressive taxation. Britain pioneered the settlement houses in working-class areas of London—a movement that soon spread to the United States as well—and, like the United States, witnessed growing challenges to the power of monopolies at both the local and national level.

In many countries, social democrats felt pressure from the rising worldwide labor movement and from the rise of socialist parties in many industrial countries as well. Strikes, sometimes violent, were common in France, Germany, Britain, and the United States in the late nineteenth century. The more militant workers became, the more unions seemed to grow. Social democrats did not always welcome the rise of militant labor movements, but they took them seriously and used them to support their own efforts at reform.

The politics of social democracy represented a great shift in the character of public life all over the industrial world. Instead of battles over the privileges of aristocrats or the power of monarchs, reformers now focused on the social problems of ordinary people and attempted to improve their lot. "The politics of the future are social politics," the British reformer Joseph Chamberlain said in the 1880s, referring to efforts to deal with the problems of ordinary citizens. That belief was fueling progressive efforts across the world in the years that Americans have come to call the "progressive era."

Commission Plan The mayor and council were replaced by an elected, nonpartisan commission. In 1907, Des Moines, Iowa, adopted its own version of the commission plan, and other cities soon followed.

Another approach to municipal reform was the city-manager plan, by which elected officials hired an outside expert—often a professionally trained business manager or engineer—to take charge of the government. **City-Manager Plan**

TOM JOHNSON As sentiment for municipal reform grew in intensity in the late nineteenth century, it became possible for progressive mayors committed to ending "boss rule" to win election over machine candidates in some of America's largest cities. One of the most prominent was Tom Johnson, the reform mayor of Cleveland. Johnson made a fortune in the steel and streetcar business, and then entered politics, partly as a result of reading Henry George's *Poverty and Progress*. He became mayor in 1901 and in his four terms waged strenuous battles against party bosses and corporate interests. He won many fights, but he lost what he considered his most important one: the struggle for municipal ownership of public utilities. *(Western Reserve Historical Society)*

The city manager would presumably remain untainted by the corrupting influence of politics. By the end of the progressive era, almost 400 cities were operating under commissions, and another 45 employed city managers.

In most urban areas, the enemies of party had to settle for less absolute victories. Some cities made the election of mayors nonpartisan (so that the parties could not choose the candidates) or moved them to years when no presidential or congressional races were in progress (to reduce the influence of the large turnouts that party organizations produced). Reformers tried to make city councilors run at large, to limit the influence of ward leaders and district bosses. They tried to strengthen the power of the mayor at the expense of the city council, on the assumption that reformers were more likely to succeed in getting a sympathetic mayor elected than they were to win control of the entire council.

Some of the most successful reformers emerged from conventional political structures that progressives came

| Tom Johnson |

to control. Tom Johnson, the celebrated reform mayor of Cleveland, waged a long war against the powerful streetcar interests in his city, fighting to lower streetcar fares to 3 cents, and ultimately to impose municipal ownership on certain basic utilities. After Johnson's defeat and death, his talented aide Newton D. Baker won election as mayor and helped maintain Cleveland's reputation as the best-governed city in America. Hazen Pingree of Detroit, Samuel

"Golden Rule" Jones of Toledo, and other mayors effectively challenged local party bosses to bring the spirit of reform into city government.

Statehouse Progressivism

The assault on boss rule in the cities did not, however, always produce results. Consequently, many progressives turned to state government as an agent for reform. They looked with particular scorn on state legislatures, whose ill-paid, relatively undistinguished members, they believed, were generally incompetent, often corrupt, and totally controlled by party bosses. Reformers began looking for ways to circumvent the boss-controlled legislatures by increasing the power of the electorate.

Two of the most important changes were innovations first proposed by Populists in the 1890s: the initiative and the referendum. The initiative allowed reformers to circumvent state legislatures by submitting | Initiative and Referendum |
new legislation directly to the voters in general elections. The referendum provided a method by which actions of the legislature could be returned to the electorate for approval. By 1918, more than twenty states had enacted one or both of these reforms.

Similarly, the direct primary and the recall were efforts to limit the power of party and improve the quality of elected officials. The primary election was an attempt to take the selection of candidates away from | Direct Primary and Recall |

the bosses and give it to the people. In the South, it was also an effort to limit black voting—since primary voting, many white southerners believed, would be easier to control than general elections. The recall gave voters the right to remove a public official from office at a special election, which could be called after a sufficient number of citizens had signed a petition. By 1915, every state in the nation had instituted primary elections for at least some offices. The recall encountered more strenuous opposition, but a few states (such as California) adopted it as well.

Other reform measures attempted to clean up the legislatures themselves. Between 1903 and 1908, twelve states passed laws restricting lobbying by business interests in state legislatures. In those same years, twenty-two states banned campaign contributions by corporations, and twenty-four states forbade public officials to accept free passes from railroads. Many states also struggled successfully to create systems of workmen's compensation for workers injured on the job. And starting in 1911, reformers successfully created pensions for widows with dependent children.

Reform efforts proved most effective in states that elevated vigorous and committed politicians to positions of leadership. In New York, Governor Charles Evans Hughes exploited progressive sentiment to create a commission to regulate public utilities. In California, Governor Hiram Johnson limited the political power of the Southern Pacific Railroad. In New Jersey, Woodrow Wilson, the Princeton University president elected governor in 1910, used executive leadership to win reforms designed to end New Jersey's widely denounced position as the "mother of trusts."

But the most celebrated state-level reformer was Robert M. La Follette of Wisconsin. Elected governor in 1900, he helped turn his state into what reformers across the nation described as a "laboratory of progressivism." Under his leadership the Wisconsin progressives won approval of direct primaries, initiatives, and referendums. They regulated railroads and utilities. They passed laws to regulate the workplace and provide compensation for laborers injured on the job. They instituted graduated taxes on inherited fortunes, and they nearly doubled state levies on railroads and other corporate interests. La Follette used his personal magnetism to widen public awareness of progressive goals. Reform was the responsibility not simply of politicians, he argued, but of newspapers, citizens' groups, educational institutions, and business and professional organizations.

Robert La Follette

Parties and Interest Groups

The reformers did not, of course, eliminate parties from American political life. But they did contribute to a

ROBERT LA FOLLETTE CAMPAIGNING IN WISCONSIN After three terms as governor of Wisconsin, La Follette began a long career in the United States Senate in 1906, during which he worked uncompromisingly for advanced progressive reforms—so uncompromisingly, in fact, that he was often almost completely isolated. He titled a chapter of his autobiography "Alone in the Senate." La Follette had a greater impact on his own state, whose politics he and his sons dominated for nearly forty years and where he was able to win passage of many reforms that the federal government resisted. *(Library of Congress)*

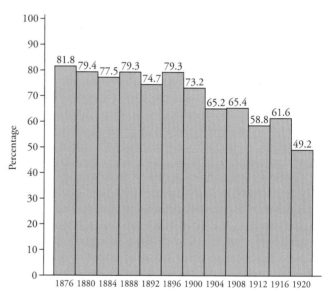

VOTER PARTICIPATION IN PRESIDENTIAL ELECTIONS, 1876–1920
One of the striking developments of early-twentieth-century politics was the significant decline in popular participation in politics. This chart shows the steady downward progression of voter turnout in presidential elections from 1876 to 1920. Turnout remained high by modern standards (except for the aberrant election of 1920, in which turnout dropped sharply because women had recently received the vote but had not yet begun to participate in elections in large numbers). But from an average rate of participation of about 79 percent in the last quarter of the nineteenth century, turnout dropped to an average of about 65 percent between 1900 and 1916.
◆ *What were some of the reasons for this decline?*

decline in party influence. Evidence of their impact came

Decline of Party Influence

from, among other things, the decline in voter turnout. In the late nineteenth century, up to 81 percent of eligible voters routinely turned out for national elections because of the strength of party loyalty. In the early twentieth century, while turnout remained high by today's standards, the figure declined markedly as parties grew weaker. In the presidential election of 1900, 73 percent of the electorate voted. By 1912, that figure had declined to about 59 percent. Never again did voter turnout reach as high as 70 percent.

At the same time that parties were declining, other power centers were beginning to replace them: what have become known as "interest groups." Beginning late in the nineteenth century and accelerating rapidly in the twentieth, new organizations emerged outside the party system: professional organizations, trade associations representing businesses and industries, labor organizations, farm lobbies, and many others. Social workers, the settlement house movement, women's clubs, and others learned to operate as interest groups to advance their demands.

SOURCES OF PROGRESSIVE REFORM

Middle-class reformers, most of them from the East, dominated the public image and much of the substance of progressivism in the late nineteenth and early twentieth centuries. But they were not alone in seeking to improve social conditions. Working-class Americans, African Americans, westerners, and even party bosses also played crucial roles in advancing some of the important reforms of the era.

Labor, the Machine, and Reform

Although the American Federation of Labor, and its leader Samuel Gompers, remained largely aloof from many of the reform efforts of the time (reflecting Gompers's firm belief that workers should not rely on government to improve their lot), some unions nevertheless played important roles in reform battles. Between 1911 and 1913, thanks to political pressure from labor groups such as the newly formed Union Labor Party, California passed a child labor law, a workmen's compensation law, and a limitation on working hours for women. Union pressures contributed to the passage of similar laws in many other states as well.

One result of the assault on the parties was a change in the party organizations themselves, which attempted to adapt to the new realities so as to preserve their influence. They sometimes allowed their machines to become vehicles of social reform. One example was New York's Tammany Hall, the nation's oldest and most notorious city machine. Its astute leader, Charles Francis Murphy, began in the early years of the century to fuse the techniques of boss rule with some of the concerns of social reformers. Tammany began to use its political power on behalf of legislation to improve working conditions, protect child laborers, and eliminate the worst abuses of the industrial economy.

In 1911, a terrible fire swept through the factory of the Triangle Shirtwaist Company in New York; 146 workers, most of them women, died. Many of them had been trapped inside

Triangle Shirtwaist Fire

the burning building because management had locked the emergency exits to prevent malingering. For the next three years, a state commission studied not only the background of the fire but also the general condition of the industrial workplace. It was responding to intense public pressure from women's groups and New York City labor unions—and to less public pressure from Tammany Hall. By 1914, the commission had issued a series of reports calling for major reforms in the conditions of modern labor. The report itself was a classic progressive document, based on the testimony of experts, filled with statistics and technical data.

Yet, when its recommendations reached the New York legislature, its most effective supporters were not middle-class progressives but two Tammany Democrats from working-class backgrounds: Senator Robert F. Wagner and Assemblyman Alfred E. Smith. With the support of Murphy and the backing of other Tammany legislators, they steered through a series of pioneering labor laws that imposed strict regulations on factory owners and established effective mechanisms for enforcement.

Western Progressives

The American West produced some of the most notable progressive leaders of the time: Hiram Johnson of California, George Norris of Nebraska, William Borah of Idaho, and others—almost all of whom spent at least some of their political careers in the United States Senate. For western states, the most important target of reform energies was not state or local governments, which had relatively little power, but the federal government, which exercised a kind of authority in the West that it had never possessed in the East. That was in part because some of the most important issues to the future of the West required action above the state level. Disputes over water, for example, almost always involved rivers and streams that crossed state lines. The question of who had the rights to the waters of the Colorado River created a political battle that no state government could resolve; the federal government had to arbitrate.

More significant, perhaps, the federal government exercised enormous power over the lands and resources of the western states and provided substantial subsidies to the

VICTIMS OF THE TRIANGLE FIRE   In this bleak photograph, victims of the fire in the factory of the Triangle Shirtwaist Company are laid out on the sidewalk near the building, as police and passersby look up at the scene of the blaze. The tragedy of the Triangle Fire galvanized New York legislators into passing laws to protect women workers.   *(Brown Brothers)*

region in the form of land grants and support for railroad and water projects. Huge areas of the West remained (and still remain) public lands, controlled by Washington—a far greater proportion than in any states east of the Mississippi; and much of the growth of the West was (and continues to be) a result of federally funded dams and water projects.

African Americans and Reform

One social question that received relatively little attention from white progressives was race. But among African Americans themselves, the progressive era produced some significant challenges to existing racial norms.

African Americans faced greater obstacles than any other group in challenging their own oppressed status and seeking reform. Thus it was not surprising, perhaps, that so many embraced the message of Booker T. Washington in the late nineteenth century, to "put down your bucket where you are," to work for immediate self-improvement rather than long-range social change. Not all African Americans, however, were content with this approach. And by the turn of the century a powerful challenge was emerging—to the philosophy of Washington and, more important, to the entire structure of race relations. The chief spokesman for this new approach was W. E. B. Du Bois.

Du Bois, unlike Washington, had never known slavery. Born in Massachusetts, educated at Fisk University in Atlanta and at Harvard, he grew to maturity with a more W. E. B. Du Bois expansive view than Washington of the goals of his race and the responsibilities of white society to eliminate prejudice and injustice. In *The Souls of Black Folk* (1903), he launched an open attack on the philosophy of Washington, accusing him of encouraging white efforts to impose segregation and of limiting the aspirations of his race. "Is it possible and probable," he asked, "that nine millions of men can make effective progress in economic lines if they are deprived of political rights, made a servile caste, and allowed only the most meager chance for developing their exceptional men? If history and reason give any distinct answer to these questions, it is an emphatic No."

Rather than content themselves with education at the trade and agricultural schools, Du Bois advocated, talented blacks should accept nothing less than a full university education. They should aspire to the professions. They should, above all, fight for their civil rights, not simply wait for them to be granted as a reward for patient striving. In 1905, Du Bois and a group of his supporters met at Niagara Falls—on the Canadian side of the border because no hotel on the American side of the Falls would have them—and launched what became known as the Niagara Movement. Four years later, after a race riot in Springfield, Illinois, they joined with white progressives sympathetic to their cause to form the National Association for the Advancement of Colored People (NAACP). Whites held most of the offices at first, but Du Bois, its director of publicity and research, was the guiding spirit. In the ensuing years, the new organization led the drive for equal rights, using as its principal weapon lawsuits in the federal courts.

NAACP Founded

Within less than a decade, the NAACP had begun to win some important victories. In *Guinn* v. *United States* (1915), the Supreme Court supported its position that the grandfather clause in an Oklahoma law was unconstitutional. (The statute denied the vote to any citizen whose ancestors had not been enfranchised in 1860.) In *Buchanan* v. *Worley* (1917), the Court struck down a Louisville, Kentucky, law requiring residential segregation. The NAACP established itself, particularly after Booker T. Washington's death in 1915, as one of the nation's leading black organizations, a position it would maintain for many years.

Among the many issues that engaged the NAACP and other African-American organizations was the phenomenon of lynching in the South. Du Bois was an outspoken critic of lynching and an advocate of a federal law making it illegal (since state courts in the South routinely refused to prosecute lynchers). But the most determined opponents of lynching were southern women. They included white women such as Jessie Daniel Ames. The most effective crusader was a black woman, Ida Wells Barnett, who worked both on her own (at great personal risk) and with such organizations as the National Association of Colored Women and the Women's Convention of the National Baptist Church to try to discredit lynching and challenge segregation.

THE YOUNG W. E. B. DU BOIS This formal photograph of W. E. B. Du Bois was taken in 1899, when he was thirty-one years old and a professor at Atlanta University. He had just published *The Philadelphia Negro*, a classic sociological study of an urban community, which startled many readers with its description of the complex class system among African Americans in the city. *(Hulton Archive/Getty Images)*

CRUSADE FOR SOCIAL ORDER AND REFORM

Reformers directed many of their energies at the political process. But they also crusaded on behalf of what they considered moral issues. There were campaigns to eliminate alcohol from national life, to curb prostitution, to limit divorce, and to restrict immigration. Proponents of each of those reforms believed that success would help regenerate society as a whole.

The Temperance Crusade

Many progressives considered the elimination of alcohol from American life a necessary step in restoring order to society. Scarce wages vanished as workers spent hours in

CRUSADING FOR TEMPERANCE This unflattering painting by Ben Shahn portrays late-nineteenth-century women demonstrating grimly in front of a saloon. It suggests the degree to which temperance and prohibition had fallen out of favor with liberals and progressives by the 1930s, when Shahn was working. In earlier years, however, temperance attracted the support of some of the most advanced American reformers. *(©Estate of Ben Shahn/Licensed by VAGA, New York, NY/Museum of the City of New York)*

the saloons. Drunkenness spawned violence, and occasionally murder, within urban families. Working-class wives and mothers hoped through temperance to reform male behavior and thus improve women's lives. Employers, too, regarded alcohol as an impediment to industrial efficiency; workers often missed time on the job because of drunkenness or came to the factory intoxicated. Critics of economic privilege denounced the liquor industry as one of the nation's most sinister trusts. And political reformers, who (correctly) looked on the saloon as one of the central institutions of the urban machine, saw an attack on drinking as part of an attack on the bosses. Out of such sentiments emerged the temperance movement.

Temperance had been a major reform movement before the Civil War, mobilizing large numbers of people in a crusade with strong evangelical overtones. In 1873, the movement developed new strength. Temperance advocates formed the Women's Christian Temperance Union (WCTU), led after 1879 by Frances Willard. By 1911, it had 245,000 members and had become the single largest women's organization in American history to that point. In 1893, the Anti-Saloon League joined the temperance movement and, along with the WCTU, began to press for a specific legislative solution: the legal abolition of saloons. Gradually, that demand grew to include the complete prohibition of the sale and manufacture of alcoholic beverages.

WCTU

Despite substantial opposition from immigrant and working-class voters, pressure for prohibition grew steadily through the first decades of the new century. By 1916, nineteen states had passed prohibition laws. But since the consumption of alcohol was actually increasing in many unregulated areas, temperance advocates were beginning to advocate a national prohibition law. America's entry into World War I, and the moral fervor it unleashed, provided the last push to the advocates of prohibition. In 1917, with the support of rural fundamentalists who opposed alcohol on moral and religious grounds, progressive advocates of prohibition steered through Congress a constitutional amendment embodying their demands. Two years later, after ratification by every state in the nation except Connecticut and Rhode Island (bastions of Catholic immigrants), the Eighteenth Amendment became law, to take effect in January 1920.

Eighteenth Amendment

Immigration Restriction

Virtually all reformers agreed that the growing immigrant population had created social problems, but there was wide disagreement on how to best respond. Some progressives believed that the proper approach was to help the new residents adapt to American society. Others argued that efforts at assimilation had failed and

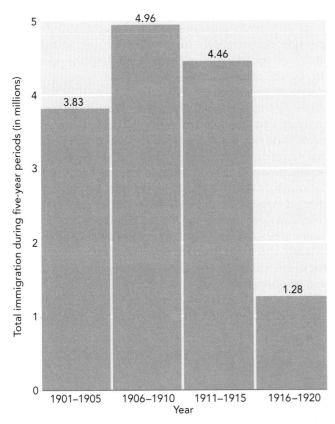

TOTAL IMMIGRATION, 1900–1920 Immigration into the United States reached the highest level in the nation's history to that point in the first fifteen years of the twentieth century. In the nineteenth century, there was no five-year period when as many as 3 million immigrants arrived in America. In the first fifteen years of the twentieth century, more than 3 million newcomers arrived in every five-year period— and in one of them, as this chart reveals, the number reached almost 5 million. ◆ *Why did the flow of immigrants drop so sharply in the period 1916–1920?*

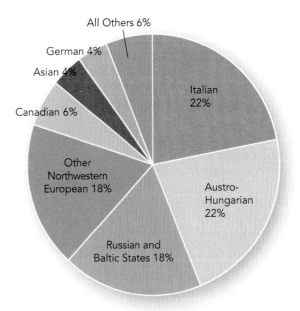

SOURCES OF IMMIGRATION, 1900–1920 At least as striking as the increase in immigration in the early twentieth century was the change in its sources. In the nineteenth century, the vast majority of immigrants to the United States had come from northern and western Europe (especially Britain, Ireland, Germany, and Scandinavia). Now, as this chart shows, the major sources were southern and eastern Europe, with over 60 percent coming from Italy, Russia, and the eastern European regions of the Austro-Hungarian empire. ◆ *What impact did these changing sources have on attitudes toward immigration in the United States?*

that the only solution was to limit the flow of new arrivals.

In the first decades of the century, pressure grew to close the nation's gates. New scholarly theories, appealing to the progressive respect for expertise, argued that the introduction of immigrants into American society was polluting the nation's racial stock. Among the theories created to support this argument was eugenics, the science of altering the reproductive processes of plants and animals to produce new hybrids or breeds. In the early twentieth century, there was an effort, funded by the Carnegie Foundation, to turn eugenics into a method of altering human reproduction as well. But the eugenics movement when applied to humans was not an effort to "breed" new people, an effort for which no scientific tools existed. It was, rather, an effort to grade races and ethnic groups according to their genetic qualities. Eugenicists advocated the forced sterilization of the mentally retarded, criminals, and others. But they also spread the belief that human inequalities were hereditary and that

Eugenics and Nativism

immigration was contributing to the multiplication of the unfit. Skillful publicists such as Madison Grant, whose *The Passing of the Great Race* (1916) established him as the nation's most effective nativist, warned of the dangers of racial "mongrelization" and of the importance of protecting the purity of Anglo-Saxon and other Nordic stock from pollution by eastern Europeans, Latin Americans, and Asians.

A special federal commission of "experts," chaired by Senator William P. Dillingham of Vermont, issued a study filled with statistics and scholarly testimony. It argued that the newer immigrant groups—largely southern and eastern Europeans—had proven themselves less assimilable than earlier immigrants. Immigration, the report implied, should be restricted by nationality. Many people who rejected these racial arguments nevertheless supported limiting immigration as a way to solve such urban problems as overcrowding, unemployment, strained social services, and social unrest.

The combination of these concerns gradually won for the nativists the support of some of the nation's leading progressives, among them former president Theodore Roosevelt. Powerful opponents—employers who saw immigration as a source of cheap labor, immigrants themselves, and their political representatives—managed to block the restriction movement for a time. But by the beginning of World War I (which itself effectively blocked immigration temporarily), the nativist tide was gaining strength.

CHALLENGING THE CAPITALIST ORDER

If there was one issue that overshadowed, and helped to shape, all others in the minds of reformers, it was the character of the dramatically growing modern industrial economy. Most of the problems that concerned progressives could be traced back, directly or indirectly, to the growing power and influence—and also, reformers believed, corruption—of corporate America. So it is not surprising that prominent among progressive concerns was reshaping or reforming the behavior of the capitalist world.

The Dream of Socialism

At no time in the history of the United States to that point, and seldom after, did radical critiques of the capitalist system attract more support than in the period between 1900 and 1914. Although never a force to rival or even seriously threaten the two major parties, the Socialist Party of America grew during these years into a force of considerable strength. In the election of 1900, it had attracted the support of fewer than 100,000 voters; in 1912, its durable leader and perennial presidential candidate, Eugene V. Debs, received nearly 1 million ballots. Strongest in urban immigrant communities, particularly among Germans and Jews, it also attracted the loyalties of a substantial number of Protestant farmers in the South and Midwest. Socialists won election to over 1,000 state and local offices. And they had the support at times of such intellectuals as Lincoln Steffens, the crusader against municipal corruption, and Walter Lippmann, the brilliant young journalist and social critic. Florence Kelley, Frances Willard, and other women reformers were attracted to socialism, too, in part because of its support for pacifism and labor organizing.

Virtually all socialists agreed on the need for basic structural changes in the economy, but they differed

Eugene Debs

MAY DAY, 1900   The American Socialist Party staged this vast rally in New York City's Union Square to celebrate May Day in 1900. The Second Socialist International had designated May Day as the official holiday for radical labor in 1899. *(Brown Brothers)*

widely on the extent of those changes and the tactics necessary to achieve them. Some socialists endorsed the radical goals of European Marxists; others envisioned a moderate reform that would allow small-scale private enterprise to survive but would nationalize major industries. Some believed in working for reform through electoral politics; others favored militant direct action. Among the militants was the radical labor union the Industrial

"Wobblies"

Workers of the World (IWW), known to opponents as the "Wobblies." Under the leadership of William ("Big Bill") Haywood, the IWW advocated a single union for all workers and abolition of the "wage slave" system; it rejected political action in favor of strikes—especially the general strike. The Wobblies were widely believed to have been responsible for the dynamiting of railroad lines and power stations and other acts of terror in the first years of the twentieth century.

The IWW was one of the few labor organizations of the time to champion the cause of unskilled workers and had particular strength in the West—where a large group of migratory laborers (miners, timbermen, and others) found it very difficult to organize or sustain conventional unions. In 1917, a strike by IWW timber workers in Washington and Idaho shut down production in the industry. That brought down upon the union the wrath of the federal government, which had just begun mobilizing for war and needed timber for war production. Federal authorities imprisoned the leaders of the union, and state governments between 1917 and 1919 passed a series of laws that effectively outlawed the IWW. The organization survived for a time, but never fully recovered.

Moderate socialists who advocated peaceful change through political struggle dominated the Socialist Party. They emphasized a gradual education of the public to the need for change and patient efforts within the system to enact it. But by the end of World War I, because the party

Socialism's Demise

had refused to support the war effort and because of a growing wave of antiradicalism that subjected the socialists to enormous harassment and persecution, socialism was in decline as a significant political force.

Decentralization and Regulation

Most progressives retained a faith in the possibilities of reform within a capitalist system. Rather than nationalize basic industries, many reformers hoped to restore the economy to a more human scale. Few envisioned a return to a society of small, local enterprises; some consolidation, they recognized, was inevitable. They did, however, argue that the federal government should work to break up the largest combinations and enforce a balance between the need for bigness and the need for competition.

This viewpoint came to be identified particularly closely with Louis D. Brandeis, a brilliant lawyer and later justice of the Supreme Court, who wrote widely (most notably in his 1913 book *Other People's Money*) about the "curse of bigness."

Brandeis and his supporters opposed bigness in part because they considered it inefficient. But their opposition had a moral basis as well. Bigness was a threat not just to efficiency but to freedom. It limited the ability of individuals to

The Problem of Corporate Centralization

control their own destinies. It encouraged abuses of power. Government must, Brandeis insisted, regulate competition in such a way as to ensure that large combinations did not emerge.

LOUIS BRANDEIS Brandeis graduated from Harvard Law School in 1877 with the best academic record of any student in the school's previous or subsequent history. His success in his Boston law practice was such that by the early twentieth century he was able to spend much of his time in unpaid work for public causes. His investigations of monopoly power soon made him a major figure in the emerging progressive movement. Woodrow Wilson nominated him for the United States Supreme Court in January 1916. He was one of the few nominees in the Court's history never to have held prior public office, and he was the first Jew ever to have been nominated. The appointment aroused five months of bitter controversy in the Senate before Brandeis was finally confirmed. For the next twenty years, he was one of the Court's most powerful members—all the while lobbying behind the scenes on behalf of the many political causes (preeminent among them Zionism, the founding of a Jewish state) to which he remained committed. *(Bettmann/Corbis)*

Other progressives were less enthusiastic about the virtues of competition. More important to them was efficiency, which they believed economic concentration encouraged. What government should do, they argued, was not to fight "bigness," but to guard against abuses of power by large institutions. It should distinguish between "good trusts" and "bad trusts," encouraging the good while disciplining the bad. Since economic consolidation was destined to remain a permanent feature of American society, continuing oversight by a strong, modernized government was essential. One of the most influential spokesmen for this emerging "nationalist" position was Herbert Croly, whose 1909 book *The Promise of American Life* became an influential progressive document.

"Good Trusts" and "Bad Trusts"

Increasingly, the attention of nationalists such as Croly focused on some form of coordination of the industrial economy. Society must act, Walter Lippmann wrote in a notable 1914 book, *Drift and Mastery*, "to introduce plan where there has been clash, and purpose into the jungles of disordered growth." To some, that meant businesses themselves learning new ways of cooperation and self-regulation. To others, the solution was for government to play a more active role in regulating and planning economic life. One of those who came to endorse that position (although not fully until after 1910) was Theodore Roosevelt, who once said: "We should enter upon a course of supervision, control, and regulation of those great corporations." Roosevelt became for a time the most powerful symbol of the reform impulse at the national level.

THEODORE ROOSEVELT AND THE MODERN PRESIDENCY

"Presidents in general are not lovable," the writer Walter Lippmann, who had known many, said near the end of his life. "They've had to do too much to get where they are. But there was one President who was lovable—Teddy Roosevelt—and I loved him."

Lippmann was not alone. To a generation of progressive reformers, Theodore Roosevelt was more than an admired public figure; he was an idol. No president before, and few since, had attracted such attention and devotion. Yet, for all his popularity among reformers, Roosevelt was in many respects decidedly conservative. He earned his extraordinary popularity less because of the extent of the reforms he championed than because he brought to his office a broad conception of its powers and invested the presidency with something of its modern status as the center of national political life.

The Accidental President

When President William McKinley suddenly died in September 1901, the victim of an assassination, Roosevelt (who had been elected vice president less than a year before) was only forty-two years old, the youngest man ever to assume the presidency. "I told William McKinley that it was a mistake to nominate that wild man at Philadelphia," party boss Mark Hanna was reported to have exclaimed. "Now look, that damned cowboy is President of the United States!"

Roosevelt's reputation as a wild man was a result less of the substance of his early political career than of its style. As a young member of the New York legislature, he had displayed an energy seldom seen in that lethargic body. As a rancher in the Dakota Badlands (where he retired briefly after the sudden death of his first wife), he had helped capture outlaws. As New York City police commissioner, he had been a flamboyant battler against crime and vice. As assistant secretary of the navy, he had been a bold proponent of American expansion. As commander of the Rough Riders, he had led a heroic, if militarily useless, charge in the battle of San Juan Hill in Cuba during the Spanish-American War.

Roosevelt's Background

THEODORE ROOSEVELT This heroic portrait of Theodore Roosevelt is by the great American portraitist John Singer Sargent. It hangs today in the White House. *(White House Historical Association)*

BOYS IN THE MINES These young boys, covered in grime and no more than twelve years old, pose for the noted photographer Lewis Hine outside the coal mine in Pennsylvania where they worked as "breaker boys," crawling into newly blasted areas and breaking up the loose coal. The rugged conditions in the mines were one cause of the great strike of 1902, in which Theodore Roosevelt intervened. *(Library of Congress)*

But Roosevelt as president never openly rebelled against the leaders of his party. He became, rather, a champion of cautious, moderate change. Reform, he believed, was a vehicle less for remaking American society than for protecting it against more radical challenges.

Government, Capital, and Labor

Roosevelt allied himself with those progressives who urged regulation (but not destruction) of the trusts. At the heart of Roosevelt's policy was his desire to win for government the power to investigate the activities of corporations and publicize the results. The new Department of Commerce and Labor, established in 1903 (later to be divided into two separate departments), was to assist in this task through its investigatory arm, the Bureau of Corporations.

Roosevelt's Vision of Federal Power

Although Roosevelt was not a trustbuster at heart, he made a few highly publicized efforts to break up combinations. In 1902, he ordered the Justice Department to invoke the Sherman Antitrust Act against a great new railroad monopoly in the Northwest, the Northern Securities Company, a $400 million enterprise pieced together by J. P. Morgan and others. To Morgan, accustomed to a warm, supportive relationship with Republican administrations, the action was baffling. He told the president, "If we have done anything wrong, send your man to my man and they can fix it up." Roosevelt proceeded with the case nonetheless, and in 1904 the Supreme Court ruled that the Northern Securities Company must be dissolved. Although he filed more than forty

Northern Securities Company

additional antitrust suits during the remainder of his presidency, Roosevelt had no serious commitment to reverse the prevailing trend toward economic concentration.

A similar commitment to establishing the government as an impartial regulatory mechanism shaped Roosevelt's policy toward labor. In the past, federal intervention in industrial disputes had almost always meant action on behalf of employers. Roosevelt was willing to consider labor's position as well. When a bitter 1902 strike by the United Mine Workers endangered coal supplies for the coming winter, Roosevelt asked both the operators and the miners to accept impartial federal arbitration. When the mine owners balked, Roosevelt threatened to send federal troops to seize the mines. The operators finally relented. Arbitrators awarded the strikers a 10 percent wage increase and a nine-hour day, although no recognition of their union—less than they had wanted but more than they would likely have won without Roosevelt's intervention. Roosevelt viewed himself as no more the champion of labor than as that of management. On several occasions, he ordered federal troops to intervene in strikes on behalf of employers.

The "Square Deal"

During Roosevelt's first years as president, he was principally concerned with winning reelection, which required that he not antagonize the conservative Republican Old Guard. By skillfully dispensing patronage to conservatives and progressives alike, and by winning the support of northern businessmen while making adroit gestures to reformers, Roosevelt had neutralized his opposition within the party by early 1904. He won its presidential nomination with ease. And in the general election, where he faced a dull conservative Democrat, Alton B. Parker, he captured over 57 percent of the popular vote and lost no states outside the South.

During the 1904 campaign, Roosevelt boasted that he had worked in the anthracite coal strike to provide everyone with a "square deal." One of his first targets after the election was the powerful railroad industry. The Interstate Commerce Act of 1887, establishing the Interstate Commerce Commission (ICC), had been an early effort to regulate the industry; but over the years, the courts had sharply limited its influence. Roosevelt asked Congress for legislation to increase the government's power to oversee railroad rates. The Hepburn Railroad Regulation Act of 1906 sought to restore some regulatory authority to the government,

Hepburn Act although the bill was so cautious that it satisfied few progressives.

Roosevelt also pressured Congress to enact the Pure Food and Drug Act, which restricted the sale of dangerous or ineffective medicines. When

Pure Food and Drug Act Upton Sinclair's powerful novel *The Jungle* appeared in 1906, featuring appalling descriptions of conditions in the meatpacking industry, Roosevelt pushed for passage of the Meat Inspection Act, which helped eliminate many diseases once transmitted in impure meat. Starting in 1907, he proposed even more stringent reforms: an eight-hour day for workers, broader compensation for victims of industrial accidents, inheritance and income taxes, regulation of the stock market, and others. He also started openly to criticize conservatives in Congress and the judiciary who were obstructing these programs. The result was a widening gulf between the president and the conservative wing of his party.

Roosevelt and Conservation

Roosevelt's aggressive policies on behalf of conservation contributed to that gulf. Using executive powers, he restricted private development on millions of acres of undeveloped government land—most of it in the West—by adding them to the previously modest national forest system. When conservatives in Congress restricted his authority over public lands in 1907, Roosevelt and his chief forester, Gifford Pinchot, seized all the forests and many of the water power sites still in the public domain before the bill became law.

Roosevelt was the first president to take an active interest in the new and struggling American conservation movement. In the early twentieth century, the idea of preserving the natural world for ecological reasons was not well established. Instead, many people who considered themselves "conservationists"—such as Pinchot, the first director of the National Forest Service (which he helped to create)—promoted policies to protect land for carefully managed development.

The Old Guard eagerly supported another important aspect

Federal Aid to the West

of Roosevelt's natural resource policy: public reclamation and irrigation projects. In 1902, the president backed the National Reclamation Act, better known as the Newlands Act (named for its sponsor, Nevada senator Francis Newlands). The Newlands Act provided federal funds for the construction of dams, reservoirs, and canals in the West—projects that would open new lands for cultivation and (years later) provide cheap electric power.

Roosevelt and Preservation

Despite his sympathy with Pinchot's vision of conservation, Roosevelt also shared some of the concerns of the naturalists—those within the conservation movement committed to protecting the natural beauty of the land and the health of its wildlife from human intrusion. Early in his presidency, Roosevelt even spent four days camping in the Sierras with John Muir, the nation's leading preservationist and the founder of the Sierra Club.

Roosevelt added significantly to the still-young National Park System, whose purpose was to protect public land from any exploitation or development at all. Congress had created the first national park—Yellowstone, in Wyoming, in 1872—and had authorized others in the 1890s: Yosemite and Sequoia in California, and Mount Rainier in Washington State. Roosevelt added land to several existing parks and also created new ones: Crater Lake in Oregon, Mesa Verde in Utah, Platt in Oklahoma, and Wind Cave in South Dakota.

The Hetch Hetchy Controversy

The contending views of the early conservation movement came to a head beginning in 1906 in a sensational controversy over the Hetch Hetchy Valley in Yosemite National Park. Hetch Hetchy (a name derived from a local Indian term meaning "grassy meadows") was a spectacular, high-walled valley popular with naturalists. But many residents of San Francisco, worried about finding enough water to serve their growing population, saw Hetch Hetchy as an ideal place for a dam, which would create a large reservoir for the city—a plan that Muir and others furiously opposed.

In 1906, San Francisco suffered a devastating earthquake and fire. Widespread sympathy for the city strengthened the case for the dam; and Theodore Roosevelt—who had initially expressed some sympathy for Muir's position—turned the decision over to his chief forester, Gifford Pinchot. Pinchot had no interest in Muir's aesthetic and spiritual arguments. He approved construction of the dam.

For over a decade, a battle raged between naturalists and the advocates of the dam, a battle that consumed the energies of John Muir for the rest of his life and that eventually, many believed, helped kill him. "Dam Hetch Hetchy!" Muir once said. "As well dam for water-

Competing Conservationist Visions

tanks the people's cathedrals and churches, for no holier

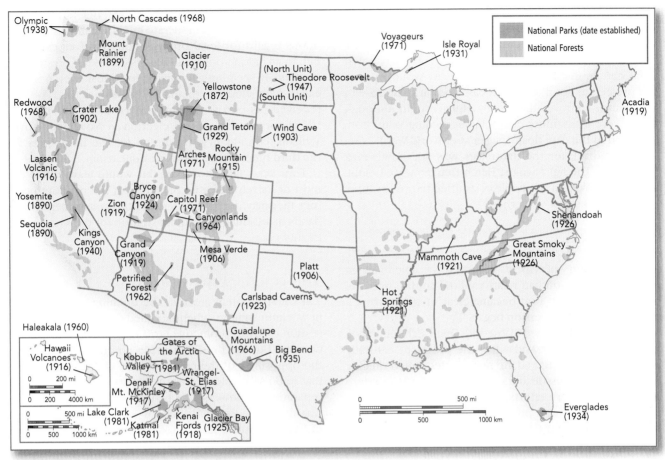

ESTABLISHMENT OF NATIONAL PARKS AND FORESTS This map illustrates the steady growth throughout the late nineteenth and twentieth centuries of the systems of national parks and national forests in the United States. Although Theodore Roosevelt is widely and correctly remembered as a great champion of national parks and forests, the greatest expansions of these systems occurred after his presidency. Note, for example, how many new areas were added in the 1920s. ◆ *What is the difference between national parks and national forests?*

ROOSEVELT AND MUIR IN YOSEMITE John Muir, founder and leader of the Sierra Club, considered Theodore Roosevelt a friend and ally—a relationship cemented by a four-day camping trip the two men took together in Yosemite National Park in 1903. Roosevelt was indeed a friend to the national park and national forest systems and added considerable acreage to both. Among other things, he expanded Yosemite (at Muir's request). But unlike Muir, Roosevelt was also committed to economic development. As a result, he was not always a reliable ally of the most committed preservationists. *(Bettmann/Corbis)*

temple has ever been consecrated by the heart of man." To Pinchot, there was no question that the needs of the city were more important than the claims of preservation. Muir helped place a referendum question on the ballot in 1908, certain that the residents of the city would oppose the project "as soon as light is cast upon it." Instead, San Franciscans approved the dam by a huge margin. Although there were many more delays in succeeding years, construction of the dam finally began after World War I.

This setback for the naturalists was not, however, a total defeat. The fight against Hetch Hetchy helped mobilize a new coalition of people committed to preservation, not "rational use," of wilderness.

The Panic of 1907

Despite the flurry of reforms Roosevelt was able to enact, the government still had relatively little control over the industrial economy. That became clear in 1907, when a serious panic and recession began.

Conservatives blamed Roosevelt's "mad" economic policies for the disaster. And while the president naturally (and correctly) disagreed, he nevertheless acted quickly to reassure business leaders that he would not interfere with their recovery efforts. J. P. Morgan, in a spectacular display of his financial power, helped construct a pool of the assets of several important New York banks to prop up shaky financial institutions. The key to the arrangement, Morgan told the president, was the purchase by U.S. Steel of the shares of the Tennessee Coal and Iron Company, currently held by a threatened New York bank. He would, he insisted, need assurances that the purchase would not prompt antitrust action. Roosevelt tacitly agreed, and the Morgan plan proceeded. Whether or not as a result, the panic soon subsided.

Roosevelt loved being president. As his years in office produced increasing political successes, as his public popularity continued to rise, more and more observers began to assume that he would run for reelection in 1908, despite the longstanding tradition of presidents serving no more than two terms. But the Panic of 1907, combined with Roosevelt's growing "radicalism" during his second term, so alienated conservatives in his own party that he might have had difficulty winning the Republican nomination. In 1904, moreover, he had made a public promise to step down four years later. And so in 1909, Roosevelt, fifty years old, retired from public life—briefly.

THE TROUBLED SUCCESSION

William Howard Taft, who assumed the presidency in 1909, had been Theodore Roosevelt's most trusted lieutenant and his hand-picked successor; progressive reformers believed him to be one of their own. But Taft had also been a restrained and moderate jurist, a man with a punctilious regard for legal process; conservatives expected him to abandon Roosevelt's aggressive use of presidential powers. By seeming acceptable to almost everyone, Taft easily won election to the White House in 1908. He received his party's nomination virtually uncontested. His victory in the general election in November—over William Jennings Bryan, running for the Democrats for the third time—was a foregone conclusion.

Four years later, however, Taft would leave office the most decisively defeated president of the twentieth century, his party deeply divided and the government in the hands of a Democratic administration for the first time in twenty years.

Taft and the Progressives

Taft's first problem arose in the opening months of the new administration, when he called Congress into special session to lower protective tariff rates, an old progressive demand. But the president made no effort to overcome the opposition of the congressional Old Guard, arguing that to do so would violate the constitutional doctrine of separation of powers. The result was the feeble Payne-Aldrich Tariff, which reduced tariff rates scarcely at all and in some areas raised them. Progressives resented the president's passivity.

Taft may not have been a champion of reform, but neither was he a consistent opponent of change. In 1912, he supported and signed legislation to create a federal Children's Bureau to investigate "all matters pertaining to the welfare of children and child life." Julia Lathrop, the first chief of the bureau, was a veteran of Hull House and a close associate of Jane Addams. She helped make the Children's Bureau a force for progressive change not just in federal policy, but also in state and local governments.

A sensational controversy broke out late in 1909 that helped destroy Taft's popularity with reformers for good. Many progressives had been unhappy when Taft replaced Roosevelt's secretary of the interior, James R. Garfield, an aggressive conservationist, with Richard A. Ballinger, a conservative corporate lawyer. Suspicion of Ballinger grew when he attempted to invalidate Roosevelt's removal of nearly 1 million acres of forests and mineral reserves from private development.

In the midst of this mounting concern, Louis Glavis, an Interior Department investigator, charged Ballinger with having once connived to turn over valuable public coal lands in Alaska to a private syndicate for personal profit. Glavis took the evidence to Gifford Pinchot, still head of the Forest Service and a critic of Ballinger's policies. Pinchot took the charges to the president. Taft investigated them and decided they were

WILLIAM HOWARD TAFT Taft could be a jovial companion in small groups, but his public image was of a dull, stolid man who stood in sharp and unfortunate contrast to his dynamic predecessor, Theodore Roosevelt. Taft also suffered public ridicule for his enormous size. He weighed as much as 350 pounds at times, and wide publicity accompanied his installation of an oversized bathtub in the White House. *(Bettmann/Corbis)*

groundless. But Pinchot was not satisfied, particularly after Taft fired Glavis for his part in the episode. He leaked the story to the press and asked Congress to investigate the scandal. The president discharged him for insubordination. The congressional committee appointed to study the controversy, dominated by Old Guard Republicans, exonerated Ballinger. But progressives throughout the country supported Pinchot. The controversy aroused as much public passion as any dispute of its time; and when it was over, Taft had alienated the supporters of Roosevelt completely and, it seemed, irrevocably.

The Return of Roosevelt

During most of these controversies, Theodore Roosevelt was far away: on a long hunting safari in Africa and an extended tour of Europe. To the American public, however, Roosevelt remained a formidable presence. His return to New York in the spring of 1910 was a major public event. Roosevelt insisted that he had no plans to reenter politics, but within a month he announced that he would embark on a national speaking tour before the end of the summer. Furious with Taft, he was becoming convinced that he alone was capable of reuniting the Republican Party.

The real signal of Roosevelt's decision to assume leadership of Republican reformers came in a speech he gave on September 1, 1910, in Osawatomie, Kansas. In it he outlined a set of principles, which he labeled the "New Nationalism," that made clear he had moved a considerable way from the cautious conservatism of the first years of his presidency. He argued that social justice was possible only through the vigorous efforts of a strong federal government whose executive acted as the "steward of the public welfare." Those who thought primarily of property rights and personal profit "must now give way to the advocate of human welfare." He supported graduated income and inheritance taxes, workers' compensation for industrial accidents, regulation of the labor of women and children, tariff revision, and firmer regulation of corporations.

"New Nationalism"

Spreading Insurgency

The congressional elections of 1910 provided further evidence of how far the progressive revolt had spread. In primary elections, conservative Republicans suffered defeat after defeat while almost all the progressive incumbents were reelected. In the general election, the Democrats, who were now offering progressive candidates of their own, won control of the House of Representatives for the first time in sixteen years and gained strength in the Senate. But Roosevelt still denied any presidential ambitions and claimed that his real purpose was to pressure Taft to return to progressive policies. Two events, however, changed his mind. The first, on October 27, 1911, was the announcement by the administration of a suit against U.S. Steel, which charged, among other things, that the 1907 acquisition of the Tennessee Coal and Iron Company had been illegal. Roosevelt had approved that acquisition in the midst of the 1907 panic, and he was enraged by the implication that he had acted improperly.

Roosevelt was still reluctant to become a candidate for president because Senator Robert La Follette, the great Wisconsin progressive, had been working since 1911 to secure the presidential nomination for himself. But La Follette's candidacy stumbled in February 1912 when, exhausted, and distraught over the illness of a daughter, he appeared to suffer a nervous breakdown during a speech in Philadelphia. Roosevelt announced his candidacy on February 22.

ROOSEVELT AT OSAWATOMIE   Roosevelt's famous speech at Osawatomie, Kansas, in 1910 was the most radical of his career and openly marked his break with the Taft administration and the Republican leadership. "The essence of any struggle for liberty," he told his largely conservative audience, "has always been, and must always be to take from some one man or class of men the right to enjoy power, or wealth, or position or immunity, which has not been earned by service to his or their fellows." *(Brown Brothers)*

Roosevelt Versus Taft

La Follette retained some diehard support. But for all practical purposes, the campaign for the Republican nomination had now become a battle between Roosevelt and Taft. Roosevelt scored overwhelming victories in all thirteen presidential primaries. Taft, however, remained the choice of most party leaders, who controlled the nominating process.

The battle for the nomination at the Chicago convention revolved around an unusually large number of contested delegates: 254 in all. Roosevelt needed fewer than half the disputed seats to clinch the nomination. But the Republican National Committee, controlled by the Old Guard, awarded all but 19 of them to Taft. At a rally the night before the convention opened, Roosevelt addressed 5,000 cheering supporters. "We stand at Armageddon," he told the roaring crowd, "and we battle for the Lord." The next day, he led his supporters out of the convention, and out of the party. The convention then quietly nominated Taft on the first ballot.

Roosevelt summoned his supporters back to Chicago in August for another convention, this one to launch the new Progressive Party and nominate himself as its presidential candidate. Roosevelt approached the battle feeling, as he put it, "fit as a bull moose" (thus giving his new party an enduring nickname).

The Progressive Party

The "Bull Moose" party was notable for its strong commitment to a wide range of progressive causes that had grown in popularity over the previous two decades. The party advocated additional regulation of industry and trusts, sweeping reforms of many areas of government, compensation by the government for workers injured on the job, pensions for the elderly and for widows with children, and (alone among the major parties) woman suffrage. The delegates left the party's convention filled with hope and excitement.

Roosevelt himself, however, entered the fall campaign aware that his cause was almost hopeless, partly because many of the insurgents who had supported him during the primaries refused to follow him out of the Republican Party. It was also because of the man the Democrats had nominated for president.

WOODROW WILSON AND THE NEW FREEDOM

The 1912 presidential contest was not simply one between conservatives and reformers. It was also one bewtween two brands of progressivism. And it matched the two most important national leaders of the early twentieth century in unequal contest.

Woodrow Wilson

Reform sentiment had been gaining strength within the Democratic as well as the Republican Party in the first years of the century. At the 1912 Democratic Convention in Baltimore in June, Champ Clark, the conservative Speaker of the House, was unable to assemble the two-thirds majority necessary for nomination because of progressive opposition. Finally, on the forty-sixth ballot, Woodrow Wilson, the governor of New Jersey and the only genuinely progressive candidate in the race, emerged as the party's nominee.

Wilson had risen to political prominence by an unusual path. He had been a professor of political science at Princeton until 1902, when he was named president of the university. Elected governor of New Jersey in 1910, he demonstrated a commitment to reform. During his two years in the statehouse, he earned a national reputation for winning passage of progressive legislation. As a presidential candidate in 1912, Wilson presented a progressive program that came

Wilson's "New Freedom"

to be called the "New Freedom." Roosevelt's New Nationalism advocated accepting economic concentration and using government to regulate and control it. But Wilson seemed to side with those who (like Louis Brandeis) believed that bigness was both unjust and inefficient, that the proper response to monopoly was not to regulate it but to destroy it.

The 1912 presidential campaign was an anticlimax. William Howard Taft, resigned to defeat, barely campaigned. Roosevelt campaigned energetically (until a gunshot wound from a would-be assassin forced him to the sidelines during the last weeks before the election), but he failed to draw any significant numbers of Democratic progressives away from Wilson. In November, Roosevelt and Taft split the Republican vote; Wilson held on to most Democrats and won. He polled only 42 percent of the vote, compared with 27 percent for Roosevelt, 23 percent for Taft, and 6 percent for the socialist Eugene Debs. But in the electoral college, Wilson won 435 of the 531 votes. Roosevelt had carried only six states, Taft two, Debs none.

The Scholar as President

Wilson was a bold and forceful president. He exerted firm control over his cabinet, and he delegated real authority only to those whose loyalty to him was beyond question. His most powerful adviser, Colonel Edward M. House, was an intelligent and ambitious Texan who held no office and whose only claim to authority was his personal intimacy with the president.

WOODROW WILSON CAMPAIGNING
Woodrow Wilson, former president of Princeton University and current governor of New Jersey, gives a political speech in Virginia (his native state) in 1912, early in his campaign for the presidency. *(Getty Images)*

In legislative matters, Wilson skillfully welded together a coalition that would support his program. Democratic majorities in both houses of Congress made his task easier. Wilson's first triumph as president was

Lowering the Tariff

the fulfillment of an old Democratic (and progressive) goal: a substantial lowering of the protective tariff. The Underwood-Simmons Tariff provided cuts substantial enough, progressives believed, to introduce real competition into American markets and thus to help break the power of trusts. To make up for the loss of revenue under the new tariff, Congress approved a graduated income tax, which the recently adopted Sixteenth Amendment to the Constitution now permitted. This first modern income tax imposed a 1 percent tax on individuals and corporations earning more than $4,000 a year, with rates ranging up to 6 percent on incomes over $500,000 annually.

Wilson held Congress in session through the summer to work on a major reform of the American banking system: the Federal Reserve Act, which Congress passed and the

Federal Reserve Act

president signed on December 23, 1913. It created twelve regional banks, each to be owned and controlled by the individual banks of its district. The regional Federal Reserve banks would hold a certain percentage of the assets of their member banks in reserve; they would use those reserves to support loans to private banks at an interest (or "discount") rate that the Federal Reserve system would set; they would issue a new type of paper currency—Federal Reserve notes—that would become the nation's basic medium of trade and would be backed by the government. Most important, they would be able to shift funds quickly to troubled areas—to meet increased demands for credit or to protect imperiled banks. Supervising and regulating the entire system was a national Federal Reserve Board, whose members were appointed by the president. Nearly half the nation's banking resources were represented in the system within a year, and 80 percent by the late 1920s.

In 1914, turning to the central issue of his 1912 campaign, Wilson proposed two measures to deal with the problem of monopoly. In the process he revealed how his own approach to the issue was beginning to change. There was a proposal to create a federal agency through which the government would help business police itself—a regulatory commission of the type Roosevelt had advocated in 1912. There were also proposals to strengthen the government's ability to break up trusts—a decentralizing approach characteristic of Wilson's 1912 campaign. The two measures took shape as the Federal Trade Commission Act and the Clayton Antitrust Act. The Federal Trade Commission Act created a regulatory agency that would help businesses determine in advance whether their actions would be acceptable to the government. The agency would also have authority to launch prosecutions against "unfair trade practices," and it would have wide power to investigate corporate behavior. Wilson signed the Federal Trade Commission Bill happily. But he seemed to lose interest in the Clayton Antitrust Bill and did little to protect it from conservative assaults, which greatly weakened it. The future, he had apparently decided, lay with government supervision.

Retreat and Advance

By the fall of 1914, Wilson believed that the program of the New Freedom was essentially complete and that agitation for reform would now subside. He refused to support the movement for national woman suffrage. Deferring to southern Democrats, and reflecting his own southern background, he condoned the reimposition of segregation in the agencies of the federal government (in contrast to Roosevelt, who had ordered the elimination of many such barriers). When congressional

Candidate (Party)	Electoral Vote	Popular Vote (%)
Woodrow Wilson (Democratic)	435	6,293,454 (41.9)
Theodore Roosevelt (Progressive/Bull Moose)	88	4,119,538 (27.4)
William H. Taft (Republican)	8	3,484,980 (23.2)
Eugene V. Debs (Socialist)	—	900,672 (6.0)
Other parties (Prohibition, Socialist Labor)	—	235,025

58.8% of electorate voting

ELECTION OF 1912 The election of 1912 was one of the most unusual in American history because of the dramatic schism within the Republican Party. Two Republican presidents—William Howard Taft, the incumbent, and Theodore Roosevelt, his predecessor—ran against each other in 1912, opening the way for a victory by the Democratic candidate, Woodrow Wilson, who won with only about 42 percent of the popular vote. A fourth candidate, the socialist Eugene V. Debs, received a significant 6 percent of the vote. ◆ *What events caused the schism between Taft and Roosevelt?*

For an interactive version of this map, go to www.mhhe.com/brinkley13ech20maps

progressives attempted to enlist his support for new reform legislation, Wilson dismissed their proposals as unconstitutional or unnecessary.

The congressional elections of 1914, however, shattered the president's complacency. Democrats suffered major losses in Congress, and voters who in 1912 had supported the Progressive Party began returning to the Republicans. Wilson would not be able to rely on a divided opposition when he ran for reelection in 1916. By the end of 1915, therefore, Wilson had begun to support a second flurry of reforms. In January 1916, he appointed Louis Brandeis to the Supreme Court, making him not only the first Jew but also the most advanced progressive to serve there. Later, he supported a measure to make it easier for farmers to receive credit and one creating a system of workers' compensation for federal employees.

Wilson was sponsoring measures that expanded the powers of the national government in important ways. In 1916, for example, Wilson supported the Keating-Owen Act, the first federal law regulating child labor. The

Child-Labor Laws

measure prohibited the shipment of goods produced by underage children across state lines, thus giving an expanded importance to the constitutional clause assigning Congress the task of regulating interstate commerce. The president similarly supported measures that used federal taxing authority as a vehicle for legislating social change. After the Court struck down Keating-Owen, a new law attempted to achieve the same goal by imposing a heavy tax on the products of child labor. (The Court later struck it down too.) And the Smith-Lever Act of 1914 demonstrated another way in which the federal government could influence local behavior; it offered matching federal grants to support agricultural extension education. Over time, these innovative uses of government overcame most of the constitutional objections and became the foundation of a long-term growth in federal power over the economy.

CONCLUSION

The powerful surge of reform efforts in the last years of the nineteenth century and the first years of the twentieth—reforms intended to help the United States deal with the extraordinary changes and the vexing problem of the modern industrial era—caused many Americans to come to identify themselves as "progressives." That label meant many different things to many different people, but at its core was a belief that human effort and government action could improve society. The reform crusades gained strength steadily, driven by both men and women, and by people of many races and ethnicities. By the early twentieth century, progressivism had become a powerful, transformative force in American life.

This great surge of reform eventually reached the federal government and national politics, as progressives began to understand the limits of state and local reform. Success, they came to believe, required the engagement of the federal government. Two national leaders—Theodore Roosevelt and Woodrow Wilson—contributed to a period of national reform that made the government in Washington a great center of power for the first time since the Civil War—a position it has never relinquished. Progressivism did not solve the nation's problems, but it gave movements, organizations, and governments new tools to deal with them.

INTERACTIVE LEARNING

The *Primary Source Investigator CD-ROM* offers the following materials related to this chapter:

- A short documentary movie, **Votes for Women,** on the story of the fight by women for the right to vote in the United States (D15).

- Interactive maps: **U.S. Elections** (M7), **Woman Suffrage** (M16), and **The United States and Latin America** (M21).

- Documents, images, and maps related to the rise of progressivism, highlighted by the presidencies of Theodore Roosevelt and Woodrow Wilson. Highlights include images and documents related to the settlement house movement; images of the Triangle Shirtwaist Company fire; the Nineteenth Amendment to the U.S. Constitution, which gave women the right to vote; images of women hanging pro-suffrage posters and a video clip of women suffragists meeting with President Roosevelt; the text of the congressional act establishing Yellowstone National Park; photographs taken of the stockyards; correspondence between President Roosevelt and Upton Sinclair; and the text of the 1906 Meat Inspection Act and an image of a promotional poster for an early movie version of *The Jungle*.

Online Learning Center (www.mhhe.com/brinkley13e)

For quizzes, Internet resources, references to additional books and films, and more, consult this book's Online Learning Center.

FOR FURTHER REFERENCE

Richard Hofstadter, *The Age of Reform: From Bryan to FDR* (1955) is a classic, and now controversial, analysis of the partly psychological origins of the Populist and progressive movements. Robert Wiebe, *The Search for Order, 1877-1920* (1967) is an important organizational interpretation of the era. Gabriel Kolko makes a distinctly revisionist argument that business conservatism was at the heart of the progressive movement in *The Triumph of Conservatism* (1963). Alan Dawley, *Struggles for Justice: Social Responsibility and the Liberal State* (1991) and Michael McGess, *A Fierce Discontent: The Rise and Fall of the Progressive Movement in America, 1870-1920* (2003) are sophisticated and contrasting synthetic accounts of progressive movements and their ideas. John Milton Cooper, *The Pivotal Decades: The United States, 1900-1920* (1990) is a good narrative history of the period. For powerful insights into pragmatism, an important philosophical underpinning to much reform, see Robert Westbrook, *John Dewey and American Democracy* (1991) and Louis Menand, *The Metaphysical Club: A Story of Ideas* (2001). Thomas L. Haskell, *The Emergence of Professional Social Science* (1977) is an important study of the social sciences and professionalism. Paul Starr, *The Social Transformation of American Medicine* (1982) is a pathbreaking study of the emergence of modern systems of health care. Richard Greenwald, *The Triangle Fire, the Protocols of Peace, and Industrial Democracy in Progressive Era New York* (2006) examines a critical event in stimulating reform.

Nancy Cott, *The Grounding of American Feminism* (1987) studies the shifting roles and beliefs of women. Kathryn Kish Sklar, *Florence Kelley and the Nation's Work: The Rise of Women's Political Culture, 1830-1900* (1995) examines the impact of female reformers on the progressive movement and the nation's political culture as a whole. Glenda Gilmore, *Gender and Jim Crow: Women and the Politics of White Supremacy in North Carolina, 1896-1920* (1996) examines the role of gender in the construction of segregation. Louis Harlan, *Booker T. Washington: The Making of a Black Leader* (1956) and *Booker T. Washington: The Wizard of Tuskegee* (1983) are parts of an outstanding multivolume biography, as are David Levering Lewis, *W. E. B. Du Bois: Biography of a Race* (1993) and *W. E. B. Du Bois: The Fight for Equality and the American Century* (2000).

John Milton Cooper Jr. compares the lives and ideas of the progressive movement's leading national politicians in *The Warrior and the Priest: Woodrow Wilson and Theodore Roosevelt* (1983). John Morton Blum, *The Republican Roosevelt* (1954) is a long-popular brief study. Donald E. Anderson, *William Howard Taft* (1973) is a useful account of this unhappy presidency. Arthur S. Link is Wilson's most important biographer and the author of *Woodrow Wilson*, 5 vols. (1947-1965). Thomas K. McCraw, *Prophets of Regulation* (1984) is an excellent examination of important figures in the making of modern state capacity. Michael McGerr, *The Decline of Popular Politics* (1986) is a perceptive examination of the decline of public enthusiasm for parties in the North in the late nineteenth and early twentieth centuries. Samuel P. Hays, *The Gospel of Efficiency: The Progressive Conservation Movement, 1890-1920* (1962) makes a pioneering argument about the organizational imperatives behind the conservation movement, and Stephen R. Fox, *The American Conservation Movement: John Muir and His Legacy* (1981) is another valuable study. John Opie, *Nature's Nation: An Environmental History of the United States* (1998) is an ambitious synthesis of environmental history.

Theodore Roosevelt, by David Grubin (1997), is a fine biographical film. *The Battle for the Wilderness* (1990) is a documentary film about the conservation movement and two of its rival leaders, Gifford Pinchot and John Muir.

CHAPTER 21

AMERICA AND THE GREAT WAR

AN APPEAL TO DUTY   This most famous of all American war posters, by the artist James Montgomery Flagg, shows a fierce-looking Uncle Sam requesting, almost demanding, Americans to join the army to fight in World War I. With the nation very divided over the wisdom of entering the war, the Wilson administration believed it needed to persuade Americans not only to support the struggle but also—something unusual for Americans—to feel a sense of obligation to the government and its overseas commitments. *(National Archives and Records Administration)*

THE GREAT WAR, AS IT WAS KNOWN to a generation unaware that another, greater war would soon follow, began relatively inconspicuously in August 1914 when forces of the Austro-Hungarian Empire invaded the tiny Balkan nation of Serbia. Within weeks, however, it had grown into a widespread conflagration, engaging the armies of almost all the major nations of Europe and shattering forever the delicate balance of power that had maintained a general peace on the Continent since the early nineteenth century.

Most Americans looked on with horror as the war became the most savage in history, but also with a conviction that the conflict had little to do with them. In that, they were profoundly mistaken. The United States in 1914 had been deeply involved in the life of the world since at least the Spanish-American War; and in the early years of the twentieth century—under three internationally active presidents—the nation took on many more international commitments and obligations. And so it should not have been surprising that the United States finally entered the war in 1917.

In doing so, it joined the most savage conflict in history. The fighting had already dragged on for two and a half years, inconclusive, almost inconceivably murderous. By 1917, the war had left Europe exhausted and on the brink of utter collapse. By the time it ended late in 1918, Germany had lost nearly 2 million soldiers in battle, Russia 1.7 million, France 1.4 million, Great Britain 900,000. A generation of European youth was decimated; centuries of political, social, and economic traditions were damaged and all but destroyed.

Total War

For America, however, the war was the source of a very different experience. As a military struggle, it was brief, decisive, and—in relative terms—without great cost. Only 112,000 American soldiers died in the conflict, half of them from influenza and other diseases rather than in combat. Economically, it was the source of a great industrial boom, which helped spark the years of prosperity that would follow. And the war propelled the United States into a position of international preeminence.

In other respects, World War I was a painful, even traumatic experience for the American people. At home, the nation became preoccupied with a search not just for victory but also for social unity—a search that continued and even intensified in the troubled years following the armistice, and that helped shatter many of the progressive ideals of the first years of the century. And abroad, once the conflict ended, the United States encountered frustration and disillusionment. The "war to end all wars," the war "to make the world safe for democracy," became neither. Instead, it led directly to twenty years of international instability that would ultimately generate another great conflict.

THE "BIG STICK": AMERICA AND THE WORLD, 1901–1917

To the general public, foreign affairs remained largely remote. Walter Lippmann once wrote: "I cannot remember taking any interest whatsoever in foreign affairs until after the outbreak of the First World War." But to Theodore Roosevelt and later presidents, that made foreign affairs even more appealing. There the president could act with less regard for the Congress or the courts. There he could free himself from concerns about public opinion. Overseas, the president could exercise power unfettered and alone.

Roosevelt and "Civilization"

Theodore Roosevelt believed in the value and importance of using American power in the world (a conviction he once described by citing the proverb "Speak softly, but carry a big stick"). But he had two different standards for using that power.

Roosevelt believed that an important distinction existed between the "civilized" and "uncivilized" nations of the world. "Civilized" nations, as he defined them, were predominantly white and Anglo-Saxon or Teutonic; "uncivilized" nations were generally nonwhite, Latin, or Slavic. But racism was only partly the basis of the distinction. Equally important was economic development. He believed, therefore, that Japan, a rapidly industrializing society, had earned admission to the ranks of the civilized. A civilized society, he argued, had the right and duty to intervene in the affairs of a "backward" nation to preserve order and stability. That belief was one important reason for Roosevelt's early support of the development of American sea power. By 1906, the American navy had attained a size and strength surpassed only by that of Great Britain (although Germany was fast gaining ground).

> Racial and Economic Basis of Roosevelt's Diplomacy

Protecting the "Open Door" in Asia

In 1904, the Japanese staged a surprise attack on the Russian fleet at Port Arthur in southern Manchuria, a

"THE NEW DIPLOMACY" This 1904 drawing by the famous *Puck* cartoonist Louis Dalrymple conveys the new image of America as a great power that Theodore Roosevelt was attempting to project to the world. Roosevelt the world policeman deals effectively with "less civilized" peoples (Asians and Latin Americans, seen clamoring at left) by using the "big stick" and deals equally effectively with the "civilized" nations (at right) by offering arbitration. *(Culver Pictures, Inc.)*

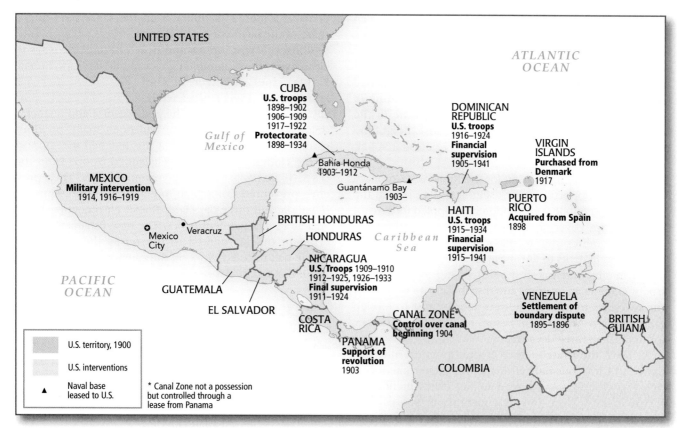

THE UNITED STATES AND LATIN AMERICA, 1895–1941 Except for Puerto Rico, the Virgin Islands, and the Canal Zone, the United States had no formal possessions in Latin America and the Caribbean in the late nineteenth century and the first half of the twentieth. But as this map reveals, the U.S. exercised considerable influence in these regions throughout this period—political and economic influence, augmented at times by military intervention. Note the particularly intrusive presence of the United States in the affairs of Cuba, Haiti, and the Dominican Republic—as well as the canal-related interventions in Colombia and Panama. ◆ *What were some of the most frequent reasons for American intervention in Latin America?*

For an interactive version of this map, go to www.mhhe.com/brinkley13ech21maps

province of China that both Russia and Japan hoped to control. Roosevelt, hoping to prevent either nation from becoming dominant there, agreed to a Japanese request to mediate an end to the conflict. Russia, faring badly in the war, had no choice but to agree. At a peace conference in Portsmouth, New Hampshire, in 1905, Roosevelt extracted from the embattled Russians a recognition of Japan's territorial gains and from the Japanese an agreement to cease the fighting and expand no further. At the same time, he negotiated a secret agreement with the Japanese to ensure that the United States could continue to trade freely in the region.

Roosevelt won the Nobel Peace Prize in 1906 for his work in ending the Russo-Japanese War. But in the years that followed, relations between the United States and Japan steadily deteriorated. Japan now emerged as the preeminent naval power in the Pacific and soon began to exclude American trade from many of the territories it controlled. To be sure the Japanese government recognized the power of the United States, he sent sixteen battleships of the new American navy (known as the "Great White Fleet"

"Great White Fleet"

because the ships were temporarily painted white for the voyage) on an unprecedented journey around the world that included a call on Japan.

The Iron-Fisted Neighbor

Roosevelt took a particular interest in events in what he (and most other Americans) considered the nation's special sphere of interest: Latin America. He established a pattern of American intervention in the region that would long survive his presidency.

Early in 1902, the financially troubled government of Venezuela began to renege on debts to European bankers. Naval forces of Britain, Italy, and Germany blockaded the Venezuelan coast in response. Then German ships began to bombard a Venezuelan port amid rumors that Germany planned to establish a permanent base in the region. Roosevelt used the threat of American naval power to pressure the German navy to withdraw.

The incident helped persuade Roosevelt that European intrusions into Latin America could result not only from aggression but also from instability or irresponsibility (such as defaulting on debts) within the Latin American nations themselves. As a result, in 1904 he announced what came to be known as the "Roosevelt Corollary" to the Monroe Doctrine. The United States, he claimed, had the right not only to oppose European intervention in the Western Hemisphere but also to intervene in the domestic affairs of its neighbors if those neighbors proved unable to maintain order and national sovereignty on their own.

"Roosevelt Corollary"

The immediate motivation for the Roosevelt Corollary, and the first opportunity for using it, was a crisis in the Dominican Republic. A revolution had toppled its corrupt and bankrupt government in 1903, but the new regime proved no better able to make good on the country's $22 million in debts to European nations. Roosevelt established, in effect, an American receivership, assuming control of Dominican customs and distributing 45 percent of the revenues to the Dominicans and the rest to foreign creditors. This arrangement lasted, in one form or another, for more than three decades.

In 1902, the United States granted political independence to Cuba, but only after the new government had agreed to the Platt Amendment to its constitution (see p. 560). The amendment gave the United States the right to prevent any other foreign power from intruding into the new nation. In 1906, when domestic uprisings seemed to threaten the internal stability of the island, American troops landed in Cuba, quelled the fighting, and remained there for three years.

Platt Amendment

The Panama Canal

The most celebrated accomplishment of Roosevelt's presidency was the construction of the Panama Canal, which linked the Atlantic and the Pacific. At first, Roosevelt and many others favored a route across Nicaragua, which would permit a sea-level canal requiring no locks. But they soon turned instead to the narrow Isthmus of Panama in Colombia, the site of an earlier, failed effort by a French company to construct a channel. Although the Panama route was not at sea level (and would thus require locks), it was shorter than the one in Nicaragua. And construction was already about 40 percent complete. When the French company lowered the price for its holdings, the United States chose Panama.

Roosevelt dispatched John Hay, his secretary of state, to negotiate an agreement with Colombian diplomats in Washington that would allow construction to begin without delay. Under heavy American pressure, the Colombian chargé d'affaires, Tomas Herrén, unwisely signed an agreement giving the United States perpetual rights to a six-mile-wide "canal zone" across Colombia. The outraged Colombian senate refused to ratify it. Colombia then sent a new representative to Washington with instructions to demand a higher payment from the Americans plus a share of the payment to the French.

Roosevelt was furious and began to look for ways to circumvent the Colombian government. Philippe Bunau-Varilla, chief engineer of the French canal project, was a ready ally. In November 1903, he helped organize and finance a revolution in Panama. There had been many previous revolts, all of them failures, but this one had the support of the United States. Roosevelt landed troops from the U.S.S. *Nashville* in Panama to "maintain order." Their presence prevented Colombian forces from suppressing the rebellion, and three days later Roosevelt recognized Panama as an independent nation. The new Panamanian government quickly agreed to the terms the Colombian senate had rejected. Work on the canal proceeded rapidly, and it opened in 1914.

Panamanian Revolt

Taft and "Dollar Diplomacy"

Like his predecessor, William Howard Taft worked to advance the nation's economic interests overseas. But he showed little interest in Roosevelt's larger vision of world stability. Taft's secretary of state, the corporate attorney Philander C. Knox, worked aggressively to extend American investments into less-developed regions. Critics called his policies "Dollar Diplomacy."

It was particularly visible in the Caribbean. When a revolution broke out in Nicaragua in 1909, the administration quickly sided with the insurgents (who had been inspired to revolt by an American mining company) and sent troops into the country to seize the customs houses. As soon as peace was restored, Knox encouraged American bankers to offer substantial loans to the new government, thus increasing Washington's financial leverage over the country. When the new pro-American government faced an insurrection less than two years later, Taft again landed troops in Nicaragua, this time to protect the existing regime. The troops remained there for more than a decade.

Intervention in Nicaragua

Diplomacy and Morality

Woodrow Wilson entered the presidency with relatively little interest or experience in international affairs. Yet he faced international challenges of a scope and gravity unmatched by those of any president before him. In many respects, he continued—and even strengthened—the Roosevelt-Taft approach to foreign policy.

Having already seized control of the finances of the Dominican Republic in 1905, the United States established a military government there in 1916. The military occupation lasted eight years. In neighboring Haiti, Wilson landed the marines in 1915 to quell a revolution, in the course of which a mob had murdered an unpopular president. American military forces remained in the country

OPENING THE PANAMA CANAL The great Miraflores locks of the Panama Canal open in October 1914 to admit the first ship to pass through the channel. The construction of the canal was one of the great engineering feats of the early twentieth century. But the heavy-handed political efforts of Theodore Roosevelt were at least equally important to its completion. *(Bettmann/Corbis)*

until 1934, and American officers drafted the new Haitian constitution adopted in 1918. When Wilson began to fear that the Danish West Indies might be about to fall into the hands of Germany, he bought the colony from Denmark and renamed it the Virgin Islands. Concerned about the possibility of European influence in Nicaragua, he signed a treaty with that country's government ensuring that no other nation would build a canal there and winning for the United States the right to intervene in Nicaragua to protect American interests.

But Wilson's view of America's role in the world was not entirely similar to the views of his predecessors, as became clear in his dealings with Mexico. For many years, under the friendly auspices of the corrupt dictator Porfirio Díaz, American businessmen had been establishing an enormous economic presence in Mexico. In 1910, however, Díaz had been overthrown by the popular leader Francisco Madero, who seemed hostile to American businesses in Mexico. The United States quietly encouraged a reactionary general, Victoriano Huerta, to depose Madero early in 1913, and the Taft administration, in its last weeks in office, prepared to recognize the new Huerta regime and welcome back a receptive envi-

Wilson's Moral Diplomacy

ronment for American investments in Mexico. Before it could do so, however, the new government murdered Madero, and Woodrow Wilson took office in Washington. The new president instantly announced that he would never recognize Huerta's "government of butchers."

At first, Wilson hoped that simply by refusing to recognize Huerta he could help topple the regime and bring to power the opposing Constitutionalists, led by Venustiano Carranza. But when Huerta, with the support of American business interests, established a full military dictatorship in October 1913, the president became more assertive. In April 1914, an officer in Huerta's army briefly arrested several American sailors from the U.S.S. *Dolphin* who had gone ashore in Tampico. The men were immediately released, but the American admiral—unsatisfied with the apology he received—demanded that the Huerta forces fire a twenty-one-gun salute to the American flag as a public display of penance. The Mexicans refused. Wilson used the trivial incident as a pretext for seizing the Mexican port of Veracruz.

Wilson had envisioned a bloodless action, but in a clash with Mexican troops in Veracruz, the Americans killed 126 of the defenders and suffered 19 casualties of their own. Now at

Veracruz

PANCHO VILLA AND HIS TROOPS Pancho Villa (fourth from left in the front row) poses with some of the leaders of his army, whose members Americans came to consider bandits once they began staging raids across the U.S. border. He was a national hero in Mexico. *(Brown Brothers)*

the brink of war, Wilson began to look for a way out. His show of force, however, had helped strengthen the position of the Carranza faction, which captured Mexico City in August and forced Huerta to flee the country. At last, it seemed, the crisis might be over.

But Wilson was not yet satisfied. He reacted angrily when Carranza refused to accept American guidelines for the creation of a new government, and he briefly considered throwing his support to still another aspirant to leadership: Carranza's erstwhile lieutenant Pancho Villa, who was now leading a rebel army of his own. When Villa's military position deteriorated, however, Wilson abandoned him and finally, in October 1915, granted preliminary recognition to the Carranza government. By now, however, he had created yet another crisis. Villa, angry at what he considered an American betrayal, retaliated in January 1916 by shooting sixteen American mining engineers in northern Mexico. Two months later, he led his soldiers (or "bandits," as the United States called them) across the border into Columbus, New Mexico, where they killed seventeen more Americans.

With the permission of the Carranza government, Wilson ordered General John J. Pershing to lead an American expeditionary force across the Mexican border in
pursuit of Villa. The American
Intervention in Mexico troops never found Villa, but they
did engage in two ugly skirmishes with Carranza's army,

in which forty Mexicans and twelve Americans died. Again, the United States and Mexico stood at the brink of war. But at the last minute, Wilson drew back. He quietly withdrew American troops from Mexico, and in March 1917, he at last granted formal recognition to the Carranza regime. By now, however, Wilson's attention was turning elsewhere—to the far greater international crisis engulfing the European continent and ultimately much of the world.

THE ROAD TO WAR

The causes of the war in Europe—indeed the question of whether there were any significant causes at all, or whether the entire conflict was the result of a tragic series of blunders—have been the subject of continued debate for more than ninety years. What is clear is that the European nations had by 1914 created an unusually precarious international system that careened into war very quickly on the basis of what most historians agree was a relatively minor series of provocations.

The Collapse of the European Peace

The major powers of Europe were organized by 1914 in two great, competing alliances. The "Triple Entente" linked Britain, France, and Russia. The
"Triple Alliance" united Germany, Competing Alliances

the Austro-Hungarian Empire, and Italy. The chief rivalry, however, was not between the two alliances, but between the great powers that dominated them: Great Britain and Germany—the former long established as the world's most powerful colonial and commercial nation, the latter ambitious to expand its own empire and become at least Britain's equal. The Anglo-German rivalry may have been the most important underlying source of the tensions that led to World War I, but it was not the immediate cause of its outbreak. The conflict emerged most directly out of a controversy involving nationalist movements within the Austro-Hungarian Empire. On June 28, 1914, the Archduke Franz Ferdinand, heir to the throne of the tottering empire, was assassinated while paying a state visit to Sarajevo. Sarajevo was the capital of Bosnia, a province of Austria-Hungary that Slavic nationalists wished to annex to neighboring Serbia; the archduke's assassin was a Serbian nationalist.

This local controversy quickly escalated through the workings of the system of alliances that the great powers had constructed. With support from Germany, Austria-Hungary launched a punitive assault on Serbia. The Serbians called on Russia to help with their defense. The Russians began mobilizing their army on July 30. Things quickly careened out of control. By August 3, Germany had declared war on both Russia and France and had invaded Belgium in preparation for a thrust across the French border. On August 4, Great Britain—ostensibly to honor its alliance with France, but more importantly to blunt the advance of its principal rival—declared war on Germany. Russia and the Austro-Hungarian Empire formally began hostilities on August 6. Italy, although an ally of Germany in 1914, remained neutral at first and later entered the war on the side of the British and French. The Ottoman Empire (centered in Turkey) and other, smaller nations all joined the fighting later in 1914 or in 1915. Within less than a year, virtually the entire European continent and part of Asia were embroiled in a major war.

Wilson's Neutrality

Wilson called on his fellow citizens in 1914 to remain "impartial in thought as well as deed." But that was impossible, for several reasons. Some Americans sympathized with the German cause (German Americans because of affection for Germany, Irish Americans because of hatred of Britain). Many more (including Wilson himself) sympathized with Britain. Wilson himself was only one of many Americans who fervently admired England—its traditions, its culture, its political system; almost instinctively, these Americans attributed to the cause of the Allies (Britain, France, Italy, Russia) a moral quality that they denied to the Central Powers (Germany, the Austro-Hungarian Empire, and the Ottoman Empire). Lurid reports of German atrocities in Belgium and France, skillfully

PROMOTING THE WAR IN AUSTRALIA   The government of Australia at times had difficulty persuading men to sign up to fight in World War I, which some Australians believed was being fought to aid the British and had nothing to do with them. This poster was part of a drive to recruit volunteers in 1915. *(Private Collection)*

exaggerated by British propagandists, strengthened the hostility of many Americans toward Germany.

Economic realities also made it impossible for the United States to deal with the belligerents on equal terms. The British had imposed a naval blockade on Germany to prevent munitions and supplies from reaching the enemy. As a neutral, the United States had the right, in theory, to trade with Germany. A truly neutral response to the blockade would have been to stop trading with Britain as well. But while the United States could survive an interruption of its relatively modest trade with the Central Powers, it could not easily weather an embargo on its much more extensive trade with the Allies, particularly when war orders from Britain and France soared after 1914, helping to produce one of the greatest economic booms in the nation's history. So America tacitly ignored the blockade of Germany and continued trading with Britain. By 1915, the United States had gradually transformed itself from a neutral power into the arsenal of the Allies.

The Germans, in the meantime, were resorting to a new and, in American eyes, barbaric tactic: submarine warfare. Unable to challenge British domination on the ocean's surface, Germany began early in 1915 to use the newly improved submarine to try to stem the flow of supplies to England. Enemy vessels, the Germans announced,

Lusitania

would be sunk on sight. Months later, on May 7, 1915, a German submarine sank the British passenger liner *Lusitania* without warning, causing the deaths of 1,198 people, 128 of them Americans. The ship was, it later became clear, carrying both passengers and munitions; but most Americans considered the attack what Theodore Roosevelt called it: "an act of piracy."

Wilson angrily demanded that Germany promise not to repeat such outrages and that the Central Powers affirm their commitment to neutral rights. The Germans finally agreed to Wilson's demands, but tensions between the nations continued. Early in 1916, in response to an announcement that the Allies were now arming merchant ships to sink submarines, Germany proclaimed that it would fire on such vessels without warning. A few weeks later it attacked the unarmed French steamer *Sussex,* injuring several American passengers. Again Wilson demanded that Germany abandon its "unlawful" tactics; again the German government relented, still hoping to keep America out of the war.

Preparedness Versus Pacifism

Despite the president's increasing bellicosity in 1916, he was still far from ready to commit the United States to war. One obstacle was American domestic politics. Facing a difficult battle for reelection, Wilson could not ignore the powerful factions that continued to oppose intervention.

The question of whether America should make military and economic preparations for war provided the first issue over which pacifists and interventionists could openly debate. Wilson at first sided with the anti-preparedness forces, denouncing the idea of an American military buildup as needless and provocative. As tensions between the United States and Germany grew, however, he changed his mind. In the fall of 1915, he endorsed an ambitious proposal for a large and rapid increase in the nation's armed forces. Amid expressions of outrage from pacifists in Congress and elsewhere, he worked hard to win approval of it, even embarking on a national speaking tour early in 1916 to arouse support for the proposal.

Still, the peace faction wielded considerable political strength, as became clear at the Democratic Convention in the summer of 1916. The convention became especially enthusiastic when the keynote speaker punctuated his

1916 Election

list of Wilson's diplomatic achievements with the chant "What did we do? What did we do? . . . We didn't go to war! We didn't go to war!" That speech helped produce one of the most prominent slogans of Wilson's reelection campaign: "He kept us out of war." During the campaign, Wilson did nothing to discourage those who argued that the Republican candidate, the progressive New York governor Charles Evans Hughes (supported by the bellicose

Theodore Roosevelt), was more likely than he to lead the nation into war. And when pro-war rhetoric became particularly heated, Wilson spoke defiantly of the nation being "too proud to fight." He ultimately won reelection by a small margin: fewer than 600,000 popular votes and only 23 electoral votes. The Democrats retained a precarious control over Congress.

A War for Democracy

The election was behind him, and tensions between the United States and Germany remained high. But Wilson still required a justification for American intervention that would unite public opinion and satisfy his own sense of morality. In the end, he created that rationale himself. The United States, Wilson insisted, had no material aims in the conflict. Rather, the nation was committed to using the war as a vehicle for constructing a new world order, one based on some of the same progressive ideals that had motivated reform in America. In a speech before Congress in January 1917, he presented a plan for a postwar order in which the United States would help maintain peace through a permanent league of nations—a peace that would ensure self-determination for all

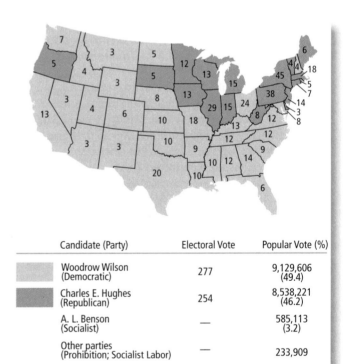

Candidate (Party)	Electoral Vote	Popular Vote (%)
Woodrow Wilson (Democratic)	277	9,129,606 (49.4)
Charles E. Hughes (Republican)	254	8,538,221 (46.2)
A. L. Benson (Socialist)	—	585,113 (3.2)
Other parties (Prohibition; Socialist Labor)	—	233,909

61.6% of electorate voting

ELECTION OF 1916 Woodrow Wilson had good reason to be concerned about his reelection prospects in 1916. He had won only about 42 percent of the vote in 1912, and the Republican Party— which had been divided four years earlier—was now reunited around the popular Charles Evans Hughes. In the end, Wilson won a narrow victory over Hughes with just under 50 percent of the vote and an even narrower margin in the electoral college. Note the striking regional character of his victory. ◆ *How did Wilson use the war in Europe to bolster his election prospects?*

nations, a "peace without victory." These were, Wilson believed, goals worth fighting for if there was sufficient provocation. Provocation came quickly.

In January, after months of inconclusive warfare in the trenches of France, the military leaders of Germany decided on one last dramatic gamble to achieve victory. They launched a series of major assaults on the enemy's lines in France. At the same time, they began unrestricted submarine warfare (against American as well as Allied ships) to cut Britain off from vital supplies. The Allied defenses would collapse, they hoped, before the United States could intervene. The new German policy made American entry into the war virtually inevitable. Two additional events helped clear the way. On February 25, the British gave Wilson a telegram intercepted from the German foreign minister, Arthur Zimmermann, to the government of Mexico. It proposed that in the event of war between Germany and the United States, the Mexicans should join with Germany against the Americans to regain their "lost provinces" (Texas and much of the rest of the American Southwest) when the war was over. Widely publicized by British propagandists and in the American press, the Zimmermann telegram inflamed public opinion and helped build popular sentiment for war. A few weeks later, in March 1917, a revolution in Russia toppled the reactionary czarist regime and replaced it with a new, republican government. The United States would now be spared the embarrassment of allying itself with a despotic monarchy.

Zimmermann Telegram

On the rainy evening of April 2, two weeks after German submarines had torpedoed three American ships, Wilson appeared before a joint session of Congress and asked for a declaration of war:

> It is a fearful thing to lead this great peaceful people into war, into the most terrible and disastrous of all wars, civilization itself seeming to be in the balance. But the right is more precious than peace, and we shall fight for the things which we have always carried nearest our hearts—for democracy, for the right of those who submit to authority to have a voice in their own Governments, for the rights and liberties of small nations, for a universal dominion of right by such a concert of free peoples as shall bring peace and safety to all nations and make the world itself at last free.

Even then, opposition remained. For four days, pacifists in Congress carried on a futile struggle. When the declaration of war finally passed on April 6, fifty representatives and six senators voted against it.

"WAR WITHOUT STINT"

Armies on both sides in Europe were decimated and exhausted by the time of Woodrow Wilson's declaration of war. The German offensives of early 1917 had failed to produce an end to the struggle, and French and British counteroffensives had accomplished little beyond adding to

Stalemate

THE WARTIME DRAFT This office in New York handled hundreds of men every day who arrived to enlist in response to draft notices. Although both the Union and the Confederacy had tried (and often failed) to use the draft during the Civil War, the World War I draft was the first centrally organized effort by the federal government to require military service from its citizens. Although some Americans evaded the draft in 1917 and 1918 (and were reviled by others as "shirkers"), most of those drafted complied with the law. *(Brown Brothers)*

the casualties. The Allies looked to the United States for help. Wilson, who had called on the nation to wage war "without stint or limit," was ready to oblige.

Entering the War

By the spring of 1917, Great Britain was suffering such vast losses from attacks by German submarines—one of every four ships setting sail from British ports never returned—that its ability to continue receiving vital supplies from across the Atlantic was in question. Within weeks of joining the war, a fleet of American destroyers began aiding the British navy in its assault on German submarines. Other American warships escorted merchant vessels across the Atlantic. Americans also helped sow anti-submarine mines in the North Sea. The results were dramatic. Sinkings of Allied ships had totaled nearly 900,000 tons in the month of April 1917; by December, the figure had dropped to 350,000, and by October 1918 to 112,000. The convoys also helped the United States protect its own soldiers en route to Europe. No American troop ship was lost at sea in World War I.

Many Americans had hoped that providing naval assistance alone would be enough to turn the tide in the war, but it quickly became clear that American ground forces would also be necessary to shore up the tottering Allies. Britain and France had few remaining reserves. By early 1918, Russia had withdrawn from the war. After the Bolshevik Revolution in November 1917, the new government, led by V. I. Lenin, negotiated a hasty and costly peace with the Central Powers, thus freeing additional German troops to fight on the western front.

Russian Revolution

The American Expeditionary Force

There were only about 120,000 soldiers in the army in 1917, and perhaps 80,000 more in the National Guard. Neither group had any combat experience; and except for the small number of officers who had participated in the Spanish-American War two decades before and the Mexican intervention of 1916, few commanders had any experience in battle either.

Some politicians urged a voluntary recruitment process to raise the needed additional forces. Among the advocates of this approach was Theodore Roosevelt, now old and ill, who swallowed his hatred of Wilson and called on him at the White House with an offer to raise a regiment to fight in Europe. But the president and his secretary of war, Newton D. Baker, decided that only a national draft could provide the needed men; and despite the protests of those who agreed with House Speaker Champ Clark that "there is precious little difference between a conscript and a convict," he won passage of the Selective Service Act in mid-May. The draft brought nearly 3 million men into the army; another 2 million joined various branches of the armed services voluntarily. Together, they formed what became known as the American Expeditionary Force (AEF).

Selective Service Act

It was the first time in American history that any substantial number of soldiers and sailors had fought overseas for an extended period. The military did its best to keep up morale among men who spent most of their time living in the trenches. They were frequently shelled and even when calm were muddy, polluted, and infested with rats. But when soldiers had time away from the front, they were usually less interested in the facilities the Red Cross

A WOMEN'S MOTOR CORPS Although the most important new role that women performed during World War I was probably working in factories that male workers had left, many women also enlisted in auxiliary branches of the military—among them these uniformed women who served as drivers for the army. *(Culver Pictures, Inc.)*

tried to make available for them than in exploring the bars and brothels of local towns. More than one in every ten American soldiers in Europe contracted venereal disease during World War I, which inspired elaborate official efforts to prevent infection and to treat it when it occurred.

In some respects, the AEF was the most diverse fighting force the United States had ever assembled. For the first time, women were permitted to enlist in the military—more than ten thousand in the navy and a few hundred in the marines. They were not allowed to participate in combat, but they served auxiliary roles in hospitals and offices.

Nearly 400,000 black soldiers enlisted in or were drafted into the army and navy as well. (The marines would not accept them.) And while most of them performed menial tasks on military bases in the United States, more than 50,000 went to France. African-American soldiers served in segregated, all-black units under white commanders; and even in Europe, most of them were assigned to noncombat duty. But some black units fought valiantly in the great offensives of 1918. Most African-American soldiers learned to live with the racism they encountered—in part because they hoped their military service would ultimately improve their status. But a few responded to provocations violently. In August 1917, a group of black soldiers in Houston, subjected to continuing abuse by people in the community, used military weapons to kill seventeen whites. Thirteen black soldiers were hanged, and another forty were sentenced to life terms in military jails.

African-American Soldiers

Having assembled this first genuinely national army, the War Department permitted the American Psychological Association to study it. The psychologists gave thousands of soldiers new tests designed to measure intelligence: the "Intelligence Quotient," or "IQ," test and other newly designed aptitude tests. In fact, the tests were less effective in measuring intelligence than in measuring education; and they reflected the educational expectations of the white middle-class people who had devised them. Half the whites and the vast majority of the African Americans taking the test scored at levels that classified them as "morons." In reality, most of them were simply people who had not had much access to education.

The Military Struggle

The engagement of these forces in combat was intense but brief. Not until the spring of 1918 were significant numbers of American ground troops available for battle. Eight months later, the war was over. Under the command of General John J. Pershing, who had only recently led the unsuccessful American pursuit of Pancho Villa, the American Expeditionary Force—although it retained a command structure independent of the other Allies—joined the existing Allied forces.

General John Pershing

The experience of American troops during World War I was very different from those of other nations, which had already been fighting for nearly four years by the time the U.S. forces arrived in significant numbers. British, French, German, and other troops had by then spent years living in the vast network of trenches that had been dug into the French countryside. Modern weapons made conventional, frontal battles a recipe for mass suicide. Instead, the two sides relied on heavy shelling of each other's trenches and occasional, usually inconclusive, and always murderous assaults across the "no-man's land" dividing them. Life

LIFE IN THE TRENCHES For most British, French, German, and ultimately American troops in France, the most debilitating part of World War I was the seeming endlessness of life in the trenches. Some young men lived in these cold, wet, muddy dugouts for months, even years, surrounded by filth, sharing their space with vermin, eating mostly rotten food. Occasional attacks to try to dislodge the enemy from its trenches usually ended in failure and became the scenes of terrible slaughters. *(National Archives and Records Administration)*

in the trenches was almost indescribably terrible. The trenches were places of extraordinary physical stress and discomfort. They were also places of intense boredom, laced with fear. By the time the Americans arrived, morale on both sides was declining, and many soldiers had come to believe that the war would be virtually endless.

Although the American forces had trench experiences of their own, they were very brief compared to those of the European armies. Instead, the United States tipped the balance of power in the battle and made it possible for the Allies at last to break out of their entrenched positions and advance against the Germans. In early June 1918, American forces at Château-Thierry assisted the French

Château-Thierry

in repelling a German offensive that had brought German forces within fifty miles of Paris. Six weeks later, after over a million American troops had flooded into France, the Americans helped turn away another assault, at Rheims, farther south. By July 18, the Allies had halted the German advance and were beginning a successful offensive of their own.

On September 26, the American fighting force joined a large assault against the Germans in the Argonne Forest that lasted nearly seven weeks. By the end of October, despite terrible weather, they had helped

Meuse-Argonne Offensive

push the Germans back toward their own border and had cut the enemy's major supply lines to the front.

Faced with an invasion of their own country, German military leaders now began to seek an armistice—an immediate cease-fire that would, they hoped, serve as a prelude to negotiations among the belligerents. Pershing wanted to drive on into Germany itself; but other Allied leaders, after first insisting on terms that made the agreement little different from a surrender, accepted the German proposal. On November 11, 1918, the Great War shuddered to a close.

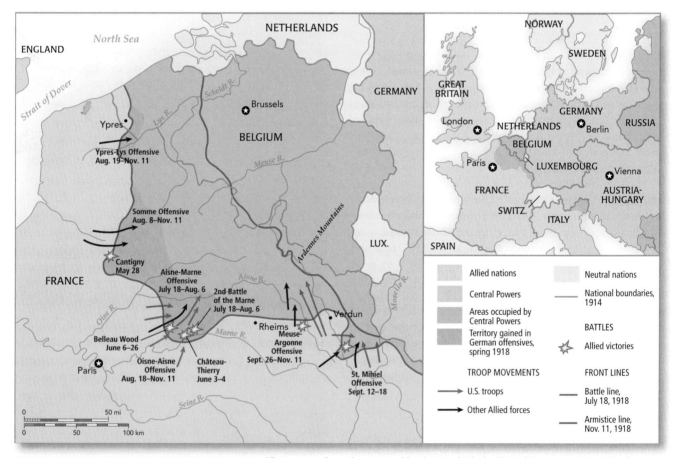

AMERICA IN WORLD WAR I: THE WESTERN FRONT, 1918 These maps show the principal battles in which the United States participated in the last year of World War I. The small map on the upper right helps locate the area of conflict within the larger European landscape. The larger map at left shows the long, snaking red line of the western front in France—stretching from the border between France and southwest Germany all the way to the northeast border between Belgium and France. Along that vast line, the two sides had been engaged in murderous, inconclusive warfare for over three years by the time the Americans arrived. Beginning in the spring and summer of 1918, bolstered by reinforcements from the United States, the Allies began to win a series of important victories that finally enabled them to begin pushing the Germans back. American troops, as this map makes clear, were decisive along the southern part of the front. ◆ *At what point did the Germans begin to consider putting an end to the war?*

For an interactive version of this map, go to www.mhhe.com/brinkley13ech21maps

The New Technology of Warfare

World War I was a proving ground for a range of military and other technologies. The trench warfare that characterized the conflict was necessary because of the enormous destructive power of newly improved machine guns and higher-powered artillery. It was no longer feasible to send troops out into an open field, or even to allow them to camp in the open. The new weaponry would slaughter them in an instant. Trenches sheltered troops while allowing limited, and usually inconclusive, fighting. But technology overtook the trenches, too, as mobile weapons—tanks and flamethrowers—proved capable of piercing entrenched positions. Most terrible of all, perhaps, new chemical weapons—poisonous mustard gas, which required troops to carry gas masks at all times—made it possible to attack entrenched soldiers without direct combat.

The new forms of technological warfare required elaborate maintenance. Faster machine guns needed more ammunition. Motorized vehicles required fuel and spare parts and mechanics capable of servicing them. The logistical difficulties of supply became a major factor in planning tactics and strategy. Late in the war, when advancing toward Germany, Allied armies frequently had to stop for days at a time to wait for their equipment to catch up with them.

World War I was the first conflict in which airplanes played a significant role. The planes themselves were relatively simple and not very maneuverable; but anti-aircraft technology was not yet highly developed either, so their effectiveness was still considerable. Planes began to be constructed to serve various functions: bombers, fighters (planes that would engage in "dogfights" with other planes), and reconaissance aircraft.

The most "modern" part of the military during World War I was the navy. New battleships emerged—of which the British *Dreadnought* was perhaps the most visible example—that made use of new technologies such as turbine propulsion, hydraulic gun controls, electric light and power, wireless telegraphy, and advanced navigational aids. Submarines, which had made a brief appearance in the American Civil War, now became significant weapons (as the German U-boat campaign in 1915 and 1916 made clear). The new submarines were driven by diesel engines, which had the advantage of being more compact than a steam engine and whose fuel was less explosive than that of a gasoline engine. The diesel engine also had a much greater range than ships powered by other fuels.

The new technologies were to a large degree responsible for the most stunning and horrible characteristic of World War I—its appalling level of casualties. A million men representing the British Empire (Britain, Canada, Australia, India, and others) died. France lost 1.7 million men; Germany, 2 million; the former Austro-Hungarian Empire,

High Casualty Rates

1.5 million; Italy, 460,000; and Russia, 1.7 million. The number of Turkish dead, which was surely large, was never known. In Britain, one-third of the men born between 1892 and 1895 died in the war. Similarly terrible percentages could be calculated for other warring nations. Even greater numbers of men returned home with injuries, some of them permanently crippling. The United States, which entered the war near its end and became engaged only in the last successful offensives, suffered very light casualties in contrast—112,000 dead, half of them victims of influenza, not battle. But the American casualties were very high in the battles in which U.S. troops were centrally involved.

THE WAR AND AMERICAN SOCIETY

The American experience in World War I was relatively brief, but it had profound effects on the government, on the economy, and on society. Mobilizing an industrial economy for total war required an unprecedented degree of government involvement in industry, agriculture, and other areas. It also required, many Americans believed, a strenuous effort to ensure the loyalty and commitment of the people.

Organizing the Economy for War

By the time the war ended, the United States government had spent $32 billion for expenses directly related to the conflict. This was a staggering sum by the standards of the time.

Financing the War

The entire federal budget had seldom exceeded $1 billion before 1915, and as recently as 1910 the nation's entire gross national product had been only $35 billion. To finance the war, the government relied on two devices. First, it launched a major drive to solicit loans from the American people by selling "Liberty Bonds" to the public. By 1920, the sale of bonds, accompanied by elaborate patriotic appeals, had produced $23 billion. At the same time, new taxes were bringing in an additional sum of nearly $10 billion—some from levies on the "excess profits" of corporations, much from new, steeply graduated income and inheritance taxes that ultimately rose as high as 70 percent in some brackets.

An even greater challenge was organizing the economy to meet war needs. In 1916, Wilson established a Council of National Defense, composed of members of his cabinet, and a Civilian Advisory Commission, which set up local defense councils in every state and locality. Economic mobilization, according to this first plan, was to rest on a dispersal of power to local communities.

But this early administrative structure soon proved unworkable. Some members of the Council of National Defense, many of them disciples of the social engineering gospel of Thorstein Veblen and the "scientific management" principles of Frederick Winslow Taylor, urged a centralized approach. Instead of dividing the economy geographically, they proposed dividing it functionally by organizing a series of planning bodies, each to supervise a specific sector of the economy. The administrative structure that slowly emerged from such proposals was dominated by a series of "war boards," one to oversee the railroads, one to supervise fuel supplies (largely coal), another to handle food (a board that helped elevate to prominence the brilliant young engineer and business executive Herbert Hoover). The boards generally succeeded in meeting essential war needs without paralyzing the domestic economy.

At the center of the effort to rationalize the economy was the War Industries Board (WIB), an agency created in War Industries Board July 1917 to coordinate government purchases of military supplies. Casually organized at first, it stumbled badly until March 1918, when Wilson restructured it and placed it under the control of the Wall Street financier Bernard Baruch. From then on, the board wielded powers greater (in theory at least) than any other government agency had ever possessed. Baruch decided which factories would convert to the production of which war materials and set prices for the goods they produced. When materials were scarce, Baruch decided to whom they should go. When corporations were competing for government contracts, he chose among them. He was, it seemed, providing the centralized regulation of the economy that some progressives had long urged.

In reality, the celebrated efficiency of the WIB was something of a myth. The agency was, in fact, plagued by mismanagement and inefficiency. Its apparent success rested in large part on the sheer extent of American resources and productive capacities. Nor was the WIB in any real sense an example of state control of the economy. Baruch viewed himself as the partner of business; and within the WIB, businessmen themselves—the so-called dollar-a-year men, who took paid leave from their corporate jobs and worked for the government for a token salary—supervised the affairs of the private economy. Baruch ensured that manufacturers who coordinated their efforts with his goals would be exempt from antitrust laws. He helped major industries earn enormous profits from their efforts.

The effort to organize the economy for war produced some spectacular accomplishments: Hoover's efficient

HARLEM BLOCK PARTY, 1915 Harlem, once a suburb of Manhattan where middle class commuters lived, became in the early twentieth century the center of African-American life in New York. By the time of this lively block party in 1915, a robust culture had begun to develop in Harlem among both adults and children. *(Brown Brothers)*

organization of domestic food supplies, William McAdoo's

Lessons of the Managed Economy

success in untangling the railroads, and others. In some areas, however, progress was so slow that the war was over before many of the supplies ordered for it were ready. Even so, many leaders of both government and industry emerged from the experience convinced of the advantages of a close, cooperative relationship between the public and private sectors. Some hoped to continue the wartime experiments in peacetime.

Labor and the War

The growing link between the public and private sectors extended, although in greatly different form, to labor. The National War Labor Board, established in April 1918 to resolve labor disputes, pressured industry to grant important concessions to workers: an eight-hour day, the maintenance of minimal living standards, equal pay for women doing equal work, recognition of the right of unions to organize and bargain collectively. In return, it insisted that workers forgo all strikes and that employers not engage in lockouts. Membership in labor unions increased by more than 1.5 million between 1917 and 1919.

The war provided workers with important, if usually temporary, gains. But it did not stop labor militancy. That was particularly clear in the West, where the Western Federation of Miners staged a series of strikes to improve the terrible conditions in the underground mines. The bloodiest of them occurred just before the war. In Ludlow, Colorado, in 1914, workers (mostly Italians, Greeks, and Slavs) walked out of coal mines owned by John D. Rockefeller. Joined by their wives and daughters, they continued the strike even after they had been evicted from company housing and had moved into hastily erected tents. The state militia was called into the town to protect the mines, but in fact (as was often the case), it actually worked to help employers defeat the strikers.

Joined by strikebreakers and others, the militia attacked the workers' tent colony; and in the battle that followed,

Ludlow Massacre

thirty-nine people died, among them eleven children. But these events, which became known as the Ludlow Massacre, were only precursors to continued conflict in the mines that the war itself did little to discourage.

Economic and Social Results of the War

Whatever its other effects, the war helped produce a remarkable period of economic growth in the United States—a boom that began in 1914 (when European demands for American products began to increase) and accelerated after 1917 (in response to demand from the United States war effort). Industrial production soared, and manufacturing activity expanded in regions that had previously had relatively little of it. The shipbuilding industry, for example, grew rapidly on the West Coast. Employment increased dramatically; and because so many white men were away at war, new opportunities for female, African-American, Mexican, and Asian workers appeared. Some workers experienced a significant growth in income, but inflation cut into the wage increases and often produced a net loss in purchasing power. The agricultural economy profited from the war as well. Farm prices rose to their highest levels in decades, and agricultural production increased dramatically as a result.

One of the most important social changes of the war years was the migration of hundreds of thousands of African Americans from the rural South into northern industrial cities. It became known as the "Great Migration." Like

"Great Migration"

most migrations, it was a result of both a "push" and a "pull." The push was the poverty, indebtedness, racism, and violence most blacks experienced in the South. The pull was the prospect of factory jobs in the urban North and the opportunity to live in communities where blacks could enjoy more freedom and autonomy. In the labor-scarce economy of the war years, northern factory owners dispatched agents to the South to recruit African-American workers. Black newspapers advertised the prospects for employment in the North. And perhaps most important, those who migrated sent word back to friends and families of the opportunities they encountered—one reason for the heavy concentration of migrants from a single area of the South in certain cities in the North. In Chicago, for example, the more than 70,000 new black residents came disproportionately from a few areas of Alabama and Mississippi.

The result was a dramatic growth in black communities in northern industrial cities such as New York, Chicago, Cleveland, and Detroit. Some older, more established black residents of these cities were unsettled by these new arrivals, with their country ways and their revivalistic religion; the existing African-American communities considered the newcomers coarse and feared that their presence would increase their own vulnerability to white racism. But the movement could not be stopped. New churches sprang up in black neighborhoods (many of them simple storefronts, from which self-proclaimed preachers searched for congregations). Low-paid black workers crowded into inadequate housing. As the black communities expanded, they inevitably began to rub up against white neighborhoods, with occa-

Race Riots

sionally violent results. In East St. Louis, Illinois, a white mob attacked a black neighborhood on July 2, 1917, burned down many houses, and shot the residents of some of them as they fled. As many as forty African Americans died.

For American women, black and white, the war meant new opportunities for employment. A million or more women worked in a wide range of industrial jobs that, in peacetime, were considered male preserves: steel,

WOMEN INDUSTRIAL WORKERS In World War II, such women were often called "Rosie the Riveter." Their presence in these previously all-male work environments was no less startling to Americans during World War I. These women are shown working with acetylene torches to bevel armor plate for tanks. *(Margaret Bourke-White/Time Life Pictures/Getty Images)*

munitions, trucking, public transportation. Most of them had been working in other, lower-paying jobs earlier. But whatever changes the war brought were temporary ones. As soon as the war was over, almost all of the women working in previously male industrial jobs quit or were fired; in fact, the percentage of women working for wages actually declined between 1910 and 1920. The government had created the Women in Industry Board to oversee the movement of these women into the jobs left behind by men. After the war, the board became the Women's Bureau, a permanent agency dedicated to protecting the interests of women in the work force.

THE SEARCH FOR SOCIAL UNITY

The idea of unity—not only in the direction of the economy but in the nation's social purpose—had been the dream of many progressives for decades. To them, the war seemed to offer an unmatched opportunity for America to close ranks behind a great common cause. In the process, they hoped, society could achieve a lasting sense of collective purpose. But the task proved impossible to achieve.

The Peace Movement

Government leaders, and many others, realized that public sentiment about American involvement in the war had been deeply divided before April 1917 and remained so even after the declaration of war.

The peace movement in the United States before 1917 had many constituencies: German Americans, Irish Americans, religious pacifists (Quakers, Mennonites, and others), intellectuals and groups on the left such as the Socialist Party and the Industrial Workers of the World, all of whom considered the war a meaningless battle among capitalist nations for commercial supremacy—an opinion many others, in America and Europe, later came to share. But the most active and widespread peace activism came from the women's movement. In 1915, Carrie Chapman Catt, a leader of the fight for woman suffrage, helped create the Woman's Peace Party, with a small but active membership. As the war in Europe intensified, the party's efforts to keep the United States from intervening grew.

Women peace activists were sharply divided once America entered the war in 1917. The National American Woman Suffrage Association, the single largest women's organization, supported the war and, more than that, presented itself as a patriotic organization dedicated to advancing the war effort. Its membership grew dramatically as a result. Catt, who was among those who abandoned the peace cause, now began calling for woman suffrage as a "war measure," to ensure that women (whose work was essential to the war effort) would feel fully a part of the nation. But many other women refused to support the war even after April 1917. Among them were Jane Addams, who was widely reviled as a result, and Charlotte Perkins Gilman, a leading feminist activist.

Women peace activists shared many of the political and economic objections to the war of the Socialist Party (to which some of them belonged). But some criticized the war on other grounds as well, arguing that as "the mother half of humanity," they had a special moral and maternal basis for their pacifism.

Selling the War and Suppressing Dissent

World War I was not as popular among the American people as World War II would be, but most of the country supported the intervention once it began. In communities all across the nation, there were outbursts of fervent patriotism, floods of voluntary enlistments in the military, and greatly increased displays of patriotism. Women joined their local Red Cross in an effort to contribute to the war effort. Children raised money for war bonds in their schools. Churches included prayers for the president and the troops in their services. Indeed, the war gave a large boost to the wave of religious revivalism that had been growing for a decade before 1917; and revivalism, in turn, became a source of support for the war. Billy Sunday, the leading revivalist of his time, dropped his early opposition to intervention in 1917 and became a fervent champion of the American military effort.

Nevertheless, government leaders (and many others) remained deeply concerned about the significant minorities who continued to oppose the war even after the United States entered it. Many believed that a crucial prerequisite for victory was an energetic, even coercive, effort to unite public opinion behind the military effort.

The most conspicuous government effort to rally public support was a vast propaganda campaign orchestrated by the new Committee on Public

CPI

Information (CPI). It was directed by the Denver journalist George Creel, who spoke openly of the importance of achieving social unity. The CPI supervised the distribution of tons of pro-war literature (75 million pieces of printed material). War posters plastered the walls of offices, shops, theaters, schools, churches, and homes. Newspapers dutifully printed official government accounts of the reasons for the war and the prospects for quick victory. Creel encouraged reporters to exercise "self-censorship" when reporting news about the struggle.

As the war continued, the CPI's tactics became increasingly crude. Government-promoted posters and films became lurid portrayals of the savagery of the Germans, bearing such titles as *The Prussian Cur* and *The Kaiser: Beast of Berlin,* encouraging Americans to think of the German people as something close to savages.

The government soon began more coercive efforts to suppress dissent. The CPI ran full-page advertisements in popular magazines like the *Saturday Evening Post*

Espionage Act

urging citizens to notify the Justice Department when they encountered "the man who spreads the pessimistic stories . . . , cries for peace, or belittles our efforts to win the war." The Espionage Act of 1917 gave the government new tools with which to respond to such reports. It created stiff penalties for spying, sabotage, or obstruction of the war effort (crimes that were often broadly defined); and it empowered the Post Office Department

WARTIME PROPAGANDA   This poster—one of many lurid images of imperial Germany used by the United States government to generate enthusiasm for American involvement in World War I—shows bloodstained German boots with the German eagle clearly visible. The demonization of Germany was at the heart of government efforts to portray the war to Americans. *(Library of Congress)*

to ban "seditious" material from the mails. Sedition, Postmaster General Albert Sidney Burleson said, included statements that might "impugn the motives of the government and thus encourage insubordination," anything that suggested "that the government is controlled by Wall Street or munitions manufacturers, or any other special interests." He included in that category all publications of the Socialist Party.

More repressive were two measures of 1918: the Sabotage Act of April 20 and the Sedition Act of May 16. These bills expanded the meaning of the Espionage Act to make illegal

Sedition Act

any public expression of opposition to the war; in practice, it allowed officials to prosecute anyone who criticized the president or the government.

The most frequent targets of the new legislation (and one of the reasons for its enactment in the first place) were such anticapitalist groups (and antiwar) groups as the Socialist Party and the Industrial Workers of the World (IWW). Many Americans had favored the repression of

BILLY SUNDAY AND MODERN REVIVALISM

Billy Sunday was a farm boy from Iowa who attended school only until the eighth grade, became a professional baseball player in his teens, and then, in 1886, at the age of twenty-four, experienced a conversion to evangelical Christianity. Over the next decade, he rose to become the most successful revivalist in America in an era when revivalism was spreading rapidly through rural and urban communities alike.

The great revival of the early twentieth century was not the first or the last in American history. But that revival—which reached a peak during the anxious years of World War I—stirred vast numbers of Americans and both reflected and helped to create a deep and lasting schism in the nation's Christian community.

The new revivalism was, among other things, an effort by conservative Christians to fight off the influence of Darwin and his theory of evolution. Conservatives deplored the impact of Darwin on religion. A great many American Protestants in the late nineteenth century—people known as modernists—had revised their faith to incorporate Darwin's teaching. In the process, they had discarded from religion some of the beliefs that many conservative Christians considered critically important: the literal truth of the Bible (including the story of Creation), the faith in personal conversion, the factuality of miracles, the strong belief in the existence of heaven and hell, and many others. Faith in these religious "fundamentals" was important to conservatives (who began to be known as "fundamentalists") because without them, they believed, religion would no longer be a vibrant, central presence in their lives. And in an age of rapid and often disorienting social change, many Americans found traditional religious belief an important source of solidity and stability.

Billy Sunday combined an instinctive feel for fundamentalist belief with an eager and skillful understanding of modern techniques of marketing and publicity and a genius for making religion entertaining. In the process, he became a prototype for the great revivalists of the later twentieth century: Aimee Semple McPherson, Billy Graham, Oral Roberts, and many others. In his own time, Sunday was as popular and successful as any of them.

Sunday enlisted the support of advertisers and public relations experts to publicize his crusades, and he developed sophisticated methods of measuring the success of his mission. He raised enormous sums of money from eager worshipers (and, at times, wealthy patrons). But while he used some of it to live and travel comfortably, most of it went to publicizing his revival meetings and constructing the elaborate, if temporary, "tabernacles" in which he spoke before up to 20,000 people at a time. Established churches canceled their services when Sunday was in town and sent their congregants to hear him. Newspapers devoted enormous attention to his sermons and their impact. People lined the streets to catch a glimpse of him as he walked or rode through towns.

Part of Sunday's success was a result of his previous career as a baseball player, which he used to create a bond with male members of his audience. And part was a result of his flamboyant oratorical style. He leaped around his platform like the athlete he was, told jokes, waved the American flag, raised and lowered his voice to create a sense of intimacy and then a sense of passion. He was a natural

BILLY SUNDAY IN ILLINOIS, 1908 This photograph shows one of the many temporary tabernacles erected to house the enormous crowds—in this case over 5,000 people—whom Billy Sunday regularly attracted. He is shown here in Bloomington, Illinois, in January 1908, but the scene repeated itself in many places through the first decades of the twentieth century. *(C. U. Williams, Bloomington, Illinois/Archives of the Billy Graham Center, Wheaton, Illinois)*

socialists and radicals even before the war; the wartime policies now made it possible to move against them legally. Eugene V. Debs, the humane leader of the Socialist Party and an opponent of the war, was sentenced to ten years in prison in 1918. Only a pardon by President Warren G. Harding ultimately won his release in 1921. Big Bill Haywood and members of the IWW were especially energetically prosecuted. Only by fleeing to the Soviet Union did Haywood avoid long imprisonment. More than 1,500 people were arrested in 1918 for the crime of criticizing the government.

BILLY SUNDAY ON THE PULPIT The artist George Bellows based this 1925 lithograph of Sunday preaching on an earlier painting of the same scene. It reveals something of the enormous energy Sunday brought to his sermons. *(Bettmann/Corbis)*

showman, and he had no inhibitions about using the techniques of showmanship to manipulate his audiences. But he was successful, too, because he combined fundamentalist religious themes with outspoken positions on social issues.

He was a highly effective advocate of prohibition and sometimes seemed to convert an entire community to temperance in a single stroke. "BURLINGTON IS DRY," an Iowa newspaper headline announced after one of his visits. "BILLY SUNDAY HAS MADE GRAVEYARD OF ONCE FAST TOWN." Sunday also spoke, at times with great fervor, about other reforms: cleaning up corrupt city governments, attacking the great trusts, fighting poverty. "I believe," he once said, "if society permits any considerable proportion of people to live in foul, unlighted rooms . . . if society allows deserving men to stagger along with less than a living wage . . . if society . . . throws the unripe strength of children into the hopper of corporate greed to be ground down into dividends, then society must share the responsibility if these people become criminals, thieves, cutthroats, drunkards, and prostitutes."

Yet he also insisted that individuals were not simply victims of society. "A man is not supposed to be the victim of his environment," he argued. Society could not explain the failures of "the individual who's got a rotten heart." Most of all, he argued, even the most degraded individuals could save themselves through Christ. An active faith would not only give them spiritual peace; it would also help them rise in the world. Religion, as Sunday presented it, was a form of self-help in a time when many Americans were searching desperately for ways to gain control over their lives and their fates.

Sunday opposed American involvement in World War I in the first years of the fighting in Europe. "A lot of fools over there are murdering each other to satisfy the damnable ambitions of a few mutts who sit on thrones," he once said. But when the United States entered the fighting, he took second place to no one in the fervor of his support and the passion of his patriotism. By then, the surge of revivalism he had helped create had spread widely through America—partly because of the ambitions of Sunday's many imitators (over a thousand of them, according to some estimates), who hoped to achieve something like his fame

POSING WITH THE BIBLE Sunday was almost never photographed in conventional portrait style. Even posed pictures usually showed him in some animated form—gesticulating, lunging, or (as here) holding up the Bible. *(Culver Pictures, Inc.)*

and fortune; and partly because of the eagerness of established congregations to bring revivalists into their communities to get people back into their churches. The war increased the appetite for revivalism in many communities, and it brought Sunday—and many others—a last great burst of success.

One of the things that made the war so important to revivalists, and their critics, was the hatred of Germany that became so powerful in American culture in those years. That hatred took several very different forms. To fundamentalists like Sunday, Germany was a source of evil because it had abandoned religion and embraced the new secular, scientific values of the modern world. To critics of fundamentalists, the problem with Germany was that it was not modern enough, that it was trapped in an older, discredited world of tribalism and savagery. This disagreement became the source of harsh charges and countercharges between fundamentalists and modernists during the war and contributed to lasting bitterness between the two groups. It also increased the fervor with which fundamentalists responded to charismatic leaders like Sunday.

Sunday's popularity faded after 1920, as he became a harsh critic of "radicalism" and "foreignness" and as the popularity of revivals declined in the face of a beckoning new consumer culture. When he died in 1935, he was attracting crowds only in scattered, rural communities of deeply conservative views. But in his heyday, Sunday provided millions of Americans with a combination of dazzling entertainment and prescriptions for renewing their religious faith. In the process, he helped sustain their belief in the possibility of personal success through a combination of faith and hard work even as the new industrial society was rapidly eroding the reality of the "self-made man."

State and local governments, corporations, universities, and private citizens contributed as well to the climate of repression. Vigilante mobs sprang up to "discipline" those who dared challenge the war. A dissident Protestant clergyman in Cincinnati was pulled from his bed one night by a mob, dragged to a nearby hillside, and whipped "in the name of the women and children of Belgium." An IWW organizer in Montana was seized by a mob and hanged from a railroad bridge.

Repressing Dissent

A cluster of citizens' groups emerged to mobilize "respectable" members of their communities to root out disloyalty. The American Protective League, probably the largest of such groups, enlisted the services of 250,000 people, who served as "agents"—prying into the activities and thoughts of their neighbors, opening mail, tapping telephones, and in general attempting to impose unity of opinion on their communities. It received government funds to support its work. Attorney General Thomas W. Gregory, a particularly avid supporter of repressing dissent, described the league and similar organizations approvingly as "patriotic organizations." Other vigilante organizations—the National Security League, the Boy Spies of America, the American Defense Society—performed much the same function.

There were many victims of such activities: socialists, labor activists, female pacifists. But the most frequent targets of repression were immigrants: Irish Americans

"100 Percent Americanism"

because of their historic animosity toward the British, Jews because many had expressed opposition to the anti-Semitic policies of the Russian government, and others. "Loyalist" citizens' groups policed immigrant neighborhoods. They monitored meetings and even conversations for signs of disloyalty. Even some settlement house workers, many of whom had once championed ethnic diversity, contributed to such efforts. The director of the National Security League described the origins of the anti-immigrant sentiment, which was producing growing support for what many were now calling "100 percent Americanism":

> The melting pot has not melted. . . . There are vast communities in the nation thinking today not in terms of America, but in terms of Old World prejudices, theories, and animosities.

The greatest target of abuse was the German-American community. Most German Americans supported the American war effort once it began. Still, public opinion turned bitterly hostile. A campaign to purge society of all things German quickly gathered speed, at times assuming ludicrous forms. Sauerkraut was renamed "liberty cabbage." Frankfurters became "liberty sausage." Performances of German music were frequently banned. German books were removed from the shelves of libraries. Courses in the German language were removed from school curricula; the California Board of Education called it "a language that disseminates the ideals of autocracy, brutality, and hatred." Germans were routinely fired from jobs in war industries, lest they "sabotage" important tasks. Some were fired from positions entirely unrelated to the war—for example, Karl Muck, the German-born conductor of the Boston Symphony Orchestra. Vigilante groups routinely subjected Germans to harassment and beatings, including a lynching in southern Illinois in 1918. Relatively few Americans favored such extremes, but many came to agree with the belief of the eminent psychologist G. Stanley Hall that "there is something fundamentally wrong with the Teutonic soul."

THE SEARCH FOR A NEW WORLD ORDER

Woodrow Wilson had led the nation into war promising a more just and stable peace at its conclusion. Well before the armistice, he was preparing to lead the fight for what he considered a democratic postwar settlement.

The Fourteen Points

On January 8, 1918, Wilson appeared before Congress to present the principles for which he claimed the nation was fighting. The war aims had fourteen distinct provisions, widely known as the Fourteen Points; but they fell into three broad categories. First, Wilson's proposals contained eight specific recommendations for adjusting postwar boundaries and for establishing new nations to replace the defunct Austro-Hungarian and Ottoman Empires. Those recommendations reflected his belief in the right of all peoples to self-determination.

Wilson's Idealistic Vision

Second, there were five general principles to govern international conduct in the future: freedom of the seas, open covenants instead of secret treaties, reductions in armaments, free trade, and impartial mediation of colonial claims. Finally, there was a proposal for a league of nations that would help implement these new principles and territorial adjustments and resolve future controversies.

There were serious flaws in Wilson's proposals. He provided no formula for deciding how to implement the "national self-determination" he promised for subjugated peoples. He said little about economic rivalries and their effect on international relations, even though such economic tensions had been in large part responsible for the war. Nevertheless, Wilson's international vision quickly came to enchant not only much of his own generation (in both America and Europe), but also members of generations to come. It reflected his belief, strongly rooted in the ideas of progressivism, that the world was as capable of just and efficient government as were individual nations; that once the international community accepted certain basic principles of conduct, and once it constructed modern institutions to implement them, the human race could live in peace.

The Fourteen Points were also an answer to the new Bolshevik government in Russia. In December 1917, Lenin issued his own statement of war aims, strikingly similar to Wilson's.

Lenin's Challenge

Wilson's announcement, which came just three weeks

later, was, among other things, a last-minute (and unsuccessful) effort to persuade the Bolshevik regime to keep Russia in the war. But Wilson also realized that Lenin was now a competitor in the effort to lead the postwar order. And he announced the Fourteen Points in part to ensure that the world looked to the United States, not Russia, for guidance.

Early Obstacles

Wilson was confident, as the war neared its end, that popular support would enable him to win Allied approval of his peace plan. But there were ominous signs both at home and abroad that his path might be more difficult than he expected. In Europe, leaders of the Allied powers, many resenting what they considered Wilson's tone of moral superiority, were preparing to resist him even before the armistice was signed. They had reacted unhappily when Wilson refused to make the United States their "ally" but had kept his distance as an "associate" of his European partners, keeping American military forces separate from the Allied armies they were joining.

Most of all, however, Britain and France, having suffered incalculable losses in their long years of war, and having stored up an enormous reserve of bitterness toward Germany as a result, were in no mood for a benign and generous peace. The British prime minister, David

Allied Intransigence

Lloyd George, insisted for a time that the German kaiser be captured and executed. He and Georges Clemenceau, president of France, remained determined to the end to gain something from the struggle to compensate them for the catastrophe they had suffered.

At the same time, Wilson was encountering problems at home. In 1918, with the war almost over, Wilson unwisely appealed to the American voters to support his peace plans by electing Democrats to Congress in the November elections. A Republican victory, he declared, would be "interpreted on the other side of the water as a repudiation of my leadership." Days later, the Republicans captured majorities in both houses. Domestic economic troubles, more than international issues, had been the most important factor in the voting; but because of the president's ill-timed appeal, the results damaged his ability to claim broad popular support for his peace plans.

The leaders of the Republican Party, in the meantime, were developing their own reasons for opposing Wilson. Some were angry that he had tried to make the 1918 balloting a referendum on his war aims, especially since many Republicans had been supporting the Fourteen Points. Wilson further antagonized them when he refused to appoint any important Republicans to the negotiating team that would represent the United States at the peace conference in Paris. But the president considered such matters unimportant. Only one member of the American negotiating party would have any real authority: Wilson himself. And once he had produced a just and moral treaty, he believed, the weight of world and American opinion would compel his enemies to support him.

The Paris Peace Conference

Wilson arrived in Europe to a welcome such as few men in history have experienced. To the war-weary people of the Continent, he was nothing less than a savior, the man who would create a new and better world. When he entered Paris on December 13, 1918, he was greeted, some observers claimed, by the largest crowd in the history of France. The negotiations themselves, however, proved less satisfying.

The principal figures in the negotiations were the leaders of the victorious Allied nations: David Lloyd George representing Great Britain; Clemenceau representing France; Vittorio Orlando, the prime minister of Italy; and Wilson, who hoped to dominate them all. From the beginning, the atmosphere of idealism Wilson had sought to

The Big Four

create was competing with a spirit of national aggrandizement. There was, moreover, a strong sense of unease about the unstable situation in eastern Europe and the threat of communism. Russia, whose new Bolshevik government was still fighting "White" counterrevolutionaries, was unrepresented in Paris; but the radical threat it seemed to pose to Western governments was never far from the minds of any of the delegates, least of all Wilson himself.

Indeed, not long before he came to Paris, Wilson ordered the landing of American troops in the Soviet Union. They were there, he claimed, to help a group of 60,000 Czech soldiers trapped in Russia to escape. But the Americans soon became involved, at least indirectly, in assisting the White Russians (the anti-Bolsheviks) in their fight against the new regime. Some American troops remained in Russia as late as April 1920. Lenin's regime survived these challenges, but Wilson refused to recognize the new government. Diplomatic relations between the United States and the Soviet Union were not restored until 1933.

In the tense and often vindictive atmosphere of the negotiations in Paris, Wilson was unable to win approval of many of the broad principles he had espoused: freedom of the seas, which the British refused even to discuss; free trade; "open covenants openly arrived at" (the Paris nego-

Wilson's Retreat

tiations themselves were often conducted in secret). Despite his support for "impartial mediation" of colonial claims, he was forced to accept a transfer of German colonies in the Pacific to Japan; the British had promised them in exchange for Japanese assistance in the war. Wilson's pledge of "national self-determination" for all peoples

THE BIG FOUR IN PARIS Surface cordiality during the Paris Peace Conference disguised serious tensions among the so-called Big Four, the leaders of the victorious nations in World War I. As the conference progressed, the European leaders developed increasing resentment of Woodrow Wilson's high (and some of them thought sanctimonious) moral posture in the negotiations. Shown here in the library of the Hotel Crillon are, from left to right, Vittorio Orlando of Italy, David Lloyd George of Great Britain, Georges Clemenceau of France, and Wilson. *(Bettmann/Corbis)*

suffered numerous assaults. Economic and strategic demands were constantly coming into conflict with the principle of cultural nationalism.

The treaty departed most conspicuously from Wilson's ideals on the question of reparations. As the conference began, the president opposed demanding compensation from the defeated Central Powers. The other Allied leaders, however, were insistent, and slowly Wilson gave way and accepted the principle of reparations, the specific sum to be set later by a commission. That figure, established in 1921, was $56 billion, supposedly to pay for damages to civilians and for military pensions. Continued negotiations over the next decade scaled the sum back considerably. In the end, Germany paid only $9 billion, which was still more than its crippled economy could afford. The reparations, combined with other territorial and economic penalties, constituted an effort to keep Germany weak for the indefinite future. Never again, the Allied leaders believed, should the Germans be allowed to become powerful enough to threaten the peace of Europe.

Wilson did manage to win some important victories in Paris in setting boundaries and dealing with former colonies. He secured approval of a plan to place many former colonies and imperial possessions (among them Palestine) in "trusteeship" under the League of Nations—the so-called mandate system. He blocked a French proposal to break up western Germany into a group of smaller states. He helped design the creation of two new nations: Yugoslavia and Czechoslovakia, which were welded together out of, among other territories, pieces of the former Austro-Hungarian Empire. Each nation contained an

Reparations

uneasy collection of ethnic groups that had frequently battled one another in the past.

But Wilson's most visible triumph, and the one most important to him, was the creation of a permanent international organization to oversee world affairs and prevent future wars. On January 25, 1919, the Allies voted to accept the "covenant" of the League of Nations; and with that, Wilson believed, the peace treaty was transformed from a disappointment into a success. Whatever mistakes and inequities had emerged from the peace conference, he was convinced, could be corrected later by the League.

League of Nations

The covenant provided for an assembly of nations that would meet regularly to debate means of resolving disputes and protecting the peace. Authority to implement League decisions would rest with a nine-member executive council; the United States would be one of five permanent members of the council, along with Britain, France, Italy, and Japan. The covenant left many questions unanswered, most notably how the League would enforce its decisions. Wilson, however, was confident that once established, the new organization would find suitable answers.

The Ratification Battle

Wilson was well aware of the political obstacles awaiting him at home. Many Americans, accustomed to their nation's isolation from Europe, questioned the wisdom of this major new commitment to internationalism. Others had serious reservations about the specific features of the treaty and the covenant. After a brief trip to

Washington in February 1919, during which he listened to harsh objections to the treaty from members of the Senate and others, he returned to Europe and insisted on several modifications in the covenant to satisfy his critics. The revisions ensured that the United States would not be obliged to accept a League mandate to oversee a territory and that the League would not challenge the Monroe Doctrine. But the changes were not enough to mollify his opponents, and Wilson refused to go further.

Wilson presented the Treaty of Versailles (which took its name from the palace outside Paris where the final negotiating sessions had taken place) to the Senate on

Wilson's Intransigence

July 10, 1919, asking, "Dare we reject it and break the heart of the world?" In the weeks that followed, he refused to consider even the most innocuous compromise. His deteriorating physical condition—he was suffering from hardening of the arteries and had apparently experienced something like a mild stroke (undiagnosed) in Paris—may have contributed to his intransigence.

The Senate, in the meantime, was raising many objections. Some senators—the fourteen so-called irreconcilables, many of them western isolationists—opposed the agreement on principle. But other opponents, with less fervent convictions, were principally concerned with constructing a winning issue for the

Henry Cabot Lodge

Republicans in 1920 and with weakening a president whom they had come to despise. Most notable of these was Senator Henry Cabot Lodge of Massachusetts, the powerful chairman of the Foreign Relations Committee. A man of stunning arrogance and a close friend of Theodore Roosevelt (who had died early in 1919, spouting hatred of Wilson to the end), Lodge loathed the president with genuine passion. "I never thought I could hate a man as I hate Wilson," he once admitted. He used every possible tactic to obstruct, delay, and amend the treaty. Wilson, for his part, despised Lodge as much as Lodge despised him.

Public sentiment clearly favored ratification, so at first Lodge could do little more than play for time. When the document reached his committee, he spent two weeks slowly reading aloud each word of its 300 pages; then he held six weeks of public hearings to air the complaints of every disgruntled minority (Irish Americans, for example, angry that the settlement made no provision for an independent Ireland). Gradually, Lodge's general opposition to the treaty crystallized into a series of "reservations"—amendments to the League covenant limiting American obligations to the organization.

At this point, Wilson might still have won approval if he had agreed to some relatively minor changes in the language of the treaty. But the president refused to yield.

When he realized the Senate would not budge, he decided to appeal to the public.

Wilson's Ordeal

What followed was a political disaster and a personal tragedy. Wilson embarked on a grueling, cross-country speaking tour to arouse public support for the treaty. In a little more than three weeks, he traveled over 8,000 miles by train, speaking as often as four times a day, resting hardly at all. Finally, he reached the end of his strength. After speaking at Pueblo, Colorado, on September 25, he collapsed with severe headaches. Canceling the rest of his itinerary, he rushed back to Washington, where, a few days later, he suffered a major stroke. For two weeks he was close to death; for six weeks more, he was so seriously ill that he could conduct virtually no public business. His wife and his doctor formed an almost impenetrable barrier around him, shielding him from any official pressures that might impede his recovery, preventing the public from receiving any accurate information about the gravity of his condition.

Wilson ultimately recovered enough to resume a limited official schedule, but he was essentially an invalid for the remaining eighteen months of his presidency. His left side was partially paralyzed; more important, like many stroke victims, he had only partial control of his mental and emotional state. His condition only intensified what had already been his strong tendency to view public issues in moral terms and to resist any attempts at compromise. When the Senate Foreign Relations Committee finally sent the treaty to the full Senate for ratification, recommending nearly fifty amendments and reservations, Wilson refused to consider any of them. When the full Senate voted in November to accept fourteen of the reservations, Wilson gave stern directions to his Democratic allies: They must vote only for a treaty with no changes whatsoever; any other version must be defeated. On November 19, 1919, forty-two Democrats,

League Membership Rejected

following the president's instructions, joined with the thirteen Republican "irreconcilables" to reject the amended treaty. When the Senate voted on the original version without any reservations, thirty-eight senators, all but one Democrats, voted to approve it; fifty-five senators (some Democrats among them) voted no.

There were sporadic efforts to revive the treaty over the next few months. But Wilson's opposition to anything but the precise settlement he had negotiated in Paris remained too formidable an obstacle. He was, moreover, becoming convinced that the 1920 national election would serve as a "solemn referendum" on the League. By now, however, public interest in the peace process had begun to fade—partly as a reaction against the tragic bitterness of the ratification fight, but more in response to a series of other crises.

A SOCIETY IN TURMOIL

Even during the Paris Peace Conference, many Americans were less concerned about international matters than about turbulent events at home. The American economy experi-

New Social Environment

enced a severe postwar recession. And much of middle-class America responded to demands for change with a fearful, conservative hostility. The aftermath of war brought not the age of liberal reform that progressives had predicted, but a period of repression and reaction.

Industry and Labor

Citizens of Washington, D.C., on the day after the armistice, found it impossible to place long-distance telephone calls: the lines were jammed with officials of the war agencies canceling government contracts. The fighting had ended sooner than anyone had anticipated, and without warning, without planning, the nation was launched into the difficult task of economic reconversion.

At first, the wartime boom continued. But the postwar prosperity rested largely on the lingering effects of the war (government deficit spending continued for some months after the armistice) and on sudden, temporary demands (a booming market for scarce consumer goods at home and a strong market for American products in the war-ravaged nations of Europe). This brief postwar boom was accompanied, however, by raging inflation, a result in part of the rapid abandonment of wartime price controls. Through most of 1919 and 1920, prices rose at an average of more than 15 percent a year.

Finally, late in 1920, the economic bubble burst, as many of the temporary forces that had created it disappeared and as inflation began killing the market for consumer goods. Between 1920 and 1921, the gross national product (GNP) declined nearly 10 percent; 100,000 businesses went bankrupt; 453,000 farmers lost their land; nearly 5 million Americans lost their jobs. In this unpromising economic environment, leaders of organized labor set out

Postwar Recession

to consolidate the advances they had made in the war, which now seemed in danger of being lost. The raging inflation of 1919 wiped out the modest wage gains workers had achieved during the war; many laborers worried about job security as hundreds of thousands of veterans returned to the work force; arduous working conditions—such as the twelve-hour workday in the steel industry—continued to be a source of discontent. Employers aggravated the resentment by using the end of the war (and the end of government controls) to rescind benefits they had been forced to give workers in 1917 and 1918—most notably recognition of unions.

The year 1919, therefore, saw an unprecedented wave of strikes—more than 3,600 in all, involving over 4 million workers. In January, a walkout by shipyard workers in Seattle, Washington, evolved into a general strike that brought the entire city to a standstill. The mayor requested and received the assistance of U.S. Marines to keep the city running, and eventually the strike failed. But the brief success of a general strike, something Americans associated with European radicals, made the Seattle incident reverberate loudly throughout the country.

In September, there was a strike by the Boston police force, which was responding to layoffs and wage cuts by demanding recognition of its

Boston Police Strike

union. Seattle had remained generally calm during its strike; but with its police off the job, Boston erupted in violence and looting. Efforts by local businessmen, veterans, and college students to patrol the streets proved ineffective; and finally Governor Calvin Coolidge called in the National Guard to restore order. (His public statement that "there is no right to strike against the public safety by anybody, anywhere, any time" attracted national acclaim.) Eventually, Boston officials dismissed the entire police force and hired a new one.

In September 1919, the greatest strike in American history began, when 350,000 steelworkers in several eastern

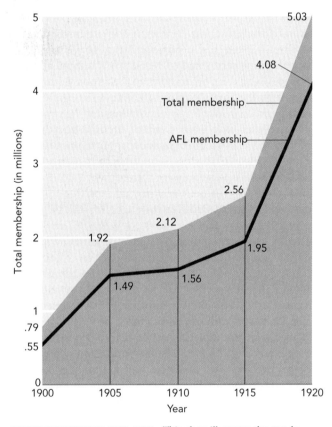

UNION MEMBERSHIP, 1900–1920 This chart illustrates the steady increase in union membership in the first part of the twentieth century—a membership dominated by unions associated with the AFL. Note the particularly sharp increase between 1915 and 1920, the years of World War I. ◆ *Why did the war years see such an expansion of union labor?*

THE BOSTON POLICE STRIKE   National Guardsmen stand guard in front of a store where broken windows suggest looting has already occurred, during the Boston Police Strike of 1919. *(Bettmann/Corbis)*

and midwestern cities walked off the job, demanding an eight-hour day and recognition of their union. The steel strike was long, bitter, and violent—most of the violence coming from employers, who hired armed guards to disperse picket lines and escort strikebreakers into factories. It climaxed in a riot in Gary, Indiana, in which eighteen strikers were killed. Steel executives managed to keep most plants running with nonunion labor, and public opinion was so hostile to the strikers that the AFL—having at first endorsed the strike—soon timidly repudiated it. By January, the strike had collapsed. It was a setback from which organized labor would not recover for more than a decade.

Steelworkers' Strike Defeated

The Demands of African Americans

The nearly 400,000 black men who had served in the armed forces during the war came home in 1919 and marched down the main streets of the industrial cities with other returning troops. And then (in New York and other cities), they marched again through the streets of black neighborhoods such as Harlem, led by jazz bands,

cheered by thousands of African Americans, worshiped as heroes. The black soldiers were an inspiration to thousands of urban African Americans, a sign, they thought, that a new age had come, that the glory of black heroism in the war would make it impossible for white society ever again to treat African Americans as less than equal citizens.

In fact, that black soldiers had fought in the war had almost no impact at all on white attitudes. But it did have a profound effect on black attitudes: it accentuated African-American bitterness—and increased black determination to fight for their rights. For soldiers, there was an expectation of some social reward for their service. For many other American blacks, the war had raised economic expectations, as they moved into industrial and other jobs vacated by white workers, jobs to which they had previously had no access. Just as black soldiers expected their military service to enhance their social status, so black factory workers regarded their move north as an escape from racial prejudice and an opportunity for economic gain.

New Black Attitudes

By 1919, however, the racial climate had become savage and murderous. In the South, there was a sudden

THE FIFTEENTH REGIMENT ON FIFTH AVENUE The all-black Fifteenth Army Regiment marches up Fifth Avenue in New York City in 1917, shortly after the United States entered World War I. They are en route to an army training camp in New York State before traveling to the front in Europe. Less than two years later, many of these same men marched through Harlem on their return from the war, and again down Fifth Avenue, before cheering crowds—convinced, wrongly, that their service in the war would win them important new freedoms at home. *(Bettmann/Corbis)*

increase in lynchings: more than seventy blacks, some of them war veterans, died at the hands of white mobs in 1919 alone. In the North, black factory workers faced widespread layoffs as returning white veterans displaced them from their jobs. Black veterans found no significant new opportunities for advancement. Rural black migrants to northern cities encountered white communities unfa-

miliar with and generally hostile to them; and as whites became convinced that black workers with lower wage demands were hurting them economically, animosity grew rapidly.

The wartime riots in East St. Louis and elsewhere were a prelude to a summer of much worse racial violence in 1919. In Chicago, a black teenager swimming in Lake

AFRICAN-AMERICAN MIGRATION, 1910–1950 Two great waves of migration produced a dramatic redistribution of the African-American population in the first half of the twentieth century—one around the time of World War I, the other during and after World War II. The map on the left shows the almost exclusive concentration of African Americans in the South as late as 1910. The map on the right shows both the tremendous increase of black populations in northern states by 1950, and the relative decline of black populations in parts of the South. Note in particular the changes in Mississippi and South Carolina. ◆ *Why did the wars produce such significant migration out of the South?*

Michigan on a hot July day happened to drift toward a white beach. Whites on shore allegedly stoned him unconscious; he sank and drowned. Angry blacks gathered in crowds and marched into white neighborhoods to retaliate; whites formed even larger crowds and roamed into black neighborhoods shooting, stabbing, and beating passersby, destroying homes and properties. For more than a week, Chicago was virtually at war. In the end, 38 people died— 15 whites and 23 blacks—and 537 were injured; over 1,000 people were left homeless. The Chicago riot was the worst but not the only racial violence during the so-called red summer of 1919; in all, 120 people died in such racial outbreaks in the space of little more than three months.

Chicago Race Riots

Racial violence, and even racially motivated urban riots, was not new. The deadliest race riot in American history had occurred in New York during the Civil War. But the 1919 riots were different in one respect: they did not just involve white people attacking blacks; they also involved blacks fighting back. The NAACP signaled this change by urging African Americans not just to demand government protection, but also to retaliate, to defend themselves. The poet Claude McKay, one of the major figures of what would shortly be known as the Harlem Renaissance, wrote a poem after the Chicago riot called "If We Must Die":

> Like men we'll face the murderous cowardly pack.
> Pressed to the wall, dying, but fighting back.

At the same time, a Jamaican, Marcus Garvey, began to attract a wide American following—mostly among poor urban blacks—with an ideology of black nationalism. Garvey encouraged African Americans to take pride in their own achievements and to develop an awareness of their African heritage—to reject assimilation into white society and develop pride in what Garvey argued was their own superior race and culture. His United Negro Improvement Association (UNIA) launched a chain of black-owned grocery stores and pressed for the creation of other black businesses. Eventually, Garvey

Marcus Garvey's Black Nationalism

MARCUS GARVEY Marcus Garvey can be seen here enthroned on an opulent stage set for the 1924 convention of his United Negro Improvement Association. He is surrounded by uniformed guards and delegates from his organization. At the organization's peak, these annual meetings attracted thousands of people from around the world and lasted for weeks. *(Marcus Garvey at Liberty Hall, 1924. Photograph by James VanDerZee. © Donna Mussendem VanDerZee.)*

began urging his supporters to leave America and "return" to Africa, where they could create a new society of their own. In the 1920s, the Garvey movement experienced explosive growth for a time; and the UNIA became notable for its mass rallies and parades, for the opulent uniforms of its members, and for the growth of its enterprises. It began to decline, however, after Garvey was indicted in 1923 on charges of business fraud. He was deported to Jamaica two years later. But the allure of black nationalism, which he helped make visible to millions of African Americans, survived in black culture long after Garvey himself was gone.

The Red Scare

To much of the white middle class at the time, the industrial warfare, the racial violence, and other forms of dissent all appeared to be frightening omens of instability and radicalism. This was in part because the Russian Revolution of November 1917 made it clear that communism was no longer simply a theory, but now an important regime.

Concerns about the communist threat grew in 1919 when the Soviet government announced the formation of the Communist International (or Comintern), whose pur-

pose was to export revolution around the world. And in America itself, there were, in addition to the great number of imagined radicals, a modest number of real ones. The American Communist Party was formed in 1919, and there were other radical groups (many of them dominated by immigrants from Europe who had been involved in radical politics before coming to America). Some of these radicals were presumably responsible for a series of bombings in the spring of 1919 that produced great national alarm. In April, the post office intercepted several dozen parcels addressed to leading businessmen and politicians that were triggered to explode when opened. Several of them reached their destinations, and one of them exploded, severely injuring a domestic servant of a public official in Georgia. Two months later, eight bombs exploded in eight cities within minutes of one another, suggesting a nationwide conspiracy. One of them damaged the façade of Attorney General A. Mitchell Palmer's home in Washington. In 1920, there was a terrible explosion in front of the Morgan bank on Wall Street, which killed thirty people (although only one clerk in the bank itself).

The bombings crystallized what was already a growing determination among many middle-class Americans (and some government officials) to fight back against radicalism—a determination steeled by the repressive

THE RED SCARE, 1919 Boston police pose for cameras holding piles of allegedly communist literature that they have gathered through raids on the offices of radical groups in the city. Such raids were already becoming common even before Attorney General A. Mitchell Palmer ordered the so-called Palmer Raids in cities all over the United States in January 1920. *(Hulton-Deutsch Collection/Corbis)*

atmosphere of the war years. This antiradicalism accompanied, and reinforced, the already strong commitment

Popular Antiradicalism

among old-stock Protestants to the idea of "100 percent Americanism." And it produced what became known as the Red Scare.

Antiradical newspapers and politicians now began to portray almost every form of instability or protest as a sign of a radical threat. Race riots, one newspaper claimed, were the work of "armed revolutionaries running rampant through our cities." The steel strike, the *Philadelphia Inquirer* claimed, was "penetrated with the Bolshevik idea . . . steeped in the doctrines of the class struggle and social overthrow." Nearly thirty states enacted new peacetime sedition laws imposing harsh penalties on those who promoted revolution; some 300 people went to jail as a result—many of them people whose "crime" had been nothing more than opposition to the war. There were spontaneous acts of violence against supposed radicals in some communities. A mob of off-duty soldiers in New York City ransacked the offices of a socialist newspaper and beat up its staff. Another mob, in Centralia, Washington, dragged an IWW agitator from jail and castrated him before hanging him from a bridge. Citizens in many communities removed "subversive" books from the shelves of libraries; administrators in some universities dismissed "radical" members from their faculties. Women's groups such as the National Consumers' League came under attack by antiradicals because so many feminists had opposed American intervention in the fighting in Europe.

Perhaps the greatest contribution to the Red Scare came from the federal government. On New Year's Day, 1920, Attorney General A. Mitchell Palmer and his ambitious assistant, J. Edgar Hoover, orchestrated a series of raids on alleged radical centers throughout the country and arrested more than 6,000 people.

The Palmer Raids had been intended to uncover large caches of weapons and explosives; they netted a total of three pistols and no dynamite.

Palmer Raids

Most of those arrested were ultimately released, but about 500 who were not American citizens were summarily deported.

The ferocity of the Red Scare soon abated, but its effects lingered well into the 1920s, most notably in the celebrated case of Sacco and Vanzetti. In May 1920, two Italian immigrants, Nicola Sacco and Bartolomeo Vanzetti, were

Sacco and Vanzetti

charged with the murder of a paymaster in Braintree, Massachusetts. The evidence against them was questionable; but because both men were confessed anarchists, they faced a widespread public presumption of guilt. They were convicted in a trial of extraordinary injudiciousness, before an openly bigoted judge, Webster Thayer, and were sentenced to death. Over the next several years, public support for Sacco and Vanzetti grew to formidable proportions. But all requests for a new trial or a pardon were denied. On August 23, 1927, amid widespread protests around the world, Sacco and Vanzetti, still proclaiming their innocence, died in the electric chair. Theirs was a cause that a generation of Americans never forgot.

SACCO AND VANZETTI The artist Ben Shahn painted this view of the anarchists Nicola Sacco and Bartolomeo Vanzetti, handcuffed together in a courtroom in 1927 waiting to hear if the appeal of their 1921 verdicts for murdering a Boston paymaster would succeed. It did not, and the two men were executed later that year. Just before his execution, Vanzetti said: "Never in our full life can we hope to do such work for tolerance, for man's understanding of man, as now we do by an accident. Our words—our lives—our pains—nothing! The taking of our lives—lives of a good shoemaker and a poor fish-peddler—all! That last moment belongs to us—that agony is our triumph." (*©Estate of Ben Shahn/ Licensed by VAGA, New York, NY. The Museum of Modern Art/Licensed by SCALA/ Art Resource, NY/Vaga*)

The Retreat from Idealism

On August 26, 1920, the Nineteenth Amendment, guaranteeing women the right to vote, became part of the Constitution. To the woman suffrage movement, this was the culmination of nearly a century of struggle. To many progressives, who had seen the inclusion of women in the electorate as a way of bolstering their political strength, it seemed to promise new support for reform. In some respects, the amendment helped fulfill that promise. Because of woman suffrage, members of Congress—concerned that women would vote as a bloc on the basis of women's issues—passed the Shepard Towner Maternity and Infancy Act in 1921, one of the first pieces of federal welfare legislation that provided funds for supporting the health of women and infants. Concern about the women's vote also appeared to create support for the 1922 Cable Act, which granted women the rights of U.S. citizenship independent of their husbands' status, and for the proposed (but never ratified) 1924 constitutional amendment to outlaw child labor.

In other ways, however, the Nineteenth Amendment marked less the beginning of an era of reform than an ending. Economic problems, feminist demands, labor unrest, racial tensions, and the intensity of the antiradicalism they helped create—all combined in the years immediately following the war to produce a general sense of disillusionment.

That became particularly apparent in the election of 1920. Woodrow Wilson wanted the campaign to be a referendum on the League of Nations, and the Democratic candidates, Ohio governor James M. Cox and Assistant Secretary of the Navy Franklin D. Roosevelt, tried to keep Wilson's ideals alive. The Republican presidential nominee, however, offered a different vision. He was Warren Gamaliel Harding, an obscure Ohio senator whom party leaders had chosen as their nominee confident that he would do their bidding once in office. Harding offered no ideals, only a vague promise of a return, as he later phrased it, to "normalcy." He won **Return to "Normalcy"** in a landslide. The Republican ticket received 61 percent of the popular vote and carried every state outside the South. The party made major gains in Congress as well. Woodrow Wilson, who had tried and failed to create a postwar order based on democratic ideals, stood repudiated. Early in 1921, he retired to a house on S Street in Washington, where he lived quietly until his death in 1924. In the meantime, for most Americans, a new era had begun.

CONCLUSION

The greatest and most terrible war in human history to that point was also an important moment in the rise of the United States to global preeminence. The powers of Europe emerged from more than four years of carnage with their societies and economies in disarray. The United States emerged from its own, much briefer, involvement in the war poised to become the most important political and economic force in the world.

For a time after the outbreak of war in Europe in 1914, most Americans—President Wilson among them—wanted to stay out of the conflict. Gradually, however, as the war dragged on and the tactics of Britain and Germany began to impinge on American trade and on freedom of the seas, the United States found itself drawn into the conflict. In April 1917, finally, Congress agreed (although not without considerable dissent) to the president's request that the United States enter the war as an ally of Britain.

American forces quickly broke the stalemate that had bogged the European forces down in years of inconclusive trench warfare. Within a few months after the arrival of substantial numbers of American troops in Europe, Germany agreed to an armistice and the war shuddered to a close. American casualties, although not inconsiderable, were negligible compared to the millions suffered by the European combatants. In the meantime, the American economy experienced an enormous industrial boom as a result of the war.

The social experience of the war in the United States was, on the whole, dismaying to reformers. Although the war enhanced some reform efforts—most notably prohibition and woman suffrage—it also introduced an atmosphere of intolerance and repression into American life, an atmosphere assisted by policies of the federal government designed to suppress dissent. The aftermath of the war was even more disheartening to progressives, both because of a brief but highly destabilizing recession, and because of a wave of repression directed against labor, radicals, African Americans, and immigrants in 1919 and 1920.

At the same time, Woodrow Wilson's bold and idealistic dream of a peace based on the principles of democracy and justice suffered a painful death. The Treaty of Versailles, which he helped to draft, was itself far from what Wilson had hoped. It did, however, contain a provision for a League of Nations, which Wilson believed could transform the international order. But the League quickly became controversial in the United States; and despite strenuous efforts by the president—efforts that hastened his own physical collapse—the treaty was defeated in the Senate. In the aftermath of that traumatic battle, the American people seemed to turn away from Wilson's ideals and entered a very different era.

INTERACTIVE LEARNING

The *Primary Source Investigator CD-ROM* offers the following materials related to this chapter:

- A short documentary, **Tulsa Race Riot of 1921** (D19).
- Interactive maps: **America in World War I** (M23) and **Influenza Pandemic** (M70).
- Documents, images, and maps related to U.S. involvement in the Great War and the significant postwar problems. Highlights include the text of Woodrow Wilson's famous Fourteen Points; the 1918 Sedition Act, which criminalized speech critical of the United

States; and images that depict a widespread fear of radicalism, such as soldiers destroying a Socialist flag and a portrait of Nicola Sacco and Bartolomeo Vanzetti, two Italian immigrants whose controversial murder trial ended with their execution.

Online Learning Center (www.mhhe.com/brinkley13e)

For quizzes, Internet resources, references to additional books and films, and more, consult this book's Online Learning Center.

FOR FURTHER REFERENCE

Ernest R. May, *The World War and American Isolation* (1959) is an authoritative account of America's slow and controversial entry into the Great War. Frank Freidel provides a sweeping account of the American soldier's battlefield experience during World War I in *Over There: The Story of America's First Great Overseas Crusade* (1964). David Kennedy, *Over Here: The First World War and American Society* (1980) is an important study of the domestic impact of the war. Robert D. Cuff, *The War Industries Board: Business-Government Relations During World War II* (1973) is a good account of mobilization for war in the United States. Ronald Schaffer, *America in the Great War: The Rise of the War Welfare State* (1991) examines the ways in which mobilization for war created new public benefits for various groups, including labor. Maureen Greenwald, *Women, War, and Work* (1980) describes the impact of World War I on women workers. John Keegan, *The First World War* (1998) is a superb military history. Thomas Knock, *To End All Wars: Woodrow Wilson and the Quest for a New World Order* (1992) is a valuable study of the battle for peace. Arno Mayer, *Wilson*

vs. Lenin (1959) and *Politics and Diplomacy of Peacemaking: Containment and Counterrevolution* (1965) are important revisionist accounts of the peacemaking process. Margaret MacMillan, *Paris 1919: Six Months That Changed the World* (2002) is an important account of the Paris Peace Conference. America's stormy debate over immigration and national identity before, during, and after World War I is best captured by John Higham, *Strangers in the Land: Patterns of American Nativism* (1955). William M. Tuttle Jr., in *Race Riot: Chicago in the Red Summer of 1919* (1970), recounts the terrible riots of 1919 that showed America violently divided along racial and ideological lines. Paul L. Murphy, *World War I and the Origins of Civil Liberties* (1979) shows how wartime efforts to quell dissent created new support for civil liberties. Beverly Gage, *The Day Wall Street Exploded* (2009) tells the story of postwar terrorism and the responses to it. *The Great War—1918* (1997) is a documentary film chronicling the experiences of American soldiers in the closing battles of World War I through their letters and diaries.

CHAPTER 22

THE "NEW ERA"

THE FLAPPER, 1927   The popular Condé Nast fashion magazine, *Vogue,* portrayed a fashionably dressed "flapper" on its cover in 1927. The short hair and the cap pulled down low over the forehead were both part of the flapper style. What had begun as a fashion among working-class women had by 1927 moved into stylish high society. *(Georges Lepape/©Vogue, The Condé Nast Publications Inc.)*

THE IMAGE OF THE 1920S in the American popular imagination is of an era of affluence, conservatism, and cultural frivolity: the "Roaring Twenties," what Warren G. Harding once called the age of "normalcy." In reality, the decade was a time of significant, even dramatic, social, economic, and

Myth and Reality

political change. It was an era in which the American economy not only enjoyed spectacular growth but developed new forms of organization as well. It was a time in which American popular culture reshaped itself in response to the urban, industrial, consumer-oriented society America was becoming. And it was a decade in which American government, for all its apparent conservatism, experimented with new approaches to public policy that helped pave the way for the important period of reform that was to follow. Contemporaries liked to refer to the 1920s as the "New Era"—an age in which America was becoming a modern nation.

To a large degree, these changes were the result of the increasing reach of industrialization, the rapid growth of cities, and the increasing size and power of the middle class. The idea of a "New Era" was primarily an urban, middle-class idea, an idea rooted in the exciting new professional, cultural, and consumerist opportunities that economic growth was creating for large groups of affluent Americans. It was also an idea that embraced the belief that the New Era was a time of liberation—in which people could reject traditional social restraints and live a freer life less constrained by tradition and propriety.

But these same challenges to traditional values and ways of life also made the 1920s a turbulent era in which the nation experienced substantial cultural conflict. Many Americans rebelled against the new customs and morals of the urban middle class and sought to defend older values. Some did so by defending traditional religion and embracing the fundamentalist movement within Protestant Christianity. Others lashed out against immigrants and minorities and called for a "purer" America in which old-stock whites were securely in charge. The vehicle for many such people was the Ku Klux Klan. Others mobilized to fight once again the power of great financial and industrial combinations, calling for a return to a more decentralized and smaller-scale society.

The intense cultural conflicts of the 1920s were evidence of how many Americans remained outside the reach of the new affluent, consumer culture—some because their economic and social circumstances barred them from it, others because they found the character of this culture alien and unfulfilling. The New Era's exuberant modernization, in short, contributed to deep divisions in both politics and culture.

SIGNIFICANT EVENTS

1914–1920 ▶	Great Migration of black southerners to northern cities
1920 ▶	First commercial radio station, KDKA in Pittsburgh, begins broadcasting
▶	Prohibition begins
▶	Warren G. Harding elected president
1921 ▶	Sheppard-Towner Act funds maternity assistance
▶	Nation experiences economic recession
▶	*Reader's Digest* founded
1922 ▶	Sinclair Lewis publishes *Babbitt*
▶	Motion Picture Association, under Will Hays, founded to regulate film industry
1923 ▶	Nation experiences mild recession
▶	Harding dies; Calvin Coolidge becomes president
▶	Teapot Dome and other scandals revealed
▶	*Time* magazine founded
1924 ▶	National Origins Act passed
▶	Ku Klux Klan reaches peak membership
▶	Coolidge elected president
1925 ▶	F. Scott Fitzgerald publishes *The Great Gatsby*
▶	Scopes trial in Dayton, Tennessee
▶	A. Philip Randolph founds Brotherhood of Sleeping Car Porters
1926 ▶	Congress passes McNary-Haugen bill; Coolidge vetoes it
1927 ▶	First feature-length sound motion picture, *The Jazz Singer*, released
▶	Charles Lindbergh makes solo transatlantic flight
1928 ▶	Congress passes, and Coolidge vetoes, McNary-Haugen bill again
▶	Herbert Hoover elected president
1929 ▶	Sheppard-Towner program terminated
▶	Ernest Hemingway publishes *A Farewell to Arms*

THE NEW ECONOMY

After the recession of 1921–1922, the United States began a long period of almost uninterrupted prosperity and economic expansion. Less visible at the time, but equally significant, was the survival (and even the growth) of inequalities and imbalances.

Technology and Economic Growth

No one could deny the remarkable, some believed miraculous, feats of the American economy in the 1920s. The nation's manufacturing output rose by more than 60 percent during the decade. Per capita income grew by a third. Inflation was negligible. A mild recession in 1923 interrupted the pattern of growth, but when it subsided early in 1924, the economy expanded with greater vigor than before.

The economic boom was a result of many factors. An immediate cause was the debilitation of European industry in the aftermath of World War I, which left the

THE STEAMFITTER Lewis Hine was among the first American photographers to recognize his craft as an art. In this photograph from the mid-1920s, Hine made a point that many other artists were making in other media: The rise of the machine could serve human beings, but might also bend them to its own needs. The steamfitter (carefully posed by the photographer) is forced to shape his body to the contours of his machine in order to complete his task. (*International Museum of Photography at George Eastman House*)

United States for a short time the only truly healthy industrial power in the world. More important in the long run was technology, and the great industrial expansion it made possible. The automobile industry, as a result of the development of the assembly line and other innovations, now became one of the most important industries in the nation. It stimulated growth in many related industries as well. Auto manufacturers purchased the products of steel, rubber, glass, and tool companies. Auto owners bought gasoline from the oil corporations. Road construction in response to the proliferation of motor vehicles became an important industry. The increased mobility that the automobile made possible increased the demand for suburban housing, fueling a boom in the construction industry.

Sources of the Boom

Other new industries benefiting from technological innovations contributed as well to the economic growth. Radio began to become a popular technology even before commercial broadcasting began in 1920. Early radio had been able to broadcast little besides pulses, which meant that radio communication could occur only through the Morse code. But with the discovery of the theory of modulation, pioneered by the Canadian scientist Reginald Fessenden, it became possible to transmit speech and music. (Modulation also eventually made possible the transmission of video signals and later helped create radar and television.) Once commercial broadcasting began, families flocked to buy conventional radio sets, which, unlike the cheaper "shortwave" or "ham" radios, could receive high-quality signals over short and medium distances. They were powered by vacuum tubes that were much more reliable than earlier models. By 1925, there were 2 million sets in American homes, and by the end of the 1920s almost every family had one.

Radio

Commercial aviation developed slowly in the 1920s, beginning with the use of planes to deliver mail. On the whole, airplanes remained curiosities and sources of entertainment. But technological advances—the development of the radial engine and the creation of pressurized cabins— were laying the groundwork for the great increase in commercial travel in the 1930s and beyond. Trains became faster and more efficient as well with the development of the diesel-electric engine. Electronics, home appliances, plastics and synthetic fibers such as nylon (both pioneered by researchers at Du Pont), aluminum, magnesium, oil, electric power, and other industries fueled by technological advances—all grew dramatically and spurred the economic boom. Telephones continued to proliferate. By the late 1930s, there were approximately 25 million telephones in the United States, approximately one for every six people.

The seeds of future widespread technologies were also visible in the 1920s and 1930s. In both England and America, scientists and engineers were working to transform primitive calculating machines into devices capable of

Early Computers

performing more complicated tasks. By the early 1930s, researchers at MIT, led by Vannevar Bush, had created an instrument capable of performing a variety of complicated tasks—the first analog computer, which became the starting point for dramatic progress over the next several decades. A few years later, Howard Aiken, with financial assistance from Harvard and MIT, built a much more complex computer with memory, capable of multiplying eleven-digit numbers in three seconds.

Genetic research had begun in Austria in the mid-nineteenth century through the work of Gregor Mendel, a Catholic monk who performed experiments on the hybridization of vegetables in the garden of his monastery. His findings attracted little attention during his lifetime, but in the early twentieth century they were discovered by several investigators and helped shape modern genetic research. Among the American pioneers was Thomas Hunt Morgan of Columbia University and later Cal Tech, whose experiments with fruit flies revealed how several genes could be transmitted together (as opposed to Mendel's belief that they could only be transferred separately). Morgan also revealed the way in which genes were arranged along the chromosome. His work helped open the path to understanding how genes could recombine—a critical discovery that led to advanced experiments in hybridization and genetics.

Economic Organization

Large sectors of American business were accelerating their drive toward national organization and consolidation. Certain industries—notably those, such as steel, dependent on large-scale mass production—seemed naturally to move toward concentrating production in a few large firms; U.S. Steel, the nation's largest corporation, was so dominant that almost everyone used the term "Little Steel" to refer to all of its competitors. Other industries, such as textiles, that were less dependent on technology and less susceptible to great economies of scale, proved more resistant to consolidation, despite the efforts of many businessmen to promote it.

In those areas where industry did consolidate, new forms of corporate organization emerged to advance the

Modern Administrative Systems

trend. General Motors, which by 1920 was not only the largest automobile manufacturer but also the fifth-largest American corporation, was a classic example. GM's founder, William Durant, had expanded the company dramatically but had never replaced the informal, personal management style with which he began. When GM foundered in the recession of the early 1920s, leadership of the company fell to Alfred P. Sloan, who created a modern administrative system with an efficient divisional organization. The new system not only made it easier for GM to control its many subsidiaries; it also made it simpler for it—and for the many other corporations that adopted similar administrative systems—to expand further.

Some industries less susceptible to domination by a few great corporations attempted to stabilize themselves not through consolidation but through cooperation. An important vehicle was the trade association—a national organization created by various members of an industry to en-

Trade Associations

courage coordination in production and marketing techniques. Trade associations worked reasonably well in the mass-production industries that had already succeeded in limiting competition through consolidation. But in more decentralized industries, such as cotton textiles, their effectiveness was limited.

The strenuous efforts by industrialists throughout the economy to find ways to curb competition through consolidation or cooperation reflected a strong fear of overproduction. Even in the booming mid-1920s, industrialists remembered how too-rapid expansion had helped produce recessions in 1893, 1907, and 1920. The great, unrealized dream of the New Era was to find a way to stabilize the economy so that such collapses would never occur again.

Labor in the New Era

The remarkable economic growth was accompanied by a continuing, and in some areas even increasing, maldistribution of wealth and purchasing power. More than two-thirds of the American people in 1929 lived at no better than what one major study described as the "minimum comfort level." Half of those languished at or below the level of "subsistence and poverty."

American industrial workers experienced both the successes and the failures of the 1920s as much as any other group. On the one hand, most workers saw their standard of living rise during the decade; many enjoyed greatly improved working conditions and other benefits. Some employers in the 1920s, eager to avoid disruptive labor unrest and the growth of independent trade unions, adopted paternalistic techniques that came to be known as "welfare

"Welfare Capitalism"

capitalism." Henry Ford, for example, shortened the workweek, raised wages, and instituted paid vacations. U.S. Steel made conspicuous efforts to improve safety and sanitation in its factories. For the first time, some workers became eligible for pensions on retirement—nearly 3 million by 1926. (Women workers in such companies tended to receive other kinds of benefits—less often pensions, more often longer rest periods and vacations.) When labor grievances surfaced despite these efforts, workers could voice them through the so-called company unions that were emerging in many industries. These were workers' councils and shop committees, organized by the corporations themselves and thus without the independence most unions demand.

Welfare capitalism brought many workers important economic benefits, but it did not help them gain any real control over their own fates. Company unions were feeble vehicles, forbidden in most industries to raise the issues most important to workers. And welfare capitalism survived only as long as industry prospered. After 1929, with the economy in crisis, the system quickly collapsed.

Welfare capitalism affected only a relatively small number of workers, in any case. Most laborers worked for employers interested primarily in keeping their labor costs to a minimum. Workers as a whole, therefore, received wage increases at a rate far below increases in production and profits. Unskilled workers, in particular, saw their wages increase almost imperceptibly—by only a little over 2 percent between 1920 and 1926. In the end, American workers in the 1920s remained a relatively impoverished and powerless group. Their wages rose; but the average annual income of a worker remained below $1,500 a year when $1,800 was considered necessary to maintain a minimally decent standard of living. Only by relying on the earnings of several family members at once could many working-class families make ends meet. And almost all such families had to live with the very real possibility of one or more members losing their jobs. Unemployment was lower in the 1920s than it had been in the previous two decades, and much lower than it would be in the 1930s. But a large proportion of the work force (estimated at 5–7 percent at any given time) was out of work for at least some period during the decade—in part because the rapid growth of industrial technology made many jobs obsolete.

Many laborers continued to regard an effective, independent union movement as their best hope. But the New Era was a bleak time for labor organization, in part because the unions themselves were generally conservative and failed to adapt to the realities of

Hard Times for Organized Labor

the modern economy. The American Federation of Labor (AFL) remained wedded to the concept of the craft union, in which workers were organized on the basis of particular skills. It continued to make no provision for the fastest-growing area of the work force: unskilled, industrial workers, who had few organizations of their own. William Green, who became president of the AFL in 1924, was committed to peaceful cooperation with employers and to strident opposition to communism and socialism. He frowned on strikes.

Women and Minorities in the Work Force

A growing proportion of the work force consisted of women, who were concentrated in what have since

"Pink-Collar" Jobs

become known as "pink-collar" jobs—low-paying service occupations with many of the same problems as manufacturing employment. Large numbers of women worked as secretaries, salesclerks, telephone operators, and in other, similarly

underpaid jobs. Because technically such positions were not industrial jobs, the AFL and other labor organizations were generally uninterested in organizing these workers.

Similarly, the half-million African Americans who had migrated from the rural South to the cities during the Great Migration after 1914 had few opportunities for union representation. The skilled crafts represented in the AFL often worked actively to exclude blacks from their trades and organizations. Most blacks worked in jobs in which the AFL took no interest at all—as janitors, dishwashers, garbage collectors, commercial laundry attendants, and domestics, and in other types of service jobs. This general reluctance to organize service sector workers was in part because AFL leaders did not want women and minorities to become union members. The Brotherhood of Sleeping Car Porters, founded in 1925 and led for years by A. Philip

A. Philip Randolph

Randolph, was a notable exception: a vigorous union, led by an African American and representing a virtually all-black work force. Over time, Randolph won some significant gains for his members—increased wages, shorter working hours, and other benefits. He also enlisted the union in battles for civil rights for African Americans.

PREPARING WOMEN FOR WORK This school was established during World War I by the Northern Pacific Telegraph Company to train new women employees to be telephone operators. Both during and after the war, telephone companies were among the largest employers of women. *(Bettmann/Corbis)*

AFRICAN-AMERICAN WORKER The frail union movement among African Americans in the 1920s, led by A. Philip Randolph and others against imposing obstacles, slowly built up a constituency within the black working class. Here an aspiring black dairy worker draws attention to the contrast between African-American patriotism in war and the discriminatory treatment African Americans faced at home. *(John Vachon/Getty Images)*

In the West and the Southwest, the ranks of the unskilled included considerable numbers of Asians and Hispanics, few of them organized, most of them actively excluded from white-dominated unions. In the wake of the Chinese Exclusion Acts of the late nineteenth century, Japanese immigrants increasingly took the place of the Chinese in menial jobs in California, despite the continuing hostility of the white population. They worked on railroads, construction sites, and farms, and in many other low-paying workplaces. Some Japanese managed to escape the ranks of the unskilled by forming their own small businesses or setting themselves up as truck farmers (farmers who grow small food crops for local sale). Many of the *Issei* (Japanese immigrants) and *Nisei* (their American-born children) enjoyed significant economic success—so much so that California passed laws in 1913 and 1920 to make it more difficult for them to buy land. Other Asians—most notably Filipinos—also swelled the unskilled work force and generated considerable hostility. Anti-Filipino riots in California beginning in 1929 helped

produce legislation in 1934 virtually eliminating immigration from the Philippines.

Mexican immigrants formed a major part of the unskilled work force throughout the Southwest and California. Nearly half a million Mexicans entered the United States in the 1920s, more than any other national group, increasing the total Mexican population to over a million. Most lived in California, Texas, Arizona, and New Mexico; and by 1930, most lived in cities. Large Mexican barrios—usually raw urban communities, often without even such basic services as plumbing and sewage—grew up in Los Angeles, El Paso, San Antonio, Denver, and many other cities and towns. Some of the residents found work locally in factories and shops; others traveled to mines or did migratory labor on farms, but returned to the cities between jobs. Mexican workers, too, faced hostility and discrimination from the Anglo population of the region; but there were few efforts actually to exclude them. Employers in the relatively underpopulated West needed this ready pool of low-paid, unskilled, and unorganized workers.

The "American Plan"

Whatever the weaknesses of the unions and of unorganized, unskilled workers, the strength of the corporations was the principal reason for the absence of effective labor organization. After the turmoil of 1919, corporate leaders worked hard to spread the doctrine that unionism was somehow subversive, that a crucial element of democratic capitalism was the protection of the open shop (a shop in which no worker could be required to join a union). The crusade for the open shop, euphemistically titled the "American Plan," received the endorsement of the National Association of Manufacturers in 1920 and became a pretext for a harsh campaign of union busting across the country.

When such tactics proved insufficient to counter union power, government assistance often made the difference. In 1921, the Supreme Court upheld a lower-court ruling that declared picketing illegal and supported the right of courts to issue injunctions against strikers. In 1922, the Justice Department intervened to quell a strike by 400,000 railroad workers. In 1924, the courts refused protection to members of the United Mine Workers Union when mine owners launched a violent campaign in western Pennsylvania to drive the union from the coal fields. As a result of these developments, union membership fell from more than 5 million in 1920 to under 3 million in 1929.

Agricultural Technology and the Plight of the Farmer

Like industry, American agriculture in the 1920s was embracing new technologies for increasing production. The number of tractors on American farms, for example,

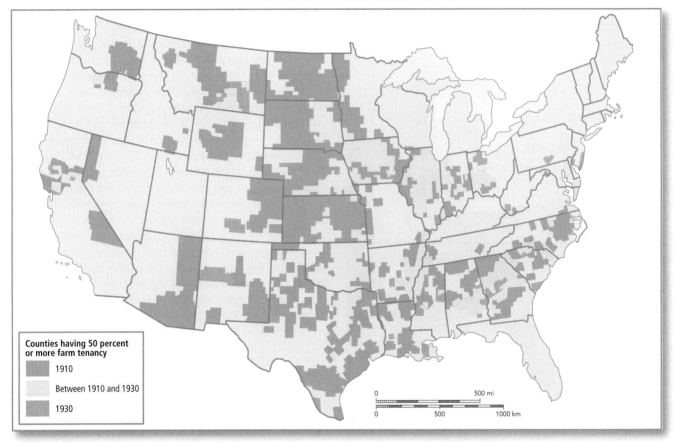

Counties having 50 percent or more farm tenancy

- 1910
- Between 1910 and 1930
- 1930

0   500 mi

0   500   1000 km

FARM TENANCY, 1910–1930 This map illustrates the significant increase in farm tenancy—that is, the number of farmers who did not own their land but worked as tenants for others—between 1910 and 1930. The dark green areas of the map show how extensive tenancy was even in 1910; over 50 percent of the land in those areas was farmed by tenants. The gold and purple parts of the map show the significant expansion of tenancy between 1910 and 1930—creating many new areas in which more than half the farmers were tenants. ◆ *How did the increasing efficiency and technological progress of agriculture in these years contribute to the growth of tenancy?*

quadrupled during the 1920s, especially after they began

Mechanized Farming

to be powered by internal combustion engines (like automobiles) rather than by the cumbersome steam engines of the past. They helped to open 35 million new acres to cultivation. Increasingly sophisticated combines and harvesters were proliferating, helping make it possible to produce more crops with fewer workers.

Agricultural researchers were already at work on other advances that would later transform food production in America and around the world: the invention of hybrid corn (made possible by advances in genetic research), which became available to farmers in 1921 but was not grown in great quantities until the 1930s; and the creation of chemical fertilizers and pesticides, which also began to have limited use in the 1920s but proliferated quickly in the 1930s and 1940s.

The new technologies greatly increased agricultural productivity, both in the United States and in other parts of the world. But the demand for agricultural goods was not rising as fast as production. The results were substantial surpluses, a disastrous decline in food prices, and a

severe drop in farmers' income beginning early in the 1920s. More than 3 million people left agriculture altogether in the course of the decade. Of those who remained, many lost ownership of their lands and had to rent instead from banks or other landlords.

In response, some farmers began to demand relief in the form of government price supports. One price-raising scheme in particular came to dominate agrarian demands: the idea of "parity." Parity was a complicated formula for setting

"Parity"

an adequate price for farm goods and ensuring that farmers would earn back at least their production costs no matter how the national or world agricultural market might fluctuate. Champions of parity urged high tariffs against foreign agricultural goods and a government commitment to buy surplus domestic crops at parity and sell them abroad at whatever the market would bring.

The legislative expression of the demand for parity was the McNary-Haugen Bill, named after its two principal sponsors in Congress and introduced repeatedly between 1924

McNary-Haugen Bill

and 1928. In 1926 and again in 1928, Congress (where

farm interests enjoyed disproportionate influence) approved a bill requiring parity for grain, cotton, tobacco, and rice, but President Coolidge vetoed it both times.

THE NEW CULTURE

The increasingly urban and consumer-oriented culture of the 1920s helped many Americans in all regions live their lives and perceive their world in increasingly similar ways. That same culture exposed them to a new set of values that reflected the prosperity and complexity of the modern economy. But the new culture could not, of course, erase the continuing, and indeed increasing, diversity of the United States. The relatively uniform mass culture reached Americans divided by region, race, religion, gender, and class, and those characteristics shaped the way individuals responded to national cultural messages.

Consumerism

Among the many changes industrialization produced in the United States was the creation of a mass consumer culture. By the 1920s, America was a society in which many men and women could afford not merely the means

Growing Mass Consumption

of subsistence, but a considerable measure of additional, discretionary goods and services; a society in which people could buy items not just because of need but for pleasure as well. Middle-class families purchased such new appliances as electric refrigerators, washing machines, electric irons, and vacuum cleaners, which revolutionized housework and had a particularly dramatic impact on the lives of women. Men and women wore wristwatches and smoked cigarettes. Women purchased cosmetics and mass-produced fashions. Above all, Americans bought automobiles. By the end of the decade, there were more than 30 million cars on American roads.

The automobile affected American life in countless ways. It greatly expanded the geographical horizons of millions of people who had previously seldom ventured very far from their homes. Rural men and women, in particular, found in the automobile a means of escaping the isolation of farm life; now they could visit friends or drive into town quickly and more or less at will, rather than spending hours traveling by horse or foot. City dwellers

Social Impact of the Automobile

found in the automobile an escape from the congestion of urban life. Weekend drives through the countryside became a staple of urban leisure. Many families escaped the city in a permanent sense: by moving to the new suburbs that were rapidly growing up around large cities in response to the ease of access the automobile had created.

The automobile also transformed the idea of vacations. In the past, the idea of traveling for pleasure had been a luxury reserved for the wealthy. Now many middle-class and even working-class people could aspire to travel

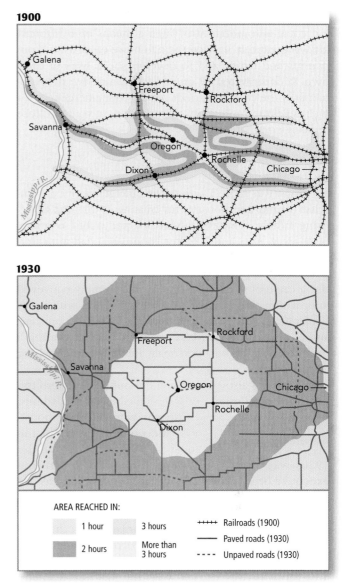

1900

1930

AREA REACHED IN:

1 hour	3 hours	┼┼┼┼ Railroads (1900)
2 hours	More than 3 hours	──── Paved roads (1930)
		┄┄┄┄ Unpaved roads (1930)

BREAKING DOWN RURAL ISOLATION: THE EXPANSION OF TRAVEL HORIZONS IN OREGON, ILLINOIS This map uses the small town of Oregon, Illinois—west of Chicago—to illustrate the way in which first railroads and then automobiles reduced the isolation of rural areas in the first decades of the twentieth century. The gold and purple areas of the two maps show the territory that residents of Oregon could reach within two hours. Note how small that area was in 1900 and how much larger it was in 1930, by which time an area of over a hundred square miles had become easily accessible to the town. Note, too, the significant network of paved roads in the region by 1930, few of which had existed in 1900. ◆ *Why did automobile travel do so much more than railroads to expand the travel horizons of small towns?*

For an interactive version of this map, go to www.mhhe.com/brinkley13ech22maps

considerable distances for vacations, which were a new concept for most men and women in this era. Many businesses and industries began to include paid vacations among their employee benefits; and many employers encouraged their vacationing workers to travel, on the assumption that a change of scene would help restore their energy and vigor at work.

For young people in families affluent enough to afford a car, the automobile was often a means of a different kind of escape. It allowed them to move easily away from parents and family and to develop social lives of their own. It contributed to one of the distinctive developments of the early twentieth century: the emergence of a well-developed and relatively independent youth culture in many communities.

Advertising

No group was more aware of the emergence of consumerism (or more responsible for creating it) than the advertising industry. The first advertising and public relations firms (N. W. Ayer and J. Walter Thompson) had appeared well before World War I; but in the 1920s, partly as a result of techniques pioneered by wartime propaganda, advertising came of age. Publicists no longer simply conveyed information; they sought to identify products with a particular lifestyle, to invest them with glamour and prestige, and to persuade potential consumers that purchasing a commodity could be a personally fulfilling and enriching experience.

Advertisers also encouraged the public to absorb the values of promotion and salesmanship and to admire those who were effective "boosters" and publicists. One of the most successful books of the 1920s was *The Man Nobody Knows,* by advertising executive Bruce Barton. It portrayed Jesus Christ as not only a religious prophet but also a "super salesman," who "picked up twelve men from the bottom ranks of business and forged them into an organization that conquered the world." The parables, Barton claimed, were "the most powerful advertisements of all time." Barton's message was fully in tune with the new spirit of the consumer culture. Jesus had been a man concerned with living a full and rewarding life in this world; twentieth-century men and women should do the same. ("Life is meant to live and enjoy as you go along," Barton once wrote.) Jesus had succeeded because he knew how to make friends, to become popular, to please others; that talent was a prescription for success in the modern era as well.

The Man Nobody Knows

The advertising industry could never have had the impact it did without the emergence of new vehicles of communication that made it possible to reach large audiences quickly and easily. Newspapers were being absorbed into national chains, and wire services were making it possible even for independent newspapers to carry nationally syndicated material.

New or expanded mass-circulation magazines also attracted broad, national audiences. *The Saturday Evening Post,* which began publication as a magazine in 1871, appealed to rural and small-town families

Mass-Circulation Magazines

with its homey stories and its conspicuous traditionalism; its popularity was, in some respects, evidence of a yearning for an earlier time. But other magazines responded directly to the realities of modern, urban life. *The Reader's Digest,* founded in 1921 by DeWitt and Lila Wallace, condensed stories and even books originally published in other places in an effort to make the expanding world of knowledge and information available in a brief, efficient form for people who would otherwise have no access to it. *Time* magazine, founded in 1923 by Henry Luce and Briton Hadden, set out to condense the news of the week into a brief, accessible, lively format for busy people who did not have the time or desire to read newspapers.

The Movies and Broadcasting

At the same time, movies were becoming an ever more popular and powerful form of mass communication. More than 100 million people saw films in 1930, as compared to 40 million in 1922. The addition of sound to motion pictures—beginning in 1927 with the first feature-length "talkie," *The Jazz Singer* with Al Jolson—created nationwide excitement. An embarrassing scandal in 1921 involving the popular comedian Fatty Arbuckle produced public outrage and political pressure to "clean up" Hollywood. In response, the film industry introduced "standards" to its films. Studio owners created the Motion Picture Association, a new trade association, and hired former postmaster general Will Hays to head it. More important, they gave Hays broad powers to review films and to ban anything likely to offend viewers (or politicians). Hays exercised his powers broadly and imposed on the film industry a safe, sanctimonious conformity for many years.

Hollywood

The most important communications vehicle was the only one truly new to the 1920s: radio. The first commercial radio station in America, KDKA in Pittsburgh, began broadcasting in 1920; and the first national radio network, the National Broadcasting Company, was formed in 1927. By 1923, there were more than 500 radio stations, covering every area of the country. The radio industry, too, feared government regulation and control, and thus monitored program content carefully and excluded controversial or provocative material. But radio was much less centralized than filmmaking. Individual stations had considerable autonomy, and even carefully monitored stations and networks could not control the countless hours of programming as effectively as the Hays office could control films. Radio programming, therefore, was more diverse—and at times more controversial and even subversive—than film.

Modernist Religion

The influence of the consumer culture, and its increasing emphasis on immediate, personal fulfillment, was visible even in religion. Theological modernists taught their

THE CINEMA

There is probably no cultural or commercial product more closely identified with the United States than motion pictures—or, as they are known in much of the world, the cinema. Although the technology of cinema emerged from the work of inventors in England and France as well as the United States, the production and distribution of films has been dominated by Americans almost from the start. The United States was the first nation to create a film "industry," and it did so at a scale vaster than that of any other country. The 700 feature films a year that Hollywood produced in the 1920s was more than ten times the number created by any other nation, and its films were dominating not only the vast American market, but much of the world's market as well. Seventy percent of the films seen in France, 80 percent of those seen in Latin America, and 95 percent of the movies viewed in Canada and Great Britain were produced in the United States in the 1920s.

As early as the 1930s, the penetration of other nations by American movies was already troubling many governments. The Soviet Union responded to the popularity of Walt Disney's Micky Mouse cartoons by inventing a cartoon hero of its own—a porcupine, designed to entertain in a way consistent with socialist values and not the capitalist ones that they believed Hollywood conveyed. During World War II, American films were banned in occupied France (prompting some anti-fascist dissidents to screen such American films as Frank Capra's *Mr. Smith Goes to Washington* in protest).

American dominance was a result in part of World War I and its aftermath, which debilitated European filmmaking just as movies were vigorously growing in the United States. By 1915, the United States had gained complete control of its own vast market and had so saturated it with movie theaters that by the end of World War I, half the theaters of the world were in America. Two decades later, after an extraordinary expansion of theaters in other nations, the United States continued to have over 40 percent of the world's cinemas. And while the spread of theaters through other areas of the world helped launch film industries in many other countries, it also increased the market (and the appetite) for American films and strengthened American supremacy in their production. "The sun, it now appears," the *Saturday Evening Post* commented in the mid-1920s, "never sets on the British empire and the American motion picture." Movies were then, and perhaps remain still, America's most influential cultural export. Even American popular music, which has enormous global reach, faces more significant local competition than American movies do in most parts of the world.

Despite this American dominance, however, filmmaking has flourished—and continues to flourish—in many countries around the world. India's fabled "Bollywood," for example, produces an enormous number of movies for its domestic market—almost as many as the American industry creates, even though few of them are widely exported. This global cinema has had a significant impact on American filmmaking, just as American films have influenced filmmakers abroad. The small British film industry had a strong early influence on American movies partly because of the quality and originality of British films, and partly because of the emigration of talented actors, directors, and screenwriters to the United States. The great Alfred Hitchcock, for example, made his first films in London before moving to Hollywood, where he spent the rest of his long career. After World War II, French "new wave" cinema helped spawn a new generation of highly individualistic directors in the United States. Asian cinema—especially the thriving film industry in Hong Kong, with its gritty realism—helped lead to some of the powerfully violent American films of the 1980s and beyond, as well as the genre of martial-arts films that has become popular around the world. German, Italian, Swedish, Dutch, Japanese, Australian, and Indian filmmakers also had influence on Hollywood—and over time perhaps even greater influence on the large and growing "independent film" movement in the United States.

VALENTINO The popularity of the film star Rudolph Valentino among American women was one of the most striking cultural phenomena of the 1920s. Valentino was slight and delicate, not at all like the conventional image of "manliness." But he developed an enormous following among women, in part—as this poster is obviously intended to suggest—by baring his body on screen. Valentino was Italian, which made him seem somehow strange and foreign to many older-stock Americans, and he was almost always cast in exotic roles, never as an American. His sudden death in 1926 (at the age of 31) created enormous outpourings of grief among many American women. *(George Kleiman/Bettmann/Corbis)*

In recent decades, as new technologies and new styles have transformed films around the world, the American movie industry has continued to dominate global cinema. But national boundaries no longer adequately describe moviemaking in the twenty-first century. It is becoming a truly globalized enterprise in the same way that so many other commercial ventures are becoming international. "American" films today are often produced abroad, often have non-American directors and actors, and are often paid for with international financing. Hollywood still dominates worldwide filmmaking, but Hollywood itself is now an increasingly global community.

"RADIO GAME" In the early 1920s, when radio was still new, many people considered it a "hobby," appropriate to people interested in technology. By the end of the decade, radio was a normal part of the everyday lives of almost everyone. But the boxed "Radio Game," whose cover is shown here and which remained popular well into the 1930s, reminded the public of radio's early days. *(From the Collections of Henry Ford)*

followers to abandon some of the traditional tenets of evangelical Christianity (literal interpretation of the Bible, belief in the Trinity, attribution of human traits to the deity) and to accept a faith that would help individuals to live more fulfilling lives in the present world.

The most influential spokesman for liberal Protestantism in the 1920s was Harry Emerson Fosdick, the pastor of Riverside Church in New York. Harry Emerson Fosdick The basis of Christian religion, he claimed, was not unexamined faith, but a fully developed personality. In his 1926 book *Abundant Religion,* he argued that Christianity would "furnish an inward spiritual dynamic for radiant and triumphant living."

Most Americans, even most middle-class Americans, stopped well short of this view of religion as a vehicle for advancing "man's abundant life" and remained faithful to traditional religious messages. But many other middle-class Americans were gradually devaluing religion altogether, assigning it a secondary role (or at times no role at all) in their lives. When the sociologists Robert and Helen Merrell Lynd studied the society of Muncie, Indiana, in the mid-1920s, they were struck by how many people there claimed that they paid less attention to religion than their parents had. They no longer devoted much time to teaching their children the tenets of their faith; they seldom prayed at home or attended church on any day but Sunday. Even the Sabbath was becoming not a day of rest and reflection, but a holiday filled with activities and entertainments.

Professional Women

In the 1920s, college-educated women were no longer pioneers. There were now two and even three generations of graduates of women's or coeducational colleges and universities; many such women were making their presence felt in professional areas that in the past they had rarely penetrated.

Still, professional opportunities for women remained limited by prevailing assumptions (prevalent among many women as well as men) about what were suitable female occupations. Although there were no-Limited Opportunities for Women table success stories about female business executives, journalists, doctors, and lawyers, most professional women remained confined to such traditionally "feminine" fields as fashion, education, social work, and nursing, or to the lower levels of business management. Some middle-class women now combined marriage and careers, but most still had to choose between work and family. The majority of the 25 percent of married women who worked outside the home in the 1920s were working class. The "new professional woman" was a vivid and widely publicized image in the 1920s. In reality, however, most middle-class married women did not work outside the home.

Changing Ideas of Motherhood

Yet the 1920s constituted a new era for middle-class women nonetheless. In particular, the decade saw a redefinition of the idea of motherhood. Shortly after World War I, an influential group of psychologists—the "behaviorists," led by John B. Watson—began to challenge the long-held assumption that women had an instinctive capacity for motherhood. Maternal affection was not, they claimed, sufficient preparation for child rearing. Instead, mothers should rely on the advice and assistance of experts and professionals: doctors, nurses, and trained educators in nursery schools and kindergartens.

For many middle-class women, these changes helped redefine what had been an all-consuming activity. Motherhood was no less important in behaviorist theory than it had been before; if anything, it was more so. But for many women it was less emotionally fulfilling, less connected to their instinctive lives, more dependent on (and tied to) people and institutions outside the family. Many attempted to compensate by devoting new attention to their roles as wives and companions, to developing what became known as "companionate marriage." The middle-class wife

"Companionate Marriages"

shared increasingly in her husband's social life; she devoted more attention to cosmetics and clothing; she was less willing to allow children to interfere with their marriage. Most of all, many women now found support for thinking of their sexual relationships with their husbands not simply as a means of procreation, as earlier generations had been taught to do, but as an important and pleasurable experience in its own right, as the culmination of romantic love.

Progress in the development of birth control was both a cause and a result of this change. The pioneer of the American birth-control movement was Margaret Sanger, who had become committed to the cause in part because of the

Birth Control

influence of Emma Goldman—a Russian immigrant and political radical who had agitated for birth control before World War I. Sanger began her career promoting the diaphragm and other birth-control devices out of a concern for working-class women, believing that large families were among the major causes of poverty and distress in poor communities. By the 1920s, partly because she had limited success in persuading working-class women to accept her teachings, she was becoming more concerned with persuading middle-class women of the benefits of birth control. Women, she argued, should be free to enjoy the pleasures of sexual activity without any connection to procreation. Birth-control devices began to find a large market among middle-class women, even though some techniques remained illegal in many states (and abortion remained illegal nearly everywhere).

THE FLAPPER By the mid-1920s, the flapper—the young woman who challenged traditional expectations—had become not only a social type but a movement in fashion as well. This drawing was one of many efforts by fashion designers to create clothes that reflected the liberated spirit the flappers had introduced into popular culture. *(Culver Pictures, Inc.)*

The "Flapper": Image and Reality

The new, more secular view of womanhood had effects on women beyond the middle class as well. Some women concluded that in the "New Era" it was no longer necessary to maintain a rigid, Victorian female "respectability." They could smoke, drink, dance, wear seductive clothes and makeup, and attend lively parties. They could strive for physical and emotional fulfillment, for release from repression and inhibition. (The wide popularity of Freudian ideas in the 1920s—often simplified and distorted for mass consumption—contributed to the growth of these attitudes.)

Such assumptions became the basis of the "flapper"— the modern woman whose liberated lifestyle found expression in dress, hairstyle, speech, and behavior. The flapper lifestyle had a particular impact on lower-middle-class and working-class single women, who were flocking to

new jobs in industry and the service sector. (The young, affluent, upper-class "Bohemian" women most often associated with the flapper image were, in fact, imitating a style that emerged first among this larger working-class group.) At night, such women flocked, often alone, to clubs and dance halls in search of excitement and companionship.

Despite the image of liberation the flapper evoked in popular culture, most women remained highly dependent on men—both in the workplace, where they were usually poorly paid, and in the home—and relatively powerless when men exploited that dependence.

Pressing for Women's Rights

The realization that the "new woman" was as much myth as reality inspired some American feminists to continue their

DANCE HALLS

In the booming, boisterous, consumerist world struggling to be born in the 1920s, many Americans—especially those living in urban areas—challenged the rules and inhibitions of traditional public culture. They looked instead for freedom, excitement, and release. Nowhere did they do so more vigorously and visibly than in the great dance halls that were proliferating in cities across the nation in these years.

The dance craze that swept urban America in the 1920s and 1930s was a result of many things. The great African-American migration during World War I had helped bring new forms of jazz out of the South and into the urban North—where the phonograph and the radio popularized it. The growth of a distinctive youth culture—and the increasing tendency of men and women to socialize together in public—created an audience for uninhibited, sexually titillating entertainment. The relative prosperity of the 1920s enabled many young

THE SAVOY The Savoy ballroom in New York's Harlem was one of the largest and most popular dance halls in America, and a regular home to many of the most noted dance bands in the 1920s and 1930s. *(Bettmann/Corbis)*

working-class people to afford to spend evenings out. And prohibition, by closing down most saloons and taverns, limited their other options.

And so, night after night, in big cities and small, young people flocked to dance halls to hear the powerful, pulsing new music; to revel in dazzling lights and ornate surroundings; to show off new clothes and hairstyles; and, of course, most of all, to dance. Some of the larger dance halls in the big cities—Roseland and the Savoy in New York, the Trianon and the Aragon in Chicago, the Raymor in Boston, the Greystone in Detroit, the Hollywood Paladium, and many others—were truly cavernous, capable of accommodating thousands of couples at once. Some were outdoors and, in warm weather, attracted even larger crowds. Many gave off some of the same sense of grandiosity and glamour that the new movie palaces, which were being built at the same time, provided. (Indeed, it was not unusual for couples to combine an evening at the movies with a visit to a dance hall.)

Many of the great ballrooms became the sites of regular radio programs—and thus enabled even isolated, rural people to experience something of the excitement of an evening of dance. In 1924, in New York City alone, 6 million people attended dance halls. Over 10 percent of the men and women between the ages of 17 and 40 in New York went dancing at least once a week, and the numbers were almost certainly comparable in other large cities.

What drew so many people to the dance halls? In large part, it was the music, which both its defenders and critics recognized as something very new in mainstream American culture. Dancing was "moral ruin," the *Ladies' Home Journal* primly warned in 1921,

JITTERBUGGERS As dance halls became more popular, dancing became more exuberant—perhaps never more so than when the "jitterbug" became popular in the 1930s. This photograph shows an acrobatic pair of dancers during a huge dance event in Los Angeles designed to raise money for the Salvation Army. More than 10,000 people attended the event, and the police on hand to keep order had to call for reinforcements as the crowd became more and more frenzied and enthusiastic. *(Bettmann/Corbis)*

prompting "carelessness, recklessness, and laxity of moral responsibility" with its "direct appeal to the body's sensory centers." Many young dancers might have agreed with the description, if not with the moral judgment. Jazz encouraged a kind of uninhibited, even frenetic dancing—expressive, athletic, sensual—that young couples, in particular, found extraordinarily exciting, a welcome release from the often staid worlds of family, school, or work. The larger dance halls also attracted crowds by showcasing the most famous bands of the day.

---

crusade for reform. The National Woman's Party, under the leadership of Alice Paul, pressed on with its campaign to make the Equal Rights Amendment, first proposed in 1923, a part of the Constitution, although it found little support in Congress (and met continued resistance from other feminist groups). Nevertheless, women's organizations and female political activities grew in many ways in the 1920s. Responding to the suffrage victory, women organized the League of Women Voters and the

League of Women Voters

DANCING AT THE SAVOY This photograph of the interior of the famous Savoy ballroom shows the hundreds of men and women who typically flocked there to dance to the great black jazz bands of the 1920s and 1930s. *(Getty Images)*

Performances by Paul Whiteman, Ben Pollack, Fletcher Henderson, Bix Beiderbecke, Louis Armstrong, or Duke Ellington—musicians already familiar to everyone through radio performances and recordings—drew enormous crowds.

Some of the less savory halls also attracted dancers for illicit reasons—as sources of bootleg liquor or as places to buy drugs. The popular "taxi-dance" ballrooms—which allowed men without their own partners to buy tickets to dance with "hostesses" and "instructresses"—were sometimes closed by municipal authorities for "lewd" dancing and prostitution. At least sixty city governments passed regulations in the 1920s restricting the styles of public dancing; and the managers of the larger ballrooms tried to distance themselves from the unsavory image of the taxi-dance halls by imposing dress codes and making at least some efforts, usually futile, to require "decorum" among their patrons.

Dance halls were particularly popular with young men and women from working-class, immigrant communities. For them, going dancing was part of becoming American, a way to escape—even if momentarily—the insular world of the immigrant neighborhood. (Their parents saw it that way too, and often tried to stop their children from going because they feared the dance halls would pull them out of the family and the community.) Going dancing was a chance to mingle with hundreds, sometimes thousands, of strangers of diverse backgrounds, and to participate in a cultural ritual that had no counterpart in ethnic cultures.

But dance halls were not melting pots. African Americans—who flocked to ballrooms at least as eagerly as whites—usually gathered at clubs in black neighborhoods, where there were only occasional white patrons. White working-class people might encounter a large number of different ethnic groups in a great hall at once, but the groups did not mix very much. In Chicago's Dreamland, for example, Italians congregated near the door, Poles near the band, and Jews in the middle of the floor. Still, the experience of the dance hall—like the experience of the movie palace or the amusement park—drew people into the growing mass culture that was competing with and beginning to overwhelm the close-knit ethnic cultures into which many young Americans had been born.

women's auxiliaries of both the Democratic and Republican Parties. Female-dominated consumer groups grew rapidly and increased the range and energy of their efforts.

Women activists won a significant triumph in 1921, when they helped secure passage in Congress of a measure in keeping with the traditional feminist goal of securing "protective" legislation for women: the Sheppard-Towner Act. It provided federal funds to states to establish prenatal and child health-care programs. From the start,

Sheppard-Towner Act

however, the bill produced controversy. Alice Paul and her supporters opposed the measure, arguing that it classified all women as mothers. Margaret Sanger's objection was that the new programs would discourage birth-control efforts. More important, the American Medical Association fought Sheppard-Towner, warning that it would introduce untrained outsiders into the health-care field. In 1929, Congress terminated the program.

Education and Youth

The growing secularism of American culture and its expanding emphasis on training and expertise found reflection in the increasingly important role of education in the lives of American youth. First, more people were going to school in the 1920s than ever before. High-school attendance more than doubled during the decade, from 2.2 million to more than 5 million. Enrollment in colleges and universities increased threefold between 1900 and 1930, with much of that increase occurring after World War I. In 1918, there had been 600,000 college students; in 1930, there were 1.2 million, nearly 20 percent of the college-age population. Attendance was increasing as well at trade and vocational schools and in other institutions providing the specialized training that the modern economy demanded. Schools were beginning to offer instruction not only in the traditional disciplines but also in modern technical skills: engineering, management, economics.

The growing importance of education contributed to the emergence of a separate youth culture. The idea of adolescence as a distinct period in the life of an individual was for the most part new to the twentieth century. In some measure it was a result of the influence of Freudian psychology. But it was a result, too, of society's recognition that a more extended period of training and preparation was necessary before a young person was ready to move into the workplace. Schools and colleges provided adolescents with a setting in which they could develop their own social patterns, their own hobbies, their own interests and activities. An increasing number of students saw school as a place not just for academic training but for organized athletics, extracurricular activities, clubs, and fraternities and sororities—that is, as an institution that allowed them to define themselves less in terms of their families and more in terms of their peer group.

Youth Culture

The Decline of the "Self-Made Man"

The sense of losing control, of becoming more dependent on rules and norms established by large, impersonal bureaucracies, created a crisis of self-identification among many American men. Robbed of the independence and control that had once defined "masculinity," many men looked for other means to do so. Theodore Roosevelt, for example, had glorified warfare and the "strenuous life" as

VASSAR STUDENTS, 1920 Although a few prominent women's colleges, Vassar among them, had been educating women since the late nineteenth century, the number of colleges and universities willing to accept women, and hence the number of women enrolled in higher education, soared in the 1920s. *(Bettmann/Corbis)*

a route to "manhood." Other men turned to fraternal societies, to athletics, and to other settings where they found confirmation of their masculinity. The "Doom of the Self-Made Man," as *Century* magazine described it, produced marked ambivalence. These mixed feelings were reflected in the identity of three men who became the most widely admired heroes of the New Era: Thomas Edison, the inventor of the electric lightbulb and many other technological marvels; Henry Ford, the creator of the assembly line and

Charles Lindbergh

one of the founders of the automobile industry; and Charles Lindbergh, the first aviator to make a solo flight across the Atlantic Ocean. All received the adulation of much of the American public. Lindbergh, in particular, became a national hero the like of which the country had never seen before.

On the one hand, all three men represented the triumphs of the modern technological and industrial society. On the other hand, all three had risen to success without the benefit of formal education and at least in part through their own efforts. They were, their admirers liked to believe, genuinely self-made men.

The Disenchanted

A generation of artists and intellectuals coming of age in the 1920s found the new society in which they lived especially disturbing. Many were experiencing a disenchantment with modern America so fundamental that they were often able to view it only with contempt. As a result, they adopted a role sharply different from that of most intellectuals of most earlier eras. Rather than trying to influence and reform their society, they isolated themselves from it and embarked on a restless search for personal fulfillment. Gertrude Stein once referred to the young Americans emerging from World War I as a "Lost Generation." For some writers and intellectuals, at least, it was an apt description.

At the heart of the Lost Generation's critique of modern society was a sense of personal alienation. This disil-

Lost Generation's Critique

lusionment had its roots in nothing so deeply as the experience of World War I. The repudiation of Wilsonian idealism, the restoration of "business as usual," the growing emphasis on materialism and consumerism suggested that the war had been a fraud; that the suffering and the dying had been in vain. Ernest Hemingway, one of the most celebrated (and most commercially successful) of the new breed of writers, expressed the generation's contempt for the war in his novel *A Farewell to Arms* (1929). Its protagonist, an American officer fighting in Europe, decides that there is no justification for his participation in the conflict and deserts the army with a nurse with whom he has fallen in love. Hemingway suggested that the officer was to be admired for doing so.

One result of this alienation was a series of savage critiques of modern society by a wide range of writers, some of whom were known as the "debunkers." Among them was

H. L. Mencken

the Baltimore journalist H. L. Mencken. His magazines—first the *Smart Set* and later the *American Mercury*—ridiculed everything most middle-class Americans held dear: religion, politics, the arts, even democracy itself. Mencken could not believe, he claimed, that "civilized life was possible under a democracy," because it was a form of government that placed power in the hands of the common people, whom he ridiculed as the "booboisie." Echoing Mencken's contempt was the novelist Sinclair Lewis, the first American to win a Nobel Prize in Literature. In a series of savage novels—*Main Street* (1920), *Babbitt* (1922), *Arrowsmith* (1925), and others—he lashed out at one aspect of modern society after another: the small town, the modern city, the medical profession, popular religion. The novelist F. Scott Fitzgerald ridiculed the American obsession with material success in *The*

Rejecting Success

Great Gatsby (1925). The novel's title character, Jay Gatsby, spends his life accumulating wealth and social prestige in order to win the woman he loves. The world to which he has aspired, however, turns out to be one of pretension, fraud, and cruelty, and it ultimately destroys him.

The Harlem Renaissance

In postwar Harlem in New York City, a new generation of black artists and intellectuals created a flourishing African-American culture widely described as the "Harlem Renaissance." There were nightclubs (among them the famous Cotton Club) featuring many of the great jazz musicians who would later become staples of national popular culture: Duke Ellington, Jelly Roll Morton, Fletcher Henderson, and others. There were theaters featuring ribald musical comedies and vaudeville acts. Many white New Yorkers traveled up to Harlem for the music and theater, but the audiences were largely black.

Harlem in the 1920s was above all a center of literature, poetry, and art that drew heavily from African roots. Black artists were trying in part to demonstrate the richness of their own racial heritage (and not incidentally, to prove to whites that their race was worthy of respect). The poet Langston Hughes captured much of the spirit of the movement in a single sentence: "I am a Negro—and beautiful." One of the lead-

African-American Pride

ers of the Harlem Renaissance was Alain Locke, who assembled a notable collection of black writings published in 1925 as *The New Negro*. Gradually, white publishers began to notice and take an interest in the writers Locke helped launch. Hughes, Zora Neale Hurston, Countee Cullen, Claude McKay, James

OPPORTUNITY
A JOURNAL OF NEGRO LIFE

JUNE 1926

THE ART OF THE HARLEM RENAISSANCE Aaron Douglas (1899–1979), one of the most significant African-American artists of the 1920s, created this cover image for *Opportunity* magazine in 1926. Douglas combined an interest in African and African-American themes with an attraction to the modernist trends in American art generally during this period. *(Schomburg Center, The New York Public Library/Art Resource, NY. Permission courtesy of the Aaron & Alta Sawyer Douglas Foundation)*

Weldon Johnson, and others gradually found readerships well beyond the black community. The painter Aaron Douglas, talented chronicler of the African-American experience, eventually found himself commissioned to create important murals in universities and public buildings.

A CONFLICT OF CULTURES

The modern, secular culture of the 1920s was not unchallenged. It grew up alongside older, more traditional cultures, with which it continually and often bitterly competed.

Prohibition

When the prohibition of the sale and manufacture of alcohol went into effect in January 1920, it had the support of most members of the middle class and most of those who considered themselves progressives. Within a year, however, it had become clear that the "noble experiment," as its defenders called it, was not working well. Prohibition did substantially reduce drinking, at least in some regions of the country. But it also produced conspicuous and growing violations that made the law an almost immediate source of disillusionment and controversy. The federal government hired only 1,500 agents to enforce the prohibition laws, and in many places they received little help from local police. Before long, it was almost as easy to acquire illegal alcohol in much of the country as it had once been to acquire legal alcohol. And since an enormous, lucrative industry was now barred to legitimate businessmen, organized crime figures took it

Failure of Prohibition

HARLEM, 1925 Well-dressed school children gather a street in Harlem, illustrating the growing affluence of the African-American elite in New York. *(Bettmann/ Corbis)*

PROHIBITION, 1921 A New York City police commissioner oversees agents pouring illegal liquor into the street. This raid occurred in the early months of prohibition, when the battle against alcohol was still popular—hence the eagerness of the commissioner to appear in the photograph. *(Library of Congress)*

over. In Chicago, Al Capone built a criminal empire based largely on illegal alcohol. He guarded it against interlopers with an army of as many as 1,000 gunmen, whose zealousness contributed to the violent deaths of more than 250 people in the city between 1920 and 1927. Other regions produced gangsters and gang wars of their own.

Alcohol and Organized Crime

Many middle-class progressives who had originally supported prohibition soon soured on the experiment. But an enormous constituency of provincial, largely rural, Protestant Americans continued vehemently to defend it. To them, prohibition had always carried implications far beyond the issue of drinking itself. It represented the effort of an older America to maintain dominance in a society in which they were becoming relatively less powerful. Drinking, which they associated with the modern city and with Catholic immigrants, became a symbol of the new culture they believed was displacing them.

Opponents of prohibition (or "wets," as they came to be known) gained steadily in influence. Not until 1933, however, when the Great Depression added weight to their appeals, were they finally able effectively to challenge the "drys" and win repeal of the Eighteenth Amendment.

Nativism and the Klan

Like that for prohibition (which was itself in part a result of old-stock Americans trying to discipline the new immigrant population), agitation for a curb on foreign immigration to the United States had begun in the nineteenth century; and like the prohibition movement, it had gathered strength in the years before the war largely because of the support of middle-class progressives. Such concerns had not been sufficient in the first years of the century to win passage of curbs on immigration; but in the troubled and repressive years immediately following the war, many old-stock Americans began to associate immigration with radicalism.

Sentiment on behalf of restriction grew rapidly as a result. In 1921, Congress passed an emergency immigration act, establishing a quota system by which annual immigration from any country could not exceed 3 percent of the number of persons of that nationality who had been in the United States in 1910. The new law cut immigration from 800,000 to 300,000 in any single year, but nativists remained unsatisfied and pushed for a harsher law. The National Origins Act of 1924 strengthened the exclusionist provision of the 1921 law. It banned immigration from east Asia entirely. That provision deeply angered Japan, which understood that the Japanese were the principal target; Chinese immigration had been illegal since 1882. The law also reduced the quota for Europeans from 3 percent to 2 percent. The quota would be based, moreover, not on the 1910 census, but on the census of 1890, a year in which there had been many fewer southern and eastern Europeans in the country. What immigration there was, in other words, would heavily favor northwestern Europeans—people of "Nordic" or "Teutonic" stock. Five years later, a further restriction set a rigid limit of

National Origins Act of 1924

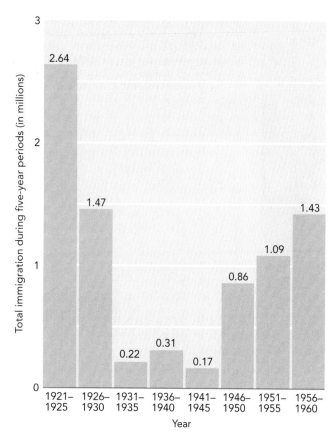

TOTAL IMMIGRATION, 1920–1960 After many years of enormous immigration from Europe and elsewhere, the United States experienced several decades of much lower immigration beginning in the 1920s. Immigration restriction legislation passed in 1921 and 1924 was one important reason for the decline. ◆ *What other factors depressed immigration in the 1930s and 1940s?*

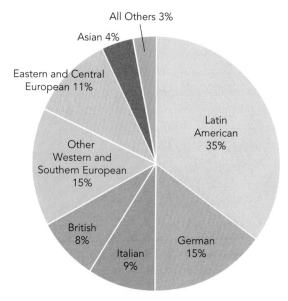

SOURCES OF IMMIGRATION, 1920–1960 This chart shows a dramatic change in the sources of immigration between 1920 and 1960, a direct result of the National Origins Act of 1924, which established national quotas for immigrants to the United States based on the number of such immigrants who had been in the country in 1890. Note the shift back toward northern and western Europe and away from Italy and other southern and eastern European nations (which had not been heavily represented in the immigration of the 1890s). But the most dramatic change was the enormous increase in the proportion of immigrants from Latin America, a region explicitly exempted from the quota system established in 1924. ◆ *Why were Latin Americans treated differently than Europeans in immigration law in these years?*

150,000 immigrants a year. In the years that followed, immigration officials seldom permitted even half that number actually to enter the country.

But the nativism of the 1920s extended well beyond restricting immigration. Among other things, this nativism helped instigate the rebirth of the Ku Klux Klan as a major force in American society.

The first Klan, founded during Reconstruction, had died in the 1870s. But in 1915, another group of white

The New Klan

southerners met on Stone Mountain near Atlanta and established a new version of the society. Nativist passions had swelled in Georgia and elsewhere in response to the case of Leo Frank, a Jewish factory manager in Atlanta convicted in 1914 (on very flimsy evidence) of murdering a female employee; a mob stormed Frank's jail and lynched him. The premiere (also in Atlanta) of D. W. Griffith's film *The Birth of a Nation,* which glorified the early Klan, also helped inspire white southerners to join a new one. At first the new Klan, like the old, was largely concerned with intimidating African Americans, who according to Klan leader William J. Simmons were becoming insub-

ordinate. And at first it remained small, obscure, and almost entirely southern. After World War I, however, concern about blacks became secondary to concern about Catholics, Jews, and foreigners. At that point, membership in the Klan expanded rapidly and dramatically, not just in the small towns and rural areas of the South, but also in industrial cities in the North and Midwest. Indiana had the largest membership of any state, and there were substantial Klans in Chicago, Detroit, and other northern industrial cities as well. The Klan was also strong in the West, with particularly large and active chapters in Oregon and Colorado. By 1924, there were reportedly 4 million members.

In some communities, where Klan leaders came from the most "respectable" segments of society, the organization operated much like a fraternal society, engaging in nothing more dangerous than occasional political pronouncements. Many Klan units (or "klaverns") tried to present themselves as patriots and community leaders. Some established women's and even children's auxiliaries to demonstrate their commitment to the family. Often, however, the Klan also operated as a brutal, even

KLAN INITIATION A Ku Klux Klan chapter in Jackson, Mississippi holds an initiation ceremony for new members in August 1923. *(Library of Congress)*

violent, opponent of "alien" groups and as a defender of traditional, fundamentalist morality. Some Klansmen systematically terrorized blacks, Jews, Catholics, and foreigners: boycotting their businesses, threatening their families, and attempting to drive them out of their communities. Occasionally, they resorted to violence: public whipping, tarring and feathering, arson, and lynching.

What the Klan feared, it soon became clear, was not simply "foreign" or "racially impure" groups; it was anyone who posed a challenge to "traditional values," as the Klan defined

Defending "Traditional Values"

them. Klansmen persecuted not only immigrants and African Americans, but also those white Protestants they considered guilty of irreligion, sexual promiscuity, or drunkenness. The Klan worked to enforce prohibition; it attempted to institute compulsory Bible reading in schools; it worked to punish divorce. It also provided its members, many of them people of modest means with little real power in society, with a sense of community and seeming authority. Its bizarre costumes, its elaborate rituals, its "secret" language, its burning crosses—all helped produce a sense of excitement and cohesion.

The Klan declined quickly after 1925, when a series of internal power struggles and several sordid scandals discredited some of its most important leaders. The most

David Stephenson

damaging episode involved David Stephenson, head of the Indiana

Klan, who raped a young secretary, kidnapped her, and watched her die rather than call a doctor after she swallowed poison. The Klan staggered on in some areas into the 1930s, but by World War II it was effectively dead. (The postwar Ku Klux Klan, which still survives, is modeled on but has no direct connection to the Klan of the 1920s and 1930s.)

Religious Fundamentalism

Another bitter cultural controversy of the 1920s was over the place of religion in contemporary society. By 1921, American Protestantism was divided into two warring camps. On one side stood the modernists: mostly urban, middle-class people who had attempted to adapt religion to the teachings of science and to the realities of their modern, secular society. On the other side stood the defenders of traditional faith: provincial, largely rural men and women, fighting to maintain the centrality of religion in American life. They became known as "fundamentalists," a term derived from an influential set of pamphlets, *The Fundamentals,* published before World War I. The fundamentalists were outraged at the abandonment of traditional beliefs in the face of scientific discoveries. They insisted the Bible was to be interpreted literally. Above all, they opposed the teachings of Charles Darwin, who had openly challenged the biblical

BRYAN AND DARROW IN DAYTON
Clarence Darrow (left) and William Jennings Bryan pose for photographers during the 1925 Scopes trial. Both men had removed their jackets because of the intense heat, and Bryan had shocked many of his admirers by revealing that he was not wearing suspenders (as most country people did), but a belt—which in rural Tennessee was a symbol of urban culture. *(Brown Brothers)*

story of the Creation. Human beings had not evolved from lower orders of animals, the fundamentalists insisted; they had been created by God, as described in Genesis.

Fundamentalism was a highly evangelical movement, interested in spreading the doctrine to new groups. Fundamentalist evangelists, among them the celebrated Billy Sunday, traveled from state to state (particularly in the South and parts of the West) attracting huge crowds to their revival meetings. (See "Patterns of Popular Culture," pp. 618–619.) Protestant modernists looked on much of this activity with condescension and amusement. But by the mid-1920s, to their great alarm, evangelical fundamentalism was gaining political strength in some states with its demands for legislation to forbid the teaching of evolution in the public schools. In Tennessee in March 1925, the legislature adopted a measure making it illegal for any public school teacher "to teach any theory that denies the story of the divine creation of man as taught in the Bible."

The Tennessee law attracted the attention of the fledgling American Civil Liberties Union, which had been founded in 1920 by men and women alarmed by the repressive legal and social climate of the war and its aftermath. The ACLU offered free counsel to any Tennessee educator willing to defy the law and become the defendant in a test case. A twenty-four-year-old biology teacher in the town of Dayton, John T. Scopes, agreed to have himself arrested. And when the ACLU decided to send the famous attorney Clarence Darrow to defend Scopes, the aging William Jennings Bryan (now an

Scopes Monkey Trial

important fundamentalist spokesman) announced that he would travel to Dayton to assist the prosecution. Journalists from across the country flocked to Tennessee to cover what became known as the "Monkey Trial," which opened in an almost circuslike atmosphere. Scopes had, of course, clearly violated the law; and a verdict of guilty was a foregone conclusion, especially when the judge refused to permit "expert" testimony by evolution scholars. Scopes was fined $100, and the case was ultimately dismissed in a higher court because of a technicality. Nevertheless, Darrow scored an important victory for the modernists by calling Bryan himself to the stand to testify as an "expert on the Bible." In the course of the cross-examination, which was broadcast by radio to much of the nation, Darrow made Bryan's stubborn defense of biblical truths appear foolish and finally tricked him into admitting the possibility that not all religious dogma was subject to only one interpretation.

The Scopes trial was a traumatic experience for many fundamentalists. It isolated and ultimately excluded them from many mainstream Protestant denominations. It helped put an end to much of their political activism. But it did not change their religious convictions. Even without connection to traditional denominations, fundamentalists continued to congregate in independent churches or new denominations of their own.

The Democrats' Ordeal

The anguish of provincial Americans attempting to defend an embattled way of life proved particularly troubling to the Democratic Party, which suffered during the 1920s as a result of tensions between its urban and rural factions. More than the Republicans, the Democrats were a diverse coalition of interest groups, linked to the party by local tradition. Among those interest groups were prohibitionists, Klansmen, and fundamentalists on one side and Catholics, urban workers, and immigrants on the other.

In 1924, the tensions between them proved devastating. At the Democratic National Convention in New York that summer, bitter conflict broke out over the platform when the party's urban wing attempted to win approval of planks calling for the repeal of prohibition and a denunciation of the Klan. Both planks narrowly failed. More damaging to the party was a deadlock in the balloting for a presidential candidate. Urban Democrats supported Alfred E. Smith, the Irish Catholic Tammanyite who had risen to become a progressive governor of New York. Rural Democrats backed William McAdoo, Woodrow Wilson's Treasury secretary (and son-in-law), later to become a senator from California; he had skillfully positioned himself to win the support of southern and western delegates suspicious of Tammany Hall and modern urban life. The convention

dragged on for 103 ballots, until finally, after both Smith and McAdoo withdrew, the party settled on a compromise: the bland corporate lawyer John W. Davis, who had served as solicitor general and ambassador to Britain under Wilson. He was easily defeated by President Calvin Coolidge.

A similar schism plagued the Democrats again in 1928, when Al Smith finally secured his party's nomination for president after a much shorter battle. Smith was not, however, able to unite his divided party—largely because of widespread anti-Catholic sentiment, especially in the South. He was the first Democrat since the Civil War not to carry the entire South. Elsewhere, although he did well in the large cities, he carried no states at all except Massachusetts and Rhode Island. Smith's opponent, and the victor in the presidential election, was a man who perhaps more than any other contemporary politician seemed to personify the modern, prosperous, middle-class society of the New Era: Herbert Hoover.

Al Smith

REPUBLICAN GOVERNMENT

For twelve years, beginning in 1921, both the presidency and the Congress rested securely in the hands of the Republican Party—a party in which the power of reformers had greatly dwindled since the heyday of progressivism before the war. For most of those years, the federal government enjoyed a warm and supportive relationship with the American business community. Yet the government of the New Era was more than the passive, pliant instrument that critics often described. It also attempted to serve as an active agent of economic change.

Harding and Coolidge

Nothing seemed more clearly to illustrate the unadventurous character of 1920s politics than the characters of the two men who served as president during most of the decade: Warren G. Harding and Calvin Coolidge.

Harding was elected to the presidency in 1920, having spent many years in public life doing little of note. An undistinguished senator from Ohio, he had received the Republican presidential nomination as a result of an agreement among leaders of his party, who considered him, as one noted, a "good second-rater." Harding appointed capable men to the most important cabinet offices, and he attempted to stabilize the nation's troubled foreign policy. But even as he attempted to rise to his office, he seemed baffled by his responsibilities, as if he recognized his own unfitness. "I am a man of limited talents from a small town," he reportedly told friends on one occasion. "I don't

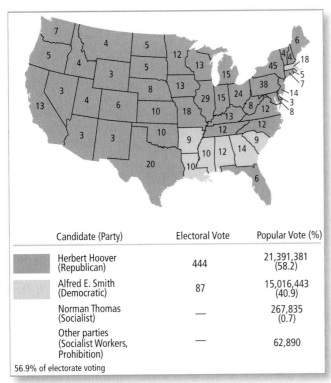

Candidate (Party)	Electoral Vote	Popular Vote (%)
Herbert Hoover (Republican)	444	21,391,381 (58.2)
Alfred E. Smith (Democratic)	87	15,016,443 (40.9)
Norman Thomas (Socialist)	—	267,835 (0.7)
Other parties (Socialist Workers, Prohibition)	—	62,890

56.9% of electorate voting

ELECTION OF 1928 The election of 1928 was, by almost any measure, highly one-sided. Herbert Hoover won over 58 percent of the vote to Alfred Smith's 41. Smith carried only Massachusetts, Rhode Island, and some traditionally Democratic states in the South. ◆ *Why did Smith do so poorly even in some of the South?*

For an interactive version of this map, go to www.mhhe.com/brinkley13ech22maps

seem to grasp that I am President." Harding's intellectual limits were compounded by personal weaknesses: his penchant for gambling, illegal alcohol, and attractive women.

Harding lacked the strength to abandon the party hacks who had helped create his political success. One of them, Harry Daugherty, the Ohio party boss principally responsible for his meteoric political ascent, he appointed attorney general. Another, New Mexico senator Albert B. Fall, he made secretary of the interior. Members of the so-called Ohio Gang filled important offices throughout the administration. Unknown to the public (and perhaps also to Harding), Daugherty, Fall, and others were engaged in fraud and corruption. The most spectacular scandal involved the rich naval oil reserves at Teapot Dome, Wyoming, and Elk Hills, California. At the urging of Fall, Harding transferred control of those reserves from the Navy Department to the Interior Department. Fall then secretly leased them to two wealthy businessmen and received in return nearly half a million dollars in "loans" to ease his private financial troubles. Fall was ultimately convicted of bribery and sentenced to a year in prison; Harry Daugherty barely avoided a similar fate for his part in another scandal.

Teapot Dome

In the summer of 1923, only months before Senate investigations and press revelations brought the scandals to light, a tired and depressed Harding left Washington for a speaking tour in the West. In Seattle late in July, he suffered severe pain, which his doctors wrongly diagnosed as food poisoning. A few days later, in San Francisco, he suffered two major heart attacks and died.

In many ways, Calvin Coolidge, who succeeded Harding in the presidency, was utterly different from his predecessor. Where Harding was genial, garrulous, and debauched, Coolidge was dour, silent, even puritanical. And while Harding was, if not perhaps personally corrupt, then at least tolerant of corruption in others, Coolidge seemed honest beyond reproach. In other ways, however, Harding and Coolidge were similar figures. Both took an essentially passive approach to their office.

Calvin Coolidge

Like Harding, Coolidge had risen to the presidency on the basis of few substantive accomplishments. Elected governor of Massachusetts in 1919, he had won national attention with his laconic response to the Boston police strike that year. That was enough to make him his party's vice presidential nominee in 1920. Three years later, after Harding's death, he took the oath of office from his father, a justice of the peace, by the light of a kerosene lamp.

If anything, Coolidge was even less active as president than Harding, partly as a result of his conviction that government should interfere as little as possible in the life of the nation. In 1924, he received his party's presidential nomination virtually unopposed. Running against John W. Davis, he won a comfortable victory: 54 percent of the popular vote and 382 of the 531 electoral votes. Robert La Follette, the candidate of the reincarnated Progressive Party, received 16 percent of the popular vote but carried only his home state of Wisconsin. Coolidge probably could have won renomination and reelection in 1928. Instead, in characteristically laconic fashion, he walked into a press room one day and handed each reporter a slip of paper containing a single sentence: "I do not choose to run for president in 1928."

HARDING AND FRIENDS President Warren G. Harding (center left, holding a rod) poses with companions during a fishing trip to Miami in 1921. He enjoyed these social and sporting events with wealthy friends and political cronies. Two of his companions here, Attorney General Harry Daugherty (to the left of Harding) and Interior Secretary Albert Fall (at far right) were later principal figures in the scandals that rocked the administration before and after Harding's death. *(Bettmann/Corbis)*

CALVIN COOLIDGE AT LEISURE Coolidge was a silent man of simple tastes. But he was not really an outdoorsman, despite his efforts to appear so. He is shown here fishing in Simsbury, Connecticut, carefully attired in suit, tie, hat, and rubber boots. *(Bettmann/ Corbis)*

Government and Business

The story of Harding and Coolidge themselves, however, is only a part—and by no means the most important part—of the story of their administrations. However passive the New Era presidents may have been, much of the federal government was working effectively and efficiently during the 1920s to adapt public policy to the widely accepted goal of the time: helping business and industry operate with maximum efficiency and productivity. The close relationship between the private sector and the federal government that had been forged during World War I continued. Secretary of the Treasury Andrew Mellon, a wealthy steel and aluminum tycoon, devoted himself to working for substantial reductions in taxes on corporate profits, personal incomes, and inheritances. Largely because of his efforts, Congress cut them all by more than half. Mellon also worked closely with President Coolidge after 1924 on a series of measures to trim dramatically the already modest federal budget. The administration even managed to retire half the nation's World War I debt.

Andrew Mellon

The most prominent member of the cabinet was Commerce Secretary Herbert Hoover, who considered himself, and was considered by others, a notable progressive. During his eight years in the Commerce Department, Hoover encouraged voluntary cooperation in the private sector as the best avenue to stability. But the idea of voluntarism did not require that the government remain passive; on the contrary, public institutions, Hoover believed, should play an active role in creating the new, cooperative order. Above all, Hoover became the champion of the concept of business "associationalism"—a concept that envisioned the creation of national organizations of businessmen in particular industries. Through these trade associations, private entrepreneurs could, Hoover believed, stabilize their industries and promote efficiency in production and marketing.

Hoover's "Associationalism"

Some progressives derived encouragement from the election of Herbert Hoover to the presidency in 1928. Hoover easily defeated Al Smith, the Democratic candidate. And he entered office promising bold new efforts to solve the nation's remaining economic problems. But Hoover had few opportunities to prove himself. Less than a year after his inauguration, the nation plunged into the severest and most prolonged economic crisis in its history—a crisis that brought many of the optimistic assumptions of the New Era crashing down and launched the nation into a period of unprecedented social innovation and reform.

CONCLUSION

The remarkable prosperity of the 1920s—a prosperity without parallel in the previous history of the United States—shaped much of what exuberant contemporaries liked to call the "New Era." In the years after World War I, America created a vibrant and extensive national culture. Its middle class moved increasingly to embrace consumerism. Its politics reorganized itself around the needs of a booming, interdependent industrial economy—rejecting many of the reform crusades of the previous generation, but also creating new institutions to help promote economic growth and stability.

Beneath the glittering surface of the New Era, however, were roiling controversies and timeless injustices clamoring for redress. Although the prosperity of the 1920s was more widely shared than at any other time in the nation's industrial history, more than half the population failed to achieve any real benefits from the growth. A new, optimistic, secular culture was attracting millions of urban, middle-class people. But many other Americans looked at this culture with alarm and fought against it with great fervor. Few eras in modern American history have seen so much political and cultural conflict.

The 1920s ended in a catastrophic economic crash that has colored the image of those years ever since. The crises of the 1930s should not obscure the real achievements of the New Era economy. Neither, however, should the prosperity of the 1920s obscure the inequity and instability in those years that helped produce the difficult years to come.

INTERACTIVE LEARNING

The *Primary Source Investigator CD-ROM* offers the following materials related to this chapter:

- Interactive maps: **Breakdown of Rural Isolation** (M22); **Areas of Population Growth** (M25); and **U.S. Elections** (M7).

- Documents, images, and maps related to America in the 1920s. Some highlights include a text excerpt from the Ku Klux Klan's Constitution and a speech by their former leader, Hiram Wesley Evans; images showing the fashions of the "flapper"; and images of the new women of the 1920s.

Online Learning Center (www.mhhe.com/brinkley13e)

For quizzes, Internet resources, references to additional books and films, and more, consult this book's Online Learning Center.

FOR FURTHER REFERENCE

Frederick Lewis Allen, *Only Yesterday* (1931) is a classic popular history of the 1920s. Michael Parrish, *Anxious Decades: America in Prosperity and Depression, 1920-1941* (1992) is a good survey. Ellis Hawley, *The Great War and the Search for a Modern Order* (1979) describes the effect of World War I on American ideas, culture, and society. William E. Leuchtenburg, *The Perils of Prosperity* (rev. ed. 1994) reveals the class divisions and culture dislocation that accompanied economic prosperity in the 1920s. David Brody, *Workers in Industrial America* (1980) includes important essays on welfare capitalism and other labor systems of the 1920s. T. J. Jackson Lears, *Fables of Abundance: A Cultural History of Advertising in America* (1994) and Roland Marchand, *Advertising the American Dream* (1985) are valuable inquiries into the role of advertising in the new consumer culture. James J. Flink, *The Car Culture* (1975) examines ways in which the automobile transformed American life. David Farber, *Sloan Rules: Alfred P. Sloan and the Triumph of General Motors* (2002) describes the consolidation of the giant automobile corporation. Susan Smulyan, *Selling Radio: The Commercialization of American Broadcasting, 1920-1934* (1994) chronicles the emergence of commercial radio. Robert Lynd and Helen Merrell Lynd, *Middletown* (1929) is a classic sociological study of how an American city encountered the consumer culture and economy of the 1920s. Ann Douglas's *Terrible Honesty: Mongrel Manhattan in the 1920s* (1995) examines the cultural and political history of the New Era in New York City. Lynn Dumenil, *The Modern Temper: America in the 1920s* (1995) examines the reactions of Americans to modern culture. George Chauncey, *Gay New York: Gender, Urban Culture, and the Making of the Gay Male World, 1890-1940* (1994) is an excellent work in a relatively new field of history. The decline of the feminist movement in the 1920s is explored in Nancy Cott, *The Grounding of American Feminism* (1987). Gary Gerstle, *American Crucible* (2000) is an important study of the changing role of race and ethnicity in defining American nationhood in the twentieth century. Nathan I. Huggins chronicles the cultural and political efflorescence of black Harlem during these years in *Harlem Renaissance* (1971). George Marsden, *Fundamentalism and American Culture* (1980) is a good study of some of the religious battles that came to a head in the 1920s. Edward J. Larson, *Summer for the Gods: The Scopes Trial and America's Continuing Debate over Science and Religion* (1997) is a valuable analysis of the Scopes Trial. Leonard Moore, *Citizen Klansmen: The Ku Klux Klan in Indiana, 1921-1928* (1991) is a challenging view of the Klan. Kathleen M. Blee, *Women and the Klan: Racism and Gender in the 1920s* (1991) re-creates the female world of the Klan. Michael Lerner, *Dry Manhattan: Prohibition in New York City* (2007) describes the impact of the Eighteenth Amendment. Kevin Boyle, *Arc of Justice: A Saga of Race, Civil Rights, and Murder in the Jazz Age* (2004) is a revealing portrait of New Era racial norms. David Burner, *The Politics of Provincialism* (1967) is a good study of the ordeal of the Democratic Party in the 1920s. Morton Keller, *Regulating a New Economy: Public Policy and Economic Change in America, 1900-1933* (1990) and *Regulating a New Society: Public Policy and Social Change in America, 1900-1933* (1994) are important studies of New Era public policy.

Coney Island (1990) is a documentary film re-creating the drama and fantasy of Coney Island. *That Rhythm, Those Blues* (1997) is a film documenting the one-night stands, makeshift housing, and poor transportation that were all a step toward the big time at the famed Apollo Theatre on Harlem's 125th Street. *Mr. Sears' Catalogue* (1997) is a film exploring how the Sears catalog became a symbol for the ambitions and dreams of a sprawling, fast-developing America.

CHAPTER 23

THE GREAT DEPRESSION

DETAIL FROM *PRIVATE CAR* (1932), BY LECONTE STEWART   Thousands of men (and some women) left their homes during the Great Depression and traveled from city to city looking for work, often hopping freight trains for a free, if illegal, ride. *(Museum of Church History & Art, Salt Lake City, Utah)*

N AUGUST 1928, NOT LONG before his election to the presidency, Herbert Hoover proclaimed: "We in America today are nearer to the final triumph over poverty than ever before in the history of any land. The poorhouse is vanishing from among us." Only fifteen months later those words would return to haunt him, as the nation plunged into the severest and most prolonged economic depression in its history—a depression that continued in one form or another for more than a decade, not only in the United States but throughout much of the rest of the world. The Depression was a traumatic experience for individual Americans, who faced unemployment, the loss of land and other property, and in some cases homelessness and starvation. It also placed great strains on the political and social fabric of the nation.

The Depression reached into every area of economic life, and thus into every area of social life as well. It destroyed the great "bull market" of the 1920s and sent stock prices into a long and steep decline from which they did not recover for years. It halted the great wave of investment in industrial plants and infrastructure that had done so much to fuel economic growth before the crash. It jeopardized the health of the national banking system. But most of all, it created massive unemployment—which rose at some points to nearly 25 percent of the work force and never fell much below 15 percent at any time between 1930 and 1941. This massive and persistent unemployment was the most visible and, to many, most frightening aspect of the Depression. It did not affect only those without jobs. It also depressed the wages of those still employed. And it created fear among almost all Americans about their own economic security.

In the midst of this crisis, Herbert Hoover used the tools of the federal government more aggressively and creatively than any president had ever used them before to address economic problems. But however much he did, it was not enough to stem the great tide of the Depression. And there were many steps that Hoover refused to consider because he believed they would violate basic principles of American life—most notably the rights and responsibilities of individuals. These values had been greatly admired through most of American history, but the crisis of the Depression called them into question, undermined Hoover's reputation, and contributed eventually to a major shift in the character of American politics.

SIGNIFICANT EVENTS

1929 ▶ Stock market crash signals onset of Great Depression
     ▶ Agricultural Marketing Act passed
1930 ▶ Hawley-Smoot Tariff enacted
     ▶ Ten-year drought begins in South and Midwest (the Dust Bowl)
     ▶ White workers in Atlanta organize Black Shirts to fight African-American competition for jobs
     ▶ Nisei form Japanese-American Citizens League
     ▶ John Dos Passos publishes *U.S.A.* trilogy
1931 ▶ Federal Reserve raises interest rates
     ▶ Depression spreads to Europe and deepens in United States
     ▶ Scottsboro defendants arrested
     ▶ Communist Party stages hunger march in Washington, D.C.
1932 ▶ Erskine Caldwell publishes *Tobacco Road*
     ▶ Reconstruction Finance Corporation established
     ▶ Farmers' Holiday Association formed in Iowa
     ▶ Bonus marchers come to Washington, D.C.
     ▶ Banking crisis begins
     ▶ Franklin D. Roosevelt elected president
1933 ▶ Franklin Roosevelt inaugurated; New Deal begins (see Chapter 24)
1934 ▶ Southern Tenant Farmers Union organized
1935 ▶ American Communist Party proclaims Popular Front
1936 ▶ Dale Carnegie publishes *How to Win Friends and Influence People*
     ▶ Margaret Mitchell publishes *Gone With the Wind*
     ▶ *Life* magazine begins publication
1939 ▶ John Steinbeck publishes *The Grapes of Wrath*
     ▶ Nazi-Soviet Pact weakens American Communist Party
1940 ▶ Richard Wright publishes *Native Son*
     ▶ Ernest Hemingway publishes *For Whom the Bell Tolls*
1941 ▶ James Agee and Walker Evans publish *Let Us Now Praise Famous Men*

THE COMING OF THE GREAT DEPRESSION

The sudden economic decline that began in 1929 came as an especially severe shock because it followed so closely a period in which the New Era seemed to be performing another series of economic miracles.

The Great Crash

In February 1928, stock prices began a steady rise that continued, with only a few temporary lapses, for a year and a half. Between May 1928 and September 1929, the average price of stocks increased over 40 percent. The stocks of the major industrials—the stocks that are used to determine the Dow Jones Industrial Average—doubled in value in that same period. Trading mushroomed from 2 or 3 million shares a day to over 5 million, and at times to as many as 10 or 12 million. There was, in short, a widespread speculative fever that grew steadily more intense, particularly once brokerage firms began encouraging the mania by recklessly offering easy credit.

Stock Market Boom

In the autumn of 1929, the great bull market began to fall apart. On October 21 and again on October 23, there were alarming declines in stock prices, in both cases followed by temporary recoveries (the second of them engineered by J. P. Morgan and Company and other big bankers, who conspicuously bought up stocks to restore public confidence). But on October 29, "Black Tuesday," all efforts to save the market failed. Sixteen million shares of stock were traded; the industrial index dropped 43 points; stocks in many companies became worthless. The market remained deeply depressed for more than four years and did not fully recover for over a decade.

"Black Tuesday"

Many people believed that the stock market crash was the beginning, and even the cause, of the Great Depres-

sion. But although October 1929 might have been the first visible sign of the crisis, the Depression had earlier beginnings and more important causes.

Causes of the Depression

Economists, historians, and others have argued for decades about the causes of the Great Depression without reaching any consensus. But most agree on several things. They agree, first, that what is remarkable about the crisis is not that it occurred; periodic recessions are a normal feature of capitalist economies. What is remarkable is that it was so severe and that it lasted so long. The important question, therefore, is not so much why there was a depression, but why it was such a bad one. Most observers agree, too, that a number of different factors account for the severity of the crisis, even if there is considerable disagreement about which was the most important.

One of those factors was a lack of diversification in the American economy in the 1920s. Prosperity had depended excessively on a few basic industries, notably construction and automobiles. In the late 1920s, those industries began to decline. Expenditures on construction fell from $11 billion to less than $9 billion between 1926 and 1929. Automobile sales fell by more than a third in the first nine months of 1929. Newer industries were emerging to take up the slack—among them petroleum, chemicals, plastics, and others oriented toward the expanding market for consumer goods—but had not yet developed enough strength to compensate for the decline in other sectors.

Lack of Diversification

A second important factor was the maldistribution of purchasing power and, as a result, a weakness in consumer demand. As industrial and agricultural production increased, the proportion of the profits going to farmers, workers, and other potential consumers was too small to create an adequate market for the goods

Maldistribution of Wealth

AFTERMATH OF THE CRASH Walter Thornton, shown here in October 1929 next to an expensive roadster he had bought not long before, was one of the affluent Americans who suffered substantial losses in the crash of the stock market in the fall of 1929. In popular mythology, many such people committed suicide in despair. In reality, very few people did. Much more common were efforts such as this to sell off assets to make up for the losses. Thornton was more fortunate than many victims of the Depression. Most had few assets to sell. *(Bettmann/Corbis)*

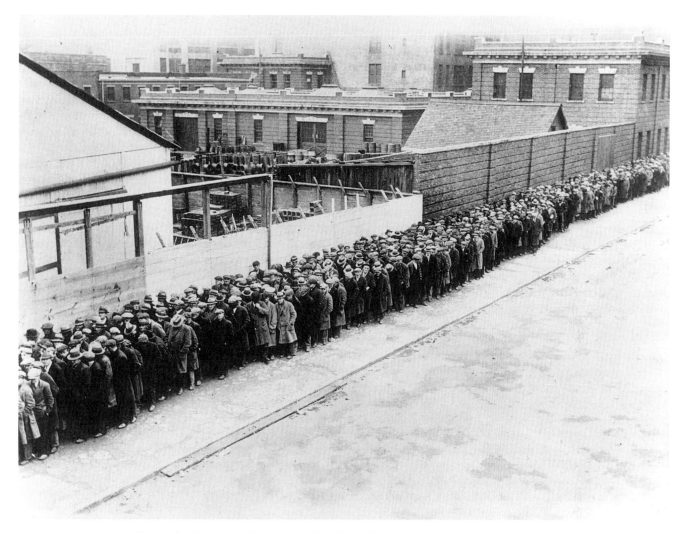

THE UNEMPLOYED, 1930 Thousands of unemployed men wait to be fed outside the Municipal Lodgers House in New York City. *(Library of Congress)*

the economy was producing. Demand was not keeping up with supply. Even in 1929, after nearly a decade of economic growth, more than half the families in America lived on the edge of or below the minimum subsistence level—too poor to buy the goods the industrial economy was producing.

As long as corporations had continued to expand their capital facilities (factories, warehouses, heavy equipment, and other investments), the economy had flourished. By 1929, however, capital investment had created more plant space than could profitably be used, and factories were producing more goods than consumers could purchase. Industries that were experiencing declining demand (construction, autos, coal, and others) began laying off workers, depleting mass purchasing power further. Even expanding industries often reduced their work forces because of new, less labor-intensive technologies; and in the sluggish economic atmosphere of 1929 and beyond, such workers had difficulty finding employment elsewhere.

A third major problem was the credit structure of the economy. Farmers were deeply in debt—their land mort-

gaged, crop prices too low to allow them to pay off what they owed. Small banks, especially those tied to the agricultural economy, were in constant trouble in the 1920s as their customers defaulted on loans; many of these small banks failed. Large banks were in trouble, too. Although most American bankers were very conservative, some of the nation's biggest banks were investing recklessly in the stock market or making unwise loans. When the stock market crashed, many of these banks suffered losses greater than they could absorb.

A fourth factor contributing to the coming of the Depression was America's position in international trade. Late in the 1920s, European demand for American goods began to decline. That was partly because European industry and agriculture were becoming more productive, and partly because some European nations (most notably Germany, under the Weimar Republic) were having financial difficulties and could not afford to buy goods from overseas. But it was also because the European economy was being destabilized by, a fifth factor contributing to

Declining Exports

CAUSES OF THE GREAT DEPRESSION

What were the causes of the Great Depression? Economists and historians have debated this question since the economic collapse began and still have not reached anything close to agreement on an answer to it. In the process, however, they have produced several very different theories about how a modern economy works.

During the Depression itself, different groups offered interpretations of the crisis that fit comfortably with their own self-interests and ideologies. Some corporate leaders claimed that the Depression was the result of a lack of "business confidence," that businessmen were reluctant to invest because they feared government regulation and high taxes. The Hoover administration, unable to solve the crisis with the tools it considered acceptable, blamed international economic forces and sought, therefore, to stabilize world currencies and debt structures. New Dealers, determined to find a domestic solution to the crisis and ideologically inclined to place limits on corporate power, argued that the Depression was a crisis of "underconsumption," that low wages and high prices had made it too difficult to buy the products of the industrial economy; and that a lack of demand had led to the economic collapse. Other groups offered equally self-serving explanations.

Scholars in the years since the Great Depression have also created interpretations that fit their views of how the economy works and which public policies are appropriate for it. One of the first important postwar interpretations came from the economists Milton Friedman and Anna Schwartz, in their *Monetary History of the United States* (1963).

(Library of Congress)

the Depression, the international debt structure that had emerged in the aftermath of World War I.

When the war came to an end in 1918, all the European nations that had been allied with the United States owed large sums of money to American banks, sums much too large to be repaid out of their shattered economies. That was one reason why the Allies had insisted (over Woodrow Wilson's objections) on reparation payments from Germany and Austria. Reparations, they believed, would provide them with a way to pay off their own debts. But Germany and Austria were themselves in economic trouble after the war; they were no more able to pay the reparations than the Allies were able to pay their debts.

Unstable International Debt Structure

The American government refused to forgive or reduce the debts. Instead, American banks began making large loans to European governments, with which they paid off their earlier loans. Thus debts (and reparations) were being paid only by piling up new and greater debts. In the late 1920s, and particularly after the American economy began to weaken in 1929, the European nations found it much more difficult to borrow money from the United States. At the same time, high American protective tariffs were making it difficult for them to sell their goods in American markets. Without any source of foreign exchange with which to repay their loans, they began to default. The collapse of the international credit structure was one of the reasons the Depression spread to Europe (and grew much worse in America) after 1931. (See "America in the World," p. 665.)

Progress of the Depression

The stock market crash of 1929 did not so much cause the Depression, then, as help trigger a chain of events that exposed longstanding weaknesses in the American economy. During the next three years, the crisis steadily worsened.

A collapse of much of the banking system followed the stock market crash. More than 9,000 American banks

In a chapter titled "The Great Contraction," they argued for what has become known as the "monetary" interpretation. The Depression, they claimed, was a result of a drastic contraction of the currency (a result of mistaken decisions by the Federal Reserve Board, which raised interest rates when it should have lowered them). These deflationary measures turned an ordinary recession into the Great Depression. The monetary argument fits comfortably with the ideas that Milton Friedman, in particular, advocated for many years: that sound monetary policy is the best way to solve economic problems—as opposed to fiscal policies, such as taxation and spending.

A second, very different argument, known as the "spending" interpretation, is identified with, among others, the economist Peter Temin, and his book *Did Monetary Forces Cause the Great Depression?* (1976). Temin's answer to his own question is "no." The cause of the crisis was not monetary contraction (although the contraction made it worse), but a drop in investment and consumer spending, which preceded the decline in the money supply and helped to cause it. Here again, there are obvious political implications. If a decline in spending was the cause of the Depression, then the proper response was an effort to stimulate demand—raising government spending, increasing purchasing power, redistributing wealth. According to this theory, the New Deal never ended the Depression because it did not spend enough. World War II did end it because it pumped so much public money into the economy. This is a liberal, Keynesian explanation, just as the "monetary hypothesis" is a conservative explanation.

Another important explanation comes from the historian Michael Bernstein. In *The Great Depression* (1987), he avoids trying to explain why the economic downturn occurred and asks, instead, why it lasted so long. The reason the recession of 1929 became the Depression of the 1930s, he argues, was the timing of the collapse. The recession began as an ordinary cyclical downturn. Had it begun a few years earlier, the basic strength of the automobile and construction industries in the 1920s would have led to a reasonably speedy recovery. Had it begun a few years later, a group of newer, emerging industries would have helped produce a recovery in a reasonably short time. But the recession began in 1929, too late for the automobile and construction industries to help (since they had already experienced a serious, long-term relative decline) and too soon for emerging new industries—aviation, petrochemicals and plastics, aluminum, electronics and electrical appliances, processed foods, and others—to help, since they were still in their infancies.

The political implications of this argument are less obvious than those for some other interpretations. But one possible conclusion is that if economic growth depends on the successful development of new industries to replace declining ones, then the most sensible economic policy for government is to target investment and other policies toward the growth of new economic sectors. One of the reasons World War II was so important to the long-term recovery of the U.S. economy, Bernstein's argument suggests, was not just that it pumped money into the economy, but that much of that money contributed to developing new industries that would help sustain prosperity after the war. This is, in other words, an explanation of the Depression that seems to support some of the economic ideas that became popular in the 1970s and 1980s calling for a more direct government role in stimulating the growth of new industries.

In the end, however, no single explanation of the Great Depression has ever seemed adequate to most scholars. The event, the economist Robert Lucas once argued, is simply "inexplicable" by any rational calculation.

---

either went bankrupt or closed their doors to avoid bankruptcy between 1930 and 1933. Depositors lost over $2.5 billion in deposits. Partly as a result of these banking closures, the total money supply of the nation

Banking Collapse

fell by more than a third between 1930 and 1933. The declining money supply meant a decline in purchasing power, and thus deflation. Manufacturers and merchants began reducing prices, cutting back on production, and laying off workers. Some economists argue that a severe depression could have been avoided if the Federal Reserve system had acted more responsibly. But the members of the Federal Reserve Board, concerned about protecting its own solvency in a dangerous economic environment, raised interest rates in 1931, which contracted the money supply even further.

The American gross national product plummeted

Severe Contraction

from more than $104 billion in 1929 to $76.4 billion in 1932—a 25 percent decline in three years. In 1929, Americans had spent $16.2 billion in capital investment; in 1933, they invested only a third of a billion. The consumer price index declined 25 percent between 1929 and 1933, the wholesale price index 32 percent. Gross farm income dropped from $12 billion to $5 billion in four years.

THE AMERICAN PEOPLE IN HARD TIMES

Someone asked the British economist John Maynard Keynes in the 1930s whether he was aware of any historical era comparable to the Great Depression. "Yes," Keynes replied. "It was called the Dark Ages, and it lasted 400 years." The Depression did not last 400 years, but it did bring unprecedented despair to the economies of the United States and much of the Western world. And it had far-reaching effects on American society and culture.

Unemployment and Relief

In the industrial Northeast and Midwest, cities were becoming paralyzed by unemployment. Cleveland, Ohio, in 1932 had an unemployment rate of 50 percent; Akron, 60 percent; Toledo, 80 percent. Many industrial workers were accustomed to periods of unemployment, but no one was prepared for the scale and duration of the joblessness of the 1930s.

Most Americans had been taught to believe that every individual was responsible for his or her own fate, that unemployment and poverty were signs of personal failure. Many adult men, in particular, felt deeply ashamed of their joblessness; the helplessness of unemployment was a challenge to traditional notions of masculinity. Unemployed workers walked through the streets day after day looking for jobs that did not exist.

Belief in Personal Responsibility

An increasing number of families were turning to state and local public relief systems, just to be able to eat. But those systems, which in the 1920s had served only a small number of indigents, were totally unequipped to handle the new demands. In many places, relief simply collapsed. Private charities attempted to supplement the public relief efforts, but the problem was far beyond their capabilities as well. State governments felt pressure to expand their own assistance to the unemployed; but tax revenues were declining along with everything else, and state leaders balked at placing additional strains on already tight budgets. Moreover, many public officials believed that an extensive welfare system would undermine the moral fiber of its clients.

Breadlines stretched for blocks outside Red Cross and Salvation Army kitchens. Thousands of people sifted through garbage cans for scraps of food or waited outside restaurant kitchens in hopes of receiving plate scrapings. Nearly 2 million men, most of them young (and a much smaller number of women), took to the roads, riding freight trains from city to city, living as nomads.

Farm income declined by 60 percent between 1929 and 1932. A third of all American farmers lost their land. In addition, a large area of agricultural settlement in the Great Plains of the South and West was suffering from a catastrophic natural disaster: one of the worst droughts in the history of the nation. Beginning in 1930, a large area of the nation, stretching north from Texas into the Dakotas, came to be known as the "Dust Bowl." It began to experience a steady decline in rainfall and an accompanying increase in heat. The drought continued for a decade, turning what

"Dust Bowl"

MIGRANT FAMILY Dorothea Lange, one of the great photographers of the twentieth century, worked in the 1930s for the photographic division of the Farm Security Administration (FSA). The FSA photographers sought to record the conditions of life in America's troubled agrarian world during the Great Depression in the hopes of stimulating reform. Lange's photograph here represents a family in transit as they, like thousands of others, moved from the Great Plains to California. *(Dorothea Lange/ Time Life Pictures/Getty Images)*

THE GLOBAL DEPRESSION

The Great Depression began in the United States. But it did not end there. The American economy was the largest in the world, and its collapse sent shock waves around the globe. By 1931, the American depression had become a world depression, with important implications for the course of global history.

The origins of the worldwide depression lay in the pattern of debts that had emerged during and after World War I, when the United States loaned billions of dollars to European nations. In 1931, with American banks staggering and in many cases collapsing, large banks in New York began desperately calling in their loans from Germany and Austria. That precipitated the failure of one of Austria's largest banks, which in turn created panic through much of central Europe. The economic collapse in Germany and Austria meant that those nations could not continue paying reparations to Britain and France (required by the Treaty of Versailles of 1919), which meant in turn that Britain and France could not continue paying off their loans to the United States.

This spreading financial crisis was accompanied by a dramatic contraction of international trade, precipitated in part by the Smoot-Hawley Tariff in the United States, which established the highest import duties in history and stifled much global commerce. Depressed agricultural prices—a result of worldwide overproduction—also contributed to the downturn. By 1932, worldwide industrial production had declined by more than a third, and world trade had plummeted by nearly two-thirds. By 1933, thirty million people in industrial nations were unemployed, five times the number four years before.

But the Depression was not confined to industrial nations. Imperialism and industrialization had drawn almost all regions of the world into the international industrial economy. Colonies and nations in Africa, Asia, and South America—critically dependent on exporting raw materials and agricultural goods to industrial countries—experienced a decline in demand for their products, which led to rising

LOOKING FOR WORK IN LONDON, 1935 An unemployed London man wears a sign that seems designed to convince passersby that he is an educated, respectable person despite his present circumstances. *(Getty Images)*

levels of poverty and unemployment. Some nations—among them the Soviet Union and China—remained relatively unconnected to the global economy and suffered relatively little from the Great Depression. But in most parts of the world, the Depression caused tremendous social and economic hardship.

It also created political turmoil. Among the countries hardest hit by the Depression was Germany, where industrial production declined by 50 percent and unemployment reached 35 percent in the early 1930s. The desperate economic conditions there contributed greatly to the rise of the Nazi Party and its leader Adolf Hitler, who became chancellor in 1932. Japan suffered greatly as well, dependent as it was on world trade to sustain its growing industrial economy and purchase essential commodities for its needs at home. And in Japan, as in Germany, economic troubles produced political turmoil and aided the rise of a new militaristic regime. In Italy, the fascist government of Benito Mussolini, which had first taken power in the 1920s, also saw militarization and territorial expansion as a way out of economic difficulties.

In other nations, governments sought solutions to the Depression through reform of their domestic economies. The most prominent example of that was the New Deal in the United States. But there were important experiments in other nations as well. Among the most common responses to the Depression around the world was substantial government investment in public works. In the United States, Britain, France, Germany, Italy, the Soviet Union, and other countries, there was substantial investment in roads, bridges, dams, public buildings, and other large projects. Another response was the expansion of government-funded relief for the unemployed. All the industrial countries of the world experimented with some form of relief, often borrowing ideas from one another in the process.

In addition, the Depression helped create new approaches to economics, in the face of the apparent failure of classical models of economic behavior to explain, or provide solutions to, the crisis. The great British economist John Maynard Keynes revolutionized economic thought in much of the world. His 1936 book *The General Theory of Employment, Interest, and Money,* despite its bland title, created a sensation by arguing that the Depression was a result not of declining production, but of inadequate consumer demand. Governments, he said, could stimulate their economies by increasing the money supply and creating investment—through a combination of lowering interest rates and public spending. Keynesianism, as Keynes's theories became known, began to have an impact in the United States in 1938, and in much of the rest of the world in subsequent years.

The Great Depression was an important turning point not only in American history, but in the history of the twentieth-century world as well. It transformed ideas of public policy and economics in many nations. It toppled old regimes and created new ones. And perhaps above all, it was a major factor—maybe the single most important factor—in the coming of World War II.

DUST STORM, SOUTHWEST PLAINS, 1937   The dust storms of the 1930s were a terrifying experience for all who lived through them. Resembling a black wall sweeping in from the western horizon, such a storm engulfed farms and towns alike, blotting out the light of the sun and covering everything with fine dirt.   *(Bettmann/Corbis)*

had once been fertile farm regions into deserts. In Kansas, the soil in some places was without moisture as far as three feet below the surface. In Nebraska, Iowa, and other states, summer temperatures were averaging over 100 degrees. Swarms of grasshoppers were moving from region to region, devouring what meager crops farmers were able to raise, often even devouring fenceposts or clothes hanging out to dry. Great dust storms—"black blizzards," as they were called—swept across the plains, blotting out the sun and suffocating livestock as well as people unfortunate or foolish enough to stay outside.

Even with these disastrous conditions, the farm economy continued through the 1930s to produce far more food than American consumers could afford to buy. Farm prices fell so low that few growers made any profit at all on their crops. As a result, many farmers, like many urban unemployed, left their homes in search of work. In the South, in particular, many dispossessed farmers—black and white—wandered from town to town, hoping to find jobs or handouts. Hundreds of thousands of families from the Dust Bowl (often known as "Okies," since many came from Oklahoma) traveled to California and other states, where they found conditions little better than those they had left. Many worked as agricultural migrants, traveling from farm to farm picking fruit and other crops at starvation wages.

"Okies"

Throughout the nation, problems of malnutrition and homelessness grew at an alarming rate. Hospitals pointed to a striking increase in deaths from starvation. On the outskirts of cities, families lived in makeshift shacks constructed of flattened tin cans, scraps of wood, abandoned crates, and other debris. Many homeless Americans simply kept moving—sleeping in freight cars, in city parks, in subways, or in unused sewer ducts.

African Americans and the Depression

As the Depression began, over half of all black Americans still lived in the South. Most were farmers. The collapse of prices for cotton and other staple crops left some with no income at all. Many left the land altogether—either by choice or forced by landlords who no longer found the sharecropping system profitable. Some migrated to southern cities. But unemployed whites in the urban South believed they had first claim to all work and began to take positions as janitors, street cleaners, and domestic servants, displacing the African Americans who formerly had occupied such jobs.

African-American Suffering

As the Depression deepened, whites in many southern cities began to demand that all blacks be dismissed from their jobs. In Atlanta in 1930, an organization calling itself the Black Shirts organized a campaign with the slogan "No Jobs for Niggers Until Every White Man Has a Job!" In other areas, whites used intimidation and violence to drive blacks from jobs. By 1932, over half the African Americans in the South were without employment. And what limited relief there was went almost invariably to whites first.

Unsurprisingly, therefore, many black southerners—perhaps 400,000 in all—left the South in the 1930s and journeyed to the cities of the North. There they generally found less blatant discrimination. But conditions were in most respects little better than in the South. In New York, black unemployment was nearly 50 percent. In other

BLACK MIGRANTS The Great Migration of blacks from the rural South into the cities had begun before World War I. But in the 1930s and 1940s the movement accelerated. Jacob Lawrence, an eminent African-American artist, created a series of paintings titled, collectively, *The Migration of the Negro,* to illustrate this major event in the history of African Americans. *(© The Jacob and Gwendolyn Lawrence Foundation, Seattle/Artists Rights Society, New York)*

cities, it was higher. Two million African Americans were on some form of relief by 1932.

Traditional patterns of segregation and disfranchisement in the South survived the Depression largely unchallenged. But a few particularly notorious examples of racism did attract national attention. The most celebrated was the Scottsboro case. In March 1931, nine black teenagers were taken off a freight train in Alabama (in a small town near Scottsboro) and arrested for vagrancy and disorder. Later, two white women who had also been riding the train accused them of rape. In fact, there was overwhelming evidence, medical and otherwise, that the women had not been raped at all; they may have made their accusations out of fear of being arrested themselves. Nevertheless, an all-white jury in Alabama quickly convicted all nine of the "Scottsboro boys" (as they were known to both friends and foes) and sentenced eight of them to death.

The Supreme Court overturned the convictions in 1932, and a series of new trials began that attracted increasing national attention. The International Labor Defense, an organization associated with the Communist Party, came to the aid of the accused youths and began to publicize the case. Later, the National Association for the Advancement of Colored People (NAACP) provided assistance as well. The trials continued throughout the 1930s. Although the white southern juries who sat on the case never acquitted any of the defendants, all of them eventually gained their freedom—four because the charges were dropped, four because of early paroles, and one because he escaped. But the last of the Scottsboro defendants did not leave prison until 1950.

The Depression was a time of important changes in the role and behavior of leading black organizations. The NAACP, for example, began to work diligently to win a position for blacks within the emerging labor movement, supporting the formation of the Congress of Industrial Organizations and helping to break down racial barriers within labor unions. Walter White, secretary of the NAACP, once made a personal appearance at an auto plant to implore blacks not to work as strikebreakers. Partly as a result of such efforts, more than half a million blacks were able to join the labor movement. In the Steelworkers Union, for example, African Americans constituted about 20 percent of the membership.

Mexican Americans in Depression America

Similar patterns of discrimination confronted the large and growing population of Mexicans and Mexican Americans, which numbered approximately 2 million in the 1930s.

Mexican Americans filled many of the same menial jobs in the West and elsewhere that blacks filled in other regions. Some farmed small, marginal tracts. Some became agricultural migrants, traveling from region to region harvesting fruit, lettuce, and other crops. But most lived in urban areas—in California, New Mexico, and Arizona, but also in Detroit, Chicago, New York, and other eastern industrial cities—and occupied the lower ranks of the unskilled labor force in such industries as steel, automobiles, and meatpacking.

As in the South, unemployed white Anglos in the Southwest demanded jobs held by Hispanics. Thus Mexican unemployment rose quickly to levels far higher than those for Anglos. Some Mexicans were, in effect, forced to leave the country by officials who arbitrarily removed them from relief rolls or simply rounded them up and transported them across the border. Perhaps half a million Chicanos left the United States for Mexico in the first years of the Depression. Most relief programs excluded Mexicans from their rolls or offered them benefits far below those available to whites. Hispanics generally had no access to American schools. Many hospitals refused them admission.

Discrimination Against Hispanics

Occasionally, there were signs of organized resistance by Mexican Americans themselves, most notably in California, where some formed a union of migrant farmworkers. But harsh repression by local growers and the public authorities allied with them prevented such organizations from having much impact. Like African-American farmworkers, many Mexicans began as a result to migrate to cities such as Los Angeles, where they lived in a poverty comparable to that of urban blacks in the South and Northeast.

Asian Americans in Hard Times

For Asian Americans, too, the Depression reinforced longstanding patterns of discrimination and economic marginalization. In California, where the largest Japanese-American and Chinese-American populations resided, even educated Asians had always found it difficult, if not impossible, to move into mainstream professions. Japanese-American college graduates often found themselves working at family fruit stands; 20 percent of all Nisei in Los Angeles worked at such stands at the end of the 1930s. For those who found jobs (usually poorly paid) in the industrial or service economy, employment was precarious; like blacks and Hispanics, they often lost jobs to white Americans desperate for work that a few years earlier they would not have

CHINATOWN, NEW YORK A Chinese man carries a "sandwich board" through the streets of New York's Chinatown bearing the latest news of the war between China and Japan, which in 1938 was already well under way. Chinese Americans had the dual challenge in the 1930s of dealing both with large-scale unemployment and with continuing news of catastrophe from China, where most still had many family members. *(Getty Images)*

considered. Japanese farmworkers, like Chicano farmworkers, suffered from the increasing competition for even these low-paying jobs from white migrants from the Great Plains.

In California, younger Nisei organized Japanese American Democratic Clubs in several cities, which worked for, among other things, laws protecting racial and ethnic minorities from discrimination. At the same time, some Japanese-American businessmen and professionals tried to overcome obstacles by encouraging the Nisei to become more assimilated, more "American." They formed the Japanese American Citizens League in 1930 to promote their goals. By 1940, it had nearly 6,000 members.

Japanese American Citizens League

Chinese Americans fared no better. The overwhelming majority continued to work in Chinese-owned laundries and restaurants. Those who moved outside the Asian community could rarely find jobs above the entry level.

Women and the Workplace in the Great Depression

The economic crisis served in many ways to strengthen the widespread belief that a woman's proper place was in the home. Most men and many women believed that what work

Popular Disapproval of Women's Employment

there was should go to men. There was a particularly strong belief that no woman whose husband was employed should accept a job.

But the widespread assumption that married women, at least, should not work outside the home did not stop them from doing so. Both single and married women worked in the 1930s, despite public condemnation of the practice, because they or their families needed the money. In fact, the largest new group of female workers consisted

Increased Female Employment

of wives and mothers. By the end of the Depression, 20 percent more women were working than had been doing so at the beginning.

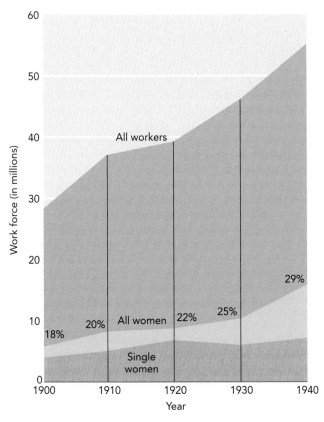

WOMEN IN THE PAID WORK FORCE, 1900–1940 The participation of women in the paid work force increased slowly but steadily in the first forty years of the twentieth century. Note, however, the general leveling off of the participation of single women—who traditionally accounted for the vast majority of women workers—after 1920, at the same time that the total number of women in the paid work force was rising. Many more married women began entering the paid work force in these years, particularly in the 1930s. ◆ *Why did so many married women begin doing paid work during the Great Depression?*

The increase occurred despite considerable obstacles. Professional opportunities for women declined because unemployed men began moving into professions, such as teaching and social work, that had previously been considered women's fields. Female industrial workers were more likely to be laid off or to experience wage reductions than their male counterparts. But white women also had certain advantages in the workplace. The nonprofessional jobs that women traditionally held—as salesclerks and stenographers, and in other service positions—were less likely to disappear than the predominantly male jobs in heavy industry. Nor were many men, even unemployed men, likely to ask for such jobs.

Black women suffered massive unemployment because of a great reduction of domestic service jobs. As many as half of all black working women lost their jobs in the 1930s. Even so, at the end of the 1930s, 38 percent of black women were employed, as compared to 24 percent of white women. That was because black women—both married and unmarried—had always been more likely to work than white women, less out of preference than out of economic necessity.

For American feminists, the Depression years were, on the whole, a time of frustration. Although economic pressures pushed more women into the work force, those same pressures helped to erode the frail support that feminists had won in the 1920s for the idea of women becoming economically and professionally independent. In the difficult years of the 1930s, such aspirations seemed to many to be less important than dealing with economic hardship.

Depression Families

The economic hardships of the Depression years placed great strains on American families, many of whom had become accustomed in the 1920s to a steadily rising standard of living but now found themselves plunged suddenly into uncertainty.

Such circumstances forced many families to retreat from the consumer patterns they had developed in the 1920s. Women often returned to sewing clothes for themselves and their families and to preserv-

Retreat from Consumerism

ing their own food rather than buying such products in stores. Others engaged in home businesses—taking in laundry, selling baked goods, accepting boarders. Many households expanded to include distant relatives. Parents often moved in with their children and grandparents with their grandchildren, or vice versa.

But the Depression also eroded the strength of many family units. There was a decline in the divorce rate, but largely because divorce was now too expensive for some. More common was the informal breakup of families, particularly the desertion of families by unemployed men bent on escaping the humiliation of being unable to earn a living. The marriage and birth rates declined simultaneously for the first time since the early nineteenth century.

THE DEPRESSION AND AMERICAN CULTURE

The Great Depression was a traumatic experience for millions of Americans, and it shook the confidence of many people in themselves or in their nation or both. Out of the crisis emerged some of the most probing criticisms of American society and the American economic system of the industrial age. At the same time, the Depression produced powerful confirmations of more traditional values and reinforced many traditional goals. There was not one Depression culture, but many.

Depression Values

American social values seemed to change relatively little in response to the Depression. Instead, many people responded to hard times by redoubling their commitment to familiar ideas and goals. The sociologists Robert Lynd and Helen Merrell Lynd, who had published a celebrated study of Muncie, Indiana, *Middletown,* in 1929, returned there in the mid-1930s to see how the city had changed. They concluded in their 1937 book, *Middletown in Transition,* that in most respects "the texture of Middletown's culture has not changed. . . . Middletown is overwhelmingly living by the values by which it lived in 1925." Above all, the men and women of "Middletown"— and by implication many other Americans—remained committed to the traditional American emphasis on the individual.

In some respects, the economic crisis worked to undermine the traditional "success ethic" in America. Many people began to look to government for assistance; many blamed corporate moguls, international bankers, "economic royalists," and others for their distress. Yet the Depression did not, in the end, seriously erode the success ethic.

Persistence of the "Success Ethic"

Some victims of the Depression expressed anger and struck out at the economic system. Many, however, seemed to blame themselves. Nothing so surprised foreign observers of America in the 1930s as the apparent passivity of the unemployed, many of whom were so ashamed of their joblessness that they refused to leave their homes.

Self-Blame

At the same time, millions of people responded eagerly to reassurances that they could, through their own efforts, restore themselves to prosperity and success. Dale Carnegie's self-help manual *How to Win Friends and Influence People* (1936) was one of the best-selling books of the decade. Carnegie's message was not only that personal initiative was the route to success; it was also that the best way for people to get ahead was to fit in and make other people feel important.

Artists and Intellectuals in the Great Depression

Just as many progressives had become alarmed when, early in the twentieth century, they "discovered" the existence of widespread poverty in the cities, so many Americans were shocked during the 1930s at their discovery of debilitating rural poverty. Among those who were most effective in conveying the dimensions of this poverty was a group of documentary photographers, many of them employed by the federal Farm Security Administration in the late 1930s, who traveled through the South recording the nature of agricultural life. Roy Stryker, Walker Evans, Arthur Rothstein, Ben Shahn, Margaret Bourke-White, Dorothea Lange, and others produced memorable studies of farm families and their surroundings, studies designed to reveal the savage impact of a hostile environment on its victims.

"Discovery" of Rural Poverty

Many writers, similarly, turned away from the personal concerns of the 1920s and devoted themselves to exposés of social injustice. Erskine Caldwell's *Tobacco Road* (1932), which later became a long-running Broadway play, was an exposé of poverty in the rural South. Richard Wright, a major African-American novelist, exposed the plight of residents of the urban ghetto in *Native Son* (1940). John Steinbeck's novels portrayed the trials of workers and migrants in California. John Dos Passos's trilogy *U.S.A.* (1930-1936) attacked modern capitalism outright. Playwright Clifford Odets provided an explicit demonstration of the appeal of political radicalism in *Waiting for Lefty* (1935).

Depression Literature

But the cultural products of the 1930s that attracted the widest popular audiences were those that diverted attention away from the Depression. And they came to Americans primarily through the two most powerful instruments of popular culture in the 1930s—radio and the movies.

Radio

Almost every American family had a radio in the 1930s. In cities and towns, radio consoles were now as familiar a part of the furnishing of parlors and kitchens as tables and chairs. Even in remote rural areas without access to electricity, many families purchased radios and hooked them up to car batteries when they wished to listen.

Unlike in later times, radio in the 1930s was often a community experience. Young people would place radios on their front porches and invite friends over to sit, talk, or dance. In poor urban neighborhoods, many people who could not afford other kinds of social activities would gather on a street or in a backyard to listen to sporting

A RADIO PLAY Among the most popular entertainments of the 1930s were live readings of plays over the radio—many of them mysteries or romances written specifically for the new medium. Here, a group of actors performs a radio comedy over WNBC in New York in the early 1930s. The actors (from left to right) are Jack Benny, George Murphy, Jean Cranford, and Reginald Gardiner. *(Hulton Archive/Getty Images)*

events or concerts. Within families, the radio often drew parents and children together in the evening to listen to favorite programs.

What did Americans hear on the radio? Although radio stations occasionally carried socially and politically provocative programs, the staple of broadcasting was escapism: comedies such as *Amos 'n Andy* (with its humorous,

Escapist Programming

if demeaning, picture of urban blacks); adventures such as *Superman, Dick Tracy,* and *The Lone Ranger;* and other entertainment programs. Radio brought a new kind of comedy—previously limited to vaudeville or to ethnic theaters—to a wide audience. Jack Benny, George Burns and Gracie Allen, and other masters of elaborately timed jokes and repartee began to develop broad followings (that they would later take with them to television).

Soap operas, also later to become staples of television programming, were enormously popular as well in the 1930s, especially with women who were alone in the house during the day. (That was one reason they became known as soap operas; soap companies—whose advertising was targeted at women—generally sponsored them.)

Almost invariably, radio programs were broadcast live; and as a result, radio spawned an enormous number of public performances. Radio comedies and dramas were often performed before audiences in theaters or studios. Band concerts were broadcast from dance halls, helping jazz and swing bands to achieve broad popularity. Classical music, too, was broadcast live from studios.

Radio provided Americans with their first direct access to important public events, and radio news and sports divisions grew rapidly to meet the demand. Some of the most dramatic moments of the 1930s were a result of radio cov-

Radio's Impact

erage of celebrated events: the World Series, major college football games, the Academy Awards, political conventions, presidential inaugurations. When the German dirigible the *Hindenburg* crashed in flames in Lakehurst, New Jersey, in 1937 after a transatlantic voyage, it produced an enormous national reaction largely because of the live radio account by a broadcaster overcome with emotion who cried out, as he watched the terrible crash, "Oh the humanity! Oh the humanity!" The actor/director Orson Welles created another memorable event in 1938 when

A NIGHT AT THE OPERA The antic comedy of the Marx Brothers provided a popular and welcome escape from the rigors of the Great Depression. The Marx Brothers, shown here in a poster for one of their most famous films, effectively lampooned dilemmas that many Americans faced in their ceaseless, and usually unsuccessful, efforts to find an easy route to wealth and comfort. *(Everett Collection)*

he broadcast "The War of the Worlds," which created panic among millions of people who believed for a while that the events it described were real. (See "Patterns of Popular Culture," pp. 718–719.)

Radio was important for the way it drew the nation together by creating the possibility of shared experiences and common access to culture and information. It was also significant for the way it helped reshape the social life of the nation, for the way it encouraged many families and individuals to center their lives more around the home than they had in the past.

Movies in the New Era

Moviegoing would seem particularly vulnerable to hard times. Families struggling to pay the rent or buy food could easily decide to forgo an evening at the movies. In the first years of the Depression, movie attendance did drop significantly. By the mid-1930s, however, most Americans had resumed their moviegoing habits—in part because movies were a less expensive entertainment option than many other possibilities, and in part because the movies themselves (all of them now with sound, and by the end of the decade many of them in color) were becoming more appealing.

Continuing Popularity of Movies

In many ways, movies were as safely conventional in the 1930s as they had been in the late 1920s. Hollywood continued to exercise tight control over its products in the 1930s through its resilient censor Will Hays, who ensured that most movies carried no sensational or controversial messages. The studio system—through which a few large movie companies exercised iron control over actors, writers, and directors, and through which a few great moguls, such as Louis B. Mayer or Jack Warner, could single-handedly

decide the fate of most projects—also worked to ensure that Hollywood films avoided controversy.

But neither the censor nor the studio system could (or wished to) prevent films from exploring social questions altogether. A few films, such as King Vidor's *Our Daily Bread* (1932) and John Ford's adaptation of *The Grapes of Wrath* (1940), did explore political themes. The director Frank Capra provided a muted social message in several of his comedies—*Mr. Deeds Goes to Town* (1936), *Mr. Smith Goes to Washington* (1939), and *Meet John Doe* (1941)—which celebrated the virtues of the small town and the decency of the common people in contrast to the selfish, corrupt values of the city and the urban rich. (See "Patterns of Popular Culture," pp. 674–675.) Gangster movies such as *Little Caesar* (1930) and *The Public Enemy* (1931) portrayed a dark, gritty, violent world with which few Americans were familiar, but their desperate stories were popular nevertheless with those engaged in their own difficult struggles.

More often, however, the commercial films of the 1930s were deliberately and explicitly escapist: lavish musicals such as *Gold Diggers of 1933* (whose theme song was "We're in the Money"), "screwball" comedies such as Capra's *It Happened One Night,* or the many films of the Marx Brothers—films designed to divert audiences from their troubles and, often, indulge their fantasies about quick and easy wealth.

The 1930s saw the beginning of Walt Disney's long reign as the champion of animation and children's entertainment. After producing cartoon shorts for theaters in the late 1920s—many of them starring the newly created character of Mickey Mouse, who made his debut in the 1928 cartoon *Steamboat Willie*—Disney began to produce feature-length animated films, starting in 1937 with *Snow White.* Other enormously popular films of the 1930s

Walt Disney

were adaptations of popular novels: *The Wizard of Oz* and *Gone With the Wind,* both released in 1939.

Popular Literature and Journalism

The social and political strains of the Great Depression found voice much more successfully in print than they did on the airwaves or the screen. Much literature and journalism in the 1930s dealt directly or indirectly with the tremendous disillusionment, and the increasing radicalism, of the era.

Not all literature, of course, was challenging or controversial. The most popular books and magazines of the time were as escapist and romantic as the most popular radio shows and movies. Two of the best-selling novels of the decade were romantic sagas set in earlier eras: Margaret Mitchell's *Gone With the Wind* (1936) and Hervey Allen's *Anthony Adverse* (1933). Leading magazines focused more on fashions, stunts, scenery, and the arts than on the social conditions of the nation. The enormously popular new photographic journal *Life,* which began publication in 1936 and quickly became one of the most successful magazines in American history, had the largest readership of any publication in the United States. It devoted some attention to politics and to the economic conditions of the Depression, more, in fact, than did many of its competitors. But it was best known for stunning photographs of sporting and theater events, natural landscapes, and impressive public projects. Its first cover was a striking picture by Margaret Bourke-White of a New Deal hydroelectric project. One of its most popular features was "*Life* Goes to a Party," which took the chatty social columns of daily newspapers and turned them into glossy photographic glimpses of the rich and famous.

Life Magazine

Other Depression writing, however, was frankly and openly challenging to the dominant values of American popular culture. In the first years of the Depression, some of the most significant literature offered corrosive portraits of the harshness and emptiness of American life: Nathanael West's *Miss Lonelyhearts* (1933), the story of an advice columnist overwhelmed by the sadness he encounters in the lives of those who consult him; Jack Conroy's *The Disinherited* (1933), a harsh portrait of the lives of coal miners; and James T. Farrell's *Studs Lonigan* (1932), a portrait of a lost, hardened working-class youth.

The Popular Front and the Left

In the later 1930s, much of the political literature adopted a more optimistic, although often no less radical, approach to society. This was in part a result of the rise of the Popular Front, a broad coalition of "antifascist" groups on the left, of which the most important was the American Communist Party. The party had long been a harsh and unrelenting critic of American capitalism and the government

it claimed was controlled by it. But in 1935, under instructions from the Soviet Union, the party softened its attitude toward Franklin Roosevelt (whom Stalin now saw as a potential ally in the coming battle against Hitler) and formed loose alliances with many other "progressive" groups. The party began to praise the New Deal and John L. Lewis, a powerful (and strongly anticommunist) labor leader, and it adopted the slogan "Communism is twentieth-century Americanism." In its heyday, the Popular Front did much to enhance the reputation and influence of the Communist Party, whose formal membership grew to perhaps 100,000 in the mid-1930s, the highest it had ever been or ever would be again. But it also helped mobilize writers, artists, and intellectuals—many of them unconnected with (and many of them uninterested in) the Communist Party—behind a pattern of social criticism.

For some intellectuals, the Popular Front offered an escape from the lonely and difficult stance of detachment and alienation they had embraced in the 1920s. The importance to many American intellectuals of the Spanish Civil War of the mid-1930s was a good example of how the left helped give meaning and purpose to individual lives. The war in Spain pitted the fascists of Francisco Franco (who was receiving support from Hitler and Mussolini) against the existing republican government. It attracted a substantial group of young Americans—more than 3,000 in all—who formed the Abraham Lincoln Brigade (directed and in part created by the American Communist Party) and traveled to Spain to join the fight against the fascists. About a third of its members died in combat. Ernest Hemingway, who spent time as a correspondent in Spain during the conflict, wrote in his novel *For Whom the Bell Tolls* (1940) of how the war provided those Americans who fought in it with "a part in something which you could believe in wholly and completely and in which you felt an absolute brotherhood with others who were engaged in it."

Spanish Civil War

The Communist Party was active as well in organizing the unemployed in the early 1930s and staged a hunger march in Washington, D.C., in 1931. Party members were among the most effective union organizers in some industries. And the party was virtually alone among political organizations in taking a firm stand in favor of racial justice; its active defense of the Scottsboro defendants was but one example of its efforts to ally itself with the aspirations of African Americans.

The American Communist Party was not, however, the open, patriotic organization it tried to appear. It was always under the close and rigid supervision of the Soviet Union. Its leaders took their orders from the Comintern in Moscow. Most members obediently followed the "party line" (although there were many areas in which Communists were active for which there was no party line, areas in which members acted independently). The subordination of the party leadership to the Soviet Union was most clearly demonstrated in 1939, when Stalin signed a nonaggression

THE FILMS OF FRANK CAPRA

Frank Capra is probably best remembered today for his last successful film, *It's a Wonderful Life* (1946), widely replayed every year at Christmas (sometimes in a new "colorized" version, but usually in its original black and white). In it, George Bailey, a kind and compassionate small-town savings-and-loan operator (played by Jimmy Stewart), is almost destroyed by a wealthy, greedy, and malicious banker. In despair and contemplating suicide, Bailey receives a visit from an angel who shows him what life in his community, Bedford Falls, would have been like had George never been born. After a few hours of wandering through a coarse, corrupt, degraded version of the town he knew, Bailey comes to understand the value of his own life. He returns to the real Bedford Falls to find that his family, friends, and neighbors have rallied together to rescue him from his financial difficulties and affirm his value to them, and theirs to him.

By the time *It's a Wonderful Life* appeared, Frank Capra had been the most famous and successful director in Hollywood for more than a decade. His films during those years had almost all been great commercial and critical successes. They had won two Academy Awards for best picture (and Capra himself had won an award as best director). Capra's popularity was a result in part of his tremendous talent as a director. But it was also a result of his vision. Most of his films expressed a vision of society, and of politics, that resonated clearly with the concerns of millions of Americans as they struggled through the years of the Great Depression.

Capra was born in 1897 in a small village in Sicily and moved with his family to America six years later. After working his way through college, he found a job in the still-young movie industry in California and eventually became a director of feature films. His great breakthrough came in 1934 with *It Happened One Night,* a now-classic comedy that won five major Academy Awards, including best picture and best director. Over the next seven years, he built on that success by making a series of more pointed films through which he established himself as a powerful voice of an old-fashioned vision of democracy and American life.

Capra made no secret of his romantic image of the small town and the common man, his distaste for cities, his contempt for opportunistic politicians, and his condemnation of what he considered the amoral (and often immoral) capitalist marketplace. In *Mr. Deeds Goes to Town* (1936), a simple man from a small town inherits a large fortune, moves to the city, and—not liking the greed and dishonesty he finds there—gives the money away

MR. DEEDS GOES TO TOWN Gary Cooper, playing the newly wealthy Longfellow Deeds, leaves the friendly, virtuous small town of Mandrake Falls en route to New York to receive the fortune he has inherited. Capra's evocation of the warmth and generosity of Mandrake Falls was part of his effort to contrast the decent America of ordinary people with the grasping and corrupt America of the wealthy and the city. *(Photofest)*

pact with Nazi Germany. Moscow then sent orders to the American Communist Party to abandon the Popular Front and return to its old stance of harsh criticism of American liberals; and Communist Party leaders in the United States immediately obeyed—although thousands of disillusioned members left the party as a result.

The Socialist Party of America, under the leadership of Norman Thomas, also cited the economic crisis as evidence of the failure of capitalism and sought vigorously to win public support for its own political program. Among other things, it attempted to mobilize support among the rural poor. The Southern Tenant Farmers Union (STFU), supported by the party and organized by a young socialist, H. L. Mitchell, attempted to create a biracial coalition of sharecroppers, tenant farmers, and others to demand economic reform. Neither the STFU nor the party itself, however, made any real progress toward establishing socialism as a major force in American politics. By 1936, membership in the Socialist Party had fallen below 20,000.

Southern Tenant Farmers Union

PROMOTING CAPRA Capra was unusual among directors of the 1930s in having a distinct following of his own. Most films attempted to attract audiences by highlighting their stars. Capra films highlighted Capra himself. *(Photofest)*

and moves back home. In *Mr. Smith Goes to Washington* (1939), a decent man from a western state is elected to the United States Senate, refuses to join in the self-interested politics of Washington, and dramatically exposes the corruption and selfishness of his colleagues. (The rugged western actor Gary Cooper portrayed Mr. Deeds, and Jimmy Stewart played Mr. Smith.) In *Meet John Doe* (1941), released on the brink of American entry into World War II, an ordinary man—played again by Gary Cooper—is manipulated by a fascist cartel to dupe the public on their behalf. He comes to his senses just in time and, by threatening suicide, rallies ordinary people to turn against the malign plans of the fascists. He then disappears into the night.

Capra was entirely conscious of the romantic populism that he brought to his films. "I would sing the songs of the working stiffs, of the short-changed Joes, the born poor, the afflicted," he once wrote (in an apparent allusion to Walt Whitman). "I would fight for their causes on the screens of the world." He was intensely patriotic, in a way characteristic of many successful immigrants, and he believed fervently that America stood for individual opportunity and was defined by the decency of ordinary people. He was not, he said (in an effort to distance himself from the communists), a "bleeding-heart with an Olympian call to 'free the masses.'" He did not like the term "masses" and found it "insulting, degrading." He saw the people, rather, as a "collection of free individuals . . . each an island of human dignity."

When America entered World War II, Capra collaborated with the government (and the Walt Disney studios) to make a series of films designed to explain to new soldiers what the war was about—a series known as *Why We Fight.* They contrasted the individualistic democracy of the American small town with the dark collectivism of the Nazis and Fascists. Capra poured into them all his skills as a filmmaker and all his romantic, patriotic images. *It's a Wonderful Life,* released a year after the war, continued his evocation of the decency of ordinary people.

In the decades that followed, Capra—although he was still a relatively young man and although he continued to work—ceased to be an important force in American cinema. The sentimental populism and comic optimism that had been so appealing

CAPRA ON THE SET Frank Capra, seated, poses with members of his camera crew and the relatively simple cameras available to filmmakers in the 1930s. *(Culver Pictures, Inc.)*

to audiences during the hard years of the Depression and the war gave way to a harder, more realistic style of filmmaking in the 1950s and 1960s; and Capra—a romantic to the end—was never fully able to adjust. But in a time of crisis, Capra had helped his audiences find solace in his romantic vision of the American past, and in the warmth and goodness of small towns and the decency of ordinary people.

Antiradicalism was a powerful force in the 1930s, just as it had been during and after World War I and would be again in the 1940s and 1950s. Hostility toward the Communist Party, in particular, was intense at many levels of government. Congressional committees chaired by Hamilton Fish of New York and Martin Dies of Texas investigated communist influence wherever they could find it (or imagine it). State and local governments harried and sometimes imprisoned communist organizers. White southerners tried to drive communist organizers out of the countryside, just as growers in California and elsewhere tried (unsuccessfully) to keep communists from organizing Mexican-American and other workers.

Even so, only a few times before in American history (and in few since) did being part of the left seem so respectable and even conventional among workers, intellectuals, and others. Thus the 1930s witnessed

The Left's Newfound Respectability

an impressive, if temporary, widening of the ideological range of mainstream art and politics. The New Deal sponsored

THE GRAPES OF WRATH This still from John Ford's 1940 film adaptation of John Steinbeck's *The Grapes of Wrath* shows the Joad family in their truck as they begin their difficult journey from Oklahoma to California. The Joad family became symbols to many Americans of the hundreds of thousands of farmers who left their lands in the Dust Bowl in the 1930s in search of greater opportunities in California. *(20th Century Fox/The Kobal Collection)*

artistic work through the Works Projects Administration that was frankly challenging to the capitalist norms of the 1920s. The filmmaker Pare Lorentz, with funding from New Deal agencies, made a series of powerful and polemical documentaries—*The Plow That Broke the Plains* (1936), *The River* (1937)—that combined a celebration of New Deal programs with a harsh critique of the exploitation of people and the environment that industrial capitalism had produced.

Perhaps the most successful chronicler of social conditions in the 1930s was the novelist John Steinbeck, particularly in his celebrated novel *The Grapes of Wrath,* published in 1939. In telling the story of the Joad family, migrants from the Dust Bowl to California who encounter

The Grapes of Wrath an unending string of calamities and failures, he offered a harsh portrait of the exploitive features of agrarian life in the West, but also a tribute to the endurance of his main characters—and to the spirit of community they represent.

THE UNHAPPY PRESIDENCY OF HERBERT HOOVER

Herbert Hoover began his presidency in March 1929 believing, like most Americans, that the nation faced a bright and prosperous future. For the first six months of his administration, he attempted to expand the policies he had advocated during his eight years as secretary of commerce, policies that would, he believed, complete a stable system of cooperative individualism and sustain a

successful economy. The economic crisis that began before the year was out forced the president to deal with a new set of problems, but for most of the rest of his term, he continued to rely on the principles that had always governed his public life.

The Hoover Program

Hoover's first response to the Depression was to attempt to restore public confidence in the economy. "The fundamental business of this country, that is, production and distribution of commodities," he said in 1930, "is on a sound and prosperous basis." He then summoned leaders of business, labor, and agriculture to the White House and urged them to adopt a program of voluntary cooperation for recovery. He implored businessmen not to cut production or lay off workers; he talked labor leaders into forgoing demands for

Failure of Voluntarism

higher wages or better hours. But by mid-1931, economic conditions had deteriorated so much that the modest structure of voluntary cooperation he had erected collapsed.

Hoover also attempted to use government spending as a tool for fighting the Depression. The president proposed to Congress an increase of $423 million—a significant sum by the standards of the time—in federal public works programs, and he exhorted state and local governments to fund public construction. But the spending was not nearly enough in the face of such devastating problems. And when economic conditions worsened, he became less willing to increase spending, worrying instead about keeping the budget balanced. In 1932, at the depth of the

HOOVER THE PATRICIAN Although Herbert Hoover grew up in a family of modest means in a small town in Iowa, his critics in the 1930s delighted in portraying him as an aloof aristocrat, fond of fancy dinners and cigars. As this photograph of a formal banquet suggests, Hoover gave them many opportunities to strengthen that image. *(Herbert Hoover Presidential Library)*

Depression, he proposed a tax increase to help the government avoid a deficit.

Even before the stock market crash, Hoover had begun to construct a program to assist the already troubled agricultural economy. In April 1929, he proposed the Agricultural Marketing Act, which established the first major government program to help farmers maintain prices. A federally sponsored Farm Board would make loans to national marketing cooperatives or establish corporations to buy surpluses and thus raise prices. At the same time, Hoover attempted to protect American farmers from international competition by raising agricultural tariffs. The Hawley-Smoot Tariff of 1930 increased protection on seventy-five farm products. But neither the Agricultural Marketing Act nor the Hawley-Smoot Tariff ultimately helped American farmers significantly.

Agricultural Marketing Act

By the spring of 1931, Herbert Hoover's political position had deteriorated considerably. In the 1930 congressional elections, Democrats won control of the House and made substantial inroads in the Senate by promising increased government assistance to the economy. Many Americans held the president personally to blame for the crisis and began calling the shantytowns that unemployed people established on the outskirts of cities "Hoovervilles." Democrats urged the president to support more vigorous programs of relief and public spending. Hoover, instead, seized on a slight improvement in economic conditions early in 1931 as proof that his policies were working.

Hoover's Declining Popularity

The international financial panic of the spring of 1931 destroyed the illusion that the economic crisis was coming to an end. Throughout the 1920s, European nations had depended on loans from American banks to allow them to make payments on their debts. After 1929, when they could no longer get such loans, the financial fabric of several European nations began to unravel. In May 1931, one of the largest banks in Austria collapsed. Over the next several months, panic gripped the financial institutions of neighboring countries. The American economy rapidly declined to new lows.

By the time Congress convened in December 1931, conditions had grown so desperate that Hoover supported a series of measures designed to keep endangered banks afloat and protect homeowners from foreclosure on their mortgages. More important was a bill passed in January 1932 establishing the Reconstruction Finance Corporation (RFC), a government agency whose purpose was to provide federal loans to troubled banks, railroads, and other businesses. It even made funds available to local governments to support public works projects and assist relief efforts. Unlike some earlier Hoover programs, it operated on a large scale. In 1932, the RFC had a budget of $1.5 billion for public works alone.

Reconstruction Finance Corporation

Nevertheless, the new agency failed to deal directly or forcefully enough with the real problems of the economy to produce any significant recovery. The RFC lent funds only to financial institutions with sufficient collateral; much of its money went to large banks and corporations. At Hoover's insistence, it helped finance only those public

HOOVERTOWN, NEVADA, 1937 Even in 1937, more than four years after he left office, Herbert Hoover remained a symbol to many Americans of the despair of the Great Depression. This shantytown for otherwise homeless people in Nevada was still known as Hoovertown by its residents and their neighbors. *(Bettmann/Corbis)*

works projects that promised ultimately to pay for themselves (toll bridges, public housing, and others). Above all, the RFC did not have enough money to make any real impact on the Depression, and it did not even spend all the money it had. Of the $300 million available to support local relief efforts, the RFC lent out only $30 million in 1932. Of the $1.5 billion public works budget, it released only about 20 percent.

Popular Protest

For the first several years of the Depression, most Americans were either too stunned or too confused to raise any effective protest. By the middle of 1932, however, dissident voices began to be heard.

In the summer of 1932, a group of unhappy farm owners gathered in Des Moines, Iowa, to establish a new organization: the Farmers' Holiday Association, which endorsed the withholding of farm products from the market—in effect a farmers' strike. The strike began in August in western Iowa, spread briefly to a few neighboring areas, and succeeded in blockading several markets, but in the end it dissolved in failure.

Farmers' Holiday Association

A more celebrated protest movement emerged from American veterans. In 1924, Congress had approved the payment of a $1,000 bonus to all those who had served in World War I, the money to be paid beginning in 1945. By 1932, however, many veterans were demanding that the bonus be paid immediately. Hoover, concerned about balancing the budget, rejected their appeal. In June, more than 20,000 veterans, members of the self-proclaimed Bonus Expeditionary Force, or "Bonus Army," marched into Washington, built crude camps around the city, and promised to stay until Congress approved legislation to pay the bonus. Some of the veterans departed in July, after Congress had voted down their proposal. Many, however, remained where they were.

Their continued presence in Washington embarrassed President Hoover. Finally, in mid-July, he ordered police to clear the marchers out of several abandoned federal buildings in which they had been staying. A few marchers threw rocks at the police, and someone opened fire; two veterans fell dead. Hoover called the incident evidence of uncontrolled violence and radicalism, and he ordered the United States Army to assist the police in clearing out the buildings.

General Douglas MacArthur, the army chief of staff, carried out the mission himself (with the assistance of his aide, Dwight D. Eisenhower) and greatly exceeded the president's orders. He led the Third Cavalry (under the command of George S. Patton), two infantry regiments, a machine-gun detachment, and six tanks down Pennsylvania Avenue in pursuit of the Bonus Army. The veterans fled in terror. MacArthur followed them across the Anacostia River, where he ordered the soldiers to burn their tent city to the ground. More than 100 marchers were injured.

Demise of the Bonus Army

The incident served as perhaps the final blow to Hoover's already battered political standing. Hoover's own cold and gloomy personality reinforced the public image of him as aloof and unsympathetic to distressed people. The Great Engineer, the personification of the optimistic days of the 1920s, had become a symbol of the nation's failure to deal effectively with its startling reversal of fortune.

CLEARING OUT THE BONUS MARCHERS In July 1932, President Hoover ordered the Washington, D.C., police to evict the Bonus marchers from some of the public buildings and land they had been occupying. The result was a series of pitched battles (one of them visible here), in which both veterans and police sustained injuries. Such skirmishes persuaded Hoover to call out the U.S. Army to finish the job. *(Bettmann/Corbis)*

The Election of 1932

As the 1932 presidential election approached, few people doubted the outcome. The Republican Party dutifully renominated Herbert Hoover for a second term of office, but the gloomy atmosphere of the convention made it clear that few delegates believed he could win. The Democrats, in the meantime, gathered jubilantly in Chicago to nominate the governor of New York, Franklin Delano Roosevelt.

FDR Nominated

Roosevelt had been a well-known figure in the party for many years already. A Hudson Valley aristocrat, a distant cousin of Theodore Roosevelt (a connection strengthened by his marriage in 1904 to the president's niece, Eleanor), and a handsome, charming young man, he progressed rapidly: from a seat in the New York State legislature to a position as assistant secretary of the navy during World War I to his party's vice presidential nomination in 1920 on the ill-fated ticket with James M. Cox. Less than a year later, he was stricken with polio. Although he never regained use of his legs (and could appear to walk only by using crutches and braces), he built up sufficient physical strength to return to politics in 1928. When Al Smith received the Democratic nomination for president that year, Roosevelt was elected to succeed him as governor. In 1930, he easily won reelection.

Roosevelt worked no miracles in New York, but he did initiate enough positive programs of government assistance to be able to present himself as a more energetic and imaginative leader than Hoover. In national politics, he avoided such divisive cultural issues as religion and prohibition and emphasized the economic grievances that most Democrats shared. He was able as a result to assemble a broad coalition within the party and win his party's nomination. In a dramatic break with tradition, he flew to Chicago to address the convention in person and accept the nomination. In the course of his acceptance speech, Roosevelt aroused the delegates with his ringing promise: "I pledge you, I pledge myself, to a new deal for the American people," giving his future program a name that would long endure. Neither then nor in the subsequent campaign did Roosevelt give much indication of what that program would be. But Herbert Hoover's unpopularity virtually ensured Roosevelt's election.

In November, to the surprise of no one, Roosevelt won by a landslide. He received 57.4 percent of the popular

Candidate (Party)	Electoral Vote	Popular Vote (%)
Franklin D. Roosevelt (Democratic)	472	22,821,857 (57.4)
Herbert Hoover (Republican)	59	15,761,841 (39.7)
Norman Thomas (Socialist)	—	881,951 (2.2)
Other candidates (Communist, Prohibition, Socialist Labor, Liberty)	—	271,355

56.9% of electorate voting

ELECTION OF 1932 Like the election of 1928, the election of 1932 was exceptionally one-sided. But this time, the landslide favored the Democratic candidate, Franklin Roosevelt, who overwhelmed Herbert Hoover in all regions of the country except New England. Roosevelt obviously benefited primarily from popular disillusionment with Hoover's response to the Great Depression. ◆ *But what characteristics of Roosevelt himself contributed to his victory?*

For an interactive version of this map, go to www.mhhe.com/brinkley13ech23maps

THE CHANGING OF THE GUARD Long before the event actually occurred, Peter Arno of *The New Yorker* magazine drew this image of Franklin D. Roosevelt and Herbert Hoover traveling together to the Capitol for Roosevelt's inauguration. It predicted with remarkable accuracy the mood of the uncomfortable ride—Hoover glum and uncommunicative, Roosevelt buoyant and smiling. This was to have been the magazine's cover for the week of the inauguration, but after an attempted assassination of the president-elect several weeks earlier in Florida (in which the mayor of Chicago was killed), the editors decided to substitute a more subdued drawing. *(Franklin Delano Roosevelt Library)*

1932 Election

vote to Hoover's 39.7. In the electoral college, the result was even more overwhelming. Hoover carried Delaware, Pennsylvania, Connecticut, Vermont, New Hampshire, and Maine. Roosevelt won everything else. Democrats won majorities in both houses of Congress. It was a broad and convincing mandate.

The "Interregnum"

The period between the election and the inauguration (which in the early 1930s lasted more than four months) was a season of growing economic crisis. Presidents-elect traditionally do not involve themselves directly in government. But in a series of brittle exchanges with Roosevelt in the months following the election, Hoover tried to exact from the president-elect a pledge to maintain policies of economic orthodoxy. Roosevelt genially refused.

In February, only a month before the inauguration, a new crisis developed when the collapse of the American banking system suddenly and rapidly accelerated. Public confidence in the banks was ebbing; depositors were withdrawing

Banking Crisis

their money in panic; and one bank after another was closing its doors and declaring bankruptcy. Hoover again asked Roosevelt to give prompt public assurances that there would be no tinkering with the currency, no heavy borrowing, no unbalancing of the budget. Roosevelt again refused.

March 4, 1933, was, therefore, a day of both economic crisis and considerable personal bitterness. On that morning, Herbert Hoover, convinced that the United States was headed for disaster, rode glumly down Pennsylvania Avenue with a beaming, buoyant Franklin Roosevelt, who would shortly be sworn in as the thirty-second president of the United States.

CONCLUSION

The Great Depression, which began so unexpectedly and spread so quickly and widely, changed many things in American life. It created unemployment on a scale never before experienced in the nation's history. It put enormous pressures on families, on communities, on state and local governments, and ultimately on Washington—which during the innovative but ultimately failed presidency of Herbert Hoover was unable to produce policies capable of dealing effectively with the crisis. In the nation's politics and culture, the Depression provoked strong currents of radicalism and protest; and many middle-class Americans came to fear (and many less affluent people to hope) that a revolution might be approaching.

In reality, while the Great Depression shook much of American society and culture, it actually toppled very little. The capitalist system survived, damaged for a time but never truly threatened. The widely shared values of materialism and personal responsibility were shaken, but never overturned. The American people in the 1930s were more receptive than they had been in the 1920s to evocations of community, generosity, and the dignity of common people. They were more open to experiments in government and business and even private lives than they had been in earlier years. But for most Americans, belief in the "American way of life"—a phrase that became widely resonant in the 1930s for the first time—remained strong throughout the long years of economic despair.

INTERACTIVE LEARNING

The *Primary Source Investigator CD-ROM* offers the following materials related to this chapter:

- A short documentary movie, **Documenting the Depression,** examining the 1930s documentary film *The River* (D17).

- Interactive maps: **U.S. Elections** (M7) and **Unemployment Relief** (M26).

- Documents, images, and maps related to the onset of the Great Depression, the suffering of the people, and the ordeal of President Herbert Hoover. Highlights include "Migrant Mother" and other striking images by

Farm Security Administration photographer Dorothea Lange; an image of the Depression-era shantytowns dubbed "Hoovervilles"; photographs of a dust storm and other images of Dust Bowl life; and an image of the Bonus Army shacks in Washington, D.C.

Online Learning Center (www.mhhe.com/brinkley13e)

For quizzes, Internet resources, references to additional books and films, and more, consult this book's Online Learning Center.

FOR FURTHER REFERENCE

Donald Worster scathingly indicts agricultural capitalism for its destruction of the plains environment in *Dust Bowl: The Southern Plains in the 1930s* (1979). Timothy Egan, *The Worst Hard Time* (2006) is a vivid portrait of the impact of the Dust Bowl. In *The Great Depression: Delayed Recovery and Economic Change in America, 1929-1939* (1987), Michael Bernstein argues that we should ask not so much why the economy crashed in 1929 but rather why the expected recovery from the crash was so slow. Richard Pells, *Radical Visions and American Dreams: Culture and Social Thought in the Depression Years* (1973) is an important survey of the cultural and intellectual history of the 1930s. Studs Terkel, *Hard Times* (1970) is an excellent oral history of the Depression. Susan Ware analyzes the effect of the Great Depression on women in *Holding Their Own: American Women in the 1930s* (1982). The Communist Party's most popular period

in the United States is the subject of Harvey Klehr's *The Heyday of American Communism: The Depression Decade* (1984) and, from quite different viewpoints, Robin D. G. Kelley, *Hammer and Hoe: Alabama Communists During the Great Depression* (1990) and Michael Denning, *The Cultural Front: The Laboring of American Culture in the Twentieth Century* (1997). Joan Hoff Wilson, *Herbert Hoover: Forgotten Progressive* (1975) argues that President Hoover was in many ways a surprisingly progressive thinker about the American social order.

The Great Depression (1993), a multipart film by Blackside Productions, is an eloquent picture of many aspects of the depression decade. *Union Maids* (1997) is a vivid film history of women organizing in the 1930s. *The Lemon Grove Incident* (1985) is a film providing a rare glimpse of Mexican-American civil rights activism over school integration in the early 1930s.

CHAPTER 24

THE NEW DEAL

ARRIVAL AT A CCC CAMP A group of boys from Idaho arrive in Andersonville, Tennessee, in October 1933, only months after the creation of the Civilian Conservation Corps earlier that year. They were there to work reforesting a watershed above the Clinch River in the area of the Tennessee Valley Authority, another newly established New Deal agency. *(Tennessee National Archives)*

F RANKLIN ROOSEVELT SERVED LONGER as president than anyone else before or since, and during his twelve years in office he became more central to the life of the nation than any chief executive before him. Most important, his administration constructed a series of programs that permanently altered the federal government and its relationship to society.

By the end of the 1930s, the New Deal (as the Roosevelt program was called) had created many of the broad outlines of the political world we know today. It had constructed the foundations of the federal welfare system. It had extended national regulation over new areas of the economy. It had presided over the birth of the modern labor movement. It had made the government a major force in the agricultural economy. It dramatically expanded the role of Washington, D.C., in supervising and funding major public works projects all over the nation, some of them of enormous size and scope, which contributed substantially to the economic growth of regions that had previously remained largely outside the new national economy. It had created a powerful coalition within the Democratic Party that would dominate American politics for most of the next thirty years. And it had produced the beginnings of a new liberal ideology that would govern reform efforts for several decades after the war.

One thing the New Deal had not done, however, was end the Great Depression. It had helped stop the disastrous downward spiral in 1933, and there had been a limited, if erratic, recovery in some areas after that. But by the end of 1939, many of the basic problems of the Depression remained unsolved. An estimated 15 percent of the work force remained unemployed. The gross national product was no larger than it had been ten years before.

The Roosevelt administration was in many ways the most politically successful presidency in American history. Franklin Roosevelt won four successive terms in office, two more than any other president, all of them by substantial margins, and two of them by landslides. His party controlled Congress throughout his presidency. He retained enormous popularity during all his time in office. But the persistence of the Depression also created many challenges to the New Deal. Dissident groups on both the right and the left—some of them of considerable size and strength—mobilized outside the conventional party system to promote alternative paths to recovery. The American Communist Party attracted more members than it had ever attracted before and had significant influence in a number of areas of American life. Significant factions of the Democratic Party, most notably southern conservatives, turned against Roosevelt's policies, joined with Republicans, and helped create a conservative coalition in Congress that was able to frustrate many of his goals.

Only the advent of World War II in 1940 and 1941 succeeded in ending the Great Depression and eliminating large-scale unemployment. It also brought to a close most of the domestic initiatives of the New Deal.

SIGNIFICANT EVENTS

1933 ▶ Franklin Roosevelt inaugurated
▶ "First New Deal" legislation enacted (see p. 704)
▶ United States officially abandons gold standard
▶ Twenty-first Amendment ends prohibition with repeal of Eighteenth Amendment
▶ Dr. Francis Townsend begins campaign for old-age pensions

1934 ▶ Conservatives create American Liberty League
▶ Huey Long establishes Share-Our-Wealth Society
▶ Labor militancy increases
▶ Indian Reorganization Act passed

1935 ▶ Supreme Court invalidates NRA
▶ "Second New Deal" legislation passed
▶ Father Charles Coughlin establishes National Union for Social Justice
▶ John L. Lewis and allies break with AFL
▶ Huey Long assassinated

1936 ▶ Supreme Court invalidates Agricultural Adjustment Act
▶ CIO established
▶ Sit-down strikes begin
▶ Roosevelt wins reelection by record margin

1937 ▶ U.S. Steel recognizes Steel Workers' Organizing Committee
▶ Roosevelt proposes "Court-packing plan"
▶ Supreme Court validates Wagner Act
▶ "Memorial Day Massacre" in Chicago
▶ Executive reorganization plan proposed
▶ New Deal spending reduced
▶ Severe recession begins

1938 ▶ Roosevelt proposes new spending measures
▶ Temporary National Economic Committee established

1939 ▶ Marian Anderson sings at Lincoln Memorial

LAUNCHING THE NEW DEAL

Roosevelt's first task upon taking office was to alleviate the panic that was threatening the financial system. He did so in part by force of personality and in part by constructing very rapidly an ambitious and diverse program of legislation.

Restoring Confidence

Much of Roosevelt's success was a result of his ebullient personality. Beginning with his inaugural address, in which he assured the American people that "the only thing we have to fear is fear itself," and promised to take drastic, even warlike, action against the emergency, he projected an infectious optimism that helped alleviate the growing despair. He was the first president to make regular use of the radio, and his friendly "fireside chats," during which he explained his programs and plans to the people, helped build public confidence in the administration. Roosevelt held frequent informal press conferences and won the respect and the friendship of most reporters. Their regard for him was such that by unwritten agreement, no journalist ever photographed the president getting into or out of his car or sitting in his wheelchair. Much of the American public remained unaware throughout the Roosevelt years that the president's legs were completely paralyzed.

Roosevelt's Personality

But Roosevelt could not rely on image alone. On March 6, 1933, two days after taking office, he issued a proclamation closing all American banks for four days until Congress could meet in special session to consider banking-reform legislation. So great was the panic about

THE RADIO PRESIDENT Franklin D. Roosevelt was the first American president to master the use of radio. Beginning in his first days in office, he regularly bypassed the newspapers (many of which were hostile to him) and communicated directly with the people through his famous "fireside chats." He is shown here speaking in 1938, urging communities to continue to provide work relief for the unemployed. *(Franklin D. Roosevelt Library)*

bank failures that the "bank holiday," as the president euphemistically described it, created a general sense of relief. Three days later, Roosevelt sent to Congress the Emergency Banking Act, a generally conservative bill (much of it drafted by Hoover administration holdovers) designed primarily to protect the larger banks from being dragged down by the weakness of smaller ones. The bill provided for Treasury Department inspection of all banks before they would be allowed to reopen, for federal assistance to some troubled institutions, and for a thorough reorganization of those in the greatest difficulty. A confused and frightened Congress passed the bill within four hours of its introduction. "I can assure you," Roosevelt told the public on March 12, in his first fireside chat, "that it is safer to keep your money in a reopened bank than under the mattress." Whatever else the new law accomplished, it helped dispel the panic. Three quarters of the banks in the Federal Reserve system reopened within the next three days, and $1 billion in hoarded currency and gold flowed back into them within a month. The immediate banking crisis was over.

"Bank Holiday"

On the morning after passage of the Emergency Banking Act, Roosevelt sent to Congress another measure—the Economy Act—designed to convince fiscally conservative Americans (and especially the business community) that the federal government was in safe, responsible hands. The act proposed to balance the federal budget by cutting the salaries of government employees and reducing pensions to veterans by as much as 15 percent. Otherwise, the president warned, the nation faced a $1 billion deficit. Like the banking bill, this one passed through Congress almost instantly—despite heated protests from some congressional progressives.

Roosevelt also moved in his first days in office to put to rest one of the divisive issues of the 1920s. He supported and then signed a bill to legalize the manufacture and sale of beer with a 3.2 percent alcohol content—an interim measure pending the repeal of prohibition, for which a constitutional amendment (the Twenty-first) was already in process. The amendment was ratified later in 1933.

Prohibition Repealed

Agricultural Adjustment

These initial actions were largely stopgaps, to buy time for comprehensive programs. The first was the Agricultural Adjustment Act, which Congress passed in May 1933. Its most important feature was its provision for reducing crop production to end agricultural surpluses and halt the downward spiral of farm prices.

Under the provisions of the act, producers of seven basic commodities (wheat, cotton, corn, hogs, rice, tobacco, and dairy products) would decide on production limits for their crops. The government, through the Agricultural Adjustment Administration (AAA), would

then tell individual farmers how much they should pro-
AAA
duce and would pay them subsidies for leaving some of their
land idle. A tax on food processing (for example, the
milling of wheat) would provide the funds for the new
payments. Farm prices were to be subsidized up to the
point of parity.

The AAA helped bring about a rise in prices for farm
commodities in the years after 1933. Gross farm income
increased by half in the first three years of the New Deal,
and the agricultural economy as a whole emerged from
the 1930s much more stable and prosperous than it had
been in many years. The AAA did, however, favor larger
farmers over smaller ones, particularly since local administration of its programs often fell into the hands of the
most powerful producers in a community. By distributing
payments to landowners, not those who worked the land,
the government did little to discourage planters who
were reducing their acreage from evicting tenants and
sharecroppers and firing field hands.

In January 1936, the Supreme Court struck down the
crucial provisions of the Agricultural Adjustment Act, arguing that the government had no constitutional authority
to require farmers to limit production. But within a few
weeks the administration had secured passage of new legislation (the Soil Conservation and Domestic Allotment
Act), which permitted the government to pay farmers to
reduce production so as to "conserve soil," prevent erosion, and accomplish other secondary goals. The Court
did not interfere with the new laws.

The administration launched several efforts to assist
poor farmers as well. The Resettlement Administration,
established in 1935, and its successor, the Farm Security
Administration, created in 1937, provided loans to help
farmers cultivating submarginal soil to relocate to better
lands. But the programs never moved more than a few
thousand farmers. More effective was the Rural Electrification Administration, created in
1935, which worked to make "Rural Electrification"
electric power available for the first time to thousands of
farmers through utility cooperatives.

Industrial Recovery

Ever since 1931, leaders of the United States Chamber of
Commerce and many others had been urging the government to adopt an antideflation scheme that would permit
trade associations to cooperate in stabilizing prices
within their industries. Existing antitrust laws clearly forbade such practices, and Herbert Hoover had refused to
endorse suspension of the laws. The Roosevelt administration was more receptive. In exchange for relaxing antitrust provisions, however, New Dealers insisted on other
provisions. Business leaders would have to make important concessions to labor—recognize the workers' right
to bargain collectively through unions—to ensure that
the incomes of workers would rise along with prices. And
to help create jobs and increase consumer buying power,
the administration added a major program of public works
spending. The result of these and many other impulses
was the National Industrial Recovery Act, which Congress
passed in June 1933.

At first, the new program appeared to work well. At its
center was a new federal agency, the National Recovery
Administration (NRA), under the
direction of the flamboyant and NRA
energetic Hugh S. Johnson. Johnson called on every business establishment in the nation to accept a temporary

SALUTING THE BLUE EAGLE Several thousand San Francisco schoolchildren assembled on a baseball field in 1933 to form the symbol of the National Recovery Administration: an eagle clutching a cogwheel (to symbolize industry) and a thunderbolt (to symbolize energy). This display is evidence of the widespread (if brief) popular enthusiasm the NRA produced. NRA administrators drew from their memories of World War I Liberty Loan drives and tried to establish the Blue Eagle as a symbol of patriotic commitment to recovery. *(Bettmann/Corbis)*

"blanket code": a minimum wage of between 30 and 40 cents an hour, a maximum workweek of thirty-five to forty hours, and the abolition of child labor. Adherence to the code, he claimed, would raise consumer purchasing power and increase employment. At the same time, Johnson negotiated another, more specific set of codes with leaders of the nation's major industries. These industrial codes set floors below which no company would lower prices or wages in its search for a competitive advantage. He quickly won agreements from almost every major industry in the country.

From the beginning, however, the NRA encountered serious difficulties. The codes themselves were hastily and often poorly written. Administering them was beyond the capacities of federal officials with no prior experience in running so vast a program. Large producers consistently dominated the code-writing process and ensured that the new regulations would work to their advantage and to the disadvantage of smaller firms. And the codes at times did more than simply set floors under prices; they actively and artificially raised them—sometimes to levels higher than the market could sustain.

Other NRA goals did not progress as quickly as the efforts to raise prices. Section 7(a) of the National Industrial Recovery Act promised workers the right to form unions and engage in collective bargaining and encouraged many workers to join unions for the first time. But Section 7(a) contained no enforcement mechanisms. Hence recognition of unions by employers (and thus the significant wage increases the unions were committed to winning) did not follow. The Public Works Administration (PWA), established in 1933 to administer the National Industrial Recovery Act's spending programs, only gradu- ally allowed the $3.3 billion in public works funds to trickle out. Not until 1938 was the PWA budget pumping an appreciable amount of money into the economy.

Perhaps the clearest evidence of the NRA's failure was that industrial production actually declined in the months after the agency's establishment—from an index of 101 in July 1933 to 71 in November—despite the rise in prices that the codes had helped to create. By the spring of 1934, the NRA was besieged by criticism, and businessmen

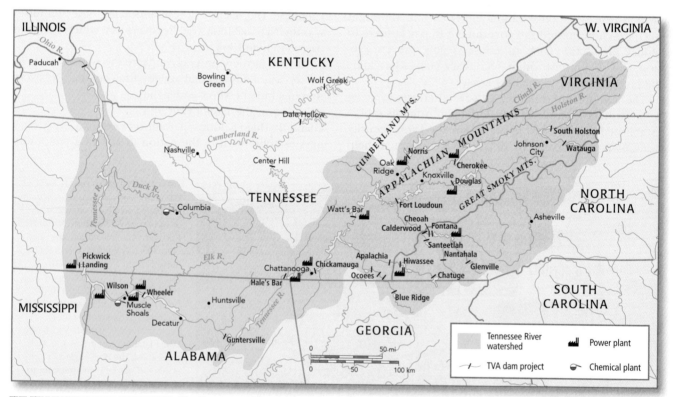

THE TENNESSEE VALLEY AUTHORITY The Tennessee Valley Authority was one of the largest experiments in government-funded public works and regional planning in American history to that point. The federal government had helped fund many projects in its history—canals, turnpikes, railroads, bridges, dams, and others. But never before had it undertaken a project of such great scope, and never before had it maintained such close control and ownership over the public works it helped create. This map illustrates the broad reach of the TVA within the Tennessee Valley region, which spanned seven states. TVA dams throughout the region helped control floods and also provided a source for hydroelectric power, which the government sold to consumers. Note the dam near Muscle Shoals, Alabama, in the bottom left of the map. It was begun during World War I, and efforts to revive it in the 1920s helped create the momentum that produced the TVA. ◆ *Why were progressives so eager to see the government enter the business of hydroelectric power in the 1920s?*

were flaunting many of its provisions. That fall, Roosevelt pressured Johnson to resign and established a new board of directors to oversee the NRA. Then, in 1935, the Supreme Court intervened.

In 1935, a case came before the Court involving alleged NRA code violations by the Schechter brothers, who operated a wholesale poultry business confined to Brooklyn, New York. The Court ruled unanimously that the Schechters were not engaged in interstate commerce (and thus not subject to federal regulation) and, further, that Congress had unconstitutionally delegated legislative power to the president to draft the NRA codes. The justices struck down the legislation establishing the agency. Roosevelt denounced the justices for their "horse-and-buggy" interpretation of the interstate commerce clause. He was rightly concerned, for the reasoning in the Schechter case threatened many other New Deal programs as well. But the Court's destruction of the NRA itself gave the New Deal a convenient excuse for ending a failed experiment.

Regional Planning

The AAA and the NRA largely reflected the beliefs of New Dealers who favored economic planning but wanted private interests (farmers or business leaders) to dominate the planning process. Other reformers believed that the government itself should be the chief planning agent in the economy. Their most conspicuous success, and one of the most celebrated accomplishments of the New Deal, was an unprecedented experiment in regional planning: the Tennessee Valley Authority (TVA).

The TVA had its roots in a political controversy of the 1920s. Progressive reformers had agitated for years for TVA public development of the nation's water resources as a source of cheap electric power. In particular, they had urged completion of a great dam at Muscle Shoals on the Tennessee River in Alabama—a dam begun during World War I but left unfinished when the war ended. But opposition from the utility companies had been too powerful to overcome.

In 1932, however, one of the great utility empires—that of the electricity magnate Samuel Insull—collapsed spectacularly, amid widely publicized exposés of corruption. Hostility to the utilities soon grew so intense that the companies were no longer able to block the public power movement. The result in May 1933 was the Tennessee Valley Authority. The TVA was authorized to complete the dam at Muscle Shoals and build others in the region, and to generate and sell electricity from them to the public at reasonable rates. It was also intended to be an agent for a comprehensive redevelopment of the entire region: for stopping the disastrous flooding that had plagued the Tennessee Valley for centuries, for encouraging the development of local industries, for supervising a substantial program of reforestation, and for helping farmers improve productivity.

The TVA revitalized the region in numerous ways. It improved water transportation, virtually eliminated flooding in the region, and provided electricity to thousands who had never before had it. Throughout the country, largely because of the "yardstick" provided by the TVA's cheap production of electricity, private power rates declined. Even so, the Tennessee Valley remained a generally impoverished region despite the TVA's efforts. And like many other New Deal programs, the TVA made no serious effort to challenge local customs and racial prejudices.

Currency, Banks, and the Stock Market

Roosevelt soon came to consider the gold standard a major obstacle to the restoration of adequate prices. On

PUBLIC WORKS Among the most visible products of the New Deal was a vast network of public works in almost all areas of the country, but concentrated particularly in the South and the West. The great dams that the government built in the Tennessee Valley and elsewhere were particularly effective at capturing the public imagination. This dramatic picture by the renowned photographer Margaret Bourke-White appeared on the cover of the very first issue of *Life* in 1936, which very quickly became the most popular and successful magazine in America. It shows the Fort Peck Dam on the Missouri River. *(Time Life Pictures/Getty Images)*

April 18, 1933, the president made the shift off the gold standard official with an executive order. By itself, the repudiation of the gold standard meant relatively little. But both before and after the April decision, the administration experimented in various ways with manipulating the value of the dollar—by making substantial purchases of gold and silver and later by establishing a new, fixed standard for the dollar (reducing its gold content substantially from the 1932 amount). The resort to government-managed currency—that is, to a dollar whose value could be raised or lowered by government policy according to economic circumstances—created an important precedent for future federal policies and permanently altered the relationship between the public and private sectors. It did not, however, have any immediate impact on the depressed American economy.

Through other legislation, the early New Deal increased federal authority over previously unregulated or weakly regulated areas of the economy. The Glass-Steagall Act of June 1933 gave the government authority to curb irresponsible speculation by banks. More important, it established the Federal Deposit Insurance Corporation, which guaranteed all bank deposits up to $2,500. Finally, in 1935, Congress passed a major banking act that transferred much of the authority once wielded by the regional Federal Reserve banks to the Federal Reserve Board in Washington.

Glass-Steagall Act

To protect investors in the stock market, Congress passed the so-called Truth in Securities Act of 1933, requiring corporations issuing new securities to provide full and accurate information about them to the public. Another act of June 1934 established the Securities and Exchange Commission (SEC) to police the stock market. Among other things, the establishment of the SEC was an indication of how far the financial establishment had fallen in public estimation. The criminal trials of a number of once-respected Wall Street figures for grand larceny and fraud (including the conviction and imprisonment of Richard Whitney, onetime head of the New York Stock Exchange and a close associate of the Morgans) eroded the public stature of the financial community still further.

SEC

The Growth of Federal Relief

Among Roosevelt's first acts in office was the establishment of the Federal Emergency Relief Administration (FERA), which provided cash grants to states to prop up bankrupt relief agencies. To administer the program, he chose the director of the New York State relief agency, Harry Hopkins, who disbursed the FERA grants widely and rapidly. But both Hopkins and Roosevelt had misgivings about establishing a government "dole."

They felt more comfortable with another form of government assistance: work relief. Thus, when it became clear that the FERA grants were not enough, the administration established a second program: the Civil Works Administration (CWA). Between November 1933 and April 1934, it put more than 4 million people to work on temporary projects. Some of the projects were of lasting value, such as the construction of roads, schools, and parks; others were little more than make-work. To Hopkins, however, the important thing was pumping money into an economy badly in need of it and providing assistance to people with nowhere else to turn.

CWA

Roosevelt's favorite relief project was the Civilian Conservation Corps (CCC). Established in the first weeks of the new administration, the CCC was designed to provide employment to the millions of young men who could find no jobs in the cities. The CCC created camps in national parks and forests and in other rural and wilderness settings. There young men (women were largely excluded from the program) worked in a semimilitary environment on such projects as planting trees, building reservoirs, developing parks, and improving agricultural irrigation. CCC camps were segregated by race. The vast majority of them were restricted to white men, but a few were available to African Americans, Mexicans, and Indians.

CCC

Mortgage relief was a pressing need for millions of farm owners and homeowners. The Farm Credit Administration, which within two years refinanced one-fifth of all farm mortgages in the United States, was one response to that problem. The Frazier-Lemke Farm Bankruptcy Act of 1933 was another. It enabled some farmers to regain their land even after foreclosure on their mortgages. Despite such efforts, however, 25 percent of all American farm owners had lost their land by 1934. Homeowners were similarly troubled, and in June 1933 the administration established the Home Owners' Loan Corporation, which by 1936 had refinanced the mortgages of more than 1 million householders. A year later, Congress established the Federal Housing Administration to insure mortgages for new construction and home repairs.

THE NEW DEAL IN TRANSITION

Seldom has an American president enjoyed such remarkable popularity as Franklin Roosevelt did during his first two years in office. But by early 1935, with no end to the Depression yet in sight, the New Deal found itself the target of fierce public criticism. In the spring of 1935, partly in response to these growing attacks, Roosevelt launched an ambitious new program of legislation that has often been called the "Second New Deal."

Critics of the New Deal

Some of the most strident attacks on the New Deal came from critics on the right. Roosevelt had tried for a time to conciliate conservatives and business leaders. By the end of 1934, however, it was clear that the American right in general, and much of the corporate world in particular, had become irreconcilably hos-

American Liberty League

tile to the New Deal. In August 1934, a group of the most fervent (and wealthiest) Roosevelt opponents, led by members of the Du Pont family, formed the American Liberty League, designed specifically to arouse public opposition to the New Deal's "dictatorial" policies and its supposed attacks on free enterprise. But the new organization was never able to expand its constituency much beyond the northern industrialists who had founded it.

Roosevelt's critics on the far left also managed to produce alarm among some supporters of the administration, but like the conservatives, they proved to have only limited strength. The Communist Party, the Socialist Party, and other radical and semiradical organizations were at times harshly critical of the New Deal. But they, too, failed to attract genuine mass support.

More menacing to the New Deal than either the far right or the far left was a group of dissident political movements that defied easy ideological classification. Some gained substantial public support within particular states and regions. And three men succeeded in mobilizing genuinely national followings. Dr. Francis E. Townsend, an elderly California physician, rose from obscurity to lead a movement of more than 5 million members with his plan for federal pensions for the elderly. According to the Townsend Plan, all Americans over the age of sixty would re-

Townsend Plan

ceive monthly government pensions of $200, provided they retired (thus freeing jobs for younger, unemployed Americans) and spent the money in full each month (which would pump needed funds into the economy). By 1935, the Townsend Plan had attracted the support of many older men and women. And while the plan itself made little progress in Congress, the public sentiment behind it helped build support for the Social Security system, which Congress did approve in 1935.

Father Charles E. Coughlin, a Catholic priest in the Detroit suburb of Royal Oak, Michigan, achieved even greater renown through his weekly sermons broadcast nationally over the radio. In later years, Coughlin became notorious for his sympathy for fascism and his outspoken anti-Semitism. But until at least 1937, he was known primarily as an advocate for changing the banking and currency systems. He proposed a series of monetary reforms—remonetization of silver, issuing of greenbacks, and nationalization of the banking system—that he insisted would restore prosperity and ensure economic justice. At first a warm supporter of Franklin Roosevelt, by late 1934 Coughlin had become disheartened by what he claimed was the president's failure to deal harshly enough with the "money powers." In the spring of 1935, he established his own political organization, the National Union for Social Justice. He was widely believed to have one of the largest regular radio audiences of anyone in America.

"AN ATTACK ON THE NEW DEAL" This cartoon by William Gropper appeared in *Vanity Fair* in 1935 to illustrate a long excerpt from an anti–New Deal editorial that had appeared a few weeks before in the Republican newspaper the New York *Herald Tribune.* The cartoon echoes the newspaper's references to Jonathan Swift's famous satire, *Gulliver's Travels.* In this case, Gulliver is Uncle Sam, and the Lilliputians who tie him down with a thousand tiny cords are New Deal agencies and laws. "Here is a giant if there ever was one," the *Herald Tribune* wrote, "the most powerful nation the world has ever seen. It has the makings of good times, [but] it does not make them. Why? Because the Lilliputians of the New Deal will not let it. These busy little folk cannot bear the thought of letting the great giant, America, escape." *(Courtesy of Vanity Fair © 1935 (renewed 1963, 1991) by The Condé Nast Publications, Inc.)*

HUEY LONG Few public speakers could arouse a crowd more effectively than Huey Long of Louisiana, known to many as "the Kingfish" (a nickname borrowed from the popular radio show *Amos 'n Andy*). It was Long's effective use of radio, however, that contributed most directly to his spreading national popularity in the early 1930s. *(Culver Pictures, Inc.)*

Most alarming of all to the administration was the growing national popularity of Senator Huey P. Long of Louisiana. Long had risen to power in his home state through his strident attacks on the banks, oil companies, and utilities and on the conservative political oligarchy allied with them. Elected governor in 1928, he launched an assault on his opponents so thorough and forceful that they were soon left with virtually no political power. Many critics in Louisiana claimed that he had, in effect, become a dictator. But he also maintained the overwhelming support of the Louisiana electorate, in part because of his flamboyant personality and in part because of his solid record of conventional progressive accomplishments: building roads, schools, and hospitals; revising the tax codes; distributing free textbooks; lowering utility rates. Barred by law from succeeding himself as governor, he

Huey Long

ran in 1930 for a seat in the United States Senate and won easily.

Long, like Coughlin, supported Franklin Roosevelt in 1932. But within six months of Roosevelt's inauguration, he had broken with the president. As an alternative to the New Deal, he advocated a drastic program of wealth redistribution, a program he ultimately named the Share-Our-Wealth Plan. The government, he claimed, could end the Depression easily by using the tax system to confiscate the surplus riches of the wealthiest men and women in America and distribute these surpluses to the rest of the population. That would, he claimed, allow the government to guarantee every family a minimum "homestead" of $5,000 and an annual wage of $2,500. In 1934, Long established his own national organization: the Share-Our-Wealth Society, which soon attracted a large following through much of the nation. A poll by the Democratic National Committee in the spring of 1935 disclosed that Long might attract more than 10 percent of the vote if he ran as a third-party candidate, possibly enough to tip a close election to the Republicans.

Share-Our-Wealth Society

The "Second New Deal"

Roosevelt launched the so-called Second New Deal in the spring of 1935 in response both to the growing political pressures and to the continuing economic crisis. The new proposals represented, if not a new direction, at least a shift in the emphasis of New Deal policy. Perhaps the most conspicuous change was in the administration's attitude toward big business. Symbolically at least, the president was now willing to attack corporate interests openly. In March, for example, he proposed to Congress an act designed to break up the great utility holding companies, and he spoke harshly of monopolistic control of their industry. The Holding Company Act of 1935 was the result, although furious lobbying by the utilities led to amendments that sharply limited its effects.

Equally alarming to affluent Americans was a series of tax reforms proposed by the president in 1935, a program conservatives quickly labeled a "soak-the-rich" scheme. Apparently designed to undercut the appeal of Huey Long's Share-Our-Wealth Plan, the Roosevelt proposals called for establishing the highest and most progressive peacetime tax rates in history—although the actual impact of these rates was limited.

The Supreme Court decision in 1935 to strike down the National Industrial Recovery Act also invalidated Section 7(a) of the act, which had guaranteed workers the right to organize and bargain collectively. A group of progressives in Congress led by Senator Robert E. Wagner of New York introduced what became the National Labor Relations Act of 1935. The new law,

National Labor Relations Board

popularly known as the Wagner Act, provided workers with a crucial enforcement mechanism missing from the 1933 law: the National Labor Relations Board (NLRB), which would have power to compel employers to recognize and bargain with legitimate unions. The president was not entirely happy with the bill, but he signed it anyway. That was in large part because American workers themselves had by 1935 become so important and vigorous a force that Roosevelt realized his own political future would depend in part on responding to their demands.

Labor Militancy

The emergence of a powerful trade union movement in the 1930s was one of the most important social and political developments of the decade. It occurred partly in response to government efforts to enhance the power of unions, but it was also a result of the increased militancy of American workers and their leaders.

The growing labor militancy first became obvious in 1934, when recently organized workers (many of them inspired by the collective bargaining provisions of the National Industrial Recovery Act) demonstrated a new assertiveness. It was soon clear, however, that without stronger legal protection, most organizing drives would end in frustration. Once the Wagner Act became law, the search for more effective forms of organization rapidly gained strength in labor ranks.

The American Federation of Labor (AFL) remained committed to the idea of the craft union: organizing workers on the basis of their skills. But that concept had little to offer unskilled laborers, who now constituted the bulk of the industrial work force. During the 1930s, therefore, a newer concept of labor organization challenged the craft union ideal: industrial unionism. Advocates of this approach argued that all workers in a particular industry should be organized in a single union, regardless of what functions the workers performed. All autoworkers should be in a single automobile union; all steelworkers should be in a single steel union. United in this way, workers would greatly increase their power.

Industrial Unionism

Leaders of the AFL craft unions for the most part opposed the new concept. But industrial unionism found a number of important advocates, most prominent among them John L. Lewis, the talented, flamboyant, and eloquent leader of the United Mine Workers. At first, Lewis and his allies attempted to work within the AFL, but friction between the new industrial organizations Lewis was promoting and the older craft unions grew rapidly. At the 1935 AFL convention, Lewis became embroiled in a series of angry confrontations (and one celebrated fistfight) with craft union leaders before finally walking out. A few weeks later, he created the Committee on Industrial Organization. When the AFL expelled the new committee and all the industrial unions it represented, Lewis renamed the committee the Congress of Industrial Organizations (CIO), established it in 1936 as an organization directly rivaling the AFL, and became its first president.

CIO

The CIO expanded the constituency of the labor movement. It was more receptive to women and to blacks than the AFL had been, in part because women and blacks were more likely to be relegated to unskilled jobs and in part because CIO organizing drives targeted previously unorganized industries (textiles, laundries, tobacco factories, and others) where women and minorities constituted much of the work force. The CIO was also a more militant organization than the AFL. By the time of the 1936 schism, it was already engaged in major organizing battles in the automobile and steel industries.

Organizing Battles

Out of several competing auto unions, the United Auto Workers (UAW) was gradually emerging preeminent in the early and mid-1930s. But although it was gaining recruits, it was making little progress in winning recognition from the corporations. In December 1936, however, autoworkers employed a controversial and effective new technique for challenging corporate opposition: the sit-down strike. Employees in several General Motors plants in Detroit simply sat down inside the plants, refusing either to work or to leave, thus preventing the company from using strikebreakers. The tactic spread to other locations, and by February 1937 strikers had occupied seventeen GM plants. While male workers remained in the factories, female supporters—relatives, friends, and co-workers of the strikers—demonstrated on behalf of the strikers, lobbied on their behalf with state and local officials, and provided food, clothing, and other necessities to the men inside. The strikers ignored court orders and local police efforts to force them to vacate the buildings. When Michigan's governor, Frank Murphy, a liberal Democrat, refused to call up the National Guard to clear out the strikers, and when the federal government also refused to intervene on behalf of employers, General Motors relented. In February 1937, it became the first major manufacturer to recognize the UAW; other automobile companies soon did the same. The sit-down strike proved effective for rubber workers and others as well, but it survived only briefly as a labor technique. Its apparent illegality aroused so much public opposition that labor leaders soon abandoned it.

Sit-Down Strike

In the steel industry, the battle for unionization was less easily won. In 1936, the Steel Workers' Organizing Committee (SWOC; later the United Steelworkers of

THE "MEMORIAL DAY MASSACRE" The bitterness of the labor struggles of the 1930s was nowhere more evident than in Chicago in 1937, when striking workers attempting to march on a Republic Steel plant were brutally attacked by Chicago police, who used clubs, tear gas, and guns to turn the marchers away. Ten strikers were killed and many others were injured. *(AP/Wide World Photos)*

America) began a major organizing drive involving thousands of workers and frequent, at times bitter, strikes. In March 1937, U.S. Steel, the giant of the industry, recognized the union rather than risk a costly strike at a time when it sensed itself on the verge of recovery from the Depression. But the smaller companies (known collectively as "Little Steel") were less accommodating. On Memorial Day 1937, a group of striking workers from Republic Steel gathered with their families for a picnic and demonstration in South Chicago. When they attempted to march peacefully (and legally) toward the steel plant, police opened fire on them. Ten demonstrators were killed; another ninety were wounded. Despite a public outcry against the "Memorial Day Massacre," the harsh tactics of Little Steel companies succeeded. The 1937 strike failed.

But the victory of Little Steel was one of the last gasps of the kind of brutal strikebreaking that had proved so effective in the past. In 1937 alone, there were 4,720 strikes—over 80 percent of them settled in favor of the unions. By the end of the year, more than 8 million workers were members of unions recognized as official bargaining units by employers (compared with 3 million in 1932). By 1941, that number had expanded to 10 million and included the workers of Little Steel, whose employers had finally recognized the SWOC.

Organized Labor's Rapid Growth

Social Security

In 1935, Roosevelt gave public support to what became the Social Security Act, which Congress passed the same year. It established several distinct programs. For the elderly, there were two types of assistance. Those who were presently destitute could receive up to $15 a month in federal assistance. More important for the future, many Americans presently working were incorporated into a pension system, to which they and their employers would contribute by paying a payroll tax; it would provide them with an income on retirement. Pension payments would not begin until 1942 and even then would provide only $10 to $85 a month to recipients. And broad categories of workers (including domestic servants and agricultural laborers, occupations with disproportionate numbers of blacks and women) were excluded from the program. But the act was a crucial first step in building the nation's most important social program for the elderly.

In addition, the Social Security Act created a system of unemployment insurance, which employers alone would finance and which made it possible for workers laid off from their jobs to receive temporary government assistance. It also established a limited system (later expanded) of federal aid to people with disabilities and a program of aid to dependent children.

Unemployment Insurance

The framers of the Social Security Act wanted to create a system of "insurance," not "welfare." And the largest programs (old-age pensions and unemployment insurance) were in many ways similar to private insurance programs, with contributions from participants and benefits available to all. But the act also provided considerable direct assistance based on need—to the elderly poor, to those with disabilities, to dependent children and their mothers. These groups were widely perceived to be small and genuinely unable to support themselves. But in later generations the programs for these groups would expand until they assumed dimensions that the planners of Social Security had neither foreseen nor desired.

New Directions in Relief

Social Security was designed primarily to fulfill long-range goals. But millions of unemployed Americans had immediate needs. To help them, the Roosevelt administration established in 1935 the Works Progress Administration (WPA). Like the Civil Works Administration and earlier efforts, the WPA established a system of work relief for the unemployed. But it was much bigger than the earlier agencies, both in the size of its budget ($5 billion at first) and in the energy and imagination of its operations.

WPA

Under the direction of Harry Hopkins, the WPA was responsible for building or renovating 110,000 public buildings (schools, post offices, government office buildings) and for constructing almost 600 airports, more than 500,000 miles of roads, and over 100,000 bridges. In the process, the WPA kept an average of 2.1 million workers employed and pumped needed money into the economy.

The WPA also displayed remarkable flexibility and imagination in offering assistance to those whose occupations did not fit into any traditional category of relief. The Federal Writers Project of the WPA, for example, gave unemployed writers a chance to do their work and receive a government salary. The Federal Arts Project, similarly, helped painters, sculptors, and others to continue their careers. The Federal Music Project and the Federal Theater Project oversaw the production of concerts and plays, creating work for unemployed musicians, actors, and directors. Other relief agencies emerged alongside the WPA. The National Youth Administration (NYA) provided work and scholarship assistance to high-school and college-age men and women. The Emergency Housing

SOCIAL SECURITY POSTER, 1935 Within months of the passage of the Social Security Act of 1935, the new Social Security Board began publicizing the benefits the new system offered to working Americans—the most dramatic of which was a monthly pension to retired Americans who had paid into the system. *(Library of Congress)*

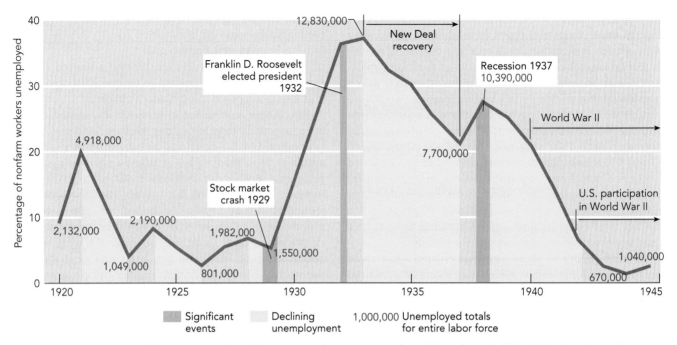

UNEMPLOYMENT, 1920–1945 This chart shows the shifting patterns of unemployment from 1920 to the end of World War II. As it reveals, unemployment was very high in the early 1920s, in the last year of the postwar recession, but remained relatively low from 1923 to 1929. The beginning of the Great Depression sent unemployment soaring—to a peak of nearly 13 million people in early 1933. The New Deal helped create a partial recovery from the Depression over the next four years, but unemployment remained very high throughout the 1930s, and spiked sharply higher again during the recession of 1937-1938, before falling rapidly after war began in Europe. ◆ *Why was the war so much more successful than the New Deal in ending unemployment?*

Division of the Public Works Administration began federal sponsorship of public housing.

Men and women alike were in distress in the 1930s (as in all difficult times). But the new welfare system dealt with members of the two sexes in very different ways. For men, the government concentrated mainly on work relief—on such programs as the CCC, the CWA, and the WPA, all of which were overwhelmingly male, and—through the Social Security Act—pensions and unemployment insurance, both structured initially to assist mostly men. The principal government aid to women was not work relief but cash assistance—most notably through the Aid to Dependent Children program of Social Security, which was designed largely to assist single mothers. This disparity in treatment reflected a widespread assumption that men constituted the bulk of the paid work force and that women needed to be treated within the context of the family. In fact, millions of women were already employed by the 1930s.

The 1936 "Referendum"

For a time in 1935 there had seemed reason to question the president's prospects for reelection. But by the middle of 1936—with the economy visibly reviving—there could be little doubt that he would win a second term. The Republican Party nominated the moderate governor of

Kansas, Alf M. Landon, who waged a generally pallid campaign. Roosevelt's dissident challengers now appeared powerless.

Alf Landon

One reason was the violent death of their most effective leader, Huey Long, who was assassinated in Louisiana in September 1935. Another reason was the ill-fated alliance among Father Coughlin, Dr. Townsend, and Gerald L. K. Smith (an intemperate henchman of Huey Long), who joined forces that summer to establish a new political movement—the Union Party, which nominated an undistinguished North Dakota congressman, William Lemke, for president.

The result was the greatest landslide in American history to that point. Roosevelt polled just under 61 percent of the vote to Landon's 36 percent and carried every state except Maine and Vermont. The Democrats increased their already large majorities in both houses of Congress. The Union Party received fewer than 900,000 votes.

The election results demonstrated the party realignment that the New Deal had produced. The Democrats now

Electoral realignment

controlled a broad coalition of western and southern farmers, the urban working classes, the poor and unemployed, and the black communities of northern cities, as well as traditional progressives and committed new liberals—a coalition that constituted a substantial majority of the electorate. It would be decades before the Republican Party could again create a lasting majority coalition of its own.

WPA WORKERS ON THE JOB The Works Progress Administration funded an enormous variety of work projects to provide jobs for the unemployed. But most WPA employees worked on construction sites of one kind or another. Here, WPA workers labor on a bridge project in the Bronx, in New York City. *(Bettmann/Corbis)*

WPA MURAL ART The Federal Arts Project of the Works Progress Administration commissioned an impressive series of public murals from the artists it employed. Many of these murals adorned post offices, libraries, and other public buildings constructed by the WPA. William Gropper's *Construction of a Dam,* a detail of which is seen here, is typical of much of the mural art of the 1930s in its celebration of the workingman. Workers are depicted in heroic poses, laboring in unison to complete a great public project. Most WPA iconography similarly portrayed workers as white men only. *(Library of Congress)*

THE GOLDEN AGE OF COMIC BOOKS

In the troubled years of the Great Depression and World War II, many Americans sought release from their anxieties in fantasy. Those who produced America's popular culture eagerly obliged them, with movies, plays, books, radio shows, and other diversions that drew people out of their own lives and into a safer or more glamorous or more exciting world. Beginning in 1938, one of the most popular forms of escape for many young Americans became the comic book. For decades after that, comic books remained a powerful force in American culture.

The modern comics began on the "funny pages" of American newspapers in the 1890s. In the first years of the twentieth century, publishers collected

SUPERMAN The most popular action figure in the history of comic books was Superman, whose superhuman powers were particularly appealing fantasies to Americans suffering through the Depression and, later, World War II. *(Superman No. 1 © 1939 DC Comics. All rights reserved. Used with permission.)*

previously published strips and began selling them in books. Seldom did these early comics make any effort to develop continuing plots or complex characters—although the popular character Dick Tracy did serve as the hero of some continuing detective stories. In the 1930s, however, some artists and businessmen began to see new and greater possibilities in the comics.

In February 1935, Malcolm Wheeler-Nicholson founded the first comics magazine—what we now know as the "comic book"—titled *New Fun,* which published entirely original material. Wheeler had little success with *New Fun,* but he continued to believe in the potential of original comic books. He founded a new company, Detective Comics, and began in 1937 to design a new magazine called *Action Comics.* Wheeler himself ran out of money before he could publish anything, but the company continued without him. In 1938, the first issue of *Action Comics* appeared with a startling and controversial cover—a powerful man in a skintight suit lifting a car over his head. His name was Superman, and he became the most popular cartoon character of all time.

Within a year, Superman had a comic book named after him, which was selling over 1.2 million copies each issue. By 1940, there was a popular Superman radio show—introduced by a breathless announcer crying, "It's a bird! It's a plane! It's . . . Superman!" And very soon, other publishers—and even Detective Comics itself—began developing new "superheroes" (a term invented by the creators of Superman) to capitalize on this growing new popular appetite. In 1939, a second great comic book publisher appeared— Marvel Comics. By the early 1940s, Superman had been joined by such

other supernatural heroes as the Human Torch, the Sub-Mariner, Batman, the Flash, and Wonder Woman, a character created in part to signal the importance of women to the war effort. None proved as popular as Superman, but many were commercially successful nevertheless.

It is not hard to imagine why superheroes would be so appealing to Americans—particularly to the teenage boys who were the largest single purchasers of comic books—in the 1930s and 1940s. Superman and other superheroes were idealized versions of the ideal boy—smart, good, "the perfect Boy Scout," as one fan put it. But they were also all-powerful, capable of righting wrong and preventing catastrophe. In a world where catastrophe was an ever-present possibility—in the lives of many families in the 1930s, and in the reality of the world at large in the 1940s—superheroes were a comforting escape from fear. Jerry Siegel and Joe Shuster, who drew and wrote the Superman comics, were themselves very young men in the late 1930s, not far removed from their own teenage fantasies. And indeed many of the early comic book writers were men in their late teens or early twenties.

Many of the creators of comic books were also Jewish, young men conscious of their outsider status in an American culture not yet wholly open to them. The characters they created almost all had alter egos, identities they used while living within the normal world. Superman was Clark Kent, a "mild-mannered reporter." Batman was Bruce Wayne, a wealthy heir. All were wholly a part of mainstream American society, and they expressed in part the outsider's dream of assimilation. At the same time, the characters as superheroes were outsiders themselves—but outsiders

THE NEW DEAL IN DISARRAY

Roosevelt emerged from the 1936 election at the zenith of his popularity. Within months, however, the New Deal was mired in serious new difficulties—a result of continuing opposition, the president's own political errors, and major economic setbacks.

The Court Fight

The 1936 mandate, Franklin Roosevelt believed, made it possible for him to do something about the problem of the Supreme Court. No program of reform, he had become convinced, could long survive the conservative justices, who had already struck down the NRA and the AAA and threatened to invalidate even more legislation.

CAPTAIN AMERICA Captain America made his comic book debut in 1941 and immediately established himself as both super-hero and super-patriot. Even before Pearl Harbor, Captain America was portrayed as a powerful foe of the Nazis and the Japanese, and as a particularly deadly enemy of spies and saboteurs who had infiltrated the United States—as in this strip where he throttles an "enemy agent." *(CAPTAIN AMERICA:TM © 2002 Marvel Characters, Inc. Used with permission.)*

THE INDUSTRY CODE Beginning in 1955, under pressure from government officials and others who charged comic books with being vulgar and dangerous, the comic book industry established its own code authority, much like the organization created to police movies that had been created in the 1920s. This stamp was the code authority's seal of approval, designed to reassure readers (and their parents) that the contents were wholesome.

endowed with special powers and abilities unavailable to ordinary people.

Even before America entered World War II, the comic books went to war with the Axis. Marvel's the Human Torch and the Sub-Mariner joined forces against the German navy. Superman fought spies and saboteurs at home. A new character created in March 1941, Captain America, was a frail young man rejected by the army who, after being given a secret serum by a military doctor, became extraordinarily powerful. Joining the army at last, he posed as an ordinary private but managed to perform extraordinary deeds. On the cover of the first issue of *Captain America*, the title character could be seen punching Hitler in his headquarters in Germany. The war also expanded the readership of the comic books. They became enormously popular among soldiers and sailors—many of whom had been reading them, as teenagers, before joining the military.

The end of the war was also the end of this first "Golden Age" of American comic books. Many super-hero magazines—including *Captain America*—ceased publication as peacetime reduced the popular appetite for fantasy. In their place emerged new comic books, which emphasized romance and even mild sexuality. A new company, Entertainment Comics, began publishing lurid horror and science-fiction comics, with levels of violence and cruelty far higher than the earlier superhero books had ever displayed. None ever reached the levels of popularity that the superhero comics had enjoyed during the Depression and war.

In the late 1940s and early 1950s, comic books began to come under attack from educators, psychiatrists, journalists, and even the federal government. In 1954, members of the United States Senate held hearings in New York to hear testimony from comic book writers and publishers. The senators

seemed unpersuaded by the claims they heard that comics were, in fact, healthy and decent. Congress took no legal action against them, but the comic book industry itself created a trade association, which produced a "Comics Code" to prevent indecency in the industry.

Comic books experienced an unexpected revival in the late 1950s and 1960s. Old superheroes—Captain America, the Human Torch, and others—reappeared. New ones—Spiderman, Iron Man, the Silver Surfer—joined them. Superman, who had never disappeared, enjoyed newfound popularity and became the hero for a time of a popular television show. But these new or revised heroes were not entirely like those of the 1930s and 1940s—not the rock-solid Boy Scouts certain of the difference between right and wrong. They were more complicated characters, plagued at times by doubt and weakness and thwarted desire. They reflected the realities of an increasingly complex and complicated world, which their characters—like their mostly young readers—were struggling to understand.

In February 1937, Roosevelt sent a surprise message to Capitol Hill proposing a general overhaul of the federal

Court Packing

court system; included among the many provisions was one to add up to six new justices to the Supreme Court. The courts were "overworked," he claimed, and needed additional manpower and younger blood to enable them to

cope with their increasing burdens. But Roosevelt's real purpose was to give himself the opportunity to appoint new, liberal justices and change the ideological balance of the Court.

Conservatives were outraged at the "Court-packing plan," and even many Roosevelt supporters were disturbed by what they considered evidence of the president's hunger for power. Still, Roosevelt might well have persuaded Congress to approve at least a compromise measure had not the Supreme Court itself intervened. Of the nine justices, three reliably supported the New Deal, and four reliably opposed it. Of the remaining two, Chief Justice Charles Evans Hughes often sided with the progressives and Associate Justice Owen J. Roberts usually voted with the conservatives. On March 29, 1937, Roberts, Hughes, and the three progressive justices voted together to uphold a state minimum-wage law—in the case of *West Coast Hotel* v. *Parrish*—thus appearing to reverse a 5-to-4 decision of the previous year invalidating a similar law. Two weeks later, again by a 5-to-4 margin, the Court upheld the Wagner Act, and in May it validated the Social Security Act. Whether or not for that reason, the Court's newly moderate position made the Court-packing bill seem unnecessary. Congress ultimately defeated it.

On one level, the affair was a significant victory for Franklin Roosevelt. The Court was no longer an obstacle to New Deal reforms, particularly after the older justices began to retire, to be replaced by Roosevelt appointees. But the Court-packing episode did lasting political damage to the administration. From 1937 on, southern Democrats and other conservatives voted against Roosevelt's measures much more often than they had in the past.

Retrenchment and Recession

By the summer of 1937, the national income, which had dropped from $82 billion in 1929 to $40 billion in 1932, had risen to nearly $72 billion. Other economic indices showed similar advances. Roosevelt seized on these improvements as an excuse to try to balance the federal budget, convinced by Treasury Secretary Henry Morgenthau and many economists that the real danger now was no longer depression but inflation. Between January and August 1937, for example, he cut the WPA in half, laying off 1.5 million relief workers. A few weeks later, the fragile boom collapsed. The index of industrial production dropped from 117 in August 1937 to 76 in May 1938. Four million additional workers lost their jobs. Economic conditions were soon almost as bad as they had been in the bleak days of 1932–1933.

The recession of 1937, known to the president's critics as the "Roosevelt recession," was a result of many factors. But to many observers at the time (including, apparently, the president himself), it seemed to be a direct result of the administration's unwise decision to reduce spending. And so in April 1938, the president asked Congress for an emergency appropriation of $5 billion for public works and relief programs, and government funds soon began pouring into the economy once again. Within a few months, another tentative recovery seemed to be

Roosevelt Recession

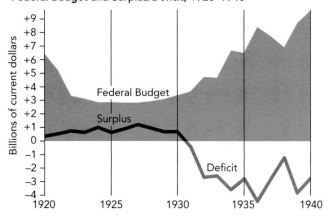

Federal Budget and Surplus/Deficit, 1920–1940

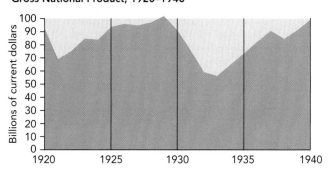

Gross National Product, 1920–1940

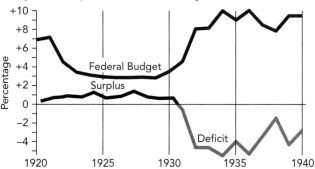

Budget and Surplus/Deficit as Percentage of GNP, 1920–1940

FEDERAL BUDGET SURPLUS/DEFICIT AND GNP, 1920–1940 Among its many other effects, the Great Depression produced dramatic changes in the fiscal condition of the federal government. In the first of these three charts, note the sharp decline in federal spending in the early 1920s (as the nation demobilized from World War I) and the appearance of significant budget surpluses. Note, too, the dramatic increase in government spending (and the appearance of significant deficits) once the Depression began and, particularly, once Franklin Roosevelt became president. The second chart illustrates the varying fortunes of the nation's economy by showing the rise and fall of gross national product—the total of goods and services produced by the economy. The GNP fell sharply in the first years of the Depression, but by the end of the 1930s was nearing its 1929 levels again. The final chart gives some perspective on these figures by illustrating the relationship between federal spending (and federal surpluses and deficits) and the total size of the economy. At its peak in these years, federal spending was never more than about 9 percent of the GNP and the deficit never more than about 5 percent. In recent decades, the federal budget has often exceeded 20 percent of the GNP, while deficits—much higher in absolute numbers than those of the 1930s—have rarely been higher as a percentage of the GNP than those of the 1930s. ◆ *Why did government deficits increase so sharply during the Great Depression?*

under way, and the advocates of spending pointed to it as proof of the validity of their approach.

At about the same time, at the urging of a group of younger, antimonopolist liberals in the administration, Roosevelt sent a stinging message to Congress, vehemently denouncing what he called an "unjustifiable concentration of economic power" and asking for the creation of a commission to examine that concentration with an eye to major reforms in the antitrust laws. In response, Congress established the Temporary National Economic Committee (TNEC), whose members included representatives of both houses of Congress and officials from several executive agencies. Also that spring, Roosevelt appointed a new head of the antitrust division of the Justice Department: Thurman Arnold, a Yale Law School professor who soon proved to be the most vigorous director ever to serve in that office.

Later in 1938, the administration successfully supported one of its most ambitious pieces of labor legislation, the Fair Labor Standards Act, which for the first time established a national minimum wage and a forty-hour workweek, and which also placed strict limits on child labor. Like Social Security, the act at first excluded from its provisions the great majority of women and minority workers.

Despite these achievements, however, by the end of 1938 the New Deal had essentially come to an end. Congressional opposition now made it difficult for the president to enact any major new programs. But more important, perhaps, the threat of world crisis hung heavy in the political atmosphere, and Roosevelt was gradually growing more concerned with persuading a reluctant nation to prepare for war than with pursuing new avenues of reform.

End of the New Deal

LIMITS AND LEGACIES OF THE NEW DEAL

In the 1930s, Roosevelt's principal critics were conservatives, who accused him of abandoning the Constitution and establishing a menacing, even tyrannical, state. In more recent years, the New Deal's most visible critics have attacked it from the left, pointing to the major problems it left unsolved and the important groups it failed to represent. A full understanding of the New Deal requires coming to terms with the sources of both critiques, by examining both its achievements and its limits.

The Idea of the "Broker State"

In 1933, many New Dealers dreamed of using their new popularity and authority somehow to remake American capitalism—to produce new forms of cooperation and control that would create a genuinely harmonious, ordered economic world. By 1939, it was clear that what they had created was in fact something quite different. But rather than bemoan the gap between their original

intentions and their ultimate achievements, New Deal liberals, both in 1939 and in later years, chose to accept what they had produced and to celebrate it—to use it as a model for future reform efforts.

What they had created was something that in later years would become known as the "broker state." Instead of forging all elements of society into a single, harmonious unit, as some reformers had once hoped to do, the real achievement of the New Deal was to elevate and strengthen new interest groups so as to allow them to compete more effectively in the national marketplace. The New Deal made the federal government a mediator in that continuous competition—a force that could intervene when necessary to help some groups and limit the power of others. In 1933, there had been only one great interest group (albeit a varied and divided one) with genuine power in the national economy: the corporate world. By the end of the 1930s, American business found itself competing for influence with an increasingly powerful labor movement, with an organized agricultural economy, and with aroused consumers. In later years, the "broker state" idea would expand to embrace other groups as well: racial, ethnic, and religious minorities; women; and many others. Thus, one of the enduring legacies of the New Deal was to make the federal government a protector of interest groups and a supervisor of the competition among them, rather than an instrument attempting to create a universal harmony of interests.

Establishment of the "Broker State"

What determines which interest groups receive government assistance in a "broker state"? The experience of the New Deal suggests that such assistance goes largely to those groups able to exercise enough political or economic power to demand it. Thus in the 1930s, farmers—after decades of organization and agitation—and workers—as the result of militant action and mass mobilization—won from the government new and important protections. Other groups, less well organized, perhaps, but politically important because so numerous and visible, won limited assistance as well: imperiled homeowners, the unemployed, the elderly.

By the same token, the interest-group democracy that the New Deal came to represent offered much less to those groups either too weak to demand assistance or not visible enough to arouse widespread public support. And yet those same groups were often the ones most in need of help from their government. One of the important limits of the New Deal, therefore, was its very modest record on behalf of several important social groups.

African Americans and the New Deal

One group the New Deal did relatively little to assist was African Americans. The administration was not hostile to black aspirations. On the contrary, the New Deal was probably more sympathetic to them than any previous government of the twentieth century. Eleanor Roosevelt

ELEANOR ROOSEVELT AND MARY MCLEOD BETHUNE
Mary McLeod Bethune was one of a small but energetic group of African-American officeholders in the Roosevelt administration. Together they formed an informal network known as the "Black Cabinet." Among their most important allies was Eleanor Roosevelt, who is shown here appearing with Bethune at a 1937 National Conference on Problems of the Negro and Negro Youth, organized by the National Youth Administration. Bethune was the NYA's director of Negro activities. *(Bettmann/Corbis)*

spoke throughout the 1930s on behalf of racial justice and put continuing pressure on her husband and others in the federal government to ease discrimination against blacks. She was also partially responsible for what was, symbolically at least, one of the most important events of the decade for African Americans. When the black singer Marian Anderson was refused permission in the spring of 1939 to give a concert in the auditorium of the Daughters of the American Revolution (Washington's only major concert hall), Eleanor Roosevelt resigned from the organization and then (along with Interior Secretary Harold Ickes, another champion of racial equality) helped secure government permission for her to sing on the steps of the Lincoln Memorial. Anderson's Easter Sunday concert attracted 75,000 people and became, in effect, one of the first modern civil rights demonstrations.

The president himself appointed a number of blacks to significant second-level positions in his administration. "Black Cabinet" Roosevelt appointees such as Robert Weaver, William Hastie, and Mary McLeod Bethune created an informal network of officeholders who consulted frequently with one another and who became known as the "Black Cabinet." Eleanor Roosevelt, Harold Ickes, and Harry Hopkins all made efforts to ensure that New Deal relief programs did not exclude blacks; and by 1935, perhaps a quarter of all African Americans were receiving some form of government assistance. One result was a historic change in black electoral behavior. As late as 1932, most African Americans were voting Republican, as they had since the Civil War. By 1936, more than 90 percent of them were voting Democratic—the beginnings of a political alliance that would endure for decades.

African Americans supported Franklin Roosevelt because they knew he was not their enemy. But they had few illusions that the New Deal represented a major turning point in American race relations. For example, the president was never willing to risk losing the backing of southern Democrats by supporting legislation to make lynching a federal crime. Nor would he endorse efforts in Congress to ban the poll tax, one of the most potent tools by which white southerners kept blacks from voting.

New Deal relief agencies did not challenge, and indeed reinforced, existing patterns of discrimination. The Civilian Conservation Corps established separate black camps. The NRA codes tolerated paying blacks less than whites doing the same jobs. African Americans were largely excluded from employment in the TVA. The Federal Housing Administration refused to provide mortgages to blacks moving into white neighborhoods, and the first public housing projects financed by the federal government were racially segregated. The WPA routinely relegated black, Hispanic, and Asian workers to the least-skilled and lowest-paying jobs, or excluded them altogether; when funding ebbed, nonwhites, like women, were among the first to be dismissed.

The New Deal was not hostile to African Americans, and it did much to help them advance. But it refused to make the issue of race a significant part of its agenda.

The New Deal and the "Indian Problem"

In many respects, government policies toward the Indian tribes in the 1930s were simply a continuation of the

HARLEM GROCERY STORE, 1940 The photographer Aaron Siskind took this picture of a community grocery store in Harlem, its manager standing proudly in the doorway. It was part of a project designed to document life in what *Look* magazine that same year called "the Negro capital of America." Siskind and other photographers worked from 1938 to 1940 to produce a series they called *The Harlem Document. (Print and Photographs Division, Library of Congress. Courtesy of The Aaron Siskind Foundation.)*

long-established effort to encourage Native Americans to assimilate into the larger society and culture.

But the principal elements of federal policy in the New Deal years worked to advance a very different goal, largely because of the efforts of the extraordinary commissioner of Indian affairs in those years, John Collier. Collier was a former social worker who had become committed to the cause of the Indians after exposure to tribal cultures in New Mexico in the 1920s. More important, he was greatly influenced by the work of twentieth-century anthropologists who promoted the idea of cultural relativism, which challenged the three-centuries-old assumption among white Americans that Indians were "savages" and that white society was inherently superior and more "civilized."

John Collier

Collier promoted legislation that would, he hoped, reverse the pressures on Native Americans to assimilate and would allow them the right to live in traditional Indian ways. Not all tribal leaders agreed with Collier; indeed, his belief in the importance of preserving Indian culture would not find its broadest support among the tribes until the 1960s. Nevertheless, Collier effectively promoted legislation—which became the Indian Reorganization Act of 1934—that restored to the tribes the right to own land collectively. (It reversed the allotment policy adopted in 1887, which encouraged the breaking up of tribal lands into individually owned plots—a policy that had led to the loss of over 90 million acres of tribal land to white specula-

Indian Reorganization Act

tors and others.) In the thirteen years after passage of the 1934 bill, tribal land increased by nearly 4 million acres, and Indian agricultural income increased from under $2 million in 1934 to over $49 million in 1947.

Even with the redistribution of lands under the 1934 act, however, Indians continued to possess, for the most part, only territory whites did not want—much of it arid, some of it desert. And as a group, they continued to constitute the poorest segment of the population. The efforts of the 1930s did not solve what some called the "Indian problem." They did, however, provide Indians with some tools for rebuilding the viability of the tribes.

Women and the New Deal

As with African Americans, the New Deal was not hostile to feminist aspirations, but neither did it do a great deal to advance them. That was largely because such aspirations did not have sufficiently widespread support (even among women) to make it politically advantageous for the administration to back them.

There were, to be sure, important symbolic gestures on behalf of women. Roosevelt appointed the first female cabinet member in the nation's history, Secretary of Labor Frances Perkins. He also named more than 100 other women to positions at lower levels of the federal bureaucracy. They created an active female network within the government and cooperated with

Symbolic Gains for Women

THE NEW DEAL

For many years, debate among historians over the nature of the New Deal mirrored the debate among Americans in the 1930s over the achievements of the Roosevelt administration. Historians struggled, just as contemporaries had done, to decide whether the New Deal was a good thing or a bad thing.

The conservative critique of the New Deal has received relatively little scholarly expression. Edgar Robinson, in *The Roosevelt Leadership* (1955), and John T. Flynn, in *The Roosevelt Myth* (1956), attacked Roosevelt as both a radical and a despot; but few other historians have taken such

(Franklin D. Roosevelt Library)

charges very seriously. By far the dominant view of the New Deal among scholars has been an approving, liberal interpretation.

The first important voice of the liberal view was Arthur M. Schlesinger Jr., who argued in the three volumes of *The Age of Roosevelt* (1957–1960) that the New Deal marked a continuation of the long struggle between public power and private interests, but that Roosevelt moved that struggle to a new level. The unrestrained power of the business community was finally confronted with an effective challenge, and what emerged was a system of reformed capitalism, with far more protection for workers, farmers, consumers, and others than in the past.

The first systematic "revisionist" interpretation of the New Deal came in 1963, in William Leuchtenburg's *Franklin D. Roosevelt and the New Deal*. Leuchtenburg was a sympathetic critic, arguing that most of the limitations of the New Deal were a result of the restrictions imposed on Roosevelt by the political and ideological realities of his time—that the New Deal prob-

ably could not have done much more than it did. Nevertheless, Leuchtenburg challenged earlier views of the New Deal as a revolution in social policy and was able to muster only enough enthusiasm to call it a "halfway revolution," one that enhanced the positions of some previously disadvantaged groups (notably farmers and factory workers) but did little or nothing for many others (including blacks, sharecroppers, and the urban poor). Ellis Hawley augmented these moderate criticisms of the Roosevelt record in *The New Deal and the Problem of Monopoly* (1966). In examining 1930s economic policies, Hawley challenged liberal assumptions that the New Deal acted as the foe of private business interests. On the contrary, he argued, New Deal efforts were in many cases designed to enhance the position of private entrepreneurs—even, at times, at the expense of some of the liberal reform goals that administration officials espoused.

Other historians in the 1960s and later, writing from the left, expressed much harsher criticisms of the New

---

one another in advancing causes of interest to women. Such appointments were in part a response to pressure from Eleanor Roosevelt, who was a committed advocate of women's rights and a champion of humanitarian causes. Molly Dewson, head of the Women's Division of the Democratic National Committee, was also influential in securing federal appointments for women as well as in increasing their role within the Democratic Party. Several women received appointments to the federal judiciary. And one, Hattie Caraway of Arkansas, became in 1934 the first woman ever elected to a full term in the U.S. Senate. (She was running to succeed her husband, who had died in office.)

But New Deal support for women operated within limits, partly because New Deal women themselves had limited views of what their aims should be. Frances Perkins and many others in the administration emerged out of the feminist tradition of the progressive era, which emphasized not so much sexual equality as special protections for women. Perkins and other women reformers were instrumental in creating support for, and shaping the character of, the Social Security Act of 1935. But they built into that bill their own notion of women's special place in a male-dominated economy. The principal provision of the

bill specifically designed for women—the Aid to Dependent Children program—was modeled on the state-level mothers' pensions that generations of progressive women had worked to pass earlier in the century.

The New Deal generally supported the prevailing belief that in hard times women should withdraw from the workplace to open up more jobs for men. New Deal relief agencies offered relatively little employment for women. The NRA sanctioned sexually discriminatory wage practices. The Social Security program at first excluded domestic servants, waitresses, and other predominantly female occupations.

> Prevailing Gender Norms Buttressed

The New Deal in the West and the South

Two regions of the United States that did receive special attention from the New Deal were the West and the South, both of which benefited disproportionately from New Deal relief and public works programs. The West received more federal funds per capita through New Deal relief programs than any other region, and parts of the South were not far behind.

Deal. Barton Bernstein, in a notable 1968 essay, compiled a dreary chronicle of missed opportunities, inadequate responses to problems, and damaging New Deal initiatives. The Roosevelt administration may have saved capitalism, Bernstein charged, but it failed to help—and in many ways actually harmed—those groups most in need of assistance. Ronald Radosh, also in 1968, portrayed the New Deal as an effective agent for the consolidation of modern corporate capitalism. Several essays by Thomas Ferguson in the 1980s and Colin Gordon's 1994 book *New Deals* took such arguments further. They cited the close ties between the New Deal and internationalist financiers and industrialists; the liberalism of the 1930s was a product of their shared interest in protecting capitalists and stabilizing capitalism.

Except for the work of Ferguson and Gordon, the attack on the New Deal from the left has not developed very far beyond its preliminary statements in the 1960s. Instead, by the 1970s and 1980s, most scholars seemed less interested in the question of whether the New Deal was a "conservative" or "revolutionary" phenomenon than in the question of the constraints within which it was operating. The sociologist Theda Skocpol, in an important series of articles, has emphasized (along with other scholars) the issue of "state capacity" as an important New Deal constraint; ambitious reform ideas often foundered, she argues, because of the absence of a government bureaucracy with sufficient strength and expertise to shape or administer them. James T. Patterson, Barry Karl, Mark Leff, and others have emphasized the political constraints the New Deal encountered. Both in Congress and among the public, conservative inhibitions about government remained strong; the New Deal was as much a product of the pressures of its conservative opponents as of its liberal supporters.

Frank Freidel, Ellis Hawley, Herbert Stein, and many others point as well to the ideological constraints affecting Franklin Roosevelt and his supporters. Alan Brinkley, in *The End of Reform* (1995), described a transition in New Deal thinking from a regulatory view of government to one that envisioned relatively little direct interference by government in the corporate world; a movement—driven in part by the need to adapt to a conservative political climate—toward an essentially "compensatory" state centered on Keynesian welfare state programs. David Kennedy, in *Freedom from Fear* (1999), argues by contrast that the more aggressive strands of early New Deal liberalism actually hampered the search for recovery, that Roosevelt's embrace of measures that unleashed the power of the market was the most effective approach to prosperity.

The phrase "New Deal liberalism" has come in the postwar era to seem synonymous with modern ideas of aggressive federal management of the economy, elaborate welfare systems, a powerful bureaucracy, and large-scale government spending. The "Reagan Revolution" of the 1980s often portrayed itself as a reaction to the "legacy of the New Deal." Many historians of the New Deal, however, would argue that the modern idea of "New Deal liberalism" bears only a limited relationship to the ideas that New Dealers themselves embraced. The liberal accomplishments of the 1930s can be understood only in the context of their own time; later liberal efforts drew from that legacy but also altered it to fit the needs and assumptions of very different eras.

Most westerners were eager for the assistance New Deal agencies provided, but their political leaders were not always as supportive. In Colorado, for example, the state legislature refused to provide the required matching funds for FERA relief in 1933. When, in response, Harry Hopkins cut Colorado off from the program, unemployed people rioted in Denver and looted food stores. Only then did the legislature reverse course and provide funding.

In the South, locally administered New Deal relief programs did not challenge prevailing racial norms. In the West, too, New Deal programs accepted existing racial and ethnic prejudices. In several states, relief agencies paid different groups at different rates: white Anglos received the most generous aid; blacks, Indians, and Mexican Americans received lower levels of support. In the CCC camps in New Mexico, Hispanics and Anglos sometimes worked in the same camps, but there were frequent tensions and occasional conflicts between them. But the main reason for the New Deal's particular impact on the West was that conditions in the region made the government's programs especially important. Federal agricultural programs had an enormous impact on the West because farming remained so much more central to the economy of the region than it did in much of the East. The largest New Deal public works programs—the great dams and power stations—were mainly in the West, both because the best locations for such facilities were there and because the West had the most need for new sources of water and power. The Grand Coulee Dam on the Columbia River was the largest public works project in American history to that point. It provided cheap electric power for much of the Northwest and, along with the construction of smaller dams and water projects nearby, created a basis for economic development in the region.

Without this enormous public investment by the federal government, much of the economic development that transformed the West after World War II would have been much more difficult, if not impossible, to achieve. But the region paid a price for the government's beneficence: For generations after the Great Depression, the federal government maintained a much greater and more visible bureaucratic presence in the West than in any other region.

Failure to Challenge Jim Crow

New Deal's Legacy in the West

The New Deal located fewer great infrastructure projects in the South than it did in the West—although the largest of them all, the TVA, was an entirely southern venture. But many of the economic development efforts the Roosevelt administration undertook were of disproportionate benefit to the South, in large part because the South was the least economically developed region of the nation in the 1930s. One example was rural electrification, which had a large impact on many agrarian areas of the nation but a particular impact on the South, where vast parts of the countryside remained without access to power lines until the REA provided them.

The New Deal also directed national attention toward the economic condition of the South in a way that no previous administration had done. Many Americans outside the South had long believed the South to be somehow "backward," but they tended to attribute that backwardness to racism, segregation, and prejudice. In a 1938 economic report sponsored by the federal government, a group of social scientists and others called the South "the nation's number one economic problem." Although the report made some reference to the South's racial customs, it spoke mostly about its lack of sufficiently developed economic institutions and facilities.

The New Deal and the National Economy

The most frequent criticisms of the New Deal involve its failure genuinely to revive or reform the American economy. New Dealers never fully recognized the value of government spending as a vehicle for recovery, and their efforts along other lines never succeeded in ending the Depression. The economic boom sparked by World War II, not the New Deal, finally ended the crisis. Nor did the New Deal substantially alter the distribution of power within American capitalism; and it had only a small impact on the distribution of wealth among the American people.

Failure to Achieve Recovery

Nevertheless, the New Deal did have a number of important and lasting effects on both the behavior and the structure of the American economy. It helped elevate new groups—workers, farmers, and others—to positions from which they could at times effectively challenge the power of the corporations. It contributed to the economic development of the West and, to a lesser degree, the South. It increased the regulatory functions of the federal government in ways that helped stabilize previously troubled areas of the economy: the stock market, the banking system, and others. And the administration helped establish the basis for new forms of federal fiscal policy, which in the postwar years would give the government tools for promoting and regulating economic growth.

The New Deal also created the basis of the federal welfare state, through its many relief programs and above all through the Social Security system. The conservative inhibitions New Dealers brought to this task ensured that the welfare system that ultimately emerged would be limited in its impact (at least in comparison with those of other industrial nations), would reinforce some traditional patterns of gender and racial discrimination, and would be expensive and cumbersome to administer. But for all its limits, the new system marked a historic break with the federal government's traditional reluctance to offer public assistance to its neediest citizens.

Federal Welfare State Established

The New Deal and American Politics

Perhaps the most dramatic effect of the New Deal was on the structure and behavior of American government itself and on the character of American politics. Franklin Roosevelt helped enhance the power of the federal government as a whole. By the end of the 1930s, state and local governments were clearly of secondary importance to the government in Washington. Roosevelt also established the presidency as the preeminent center of authority within the federal government.

MAJOR LEGISLATION OF THE NEW DEAL

1933	Emergency Banking Act		**1935**	Works Progress Administration
	Economy Act			National Youth Administration
	Civilian Conservation Corps			Social Security Act
	Agricultural Adjustment Act			National Labor Relations Act
	Tennessee Valley Authority			Public Utilities Holding Company Act
	National Industrial Recovery Act			Resettlement Administration
	Banking Act			Rural Electrification Administration
	Federal Emergency Relief Act			Revenue Act ("wealth tax")
	Home Owners' Refinancing Act		**1936**	Soil Conservation and Domestic Allotment Act
	Civil Works Administration		**1937**	Farm Security Administration
	Federal Securities Act			National Housing Act
1934	National Housing Act		**1938**	Second Agricultural Adjustment Act
	Securities and Exchange Act			Fair Labor Standards Act
	Home Owners' Loan Act		**1939**	Executive Reorganization Act

Finally, the New Deal had a profound impact on how the American people defined themselves politically. It

New Expectations of Government

took a weak, divided Democratic Party, which had been a minority force in American politics for many decades, and turned it into a mighty coalition that would dominate national party competition for more than forty years. It turned the attention of many voters away from some of the cultural issues that had preoccupied them in the 1920s and awakened in them an interest in economic matters of direct importance to their lives. And it created among the American people greatly increased expectations of government—expectations that the New Deal itself did not always fulfill but that survived to become the basis of new liberal crusades in the postwar era.

CONCLUSION

The New Deal was the most dramatic and important moment in the modern history of American government. From the time of Franklin Roosevelt's inauguration in 1933 to the beginning of World War II eight years later, the federal government engaged in a broad and diverse series of experiments designed to relieve the distress of unemployment and poverty, to reform the economy to prevent future crises, and to bring the Great Depression itself to an end. It had only partial success in all those efforts.

Unemployment and poverty remained high throughout the New Deal, although many federal programs provided assistance to millions of people who would otherwise have had none. The structure of the American economy remained essentially the same as it had been in earlier years, although there were by the end of the New Deal some important new regulatory agencies in Washington—and an important new role for organized labor, enforced by a new federal law. Nothing the New Deal did ended the Great Depression, but some of its policies kept it from getting worse—and some of them pointed the way toward more effective economic policies in the future.

Perhaps the most important legacy of the New Deal was the creation of a sense of possibilities among many Americans, to persuade them that the fortunes of individuals need not be left entirely to chance or to the workings of the market. Many Americans emerged from the 1930s convinced that individuals deserved some protections from the unpredictability and instability of the modern economy, and that the New Deal—for all its limitations—had demonstrated the value of enlisting government in the effort to provide those protections.

INTERACTIVE LEARNING

The *Primary Source Investigator CD-ROM* offers the following materials related to this chapter:

- Interactive maps: **U.S. Elections** (M7) and **Unemployment Relief** (M26).
- Documents, images, and maps related to Roosevelt and the policies and politics of his New Deal. Highlights include excerpts from some of the major legislation of the New Deal era, including the Tennessee Valley Authority Act and the Social Security Act; lyrics and audio clips of Depression-era songs; a 1936 "fireside chat"; and excerpts from the WPA slave narratives, as documented by the Federal Writers Project.

Online Learning Center (www.mhhe.com/brinkley13e)

For quizzes, Internet resources, references to additional books and films, and more, consult this book's Online Learning Center.

FOR FURTHER REFERENCE

William E. Leuchtenburg, *Franklin D. Roosevelt and the New Deal* (1963) is a classic short history of the New Deal. Anthony Badger, *The New Deal: The Depression Years* (1989) is another fine overview. David Kennedy, *Freedom from Fear: The American People in Depression and War, 1929–1945* (1999) is an important narrative history, a volume in the Oxford History of the United States. Geoffrey Ward, *Before the Trumpet: Young Franklin Roosevelt, 1882–1905* (1985) and *A First-Class Temperament: The Emergence of Franklin Roosevelt* (1989) are superb biographical accounts of the pre-presidential FDR. Frank Freidel, *Franklin D. Roosevelt: A Rendezvous with Destiny* (1990) is a one-volume biography by one of FDR's important biographers. Jonathan Alter, *The Defining Moment* (2006) and Anthony Badger *FDR: The First Hundred Days* (2008) portray the first months of the New Deal. Ellis Hawley, *The New Deal and the Problem of Monopoly* (1967) is a classic examination of the economic policies of the Roosevelt administration in its first five years. Colin Gordon, *New Deals: Business, Labor, and Politics in America, 1920–1935* (1994) is a challenging reinterpretation of the early New Deal years. Michael Janeway, *The Fall of the House of Roosevelt* (2004) is an engaging account of the complex group of New Dealers who shaped not only Roosevelt's government, but policy and politics beyond the New Deal. The transformation of liberalism after 1937 is the subject of Alan Brinkley, *The End of Reform: New Deal Liberalism in Recession and War* (1995). Jennifer Klein, *For All These Rights: Business, Labor, and the Shaping of America's Public-Private Welfare State* (2003) sees the origin of the modern welfare state as a product in part of struggles between labor and capital. Linda Gordon, *Pitied but Not Entitled: Single Mothers and the History of Welfare* (1994) is a pioneering work on women as the recipients and also the authors of government welfare policies. Alice Kessler-Harris, *In Pursuit of Equity: Women, Men, and the Quest for Economic Citizenship in Twentieth-Century America* (2001) is an important study of the intersection of gender and economic rights. The efforts of Chicago workers to protest and organize is the subject of Lizabeth Cohen, *Making a New Deal: Industrial Workers in Chicago, 1919–1939* (1990). Nelson Lichtenstein, *The Most Dangerous Man in Detroit: Walter Reuther and the Fate of American Labor* (1995) is a valuable study of one of the early leaders of the CIO. Richard Lowitt, *The New Deal and the West* (1984) pays particular attention to water policy and agriculture in the New Deal years. Jordan Schwarz, *The New Dealers: Power Politics in the Age of Roosevelt* (1993) examines the proponents of state-funded economic development of the South and West. Alan Brinkley, *Voices of Protest: Huey Long, Father Coughlin, and the Great Depression* (1982) examines some of the most powerful challenges to the New Deal. Bruce Shulman, *From Cotton Belt to Sunbelt* (1991) explores the New Deal's effort to transform the region Roosevelt and others considered the nation's number one economic problem, the American South. Harvard Sitkoff, *A New Deal for Blacks* (1978) and Nancy J. Weiss, *Farewell to the Party of Lincoln: Black Politics in the Age of FDR* (1983) take contrasting positions on what the New Deal did for African Americans.

FDR (1994), a documentary by David Grubin, gives viewers a fine view of the private and public life of Franklin D. Roosevelt. One of the president's most vocal and powerful critics is featured in another film, by Ken Burns, *Huey Long* (1986). *The World of Tomorrow* (1984) is a provocative documentary on the 1939 World's Fair.

CHAPTER 25

THE GLOBAL CRISIS, 1921–1941

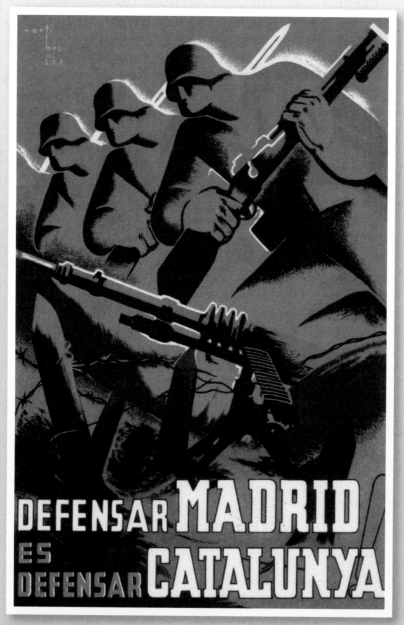

"DEFENDING MADRID"   The Spanish Civil War, in which fascist forces led by Francisco Franco overturned the existing republican government, was an early signal to many Americans of the dangers of fascism and the threat to democracy. Although the United States government remained aloof from the conflict, several thousand Americans volunteered to fight on behalf of the republican forces. This 1938 Spanish war poster contains the words "Defending Madrid Is Defending Catalonia," an effort by the government in Madrid to enlist the support of the surrounding regions to defend the capital against the fascists. *(Getty Images)*

Henry Cabot Lodge of Massachusetts, chairman of the Senate Foreign Relations Committee and one of the most powerful figures in the Republican Party, led the fight against ratification of the Treaty of Versailles in 1918 and 1919. In part because of his efforts, the Senate defeated the treaty; the United States failed to join the League of Nations; and American foreign policy embarked on an independent course that for the next two decades would attempt, but ultimately fail, to expand American influence and maintain international stability without committing the United States to any lasting relationships with other nations.

Lodge was not an isolationist. He recognized that America had emerged from World War I the most powerful nation in the world. He believed the United States should use that power and should exert its influence internationally. But he believed, too, that America's expanded role in the world should reflect the nation's own interests and its own special virtues; it should leave the nation unfettered with obligations to anyone else. He said in 1919:

> We are a great moral asset of Christian civilization. . . . How did we get there? By our own efforts. Nobody led us, nobody guided us, nobody controlled us. . . . I would keep America as she has been—not isolated, not prevent her from joining other nations for . . . great purposes—but I wish her to be master of her own fate.

Lodge was not alone in voicing such sentiments. Throughout the 1920s, those controlling American foreign policy attempted to increase America's role in the world while at the same time keeping the nation free of burdensome commitments that might limit its own freedom of action. In 1933, Franklin Roosevelt became president, and brought with him his own legacy as a leading Wilsonian internationalist and erstwhile supporter of the League of Nations. But for more than six years, Roosevelt also attempted to keep America the "master of her own fate," to avoid important global commitments that might reduce the nation's ability to pursue its own ends.

In the end, the cautious, limited American internationalism of the interwar years proved insufficient to protect the interests of the United States, to create global stability, or to keep the nation from becoming involved in the greatest war in human history.

SIGNIFICANT EVENTS

1921 ▶	Washington Conference leads to reductions in naval armaments
1922 ▶	Fordney-McCumber tariff passed
1924 ▶	Dawes Plan renegotiates European debts, reparations
1928 ▶	Kellogg-Briand Pact signed
1931 ▶	Economic crisis spreads worldwide
▶	Japan invades Manchuria
1932 ▶	World Disarmament Conference held in Geneva
1933 ▶	Adolf Hitler becomes chancellor of Germany
▶	United States scuttles World Economic Conference
▶	United States establishes diplomatic relations with Soviet Union
▶	Roosevelt proclaims Good Neighbor Policy
1935 ▶	Senate defeats World Court treaty
▶	Neutrality Act passed
▶	Italy invades Ethiopia
1936 ▶	Spanish Civil War begins
▶	Germany reoccupies Rhineland
▶	Second Neutrality Act passed
1937 ▶	Japan launches new invasion of China
▶	Roosevelt gives "quarantine" speech
▶	Japan attacks U.S. gunboat Panay
▶	Third Neutrality Act passed
1938 ▶	Germany annexes Austria (the Anschluss)
▶	Munich Conference
1939 ▶	Nazi-Soviet nonaggression pact signed
▶	Germany invades Czechoslovakia
▶	Germany invades Poland
▶	World War II begins
1939–1940 ▶	Soviet Union invades Baltic nations, Finland
1940 ▶	German blitzkrieg conquers most of western Europe
▶	Germany, Italy, Japan sign Tripartite Pact
▶	Fight for Freedom Committee founded
▶	America First Committee founded
▶	Roosevelt reelected president
▶	United States makes destroyers-for-bases deal with Britain
1941 ▶	Lend-lease plan provides aid to Britain
▶	American ships confront German submarines in North Atlantic
▶	Germany invades Soviet Union
▶	Atlantic Charter signed
▶	Japan attacks Pearl Harbor
▶	United States declares war on Japan
▶	Germany declares war on United States
▶	United States declares war on Germany

THE DIPLOMACY OF THE NEW ERA

Critics of American foreign policy in the 1920s often used a single word to describe the cause of their disenchantment: isolationism. Having rejected the Wilsonian vision of a new world order, they claimed, the nation had turned its back on the rest of the globe and repudiated its international responsibilities. In fact,

Myth of Isolationism

the United States played a more active role in world affairs in the 1920s than it had at almost any previous time in its history—even if not the role the Wilsonians had prescribed.

Replacing the League

It was clear when the Harding administration took office in 1921 that American membership in the League of Nations was no longer a realistic possibility. As if finally to bury the issue, Secretary of State Charles Evans Hughes secured legislation from Congress in 1921 declaring the war with Germany at an end, and then proceeded to negotiate separate peace treaties with the former Central Powers. Through these treaties, American policymakers believed, the United States would receive all the advantages of the Versailles Treaty with none of the burdensome responsibilities. But Hughes was also committed to finding something to replace the League as a guarantor of world peace and stability. He embarked, therefore, on a series of efforts to build safeguards against future wars—but safeguards that would not hamper American freedom of action in the world.

The most important such effort was the Washington Conference of 1921—an attempt to prevent what was

Washington Conference of 1921

threatening to become a costly and destabilizing naval armaments race between America, Britain, and Japan. In his opening speech, Hughes startled the delegates by proposing a plan for dramatic reductions in the fleets of all three nations and a ten-year moratorium on the construction of large warships. He called for the scrapping of nearly 2 million tons of existing shipping. Far more surprising than the proposal was the fact that the conference ultimately agreed to accept most of its terms, something that Hughes himself apparently had not anticipated. The Five-Power Pact of February 1922 established both limits for total naval tonnage and a ratio of armaments among the signatories. For every 5 tons of American and British warships, Japan would maintain 3 and France and Italy 1.75 each. (Although the treaty seemed to confirm the military inferiority of Japan, in fact it sanctioned Japanese dominance in East Asia. America and Britain had to spread their fleets across the globe; Japan was concerned only with the Pacific.) The Washington Conference also produced two other, related treaties: the Nine-Power Pact, pledging a continuation of the Open Door policy in China, and the Four-Power Pact, by which the United States, Britain, France, and Japan promised to respect one another's Pacific territories and cooperate to prevent aggression.

The Washington Conference began the New Era effort to protect the peace (and the international economic interests of the United States) without accepting active international duties. The Kellogg-Briand Pact of 1928 concluded

Kellogg-Briand Pact

it. When the French foreign minister, Aristide Briand, asked the United States in 1927 to join an alliance against Germany, Secretary of State Frank Kellogg (who had replaced Hughes in 1925) instead proposed a multilateral treaty outlawing war as an instrument of national policy. Fourteen nations signed the agreement in Paris on August 27, 1928, amid great solemnity and wide international acclaim. Forty-eight other nations later joined the pact. It contained no instruments of enforcement but rested, as Kellogg put it, on the "moral force" of world opinion.

Debts and Diplomacy

The first responsibility of diplomacy, Hughes, Kellogg, and others agreed, was to ensure that American overseas trade faced no obstacles to expansion and would remain free of interference. Preventing a dangerous armaments race and reducing the possibility of war were steps to that end. So were new financial arrangements that emerged at the same time.

The United States was most concerned about Europe, on whose economic health American prosperity in large part depended. Not only were the major European industrial powers suffering from the devastation World War I had produced; they were also staggering under a heavy burden of debt. The Allied powers were struggling to repay $11 billion in loans they had contracted with the United States during and shortly after the war, loans that the Republican administrations were unwilling to reduce or forgive. "They hired the money, didn't they?" Calvin Coolidge once replied when asked if he favored offering Europe relief from their debts. At the same time, an even more debilitated Germany was attempting to pay the reparations levied against it by the Allies. With the financial structure of Europe on the brink of collapse, the United States stepped in with a solution.

In 1924 Charles G. Dawes, an American banker and diplomat, negotiated an agreement under which American banks would provide enormous loans to the Germans, enabling them to meet their reparations payments; in return, Britain and France would agree to reduce the amount of those payments. Dawes won the Nobel Peace Prize for his efforts, but in fact the Dawes Plan did little to solve the problems it addressed.

It led to a troubling circular pattern in international finance.

Circular Loans

America would lend money to Germany, which would use that money to pay reparations to France and England, which would in turn use

A FORD PLANT IN RUSSIA The success of Henry Ford in creating affordable, mass-produced automobiles made him famous around the world, and particularly popular in the Soviet Union in the 1920s and early 1930s, as the communist regime strove to push the nation into the industrial future. Russians called the system of large-scale factory production "Fordism," and they welcomed assistance from the Ford Motor Company itself, which sent engineers and workers over to Russia to help build large automobile plants such as this one. *(Bettmann/Corbis)*

those funds (as well as large loans they themselves were receiving from American banks) to repay war debts to the United States. The flow was able to continue only by virtue of the enormous debts Germany and the other European nations were accumulating to American banks and corporations.

Those banks and corporations were doing more than providing loans. They were becoming a daily presence in the economic life of Europe. American automobile manufacturers were opening European factories, capturing a large share of the overseas market. Other industries in the 1920s were establishing subsidiaries worth more than $10 billion throughout the Continent, taking advantage of the devastation of European industry and the inability of domestic corporations to recover. Some groups within the American government warned that the reckless expansion of overseas loans and investments, many in enterprises of dubious value, threatened disaster; that the United States was becoming too dependent on unstable European economies.

The high tariff barriers that the Republican Congress had erected (through the Fordney-McCumber Act of 1922) were creating additional problems, such skeptics warned. European nations, unable to export their goods to the United States, were finding it difficult to earn the money necessary to repay their loans. Such warnings fell for the most part on deaf ears, and American economic expansion in Europe continued until disaster struck in 1931.

The United States government felt even fewer reservations about assisting American economic expansion in

Latin America. During the 1920s, American military forces maintained a presence in numerous

Economic Expansion in Latin America

countries in the region. United States investments in Latin America more than doubled between 1924 and 1929; American corporations built roads and other facilities in many areas—partly, they argued, to weaken the appeal of revolutionary forces in the region, but at least equally to increase their own access to Latin America's rich natural resources. American banks were offering large loans to Latin American governments, just as they were in Europe; and just as in Europe, the Latin Americans were having great difficulty earning the money to repay them in the face of the formidable United States tariff barrier. By the end of the 1920s, resentment of "Yankee imperialism" was growing rapidly. The economic troubles after 1929 would only accentuate such problems.

Hoover and the World Crisis

After the relatively placid international climate of the 1920s, the diplomatic challenges facing the Hoover administration must have seemed ominous and bewildering. The world financial crisis that began in 1929 and greatly intensified after 1931 was not only creating economic distress; it was producing a dangerous nationalism that threatened the weak international agreements established during the previous decade. Above all, the Depression was toppling some existing political leaders and replacing them with powerful, belligerent governments bent on expansion as a solution to their economic problems. Hoover was confronted, therefore, with the beginning of a process that would ultimately lead to war. He lacked sufficient tools for dealing with it.

In Latin America, Hoover worked studiously to repair some of the damage created by earlier American policies. He made a ten-week goodwill tour through the region before his inauguration. Once in office, he tried to abstain from intervening in the internal affairs of neighboring nations and moved to withdraw American troops from Haiti. When economic distress led to the collapse of one Latin American regime after another, Hoover announced a new policy: America would grant diplomatic recognition to any sitting government in the region without questioning the means it had used to obtain power. He even repudiated the Roosevelt corollary to the Monroe Doctrine by refusing to permit American intervention when several Latin American countries defaulted on debt obligations to the United States in October 1931.

In Europe, the administration enjoyed few successes in its efforts to promote economic stability. When Hoover's proposed moratorium on debts in 1931 failed to attract broad support or produce financial stability (see pp. 661–662), many economists and political leaders appealed to the president to cancel all war debts to the United States. Like his predecessors, Hoover refused;

HITLER AND MUSSOLINI IN BERLIN The German and Italian dictators (shown here reviewing Nazi troops in Berlin in the mid-1930s) acted publicly as if they were equals. Privately, Hitler treated Mussolini with contempt, and Mussolini complained constantly of being a junior partner in the relationship. *(Bettmann/Corbis)*

and several European nations promptly went into default, severely damaging an already tense international climate.

The ineffectiveness of diplomacy in Europe was particularly troubling in view of some of the new governments coming to power on the Continent. Benito Mussolini's Fascist Party had been in control of Italy since the early 1920s; by the 1930s, the regime was growing increasingly nationalistic and militaristic, and Fascist leaders were loudly threatening an active campaign of imperial expansion. Even more ominous was the growing power of the National Socialist (or Nazi) Party in Germany. By the late 1920s, the Weimar Republic, the nation's government since the end of World War I, had lost virtually all popular support, discredited by, among other things, a ruinous inflation. Adolf Hitler, the stridently nationalistic leader of the Nazis, was rapidly growing in popular favor. Although he lost a 1932 election for chancellor, Hitler would sweep into power less than a year later. His belief in the racial superiority of the Aryan (German) people, his commitment to providing *Lebensraum* (living space) for his "master race," his pathological anti-Semitism, and his passionate militarism—all posed a threat to European peace.

More immediately alarming to the Hoover administration was a major crisis in Asia—another early step toward World War II. The Japanese, reeling from an economic depression of their own, were concerned about the increasing strength of the Soviet Union and of Chiang Kai-shek's nationalist China. In particular, they were alarmed at Chiang's insistence on expanding his government's power in Manchuria, which remained officially a part of China but over which the Japanese had maintained effective economic control since 1905. When the moderate government of Japan failed to take forceful steps to counter Chiang's ambitions, Japan's military leaders staged what was, in effect, a coup in the autumn of 1931—seizing control of foreign policy from the weakened liberals. Weeks later, they launched a major invasion of northern Manchuria. (See "America in the World," p. 716.)

The American government had few options. For a while, Secretary of State Henry Stimson (who had served as secretary of war under Taft) continued to hope that Japanese moderates would regain control of the Tokyo government and halt the invasion. The militarists, however, remained in command; and by the beginning of 1932, the conquest of Manchuria was complete. Stimson

THE BOMBING OF CHUNGKING, 1940 Chungking (now Chongqing) was the capital of China under the Nationalist government of Chiang Kai-shek during World War II. It was also the site of some of the most savage fighting of the Sino-Japanese War. This photograph shows buildings in Chungking burning after Japanese bombing in 1940. *(Getty Images)*

issued stern (but essentially toothless) warnings to Japan and tried to use moral suasion to end the crisis. But Hoover forbade him to cooperate with the League of Nations in imposing economic sanctions against the Japanese. Stimson's only real tool in dealing with the Manchurian invasion was a refusal to grant diplomatic recognition to the new Japanese territories. Japan was unconcerned and early in 1932 expanded its aggression farther into China, attacking the city of Shanghai and killing thousands of civilians.

By the time Hoover left office early in 1933, it was clear that the international system the United States had attempted to create in the 1920s—a system based on voluntary cooperation among nations and on an American refusal to commit itself to the interests of other countries—had collapsed. The United States faced a choice. It could adopt a more energetic form of internationalism and enter into firmer and more meaningful associations with other nations. Or it could resort to nationalism and rely on its own devices for dealing with its (and the world's) problems. For the next six years, it experimented with elements of both approaches.

Failure of America's Interwar Diplomacy

ISOLATIONISM AND INTERNATIONALISM

The administration of Franklin Roosevelt faced a dual challenge as it entered office in 1933. It had to deal with the worst economic crisis in the nation's history, and it had to deal with the effects of a decaying international structure. The two problems were not unrelated. It was the worldwide Depression itself that was producing much of the political chaos throughout the globe.

Through most of the 1930s, however, the United States was unwilling to make more than faint gestures toward restoring stability to the world. Like many other peoples suffering economic hardship, most Americans were turning inward. Yet the realities of world affairs were not to allow the nation to remain isolated for very long—as Franklin Roosevelt realized earlier than many other Americans.

Depression Diplomacy

Perhaps Roosevelt's sharpest break with the policies of his predecessor was on the question of American economic relations with Europe. Hoover had argued that only by resolving the question of war debts and reinforcing the gold standard could the American economy hope to recover. He had therefore agreed to participate in the World Economic Conference, to be held in London in June 1933, to try to resolve these issues. By the time the conference assembled, however, Roosevelt had already decided to allow the gold value of the dollar to fall to enable American goods to compete in world markets. Shortly after the conference convened, Roosevelt released a famous "bombshell" message repudiating the orthodox views of most of the delegates and rejecting any agreement on currency stabilization. The conference quickly dissolved without reaching agreement, and not until 1936 did the administration finally agree to new negotiations to stabilize Western currencies.

FDR's "Bombshell"

At the same time, Roosevelt abandoned the commitments of the Hoover administration to settle the issue of war debts through international agreement. In effect, he simply let the issue die. In April 1934, he signed a bill to forbid American banks to make loans to any nation in default on its debts. The result was to stop the old, circular system; within months, war-debt payments from every nation except Finland stopped for good.

Although the new administration had no interest in international currency stabilization or settlement of war debts, it did have an active interest in improving America's position in world trade. Roosevelt approved the Reciprocal Trade Agreement Act of 1934, authorizing the administration to negotiate treaties lowering tariffs by as much as 50 percent in return for reciprocal reductions by other nations. By 1939, Secretary of State Cordell Hull, a devoted free trader, had negotiated new treaties with twenty-one countries. The result was an increase in American exports to them of nearly 40 percent. But most of the agreements admitted only products not competitive with American industry and agriculture, so imports into the United States continued to lag. Thus other nations were not obtaining the American currency needed to buy American products or pay off debts to American banks.

Reciprocal Trade Agreement Act

America and the Soviet Union

America's hopes of expanding its foreign trade helped produce efforts by the Roosevelt administration to improve relations with the Soviet Union. The United States and Russia had viewed each other with mistrust and even hostility since the Bolshevik Revolution of 1917, and the American government still had not officially recognized the Soviet regime by 1933. But powerful voices within the United States were urging a change in policy—less because the revulsion with which most Americans viewed communism had diminished than because the Soviet Union appeared to be a possible source of trade. The Russians, too, were eager for a new relationship. They were hoping in particular for American cooperation in

containing the power of Japan, which Soviet leaders feared as a threat to Russia from the southeast. In November 1933, therefore, Soviet foreign minister Maxim Litvinov reached an agreement with the president in Washington. The Soviets would cease their propaganda efforts in the United States and protect American citizens in Russia; in return, the United States would recognize the communist regime.

Despite this promising beginning, however, relations with the Soviet Union soon soured once again. American trade failed to establish much of a foothold in Russia; and the Soviets received no reassurance from the United States that it was interested in stopping Japanese expansion in Asia. By the end of 1934, as a result of these disappointed hopes on both sides, the Soviet Union and the United States were once again viewing each other with considerable mistrust.

The Good Neighbor Policy

Somewhat more successful were American efforts to enhance both diplomatic and economic relations with Latin America through what became known as the "Good Neighbor Policy." Latin America was one of the most important targets of the new policy of trade reciprocity. During the 1930s, the United States succeeded in increasing both exports to and imports from the other nations of the Western Hemisphere by over 100 percent. Closely tied to these new economic relationships was a new American attitude toward intervention in Latin America. The Hoover administration had unofficially abandoned the earlier American practice of using military force to compel Latin American governments to repay debts, respect foreign investments, or otherwise behave "responsibly." The Roosevelt administration went further. At the Inter-American Conference in Montevideo in December 1933, Secretary of State Hull signed a formal convention declaring: "No state has the right to intervene in the internal or external affairs of another." Roosevelt respected that pledge throughout his years in office. The Good Neighbor Policy did not mean, however, that the United States had abandoned its influence in Latin America. Instead of military force, Americans now tried to use economic influence. The new reliance on economic pressures eased tensions between the United States and its neighbors considerably. It did nothing to stem the growing American domination of the Latin American economies.

Inter-American Conference

The Rise of Isolationism

The first years of the Roosevelt administration marked not only the death of Hoover's hopes for international economic agreements, but the end of any hopes for world peace through treaties and disarmament as well.

The arms control conference in Geneva had been meeting, without result, since 1932; and in May 1933, Roosevelt attempted to spur it to action by submitting a new American proposal for arms reductions. Negotiations stalled and then broke down; and only a few months later, first Hitler and then Mussolini withdrew from the talks altogether. Two years later, Japan withdrew from the London Naval Conference, which was attempting to draw up an agreement to continue the limitations on naval armaments negotiated at the Washington Conference of 1921.

Faced with a choice between more active efforts to stabilize the world or more energetic attempts to isolate the nation from it, most Americans unhesitatingly chose the latter. Support for isolationism emerged from many quarters. Old Wilsonian internationalists had grown disillusioned

Sources of Isolationism

with the League of Nations and its inability to stop Japanese aggression in Asia. Other Americans were listening to the argument (popular among populist-minded politicians in the Midwest and West) that powerful business interests—Wall Street, munitions makers, and others—had tricked the United States into participating in World War I. An investigation by a Senate committee chaired by Senator Gerald Nye of North Dakota revealed exorbitant profiteering and blatant tax evasion by many corporations during the war, and it suggested (on the basis of little evidence) that bankers had pressured Wilson to intervene in the war so as to protect their loans abroad. Roosevelt himself shared some of the suspicions voiced by the isolationists and claimed to be impressed by the findings of the Nye investigation. Nevertheless, he continued to hope for at least a modest American role in maintaining world peace. In 1935, he asked the Senate to ratify a treaty to make the United States a member of the World Court—a treaty that would have expanded America's symbolic commitment to internationalism without increasing its actual responsibilities in any important way. Nevertheless, isolationist opposition (spurred by unrelenting hostility from the Hearst newspapers and a passionate broadcast by Father Charles Coughlin on the eve of the Senate vote) resulted in the defeat of the treaty. It was a devastating political blow to the president, and he did not soon again attempt to challenge the isolationist tide.

That tide seemed to grow stronger in the following months. Through the summer of 1935, it became clear that Mussolini's Italy was preparing to invade Ethiopia in an effort to expand its colonial holdings in Africa. Fearing that a general European war would result, American legislators began to design legal safeguards to prevent the United States from being dragged into the conflict. The result was the Neutrality Act of 1935.

The 1935 act, and the Neutrality Acts of 1936 and 1937 that followed, was designed to prevent a recurrence of the events that many Americans now believed had pressured the United

Neutrality Acts

States into World War I. The 1935 law established a mandatory arms embargo against both victim and aggressor in any military conflict and empowered the president to warn American citizens that they might travel on the ships of warring nations only at their own risk. Thus, isolationists believed, the "protection of neutral rights" could not again become an excuse for American intervention in war. The 1936 Neutrality Act renewed these provisions. And in 1937, with world conditions growing even more precarious, Congress passed a new Neutrality Act that established the so-called cash-and-carry policy, by which belligerents could purchase only nonmilitary goods from the United States and had to pay cash and carry the goods away on their own vessels.

THE SPANISH CIVIL WAR Less than a year before the beginning of World War II, American volunteers were in Spain serving as Republican soldiers in the country's civil war. Most of the Americans were members of the Abraham Lincoln Brigade, members of which are shown here in October 1938 near Barcelona. Because many members of the brigade were communists, they were dismissed by the government in 1939 after the Nazi-Soviet pact ended Stalin's support of the Spanish Republicans. *(Magnum Photos)*

THE SINO-JAPANESE WAR, 1931–1941

Long before Pearl Harbor, well before war broke out in Europe in 1939, the first shots of what would become World War II had been fired in the Pacific in a conflict between Japan and China.

Having lived in almost complete isolation from the world until the nineteenth century, Japan emerged from World War I as a great world power, with a proud and powerful military and growing global trade. But the Great Depression created severe economic problems for the Japanese (in part because of stiff new American tariffs on silk imports); and as in other parts of the world, the crisis strengthened the political influence of highly nationalistic and militaristic leaders. Out of the Japanese military emerged dreams of a new empire in the Pacific. Such an empire would, its proponents believed, give the nation access to fuel, raw materials, and markets for its industries, as well as land for its agricultural needs and its rapidly increasing population. Such an empire, they argued, would free Asia from exploitation by Europe and America and would create a "new world order based on moral principles."

During World War I, Japan had seized territory and economic concessions in China and had created a particularly strong presence in the northern Chinese region of Manchuria. There, in September 1931, a group of militant young army officers seized on a railway explosion to justify a military campaign through which they conquered the entire province. Both the United States government and the League of Nations demanded that Japan evacuate Manchuria. The Japanese ignored them, and for the next six years consolidated their control over their new territory.

On July 7, 1937, Japan began a wider war when it attacked Chinese troops at the Marco Polo Bridge outside Beijing. Over the next few weeks, Japanese forces overran a large part of southern China, including most of the port cities, killing many Chinese soldiers and civilians in the process. Particularly notorious was the Japanese annihilation of many thousands of civilians in the city of Nanjing (the number has long been in dispute, but estimates range from 80,000 to more than 300,000) in an event that became known in China and

ENTERING MANCHURIA, 1931 Japanese troops pour into Mukden (now Shenyang), the capital of the Chinese province of Manchuria, in 1931—following a staged incident that allowed Japan to claim that its troops had been attacked. The so-called Mukden Incident marked the beginning of the long Sino-Japanese War. *(Getty Images)*

the West as the Nanjing Massacre. The Chinese government fled to the mountains. As in 1931, the United States and the League of Nations protested in vain.

The China that the Japanese had invaded was a nation in turmoil. It was engaged in a civil war of its own—between the so-called Kuomintang, a nationalist party led by Chiang Kai-shek, and the Chinese Communist Party, led by Mao Zedong; and this internal struggle weakened China's capacity to resist invasion. But beginning in 1937, the two Chinese rivals agreed to an uneasy truce and began fighting the Japanese together, with some success—bogging the Japanese military down in a seemingly endless war and imposing hardships on the Japanese people at home. The Japanese government and the military, however, remained determined to continue the war against China, whatever the sacrifices.

One result of the costs of the war in China was a growing Japanese dependence on the United States for

steel and oil to meet civilian and military needs. In July 1941, in an effort to pressure the Japanese to stop their expansion, the Roosevelt administration made it impossible for the Japanese to continue buying American oil. Japan now faced a choice between ending its war in China or finding other sources of fuel to keep its war effort (and its civilian economy) going. It chose to extend the war beyond China in a search for oil. The best available sources were in the Dutch East Indies; but the only way to secure that European colony, the Japanese believed, would be to neutralize the increasingly hostile United States in Asia. Visionary military planners in Japan began advocating a daring move to immobilize the Americans in the Pacific before expanding the war elsewhere—with an attack on the American naval base at Pearl Harbor. The first blow of World War II in America, therefore, was the culmination of more than a decade of Japanese efforts to conquer China.

716

The American stance of militant neutrality gained support in October 1935 when Mussolini finally launched his long-anticipated attack on Ethiopia. When the League of Nations protested, Italy simply resigned from the organization, completed its conquest of Ethiopia, and formed an alliance (the "Axis") with Nazi Germany. Most Americans responded to the news with renewed determination to isolate themselves from European instability. Two-thirds of those responding to public opinion polls at the time opposed any American action to deter aggression. Isolationist sentiment showed its strength once again in 1936–1937 in response to the civil war in Spain. The Falangists, a group much like the Italian fascists, revolted in July 1936 against the existing republican government. Hitler and Mussolini supported General Francisco Franco, who became the leader of the Falangists in 1937, both vocally and with weapons and supplies. Some individual Americans traveled to Spain to assist the republican cause; but the United States government joined with Britain and France in an agreement to offer no assistance to either side—although all three governments were sympathetic to the republicans.

Particularly disturbing was the deteriorating situation in Asia. Japan's aggressive designs against China had been clear since the invasion of Manchuria in 1931. In the summer of 1937, Tokyo launched an even broader assault, attacking China's five northern provinces. (See "America in the World," p. 716.) The United States, Roosevelt believed, could not allow the Japanese aggression to go unremarked or unpunished. In a speech in Chicago in October 1937, therefore, the president warned forcefully of the dangers that Japanese aggression posed to world peace. Aggressors, he proclaimed, should be "quarantined" by the international community to prevent the contagion of war from spreading. The president was deliberately vague about what such a "quarantine" would mean. Nevertheless, public response to the speech was disturbingly hostile. As a result, Roosevelt drew back.

Only months later, another episode provided renewed evidence of how formidable the obstacles to Roosevelt's efforts remained. On December 12, 1937, Japanese aviators bombed and sank the U.S. gunboat *Panay* as it sailed the Yangtze River in China. The attack was almost undoubtedly deliberate. It occurred in broad daylight, with clear visibility. A large American flag had been painted conspicuously on the *Panay*'s deck. Even so, isolationists seized eagerly on Japanese protestations that the bombing had been an accident and pressured the administration to accept Japan's apologies.

The Failure of Munich

Hitler's determination to expand German power became fully visible in 1936, when he moved the revived German army into the Rhineland, violating the Versailles Treaty and rearming an area that France had, in effect, controlled since World War I. In March 1938, German forces marched into Austria, and Hitler proclaimed a union (or *Anschluss*) between Austria, his native land, and Germany, his adopted one—thus fulfilling his longtime dream of uniting the German-speaking peoples in one great nation. Neither in America nor in most of Europe was there much more than a murmur of opposition. The Austrian invasion, however, soon created another crisis, for Hitler had by now occupied territory surrounding three sides of western Czechoslovakia, a region he dreamed of annexing to provide Germany with the *Lebensraum* he believed it needed. In September 1938, he demanded that Czechoslovakia cede to him part of that region, the Sudetenland, an area on the Austro-German border in which many ethnic Germans lived. Czechoslovakia, which possessed substantial military power of its own, was prepared to fight rather than submit. But it realized it could not hope for success without help from other European nations. It received none. Most Western nations were appalled at the prospect of another war and were willing to pay almost any price to settle the crisis peacefully. Anxiety ran almost as high in the United States as it did in Europe during and after the crisis, and helped produce such strange expressions of fear as the hysterical response to the famous "War of the Worlds" radio broadcast in October. (See "Patterns of Popular Culture," pp. 718–719.)

On September 29, Hitler met with the leaders of France and Great Britain at Munich in an effort to resolve the crisis. The French and British agreed to accept the German demands for Czechoslovakia in return for Hitler's promise to expand no farther. "This is the last territorial claim I have to make in Europe," the Führer solemnly declared. And Prime Minister Neville Chamberlain returned to England to a hero's welcome, assuring his people that the agreement ensured "peace in our time." Among those who had cabled him with encouragement at Munich was Franklin Roosevelt.

The Munich accords were the most prominent element of a policy that came to be known as "appeasement" and that came to be identified (not altogether fairly) almost exclusively with Chamberlain. Whoever was to blame, however, it became clear almost immediately that the policy was a failure. In March 1939, Hitler occupied the remaining areas of Czechoslovakia, violating the Munich agreement unashamedly. And in April, he began issuing threats against Poland. At that point, both Britain and France gave assurances to the Polish government that they would come to its assistance in case of an invasion; they even flirted, too late, with the Stalinist regime in Russia, attempting to draw it into a mutual defense agreement. Stalin, however, had already decided that he could expect no protection from the

ORSON WELLES AND THE "WAR OF THE WORLDS"

On the evening of October 30, 1938, about 6 million Americans were listening to the weekly radio program *The Mercury Theater of the Air,* produced by the actor/filmmaker Orson Welles and broadcast over the CBS network. A few minutes into the show, an announcer broke in and interrupted some dance music with a terrifying report:

> At least forty people, including six state troopers, lie dead in a field east of Grover's Mill [New Jersey], their bodies burned and distorted beyond recognition. . . . Good heavens, something's

wriggling out of the shadow like a gray snake! Now it's another one and another. . . . It's large as a bear and it glistens like black leather. But that face . . . it's indescribable! I can hardly force myself to keep looking at it.

The panicky announcer was describing the beginning of an alien invasion of earth and the appearance of Martians armed with "death rays," determined to destroy the planet. Later in the evening, an announcer claiming to be broadcasting from Times Square reported the destruc-

tion of New York City before falling dead at the microphone. Other statements advised citizens of surrounding areas to flee.

The dramatic "news bulletins" were part of a radio play by Howard Koch, loosely adapted from H. G. Wells's 1898 novel *The War of the Worlds.* Announcers reminded the audience repeatedly throughout the broadcast that they were listening to a play, not reality. But many people either did not hear or did not notice the disclaimers. By the end of the hour, according to some estimates, as many as a million

THE MERCURY THEATER OF THE AIR
Orson Welles, the founder and director of the *Mercury Theater of the Air,* directs a corps of actors during a rehearsal for one of the show's radio plays. *(Culver Pictures, Inc.)*

WELLES ON THE AIR   Welles is shown here during the broadcast of the "War of the Worlds" in 1938. Although he was careful to note that the broadcast was fiction, he came under intense criticism in following days for the panic it caused among many listeners. *(Bettmann/Corbis)*

West; after all, he had not even been invited to attend the Munich Conference. Accordingly, he signed a nonaggression pact with Hitler in August 1939, freeing the Germans for the moment from the danger of a two-front war. For a few months, Hitler had been trying to frighten the Poles into submitting to German demands. When that failed, he staged an incident on the Polish border to allow him to claim that Germany had been attacked; and on September 1, 1939, he launched a full-scale invasion of Poland. Britain and France, true to their pledges, declared war on Germany two days later. World War II had begun.

FROM NEUTRALITY TO INTERVENTION

"This nation will remain a neutral nation," the president declared shortly after the hostilities began in Europe, "but I cannot ask that every American remain neutral in thought as well." It was a statement that stood in stark and deliberate contrast to Woodrow Wilson's 1914 plea that the nation remain neutral in both deed and thought; and it was clear from the start that among those whose opinions were decidedly unneutral in 1939 was the president himself.

Americans were flying into panics, convinced that the end of the world was imminent.

Thousands of listeners in New York and New Jersey actually fled their homes and tried to drive along clogged highways into the hills or the countryside. Others rushed into the streets, huddled in parks, or hid under bridges. In Newark, people ran from their buildings with wet towels wrapped around their faces or wearing gas masks—as if defending themselves against the chemical warfare that many remembered from the trenches in World War I. In cities across the country, people flocked into churches to pray; called police and hospitals for help; flooded the switchboards of newspapers, magazines, and radio stations desperate for information. "I never hugged my radio so closely as I did last night," one woman later explained. "I held a crucifix in my hand and prayed while looking out of my open window for falling meteors." The New York Times described it the next day as "a wave of mass hysteria." Other papers wrote of a "tidal wave of terror that swept the nation." For weeks thereafter, Orson Welles and other producers of the show were the focus of a barrage of criticism for what many believed had been a deliberate effort to create public fear. For years, sociologists and other scholars studied the episode for clues about mass behavior.

Welles and his colleagues claimed to be surprised by the reaction their show created. It had never occurred to them, they insisted, that anyone would consider it real. But the broadcast proved more effective than they

MASS HYSTERIA A *New York Times* headline the morning after the famous "War of the Worlds" broadcast of the *Mercury Theater of the Air* reports on the panic the radio show had caused the night before. "A wave of mass hysteria seized thousands of radio listeners throughout the nation between 8:15 and 9:30 o'clock last night," the paper reported, "when a broadcast of H. G. Wells's fantasy 'The War of the Worlds,' led thousands to believe that an interplanetary conflict had started with invading Martians spreading wide death and destruction in New Jersey and New York." *(Copyright © 1938 by the New York Times Co. Reprinted by Permission)*

had expected because it touched on a cluster of anxieties and assumptions that ran deep in American life at the time—anxieties similar to those that ran deep again in the aftermath of the September 2001 attacks on New York and Washington. The show aired only a few weeks after the war fever that had preceded the Munich pact among Germany, Britain, and France; Americans already jittery about the possibility of war proved easy prey to fears of another kind of invasion. The show also tapped longer-standing anxieties about the fragility of life that afflicted many Americans during the long depression of the 1930s, and it seemed to frighten working-class people—those most vulnerable to unexpected catastrophes—in particular.

Most of all, however, "The War of the Worlds" unintentionally exploited the enormous power that radio had come to exercise in American life, and the great trust many people had developed in what they heard over the air. Over 85 percent of American families had radios in 1938. For many of them, the broadcasts they received had become their principal, even their

only, source of information about the outside world. When the actors from the *Mercury Theater* began to use the familiar phrases and cadences of radio news announcers, it was all too easy for members of their audience to assume that they were hearing the truth.

Welles concluded the broadcast by describing the play as "the Mercury Theater's own radio version of dressing up in a sheet and jumping out of a bush and saying Boo! . . . So good-bye everybody, and remember, please, for the next day or so, the terrible lesson you learned tonight. The grinning, glowing, globular invader of your living room is an inhabitant of the pumpkin patch, and if your doorbell rings and there's no one there, that was no Martian . . . it's Halloween." But the real lesson of "The War of the Worlds" was not Welles's jocular one. It was the lesson of the enormous, and at times frightening, power of the medium of broadcasting.

Neutrality Tested

There was never any question that both the president and the majority of the American people favored Britain, France, and the other Allied nations in the conflict. The question was how much the United States was prepared to do to assist them. At the very least, Roosevelt believed, the United States should make armaments available to the Allied armies to help them counter the highly productive German munitions industry. In September 1939, he asked Congress for a revision of the Neutrality Acts. The original measures had forbidden the sale of American weapons to

any nation engaged in war; Roosevelt wanted the arms embargo lifted. Powerful isolationist opposition forced him to accept a weaker revision than he would have liked; as passed by Congress, the 1939 measure maintained the prohibition on American ships entering war zones. It did, however, permit belligerents to purchase arms on the same cash-and-carry basis that the earlier Neutrality Acts had established for the sale of nonmilitary materials.

Cash-and-Carry

After the German armies had quickly subdued Poland, the war in Europe settled into a long, quiet lull that

THE OCCUPATION OF POLAND, 1939 A German motorized detachment enters a Polish town that has already been battered by heavy bombing from the German air force (the *Luftwaffe*). The German invasion of Poland, which began on September 1, 1939, sparked the formal beginning of World War II. *(Bettmann/Corbis)*

lasted through the winter and spring—a "phony war," many people called it. The only real fighting during this period occurred not between the Allies and the Axis, but between Russia and its neighbors. Taking advantage of the situation in the West, the Soviet Union overran and annexed the small Baltic republics of Latvia, Estonia, and Lithuania and then, in late November, invaded Finland. Most Americans were outraged, but neither Congress nor the president was willing to do more than impose an ineffective "moral embargo" on the shipment of armaments to Russia. By March 1940, the Soviet advance was complete.

Whatever illusions anyone may have had about the reality of the war in western Europe were shattered in the spring of 1940 when Germany launched an invasion to the west—first attacking Denmark and Norway, sweeping next across the Netherlands and Belgium, and driving finally deep into the heart of France. Allied efforts proved futile against the Nazi blitzkrieg. One western European stronghold after another fell into German hands. On June 10, Mussolini brought Italy into the war, invading France from the south as Hitler was attacking from the north. On June 22, finally, France fell to the German onslaught. Nazi troops marched into Paris; a new collaborationist regime assembled in Vichy; and in all Europe, only the shattered remnants of the British army, rescued from the beaches of Dunkirk | Fall of France | by a flotilla of military and civilian vessels assembled miraculously quickly, remained to oppose the Axis forces.

Roosevelt had already begun to increase American aid to the Allies. He also began preparations to resist a possible Nazi invasion of the United States. On May 16, he asked Congress for an additional $1 billion for defense (much of it for the construction of an enormous new fleet of warplanes) and received it quickly. With France tottering a few weeks later, he proclaimed that the United States would "extend to the opponents of force the material resources of this nation." And on May 15, Winston Churchill, the new British prime minister, sent Roosevelt the first of many long lists of requests for ships, armaments, and other assistance without which, he insisted, England could not long survive. Many Americans (including the United States ambassador to London, Joseph P. Kennedy) argued that the British

THE BLITZ, LONDON The German *Luftwaffe* terrorized London and other British cities in 1940–1941 and again late in the war by bombing civilian areas indiscriminately in an effort to break the spirit of the English people. The effort failed, and the fortitude of the British in the face of the attack did much to arouse support for their cause in the United States. St. Paul's Cathedral, largely undamaged throughout the raids, looms in the background of this photograph, as other buildings crumble under the force of German bombs. (*Brown Brothers*)

plight was already hopeless, that any aid to the English was a wasted effort. The president, however, made the politically dangerous decision to make war materials available to Churchill. He even circumvented the cash-and-carry provisions of the Neutrality Act by trading fifty American destroyers (most of them left over from World War I) to England in return for the right to build American bases on British territory in the Western Hemisphere; and he returned to the factories a number of new airplanes purchased by the American government so that the British could buy them instead.

Roosevelt was able to take such steps in part because of a major shift in American public opinion. Before the invasion of France, most Americans had believed that a German victory in the war would not be a threat to the United States. By July, with France defeated and Britain threatened, more than 66 percent of the public (according to opinion polls) believed that Germany posed a direct threat to the United States. Congress was aware of the change

Shifting Public Opinion

and was becoming more willing to permit expanded American assistance to the Allies. It was also becoming more concerned about the need for internal preparations for war, and in September it approved the Burke-Wadsworth Act, inaugurating the first peacetime military draft in American history.

But while the forces of isolation may have weakened, they were far from dead. A spirited and at times vicious debate began in the spring of 1940 between those activists who advocated expanded American involvement in the war (who were termed, often inaccurately, "interventionists") and those who continued to insist on neutrality. The celebrated journalist William Allen White served as chairman of a new Committee to Defend America, whose members lobbied actively for increased American assistance to the Allies but opposed actual intervention. Others went so far as to urge an immediate declaration of war (a position that as yet had little public support) and in April 1941 created an organization of their own, the Fight for Freedom Committee.

Opposing them was a powerful new lobby called the America First Committee, which attracted some of America's most prominent leaders. Its chairman was General Robert E. Wood, until recently the president of Sears Roebuck; and its membership included Charles Lindbergh, General Hugh Johnson, Senator Gerald Nye, and Senator Burton Wheeler. It won the editorial support of the Hearst chain and other influential newspapers, and it had at least the indirect support of a large proportion of the Republican Party. (It also, inevitably, attracted a fringe of Nazi sympathizers and anti-Semites.) The debate between the two sides was loud and bitter. Through the summer and fall of 1940, moreover, it was complicated by a presidential campaign.

America First Committee

The Third-Term Campaign

For many months, the politics of 1940 revolved around the question of Franklin Roosevelt's intentions. Would he break with tradition and run for an unprecedented third term? The president himself never publicly revealed his own wishes. But by refusing to withdraw from the contest, he made it impossible for any rival Democrat to establish a foothold within the party. Just before the Democratic Convention in July, he let it be known that he would accept a "draft" from his party. The Democrats quickly renominated him and even reluctantly swallowed his choice for vice president: Agriculture Secretary Henry A. Wallace, a man too liberal for the taste of many party leaders.

With Roosevelt effectively straddling the center of the defense debate, favoring neither the extreme isolationists nor the extreme interventionists, the Republicans had few obvious alternatives. Succumbing to a remarkable popular movement (carefully orchestrated by, among others, *Time* and *Life* magazines), they nominated a dynamic and attractive but politically inexperienced businessman, Wendell Willkie.

Wendell Willkie

Willkie took positions little different from Roosevelt's: he would keep the country out of war but would extend generous assistance to the Allies. An appealing figure and a vigorous campaigner, he managed to evoke more public enthusiasm than any Republican candidate in decades. In the end, however, he was no match for Franklin Roosevelt. The election was closer than it had been in either 1932 or 1936, but Roosevelt nevertheless won decisively. He received 55 percent of the popular vote to Willkie's 45 percent, and won 449 electoral votes to Willkie's 82.

Neutrality Abandoned

In the last weeks of 1940, with the election behind him, Roosevelt began to make subtle but profound changes in the American role in the war. More than aiding Britain, he was moving the United States closer to war.

In December 1940, Great Britain was virtually bankrupt. No longer could the British meet the cash-and-carry requirements imposed by the Neutrality Acts; yet England's needs, Churchill insisted, were greater than ever. The president, therefore, suggested a method that would "eliminate the dollar sign" from all arms transactions. The new system was labeled "lend-lease." It would allow the government not only to sell but also to lend or lease armaments to any nation deemed "vital to the defense of the United States." In other words, America could funnel weapons to England on the basis of no more than Britain's promise to return or pay for them when the war was over. Isolationists attacked the measure bitterly, arguing (correctly) that it was simply a device to tie the United States more closely to the Allies; but Congress enacted the bill by wide margins.

Lend-Lease

With lend-lease established, Roosevelt soon faced another serious problem: ensuring that the American supplies would actually reach Great Britain. Shipping lanes in the Atlantic had become extremely dangerous; German submarines destroyed as much as a half-million tons of shipping each month. The British navy was losing ships more rapidly than it could replace them and was finding it difficult to transport materials across the Atlantic from America. Secretary of War Henry Stimson (who had been Hoover's secretary of state and who returned to the cabinet at Roosevelt's request in 1940) argued that the United States should itself convoy vessels to England; but Roosevelt decided to rely instead on the concept of "hemispheric defense," by which the United States navy would defend transport ships only in the western Atlantic—which he argued was a neutral zone and the responsibility of the American nations. By July 1941, American ships were patrolling the ocean as far east as Iceland, escorting convoys of merchant ships, and radioing information to British vessels about the location of Nazi submarines.

At first, Germany did little to challenge these obviously hostile American actions. By the fall of 1941, however, events in Europe changed its position. German forces had invaded the Soviet Union in June of that year, shattering the 1939 Nazi-Soviet pact. The Germans drove quickly and forcefully deep into Russian territory. When the Soviets did not surrender, as many military observers had predicted they would, Roosevelt persuaded Congress to extend lend-lease privileges to them—the first step toward creating a new relationship with Stalin that would ultimately lead to a formal Soviet-American alliance. Now American industry was providing crucial assistance to Hitler's foes on two fronts, and the navy was playing a more active role than ever in protecting the flow of goods to Europe.

Germany Invades the USSR

In September, Nazi submarines began a concerted campaign against American vessels. Early that month, a

German U-boat fired on the American destroyer *Greer* (which was radioing the U-boat's position to the British at the time). Roosevelt responded by ordering American ships to fire on German submarines "on sight." In October, Nazi submarines hit two American destroyers and sank one of them, the *Reuben James,* killing many American sailors. Enraged members of Congress now voted approval of a measure allowing the United States to arm its merchant vessels and to sail all the way into belligerent ports. The United States had, in effect, launched a naval war against Germany.

At the same time, a series of meetings, some private and one public, were tying the United States and Great Britain more closely together. In April 1941, senior military officers of the two nations met in secret and agreed on the joint strategy they would follow were the United States to enter the war. In August, Roosevelt met with Churchill aboard a British vessel anchored off the coast of Newfoundland. The president made no military commit-

Atlantic Charter

ments, but he did join the prime minister in releasing a document that became known as the Atlantic Charter, in which the two nations set out "certain common principles" on which to base "a better future for the world." It was, in only vaguely disguised form, a statement of war aims that called openly for, among other things, "the final destruction of the Nazi tyranny."

By the fall of 1941, it seemed only a matter of time before the United States became an official belligerent. Roosevelt remained convinced that public opinion would support a declaration of war only in the event of an actual enemy attack. But an attack seemed certain to come, if not in the Atlantic, then in the Pacific.

The Road to Pearl Harbor

Japan took advantage of the crisis that had preoccupied the Soviet Union and the two most powerful colo-

Tripartite Pact

nial powers in Asia, Britain and France, to extend its empire in the Pacific. In September 1940, Japan signed the Tripartite Pact, a loose defensive alliance with Germany and Italy that seemed to extend the Axis into Asia. (In reality, the European Axis powers never developed a strong relationship with Japan, and the wars in Europe and the Pacific were largely separate conflicts.)

Roosevelt had already displayed his animosity toward Japanese policies by harshly denouncing their continuing assault on China and by terminating a longstanding American commercial treaty with the Tokyo government. Still the Japanese drive continued. In July 1941, imperial troops moved into Indochina and seized the capital of Vietnam, a colony of France. The United States, having broken the Japanese codes, knew that Japan's next target would be the Dutch East Indies; and when Tokyo failed to respond to Roosevelt's stern warnings,

the president froze all Japanese assets in the United States and established a complete trade embargo, severely limiting Japan's ability to purchase essential supplies (including oil). American public opinion, shaped by strong anti-Japanese prejudices developed over several decades, generally supported these hostile actions.

Tokyo now faced a choice. Either it would have to repair relations with the United States to restore the flow of supplies, or it would have to find those supplies elsewhere, most notably by seizing British and Dutch possessions in the Pacific. At first the Japanese prime minister, Prince Konoye, seemed willing to compromise. In October, however, militants in Tokyo forced Konoye out of office and replaced him with the leader of the war party, General Hideki Tojo. With Japan's need for new sources of fuel becoming desperate, there now seemed little alternative to war.

For several weeks, the Tojo government kept up a pretense of wanting to continue negotiations. On November 20, 1941, Tokyo proposed a modus vivendi highly favorable to itself and sent its diplomats in Washington to the State Department to discuss it. But Tokyo had already decided that it would not yield on the question of China, and Washington had made clear that it would accept nothing less than a reversal of that policy. Secretary of State Cordell Hull rejected the Japanese overtures out of hand; on November 27, he told Secretary of War Henry Stimson, "I have washed my hands of the Japanese situation, and it is now in the hands of you and [Secretary of the Navy Frank]

Tokyo's Decision for War

Knox, the Army and Navy." He was not merely speculating. American intelligence had already decoded Japanese messages, which made clear that war was imminent, that after November 29 an attack would be only a matter of days.

But Washington did not know where the attack would take place. Most officials were convinced that the Japanese would move first not against American territory but against British or Dutch possessions to the south. American intelligence took note of a Japanese naval task force that began sailing east from the Kuril Islands in the general direction of Hawaii on November 25, and radioed a routine warning to the United States naval facility at Pearl Harbor, near Honolulu. But officials were paying more attention to a large Japanese convoy moving southward through the China Sea. A combination of confusion and miscalculation led the government to overlook indications that Japan intended a direct attack on American forces—partly because Hawaii was so far from Japan that few officials believed such an attack possible.

At 7:55 A.M. on Sunday, December 7, 1941, a wave of Japanese bombers—taking off from aircraft carriers hundreds of miles away—attacked the United States naval base at Pearl Harbor. A second wave came an hour later.

THE QUESTION OF PEARL HARBOR

The phrase "Remember Pearl Harbor!" became a rallying cry during World War II—reminding Americans of the surprise Japanese attack on the American naval base in Hawaii and arousing the nation to exact revenge. But within a few years of the end of hostilities, some Americans remembered Pearl Harbor for very different reasons. They began to challenge the official version of the attack on December 7, 1941, and their charges sparked a debate that has never fully subsided. Was the Japanese attack on Pearl Harbor unprovoked, and did it come without warning, as the Roosevelt administration claimed at the time? Or was it part of a deliberate plan by the president to make the Japanese force a reluctant United States into the war? Most controversial of all, did the administration know of the attack in advance? Did Roosevelt deliberately refrain from warning the commanders in Hawaii so that the air raid's effect on the American public would be more profound?

Among the first to challenge the official version of Pearl Harbor was the historian Charles A. Beard, who maintained in *President Roosevelt and the Coming of the War* (1948) that the United States had deliberately forced the Japanese into a position whereby they had no choice but to attack. By cutting off Japan's access to the raw materials it needed for its military adventure in China, by stubbornly refusing to compromise, the United States ensured that the Japanese would strike out into the southwest Pacific to take the needed supplies by force—even at the risk of war with the United States. Not only was American policy provocative in effect, Beard suggested; it was deliberately provocative. More than that, the administration, which had some time before cracked the Japanese code, must have known weeks in advance of Japan's plan to attack—although Beard did not claim that

PEARL HARBOR, DECEMBER 7, 1941 The destroyer U.S.S. *Shaw,* immobilized in a floating drydock in Pearl Harbor in December 1941, survived the first wave of Japanese bombers unscathed. But in the second attack, the Japanese scored a direct hit and produced this spectacular explosion, which blew off the ship's bow. Damage to the rest of the ship, however, was slight. Just a few months later the *Shaw* was fitted with a new bow and rejoined the fleet. *(U.S. Navy Photo)*

Pearl Harbor

Military commanders in Hawaii had taken no precautions against such an attack and had allowed ships to remain bunched up defenselessly in the harbor and airplanes to remain parked in rows on airstrips. The consequences of the raid were disastrous for America. Within two hours, the United States lost 8 battleships, 3 cruisers, 4 other vessels, 188 airplanes, and several vital shore installations. More than 2,000 soldiers and sailors died, and another 1,000 were injured. The Japanese suffered only light losses.

American forces were now greatly diminished in the Pacific (although by a fortunate accident, none of the American aircraft carriers—the heart of the Pacific fleet—had been at Pearl Harbor on December 7). Nevertheless, the raid on Pearl Harbor did virtually overnight what more than two years of effort by Roosevelt and others had been unable to do: it unified the American people in a fervent commitment to war. On December 8, the president traveled to Capitol Hill, where he grimly addressed a joint session of Congress: "Yesterday, December 7, 1941—a date which will live in infamy—the United States of America was suddenly and deliberately attacked by the naval and air forces of the Empire of Japan." Within four hours, the Senate unanimously and the House 388 to 1 (the lone dissenter being Jeanette Rankin of Montana, who had voted against war in 1917 as well) approved a declaration of war against Japan. Three days later, Germany and Italy, Japan's European allies, declared war on the United States; and on the same day, December 11, Congress reciprocated without a dissenting vote. For the second time in twenty-five years, the United States was engaged in a world war.

officials knew the attack would come at Pearl Harbor. Beard supported his argument by citing Secretary of War Henry Stimson's comment in his diary: "The question was how we should maneuver them into the position of firing the first shot." This view has reappeared more recently in Thomas Fleming, *The New Dealers' War* (2001), which also argues that Roosevelt deliberately (and duplicitously) maneuvered the United States into war with Japan.

A partial refutation of the Beard argument appeared in 1950 in Basil Rauch's *Roosevelt from Munich to Pearl Harbor*. The administration did not know in advance of the planned attack on Pearl Harbor, he argued. It did, however, expect an attack somewhere; and it made subtle efforts to "maneuver" Japan into firing the first shot in the conflict. But Richard N. Current, in *Secretary Stimson: A Study in Statecraft* (1954), offered an even stronger challenge to Beard. Stimson did indeed anticipate an attack, Current argued, but not an attack on American territory; rather, he anticipated an assault on British or Dutch possessions in the Pacific. The problem confronting the administration was not how to maneuver the Japanese into attacking the United States, but how to find a way to make a Japanese attack on British or Dutch territory appear to be an attack on America. Only thus, Stimson believed, could Congress be persuaded to approve a declaration of war.

Roberta Wohlstetter took a different approach to the question in *Pearl Harbor: Warning and Decision* (1962), the most thorough scholarly study to appear to that point. De-emphasizing the question of whether the American government wanted a Japanese attack, she undertook to answer the question of whether the administration knew of the attack in advance. Wohlstetter concluded that the United States had ample warning of Japanese intentions and should have realized that the Pearl Harbor raid was imminent. But government officials failed to interpret the evidence correctly, largely because their preconceptions about Japanese intentions were at odds with the evidence they confronted. Admiral Edwin T. Layton, who had been a staff officer at Pearl Harbor in 1941, also blamed political and bureaucratic failures for the absence of advance warning of the attack. In a 1985 memoir, *And I Was There,* he argued that the Japanese attack was a result not only of "audacious planning and skillful execution" by the Japanese, but of "a dramatic breakdown in our intelligence process . . . related directly to feuding among high-level naval officers in Washington."

The most thorough study of Pearl Harbor to date appeared in 1981: Gordon W. Prange's *At Dawn We Slept.* Like Wohlstetter, Prange concluded that the Roosevelt administration was guilty of a series of disastrous blunders in interpreting Japanese strategy; the American government had possession of enough information to predict the attack, but failed to do so. But Prange dismissed the arguments of the "revisionists" (Beard and his successors) that the president had deliberately maneuvered the nation into the war by permitting the Japanese to attack. Instead, he emphasized the enormous daring and great skill with which the Japanese orchestrated an ambitious operation that few Americans believed possible.

But the revisionist claims have not been laid to rest. John Toland revived the charges of a Roosevelt betrayal in 1982, in *Infamy: Pearl Harbor and Its Aftermath,* claiming to have discovered new evidence (the testimony of an unidentified seaman) that proves the navy knew at least five days in advance that Japanese aircraft carriers were heading toward Hawaii. From that, Toland concluded that Roosevelt must have known that an attack was forthcoming and that he allowed it to occur in the belief that a surprise attack would arouse the nation. But like the many other writers who have made the same argument, Toland was unable to produce any direct evidence of Roosevelt's knowledge of the planned attack.

CONCLUSION

American foreign policy in the years after World War I attempted something that ultimately proved impossible. The United States was determined to be a major power in the world, to extend its trade broadly around the globe, and to influence other nations in ways Americans believed would be beneficial to their own, and the world's, interests. But the United States was also determined to do nothing that would limit its own freedom of action. It would not join the League of Nations. It would not join the World Court. It would not form alliances with other nations. It would operate powerfully—and alone.

But ominous forces were at work in the world that would gradually push the United States into greater engagement with other nations. The economic disarray that the Great Depression created all around the world; the rise of totalitarian regimes in Europe and Asia; the expansionist ambitions of powerful new leaders—all worked to destroy the uneasy stability of the post–World War I international system. America's own interests, economic and otherwise, were now imperiled. And America's go-it-alone foreign policy seemed powerless to change the course of events.

Franklin Roosevelt tried throughout the later years of the 1930s to push the American people slowly into a greater involvement in international affairs. In particular, he tried to nudge the United States toward taking a more forceful stand against dictatorship and aggression. A powerful isolationist movement helped stymie him for a time, even after war broke out in Europe. Gradually, however, public opinion shifted toward support of the Allies (Britain, France, and eventually Russia) and against the Axis (Germany, Italy, and Japan). The nation began to mobilize for war, to supply ships and munitions to Britain, even to engage in naval combat with German forces in the Atlantic. Finally, on December 7, 1941, a surprise Japanese attack on the American base at Pearl Harbor in Hawaii ended the last elements of uncertainty and drove the United States—now united behind the war effort—into the greatest conflict in human history.

INTERACTIVE LEARNING

The *Primary Source Investigator CD-ROM* offers the following materials related to this chapter:

- Documents, images, and maps related to the rising world tensions in the 1920s and 1930s, and the outbreak of World War II. Highlights include an excerpt from the Lend-Lease Act of 1941 providing U.S. aid to Britain, a 1941 "fireside chat" in which President Roosevelt makes the case for expanded powers during wartime, and a video clip showing the destruction from the Japanese attack on Pearl Harbor.

Online Learning Center (www.mhhe.com/brinkley13e)

For quizzes, Internet resources, references to additional books and films, and more, consult this book's Online Learning Center.

FOR FURTHER REFERENCE

Robert Dallek, *Franklin D. Roosevelt and American Foreign Policy, 1932-1945* (1979) is a comprehensive study of Roosevelt's foreign policy. Akira Iriye, *The Cambridge History of American Foreign Relations, vol. 3: The Globalizing of America, 1913-1945* (1993) is another important study. In *Inevitable Revolutions* (1983), Walter LaFeber recounts America's attempts to halt revolutionary movements throughout the world. James MacGregor Burns, *Roosevelt: the Soldier of Freedom* (1970) and Warren F. Kimball, *The Juggler: Franklin Roosevelt as Wartime Statesman* (1991) are two important studies of the president. Wayne S. Cole, *Charles A. Lindbergh and the Battle Against American Intervention in World War II* (1974) and *Roosevelt and the Isolationists, 1932-1945* (1983) examine prewar isolationism. A. Scott Berg, *Lindbergh* (1998) is an excellent biography of the aviation hero who became such a controversial figure in the 1930s. Charles DeBenedetti, *Origins of the Modern American Peace Movement, 1915-1929* (1978) and *The Peace Reform in American History* (1980) examine antiwar movements in American history, including prior to World War II. Joseph Lash's *Roosevelt and Churchill* (1976) explores the dynamic relationship between the two leaders of the United States and England. Akira Iriye, *The Origins of the Second World War in Asia and the Pacific* (1988) examines the conflict between China and Japan that preceded American intervention in the Pacific war. Gordon Prange, *At Dawn We Slept* (1981) examines the controversial attack on Pearl Harbor from both the Japanese and American sides.

CHAPTER 26

AMERICA IN A WORLD AT WAR

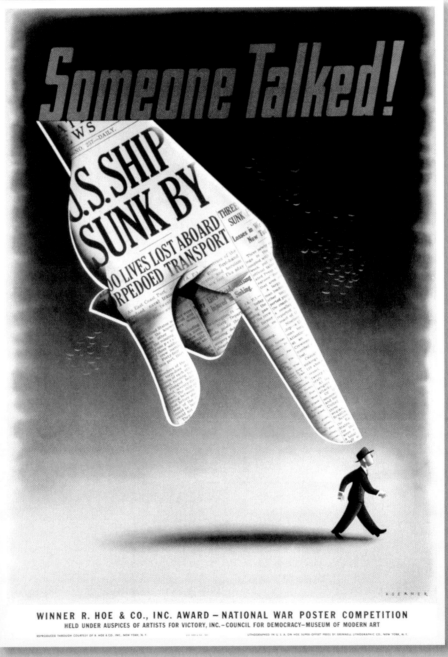

"SOMEONE TALKED"   This World War II poster, created by the graphic artist Henry Koerner, was one of many stern reminders to Americans from the government of the dangers of disclosing military secrets. In particular, wartime leaders were worried about soldiers and their families talking loosely about troop and ship locations (hence the title of another such poster: "Loose Lips Sink Ships"). *(K. J. Historical/Corbis)*

THE ATTACK ON PEARL HARBOR thrust the United States into the greatest and most terrible war in the history of humanity. World War I had cost many lives and had destroyed centuries-old European social and political institutions. But World War II created even greater carnage and horror in Europe and in much of the rest of the globe. In the end, it changed the world as profoundly as any event of the twentieth century, perhaps of any century.

For the United States, World War II was a shorter and less costly conflict than it was for the other principal combatant nations. America did not enter the war until it had already been in progress for two years in Europe and at least seven years in Asia. Except for the 1941 Japanese attack on Pearl Harbor, no battles were fought on American soil. Although more than 300,000 Americans died in World War II, many more than had died in World War I, casualties were still far fewer than for the other major participants in the war (Russia, Germany, Italy, Britain, and Japan).

In other ways, however, the United States fought a larger war than any other nation. It joined Britain, Russia, and other allies in the great struggle against Nazi Germany and Fascist Italy in Europe and North Africa, and ultimately played a decisive role in securing the victory of that effort. Simultaneously, the United States was fighting one of the greatest naval wars in history as well as a series of land campaigns against the Japanese Empire, and was doing so with only limited assistance from other nations. Only a few years before, the United States had possessed one of the smallest militaries in the world. It emerged during World War II as the most powerful military nation in history—a role that it has continued to play ever since. The war, in short, profoundly transformed America's relationship to the rest of the world.

The war also changed America at home—its society, its politics, and its image of itself. Except for the combatants themselves, most Americans experienced the war at a remove of several thousand miles. They endured no bombing, no invasion, no massive dislocations, no serious material shortages. Veterans returning home in 1945 and 1946 found a country that looked very much like the one they had left—something that clearly could not be said of veterans returning home to Britain, France, Germany, Russia, or Japan.

But World War II did transform the United States in profound, if not always readily visible, ways. As the poet Archibald MacLeish said in 1943: "The great majority of the American people understand very well that this war is not a war only, but an end and a beginning—an end to things known and a beginning of things unknown. We have smelled the wind in the streets that changes weather. We know that whatever the world will be when the war ends, the world will be different." The story of American involvement in the war is not just the story of how the military forces and the industrial might of the United States helped defeat Germany, Italy, and Japan. It is also the story of the creation of a new world, both abroad and at home.

WAR ON TWO FRONTS

Whatever political disagreements and social tensions may have existed among the American people during World War II, there was striking unity of opinion about the conflict itself—"a unity," as one member of Congress proclaimed shortly after Pearl Harbor, "never before witnessed in this country." America's unity and confidence were severely tested in the first, troubled months of 1942. Despite the impressive display of patriotism and the dramatic flurry of activity, the war was going very badly. Britain appeared ready to collapse. The Soviet Union was staggering. One after another, Allied strongholds in the Pacific were falling to the forces of Japan. The first task facing the United States, therefore, was less to achieve victory than to stave off defeat.

America Unified

Containing the Japanese

Ten hours after the strike at Pearl Harbor, Japanese airplanes attacked the American airfields at Manila in the Philippines, destroying much of America's remaining air power in the Pacific. Three days later Guam, an American possession, fell to Japan; then Wake Island and the British colony Hong Kong. The great British fortress of Singapore surrendered in February 1942, the Dutch East Indies in March, Burma in April. In the Philippines, exhausted Filipino and American troops gave up their defense of the islands on May 6.

American strategists planned two broad offensives to turn the tide against the Japanese. One, under the command of General Douglas MacArthur, would move north from Australia, through New Guinea, and eventually back to the Philippines. The other, under Admiral Chester Nimitz, would move west from Hawaii toward major Japanese island outposts in the central Pacific. Ultimately, the two offensives would come together to invade Japan itself.

The Allies achieved their first important victory in the Battle of Coral Sea, just northwest of Australia, on May 7-8, 1942, when American forces turned back the previously unstoppable Japanese fleet. A month later, there was an even more important turning point northwest of Hawaii. An enormous battle raged for four days, June 3-6, 1942, near the small American outpost at Midway Island, at the end of which the United States, despite great losses, was clearly victorious. The American navy destroyed four Japanese aircraft carriers while losing only one, and regained control of the central Pacific for the United States.

Midway

The Americans took the offensive for the first time several months later in the southern Solomon Islands, to the east of New Guinea. In August 1942, American forces assaulted three of the islands: Gavutu, Tulagi, and Guadalcanal. A struggle of terrible ferocity (and, before it was over, terrible savagery) developed at Guadalcanal and continued for six months, inflicting heavy losses on both sides. In the end, however, the Japanese were forced to abandon the island—and with it their last chance of launching an effective offensive to the south.

Guadalcanal

Thus, in both the southern and central Pacific, the initiative had shifted to the United States by mid-1943. The Japanese advance had come to a stop. With aid from Australians and New Zealanders, the Americans now began the slow, arduous process of moving toward the Philippines and Japan itself.

Holding Off the Germans

In the European war, the United States had less control over military operations. It was fighting in cooperation with Britain and with the exiled "Free French" forces in the west; and it was trying also to conciliate its new ally, the Soviet Union, which was fighting Hitler in the east. The army chief of staff, General George C. Marshall, supported a plan for a major Allied invasion of France across the English Channel in the spring of 1943. But the American plan faced challenges from the Allies. The Soviet Union, which was absorbing (as it would throughout the war) the brunt of the German effort, wanted the Allied invasion to proceed at the earliest possible moment. The British, on the other hand, wanted first to launch a series of Allied offensives around the edges of the Nazi empire—in northern Africa and southern Europe—before undertaking the major invasion of France.

Roosevelt realized that to support the British plan would antagonize the Soviets and might delay the important cross-channel invasion. But he also knew that the invasion of Europe would take a long time to prepare, and he was reluctant to wait so long before getting American forces into combat. And so, over the objections of some of his most important advisers, he decided to support the British plan. At the end of October 1942, the British opened a counteroffensive against Nazi forces in North Africa under General Erwin Rommel, who was threatening the Suez Canal at El Alamein, and forced the Germans to retreat from Egypt. On November 8, Anglo-American forces landed at Oran and Algiers in Algeria and at Casablanca in Morocco—areas under the Nazi-controlled French government at Vichy—and began moving east toward Rommel.

The Germans threw the full weight of their forces in Africa against the inexperienced Americans and inflicted a serious defeat on them at the Kasserine Pass in Tunisia. General George S. Patton, however, regrouped the American troops and began an effective counteroffensive. With the help of Allied air and naval power and of British forces attacking from the east under General Bernard Montgomery (the hero of El Alamein), the American offensive finally drove the last Germans from Africa in May 1943.

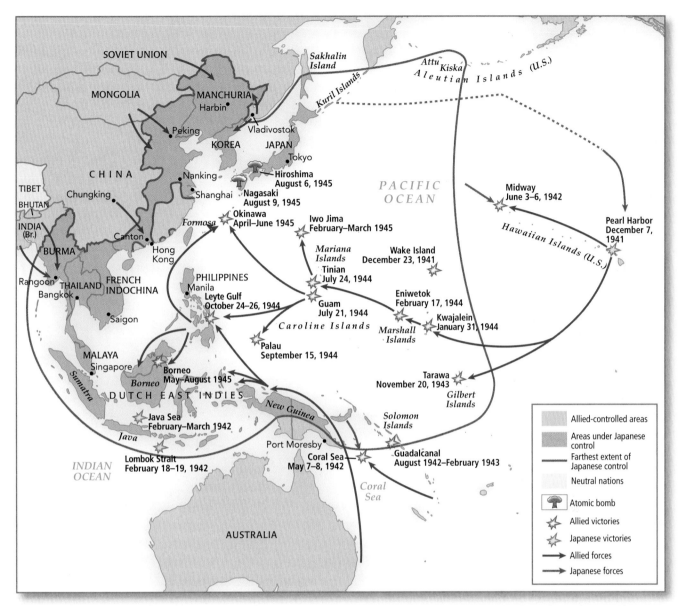

WORLD WAR II IN THE PACIFIC This map illustrates the changing fortunes of the two combatants in the Pacific phase of World War II. The long red line stretching from Burma around to Manchuria represents the eastern boundary of the vast areas of the Pacific that had fallen under Japanese control by the summer of 1942. The blue lines illustrate the advance of American forces back into the Pacific beginning in May 1942 and accelerating in 1943 and after, which drove the Japanese forces back. The American advance was a result of two separate offensives—one in the central Pacific, under the command of Chester Nimitz, which moved west from Hawaii; the other, under the command of Douglas MacArthur, which moved north from Australia. By the summer of 1945, American forces were approaching the Japanese mainland and were bombing Tokyo itself. The dropping of two American atomic bombs, on Hiroshima and Nagasaki, finally brought the war to an end. ◆ *Why did the Soviet Union enter the Pacific war in August 1945, as shown in the upper left corner of the map?*

The North Africa campaign had tied up a large proportion of the Allied resources and contributed to the postponement of the planned May 1943 cross-channel invasion of France. That produced angry complaints from the Soviet Union. By now, however, the threat of a Soviet collapse seemed much diminished, for during the winter of 1942–1943 the Red Army had successfully held off a major German assault at Stalingrad in southern Russia. Hitler had committed such enormous forces to the battle, and had

Stalingrad

suffered such appalling losses, that he could not continue his eastern offensive.

The Soviet victory had come at a terrible cost. The German siege of Stalingrad had decimated the civilian population of the city and devastated the surrounding countryside. Indeed, throughout the war, the Soviet Union absorbed losses far greater than any other warring nation (up to 20 million casualties)—a fact that continued to haunt the Russian memory and affect Soviet policy generations later. But the Soviet success in beating back the

AUSCHWITZ, DECEMBER 1944 This photograph, taken near the end of World War II, shows a group of imprisoned children behind a barbed wire fence in one of the most notorious Nazi concentration camps. By the time this picture was taken, the Nazis had been driven out of Auschwitz and were under the control of Allied soldiers. *(Keystone/Getty Images)*

German offensive persuaded Roosevelt to agree, in a January 1943 meeting with Churchill in Casablanca, to an Allied invasion of Sicily. General Marshall opposed the plan, arguing that it would further delay the vital invasion of France. But Churchill prevailed with the argument that the operation in Sicily might knock Italy out of the war and tie up German divisions that might otherwise be stationed in France. On the night of July 9, 1943, American and British armies landed in southeast Sicily; thirty-eight days later they had conquered the island and were moving onto the Italian mainland. In the face of these setbacks, Mussolini's government collapsed and the dictator fled north to Germany. But although Mussolini's successor, Pietro Badoglio, quickly committed Italy to the Allies, Germany moved eight divisions into the country and established a powerful defensive line south of Rome. The Allied offensive on the Italian peninsula, which began on September 3, 1943, soon bogged down, especially after a

serious setback at Monte Cassino that winter. Not until May 1944 did the Allies resume their northward advance. On June 4, 1944, they captured Rome.

The invasion of Italy contributed to the Allied war effort in several important ways. But it postponed the invasion of France by as much as a year, deeply embittering the Soviet Union, many of whose leaders believed that the United States and Britain were deliberately delaying the cross-channel invasion in order to allow the Russians to absorb the brunt of the fighting. The postponement also gave the Soviets time to begin moving toward the countries of eastern Europe.

> Dispute over the Second Front

America and the Holocaust

In dealing with the global crisis, the leaders of the American government were confronted with one of history's great horrors: the Nazi campaign to exterminate the Jews of Europe—the Holocaust. As early as 1942, high officials in Washington had incontrovertible evidence that Hitler's forces were rounding up Jews and others (including non-Jewish Poles, gypsies, homosexuals, and communists) from all over Europe, transporting them to concentration camps in eastern Germany and Poland, and systematically murdering them. (The death toll would ultimately reach 6 million Jews and approximately 4 million others.) News of the atrocities was reaching the public as well, and public pressure began to build for an Allied effort to end the killing or at least to rescue some of the surviving Jews.

The American government consistently resisted almost all such entreaties. Although Allied bombers were flying missions within a few miles of the most notorious death camp at Auschwitz in Poland, pleas that the planes try to destroy the crematoria at the camp were rejected as militarily unfeasible. So were similar requests that the Allies try to destroy railroad lines leading to the camps.

The United States also resisted entreaties that it admit large numbers of the Jewish refugees attempting to escape Europe—a pattern established well before Pearl Harbor. One ship, the German passenger liner *St. Louis,* had arrived off Miami in 1939 (after having already been turned away from Havana, Cuba) carrying nearly 1,000 escaped German Jews, only to be refused entry and forced to return to Europe. Both before and during the war, the State Department did not even use up the number of visas permitted by law; almost 90 percent of the quota remained untouched. This disgraceful record was not a result of inadvertence. There was a deliberate effort by officials in the State Department—spearheaded by Assistant Secretary Breckinridge Long, a genteel anti-Semite—to prevent Jews | Official Anti-Semitism from entering the United States in large numbers. One opportunity after another to assist imperiled Jews was either ignored or rejected.

After 1941, there was probably little American leaders could have done, other than defeat Germany, to save most

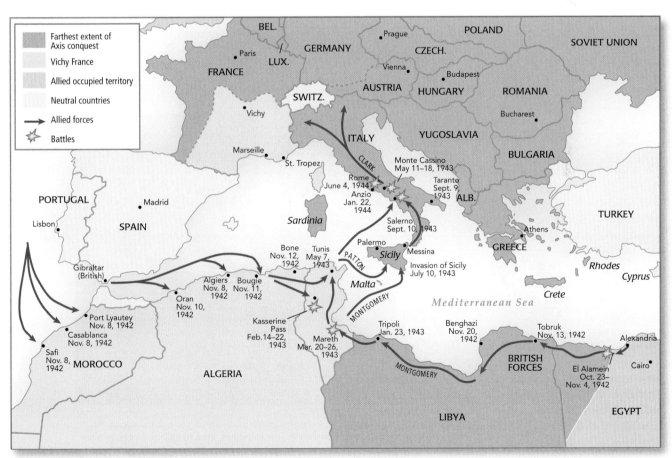

WORLD WAR II IN NORTH AFRICA AND ITALY: THE ALLIED COUNTEROFFENSIVE, 1942–1943 The United States and Great Britain understood from the beginning that an invasion of France across the English Channel would eventually be necessary for a victory in the European war. In the meantime, however, they began a campaign against Axis forces in North Africa, and in the spring of 1943 they began an invasion across the Mediterranean into Italy. This map shows the points along the coast of North Africa where Allied forces landed in 1942—with American forces moving east from Morocco and Algeria, and British forces moving west from Egypt. The two armies met in Tunisia and moved into Italy from there. ◆ *Why were America and Britain reluctant to launch the cross-channel invasion in 1942 or 1943?*

For an interactive version of this map, go to www.mhhe.com/brinkley13ech26maps

of Hitler's victims. But more forceful action by the United States (and Britain, which was even less amenable than America to Jewish requests for assistance) before and even during the war might well have saved some lives. Policymakers at the time justified their inaction by arguing that most of the proposed actions—bombing the railroads and the death camps, for example—would have had little effect. They insisted that the most effective thing they could do for the victims of the Holocaust was to concentrate their attention solely on the larger goal of winning the war.

THE AMERICAN PEOPLE IN WARTIME

"War is no longer simply a battle between armed forces in the field," an American government report of 1939 concluded. "It is a struggle in which each side strives to bring to bear against the enemy the coordinated power of every individual and of every material resource at its command. The conflict extends from the soldier in the front line to the citizen in the remotest hamlet in the rear." The United States had experienced wars before. But not since the Civil War had the nation undergone so consuming a military experience as World War II. American armed forces engaged in combat around the globe for nearly four years. American society, in the meantime, underwent changes that reached into virtually every corner of the nation.

Prosperity

World War II had its most profound impact on American domestic life by at last ending the Great Depression. By the middle of 1941, the economic problems of the 1930s— unemployment, deflation, industrial sluggishness—had virtually vanished before the great wave of wartime industrial expansion.

War-Induced Economic Recovery

The most important agent of the new prosperity was federal spending, which after 1939 was pumping more money into the economy each year than all the New Deal relief agencies combined had done. In 1939, the federal

THE *ST. LOUIS* The fate of the German liner *St. Louis* has become a powerful symbol of the indifference of the United States and other nations to the fate of European Jews during the Holocaust, even though its forlorn journey preceded both the beginning of World War II and the beginning of systematic extermination of Jews by the Nazi regime. The *St. Louis* carried a group of over 900 Jews fleeing from Germany in 1939, carrying exit visas of dubious legality cynically sold to them by members of Hitler's Gestapo. It became a ship without a port as it sailed from country to country—Mexico, Paraguay, Argentina, Costa Rica, and Cuba—where its passengers were refused entry time and again. Most of the passengers were hoping for a haven in the United States, but the American State Department refused to allow the ship even to dock as it sailed up the American eastern seaboard. Eventually, the *St. Louis* returned to Europe and distributed its passengers among Britain, France, Holland, and Belgium (where this photograph was taken showing refugees smiling and waving as they prepare to disembark in Antwerp in June 1939). Less than a year later, all those nations except Britain fell under Nazi control. *(Bettmann/Corbis)*

budget had been $9 billion, the highest level it had ever reached in peacetime; by 1945, it had risen to $100 billion. Largely as a result, the gross national product soared: from $91 billion in 1939 to $166 billion in 1945. Personal incomes in some areas grew by as much as 100 percent or more. The demands of wartime production created a shortage of consumer goods, so many wage earners diverted much of their new affluence into savings, which would help keep the economic boom alive in the postwar years.

The War and the West

The impact of government spending was perhaps most dramatic in the West, which had long relied on federal largesse more than other regions. The West Coast, naturally, became the launching point for most of the naval war against Japan; and the government created large manufacturing facilities in California and elsewhere to serve the needs of its military. Altogether, the government made almost $40 billion worth of capital investments (factories, military and transportation facilities, highways, power plants) in the West during the war, more than in any other region. Ten percent of all the money the federal government spent between 1940 and 1945 went to California. Other western states also shared disproportionately in war contracts and government-funded capital investments.

By the end of the war, the economy of the Pacific Coast and, to a lesser extent, other areas of the West had been transformed. The Pacific Coast had become the center of the growing American aircraft industry. New yards in southern California, Washington State, and elsewhere made the West a center of the shipbuilding industry. Los Angeles, formerly a medium-sized city notable chiefly for its film industry, now became a major industrial center as well.

Once a lightly industrialized region, parts of the West were now among the most important manufacturing areas in the country. Once a region without adequate facilities to support substantial economic growth, the West now stood poised to become the fastest-growing region in the nation after the war.

Labor and the War

Instead of the prolonged and debilitating unemployment that had been the most troubling feature of the Depression economy, the war created a serious labor shortage. The armed forces took more than 15 million men and women out of the civilian work force at the same time that the demand for labor was rising rapidly. Nevertheless, the civilian work force increased by almost 20 percent during the war. The 7 million people who had previously been unemployed accounted for some of the increase; the employment of many people previously considered inappropriate for the work force—the very young, the elderly, and, most important, several million women—accounted for the rest.

The war gave an enormous boost to union membership, which rose from about 10.5 million members in 1941 to more than 13 million in 1945. But it also created important new restrictions on the ability of unions to fight for their members' demands. The government was principally interested in preventing inflation and in keeping production moving without disruption. It managed to win important concessions from union leaders on both scores. One was the so-called Little Steel formula, which set a 15 percent limit on wartime wage increases. Another was the "no-strike" pledge, by which unions agreed not to stop production in wartime. In return, the government provided labor with a "maintenance-of-membership" agreement, which insisted that the thousands of new workers pouring into unionized defense plants would be automatically enrolled in the unions. The agreement ensured the continued health of the union organizations, but in return workers had to give up the right to demand major economic gains during the war.

Union Gains

Many rank-and-file union members, and some local union leaders, resented the restrictions imposed on them by the government and the labor movement hierarchy. Despite the no-strike pledge, there were nearly 15,000 work stoppages during the war, mostly wildcat strikes (strikes unauthorized by the union leadership). When the United Mine Workers defied the government by striking in May 1943, Congress reacted by passing, over Roosevelt's veto, the Smith-Connally Act (or the War Labor Disputes Act), which required unions to wait thirty days before striking and empowered the president to seize a struck war plant. In the meantime, public animosity toward labor rose rapidly, and many states passed laws to limit union power.

Stabilizing the Boom

The fear of deflation, the central concern of the 1930s, gave way during the war to a fear of inflation, particularly after prices rose 25 percent in the two years before Pearl Harbor. In October 1942, Congress grudgingly responded to the president's request and passed the Anti-Inflation Act, which gave the administration authority to freeze agricultural prices, wages, salaries, and rents throughout the country. Enforcement of these provisions was the task of the Office of Price Administration (OPA), led first by Leon Henderson and then by Chester Bowles. In part because of its success, inflation was a much less serious problem during World War II than it had been during World War I.

Office of Price Administration

Even so, the OPA was never popular. There was widespread resentment of its controls over wages and prices. And there was only grudging acquiescence in its complicated system of rationing scarce consumer goods: coffee, sugar, meat, butter, canned goods, shoes, tires, gasoline, and fuel oil. Black-marketing and overcharging grew to proportions far beyond OPA policing capacity.

From 1941 to 1945, the federal government spent a total of $321 billion—twice as much as it had spent in the entire 150 years of its existence to that point, and ten times as much as the cost of World War I. The national debt rose from $49 billion in 1941 to $259 billion in 1945. The government borrowed about half the revenues it needed by selling $100 billion worth of bonds. Much of the rest it raised by radically increasing income taxes through the Revenue Act of 1942, which established a 94 percent rate for the highest brackets and, for the first time, imposed taxes on the lowest-income families as well. To simplify collection, Congress enacted a withholding system of payroll deductions in 1943.

Mobilizing Production

The search for an effective mechanism to mobilize the economy for war began as early as 1939 and continued for nearly four years. One failed agency after another attempted to bring order to the mobilization effort. Finally, in January 1942, the president responded to widespread criticism by creating the War Production Board (WPB),

War Production Board

under the direction of former Sears Roebuck executive Donald Nelson. In theory, the WPB was to be a "superagency," with broad powers over the economy. In fact, it never had as much authority as its World War I equivalent, the War Industries Board. And the genial Donald Nelson never displayed the administrative or political strength of his 1918 counterpart, Bernard Baruch.

The WPB was never able to win control over military purchases; the army and navy often circumvented the board entirely in negotiating contracts with producers. It was never able to satisfy the complaints of small business, which charged (correctly) that most contracts were going to large corporations. Gradually, the president transferred much of the WPB's authority to a new office located within the White House: the Office of War Mobilization, directed by former Supreme Court justice and South Carolina senator James F. Byrnes. But the OWM was only slightly more successful than the WPB.

Despite the administrative problems, the war economy managed to meet almost all the nation's critical war needs. Enormous new factory complexes sprang up in the space of a few months, many of them funded by the federal government's Defense Plants Corporation. An entire new industry producing synthetic rubber emerged, to make up for the loss of access to natural rubber in the Pacific. By the beginning of 1944, American factories were, in fact, producing more of most goods than the government needed. Their output was twice that of all the Axis countries combined. There were even complaints late in the war from some officials that military production was becoming excessive, that a limited resumption of civilian

production should begin before the fighting ended. The military staunchly and successfully opposed almost all such demands.

Wartime Science and Technology

More than any previous American war, World War II was a watershed for technological and scientific innovation. That was partly because the American government poured substantial funds into research and development beginning in 1940. In that year the government created the National Defense Research Committee, headed by the MIT scientist Vannevar Bush, who had been

National Defense Research Committee

a pioneer in the early development of the computer. By the end of the war, the new agency had spent more than $100 million on research, more than four times the amount spent by the government on military research and development in the previous forty years.

In the first years of the war, all the technological advantages seemed to lie with the Germans and Japanese. Germany had made great advances in tanks and other mechanized armor in the 1930s, particularly during the Spanish Civil War, when it had helped arm Franco's fascist forces. It used its armor effectively during its blitzkrieg in Europe in 1940 and again in North Africa in 1942. German submarine technology was significantly advanced compared to British and American capabilities in 1940, and German U-boats were, for a time, devastatingly effective in disrupting Allied shipping. Japan had developed extraordinary capacity in its naval-air technology. Its highly sophisticated fighter planes, launched from distant aircraft carriers, conducted the successful raid on Pearl Harbor in December 1941.

But Britain and America had advantages of their own, which quickly helped redress these imbalances. American techniques of mass production—the great automotive assembly lines in particular—were converted efficiently to military production in 1941 and 1942 and soon began producing airplanes, ships, tanks, and other armaments in much greater numbers than the Germans and Japanese could produce. Allied scientists and engineers moved quickly as well to improve Anglo-American aviation and naval technology, particularly to improve the performance of submarines and tanks. By late 1942, Allied weaponry was at least as advanced as, and coming to be more plentiful than, that of the enemy.

In addition, each technological innovation by the enemy produced a corresponding innovation to limit the damage of the new techniques. American and British physicists made rapid advances in improving radar and sonar technology—

Radar and Sonar

taking advantage of advances in radio technology in the 1920s and beyond—which helped Allied naval forces decimate German U-boats in 1943 and effectively end their effectiveness in the naval war. Particularly important was

RADAR SCOPE, 1944 Navy technicians are shown here demonstrating the new radar scopes that revolutionized the tracking of ships and planes during World War II. *(National Archives and Records Administration)*

the creation in 1940 of "centimetric radar," which used narrow beams of short wavelength that made radar more efficient and effective than ever before—as the British navy discovered in April 1941 when the instruments on one of its ships detected a surfaced submarine ten miles away at night and, on another occasion, spotted a periscope at three-quarters of a mile range. With earlier technologies, the sub and periscope would have been undetectable. This new radar could also be effectively miniaturized, which was critical to its use on airplanes and submarines in particular. It required only a small rotating aerial, and it used newly advanced cavity magnetron valves of great power. These innovations put the Allies far in advance of Germany and Japan in radar technology. The Allies also learned early how to detect and disable German naval mines; and when the Germans tried to counter this progress by introducing an "acoustic" mine, which detonated when a ship came near it, not necessarily just on contact, the Allies developed acoustical countermeasures of their own, which transmit-

ted sounds through the water to detonate mines before ships came near them.

Anglo-American antiaircraft technology—both on land and on sea—also improved, although never to the point where it could stop bombing raids. Germany made substantial advances in the development of rocket technology in the early years of the war, and it managed to launch some rocket-propelled bombs (the V1s and V2s) across the English Channel, aimed at London. The psychological effects of the rockets on the British people were considerable. But the Germans were never able to create a production technology capable of building enough such rockets to make a real difference in the balance of military power.

Beginning in 1942, British and American forces seized the advantage in the air war by producing new and powerful four-engine bombers in great numbers—among them the British Lancaster B1 and the American Boeing B17F, capable of flying a bomb load of 6,000 pounds for

1,300 miles, and capable of reaching 37,500 feet. Because they were able to fly higher and longer than the German equivalents, they were able to conduct extensive bombing missions over Germany (and later Japan) with much less danger of being shot down. But the success of the bombers rested heavily as well on new electronic devices capable of guiding their bombs to their targets. The Gee navigation system, which was also valuable to the navy, used electronic pulses to help pilots plot their exact location—something that in the past only a highly skilled navigator could do, and then only in good weather. In March 1942, eighty Allied bombers fitted with Gee systems staged a devastatingly effective bombing raid on German industrial and military installations in the Ruhr Valley. Studies showed that the Gee system doubled the accuracy rate of night bombing raids. Also effective was the Oboe system, a radio device that sent a sonic message to airplanes to tell them when they were within twenty yards of their targets, first introduced in December 1942.

The area in which the Allies had perhaps the greatest advantages in technology and knowledge was the gathering of intelligence, much of it through Britain's top-secret Ultra project. Some of the advantages the Allies enjoyed came from successful efforts to capture or steal German and Japanese intelligence devices. More important, however, were the efforts of cryptologists to puzzle out the enemy's systems, and advances in computer technology that helped the Allies decipher coded messages sent by the Japanese and the Germans. Much of Germany's coded communication made use of the so-called Enigma machine, which was effective because it constantly changed the coding systems it used.

In the first months of the war, Polish intelligence had developed an electro-mechanical computer, which it called the "Bombe," that could decipher some Enigma messages. After the fall of Poland, British scientists, led by the brilliant computer pioneer Alan Turing, took the Bombe, which was too slow to keep up with the increasingly frequent changes of coding the Germans were using, and greatly improved it. On April 15, 1940, the new, improved, high-speed Bombe broke the coding of a series of German messages within hours (not days, as had previously been the case). A few weeks later, it began decrypting German messages at the rate of 1,000 a day, providing the British (and later the Americans) with a constant flow of information about enemy operations that continued—unknown to the Germans—until the end of the war.

Later in the war, British scientists working for the intelligence services built the first real programmable, digital computer—the Colossus II, which became operational less than a week before the beginning of the Normandy invasion. It was able to decipher an enormous number of intercepted German messages almost instantly.

The United States also had some important intelligence breakthroughs, including, in 1941, a dramatic success by the American Magic operation (the counterpart to the British Ultra) in breaking a Japanese coding system not unlike the German Enigma, a mechanical device known to the Allies as Purple. The result was that Americans had access to intercepted information that, if properly interpreted, could have alerted them to the Japanese raid on Pearl Harbor in December 1941. But because such a raid had seemed entirely inconceivable to most American officials prior to its occurrence, those who received the information failed to understand or disseminate it in time.

African Americans and the War

During World War I, many African Americans had eagerly seized the chance to serve in the armed forces, believing that their patriotic efforts would win them an enhanced position in postwar society. They had been cruelly disappointed. As World War II approached, blacks were again determined to use the conflict to improve their position in society—this time, however, not by currying favor but by making demands.

In the summer of 1941, A. Philip Randolph, president of the predominantly black Brotherhood of Sleeping Car Porters, began to insist that the government require companies receiving defense contracts to integrate their work forces. To mobilize support for the demand, Randolph planned a massive march on Washington, which would, he promised, bring over 100,000 demonstrators to the capital. Roosevelt was afraid of both the possibility of violence and the certainty of political embarrassment. He finally persuaded Randolph to cancel the march in return for a promise to establish a Fair Employment Practices Commission to investigate discrimination in war industries. The FEPC's enforcement powers, and thus its effectiveness, were limited, but its creation was a rare symbolic victory for African Americans making demands of the government.

The demand for labor in war plants greatly increased the migration of blacks from the rural areas of the South into industrial cities—a migration that continued for more than a decade after the war and brought many more African Americans into northern cities than the Great Migration of 1914–1919 had done. The migration bettered the economic condition of many African Americans, but it also created urban tensions. On a hot June day in Detroit in 1943, a series of altercations between blacks and whites at a city park led to two days of racial violence in which thirty-four people died, twenty-five of them African Americans.

Despite such tensions, the leading black organizations redoubled their efforts during the war to challenge the system of segregation. The Congress of Racial Equality (CORE), organized in 1942, mobilized mass popular resistance to discrimination in a way that the older, more conservative organizations had never done. Randolph, Bayard Rustin,

James Farmer, and other, younger black leaders helped organize sit-ins and demonstrations in segregated theaters and restaurants. In 1944, CORE won a much-publicized victory by forcing a Washington, D.C., restaurant to agree to serve African Americans. Its defiant spirit would survive into the 1950s and help produce the civil rights movement.

Pressure for change was also growing within the military. At first, the armed forces maintained their traditional practice of limiting blacks to the most menial assignments, keeping them in segregated training camps and units, and barring them entirely from the Marine Corps and the Army Air Force. Gradually, however, military leaders were forced to make adjustments—in part because of public and political pressures, but also because they recognized that these forms of segregation were wasting manpower. By the end of the war, the number of black servicemen had increased sevenfold, to 700,000; some training camps were being at least partially integrated; African Americans were beginning to serve on ships with white sailors; and more black units were being sent into combat. But tensions remained. In some of the partially integrated army bases—Fort Dix, New Jersey, for example—riots occasionally broke out when African Americans protested having to serve in segregated divisions. Substantial discrimination survived in all the services until well after the war. But within the military, as within the society at large, the traditional pattern of race relations was slowly eroding.

Native Americans and the War

Approximately 25,000 Native Americans performed military service during World War II. Many of them served in combat (among them Ira Hayes, one of the men who memorably raised the American flag at Iwo Jima). Others worked as "code-talkers," working in military communications and speaking their own languages (which enemy forces would be unlikely to understand) over the radio and the telephones.

"Code-Talkers"

The war had important effects, too, on those Native Americans who remained civilians. Little war work reached the tribes, and government subsidies dwindled. Many talented young people left the reservations, some to serve in the military, others (more than 70,000) to work in war plants. This brought many Indians into close contact with white society for the first time and awakened in some of them a taste for the material benefits of life in capitalist America that they would retain after the war. Some never returned to the reservations, but chose to remain in the non-Indian world and assimilate to its ways. Others found that after the war, employment opportunities that had been available to them during the fighting became unavailable once again, drawing them back to the reservations.

The wartime emphasis on national unity undermined support for the revitalization of tribal autonomy that the

Indian Reorganization Act of 1934 had launched. New pressures emerged to eliminate the reservation system and require the tribes to assimilate into white society—pressures so severe that John Collier, the director of the Bureau of Indian Affairs who had done so much to promote the reinvigoration of the reservations, resigned in 1945.

Mexican-American War Workers

Large numbers of Mexican workers entered the United States during the war in response to labor shortages on the Pacific Coast, in the Southwest, and eventually in almost all areas of the nation. The American and Mexican governments agreed in 1942 to a program by which *braceros* (contract laborers) would be admitted to the United States for a limited time to work at specific jobs, and American employers in some parts of the Southwest began actively recruiting Hispanic workers.

During the Depression, many Mexican farmworkers had been deported to make room for unemployed white workers. The wartime labor shortage caused farm owners to begin hiring Mexicans again. More important, however, Mexicans were able for the first time to find significant numbers of factory jobs. They formed the second-largest group of migrants (after African

Employment Gains for Mexican Americans

YOUNG STREET, LOS ANGELES Although the Anglo image of Mexican Americans in wartime southern California was dominated by the culture of the "zoot-suiters," there was a longstanding and thriving Mexican-American middle class. Here two friends, Richard Garcia and John Urrea, pose in front of the Urrea home in the early 1940s. *(Shades of L.A. Archives/Los Angeles Public Library)*

Americans) to American cities in the 1940s. Over 300,000 of them served in the United States military.

The sudden expansion of Mexican-American neighborhoods created tensions and occasionally conflict in some American cities. Some white residents of Los Angeles became alarmed at the activities of Mexican-American teenagers, many of whom were joining street gangs (pachucos). The pachucos were particularly distinctive because of their members' style of dress, which whites considered outrageous. They wore "zoot suits"—long, loose jackets with padded shoulders, baggy pants tied at the ankles—long watch chains, broad-brimmed hats, and greased, ducktail hairstyles. (It was a style borrowed in part from fashions in Harlem.) For some of those who wore them, the style of dress served as a symbol of rebellion against and defiance toward conventional white, middle-class society.

In June 1943, animosity toward the zoot-suiters produced a four-day riot in Los Angeles, during which white | **Zoot-Suit Riots** | sailors stationed at a base in Long Beach invaded Mexican-American communities and attacked zoot-suiters (in response to alleged attacks). The city police did little to restrain the sailors, who grabbed Hispanic teenagers, tore off and burned their clothes, cut off their ducktails, and beat them. But when Hispanics tried to fight back, the police moved in and arrested them. In the aftermath of the "zoot-suit riots," Los Angeles passed a law prohibiting the wearing of zoot suits.

Women and Children at War

The war drew increasing numbers of women into roles from which, by either custom or law, they had been largely barred. The number of women in the work force increased | **Dramatic Increase in Female Employment** | by nearly 60 percent, and women accounted for a third of paid workers in 1945 (as opposed to a quarter in 1940). These wage-earning women were more likely to be married and older than most women who had entered the work force in the past.

Many women entered the industrial work force to replace male workers serving in the military. But while economic and military necessity eroded some of the popular objections to women in the workplace, obstacles remained. Many factory owners continued to categorize jobs by gender. (Female work, like male work, was also categorized by race: black women were usually assigned more menial tasks, and paid at a lower rate, than their white counterparts.) Employers also made substantial investments in automated assembly lines to reduce the need for heavy labor.

Many employers treated women in the war plants with a combination of solicitude and patronization, which was also an obstacle to winning genuine equality within the work force. Special recruiting materials presented factory work to women through domestic analogies that male employers assumed females would find

easily comprehensible: cutting airplane wings was compared to making a dress pattern, mixing chemicals to making a cake. Still, women did make important inroads in industrial employment during the war. Women had been working in industry for over a century, but some began now to take on heavy industrial jobs that had long been considered "men's work." The famous wartime image of "Rosie the Riveter" symbolized the new importance of the female industrial work force. Women workers | **"Rosie the Riveter"** | joined unions in substantial numbers, and they helped erode at least some of the prejudice, including the prejudice against working mothers, that had previously kept many of them from paid employment.

Most women workers during the war were employed not in factories but in service-sector jobs. Above all, they worked for the government, whose bureaucratic needs expanded dramatically alongside its military and industrial needs. Washington, D.C., in particular, was flooded with young female clerks, secretaries, and typists—known as "government girls"—most of whom lived in cramped quarters in boardinghouses, private homes, and government dormitories and worked long hours in the war agencies. Public and private clerical employment for women expanded in other urban areas as well, creating high concentrations of young women in places largely depleted of young men. The result was the development of distinctively female communities, in which women, often separated for the first time from home and family, adjusted to life in the work force through their association with other female workers. Even within the military, which enlisted substantial numbers of women as WACs (army) and WAVEs (navy), most female work was clerical.

The new opportunities produced new problems. Many mothers whose husbands were in the military had to combine working with caring for their children. The scarcity of | **Limited Child Care** | child-care facilities or other community services meant that some women had no choice but to leave young children—often known as "latchkey children" or "eight-hour orphans"—at home alone (or sometimes locked in cars in factory parking lots) while they worked.

Perhaps in part because of the family dislocations the war produced, juvenile crime rose markedly in the war years. Young boys were arrested at rapidly increasing rates for car theft and other burglary, vandalism, and vagrancy. The arrest rate for prostitutes, many of whom were teenage girls, rose too, as did the incidence of sexually transmitted disease. For many children, however, the distinctive experience of the war years was not crime but work. More than a third of all teenagers between the ages of fourteen and eighteen were employed late in the war, causing some reduction in high-school enrollments.

The return of prosperity during the war helped increase the rate and lower the age of marriage, but many of these young marriages were unable to survive the

SOLDIERS *without guns*

Beginning of the "Baby Boom" pressures of wartime separation. The divorce rate rose rapidly. The rise in the birth rate that accompanied the increase in marriages was the first sign of what would become the great postwar "baby boom."

Wartime Life and Culture

The war created considerable anxiety in American life. Families worried about loved ones at the front and struggled to adjust to the absence of husbands, fathers, brothers, sons—and to the new mobility of women, which also drew family members away from home. Businesses and communities struggled to compensate for shortages of goods and the absence of men.

But the abundance of the war years also created a striking buoyancy in American life that the conflict itself only partially subdued. Suddenly, people had money to spend again and—despite the many shortages of consumer goods—at Economic Good Times least some things to spend it on. Audiences equal to about half the population attended movies each week, often to watch heroic war films. Magazines, particularly pictorial ones such as *Life,* reached the peak of their popularity, satisfying the seemingly insatiable hunger of readers for pictures of and stories about the war. Radio ownership and listening also increased, for the same reason.

Resort hotels, casinos, and racetracks were jammed with customers. Dance halls were packed with young people drawn to the seductive music of swing bands; soldiers and sailors home on leave, or awaiting shipment overseas, were especially attracted to the dances and the big bands, which became to many of them a symbol of the life they were leaving and that they believed they were fighting to defend. (See "Patterns of Popular Culture," pp. 742–743.)

Advertisers, and at times even the government, exhorted Americans to support the war effort to ensure a future of material comfort and consumer choice for themselves and their children. "Your people are giving their lives in useless sacrifice," the *Saturday Evening Post*

THE AGE OF SWING

To many young Americans during World War II—both those who went off to the front and those who stayed at home—nothing more strongly evoked the image of life as they remembered it and wished it to be again than the big bands, the most popular musical groups of the era. The smooth, romantic sound of brass and woodwinds, the sultry voices of the mostly female singers, the swaying bodies of hundreds—in some places thousands—of dancers moving to the music: that, in wartime, represented to many people what the good life was all about.

The big bands always played several different kinds of jazz, but from the mid-1930s to the mid-1940s, they played "swing" above all—a new form of jazz that, as its name implied, seemed made for dancing. And although swing quickly became extremely popular with white,

THE KING OF SWING This poster advertises a 1944 film highlighting the music of the great Swing musician Benny Goodman. *(© 20th Century Fox Film Corp. All Rights Reserved. Courtesy Everett Collection)*

STARS OF THE AGE OF SWING This 1939 photograph shows a group of extraordinary musical artists who contributed to the emergence of Swing as the most popular music in America. Duke Ellington is at the piano, Cab Calloway is playing a guitar, and other guests gather around to listen at a party hosted by a political cartoonist for the Hearst newspapers. *(Charles Peterson/ Hulton Archive/Getty Images)*

middle-class audiences, it had its origins—like other kinds of jazz and like the rock music that would later help displace it—in the African-American musical world. The black musician Fletcher Henderson began experimenting with swing in Harlem in the 1920s; he called it "hot jazz." In 1934, he began working with the white jazz musician

wrote in a mock letter to the leaders of wartime Japan. "Ours are fighting for a glorious future of mass employment, mass production and mass distribution and ownership." Even troops at the front seemed at times to justify their efforts with reference to the comforts of home more than to the character of the enemy or the ideals America claimed to be defending. "They are fighting for home," the writer John Hersey once wrote from Guadalcanal (with at least a trace of dismay), because "Home is where the good things are—the generosity, the good pay, the comforts, the democracy, the pie."

Fighting for Future Prosperity

For men at the front, the image of home was a powerful antidote to the rigors of wartime. They dreamed of music, food, movies, material comforts. Many also dreamed of women—wives and girlfriends, but also movie stars

and others who became the source of one of the most popular icons of the front: the pinup.

For the servicemen who remained in America during the war, and for soldiers and sailors in cities far from home in particular, the company of friendly, "wholesome" women was, the military believed, critical to maintaining morale. USOs recruited thousands of young women to serve as hostesses in their clubs—women who were expected to dress nicely, dance well, and chat happily with lonely men. Other women joined "dance brigades" and traveled by bus to military bases for social evenings with servicemen. They, too, were expected to be pretty, to dress attractively (and conservatively), and to interact comfortably with men they had never met before and would likely never see again. The USO forbade women to have dates with soldiers after parties in the

USO

Benny Goodman, arranging numbers for Goodman's own band. And in 1935, when Goodman played several of Henderson's arrangements to a wildly enthusiastic crowd of dancers in the Palomar Ballroom in Los Angeles, the "swing era"—the era of the new music's popularity among a broad, multiracial public—began. After his success at the Palomar, Goodman—soon to be known as the "King of Swing"—began playing more and more often on the radio, spreading the popularity of the music.

Soon new big bands were springing up, both black and white, seizing the style, modifying it at times, and spreading it further: Count Basie ("One O'Clock Jump"), who emerged from the relative obscurity of the Kansas City jazz scene in 1936 and became one of the great innovators in modern jazz; Tommy Dorsey ("Marie"); Artie Shaw ("Begin the Beguine"); the incomparable Duke Ellington ("In a Mellotone"), probably the most gifted and inventive jazz musician of his era; and—perhaps the performer etched most vividly in the memory of fighting men during World War II—Glenn Miller, whose "In the Mood" was one of the most popular songs of the 1940s, and whose early death while traveling to entertain troops made him something of a national hero.

During the heyday of swing, band leaders were among the most recognized and popular figures in American popular culture, rivaling movie stars in their celebrity. Swing dominated the radio. It drew huge audiences to dance

THE COUNT BASIE BAND Count Basie, one of the most renowned swing musicians, plays the piano here, accompanied by Lester Young on saxophone. Surrounding them are other musicians, fans, and students. *(Photo by Gjon Mili/Time Life Pictures/Getty Images)*

halls everywhere. It sold more records than any other kind of music. And it became one of the first forms of popular music to challenge racial taboos. Benny Goodman hired the black pianist Teddy Wilson to play with his band in 1935; other white band leaders followed.

Swing was not without its critics: people who recoiled at its black roots and at its interracial culture; and others who abhorred its openly sensual style and the romantic, at times overtly sexual, dancing it inspired. It had a "dangerously hypnotic influence," the *New York Times* complained in 1938 (in a critique that echoed earlier attacks on jazz in the 1920s and resembled later ones on rock and rap music in the postwar years) and led dancers toward "moral weakness" and "the breakdown of conventions." But young men and women in the anxious years of depression and war found in swing an avenue to escape, romance, and excitement. "It don't mean a thing if it ain't got that swing," the lyrics of a celebrated 1932 Duke Ellington song said. Until at least 1945, when swing began to give way to other forms of jazz, millions of Americans agreed.

clubs, and the members of the "dance brigades" were expected to have no contact with servicemen except during the dances. Clearly, such regulations were sometimes violated. But while the military took elaborate measures to root out homosexuals and lesbians from their ranks (unceremoniously dismissing many of them with undesirable discharges), it quietly tolerated "healthy heterosexuality."

The Internment of Japanese Americans

World War I had produced widespread hatred, vindictiveness, and hysteria in America, as well as widespread and flagrant violations of civil liberties. World War II did not produce a comparable era of repression. The government barred from the mails a few papers it considered seditious, among them Father Coughlin's anti-Semitic and pro-fascist *Social Justice,* but there was no general censorship of dissident publications. The most ambitious effort to punish domestic fascists, a sedition trial of twenty-eight people, ended in a mistrial, and the defendants went free. Unlike during World War I, the government generally left socialists and communists (most of whom strongly supported the war effort) alone.

Nor was there much of the ethnic or cultural animosity that had shaped the social climate of the United States during World War I. The "zoot-suit" riots in Los Angeles and occasional racial conflicts in American cities and on military bases made clear that traditional racial and ethnic hostilities had not disappeared. So did wartime restrictions imposed on some Italians—including provisions forbidding many of them to travel and the imprisonment of

Ethnic Distinctions Blurred

several hundred, including the great opera singer Ezio Pinza, as "enemy aliens." But on the whole, the war worked more to blur ethnic distinctions than to heighten them. Americans continued to eat sauerkraut without calling it "liberty cabbage." They displayed little hostility toward German or Italian Americans. Instead, they seemed on the whole to share the view of their government's propaganda: that the enemy was less the German and Italian people than the vicious political systems to which they had succumbed. In popular culture, and in everyday interactions, ethnicity began to seem less a source of menacing difference—as it often had in the past—than evidence of healthy diversity. The participation of, and frequent heroism from, American soldiers of many ethnic backgrounds encouraged this change.

But there was a glaring exception to the general rule of tolerance: the treatment of the small, politically powerless group of Japanese Americans. From the beginning, Americans adopted a different attitude toward their Asian enemy than they did toward their European foes. The Japanese, both government and private propaganda encouraged Americans to believe, were a devious, malign, and cruel people. The infamous attack on Pearl Harbor seemed to many to confirm that assessment.

This racial animosity soon extended to Americans of Japanese descent. There were not many Japanese Americans in the continental United States—only about 127,000, most of them concentrated in a few areas in California. About a third of them were unnaturalized, first-generation immigrants (Issei); two-thirds were naturalized or native-born citizens of the United States (Nisei). The Japanese in America, like the Chinese, had long been the target of ethnic and racial animosity; and unlike members of European ethnic groups,

Anti-Japanese Prejudice

who had encountered similar resentment, Asians seemed unable to dispel prejudice against them no matter how assimilated they became. Many white Americans continued to consider Asians (even native-born citizens) so "foreign" that they could never become "real" Americans. Partly as a result, much of the Japanese-American population in the West continued to live in close-knit, to some degree even insular, communities, which reinforced the belief that they were alien and potentially menacing.

Pearl Harbor inflamed these longstanding suspicions and turned them into active animosity. Wild stories circulated about how the Japanese in Hawaii had helped sabotage Pearl Harbor and how Japanese Americans in California were conspiring to aid an enemy landing on the Pacific coast. There was no evidence to support any of these charges; but according to Earl Warren, then attorney general of California, the apparent passivity of the Japanese Americans was itself evidence of the danger they posed. Because they did nothing to allow officials to gauge their intentions, Warren claimed, it was all the more important to take precautions against conspiracies.

Although there was some public pressure in California to remove the Japanese "threat," on the whole popular senti-

ment was more tolerant of the Nisei and Issei (and more willing to make distinctions between them and the Japanese in Japan) than was official sentiment. The real impetus for taking action came from the government. Secretary of the Navy Frank Knox, for example, said shortly after Pearl Harbor that "the most effective fifth column [a term for internal sabotage] work of the entire war was done in Hawaii," a statement—clearly referring to the large Japanese population there—that later investigations proved to be entirely false. General John L. DeWitt, the senior military commander on the West Coast, claimed to have "no confidence in [Japanese-American] loyalty whatsoever." When asked about the distinction between unnaturalized Japanese immigrants and American citizens, he said, "A Jap is a Jap. It makes no difference whether he is an American citizen or not."

In February 1942, in response to such pressure (and over the objections of the attorney general and J. Edgar Hoover, the director of the FBI), President Roosevelt authorized the army to "intern" the Japanese Americans. He created the War Relocation Authority (WRA) to oversee the project. More than 100,000 people (Issei and Nisei alike) were rounded up, told to dispose of their property however they could (which often meant simply abandoning it), and taken to what the

"Relocation Centers"

government euphemistically termed "relocation centers" in the "interior." In fact, they were facilities little different from prisons, many of them located in the western mountains and the desert. Conditions in the internment camps were not brutal, but they were harsh and uncomfortable. Government officials talked of them as places where the Japanese could be socialized and "Americanized," much as many officials had at times considered Indian reservations as places for training Native Americans to become more like whites.

But like Indian reservations, the internment camps were more a target of white economic aspirations than of missionary work. The governor of Utah, where many of the internees were located, wanted the federal government to turn over thousands of Japanese Americans to serve as forced laborers. Washington did not comply, but the WRA did hire out many inmates as agricultural laborers.

The internment never produced significant popular opposition. For the most part, once the Japanese were in the camps, other Americans (including their former neighbors on the West Coast) largely forgot about them—except to make strenuous efforts to acquire the property they had abandoned. Even so, beginning in 1943 conditions slowly improved. Some young Japanese Americans left the camps to attend colleges and universities (mostly in the East—the WRA continued to be wary of letting Japanese return to the Pacific Coast). Others were permitted to move to cities to take factory and service jobs (although, again, not on the West Coast). Some young men joined and others were drafted into the American military; a Nisei army unit fought with distinction in Europe.

In 1944, the Supreme Court ruled in *Korematsu* v. *U.S.* that the relocation was constitutionally permissible. In

MANZANAR RELOCATION CENTER Dorothea Lange, the great documentary photographer, took a series of photographs to record the experiences of Japanese Americans who were evacuated from their homes on the California coast during World War II. Here she captures a Japanese-American woman in the Manzanar Relocation Center in eastern California as she works in a vegetable garden at the center in which residents grew food for their own use. *(Courtesy of the Bancroft Library, University of California, Berkeley, WRA no. C-685)*

another case the same year, it barred the internment of "loyal" citizens, but left the interpretation of "loyal" to the discretion of the government. Nevertheless, by the end of 1944, most of the internees had been released; and in early 1945, they were finally permitted to return to the West Coast—where they faced continuing harassment and persecution, and where many found their property and businesses irretrievably lost. In 1988, they won some compensation for their losses, when, after years of agitation by survivors of the camps and their descendants, Congress voted to award them reparations. But by then, many of the internees had died.

Korematsu v. U.S.

Chinese Americans and the War

Just as America's conflict with Japan undermined the position of Japanese Americans, the American alliance with China during World War II significantly enhanced both the legal and social status of Chinese Americans. In 1943, partly to improve relations with the government of China, Congress finally repealed the Chinese Exclusion Acts, which had barred almost all Chinese immigration since 1892. The new quota for Chinese immigrants was minuscule (105 a year), but a substantial number of Chinese women managed to gain entry into the country through other provisions covering war brides and fiancées. Over 4,000 Chinese women entered the United States in the first three years after the war. Permanent residents of the United States who were of Chinese descent were finally permitted to become citizens.

Chinese Exclusion Acts Repealed

Racial animosity toward the Chinese did not disappear, but it did decline—in part because government propaganda and popular culture began presenting positive images of the Chinese (partly to contrast them with the Japanese); in part because Chinese Americans (like African Americans and other previously marginal groups) began taking jobs in war plants and other booming areas suffering from labor shortages and hence moving out of the isolated world of the Chinatowns. A higher proportion of Chinese Americans (22 percent of all adult males) were drafted than of any other national group, and the entire Chinese community in most cities worked hard and conspicuously for the war effort.

The Retreat from Reform

Late in 1943, Franklin Roosevelt publicly suggested that "Dr. New Deal," as he called it, had served its purpose and should now give way to "Dr. Win-the-War." The statement reflected the president's own genuine shift in concern: that victory was now more important than reform. But it also reflected the political reality that had emerged during the first two years of war. Liberals in government were finding themselves unable to enact new programs. They were even finding it difficult to protect existing ones from conservative assault.

Within the administration itself, many liberals found themselves displaced by the new managers of the wartime agencies, who came overwhelmingly from large corporations and conservative Wall Street law firms. But the greatest assault on New Deal reforms came from

Dismantling the New Deal

conservatives in Congress, who seized on the war as an excuse to do what many had wanted to do in peacetime: dismantle many of the achievements of the New Deal. They were assisted by the end of mass unemployment, which decreased the need for such relief programs as the Civilian Conservation Corps and the Works Progress Administration (both of which were abolished by Congress). They were assisted, too, by their own increasing numbers. In the congressional elections of 1942, Republicans gained 47 seats in the House and 10 in the Senate. Roosevelt continued to talk at times about his commitment to social progress and liberal reform, in part to bolster the flagging spirits of his traditional supporters. But increasingly, the president quietly accepted the defeat or erosion of New Deal measures in order to win support for his war policies and peace plans. He also accepted the changes because he realized that his chances for reelection in 1944 depended on his ability to identify himself less with domestic issues than with world peace.

Republicans approached the 1944 election determined to exploit what they believed was resentment of wartime regimentation and privation and unhappiness with Democratic reform. They nominated as their candidate the young and vigorous governor of New York, Thomas E. Dewey. Roosevelt was unopposed within his party, but Democratic leaders pressured him to abandon the controversial Vice President Henry Wallace, an outspoken liberal and hero of the CIO. Roosevelt, tired and ill, seemed to take little interest in the matter and passively acquiesced in the selection of Senator Harry S. Truman of Missouri, a man he barely knew. Truman was not a prominent figure in the party, but he had won acclaim as chairman of the Senate War Investigating Committee (known as the Truman Committee), which had compiled an impressive record uncovering waste and corruption in wartime production.

The conduct of the war was not an issue in the campaign. Instead, the election revolved around domestic economic issues and, indirectly, the president's health. The president was in fact gravely ill, suffering from, among other things, arteriosclerosis. But the campaign seemed momentarily to revive him. He made several strenuous public appearances late in October, which dispelled popular doubts about his health and ensured his reelection. He captured 53.5 percent of the popular vote to Dewey's 46 percent, and won 432 electoral votes to Dewey's 99. Democrats lost 1 seat in the Senate, gained 20 in the House, and maintained control of both.

1944 Election

THE DEFEAT OF THE AXIS

By the middle of 1943, America and its allies had succeeded in stopping the Axis advance both in Europe and in the Pacific. In the next two years, the Allies themselves seized the offensive and launched a series of powerful drives that rapidly led the way to victory.

The Liberation of France

By early 1944, American and British bombers were attacking German industrial installations and other targets almost around the clock, drastically cutting production and impeding transportation. Especially devastating was the massive bombing of such German cities as Leipzig, Dresden, and Berlin. A February 1945 incendiary raid on Dresden created a great firestorm that destroyed three-fourths of the previously undamaged city and killed approximately 135,000 people, almost all civilians.

Strategic Bombing

Military leaders claimed that the bombing destroyed industrial facilities, demoralized the population, and cleared the way for the great Allied invasion of France planned for the late spring. In fact, the greatest contribution of the bombing to the military struggle was to force the German air force (the *Luftwaffe*) to relocate much of its strength in Germany itself and to engage Allied forces in the air. The air battles over Germany considerably weakened the *Luftwaffe* and made it a less formidable obstacle to the Allied invasion than it might once have been. Preparations for the invasion were also assisted by the breaking of the Enigma code.

An enormous invasion force had been gathering in England for two years: almost 3 million troops, and perhaps the greatest array of naval vessels and armaments ever assembled in one place. On the morning of June 6, 1944, D-Day, General Dwight D. Eisenhower, the Supreme Commander of the Allied forces, sent this vast armada into action. The landing came not at the narrowest part of the English Channel, where the Germans had expected and prepared for it, but along sixty miles of the Cotentin Peninsula on the coast of Normandy. While airplanes and battleships offshore bombarded the Nazi defenses, 4,000 vessels landed troops and supplies on the beaches. (Three divisions of paratroopers had been dropped behind the German lines the night before, amid scenes of great confusion, to seize critical roads and bridges for the push inland.) Fighting was intense along the beach, but the superior manpower and equipment of the Allied forces gradually prevailed. Within a week, the German forces had been dislodged from virtually the entire Normandy coast.

D-Day

For the next month, further progress remained slow. But in late July in the Battle of Saint-Lô, General Omar Bradley's First Army smashed through the German lines. George S. Patton's Third Army, spearheaded by heavy tank attacks, then moved through the hole Bradley had created and began a drive into the heart of France. On August 25, Free French forces arrived in Paris and liberated the city from four years of German occupation. And by mid-September, the Allied armies had driven the Germans almost entirely out of France and Belgium.

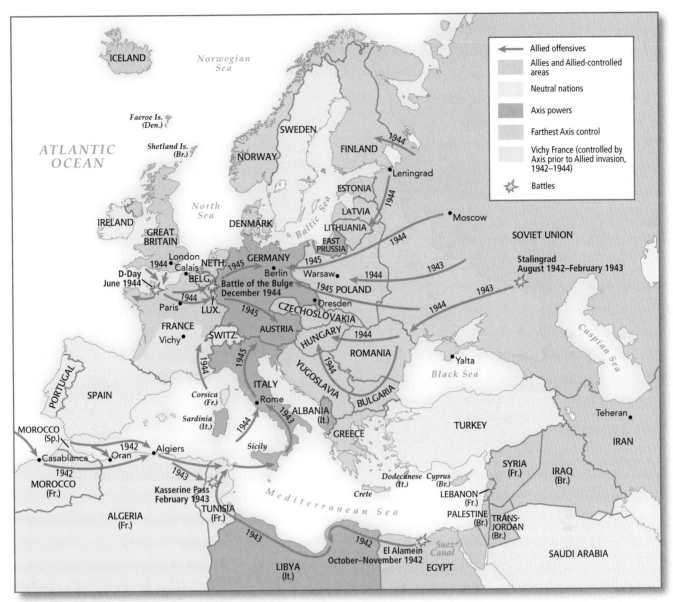

WORLD WAR II IN EUROPE: THE ALLIED COUNTEROFFENSIVE, 1943–1945 This map illustrates the final, climactic movements in the war in Europe—the two great offensives against Germany that began in 1943 and culminated in 1945. From the east, the armies of the Soviet Union, having halted the Germans at Stalingrad and Moscow, swept across eastern Europe toward Germany. From the west and the south, American, British, and other Allied forces moved toward Germany through Italy and—after the Normandy invasion in June 1944—through France. The two offensives met in Berlin in May 1945. Note, too, the northern routes that America and Britain used to supply the Soviet Union during the war.

◆ *What problems did the position of the Allied forces at the end of the war help to produce?*

For an interactive version of this map, go to www.mhhe.com/brinkley13ech26maps

The great Allied drive came to a halt, however, at the Rhine River in the face of a firm line of German defenses and a period of cold weather, rain, and floods. In mid-December, German forces struck in desperation along fifty miles of front

Battle of the Bulge

in the Ardennes Forest. In the Battle of the Bulge (named for a large bulge that appeared in the American lines as the Germans pressed forward), they drove fifty-five miles toward Antwerp before they were finally stopped at Bastogne. The battle ended serious German resistance in the west.

While the Allies were fighting their way through France, Soviet forces were sweeping westward into central Europe and the Balkans. In late January 1945, the Russians launched a great offensive toward the Oder River inside Germany. In early spring, they were ready to launch a final assault against Berlin. By then, Omar Bradley's First Army was pushing into Germany from the west. Early in March, his forces captured the city of Cologne, on the west bank of the Rhine. The next day, in a remarkable stroke of good fortune, he discovered and seized an undamaged bridge

THE NORMANDY INVASION This photograph, taken from a landing craft, shows American troops wading ashore and onto the Normandy beaches, where one of the decisive battles of World War II was taking shape. The invasion was launched despite threatening weather and rough seas. *(Popperfoto/Getty Images)*

over the river at Remagen; Allied troops were soon pouring across the Rhine. In the following weeks the British field marshal Bernard Montgomery, commander of Allied ground operations on D-Day and after, pushed into northern Germany with a million troops, while Bradley's army, sweeping through central Germany, completed the encirclement of 300,000 German soldiers in the Ruhr.

The German resistance was now broken on both fronts. American forces were moving eastward faster than they had anticipated and could have beaten the Russians to Berlin and Prague. Instead, the American and British high commands decided to halt the advance along the Elbe River in central Germany to await the Russians. That decision enabled the Soviets to occupy eastern Germany and Czechoslovakia.

On April 30, with Soviet forces on the outskirts of Berlin, Adolf Hitler killed himself in his bunker in the capital.

Germany Defeated And on May 8, 1945, the remaining German forces surrendered unconditionally. V-E (Victory in Europe) Day prompted great celebrations in western Europe and in the United States, tempered by the knowledge of the continuing war against Japan.

The Pacific Offensive

In February 1944, American naval forces under Admiral Chester Nimitz won a series of victories in the Marshall Islands and cracked the outer perimeter of the Japanese Empire. Within a month, the navy had destroyed other vital Japanese bastions. American submarines, in the meantime, were decimating Japanese shipping and crippling the nation's domestic economy. By the summer of 1944, the already skimpy food rations for the Japanese people had been reduced by nearly a quarter; there was also a critical gasoline shortage.

Meanwhile, a frustrating struggle was in progress on the Asian mainland. In 1942, the Japanese had forced General Joseph W. Stilwell of the United States out of Burma and had moved their own troops as far west as the mountains bordering India. For a time, Stilwell supplied the isolated Chinese forces that were continuing to resist Japan with an aerial ferry over the Himalayas. In 1943, finally, he led Chinese, Indian, and a few American troops back through northern Burma, constructing a road and pipeline across the mountains into China (the Burma Road, also known as the Ledo Road or Stilwell Road), which finally opened in the fall of 1944. By then,

COMING HOME Euphoric American soldiers arrive in New York harbor back aboard the *Queen Elizabeth* after the end of the war in Europe in 1945. *(AP Images)*

however, the Japanese had launched a major counteroffensive and had driven so deep into the Chinese interior that they threatened the terminus of the Burma Road and the center of Chinese government at Chungking. The Japanese offensive precipitated a long-simmering feud between General Stilwell and Premier Chiang Kai-shek of China. Stilwell was indignant because Chiang (whom he called, contemptuously, the "Peanut") was using many of his troops to maintain an armed frontier against the Chinese communists and would not deploy those troops against the Japanese.

The decisive battles of the Pacific war, however, occurred at sea. In mid-June 1944, an enormous American armada struck the heavily fortified Mariana Islands and, after some of the bloodiest operations of the war, captured Tinian, Guam, and Saipan, 1,350 miles from Tokyo. In September, American forces landed on the western Carolines. And on October 20, General MacArthur's troops landed on Leyte Island in the Philippines. As the American forces pushed closer to Japan itself, the Japanese used their entire fleet against the Allied invaders in three major encounters—which together constituted the decisive Battle of

Battle of Leyte Gulf

Leyte Gulf, the largest naval engagement in history. American forces held off the Japanese onslaught and sank four Japanese carriers, all but destroying Japan's capacity to continue a serious naval war.

Nevertheless, the imperial forces seemed only to increase their resistance. In February 1945, American marines seized the tiny volcanic island of Iwo Jima, only 750 miles from Tokyo, but only after the costliest single battle in the history of the Marine Corps. The marines suffered over 20,000 casualties, and the Japanese forces suffered even greater losses.

The battle for Okinawa, an island only 370 miles south of Japan, was further evidence of the strength of the Japanese resistance in those last desperate months. Week after week, the Japanese sent kamikaze (suicide) planes against American and British ships, sacrificing 3,500 of them while inflicting great damage. Japanese troops on shore launched desperate nighttime attacks on the American lines. The United States and its allies suffered nearly 50,000 casualties before finally capturing Okinawa in late June 1945. More than 100,000 Japanese died in the siege.

Okinawa

OKINAWA The invasion of Okinawa, an island near Japan, was one of the last major battles of World War II. In this photograph, taken June 18, 1945, a bullet-scarred monument provides shelter to members of the 7th Infantry of the U.S. Tenth Army as they look ahead at Japanese action. Over 11,000 Americans (and more than 80,000 Japanese) died in the rugged battle for the island, which consumed nearly three months. It ended three days after this photograph was taken. Two months later—after the bombing of Hiroshima and Nagasaki—Japan surrendered. *(Bettmann/Corbis)*

The same kind of bitter fighting seemed to await the Americans in Japan. But there were also signs early in 1945 that such an invasion might not be necessary. The Japanese had almost no ships or planes left with which to fight. In July 1945, for example, American warships stood off the shore of Japan and shelled industrial targets (many already in ruins from aerial bombings) with impunity. A brutal firebombing of Tokyo in March, in which American bombers dropped napalm on the city and created a firestorm in which more than 80,000 people died, further weakened the Japanese will to resist. Moderate Japanese leaders, who had long since decided that the war was lost, were struggling for power within the government and were looking for ways to bring the war to an end. After the invasion of Okinawa, Emperor Hirohito appointed a new premier and gave him instructions to sue for peace; but the new leader could not persuade military leaders to give up the fight. He did try, along with the emperor himself, to obtain mediation through the Soviet Union. The Russians, however, showed little interest in playing the role of arbitrator.

Whether the moderates could ultimately have prevailed is a question about which historians and others continue to disagree. In any case, the question eventually became moot. In mid-July, American scientists conducted a successful test of a new atomic bomb, which led to a major event in world history, significant only in part because it ended World War II.

The Manhattan Project

Reports had reached the United States in 1939 that Nazi scientists had taken the first step toward the creation of an atomic bomb. The United States and Britain immediately began a race to develop the weapon before the Germans did.

The search for the new weapon emerged from theories developed by atomic physicists, beginning early in the century, and particularly from some of the founding ideas of modern science developed by Albert Einstein. Einstein's famous theory of relativity had revealed the relationships between mass and energy. More precisely, he had argued that, in theory at least, matter could be converted into a tremendous force of energy. It was Einstein himself, by then living in the United States, who warned Franklin Roosevelt that the Germans were developing atomic weapons and that the United States must begin trying to do the same. The effort to build atomic weapons centered on the use of uranium, whose atomic structure made possible the creation of a nuclear chain reaction. A nuclear chain reaction occurs when the atomic nuclei in radioactive matter are split (a process known as nuclear fission) by neutrons. Each fission creates new neutrons that produce fissions in additional atoms at an ever-increasing and self-sustaining pace.

The construction of atomic weapons had become feasible by the 1940s because of the discovery of the

Enrico Fermi

radioactivity of uranium in the 1930s by Enrico Fermi in Italy. In 1939, the great Danish physicist Niels Bohr sent news of German experiments in radioactivity to the United States. In 1940, scientists at Columbia University began chain-reaction experiments with uranium and produced persuasive evidence of the feasibility of using uranium as fuel for a weapon. The Columbia experiments stalled in 1941, and the work moved to UC Berkeley and the University of Chicago, where Enrico Fermi (who had emigrated to the United States in 1938) achieved the first controlled fission chain reaction in December 1942.

By then, the army had taken control of the research and appointed General Leslie Groves to reorganize the project—which soon became known as the Manhattan Project (because it was devised in the Manhattan Engineer District Office of the Army Corps of Engineers). Over the next three years, the U.S. government secretly poured

nearly $2 billion into the Manhattan Project—a massive scientific and technological effort conducted at hidden laboratories in Oak Ridge, Tennessee; Los Alamos, New Mexico; Hanford, Washington; and other sites. Scientists in Oak Ridge, who were charged with finding a way to create a nuclear chain reaction that could be feasibly replicated within the confined space of a bomb, began experimenting with plutonium—a derivative of uranium first discovered by scientists at UC Berkeley. Plutonium proved capable of providing a practical fuel for the weapon. Scientists in Los Alamos, under the direction of J. Robert Oppenheimer, were charged with the construction of the actual atomic bomb.

Despite many unforeseen problems, the scientists pushed ahead much faster than anyone had predicted. Even so, the war in Europe ended before they were ready to test the first weapon. Just before dawn on July 16, 1945, in the desert near Alamogordo, New Mexico, the scientists gathered to witness the first atomic explosion in history: the detonation of a plutonium-fueled bomb that its creators had named Trinity. The explosion—a blinding flash of light, probably brighter than any

The Trinity Bomb

ever seen on earth, followed by a huge, billowing mushroom cloud—created a vast crater in the barren desert.

Atomic Warfare

News of the explosion reached President Harry S. Truman (who had taken office in April on the death of Roosevelt) in Potsdam, Germany, where he was attending a conference of Allied leaders. He issued an ultimatum to the Japanese (signed jointly by the British) demanding that they surrender by August 3 or face complete devastation. The Japanese premier wanted to accept the Allied demand, but he could not persuade the military leaders to agree. There was a hint from Tokyo that the government might agree to surrender, in return for a promise that the Japanese could retain their emperor. The American government, firmly committed to the idea of "unconditional surrender," dismissed those proposals, convinced (perhaps correctly) that the moderates who were making them did not have the power to deliver them. When the deadline passed with no surrender, Truman ordered the air force to use the new atomic weapons against Japan.

Controversy has raged for decades over whether Truman's decision to use the bomb was justified and what his motives were. (See "Where Historians Disagree," pp. 752–753.) Some have argued that the atomic attack was unnecessary, that had the United States agreed to the survival of the emperor (which it

Debating the Bomb's Use

ultimately did agree to, in any case), or waited only a few more weeks, the Japanese would have surrendered. Others argue that nothing less than the atomic bombs could have persuaded the hard-line military leaders of Japan to

THE MANHATTAN PROJECT J. Robert Oppenheimer, wearing the broad-brimmed hat, was one of the scientific leaders of the Manhattan Project, which developed the atomic bomb during World War II. The military commander of the project was General Leslie Groves. The two men are shown here after the war, examining the charred landscape of the Trinity site in New Mexico, where the first successful detonation of the new weapon occurred in July 1945. *(Bettmann/Corbis)*

THE DECISION TO DROP THE ATOMIC BOMB

In the fall of 1994, the Air and Space Museum of the Smithsonian Institution in Washington, D.C., installed in its main hall the fuselage of the *Enola Gay,* the airplane that dropped the first atomic bomb ever used in warfare on Hiroshima in 1945. Originally, the airplane was to have been accompanied by an exhibit that would include discussions of the many popular and academic controversies over whether the United States should have used the bomb. But a powerful group of critics—led by veterans' groups and aided by many members of Congress—organized to demand that the exhibit be altered and that it reflect only the "official" explanation of the decision. In the end, the museum decided to mount no exhibit at all. The *Enola Gay* hangs in the Smithsonian today entirely without explanation for the millions of tourists who see it each year.

The furor that surrounded the Air and Space Museum installation reflects the passions that the bombing of Hiroshima and Nagasaki continue to arouse among people around the world, and people in the United States and Japan in particular. It also reflects the continuing debate among historians about how to explain, and evaluate, President Truman's decision to use the atomic bomb in the war against Japan.

Truman himself, both at the time and in his 1955 memoirs, insisted that the decision was a simple and straightforward one. The alternative to using atomic weapons, he claimed,

NAGASAKI SURVIVORS A Japanese woman and child look grimly at a photographer as they hold pieces of bread in the aftermath of the dropping of the second American atomic bomb—this one on Nagasaki. *(Bettmann/Corbis)*

surrender without a costly American invasion. Some critics of the decision, including some of the scientists involved in the Manhattan Project, have argued that whatever the Japanese intentions, the United States, as a matter of morality, should not have used the terrible new weapon. One horrified physicist wrote the president shortly before the attack: "This thing must not be permitted to exist on this earth. We must not be the most hated and feared people in the world."

The nation's military and political leaders, however, showed little concern about such matters. Truman, who

had not even known of the existence of the Manhattan Project until he became president, was apparently making what he believed to be a simple military decision. A weapon was available that would end the war quickly; he could see no reason not to use it.

Still more controversy has existed over whether there were other motives at work behind Truman's decision. With the Soviet Union poised to enter the war in the Pacific, did the United States want to end the conflict quickly to forestall an expanded communist presence in Asia? Did Truman use the bomb to intimidate Stalin, with

American invasion of mainland Japan that might have cost as many as a million lives. Given that choice, he said, the decision was easy. "I regarded the bomb as a military weapon and never had any doubt that it should be used." Truman's explanation of his decision has been supported by the accounts of many of his contemporaries: by Secretary of War Henry Stimson, in his 1950 memoir, *On Active Service in Peace and War;* by Winston Churchill; by Truman's senior military advisers. It has also received considerable support from historians. Herbert Feis argued in *The Atomic Bomb and the End of World War II* (1966) that Truman had made his decision on purely military grounds—to ensure a speedy American victory. David McCullough, the author of a popular biography of Truman published in 1992, also accepted Truman's own account of his actions largely uncritically, as did Alonzo L. Hamby in *Man of the People* (1995), an important scholarly study of Truman. "One consideration weighed most heavily on Truman," Hamby concluded. "The longer the war lasted, the more Americans killed." Robert J. Donovan, author of an extensive history of the Truman presidency, *Conflict and Crisis* (1977), reached the same conclusion: "The simple reason Truman made the decision to drop the bomb was to end the war quickly and save lives."

Other scholars have strongly disagreed. As early as 1948, a British physicist, P. M. S. Blackett, wrote in *Fear, War, and the Bomb* that the destruction of Hiroshima and Nagasaki was "not so much the last military act of the second World War as the first major operation of the cold diplomatic war with Russia." The most important critic of Truman's decision is the historian Gar Alperovitz, the author of two influential books on the subject: *Atomic Diplomacy: Hiroshima and Potsdam* (1965) and *The Decision to Use the Atomic Bomb and the Architecture of an American Myth* (1995). Alperovitz dismisses the argument that the bomb was used to shorten the war and save lives. Japan was likely to have surrendered soon even if the bomb had not been used, he claims; large numbers of American lives were not at stake in the decision. Instead, he argues, the United States used the bomb less to influence Japan than to intimidate the Soviet Union. Truman made his decision to bomb Hiroshima in the immediate aftermath of a discouraging meeting with Stalin at Potsdam. He was heavily influenced, therefore, by his belief that America needed a new way to force Stalin to change his behavior, that, as Alperovitz has argued, "the bomb would make Russia more manageable in Europe."

Martin J. Sherwin, in *A World Destroyed* (1975), is more restrained in his criticism of American policymakers. But he too argues that a rapidly growing awareness of the danger Stalin posed to the peace made leaders aware that atomic weapons—and their effective use—could help strengthen the American hand in the nation's critical relationship with the Soviet Union. Truman, Sherwin said, "increasingly came to believe that America's possession of the atomic bomb would, by itself, convince Stalin to be more cooperative."

John W. Dower's *War Without Mercy* (1986) contributed, by implication at least, to another controversial explanation of the American decision: racism. Throughout World War II, most Americans considered the Germans and the Italians to be military and political adversaries. They looked at the Japanese very differently: as members of a very different and almost bestial race. They were, many Americans came to believe, almost a subhuman species. And while Dower himself stops short of saying so, other historians have suggested that this racialized image of Japan contributed to American willingness to drop atomic bombs on Japanese cities. Even many of Truman's harshest critics, however, note that it is, as Alperovitz has written, "all but impossible to find specific evidence that racism was an important factor in the decision to attack Hiroshima and Nagasaki."

The debate over the decision to drop the atomic bomb is an unusually emotional one—driven in part by the tremendous moral questions that the destruction of so many lives raises—and it has inspired bitter professional and personal attacks on advocates of almost every position. It illustrates clearly how history has often been, and remains, a powerful force in the way societies define their politics, their values, and their character.

whom he was engaged in difficult negotiations, so the Soviet leader would accept American demands? Little direct evidence is available to support (or definitively refute) either of these accusations.

On August 6, 1945, an American B-29, the *Enola Gay,* dropped an atomic weapon on the Japanese industrial center at Hiroshima. With a single bomb, the United States completely incinerated a four-square-mile area at the center of the previously undamaged city. More than 80,000 civilians died, according to later American estimates. Many more

Hiroshima

survived to suffer the crippling effects of radioactive fallout or to pass those effects on to their children in the form of birth defects.

The Japanese government, stunned by the attack, was at first unable to agree on a response. Two days later, on August 8, the Soviet Union declared war on Japan. And the following day, the United States sent another American plane to drop another atomic weapon—this time on the city of Nagasaki—inflicting more horrible damage and causing more than 100,000 deaths in another unfortunate community.

Nagasaki

THE EMPEROR SURVEYS THE RUINS   In the aftermath of the American firebombing of Tokyo, which caused as much damage and death as the atomic bomb attacks on Hiroshima and Nagasaki, and just before the formal Japanese surrender in September 1945, Emperor Hirohito—previously visible to most Japanese only in formal portraits—walked through the ruins of the city and allowed himself to be photographed. This photograph is widely considered the first picture of the emperor to reveal any expression on his face. It was taken by Carl Mydans, a photographer for *Life* magazine. *(Time Life Pictures/Getty Images)*

Finally, the emperor intervened to break the stalemate in the cabinet, and on August 14 the government announced that it was ready to give up. On September 2, 1945, on board the American battleship *Missouri,* anchored in Tokyo Bay, Japanese officials signed the articles of surrender.

The most catastrophic war in the history of mankind had come to an end, and the United States had emerged not only victorious but in a position of unprecedented power, influence, and prestige. It was a victory, however, that few could greet with unambiguous joy. Fourteen million combatants had died in the struggle. Many more

civilians had perished, from bombings, from disease and starvation, from genocidal campaigns of extermination. The United States had suffered only light casualties in comparison with many other nations, but the cost had still been high: 322,000 dead, another 800,000 injured. And despite the sacrifices, the world continued to face an uncertain future, menaced by the threat of nuclear warfare and by the emerging antagonism between the world's two strongest nations—the United States and the Soviet Union—that would darken the peace for many decades to come.

CONCLUSION

The United States played a critical, indeed decisive, role in the war against Germany and Italy; and it defeated Imperial Japan in the Pacific largely alone. But America's sacrifices in the war paled next to those of the nation's most important allies. Britain, France, and, above all, the Soviet Union paid a staggering price—in lives, infrastructure, and social unity—that had no counterpart in

the United States, most of whose citizens experienced a booming prosperity and only modest privations during the four years of American involvement in the conflict. There were, of course, jarring social changes during the war that even prosperity could not entirely offset: shortages, restrictions, regulations, family dislocations, and perhaps most of all the absence of millions of men, and considerable numbers of women, who went overseas to work and fight.

American fighting men and women, of course, had very different experiences than those Americans who remained at home. They endured tremendous hardships, substantial casualties, and great loneliness. They fought effectively and bravely. They helped liberate North Africa and Italy from German occupation. And in June 1944, finally, they joined British, French, and other forces in a great and successful invasion of France, which led less than a year later to the destruction of the Nazi regime and the end of the European war. In the Pacific, they turned back the Japanese offensive through a series of difficult naval and land battles. But in the end, it was not the American army and navy that brought the war against Japan to a close. It was the unleashing of the most destructive weapon mankind had ever created—the atomic bomb—on the people of Japan that finally persuaded the leaders of that nation to surrender.

INTERACTIVE LEARNING

The *Primary Source Investigator CD-ROM* offers the following materials related to this chapter:

- A short documentary movie, **Dawn of the Nuclear Age**, on the Manhattan Project and the decision to use the atomic bomb against Japan (D18).

- Interactive maps: **U.S. Elections** (M7) and **World War II** (M27).

- Documents, images, and maps related to the massive U.S. effort in World War II and the effects of the war on the home front. Highlights include images of the soldiers' experience in World War II, government posters encouraging women to join the wartime work force, and images and documents relating to the development of the atomic bomb.

Online Learning Center (www.mhhe.com/brinkley13e)

For quizzes, Internet resources, references to additional books and films, and more, consult this book's Online Learning Center.

FOR FURTHER REFERENCE

John Morton Blum, *V Was for Victory: Politics and American Culture During World War II* (1976) and Richard Polenberg, *War and Society* (1972) are important studies of the home front during World War II. David Kennedy, *Freedom from Fear: The American People in Depression and War, 1929-1945* (1999) is an important narrative of both the American military experience in the war and the war's impact on American politics and society. Alan Brinkley, *The End of Reform: New Deal Liberalism in Recession and War* (1995) examines the impact of the war on liberal ideology and political economy. Doris Kearns Goodwin, *No Ordinary Time: Franklin and Eleanor Roosevelt: The Home Front in World War II* (1994) is an engaging portrait of the Roosevelts during the war. Susan Hartmann examines the transformation in women's work and family roles during and after the war in *The Homefront and Beyond: American Women in the 1940s* (1982). Richard M. Dalfiume, *Desegregation of the U.S. Armed Forces: Fighting on Two Fronts, 1939-1953* (1969) discusses race relations in the military during World War II and beyond. Maurice Isserman, *Which Side Were You On? The American Communist Party During World War II* (1982) portrays the dramatic shifts in Communist Party strategy and status during the war. John W. Dower, *War Without Mercy: Race and Power in the Pacific War* (1986) examines the intense racism that shaped both sides of the war between the United States and Japan. Peter Irons, *Justice at War* (1983) and Roger Daniels, *Concentration Camps USA: Japanese-Americans and World War II* (1981) examine the internment of Japanese Americans. John Keegan, *Six Armies in Normandy: From D-Day to the Liberation of Paris, June 6-August 25, 1944* (1982) is a superb account of the Normandy invasion, as is Paul Fussell, *The Boys' Crusade: The American Infantry in Northwestern Europe, 1944-1945* (2003). David S. Wyman, *The Abandonment of the Jews: America and the Holocaust, 1941-1945* (1984) is sharply critical of American policy toward the victims of the Holocaust. Richard Rhodes, *The Making of the Atomic Bomb* (1987) is an excellent account of one of the great scientific projects of the twentieth century. Gar Alperovitz, *The Decision to Use the Atomic Bomb and the Architecture of an American Myth* (1995) is an exhaustive and highly critical study of why the United States used atomic weapons in 1945. A sharply different view is visible in Herbert Feis, *The Atomic Bomb and the End of World War II* (1966) and Robert Maddox, *Hiroshima in History* (2007). John Hersey's *Hiroshima* (1946) reconstructs in minute detail the terrifying experience of the American atomic bomb attack on that Japanese city.

CHAPTER 27

THE COLD WAR

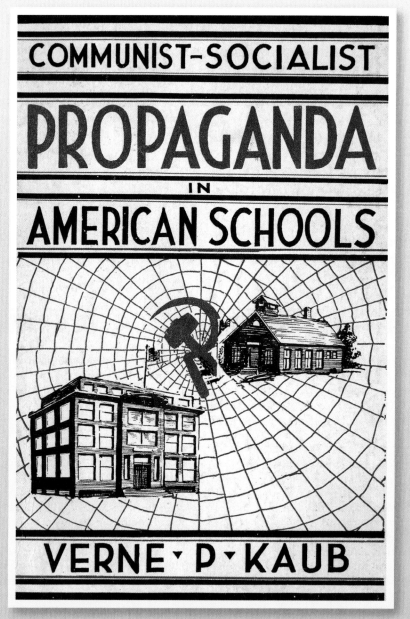

THE COMMUNIST THREAT Verne P. Kaub, a retired journalist and head of the American Council of Christian Laymen, became—like many Americans—concerned about the dangers of communist infiltration of the United States in the years after World War II. This book, published in 1953, accused the National Education Association and its "self-styled progressive educators" of preparing the way for communism. "No technique of the propagandists for Communism-Socialism," he wrote, "is . . . more effective in preparing the minds of both adults and young people for acceptance of the Marxian ideology than the 'debunking' of American history." *(Michael Barson Collection)*

EVEN BEFORE THE END OF WORLD WAR II, in which the United States and the Soviet Union had fought together as allies, there were signs of tension between the two nations. Once the hostilities were over, those tensions quickly grew to create what became known as the "Cold War"—a tense and dangerous rivalry that would cast its shadow over international affairs for decades.

The Cold War was a profound event in the history of the twentieth century and, like World War II, reshaped the world order in important ways. The intense rivalry between the United States and the Soviet Union—and between democratic capitalism and communism—divided much of the world into two not-quite-warring camps. Out of this rivalry came a series of new military alliances on both sides of the conflict. Because of the rivalry, the newly created atomic bomb quickly became a central weapon in the arsenals of both the United States and the Soviet Union—a development that greatly increased the danger of the tense relationship between the two nations. A new conception of American foreign policy, known as containment, also emerged, based on the belief that the principal international goal of the United States should be to contain communism within its present boundaries. Containment helped keep the tensions between the rival blocs at a low enough level to avoid a catastrophic nuclear war. But the Cold War world was far from stable—as two major wars (in Korea and Vietnam) and countless smaller conflicts all over the world made clear.

The Cold War was also a major event in the domestic history of the United States. It transformed American politics—weakening the grip of the Democratic Party on the electorate and making the issue of communism a central part of postwar political life. The competition between the Democratic and Republican Parties to prove that they were the most reliable enemies of communism helped produce a great anticommunist frenzy in the late 1940s and early 1950s that had corrosive effects on American life. Known to many as "McCarthyism," after the Wisconsin senator who became the most famous and notorious voice of anticommunism for a time, the post–World War II Red Scare was a widespread phenomenon that affected almost every area of American life.

The early years of the Cold War coincided with a time of economic anxiety as the nation attempted to adjust to conversion from war to peace; but by the early 1950s, the American economy had entered a period of economic growth and stability. The 1950s became a time not only of anxiety about the world but also of an exuberant new consumerism.

ORIGINS OF THE COLD WAR

Few issues in twentieth-century American history have aroused more debate than the question of the origins of the Cold War. Some historians have claimed that Soviet duplicity and expansionism created the international tensions, while others have proposed that American provocations and imperial ambitions were at least equally to blame. Most historians agree, however, that wherever the preponderance of blame may lie, both the United States and the Soviet Union contributed to the atmosphere of hostility and suspicion that quickly clouded the peace. (See "Where Historians Disagree," pp. 760–761.)

Sources of Soviet-American Tension

At the heart of the rivalry between the United States and the Soviet Union in the 1940s was a fundamental difference in the ways the great powers

America's Postwar Vision

envisioned the postwar world. One vision, first openly outlined in the Atlantic Charter in 1941, was of a world in which nations abandoned their traditional beliefs in military alliances and spheres of influence and governed their relations with one another through democratic processes, with an international organization serving as the arbiter of disputes and the protector of every nation's right of self-determination. That vision appealed to many Americans, including Franklin Roosevelt.

The other vision was that of the Soviet Union and to some extent, it gradually became clear, of Great Britain. Both Stalin and Churchill had signed the Atlantic Charter. But Britain had always been uneasy about the implications of the self-determination

Spheres of Influence

ideal for its own enormous empire. And the Soviet Union was determined to create a secure sphere for itself in Central and Eastern Europe as protection against possible future aggression from the West. Both Churchill and Stalin, therefore, tended to envision a postwar structure in which the great powers would control areas of strategic interest to them, in which something vaguely similar to the traditional European balance of power would reemerge. Gradually, the differences between these two positions would turn the peacemaking process into a form of warfare.

Wartime Diplomacy

Serious strains had already begun to develop in the alliance with the Soviet Union in January 1943, when Roosevelt and Churchill met in Casablanca, Morocco, to discuss Allied strategy. (Stalin had declined Roosevelt's invitation to attend.) The two leaders could not accept Stalin's most important demand—the immediate opening of a second front in western Europe. But they tried to reassure Stalin by announcing that they would accept nothing less than the unconditional surrender of the Axis powers, thus indicating that they would not negotiate a separate peace with Hitler and leave the Soviets to fight on alone.

In November 1943, Roosevelt and Churchill traveled to Teheran, Iran, for their first meeting with Stalin. By now, however, Roosevelt's most effective bargaining tool—Stalin's need for American assistance in his struggle against Germany—had been largely removed. The German advance against Russia had been halted; Soviet forces were now launching their own westward offensive. Nevertheless, the Teheran Conference seemed in most respects a success. Roosevelt and Stalin established a cordial personal relationship. Stalin agreed to an American request that the Soviet Union enter the war in the Pacific soon after the end of hostilities in Europe. Roosevelt, in turn, promised that an Anglo-American second front would be established within six months.

On other matters, however, the origins of future disagreements were already visible. Most important was the question of the future of Poland. Roosevelt and Churchill

Dispute over Poland

were willing to agree to a movement of the Soviet border westward, allowing Stalin to annex some historically Polish territory. But on the nature of the postwar government in the rest of Poland, there were sharp differences. Roosevelt and Churchill supported the claims of the Polish government-in-exile that had been functioning in London since 1940; Stalin wished to install another procommunist exiled government that had spent the war in Lublin, in the Soviet Union. The three leaders avoided a bitter conclusion to the Teheran Conference only by leaving the issue unresolved.

Yalta

More than a year later, in February 1945, Roosevelt joined Churchill and Stalin for a great peace conference in the Soviet city of Yalta. On a number of issues, the Big Three reached agreements. In return for Stalin's renewed promise to enter the Pacific war, Roosevelt agreed that the Soviet Union should receive some of the territory in the Pacific that Russia had lost in the 1904 Russo-Japanese War.

The negotiators also agreed to a plan for a new international organization, a plan that had been hammered out the previous summer at a conference in Washington, D.C., at the Dumbarton Oaks estate. The new United Nations would

United Nations

contain a General Assembly, in which every member would be represented, and a Security Council, with permanent representatives of the five major powers (the United States, Britain, France, the Soviet Union, and China), each of which would have veto power. The Security Council would also have temporary delegates from several other nations. These agreements became the basis of the United Nations charter, drafted at a conference of fifty nations beginning April 25, 1945, in San Francisco. The

YALTA Churchill, Roosevelt, and Stalin (known during the war as the "Big Three") meet at Yalta in the Crimea in February 1945 to try to agree on the outlines of the peace that they knew was soon to come. Instead, they settled on a series of vague compromises that ultimately left all parties feeling betrayed. *(Bettmann/Corbis)*

United States Senate ratified the charter in July by a vote of 80 to 2 (in striking contrast to the slow and painful defeat it had administered to the charter of the League of Nations twenty-five years before).

On other issues, however, the Yalta Conference produced no real accord. Basic disagreement remained about the postwar Polish government. Stalin, whose armies now occupied Poland, had already installed a government composed of the pro-communist "Lublin" Poles. Roosevelt and Churchill insisted that the pro-Western "London" Poles must be allowed a place in the Warsaw regime. Roosevelt envisioned a government based on free, democratic elections—which both he and Stalin recognized the pro-Western forces would win. Stalin agreed only to a vague compromise by which an unspecified number of pro-Western Poles would be granted a place in the government. He reluctantly consented to hold "free and unfettered elections" in Poland on an unspecified future date. They did not take place for more than forty years.

Nor was there agreement about the future of Germany. Roosevelt seemed to want a reconstructed and reunited Germany. Stalin wanted to impose heavy reparations on Germany and to ensure a perma-

Disagreements over Germany

nent dismemberment of the nation. The final agreement was, like the Polish accord, vague and unstable. The decision on reparations would be referred to a future commission. The United States, Great Britain, France, and the Soviet Union would each control its own "zone of occupation" in Germany—the zones to be determined by the position of troops at the end of the war. Berlin, the German capital, was already well inside the Soviet zone, but because of its symbolic importance it would itself be divided into four sectors, one for each nation to occupy. At an unspecified date, Germany would be reunited; but there was no agreement on how the reunification would occur. As for the rest of Europe, the conference produced a murky accord on the establishment of governments "broadly representative of all democratic elements" and "responsible to the will of the people."

The Yalta accords, in other words, were less a settlement of postwar issues than a set of loose principles that sidestepped the most difficult questions. Roosevelt, Churchill, and Stalin returned home from the conference each apparently convinced that he had signed an important agreement. But the Soviet interpretation of the accords differed so sharply from the Anglo-American interpretation that the illusion endured only briefly. In the weeks following the Yalta Conference, Roosevelt watched with growing alarm as the Soviet Union moved systematically to establish pro-communist governments in one Central or Eastern European nation after another and as Stalin refused to make the changes in Poland that the president believed he had promised.

But Roosevelt did not abandon hope. Still believing the differences could be settled, he left Washington early in the spring for a vacation at his retreat in Warm Springs, Georgia. There, on April 12, 1945, he suffered a sudden, massive stroke and died.

ORIGINS OF THE COLD WAR

No issue in recent American history has produced more controversy than that of the origins of the Cold War, between the United States and the Soviet Union. Historians have disagreed, often sharply, over the question of who was responsible for the breakdown

(National Archives and Records Administration)

of American-Soviet relations, and on whether the conflict between the two superpowers was inevitable or could have been avoided. The Cold War may now be over, but the debate over its origins is not.

For more than a decade after the end of World War II, few historians in the United States saw any reason to challenge the official American interpretation of the beginnings of the Cold War. Thomas A. Bailey spoke for most students of the conflict when he argued, in *America Faces Russia* (1950), that the breakdown of relations was a direct result of aggressive Soviet policies of expansion in the immediate postwar years. Stalin's government violated its solemn promises in the Yalta accords, imposed Soviet-dominated governments on the unwilling nations of Eastern Europe, and schemed to spread communism throughout the world. American policy was the logical and necessary response.

The American involvement in Vietnam disillusioned many historians with the premises of the containment policy and, thus, with the traditional view of the origins of the Cold War.

But even before the conflict in Asia had reached major proportions, the first works in what would become known as the "revisionist" interpretation began to appear. William Appleman Williams challenged the accepted wisdom in 1959 in *The Tragedy of American Diplomacy*. The United States had operated in world affairs, Williams argued, in response to one overriding concern: its commitment to maintaining an "open door" for American trade in world markets. The confrontation with the Soviet Union, therefore, was less a response to Russian aggressive designs than an expression of the American belief in the necessity of capitalist expansion.

Later revisionists modified many of Williams's claims, but most accepted some of the basic outlines of his thesis: that the United States had been primarily to blame for the Cold War; that the Soviet Union had displayed no aggressive designs toward the West (and was too weak and exhausted at the end of World War II to be able to pose a serious threat to America in any case); that the United States had used its nuclear monopoly to

THE COLLAPSE OF THE PEACE

Harry S. Truman, who succeeded Roosevelt in the presidency, had almost no familiarity with international issues. Nor did he share Roosevelt's apparent faith in the flexibility of the Soviet Union. Roosevelt had apparently believed that Stalin was, essentially, a reasonable man with whom an ultimate accord might be reached. Truman, in contrast, sided with those in the government (and there were many) who considered the Soviet Union fundamentally untrustworthy and viewed Stalin himself with suspicion and even loathing.

The Failure of Potsdam

Truman had been in office only a few days before he decided to "get tough" with the Soviet Union. Truman met on April 23 with Soviet foreign minister Molotov and sharply chastised him for violations of the Yalta accords. In fact, Truman had only limited leverage by which to compel the Soviet Union to carry out its agreements. He insisted that the United States should be able to get

"85 percent" of what it wanted, but he was ultimately forced to settle for much less.

Truman's "Get Tough" Policy

Truman conceded first on Poland. When Stalin made a few minor concessions to the pro-Western exiles, Truman recognized the Warsaw government, hoping that non-communist forces might gradually expand their influence there. Until the 1980s, they did not. Other questions remained, above all the question of Germany. To settle them, Truman met in July at Potsdam, in Russian-occupied Germany, with Churchill (who, after elections in Britain in the midst of the talks, was replaced as prime minister by Clement Attlee) and Stalin. Truman reluctantly accepted the adjustments of the Polish-German border that Stalin had long demanded; he refused, however, to permit the Russians to claim any reparations from the American, French, and British zones of Germany. This stance effectively confirmed that Germany would remain divided, with the western zones united into one nation, friendly to the United States, and the Russian zone surviving as another nation, with a pro-Soviet, communist government.

attempt to threaten and intimidate Stalin; that Harry Truman had recklessly abandoned the conciliatory policies of Franklin Roosevelt and taken a provocative hard line against the Russians; and that the Soviet response had reflected a legitimate fear of capitalist encirclement. Walter LaFeber, in *America, Russia, and the Cold War, 1945–1967* (1967 and many later editions), maintained that America's supposedly idealistic internationalism at the close of the war—its vision of "One World," with every nation in control of its own destiny—was in reality an effort to ensure a world shaped in the American image, with every nation open to American influence (and American trade).

Ultimately, the revisionist interpretation began to produce a reaction of its own, a "post-revisionist" view of the conflict. Some manifestations of this reaction consisted of little more than a reaffirmation of the traditional view of the Cold War. Arthur M. Schlesinger Jr., for example, admitted in a 1967 article that the Soviets may not have been committed to world conquest, as most earlier accounts had claimed. Nevertheless, the Soviets (and Stalin in particular) were motivated by a deep-seated paranoia about the West, which made them insistent on dominating Eastern Europe and rendered any amicable relationship between them and the United States impossible.

But the dominant works of post-revisionist scholarship attempted to strike a balance between the two camps, to identify areas of blame and misperception on both sides of the conflict. Thomas G. Paterson, in *Soviet-American Confrontation* (1973), viewed Russian hostility and American efforts to dominate the postwar world as equally responsible for the Cold War. John Lewis Gaddis, in *The United States and the Origins of the Cold War, 1941–1947* (1972) and other works, similarly maintained that "neither side can bear sole responsibility for the onset of the Cold War." American policymakers, he argued, had only limited options because of the pressures of domestic politics. And Stalin was immobilized by his obsessive concern with maintaining his own power and ensuring absolute security for the Soviet Union. But if neither side was entirely to blame, Gaddis concluded, the Soviets must be held at least slightly more accountable for the problems, for Stalin was in a much better position to compromise, given his broader power within his own government, than the politically hamstrung Truman. Melvyn Leffler's *Preponderance of Power* (1991) argued similarly that American policymakers genuinely believed in the existence of a Soviet threat and were determined to remain consistently stronger than the Soviets in response.

Out of the postrevisionist literature has begun to emerge a more complex view of the Cold War, which de-emphasizes the question of who was to blame and adopts a more detached view of the conflict. The Cold War, historians now suggest, was not so much the fault of one side or the other as it was the natural, perhaps inevitable, result of tensions between the world's two most powerful nations—nations that had been suspicious of, if not hostile toward, one another for nearly a century. As Ernest May wrote in a 1984 essay:

> After the Second World War, the United States and the Soviet Union were doomed to be antagonists. . . . There probably was never any real possibility that the post-1945 relationship could be anything but hostility verging on conflict. . . . Traditions, belief systems, propinquity, and convenience . . . all combined to stimulate antagonism, and almost no factor operated in either country to hold it back.

The China Problem

Central to American hopes for an open, peaceful world "policed" by the great powers was a strong, independent China. But even before the war ended, the American government was aware that those hopes faced a major, perhaps insurmountable, obstacle: the Chinese government of Chiang Kai-shek. Chiang was generally friendly to the United States, but his government was corrupt and incompetent with feeble popular support, and Chiang was himself unable or unwilling to face the problems that were threatening to engulf him. Since 1927, the nationalist government he headed had been engaged in a prolonged and bitter rivalry with the communist armies of Mao Zedong. So successful had the communist challenge grown that Mao was in control of one-fourth of the population by 1945.

Chiang Kai-shek

Some Americans urged the government to try to find a "third force" to support as an alternative to either Chiang or Mao. A few argued that the United States should try to reach some accommodation with Mao. Truman, however, decided reluctantly that he had no choice but to continue supporting Chiang. For the next several years, as the long struggle between the nationalists and the communists erupted into a full-scale civil war, the United States continued to send money and weapons to Chiang, even as it was becoming clear that the cause was lost. But Truman was not prepared to intervene militarily to save the nationalist regime.

Instead, the American government was beginning to consider an alternative to China as the strong, pro-Western force in Asia: a revived Japan. Abandoning the strict occupation policies of the first years after the war (when General Douglas MacArthur had governed the nation), the United States lifted all restrictions on industrial development and encouraged rapid economic growth in Japan. The vision of an open, united world was giving way in Asia, as it was in Europe, to an acceptance of a divided world with a strong, pro-American sphere of influence.

Restoring Japan

The Containment Doctrine

By the end of 1945, any realistic hope of a postwar world constructed according to the Atlantic Charter ideals

Roosevelt and others had supported was in shambles. Instead, a new American policy, known as containment, was slowly emerging. Rather than attempting to create a unified, "open" world, the United States and its allies would work to "contain" the threat of further Soviet expansion.

The new doctrine emerged in part as a response to events in Europe in 1946. In Turkey, Stalin was trying to win control over the vital sea lanes to the Mediterranean. In Greece, communist forces were threatening the pro-Western government. The British had announced they could no longer provide assistance. Faced with these

Truman Doctrine

challenges, Truman decided to enunciate a firm new policy. In doing so, he drew from the ideas of the influential American diplomat George F. Kennan, who had warned not long after the war that the only appropriate diplomatic approach to dealing with the Soviet Union was "a long-term, patient but firm and vigilant containment of Russian expansive tendencies." On March 12, 1947, Truman appeared before Congress and used Kennan's warnings as the basis of what became known as the Truman Doctrine. "I believe," he argued, "that it must be the policy of the United States to support free peoples who are resisting attempted subjugation by armed minorities or by outside pressures." In the same speech he requested $400 million—part of it to bolster the armed forces of Greece and Turkey, another part to provide economic assistance to Greece. Congress quickly approved the measure.

The American commitment ultimately helped ease Soviet pressure on Turkey and helped the Greek government defeat the communist insurgents. More important, it established a basis for American foreign policy that would survive for more than forty years.

The Marshall Plan

An integral part of the containment policy was a proposal to aid in the economic reconstruction of Western Europe.

Rebuilding Europe

There were many motives: humanitarian concern for the European people; a fear that Europe would remain an economic drain on the United States if it could not quickly rebuild and begin to feed itself; a desire for a strong European market for American goods. But above all, American policymakers believed that unless something could be done to strengthen the shaky pro-American governments in Western Europe, those governments might fall under the control of rapidly growing domestic communist parties.

In June 1947, therefore, Secretary of State George C. Marshall announced a plan to provide economic assistance to all European nations (including the Soviet Union) that would join in drafting a program for recovery. Although Russia and its Eastern satellites quickly and

A BENEFICIARY OF THE MARSHALL PLAN A young boy in Austria enthusiastically embraces a pair of shoes provided to him, indirectly, by the Marshall Plan—the $13 billion program of assistance to the nations of postwar Western Europe to help them recover from the war and, of at least equal importance, resist the allure of communism. *(Red Cross Museum)*

predictably rejected the plan, sixteen Western European nations eagerly participated. Whatever domestic opposition to the plan there was in the United States largely vanished after a sudden coup in Czechoslovakia in February 1948 that established a Soviet-dominated communist government there. In April, Congress approved the creation of the Economic Cooperation Administration, the agency that would administer the Marshall Plan, as it became known. Over the next three years, the Marshall Plan channeled over $12 billion of American aid into Europe, helping to spark a substantial economic revival. By the end of 1950, European industrial production had risen 64 percent, communist strength in the member nations had declined, and opportunities for American trade had revived.

Survival Secrets for Atomic Attacks

ALWAYS PUT FIRST THINGS FIRST

Try to Get Shielded

If you have time, get down in a basement or subway. Should you unexpectedly be caught out-of-doors, seek shelter alongside a building, or jump in any handy ditch or gutter.

Drop Flat on Ground or Floor

To keep from being tossed about and to lessen the chances of being struck by falling and flying objects, flatten out at the base of a wall, or at the bottom of a bank.

Bury Your Face in Your Arms

When you drop flat, hide your eyes in the crook of your elbow. That will protect your face from flash burns, prevent temporary blindness and keep flying objects out of your eyes.

NEVER LOSE YOUR HEAD

SURVIVING NUCLEAR WAR Preoccupation with the possibility of a nuclear war reached a fever pitch in the first years of the atomic era. The Federal Civil Defense Agency, which in 1950 issued these simple rules for civilians to follow in dealing with an atomic attack, was one of many organizations attempting to convince the American public that a nuclear war was survivable. *(Federal Civil Defense Agency)*

Mobilization at Home

That the United States had fully accepted a continuing commitment to the containment policy became clear in 1947 and 1948 through a series of measures designed to maintain American military power at near wartime levels. In 1948, at President Truman's request, Congress approved a new military draft and revived the Selective Service System. In the meantime, the United States, having failed to reach agreement with the Soviet Union on international control of nuclear weapons, redoubled its own efforts in atomic research, elevating nuclear weaponry to a central place in its military arsenal. The Atomic Energy Commission, established in 1946, became the supervisory body charged with overseeing all nuclear research, civilian and military alike. And in 1950, the Truman administration approved the development of the new hydrogen bomb, a nuclear weapon far more powerful than the bombs the United States had used in 1945.

The National Security Act of 1947 reshaped the nation's major military and diplomatic institutions. It created a new Department of Defense to oversee all branches of the armed services, combining functions previously performed separately by the War and Navy Departments. A National

National Security Act of 1947

Security Council (NSC), operating out of the White House, would oversee foreign and military policy.

A Central Intelligence Agency (CIA) would replace the wartime Office of Strategic Services and would be responsible for collecting information through both open and covert methods; as the Cold War continued, the CIA would also engage secretly in political and military operations on behalf of American goals. The National Security Act, in other words, gave the president expanded powers with which to pursue the nation's international goals.

The Road to NATO

At about the same time, the United States was moving to strengthen the military capabilities of Western Europe. Convinced that a reconstructed Germany was essential to the hopes of the West, Truman reached an agreement with England and France to merge the three western zones of occupation into a new West German republic (which would include the American, British, and French sectors of Berlin, even though that city lay well within the Soviet zone). Stalin responded quickly. On June 24, 1948, he imposed a tight blockade around the western sectors of Berlin. If Germany was to be officially divided, he was implying, then the country's western government would have to abandon its outpost in the heart of the Soviet-controlled eastern zone. Truman refused to do so. Unwilling to risk war through a military challenge to the blockade, he ordered a massive airlift to supply the city with food, fuel, and other needed

DIVIDED EUROPE AFTER WORLD WAR II This map shows the sharp division that emerged in Europe after World War II between the area under the control of the Soviet Union and the area allied with the United States. In the east, Soviet control or influence extended into all the nations shaded brown—including the eastern half of Germany. In the west and south, the green-shaded nations were allied with the United States as members of the North Atlantic Treaty Organization (NATO). The countries shaded gold were aligned with neither of the two superpowers. The small map in the upper right shows the division of Berlin among the various occupying powers at the end of the war. Eventually, the American, British, and French sectors were combined to create West Berlin, a city governed by West Germany but entirely surrounded by communist East Germany. ◆ *How did the West prevent East Germany from absorbing West Berlin?*

goods. The airlift continued for more than ten months, transporting nearly 2.5 million tons of material, keeping a city of 2 million people alive, and transforming West Berlin into a symbol of the West's resolve to resist communist expansion. In the spring of 1949, Stalin lifted the now ineffective blockade. And in October, the division of Germany into two nations—the Federal Republic in the west and the Democratic Republic in the east—became official.

The crisis in Berlin accelerated the consolidation of what was already in effect an alliance among the United States and the countries of Western Europe. On April 4,

1949, twelve nations signed an agreement establishing the North Atlantic Treaty Organization (NATO) and declaring that an

NATO

armed attack against one member would be considered an attack against all. The NATO countries would, moreover, maintain a standing military force in Europe to defend against what many policymakers believed was the threat of a Soviet invasion. The formation of NATO eventually spurred the Soviet Union to create an alliance of its own with the communist governments in Eastern Europe—an alliance formalized in 1955 by the Warsaw Pact.

Reevaluating Cold War Policy

A series of events in 1949 propelled the Cold War in new directions. An announcement in September that the Soviet Union had successfully exploded its first atomic weapon, years earlier than predicted, shocked and frightened many Americans. So did the collapse of Chiang Kai-shek's nationalist government in China, which occurred with startling speed in the last months of 1949. Chiang fled with his political allies and the remnants of his army to the offshore island of Formosa (Taiwan), and the entire Chinese mainland came under the control of a communist government that many Americans believed to be an extension of the Soviet Union. The United States refused to recognize the new communist regime, and instead devoted increased attention to the revitalization of Japan as a buffer against Asian communism, ending the American occupation in 1952.

PROCLAIMING THE VICTORY OF THE REVOLUTION Chairman Mao Zedong, standing on the rostrum of the Tiananmen Square Gate in Beijing, speaks by radio to the Chinese people on October 1, 1949, to proclaim the founding of the People's Republic of China. This was shortly after the communist victory in the nation's civil war and the departure of Chiang Kai-shek and his followers to the island of Taiwan. *(AP Images)*

In this atmosphere of escalating crisis, Truman called for a thorough review of American foreign policy. The result was a National Security Council report, issued in 1950 and commonly known as NSC-68, which outlined a shift in the American position. The first statements of the containment doctrine—the writings of George Kennan, the Truman Doctrine speech—had made at least some distinctions between areas of vital interest to the United States and areas of less importance to the nation's foreign policy and called on America to share the burden of containment with its allies. But the April 1950 document argued that the United States could no longer rely on other nations to take the initiative in resisting communism. It must itself establish firm and active leadership of the non-communist world. And it must move to stop communist expansion virtually anywhere it occurred, regardless of the intrinsic strategic or economic value of the lands in question. Among other things, the report called for a major expansion of American military power, with a defense budget almost four times the previously projected figure.

NSC-68

AMERICAN SOCIETY AND POLITICS AFTER THE WAR

The crises overseas were not the only frustrations the American people encountered after the war. The nation also faced serious economic difficulties in adapting to the peace. The resulting instability contributed to an increasingly heated political climate.

The Problems of Reconversion

The bombs that destroyed Hiroshima and Nagasaki ended the war months earlier than almost anyone had predicted and propelled the nation precipitously into a process of reconversion.

There had been many predictions that peace would bring a return of Depression unemployment, as war production ceased and returning soldiers flooded the labor market. But there was no general economic collapse in 1946—for several reasons. Government spending dropped sharply and abruptly, to be sure; $35 billion of war contracts were canceled within weeks of the Japanese surrender. But increased consumer demand soon compensated. Consumer goods had been generally unavailable during the war, so many workers had saved a substantial portion of their wages and were now ready to spend. A $6 billion tax cut pumped additional money into general circulation. The Servicemen's Readjustment Act of 1944, better known as the GI Bill of Rights, provided economic and educational assistance to veterans, increasing spending even further.

GI Bill

This flood of consumer demand ensured that there would be no new depression, but it contributed to more

A GI BILL STUDENT Joe Heinrich, recently returned from service in World War II, was an aspiring artist and used the benefits available to him under the GI Bill to enroll in art classes in San Francisco in 1946. Heinrich had not yet benefited from one of the other provisions of the GI Bill—housing assistance. Unable to find housing in San Francisco, he hitchhiked 100 miles each way every day from Sacramento to school. *(Bettmann/Corbis)*

than two years of serious inflation, during which prices rose at rates of 14 to 15 percent annually. In the summer of 1946, President Truman vetoed an extension of the authority of the wartime Office of Price Administration, thus eliminating price controls. (He was opposed not to the controls, but to congressional amendments that had weakened the OPA.) Inflation soared to 25 percent before he relented a month later and signed a bill little different from the one he had rejected.

Compounding the economic difficulties was a sharp rise in labor unrest, driven in part by the impact of inflation. By the end of 1945, there had already been major strikes in the automobile, electrical, and steel industries. In April 1946, John L. Lewis led the United Mine Workers out on strike, shutting down the coal fields for forty days. Fears grew rapidly that without vital coal supplies, the entire nation might virtually grind to a halt. Truman finally forced the miners to return to work by ordering government seizure of the mines. But in the process, he pressured mine owners to grant the union most of its demands, which he had earlier denounced as inflationary. Almost simultaneously, the nation's railroads suffered a total shutdown—the first in the nation's history—as two major unions walked out on strike. By threatening to use the army to run the trains, Truman pressured the workers back to work after only a few days.

Reconversion was particularly difficult for the millions of women and minorities who had entered the work force during the war. With veterans returning home and looking for jobs in the industrial economy, employers tended to push women, blacks, Hispanics, Chinese, and others out of the plants to make room for white males. Some of the war workers, particularly women, left the work force voluntarily,

out of a desire to return to their former domestic lives. But as many as 80 percent of women workers, and virtually all black, Hispanic, and Asian males, wanted to continue working. The postwar inflation, the pressure to meet the rising expectations of a high-consumption society, the rising divorce rate, which left many women responsible for their own economic well-being—all combined to create among women a high demand for paid employment. As they found themselves excluded from industrial jobs, therefore, women workers moved increasingly into other areas of the economy (above all, the service sector).

The Fair Deal Rejected

Days after the Japanese surrender, Truman submitted to Congress a twenty-one-point domestic program outlining what he later termed the "Fair Deal." It called for expansion of Social Security benefits, the raising of the legal minimum wage from 40 to 65 cents an hour, a program to ensure full employment through aggressive use of federal spending and investment, a permanent Fair Employment Practices Act, public housing and slum clearance, long-range environmental and public works planning, and government promotion of scientific research. Weeks later he added other proposals: federal aid to funding for the St. Lawrence Seaway, nationalization of atomic energy, and, perhaps most important, national health insurance—a dream of welfare-state liberals for decades, but one deferred in 1935 when the Social Security Act was written. The president was declaring an end to the wartime moratorium on liberal reform. He was also symbolizing, as he later wrote, "my assumption of the office of President in my own right."

But the Fair Deal programs fell victim to the same public and congressional conservatism that had crippled the last years of the New Deal. Indeed, that conservatism seemed to be intensifying, as the November 1946 congressional elections suggested. Using the simple but devastating slogan "Had Enough?," the Republican Party won control of both houses of Congress.

The new Republican Congress quickly moved to reduce government spending and chip away at New Deal reforms. The president bowed to what he claimed was the popular mandate to lift most remaining wage and price controls, and Congress moved further to deregulate the economy. Inflation rapidly increased. When a public outcry arose over the soaring prices for meat, Senator Robert Taft, perhaps the most influential Republican conservative in Congress, advised consumers to "eat less," and added, "We have got to break with the corrupting idea that we can legislate prosperity, legislate equality, legislate opportunity." True to the spirit of Taft's words, the Republican Congress refused to appropriate funds to aid education, increase Social Security, or support reclamation and power projects in the West. It defeated a proposal to raise the minimum wage. It passed tax measures that cut rates

Postwar Labor Unrest

Truman's "Fair Deal"

HARRY AND BESS TRUMAN AT HOME
Senator Harry Truman and his wife, Bess, pose for photographers in the kitchen of their Washington apartment, suggesting the "common man" image that Truman retained throughout his public life. The picture was taken shortly before the 1944 Democratic National Convention, which would nominate Truman for vice president. Less than a year later, the Trumans would be living in the White House. *(Bettmann/Corbis)*

dramatically for high-income families and moderately for those with lower incomes. Only vetoes by the president finally forced a more progressive bill.

The most notable action of the new Congress was its assault on the Wagner Act of 1935. Conservatives had always resented the new powers the legislation had granted unions; and in light of the labor difficulties during and after the war, such resentments intensified sharply. The result was the Labor-Management Relations Act of 1947, better known as the Taft-Hartley Act. It made illegal the so-called closed shop (a workplace in which no one can be hired without first being a member of a union). And although it continued to permit the creation of so-called union shops (in which workers must join a union after being hired), it permitted states to pass "right-to-work" laws prohibiting even that. Repealing this provision, the controversial Section 14(b), would remain a goal of the labor movement for decades. Outraged workers and union leaders denounced the measure as a "slave labor bill." Truman vetoed it, but both houses easily overruled him the same day.

The Taft-Hartley Act did not destroy the labor movement, as many union leaders had predicted. But it did damage weaker unions in relatively lightly organized industries such as chemicals and textiles; and it made more difficult the organizing of workers who had never been union members at all, especially women, minorities, and most workers in the South.

The Election of 1948

Truman and his advisers believed the American public was not ready to abandon the achievements of the New Deal, despite the 1946 election results. As they planned strategy for the 1948 campaign, therefore, they placed their hopes in an appeal to enduring Democratic loyalties. Throughout 1948, Truman proposed one reform measure after another. Although Congress ignored or defeated them all, the president was building campaign issues for the fall.

There remained, however, the problems of Truman's personal unpopularity—the belief among much of the electorate that he and his administration were weak and inept— and the deep divisions within the Democratic Party. At the Democratic Convention that summer, two factions abandoned the party altogether. Southern conservatives reacted angrily to Truman's proposed civil rights bill (the first major one of the century) and to the approval at the convention of a civil rights plank in the platform (engineered by Hubert Humphrey, the mayor of Minneapolis). They walked out and formed the States' Rights (or "Dixiecrat") Party, with Governor Strom Thurmond of South Carolina as its presidential nominee. At the same time, the party's left wing formed a new Progressive Party, with Henry A. Wallace as its candidate. Wallace supporters objected to what they considered the slow and ineffective domestic policies of the Truman administration, but they resented even more the president's confrontational stance toward the Soviet Union.

In addition, many Democratic liberals unwilling to leave the party attempted to dump the president in 1948. The Americans for Democratic Action (ADA), a coalition of liberals, tried to entice Dwight D. Eisenhower, the popular war hero, to contest the nomination. Only after Eisenhower had refused did liberals bow to the inevitable and concede the nomination to Truman. The Republicans, in the meantime, had once again nominated Governor Thomas E. Dewey of New York, whose substantial reelection victory in 1946 had made him one of the nation's leading political figures. Austere, dignified, and competent, he seemed to offer an unbeatable alternative to the president. Polls showed Dewey with an apparently insurmountable lead in September, so much so that some opinion analysts stopped taking surveys. Dewey conducted a subdued, statesmanlike campaign and tried to avoid antagonizing anyone. Only Truman, it seemed, believed he could win. As the campaign gathered momentum, he became ever more aggressive, turning the fire away from himself and toward Dewey and the "do-nothing, good-for-nothing" Republican Congress, which was, he told the voters, responsible for fueling inflation and abandoning workers and common people. To dramatize his point, he called Congress into a special session in July to give it a chance, he said, to enact the liberal measures the Republicans had recently written into their platform. Congress met for two weeks and, predictably, did almost nothing.

The president traveled nearly 32,000 miles and made 356 speeches, delivering blunt, extemporaneous attacks. He had told Senator Alben Barkley of Kentucky, his running mate, "I'm going to fight hard. I'm going to give them hell." He called for repeal of the Taft-Hartley Act, increased price supports for farmers, and strong civil rights protection for blacks. (He was the first president to campaign in Harlem.) He sought, in short, to re-create much of Franklin Roosevelt's New Deal coalition. To the surprise of virtually everyone, he succeeded. On election night, he won a narrow but decisive victory: 49.5 percent of the popular vote to Dewey's 45.1 percent (with the two splinter parties dividing the small remainder between them), and an electoral vote margin of 303 to 189. Democrats, in the meantime, had regained both houses of Congress by substantial margins.

Truman's Surprising Victory

The Fair Deal Revived

Despite the Democratic victories, the Eighty-first Congress was little more hospitable to Truman's Fair Deal reform than its Republican predecessor. Truman did win some important victories. Congress raised the legal minimum wage from 40 cents to 75 cents an hour. It approved an important expansion of the Social Security system, increasing benefits by 75 percent and extending them to 10 million additional people. And it passed the National Housing Act of 1949, which provided for the construction of 810,000 units of low-income housing, accompanied by long-term rent subsidies. (Inadequate funding plagued the program for years, and it reached its initial goal only in 1972.)

But on other issues—among them national health insurance and aid to education—he made no progress. Nor was he able to persuade Congress to accept the civil

Truman Stymied

rights legislation he proposed in 1949, which would have made lynching a federal crime, provided federal protection of black voting rights, abolished the poll tax, and established a new Fair Employment Practices Commission to curb discrimination in hiring (to replace the wartime commission Roosevelt had established in 1941). Southern Democrats filibustered to kill the bill.

Truman did proceed on his own to battle several forms of racial discrimination. He ordered an end to discrimination in the hiring of government employees. He began to dismantle segregation within the armed forces. And he allowed the Justice Department to become actively involved in court battles against discriminatory statutes. In the meantime, the Supreme Court signaled its own growing awareness of the issue by ruling, in *Shelley* v. *Kraemer* (1948), that the courts could not be used to enforce private "covenants" meant to bar blacks from residential neighborhoods.

Candidate (Party)	Electoral Vote	Popular Vote (%)
Harry S. Truman (Democratic)	303	24,105,695 (49.5)
Thomas E. Dewey (Republican)	189	21,969,170 (45.1)
Strom Thurmond (States' Rights)	39	1,169,021 (2.4)
Henry A. Wallace (Progressive)	—	1,156,103 (2.4)
Other Candidates (Prohibition, Socialist Labor, Socialist, Socialist Workers)	—	272,713

53% of electorate voting

ELECTION OF 1948 Despite the widespread expectation that the Republican candidate, Thomas Dewey, would easily defeat Truman in 1948, the president in fact won a substantial reelection victory that year. This map shows the broad geographic reach of Truman's victory. Dewey swept most of the Northeast, but Truman dominated almost everywhere else. Strom Thurmond, the States' Rights candidate, carried four states in the South. ◆ *What had prompted Thurmond to desert the Democratic party and run for president on his own?*

For an interactive version of this map, go to www.mhhe.com/brinkley13ech27maps

The Nuclear Age

Looming over the political, economic, and diplomatic struggles of the postwar years was the image of the great and terrible mushroom clouds that had risen over Alamogordo, Hiroshima, and Nagasaki. Americans greeted these terrible new instruments of destruction with fear and awe, but also with expectation. Postwar culture, therefore, was torn in many ways between a dark image of the nuclear war that many Americans feared would be a result of the rivalry with the Soviet Union, and the bright image of a dazzling technological future that atomic power might help to produce.

Conflicting Views of Nuclear Power

The fear of nuclear weapons was not hard to find in popular culture, even if it was often disguised in other ways. The late 1940s and early 1950s were the heyday of the *film noir,* a kind of filmmaking that had originated in France and had been named for the dark lighting that was characteristic of the genre. American *film noir* movies portrayed the loneliness of individuals in an impersonal world—a staple of American culture for many decades—but also suggested the menacing character of the age, the looming possibility of vast destruction. Sometimes, films and television programs addressed nuclear fear explicitly—for example, the celebrated television show of the 1950s and early 1960s *The Twilight Zone,* which frequently featured dramatic portrayals of the aftermath of nuclear war; or postwar comic books, which depicted powerful superheroes saving the world from destruction.

Such images resonated with the public because awareness of nuclear weapons was increasingly built into their daily lives. Schools and office buildings had regular air raid drills, to prepare people for the possibility of nuclear attack. Radio stations regularly tested the emergency broadcast systems. Fallout shelters sprang up in public buildings and private homes, stocked with water and canned goods. America was a nation filled with anxiety.

And yet at the same time, the United States was also an exuberant nation, dazzled by its own prosperity and excited by the technological innovations that were transforming the world. Among those innovations was nuclear power—which offered the possibility that the same scientific knowledge that could destroy the world might also lead it into a dazzling future. A Gallup poll late in 1948 revealed that approximately two-thirds of those who had an opinion on the subject believed that, "in the long run," atomic energy would "do more good than harm." Nuclear power plants began to spring up in many areas of the country, welcomed as the source of cheap and unlimited electricity, their potential dangers scarcely even discussed by those who celebrated their creation.

Promise of Cheap Nuclear Power

THE KOREAN WAR

On June 24, 1950, the armies of communist North Korea swept across their southern border and invaded the pro-Western half of the Korean peninsula to the south. Within days, they had occupied much of South Korea, including Seoul, its capital. Almost immediately, the United States committed itself to the conflict. It was the nation's first military engagement of the Cold War.

The Divided Peninsula

By the end of 1945, both the United States and the Soviet Union had sent troops into Korea, and neither was willing to leave. Instead, they had divided the nation, supposedly temporarily, along the 38th parallel. The Russians finally departed in 1949, leaving behind a communist government in the north with a strong, Soviet-equipped army. The Americans left a few months later, handing control to the pro-Western government of Syngman Rhee, who was anticommunist but only nominally democratic. He had a relatively small military, which he used primarily to suppress internal opposition.

Syngman Rhee

The relative weakness of the south offered a strong incentive to nationalists in the North Korean government who wanted to reunite the country. The temptation to invade grew stronger when the American government implied that it did not consider South Korea within its own "defense perimeter." The role of the Soviet Union in North Korea's calculations prior to the 1950 invasion remains unclear; there is reason to believe that the North Koreans acted without Stalin's prior approval. But the Soviets supported the offensive once it began.

The Truman administration responded quickly to the invasion. On June 27, 1950, the president appealed to the United Nations to intervene. The Soviet Union was boycotting the Security Council at the time (to protest the council's refusal to recognize the new communist government of China) and thus was unable to exercise its veto power. As a result, American delegates were able to win UN agreement to a resolution calling for international assistance to the Rhee government. On June 30, the United States ordered its own ground forces into Korea, and Truman appointed General Douglas MacArthur to command the (overwhelmingly American) UN operations there.

The intervention in Korea was the first expression of the newly expansive American foreign policy outlined in NSC-68. But the administration quickly went beyond NSC-68 and decided that the war would be an effort not simply at containment but also at "liberation." After a surprise American invasion at Inchon in September had routed the North Korean forces from the south and sent them fleeing back across the 38th parallel, Truman gave MacArthur permission to pursue the communists into their own territory. His aim, as an American-sponsored UN resolution

"Liberation"

DISARRAY IN KOREA This disturbing picture by a noted *Life* magazine photographer conveys something of the air of catastrophe that surrounded the rout of Americans from North Korea by the Chinese in 1951. Having approached the Chinese border, the Americans confronted a massive invasion of Korea by Chinese troops, who soon pushed them back below the border between the North and the South and well beyond. Shown here are Marines following a vehicle carrying corpses after a battle with Chinese and North Korean troops. They had been trapped by the enemy in North Korea and had fought their way forty miles south before being rescued. *(Carl Mydans/Time Life Pictures/Getty Images)*

proclaimed in October, was to create "a unified, independent and democratic Korea."

From Invasion to Stalemate

For several weeks, MacArthur's invasion of North Korea proceeded smoothly. On October 19, the capital, Pyongyang, fell to the UN forces. Victory seemed near—until the new communist government of China, alarmed by the movement of American forces toward its border, intervened. By November 4, eight divisions of the Chinese army had entered the war. The UN offensive stalled and then collapsed. Through December 1950, outnumbered American forces fought a bitter, losing battle against the Chinese divisions, retreating at almost every juncture. Within weeks, communist forces had pushed the Americans back below the 38th parallel once again and had captured the South Korean capital of Seoul a second time. By mid-January 1951 the rout had ceased; and by March the UN armies had managed to regain much of the territory they had

recently lost, taking back Seoul and pushing the communists north of the 38th parallel once more. But with that, the war degenerated into a protracted stalemate.

From the start, Truman was determined to avoid a direct conflict with China, which he feared might lead to a new world war. Once China entered the war, he began seeking a negotiated solution to the struggle, and for the next two years he insisted that there be no wider war. But he faced a formidable opponent in General MacArthur, who resisted any limits on his military discretion. The United States was fighting the Chinese, he argued. It should therefore attack China itself, if not through an actual invasion, then at least by bombing communist forces massing north of the Chinese border. In March 1951, he indicated his unhappiness in a public letter to House Republican leader Joseph W. Martin that concluded: "There is no substitute for victory." His position had wide popular support.

The Martin letter came after nine months during which MacArthur had resisted Truman's decisions. More

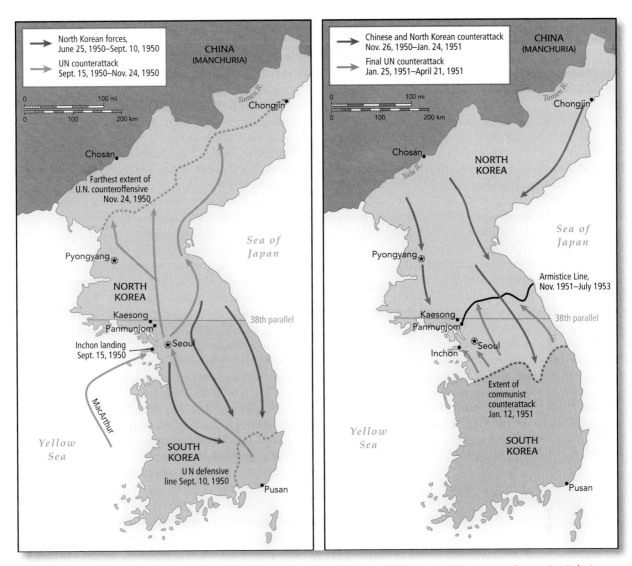

THE KOREAN WAR, 1950–1953 These two maps illustrate the changing fortunes of UN forces (which were mostly American) during the 1950-1953 Korean War. The map at the left shows the extent of the North Korean invasion of the South in 1950; communist forces for a time controlled all of Korea except a small area around Pusan in the southeast. On September 15, 1950, UN troops under Douglas MacArthur landed in force at Inchon and soon drove the North Koreans well into their own territory. MacArthur then pursued the North Koreans well into their own territory. The map at right shows the very different circumstances once the Chinese entered the war in November 1950. Chinese forces drove the UN army back below the 38th parallel and, briefly, deep into South Korea, below Seoul. The UN troops fought back to the prewar border between North and South Korea late in 1951, but the war then bogged down into a stalemate that continued for a year and a half. ◆ *What impact did the Korean War have on American politics in the early 1950s?*

Truman-MacArthur Controversy

than once, the president had warned the general to keep his objections to himself. The release of the Martin letter, therefore, struck the president as intolerable insubordination. On April 11, 1951, he relieved MacArthur of his command.

There was a storm of public outrage. Sixty-nine percent of the American people supported MacArthur, a Gallup poll reported. When the general returned to the United States later in 1951, he was greeted with wild enthusiasm. His televised farewell appearance before a joint session of Congress—which he concluded by saying, "Old soldiers never die, they just fade away"—attracted an audience of millions. Public criticism of Truman finally abated somewhat when a number of prominent military figures, including General Omar Bradley, publicly supported the president's decision. But substantial hostility toward Truman remained. In the meantime, the Korean stalemate continued. Negotiations between the opposing forces began at Panmunjom in July 1951, but the talks—and the war—dragged on until 1953.

Limited Mobilization

Just as the war in Korea produced only a limited American military commitment abroad, so it created only a limited economic mobilization at home. Still, the government did try to control the wartime economy in several important ways.

First, Truman set up the Office of Defense Mobilization to fight inflation by holding down prices and discouraging high union wage demands. When these cautious regulatory efforts failed, the president took more drastic action. Railroad workers walked off the job in 1951, and Truman ordered the government to seize control of the railroads. That helped keep the trains running, but it had no effect on union demands. Workers ultimately got most of what they had demanded. In 1952, during a nationwide steel strike, Truman seized the steel mills, citing his powers as commander in chief. But in a 6-to-3 decision, the Supreme Court ruled that the president had exceeded his authority, and Truman was forced to relent.

Wartime Economic Regulation

The Korean War gave a significant boost to economic growth by pumping new government funds into the economy at a point when many believed a recession was about to begin. But as the long stalemate continued, leaving 140,000 Americans dead or wounded, frustration turned to anger. Many began to believe that something must be deeply wrong—not only in Korea but within the United States as well. Such fears contributed to the rise of the second major campaign of the century against domestic communism.

THE CRUSADE AGAINST SUBVERSION

Why did the American people develop a growing fear of internal communist subversion that by the early 1950s had reached the point of near hysteria? There are many possible answers, but no single definitive explanation.

One factor was obvious. Communism was not an imagined enemy in the 1950s. It had tangible shape, in Joseph Stalin and the Soviet Union. In addition, America had encountered setbacks in its battle against communism: the Korean stalemate, the "loss" of China, the Soviet development of an atomic bomb. Searching for someone to blame, many people were attracted to the idea of a communist conspiracy within American borders. But there were other factors as well, rooted in American domestic politics.

Sources of the Red Scare

HUAC and Alger Hiss

Much of the anticommunist furor emerged out of the Republican Party's search for an issue with which to attack the Democrats, and out of the Democrats' efforts to stifle that issue. Beginning in 1947 (with Republicans temporarily in control of Congress), the House Un-American Activities Committee (HUAC) held widely publicized investigations to prove that, under Democratic rule, the government had tolerated (if not actually encouraged) communist subversion. The committee turned first to the movie industry, arguing that communists had infiltrated Hollywood. Writers and producers, some of them former communists, were called to testify; and when some of them ("the Hollywood Ten") refused to answer questions about their own political beliefs and those of their colleagues, they were jailed for contempt. Others were barred from employment in the industry when Hollywood, attempting to protect its public image, adopted a blacklist of those of "suspicious loyalty."

More alarming to the public was HUAC's investigation into charges of disloyalty leveled against a former high-ranking member of the State Department: Alger Hiss. In 1948, Whittaker Chambers, a self-avowed former communist agent who had turned vehemently against the party and become an editor at *Time* magazine, told the committee that Hiss had passed classified State Department documents through him to the Soviet Union in 1937 and 1938. When Hiss sued him for slander, Chambers produced microfilms of the documents (called the "pumpkin papers," because Chambers had kept them hidden in a pumpkin in his garden). Hiss could not be tried for espionage because of the statute of limitations (a law that protects individuals from prosecution for most crimes after seven years have passed). But largely because of the relentless efforts of Richard M. Nixon, a freshman Republican congressman from California and a member of HUAC, Hiss was convicted of perjury and served several years in prison. The Hiss case not only discredited a prominent young diplomat; it also cast suspicion on a generation of liberal Democrats and made it possible for many Americans to believe that communists had actually infiltrated the government.

Alger Hiss

The Federal Loyalty Program and the Rosenberg Case

Partly to protect itself against Republican attacks, partly to encourage support for the president's foreign policy initiatives, the Truman administration in 1947 initiated a widely publicized program to review the loyalty of federal employees. In August 1950, the president authorized sensitive agencies to fire people deemed no more than "bad security risks." By 1951, more than 2,000 government employees had resigned under pressure and 212 had been dismissed.

The employee loyalty program launched a major assault on subversion. The attorney general established a widely cited list of supposedly subversive organizations. The director of the Federal Bureau of Investigation (FBI), J. Edgar Hoover, investigated and harassed alleged radicals. In 1950, Congress passed the McCarran Internal Security

The McCarran Internal Security Act

Act, requiring all communist organizations to register with the government. Truman vetoed the bill. Congress easily overrode his veto.

The successful Soviet detonation of a nuclear weapon in 1949, earlier than generally expected, convinced many people that there had been a conspiracy to pass American atomic secrets to the Russians. In 1950, Klaus Fuchs, a young British scientist, seemed to confirm those fears when he testified that he had delivered to the Russians details of the manufacture of the bomb. The case ultimately settled on an obscure New York couple, Julius and Ethel Rosenberg, members of the Communist Party, whom the federal government claimed had been the masterminds of the conspiracy. The case against them rested in large part on testimony by Ethel's brother, David Greenglass, a machinist who had worked on the Manhattan Project. Greenglass admitted to channeling secret information to the Soviet Union through other agents (including Fuchs). His sister and brother-in-law had, he claimed, planned and orchestrated the espionage. The Rosenbergs were convicted and, on April 5, 1951, sentenced to death. After two years of appeals and protests by sympathizers, they died in the electric chair on June 19, 1953.

All these factors—the HUAC investigations, the Hiss trial, the loyalty investigations, the McCarran Act, the Rosenberg case—combined with concern about international events to create a fear of communist subversion that by the early 1950s seemed to have gripped virtually the entire country. State and local gov-

Anticommunist Hysteria

ernments, the judiciary, schools and universities, labor unions—all sought to purge themselves of real or imagined subversives. A pervasive fear settled on the country—not only the fear of communist infiltration but also the fear of being suspected of communism. It was a climate that made possible the rise of an extraordinary public figure, whose behavior at any other time might have been dismissed as preposterous.

McCarthyism

Joseph McCarthy was an undistinguished first-term Republican senator from Wisconsin when, in February 1950, he suddenly burst into national prominence. In the midst of a speech in Wheeling, West Virginia, he raised a sheet of paper and claimed to "hold in my hand" a list of 205 known communists currently working in the American State Department. No person of comparable stature had ever made so bold a charge against the federal government; and in the weeks to come, as McCarthy repeated and expanded on his accusations, he emerged as the nation's most prominent leader of the crusade against domestic subversion.

Within weeks of his charges against the State Department, McCarthy was leveling accusations at other agencies. After 1952, with the Republicans in control of the Senate and McCarthy the chairman of a special subcommittee, he conducted highly publicized investigations of subversion in many areas of the government. His unprincipled assistants, Roy Cohn and David Schine, sauntered arrogantly through federal offices and American embassies

MCCARTHYISM

When the American Civil Liberties Union warned in the early 1950s, at the peak of the anticommunist fervor that is now known as McCarthyism, that "the threat to civil liberties today is the most serious in the history of our country," it was expressing a view with which many Americans wholeheartedly agreed. But while almost everyone accepts that there were unusually powerful challenges to freedom of speech and association in the late 1940s and early 1950s, there is wide disagreement about the causes and meaning of those challenges.

The simplest argument—and one that continues to attract scholarly support—is that the postwar Red Scare expressed real and legitimate concerns about communist subversion in the United States. William O'Neill, in *A Better World* (1982), and Richard Gid Powers, in *Not Without Honor* (1995), have both argued that anticommunism was a serious, intelligent, and patriotic

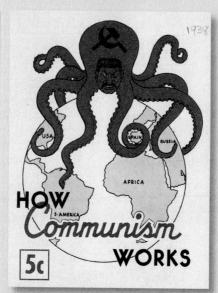

(Rare Book and Special Collections Division, Library of Congress)

movement, despite its excesses. The American Communist Party, according to this view, was an agent of Stalin and the Soviet Union within the United States, actively engaged in espionage and subversion. The effort to root communists out of public life was both understandable and justifiable—and the hysteria it sometimes produced was an unhappy but predictable by-product of an essentially rational and justifiable effort. "Anticommunism," Powers wrote, "expressed the essential American determination to stand against attacks on human freedom and foster the growth of democracy throughout the world.... To superimpose on this rich history the cartoon features of Joe McCarthy is to reject history for the easy comforts of moralism."

Most interpretations, however, have been much less charitable. In the 1950s, in the midst of the Red Scare itself, an influential group of historians and social scientists began to portray the anticommunist fervor of their time as an expression of deep social maladjustment—an argument perhaps most

---

overseas looking for evidence of communist influence. One hapless government official after another appeared before McCarthy's subcommittee, where the senator belligerently and often cruelly badgered witnesses and destroyed public careers. McCarthy never produced solid evidence that any federal employee had communist ties. But a growing constituency adored him nevertheless for his coarse, "fearless" assaults on a government establishment that many considered arrogant, effete, even traitorous. Republicans, in particular, rallied to his claims that the Democrats had been responsible for "twenty years of treason," that only a change of parties could rid the country of subversion. McCarthy, in short,

McCarthyism's Appeal

provided his followers with an issue into which they could channel a wide range of resentments: fear of communism, animosity toward the country's "eastern establishment," and frustrated partisan ambitions.

For a time, McCarthy intimidated all but a few people from opposing him. Even the highly popular Dwight D. Eisenhower, running for president in 1952, did not speak out against him, even though he disliked McCarthy's tactics and was outraged at, among other things, McCarthy's attacks on General George Marshall.

The Republican Revival

Public frustration over the stalemate in Korea and popular fears of internal subversion combined to make 1952 a bad year for the Democratic Party. Truman, whose own popularity had greatly diminished, wisely withdrew from the presidential contest. The party united instead behind Governor Adlai E. Stevenson of Illinois. Stevenson's dignity, wit, and eloquence made him a beloved figure to many liberals and intellectuals. But Republicans charged that Stevenson lacked the strength or the will to combat communism sufficiently. McCarthy described him as "soft" and took delight in deliberately confusing him with Alger Hiss.

Stevenson's greatest problem, however, was the Republican candidate opposing him. Rejecting the efforts of conservatives to nominate Robert Taft or Douglas MacArthur, the Republicans turned to a man who had no previous identification with the party: General Dwight D. Eisenhower, military hero, commander of NATO, president of Columbia University in New York, who won nomination on

Dwight Eisenhower

the first ballot. He chose as his running mate the young California senator who had gained national prominence closely associated with a famous essay by Richard Hofstadter, "The Paranoid Style in American Politics." There was, they argued, no logical connection between the modest power of actual communists in the United States and the hysterical form these scholars believed anticommunism was assuming. The explanation, therefore, had to lie in something other than reality, in a deeper set of social and cultural anxieties that had only an indirect connection with the political world as it existed. Extreme anticommunism, they claimed, was something close to a pathology; it expressed fear of and alienation from the modern world. A person afflicted with the "paranoid style," Hofstadter wrote:

> believes himself to be living in a world in which he is spied upon, plotted against, betrayed, and very likely destined for total ruin. He feels that his liberties have been arbitrarily and outrageously invaded. He is opposed to almost everything that has happened in American politics in the past twenty years.

Other scholars, writing not long after the decline of McCarthyism, rejected the sociocultural arguments of Hofstadter and others but shared the belief that the crusade against subversion was a distortion of normal public life. They saw the anticommunist crusade as an example of party politics run amok. Richard Freeland, in *The Truman Doctrine and the Origins of McCarthyism* (1971), argued that the Democrats began the effort to purge the government of radicals to protect themselves from attacks by the Republicans. Nelson Polsby, Robert Griffith, and others have noted how Republicans seized on the issue of communism in government in the late 1940s to reverse their nearly twenty-year exclusion from power. With each party trying to outdo the other in its effort to demonstrate its anticommunist credentials, it was hardly surprising that the crusade reached extraordinarily intense proportions.

Still other historians have emphasized the role of powerful government officials and agencies with a strong commitment to anticommunism—most notably J. Edgar Hoover and the FBI. Athan Theoharis and Kenneth O'Reilly introduced the idea of an anticommunist bureaucracy in work published in the 1970s and 1980s. Ellen Schrecker's *Many Are the Crimes* (1998) offers the fullest argument that the Red Scare was, at its heart, directed largely against communists (and not very often against people without any connection to the Communist Party) and that it was orchestrated by an interlocking cluster of official agencies with a deep commitment to the project.

Several scholars, finally, have presented an argument that does not so much challenge other interpretations as complement them. Anticommunist zealots were not alone to blame for the excesses of McCarthyism, they argue. It was also the fault of liberals—in politics, in academia, and perhaps above all in the media—who were so intimidated by the political climate, or so imprisoned within the conventions of their professions, that they found themselves unable to respond effectively to the distortions and excesses that they recognized around them.

through his crusade against Alger Hiss: Richard M. Nixon. Eisenhower and Nixon were a powerful combination in the autumn campaign. While Eisenhower attracted support through his geniality and his statesmanlike pledges to settle the Korean conflict (at one point dramatically promising to "go to Korea" himself), Nixon effectively exploited the issue of domestic subversion. After surviving early accusations of financial improprieties (which he effectively neutralized in a famous television address, the "Checkers speech"), Nixon went on to launch harsh attacks on Democratic "cowardice," "appeasement," and "treason."

Eisenhower won by both a popular and electoral landslide: 55 percent of the popular vote to Stevenson's 44 percent, 442 electoral votes to Stevenson's 89. Republicans gained control of both houses of Congress for only the second time in two decades. The election of 1952 ended twenty years of Democratic government. And while it might not have seemed so at the time, it also signaled the end of some of the worst turbulence of the postwar era.

CONCLUSION

Even during World War II itself, when the United States and the Soviet Union were allies, it was evident to leaders in both nations that America and Russia had quite different visions of what the postwar world should look like. Very quickly after the war ended, those differences became visible to almost everyone, and the once fruitful relationship between the world's two greatest powers quickly soured. Americans came to believe that the Soviet Union was an expansionist tyranny little different from Hitler's Germany, that Josef Stalin, the Soviet leader, was bent on world conquest. Soviets came to believe that the United States was trying to protect its own dominance in the world by encircling the Soviet Union and trying to limit its ability to operate as a great power. The result of these tensions was what became known by the end of the 1940s as the Cold War.

Actual conflicts in the early years of the Cold War were relatively few. Instead, the United States engaged in a series of policies designed to prevent both war and Soviet aggression. It helped rebuild the shattered nations of Western Europe with substantial economic aid, through the Marshall Plan, to stabilize those nations and prevent them from becoming communist. America announced a new foreign policy—known as containment—that committed it to an effort to keep the Soviet Union from expanding its influence further into the world. The United States and Western Europe formed a strong and enduring alliance, NATO, to defend Europe against possible Soviet advances.

In 1950, however, the armed forces of communist North Korea launched an invasion of the noncommunist South; and to most Americans—including, most importantly, President Truman—the conflict quickly came to be seen as a test of American resolve in the Cold War. The Korean War was long, costly, and unpopular, with many military setbacks and frustrations. In the end, however, the United States—working through the United Nations—managed to drive the North Koreans out of the south and stabilize the original division of the peninsula.

The Korean War had other effects on the domestic life of the United States. It hardened American foreign policy into a much more rigidly anticommunist form. It undermined the Truman administration, and the Democratic Party, and helped strengthen conservatives and Republicans. It greatly strengthened an already powerful crusade against communists, and those believed to be communists, within the United States—a crusade often known as McCarthyism, because of the notoriety of Senator Joseph McCarthy of Wisconsin, the most celebrated leader of the effort.

America after World War II was indisputably the wealthiest and most powerful nation in the world. But in the harsh climate of the Cold War, neither wealth nor power could obscure deep anxieties and bitter divisions.

INTERACTIVE LEARNING

The *Primary Source Investigator CD-ROM* offers the following materials related to this chapter:

- Interactive maps: **U.S. Elections** (M7) and **The Cold War** (M67).
- Documents, images, and maps related to the early years of the Cold War, the rise of McCarthyism, and the Korean War, including the Marshall Plan and the treaty that established NATO, as well as the charter for the establishment of the United Nations; a film clip of an early nuclear test and students practicing a "duck and cover" drill; and images from the Korean War.

Online Learning Center (www.mhhe.com/brinkley13e)

For quizzes, Internet resources, references to additional books and films, and more, consult this book's Online Learning Center.

FOR FURTHER REFERENCE

Several books by John Lewis Gaddis, *Strategies of Containment* (1982), *The United States and the Origins of the Cold War, 1941-1947* (1972), and *The Cold War: A New History* (2005), provide an introduction to Cold War history. Walter LaFeber, *America, Russia, and the Cold War, 1945-1967* (7th ed. 1993) is a classic survey of American-Soviet relations. Melvyn P. Leffler, *A Preponderance of Power: National Security, the Truman Administration, and the Cold War* (1992) is a superb, densely researched history of the policies of the 1940s, and his *For the Soul of Mankind: The United States, the Soviet Union, and the Cold War* (2008) is a reconsideration in light of the end of the Cold War. Warren I. Cohen, *The Cambridge History of American Foreign Relations, Vol. 4: America in the Age of Soviet Power, 1945-1991* (1991) is a good general history. Michael Hogan, *The Marshall Plan* (1987) is a provocative interpretation of one of the pillars of the early containment doctrine. Philip Taubman, *Secret Empire: Eisenhower, the CIA, and the Hidden Story of America's Space Espionage* (2002) provides an unusual window onto the impact of the Cold War on American intelligence efforts. David McCullough, *Truman* (1992) is an elegant popular biography, while Alonzo Hamby, M*an of the People: A Life of Harry S. Truman* (1995) is a fine scholarly one. Bruce Cumings, *The Origins of the Korean War* (1980) is an important study of the context for America's first armed conflict of the Cold War. Ellen Schrecker, *Many Are the Crimes: McCarthyism in America* (1998) is an important recent interpretation of McCarthyism, and David Oshinsky, *A Conspiracy So Immense: The World of Joe McCarthy* (1983) is a fine biography. Richard Fried, *Nightmare in Red* (1990) is a good, short overview of the Red Scare. Michael Ybarra, *Washington Gone Crazy: Senator Pat McCarran and the Great American Communist Hunt* (2004) is a study of another important figure in the Red Scare. Richard Pells, *The Liberal Mind in a Conservative Age: American Intellectuals in the 1940s and 1950s* (1985) is a valuable survey of postwar intellectual life.

The Spy in the Sky (1996) is a documentary film that tells the story of a team of engineers and pilots racing to design, perfect, and deploy the high-flying U2 spy plane in the 1950s. *Truman* (1997) is an excellent documentary about the 33rd president.

CHAPTER 28

THE AFFLUENT SOCIETY

SUBURBAN LIFE In the aftermath of World War II, suburban development experienced explosive growth—a result of the absence of housing construction during the war and the rapid population growth after it. This 1952 photograph, commissioned by *Life* magazine, shows a traffic jam of moving vans helping families settle in a new suburban development in Lakewood, California. (*J.R. Eyerman/Time Life Pictures/Getty Images*)

I F AMERICA WAS EXPERIENCING a golden age in the 1950s and early 1960s, as many Americans believed at the time and many continue to believe today, it was largely a result of two developments. One was a booming national prosperity, which profoundly altered the social, economic, and even physical landscape of the United States as well as the way many Americans thought about their lives and their world. The other was the continuing struggle against communism, a struggle that created considerable anxiety but that also encouraged some Americans to look even more approvingly at their own society.

The politics of the 1950s seemed in many ways to reflect the combination of self-satisfaction and anxiety that affluence and the Cold War had encouraged. Differences between the two major parties were muted, and voters crossed party lines in their affection for the man who led the nation through most of the fifties: Dwight D. Eisenhower, the former war hero who, as president, wanted nothing so much as to avoid conflict and create stability. There were, to be sure, many critics of American life in these years, but their influence was mostly limited to the margins of the nation's culture and did not significantly disturb the calm at the center.

In retrospect, many of these marginalized critics appear to have understood the state of American life far better than those who so confidently celebrated the national purpose, for there were serious social problems that most Americans failed to see. More than 30 million Americans (20 percent of the population) continued to live in poverty in the 1950s, according to some measurements. Significant minorities—most prominently the 10 percent of the American people

Affluence and Inequality

who were black, but also Latinos, Asians, Indians, gays and lesbians, and others—continued to suffer social, political, and economic discrimination. Many American women were beginning to chafe at the obstacles to their personal and professional growth. The very things that made America seem so successful in the 1950s also contributed, in the end, to bringing the nation's social problems more sharply into focus. Gunnar Myrdal, a Swedish sociologist who had spent years studying life in the United States, wrote in 1944: "American affluence is heavily mortgaged. America carries a tremendous burden of debt to its poor people." The efforts to pay that debt, and others, would ultimately help move the nation into the more turbulent era of the 1960s.

But even in the 1950s, the first signs of the changes to come could be seen. A growing number of young Americans began to express their disillusionment with what they saw as the shallowness and oppressiveness of their culture. Women moved into the work force in increasing numbers. The Supreme Court confronted some of the most profound injustices in American history, and at the same time African Americans became increasingly vocal and active in their criticism of racial injustice and inequality. The smooth surface of American public life could not always obscure a growing restlessness.

"THE ECONOMIC MIRACLE"

Among the most striking features of American society in the 1950s and early 1960s was a booming economic growth that made even the heady 1920s seem pale by comparison. It was a better balanced and more widely distributed prosperity than that of thirty years earlier, but it was not as universal as some Americans liked to believe.

Sources of Economic Growth

Between 1945 and 1960, the gross national product grew by 250 percent, from $200 billion to over $500 billion. Unemployment, which during the Depression had averaged between 15 and 25 percent, remained throughout the 1950s and early 1960s at about 5 percent or lower. Inflation, in the meantime, hovered around 3 percent a year or less.

The causes of this growth and stability were varied. Government spending, which had ended the Depression in the 1940s, continued to stimulate growth through public funding of schools, housing, veterans' benefits, welfare, the $100 billion interstate highway program, which began in 1956, and above all, military spending. Economic growth was at its peak (averaging 4.7 percent a year) during the first half of the 1950s, when military spending was highest because of the Korean War. In the late 1950s, with spending on armaments in decline, the annual rate of growth declined by more than half, to 2.25 percent.

The national birth rate reversed a long pattern of decline with the so-called baby boom, which had begun during the war and peaked in 1957. The nation's population rose almost 20 percent in the decade, from 150 million in 1950 to 179 million in 1960. The baby boom contributed to increased consumer demand and expanding economic growth.

The rapid expansion of suburbs—the suburban population grew 47 percent in the 1950s, more than twice as fast as the population as a whole—helped stimulate growth in several important sectors of the economy. The number of privately owned cars (essential for most suburban living) more than doubled in a decade, sparking a great boom in the automobile industry. Demand for new homes helped sustain a vigorous housing industry. The construction of roads and highways stimulated the economy as well.

Because of this unprecedented growth, the economy grew nearly ten times as fast as the population in the thirty years after the war. And while that growth was far from equally distributed, it affected most of society. The average American in 1960 had over 20 percent more purchasing power than in 1945, and more than twice as much as during the prosperous 1920s. By 1960, per capita income was over $1,800, $500 more than it had been in 1945. The American people had achieved the highest standard of living of any society in the history of the world.

Government Spending

Suburban Growth

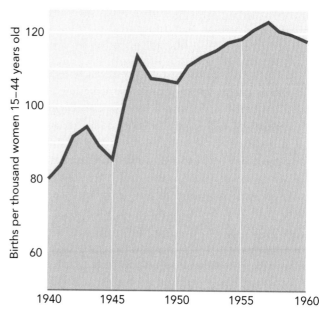

THE AMERICAN BIRTH RATE, 1940–1960   This chart shows how the American birth rate grew rapidly during and after World War II (after a long period of decline in the 1930s) to produce what became known as the "baby boom." At the peak of the baby boom, during the 1950s, the nation's population grew by 20 percent.   ◆ *What impact did the baby boom have on the nation's economy?*

The Rise of the Modern West

No region of the country experienced more dramatic changes as a result of the new economic growth than the American West. Its population expanded dramatically; its cities boomed; its industrial economy flourished. Before World War II, most of the West had been, economically at least, an appendage of the great industrial economy of the East—providing it with raw materials and agricultural goods. By the 1960s, some parts of the West were among the most important (and populous) industrial and cultural centers of the nation in their own right. As during World War II, much of the growth of the West was a result of federal spending and investment—on the dams, power stations, highways, and other infrastructure projects that made economic development possible; and on the military contracts that continued to flow disproportionately to factories in California and Texas, many of them built with government funds during the war. But other factors played a role as well. The enormous increase in automobile use after World War II—a result, among other things, of suburbanization and improved highway systems—gave a large stimulus to the petroleum industry and contributed to the rapid growth of oil fields in Texas and Colorado, and also to the metropolitan centers serving them: Houston, Dallas, and Denver. State governments in the West invested heavily in their universities. The University of Texas and University of California systems, in particular, became among the nation's largest and best; as centers of research, they helped attract technology-intensive industries to the region.

Climate also contributed. California, Nevada, and Arizona, in particular, attracted many
Favorable Climate
migrants from the East because of their warm, dry climates. The growth of Los Angeles after World War II was a particularly remarkable phenomenon. More than 10 percent of all new businesses in the United States between 1945 and 1950 began in Los Angeles. Its population rose by over 50 percent between 1940 and 1960.

The New Economics

The exciting (and to some, surprising) discovery of the power of the American economic system was a major cause of the confident tone of much American political life in the 1950s. During the Depression, politicians, intellectuals, and others had often questioned the viability of capitalism. In the 1950s, such doubt virtually vanished. Two features in particular made the postwar economy a source of national confidence.

First was the belief that Keynesian economics made it possible for government to regulate and stabilize the economy without intruding
Keynesian Economics
directly into the private sector. The British economist John Maynard Keynes had argued as early as the 1920s that by varying the flow of government spending and taxation (fiscal policy) and managing the supply of currency (monetary policy), the government could stimulate the economy to cure recession, and dampen growth to prevent inflation. The experience of the last years of the Depression and the first years of the war had seemed to confirm this argument. By the mid-1950s, Keynesian theory was rapidly becoming a fundamental article of faith—not only among professional economists but also among much of the public.

The "new economics," as its supporters came to call it, finally won official acceptance in 1963, when John Kennedy proposed a tax cut to stimulate economic growth. Although it took Kennedy's death and the political skills of Lyndon Johnson to win passage of the measure in 1964, the result seemed to confirm all that the Keynesians had predicted: an increase in private demand, which stimulated economic growth and reduced unemployment.

As the economy continued to expand far beyond what any observer had predicted was possible only a few years before, more and more Americans assumed that such growth was now without bounds. By the mid-1950s,
Ending Poverty Through Economic Growth
reformers concerned about poverty were arguing that the solution lay not in redistribution but in economic growth. The affluent would not have to sacrifice in order to eliminate poverty; the nation would simply have to produce more abundance, thus raising the quality of life of even the poorest citizens to a level of comfort and decency.

Capital and Labor

Over 4,000 corporate mergers took place in the 1950s; and more than ever before, a relatively small number of large-scale organizations controlled an enormous proportion of the nation's economic activity. This was particularly true in industries benefiting from government defense spending. As during World War II, the federal government tended to award mili-
Corporate Consolidation
tary contracts to large corporations. In 1959, for example, half of all defense contracts went to only twenty firms. By the end of the decade, half the net corporate income in the nation was going to only slightly more than 500 firms, or one-tenth of 1 percent of the total number of corporations.

A similar consolidation was occurring in the agricultural economy. As increasing mechanization reduced the need for farm labor, the agricultural work force declined by more than half in the two decades after the war. Mechanization also endangered one of the most cherished American institutions: the family farm. By the 1960s, relatively few individuals could any longer afford to buy and equip a modern farm, and much of the nation's most productive land had been purchased by financial institutions and corporations.

Corporations enjoying booming growth were reluctant to allow strikes to interfere with their operations. As a result, business leaders made important concessions to unions. As early as 1948, Walter Reuther, president of the United Automobile Workers, obtained a contract from General Motors that included a built-in "escalator clause"—an automatic cost-of-living increase pegged to the consumer price index. In 1955, Reuther received a guarantee from Ford Motor Company of continuing wages to auto workers even during layoffs. By the mid-1950s, factory wages in all industries had risen substantially, to an average of $80 per week.

By the early 1950s, large labor unions had developed a new kind of relationship with employers, a relationship sometimes known as the "post-war contract." Workers in steel,
The "Postwar Contract"
automobiles, and other large unionized industries were receiving generous increases in wages and benefits; in return, the unions tacitly agreed to refrain from raising other issues—issues involving control of the workplace and a voice for workers in the planning of production.

The economic successes of the 1950s helped pave the way for a reunification of the labor movement. In December 1955, the American Federation of Labor and the Congress of Industrial Organizations
AFL-CIO
ended their twenty-year rivalry and merged to create the AFL-CIO, under the leadership of George Meany. Relations between the leaders of the former AFL and the former CIO were not always comfortable. CIO leaders believed (correctly) that the AFL hierarchy was

dominating the relationship. AFL leaders were suspicious of what they considered the radical past of the CIO leadership. Even so, the union of the two great labor movements of the 1930s survived; and gradually tensions subsided.

Success bred corruption in some union bureaucracies. In 1957, the powerful Teamsters Union became the subject of a congressional investigation, and its president, David Beck, was charged with misappropriation of union funds. Beck ultimately stepped down to be replaced by Jimmy Hoffa, whom government investigators pursued for nearly a decade before finally winning a conviction against him (for tax evasion) in 1967. The United Mine Workers, the union that had spearheaded the industrial movement in the 1930s, similarly became tainted by suspicions of corruption and by violence. John L. Lewis's last years as head of the union were plagued with scandals and dissent within the organization. His successor, Tony Boyle, was ultimately convicted of complicity in the 1969 murder of the leader of a dissident faction within the union.

While the labor movement enjoyed significant success in winning better wages and benefits for workers already organized in strong unions, the majority of laborers who were as yet unorganized made fewer advances. Total union membership remained relatively stable throughout the 1950s, at about 16 million; and while this was in part a result of a shift in the work force from blue-collar to white-collar jobs, it was also a result of new obstacles to organization. The Taft-Hartley Act and the state right-to-work

Limited Gains for Unorganized Workers

laws that it spawned made the creation of new unions more difficult. The CIO launched a major organizing drive in the South shortly after World War II, targeting the poorly paid workers in textile mills in particular. But "Operation Dixie," as it was called, was a failure—as were most other organizing drives for at least thirty years after World War II.

THE EXPLOSION OF SCIENCE AND TECHNOLOGY

In 1961, *Time* magazine selected as its "man of the year" not a specific person but "the American Scientist." The choice was an indication of the widespread fascination with which Americans in the age of atomic weapons viewed science and technology. But it was also a sign of the remarkable, and remarkably rapid, scientific and technological advances in many areas during the postwar years.

Medical Breakthroughs

A particularly important advance in medical science was the development of new antibacterial drugs capable of fighting infections that in the past had been all but untreatable.

The development of antibiotics had its origins in the discoveries of Louis Pasteur and Jules-François Joubert. Working in France in the 1870s, they produced the first conclusive evidence that virulent bacterial infections could be defeated by other, more ordinary bacteria. Using their discoveries, the English physician Joseph Lister revealed the value of antiseptic solutions in preventing infection during surgery.

Antibiotics

But the practical use of antibacterial agents to combat disease did not begin until many decades later. In the 1930s, scientists in Germany, France, and England demonstrated the power of so-called sulfa drugs—drugs derived from an antibacterial agent known as sulfanilamide—which could be used effectively to treat streptococcal blood infections. New sulfa drugs were soon being developed at an astonishing rate, and were frequently improved, with dramatic results in treating what had once been a major cause of death.

In 1928, in the meantime, Alexander Fleming, an English medical researcher, accidentally discovered the antibacterial properties of an organism that he named penicillin. There was little progress in using penicillin to treat human illness, however, until a group of researchers at Oxford University, directed by Howard Florey and Ernest Chain, learned how to produce stable, potent penicillin in sizable enough quantities to make it a practical weapon against

Penicillin

bacterial disease. The first human trials of the new drug, in 1941, were dramatically successful, but progress toward the mass availability of penicillin was stalled in England because of World War II. American laboratories took the next crucial steps in developing methods for the mass

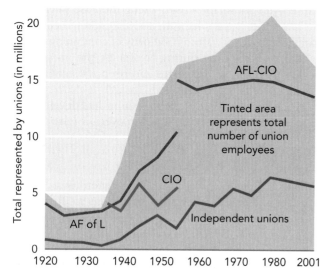

WORKERS REPRESENTED BY UNIONS, 1920–2001 This chart shows the number of workers represented by unions over an eighty-year period. Note the dramatic rise in the unionized work force during the 1930s and 1940s, the slower but still significant rise in the 1960s and 1970s, and the steady decline that began in the 1980s. The chart, in fact, understates the decline of unionized labor in the postwar era, since it shows union membership in absolute numbers and not as a percentage of the rapidly growing work force. ◆ *Why did unions cease recruiting new members successfully in the 1970s, and why did they begin actually losing members in the 1980s?*

production and commercial distribution of penicillin, which became widely available to doctors and hospitals around the world by 1948. Since then, a wide range of new antibiotics of highly specific character have been developed so that bacterial infections are now among the most successfully treated of all human illnesses.

There was also dramatic progress in immunization. The first great triumph was the development of the smallpox vaccine by the English researcher Edward Jenner in the late eighteenth century. A vaccine effective against typhoid was developed by an English bacteriologist, Almorth Wright, in 1897, and was in wide use by World War I. Vaccination against tetanus became widespread just before and during World War II. Medical scientists also developed a vaccine, BCG, against another major killer, tuberculosis, in the 1920s; but controversy over its safety stalled its adoption, especially in the United States, for many years. It was not widely used in the United States until after World War II, when it largely eliminated tuberculosis.

Viruses are much more difficult to prevent and treat than bacterial infections, and progress toward vaccines against viral infections—except for smallpox—was relatively slow. Not until the 1930s, when scientists discovered how to grow viruses in laboratories in tissue cultures, could researchers study them with any real effectiveness. Gradually, they discovered how to produce forms of a virus incapable of causing a disease but capable of triggering antibodies in vaccinated people that would protect them from contracting the disease. An effective vaccine against yellow fever was developed in the late 1930s, and one against influenza—one of the great killers of the first half of the twentieth century—appeared in 1945.

A particularly dramatic postwar triumph was the development of a vaccine against polio. In 1954, the American scientist Jonas Salk introduced an Salk Vaccine effective vaccine against the virus that had killed and crippled thousands of children and adults (among them Franklin Roosevelt). It was provided free to the public by the federal government beginning in 1955. After 1960, an oral vaccine developed by Albert Sabin—usually administered in a sugar cube—made widespread vaccination even easier. By the early 1960s, these vaccines had virtually eliminated polio from American life and much of the rest of the world.

As a result of these and many other medical advances, both infant mortality and the death rate among young children declined significantly in the first twenty-five years after the war (although not by as much as in Western Europe). Average life expectancy in that same period rose by five years, to seventy-one.

Pesticides

At the same time that medical researchers were finding cures for and vaccines against infectious diseases, other scientists were developing new kinds of chemical pesticides, which they hoped would protect crops from destruction by insects and protect humans from such insect-carried diseases DDT as typhus and malaria. The most famous of the new pesticides was dichlorodiphenyltrichloroethane, generally known as DDT, a compound discovered in 1939 by a Swiss chemist named Paul Muller. He had found that although DDT seemed harmless to human beings and other mammals, it was extremely toxic to insects. American scientists learned of Muller's discovery in 1942, just as the army was grappling with the insect-borne tropical diseases—especially malaria and typhus—that threatened American soldiers.

Under these circumstances, DDT seemed a godsend. It was first used on a large scale in Italy in 1943–1944 during a typhus outbreak, which it quickly helped end. Soon it was being sprayed in mosquito-infested areas of Pacific islands where American troops were fighting the Japanese. No soldiers suffered any apparent ill effects from the sprayings, and the incidence of malaria dropped precipitously. DDT quickly gained a reputation as a miraculous tool for controlling insects, and it undoubtedly saved thousands of lives. Only later did scientists recognize that DDT had long-term toxic effects on animals and humans.

Postwar Electronic Research

The 1940s and 1950s saw dramatic new developments in electronic technology. Researchers in the 1940s produced the first commercially viable televisions and created a technology that made it possible Invention of Television to broadcast programming over large areas. Later, in the late 1950s, scientists at RCA's David Sarnoff Laboratories in New Jersey developed the technology for color television, which first became widely available in the early 1960s.

In 1948 Bell Labs, the research arm of AT&T, produced the first transistor, a solid-state device capable of amplifying electrical signals, which was much smaller and more efficient than the cumbersome vacuum tubes that had powered most electronic equipment in the past. Transistors made possible the miniaturization of many devices (radios, televisions, audio equipment, hearing aids) and were also important in aviation, weaponry, and satellites. They contributed as well to another major breakthrough in electronics: the development of integrated circuitry in the late 1950s.

Integrated circuits combined a number of once-separate electronic elements (transistors, resistors, diodes, and others) and embedded them into a single, microscopically small device. They made it possible to create increasingly complex electronic devices requiring complicated circuitry that would have been impractical to produce through other means. Most of all, integrated circuits helped advance the development of the computer.

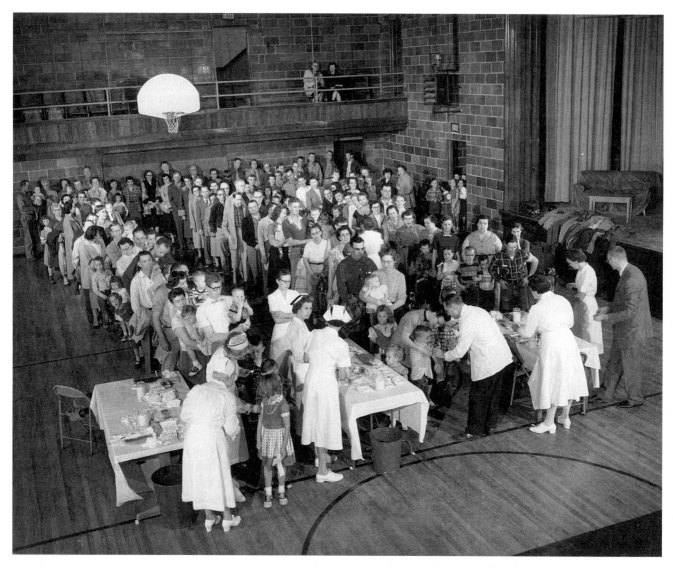

THE SALK VACCINE Dr. Jonas Salk, a medical researcher at the University of Pittsburgh, developed in the mid-1950s the first vaccine that proved effective in preventing polio. In its aftermath, scenes similar to this one—a mass inoculation of families in a school gymnasium in Kansas— repeated themselves all over the country. A few years later, Dr. Albert Sabin of the University of Cincinnati created a vaccine that could be administered more easily, through sugar cubes. *(March of Dimes Birth Defects Foundation)*

Postwar Computer Technology

Prior to the 1950s, computers had been constructed mainly to perform complicated mathematical tasks, such as those required to break military codes. In the 1950s, they began to perform commercial functions for the first time, as data-processing devices used by businesses and other organizations.

The first significant computer of the 1950s was the Universal Automatic Computer (or UNIVAC), which was developed initially for the U.S. Bureau of the Census by the Remington Rand Company. It was the first computer able to handle both alphabetical and numerical information easily. It used tape storage and could perform calculations and other functions much faster than its predecessor, the ENIAC, developed in 1946 by the same researchers

UNIVAC

at the University of Pennsylvania who were responsible for the UNIVAC. Searching for a larger market than the census for their very expensive new device, Remington Rand arranged to use a UNIVAC to predict the results of the 1952 election for CBS television news. It would, they believed, produce valuable publicity for the machine. Analyzing early voting results, the UNIVAC accurately predicted an enormous landslide victory for Eisenhower over Stevenson. Few Americans had ever heard of a computer before that night, and the UNIVAC's television debut became, therefore, a critical breakthrough in public awareness of computer technology.

Remington Rand had limited success in marketing the UNIVAC, but in the mid-1950s the International Business Machines Company (IBM) introduced its first major data-processing computers and began to find a wide market

THE DAWN OF THE COMPUTER AGE This massive computer, powered by tubes, was part of the first generation of mainframes developed after World War II. They served mostly government agencies and large corporations. By the 1990s, a small desktop computer could perform all the functions of this huge computer at much greater speed. *(Hagley Museum and Library)*

for them among businesses in the United States and abroad. These early successes, combined with the enormous amount of money IBM invested in research and development, made the company the worldwide leader in computers for many years.

Bombs, Rockets, and Missiles

In 1952, the United States successfully detonated the first hydrogen bomb. (The Soviet Union tested its first H-bomb a year later.) Unlike the plutonium and uranium bombs developed during World War II, the hydrogen bomb derives its power not from fission (the splitting of atoms) but from fusion (the joining of lighter atomic elements with heavier ones). It is capable of producing explosions of vastly greater power than the earlier, fission bombs.

The Hydrogen Bomb

The development of the hydrogen bomb gave considerable impetus to a stalled scientific project in both the United States and the Soviet Union—the effort to develop unmanned rockets and missiles capable of carrying the new weapons, which were not suitable for delivery by airplanes, to their targets. Both nations began to put tremendous resources into their development. The United States, in particular, benefited from the emigration to America of some of the German scientists who had helped develop rocketry for Germany during World War II.

In the United States, early missile research was conducted almost entirely by the Air Force, and there were significant early successes in developing rockets capable of traveling several hundred miles. But American and Soviet leaders were both struggling to build longer-range missiles that could cross oceans and continents—intercontinental

LAUNCHING A SATELLITE, 1961 Four years after the successful Russian launching of the satellite *Sputnik* in 1957 threw Americans into something close to a panic, a Thor-Able Star rocket takes off from Cape Canaveral, Florida, carrying an American satellite. The satellite contained a nuclear generator capable of providing it with continuous power for its radio transmitters. *(National Archives and Records Administration)*

ballistic missiles, or ICBMs, capable of traveling through space to distant targets. American scientists experimented in the 1950s with first the Atlas and then the Titan ICBM. There were some early successes, but there were also many setbacks, particularly because of the difficulty of massing sufficient, stable fuel to provide the tremendous power needed to launch missiles beyond the atmosphere. By 1958, scientists had created a solid fuel to replace the volatile liquid fuels of the early missiles; and they had also produced miniaturized guidance systems capable of ensuring that missiles could travel to reasonably precise destinations. Within a few years, a new generation of missile, known as the Minuteman, with a range of several thousand miles, became the basis of the American atomic weapons arsenal. American scientists also developed a nuclear missile capable of being carried and fired by submarines—the Polaris, which could launch from below the surface of the ocean by compressed air. A Polaris was first successfully fired from underwater in 1960.

The Space Program

The origins of the American space program can be traced most directly to a dramatic event in 1957, when the Soviet Union announced that it had launched an earth-orbiting satellite—*Sputnik*—into outer space. The United States had yet to perform any similar feats, and the American government (and much of American society) reacted to the announcement with alarm, as if the Soviet achievement was also a massive American failure. Federal policy began encouraging (and funding) strenuous efforts to improve scientific education in the schools, to create more research laboratories, and, above all, to speed the development of America's own exploration of outer space. The United States launched its first satellite, *Explorer I,* in January 1958.

The Shock of *Sputnik*

The centerpiece of space exploration, however, soon became the manned space program, established in 1958 through the creation of a new agency, the National Aeronautics and Space Administration (NASA), and through the selection of the first American space pilots, or "astronauts." They quickly became among the nation's most revered heroes. NASA's initial effort, the Mercury Project, was designed to launch manned vehicles into space to orbit the earth. On May 5, 1961, Alan Shepard became the first American launched into space. But his short, suborbital

APOLLO 11 Edwin ("Buzz") Aldrin is photographed by his fellow astronaut Neil Armstrong in August 1969, when they became the first humans ever to set foot on the surface of the moon. They traveled into orbit around the moon in the spaceship *Apollo 11,* and then traveled from the spaceship to the moon itself in a "lunar module," which they then used to return to the ship for the journey home. *(NASA)*

flight came several months after a Soviet "cosmonaut," Yuri Gagarin, had made a flight in which he had actually orbited the earth. On February 2, 1962, John Glenn (later a United States senator) became the first American to orbit the globe. NASA later introduced the Gemini program, whose spacecraft could carry two astronauts at once.

Mercury and Gemini were followed by the Apollo program, whose purpose was to land men on the moon. It had some catastrophic setbacks, most notably a fire in January 1967 that killed three astronauts. But on July 20, 1969, Neil Armstrong, Edwin Aldrin, and Michael Collins successfully traveled in a space capsule into orbit around the moon. Armstrong and Aldrin then detached a smaller craft from the capsule, landed on the surface of the moon, and became the first men to walk on a body other than earth. Six more lunar missions followed, the last in 1972. Not long after that, however, the government began to cut the funding for missions, and popular enthusiasm for the program began to wane.

The Apollo Program

The future of the manned space program did not lie primarily in efforts to reach distant planets, as originally envisioned. Instead, the program became a modest effort to make travel in near space easier and more practical through the development of the "space shuttle," an airplane-like device launched by a missile but capable of both navigating in space and landing on earth much like a conventional aircraft. The first space shuttle was successfully launched in 1982. The explosion of one shuttle, *Challenger,* in January 1986 shortly after takeoff, killing all seven astronauts, stalled the program for two years. Missions resumed in the late 1980s, driven in part by commercial purposes. The space shuttle launched and repaired communications satellites, and inserted the Hubble Space Telescope into orbit in 1990 (and later repaired its flawed lens). But problems continued to plague the program into the early twenty-first century.

The space program, like the military development of missiles, gave a tremendous boost to the American aeronautics industry and was responsible for the development of many technologies that proved valuable in other areas.

PEOPLE OF PLENTY

Among the most striking social developments of the postwar era was the rapid expansion of a middle-class lifestyle and outlook to large groups of the population previously insulated from it. The new prosperity of social groups that had previously lived on the margins; the growing availability of consumer products at affordable prices and the rising public fascination with such products; and the massive population movement from the cities to the suburbs—all helped make the American middle class a larger, more powerful, more homogeneous, and more dominant force than ever before.

The Consumer Culture

At the center of middle-class culture in the 1950s, as it had been for many decades before, was a growing absorption with consumer goods. That was a result of increased prosperity, of the increasing variety and availability of products, and of advertisers' adeptness in creating a demand for those products. It was also a result of the growth of consumer credit, which increased by 800 percent between 1945 and 1957 through the development of credit cards, revolving charge accounts, and easy-payment plans. Prosperity fueled the automobile industry, and Detroit responded to the boom with ever-flashier styling and accessories. Consumers also responded eagerly to the development of such new products as dishwashers,

garbage disposals, televisions, hi-fis, and stereos. To a large degree, the prosperity of the 1950s and 1960s was consumer driven (as opposed to investment driven).

Because consumer goods were so often marketed (and advertised) nationally, the 1950s were notable for the rapid spread of great national consumer crazes. For example, children, adolescents, and even some adults became entranced in the late 1950s with the hula hoop—a large plastic ring kept spinning around the waist. The popularity of the Walt Disney–produced children's television show *The Mickey Mouse Club* created a national demand for related products such as Mickey Mouse watches and hats. It also helped produce the stunning success of Disneyland, an amusement park near Los Angeles that re-created many of the characters and events of Disney entertainment programs.

The Landscape and the Automobile

The success of Disneyland depended largely on the ease of highway access from the dense urban areas around it, as well as the vast parking lots that surrounded the park. It was, in short, a symbol of the overwhelming influence of automobiles on American life and on the American

THE FIFTIES FAMILY This advertisement for a combination television and record player presents a popular image of the middle-class family of the 1950s—a professional father relaxing in front of the television with two well-dressed children, his glamorous wife serving drinks and presiding happily and benignly over the evening. Television marketing stressed the power of the new medium to bring families together for shared entertainment experiences. *(Gaslight Archives)*

INTERSTATES The interstate highway system changed the physical landscape of the United States. Its great, sprawling ribbons of concrete—such as this one on Long Island—sliced through cities, towns, and rural areas. But its biggest impact was in facilitating the movement of urban populations out of cities and into increasingly distant suburbs. *(Ewing Galloway)*

landscape in the postwar era. Between 1950 and 1980, the nation's population increased by 50 percent, but the numbers of automobiles owned by Americans increased by 400 percent.

The Federal Highway Act of 1956, which appropriated $25 billion for highway construction, was one of the most important alterations of the national landscape in modern history. Great ribbons of concrete—40,000 miles of them—spread across the nation, spanning rivers and valleys, traversing every state, and providing links to every major city (and between cities and their suburbs). These highways dramatically reduced the time necessary to travel from one place to another. They also made trucking a more economical way than railroads to transport goods to markets. They made travel by automobile and bus as fast as or faster than travel by passenger trains, resulting in the long, steady decline of railroads.

Interstate Highways

Highways also encouraged the movement of economic activities—manufacturing in particular—out of cities and into suburban and rural areas where land was cheaper. The decline of many traditional downtowns followed. So did the growth of what eventually became known as "edge cities" and other new centers of industry and commerce outside traditional city centers.

The proliferation of automobiles and the spread of highways also made it easier for families to move into homes that were significant distances from where they worked. This enabled many people to live in larger houses with larger lots than they could have afforded previously.

Garages began to be built onto houses in great numbers after World War II, and such suburban amenities as swing sets, barbecues, and private swimming pools became more common as backyards became more the norm. The shift of travel from train to automobile helped spawn a tremendous proliferation of motels—26,000 by 1948, 60,000 by 1960, well over 100,000 by 1970. The first Holiday Inn (launching what would soon become the largest motel chain in America) opened along a highway connecting Memphis and Nashville, Tennessee, in 1952. Drive-in theaters—a distinctively American phenomenon that had begun to appear in the 1930s—spread rapidly after the war. There were 4,000 drive-ins by 1958.

The automobile also transformed the landscape of retailing. It encouraged the creation of fast-food chains, many of which began with drive-in restaurants, where customers could be served and eat in their cars. The first drive-in restaurant (Royce Hailey's Pig Stand) opened in Dallas in 1921, followed later in the decade by White Tower, the first fast-food company to create franchises. Ray Kroc's McDonald's opened its first outlets in Des Plaines, Illinois, and southern California in 1955. Five years later, there were 228 McDonald's outlets; and over the decades that followed, McDonald's franchises spread throughout the nation and abroad—making the "golden arches" the most recognizable symbol of food in the world. Large supermarket chains—catering to customers with automobiles—replaced smaller, family-owned markets in town centers. Large shopping centers and malls moved

Fast Food

the center of retailing out of cities and into widely separate complexes surrounded by large parking lots.

The Suburban Nation

By 1960, a third of the nation's population was living in suburbs. Suburbanization was partly a result of important innovations in home-building, which made single-family houses affordable to millions of people. The most famous of the postwar suburban developers, William Levitt, made use of mass-production techniques to construct a large housing development on Long Island, near New York City. This first "Levittown" (there would later be others in New Jersey and Pennsylvania) consisted of several thousand two-bedroom Cape Cod–style houses, with identical interiors and only slightly varied facades, each perched on its own concrete slab (to eliminate excavation costs), facing curving, treeless streets. Levittown houses sold for under $10,000, and they helped meet an enormous and growing demand for housing. Young couples—often newly married war veterans eager to start a family, assisted by low-cost, government-subsidized mortgages provided by the GI Bill (see p. 765)—rushed to purchase the inexpensive homes, not only in the Levittowns but in similar developments that soon began appearing throughout the country.

"Levittown"

Why did so many Americans want to move to the suburbs? One reason was the enormous importance postwar Americans placed on family life after five years of disruptive war. Suburbs provided families with larger homes than they could find (or afford) in the cities. Many people were attracted by the idea of living in a community populated largely by people of similar age and background and found it easier to form friendships and social circles there than in the city. Women in particular often valued the presence of other nonworking mothers living nearby to share the tasks of child raising. Another factor motivating white Americans to move to the suburbs was race. There were some African-American suburbs, but most suburbs were restricted to whites—both because relatively few blacks could afford to live in them and because formal and informal barriers kept

AN EARLY McDONALD'S   The new automobile-centered landscape of postwar America transformed many patterns of life, including eating, as this early McDonald's in Des Plaines, Illinois, suggests. Ray Kroc bought the company in 1955 from the McDonald brothers, who had founded it several years earlier, and expanded it to create fast, convenient restaurants for people moving from place to place by automobile. (The early competition was the older drive-ins.) Today, McDonald's operates restaurants in most countries in the world, many of them in cities. But it remains a fixture of American car culture as well.   *(Hulton Archive/Getty Images)*

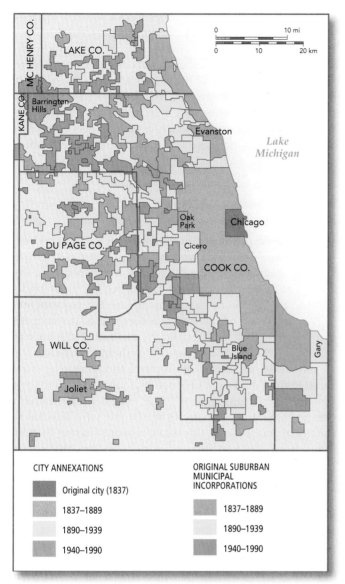

CITY ANNEXATIONS

Original city (1837)

1837–1889

1890–1939

1940–1990

ORIGINAL SUBURBAN MUNICIPAL INCORPORATIONS

1837–1889

1890–1939

1940–1990

CHICAGO'S ANNEXATIONS AND THE SUBURBAN NOOSE This map uses Chicago as an example of two important processes in the growth of American cities—municipal consolidation and suburbanization. In 1837, Chicago consisted of a small area on the shore of Lake Michigan (represented by the small dark orange area on the right center of the map. Over the next fifty years, Chicago annexed an enormous amount of additional land around its original borders, followed by a few smaller annexations in the twentieth century. At the same time, however, many of the areas around Chicago were separating themselves from the city by incorporating as independent communities—suburbs—with a particular wave of such incorporations in the first decades of the twentieth century, continuing into the 1990s. A map of New York, and of many other cities, would reveal a similar pattern. ◆ *What were the consequences for the city of its legal and financial separation from so many suburban communities?*

out even prosperous African Americans. In an era when the black population of most cities was rapidly growing, many white families fled to the suburbs to escape the integration of urban neighborhoods and schools.

Suburban neighborhoods had many things in common with one another. But they were not uniform. A famous study of one Levittown revealed a striking variety of occupations, ethnic backgrounds, and incomes there. Still, the Levittowns and inexpensive developments like them ultimately became the homes of mainly lower-middle-class people one step removed from the inner city. Other, more affluent suburbs became enclaves of wealthy families. In virtually every city, a clear hierarchy emerged of upper-class suburban neighborhoods and more modest ones, just as such gradations had emerged years earlier among urban neighborhoods.

The Suburban Family

For professional men (many of whom worked in the city, at some distance from their homes), suburban life generally meant a rigid division between their working and personal worlds. For many middle-class, married women, it meant increased isolation from the workplace. The enormous cultural emphasis on family life in the 1950s strengthened popular prejudices against women entering the professions, or occupying any paid job at all. Many middle-class husbands considered it demeaning for their wives to be employed. And many women themselves shied away from the workplace when they could afford to, in part because of prevailing ideas about motherhood that seemed to require women to stay at home full-time with their children.

Prevailing Gender Roles Reinforced

One of the most influential books in postwar American life was a famous guide to child rearing: Dr. Benjamin Spock's *Baby and Child Care,* first published in 1946 and reissued (and revised) repeatedly for decades thereafter. Dr. Spock's approach to raising babies was child-centered, as opposed to parent-centered. The purpose of motherhood, he taught, was to help children learn and grow and realize their potential. All other considerations, including the mother's own physical and emotional requirements, should be subordinated to the needs of the child. Dr. Spock at first envisioned only a very modest role for fathers in the process of child rearing, although he changed his views on this (and on many other issues) over time.

Dr. Benjamin Spock

Women who could afford not to work faced heavy pressures to remain in the home and concentrate on raising their children. But as expectations of material comfort rose, many middle-class families needed a second income to maintain the standard of living they desired. As a result, the number of married women working outside the home actually increased in the postwar years—even as the social pressure for them to stay out of the workplace grew. By 1960, nearly a third of all married women were part of the paid work force.

The Birth of Television

Television, perhaps the most powerful medium of mass communication in history, was central to the culture of the postwar era. Experiments in broadcasting pictures (along with sound) had begun as early as the 1920s, but commercial television began only shortly after World War II. Its growth was phenomenally rapid. In 1946, there were only 17,000 sets in the country; by 1957, there were 40 million television sets in use—almost as many sets as there were families. More people had television sets, according to one report, than had refrigerators.

The television industry emerged directly out of the radio industry, and all three of the major networks—the National Broadcasting Company, the Columbia Broadcasting System, and the American Broadcasting Company—had started as radio companies. Like radio, the television business was driven by advertising. The need to attract advertisers determined most programming decisions; and in the early days of television, sponsors often played a direct, powerful, and continuing role in determining the content of the programs they chose to sponsor. Many early television shows bore the names of the corporations that were paying for them: the GE Television Theater, the Chrysler Playhouse, the Camel News Caravan, and others. Some daytime serials were actually written and produced by Procter & Gamble and other companies.

The impact of television on American life was rapid, pervasive, and profound. By the late 1950s, television news had replaced newspapers, magazines, and radios as the nation's most important vehicle of information. Television advertising helped create a vast market for new fashions and products. Televised athletic events gradually made professional and college sports one of the most important sources of entertainment (and one of the biggest businesses) in America. Television entertainment programming—almost all of it controlled by the three national networks and their corporate sponsors—replaced movies and radio as the principal source of diversion for American families.

Much of the programming of the 1950s and early 1960s created a common image of American life—an image that was predominantly white, middle-class, and suburban, and that was epitomized by such popular situation comedies as *Ozzie and Harriet* and *Leave It to Beaver*. Programming also reinforced the concept of gender roles that most men (and many women) unthinkingly embraced. Most situation comedies, in particular, showed families in which, as the title of one of the most popular put it, *Father Knows Best,* and in which most women were mothers and housewives striving to serve their children and please their husbands. But television also conveyed other images: gritty, urban, working-class families in Jackie Gleason's *The Honeymooners;* the childless show-business family of the early *I Love Lucy;* unmarried professional women in *Our Miss Brooks* and *My Little Margie;* hapless African Americans in *Amos 'n' Andy.* Television not only sought to create an idealized image of a homogeneous suburban America. It

Social Consequences of Television

Television's Homogenizing Message

also sought to convey experiences at odds with that image—but to convey them in warm, unthreatening terms.

Yet television also, inadvertently, created conditions that could accentuate social conflict. Even those unable to share in the affluence of the era could, through television, acquire a vivid picture of how the rest of their society lived. Thus at the same time that television was reinforcing the homogeneity of the white middle class, it was also contributing to the sense of alienation and powerlessness among groups excluded from the world it portrayed.

Travel, Outdoor Recreation, and Environmentalism

The idea of a paid vacation for American workers, and the association of that idea with travel, had entered American culture beginning in the 1920s. But it was not until the postwar years that vacation travel became truly widespread among middle-income Americans. The construction of the interstate highway system contributed dramatically to the growth of travel. So did the increasing affluence of workers, which made it possible for them to buy cars.

Nowhere was this surge in travel and recreation more visible than in the nation's national parks, which experienced the beginnings of what became a permanent surge in attendance in the 1950s. People who traveled to national parks did so for many reasons—some to hike and camp; some to fish and hunt (activities that themselves grew dramatically in the 1950s and spawned a large number of clubs); some simply to look in awe at the landscape. But whatever their motives, most visitors to national parks came in search less of conventional recreation than of wilderness. The importance of that search became clear in the early 1950s in the first of many battles over development of wilderness areas: the fight to preserve Echo Park.

Echo Park

Echo Park is a spectacular valley in the Dinosaur National Monument, on the border between Utah and Colorado, near the southern border of Wyoming. In the early 1950s, the federal government's Bureau of Reclamation—which had been created early in the century to encourage irrigation, develop electric power, and increase water supplies—proposed building a dam across the Green River, which runs through Echo Valley, so as to create a lake for recreation and a source of hydroelectric power. The American environmental movement had been relatively quiet since its searing defeat early in the century in its effort to stop a similar dam in the Hetch Hetchy Valley at Yosemite National Park (see p. 590). But the Echo Park proposal helped rouse it from its slumber.

In 1950, Bernard DeVoto—a well-known writer and a great champion of the American West—published an essay in *The Saturday Evening Post* titled "Shall We Let Them Ruin Our National Parks?" It had a sensational impact, arousing opposition to the Echo Valley dam from many areas of the country. The Sierra Club, relatively quiet in previous decades, moved into action; the controversy

Sierra Club Reborn

helped elevate a new and aggressive leader, David Brower, who eventually transformed the club into the nation's leading environmental organization. By the mid-1950s, a large coalition of environmentalists, naturalists, and wilderness vacationers had been mobilized in opposition to the dam, and in 1956 Congress—bowing to the public pressure— blocked the project and preserved Echo Park in its natural state. The controversy was a major victory for those who wished to preserve the sanctity of the national parks, and it was an important impetus to the dawning environmental consciousness that would become so important a decade and more later.

Organized Society and Its Detractors

White-collar workers came to outnumber blue-collar laborers for the first time in the 1950s, and an increasing proportion of them worked in corporate settings with rigid hierarchical structures. Industrial workers also confronted large bureaucracies, both in the workplace and in their own unions. Consumers discovered the frustrations of bureaucracy in dealing with the large national companies from whom they bought goods and services. More and more Americans were becoming convinced that the key to a successful future lay in acquiring the specialized training and skills necessary for work in large organizations.

The American educational system responded to the demands of this increasingly organized society by experimenting with changes in curriculum and philosophy. Elementary and secondary schools gave increased attention to the teaching of science, mathematics, and foreign lan-

Growth of Specialized Education

guages (particularly after the launching of the Soviet Union's *Sputnik*)—all of which educators considered important for the development of skilled, specialized professionals. Universities in the meantime were expanding their curricula to provide more opportunities for students to develop specialized skills. The idea of the "multiversity"—a phrase first coined by the chancellor of the University of California at Berkeley to describe his institution's diversity—represented a commitment to making higher education a training ground for specialists in a wide variety of fields.

The debilitating impact of bureaucratic life on the individual slowly became a central theme of popular and scholarly debate. William H. Whyte Jr. produced one of the most widely discussed books of the decade: *The Organization Man* (1956), which attempted to describe the special mentality of the worker in a large, bureaucratic setting. Self-reliance, Whyte claimed, was losing place to the ability to "get along" and "work as a team" as the most valued trait

in the modern character. Sociologist David Riesman had made similar observations in *The Lonely Crowd* (1950), in which he argued that the traditional "inner-directed" man, who judged himself on the basis of his own values and the esteem of his family, was giving way to a new "other-directed" man, more concerned with winning the approval of the larger organization or community.

Novelists, too, expressed misgivings in their work about the enormity and impersonality of modern society. Saul Bellow produced a series of novels—*The Adventures of Augie March* (1953), *Seize the Day* (1956), *Herzog* (1964), and many others—that chronicled the difficulties American Jewish men had in finding fulfillment in modern urban America. J. D. Salinger wrote in *The Catcher in the Rye* (1951) of a prep-school student, Holden Caulfield, who was unable to find any area of society—school, family, friends, city—in which he could feel secure or committed.

The Beats and the Restless Culture of Youth

The most caustic critics of bureaucracy, and of middle-class society in general, were a group of young poets, writers, and artists generally known as the "beats" (or, derisively, as "beatniks"). They wrote

The Beat Generation's Critiques

harsh critiques of what they considered the sterility and conformity of American life, the meaninglessness of American politics, and the banality of popular culture. Allen Ginsberg's dark, bitter poem "Howl" (1955) decried the "Robot apartments! invincible suburbs! skeleton treasuries! blind capitals! demonic industries!" of modern life. Jack Kerouac produced what may have been the bible of the Beat Generation in his novel *On the Road* (1957)—an account of a cross-country automobile trip that depicted the rootless, iconoclastic lifestyle of Kerouac and his friends.

The beats were the most visible evidence of a widespread restlessness among young Americans in the 1950s. In part, that restlessness was a result of prosperity itself— of a growing sense among young people of limitless possibilities, and of the declining power of such traditional values as thrift, discipline, and self-restraint. Young middle-class Americans were growing up in a culture that encouraged them to expect wholly fulfilling lives; but of course they were living in a world in which almost all of them experienced obstacles to complete fulfillment. Yet, youth in the 1950s never staged rebellions as widespread or as bitter as those of the 1960s.

Tremendous public attention was directed at the phenomenon of "juvenile delinquency," and in both politics and popular culture there were dire warnings about the growing criminality of American youth. The 1955 film *Blackboard Jungle*, for example, was a frightening depiction of crime and violence in city schools. Scholarly studies, presidential commissions, and journalistic exposés all contributed to the sense of alarm about the spread of

LUCY AND DESI

The most popular show in the history of television began as an effort by a young comedian to strengthen a difficult marriage. In 1950, 38-year-old Lucille Ball—whose fifteen-year movie career had never quite launched her to stardom—was performing in a popular weekly CBS radio comedy, *My Favorite Husband,* in which she portrayed a slightly zany housewife who tangled frequently with her banker husband, played by Richard Denning. The network proposed to transfer the show from radio to television. Lucy said she would do so only if she could replace

VITAMEATAVEGAMIN   One of the most popular episodes of *I Love Lucy* portrays Lucy at a trade show promoting a new health product called "Vitameatavegamin." In the course of the show, she herself drinks a great deal of the concoction, which has a high alcohol content and leaves her hilariously drunk. *(Photofest)*

LUCY AT HOME   Although Lucy and Desi at first portrayed a childless, ethnically mixed couple living in a Manhattan apartment, many of the comic situations in the early years of the show were purely domestic. Here, Lucy, wearing an apron, deals with one of her many household predicaments with the extraordinary physical comedy that was part of her great success. Desi, watching skeptically, was a talented straight man to Lucy's zaniness. *(Photofest)*

Denning with her real-life husband of ten years, Desi Arnaz—a celebrated, Cuban-born bandleader whose almost constant traveling was putting a strain on their marriage. Network officials tried in vain to talk her out of the idea. Arnaz had no acting experience, they told her. Lucy herself recognized another reason for their reluctance: the radicalism of portraying an ethnically mixed marriage on the air. Her radio show, she later said, had "firmly established my type of man . . . as a nice gent from Minneapolis . . . a typical Midwestern American . . . not—great heavens—Desi Arnaz from Cuba." But she held her ground.

On Monday, October 15, 1951, in the 9 P.M. time slot that Lucille Ball would dominate for years, the first episode of *I Love Lucy* was broadcast over CBS. Desi Arnaz played Ricky Ricardo, a Cuban bandleader and singer who spoke, at times, with a comically exaggerated Latin accent. Lucille Ball was Lucy Ricardo, his stage-struck and slightly dizzy wife. Performing with them were William

delinquency—although in fact youth crime did not dramatically increase in the 1950s.

Many young people began to wear clothes and adopt hairstyles that mimicked popular images of juvenile criminal gangs. The culture of alienation that the beats so vividly represented had counterparts even in ordinary middle-class behavior: teenage rebelliousness toward parents, youthful fascination with fast cars and motorcy-

cles, and the increasing visibility of teenage sex, assisted by the greater availability of birth-control devices. The popularity of James Dean, in such movies as *Rebel Without a Cause* (1955), *East of Eden* (1955), and *Giant* (1956), conveyed a powerful image of youth culture in the 1950s. Both in the roles he played (moody, alienated teenagers and young men with a streak of self-destructive violence) and in the way he lived his own life (he died

Frawley and Vivian Vance, who played their neighbors and close friends, Fred and Ethel Mertz. In the premiere episode, "The Girls Want to Go to a Nightclub," Ricky and Fred want to go to a boxing match on the night of Fred and Ethel's anniversary, while the wives are arranging an evening at a nightclub. The men and women battle each other ridiculously, but no one really wins.

The opening episode contained many of the elements that characterized the show throughout its long run and ensured its extraordinary success: the remarkable chemistry among the four principal actors, the unexpected comedic talent of Desi Arnaz, and most of all the brilliance of Lucille Ball—who proved herself one of the great comic actors of her time. She was a master of physical comedy, and many of her funniest moments involved scenes of absurdly incongruous situations (Lucy working an assembly line, Lucy stomping grapes in Italy). She had a remarkably variable voice, and her characteristic yowl of frustration became one of the most familiar sounds in American culture. She was a beautiful woman, but she never hesitated to make herself look ridiculous. "She was everywoman," her longtime writer Jess Oppenheim once wrote; "her little expressions and inflections stimulated the shock of recognition in the audience."

But it was not just the great talents of its cast that made *I Love Lucy* such a phenomenon. It was the skill of its writers in evoking some of the most common experiences and desires of television viewers in the 1950s. The wives demanded more attention from their husbands and more glamour in their lives. Lucy, in particular, mined the frustrations of domestic life for all

PROMOTING THE SHOW   The marriage of Lucille Ball and Desi Arnaz, which paralleled the television marriage of Lucy and Ricky Ricardo, was one of the most effective promotional devices for *I Love Lucy*. Here, Lucy and Desi pose for a promotional still— one of many they made for advertisements, magazine covers, and posters until their marriage (and the show) dissolved in 1960. *(Photofest)*

they were worth, constantly engaging in zany and hilarious schemes to break into show business or somehow expand her world. The level-headed husbands wanted calm and conventional domestic lives—and time to themselves for conspicuously male activities: boxing, fishing, baseball. In the first seasons, the fictional couples lived as neighbors, without children, in a Manhattan apartment building. Later, like so many of the show's viewers, Lucy had a child and they all moved to the suburbs. (The show used Lucy's real-life pregnancy on the air; and on January 19, 1953—only hours after Lucille Ball

gave birth to her real son and second child—CBS aired a previously filmed episode of the fictional Lucy giving birth to a fictional son, "Little Ricky" Ricardo, before one of the largest audiences in television history. "Little Ricky" became a continuing character in the show.)

I Love Lucy (and its successor, *The Lucille Ball–Desi Arnaz Comedy Hour*) was the most-watched show on television from its first weeks in 1951 until the final episode in 1960. Organizations rescheduled meetings, politicians postponed speeches, taxi drivers and other workers changed their shifts to avoid competing with Lucy. The great Marshall Field department store in Chicago posted a sign in its window stating: "We love Lucy, too, so we're closing on Monday nights." During a typical broadcast, up to two-thirds of the televisions in America were tuned to Lucy.

Lucille Ball remained a major television star for nearly twenty years after *I Love Lucy* left the air. She died in 1989. Desi Arnaz, whom Lucy divorced in 1960, remained for a time one of Hollywood's most powerful and successful studio executives as the head of Desilu Productions. And nearly sixty years after the first episode of *I Love Lucy* aired, the series remains extraordinarily popular all over the world— shown so frequently in reruns that in some American cities it is sometimes possible to see six Lucy episodes in a single evening. "People identified with the Ricardos," Lucille Ball once said, "because we had the same problems they had. We just took ordinary situations and exaggerated them." In the process, *I Love Lucy* revealed many of the dilemmas of 1950s domestic life and established the pattern for the long and popular history of television situation comedies.

in 1955, at the age of 24, in a car accident), Dean became an icon of the unfocused rebelliousness of American youth in his time.

Rock 'n' Roll

One of the most powerful signs of the restiveness of American youth was the enormous popularity of rock 'n' roll—and of the greatest early rock star, Elvis Presley. Pres-

ley became a symbol of a youthful determination to push at the borders of the conventional and acceptable. His sultry good looks; his self-conscious effort to dress in the vaguely rebellious style of urban gangs (motorcycle jackets and slicked-back hair, even though Presley himself was a product of the rural South); and most of all, the open sexuality of his music and his public performances

Elvis Presley

made him wildly popular among young Americans in the 1950s. His first great hit, "Heartbreak Hotel," established him as a national phenomenon in 1956, and he remained a powerful figure in American popular culture until—and indeed beyond—his death in 1977.

Presley's music, like that of most early white rock musicians, drew heavily from black rhythm and blues traditions, which appealed to some white youths in the early 1950s because of their pulsing, sensual rhythms and their hard-edged lyrics. Sam Phillips, a local record promoter who had recorded some of the important black rhythm and blues musicians of his time (among them B. B. King), reportedly said in the early 1950s: "If I could find a white man with a Negro sound, I could make

Rock 'n' Roll's Black Roots

a billion dollars." Soon after that, he found Presley. But there were others as well, among them Buddy Holly and Bill Haley (whose 1955 song "Rock Around the Clock"—used in the film *Blackboard Jungle*—served to announce the arrival of rock 'n' roll to millions of young people), who were closely connected to African-American musical traditions. Rock drew from other sources too: from country western music (another strong influence on Presley), from gospel music, even from jazz. But its most important influence was its roots in rhythm and blues.

The rise of such white rock musicians as Presley was a result in part of the limited willingness of white audiences to accept black musicians. But the 1950s did see a growth in the popularity of African-American bands and singers among both black and white audiences. Chuck

AMERICAN BANDSTAND One of the most popular television programs among young people in the 1950s (and into the 1960s) was *American Bandstand*, which combined the new popularity of television with the new popularity of rock 'n' roll. Dick Clark, the engaging host of the show, shown here holding a microphone and sitting among members of his audience, became one of the best-known promoters of rock music in America. *(Hulton/Archive/Getty Images)*

Berry, Little Richard, B. B. King, Chubby Checker, the Temptations, and others—many of them recorded by the black producer Berry Gordy, the founder and president of Motown Records in Detroit—never rivaled Presley in their popularity among white youths. But they did develop a significant multiracial audience of their own.

The rapid rise and enormous popularity of rock owed a great deal to innovations in radio and television programming. By the 1950s, radio stations no longer felt obliged to present mostly live programming. Instead, many radio stations devoted themselves almost entirely to playing recorded music. Early in the 1950s, a new breed of radio announcers, known now as "disk jockeys," began to create programming aimed specifically at young fans of rock music; and when those programs became wildly successful, other stations followed suit. *American Bandstand,* a televised showcase for rock 'n' roll hits that began in 1957, featured a live audience dancing to recorded music. The show helped spread the popularity of rock—and made its host, Dick Clark, one of the best-known figures in America among young Americans.

Radio and television were important to the recording industry, of course, because they encouraged the sale of records, which was increasing rapidly in the mid- and late 1950s, especially in the inexpensive and popular 45 rpm format—small disks that contained one song on each side. Also important were jukeboxes, which played individual songs on 45s and proliferated in soda fountains, diners, bars, and other places where young people were likely to congregate. Sales of records increased threefold—from $182 million to $521 million— | "Payola" Scandals | between 1954 and 1960. The popularity of rock music was the driving force behind that increase. So eager were record promoters to get their songs on the air that they routinely made secret payments to station owners and disk jockeys to encourage them to showcase their artists. These payments, which became known as "payola," produced a briefly sensational series of scandals when they were exposed in the late 1950s and early 1960s.

THE "OTHER AMERICA"

It was relatively easy for white, middle-class Americans in the 1950s to believe that the world they knew—a world of economic growth, personal affluence, and cultural homogeneity—was the world virtually all Americans knew; that the values and assumptions they shared were ones that most other Americans shared too. But such assumptions were false. Even within the middle class, there was considerable restiveness—among women, intellectuals, young people, and others who found the middle-class consumer culture somehow unsatisfying, even stultifying. More importantly, large groups of Americans remained outside the circle of abundance and shared in neither the affluence of the middle class nor its values.

On the Margins of the Affluent Society

In 1962, the socialist writer Michael Harrington created a sensation by publishing a book called *The Other America,* in | The Other America | which he chronicled the continuing existence of poverty in America. The conditions he described were not new. Only the attention he was bringing to them was.

The great economic expansion of the postwar years reduced poverty dramatically but did not eliminate it. In 1960, at any given moment, more than a fifth of all American families (over 30 million people) continued to live below what the government defined as the poverty line (down from a third of all families fifteen years before). Many millions more lived just above the official poverty line, but with incomes that gave them little comfort and no security.

Most of the poor experienced poverty intermittently and temporarily. Eighty percent of those classified as poor at any particular moment were likely to have moved into poverty relatively recently and might move out of it again as soon as they found a job—an indication of how unstable employment could be at the lower levels of the job market. But approximately 20 percent of the poor were people for whom poverty was a continuous, debilitating reality, | Persistent Poverty | from which there was no easy escape. That included approximately half the nation's elderly and a large proportion of African Americans and Hispanics. Native Americans constituted the single poorest group in the country, a result of government policies that undermined the economies of the reservations and drove many Indians into cities, where some lived in a poverty worse than that they had left. These were the people Harrington had written about in *The Other America,* people who suffered from what he called "a system designed to be impervious to hope."

This "hard-core" poverty rebuked the assumptions of those who argued that economic growth would eventually lead everyone into prosperity; that, as many claimed, "a rising tide lifts all boats." It was a poverty that the growing prosperity of the postwar era seemed to affect hardly at all.

Rural Poverty

Among those on the margins of the affluent society were many rural Americans. In 1948, farmers had received 8.9 percent of the national income; in 1956, they received only 4.1 percent. In part, this decline reflected the steadily shrinking farm population; in 1956 alone, nearly 10 percent of the rural population moved into or was absorbed by cities. But it also reflected declining farm prices. Because of enormous surpluses in basic staples, prices fell 33 percent in those years, even | Declining Agricultural Prices |

though national income as a whole rose 50 percent at the same time. Even most farmers who managed to survive experienced substantial losses of income at the same time that the prices of many consumer goods rose.

Not all farmers were poor. Some substantial landowners weathered, and even managed to profit from, the changes in American agriculture. Others moved from considerable to only modest affluence. But the agrarian economy did produce substantial numbers of genuinely impoverished people. Black sharecroppers and tenant farmers continued to live at or below subsistence level throughout the rural South—in part because of the mechanization of cotton picking beginning in 1944, in part because of the development of synthetic fibers that reduced demand for cotton. (Two-thirds of the cotton acreage of the South went out of production between 1930 and 1960.) Migrant farmworkers, a group concentrated especially in the West and Southwest and containing many Mexican-American and Asian-American workers, lived in similarly dire circumstances. In rural areas without much commercial agriculture—such as the Appalachian region in the East, where the decline of the coal economy reduced the one significant source of support for the region— whole communities lived in desperate poverty, increasingly cut off from the market economy. All these groups were vulnerable to malnutrition and even starvation.

The Inner Cities

As white families moved from cities to suburbs in vast numbers, more and more inner-city neighborhoods became vast repositories for the poor, "ghettos" from which there was no easy escape. The growth of these neighborhoods owed much to a vast migration of African Americans out of the countryside (where the cotton economy was in decline) and into industrial cities. More than 3 million black men and women moved from the South to northern cities between 1940 and 1960. Chicago, Detroit, Cleveland, New York, and other eastern and midwestern industrial cities experienced a great expansion of their black populations—both in absolute numbers and, even more, as a percentage of the whole, since so many whites were leaving at the same time.

Black Urban Migration

Similar migrations from Mexico and Puerto Rico expanded poor Hispanic neighborhoods at the same time. Between 1940 and 1960, nearly a million Puerto Ricans moved into American cities (the largest group to New York). Mexican workers crossed the border in Texas and California and swelled the already substantial Latino communities of such cities as San Antonio, Houston, San Diego, and Los Angeles (which by 1960 had the largest Mexican-American population of any city, approximately 500,000 people).

Why these inner-city communities, populated largely by racial and ethnic minorities, remained so poor in the midst of growing affluence has been the subject of considerable debate. Some critics have argued that the new migrants were victims, in part, of their own pasts, that the work habits, values, and family structures they brought with them from their rural homes were poorly adapted to the needs of the modern industrial city. Others have argued that the inner city itself—its crippling poverty, its crime, its violence, its apparent hopelessness—created a "culture of poverty" that made it difficult for individuals to advance.

Many others argue that a combination of declining blue-collar jobs, inadequate support for minority-dominated public schools, and barriers to advancement

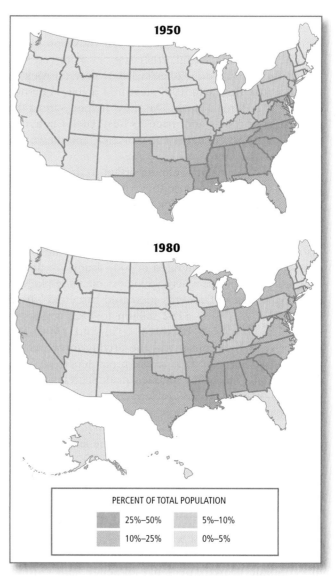

AFRICAN-AMERICAN MIGRATION, 1950–1980 Although there had been a substantial migration of African Americans out of the South and into northern industrial cities around the time of World War I and again during World War II, that process accelerated in the thirty years after 1950. By 1980, fewer southern states had black populations that accounted for 25 percent or more of their total population than in 1950. In the rest of the country, the number of states whose black populations exceeded 5 and 10 percent (the states shaded orange and purple) greatly increased. ♦ *What were some of the factors that produced the African-American migration in this period?*

rooted in racism—not the culture and values of the poor themselves—was the source of inner-city poverty. It is indisputable that inner cities were filling up with poor minority residents at the same time that the unskilled industrial jobs they were seeking were diminishing. Employers were relocating factories and mills from old industrial cities to new locations in suburbs, smaller cities, and even abroad—places where the cost of labor was lower. Even in the factories that remained, automation was reducing the number of unskilled jobs. The economic opportunities that had helped earlier immigrant groups to rise up from poverty were unavailable to most of the postwar migrants. Nor can there be any doubt that historic patterns of racial discrimination in hiring, education, and housing doomed many members of these communities to continuing, and in some cases increasing, poverty.

For many years, the principal policy response to the poverty of inner cities was "urban renewal": the effort to tear

"Urban Renewal"

down buildings in the poorest and most degraded areas. In the twenty years after World War II, urban renewal projects destroyed over 400,000 buildings, among them the homes of nearly 1.5 million people. In some cases, urban renewal provided new public housing for poor city residents. Some of it was considerably better than the housing they left; some of it was poorly designed and constructed, and deteriorated rapidly into dismal and dangerous slums. Urban renewal was, on the whole, better at eliminating "blights" than at helping the people who lived in them. In many cases, urban renewal projects replaced "slums" with middle- and upper-income housing (part of an often futile attempt to keep middle-class people from leaving), office towers, or commercial buildings; in Los Angeles, a baseball stadium for the Los Angeles Dodgers, recently relocated from Brooklyn, was erected on the site of a Mexican barrio.

THE RISE OF THE CIVIL RIGHTS MOVEMENT

After decades of skirmishes, an open battle began in the 1950s against racial segregation and discrimination. Although white Americans played an important role in the civil rights movement, pressure from African Americans themselves was the crucial element in raising the issue of race to prominence.

The *Brown* Decision and "Massive Resistance"

On May 17, 1954, the Supreme Court announced its decision in the case of *Brown* v. *Board of Education of Topeka*. In considering the legal segregation of a Kansas public school

Brown v. Board of Education

system, the Court rejected its own 1896 *Plessy* v. *Ferguson* decision, which had ruled that communities

could provide blacks with separate facilities as long as the facilities were equal to those of whites.

The *Brown* decision was the culmination of many decades of effort by black opponents of segregation, and particularly by a group of talented NAACP lawyers, many of them trained at Howard University in Washington by the great legal educator Charles Houston. Thurgood Marshall, William Hastie, James Nabrit, and others spent years filing legal challenges to segregation in one state after another, nibbling at the edges of the system, and accumulating precedents to support their assault on the "separate but equal" doctrine itself. The same lawyers filed the suits against the school boards of Topeka, Kansas, and several other cities that became the basis for the *Brown* decision.

The Topeka suit involved the case of an African-American girl who had to travel several miles to a segregated public school every day even though she lived virtually next door to a white elementary school. When the case arrived before the Supreme Court, the justices examined it not simply in terms of legal precedent but in terms of history, sociology, and psychology. They concluded that school segregation inflicted unac-

"Separate but Equal" Doctrine Overturned

ceptable damage on those it affected, regardless of the relative quality of the separate schools. Chief Justice Earl Warren explained the unanimous opinion of his colleagues: "We conclude that in the field of public education the doctrine of "separate but equal" has no place. Separate educational facilities are inherently unequal." The following year, the Court issued another decision (known as *Brown* II) to provide rules for implementing the 1954 order. It ruled that communities must work to desegregate their schools "with all deliberate speed," but it set no timetable and left specific decisions up to lower courts.

In some communities—for example, Washington, D.C.—compliance came relatively quickly and quietly. More often, however, strong local opposition (what came to be known in the South as "massive resistance") produced

"Massive Resistance"

long delays and bitter conflicts. Some school districts ignored the ruling altogether. Others attempted to circumvent it with purely token efforts to integrate. More than 100 southern members of Congress signed a "manifesto" in 1956 denouncing the *Brown* decision and urging their constituents to defy it. Southern governors, mayors, local school boards, and nongovernmental pressure groups (including hundreds of "White Citizens' Councils") all worked to obstruct desegregation. Many school districts enacted "pupil placement laws" allowing school officials to place students in schools according to their scholastic abilities and social behavior. Such laws were transparent devices for maintaining segregation; but in 1958, the Supreme Court (in *Shuttlesworth* v. *Birmingham Board of Education*) refused to declare them unconstitutional.

LITTLE ROCK   An African-American student passes by jeering whites in Arkansas on her way to Little Rock Central High School, newly integrated by federal court order. The black students later admitted that they had been terrified during the first difficult weeks of integration. But in public, most of them acted with remarkable calm and dignity. *(Bettmann/Corbis)*

By the fall of 1957, only 684 of 3,000 affected school districts in the South had even begun to desegregate their schools. In those that had complied, white resistance often produced angry mob actions and other violence. Many white parents simply withdrew their children from the public schools and enrolled them in all-white "segregation academies"; some state and local governments diverted money from newly integrated public schools and used it to fund the new, all-white academies. The *Brown* decision, far from ending segregation, had launched a prolonged battle between federal authority and state and local governments, and between those who believed in racial equality and those who did not.

The Eisenhower administration was not eager to commit itself to that battle. The president himself had greeted the *Brown* decision with skepticism (and once said it had set back progress on race relations "at least fifteen years"). But in September 1957, he faced a case of direct state defiance of federal authority and felt compelled to act. Federal courts had ordered the desegregation of Central High School in Little Rock, Arkansas. An angry white mob tried to prevent implementation of the order by blockading the entrances to the school, and Governor Orval Faubus refused to do anything to stop the obstruction. President Eisenhower finally responded by federalizing the National Guard and sending troops to Little Rock to restore order and ensure that the court orders would be obeyed. Only then did Central High School admit its first black students.

Little Rock

The Expanding Movement

The *Brown* decision helped spark a growing number of popular challenges to segregation in the South. On December 1, 1955, Rosa Parks, a black woman, was arrested in Montgomery, Alabama, when she refused to give up her seat on a Montgomery bus to a white passenger. Parks, an active civil rights leader in the community, had apparently decided spontaneously to resist the order to move. Her feet were tired, she later explained. But black leaders in Montgomery had been waiting for such an incident, which they wanted to use to challenge the segregation of the buses. The arrest of this admired woman produced outrage in the city's African-American community and helped local leaders organize a successful boycott of the bus system to demand an end to segregated seating.

The bus boycott owed much of its success to the prior existence of well-organized black citizens' groups. A black women's political caucus had, in fact, been developing plans for a boycott of the segregated buses for some time. They seized on Rosa Parks as a symbol of the movement. Once launched, the boycott was almost completely effective. Black workers who needed to commute to their jobs (of whom the largest group consisted of female domestic servants) formed car pools to ride back and forth to work, or simply walked, even at times over long distances. The boycott put economic pressure not only on the bus company (a private concern) but on many Montgomery merchants as well. The bus boycotters found it difficult to get to downtown stores and tended to shop instead in their own neighborhoods. Still, the boycott might well have failed had it not been for a Supreme Court decision late in 1956, inspired in part by the protest, that declared segregation in public transportation to be illegal. The buses in Montgomery abandoned their discriminatory seating policies, and the boycott came to a close.

Montgomery Bus Boycott

As important as the immediate victories of the Montgomery boycott was its success in elevating to prominence a new figure in the movement for civil rights. The man chosen to head the boycott movement after its launching was a local Baptist pastor, Martin Luther King Jr., the son of a prominent Atlanta minister, a powerful orator, and a gifted leader. At first King was reluctant to accept responsibility for the movement. But once he accepted the role, he became consumed by it.

King's approach to black protest was based on the doctrine of nonviolence—that is, of passive resistance even in the face of direct attack. He drew from the teachings of Mahatma Gandhi, the Indian nationalist leader; from Henry David Thoreau and his doctrine of civil disobedience; and from Christian doctrine. And he produced an approach to racial struggle that captured the moral high ground for his supporters. He urged African Americans to engage in peaceful demonstrations; to allow themselves to be arrested, even beaten, if necessary; and to respond to hate with love. For the next thirteen years—as leader of the Southern Christian Leadership Conference, an interracial group he founded shortly after the bus boycott—he was the most influential and most widely admired black leader in the country. The popular movement he came to represent soon spread throughout the South and throughout the country.

Martin Luther King's Strategy

Pressure from the courts, from northern liberals, and from African Americans themselves also speeded the pace of racial change in other areas. One important color line had been breached as early as 1947, when the Brooklyn Dodgers signed the great Jackie Robinson as the first African American to play Major League baseball. By the mid-1950s, blacks had established themselves as a powerful force in almost all professional sports. Within the government, President Eisenhower completed the integration of the armed forces, attempted to desegregate the federal work force, and in 1957 signed a civil rights act (passed, without active support from the White House, by a Democratic Congress) providing federal protection for African Americans who wished to register to vote. It was a weak bill, with few mechanisms for enforcement, but it was the first civil rights bill of any kind to win passage since the end of Reconstruction, and it served as a signal that the executive and legislative branches were beginning to join the judiciary in the federal commitment to the "Second Reconstruction."

Causes of the Civil Rights Movement

Why did a civil rights movement begin to emerge at this particular moment? The injustices it challenged and the goals it promoted were hardly new; in theory, African Americans could have launched the same movement fifty or a hundred years earlier, or decades later. Why did they do so in the 1950s and 1960s?

Several factors contributed to the rise of African-American protest in these years. The legacy of World War II was one of the most important. Millions of black men and women had served in the military or worked in war plants during the war and had derived from the experience a broader view of the world, and of their place in it.

Legacy of World War II

Another factor was the growth of an urban black middle class, which had been developing for decades but which began to flourish after the war. Much of the impetus for the civil rights movement came from the leaders of urban black communities—ministers, educators, professionals—and much of it came as well from students at black colleges and universities, which had expanded significantly in the previous decades. Men and women with education and a stake in society were often more aware of the obstacles to their advancement than poorer and more oppressed people, to whom the possibility of advancement may have seemed too remote even to consider. And urban blacks had considerably more freedom to associate with one another and to develop independent institutions than did rural blacks, who were often under the very direct supervision of white landowners.

Urban Black Middle Class

Television and other forms of popular culture were another factor in the rising consciousness of racism among blacks. More than any previous generation, postwar African Americans had constant, vivid reminders of how the white majority lived—of the world from which they were effectively excluded. Television also conveyed the activities of demonstrators to a national audience, ensuring that activism in one community would inspire similar protests in others. In addition to the forces that were inspiring African Americans to mobilize, other forces were at work mobilizing many white Americans to support the movement once it began. One was the Cold War, which made racial injustice an embarrassment to Americans trying to present their nation as a model to the world. Another was the political mobilization of northern blacks, who were now a substantial voting bloc within the Democratic Party; politicians from northern industrial states could not ignore their views. Labor unions with substantial black memberships also played an important part in supporting (and funding) the civil rights movement.

EISENHOWER REPUBLICANISM

Dwight D. Eisenhower was the least experienced politician to serve in the White House in the twentieth century. He was also among the most popular and politically successful presidents of the postwar era. At home, he pursued essentially moderate policies, avoiding most new initiatives but accepting the work of earlier reformers. Abroad, he continued and even intensified American commitments to oppose communism but brought to some of those commitments a measure of restraint that his successors did not always match.

"What Was Good for . . . General Motors"

The first Republican administration in twenty years staffed itself with men drawn from the same quarter as those who had staffed Republican administrations in the 1920s: the business community. But by the 1950s, many business leaders had acquired a social and political outlook very different from that of their predecessors. Above all, many had reconciled themselves to at least the broad outlines of the Keynesian welfare state the New Deal had launched. Indeed, some corporate leaders had come to see it as something that actually benefited them—by helping maintain social order, by increasing mass purchasing power, and by stabilizing labor relations.

Business Leaders' New Outlook

To his cabinet, Eisenhower appointed wealthy corporate lawyers and business executives who were not apologetic about their backgrounds. Charles Wilson, president of General Motors, assured senators considering his nomination for secretary of defense that he foresaw no conflict of interest because he was certain that "what was good for our country was good for General Motors, and vice versa."

Eisenhower's consistent inclination was to limit federal activities and encourage private enterprise. He supported the private rather than public development of natural resources. To the chagrin of farmers, he lowered federal support for farm prices. He also removed the last limited wage and price controls maintained by the Truman administration. He opposed the creation of new social service programs such as national health insurance. He strove constantly to reduce federal expenditures (even during the recession of 1958) and balance the budget. He ended 1960, his last full year in office, with a $1 billion budget surplus.

The Survival of the Welfare State

The president took few new initiatives in domestic policy, but he resisted pressure from the right wing of his party to dismantle those welfare policies of the New Deal that had survived the conservative assaults of the war years and after. Indeed, during his term, he agreed to extend the Social Security system to an additional 10 million people and unemployment compensation to an additional 4 million, and he agreed to increase the minimum hourly wage from 75 cents to $1. Perhaps the most significant legislative accomplishment of the Eisenhower administration was the Federal Highway Act of 1956, which authorized $25 billion for a ten-year project that built over 40,000 miles of interstate highways—the largest public works project in American history. The program was to be funded through a highway "trust fund," whose revenues would come from new taxes on the purchase of fuel, automobiles, trucks, and tires.

Federal Highway Act of 1956

In 1956, Eisenhower ran for a second term, even though he had suffered a serious heart attack the previous year. With Adlai Stevenson opposing him once again, he won by another, even greater landslide, receiving nearly 57 percent of the popular vote and 457 electoral votes to Stevenson's 73. Democrats retained the control of both houses of Congress they had won back in 1954. And in 1958—during a serious recession—they increased that control by substantial margins.

The Decline of McCarthyism

The Eisenhower administration did little in its first years in office to discourage the anticommunist furor that had gripped the nation. By 1954, however, the crusade against subversion was beginning to produce significant popular opposition—an indication that the anticommunist passion of several years earlier was beginning to abate. The clearest signal of that change was the political demise of Senator Joseph McCarthy.

During the first year of the Eisenhower administration, McCarthy continued to operate with impunity. But in January 1954 he overreached himself when he attacked Secretary of the Army Robert Stevens and the armed services in general. At that point, the administration and influential members of Congress organized a special investigation of the charges, which became known as the Army-McCarthy

THE ARMY-MCCARTHY HEARINGS Senator Joseph McCarthy uses a map to show the supposed distribution of communists throughout the United States during the televised 1954 Senate hearings to mediate the dispute between McCarthy and the U.S. Army. Joseph Welch, chief counsel for the army, remains conspicuously unimpressed. *(Bettmann/Corbis)*

Army-McCarthy Hearings

hearings. They were among the first congressional hearings to be nationally televised. The result was devastating to McCarthy. Watching McCarthy in action—bullying witnesses, hurling groundless (and often cruel) accusations, evading issues—much of the public began to see him as a villain, and even a buffoon. In December 1954, the Senate voted 67 to 22 to condemn him for "conduct unbecoming a senator." Three years later, with little public support left, he died—a victim, apparently, of complications arising from alcoholism.

EISENHOWER, DULLES, AND THE COLD WAR

The threat of nuclear war with the Soviet Union created a sense of high anxiety in international relations in the 1950s. But the nuclear threat had another effect as well. With the potential devastation of an atomic war so enormous, both superpowers began to edge away from direct confrontations. The attention of both the United States and the Soviet Union began to turn to the rapidly escalating instability in the nations of the Third World.

Dulles and "Massive Retaliation"

Eisenhower's secretary of state, and (except for the president himself) the dominant figure in the nation's foreign policy in the 1950s, was John Foster Dulles, an aristocratic corporate lawyer with a stern moral revulsion to communism. He entered office denouncing the containment policies of the Truman years as excessively passive, arguing that the United States should pursue an active program of "liberation," which would lead to a "rollback" of communist expansion. Once in power, however, he had to defer to the more moderate views of the president himself.

The most prominent of Dulles's innovations was the policy of "massive retaliation," which Dulles announced early in 1954. The United States would, he explained, respond to communist threats to its allies not by using conventional forces in local conflicts (a policy that had led to so much frustration in Korea) but by relying on "the deterrent of massive retaliatory power" (by which he meant nuclear weapons). In part, the new doctrines reflected Dulles's inclination for tense confrontations, an approach he once defined as "brinksmanship"—pushing the Soviet Union to the brink of war in order to exact concessions. But the real force behind

Economic Benefits of "Massive Retaliation"

EISENHOWER AND DULLES Although President Eisenhower himself was a somewhat colorless television personality, his was the first administration to make extensive use of the new medium to promote its policies and dramatize its actions. The president's press conferences were frequently televised, and on several occasions Secretary of State John Foster Dulles reported to the president in front of the cameras. Dulles is shown here in the Oval Office on May 17, 1955, reporting after his return from Europe, where he had signed the treaty restoring sovereignty to Austria. *(AP/Wide World Photos)*

the massive-retaliation policy was economics. With pressure growing both in and out of government for a reduction in American military expenditures, an increasing reliance on atomic weapons seemed to promise, as some advocates put it, "more bang for the buck."

France, America, and Vietnam

What had been the most troubling foreign policy concern of the Truman years—the war in Korea—plagued the Eisenhower administration only briefly. On July 27, 1953, negotiators at Panmunjom finally signed an agreement ending the hostilities. Each antagonist was to withdraw its troops a mile and a half from the existing battle line, which ran roughly along the 38th parallel, the prewar border between North and South Korea. A conference in Geneva was to consider means by which to reunite the nation peacefully—although in fact the 1954 meeting produced no agreement and left the cease-fire line as the apparently permanent border between the two countries.

Almost simultaneously, however, the United States was being drawn into a long, bitter struggle in Southeast Asia. Ever since 1945, France had been attempting to restore its authority over Vietnam, its one-time colony, which it had been forced to abandon to the Japanese toward the end of World War II. Opposing the French, however, were the

powerful nationalist forces of Ho Chi Minh, a communist determined to win independence for his nation.

Early in 1954, 12,000 French troops became surrounded in a disastrous siege at the village of Dien Bien Phu. Only American intervention, it was clear, could prevent the total collapse of the French military effort. Yet despite the urgings of Secretary of State Dulles, Vice President Nixon, and others, Eisenhower refused to permit direct American military intervention in Vietnam, claiming that neither Congress nor America's other allies would support such action.

Without American aid, the French defense of Dien Bien Phu finally collapsed on May 7, 1954, and France quickly agreed to a settlement of the conflict at the same international conference in Geneva that summer that was considering the Korean settlement. The agreement marked the end of the French commitment to Vietnam and the beginning of an expanded American presence there (see pp. 826–827).

Cold War Crises

American foreign policy in the 1950s rested on a reasonably consistent foundation: the containment policy, as revised by the Eisenhower administration. But the nation's leaders spent much of their time reacting to both real and imagined crises in far-flung areas of the world. Among the

THE STATE OF ISRAEL The prime minister of Israel, David Ben-Gurion (left), watches the departure of the last British troops from Palestine shortly after the United Nations approved (and the United States recognized) in 1948 the existence of a new Jewish state in part of the region. *(Bettmann/Corbis)*

Cold War challenges the Eisenhower administration confronted were a series of crises in the Middle East, a region in which the United States had been little involved until after World War II.

On May 14, 1948, after years of Zionist efforts and a dramatic decision by the new United Nations, the nation

Recognizing Israel

of Israel proclaimed its independence. President Truman recognized the new Jewish homeland the next day. But the creation of Israel, while it resolved some conflicts, created others. Palestinian Arabs, unwilling to accept being dis-

placed from what they considered their own country, joined with Israel's Arab neighbors and fought determinedly against the new state in 1948—the first of several Arab-Israeli wars.

Committed as the American government was to Israel, it was also concerned about the stability and friendliness of the Arab regimes in the oil-rich Middle East, in which American petroleum companies had major investments. Thus the United States reacted with alarm as it watched Muhammad Mossadegh, the nationalist prime minister of Iran, begin to resist the presence of Western corporations in his nation in the early 1950s. In 1953, the American CIA joined forces with conservative Iranian military leaders to engineer a coup that drove Mossadegh from office. To replace him, the CIA helped elevate the young Shah of Iran, Muhammad Reza Pahlevi, from his position as token constitutional monarch to that of virtually absolute ruler. The Shah remained closely tied to the United States for the next twenty-five years.

American policy was less effective in dealing with the nationalist government of Egypt, under the leadership of General Gamal Abdel Nasser, which began to develop a trade relationship with the Soviet Union in the early 1950s. In 1956, to punish Nasser for his friendliness toward the communists, Dulles withdrew American offers to

Suez Crisis

assist in building the great Aswan Dam across the Nile. A week later, Nasser retaliated by seizing control of the Suez Canal from the British, saying that he would use the income from it to build the dam himself.

On October 29, 1956, Israeli forces attacked Egypt. The next day the British and French landed troops in the Suez to drive the Egyptians from the canal. Dulles and Eisenhower feared that the Suez crisis would drive the Arab states toward the Soviet Union and precipitate a new world war. By refusing to support the invasion, and by joining in a United Nations denunciation of it, the United States helped pressure the French and British to withdraw and helped persuade Israel to agree to a truce with Egypt.

Cold War concerns affected American relations in Latin America as well. In 1954, the Eisenhower administration ordered the CIA to help topple the new, leftist government of Jacobo Arbenz Guzmán in Guatemala, a regime that Dulles (responding to the entreaties of the United Fruit Company, a major investor in Guatemala fearful of Arbenz) argued was potentially communist.

No nation in the region had been more closely tied to America than Cuba. Its leader, Fulgencio Batista, had ruled as a military dictator since 1952, when with American assistance he had toppled a more moderate government. Cuba's relatively prosperous economy had become a virtual fiefdom of American corporations, which controlled almost all the island's natural resources and had cornered over half the vital sugar crop. American organized-crime syndicates controlled much of Havana's lucrative hotel and nightlife business. In 1957, a popular movement of

THE CUBAN REVOLUTION   Fidel Castro is shown here in the Cuban jungle in 1957 with a small group of his staff and their revolutionary forces. Kneeling in the foreground is Castro's brother Raoul. Two years later, Castro's forces toppled the existing government and elevated Fidel to the nation's leadership, where he remained for almost fifty years.   *(Bettmann/Corbis)*

resistance to the Batista regime began to gather strength

Fidel Castro

under the leadership of Fidel Castro. On January 1, 1959, with Batista having fled to exile in Spain, Castro marched into Havana and established a new government.

Castro soon began implementing drastic policies of land reform and expropriating foreign-owned businesses and resources. Cuban-American relations deteriorated rapidly as a result. When Castro began accepting assistance from the Soviet Union in 1960, the United States cut back the "quota" by which Cuba could export sugar to America at a favored price. Early in 1961, as one of its last acts, the Eisenhower administration severed diplomatic relations with Castro. Isolated by the United States, Castro soon cemented an alliance with the Soviet Union.

Europe and the Soviet Union

Although the problems of the Third World were moving slowly toward the center of American foreign policy, the direct relationship with the Soviet Union and the effort to resist communist expansion in Europe remained the principal concerns of the Eisenhower administration. In 1955, Eisenhower and other NATO leaders met with the Soviet premier, Nikolai Bulganin, at a cordial summit conference in Geneva. But when a subsequent conference of foreign ministers met to try to resolve specific issues, they could find no basis for agreement. Relations between the Soviet Union and the West soured further in 1956 in response to the Hungarian Revolution. Hungarian dissidents had launched a popular uprising in November to demand democratic reforms. Before the month was out, Soviet tanks and troops entered Budapest to crush the uprising and restore

Hungarian Revolution of 1956

an orthodox, pro-Soviet regime. The Eisenhower administration refused to intervene.

The U-2 Crisis

In November 1958, Nikita Khrushchev, who had succeeded Bulganin as Soviet premier and Communist

Party chief earlier that year, renewed the demands of his predecessors that the NATO powers abandon West Berlin. When the United States and its allies predictably refused, Khrushchev suggested that he and Eisenhower discuss the issue personally, both in visits to each other's countries and at a summit meeting in Paris in 1960. The United States agreed. Khrushchev's 1959 visit to America produced a cool but polite public response. Plans proceeded for the summit conference and for Eisenhower's visit to Moscow shortly thereafter. Only days before the scheduled beginning of the Paris meeting, however, the Soviet Union announced that it had shot down an American U-2, a high-altitude spy plane, over Russian territory. Its pilot, Francis Gary Powers, was in captivity. Khrushchev lashed out angrily at the American incursion into Soviet air space, breaking up the Paris summit almost before it could begin and with-drawing his invitation to Eisenhower to visit the Soviet Union.

After eight years in office, Eisenhower had failed to eliminate, and in some respects had actually increased, the tensions between the United States and the Soviet Union. Yet Eisenhower had brought to the Cold War his own sense of the limits of American power. He had resisted military intervention in Vietnam. And he had placed a measure of restraint on those who urged the creation of an enormous American military establishment. In his farewell address in January 1961, he warned of the "unwarranted influence" of a vast "military-industrial complex." His caution, in both domestic and international affairs, stood in marked contrast to the attitudes of his successors, who argued that the United States must act more boldly and aggressively on behalf of its goals at home and abroad.

Eisenhower's Restraint

CONCLUSION

The booming economic growth of the 1950s—and the anxiety over the Cold War that formed a backdrop to it—shaped the politics and the culture of the decade. For most Americans, the 1950s were years of increasing personal prosperity. Sales of private homes increased dramatically; suburbs grew precipitously; young families had children at an astounding rate—creating what came to be known as the postwar "baby boom." After the end of the divisive Korean War, the nation's politics entered a period of relative calm, symbolized by the genial presence in the White House of Dwight D. Eisenhower, who provided moderate and undemanding leadership through most of the decade.

The nation's culture, too, helped create a broad sense of stability and calm. Television, which emerged in the 1950s as the most powerful medium of mass culture, presented largely uncontroversial programming dominated by middle-class images and traditional values. Movies, theater, popular magazines, and newspapers all generally contributed to a broad sense of well-being.

But the 1950s were not, in the end, as calm and contented as the politics and popular culture of the time suggested. A powerful youth culture emerged in these years that displayed a considerable level of restiveness and even disillusionment. African Americans began to escalate their protests against segregation and inequality. The continuing existence of widespread poverty among large groups of Americans attracted increasing attention as the decade progressed. These pulsing anxieties, combined with frustration over the continuing tensions of the Cold War, produced by the late 1950s a growing sense of impatience with the calm, placid public culture of the time. That was one reason for the growing desire for action and innovation as the 1960s began.

INTERACTIVE LEARNING

The *Primary Source Investigator CD-ROM* offers the following materials related to this chapter:

• Interactive maps: **U.S. Elections** (M7) and **Middle East** (M28).

• Documents, images, and maps related to American culture and politics in the 1950s, including the Eisenhower presidency and the growing civil rights movement. Some highlights include Jackie Robinson's letter to President Dwight Eisenhower regarding civil rights; images of integration in Little Rock; excerpts from the Supreme Court's ruling in *Brown* v. *Board of Education;* images of Levittown; and images and documents of the *Apollo 11* mission.

Online Learning Center (www.mhhe.com/brinkley13e)

For quizzes, Internet resources, references to additional books and films, and more, consult the book's Online Learning Center.

FOR FURTHER REFERENCE

James T. Patterson, *Grand Expectations: Postwar America, 1945–1974* (1996), a volume in the Oxford History of the United States, is an important general history of the postwar era. John P. Diggins, *The Proud Decades: America in War and Peace, 1941–1960 (1989)* and Godfrey Hodgson, *America in Our Time* (1976) are other important surveys. Kenneth T. Jackson, *The Crabgrass Frontier: The Suburbanization of the United States* (1985) is a classic history of a major social movement. Karal Ann Marling, *As Seen on TV: The Visual Culture of Everyday Life in the 1950s* (1995) is a study of the new medium. Lizabeth Cohen, *A Consumer's Republic: The Politics of Mass Consumption in Postwar America* (2003) examines the power of consumerism in postwar America. Elaine Tyler May, *Homeward Bound: American Families in the Cold War* (1988) is a challenging cultural history. Paul Boyer, *By the Bomb's Early Light: American Thought and Culture at the Dawn of the Atomic Age* (1985) examines the impact of the atomic bomb on American social thought. Stephen Ambrose, *Eisenhower the President* (1984) is a good biography, and Fred Greenstein, *The Hidden-Hand Presidency* (1982) is a challenge to earlier, dismissive views of Eisenhower's leadership style. Richard Kluger, *Simple Justice* (1975) is a classic history of the *Brown* decision. John Egerton, *Speak Now Against the Day: The Generation Before the Civil Rights Movement in the South* (1994) is a history of struggles over white supremacy in the first years after World War II.

CHAPTER 29

CIVIL RIGHTS, VIETNAM, AND THE ORDEAL OF LIBERALISM

KHE SANH, VIETNAM, 1968 A beleaguered American soldier shows his exhaustion during the 76-day siege of the American marine base at Khe Sanh, which began shortly before the 1968 Tet offensive in Vietnam. American forces sustained record casualties in the fierce fighting at Khe Sanh; the Vietnamese communist forces suffered far more. *(Robert Ellison/Black Star)*

By THE LATE 1950S, a growing restlessness was becoming apparent beneath the placid surface of American society. Anxiety about America's position in the world, growing pressures from African Americans and other minorities, the increasing visibility of poverty, the rising frustrations of women, and other long-suppressed discontents were beginning to shake the nation's public life. Ultimately, that restlessness would make the 1960s one of the most turbulent eras of the twentieth century. But at first, it contributed to a bold and confident effort by political leaders and popular movements to attack social and international problems within the framework of conventional liberal politics.

The decade began with the election of John F. Kennedy, a young and magnetic new president who—although in many ways a cautious and pragmatic leader—seemed to millions of Americans to be a symbol of energy and idealism. His assassination in 1963 later came to symbolize the end of an era. But at the time, Kennedy's death—traumatic as it was—seemed to confirm the power of the confident, moderate liberalism that Kennedy himself had begun to express. His successor, Lyndon Johnson, took Kennedy's legacy, enlarged it, and made it his own, accumulating a record of legislative achievement unmatched by any president since Franklin Roosevelt.

But this high tide of liberal success overlapped with the emergence of a series of challenges to liberalism from both the left and the right. The civil rights movement that began in the 1950s grew rapidly in the early 1960s, met with an at-times violent response from conservative whites in the South, and quickly evolved into a diverse set of movements, some of which adopted radical and even revolutionary goals. The student disenchantment that was sometimes visible in the 1950s grew dramatically in the 1960s, becoming a powerful and increasingly disruptive force on campuses, and beyond.

Perhaps most of all, the United States in the 1960s became deeply involved in one of the most disastrous wars in the nation's history—a conflict in Vietnam that eventually led to a commitment of over half a million American troops, resulted in over 55,000 American deaths (and hundreds of thousands of Vietnamese casualties), and produced an unprecedentedly large opposition movement in the United States.

By the end of the 1960s, the United States had entered what was in many ways a fundamentally new period in its history. The 1960s produced both a searing critique of American life, which greatly transformed both the politics and culture of the nation, and a powerful conservative backlash that, over time, was at least equally successful in putting its stamp on society. The moderate center had dominated American life for decades before the 1960s. In the aftermath of the decade, American society became increasingly fragmented and, at times, polarized.

SIGNIFICANT EVENTS

1959 ▶ Soviet Comintern urges wars of "national liberation" in the Third World
▶ National Liberation Front (Viet Cong) created in Vietnam
1960 ▶ John F. Kennedy elected president
▶ Greensboro sit-ins
1961 ▶ Freedom rides
▶ United States supports failed invasion of Bay of Pigs
▶ Kennedy meets Khrushchev in Vienna
▶ Berlin Wall erected
▶ Peace Corps established
▶ Alliance for Progress established
1962 ▶ Steel price increase provokes controversy
▶ Kennedy proposes tax cut to stimulate economy
▶ Desegregation crisis at University of Mississippi
▶ Cuban missile crisis
1963 ▶ Martin Luther King Jr. begins Birmingham campaign
▶ Desegregation crisis at University of Alabama
▶ Kennedy proposes civil rights bill
▶ March on Washington; King gives "I have a dream" speech
▶ Test ban treaty signed
▶ Buddhist crisis in Vietnam; Diem toppled by coup
▶ Kennedy assassinated; Lyndon B. Johnson becomes president
1964 ▶ Johnson launches war on poverty
▶ "Freedom summer" campaign in Mississippi
▶ Congress passes Civil Rights Act
▶ Gulf of Tonkin Resolution passed
▶ United States bombs North Vietnam for first time
▶ Johnson elected president by record margin
1965 ▶ Medicare enacted
▶ Selma campaign for voting rights
▶ Race riot breaks out in Watts, Los Angeles
▶ Malcolm X assassinated
▶ *Autobiography of Malcolm X* published
▶ Congress passes Voting Rights Act
▶ United States intervenes in Dominican Republic
▶ American combat troops sent to Vietnam
▶ Antiwar activities begin on university campuses
▶ Immigration Reform Act passed
1966 ▶ Medicaid enacted
▶ King leads Chicago campaign
▶ Senate Foreign Relations Committee holds hearings on Vietnam
1967 ▶ Race riot breaks out in Detroit
▶ Antiwar movement intensifies
1968 ▶ Viet Cong launch Tet offensive
▶ Johnson withdraws from presidential contest
▶ Martin Luther King Jr. assassinated
▶ Racial violence breaks out in American cities
▶ Robert Kennedy assassinated
▶ Demonstrators clash with police at Democratic National Convention
▶ George Wallace launches third-party presidential campaign
▶ Richard M. Nixon elected president

EXPANDING THE LIBERAL STATE

Those who yearned for a more active government in the late 1950s, and who accused the Eisenhower administration of allowing the nation to "drift," looked above all to the presidency for leadership. The two men who served in the White House through most of the 1960s—John Kennedy and Lyndon Johnson—seemed for a time to be the embodiment of these liberal hopes.

John Kennedy

The presidential campaign of 1960 produced two young candidates who claimed to offer the nation active leadership. The Republican nomination went almost uncontested to Vice President Richard Nixon, who promised moderate reform. The Democrats, in the meantime, emerged from a spirited primary campaign united, somewhat uneasily, behind John Fitzgerald Kennedy, an attractive and articulate senator from Massachusetts who had narrowly missed being the party's vice presidential candidate in 1956.

John Kennedy was the son of the wealthy, powerful, and highly controversial Joseph P. Kennedy, former American ambassador to Britain. But while he had grown up in a world of ease and privilege, he became a spokesman for energy and sacrifice. His appealing public image was at least as important as his political positions in attracting popular support. He overcame doubts about his youth (he turned forty-three in 1960) and religion (he was Catholic) to win with a tiny plurality of the popular vote (49.7 percent to Nixon's 49.6 percent) and only a slightly more comfortable electoral majority (303 to 219).

Election of 1960

Kennedy had campaigned promising a set of domestic reforms more ambitious than any since the New Deal, a program he described as the "New Frontier." But his thin popular mandate and a Congress dominated by a coalition of Republicans and conservative Democrats frustrated many of his hopes. Kennedy did manage to win approval of tariff reductions his administration had negotiated, and he began to build an ambitious legislative agenda that he hoped he might eventually see enacted—including a call for a significant tax cut to promote economic growth.

More than any other president of the century (except perhaps the two Roosevelts and, later, Ronald Reagan), Kennedy made his own personality an integral part of his presidency and a central focus of national attention. Nothing illustrated that more clearly than the popular reaction to the tragedy of November 22, 1963. Kennedy had traveled to Texas with his wife and Vice President Lyndon Johnson for a series of political appearances. While the presidential motorcade rode slowly through the streets of Dallas,

Kennedy Assassinated

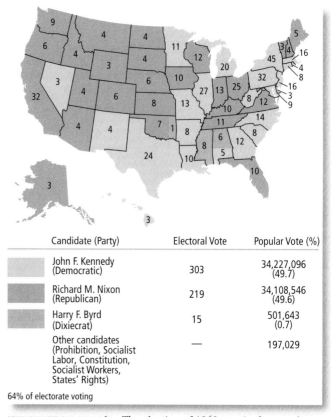

Candidate (Party)	Electoral Vote	Popular Vote (%)
John F. Kennedy (Democratic)	303	34,227,096 (49.7)
Richard M. Nixon (Republican)	219	34,108,546 (49.6)
Harry F. Byrd (Dixiecrat)	15	501,643 (0.7)
Other candidates (Prohibition, Socialist Labor, Constitution, Socialist Workers, States' Rights)	—	197,029

64% of electorate voting

THE ELECTION OF 1960 The election of 1960 was, in the popular vote at least, one of the closest in American history. John Kennedy's margin over Richard Nixon was less than one-third of 1 percent of the total national vote, but greater in the electoral college. Note the distribution of electoral strength of the two candidates. Kennedy was strong in the industrial Northeast and the largest industrial states of the Midwest, and he retained at least a portion of his party's traditional strength in the South and Southwest. But Nixon made significant inroads into the upper South, carried Florida, and swept most of the Plains and Mountain states. ◆ *What was the significance of this distribution of strength to the future of the two parties?*

For an interactive version of this map, go to www.mhhe.com/brinkley13ech29maps

shots rang out. Two bullets struck the president—one in the throat, the other in the head. He was sped to a nearby hospital, where minutes later he was pronounced dead. Lee Harvey Oswald, who appeared to be a confused and embittered Marxist, was arrested for the crime later that day, and then mysteriously murdered by a Dallas nightclub owner, Jack Ruby, two days later. Most Americans at the time accepted the conclusions of a federal commission, appointed by President Johnson and chaired by Chief Justice Earl Warren, which found that both Oswald and Ruby had acted alone, that there was no larger conspiracy. In later years, however, many Americans came to believe that the Warren Commission report had ignored evidence of a wider conspiracy behind the murders. Controversy over the truth about the assassination has continued ever since.

JOHN KENNEDY The new president and his wife, Jacqueline, attend one of the five balls in Washington marking Kennedy's inauguration in 1961. *(Time Life Pictures/Getty Images)*

Lyndon Johnson

The Kennedy assassination was a national trauma—a defining event for almost everyone old enough to be aware of it. At the time, however, much of the nation took comfort in the personality and performance of Kennedy's successor in the White House, Lyndon Baines Johnson. Johnson was a native of the poor "hill country" of west Texas and had risen to become majority leader of the U.S. Senate by dint of extraordinary, even obsessive, effort and ambition. Having failed to win the Democratic nomination for president in 1960, he surprised many who knew him by agreeing to accept the second position on the ticket with Kennedy. The events in Dallas thrust him into the White House.

Johnson's rough-edged, even crude personality could hardly have been more different from Kennedy's. But like Kennedy, Johnson was a man who believed in the active use of power. Between 1963 and 1966, he compiled the

most impressive legislative record of any president since Franklin Roosevelt. He was aided by the tidal wave of emotion that followed the death of President Kennedy, which helped win support for many New Frontier proposals. But Johnson also constructed a remarkable reform program of his own, one that he ultimately labeled the "Great Society." And he won approval of much of it through the same sort of skillful lobbying in Congress that had made him an effective majority leader.

The "Great Society"

Johnson envisioned himself as a great "coalition builder." He wanted the support of everyone, and for a time he very nearly got it. His first year in office was, by necessity, dominated by the campaign for reelection. There was little doubt that he would win—particularly after the Republican Party fell under the sway of its right wing and nominated the conservative Senator Barry Goldwater of Arizona. In the November 1964 election, the president received a larger plurality, over 61 percent, than any candidate before or since. Goldwater managed to carry only his home state of Arizona and five states in the Deep South. Record Democratic majorities in both houses of Congress, many of whose members had been swept into office only because of the margin of Johnson's victory, ensured that the president would be able to fulfill many of his goals.

The Assault on Poverty

For the first time since the 1930s, the federal government took steps in the 1960s to create important new social welfare programs. The most important of these, perhaps, was Medicare: a program to provide federal aid to the elderly for medical expenses. Its enactment in 1965 came at the end of a bitter, twenty-year debate between those who believed in the concept of national health assistance and those who denounced it as "socialized medicine." But the program as it went into effect pacified many critics. For one thing, it avoided the stigma of "welfare" by making Medicare benefits available to all elderly Americans, regardless of need (just as Social Security had done with pensions). That created a large middle-class constituency for the program. The program also defused the opposition of the medical community by allowing doctors serving Medicare patients to practice privately and to charge their normal fees; Medicare simply shifted responsibility for paying those fees from the patient to the government. In 1966, Johnson steered to passage the Medicaid program, which extended federal medical assistance to welfare recipients and other indigent people of all ages.

Medicare and Medicaid

Medicare and Medicaid were early steps in a much larger assault on poverty—one that Kennedy had been planning in the last months of his life and that Johnson launched only weeks after taking office. The centerpiece

RETROACTIVE I, 1964 Within months of his death, John Kennedy had become a figure larger than life, a symbol of the nation's thwarted aspirations. The artist Robert Rauschenberg gave evidence of Kennedy's new mythological importance by making him the centerpiece of this evocation of contemporary American society. *(© Robert Rauschenberg/Licensed by VAGA, New York, N.Y. Wadsworth Atheneum Museum of Art, Hartford, CT. Gift of Susan Morse Hilles)*

of this "war on poverty," as Johnson called it, was the Office of Economic Opportunity (OEO), which created an array of new educational, employment, housing, and health-care programs. But the OEO was controversial from the start, in part because of its commitment to the idea of "Community Action."

Community Action was an effort to involve members of poor communities themselves in the planning and administration of the programs designed to help them. The Community Action programs provided jobs for many poor people and gave them valuable experience in administrative and political work. Many men and women who went on to significant careers in politics or community organizing, including many black and Hispanic politicians, as well as many Indians, got their start in Community Action programs. But despite its achievements, the Community Action approach proved impossible to

Community Action Program

sustain, both because of administrative failures and because the apparent excesses of a few agencies damaged the popular image of the Community Action programs and, indeed, the war on poverty as a whole.

The OEO spent nearly $3 billion during its first two years of existence, and it helped reduce poverty in some areas. But it fell far short of eliminating poverty. That was in part because of the weaknesses of the programs themselves and in part because funding for them, inadequate from the beginning, dwindled as the years passed and a costly war in Southeast Asia became the nation's first priority.

Cities, Schools, and Immigration

Closely tied to the antipoverty program were federal efforts to promote the revitalization of decaying cities and to strengthen the nation's schools. The Housing Act of 1961 offered $4.9 billion in federal grants to cities for

THE JOHNSON TREATMENT Lyndon Johnson was legendary for his powers of persuasion—for a combination of charm and intimidation that often worked on even the most experienced politicians. He is shown here in the Oval Office meeting with his old friend Senator Richard Russell of Georgia and demonstrating one of his most powerful and unsettling techniques of persuasion: moving so close to the person with whom he was talking as to be almost touching him. *(Photo by Yoichi Okamoto. Lyndon Baines Johnson Library & Museum)*

the preservation of open spaces, the development of mass-transit systems, and the subsidization of middle-income housing. In 1966, Johnson established a new cabinet agency, the Department of Housing and Urban Development (whose first secretary, Robert Weaver, was the first African American ever to serve in the cabinet). Johnson also inaugurated the Model Cities program, which offered federal subsidies for urban redevelopment pilot programs.

Housing and Urban Development

Kennedy had long fought for federal aid to public education, but he had failed to overcome two important obstacles: Many Americans feared that aid to education was the first step toward federal control of the schools, and Catholics insisted that federal assistance must extend to parochial as well as public schools. Johnson managed to circumvent both objections with the Elementary and Secondary Education Act of 1965 and a series of subsequent measures. The bills extended aid to both private and parochial schools and based the aid on the economic conditions of the students, not on the needs of the schools themselves. Total federal expenditures for education and technical training rose from $5 billion to $12 billion between 1964 and 1967.

The Johnson administration also supported the Immigration Act of 1965, one of the most important pieces of legislation of the 1960s. The law maintained a strict limit on the number of newcomers admitted to the country each year (170,000), but it eliminated the "national origins" system established in the 1920s, which gave preference to immigrants from northern Europe over those from other parts of the world. It continued to restrict immigration from some parts of Latin America, but it allowed

Immigration Act of 1965

people from all parts of Europe, Asia, and Africa to enter the United States on an equal basis. By the early 1970s, the character of American immigration had changed, with members of new national groups—and particularly large groups of Asians—entering the United States and changing the character of the American population.

Legacies of the Great Society

Taken together, the Great Society reforms meant a significant increase in federal spending. For a time, rising tax revenues from the growing economy nearly compensated for the new expenditures. In 1964, Johnson managed to win passage of the $11.5 billion tax cut that Kennedy had first proposed in 1962. The cut increased the federal deficit, but substantial economic growth over the next several years made up for much of the revenue initially lost. As Great Society programs began to multiply, however, and particularly as they began to compete with the escalating costs of America's military ventures, federal spending rapidly outpaced increases in revenues. In 1961, the federal government had spent $94.4 billion. By 1970, that sum had risen to $196.6 billion.

The high costs of the Great Society programs, the deficiencies and failures of many of them, and the inability of the government to find the revenues to pay for them contributed to a growing disillusionment in later years with the idea of federal efforts to solve social problems. By the 1980s, many Americans had become convinced that the Great Society experiments had not worked and that, indeed, government programs to solve social problems could not work. But the

Failures and Achievements of the Great Society

Great Society, despite many failures, was also responsible for some significant achievements. It substantially reduced hunger in America. It made medical care available to millions of elderly and poor people who would otherwise have had great difficulty affording it. It contributed to the greatest reduction in poverty in American history. In 1959, according to the most widely accepted estimates, 21 percent of the American people lived below the official poverty line. By 1969, only 12 percent remained below that line. The improvements affected blacks and whites in about the same proportion: 56 percent of the black population had lived in poverty in 1959, while only 32 percent did so ten years later—a 42 percent reduction; 18 percent of all whites had been poor in 1959, but only 10 percent were poor a decade later—a 44 percent reduction. Much of that progress was a result of economic growth, but some of it was a result of Great Society programs.

THE BATTLE FOR RACIAL EQUALITY

The nation's most important domestic initiative in the 1960s was the effort to provide justice and equality to African Americans. It was the most difficult commitment, the one that produced the severest strains on American society. It was also unavoidable. Black Americans were themselves ensuring that the nation would have to deal with the problem of race.

Expanding Protests

John Kennedy had long been vaguely sympathetic to the cause of racial justice, but he was hardly a committed crusader. His intervention during the 1960 campaign to help win the release of Martin Luther King Jr. from a Georgia prison won him a large plurality of the black vote. But like many presidents before him, he feared alienating southern Democratic voters and congressmen. His administration set out to contain the racial problem by expanding enforcement of existing laws and supporting litigation to overturn existing segregation statutes, hoping to make modest progress without creating politically damaging divisions.

But the pressure for more fundamental change could not be contained. In February 1960, black college students in Greensboro, North Carolina, staged a sit-in at a segregated Woolworth's lunch counter; and in the following weeks, similar demonstrations spread throughout the South, forcing many merchants to integrate their facilities. In the fall of 1960, some of those who had participated in the sit-ins formed the Student Nonviolent Coordinating Com-

SNCC

mittee (SNCC), which worked to keep the spirit of resistance alive.

In 1961, an interracial group of students, working with the Congress of Racial Equality (CORE), began what they called "freedom rides" (reviving a tactic CORE had tried, without much success, in the 1940s). Traveling by bus throughout the South, the freedom riders tried to force the desegregation of bus stations. In some places, they met with such savage violence at the hands of enraged whites that the president finally dispatched federal marshals to help keep the peace. Kennedy also ordered the integration of all bus and train stations. In the meantime, SNCC workers began fanning out through black communities and even into remote rural areas to encourage blacks to challenge the obstacles to voting that the Jim Crow laws had created and that powerful social custom sustained. The Southern Christian Leadership Conference (SCLC) also created citizen-education and other programs—many of them organized by Ella Baker, one of the great grassroots leaders of the movement—to mobilize black workers, farmers, housewives, and others to challenge segregation, disfranchisement, and discrimination.

"Freedom Rides"

Continuing judicial efforts to enforce the integration of public education increased the pressure on national leaders to respond to the civil rights movement. In October 1962, a federal court ordered the University of Mississippi to enroll its first black student, James Meredith; Governor Ross Barnett, a strident segregationist, refused to enforce the order. When angry whites in Oxford, Mississippi, began rioting to protest the court decree, President Kennedy sent federal troops to the city to restore order and protect Meredith's right to attend the university.

Events in Alabama in 1963 helped bring the growing movement to something of a climax. In April, Martin Luther King Jr. helped launch a series of nonviolent demonstrations in Birmingham, Alabama, a city unsurpassed in its commitment to segregation. Police Commissioner Eugene "Bull" Connor supervised a brutal effort to break up the peaceful marches, arresting hundreds of demonstrators and using attack dogs, tear gas, electric cattle prods, and fire hoses—at times even against small children—as much of the nation watched televised reports in horror. Two months later, Governor George Wallace—who had won election in 1962 pledging staunch resistance to integration—pledged to stand in the doorway of a building at the University of Alabama to prevent the court-ordered enrollment of several black students. Only after the arrival of federal marshals and a visit from Attorney General Robert Kennedy did Wallace give way. His stand won him wide popularity among whites throughout the nation who were growing uncomfortable with the pace of integration. That same night, NAACP official Medgar Evers was murdered in Mississippi.

Birmingham

BIRMINGHAM, 1963 In one of the scenes that horrified many Americans watching on television, police in Birmingham, Alabama, turn fire hoses full force on civil rights demonstrators, knocking many of them to the ground. *(AP/Wide World Photos)*

A National Commitment

The events in Alabama and Mississippi were a warning to the president that he could no longer contain or avoid the issue of race. In an important television address the night of the University of Alabama confrontation (and the murder of Evers), Kennedy spoke eloquently of the "moral issue" facing the nation. "If an American," he asked, "because his skin is dark, . . . cannot enjoy the full and free life which all of us want, then who among us would be content to have the color of his skin changed and stand in his place? Who among us would then be content with the counsels of patience and delay?" Days later, he introduced a series of new legislative proposals prohibiting segregation in "public accommodations" (stores, restaurants, theaters, hotels), barring discrimination in employment, and increasing the power of the government to file suits on behalf of school integration.

To generate support for the legislation, and to dramatize the power of the growing movement, more than 200,000 demonstrators marched down the Mall in Washington, D.C., in August 1963 and gathered before the Lincoln Memorial for the greatest civil rights demonstration in the nation's history. President Kennedy, who had at first opposed the idea of the march, in the end gave it his open support after receiving pledges from organizers that speakers would not criticize the administration. Martin Luther King Jr. in one of the greatest speeches of his distinguished oratorical career, roused the crowd with a litany of images prefaced again and again by the phrase "I have a dream." The march was the high-water mark of the peaceful, interracial civil rights movement.

The assassination of President Kennedy three months later gave new impetus to the battle for civil rights

March on Washington

THE CIVIL RIGHTS MOVEMENT

The civil rights movement was one of the most important events in the modern history of the United States. It helped force the dismantling of legalized segregation and disfranchisement of African Americans, and also served as a model for other groups mobilizing to demand dignity and rights. And like all important events in history, it has produced scholarship that examines the movement in a number of different ways.

The early histories established a view of the civil rights movement that remains the most widely accepted. They rest on a heroic narrative of moral purpose and personal courage by which great men and women inspired ordinary people to rise up and struggle for their rights. This narrative generally begins with the *Brown* decision of 1954 and the Montgomery bus boycott of 1955, continues through the civil rights campaigns of the early 1960s, and culminates in the Civil Rights Acts of 1964 and 1965. Among the central events in this narrative are the March on Washington of 1963, with Martin Luther King Jr.'s famous "I Have a Dream" speech, and the assassination of King in 1968, which has often symbolized the end of the movement and the beginning of a different, more complicated period of the black freedom struggle. The key element of these

narratives is the central importance to the movement of a few great leaders, most notably King himself. Among the best examples of this kind of narrative are Taylor Branch's powerful studies of the life and struggles of King, *Parting the Waters* (1988), *Pillar of Fire* (1998), and *At Canaan's Edge* (2006), as well as David Garrow's important study, *Bearing the Cross* (1986).

Few historians would deny the importance of King and other leaders to the successes of the civil rights movement. But a number of scholars have argued that the leader-centered narrative obscures the vital contributions of ordinary people in communities throughout the South, and the nation, to the struggle. John Dittmer's *Local People: The Struggle for Civil-Rights in Mississippi* (1994) and Charles Payne's *I've Got the Light of Freedom* (1995) both examine the day-to-day work of the movement's rank and file in the early 1960s and argue that their efforts were at least as important as those of King and other leaders. The national leadership helped bring visibility to these struggles, but King and his circle were usually present only briefly, if at all, for the actual work of communities in challenging segregation. Only by understanding the local origins of the movement, these and other scholars argue, can we understand its true character.

BROWN V. BOARD OF EDUCATION This photograph, taken for an Atlanta newspaper, illustrated the long and dangerous walk that Linda Brown, one of the plaintiffs in the famous desegregation case that ultimately reached the Supreme Court, had to travel each day on her way to a segregated school in Topeka, Kansas. An all-white school was located close to her home, but to reach the black school she had to attend required a long walk and a long bus ride each day. Not only does the picture illustrate the difficulties segregation created for Linda Brown, it was also a part of a broad publicity campaign launched by the supporters of the case. *(Carl Iwasaki/Time Life Pictures/Getty Images)*

legislation. The ambitious measure that Kennedy had proposed in June 1963 had stalled in the Senate after having passed through the House of Representatives with relative ease. Early in 1964, after Johnson applied both public and private pressure, supporters of the measure finally mustered the two-thirds majority necessary to close debate and end a filibuster by southern senators; and the Senate passed the most comprehensive civil rights bill in the nation's history.

The Battle for Voting Rights

Having won a significant victory in one area, the civil rights movement shifted its focus to another: voting rights. During the summer of 1964, thousands of civil rights workers, black and white, northern and southern, spread out through the South, but primarily in Mississippi, to work on

behalf of black voter registration and participation. The campaign was known as "freedom summer," and it produced a violent response from some southern whites. Three of the first freedom workers to arrive in the South—two whites, Andrew Goodman and Michael Schwerner, and one black, James Chaney—were brutally murdered by Ku Klux Klan members with the support of local police and others.

"Freedom Summer"

The "freedom summer" also produced the Mississippi Freedom Democratic Party (MFDP), an integrated alternative to the regular state party organization. Under the leadership of Fannie Lou Hamer and others, the MFDP challenged the regular party's right to its seats at the Democratic National Convention that summer. President Johnson, eager to avoid antagonizing anyone (even southern white Democrats who seemed likely to support his Republican opponent), enlisted King's help to broker a compromise.

Scholars also disagree about the time frame of the movement. Rather than beginning the story in 1954 or 1955 (as in Robert Weisbrot's excellent 1991 synthesis *Freedom Bound* or William Chafe's remarkable 1981 local study *Civilities and Civil Rights,* which examined the Greensboro sit-ins of 1961), a number of scholars have tried to move the story into both earlier periods and later ones. Robin Kelley's *Race Rebels* (1994) emphasizes the important contributions of working-class African Americans, some of them allied for a time with the Communist Party, to the undermining of racist assumptions. These activists, Kelley shows, organized some of the earliest civil rights demonstrations—sit-ins, marches, and other efforts to challenge segregation—long before the conventional dates for the beginning of the movement. Gail O'Brien's *The Color of the Law* (1999) examines a 1946 "race riot" in Columbia, Tennessee, arguing for its importance as a signal of the early growth of African-American militancy, and the movement of that militancy from the streets into the legal system.

Other scholars have looked beyond the 1960s and have incorporated events outside the orbit of the formal "movement" to explain the history of the civil rights struggle. A growing literature on northern, urban, and relatively radical activists has suggested that focusing too much on mainstream leaders and the celebrated efforts in the South in the 1960s diverts our view from the equally important challenges facing northern African Americans and the very different tactics and strategies that they often chose to pursue their goals. The enormous attention historians have given to the life and legacy of Malcolm X—among them Alex Haley's influential *Autobiography of Malcolm X* (1965) and Michael Eric Dyson's *Making Malcolm* (1996)—is one example of this, as is the increasing attention scholars have given to black radicalism in the late 1960s and beyond and to such militant groups as the Black Panthers. Other literature has extended the civil rights struggle even further, into the 1980s and beyond, and has brought into focus such issues as the highly disproportionate number of African Americans sentenced to death within the criminal justice system. Randall Kennedy's *Race, Crime, and the Law* (1997) is a particularly important study of this issue.

Even *Brown* v. *Board of Education* (1954), the great landmark of the legal challenge to segregation, has been subject to reexamination. Richard Kluger's narrative history of the *Brown* decision, *Simple Justice* (1975), is a classic statement of the traditional view of *Brown* as a triumph over injustice. But others have been less certain of the dramatic success of the ruling. James T. Patterson's *Brown* v. *Board of Education: A Civil Rights Milestone and Its Troubled Legacy* (2001) argues that the *Brown* decision long preceded any national consensus on the need to end segregation and that its impact was far less decisive than earlier scholars have suggested. Michael Klarman's *From Jim Crow to Civil Rights* (2004) examines the role of the Supreme Court in advancing civil rights and suggests, among other things, that the *Brown* decision may actually have retarded racial progress in the South for a time because of the enormous backlash it created. Charles Ogletree's *All Deliberate Speed* (2004) and Derrick Bell's *Silent Covenants* (2004) both argue that the Court's decision did not provide an effective enforcement mechanism for desegregation and in many other ways failed to support measures that would have made school desegregation a reality. They note as evidence for this view that American public schools are now more segregated—even if not forcibly by law—than they were at the time of the *Brown* decision.

As the literature on the African-American freedom struggles of the twentieth century has grown, historians have begun to speak of civil rights *movements,* rather than a single, cohesive movement. In this way, scholars recognize that struggles of this kind take many more forms, and endure through many more periods of history, than the traditional accounts suggest.

It permitted the MFDP to be seated as observers, with promises of party reforms later on, while the regular party retained its official standing. Both sides grudgingly accepted the agreement. Both were embittered by it.

A year later, in March 1965, King helped organize a major demonstration in Selma, Alabama, to press the demand for the right of blacks to register to vote. Selma sheriff Jim Clark led local police in a brutal attack on the demonstrators—which, as in Birmingham, received graphic television coverage and horrified many viewers across the nation. Two northern whites participating in the Selma march were murdered in the course of the effort there—one, a minister, beaten to death in the streets of the town; the other, a Detroit housewife, shot as she drove along a highway at night with a black passenger in her car. The national outrage that followed the events in Alabama helped push Lyndon Johnson to propose and win passage of the Civil Rights Act of 1965, better known as the Voting Rights Act, which provided federal protection to blacks attempting to exercise their right to vote. But important as such gains were, they failed to satisfy the rapidly rising expectations of African Americans as the focus of the movement began to move from political to economic issues.

Voting Rights Act

The Changing Movement

For decades, the nation's African-American population had been undergoing a major demographic shift; and by the 1960s, the problem of racial injustice was no longer primarily southern and rural, as it had been earlier in the century. By 1966, 69 percent of American blacks were living in metropolitan areas and 45 percent outside the South. Although the economic condition of much of American

MARTIN LUTHER KING JR. IN WASHINGTON Moments after completing his memorable speech during the August 1963 March on Washington, King waves to the vast and enthusiastic crowd that has gathered in front of the Lincoln Memorial to demand "equality and jobs." *(AP/Wide World Photos)*

society was improving, in the poor urban communities in which the black population was concentrated, things were getting significantly worse. Well over half of all American nonwhites lived in poverty at the beginning of the 1960s; black unemployment was twice that of whites.

By the mid-1960s, therefore, the issue of race was moving out of the South and into the rest of the nation. The battle against school desegregation had moved beyond the initial assault on de jure segregation (segregation by law) to an attack on de facto segregation (segregation in practice, as through residential patterns), thus carrying the fight into northern cities. Many African-American leaders (and their white supporters) were demanding, similarly, that the battle against job discrimination move to a new level. Employers not only should abandon negative measures to deny jobs to blacks; they also should adopt positive measures to recruit minorities,

De jure and De facto Segregation

thus compensating for past injustices. Lyndon Johnson gave his tentative support to the concept of "affirmative action" in 1965. Over the next decade, affirmative action guidelines gradually extended to all institutions doing business with or receiving funds from the federal government (including schools and universities)—and to many others as well.

A symbol of the movement's new direction, and of the problems it would cause, was a major campaign in the summer of 1966 in Chicago, in which King played a prominent role. Organizers of the Chicago campaign hoped to direct national attention to housing and employment discrimination in northern industrial cities in much the same way similar campaigns had exposed legal racism in the South. But the Chicago campaign not only evoked vicious and at times violent opposition from white residents of that city; it also failed to arouse the national conscience in the way events in the South had.

Urban Violence

Well before the Chicago campaign, the problem of urban poverty was thrust into national attention when violence broke out in black neighborhoods in major cities. There were a few scattered disturbances in the summer of 1964, most notably in Harlem. The first large race riot

Watts Riot

since the end of World War II occurred the following summer in the Watts section of Los Angeles. In the midst of a seemingly routine traffic arrest, a white police officer struck a protesting black bystander with his club. The incident triggered a storm of anger and a week of violence (and revealed how deeply African Americans in Los Angeles, and in other cities, resented their treatment at the hands of local police). As many as 10,000 people were estimated to have participated in the violence—attacking white motorists, burning buildings, looting stores, and sniping at policemen. Thirty-four people died during the Watts uprising, which was eventually quelled by the National Guard; twenty-eight of the dead were black. In the summer of 1966, there were forty-three additional outbreaks, the most serious of them in Chicago and Cleveland. And in the summer of 1967, there were eight major outbreaks, including the largest of

them all—a racial clash in Detroit in which forty-three people (thirty-three of them black) died.

Televised reports of the violence alarmed millions of Americans and created both a new sense of urgency and a growing sense of doubt among many of those whites who had embraced the cause of racial justice only a few years before. A special Commission on Civil Disorders, created by the president in response to the disturbances, issued a celebrated report in the spring of 1968 recommending massive spending to eliminate the abysmal conditions of the ghettos. "Only a commitment to national action on an unprecedented scale," the commission concluded, "can shape a future compatible with the historic ideals of American society." To many white Americans, however, the lesson of the riots was the need for stern measures to stop violence and lawlessness.

Black Power

Disillusioned with the ideal of peaceful change in cooperation with whites, an increasing number of African Americans were turning to a new approach to the racial issue: the philosophy of "black power." Black power could mean many different things. But in all

Shift from Integration to Racial Distinction

"TURN LEFT OR GET SHOT" This chilling sign, erected at an intersection in the Watts neighborhood in Los Angeles during the 1965 riot there, illustrates the escalating racial tensions that were beginning to explode in American cities in the mid-1960s. *(Bettmann/Corbis)*

its forms, it suggested a move away from interracial cooperation and toward increased awareness of racial distinctiveness. It was part of a long nationalist tradition among African Americans that extended back into slavery and that had its most visible twentieth-century expression in the Garvey movement of the 1920s.

Perhaps the most enduring impact of the black-power ideology was a social and psychological one: instilling racial pride in African Americans, who lived in a society whose dominant culture generally portrayed African Americans as inferior to whites. It encouraged the growth of black studies in schools and universities. It helped stimulate important black literary and artistic movements. It produced a new interest among many African Americans in their African roots. It led to a rejection by some blacks of certain cultural practices borrowed from white society: "Afro" hairstyles began to replace artificially straightened hair; some blacks began to adopt African styles of dress, even to change their names.

But black power had political manifestations as well, most notably in creating a deep schism within the civil rights movement. Traditional black organizations that had emphasized cooperation with sympathetic whites—groups such as the NAACP, the Urban League, and King's Southern Christian Leadership Conference—now faced competition from radical groups. The Student Nonviolent Coordinating Committee and the Congress of Racial Equality had both begun as moderate, interracial organizations; SNCC, in fact, was originally a student branch of the SCLC. By the mid-1960s, however, these and other groups were calling for radical and occasionally even violent action against the racism of white society and were openly rejecting the approaches of older, more established black leaders.

An Increasingly Divided Civil Rights Movement

Particularly alarming to many whites (and to some African Americans as well) were organizations that existed entirely outside the mainstream civil rights movement. In Oakland, California, the Black Panther Party (founded by Huey Newton and Bobby Seale) promised to defend black rights even if that required violence. Black Panthers organized along semimilitary lines and wore weapons openly and proudly. They were, in fact, more the victims of violence from the police than they were practitioners of violence themselves. But they created an image, quite deliberately, of militant radicals willing to fight for justice, in Newton's words, "through the barrel of a gun."

Malcolm X

In Detroit, a once-obscure black nationalist group, the Nation of Islam, gained new prominence. Founded in 1931 by Elijah Poole (who converted to Islam and renamed himself Elijah Muhammed), the movement taught blacks

Nation of Islam

MALCOLM X Malcolm X, a leader of the militant Nation of Islam, arrives in Washington, D.C., in May 1963 to set up a headquarters for the organization there. Malcolm was hated and feared by many whites during his lifetime. After he was assassinated in 1965, he became a widely revered hero among African Americans. *(Bettmann/ Corbis)*

to take responsibility for their own lives, to live by strict codes of behavior, and to reject any dependence on whites. The most celebrated of the Black Muslims, as whites often termed them, was Malcolm Little, a former drug addict and pimp who had spent time in prison and had rebuilt his life after joining the movement. He adopted the name Malcolm X ("X" to denote his lost African surname).

Malcolm became one of the movement's most influential spokesmen, particularly among younger blacks, as a result of his intelligence, his oratorical skills, and his harsh, uncompromising opposition to all forms of racism and oppression. He did not advocate violence, as his critics often claimed; but he insisted that black people had the right to defend themselves, violently if necessary, from those who assaulted them. Malcolm died in

1965 when black gunmen, presumably under orders from rivals within the Nation of Islam, assassinated him in New York.

But Malcolm's influence did not die with him. A book he had been working on before his death with the writer Alex Haley *(The Autobiography of Malcolm X)* attracted wide attention after its publication in 1965 and spread his reputation broadly through the nation. Years after his death, he was to many African Americans as important and revered a symbol as Martin Luther King Jr.

"FLEXIBLE RESPONSE" AND THE COLD WAR

In international affairs as much as in domestic reform, the optimistic liberalism of the Kennedy and Johnson administrations dictated a more positive, more active approach to dealing with the nation's problems than in the past. And just as the new activism in domestic reform proved more difficult and divisive than liberals had imagined, so too it created frustrations and failures in foreign policy.

Diversifying Foreign Policy

The Kennedy administration entered office convinced that the United States needed to be able to counter communist aggression in more flexible ways than the atomic-weapons-oriented defense strategy of the Eisenhower years had permitted. In particular, Kennedy was unsatisfied with the nation's ability to meet communist threats in "emerging areas" of the Third World—the areas in which, Kennedy believed, the real struggle against communism would be waged in the future. He gave enthusiastic support to the expansion of the Special Forces (or "Green Berets," as they were soon known)—soldiers trained specifically to fight guerrilla conflicts and other limited wars.

"Flexible Response"

Kennedy also favored expanding American influence through peaceful means. To repair the badly deteriorating relationship with Latin America, he proposed an "Alliance for Progress": a series of projects for peaceful development and stabilization of the nations of that region. Kennedy also inaugurated the Agency for International Development (AID) to coordinate foreign aid. And he established what became one of his most popular innovations: the Peace Corps, which sent young American volunteers abroad to work in developing areas.

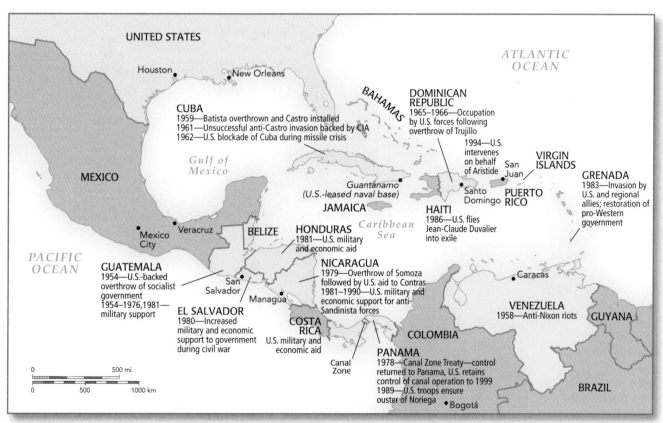

THE UNITED STATES IN LATIN AMERICA, 1954–1996 The Cold War greatly increased the readiness of the United States to intervene in the affairs of its Latin American neighbors. This map presents the many times and ways in which Washington ordered interventions in Central America, the Caribbean, and the northern nations of South America. During much of this period, the interventions were driven by Cold War concerns—by fears that communists might take over nations near the United States as they had taken over Cuba in the early 1960s. ◆ *What other interests motivated the U.S. to exert influence in Latin America, even after the end of the Cold War?*

Among the first foreign policy ventures of the Kennedy administration was a disastrous assault on the Castro government in Cuba. The Eisenhower administration had begun the project; and by the time Kennedy took office, Bay of Pigs the CIA had been working for months to train a small army of anti-Castro Cuban exiles in Central America. On April 17, 1961, with the approval of the new president, 2,000 of the armed exiles landed at the Bay of Pigs in Cuba, expecting first American air support and then a spontaneous uprising by the Cuban people on their behalf. They received neither. At the last minute, as it became clear that things were going badly, Kennedy withdrew the air support, fearful of involving the United States too directly in the invasion. The expected uprising did not occur. Instead, well-armed Castro forces easily crushed the invaders, and within two days the entire mission had collapsed.

Confrontations with the Soviet Union

In the grim aftermath of the Bay of Pigs, Kennedy traveled to Vienna in June 1961 for his first meeting with Soviet premier Nikita Khrushchev. Their frosty exchange of views did little to reduce tensions between the two nations—nor did Khrushchev's veiled threat of war if the United States continued to support a noncommunist West Berlin in the heart of East Germany.

Khrushchev was particularly unhappy about the mass exodus of residents of East Germany to the West through the easily traversed border in the center of Berlin. But he ultimately found a method short of war to stop it. Before dawn on August 13, 1961, the East German government, complying with directives from Moscow, began constructing a wall between East and West Berlin. Guards fired on those who continued to try to escape. For nearly thirty years, the Berlin Wall served as the most potent physical symbol of the conflict between the communist and noncommunist worlds.

The rising tensions culminated the following October in the most dangerous and dramatic crisis of the Cold War. On October 14, aerial reconnaissance photos produced clear evidence that the Soviets were constructing sites in Cuba for offensive nuclear weapons. To the Soviets, placing missiles in Cuba probably seemed a reasonable—and relatively inexpensive—way to counter the presence of

REPAIRING THE BERLIN WALL First erected in 1961, the Berlin Wall became steadily higher and more elaborately fortified over the next several years. *(AP/Wide World Photos)*

American missiles in Turkey (and a way to deter any future American invasion of Cuba). But to Kennedy and most other Americans, the missile sites represented an act of aggression by the Soviets toward the United States. Almost immediately, the president decided that the weapons could not be allowed to remain. On October 22, he ordered a naval and air blockade around Cuba, a "quarantine" against all offensive weapons. Preparations were under way for an American air attack on the missile sites when, late in the evening of October 26, Kennedy received a message from Khrushchev implying that the Soviet Union would remove the missile bases in exchange for an American pledge not to invade Cuba. Ignoring other, tougher Soviet messages, the president agreed. The crisis was over.

Johnson and the World

Lyndon Johnson entered the presidency lacking even John Kennedy's limited prior experience with international affairs. He was eager, therefore, not only to continue the policies of his predecessor but also to prove quickly that he too was a strong and forceful leader.

An internal rebellion in the Dominican Republic gave him an early opportunity to do so. A 1961 assassination had toppled the repressive dictatorship of General Rafael Trujillo, and for the next four years various factions in the country had struggled for dominance. In the spring of 1965, a conservative military regime began to collapse in

Intervention in the Dominican Republic

the face of a revolt by a broad range of groups on behalf of the left-wing nationalist Juan Bosch. Arguing (without any evidence) that Bosch planned to establish a pro-Castro, communist regime, Johnson dispatched 30,000 American troops to quell the disorder. Only after a conservative candidate defeated Bosch in a 1966 election were the forces withdrawn.

From Johnson's first moments in office, however, his foreign policy was almost totally dominated by the bitter civil war in Vietnam and by the expanding involvement of the United States there.

THE AGONY OF VIETNAM

George Kennan, who helped devise the containment doctrine that drew America into war in Vietnam, once called the conflict "the most disastrous of all America's undertakings over the whole 200 years of its history." Yet at first, the Vietnam War seemed simply one more Third World struggle on the periphery of the Cold War, a struggle in which the United States would try to tip the balance against communism without becoming too deeply or directly engaged. No single president really "decided" to go to war in Vietnam. Rather, the American involvement there emerged from years of gradually increasing commitments that slowly and almost imperceptibly expanded.

The First Indochina War

Vietnam had a long history both as an independent kingdom and a major power in its region, and as a subjugated province of China; its people were both proud of their past glory and painfully aware of their many years of subjugation. In the mid-nineteenth century, Vietnam became a colony of France. And like other European possessions in Asia, it fell under the control of Japan during World War II. After the defeat of Japan, the question arose of what was to happen to Vietnam in the postwar world. There were two opposing forces attempting to answer that question, both of them appealing to the United States for help. The French wanted to reassert their colonial control

HARVARD ON STRIKE, 1969 The poster, one of several versions of the same image, was designed by architecture students at Harvard in the spring of 1969 during a strike that threw the university into turmoil. As at other universities, students occupied an administration building; police were called in to clear them out; and a crisis followed that at Harvard, as at Columbia the year before, led to the resignation of the president. Another version of this poster superimposed a list of reasons for the strike, among them, "Strike because you hate cops/strike because your roommate was clubbed . . ./strike to seize control of your life/strike to become more human . . ./strike because there's no poetry in your lectures/strike because classes are a bore/strike for power/strike to smash the corporation/strike to make yourself free/. . . strike because they are trying to squeeze the life out of you." *(Courtesy of the Harvard University Archives, HUA 969.100.2 pf)*

over Vietnam. Challenging them was a powerful nationalist movement within Vietnam committed to creating an independent country. The nationalists were organized into a political party, the Vietminh, which had been created in 1941 and led ever since by Ho Chi Minh, a communist educated in Paris and Moscow, and a fervent Vietnamese nationalist. The Vietminh had fought against Japan throughout World War II. In the fall of 1945, after the collapse of Japan and before the Western powers had time to return, the Vietminh declared Vietnam an independent nation and set up a nationalist government under Ho Chi Minh in Hanoi.

Ho had worked closely during the war with American intelligence forces in Indochina in fighting the Japanese; he apparently considered the United States something like an ally. When the war ended in 1945, he began writing President Truman asking for support in his struggle against the French. He received no reply to his letters, probably because no one in the State Department had heard of him. At the same time, Truman was under heavy pressure from both the British and the French to support France in its effort to reassert its control over Vietnam. The French argued that without Vietnam, their domestic economy would collapse. And since the economic revival of Western Europe was quickly becoming one of the Truman administration's top priorities, the United States did nothing to stop (although, at first, also relatively little to encourage) the French as they moved back into Vietnam in 1946 and began a struggle with the Vietminh to reestablish control over the country.

At first, the French had little difficulty reestablishing control. They drove Ho Chi Minh out of Hanoi and into hiding in the countryside; and in 1949, they established a nominally independent national government under the leadership of the former emperor, Bao Dai—an ineffectual, Westernized playboy unable to assert any real independent authority. The real power remained in the hands of the French. But the Vietminh continued to challenge the French-dominated regime and slowly increased its control over large areas of the countryside. The French appealed to the United States for support; and in February 1950, the Truman administration formally recognized the Bao Dai regime and agreed to provide it with direct military and economic aid.

For the next four years, during what has become known as the First Indochina War, Truman and then Eisenhower continued to support the French military campaign against the Vietminh; by 1954, by some calculations, the United States was paying 80 percent of France's war costs. But the war went badly for the French in spite of the American support. Finally, late in 1953, Vietminh forces engaged the French in a major battle in the far northwest corner of the country, at Dien Bien Phu, an isolated and almost indefensible site. The French were surrounded, and the battle turned into a prolonged and horrible siege, with the French position steadily deteriorating. It was at this point that the Eisenhower administration decided not to intervene to save the French (see p. 804). The defense of Dien Bien Phu collapsed and the French government decided the time had come to get out. The First Indochina War had come to an end.

Geneva and the Two Vietnams

An international conference at Geneva, planned many months before to settle the Korean dispute and other controversies, now took up the fate of Vietnam as well. The United States was only indirectly involved in the Vietnam phase of the Geneva Conference. Secretary of State Dulles, who did not really believe in negotiating with communists, reluctantly attended but left early; the United States was not a party to the accords. Even so, the Geneva Conference produced an agreement to end the Vietnam conflict. There would be an immediate cease-fire in the war; Vietnam would be temporarily partitioned along the 17th parallel, with the Vietminh in control of North Vietnam and a pro-Western regime in control of the South. In 1956, elections would be held to reunite the country under a single government.

The partition of Vietnam was essentially artificial. But there were, in fact, real and important differences between North and South Vietnam. North Vietnam, the area now to be controlled by the Vietminh, was the heart of traditional Vietnamese society, the area where French influence had been the weakest. The North had remained a reasonably stable, reasonably homogeneous culture, most of whose people lived in very close-knit, traditional villages. North Vietnam was also the poorest region of the country—overpopulated, plagued by a serious maldistribution of scarce land, and hit by a serious famine at the end of the war. The Vietminh had worked effectively to alleviate the great famine and had won strong popular allegiance to the regime as a result. (Later, in the early 1950s, it launched a disastrous land reform policy, which it soon repudiated.) The Hanoi government was also strengthened by the mass exodus—in 1954, at the time of the partition—of many Catholics and others in the north who might have opposed them had they stayed. The North Vietnamese were passionately committed to the unification of the nation, a commitment with deep roots in Vietnamese history.

South Vietnam, by contrast, was a much more recently settled area. Until the early nineteenth century, in fact, very few Vietnamese had lived there; most of the sparse population had consisted of Khmer (Cambodians). Even in the 1950s, most of its people had been there only three generations or less. For many years it had been something like the American West in the nineteenth century—the place where adventurous, or opportunistic, or disenchanted people from the poor, overpopulated North would move in search of a new beginning, and in search of land (which was scarce in the north but plentiful in the south). It was a looser, more heterogeneous, more individualistic society. It was highly factionalized—religiously, politically, and ethnically—with powerful sects (and even a

The Vietminh

Geneva Conference

South Vietnamese Society

powerful mafia) all competing for power. It was also more prosperous and fertile than the North. It was not overpopulated. It had experienced no famine. It was the only region of the country producing a surplus for export.

South Vietnam had no legacy of strong commitment to the Vietminh and much less fervent commitment to national unification than did North Vietnam. It was the area where the influence of the French (their language, culture, and values) had been strongest and where there was a substantial, Westernized middle class. It was, in other words, a society much more difficult to unite and to govern than was the society of the North.

America and Diem

As soon as the Geneva accords established the partition, the French finally left Vietnam. The United States almost immediately stepped into the vacuum and became the principal benefactor of the new government in the South,

Ngo Dinh Diem

led by Ngo Dinh Diem. Diem was an aristocratic Catholic from central Vietnam, an outsider in the South. But he was also a nationalist, uncontaminated by collaboration with the French. And he was, for a time, successful. With the help of the American CIA, Diem waged an effective campaign against some of the powerful religious sects and the South Vietnamese mafia, which had challenged the authority of the central government. As a result, the United States came to regard Diem as a powerful and impressive alternative to Ho Chi Minh. Lyndon Johnson once called him the "Churchill of Southeast Asia."

The American government supported South Vietnamese president Ngo Dinh Diem's refusal in 1956 to permit the elections called for by the Geneva accords (see p. 826), reasoning, correctly, that Ho Chi Minh would easily win any such election. Ho could count on 100 percent of the vote in the north, with its much larger population, and at least some support in the south. In the meantime, the United States poured military and economic aid into South Vietnam. By 1956, it was the second largest recipient of American military aid in the world, after Korea.

Diem's early successes in suppressing the sects in Vietnam led him in 1959 to begin a similar campaign to eliminate the Vietminh supporters who had stayed behind in the south after the partition. He was quite successful for a time, so successful, in fact, that the North Vietnamese found it necessary to respond. A new policy emanating from Moscow beginning in 1959, emphasizing communist wars of national liberation (as opposed to direct Soviet confrontations with the United States and NATO), also encouraged Ho Chi Minh to resume his armed struggle for national unification. In 1959, the Vietminh cadres in the south created the National

The NLF

Liberation Front (NLF), known to many Americans as the Viet Cong—an organization closely allied with the North Vietnamese government. It was committed to over-

throwing the "puppet regime" of Diem and reuniting the nation. In 1960, under orders from Hanoi, and with both material and manpower support from North Vietnam, the NLF began military operations in the South.

By 1961, NLF forces were very successfully destabilizing the Diem regime. They were killing over 4,000 government officials a year (mostly village leaders) and establishing effective control over many areas of the countryside. Diem was also by now losing the support of many other groups in South Vietnam, and he was even losing support within his own military. In 1963, the Diem regime precipitated a major crisis by trying to discipline and repress the South Vietnamese Buddhists in an effort to make Catholicism the dominant religion of the country. The Buddhists began to stage enormous antigovernment demonstrations; and after Diem launched a series of heavy-handed military and police actions against them—which included several massacres of demonstrators and violent government raids on their sacred pagodas—the demonstrations grew much larger. Several Buddhist monks doused themselves with gasoline, sat cross-legged in the streets of downtown Saigon, and set themselves on fire—in view of photographers and television cameras.

The Buddhist crisis was alarming and embarrassing to the Kennedy administration. It caused the American government to reconsider its commitment to Diem—although not to the survival of South Vietnam.

Diem Overthrown

American officials pressured Diem to reform his government, but Diem made no significant concessions. As a result, in the fall of 1963, Kennedy gave his tacit approval to a plot by a group of South Vietnamese generals to topple Diem. In early November 1963, the generals staged the coup, assassinated Diem and his brother and principal adviser, Ngo Dinh Nhu (killings the United States had not wanted or expected), and established the first of a series of new governments, which were, for over three years, even less stable than the one they had overthrown. A few weeks after the coup, John Kennedy too was dead.

From Aid to Intervention

Lyndon Johnson thus inherited what was already a substantial American commitment to the survival of an anticommunist South Vietnam. During his first two years in office, he expanded that commitment into a full-scale American war. Why he did so has long been a subject of debate (see "Where Historians Disagree," pp. 828–829).

Many factors played a role in Johnson's decision. But the most obvious explanation is that the new president faced many pressures to expand the American involvement and very few to limit it. As the untested successor to a revered and martyred president, he felt obliged to prove his worthiness for the office by continuing the policies of his predecessor. Aid to South Vietnam

Pressure for American Intervention

had been one of the most prominent of those policies.

THE VIETNAM COMMITMENT

In 1965, the Department of Defense released a film intended for American soldiers about to embark for service in Vietnam and designed to explain why the United States had found it necessary to commit so many lives and resources to the defense of a small and distant land. The film was titled *Why Vietnam?*—a question many Americans have pondered and debated in the decades since. The debate has proceeded on two levels. At one level is an effort to assess the broad objectives Americans believed they were pursuing in Vietnam. At another is an effort to explain how and why policymakers made the specific decisions that led to the American commitment.

The Defense Department film itself offered one answer to the question of America's broad objectives, an answer that for a time most Americans tended to accept: The United States was fighting in Vietnam to defend freedom and stop aggression; and it was fighting in Vietnam to prevent the spread of communism into a new area of the world, to protect not only Vietnam but also the other nations of the Pacific that would soon be threatened if Vietnam itself were to fall. This explanation—that America intervened in Vietnam to defend its ideals and its legitimate interests—continued to attract support well after the war ended. Political scientist Guenter Lewy contended, in *America in Vietnam* (1978), that the

United States entered Vietnam to help an ally combat "foreign aggression." R. B. Smith argued that Vietnam was a vital American interest, that the global concerns of the United States required a commitment there. And historian Ernest R. May stated: "The paradox is that the Vietnam War, so often condemned by its opponents as hideously immoral, may well have been the most moral or at least the most selfless war in all of American history. For the impulse guiding it was not to defeat an enemy or to serve a national interest; it was simply not to abandon friends."

Other scholars have taken a starkly different view: that America's broad objectives in Vietnam were not altruistic, that the intervention was a form of imperialism—part of a larger effort by the United States after World War II to impose a particular political and economic order on the world. "The Vietnam War," historian Gabriel Kolko wrote in *Anatomy of a War* (1985), "was for the United States the culmination of its frustrating postwar effort to merge its arms and politics to halt and reverse the emergence of states and social systems opposed to the international order Washington sought to establish." Economist Robert Heilbroner, writing in 1967, saw the American intent as somewhat more defensive; the intervention in Vietnam was a response to "a fear of losing our place in the sun," to a fear that a communist victory "would signal the end of capitalism as the dominant world order and would force the acknowledgment that America no longer constituted the model on which the future of world civilization would be mainly based."

(National Archives/AFP/Getty Images)

Johnson also felt it necessary to retain in his administration many of the important figures of the Kennedy years. In doing so, he surrounded himself with a group of foreign policy advisers—Secretary of State Dean Rusk, Secretary of Defense Robert McNamara, National Security Adviser McGeorge Bundy, and others—who firmly believed that the United States had an obligation to resist communism in Vietnam. A compliant Congress raised little protest to, and indeed at one point openly endorsed, Johnson's use of executive powers to lead the nation into war. And for sev-

eral years at least, public opinion remained firmly behind him—in part because Barry Goldwater's bellicose remarks about the war during the 1964 campaign made Johnson seem by comparison to be a moderate on the issue.

Above all, intervention in South Vietnam was fully consistent with nearly twenty years of American foreign policy. An anticommunist ally was appealing to the United States for assistance; all the assumptions of the containment doctrine, as it had come to be defined by the 1960s, seemed to require the nation to oblige. Vietnam, Johnson believed,

And Marilyn Young, in *The Vietnam Wars, 1945–1990* (1991), argues that the United States intervened in Vietnam as part of a broad and continuing effort to organize the post–World War II world along lines compatible with American interests and ideals.

Those who looked less at the nation's broad objectives than at the internal workings of the policy-making process likewise produced competing explanations. Journalist David Halberstam's *The Best and the Brightest* (1972) argued that policy-makers deluded themselves into thinking they could achieve their goals in Vietnam by ignoring, suppressing, or dismissing the information that might have suggested otherwise. The foreign policy leaders of the Kennedy and Johnson administrations were so committed to the idea of American activism and success that they refused to consider the possibility of failure; the Vietnam disaster was thus, at least in part, a result of the arrogance of the nation's leaders.

Larry Berman, a political scientist, offered a somewhat different view in *Planning a Tragedy* (1982) and *Lyndon Johnson's War* (1989). Lyndon Johnson never believed that American prospects in Vietnam were bright or that a real victory was within sight, Berman argued. Johnson was not misled by his advisers. He committed American troops to the war in Vietnam in 1965 not because he expected to win but because he feared that allowing Vietnam to fall would ruin him politically. To do otherwise, Johnson believed, would destroy his hopes for winning approval of his Great Society legislation at home.

Leslie H. Gelb and Richard K. Betts produced another, related explanation

(Leif Skoogfors/Corbis)

for American intervention, which saw the roots of the involvement in the larger imperatives of the American foreign policy system. In *The Irony of Vietnam: The System Worked,* published in 1979 and written in collaboration with political scientist Richard K. Betts, Gelb argued that intervention in Vietnam was the logical, perhaps even inevitable, result of a political and bureaucratic order shaped by the doctrine of containment. American foreign policy operated in response to a single, overriding imperative: the need to prevent the expansion of communism. However high the costs of intervention, policymakers believed, the costs of not intervening, of allowing South Vietnam to fall, would be higher. Only when the national and international political situation had shifted to the point where it was possible for American policymakers to reassess the costs of the commitment—to conclude

that the costs of allowing Vietnam to fall were less than the costs of continuing the commitment (a shift that began to occur in the early 1970s)—was it possible for the United States to begin disengaging.

More recent studies have questioned the idea that intervention was inevitable or that there were no viable alternatives. David Kaiser, in *American Tragedy* (2000), argues that John Kennedy was not, in fact, the hawkish supporter of escalation that he has often been portrayed as, but a man whose deep skepticism about the judgment of his military advisers had led him to believe that the United States should find a negotiated settlement to the war. His successor, Lyndon Johnson, harbored no such skepticism and sided with those who favored a military solution. The death of John Kennedy, therefore, becomes a vital event in the history of America in Vietnam. Fredrik Logevall, in *Choosing War: The Lost Chance for Peace and the Escalation of the War in Vietnam* (1999), argues that there were significant opportunities for a negotiated settlement of the war in the early 1960s, but that American leaders (including both Kennedy and Johnson) chose a military response instead—in part to protect themselves politically from charges of weakness.

That the debate over the Vietnam War has been so continuous over the past quarter-century is a reflection of the enormous role the United States's failure there has played in shaping the way Americans have thought about politics and policy ever since. Because the "lessons of Vietnam" remain a subject of intense popular concern, the debate over the history of Vietnam is likely to continue.

was a test of American willingness to fight communist aggression, a test he was determined not to fail.

During his first months in office, Johnson expanded the American involvement in Vietnam only slightly, sending an additional 5,000 military advisers there and preparing to send 5,000 more. Then, early in August 1964, the president announced that American destroyers on patrol in international waters in the Gulf of Tonkin had been attacked by North Vietnamese torpedo boats. Later information raised serious doubts as to whether the administration reported the attacks accurately. At the time, however, virtually no one questioned Johnson's portrayal of the incident as a serious act of aggression, or his insistence that the United States must respond.

Gulf of Tonkin Resolution

By a vote of 416 to 0 in the House and 88 to 2 in the Senate, Congress hurriedly passed the Gulf of Tonkin Resolution, which authorized the president to "take all necessary measures" to protect American forces and "prevent further aggression" in Southeast Asia. The resolution became,

THE WAR IN VIETNAM AND INDOCHINA, 1964–1975 Much of the Vietnam War was fought in small engagements in widely scattered areas and did not conform to traditional notions of combat. But as this map shows, there were traditional battles and invasions and supply routes as well. The red arrows in the middle of the map show the general path of the Ho Chi Minh Trail, the main supply route by which North Vietnam supplied its troops and allies in the South. The blue arrow in southern South Vietnam indicates the point at which American troops invaded Cambodia in 1970. ♦ *What is there in the geography of Indochina, as presented on this map, that helps to explain the great difficulty the American military had in securing South Vietnam against communist attacks?*

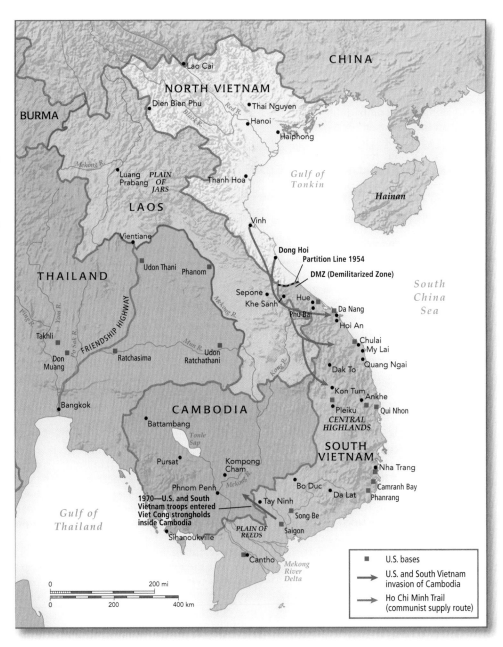

in Johnson's view at least, an open-ended legal authorization for escalation of the conflict.

With the South Vietnamese leadership still in disarray, more and more of the burden of opposition to the Viet Cong fell on the United States. In February 1965, seven marines died when communist forces attacked an American military base at Pleiku. Johnson retaliated by ordering the first American bombings of the north since the 1964 Tonkin crisis in an attempt to destroy the depots and transportation lines responsible for the flow of North Vietnamese soldiers and supplies into South Vietnam. The bombing continued intermittently until 1972. A month later, in March 1965, two battalions of American marines landed at Da Nang in South Vietnam. There were now more than 100,000 American troops in Vietnam.

Four months later, the president finally admitted that the character of the war had changed. American soldiers would now, he announced, begin playing an active combat role in the conflict. By the end of the year, there were more than 180,000 American combat troops in Vietnam; in 1966, that number doubled; and by the end of 1967, there were over 500,000 American soldiers there—along with a considerable number of civilian personnel working in various capacities and many American women (some enlisted, some not) who worked as nurses in military hospitals. In the meantime, the air war had intensified; ultimately the tonnage of bombs dropped on North Vietnam would exceed that in all theaters during World War II. And American casualties were mounting. In 1961, 14 Americans had died in Vietnam. By the spring of 1966, more than 4,000 Americans had been killed.

Mounting Casualties

SEARCH AND DESTROY   U.S. troops in Vietnam, often unable to distinguish enemy forces from the civilian population, increasingly sought to destroy places they considered possible enemy sanctuaries. Here an American soldier watches the burning of a village, one of many that U.S. troops destroyed.   *(Topham/The Image Works)*

Yet the gains resulting from the carnage were negligible. The United States had finally succeeded in 1965 in creating a reasonably stable government in the south under General Nguyen Van Thieu. But the new regime was hardly less corrupt or brutal than its predecessors, and no more able than they to establish its authority in its own countryside. The Viet Cong, not the Thieu regime, controlled the majority of South Vietnam's villages and hamlets.

The Quagmire

Central to the American war effort was a commitment to what the military called "attrition," a strategy premised

Strategy of "Attrition"

on the belief that the United States could inflict so many casualties and so much damage on the enemy that eventually they would be unable and unwilling to continue the struggle. But the attrition strategy failed because the North Vietnamese proved willing to commit many more soldiers to the conflict than the United States had expected (and many more than America itself was willing to send).

It failed, too, because the United States relied heavily on its bombing of the north to eliminate the communists' war-making capacity. American bombers struck at strategic targets (factories, bridges, railroads, shipyards, oil storage depots, etc.) in North Vietnam to weaken the material capacity of the communists to continue the war; and they bombed jungle areas of Vietnam, Laos, and Cambodia to cut off the "Ho Chi Minh Trail," the infiltration routes by which Hanoi sent troops and supplies into the south. In addition, the Americans hoped bombing would weaken the will of North Vietnam to continue the war.

By the end of 1967, virtually every identifiable target of any strategic importance in North Vietnam had been destroyed. The bombing had badly damaged the North Vietnamese economy, killed many soldiers and civilians, and made life difficult for those who survived, but it had produced none of the effects that the United States had expected. North Vietnam was not a modern, industrial society; it had few of the sorts of targets against which bombing is effective. And in any case, the North Vietnamese responded to the air raids with enormous ingenuity: They created a great network of underground tunnels, shops, and factories. They also secured increased aid from the Soviet Union and

THE FOLK-MUSIC REVIVAL

Two impulses of the 1960s—the renewed interest among young people in the politics of the left, and the search for an "authentic" alternative to what many considered the artificial, consumerist culture of modern America—helped produce the revived popularity of folk music in that turbulent era. Although the harder, harsher, and more sensual music of rock 'n' roll was more visible and more popular in the 1960s, folk music more clearly expressed many of the political ideas and aspirations that were welling up in the youth culture of the time.

The folk-music tradition, like most American musical traditions, had many roots. It drew from some of the black musical traditions of the South, and from the white country music of Appalachia. And it drew most immediately from a style of music developed by musicians associated with the Communist Party's Popular Front in the 1930s. Woody Guthrie, Pete Seeger, the Weavers, and others whose music would become popular again in the 1960s began their careers singing in Popular Front and union rallies during the Great Depression. Their music, like the Popular Front itself, set out to seem entirely American, rooted in the nation's folk traditions.

Folk music remained alive in the 1940s and 1950s, but it had only

DYLAN AND BAEZ This poster, created by the artist Eric Von Schmidt for a concert in 1961 by Joan Baez and Bob Dylan, evokes the gentle, vaguely spiritual character of folk music, which both differentiated it from rock and made it an appropriate vehicle for the idealistic political impulses that were emerging among many young people in the early 1960s. *(Getty Images)*

a modest popular following. Pete Seeger and the Weavers continued to perform and to attract attention on college campuses. Harry Belafonte

and the Kingston Trio recorded slick, pop versions of folk songs in an effort to bring them to mass audiences. In 1952, Folkway Records released the *Anthology of American Folk Music,* a collection of eighty-four performances recorded in the 1920s and 1930s that became an inspiration and an important source of material to many younger folk musicians. Folk-music festivals—at Berkeley, Newport, and Chicago—began to proliferate beginning in 1959. And an important community of folk musicians lived and performed together in the 1950s and early 1960s in New York's Greenwich Village.

As the politics of the 1960s became more heated, and as young people in particular became politically aroused, it was folk music that most directly reflected their new values and concerns. Peter, Paul, and Mary—although only intermittently political—became icons to much of the New Left, beginning with their 1962 recording of "If I Had a Hammer," a song first performed at Communist Party rallies in the 1940s by Pete Seeger and the Weavers. Bob Dylan, whose own politics were never wholly clear to the public, had a large impact on the 1960s left, even inadvertently providing a name to the most radical offshoot of Students for a Democratic Society (SDS), the Weathermen, who named themselves

---

China. Infiltration of the south was unaffected; the North Vietnamese just kept moving the Ho Chi Minh Trail. Nor did the bombing weaken North Vietnam's will to continue fighting. On the contrary, it seemed to increase the nation's resolve and strengthen its hatred of the United States.

Another crucial part of the American strategy was the "pacification" program, which was intended to push the Viet Cong from particular regions and then "pacify" those regions by winning the "hearts and minds" of the people. Routing the Viet Cong was often possible, but the subsequent pacification was more difficult. American forces were not adept at establishing the same kind of rapport with provincial Vietnamese that the Viet Cong had created; and the American military never gave that part of the program a high priority in any case.

"Hearts and Minds"

Gradually, the pacification program gave way to a heavy-handed relocation strategy, through which American troops uprooted villagers from their homes, sent them fleeing to refugee camps or into the cities (producing by 1967 more than 3 million refugees), and then destroyed the vacated villages and surrounding countryside. Saturation bombings (using conventional weapons and such incendiary devices as napalm), bulldozing of settlements, chemical defoliation of fields and jungles—all were designed to eliminate possible Viet Cong sanctuaries. But the Viet Cong responded by moving to new sanctuaries elsewhere. The futility of the United States's effort was suggested by the statement of an American officer after flattening one such hamlet that it had been "necessary to destroy [the village] in order to save it."

As the war dragged on and victory remained elusive, some American officers and officials began to urge the

COFFEE HOUSE MUSIC The Feejon Coffee House in Manhattan was popular among young writers, poets, and others in the late 1950s, in part because it was a gathering place for folk musicians, two of whom are shown here performing at right. *(Getty Images)*

PETE SEEGER Pete Seeger was one of several folk musicians who provided a link between the Popular Front–labor movement folk music of the 1930s and the folk revival of the 1960s. He is shown here in concert in 1966. *(Getty Images)*.

after a line from one of his songs: "You don't need a weatherman to know which way the wind blows."* Joan Baez, whose politics were no secret to anyone, was actively engaged in the antiwar movement and was arrested several times for participating in militant protests.

But it was not just the overt political messages of folk musicians that made them so important to young Americans in the 1960s. In addition, folk was a kind of music that seemed to reflect the "authenticity" the youth culture was attempting to find. In truth, neither the musicians themselves nor the young Americans attracted to them had much real connection with the traditions they were trying to evoke. The audiences for folk music—a product of rural and working-class traditions—were overwhelmingly urban, middle-class people. But the message of folk music—that there is a "real" America rooted in values of sharing and community, hidden beneath the crass commercialism of modern culture—resonated with the yearnings of many people in the 1960s (and beyond) for an alternative to their own troubled world. When young audiences responded to Woody Guthrie's famous ballad "This Land Is Your Land," they were expressing a hope for a different America—more democratic, more honest, and more natural than the land they knew.

*Bob Dylan, "Subterranean Homesick Blues." Copyright © 1965 by Warner Bros. Music. Copyright renewed 1993 by Special Rider Music. All rights reserved. International copyright secured. Reprinted by permission.

president to expand the military efforts. The Johnson administration, however, resisted. Unwilling to abandon its commitment to South Vietnam for fear of destroying American "credibility" in the world, the government was also unwilling to expand the war too far, for fear of provoking direct intervention by the Chinese, the Soviets, or both. In the meantime, the president began to encounter additional obstacles and frustrations at home.

The War at Home

As late as the end of 1965, few Americans, and even fewer influential ones, had protested the American involvement in Vietnam. But as the war dragged on and its futility became apparent, political support for it began to erode. A series of "teach-ins" on university campuses, beginning at the University of Michigan in 1965, sparked a national debate over the war. By the end of 1967, American students opposed to the war had become a significant political force. Enormous peace marches in New York, Washington, D.C., and other cities drew broad public attention to the antiwar movement. Opposition to the war had become a central issue in left-wing politics and in the culture of colleges and universities. It had penetrated popular cultures as well—most visibly in the rising popularity of folk musicians, many of whom used their songs to express opposition to the war. In the meantime, a growing number of journalists, particularly reporters who had spent time in Vietnam, helped sustain the movement with their frank revelations about the brutality and apparent futility of the war. The growing chorus

Growing Opposition to the War

1968

The year 1968 was one of the most turbulent in the postwar history of the United States. Much of what caused these upheavals were specifically American events—the growing controversy over the war in Vietnam, the assassinations of Martin Luther King Jr. and Robert Kennedy, racial unrest in the nation's cities, student protests on campuses throughout America. But the turmoil of 1968 was not confined to the United States. There were tremendous upheavals in many parts of the world that year.

The most common form of turbulence around the world in 1968 was student unrest. In France, in May 1968, there was a student uprising that far exceeded in size and ferocity anything that occurred in the United States. It attracted the support of French workers, briefly paralyzed Paris and other cities, and contributed to the downfall of the government of Charles de Gaulle a year later. In England, Ireland, Germany, Italy, the Netherlands, Mexico, Canada, Japan, and South Korea, students and other young people also demonstrated in great numbers, and at times with

PRAGUE SPRING Czech demonstrators march through Wenceslaus Square in Prague following a radio address by their reform president, Alexander Dubcek, in August 1968. By this time, the great hopes awakened by Dubcek's reforms during the "Prague Spring" of several months ago had been crushed by Soviet pressure, including the arrival of Soviet tanks in the streets of Prague. These demonstrators are demanding the "brutal truth" from their leaders about the price Czechoslovakia paid to keep Dubcek in power. *(Bettmann/Corbis)*

of popular protest soon began to stimulate opposition to the war from within the government.

Senator J. William Fulbright of Arkansas, chairman of the powerful Senate Foreign Relations Committee, turned against the war and in January 1966 began to stage highly publicized and occasionally televised congressional hearings to air criticisms of it. Distinguished figures such as George F. Kennan and retired general James Gavin testified against the conflict, giving opposition to the war greater respectability in the minds of many Americans generally unwilling to question the government or the military. Other members of Congress joined Fulbright in opposing Johnson's policies—including, in 1967, Robert F. Kennedy, brother of the slain president, now a senator from New York. Even within the administration, the consensus seemed to be crumbling. Robert McNamara, who had done much to help extend the American involvement in Vietnam, quietly left the government, disillusioned, in 1968. His successor as secretary of defense, Clark Clifford, became a quiet but powerful voice within the administration on behalf of a cautious scaling down of the commitment.

In the meantime, the American economy was beginning to suffer. Johnson's commitment to fighting the war while continuing his Great Society reforms—his promise of "guns and butter"—proved impossible to maintain. The inflation rate, which had remained at 2 percent through most of the early 1960s, rose to 3 percent in 1967, 4 percent in 1968, and 6 percent in 1969. In August 1967, Johnson asked Congress for a tax increase—a 10 percent surcharge that was widely labeled a "war tax"—which he knew was necessary if the nation was to avoid even more ruinous inflation. In return, congressional conservatives demanded and received a $6 billion reduction in the funding for Great Society programs.

War-Induced Inflation

THE TRAUMAS OF 1968

By the end of 1967, the twin crises of the war in Vietnam and the deteriorating racial situation at home—crises that fed upon and inflamed each other—had produced profound social and political tensions. In the course of 1968,

834

some violence, against governments and universities and other structures of authority. Elsewhere, 1968 created more widespread protest, as in Czechoslovakia, where hundreds of thousands of citizens took to the streets in support of what became known as "Prague Spring"—a demand for greater democracy and a repudiation of many of the oppressive rules and structures imposed on the nation by its Soviet-dominated communist regimes—until Russian tanks rolled into the city to crush the uprising. For over thirty years, many people have tried to explain why so much instability emerged in so many nations at the same time.

One factor that contributed to the worldwide turbulence of 1968 was simple numbers. The postwar baby boom, which occurred in many nations, had created a very large age cohort that by the late 1960s was reaching adulthood. In Western industrial nations, in particular, this rising generation was a powerful new social force. The sheer size of the new generation produced a tripling of the number of people attending colleges and universities in fewer than twenty years, and a heightened sense of the power of youth. The long period of postwar prosperity and relative peace in which this generation had grown up contributed to heightened expectations of what the world should offer them—and a greater level of impatience than previous generations had demonstrated with the obstacles that stood in the way of their hopes. A new global youth culture emerged that was in many ways at odds with the dominant culture of older generations. It valued nonconformity, personal freedom, and even rebellion.

A second force contributing to the widespread turbulence of 1968 was the power of global media. Satellite technology introduced in the early 1960s made it possible to transmit live news instantly across the world. Videotape technology and the creation of lightweight portable television cameras enabled media organizations to respond to events much more quickly and flexibly than in the past. And the audience for these televised images was by now global and enormous, particularly in industrial nations but even in the poorest areas of the world. Protests in one country were suddenly capable of inspiring protests in others. Demonstrators in Paris, for example, spoke openly of how campus protests in the United States in 1968—for example, the student uprising at Columbia University in New York—had helped motivate French students to rise up as well. Just as American students were protesting against what they considered the antiquated paternalistic features of their universities, French students demanded an end to the rigid, autocratic character of their own academic world.

In most parts of the world, the 1968 uprisings came and went without fundamentally altering the institutions and systems they were attacking. But many changes came in the wake of these protests. Universities around the globe undertook significant reforms. Religious observance in mainstream churches and synagogues in the West declined dramatically after 1968. New concepts of personal freedom gained legitimacy, helping to inspire new social movements in the years that followed—among them the dramatic growth of feminism in many parts of the world. The events of 1968 did not produce a revolution, in the United States or in most of the rest of the world, but they did help launch a period of dramatic social, cultural, and political change that affected the peoples of many nations.

those tensions seemed suddenly to burst to the surface and to threaten the nation with genuine chaos. Not since World War II had the United States experienced so profound a sense of crisis.

The Tet Offensive

On January 31, 1968, the first day of the Vietnamese New Year (Tet), communist forces launched an enormous, concerted attack on American strongholds throughout South Vietnam. A few cities fell to the communists. During their occupation of the provincial capital, Hue, the communist forces rounded up supporters of the Saigon regime and massacred them. Other cities suffered major disruptions.

Few Americans were aware of the events in Hue. But they did see vivid reports on television of communist forces in the heart of Saigon, setting off bombs, shooting down South Vietnamese officials and troops, and holding down fortified areas (including, briefly, the grounds of the American embassy). Such images shocked many Americans and proved devastating to popular support for the war.

The Tet offensive also suggested to the American public something of the brutality of the struggle in Vietnam. In the midst of the fighting, television cameras recorded the sight of a captured Viet Cong soldier being led up to a South Vietnamese officer in the streets of Saigon. Without a word, the officer pulled out his pistol and shot the young man in the head, leaving him lying dead in the street, his blood pouring onto the pavement. Perhaps no single event did more to galvanize support for the war in the United States.

American forces soon dislodged the Viet Cong from most of the positions they had seized, and the Tet offensive in the end cost the communists such appalling casualties that they were significantly weakened for months to come. Indeed, the Tet defeats permanently depleted the ranks of the NLF and forced North Vietnamese troops to take on a much larger share of the subsequent fighting. But all that had little impact on American opinion. Tet may have been a military victory for the United States, but it was a political defeat for the administration, a defeat from which it would never fully recover.

Political and Psychological Defeat

835

In the following weeks, opposition to the war grew substantially. Leading newspapers and magazines, television commentators, and mainstream politicians began taking public stands in favor of de-escalation of the conflict. Within weeks of the Tet offensive, public opposition to the war had almost doubled. And Johnson's personal popularity rating had slid to 35 percent, the lowest of any president since Harry Truman.

The Political Challenge

Beginning in the summer of 1967, dissident Democrats (led by the talented activist Allard Lowenstein) tried to mobilize support behind an antiwar candidate who would challenge Lyndon Johnson in the 1968 primaries. When Robert Kennedy declined their invitation, they turned to Senator Eugene McCarthy of Minnesota. A brilliantly orchestrated campaign by Lowenstein and thousands of young volunteers in the New Hampshire primary produced a startling showing by McCarthy in March; he nearly defeated the president.

A few days later, Robert Kennedy finally entered the campaign, embittering many McCarthy supporters, but bringing his own substantial strength among blacks, the poor, and workers to the antiwar cause. Polls showed the president trailing badly in the next scheduled primary, in Wisconsin. Indeed, public animosity toward the president was now so intense that Johnson did not even dare leave the White House to campaign. On March 31, Johnson went on television to announce a limited halt in the bombing of North Vietnam—his first major concession to the antiwar forces—and, more surprising, his withdrawal from the presidential contest.

For a moment, it seemed as though the antiwar forces had won. Robert Kennedy quickly established himself as the champion of the Democratic primaries, winning one election after another. In the meantime, however, Vice President Hubert Humphrey, with the support of President Johnson, entered the contest and began to attract the support of party leaders and of the many delegations that were selected not by popular primaries but by state party organizations. He soon appeared to be the front-runner in the race.

The King and Kennedy Assassinations

In the midst of this bitter political battle, in which the war had been the dominant issue, attention suddenly turned back to the nation's bitter racial conflicts. On April 4, Martin Luther King Jr., who had traveled to Memphis, Tennessee, to lend his support to striking black sanitation workers in the city, was shot and killed while standing on the balcony of his motel. The presumed assassin, James Earl Ray, who was captured days later in London and eventually convicted, had no apparent motive. Later evidence suggested that he had been hired by others to do the killing, but he himself never revealed the identity of his employers and doubts about his role in the assassination continued after his death in prison in 1998.

King's tragic death produced an outpouring of grief matched in recent memory only by the reaction to the death of John Kennedy. Among African Americans, it also produced anger. In the days after the assassination, major riots broke out in more than sixty American cities. Forty-three people died; more than 3,000 suffered injuries; as many as 27,000 people were arrested.

For two months following the death of King, Robert Kennedy continued his campaign for the presidential nomination. Late on the night of June 6, he appeared in the ballroom of a Los Angeles hotel to acknowledge his victory in that day's California primary. As he left the ballroom after his victory statement, Sirhan Sirhan, a young Palestinian apparently enraged by pro-Israeli remarks Kennedy had recently made, emerged from a crowd and shot him in the head. Early the next morning, Kennedy died.

By the time of his death, Robert Kennedy—who earlier in his career had been widely considered a cold, ruthless agent of his more appealing brother—had emerged as a figure of enormous popular appeal. More than John Kennedy, Robert identified his hopes with the American "underclass"—with blacks, Hispanics, Native Americans, the poor. Indeed, Robert Kennedy, much more than John, shaped what some would later call the "Kennedy legacy," a set of ideas that would for a time become central to American liberalism: the fervent commitment to using government to help the powerless. In addition, Robert had an impassioned following among many people who saw in him (and his family) the kind of glamour and hopefulness they had come, at least in retrospect, to identify with the martyred president. His campaign appearances inspired outbursts of public enthusiasm rarely seen in political life. The passions Kennedy had aroused made his violent death a particularly shattering experience for many Americans.

The presidential campaign continued gloomily during the last weeks before the convention. Hubert Humphrey, who had seemed likely to win the nomination even before Robert Kennedy's death, now faced only minor opposition—despite the embittered claims of many Democrats that Humphrey would simply continue the bankrupt policies of the Johnson administration. The approaching Democratic Convention, therefore, began to take on the appearance of an exercise in futility; and antiwar activists, despairing of winning any victories within the convention, began to plan major demonstrations outside it.

When the Democrats finally gathered in Chicago in August, even the most optimistic observers were predicting a turbulent convention. Inside the hall, delegates bitterly debated an antiwar plank in the party platform that both Kennedy and McCarthy supporters favored. Miles away, in a downtown park, thousands of antiwar protesters were staging demonstrations. On the third night of the convention, as the delegates were beginning their balloting on the now inevitable nomination of Hubert Humphrey, demonstrators and police clashed in a bloody riot in the streets of Chicago. Hundreds of protesters were injured as police attempted to disperse them with tear gas and billy clubs. Aware that the violence was being televised to the nation, the demonstrators taunted the authorities with the chant, "The whole world is watching!" And Hubert Humphrey, who had spent years dreaming of becoming his party's candidate for president,

Democratic National Convention

received a nomination that appeared at the time to be almost worthless.

The Conservative Response

The turbulent events of 1968 persuaded many observers that American society was in the throes of revolutionary change. In fact, however, the response of most Americans to the turmoil was a conservative one.

The most visible sign of the conservative backlash was the surprising success of the campaign of the segregationist Alabama governor George Wallace for the presidency. In 1964, he had run in a few Democratic presidential primaries and had done surprisingly well, even in several states outside the South. In 1968, he became a

George Wallace

CHICAGO, 1968 Demonstrators climb on a statue in a Chicago park during the 1968 Democratic National Convention, protesting both the Vietnam War and the harsh treatment they had received from Mayor Richard Daley's Chicago police. *(Dennis Brack/Black Star)*

third-party candidate for president, basing his campaign on a host of conservative grievances, not all of them connected to race. He denounced the forced busing of students, the proliferation of government regulations and social programs, and the permissiveness of authorities toward race riots and antiwar demonstrations. There was never any serious chance that Wallace would win the election; but his standing in the polls at times rose to over 20 percent.

A more effective effort to mobilize the "silent majority" in favor of order and stability was under way within the Republican Party. Richard Nixon, whose political career had seemed at an end after his losses in the presidential race of 1960 and a California gubernatorial campaign two years later, reemerged as the preeminent spokesman for what he called "Middle America." Nixon recognized that many Americans were tired of hearing about their obligations to the poor, tired of hearing about the sacrifices necessary to achieve racial justice, tired of judicial reforms that seemed designed to help criminals. By offering a vision of stability, law and order, government retrenchment, and "peace with honor" in Vietnam, he easily captured the Republican presidential nomination. And after the spectacle of the Democratic Convention, he enjoyed a commanding lead in the polls as the November election approached.

That lead diminished greatly in the last weeks before the voting. Old doubts about Nixon's character continued to haunt the Republican candidate. A skillful last-minute surge by Hubert Humphrey, who managed to restore a tenuous unity to the Democratic Party, narrowed the gap further. And the Wallace campaign appeared to be hurting the Republicans more than the Democrats. In the end, however, Nixon eked out a victory almost as narrow as

Nixon Victorious

his defeat in 1960. He received 43.4 percent of the popular vote to Humphrey's 42.3 percent (a margin of only about 800,000 votes), and 301 electoral votes to Humphrey's 191. George Wallace, who like most third-party candidates faded in the last weeks of the campaign, still managed to poll 13.5 percent of the popular vote and to carry five

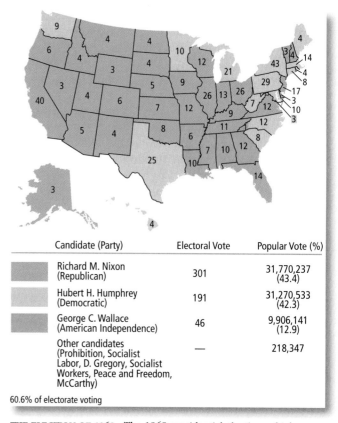

Candidate (Party)	Electoral Vote	Popular Vote (%)
Richard M. Nixon (Republican)	301	31,770,237 (43.4)
Hubert H. Humphrey (Democratic)	191	31,270,533 (42.3)
George C. Wallace (American Independence)	46	9,906,141 (12.9)
Other candidates (Prohibition, Socialist Labor, D. Gregory, Socialist Workers, Peace and Freedom, McCarthy)	—	218,347

60.6% of electorate voting

THE ELECTION OF 1968   The 1968 presidential election, which Richard Nixon won, was almost as close as the election of 1960, which he lost. Nixon might have won a more substantial victory had it not been for the independent candidacy of Governor George C. Wallace, who attracted many of the same conservative voters to whom Nixon appealed.   ◆ *How does the distribution of Democratic and Republican strength in this election compare to that in 1960?*

For an interactive version of this map, go to www.mhhe.com/brinkley13ech29maps

southern states with a total of 46 electoral ballots—the best showing by a third-party candidate since the 1920s. Nixon had not won a decisive personal mandate. But the election made clear that a majority of the American electorate was more interested in restoring stability than in promoting social change.

CONCLUSION

No decade of the twentieth century has created more powerful and enduring images than the 1960s. It began with the election—and then the traumatic assassination—of an attractive and energetic young president, John Kennedy, who captured the imagination of millions and seemed to symbolize the rising idealism of the time. It produced a dramatic period of political innovation, christened the "Great Society" by President Lyndon Johnson, which greatly expanded the size and functions of the

federal government and its responsibility for the welfare of the nation's citizens. It saw the emergence of a sustained and enormously powerful civil rights movement that won a series of important legal victories, including two civil rights acts that dismantled the Jim Crow system constructed in the late nineteenth and early twentieth centuries.

The very spirit of dynamism and optimism that shaped the early 1960s also helped bring to the surface problems and grievances that had no easy solutions. The civil rights movement ended legalized segregation and disfranchisement, but it also awakened expectations of social and economic equality that laws alone could not provide and that remained in many respects unfulfilled. The peaceful, interracial crusade of the early 1960s gradually turned into a much more militant, confrontational, and increasingly separatist movement toward the decade's end. The idealism among white youths that began the 1960s, and played an important role in the political success of John Kennedy, evolved into an angry rebellion against many aspects of American culture and politics and produced a large upsurge of student protest that rocked the nation at the decade's end. Perhaps most of all, a small and largely unnoticed Cold War commitment to defend South Vietnam against communist aggression from the north led to a large and disastrous American military commitment that destroyed the presidency of Lyndon Johnson, shook the faith of millions in their leaders and their political system, sent thousands of young American men to their deaths, and showed no signs of producing a victory. A decade that began with high hopes and soaring ideals ended with ugly and at times violent division, and deep disillusionment.

INTERACTIVE LEARNING

The *Primary Source Investigator CD-ROM* offers the following materials related to this chapter:

- Interactive maps: **U.S. Elections** (M7); **The Vietnam War** (M29); and **Patterns of Protest** (M30).
- Documents, images, and maps related to the turbulent decade of the 1960s, including the Kennedy and Johnson presidencies and the escalation of the Vietnam War. Highlights include the text of the Gulf of Tonkin Resolution authorizing massive force in Vietnam, images of missile sites in Cuba, and images of soldiers in Vietnam.

Online Learning Center (www.mhhe.com/brinkley13e)

For quizzes, Internet resources, references to additional books and films, and more, consult this book's Online Learning Center.

FOR FURTHER REFERENCE

Allen J. Matusow, *The Unraveling of America: A History of Liberalism in the 1960s* (1984) is a provocative history of this turbulent decade. David Farber, *The Age of Great Dreams: America in the 1960s* (1994) is an intelligent and lively general history. Robert Dallek, *Lone Star Rising: Lyndon Johnson and His Times, 1908-1960* (1991), *Flawed Giant: Lyndon B. Johnson, 1960-1973* (1998), and *An Unfinished Life: John F. Kennedy, 1917-1963* (2003) are important biographies. Raymond Arsenault, *Freedom Riders: 1961 and the Struggle for Justice* (2006) is an important study. John Dittmer, *Local People: The Struggle for Civil Rights in Mississippi* (1994) is a study of the grassroots origins of the movement. William Chafe, *Civilities and Civil Rights: Greensboro, North Carolina, and the Black Struggle for Freedom* (1980) examines the southern civil rights movement and the white reaction to it. Taylor Branch, *Parting the Waters: America in the King Years, 1959-1963* (1988), *Pillar of Fire: America in the King Years, 1963-1965*, and *At Canaan's Edge: America in the King Years, 1965-68* (2006) are good narrative histories of the movement (1998). Nicholas Lemann, *The Promised Land: The Great Black Migration and How It Changed America* (1991) is a challenging study of the postwar African-American migration to northern cities and of the Great Society's response to it. Graham T. Allison, *The Essence of Decision: Explaining the Cuban Missile Crisis* (1971) is an important interpretation of the greatest crisis of the Cold War. Ernest R. May and Philip D. Zelikow, *The Kennedy Tapes: Inside the White House During the Cuban Missile Crisis* (1997) provides the annotated transcripts of the taped meetings of Kennedy's inner circle during the crisis. Robert D. Schulzinger, *A Time for War: The United States and Vietnam, 1945-1975* (1997) is a good general history of the war. Neil Sheehan, *A Bright Shining Lie: John Paul Vann and America in Vietnam* (1988) is a compelling picture of the war as experienced by a significant military figure of the 1960s. Christian J. Appy, *Working-Class War: American Combat Soldiers and Vietnam* (1993) examines the class basis of the army that fought in Vietnam. Larry Berman, *Planning a Tragedy* (1982) and *Lyndon Johnson's War* (1989); Leslie Gelb and Richard Betts, *The Irony of Vietnam: The System Worked* (1979); and David Halberstam, *The Best and the Brightest* (1972) are important interpretations of the American decision to intervene and stay in Vietnam. Dan T. Carter, *The Politics of Rage: George Wallace, The Origins of the New Conservatism, and the Transformation of American Politics* (1995) is a good study of the career of George Wallace. David Farber, *Chicago '68* (1988) examines the turbulent Democratic Convention and, through it, the passions that shaped a traumatic year in American history. Mark Kurlansky, *1968: The Year That Rocked the World* (2003) is a broader history of that turbulent year.

CHAPTER 30

THE CRISIS OF AUTHORITY

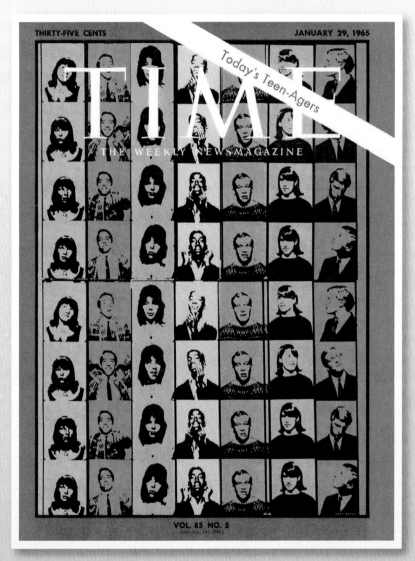

"TODAY'S TEEN-AGERS" The coming of age of the "baby-boom" generation, and the rise of youthful activism, led *Time* magazine to devote a 1965 cover story to "Today's Teen-Agers." As notable as the choice of subject was the choice of artist for the cover image: Andy Warhol, the great pop artist whose serial portraits of both famous and unknown people helped define his era. Warhol's work was instrumental in breaking down barriers between serious art and popular culture, both in its subject matter (celebrities, commercial products) and in its techniques, which drew heavily from commercial art. This series of silk-screened photographs made use of one of his trademark media. *(Reprinted through the courtesy of the Editors of TIME Magazine © 2008 Time Inc.)*

RICHARD NIXON'S ELECTION in 1968 was the result of more than the unpopularity of Lyndon Johnson and the war. It was the result, too, of a strong popular reaction against what many Americans considered a frontal assault on the foundations of their culture.

Throughout the late 1960s and early 1970s, new movements and interest groups were mobilizing to demand protections and benefits. New values and assumptions were emerging to challenge traditional patterns of thought and behavior. The United States was in the throes, it sometimes seemed, of a cultural revolution.

Some Americans welcomed the changes. But the 1968 election returns suggested that more people feared them. There was growing resentment against the attention directed toward minorities and the poor, against the federal social programs that were funneling billions of dollars into the inner cities to help the poor and unemployed, against the increasing tax burden on the middle class, against the "hippies" and radicals who were dominating public discourse with their bitter critiques of values that many middle-class Americans revered. It was time, their critics believed, for a restoration of stability and a relegitimization of traditional centers of authority.

In Richard Nixon they found a man who seemed to match their mood. Himself a product of a hardworking, middle-class family, he had risen to prominence on the basis of his own unrelenting efforts. He projected an image of stern dedication to traditional values. Yet the presidency of Richard Nixon, far from returning calm and stability to American politics, coincided with, and in many ways helped to produce, more years of crisis.

Several crises were not wholly of Nixon's making. He inherited an unpopular war in Vietnam. Nixon attempted to reduce opposition to the war by withdrawing some American troops and replacing them with Vietnamese soldiers. But in other ways he escalated the war, through higher levels of bombing and through an incursion into Cambodia in the spring of 1970. Nixon also inherited an economy that was beginning to weaken and that, by the beginning of his second term, was reeling under rapidly rising energy prices and growing inflation.

One crisis, at least, was attributable to Nixon and the people in his administration. An obscure break-in at the Democratic National Committee headquarters in Washington, D.C., in June 1972, hardly noticed at the time, gradually expanded to create one of the most serious crises in the history of the presidency—and the first such crisis to drive a president from office. Having won election by railing against crises of authority that threatened social stability, Nixon left office having created a major crisis of authority himself.

THE YOUTH CULTURE

Perhaps most alarming to conservative Americans in the 1960s and 1970s was a pattern of social and cultural protest that was emerging from younger Americans, who were giving vent to two related impulses. One was the impulse, originating with the political left, to create a great new community of "the people," which would rise up to break the power of elites and force the nation to end the war, pursue racial and economic justice, and transform its political life. The other, at least equally powerful, impulse was

"Liberation"

the vision of "liberation." It found expression, in part, through the efforts of particular groups—African Americans, Native Americans, Hispanics, women, gays and lesbians, and others—to define and assert themselves and make demands on the larger society. It also found expression through the efforts of individuals to create a new culture—one that would allow them to escape from what they considered the dehumanizing pressures of what some called the modern "technocracy."

The New Left

In retrospect, it seems unsurprising that young Americans became so assertive and powerful in American culture and politics in the 1960s. The postwar baby-boom generation, the unprecedented number of people born in a few years just after World War II, was growing up. By 1970, more than half the American population was under thirty years old; more than 8 million Americans—eight times the number in 1950—were attending college. This was the largest generation of youth in American history, and it was coming to maturity in a time of unprecedented affluence, opportunity, and—for many—frustration.

One of the most visible results of the increasingly assertive youth movement was a radicalization of many American college and university students, who in the course of the 1960s formed what became known as the New Left—a large, diverse group of men and women energized by the polarizing developments of their time. The New Left

Sources of the New Left

embraced the cause of African Americans and other minorities, but its own ranks consisted overwhelmingly of white people. Blacks and minorities formed political movements of their own. Some members of the New Left were the children of radical parents (members of the so-called Old Left of the 1930s and 1940s).

The New Left drew from the writings of some of the important social critics of the 1950s—among them C. Wright Mills, a sociologist at Columbia University who wrote a series of scathing and brilliant critiques of modern bureaucracies. Relatively few members of the New Left were communists, but many were drawn to the writings of Karl Marx and of contemporary Marxist theorists. Some came to revere Third World Marxists such as Che

Guevara, the South American revolutionary and guerrilla leader; Mao Zedong; and Ho Chi Minh. But the New Left drew its inspiration above all from the civil rights movement, in which many idealistic young white Americans had become involved in the early 1960s.

In 1962, a group of students, most of them from prestigious universities, gathered in Michigan to form an organization to give voice to their

SDS

demands: Students for a Democratic Society (SDS). Their declaration of beliefs, the Port Huron Statement, expressed their disillusionment with the society they had inherited and their determination to build a new politics.

Some members of SDS moved into inner-city neighborhoods and tried for a time, without great success, to mobilize poor, working-class people politically. But most members of the New Left were students, and their radicalism centered in part on issues related to the modern university. A 1964 dispute at the University of California at Berkeley over the rights of students to engage in political activities on campus gained national attention. The Free Speech Movement, as it called itself, created turmoil at Berkeley

Free Speech Movement

as students challenged campus police, occupied administrative offices, and produced a strike in which nearly three-quarters of the Berkeley students participated. The immediate issue was the right of students to pass out literature and recruit volunteers for political causes on campus. But the protest quickly became as well an expression of a more basic critique of the university, and the society it seemed to represent.

The revolt at Berkeley was the first outburst of what was to be nearly a decade of campus turmoil. Students at Berkeley and elsewhere protested the impersonal character of the modern university, and they denounced the role of educational institutions in sustaining what they considered corrupt or immoral public policies. The antiwar movement greatly inflamed the challenge and expanded it to the universities; and beginning in 1968, campus demonstrations, riots, and building seizures became almost commonplace. At Columbia University in New York, students seized several buildings, including the offices of the president, and occupied them for days until local police forcibly and violently ejected them. Harvard University had a similar, and even more violent, experience a year later.

Also in 1969, Berkeley became the scene of perhaps the most prolonged and traumatic conflict of any American college campus in the 1960s: a battle over the efforts of a few students to build a "People's Park" on a vacant lot the university planned to use to build a parking garage. This seemingly minor event precipitated weeks of impassioned and often violent conflicts between the university administration, which sought to evict the intruders from the land, and the students, many of whom supported the advocates of the park and who saw the university's efforts to close it as a symbol of the struggle between liberation and oppression.

By the end of the People's Park battle, which lasted for more than a week, the Berkeley campus was completely polarized; even students who had not initially supported or even noticed the People's Park (the great majority) were, by the end, committed to its defense; 85 percent of the 15,000 students voted in a referendum to leave the park alone. Student radicals were, for the first time, winning large audiences for their extravagant rhetoric linking university administrators, the police, and the larger political and economic system, describing them all as part of one united, oppressive force.

People's Park

Most campus radicals were rarely if ever violent (except at times in their rhetoric). But the image of student radicalism in mainstream culture was one of chaos and disorder, based in part on the disruptive actions of relatively small groups of militants, among them the "Weathermen," a violent offshoot of SDS. The Weathermen were responsible for a few cases of arson and bombing that destroyed campus buildings and claimed several lives. Not many people, not even many students, ever accepted the radical political views that lay at the heart of the New Left. But many supported the position of SDS and other groups on particular issues and, above all, on the Vietnam War. Student activists tried to drive out training programs for military officers (ROTC) and bar military recruiters from college campuses. They attacked the laboratories and corporations that were producing weapons for the war. And between 1967 and 1969, they organized some of the largest political demon-strations in American history. The October 1967 march on the Pentagon, where demonstrators were met by a solid line of armed troops; the "spring mobilization" of April 1968, which attracted hundreds of thousands of demonstrators in cities around the country; the Vietnam "moratorium" of the fall of 1969, during which millions of opponents of the war gathered in major rallies across the nation; and countless other demonstrations, large and small—all helped thrust the issue of the war into the center of American politics.

Closely related to opposition to the war was opposition to the military draft. The gradual abolition of many traditional deferments—for graduate students, teachers, husbands, fathers, and others—swelled the ranks of those faced with conscription (and thus of those likely to oppose it). Some draft-age Americans simply refused induction, accepting what occasionally were long terms in jail as a result. Others fled to Canada, Sweden, and elsewhere (where they were joined by deserters from the armed forces) to escape conscription. Not until 1977, when President Jimmy Carter issued a general pardon to draft resisters and a more limited amnesty for deserters, did the Vietnam exiles begin to return to the country in substantial numbers.

The Counterculture

Closely related to the New Left was a new youth culture openly scornful of the values and conventions of middle-class society. As if to display their contempt for conven-

BERKELEY, 1969 The People's Park controversy at the University of California at Berkeley turned the campus and the town into something close to a war zone. In this photograph, National Guardsmen with fixed bayonets stand in the way of a planned march to protest the closing of People's Park on May 30, 1969, more than two weeks after they first arrived to keep peace in Berkeley. *(AP/Wide World Photos)*

ROCK MUSIC IN THE SIXTIES

While folk music often expressed the ideals of young people in the 1960s, rock music expressed their desires. The rock music of the late 1960s and 1970s, even more than the rock 'n' roll of the 1950s and early 1960s, emphasized release. It gave vent to impulse and instinct, to physical and emotional (as opposed to intellectual) urges. That was one reason it was so enormously popular among young people in an age of cultural and sexual revolution. It was also why it seemed so menacing and dangerous to many more conservative Americans seeking to defend more traditional values and behavior.

Rock in the late 1960s seemed simultaneously subversive and liberating. That was partly because of the behavior and lifestyles of rock musicians. They were no longer clean-cut young men wearing red blazers, as many rock performers had been in the 1950s, but men and women whose appearance and behavior were often deliberately outrageous. Rock musicians were connected at times to the drug culture of the 1960s (especially through the so-called psychedelic-rock groups inspired by experiences with the hallucinogen LSD). They had links to mystical Eastern religions (most notably the Beatles, who had spent time in India studying Transcendental Meditation and who, beginning in 1967 with their album *Sergeant Pepper's Lonely Hearts Club Band,* incorporated those themes into their music). And they often reveled in flouting social conventions, begin-

WOODSTOCK MUSIC & ART FAIR
presents
AN AQUARIAN EXPOSITION
in
WHITE LAKE, N.Y.*

3 DAYS ᴏꜰ PEACE & MUSIC

WITH

Joan Baez	Keef Hartley	The Band
Arlo Guthrie	Canned Heat	Jeff Beck Group
Tim Hardin	Creedence Clearwater	Blood, Sweat and Tears
Richie Havens	Grateful Dead	Joe Cocker
Incredible String Band	Janis Joplin	Crosby, Stills and Nash
Ravi Shankar	Jefferson Airplane	Jimi Hendrix
Sly And The Family Stone	Mountain	Iron Butterfly
Bert Sommer	Quill	Ten Years After
Sweetwater	Santana	Johnny Winter
	The Who	

FRI.	SAT.	SUN.
AUG. 15	**AUG. 16**	**AUG. 17**

All programs subject to change without notice
*White Lake, Town of Bethel, Sullivan County, N.Y.

ADVERTISING WOODSTOCK Even before the thousands of spectators gathered for the famous rock concert at Woodstock in 1969, organizers envisioned it as something more than a performance. It would, this poster claims, be a search for peace as well as for music. *(Getty Images)*

ning with the Rolling Stones and culminating, perhaps, in the extreme and self-destructive behavior of Jimi

HIPPIES MIRED IN SEA OF MUD

They Don't Melt . . .

REPORTING WOODSTOCK The *New York Daily News,* whose largely working-class readership was not notably sympathetic toward the young people at Woodstock, ran this slightly derisive front-page story on the concert as heavy rains turned the concert site into a sea of mud. ["They Don't Melt," the caption said.] *(© New York Daily News, L.P. Reprinted with Permission)*

Hendrix, Jim Morrison, and Janis Joplin, all of whom died very young of drug-related causes.

Late-sixties rock was among many expressions of the impulses that came to be known as the counterculture; and like the counterculture itself, it inspired widely varying reactions. To its defenders, the new rock, with its emphasis on emotional release, was a healthy rebuke to the repressive norms of mainstream culture. To

"Hippies"

tional standards, young Americans flaunted long hair, shabby or flamboyant clothing, and a rebellious disdain for traditional speech and decorum. Also central to the counterculture, as it became known, were drugs: marijuana—which after 1966 became almost as common a youthful diversion as beer drinking—and the less widespread but still substantial use of other, more potent hallucinogens, such as LSD.

There was also a new, more permissive view of sexual behavior—the beginnings of what came to be known as a sexual revolution. To some degree, the emergence of

relaxed approaches to sexuality was a result less of the counterculture than of the new accessibility of effective contraceptives, most notably the birth-control pill and, after 1973, legalized abortion. But the new sexuality also reflected the counterculture's belief that individuals should strive for release from inhibitions and give vent to their instincts.

The counterculture challenged the structure of modern American society, attacking its banality, hollowness, artificiality, materialism, and isolation from nature. The most committed

Haight-Ashbury

them, its virtues were symbolized by the great rock festival at Woodstock, New York, in August 1969, where over 400,000 young people gathered on a remote piece of farmland for several days to hear performances by such artists as the Who, Jimi Hendrix, the Grateful Dead, Janis Joplin, Joe Cocker, the Jefferson Airplane, and many others. The festival was marred by heavy rains that produced a sea of mud, and by supplies and facilities completely inadequate for the unexpectedly large crowd. Drugs were everywhere in evidence, as was a kind of open sexual freedom that a decade earlier would have seemed unthinkable to all but a few Americans. But Woodstock remained through it all peaceful, friendly, and harmonious. There was rhapsodic talk at the time of how Woodstock represented the birth of a new youth culture, the "Woodstock nation."

Critics of the new rock, and the counterculture with which they associated it, were not impressed with the idea of the "Woodstock nation." To them, the essence of the counterculture was a kind of numbing hopelessness and despair, with a menacing and violent underside. To them, the appropriate symbol was not Woodstock, but another great rock concert, which more than 300,000 people attended only four months after Woodstock, at the Altamont Speedway east of San Francisco. The concert featured many of the groups that had been at Woodstock, but the Rolling Stones, who had organized the event, were the main attraction. As at Woodstock, drugs were plentiful and sexual exhibitionism was frequent. But

ALTAMONT Hell's Angels "security guards" club a spectator near the stage during the rock concert at Altamont as other concertgoers—some curious, some aghast—watch. One spectator died as a result of the beatings. *(Photofest)*

unlike Woodstock, Altamont was far from peaceful. Instead, it became ugly, brutal, and violent, and resulted in the deaths of four people. Several of them died accidentally, one, for example, from a bad drug trip, during which he fell into a stream and drowned. But numerous people were brutally beaten by members of the Hell's Angels motorcycle gang, who had been hired by the Rolling Stones as security guards. One man was beaten and stabbed to death in front of the stage while the Stones were playing "Sympathy for the Devil."

Woodstock and Altamont, then, became symbols of two aspects of the counterculture of the late 1960s and early 1970s, and of the rock music that created its anthems. The beat poet Allen Ginsberg wrote an

ecstatic poem proclaiming that at Woodstock "a new kind of man has come to his bliss/to end the cold war he has borne/against his own kind of flesh." The festival and its music, many claimed, had shown the path to an age of love and peace and justice. Altamont, however, suggested a dark underside of the rock culture, its potential for destruction and violence. "As far as I was concerned," one participant said, "Altamont was the death knell of all those things that we thought would last forever. I personally felt like the sixties had been an extravagant stage show and I had been a spectator in the audience. Altamont had rung down the curtain to no applause."*

*Allen Ginsberg's estate is affiliated with the Naropa Institute, Boulder, CO.

adherents of the counterculture—the hippies, who came to dominate the Haight-Ashbury neighborhood of San Francisco and other places, and the social dropouts, some of whom retreated to rural communes—rejected modern society and attempted to find refuge in a simpler, more "natural" existence. But even those whose commitment to the counterculture was less dramatic shared a commitment to the idea of personal fulfillment through rejecting the inhibitions and conventions of middle-class culture. In a corrupt and alienating society, the new creed seemed to suggest, the first responsibility of the individual was culti-

vation of the self, the unleashing of one's own full potential for pleasure and fulfillment.

The effects of the counterculture reached out to the larger society and helped create a new set of social norms that many young people (and some adults) chose to imitate. Long hair and freakish clothing became the badge not only of hippies and radicals but of an entire generation as well. The use of marijuana, the freer attitudes toward sex, the iconoclastic (and sometimes obscene) language—all spread far beyond the realm of the true devotees of the counterculture.

WOODSTOCK In the summer of 1969, more than 400,000 people gathered for a rock concert on a farm near Woodstock, New York. Despite mostly terrible weather, the gathering was remarkably peaceful—sparking talk among some enthusiasts of the new youth culture about the "Woodstock nation." *(Shelly Rustin/Black Star/Stock Photo)*

Perhaps the most pervasive element of the new youth society was one that even the least radical members of the generation embraced: rock music. Rock 'n' roll first achieved wide popularity in the 1950s, on the strength of such early performers as Buddy Holly and, above all, Elvis Presley. Early in the 1960s, its influence began to spread, largely a result of the phenomenal popularity of the Beatles, the English group whose first visit to the United States in 1964 created a remarkable sensation, "Beatlemania." For

Growing Influence of Rock 'n' Roll

a time, most rock musicians—like most popular musicians before them—concentrated largely on uncontroversial, romantic themes. By the late 1960s, however, rock had begun to reflect many of the new iconoclastic values of its time. The Beatles, for example, abandoned their once simple and seemingly innocent style for a new, experimental, even mystical approach that reflected the growing popular fascination with drugs and Eastern religions. Other groups, such as the Rolling Stones, turned even more openly to themes of anger, frustration, and rebelliousness. Rock's driving rhythms, its undisguised sensuality, its often harsh and angry tone—all made it an appropriate vehicle for expressing the themes of the social and political

unrest of the late 1960s. A powerful symbol of the fusion of rock music and the counterculture was the great music festival at Woodstock, New York, in the summer of 1969. (See "Patterns of Popular Culture," pp. 844–845.)

THE MOBILIZATION OF MINORITIES

The growth of African-American protest encouraged other minorities to assert themselves and demand redress of their grievances. For Native Americans, Hispanic Americans, gay men and women, and others, the late 1960s and the 1970s were a time of growing self-expression and political activism.

Seeds of Indian Militancy

Few minorities had deeper or more justifiable grievances against the prevailing culture than American Indians—or Native Americans, as some began to call themselves in the 1960s. Indians were the least prosperous, least healthy, and least stable group in the nation. They were also one of

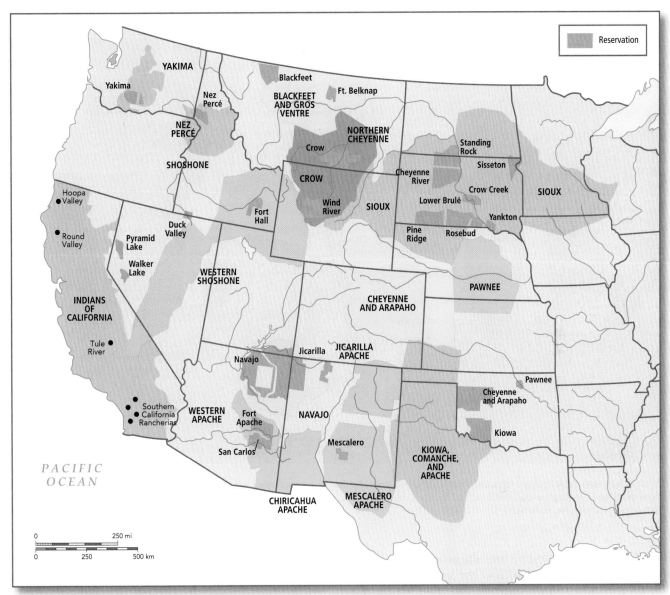

ABORIGINAL TERRITORIES AND MODERN RESERVATIONS OF WESTERN INDIAN TRIBES This map shows the rough distribution of the Native American population in the western United States before the establishment of reservations by the federal government in the nineteenth century. The large shaded regions in colors other than light green represent the areas in which the various tribes were dominant a century and more ago. The purple shaded areas show the much smaller areas set aside for them as reservations after the Indian wars of the late nineteenth century. ◆ *What impact did life on the reservations have on the rise of Indian activism in the 1960s and 1970s?*

the smallest. They constituted less than 1 percent of the population. Average annual family income for Indians was $1,000 less than that for blacks. The Native American unemployment rate was ten times the national rate. Joblessness was particularly high on the reservations, where

Native American Grievances

nearly half the Indians lived. But even most Indians living in cities suffered from their limited education and training and could find only menial jobs. Life expectancy among Indians was more than twenty years less than the national average. Suicides among Indian youths were a hundred times more frequent than among white youths. And while black Americans attracted the

attention (for good or for ill) of many whites, Indians for many years remained largely ignored.

For much of the postwar era, particularly after the resignation of John Collier as commissioner of Indian Affairs in 1946, federal policy toward the tribes had been shaped by a determination to incorporate Indians into mainstream American society, whether Indians wanted to assimilate or not. Two laws passed in 1953 established the basis of a new policy, which became known as "termination." Through termination, the federal government withdrew all official recognition of the tribes as legal entities, administratively separate from state governments, and made them subject to the same local jurisdictions as

THE OCCUPATION OF ALCATRAZ Alcatraz is an island in San Francisco Bay that once housed a large federal prison that by the late 1960s had been abandoned. In 1969, a group of Indian activists occupied the island and claimed it as Indian land—precipitating a long standoff with authorities. *(AP/Wide World Photos)*

white residents. At the same time, the government encouraged Indians to assimilate into the larger society and worked to funnel Native Americans into cities, where, presumably, they would adapt themselves to the white world and lose their cultural distinctiveness.

To some degree, the termination and assimilation policies achieved their objectives. The tribes grew weaker as legal and political entities. Many Native Americans adapted to life in the cities, at least to a degree. On the whole, however, the new policies were a disaster for the tribes and a failure for the reformers who had promoted them. Termination led to widespread corruption and abuse. And Indians themselves fought so bitterly against it that in 1958 the Eisenhower administration barred further "terminations" without the consent of the affected tribes. In the meantime, the struggle against termination had mobilized a new generation of Indian militants and had breathed life into the principal Native American organization, the National Congress of American Indians (NCAI), which had been created in 1944. The new militancy also benefited from the rapid increase in the Indian population, which was growing

Failure of "Termination"

much faster than that of the rest of the nation (nearly doubling between 1950 and 1970, to a total of about 800,000).

The Indian Civil Rights Movement

In 1961, more than 400 members of 67 tribes gathered in Chicago to discuss ways of bringing all Indians together in an effort to redress common wrongs. The manifesto they issued, the Declaration of Indian Purpose, stressed the "right to choose our own way of life." One result of the movement was a gradual change in the way popular culture depicted Indians. By the 1970s, almost no films or television westerns any longer portrayed Indians as brutal savages attacking peaceful white people. And Indian activists even persuaded some white institutions to abandon what they considered demeaning references to them; Dartmouth College, for example, ceased referring to its athletic teams as the "Indians." In 1968, a group of young militant Indians established the American Indian Movement (AIM), which drew its greatest support from those Indians who lived in urban areas but soon established a significant presence on the reservations as well.

AIM

The new activism had some immediate political results. In 1968, Congress passed the Indian Civil Rights Act, which recognized the legitimacy of tribal laws within the reservations. But leaders of AIM and other insurgent groups were not satisfied and turned increasingly to direct action. In 1968, Indian fishermen clashed with Washington State officials on the Columbia River and in Puget Sound, where Indians claimed that treaties gave them the exclusive right to fish. The following year, members of several tribes made a symbolic protest by occupying the abandoned federal prison on Alcatraz Island in San Francisco Bay and claiming the site "by right of discovery."

In response to the growing pressure, the new Nixon administration appointed a Mohawk-Sioux to the position of commissioner of Indian Affairs in 1969; and in 1970, the president promised both increased tribal self-determination and an increase in federal aid. But the protests continued. In November 1972, nearly a thousand demonstrators, most of them Sioux, forcibly occupied the building of the Bureau of Indian Affairs in Washington, D.C., for six days.

A more celebrated protest occurred in February 1973 at

Occupation
of Wounded Knee

Wounded Knee, South Dakota, the site of the 1890 massacre of Sioux by federal troops. Members of AIM seized and occupied the town of Wounded Knee for two months, demanding radical changes in the administration of the reservation and insisting that the government honor its long-forgotten treaty obligations. A brief clash between the occupiers and federal forces left one Indian dead and another wounded.

More immediately effective than these militant protests were the victories that various tribes were achieving in the federal courts. In *United States* v. *Wheeler* (1978), the Supreme Court confirmed that tribes had independent legal standing and could not be "terminated" by Congress. Other decisions ratified the authority of tribes to impose taxes on businesses within their reservations and to perform other sovereign functions. In 1985, the U.S. Supreme Court, in *County of Oneida* v. *Oneida Indian Nation,* supported Indian claims to 100,000 acres in upstate New York that the Oneida tribe claimed by virtue of treaty rights long forgotten by whites.

The Indian civil rights movement, like other civil rights movements of the same time, fell far short of winning full justice and equality for its constituents. To some Indians, the principal goal was to defend tribal autonomy, to protect the right of Indians (and, more to the point, individual tribal groups) to remain separate and distinct. To others, the goal was equality—to win for Indians a place in society equal to that of other groups of Americans. Because there was no single Indian culture or tradition in America, the movement never united all Indians.

For all its limits, however, the Indian civil rights move-

Important Legal
Victories

ment helped the tribes win a series of new legal rights and protections that gave them a stronger position than they had enjoyed at any previous time in the twentieth century.

Latino Activism

Far more numerous than Indians were Latinos (or Hispanic Americans), the fastest-growing minority group in the United States. They were no more a single, cohesive group than the Indians were. Some—including the descendants of early Spanish settlers in New Mexico—had roots as deep in American history as those of any other group. Others were men and women who had immigrated since World War II.

Large numbers of Puerto Ricans had migrated to eastern cities, particularly New York. South Florida's substantial Cuban population began with a wave of middle-class refugees fleeing the Castro regime in the early 1960s, followed by a second, much poorer wave of Cuban immigrants in 1980—the so-called Marielitos, named for the port from which they left Cuba. Later in the 1980s, large numbers of immigrants (both legal and illegal) began to arrive from the troubled nations of Central and South America—from Guatemala, Nicaragua, El Salvador, Peru, and others. But the most numerous and important Latino group in the United States was Mexican Americans.

During World War II, large numbers of Mexican Americans had entered the country in response to the labor shortage, and many had remained in the cities of the Southwest and the Pacific Coast. After the war, when the legal agreements that had allowed Mexican contract workers to enter the country expired, large numbers of immigrants continued to move to the United States illegally. In 1953, the government launched what it called Operation Wetback to deport the illegals, but the effort failed to stem the flow of new arrivals. By 1960, there were substantial Mexican-American neighborhoods (barrios) in American cities from El Paso to Detroit. The largest (with more than 500,000 people, according to census figures) was in Los Angeles, which by then had a bigger Mexican population than any other place except Mexico City.

But the greatest expansion in the Mexican-American population was yet to come. In 1960, the census reported slightly more than 3 million Latinos living in the United States (the great majority of them

Mexican Americans). By 1970,

Surging Latino
Immigration

that number had grown to 9 million, and by 2006 to 44 million. Since there was also an uncounted but very large number of illegal immigrants in those years, the real number was undoubtedly much larger.

By the late 1960s, therefore, Mexican Americans were one of the largest population groups in the West—outnumbering African Americans—and had established communities in most other parts of the nation as well. They were also among the most urbanized groups in the population; almost 90 percent lived and worked in cities. Many

KENNEDY AND CHAVEZ Cesar Chavez, the magnetic leader of the largely Mexican-American United Farm Workers Union, which represented mostly migrant workers, staged a hunger strike in 1968 to demand that union members receive better treatment by growers. Robert F. Kennedy, just beginning his campaign for the presidency, paid him a visit in Delano, California, to show his support. Chavez, who had by then been fasting for many weeks, looks visibly weak here. Kennedy's visit helped persuade him to end the fast. *(Time Life Pictures/Getty Images)*

of them (particularly members of the older and more assimilated families of Mexican descent) were affluent and successful people. Wealthy Cubans in Miami filled influential positions in the professions and local government; in the Southwest, Mexican Americans elected their own leaders to seats in Congress and to governorships.

But most newly arrived Mexican Americans and other Hispanics were less well educated than either "Anglo" or African Americans and hence less well prepared for high-paying jobs. Some of them found good industrial jobs in unionized industries, and some Mexican Americans became important labor organizers in the AFL-CIO. But many more (including the great majority of illegal immigrants) worked in low-paying service jobs, with few if any benefits and no job security.

Partly because of language barriers, partly because the family-centered culture of many Latino communities discouraged effective organization, and partly because of discrimination, Mexican Americans and others were slower to develop political influence than other minorities. But some did respond to the highly charged climate of the 1960s by strengthening their ethnic identification

and organizing for political and economic power. Young Mexican-American activists began to call themselves "Chicanos" (once a term of derision used by whites) as a way of

"Chicano" Activism

emphasizing the shared culture of Spanish-speaking Americans. Some Chicanos advocated a form of nationalism not unlike the ideas of black power advocates. The Texas leaders of La Raza Unida, a Chicano political party in the Southwest, called for the creation of something like an autonomous Mexican-American state within a state; it demonstrated significant strength at the polls in the 1970s.

One of the most visible efforts to organize Mexican Americans occurred in California, where an Arizona-born Latino farmworker, Cesar Chavez,
created an effective union of

Cesar Chavez

itinerant farmworkers. In 1965, his United Farm Workers (UFW), a largely Mexican organization, launched a prolonged strike against growers to demand recognition of their union and increased wages and benefits. When employers resisted, Chavez enlisted the cooperation of college students, churches, and civil rights groups (including CORE and SNCC) and organized a nationwide boycott, first of table grapes and then of lettuce. In 1968, Chavez campaigned openly for Robert Kennedy. Two years later, he won a substantial victory when the growers of half of California's table grapes signed contracts with his union.

Latino Americans were at the center of another controversy of the 1970s and beyond: the issue of bilingualism. It was a question that aroused the opposition not only of many whites but of some Hispanics as well. Supporters of bilingualism in education argued that non-English-speaking Americans were entitled to schooling in their own language, that otherwise they would be at a grave disadvantage in comparison with native English speakers. The United States Supreme Court confirmed the right of non-English-speaking students to schooling in their native language in 1974. Opponents cited not only the cost and difficulty of bilingualism but the dangers it posed to students' ability to assimilate into the mainstream of American culture.

Challenging the "Melting Pot" Ideal

The efforts of African Americans, Latinos, Indians, Asians, and others to forge a clearer group identity challenged a longstanding premise of American political thought: the idea of the "melting pot." Older, European immigrant groups liked to believe that they had advanced in American society by adopting the values and accepting the rules of the country to which they had moved. The newly assertive ethnic groups of the 1960s and after appeared less willing to accept the standards of the larger society and were more likely to demand recognition of their own ethnic identities. Some, although far from all, African Americans, Indians, Latinos, and Asians challenged the assimilationist idea. They advocated instead a culturally pluralistic society, in which racial and ethnic groups would preserve a sense of their own heritage and their own social and cultural norms.

To a considerable degree, the advocates of cultural pluralism succeeded. Recognition of the special character of particular groups was embedded in federal law through a wide range of affirmative action programs, which extended not only to blacks, but to Indians, Latinos, Asians, and others as well. Ethnic studies programs proliferated in schools and universities. Beginning in the 1980s, this impulse led to an even more assertive (and highly controversial) cultural movement that became known as "multiculturalism," which, among other things, challenged the "Eurocentric" basis of American education and culture and demanded that non-European civilizations be accorded equal attention.

Cultural Pluralism

Gay Liberation

The most recent important liberation movement to make major gains in the 1960s, and the most surprising to many Americans, was the effort by homosexuals to win political and economic rights and, equally important, social acceptance. Homosexuality and lesbianism had been unacknowledged realities throughout American history; not until many years after their deaths did many Americans know, for example, that revered cultural figures such as Walt Whitman and Horatio Alger were homosexuals. But by the late 1960s, the liberating impulses that had affected other groups helped mobilize gay men and women to fight for their own rights.

On June 27, 1969, police officers raided the Stonewall Inn, a gay nightclub in New York City's Greenwich Village, and began arresting patrons simply for frequenting the place. The raid was not unusual; police had been harassing gay bars (and homosexual men and women) for years. It was, in fact, the accumulated resentment of this long history of assaults and humiliations that caused the extraordinary response that summer night. Gay onlookers taunted the police, then attacked them. Someone started a blaze in the Stonewall Inn itself, almost trapping the policemen inside. Rioting continued throughout Greenwich Village (a center of New York's gay community) through much of the night.

"Stonewall Riot"

The "Stonewall Riot" helped mark the beginning of the gay liberation movement—one of the most controversial challenges to traditional values and assumptions of its time. New organizations sprang up around the country. Public discussion and media coverage of homosexuality, long subject to an unofficial taboo, quickly and dramatically increased. Gay and lesbian activists had some success in challenging the longstanding assumption that homosexuality was "aberrant" behavior. They argued that no sexual preference was any more "normal" than another.

Most of all, however, the gay liberation movement transformed the outlook of gay men and lesbians themselves. It helped them to "come out," to express their preferences openly and unapologetically, and to demand from society a recognition that gay relationships could be as significant and worthy of respect as heterosexual ones. Even the ravages of the AIDS epidemic (see pp. 907–908), which affected the gay community more disastrously than it affected any other group, failed to halt the growth of gay liberation. In many ways, it strengthened it.

Impact of the Gay Liberation Movement

By the early 1990s, gay men and lesbians were achieving some of the same milestones that other oppressed minorities had attained in earlier decades. Some openly gay politicians won election to public office. Universities were establishing gay and lesbian studies programs. And laws prohibiting discrimination on the basis of sexual preference were making slow, halting progress at the local level.

THE QUILT In the early years of gay liberation, the movement focused mostly on ending discrimination and harassment. By the 1990s, however, with the AIDS epidemic sweeping through large numbers of gay men, activists shifted much of their attention to pressing for a cure and to remembering those who had died. One of the most remarkable results of that effort was the AIDS Quilt. Friends and relatives of victims of the disease made individual patches in memory of those they had lost. Then, in many different cities, thousands of quilters would join their pieces to create a vast testament to bereavement and memory. The enormity of the project was most visible in October 1996, when hundreds of thousands of pieces of the quilt were laid out on the Mall in Washington, stretching from the Washington Monument to the Capitol. (*Ron Edmunds /AP/Wide World Photos*)

But gay liberation also produced a powerful backlash. This became especially evident in 1993, when President Bill Clinton's effort to lift the ban on gays and lesbians serving in the military met a storm of criticism from members of Congress and from within the military itself. The backlash proved so strong that the administration retreated from its position and settled for a weak compromise ("Don't ask, don't tell") by which the military would not ask recruits about their sexual preferences, while those who enlisted in the military were expected not to reveal them.

A decade later, in the prelude to the 2004 presidential election, issues involving gays and lesbians reached a high level of intensity again, sparked in part by the efforts of several cities and states to legalize same-sex marriage. President George W. Bush proposed a constitutional amendment to ban same-sex marriage, and the issue became a major element of the Republican campaign. Many states put referenda on their ballots in 2004 banning gay marriage, and almost all such referenda were decisively approved by the voters.

THE NEW FEMINISM

American women constitute a slight majority of the population. But during the 1960s and 1970s, many women began to identify with minority groups and to demand a liberation of their own. As a result, the role of women in American life changed more dramatically than that of any other group in the nation.

The Rebirth

Feminism had been a weak and often embattled force in American life for more than forty years after the adoption of the woman suffrage amendment in 1920. Yet in the 1960s and 1970s, it evolved very quickly from an almost invisible remnant to one of the most powerful social movements in American history.

The 1963 publication of Betty Friedan's *The Feminine Mystique* is often cited as an important early event of contemporary women's liberation. Friedan, a magazine journalist, had traveled around the country interviewing the women who had graduated with her from Smith College in 1947. Most of these women were living out the dream that postwar American society had created for them: they were affluent wives and mothers living in comfortable suburbs. And yet many of them were deeply frustrated and unhappy. The suburbs, Friedan claimed, had become a "comfortable concentration camp," providing the women who inhabited them with no outlets for their intelligence, talent, and education. The "feminine mystique" was responsible for "burying millions of women alive." By chronicling their unhappiness and frustration, Friedan did not so much cause the revival of feminism as help give voice to a movement that was already stirring.

The Feminine Mystique

By the time *The Feminine Mystique* appeared, John Kennedy had established the President's Commission on the Status of Women; it brought national attention to sexual discrimination and helped create important networks of feminist activists who would lobby for legislative redress. Also in 1963, the Kennedy administration helped win passage of the Equal Pay Act, which barred the pervasive practice of paying women less than men for equal work. A year later, Congress incorporated into the Civil Rights Act of 1964 an amendment—Title VII—that extended to women many of the same legal protections against discrimination that were being extended to African Americans.

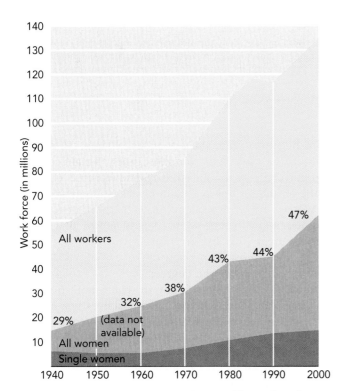

WOMEN IN THE PAID WORK FORCE, 1940–2000 The number of women working for wages steadily expanded from 1940 on, to the point that in 2000, they constituted just under half the total work force. ◆ *What role did this growing participation in the paid work force have on the rise of feminism in the 1960s and beyond?*

The events of the early 1960s helped expose a contradiction that had been developing for decades between the image of happy domesticity, what Friedan had called the "feminine mystique," and the reality of women's roles in America. The reality was that increasing numbers of women (including, by 1963, over a third of all married women) had already entered the workplace and were encountering widespread discrimination there; and that many other women were finding their domestic lives suffocating and frustrating.

In 1966, Friedan joined with other feminists to create the National Organization for Women (NOW), which soon became the nation's largest and most influential feminist organization. Like other movements for liberation, feminism drew much of its inspiration from the black struggle for freedom.

NOW Founded

The new organization responded to the complaints of the women Friedan's book had examined—affluent suburbanites with no outlet for their interests—by demanding greater educational opportunities for women and denouncing the domestic ideal and the traditional concept of marriage. But the heart of the movement, at least in the beginning, was directed toward the needs of women already in the workplace. NOW denounced the exclusion of women from professions, from politics, and from countless other areas of American life. It decried legal and economic discrimination, including the practice of paying women less than men for equal work (a practice the Equal Pay Act had not effectively eliminated). The organization called for "a fully equal partnership of the sexes, as part of the worldwide revolution of human rights."

Women's Liberation

By the late 1960s, new and more radical feminist demands were also attracting a large following. The new feminists were mostly younger, the vanguard of the baby-boom generation. Many of them drew inspiration from the New Left and the counterculture. Some were involved in the civil rights movement, others in the antiwar crusade. Many had found that even within those movements, they faced discrimination and exclusion or subordination to male leaders.

New Directions in the Women's Movement

By the early 1970s, a significant change was visible in the tone and direction of the women's movement. New books by younger feminists expressed a harsher critique of American society than Friedan had offered. Kate Millett's *Sexual Politics* (1969) signaled the new direction by arguing that "every avenue of power within the society is entirely within male hands." The answer to women's problems, in other words, was not, as Friedan had suggested, for individual women to search for greater personal fulfillment; it was for women to band together to

MARCHING FOR WOMEN'S RIGHTS By the end of the 1960s, the struggle for individual rights—which the African-American civil rights movement had helped push to the center of national consciousness—had inspired a broad range of movements. Perhaps the most important in the long run was the drive for women's rights, which was already formidable in the summer of 1970, when thousands of women joined this march through New York City. *(Werner Wolff/Black Star/Stock Photo)*

assault the male power structure. Shulamith Firestone's *The Dialectic of Sex* (1970) was subtitled "The Case for Feminist Revolution."

In its most radical form, the new feminism rejected the whole notion of marriage, family, and even heterosexual intercourse. By the early 1970s, large numbers of women were coming to see themselves as an exploited group organizing against oppression and developing a culture and communities of their own.

Expanding Achievements

By the early 1970s, the public and private achievements of the women's movement were already substantial. In 1971, the government extended its affirmative action guidelines to include women—linking sexism with racism as an officially acknowledged social problem. In the meantime, women were making rapid progress in their efforts to move into the economic and political mainstream. The nation's major all-male educational institu-

tions began to open their doors to women. (Princeton and Yale did so in 1969, and most other all-male colleges and universities soon followed.) Some women's colleges, in the meantime, began accepting male students.

Women were also becoming an important force in business and the professions. Nearly half of all married women held jobs by the mid-1970s, and almost 90 percent of all women with college degrees worked. The two-career family, in which both husband and wife maintained active professional lives, was becoming a widely accepted norm; many women were postponing marriage or motherhood for the sake of their careers. There were also important symbolic changes, such as the refusal of many women to adopt their husbands' names when they married and the use of the term "Ms." in place of "Mrs." or "Miss" to denote the irrelevance of a woman's marital status in the public world. In politics, women were beginning to compete effectively with men for both elected and appointive positions. By the end of the

Political and Economic Success

twentieth century, considerable numbers of women were serving in both houses of Congress, in numerous federal cabinet positions, as governors of several states, and in many other positions. Ronald Reagan named the first female Supreme Court justice, Sandra Day O'Connor, in 1981; in 1993, Bill Clinton named the second, Ruth Bader Ginsburg. In 1984, the Democratic Party chose a woman, Representative Geraldine Ferraro of New York, as its vice presidential candidate, and in 2008, Hillary Clinton became a formidable candidate in the race for the Democratic presidential nomination. In academia, women were expanding their presence in traditional scholarly fields; they were also creating a field of their own—women's studies, which in the 1980s and early 1990s was among the fastest-growing areas of American scholarship.

In professional athletics, in the meantime, women were beginning to compete with men both for attention and for an equal share of prize money. By the late 1970s, the federal government was pressuring colleges and universities to provide women with athletic programs equal to those available to men.

In 1972, Congress approved the Equal Rights Amendment to the Constitution, which some feminists had been promoting since the 1920s, and sent it to the states. For a while, ratification seemed almost certain. By the late 1970s, however, the momentum behind the amendment had died. The ERA was in trouble not because of indifference but because of a rising chorus of objections to it from people (including many antifeminist women) who feared it would disrupt traditional social patterns. In 1982, the amendment finally died when the time allotted for ratification expired.

Failure of ERA

The Abortion Controversy

A vital element of American feminism since the 1920s has been women's effort to win greater control of their own sexual and reproductive lives. In its least controversial form, this impulse helped produce an increasing awareness in the 1960s and 1970s of the problems of rape, sexual abuse, and wife beating. There continued to be some controversy over the dissemination of contraceptives and birth-control information; but that issue, at least, seemed to have lost much of the explosive character it had had in the 1920s. A related issue, however, stimulated as much popular passion as any question of its time: abortion.

Abortion had once been legal in much of the United States, but by the beginning of the twentieth century it was banned by statute in most of the country and remained so into the 1960s (although many abortions continued to be performed quietly, and often dangerously, out of sight of the law). But the women's movement created strong new pressures on behalf of legalizing abortion. Several states had abandoned restrictions on abortion by the end of the 1960s. And in 1973, the Supreme Court's

decision in *Roe* v. *Wade,* based on a relatively new theory of a constitutional "right to privacy," first recognized by the Court only a few years earlier in *Griswold* v. *Connecticut* (1965), invalidated all laws prohibiting abortion during the "first trimester"—the first three months of pregnancy. The decision would become the most controversial ruling of the century.

Roe v. Wade

ENVIRONMENTALISM IN A TURBULENT SOCIETY

Like feminism, environmentalism entered the 1960s with a long history and relatively little public support. Also like feminism, environmentalism both profited from and transcended the turbulence of the era and emerged by the 1970s as a powerful and enduring force in American and global life.

The rise of this new movement was in part a result of the environmental degradation that had become increasingly evident in the advanced industrial society of the late twentieth century. It was a result, too, of the growth of the science of ecology, which provided environmentalists with new and powerful arguments. And it was a product as well of some of the countercultural movements of the time: movements that rejected aspects of the modern, industrial, consumer society and called for a return to a more natural existence.

The New Science of Ecology

Until the mid-twentieth century, most people who considered themselves environmentalists (or, to use the more traditional term, conservationists) based their commitment on aesthetic or moral grounds. They wanted to preserve nature because it was too beautiful to despoil, or because it was a mark of divinity on the world. In the course of the twentieth century, however, scientists in the United States and other nations—drawing from earlier, relatively obscure scientific writings—began to create a new rationale for environmentalism. They called it ecology.

Ecology is the science of the interrelatedness of the natural world. It rests on an assumption—as the American zoologist Stephan A. Forbes wrote as early as 1880—that "primeval nature . . . presents a settled harmony of interaction among organic groups," and that this harmony "is in strong contrast with the many serious maladjustments of plants and animals found in countries occupied by man." Such problems as air and water pollution, the destruction of forests, the extinction of species, and toxic wastes are not, ecology teaches, separate, isolated problems. All elements of the earth's environment are intimately and delicately linked. Damaging any one of those elements, therefore, risks damaging all the others.

Idea of an Interrelated World

A number of American scientists built on Forbes's ideas in the early twentieth century, but perhaps the greatest early contribution to popular knowledge of ecology came not from a scientist, but from the writer and naturalist Aldo Leopold. During a career in forest management, Leopold sought to apply the new scientific findings on ecology to his interactions with the natural world. And in 1949, he published a classic of environmental literature, *The Sand County Almanac,* in which he argued that humans have a responsibility to understand and maintain the balance of nature, that they should behave in the natural world according to a code that he called the "land ethic." By then, the science of ecology was spreading widely in the scientific community. Among the findings of ecologists were such now-common ideas as the "food chain," the "ecosystem," "biodiversity," and "endangered species."

The influence of these emerging ideas of ecology could be seen especially clearly in the sensational 1962 book by Rachel Carson, *Silent Spring.* Carson was a marine biologist who had become a successful science writer. In 1957, she received a letter from a friend reporting the deaths of songbirds in her yard after the area had been sprayed with the insecticide DDT—the chemical developed in the 1930s to kill mosquitos. Carson began investigating the impact of DDT and discovered growing signs of danger. DDT was slowly being absorbed into the food chain

through water and plants, and the animals who ate and drank them. It was killing some animals (especially birds and fish) and inhibiting the ability of others to reproduce. Carson wrote eloquently about the growing danger of a "silent spring," in which birds would no longer sing and in which sickness and death would soon threaten large numbers of animals and, perhaps, people.

Silent Spring was an enormously influential book and had a direct, if delayed, influence on the decision to ban DDT in the United States in 1972. It was evidence of the growing power of environmentalism, and of the science of ecology, on public policy and national culture. But *Silent Spring* was also a very controversial book, which enraged the chemical industry. Critics of Carson attempted to suppress the book and, when that effort failed, to discredit its findings. Both the future power of environmentalism and the future challenges to it could be seen in the history of Carson's book.

Between 1945 and 1960, the number of ecologists in the United States grew rapidly, and that number doubled again between 1960 and 1970. Funded by government agencies, by universities, by foundations, and eventually even by some corporations, ecological science gradually established itself as a significant field of its own. By the early twenty-first century, there were programs in and departments of ecological science in major universities throughout the United States and in many other nations.

> Ecology's Postwar Growth

Much more than other scientists, however, ecologists tend to fuse their commitment to research with a commitment to publicizing their work and promoting responsible public action to deal with environmental crises.

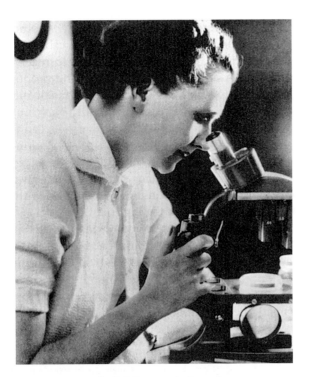

RACHEL CARSON Rachel Carson, who began her career as a marine biologist, wrote the world's best-selling book about the ocean environment in the 1950s. Carson's abiding love for the creatures of shore and surf led to her concern about the harm pesticides might do them. *(Bettmann/Corbis)*

Environmental Advocacy

Among the most important environmental organizations of the late twentieth and early twenty-first centuries were the Wilderness Society, the Sierra Club, the National Audubon Society, the Nature Conservancy, the National Wildlife Federation, and the National Parks and Conservation Association. All of these organizations predated the rise of modern ecological science, but all of them entered the twenty-first century reenergized and committed to the new concepts of environmentalism. They found allies among other not-for-profit organizations that had no previous experience with environmentalism but now chose to join the battle—among them such groups as the American Civil Liberties Union, the League of Women Voters, the National Council of Churches, and even the AFL-CIO.

Out of these organizations emerged a new generation of professional environmental activists able to contribute to the legal and political battles of the movement. Scientists provided the necessary data. Lawyers fought battles with government

> New Professional Environmental Activists

agencies and in the courts. Lobbyists used traditional techniques of political persuasion with legislators and other officials—knowing that many corporations and other opponents of environmental efforts would be doing the same in opposition to their goals. Perhaps most of all, these organizations learned how to mobilize public opinion on their behalf.

Environmental Degradation

Perhaps the greatest force behind environmentalism was the condition of the environment itself. By the 1960s, the damage to the natural world from the dramatic economic growth of the postwar era was becoming impossible to ignore. Water pollution—which had been a problem in some areas of the country for many decades—was becoming so widespread that almost every major city was dealing with the unpleasant sight and odor, as well as the very real health risks, of polluted rivers and lakes.

Water and Air Pollution

In Cleveland, Ohio, for example, the Cuyahoga River actually burst into flame from time to time beginning in the 1950s from the petroleum waste being dumped into it.

Perhaps more alarming was the growing awareness that the air itself was becoming unhealthy, that toxic fumes from factories and power plants and, most of all, automobiles were poisoning the atmosphere. Weather forecasts and official atmospheric information began to refer to "smog" levels—using a new word formed from a combination of "smoke" and "fog." In some large cities—Los Angeles and Denver among them—smog became a perpetual fact of life, rising steadily through the day, blotting out the sun, and creating respiratory difficulties for many citizens.

Environmentalists also brought to public attention some longer-term dangers of unchecked industrial development: the rapid depletion of oil and other irreplaceable fossil fuels; the destruction of lakes and forests as a result of "acid rain" (rainfall polluted by chemical contaminants); the rapid destruction of vast rain forests, in Brazil and elsewhere, which limited the earth's capacity to replenish its oxygen supply; the depletion of the ozone layer as a result of the release of chlorofluorocarbons into the atmosphere, which threatened to limit the earth's protection from dangerous ultraviolet rays from the sun; and most alarming, global warming, which if unchecked would create dramatic changes in the earth's climate and would threaten existing cities and settlements in coastal areas all over the world by causing a rise in ocean levels. Many of these claims became controversial, with skeptics arguing that environmentalists had not conclusively proven their cases. But most environmentalists—and many scientists—came to believe that the problems were real and deserving of immediate, urgent attention.

Earth Day and Beyond

On April 22, 1970, people all over the United States gathered in schools and universities, in churches and clubs, in parks and auditoria, for the first "Earth Day." Originally proposed by Wisconsin senator Gaylord Nelson as a series of teach-ins on college campuses, Earth Day gradually took on a much larger life. Carefully managed by people who wanted to avoid associations with the radical left, it had an unthreatening quality that made it appealing to many people for whom antiwar demonstrations and civil rights rallies seemed threatening. According to some estimates, over 20 million Americans participated in some part of the Earth Day observances, which may have made it the largest single demonstration in the nation's history.

The First "Earth Day"

The cautious, centrist character of Earth Day and related efforts to popularize environmentalism helped

EARTH DAY, 1970 The first "Earth Day," April 22, 1970, was an important event in the development of the environmental movement. Conceived by Wisconsin senator Gaylord Nelson, Earth Day quickly gathered support in many areas of the United States and produced large demonstrations such as this one in New York City, where crowds surround a large banner portraying the earth crying out for help. *(Getty Images)*

create a movement that had little of the divisiveness of other, more controversial causes. Gradually, environmentalism became more than simply a series of demonstrations and protests. It became part of the consciousness of the vast majority of Americans—absorbed into popular culture, built into primary and secondary education, endorsed by almost all politicians (even if many of them opposed some environmental goals).

It also became part of the fabric of public policy. In 1970, Congress passed and President Nixon signed the National Environmental Protection Act, which created a new agency—the Environmental Protection Agency—to

EPA Established

enforce antipollution standards on businesses and consumers. The Clean Air Act, also passed in 1970, and the Clean Water Act, passed in 1972, added tools to the government's arsenal of weapons against environmental degradation.

NIXON, KISSINGER, AND THE WAR

Richard Nixon assumed office in 1969 committed not only to restoring stability at home but also to creating a new and more stable order in the world. Central to his hopes was a resolution of the stalemate in Vietnam. Yet the new president felt no freer than his predecessor to abandon the American commitment there. He realized that the war was threatening both the nation's domestic stability and its position in the world. But he feared that a precipitous retreat would destroy American honor and "credibility." American involvement in Indochina continued for four more years, during which the war expanded both in its geographic scope and in its bloodiness.

Vietnamization

Despite Nixon's own passionate interest in international affairs, he brought with him into government a man who ultimately seemed to overshadow him in the conduct of diplomacy: Henry Kissinger, a Harvard professor whom

Henry Kissinger

the president appointed as his national security adviser. Kissinger quickly established dominance over both the secretary of state, William Rogers, and the secretary of defense, Melvin Laird, who were both more experienced in public life than Kissinger was. That was in part a result of Nixon's passion for concentrating decision making in the White House. But Kissinger's keen intelligence, his bureaucratic skills, and his success in handling the press were at least equally important. Together, Nixon and Kissinger set out to find an acceptable solution to the stalemate in Vietnam.

The new Vietnam policy moved along several fronts. One was an effort to limit domestic opposition to the war. Aware that the military draft was one of the most visible

targets of dissent, the administration devised a new "lottery" system, through which only a limited group—those nineteen-year-olds with low lottery numbers—would be subject to conscription. Later, the president urged the creation of an all-volunteer army. By 1973, the Selective Service System was on its way to at least temporary extinction.

More important in stifling dissent, however, was the new policy of "Vietnamization" of the war—the training and equipping of the South Vietnamese military to take over the burden of combat from American forces. In the fall of 1969, Nixon announced reduction of American ground troops from Vietnam by 60,000,

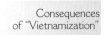
Consequences of "Vietnamization"

the first reduction in U.S. troop strength since the beginning of the war. The reductions continued steadily for more than three years. From a peak of more than 540,000 American troops in 1969, the number had dwindled to about 60,000 by 1972.

Vietnamization helped quiet domestic opposition to the war. But it did nothing to break the stalemate in the negotiations with the North Vietnamese in Paris. The new administration quickly decided that new military pressures would be necessary to do that.

Escalation

By the end of their first year in office, Nixon and Kissinger had concluded that the most effective way to tip the military balance in America's favor was to destroy the bases in Cambodia from which, the American military believed, the North Vietnamese were launching many of their attacks. Very early in his presidency, Nixon ordered the air force to begin bombing Cambodian territory to destroy the enemy sanctuaries. He kept the raids secret from Congress and the public. In the spring of 1970, possibly with U.S. encouragement and support, conservative military leaders overthrew the neutral government of Cambodia and established a new, pro-American regime under General Lon Nol. Lon Nol quickly gave his approval to American incursions into his territory; and on April 30, Nixon went on television to announce that he was ordering American troops across the border into Cambodia to "clean out" the bases that the enemy had been using for its "increased military aggression."

Literally overnight, the Cambodian invasion restored the dwindling antiwar movement to vigorous life. The first days of May saw the most widespread and vocal antiwar demonstrations since the beginning of the war. Hundreds of thousands of protesters gathered in Washington, D.C., to denounce the president's policies. Millions, perhaps, participated in countless other demonstrations on campuses nationwide. The mood of crisis intensified greatly on May 4, when four college students were killed and nine others injured when members of the National Guard opened fire on antiwar demonstrators at Kent

Kent State State University in Ohio. Ten days later, police killed two black students at Jackson State University in Mississippi during a demonstration there.

The clamor against the war quickly spread into the government and the press. Congress angrily repealed the Gulf of Tonkin Resolution in December, stripping the president of what had long served as the legal basis for the war. Nixon ignored the action. Then, in June 1971, first the *New York Times* and later other newspapers began publishing excerpts from a secret study of the war prepared by the Defense Department during the Johnson administration. What came to be known as the Pentagon Papers, leaked to the press by former Defense official Daniel Ellsberg, provided evidence of what many had long believed: that the government had been dishonest, both in reporting the military progress of the war and in explaining its own motives for American involvement. The administration went to court to suppress the documents, but the Supreme Court finally ruled that the press had the right to publish them.

Morale and discipline were rapidly deteriorating among U.S. troops in Vietnam, who had been fighting a savage and inconclusive war for more than five years. The trial and conviction in 1971 of Lieutenant William Calley, who was charged with overseeing a massacre of more than 300 unarmed South Vietnamese civilians, attracted wide public attention. Many Americans believed that the My Lai tragedy was not an isolated incident, that it suggested the dehumanizing impact **My Lai Massacre** of the war on those who fought it—and the terrible consequences for the Vietnamese people of that dehumanization. Less publicized were other, more widespread problems among American troops in Vietnam: desertion, drug addiction, racial hostilities, refusal to obey orders, even the killing of unpopular officers by enlisted men.

By 1971, nearly two-thirds of those interviewed in public opinion polls were urging American withdrawal from Vietnam. But Richard Nixon showed no sign of retreat. With the approval of the White House, both the FBI and the CIA intensified their surveillance and infiltration of antiwar and radical groups. Administration officials sought to discredit prominent critics of the war by leaking damaging personal information about them. At one point, White House agents broke into the office of a psychiatrist in an unsuccessful effort to steal files on Daniel Ellsberg. During the congressional campaign of 1970, Vice President Spiro Agnew, using the acid rhetoric that had already made him the hero of many conservatives, stepped up his attack on the "effete" and "impudent" critics of the administration. The president himself once climbed on top of an automobile to taunt a crowd of angry demonstrators.

In March 1972, the North Vietnamese mounted their biggest offensive since 1968 (the **Easter Offensive** so-called Easter offensive). American and South Vietnamese forces managed to halt the communist advance, but it was clear that without American support the offensive would have succeeded. At the same time, Nixon ordered American planes to bomb targets near Hanoi, the capital of North Vietnam, and Haiphong, its principal port, and called for the mining of seven North Vietnamese harbors (including Haiphong) to stop the flow of supplies from China and the Soviet Union.

"Peace with Honor"

As the 1972 presidential election approached, the administration stepped up its efforts to produce a breakthrough in negotiations with the North Vietnamese. In April 1972, the president dropped his longtime insistence on a removal of North Vietnamese troops from the south before any American withdrawal. Meanwhile, Henry Kissinger was meeting privately in Paris with the North Vietnamese foreign secretary, Le Duc Tho, to work out terms for a cease-fire. On October 26, only days before the presidential election, Kissinger announced that "peace is at hand." Several weeks later (after the election), negotiations broke down once again. The American and the North Vietnamese governments appeared ready to accept the Kissinger-Tho plan for a cease-fire, but the Thieu regime balked, still insisting on a full withdrawal of North Vietnamese forces from the south. Kissinger tried to win additional concessions from the communists to meet Thieu's objections, but on December 16 talks broke off.

The next day, December 17, American B-52s began the heaviest and most destructive air raids of the entire war on Hanoi, Haiphong, and other North Vietnamese targets. Civilian casualties were high, and fifteen American B-52s were shot **"Christmas Bombing"** down by the North Vietnamese; in the entire war to that point, the United States had lost only one of the giant bombers. On December 30, Nixon terminated the "Christmas bombing." The United States and the North Vietnamese returned to the conference table. And on January 27, 1973, they signed an "agreement on ending the war and restoring peace in Vietnam." Nixon claimed that the Christmas bombing had forced the North Vietnamese to relent. At least equally important, however, was the enormous American pressure on Thieu to accept the cease-fire.

The terms of the Paris accords were little different from those Kissinger and Tho had accepted in principle a few months before. There would be an immediate cease-fire. The North Vietnamese would release several hundred American prisoners of war. The Thieu regime would survive for the moment—the principal North Vietnamese concession to the United States—but North Vietnamese forces already in the south would remain there. An undefined committee would work out a permanent settlement.

Defeat in Indochina

American forces were hardly out of Indochina before the Paris accords collapsed. During the first year after the cease-fire, the contending Vietnamese armies suffered greater battle losses than the Americans had absorbed during ten years of fighting. Finally, in March 1975, the North Vietnamese launched a full-scale offensive against the now greatly weakened forces of the south. Thieu appealed to Washington for assistance; the president (now Gerald Ford; Nixon had resigned in 1974) appealed to Congress for additional funding; Congress refused. Late in April 1975, communist forces marched into Saigon, shortly after officials of the Thieu regime and the staff of the American embassy had fled the country in humiliating disarray. Communist forces quickly occupied the capital, renamed it Ho Chi Minh City, and began the process of reuniting Vietnam under the

Fall of Saigon

Hanoi government. At about the same time, the Lon Nol regime in Cambodia fell to the murderous communists of Pol Pot and the Khmer Rouge—whose genocidal policies led to the deaths of more than a third of the country's people over the next several years. That was the grim end of over a decade of direct American military involvement in Vietnam. More than 1.2 million Vietnamese soldiers had died in combat, along with countless civilians throughout the region. A beautiful land had been ravaged, its agrarian economy left in ruins; for many years after, Vietnam remained one of the poorest and most politically oppressive nations in the world. The United States had paid a heavy price as well. The war had cost the nation almost $150 billion in direct costs and much more indirectly. It had resulted in the deaths of over 55,000 young Americans and the injury of 300,000 more. And the nation had suffered a heavy blow to its confidence and self-esteem.

THE EVACUATION OF SAIGON   A harried U.S. official struggles to keep panicking Vietnamese from boarding an already overburdened helicopter on the roof of the American embassy in Saigon. The hurried evacuation of Americans took place only hours before the arrival of North Vietnamese troops, signaling the final defeat of South Vietnam. *(AP/Wide World Photos)*

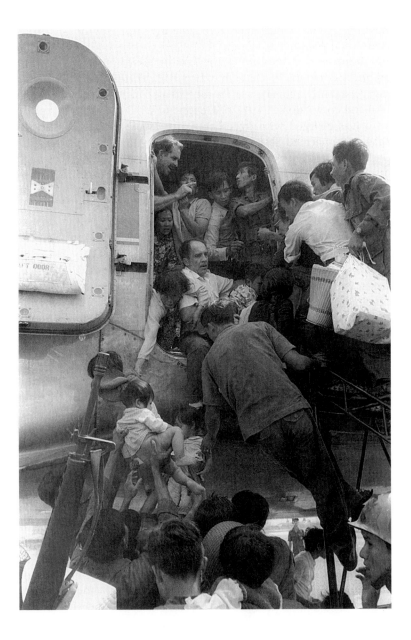

NIXON, KISSINGER, AND THE WORLD

The continuing war in Vietnam provided a dismal backdrop to what Nixon considered his larger mission in world affairs: the construction of a new international order. The president had become convinced that old assumptions of a "bipolar" world—in which the United States and the Soviet Union were the only truly great powers—were now obsolete. America must adapt to the new "multipolar"

Toward a "Multipolar" World

international structure, in which China, Japan, and Western Europe would become major, independent forces. "It will be a safer world and a better world," he said in 1971, "if we have a strong, healthy United States, Europe, Soviet Union, China, Japan—each balancing the other, not playing one against the other, an even balance."

China and the Soviet Union

For more than twenty years, ever since the fall of Chiang Kai-shek in 1949, the United States had treated China, the second-largest nation on earth, as if it did not exist. Instead, America recognized the regime-in-exile on Taiwan as the legitimate government of mainland China. Nixon and Kissinger wanted to forge a new relationship with the Chinese communists—in part to strengthen them as a counterbalance to the Soviet Union. The Chinese, for their part, were eager to forestall what they feared was the possibility of a Soviet-American alliance against China and to end China's own isolation from the international arena.

In July 1971, Nixon sent Henry Kissinger on a secret mission to Beijing. When Kissinger returned, the president made the startling announcement that he would visit China himself within the next few months. That fall, with American approval, the United Nations admitted the communist government of China and expelled the representatives of the Taiwan regime. Finally, in February 1972, Nixon paid a formal visit to China, which erased much of the deep American ani-

Nixon's China Visit

mosity toward the Chinese communists. Nixon did not yet formally recognize the communist regime, but in 1972 the United States and China began low-level diplomatic relations.

The initiatives in China coincided with (and probably assisted) an effort by the Nixon administration to improve relations with the Soviet Union. In 1969, American and Soviet diplomats met in Helsinki, Finland, to begin talks on limiting nuclear weapons. In 1972, they produced the first Strategic Arms Limitation Treaty (SALT I), which froze

SALT I

the nuclear missiles (ICBMs) of both sides at present levels.

The Problems of Multipolarity

Nixon and Kissinger believed that great-power relationships could not alone ensure international stability, for the

"Third World" remained the most volatile and dangerous source of international tension.

Central to the Nixon-Kissinger policy toward the Third World was the effort to maintain a stable status quo without involving the United States too deeply in local disputes. In 1969 and 1970, the president described what became

Nixon Doctrine

known as the Nixon Doctrine, by which the United States would "participate in the defense and development of allies and friends" but would leave the "basic responsibility" for the future of those "friends" to the nations themselves. In practice, the Nixon Doctrine meant a declining American interest in contributing to Third World development; a growing contempt for the United Nations, where

DÉTENTE AT HIGH TIDE The visit of Soviet premier Leonid Brezhnev to Washington in 1973 was a high-water mark in the search for détente between the two nations, a search that had begun as early as 1962, that continued through parts of five presidential administrations, and that collapsed in disarray in the late 1970s. Here, Brezhnev and Nixon share friendly words while standing on the White House balcony. *(J. P. Laffont/Corbis Sygma)*

less-developed nations were gaining influence through their sheer numbers; and increasing support to authoritarian regimes attempting to withstand radical challenges from within.

In 1970, for example, the CIA poured substantial funds into Chile to help support the established government against a communist challenge. When the Marxist candidate for president, Salvador Allende, came to power through an honest election, the United States began funneling more money to opposition forces in Chile to help "destabilize" the new government. In 1973, a military junta seized power from Allende, who was subsequently murdered. The United States developed a friendly relationship with the new, repressive military government of General Augusto Pinochet.

In the Middle East, conditions were growing more volatile in the aftermath of the 1967 "Six-Day War," in which

"Six-Day War"

Israel routed Egyptian, Syrian, and Jordanian forces, gained control of the whole of the long-divided city of Jerusalem, and occupied substantial new territories: on the west bank of the Jordan River, the Gaza Strip, the Golan Heights, and elsewhere. The war also increased the number of refugee Palestinians—Arabs who claimed the lands now controlled by Israel and who, dislodged from their homes, became a source of considerable instability in Jordan, Lebanon, and the other surrounding countries into which they now moved. Jordan's ruler, King Hussein, was particularly alarmed by the influx of Palestinians and by the activities of the Palestinian Liberation Organization (PLO) and other radical groups, which he feared would threaten Jordan's important relationship with the United States. After a series of uprisings in 1970, Hussein ordered the Jordanian army to expel the Palestinians. Many of them moved to Lebanon, where they became part of many years of instability and civil war.

In October 1973, on the Jewish High Holy Day of Yom Kippur, Egyptian and Syrian forces attacked Israel. For ten days, the Israelis struggled to recover from the surprise attack; finally, they launched an effective counteroffensive against Egyptian forces in the Sinai. At that point, the United States intervened, placing heavy pressure on Israel to accept a cease-fire rather than press its advantage.

The imposed settlement of the Yom Kippur War demonstrated the growing dependence of the United States and its allies on Arab oil. Permitting Israel to continue its drive into Egypt might have jeopardized the ability of the United States to purchase needed petroleum from the

Arab Oil Embargo

Arab states. A brief but painful embargo by the Arab governments on the sale of oil to supporters of Israel (including America) in 1973 provided an ominous warning of the costs of losing access to the region's resources. The lesson of the Yom Kippur War, therefore, was that the United States could not ignore the interests of the Arab nations in its efforts on behalf of Israel.

A larger lesson of 1973 was that the nations of the Third World could no longer be expected to act as passive, cooperative "client states." The United States could no longer depend on cheap, easy access to raw materials as it had in the past.

POLITICS AND ECONOMICS UNDER NIXON

For a time in the late 1960s, it had seemed to many Americans that the forces of chaos and radicalism were taking control of the nation. The domestic policy of the Nixon administration was an attempt to restore balance: between the needs of the poor and the desires of the middle class, between the power of the federal government and the interests of local communities. In the end, however, economic and political crises—some beyond the administration's control, some of its own making—sharply limited Nixon's ability to fulfill his domestic goals.

Domestic Initiatives

Many of Nixon's domestic policies were a response to what he believed to be the demands of his own constituency—conservative, middle-class people whom he liked to call the "silent majority" and who wanted to reduce federal "interference" in local affairs. He tried, unsuccessfully, to persuade Congress to pass legislation prohibiting the use of forced busing to achieve school desegregation. He forbade the Department of Health, Education, and Welfare to cut off federal funds from school districts that had failed to comply with court orders to integrate. At the same time, he began to reduce or dismantle many of the social programs of the Great Society and the New Frontier. In 1973, for example, he

Dismantling the Great Society

abolished the Office of Economic Opportunity, the centerpiece of the antipoverty program of the Johnson years.

Yet Nixon's domestic efforts were not entirely conservative. One of the administration's boldest efforts was an attempt to overhaul the nation's enormous welfare system. Nixon proposed replacing the existing system, which almost everyone agreed was cumbersome, expensive, and inefficient, with what he called the Family Assistance Plan (FAP). It would in effect have created a guaranteed annual income for all Americans: $1,600 in federal grants, which could be supplemented by outside earnings up to $4,000. Even many liberals applauded the proposal as an important step toward expanding federal responsibility for the poor. Nixon, however, presented the plan in conservative terms: as something that would reduce the role of government and transfer to welfare recipients themselves daily responsibility for their own lives. Although the FAP won approval in the House in 1970, concerted attacks by welfare recipients (who considered the benefits inadequate), members of the welfare bureaucracy (whose own influence stood to be sharply diminished by the bill), and conservatives (who opposed a guaranteed income on principle) helped kill it in the Senate.

From the Warren Court to the Nixon Court

Of all the liberal institutions that had aroused the enmity of the "silent majority" in the 1950s and 1960s, none had evoked more anger and bitterness than the Supreme Court. Not only had its rulings on racial matters disrupted traditional social patterns, but its staunch defense of civil liberties had, in the opinions of many Americans, contributed to the increase in crime, disorder, and moral decay. In *Engel* v. *Vitale* (1962), the Court ruled that prayers in public schools violated the constitutional separation of church and state, sparking outrage among religious fundamentalists and others. In *Roth* v. *United States* (1957), the Court had sharply limited the authority of local governments to curb pornography. In a series of other decisions, the Court greatly strengthened the civil rights of criminal defendants and, many Americans believed, greatly weakened the power of law enforcement officials to do their jobs. In *Gideon* v. *Wainwright* (1963), the Court ruled that every felony defendant was entitled to a lawyer regardless of his or her ability to pay. In *Escobedo* v. *Illinois* (1964), it ruled that a defendant must be allowed access to a lawyer before questioning by police. In *Miranda* v. *Arizona* (1966), the Court confirmed the obligation of authorities to inform a criminal suspect of his or her rights. By 1968, the Warren Court had become the target of Americans of all kinds who felt the balance of power in the United States had shifted too far toward the poor and dispossessed at the expense of the middle class, and toward criminals at the expense of law-abiding citizens.

One of the most important decisions of the Warren Court in the 1960s was *Baker* v. *Carr* (1962), which

Baker v. *Carr*

required state legislatures to apportion electoral districts so that all citizens' votes would have equal weight. In dozens of states, systems of legislative districting had given disproportionate representation to sparsely populated rural areas, hence diminishing the voting power of urban residents. The reapportionment that the decision required greatly strengthened the voting power of African Americans, Hispanics, and other groups concentrated in cities.

Nixon was determined to use his judicial appointments to give the Court a more conservative cast. His first opportunity came almost as soon as he entered office. When Chief Justice Earl Warren resigned early in 1969, Nixon replaced him with a federal appeals court judge of conservative leanings, Warren Burger. A few months later, Associate Justice Abe Fortas resigned after allegations of financial improprieties. To replace him, Nixon named Clement F. Haynsworth, a respected federal circuit court judge from South Carolina. But Haynsworth came under fire from Senate liberals, black organizations, and labor unions for his conservative record on civil rights and for what some claimed was a conflict of interest in several of the cases on which he had sat. The Senate rejected him. Nixon's next choice was G. Harrold Carswell, a judge of the Florida federal appeals court of little distinction and widely considered unfit for the Supreme Court. The Senate rejected his nomination too.

Nixon angrily denounced the votes, calling them expressions of prejudice against the South. But he was careful thereafter to choose men of standing within the legal community to fill vacancies on the Supreme Court: Harry Blackmun, a moderate jurist from Minnesota; Lewis F. Powell Jr., a respected judge from Virginia; and William Rehnquist, a member of the Nixon Justice Department.

The new Court, however, fell short of what many conservatives had expected. Rather than retreating from its commitment to social reform, the Court in many areas actually became more committed. In *Swann* v. *Charlotte-Mecklenburg Board of Education* (1971), it ruled in favor of the use of forced busing to achieve racial balance in schools. In *Furman* v. *Georgia* (1972), the Court overturned existing capital punishment statutes and established strict new guidelines for such laws in the future. In *Roe* v. *Wade* (1973), it struck down laws forbidding abortions. In other decisions, however, the Burger Court was more moderate. Although the justices approved busing as a tool for achieving integration, they rejected, in *Milliken* v. *Bradley* (1974), a plan to transfer students across district lines (in this case, between Detroit and its suburbs) to achieve racial balance. While the Court upheld the principle of affirmative action in its celebrated 1978 decision *Bakke* v. *Board of Regents of California,* it established restrictive new guidelines for such programs in the future.

Bakke v. *Board of Regents of California*

The Election of 1972

However unsuccessful his administration may have been in achieving some of its specific goals, Nixon entered the presidential race in 1972 with a substantial reserve of strength. His energetic reelection committee collected enormous sums of money to support the campaign. The president himself used the powers of incumbency with great effect, refraining from campaigning and concentrating on highly publicized international decisions and state visits. Agencies of the federal government dispensed funds and favors to strengthen Nixon's political standing in critical areas.

Nixon was most fortunate in 1972, however, in his opposition. The return of George Wallace to the presidential fray caused some early concern. Nixon was delighted to see Wallace run in the Democratic primaries and quietly encouraged him to do so. But he feared that Wallace would again launch a third-party campaign; Nixon's own reelection strategy rested on the same appeals to the troubled middle class that Wallace was expressing. The possibility of such a campaign vanished in May, when a would-be assassin shot the Alabama governor during a rally at a Maryland shopping center. Paralyzed from the waist down, Wallace was unable to continue campaigning.

The Democrats, in the meantime, were making their own contributions to the Nixon cause by nominating for president a representative of their most liberal wing: Senator George S. McGovern of South Dakota. An outspoken critic of the war, a forceful advocate of advanced liberal positions on most social and economic issues, McGovern seemed to embody many aspects of the turbulent 1960s that middle-class Americans were most eager to reject. McGovern profited greatly from party reforms (which he himself had helped to draft) that reduced the power of party leaders and gave increased influence to women, blacks, and young people in the selection of the Democratic ticket. But those same reforms helped make the Democratic Convention of 1972 an unappealing spectacle to much of the public.

George McGovern

On election day, Nixon won reelection by one of the largest margins in history: 60.7 percent of the popular vote compared with 37.5 percent for the forlorn McGovern, and an electoral margin of 520 to 17.

Nixon's Landslide

The Troubled Economy

For three decades, the American economy had been the envy of the world. It had produced as much as a third of the world's industrial goods and had dominated international trade. The American dollar had been the strongest currency in the world, and the American standard of living had risen steadily from its already substantial heights. Many Americans assumed that this remarkable prosperity was the normal condition of their society. In fact, however, it rested in part on several advantages that were rapidly disappearing by the late 1960s: above all, the absence of significant foreign competition and easy access to raw materials in the Third World.

Inflation, which had been creeping upward for several years when Richard Nixon took office, soon began to soar; it would be the most disturbing economic problem of the 1970s. Its most visible cause was a significant increase in federal deficit spending that began in the 1960s, when the Johnson administration tried to fund the war in Vietnam and its ambitious social programs without raising taxes. But there were other, equally important causes. No longer did the United States have exclusive access to cheap raw materials around the globe; not only were other industrial nations now competing for increasingly scarce raw materials, but Third World suppliers of those materials were beginning to realize their value and to demand higher prices for them.

Inflation

The greatest immediate blow to the American economy was the increasing cost of energy. More than any nation on earth, the United States based its economy on the easy availability of cheap and plentiful fossil fuels. No society was more dependent on the automobile; none was more wasteful in its use of oil and gas in its homes, schools, and factories. Domestic petroleum reserves were no longer sufficient to meet this demand, and the nation was heavily dependent on imports from the Middle East and Africa.

For many years, the Organization of Petroleum Exporting Countries (OPEC) had operated as an informal bargaining unit for the sale of oil by Third World nations, but had seldom managed to exercise any real strength. But in the early 1970s, OPEC began to use its oil both as an economic tool and as a political weapon. In 1973, in the midst of the Yom Kippur War, Arab members of OPEC announced that they would no longer ship petroleum to nations supporting Israel—which meant the United States and its allies in Western Europe. At about the same time, the OPEC nations agreed to raise their prices 400 percent. These twin shocks produced momentary economic chaos in the West. The United States suffered its first fuel shortage since World War II. And although the boycott ended a few months later, the price of energy continued to skyrocket both because of OPEC's new militant policies and because of the weakening competitive position of the dollar in world markets.

OPEC

But inflation was only one of the new problems facing the American economy. Another was the decline of the

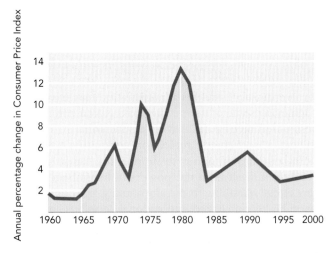

INFLATION, 1960–2000 Inflation was the biggest economic worry of most Americans in the 1970s and early 1980s, and this chart shows why. Having remained very low through the early 1960s, inflation rose slowly in the second half of the decade and then dramatically in the mid- and late 1970s, before beginning a long and steady decline in the early 1980s. ◆ *What caused the great spike in inflation in the 1970s?*

nation's manufacturing sector. American industry had flourished in the immediate aftermath of World War II, in part because of the new plant capacity the war had created, in part because the country faced almost no competition from other industrial nations. American workers in unionized industries had profited from this postwar success by winning some of the most generous wage and benefits packages in the world.

By the 1970s, however, the climate for American manufacturing had changed significantly. Many of the great industrial plants were now many decades old, much less efficient than the newer plants that Japan and European industrial nations had constructed after the war. In some industries (notably steel and automobiles), management had become complacent and stultifyingly bureaucratic. Most important, U.S. manufacturing now faced major competition from abroad—not only in world trade (which still constituted only a small part of the American economy) but also at home. Automobiles, steel, and many other manufactured goods from Japan and Europe established major footholds in the United States markets. Some of America's new competitors benefited from lower labor costs than their U.S. counterparts; but that was only one of many reasons for their success.

Thus the 1970s marked the beginning of a long, painful process of deindustrialization, during which thousands of

Deindustrialization

factories across the country closed their gates and millions of workers lost their jobs. New employment opportunities were becoming available in other, growing areas of the economy: technology, information systems, and many other more "knowledge-based" industries that would ultimately drive an extraordinary (if unbalanced) economic revival in the 1980s and 1990s. But many industrial workers were poorly equipped to move into those jobs. The result was a growing pool of unemployed and underemployed workers; the virtual disappearance of industrial jobs from many inner cities, where large numbers of minorities lived; and the impoverishment of communities dependent on particular industries. Some of the nation's manufacturing sectors ultimately revived, but few regained the size and dominance they had enjoyed in the 1950s and 1960s; and few employed a work force as large or as relatively well paid as they once had.

The Nixon Response

The Nixon administration responded to these mounting economic problems by focusing on the one thing it thought it could control: inflation. Nixon came to focus on control of the currency. Placing conservative economists at the head of the Federal Reserve Board, he ensured sharply higher interest rates and a contraction of the money supply. But the tight money policy did little to

"Stagflation"

curb inflation: the cost of living rose a cumulative 15 percent dur-

ing Nixon's first two and a half years in office. Economic growth, in the meantime, declined. The United States was encountering a new and puzzling dilemma: "stagflation," a combination of rising prices and general economic stagnation.

In the summer of 1971, Nixon imposed a ninety-day freeze on all wages and prices at their existing levels. Then, in November, he launched what he called Phase II of his economic plan: mandatory guidelines for wage and price increases, to be administered by a federal agency. Inflation subsided temporarily, but the recession continued. Fearful that the recession would be more damaging than inflation in an election year, the administration reversed itself late in 1971: interest rates were allowed to drop sharply, and government spending was increased—producing the largest budget deficit since World War II. The new tactics helped revive the economy in the short term, but inflation rose substantially—particularly after the administration abandoned the strict Phase II controls.

In 1973, prices rose 9 percent; in 1974, after the Arab oil embargo and the OPEC price increases, they rose 12 percent—the highest rate since the relaxation of price controls shortly after World War II. The value of the dollar continued to slide, and the nation's international trade continued to decline.

The erratic economic programs of the Nixon administration were a sign of a broader national confusion about the prospects for American prosperity. The Nixon pattern—of moving from a tight money policy to curb inflation at one moment, to a spending policy to cure recession at the next—repeated itself during the two administrations that followed him.

THE WATERGATE CRISIS

Although economic problems greatly concerned the American people in the 1970s, another stunning development almost entirely preoccupied the nation beginning early in 1973: the fall of Richard Nixon.

The Scandals

Nixon's crisis was in part a culmination of long-term changes in the presidency. Public expectations of the president had increased dramatically in the years since World War II; yet the constraints placed

The Changing Presidency

on the authority of the office had grown as well. In response, a succession of presidents had sought new methods for the exercise of power, often stretching the law, occasionally breaking it. Nixon greatly accelerated these trends. Facing a Democratic Congress hostile to his goals, he attempted to find ways to circumvent the legislature whenever possible. Saddled with a federal bureaucracy

WATERGATE

More than three decades after Watergate—one of the most famous political scandals in American history—historians and others continue to argue about its causes and significance. Their interpretations fall into several broad categories.

One argument emphasizes the evolution of the institution of the presidency over time and sees Watergate as the result of a much larger pattern of presidential usurpations of power that stretched back at least several decades. Arthur Schlesinger Jr. helped develop this argument in his 1973 book *The Imperial Presidency,* which argues that ever since World War II, Americans have believed that the nation was in a state of permanent crisis, threatened from abroad by the menace of communism, threatened from within by the danger of insufficient will. The

(Bettmann/Corbis)

belief of a succession of presidents in the urgency of this crisis, and in their duty to take whatever measures might

be necessary to combat it, led them gradually to usurp more and more power from Congress, from the courts, and from the public. Initially, this expansion of presidential power came in the realm of international affairs: covert and at times illegal activities overseas.

But in the postwar world, domestic politics began to seem inseparable from international politics. Gradually, presidents began to look for ways to circumvent constraints in domestic matters as well. Nixon's actions in the Watergate crisis were, in other words, a culmination of this long and steady expansion of covert presidential power. Jonathan Schell, in *The Time of Illusion* (1975), offers a variation of this argument, tying the crisis of the presidency to the pressure that nuclear weapons place on presidents to

unresponsive to his wishes, he constructed a hierarchy in which virtually all executive power became concentrated in the White House. Operating within a rigid, even autocratic staff structure, the president became a solitary, at times brooding figure. Unknown to all but a few intimates, he also became mired in a pattern of illegalities and abuses of power that in late 1972 began to break through to the surface.

Early on the morning of June 17, 1972, police arrested five men who had broken into the offices of the Democratic National Committee in the Watergate office building in Washington, D.C. Two others were seized a short time later and charged with supervising the break-in. When reporters for the *Washington Post* began researching the backgrounds of the culprits, they discovered that among those involved in the burglary were former employees of the Committee for the Re-election of the President. One of them had worked in the White House itself. Moreover, they had been paid to execute the break-in from a secret fund of the reelection committee, a fund controlled by members of the White House staff.

The Watergate Break-In

Public interest in the disclosures grew slowly in the last months of 1972. Early in 1973, however, the Watergate burglars went on trial; and under relentless prodding from federal judge John J. Sirica, one of the defendants, James W. McCord, agreed to cooperate both with the grand jury and with a special Senate investigating committee. McCord's testimony opened a floodgate of confessions,

and for months a parade of White House and campaign officials exposed one illegality after another. Foremost among them was a member of the inner circle of the White House, counsel to the president John Dean, who leveled allegations against Nixon himself.

Two different sets of scandals emerged from the investigations. One was a general pattern of abuses of power involving both the White House and the Nixon campaign committee, which included, but was not limited to, the Watergate break-in. The other scandal, and the one that became the major focus of public attention for nearly two years, was the way in which the administration tried to manage the investigations of the Watergate break-in and other abuses—a pattern of behavior that became known as the "cover-up." There was never any conclusive evidence that the president had planned or approved the Watergate burglary in advance.

But there was mounting evidence that he had been involved in illegal efforts to obstruct investigations and withhold information. Testimony before the Senate provided evidence of the complicity of Dean, Attorney General John Mitchell, top White House assistants H. R. Haldeman and John Ehrlichman, and others. As interest in the case grew to something approaching a national obsession, the investigation focused increasingly on a single question: in the words of Senator Howard Baker of Tennessee, a member of the Ervin committee, "What did the President know and when did he know it?"

"Cover-Up"

protect the nation's—and their own— "credibility." Other commentators (but few serious historical studies) go even further and argue that what happened to produce the Watergate scandals was not substantively different from the normal patterns of presidential behavior, that Nixon simply got caught where others had not, and that a long-standing liberal hostility toward Nixon ensured that he would pay a higher price for his behavior than other presidents would.

A second explanation of Watergate emphasizes the difficult social and political environment of the late 1960s and early 1970s. Nixon entered office, according to this view, facing an unprecedentedly radical opposition that would stop at nothing to discredit the war and destroy his authority. He found himself, therefore, drawn into taking similarly desperate measures of his own to defend himself from these extraordinary challenges. Nixon made this argument in his own 1975 memoirs:

> It was this epidemic of unprecedented domestic terrorism that prompted our efforts to discover the best means by which to deal with this new phenomenon of highly organized and highly skilled revolutionaries dedicated to the violent destruction of our democratic system.*

The historian Herbert Parmet echoes parts of this argument in *Richard Nixon and His America* (1990). Stephen Ambrose offers a more muted version of the same view in *Richard Nixon* (1989).

Most of those who have written about Watergate, however, search for the explanation not in institutional or social forces, but in the personalities of the people involved and, most notably, in the personality of Richard Nixon. Even many of those who have developed structural explanations (Schlesinger, Schell, and Ambrose, for example) return eventually to Nixon himself as the most important explanation for Watergate. Others begin there, perhaps most notably Stanley I. Kutler, in *The Wars of Watergate* (1990) and, later, *Abuse of Power* (1997), in which he presents extensive excerpts from conversations about Watergate taped in the Nixon White House. Kutler emphasizes Nixon's lifelong resort to vicious political tactics and his long-standing belief that he was a special target of unscrupulous enemies and had to "get" them before they got him. Watergate was rooted, Kutler argues, "in the personality and history of Nixon himself." A "corrosive hatred," he claims, "decisively shaped Nixon's own behavior, his career, and eventually his historical standing."

Nixon accepted the departure of those members of his administration implicated in the scandals. But he continued to insist that he himself was innocent. There the matter might have rested, had it not been for the disclosure during the Senate hearings of a White House taping system that had recorded virtually every conversation in the president's office during the period in question. All the groups investigating the scandals sought access to the tapes; Nixon, pleading "executive privilege," refused to release them. A special prosecutor appointed by the president to handle the Watergate cases, Harvard law professor Archibald Cox, took Nixon to court in October 1973 in an effort to force him to relinquish the recordings. Nixon fired Cox and suffered the humiliation of watching both Attorney General Elliot Richardson and his deputy resign

"Saturday Night Massacre"

in protest. This "Saturday night massacre" made the president's predicament infinitely worse. Not only did public pressure force him to appoint a new special prosecutor, Texas attorney Leon Jaworski, who proved just as determined as Cox to subpoena the tapes; but the episode precipitated an investigation by the House of Representatives into the possibility of impeachment.

The Fall of Richard Nixon

Nixon's situation deteriorated further in the following months. Late in 1973, Vice President Spiro Agnew became embroiled in a scandal of his own when evidence surfaced that he had accepted bribes and kickbacks while serving as governor of Maryland and even as vice president. In return for a Justice Department agreement not to press the case, Agnew pleaded no contest to a lesser charge of income-tax evasion and resigned from the government. With the controversial Agnew no longer in line to succeed to the presidency, the prospect of removing Nixon from the White House became less worrisome to his opponents. The new vice president (the first appointed under the terms of the Twenty-fifth Amendment, which had been adopted in 1967) was House Minority Leader Gerald Ford, an amiable and popular Michigan congressman.

In April 1974, in an effort to head off further subpoenas of the tapes, the president released transcripts of a number of relevant conversations, claiming that they proved his innocence. But even these edited tapes seemed to suggest Nixon's complicity in the cover-up. In July, the crisis reached a climax. First the Supreme Court ruled unanimously, in *United States* v. *Richard M. Nixon,* that the president must relinquish the tapes to Special Prosecutor Jaworski. Days later, the House Judiciary Committee voted

U.S. v. Richard M. Nixon

to recommend three articles of impeachment, charging that Nixon had, first, obstructed justice in the Watergate cover-up; second, misused federal agencies to violate the rights of citizens; and third, defied the authority of Congress by refusing to deliver tapes and other materials subpoenaed by the committee.

NIXON'S FAREWELL   Only moments before, Nixon had been in tears saying good-bye to his staff in the East Room of the White House. But as he boarded a helicopter to begin his trip home to California shortly after resigning as president, he flashed his trademark "victory" sign to the crowd on the White House lawn. *(Bettmann/Corbis)*

Even without additional evidence, Nixon might well have been impeached by the full House and convicted by the Senate. Early in August, however, he provided at last what many wavering members of Congress had begun to call the "smoking gun." Among the tapes that the Supreme Court compelled Nixon to relinquish were several that offered apparently incontrovertible evidence of his involvement in the Watergate cover-up. Only days after the burglary, the recordings disclosed, the president had ordered the FBI to stop investigating the break-in. Impeachment and conviction now seemed inevitable.

For several days, Nixon brooded in the White House. Finally, on August 8, 1974, he announced his resignation—the first president in American history ever to do so. At noon the next day, while Nixon and his family were flying west to their home in California, Gerald Ford took the oath of office as president.

Nixon Resigns

Many Americans expressed relief and exhilaration that, as the new president put it, "Our long national nightmare is over." But the wave of good feeling could not obscure the deeper and more lasting damage of the Watergate crisis. In a society in which distrust of leaders and institutions of authority was already widespread, the fall of Richard Nixon seemed to confirm the most cynical assumptions about the character of American public life.

CONCLUSION

The victory of Richard Nixon in the 1968 presidential election represented a popular repudiation of turbulence and radicalism. It was a call for a restoration of order and stability. But order and stability were not the dominant characteristics of Nixon's troubled years in office. Nixon entered office, rather, when the forces of the left and the counterculture were approaching the peak of their influence. American culture and society in the late 1960s and early 1970s were shaped decisively by, and were deeply divided over, the challenges of young people to the norms by which most Americans had lived. Also in those years, a host of new liberation movements joined the drive for racial equality, and women mobilized effectively and powerfully to demand changes in the way their society treated gender differences.

Nixon had run for office attacking the failure of his predecessor to end the war in Vietnam. But during the first four years of his presidency, the war—and the protests against it—continued and even in some respects escalated. The division of opinion over the war was as deep as any of the many other divisions in national life. It continued to poison the nation's politics and social fabric until the American role in the conflict finally shuddered to a close in 1973.

But much of the controversy and division in the 1970s was a product of the Nixon presidency itself. Nixon was in many ways a dynamic and even visionary leader, who proposed (but rarely succeeded in enacting) some important domestic reforms and who made important changes in American foreign policy, most notably making overtures to communist China and forging détente

with the Soviet Union. He was also, however, a devious and secretive man whose White House staff became engaged in a series of covert activities—many of them connected with the president's reelection campaign in 1972—that produced the most dramatic political scandal in American history. Watergate, as it was called, preoccupied much of the nation for nearly two years beginning in 1972; and ultimately, in the summer of 1974, the scandal forced Richard Nixon—who had been reelected to office only two years before by one of the largest majorities in modern history—to become the first president in American history to resign. He was a victim in part of the passions and divisions of his time and of the Vietnam War, which he had inherited but had not been able to end quickly. He was a victim as well of his own insecurities and resentments. Whatever the causes of his fall, however, the greatest cost of Watergate was not what it did to Nixon himself, but how it damaged the faith of the American people in their leaders and their government. That faith would remain weak through the remainder of the century and beyond.

INTERACTIVE LEARNING

The *Primary Source Investigator CD-ROM* offers the following materials related to this chapter:

- Interactive maps: **U.S. Elections** (M7); **Patterns of Protest** (M30); and **Middle East** (M28).

- Documents, images, and maps related to the social changes in the late 1960s and 1970s, the presidency of Richard Nixon, and the Watergate scandal. Highlights include documents related to the Watergate crisis, the ensuing investigation, and the resignation

of President Nixon; the text of the legislation that established the Environmental Protection Agency; and images related to the women's liberation movement.

Online Learning Center (www.mhhe.com/brinkley13e)

For quizzes, Internet resources, references to additional books and films, and more, consult this book's Online Learning Center.

FOR FURTHER REFERENCE

John Morton Blum, *Years of Discord: American Politics and Society, 1961-1974* (1991) is a good overview. James Miller, *"Democracy in the Streets": From Port Huron to the Siege of Chicago* (1987) is a perceptive history of the New Left through its leading organization, SDS. Kristin Luker, *Abortion and the Politics of Motherhood* (1984) is an excellent account of this central battle over the nature of feminism. Margaret Cruikshank, *The Rise of a Gay and Lesbian Liberation Movement* (1992) and David Eisenbach, *Gay Power: An American Revolution* (2006) recount another important struggle of the 1960s and beyond. Ronald Takaki, *Strangers from a Distant Shore: A History of Asian Americans* (1989) examines the growing Asian community in postwar America. Stephen Ambrose, *Nixon: The Triumph of a Politician, 1962-1972* (1989) and *Nixon, Ruin*

and Recovery, 1973-1990 (1992) provides a thorough chronicle of this important presidency. Joan Hoff, *Nixon Reconsidered* (1994) is a sympathetic account of Nixon's presidency before Watergate. Margaret MacMillan, *Nixon and Mao: The Week That Changed the World* (2007) examines Nixon's most famous diplomatic effort. Stanley J. Kutler, *The Wars of Watergate* (1990) is a scholarly study of the great scandal, and Jonathan Schell, *The Time of Illusion* (1975) is a perceptive contemporary account. David Greenberg, *Nixon's Shadow* (2003) is a perceptive examination of Nixon's place in American culture. Marilyn Young, *The Vietnam Wars, 1945-1990* (1991) provides, among other things, a full account of the last years of American involvement in Vietnam and of the conflicts in the region that followed the American withdrawal.

CHAPTER 31

FROM THE "AGE OF LIMITS" TO THE AGE OF REAGAN

"MORNING IN AMERICA, 1984" Ronald Reagan displays his legendary charm while speaking to supporters in Pennsylvania Dutch country during his successful campaign for reelection in 1984. Reagan avoided attacks on his Democratic opponent, Walter Mondale, and spoke instead mostly about what he called the "morning in America" that he claimed his policies had helped to produce. *(Time Life Pictures/Getty Images)*

THE FRUSTRATIONS OF THE early 1970s—the defeat in Vietnam, the Watergate crisis, the problems of the American economy—inflicted serious blows on the confident nationalism and muscular liberalism that had shaped so much of the postwar era. Many Americans began to wonder whether the future might be considerably bleaker than the past, whether the age of a growing economy and growing expectations might be over. Some vocal critics were writing of the dawn of an "age of limits," in which America would have to learn to survive with less of everything—money, energy, possibilities, global power—and thus would have to accept constricted expectations. The presidency of Jimmy Carter, which coincided with some of the nation's most serious economic difficulties, appeared at times to reflect these assumptions and eventually contributed to Carter's political demise.

At the end of the decade, however, the idea of an "age of limits" met a powerful and ultimately decisive challenge. That challenge combined a conservative rejection of some of the heady visions of the 1960s with a reinforced commitment to economic growth, international power, and American virtue. The effort to combat the "defeatism" of the 1970s took many forms and could be seen in intellectual life, popular culture, and, of course, politics. Throughout the 1970s, a powerful, grassroots conservative movement grew rapidly in many parts of the United States. This movement brought together those who wanted a more conservative economic policy with those who were most concerned about such cultural questions as religion and sexuality. It developed an impressive set of institutions and a remarkable ability to raise money for political campaigns.

The most potent symbol of this growing movement was Ronald Reagan, who was elected president in 1980 and who, for the next eight years, became a symbol of a new kind of confident conservatism that would soon have enormous influence in the United States and in many other parts of the world. Reagan helped re-legitimize a belief that trusting the power of the "free market" was a far more reliable recipe for economic success than trusting government economic policies. He also gathered support for a new American commitment to the Cold War and for a more active American role in the world. His presidency was less notable for broad legislative accomplishments than for the power of the ideas it expressed. Reagan's personal popularity was an important part of his success, but so was an impressive economic revival that helped win support for his ideas.

POLITICS AND DIPLOMACY AFTER WATERGATE

In the aftermath of Richard Nixon's ignominious departure from office, many Americans wondered whether faith in the presidency, and in the government as a whole, could easily be restored. The administrations of the two presidents who succeeded Nixon did little to answer those questions.

The Ford Custodianship

Gerald Ford inherited the presidency under unenviable circumstances. He had to try to rebuild confidence in government after the Watergate scandals and to restore economic prosperity in the midst of difficult domestic and international conditions. He enjoyed some success in the first of these efforts but very little in the second.

The new president's effort to establish himself as a symbol of political integrity suffered a setback only a

Nixon Pardoned

month after he took office, when he granted Richard Nixon "a full, free, and absolute pardon" for any crimes he may have committed during his presidency. Ford explained that he was attempting to spare the nation the ordeal of years of litigation and to spare Nixon himself any further suffering. But much of the public suspected a secret deal with the former president. The pardon caused a decline in Ford's popularity from which he never fully recovered. Nevertheless, most Americans considered him a decent man; his honesty and amiability did much to reduce the bitterness and acrimony of the Watergate years.

The Ford administration enjoyed less success in its effort to solve the problems of the American economy. In his efforts to curb inflation, the president rejected the idea of wage and price controls and called instead for largely ineffective voluntary efforts. After supporting high interest rates, opposing increased federal spending (through liberal use of his veto power), and resisting pressures for a tax reduction, Ford had to deal with a serious recession in 1974 and 1975. The continuing energy crisis made his task more difficult. In the aftermath of the Arab oil embargo of 1973, the OPEC cartel began to raise the price of oil—by 400 percent in 1974 alone, one of the principal reasons why inflation reached 11 percent in 1976.

Ford retained Henry Kissinger as secretary of state and

Ford's Diplomatic Successes

continued the general policies of the Nixon years. Late in 1974, Ford met with Soviet premier Leonid Brezhnev at Vladivostok in Siberia and signed an arms control accord that was to serve as the basis for SALT II, thus achieving a goal the Nixon administration had long sought. Meanwhile, in the Middle East, Henry Kissinger helped produce a new accord, by which Israel agreed to return large portions of the occupied Sinai to

Egypt, and the two nations pledged not to resolve future differences by force.

Nevertheless, as the 1976 presidential election approached, Ford's policies were coming under attack from both the right and the left. In the Republican primary campaign, Ford faced a powerful challenge from former California governor Ronald Reagan, leader of the party's conservative wing, who spoke for many on the right who were unhappy with any conciliation of communists. The president only barely survived the assault to win his party's nomination. The Democrats, in the meantime, were gradually uniting behind a new and, before 1976, little known candidate: Jimmy Carter, a former governor of Georgia who organized a brilliant primary campaign and appealed to the general unhappiness with Washington by offering honesty, piety, and an outsider's skepticism of the federal government. And while Carter's mammoth lead in opinion polls dwindled by election day, unhappiness with the economy and a general disenchantment with Ford enabled the Democrat to hold on for a narrow victory. Carter emerged with 50 percent of the popular vote to Ford's 47.9 percent and 297 electoral votes to Ford's 240.

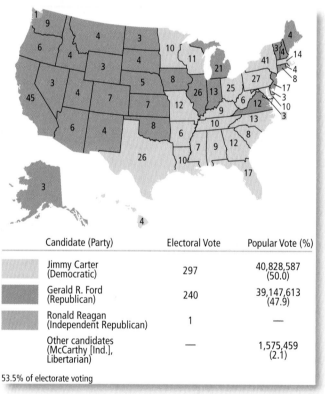

Candidate (Party)	Electoral Vote	Popular Vote (%)
Jimmy Carter (Democratic)	297	40,828,587 (50.0)
Gerald R. Ford (Republican)	240	39,147,613 (47.9)
Ronald Reagan (Independent Republican)	1	—
Other candidates (McCarthy [Ind.], Libertarian)	—	1,575,459 (2.1)

53.5% of electorate voting

THE ELECTION OF 1976 Jimmy Carter, a former governor of Georgia, swept the South in the 1976 election and carried enough of the industrial states of the Northeast and Midwest to win a narrow victory over President Gerald R. Ford. His showing indicated the importance to the Democratic Party of having a candidate capable of attracting support in the South, which was becoming increasingly Republican by the 1970s. ◆ *What drove so many southerners into the Republican Party?*

The Trials of Jimmy Carter

Like Ford, Jimmy Carter assumed the presidency at a moment when the nation faced problems of staggering complexity and difficulty. Perhaps no leader could have thrived in such inhospitable circumstances. But Carter seemed at times to make his predicament worse by a style of leadership that many considered self-righteous and inflexible. He left office in 1981 one of the least popular presidents of the century.

Carter had campaigned for the presidency as an "outsider," representing Americans suspicious of entrenched bureaucracies and complacent public officials. He carried much of that suspiciousness with him to Washington. He surrounded himself in the White House with a group of close-knit associates from Georgia; and in the beginning, at least, he seemed deliberately to spurn assistance from more experienced political figures. Carter was exceptionally intelligent, but his critics charged that he provided no overall vision or direction to his government. His ambitious legislative agenda included major reforms of the tax and welfare systems; Congress passed virtually none of it.

Carter's Lack of Direction

Carter devoted much of his time to the problems of energy and the economy. Entering office in the midst of a recession, he moved first to reduce unemployment by raising public spending and cutting federal taxes. Unemployment declined, but inflation soared—less because of the fiscal policies he implemented than because of the continuing, sharp increases in energy prices imposed on the West by OPEC. During Carter's last two years in office, prices rose at well over a 10 percent annual rate. Like Nixon and Ford before him, Carter responded with a combination of tight money and calls for voluntary restraint. He appointed first G. William Miller and then Paul Volcker, both conservative economists, to head the Federal Reserve Board, thus ensuring a policy of high interest rates and reduced currency supplies. By 1980, interest rates had risen to the highest levels in American history; at times, they exceeded 20 percent.

High Interest Rates

The problem of energy also grew steadily more troublesome in the Carter years. In the summer of 1979, instability in the Middle East produced a second major fuel shortage in the United States. In the midst of the crisis, OPEC announced another major price increase, clouding the economic picture further. Faced with increasing pressure to act (and with a dismal approval rating of 26 percent), Carter retreated to Camp David, the presidential retreat in the Maryland mountains. Ten days later, he emerged to deliver a remarkable television address. It included a series of proposals for resolving the energy crisis. But it was most notable for Carter's bleak assessment of the national condition. Speaking with unusual fervor, he complained of a "crisis of confidence" that had struck "at the very heart and soul of our national will." The address became known as the "malaise" speech (although

CARTER IN THE WHITE HOUSE Jimmy Carter made a strenuous effort to bring a sense of informality to the presidency, in contrast to the "imperial" style many had complained about during the Nixon years. He began on his inauguration day, when he and his family walked down Pennsylvania Avenue from the Capitol to the White House instead of riding in the traditional limousines. Here, Carter sits in a room in the White House preparing for a television address. He is sitting in front of a fire wearing a cardigan sweater, with his notes in his lap rather than on a desk. *(Bettmann/Corbis)*

Carter himself had never used that word), and it helped fuel charges that the president was trying to blame his own problems on the American people. Carter's sudden firing of several members of his cabinet a few days later deepened his political problems.

Human Rights and National Interests

Among Jimmy Carter's most frequent campaign promises was a pledge to build a new basis for American foreign policy, one in which the defense of "human rights" would replace the pursuit of "selfish interests." Carter spoke out sharply and often about violations of human rights in many countries (including, most prominently, the Soviet Union). Beyond that general commitment, the Carter administration focused on several more traditional concerns.

Carter completed negotiations begun several years earlier on a pair of treaties to turn over control of the Panama Canal to the government of Panama. Domestic opposition to the treaties was intense. After an acrimonious debate, the Senate ratified the treaties by 68 to 32, only one vote more than the necessary two-thirds majority.

Carter's greatest achievement was his success in arranging a peace treaty between Egypt and Israel. Middle East negotiations between Egyptian president Anwar Sadat and Israeli prime minister Menachem Begin had begun in 1977. When those talks stalled, Carter invited Sadat and Begin to a summit conference at Camp David in September 1978, and persuaded them to remain there for two weeks while he and others helped mediate the disputes between them. On September 17, Carter Camp David Accords | announced agreement on a "framework" for an Egyptian-Israeli peace treaty. On March 26, 1979, Begin and Sadat returned together to the White House to sign a formal peace treaty—known as the Camp David accords—between their two nations.

In the meantime, Carter tried to improve relations with China and the Soviet Union and to complete a new arms agreement. He responded eagerly to the overtures of Deng Xiaoping, the new Chinese leader who was attempting to open his nation to the outside world. On December 15, 1978, Washington and Beijing announced the resumption of formal diplomatic relations. A few months later, Carter traveled to Vienna to meet with the aging and visibly ailing Brezhnev to finish drafting the new SALT II arms control agreement. The treaty set limits on the number of long-range missiles, bombers, and nuclear warheads for both the United States and the USSR. Almost immediately, however, SALT II met with fierce conservative opposition in the United States.

The Year of the Hostages

Ever since the early 1950s, the United States had provided political support and, more recently, massive military assistance to the government of the Shah of Iran, hoping to make his nation a bulwark against Soviet expansion in the Middle East. By 1979, however, the Shah was in deep trouble with his own people. Many Iranians resented the repressive, authoritarian tactics through | Iranian Revolution | which the Shah had maintained his autocratic rule. At the same time, Islamic clergy (and much of the fiercely religious populace) opposed his efforts to modernize and Westernize a fundamentalist society. The combination of resentments produced a powerful revolutionary movement. In January 1979, the Shah fled the country.

The United States made cautious efforts in the first months after the Shah's abdication to establish cordial relations with the succession of increasingly militant regimes that followed. By late 1979, however, revolutionary chaos in Iran was making any normal relations impossible. What power there was resided with a zealous religious leader, the Ayatollah Ruhollah Khomeini, whose hatred of the West in general and the United States in particular was intense. In late October 1979, the deposed Shah arrived in New York to be treated for cancer. Days later, on November 4, an armed mob invaded the American embassy in Teheran, seized the diplomats and military personnel inside, and demanded the return of the Shah to Iran in exchange for their freedom. Fifty-three

SIGNING THE CAMP DAVID ACCORDS
Jimmy Carter experienced many frustrations during his presidency, but his successful efforts in 1978 to negotiate a peace treaty between Israel and Egypt was undoubtedly his finest hour. Egyptian president Anwar Sadat and Israeli prime minister Menachem Begin join Carter here in the East Room of the White House in March 1979 to sign the accords they had begun to hammer out during two weeks at the president's retreat at Camp David several months before. *(D. B. Owen/Black Star)*

WAITING FOR KHOMEINI Iranian women, dressed in traditional Islamic garb, stand in a crowd in Teheran waiting for a glimpse of the Ayatollah Khomeini, the spiritual and eventually also political leader of the Iranian Revolution, which created so many difficulties for the United States. *(David Burnett/Contact Press Images)*

Americans remained hostages in the embassy for over a year.

Only weeks after the hostage seizure, on December 27, 1979, Soviet troops invaded Afghanistan, the mountainous Islamic nation lying between the USSR and Iran. The Soviet Union had in fact been a power in Afghanistan for years, and the dominant force since April 1978, when a coup had established a Marxist government there with close ties to the Kremlin. But while some diplomats claimed that the Soviet invasion was a Russian attempt to secure the status quo, Carter called it the "gravest threat to world peace since World War II" and angrily imposed a series of economic sanctions on the Russians, canceled American participation in the 1980 summer Olympic Games in Moscow, and announced the withdrawal of SALT II from Senate consideration.

The combination of domestic economic troubles and international crises created widespread anxiety, frustra-

Carter's Falling Popularity

tion, and anger in the United States—damaging President Carter's already low standing with the public and giving added strength to an alternative political force that had already made great strides.

THE RISE OF THE NEW AMERICAN RIGHT

Much of the anxiety that pervaded American life in the 1970s was a result of jarring public events that left many men and women shaken and uncertain about their leaders and their government. But much of it was a result, too, of significant changes in the character of America's economy, society, and culture. Together these changes provided the right with its most important opportunity in generations to seize a position of authority in American life.

The Sunbelt and Its Politics

The most widely discussed demographic phenomenon of the 1970s was the rise of what became known as the "Sunbelt"—a term coined by the political analyst Kevin Phillips. The Sunbelt included the Southeast (particularly Florida), the Southwest (particularly Texas), and above all, California, which became the nation's most populous state, sur-

Rise of the "Sunbelt"

passing New York, in 1964, and continued to grow dramatically in the years that followed. By 1980, the

THE MALL

In the late nineteenth century, it was the department store that tried to create a magical world, attracting patrons by arousing consumer fantasies. By the late twentieth century, it was the mall that was fusing consumption, entertainment, and desire. In cities and towns in every part of America, malls became not just places for shopping, but often centers of a much-altered community life as well.

MAIN STREET   This photograph of the Main Street of Henderson, Kentucky, in the 1940s was a popular image for advertisers and others trying to evoke the character of urban shopping in small cities—a kind of shopping soon to be displaced by shopping centers and malls outside the center of town. *(Ewing Galloway, N.Y.)*

The modern mall is the direct descendant of an earlier retail innovation, the automobile-oriented shopping center, which strove to combine a number of different shops in a single structure, with parking for customers. The first modern shopping center, the Country Club Plaza, opened in Kansas City in 1924. By the mid-1950s, shopping centers—ranging from small "strips" to large integrated complexes—had proliferated throughout the country and were challenging traditional downtown shopping districts, which suffered from lack of parking and from the movement of middle-class residents to the suburbs.

In 1956, the first enclosed, climate-controlled shopping mall—the Southdale Shopping Center—opened in Minneapolis, followed quickly by similar ventures in New York, New Jersey, Illinois, North Carolina, and Tennessee. As the malls spread, they grew larger and more elaborate. They also began self-consciously to emulate some aspects of the older downtowns that they were rapidly displacing. At the same time, they tried to insulate customers from the dangers and aggravations of traditional urban shopping.

SHOPPING CENTER, NORTHERN VIRGINIA
This small shopping center near Washington, D.C., was characteristic of the new "strip malls" that were emerging in the 1950s to serve suburban customers who traveled almost entirely by automobile. *(Charles Fenno Jacobs/Time Life Pictures/Getty Images)*

By the 1970s, vast "regional malls" were emerging—Tyson's Corner in Fairfax, Virginia; Roosevelt Field on Long Island; the Galleria in Houston, and many others—that drew customers from great distances and dazzled them not only with acres of varied retail space, but also with restaurants, movie theaters, skating rinks, bowling alleys, hotels, video arcades, and large public spaces with fountains, benches, trees, gardens, and concert spaces. "The more needs you fulfill,

---

population of the Sunbelt had risen to exceed that of the older industrial regions of the North and the East.

In addition to shifting the nation's economic focus from one region to another, the rise of the Sunbelt helped produce a change in the political climate. The strong populist traditions in the South and the West were capable of producing progressive and even radical politics; but more often in the late twentieth century, they produced a strong opposition to the growth of government and a resentment of the proliferating regulations and restrictions that the liberal state was producing. Many of those regulations and restrictions—environmental laws, land-use restrictions, even the 55-mile-per-hour speed limit created during the energy crisis to force motorists to conserve fuel—affected the West more than any other region. Both the South and the West, moreover, embraced myths about their own pasts that reinforced hostility to liberal government.

White southerners equated the federal government's effort to change racial norms in the region with what they believed was the tyranny of Reconstruction. Westerners embraced an image of their region as a refuge of "rugged individualism" and resisted what they considered efforts by the government to impose new standards of behavior on them. Thus, the same impulses and rhetoric that populists had once used to denounce banks and corporations, the new conservative populists of the postwar era now used to attack the government—and the liberals, radicals, and minorities whom they believed were driving its growth.

The so-called Sagebrush Rebellion, which emerged in parts of the West in the late 1970s, mobilized conservative opposition to environmental laws and restrictions on development. It also sought to portray the West (which had probably benefited more than any other region from federal investment) as a victim of government control. Its members complained about the very large amounts of land the federal government owned in many western states and demanded that the land be opened for development.

Suburbanization also fueled the rise of the right. Not all suburbs bred conservative politics, of course; but the

Sagebrush Rebellion

the longer people stay," one developer observed.

Malls had become self-contained imitations of cities—but in a setting from which many of the troubling and abrasive features of downtowns had been eliminated. Malls were insulated from the elements. They were policed by private security forces, who (unlike real police) could and usually did keep "undesirable" customers off the premises. They were purged of bars, pornography shops, and unsavory businesses. They were off limits to beggars, vagrants, the homeless, and anyone else the managers considered unattractive to their customers. Malls set out to "perfect" urban space, recasting the city as a protected, controlled, and socially homogeneous site attractive to, and in many cases dominated by, white middle-class people.

Some malls also sought to become community centers in sprawling suburban areas that had few real community spaces of their own. A few malls built explicitly civic spaces—meeting halls and conference centers, where community groups could gather. Some published their own newspapers. Many staged concerts, plays, and dances. But civic activities had a difficult time competing with the principal attraction of the malls: consumption.

THE NORTHLAND MALL Constructed in 1960, and designed by architect Victor Gruen, who was one of the pioneers in designing indoor shopping malls, this vast shopping center in Northland, near Detroit, immediately attracted enormous crowds. *(Courtesy of Victor Gruen Collection, American Heritage Center, University of Wyoming)*

Malls were designed with women, the principal consumers in most families, mainly in mind. "I wouldn't know how to design a center for a man," one architect said of the complexes he built. They catered to the concerns of mothers about their own and their children's safety, and they offered products of particular interest to them. (Male-oriented stores—men's clothing, sporting goods, hardware stores—were much less visible in most malls than shops marketing women's and

children's clothing, jewelry, lingerie, and household goods.)

Malls also became important to teenagers, who flocked to them in the way that earlier generations had flocked to street corners and squares in traditional downtowns. The malls were places for teenagers to meet friends, go to movies, avoid parents, hang out. They were places to buy records, clothes, or personal items. And they were places to work. Low-paying retail jobs, plentiful in malls, were typical first working experiences for many teens.

The proliferation of malls has dismayed many people, who see in them a threat to the sense of community in America. By insulating people from the diversity and conflict of urban life, critics argue, malls divide groups from one another and erode the bonds that make it possible for those groups to understand one another. But malls, like the suburbs they usually serve, also create a kind of community. They are homogeneous and protected, to be sure, but they are also social gathering places in many areas where the alternative is not the rich, diverse life of the downtown but the even more isolated experience of shopping in isolated strips—or through catalogs, telephone, and the Internet.

Suburban Conservatism

most militantly conservative communities in America—among them Orange County in southern California—were mostly suburbs. Suburbs tended to attract people who wished to flee the problems and the jarring diversity of cities, who preferred stable, homogeneous surroundings. Many suburbs insulated their residents from contact with diverse groups—through the relative homogeneity of the population, through the transferring of retail and even work space into suburban office parks and shopping malls.

Religious Politics

In the 1960s, many social critics had predicted the extinction of religious influence in American life. *Time* magazine had reported such assumptions in 1966 with a celebrated cover emblazoned with the question "Is God Dead?" But religion in America was far from dead. Indeed, in the 1970s the United States experienced the beginning of a major religious revival, perhaps the most powerful since

the Second Great Awakening of the early nineteenth century. It continued in various forms into the early twenty-first century.

Some of the new religious enthusiasm found expression in the rise of various cults and pseudo-faiths: the Church of Scientology; the Unification Church of the Reverend Sun Myung Moon; even the tragic People's Temple, whose members committed mass suicide in their jungle retreat in Guyana in 1978. But the most important impulse of the religious revival was the growth of evangelical Christianity.

Evangelical Christianity

Evangelicalism is the basis of many forms of Christian faith, but evangelicals have in common a belief in personal conversion (being "born again") through direct communication with God. Evangelical religion had been the dominant form of Christianity in America through much of its history, and a substantial subculture since the late nineteenth century. In its modern form, it became increasingly visible during the early 1950s, when evangelicals such as Billy Graham and Pentecostals such as Oral

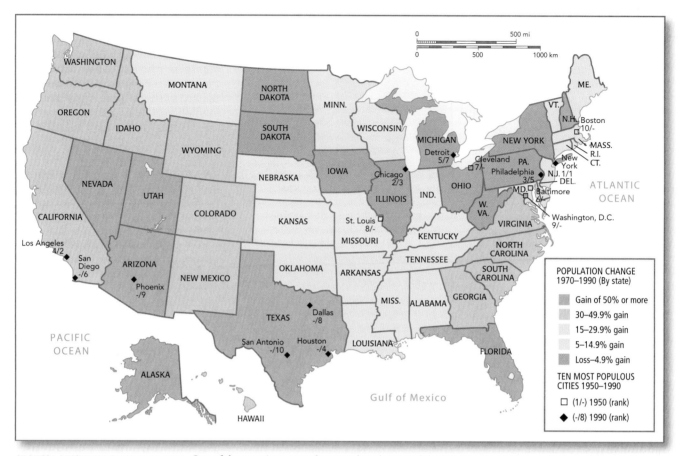

GROWTH OF THE SUNBELT, 1970–1990 One of the most important demographic changes of the last decades of the twentieth century was the shift of population out of traditional population centers in the Northeast and Midwest and toward the states of the so-called Sunbelt—most notably the Southwest and the Pacific Coast. This map gives a dramatic illustration of the changing concentration of population between 1970 and 1990. The orange/brown states are those that lost population, while the purple and blue states are those that made very significant gains (30 percent or more).   ◆ *What was the impact of this population shift on the politics of the 1980s?*

Roberts began to attract huge national (and international) followings for their energetic revivalism.

Earlier in the century, many (although never all) evangelicals had been poor rural people, isolated from the mainstream of American culture. But the great capitalist expansion after World War II had lifted many of these people out of poverty and into the middle class, where they were more visible and more assertive. More than 70 million Americans now described themselves as "born-again" Christians—men and women who had established a "direct personal relationship with Jesus." Christian evangelicals owned their own newspapers, magazines, radio stations, and television networks. They operated their own schools and universities.

For some evangelicals, Christianity had formed the basis for a commitment to racial and economic justice and to world peace. For many other evangelicals, however, the message of the new religion was very different— but no less political. In the 1970s, some Christian evangelicals became active on the political and cultural right. They were alarmed by what they considered the spread of immorality and disorder in American life. Many

evangelical men and women feared the growth of feminism and the threat they believed it posed to the traditional family, and they resented the way in which government policies advanced the goals of the women's movement. Particularly alarming to them were Supreme Court decisions eliminating religious observance from schools and, later, the decision guaranteeing women the right to an abortion.

By the late 1970s, the "Christian right" had become a visible and increasingly powerful political force. Jerry Falwell, a fundamentalist minister in Virginia with a substantial television audience, launched a movement he called the Moral Majority, which attacked the rise of "secular humanism"—a term many conservative evangelicals used to describe the rejection of religion in American culture. The Pentecostal minister Pat Robertson began a political movement of his own and, in the 1990s, launched an organization known as the Christian Coalition.

The Moral Majority and the Christian Coalition

Despite the historic antagonism between many evangelical Protestants and the Catholic Church, the growing politicization of religion in the 1970s and beyond brought some former rivals together. Catholics were the first major opponents of the Supreme Court's decision legalizing abortion in *Roe* v. *Wade,* but evangelical Protestants soon joined them in the battle against abortion. The rapidly growing Mormon Church, long isolated from both Catholics and traditional Protestants, also became increasingly engaged with the political struggles of other faiths. Mormons were instrumental in the 1982 defeat of the Equal Rights Amendment to the Constitution, which would have guaranteed women the same rights as men. And they too supported the evangelical agenda of opposition to abortion and homosexuality.

The New Right

Conservative Christians were an important part, but only a part, of what became known as the New Right—a diverse but powerful movement that enjoyed rapid growth in the 1970s and early 1980s. Its origins lay in part in the 1964 presidential election. After Republican senator Barry Goldwater's shattering defeat, Richard Viguerie, a remarkable conservative activist and organizer, took a list of 12,000 contributors to the Goldwater campaign and used it to begin a formidable conservative communications and fund-raising organization. Beginning in the 1970s, largely because of these and other organizational advances, conservatives usually found themselves better funded and organized than their opponents. Gradually these direct-mail operations helped create a much larger conservative infrastructure. By the late 1970s, there were right-wing think tanks, consulting firms, lobbyists, foundations, and schools.

Another factor in the revival of the right was the emergence of a credible right-wing leadership to replace the defeated conservative hero, Barry Goldwater. Chief among this new

Ronald Reagan

generation of conservative leaders was Ronald Reagan, a well-known film actor turned political activist. As a young man, he had been a liberal and a fervent admirer of Franklin Roosevelt. But he moved decisively to the right after his second marriage, to Nancy Davis, a woman of strong conservative convictions, and after he became embroiled, as president of the Screen Actors Guild, in battles with communists in the union. In the early 1950s, Reagan became a corporate spokesman for General Electric and won a wide following on the right with his smooth, eloquent speeches in defense of individual freedom and private enterprise.

In 1964, Reagan delivered a memorable television speech on behalf of Goldwater. After Goldwater's defeat, he worked quickly to seize the leadership of the conservative wing of the Republican Party. In 1966, with the support of a group of wealthy conservatives, Reagan won the first of two terms as governor of California—which gave him a much more visible platform for promoting himself and his ideas.

The presidency of Gerald Ford also played an important role in the rise of the right, by destroying the fragile equilibrium that had enabled the right wing and the moderate wing of the Republican Party to coexist. Ford, probably without realizing it, touched on some of the right's rawest nerves. He appointed as vice president Nelson Rockefeller, the liberal Republican governor of New York and an heir to one of America's great fortunes; many conservatives had been demonizing Rockefeller and his family for more than twenty years. Ford proposed an amnesty program for draft resisters, embraced and even extended the Nixon-Kissinger policies of détente, presided over the fall of Vietnam, and agreed to cede the Panama Canal to Panama. When Reagan challenged Ford in the 1976 Republican primaries, the president survived, barely, only by dumping Nelson Rockefeller from the ticket and agreeing to a platform largely written by one of Reagan's allies.

The Tax Revolt

Equally important to the success of the New Right was a new and potent conservative issue: the tax revolt. It had its public beginnings in 1978, when Howard Jarvis, a conservative activist in California, launched the first successful major citizens' tax revolt in California with Proposition 13, a

Proposition 13

referendum question on the state ballot rolling back property tax rates. Similar antitax movements soon began in other states and eventually spread to national politics.

The tax revolt helped the right solve one of its biggest problems. For more than thirty years after the New Deal, Republican conservatives had struggled to halt and even reverse the growth of the federal government. But attacking government programs directly, as right-wing politicians from Robert Taft to Barry Goldwater discovered, was not often the way to attract majority support. Every federal program had a political constituency. The biggest and most expensive programs—Social Security, Medicare, Medicaid, and others—had the broadest support.

In Proposition 13 and similar initiatives, members of the right separated the issue of taxes from the issue of what

Attacking Taxes

taxes supported. That helped them achieve some of the most controversial elements of the conservative agenda (eroding the government's ability to expand and launch new programs) without openly antagonizing the millions of voters who supported specific programs. Virtually no one liked to pay taxes, and as the economy weakened and the relative burden of paying taxes grew heavier, that resentment naturally rose. The right exploited that resentment and, in the process, greatly expanded its constituency.

The Campaign of 1980

By the time of the crises in Iran and Afghanistan, Jimmy Carter was in desperate political trouble—his standing in popularity polls lower than that of any president in history. Senator Edward Kennedy, younger brother of John and Robert Kennedy, challenged him in the primaries. And while Carter managed to withstand the confrontation with Kennedy and win his party's nomination, he entered the fall campaign badly weakened.

The Republican Party, in the meantime, rallied enthusiastically behind Ronald Reagan. He linked his campaign to the spreading tax revolt (something to which he had paid relatively little attention in the past) by promising substantial tax cuts. Equally important, he championed a restoration of American "strength" and "pride" in the world. Reagan clearly benefited from the continuing popular frustration at Carter's inability to resolve the Iranian hostage crisis. In a larger sense, he benefited as well from the accumulated frustrations of more than a decade of domestic and international disappointments.

On election day 1980, the one-year anniversary of the seizure of the hostages in Iran, Reagan swept to victory, winning 51 percent of the vote to 41 percent for Jimmy Carter, and 7 percent for John Anderson—a moderate Republican congressman from Illinois who had mounted an independent campaign. Carter carried only five states and the District of Columbia, for a total of 49 electoral votes to Reagan's 489. The Republican Party won control of the Senate for the first time since 1952; and although the Democrats retained a modest majority in the House, the lower chamber too seemed firmly in the hands of conservatives.

1980 Election

On the day of Reagan's inauguration, the American hostages in Iran were released after their 444-day ordeal. The government of Iran, desperate for funds to support its floundering war against neighboring Iraq, had ordered the hostages freed in return for a release of billions in Iranian assets that the Carter administration had frozen in American banks.

THE "REAGAN REVOLUTION"

Ronald Reagan assumed the presidency in January 1981, promising a change in government more fundamental than any since the New Deal of fifty years before. Reagan had only moderate success in redefining public policy. But he succeeded brilliantly in making his own engaging personality the central fact of American politics in the 1980s.

The Reagan Coalition

Reagan owed his election to widespread disillusionment with Carter and to the crises and disappointments that many voters, perhaps unfairly, associated with him. But he owed it as well to the emergence of a powerful coalition of conservative groups. That coalition was not a single, cohesive movement. It was an uneasy and generally temporary alliance among several very different movements.

The Reagan coalition included a relatively small but highly influential group of wealthy Americans associated with the corporate and financial world. What united this group was a firm commitment to capitalism and to unfettered economic growth; a belief that the market offers the best solutions to most problems; a deep hostility to most (although not all) government interference in markets. Central to this group's agenda in the 1980s was opposition to what it considered the "redistributive" politics of the federal government (especially its highly progressive tax structure) and hostility to the rise of what it believed were "antibusiness" government regulations. Reagan courted these free-market conservatives carefully and effectively, and in the end it was their interests his administration most effectively served.

Corporate Elites

A second element of the Reagan coalition was even smaller, but also disproportionately influential: a group of intellectuals commonly known as "neo-conservatives," who gave to the right something it had not had in many years—a firm base among "opinion leaders." Many of these people had

"Neo-conservatives"

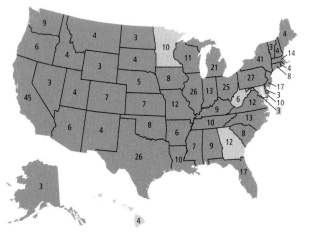

Candidate (Party)	Electoral Vote	Popular Vote (%)
Ronald Reagan (Republican)	489	43,901,812 (50.7)
Jimmy Carter (Democratic)	49	35,483,820 (41.0)
John B. Anderson (Independent)	—	5,719,722 (6.6)
Other candidates (Libertarian)	—	921,299 (1.1)

52.6% of electorate voting

THE ELECTION OF 1980 Although Ronald Reagan won only slightly more than half of the popular vote in the 1980 presidential election, his electoral majority was overwhelming—a reflection to a large degree of the deep unpopularity of President Jimmy Carter in 1980. ◆ *What had made Carter so unpopular?*

For an interactive version of this map, go to www.mhhe.com/brinkley13ech31maps

once been liberals and, before that, socialists. But during the turmoil of the 1960s, they had become alarmed by what they considered the dangerous and destructive radicalism that was destabilizing American life, weakening the liberal ardor in the battle against communism. Neo-conservatives were sympathetic to the complaints and demands of capitalists, but their principal concern was to reaffirm Western democratic, anticommunist values and commitments. Some neo-conservative intellectuals went on to become important figures in the battle against multiculturalism and "political correctness" within academia.

These two groups joined in an uneasy alliance in 1980 with the growing New Right. But several things differentiated the New Right from the corporate conservatives and the neo-conservatives. Perhaps the most important was the New Right's fundamental distrust of the "eastern establishment": a

Populist Conservatives

suspicion of its motives and goals; a sense that it exercised a dangerous, secret power in American life; a fear of the hidden influence of such establishment institutions and people as the Council on Foreign Relations, the Trilateral Commission, Henry Kissinger, and the Rockefellers.

These populist conservatives expressed the kinds of concerns that outsiders, non-elites, have traditionally voiced in American society: an opposition to centralized power and influence, a fear of living in a world where distant, hostile forces are controlling society and threatening individual freedom and community autonomy. It was a testament to Ronald Reagan's political skills and personal charm that he was able to generate enthusiastic support from these populist conservatives while appealing to elite conservative groups whose concerns were in some ways antithetical to those of the New Right.

RONALD AND NANCY REAGAN The president and the first lady greet guests at a White House social event. Nancy Reagan was most visible in her efforts to make the White House, and her husband's presidency, seem more glamorous than those of most recent administrations. But she also played an important, if quiet, policy role in the administration. *(Dirck Halstead/Time Life Pictures/Getty images)*

Reagan in the White House

Even many people who disagreed with Reagan's policies found themselves drawn to his attractive and carefully honed public image. Reagan was a master of television, a gifted public speaker, and—in public at least—rugged, fearless, and seemingly impervious to danger or misfortune. He turned seventy weeks after taking office and was the oldest man ever to serve as president. But through most of his presidency, he appeared to be vigorous, resilient, even youthful. He spent his many vacations on a California ranch, where he chopped wood and rode horses. When he was wounded in an assassination attempt in 1981, he joked with doctors on his way into surgery and appeared to bounce back from the ordeal with remarkable speed.

Reagan was not much involved in the day-to-day affairs of running the government; he surrounded himself with tough, energetic administrators who insulated him from many of the pressures of the office. At times, the president revealed a startling ignorance about the nature of his own policies or the actions of his subordinates. But Reagan did make active use of his office to generate support for his

administration's programs by fusing his proposals with a highly nationalistic rhetoric.

"Supply-Side" Economics

Reagan's 1980 campaign for the presidency had promised to restore the economy to health by a bold experiment that became known as "supply-side" economics or, to some, "Reagan-omics." Supply-side economics operated from the assumption that the woes of the American economy were in large part a result of excessive taxation, which left inadequate capital available to investors to stimulate growth. The solution, therefore, was to reduce taxes, with particularly generous benefits to corporations and wealthy individuals, in order to encourage new investments. Because a tax cut would reduce government revenues (at least at first), it would also be necessary to reduce government expenses. A cornerstone of the Reagan economic program, therefore, was a significant reduction of the federal budget.

"Reaganomics"

In its first months in office, the new administration proposed $40 billion in budget reductions and managed to win congressional approval of almost all of them. In addition, the president proposed a bold three-year, 30 percent reduction on both individual and corporate tax rates. In the summer of 1981, Congress passed it too, after lowering the reductions to 25 percent. Reagan was successful because he had a disciplined Republican majority in the Senate, and because the Democratic majority in the House was weak and riddled with defectors.

Men and women whom Reagan appointed fanned out through the executive branch of government committed to reducing the role of government in American economic life. Secretary of the Interior James Watt, previously a major figure in the Sagebrush Rebellion, opened up public lands and water to development. The Environmental Protection Agency (before its directors were indicted for corruption) relaxed or entirely eliminated enforcement of major environmental laws and regulations. The Civil Rights Division of the Justice Department eased enforcement of civil rights laws. The Department of Transportation slowed implementation of new rules limiting automobile emissions and imposing new safety standards on cars and trucks. By getting government "out of the way," Reagan officials promised, they were ensuring economic revival.

"Deregulation"

By early 1982, the nation had sunk into a severe recession. In 1982 unemployment reached 11 percent, its highest level in over forty years. But the economy recovered relatively rapidly. By late 1983, unemployment had fallen to 8.2 percent, and it declined steadily for several years after that. The gross national product had grown 3.6 percent in a year, the largest one-year increase since the mid-1970s. Inflation had fallen below 5 percent. The economy continued to grow, and both inflation and unemployment remained low through most of the decade.

The recovery was a result of many things. The years of tight money policies by the Federal Reserve Board, painful and destructive as they may have been in many ways, had helped lower inflation; perhaps equally important, the board had lowered interest rates early in 1983 in response to the recession. A worldwide "energy glut" and the collapse of the OPEC cartel had produced at least a temporary end to the inflationary pressures of spiraling fuel costs. And large federal budget deficits were pumping billions of dollars into the flagging economy. As a result, consumer spending and business investment both increased. The stock market rose from its doldrums of the 1970s and began a sustained boom. In August 1982, the Dow Jones Industrial Average stood at 777. Five years later it had passed 2,000. Despite a frightening crash in the fall of 1987, the market continued to grow.

Sources of the Recovery

The Fiscal Crisis

The economic revival did little at first to reduce federal budget deficits or to slow the growth in the national debt

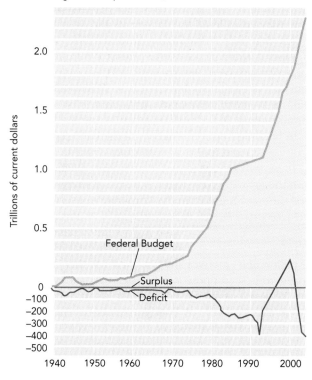

Federal Budget and Surplus/Deficit, 1940–2004

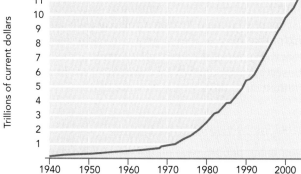

Gross National Product, 1940–2004

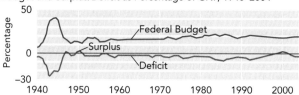

Budget and Surplus/Deficit as Percentage of GNP, 1940–2004

FEDERAL BUDGET SURPLUS/DEFICIT, 1940–2004 These charts help illustrate why the pattern of federal deficits seemed so alarming to Americans in the 1980s, and also why those deficits proved much less damaging to the economy than many economists had predicted. The upper chart shows a dramatic increase in the federal budget from the mid-1960s on. It shows as well a corresponding, and also dramatic, increase in the size of federal deficits. Gross national product also increased dramatically, especially in the 1980s and 1990s, as the middle chart shows. When the federal budgets and deficits of these years are calculated not in absolute numbers, but as a percentage of GNP, they seem much more stable and much less alarming. ◆ *What factors contributed to the increasing deficits of the 1980s? How were those deficits eliminated in the 1990s?*

(the debt the nation accumulates over time as a result of its annual deficits). By the mid-1980s, the popular sense of a growing fiscal crisis had become one of the central issues in American politics. Having entered office promis-

Soaring National Debt

ing a balanced budget within four years, Reagan presided over record budget deficits and accumulated more debt in his eight years in office than the American government had accumulated in its entire previous history.

The enormous deficits had many causes, some of them stretching back over decades of American public policy

Welfare Benefits Cut

decisions. In particular, the budget suffered from enormous increases in the costs of "entitlement" programs (especially Social Security and Medicare), a result of the aging of the population and dramatic increases in the cost of health care. But some of the causes of the deficit lay in the policies of the Reagan administration. The 1981 tax cuts, the largest in American history to that point, contributed to the deficit. The massive increase in military spending by the Reagan administration added much more to the federal budget than its cuts in domestic spending removed.

In the face of these deficits, the administration's answer to the fiscal crisis was further cuts in "discretionary" domestic spending, which included many programs aimed at the poorest (and politically weakest) Americans. There were reductions in funding for food stamps; a major cut in federal subsidies for low-income housing; strict new limitations on Medicare and Medicaid payments; reductions in student loans, school lunches, and other educational programs; and an end to many forms of federal assistance to the states and cities—which helped precipitate years of local fiscal crises as well.

By the late 1980s, many fiscal conservatives were calling for a constitutional amendment mandating a balanced budget—a provision the president himself claimed to support. (Congress came within a few votes of passing such an amendment in 1994 and again in 1996, but by then deficits had begun to decline and the momentum behind the amendment gradually faded.)

POVERTY IN AMERICA The American poverty rate declined sharply beginning in the 1950s and reached a historic low in the late 1970s. But the dramatic increase in income and wealth inequality that began in the mid-1970s gradually pushed the poverty rate upward again. By the mid-1980s, the poverty rate was approaching 15 percent, the highest in twenty years. In the image above, a group of children huddle against a barrier at an emergency center for homeless families in New York City in 1987. *(Richard Falco/Black Star/Stock Photo)*

CONTRAS IN TRAINING The Reagan administration's support for the Nicaraguan "contras," who opposed the leftist Sandinista regime, was the source of some of its greatest problems. Here, a small band of contras train in the Nicaraguan jungle. *(Piovano/SIPA Press)*

Reagan and the World

Reagan encountered a similar combination of triumphs and difficulties in international affairs. Determined to restore American pride and prestige in the world, he argued that the United States should once again become active and assertive in opposing communism and in supporting friendly governments whatever their internal policies.

Relations with the Soviet Union, which had been steadily deteriorating in the last years of the Carter administration, grew still more chilly in the first years of the Reagan presidency. The president spoke harshly of the Soviet regime (which he once called the "evil empire"), accusing it of sponsoring world terrorism and declaring that any armaments negotiations must be linked to negotiations on Soviet behavior in other areas. Relations with the Russians deteriorated further after the government of Poland (under strong pressure from Moscow) imposed martial law on the country in the winter of 1981 to crush a growing challenge from an independent labor organization, Solidarity.

Although the president had long denounced the SALT II arms control treaty as unfavorable to the United States, he continued to honor its provisions. But Reagan remained skeptical about arms control. In fact, the president proposed the most ambitious (and potentially most expensive) new military program in many years: the Strategic Defense Initiative (SDI), widely known as "Star Wars." Reagan claimed that SDI, through the use of lasers and satellites, could provide an effective shield against incoming missiles and thus make nuclear war obsolete. The Soviet Union claimed

SDI

that the new program would elevate the arms race to new and more dangerous levels (a complaint many domestic critics of SDI shared) and insisted that any arms control agreement begin with an American abandonment of SDI.

The escalation of Cold War tensions and the slowing of arms control initiatives helped produce an important popular movement in Europe and the United States calling for an end to nuclear weapons buildups. In America, the principal goal of the movement was a "nuclear freeze," an agreement between the two superpowers not to expand their atomic arsenals.

Rhetorically at least, the Reagan administration supported opponents of communism anywhere in the world, whether or not they had any direct connection to the Soviet

Reagan Doctrine

Union. This new policy became known as the Reagan Doctrine, and it meant, above all, a new American activism in the Third World. In October 1982, the administration sent American soldiers and marines into the tiny Caribbean island of Grenada to oust an anti-American Marxist regime that showed signs of forging a relationship with Moscow. In Nicaragua, a pro-American dictatorship had fallen to the revolutionary "Sandinistas" in 1979; the new government had grown increasingly anti-American (and increasingly Marxist) throughout the early 1980s. The Reagan administration supported to the so-called contras, a guerrilla movement drawn from several antigovernment groups and trying to topple the Sandinista regime.

In other parts of the world, the administration's tough rhetoric sometimes obscured an instinctive restraint. In June 1982, the Israeli army launched an invasion of Lebanon in an effort to drive guerrillas of the Palestinian Liberation

Organization from the country. An American peacekeeping force entered Beirut to supervise the evacuation of PLO forces from Lebanon. American marines then remained in the city to protect the fragile Lebanese government. Americans became the targets in 1983 of a terrorist bombing of a U.S. military barracks in Beirut that left 241 marines dead. Rather than become more deeply involved in the Lebanese struggle, Reagan withdrew American forces.

The tragedy in Lebanon was an example of the changing character of Third World struggles: an increasing reliance on terrorism by otherwise powerless groups to advance their political aims. A series of terrorist acts in the 1980s—attacks on airplanes, cruise ships, commercial and diplomatic posts; the seizing

| Terrorism |

of American and other Western hostages—alarmed and frightened much of the Western world.

The Election of 1984

Reagan approached the campaign of 1984 at the head of a united Republican Party firmly committed to his candidacy. The Democrats followed a more fractious course. Former vice president Walter Mondale, the early front-runner, fought off challenges from Senator Gary Hart of Colorado and the magnetic Jesse Jackson, who had

Candidate (Party)	Electoral Vote	Popular Vote (%)
Ronald Reagan (Republican)	525	54,455,075 (59.0)
Walter Mondale (Democratic)	13	37,577,185 (41.0)

53.3% of electorate voting

THE ELECTION OF 1984 In 1984, Ronald Reagan repeated (and slightly expanded) his electoral landslide of 1980 and added to it the popular landslide that had eluded him four years earlier. As this map shows, Mondale succeeded in carrying only his home state of Minnesota and the staunchly Democratic District of Columbia. ◆ *What were some of the factors that made Reagan so popular in 1984?*

For an interactive version of this map, go to www.mhhe.com/brinkley13ech31maps

established himself as the nation's most prominent spokesman for minorities and the poor. Mondale brought momentary excitement to the Democratic campaign by selecting a woman, Representative Geraldine Ferraro of New York, to be his running mate and the first female candidate to appear on a national ticket.

In the campaign that fall, Reagan scarcely took note of his opponents and spoke instead of what he claimed was the remarkable revival of American fortunes and spirits under his leadership. His campaign emphasized such phrases as "It's Morning in America" and "America Is Back." Reagan's victory in 1984 was decisive. He won approximately 59 percent of the vote and carried every state but Mondale's native Minnesota and the District of Columbia. But Reagan was much stronger than his party. Democrats gained a seat in the Senate and maintained only slightly reduced control of the House of Representatives.

AMERICA AND THE WANING OF THE COLD WAR

Many factors contributed to the collapse of the Soviet empire. The long, stalemated war in Afghanistan proved at least as disastrous to the Soviet Union as the Vietnam War had been to America. The government in Moscow had failed to address a long-term economic decline in the Soviet republics and the Eastern-bloc nations. Restiveness with the heavy-handed policies of communist police states was growing throughout much of the Soviet empire. But the most visible factor at the time was the emergence of Mikhail Gorbachev, who succeeded to the leadership of the Soviet Union in 1985 and, to the surprise of almost everyone, very quickly became the most revolutionary figure in world politics in several decades.

The Fall of the Soviet Union

Gorbachev quickly transformed Soviet politics with two dramatic new initiatives. The first he called *glasnost* (openness): the dismantling of many of the repressive mecha-

| Mikhail Gorbachev |

nisms that had been conspicuous features of Soviet life for over half a century. The other policy Gorbachev called *perestroika* (reform): an effort to restructure the rigid and unproductive Soviet economy by introducing, among other things, such elements of capitalism as private ownership and the profit motive.

The severe economic problems at home evidently convinced Gorbachev that the Soviet Union could no longer sustain its extended commitments around the world. As early as 1987, he began reducing Soviet influence in Eastern Europe. And in 1989, in the space of a few months, every communist state in Europe—Poland, Hungary, Czechoslovakia, Bulgaria, Romania, East Germany, Yugoslavia, and

Albania—either overthrew its government or forced it to transform itself into an essentially noncommunist (and in some cases, actively anticommunist) regime. The Communist Parties of Eastern Europe collapsed or redefined themselves into more conventional left-leaning social democratic parties.

The challenges to communism were not successful everywhere. In May 1989, students in China launched a mass movement calling for greater democratization. But in June, hard-line leaders seized control of the government and sent military forces to crush the uprising. The result was a bloody massacre on June 3, 1989, in Tiananmen Square in Beijing, in which a still-unknown number of demonstrators died. The assault crushed the democracy movement and restored the hard-liners to power. It did not, however, stop China's efforts to modernize and even Westernize its economy.

Tiananmen Square

But China was an exception to the worldwide movement toward democratization. Early in 1990, the government of South Africa, long an international pariah for its rigid enforcement of "apartheid" (a system designed to protect white supremacy), began a cautious retreat from its traditional policies. Among other things, it legalized the chief black party in the nation, the African National Congress (ANC), which had been banned for decades; and on February 11, 1990, it released from prison the leader of the ANC, and a revered hero to black South Africans, Nelson Mandela, who had been in jail for twenty-seven years. Over the next several years, the South African government repealed its apartheid laws. And in 1994, after national elections in which all South Africans could participate, Nelson Mandela became the first black president of South Africa.

In 1991, communism began to collapse at the site of its birth: the Soviet Union itself. An unsuccessful coup by hard-line Soviet leaders on August 19 precipitated a dramatic unraveling of communist power. Within days, the coup itself collapsed in the face of resistance from the public and, more important, crucial elements within the military. Mikhail Gorbachev returned to power, but it soon became evident that the legitimacy of both the Communist Party and the central Soviet government had been fatally injured. By the end of August, many of the republics of the Soviet Union had declared independence; the Soviet government was clearly powerless to stop the fragmentation. Gorbachev himself finally resigned as leader of the now virtually powerless Communist Party and Soviet government, and the Soviet Union ceased to exist.

Dissolution of the USSR

Reagan and Gorbachev

Reagan was skeptical of Gorbachev at first, but he gradually became convinced that the Soviet leader was sincere in his desire for reform. At a summit meeting with Reagan in Reykjavik, Iceland, in 1986, Gorbachev proposed reducing the nuclear arsenals of both sides by 50 percent or more, although continuing disputes over Reagan's commitment to the SDI program prevented agreements. But in 1988, after Reagan and Gorbachev exchanged cordial visits to each other's capitals, the two superpowers signed a treaty eliminating American and Soviet intermediate-range nuclear forces (INF) from Europe—the most significant arms control agreement of the nuclear age. At about the same time, Gorbachev ended the Soviet Union's long and frustrating military involvement in Afghanistan.

TIANANMEN SQUARE, 1989 The democracy movement in China accelerated rapidly in the spring of 1989 and was most visible through the vast crowds of students who began demonstrating in Tiananmen Square in Beijing. On June 3, the government sent troops into the square to clear out and arrest the demonstrating students. Hundreds, perhaps thousands, were killed in the violence that resulted from that decision. *(AP Images/Sadayuki Mikami)*

The Fading of the Reagan Revolution

For a time, the dramatic changes around the world and Reagan's personal popularity deflected attention from a series of political scandals. There were revelations of illegality, corruption, and ethical lapses in the Environmental Protection Agency, the CIA, the Department of Defense, the Department of Labor, the Department of Justice, and the Department of Housing and Urban Development. A more serious scandal emerged within the savings and loan industry, which the Reagan administration had helped deregulate in the early 1980s. By the end of the decade the industry was in chaos, and the government was forced to step in to prevent a complete collapse.

Savings and Loan Crisis

But the most politically damaging scandal of the Reagan years came to light in November 1986, when the White House conceded that it had sold weapons to the revolutionary government of Iran as part of a largely unsuccessful effort to secure the release of several Americans being held hostage by radical Islamic groups in the Middle East. Even more damaging was the revelation that some of the money from the arms deal with Iran had been covertly and illegally funneled into a fund to aid the contras in Nicaragua.

In the months that followed, aggressive reporting and a highly publicized series of congressional hearings exposed a widespread pattern of illegal covert activities orchestrated by the White House and dedicated to advancing the administration's foreign policy aims. The Iran-contra scandal, as it became known, did serious damage to the Reagan presidency—even though the investigations were never able decisively to tie the president himself to the most serious violations of the law.

Iran-Contra Scandal

The Election of 1988

The fraying of the Reagan administration helped the Democrats regain control of the United States Senate in 1986 and fueled hopes in the party for a presidential victory in 1988. Even so, several of the most popular figures in the Democratic Party refused to run, and the nomination finally went to a previously little-known figure: Michael Dukakis, a three-term governor of Massachusetts. Dukakis was a dry, even dull campaigner. But Democrats were optimistic about their prospects in 1988, largely because their opponent, Vice President George Bush, had failed to spark public enthusiasm. He entered the last months of the campaign well behind Dukakis.

Beginning at the Republican Convention, however, Bush staged a remarkable turnaround by making his campaign a long, relentless attack on Dukakis, tying him to all the unpopular social and cultural stances Americans had come to identify with "liberals." Indeed, the Bush campaign was almost certainly the most

Bush's Negative Campaign

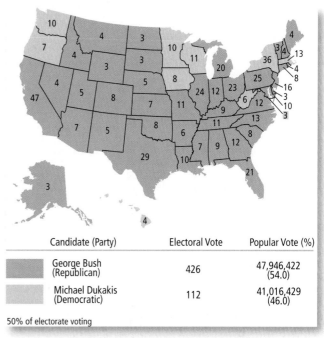

Candidate (Party)	Electoral Vote	Popular Vote (%)
George Bush (Republican)	426	47,946,422 (54.0)
Michael Dukakis (Democratic)	112	41,016,429 (46.0)

50% of electorate voting

THE ELECTION OF 1988 Democrats had high hopes going into the election of 1988, but Vice President George Bush won a decisive victory over Michael Dukakis, who did only slightly better than Walter Mondale had done four years earlier. ◆ *What made it so difficult for a Democrat to challenge the Republicans in 1988 after eight years of a Republican administration?*

negative of the twentieth century; and even more than Reagan's campaigns, it revealed the new political aggressiveness of the Republican right. It was very effective. Bush won a substantial victory in November: 54 percent of the popular vote to Dukakis's 46 percent, and 426 electoral votes to Dukakis's 112. But the Democrats retained secure majorities in both houses of Congress.

The Bush Presidency

The Bush presidency was notable for the dramatic developments in international affairs with which it coincided and at times helped to advance, and for the absence of important initiatives or ideas on most domestic issues.

The broad popularity Bush enjoyed during his first three years in office was partly a result of his subdued, unthreatening public image. But it was primarily because of the wonder and excitement with which Americans viewed the dramatic events in the rest of the world. Bush moved cautiously at first in dealing with the changes in the Soviet Union. But like Reagan, he eventually cooperated with Gorbachev and reached a series of significant agreements with the Soviet Union in its waning years. In the three years after the INF agreement in 1988, the United States and the Soviet Union moved rapidly toward even more far-reaching arms reduction agreements.

On domestic issues, the Bush administration was less successful. His administration inherited a heavy burden of

THE BUSH CAMPAIGN, 1988 Vice President George Bush had never been an effective campaigner, but in 1988 he revived his candidacy with an unabashed attack on his opponent's values and patriotism. Bush himself missed no chance to surround himself with patriotic symbols, including this red, white, and blue hot-air balloon in Kentucky. *(Time Life Pictures/Getty Images)*

debt and a federal deficit that had been growing for nearly a decade. The president's pledge to reduce the deficit and his 1988 campaign promise of "no new taxes" were in conflict with one another. Bush faced a Democratic Congress with an agenda very different from his own.

Despite this political stalemate, Congress and the White House managed on occasion to agree on significant measures. They cooperated in producing the plan to salvage the floundering savings and loan industry. In 1990, the president bowed to congressional pressure and agreed to a significant tax increase as part of a multiyear "budget package" designed to reduce the deficit—thus violating his own 1988 campaign pledge.

But the most serious domestic problem facing the Bush administration was one for which neither the president nor Congress had any answer: a recession that began late in 1990

Political Gridlock

1990 Recession

and slowly increased its grip on the national economy in 1991 and 1992. Because of the enormous level of debt that corporations (and individuals) had accumulated in the 1980s, the recession caused an unusual number of bankruptcies. It also increased the fear and frustration among middle- and working-class Americans and put pressure on the government to address such problems as the rising cost of health care.

The First Gulf War

The events of 1989–1991 had left the United States in the unanticipated position of being the only real superpower in the world. The Bush administration, therefore, had to consider what to do with America's formidable political and military power in a world in which the major justification for that power—the Soviet threat—was now gone.

The events of 1989–1991 suggested two possible answers, both of which had some effect on policy. One was that the United States would reduce its military strength and concentrate its energies and resources on pressing domestic problems. There was, in fact, movement in that direction both in Congress and within the administration. The other was that America would continue to use its power actively, not to fight communism but to defend its regional and economic interests. In 1989, that led the administration to order an invasion of Panama, which overthrew the unpopular military leader Manuel Noriega (under indictment in the United States for drug trafficking) and replaced him with an elected, pro-American regime.

On August 2, 1990, the armed forces of Iraq invaded and quickly overwhelmed their small, oil-rich neighbor, the emirate of Kuwait. Saddam Hussein, the militaristic leader of Iraq, soon announced that he was annexing Kuwait and set out to entrench his forces there. After some initial indecision, the Bush administration agreed to lead other nations in a campaign to force Iraq out of Kuwait—through the pressure of economic sanctions if possible, through military force if necessary. Within a few weeks, Bush had persuaded virtually every important government in the world, including the Soviet Union and almost all the Arab and Islamic states, to join in a United Nations–sanctioned trade embargo of Iraq.

Invasion of Kuwait

At the same time, the United States and its allies (including the British, French, Egyptians, and Saudis) began deploying a large military force along the border between Kuwait and Saudi Arabia, a force that ultimately reached 690,000 troops (425,000 of them American). On November 29, the United Nations, at the request of the United States, voted to authorize military action to expel Iraq from Kuwait if Iraq did not leave by January 15, 1991. On January 12, both houses of Congress voted to authorize the use of force against Iraq. And on January 16, American and allied air forces began a massive bombardment of

THE FIRST GULF WAR This photograph, taken in the Saudi desert, shows U.S. marines in Hummers lining up to enter Kuwait in the 1991 war that expelled Iraqi troops from Kuwait. The wind, dust, and heat of the desert made the Gulf War a far more difficult experience for American troops than the relatively brief fighting would suggest. *(Peter Turnley/Corbis)*

Iraqi forces in Kuwait and of military and industrial installations in Iraq itself.

The allied bombing continued for six weeks. On February 23, allied (primarily American) forces under the command of General Norman Schwarzkopf began a major ground offensive—not primarily against the heavily entrenched Iraqi forces along the Kuwait border, as expected, but to the north of them into Iraq itself. The allied armies encountered almost no resistance and suffered relatively few casualties (141 fatalities). Estimates of Iraqi deaths in the war were 100,000 or more. On February 28, Iraq announced its acceptance of allied terms for a cease-fire, and the brief Persian Gulf War came to an end.

The quick and (for America) relatively painless victory over Iraq was highly popular in the United States. But the tyrannical regime of Saddam Hussein survived, weakened but still ruthless.

The Election of 1992

President Bush's popularity reached a record high in the immediate aftermath of the Gulf War. But the glow of that victory faded quickly as the recession worsened in late 1991, and as the administration declined to propose any policies for combating it.

Because the early maneuvering for the 1992 presidential election occurred when President Bush's popularity remained high, many leading Democrats declined to run. That gave Bill Clinton, the young five-term governor of

Bill Clinton

Arkansas, an opportunity to emerge early as the front-runner, as a result of a skillful campaign that emphasized broad

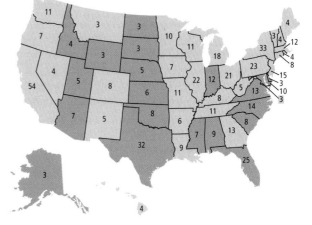

Candidate (Party)	Electoral Vote	Popular Vote (%)
Bill Clinton (Democratic)	370	44,909,889 (43.0)
George Bush (Republican)	168	39,104,545 (37.5)
Ross Perot (Independent)	0	19,742,267 (18.9)
Other candidates	—	669,958 (0.6)

55.2% of electorate voting

THE ELECTION OF 1992 In the 1992 election, for the first time since 1976, a Democrat captured the White House. And although the third-party candidacy of Ross Perot deprived Bill Clinton of an absolute majority, he nevertheless defeated George Bush by a decisive margin in both the popular and electoral vote. ◆ *What factors had eroded President Bush's once-broad popularity by 1992? What explained the strong showing of Ross Perot?*

For an interactive version of this map, go to www.mhhe.com/brinkley13ech31maps

economic issues instead of the racial and cultural questions that had so divided the Democrats in the past.

Complicating the campaign was the emergence of Ross Perot, a blunt, forthright Texas billionaire who became an independent candidate by tapping popular resentment of the federal bureaucracy and by promising tough, uncompromising leadership to deal with the fiscal crisis. At several moments in the spring, Perot led both Bush and Clinton in public opinion polls. In July, as he began to face hostile scrutiny from the media, he abruptly withdrew

Ross Perot

from the race. But early in October, he reentered and soon regained much (although never all) of his early support.

After a campaign in which the economy and the president's unpopularity were the principal issues, Clinton won a clear, but hardly overwhelming, victory over Bush and Perot. He received 43 percent of the vote in the three-way race, to the president's 38 percent and Perot's 19 percent (the best showing for a third-party or independent candidate since Theodore Roosevelt in 1912). Clinton won 370 electoral votes to Bush's 168; Perot won none. Democrats retained control of both houses of Congress.

CONCLUSION

America in the late 1970s was, by the standards of its own recent history, an unusually troubled nation: numbed by the Watergate scandals, the fall of Vietnam, and perhaps most of all the nation's increasing economic difficulties. The unhappy presidencies of Gerald Ford and Jimmy Carter provided little relief from these accumulating problems and anxieties. Indeed, in the last year of the Carter presidency, the nation's prospects seemed particularly grim in light of severe economic problems, a traumatic seizure of American hostages in Iran, and a Soviet invasion of Afghanistan.

In the midst of these problems, American conservatives were slowly and steadily preparing for an impressive revival. A coalition of disparate but impassioned groups on the right—including a large movement known as the "New Right," with vaguely populist impulses—gained strength from the nation's troubles and from their own success in winning support for a broad-ranging revolt against taxes. Their efforts culminated in the election of 1980, when Ronald Reagan became the most conservative man in at least sixty years to be elected president of the United States.

Reagan's first term was a dramatic contrast to the troubled presidencies that had preceded it. He won substantial victories in Congress (cutting taxes, reducing spending on domestic programs, building up the military). Perhaps equally important, he made his own engaging personality one of the central political forces in national life. Easily reelected in 1984, he seemed to have solidified the conservative grip on national political life. In his second term, a series of scandals and misadventures—and the president's own declining energy—limited the administration's effectiveness. Nevertheless, Reagan's personal popularity remained high, and the economy continued to prosper—factors that helped his vice president, George H. W. Bush, to succeed him in 1989.

Bush's presidency was defined not by domestic initiatives, as Reagan's had been—and the perception of its disengagement with the nation's growing economic problems contributed to Bush's defeat in 1992. But a colossal historic event overshadowed domestic concerns during much of Bush's term in office: the collapse of the Soviet Union and the fall of communist regimes all over Europe and in other parts of the world. The United States was to some degree a dazzled observer of this process. But the end of the Cold War also propelled the United States into the possession of unchallenged global preeminence—and drew it increasingly into the role of international arbiter and peacemaker. The Gulf War of 1991 was only the most dramatic example of the new global role the United States would now increasingly assume.

INTERACTIVE LEARNING

The *Primary Source Investigator CD-ROM* offers the following materials related to this chapter:

- Interactive maps: **U.S. Elections** (M7) and **Middle East** (M28).
- Documents, images, and maps related to politics and society in the late 1970s through the early 1990s, the Reagan presidency, and the collapse of the Soviet Union. Some highlights include Jimmy Carter's speech regarding the "crisis of confidence" of the nation; the text of Ronald Reagan's speech referring to the Soviet

Union as an "evil empire"; an excerpt from the transcripts of the Senate Judiciary Committee hearings into confirming Clarence Thomas to serve on the Supreme Court; and excerpts from President George H. W. Bush's diary during the Gulf War in 1991.

Online Learning Center (www.mhhe.com/brinkley13e)

For quizzes, Internet resources, references to additional books and films, and more, consult this book's Online Learning Center.

FOR FURTHER REFERENCE

Bruce J. Schulman, *The Seventies: The Great Shift in American Culture, Society, and Politics* (2001) is a good general history of the period. James M. Cannon, *Time and Chance: Gerald Ford's Appointment with History* (1994) is a journalist's account of the Ford presidency, and Yanek Mieczkowski, *Gerald Ford and the Challenges of the 1970s* (2005) is an excellent scholarly study. Gaddis Smith, *Morality, Reason, and Power* (1986) examines the Carter foreign policy. Steven Gillon, *The Democrats' Dilemma: Walter Mondale and the Liberal Legacy* (1992) is a good discussion of the travails of the Democrats in the 1970s. Jerome L. Himmelstein, *To the Right: The Transformation of American Conservatism* (1990) and Godfrey Hodgson, *The World Turned Upside Down: A History of the Conservative Ascendancy in America* (1996) are good introductions to the subject. Kevin Kruse, *White Flight: Atlanta and the Making of Modern Conservatism* (2005) is a valuable study. Lou Cannon, *President Reagan: The Role of a Lifetime* (1990) and Haynes Johnson, *Sleepwalking Through History* (1991) are accounts by journalists who covered the Reagan White House. Gil Troy, *Morning in America: How Ronald Reagan Invented the 1980s* (2005) is an excellent scholarly study. John Lewis Gaddis, *The United States and the End of the Cold War* (1992) and *We Now Know: Rethinking Cold War History* (1997) examine the transformation of the world order after 1989. Richard Rhodes, *Arsenals of Folly* (2007) is a passionate account of the nuclear arms race. Herbert Parmet, *George Bush: The Life of a Lone Star Yankee* (1997) is the first major scholarly study of the 41st president.

CHAPTER 32

THE AGE OF GLOBALIZATION

BAGHDAD, MARCH 21, 2003 At the beginning of the American invasion of Iraq in spring 2003, the United States military used techniques honed in the first Gulf War in Kuwait—the use of heavy bombing of Iraqi targets before deploying troops in the field. This photograph shows explosions in downtown Baghdad at the beginning of the war as American bombers tried to hit strategic targets in the city. *(Getty Images)*

A T 8:45 A.M. ON THE BRIGHT, SUNNY MORNING of September 11, 2001, as tens of thousands of workers—executives and financiers, secretaries and clerks, security guards and maintenance workers, chefs and waiters, citizens of dozens of nations—were beginning a day's work in lower Manhattan, a commercial airliner crashed into the side of one of the two towers of the World Trade Center, the tallest buildings in New York. The collision created a huge explosion and a great fire of extraordinary intensity. Less than half an hour later, as thousands of workers fled the burning building, another commercial airliner rammed into the companion tower, creating a second fireball. Within an hour after that, the burning floors of both towers gave way and fell onto the floors below them, pulling one of New York's (and America's) most famous symbols to the ground. At about the same time, in Washington, D.C., another commercial airliner crashed into a side of the Pentagon—the headquarters of the nation's military—turning part of the building's façade into rubble. And several hundred miles away, still another airplane crashed in a field not far from Pittsburgh.

September 11, 2001

These four almost simultaneous catastrophes—in which nearly 3,000 people died—were the result of a single, orchestrated plan by members of Al Qaeda, a previously little-known Middle Eastern terrorist group. The attacks they launched profoundly affected the United States and the world. They made what came to be known as the "war on terrorism" a central issue in American life. They turned George W. Bush, who had won the presidency in a bitterly controversial election, into a war leader with broad public support. They led to an American invasion of Afghanistan and, two years later, of Iraq, and they legitimized a major change in the foundations of American foreign policy. The dramatic new initiatives of the Bush administration were not without their critics. American foreign policy in the aftermath of 2001 was bitterly opposed by much of the rest of the world and attracted sharp criticism within the United States as well. But Bush survived the unpopularity of many of his initiatives to win reelection in 2004 by a thin margin.

The attacks of September 11, 2001, seemed to many Americans at the time to change everything—to alter fundamentally how they thought about the world, and to change decisively the way Americans would have to live. In fact, most aspects of life in the United States quickly returned to their normal patterns. And in many ways, September 11, rather than being an aberration in American life, was an example of one of the most important realities of the age. The United States, more than at any other time in its history, was becoming deeply entwined in a new age of globalism—an age that combined great promise with great peril.

SIGNIFICANT EVENTS

1977 ▶	Apple introduces first personal computer
1979 ▶	Nuclear accident at Three Mile Island
1981 ▶	Existence of AIDS first reported in United States
1985 ▶	Crack cocaine appears in American cities
1989 ▶	Human genome project launched
1991 ▶	Controversy surrounds confirmation of Clarence Thomas to Supreme Court
1992 ▶	Major race riot in Los Angeles
▶	Bill Clinton elected president
1993 ▶	Congress approves tax increase as part of deficit reduction
▶	Congress ratifies North American Free Trade Agreement
▶	Clinton proposes national health-care system
1994 ▶	Congress rejects health-care reform
▶	Republicans win control of both houses of Congress
1995 ▶	New Republican Congress attempts to enact "Contract with America"
▶	Showdown between president and Congress leads to shutdown of federal government
▶	National crime rates show dramatic decline
▶	O. J. Simpson trial
1996 ▶	Congress passes and president signs major welfare reform bill, minimum wage increase, and health-insurance reform
▶	Clinton reelected president; Republicans retain control of Congress
1997 ▶	President and Congress agree on plan to balance budget
▶	Justice Department files antitrust suits against Microsoft
1998 ▶	Lewinsky scandal rocks Clinton presidency
▶	Democrats gain in congressional elections
▶	Clinton impeached by House
1999 ▶	Senate acquits Clinton in impeachment trial
2000 ▶	George W. Bush wins contested presidential election
2001 ▶	Terrorists destroy World Trade Center and damage Pentagon
▶	United States begins military action against Afghanistan
2002 ▶	Corporate scandals rock business world
2003 ▶	United States invades Iraq
2004 ▶	Prison abuse scandal in Iraq
▶	Bush defeats Kerry in presidential election
2005 ▶	Hurricane Katrina devastates New Orleans and the Gulf Coast
2006 ▶	Democrats gain control of both houses of Congress
2007 ▶	Troop "surge" in Iraq
▶	Mortgage crisis weakens economy
2008 ▶	Barack Obama wins Democratic nomination for president
▶	John McCain wins Republican nomination for president

A RESURGENCE OF PARTISANSHIP

Bill Clinton took the oath of office in January 1993 with a domestic agenda more ambitious than that of any other president in nearly thirty years. He entered the presidency carrying the extravagant expectations of liberals who had spent a generation in exile. But Clinton also had signifi-

William Jefferson Clinton

cant political weaknesses. Having won the votes of well under half the electorate, he had no powerful mandate. Democratic majorities in Congress were frail, and Democrats in any case had grown unaccustomed to bowing to presidential leadership. The Republican leadership in Congress was highly adversarial and opposed the president with unusual unanimity on many issues. A tendency toward reckless personal behavior, both before and during his presidency, caused the president continuing problems and gave his many enemies repeated opportunities to discredit him.

Launching the Clinton Presidency

The new administration compounded its problems with a series of missteps and misfortunes in its first months. The president's failed effort to end the longtime ban on gay men and women serving in the military met with ferocious resistance from the armed forces themselves and from many conservatives in both parties. Several of his early appointments became so controversial he had to withdraw them. The suicide of a longtime friend of the president, Vince Foster, helped spark an escalating inquiry into some banking and real estate ventures involving the president and his wife in the early 1980s, in what became known as the Whitewater affair. An independent counsel began examining these issues in 1993 (the Clintons were eventually cleared of wrongdoing in 2000).

Despite its many problems, the Clinton administration could boast of some significant achievements in its first year. The president narrowly won approval of a budget that marked a significant turn away from the policies of the Reagan-Bush years. It included a substantial tax increase on the wealthiest Americans, a significant reduction in many areas of government spending, and a major expansion of tax credits to low-income working people.

Clinton was a committed advocate of free trade and a proponent of many aspects of what came to be known as globalism. He made that clear through his strong support of a series of new and controversial free trade agreements. After a long and difficult battle, he won approval of the

NAFTA

North American Free Trade Agreement (or NAFTA), which eliminated most trade barriers among the United States, Canada, and Mexico. Later he won approval of other far-reaching trade agreements negotiated in the General Agreement on Trade and Tarriffs (or GATT).

The president's most important and ambitious initiative was a major reform of the nation's health-care system. Early in 1993, he appointed a task force

Failure of Health-Care Reform

chaired by his wife, Hillary Rodham Clinton, which proposed a sweeping reform designed to guarantee coverage to every American and hold down the costs of medical care. Substantial opposition from the right, from insurance companies, and from Republican leaders in Congress doomed the plan. In September 1994, Congress abandoned the health-care reform effort.

The foreign policy of the Clinton administration was at first cautious and even tentative, but not without some successes. The small Balkan nation Bosnia was embroiled in a bloody civil war between its two major ethnic groups: one Muslim, the other Serbian and Christian. The American negotiator Richard Holbrooke finally brought the warring parties together in 1995 and crafted an agreement to partition Bosnia. The United States was among the nations to send peacekeeping troops to Bosnia to police the fragile settlement, which—despite many pessimistic predictions—was still largely in place over a decade later.

The Republican Resurgence

The trials of the Clinton administration, and the failure of health-care reform in particular, damaged the Democratic Party as it faced the congressional elections of 1994. For the first time in forty years, Republicans gained control of both houses of Congress.

Throughout 1995, the Republican Congress worked at a sometimes feverish pace to construct one of the most ambitious and even radical legislative programs in modern times. The members proposed a series of measures to transfer important powers from the federal government to the states. They proposed dramatic reductions in federal spending, including a major restructuring of the once-sacrosanct Medicare program to reduce costs. They attempted to scale back a wide range of federal regulatory functions. In all these efforts, they could count on a disciplined Republican majority in the House and an only slightly less united Republican majority in the Senate.

President Clinton responded to the 1994 election results by proclaiming that "the era of big government is over" and shifting his own agenda conspicuously to the center. He announced his own plan to cut taxes and balance the budget. Indeed, the gap between the Democratic White House and the Republican Congress on many major issues was relatively small. But compromise between the president and the highly partisan Republicans in Congress became difficult. In November 1995 and again in January 1996, the federal government shut down for several days because the president and Congress could not agree on a budget. Republican leaders had refused to pass a "continuing resolution" (to allow government operations to continue during negotiations) in hopes of pressuring the

BREAKING PRECEDENT Bill Clinton broke with precedent in 1993 when he appointed his wife, Hillary Rodham Clinton, to head a task force on health care reform. The prominent role of the first lady in the Clinton administration surprised many Americans, pleasing some and angering others. Here she campaigns for her plan at Johns Hopkins University in 1993. Hillary Clinton broke precedent again in 2000 when she was elected to the United States Senate from New York and when she was a candidate for president in 2008. *(AP Images/Joe Marquette)*

president to agree to their terms. That proved to be an epic political blunder. Public opinion turned quickly and powerfully against the Republican leadership, and against much of its agenda. House Speaker Newt Gingrich quickly became one of the most unpopular political leaders in the nation, while President Clinton slowly improved his standing in the polls.

The Election of 1996

By the time the 1996 presidential campaign began in earnest, President Clinton was in a commanding position to win reelection. Unopposed for the Democratic nomination, he faced a Republican opponent—Senator Robert Dole of Kansas—who inspired little enthusiasm even within his own party. Clinton's revival was in part a result of his adroitness in taking centrist positions that undermined the Republicans and in championing traditional

Clinton Versus Dole

Democratic issues—such as raising the minimum wage—that were broadly popular. But his greatest strength came from the remarkable success of the American economy and the marked reduction in the federal deficit that had occurred during his presidency. Like Reagan in 1984, he could campaign as the champion of peace, prosperity, and national well-being.

As the election approached, the Congress passed several important bills. It raised the minimum wage for the first time in more than a decade. Most dramatically of all, the Congress passed a welfare reform bill, which President Clinton somewhat reluctantly signed, that marked the most important change in aid to the poor since the Social Security Act of 1935. It ended the fifty-year federal guarantee of assistance to families with dependent children and turned most of the responsibility for allocating federal welfare funds (now greatly reduced) to the states. Most of all, it shifted the bulk of welfare benefits away from those without jobs and toward support for low-wage workers.

Candidate (Party)	Electoral Vote	Popular Vote (%)
Bill Clinton (Democratic)	379	47,401,185 (49.3)
Robert Dole (Republican)	159	39,197,469 (40.7)
Ross Perot (Reform)	0	8,085,294 (8.4)

49% of electorate voting

THE ELECTION OF 1996 Ross Perot did much less well in 1996 than he had in 1992, and President Clinton came much closer than he had four years earlier to winning a majority of the popular vote. Once again, Clinton defeated his Republican opponent, this time Robert Dole, by a decisive margin in both the popular and electoral vote. After the 1994 Republican landslide in the congressional elections, Bill Clinton had seemed permanently weakened. ◆ *What explains his political revival?*

For an interactive version of this map, go to www.mhhe.com/brinkley13ech32maps

Clinton's buoyant campaign flagged slightly in the last weeks, but the president nevertheless received just over 49 percent of the popular vote to Dole's 41 percent; Ross Perot, running now as the candidate of what he called the Reform Party, received just over 8 percent of the vote. Clinton won 379 electoral votes to Dole's 159. But other Democrats made only modest gains and failed to regain either house of Congress.

Clinton Triumphant and Embattled

Bill Clinton was the first Democratic president to win two terms as president since Franklin Roosevelt. Facing a somewhat chastened but still hostile Republican Congress, he proposed a modest domestic agenda, consisting primarily of tax cuts and tax credits targeted at middle-class Americans to help them educate their children. He also negotiated effectively with the Republican leadership on a plan for a balanced budget, which passed with much fanfare late in 1997. By the end of 1998, the federal budget was generating its first surplus in thirty years.

Budget Surpluses

Clinton's popularity would be important to him in the turbulent year that followed, when the most serious crisis of his presidency suddenly erupted. Clinton had been bedeviled by alleged scandals almost from his first weeks in office, including a civil suit for sexual harassment filed against the president by a former state employee in Arkansas, Paula Jones.

In early 1998, inquiries associated with the Paula Jones case led to charges that the president had had a sexual relationship with a young White House intern, Monica Lewinsky, and that he had lied about it in his deposition before Jones's attorneys. Those revelations produced a new investigation by the independent counsel in the Whitewater case, Kenneth Starr, a former judge and official in the Reagan Justice Department. Clinton forcefully denied the charges, and the public strongly backed him. His popularity soared to record levels and remained high throughout the year that followed.

Monica Lewinsky

The Lewinsky scandal revived again in August 1998, when Lewinsky struck a deal with the independent counsel and testified about her relationship with Clinton. Starr then subpoenaed Clinton himself, who finally admitted that he and Lewinsky had had what he called an "improper relationship." A few weeks later, Starr recommended that Congress impeach the president.

Republican conservatives were determined to pursue the case. First the House Judiciary Committee and then, on December 19, 1998, the full House, both voting on strictly partisan lines, approved two counts of impeachment: lying to the grand jury and obstructing justice. The matter then moved to the Senate, where a trial of the president—the first since the trial of Andrew Johnson in 1868—began in early January. The trial ended with a decisive acquittal of the president. Neither of the charges attracted even a majority of the votes, let alone the two-thirds necessary for conviction.

Impeachment

Kosovo

In 1999, the president faced the most serious foreign policy crisis of his presidency, once again in the Balkans. This time, the conflict involved a province of Serbian-dominated Yugoslavia—Kosovo—most of whose residents were Albanian Muslims. A long-simmering conflict between the Serbian government of Yugoslavia and Kosovo separatists erupted into a savage civil war in 1998. Numerous reports of Serbian atrocities against the Kosovans slowly roused world opinion. In May 1999, NATO forces—dominated and led by the United States—began a bombing campaign against the Serbians, which after little more than a week led the leader of Yugoslavia, Slobodan Milosevic, to agree to a cease-fire. Serbian troops withdrew from Kosovo entirely, replaced by NATO peacekeeping forces. A precarious peace returned to the region.

Clinton finished his eight years in office with his popularity higher than it had been when he had begun. Indeed, public approval of Clinton's presidency—a presidency marked by astonishing prosperity and general world stability—was consistently among the highest of any postwar president—despite the many scandals and setbacks he suffered in the White House. But his personal recklessness continued to trouble voters—and burden the Democratic Party.

The Election of 2000

The 2000 presidential election was one of the most extraordinary in American history—not because of the campaign that preceded it, but because of the sensational controversy over its results.

The two men who had been the front-runners for their parties' nominations a year before the election captured those nominations with only slight difficulty: George W.

George W. Bush Versus Al Gore

Bush—son of the former president and a second-term governor of Texas—and Vice President Al Gore.

Both men ran cautious, centrist campaigns, making much of their relatively modest differences over how to use the large budget surpluses forecast for the years ahead. Polls showed an exceptionally tight race right up to the end. In the congressional races, Republicans maintained control of the House of Representatives by five seats, while the Senate split evenly between Democrats and Republicans. (Among the victors in the Senate was First Lady Hillary Rodham Clinton, who won a highly publicized race in New York.) In the presidential race, Gore won the national popular vote by the thin margin of about 540,000 votes out of about 100 million cast (or .05%). But

Florida

on election night, both candidates remained short of the 270 electoral votes needed for victory because no one could determine who had won Florida. After a mandatory recount over the next two days, Bush led Gore in the state by fewer than 300 votes.

In a number of Florida counties, including some of the most heavily Democratic ones, votes were cast by notoriously inaccurate punch-card ballots, which were then counted by machines. Many voters failed fully to punch out the appropriate holes, leaving the machines unable to read them. Into this morass, the Gore campaign moved quickly with a demand—sanctioned by Florida law—for hand recounts of punch-card ballots in three critical counties.

When a court-ordered deadline arrived, the recount was not yet complete. The Florida secretary of state, a Republican, then certified Bush the winner in Florida by a little more than 500 votes. The Gore campaign immediately contested the results in the Florida Supreme Court, which ordered hand recounts of all previously uncounted ballots in all Florida counties.

In the meantime, the Bush campaign appealed to the United States Supreme Court. Late on December 12, the

ELECTION NIGHT, 2000 The electronic billboard in New York City's Times Square, showing network coverage of the presidential contest, reports George Bush the winner of the 2000 presidential race late on election night. A few hours later, the networks retracted their projections because of continuing uncertainty over the results in Florida. Five weeks later, and then only because of the controversial intervention of the Supreme Court, Bush finally emerged the victor. *(Chris Hondros/Getty Images)*

Court issued one of the most unusual and controversial decisions in its history. In a 5–4 vote,

The Supreme Court's Decision

divided sharply along party and ideological lines, the conservative majority overruled the Florida Supreme Court and insisted that any revised recount order be completed by December 12 (an obviously impossible demand, since the Court issued its ruling late at night on the 12th). The Court had decided the election. Absent a recount, the original certification of Bush's victory stood.

The Second Bush Presidency

George W. Bush assumed the presidency in January 2001 burdened by both the controversies surrounding his

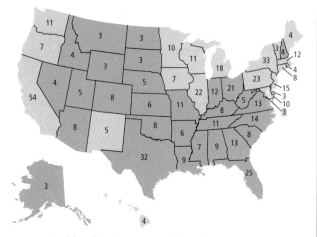

Candidate (Party)	Electoral Vote	Popular Vote (%)
Al Gore (Democratic)	266	51,003,894 (48)
George W. Bush (Republican)	271	50,459,211 (48)

51% of electorate voting

THE ELECTION OF 2000 The 2000 presidential election was one of the closest and most controversial in American history. It also starkly revealed a new pattern of party strength, which had been developing over the previous decade. Democrats swept the Northeast and most of the industrial Midwest and carried all the states of the Pacific Coast. Republicans swept the South, the plains states, and the mountain states (with the exception of New Mexico) and held on to a few traditional Republican strongholds in the Midwest. Compare this map to those of earlier elections, in particular the election of 1896, and ask how the pattern of party support changed over the course of the twentieth century.

election and the widespread perception, even among some of his own supporters, that he was ill prepared for the office.

Bush's principal campaign promise had been that he would use the predicted budget surplus to finance a massive tax reduction. By relying on his own party's control of both houses of Congress, he won passage of the largest tax cut in American history—$1.35 trillion over several years.

Bush Tax Cuts

Having campaigned as a moderate adept at building coalitions across party lines, Bush governed as a staunch conservative, relying on the most orthodox members of his own party for support. As preparation for the 2004 election, the president's political adviser, Karl Rove, encouraged the administration to take increasingly conservative positions on a number of divisive social issues. The president appealed to the gun lobby by refusing to support a renewal of the assault weapons ban that Clinton had enacted. He proposed a constitutional amendment to ban gay marriage, thus making the debate over the rights of homosexuals a potent issue in the campaign. The Bush administration's proposals for incorporating "faith-based" organizations into the circle of institutions that administer federally funded social programs was part of a broad and successful effort to mobilize evangelical

Christians as an active part of the Republican coalition. But almost from the beginning, the aftermath of the September 11 attacks dominated both Bush's presidency and the nation's politics.

The Election of 2004

The 2004 election pitted President Bush, who was unopposed within his party, against John Kerry, a senator from Massachusetts who won the Democratic nomination. Throughout the months before the election, the electorate was almost evenly divided.

The election itself, although very close, was more decisive than the election of 2000. Bush won 51 percent

RELIGION AND POLITICS, 2004 Although many issues were at stake in the election of 2004, the campaign of that year was distinctive in the degree to which religion became a major issue. For many evangelical Christians, in particular, the reelection of President George W. Bush became a religious as well as a political cause, in part because of Bush's stances on such religiously charged subjects as abortion, gay rights, stem-cell research, and the role of "faith-based" institutions in public life. These participants in a Bush campaign rally carry crosses made out of Bush campaign posters. *(Bill O'Leary/The Washington Post)*

Candidate (Party)	Electoral Vote	Popular Vote (%)
George W. Bush (Republican)	286	62,040,606 (51)
John F. Kerry (Democratic)	251	59,028,109 (48)

60% of electorate voting

THE ELECTION OF 2004 The 2004 election repeated the pattern established in 2000. The Democrats, led this time by Massachusetts senator John F. Kerry, swept the Northeast, most of the industrial Midwest, and the Pacific Coast. The Republicans, led by President Bush, carried almost everything else. Although Bush's popular and electoral margins were both larger than they had been in 2000, the election remained extremely close. The shift of about 100,000 votes from Bush to Kerry in Ohio would have produced a Democratic victory.

of the popular vote to Kerry's 48. The electoral vote was much closer, 286 for Bush, 252 for Kerry. A Kerry victory in Ohio, a hotly contested state that Bush won by a very narrow margin, would have given him the presidency.

THE ECONOMIC BOOM

The last two decades of the twentieth century and the first decade of the twenty-first saw remarkable changes in American life—some a result of the end of the Cold War, some the changing character of the American population, and some a product of a rapidly evolving culture. But most of these changes were at least in part a product of the dramatic transformation of the American economy.

From "Stagflation" to Growth

The roots of the economic growth of the 1980s and 1990s lay in part in the troubled years of the 1970s, when the United States seemed for a time to be losing its ability to produce long-term prosperity. In the face of the sluggish growth and persistent inflation of those years, however, many American corporations began making important

changes in the way they ran their businesses—changes that contributed to both the prosperity of the last decades of the twentieth century and the growing inequality that accompanied it. Businesses invested heavily in new technology, to make themselves more efficient and productive. Corporations began to consider mergers to provide themselves with a more diversified basis for growth. Many enterprises—responding to the energy crises of the 1970s—created more energy-efficient plants and offices. Perhaps most of all, American businesses sought to reduce their labor costs, which were among the highest in the world and which many economists and business leaders believed had made the United States uncompetitive against the many emerging economies that relied on low-wage workers.

New Business Practices

Businesses cut labor costs in many ways. They took a much harder line against unions. Nonunion companies became more successful in staving off unionization drives. Companies already unionized won important concessions from their union members on wages and benefits in exchange for preserving jobs. Some companies moved their operations to areas of the country where unions were weak and wages low—the American South and West in particular. And many companies moved much of their production out of the United States entirely, to such nations as Mexico and China, where there were large available pools of cheaper labor.

Another important driver of the new economy was the growth of technology industries. Digital technology made possible an enormous range of new products: computers, the Internet, cellular phones, digital music, video, and cameras, personal digital assistants, and many other products. The technology industries created many new jobs and produced new consumer needs and appetites.

Technology Industries

For these and many other reasons, the American economy experienced rapid growth in the last decades of the twentieth century. The gross national product (the total of goods and services produced by the United States) quadrupled in twenty years—from $2.7 trillion in 1980 to over $9.8 trillion in 2000. Inflation was low throughout these decades, never rising above 3 percent in any year. Stock prices soared to unprecedented levels, and with few interruptions, from the mid-1980s to the end of the century. The Dow Jones Industrial Average, the most common index of stock performance, stood at 1,000 in late 1980. Late in 1999, it passed 11,000. Economic growth was particularly robust in the last years of the 1990s. In 1997 and 1998, annual growth rates reached 5 percent for the first time since the 1960s. Most impressive of all was the longevity of the boom. From 1994 to 2000, the economy recorded growth—at times very substantial growth—in every year, indeed in every quarter, something that had never before happened so continuously in peacetime. Except for the brief recession of 1992–1993, the period of dramatic growth actually extended unbroken from late 1983 until an economic downturn began in spring 2000.

Downturns

Alan Greenspan, chairman of the Federal Reserve Board, warned in 1999 of the "irrational exuberance" with which Americans were pursuing profits in the stock market. A few months later, the market vindicated his concerns when, in April 2001, there was a sudden and disastrous collapse of a booming new "dot.com" sector of the economy, made up of start-up companies and new, profitable businesses making use of the Internet.

At first, the bursting of the "tech bubble" seemed to have few effects on the larger economy. But by the beginning of 2001, the stock market—a great engine of growth over the previous decade—began a substantial decline, which continued for almost a year. Even when it recovered, beginning in 2002, it could not match the booming growth of the 1990s. In the fall of 2001, the economy as a whole slipped into a recession. Even after recovery in 2002, stock market growth remained relatively slow. And

in early 2008, a disastrous collapse of the home mortgage market drove both the stock market and the national economy into a recession.

The Two-Tiered Economy

Although the American economy revived from the sluggishness that had characterized it in the 1970s and early 1980s, the benefits of the new economy were less widely shared than those of earlier boom times. The increasing abundance of the late twentieth and early twenty-first centuries created enormous new wealth that enriched those talented, or lucky, enough to profit from the areas of booming growth. The rewards for education—particularly in such areas as science and engineering—increased substantially. Between 1980 and 2000, the average family incomes of the wealthiest 20 percent of the population grew by nearly 20 percent (to over $100,000 a year); the average family income of the next 20 percent of the population grew by more than 8 percent. Incomes remained flat for most of the remaining 60 percent of the public, and actually declined for many in the bottom 20 percent.

Rising Income Inequality

ENRON FIELD In happier days, Enron was a high-profile corporation eager to spread its reputation widely. It built a gleaming curved skyscraper in downtown Houston and was nearing completion of a second tower when bankruptcy stopped construction in December 2001. It also paid to have the new Houston baseball stadium named Enron Field. In spring 2002, as scandal tarnished the reputation of the company and its leaders, the Houston Astros paid several million dollars to allow itself to remove the now-notorious Enron name from its stadium. *(David J. Phillip/AP/Wide World Photos)*

The jarring changes in America's relationship to the world economy that had begun in the 1970s—the loss of cheap and easy access to raw materials, the penetration of the American market by foreign competitors, the restructuring of American heavy industry so that it produced fewer jobs and paid lower wages—continued and in some respects accelerated in the following decades. For families and individuals outside the circle of knowledgeable people benefiting from the new technologies, the results of these contractions were often devastating.

Poverty in America had declined steadily and at times dramatically in the years after World War II, so that by the end of the 1970s the percentage of people living in poverty had fallen to 12 percent (from about 20 percent in preceding decades). But the decline in poverty did not continue. In the 1980s, the poverty rate rose again, at times as high as 15 percent. By 2005, it had dropped to

Growing Poverty Rates

13.3 percent, about the same as it had been twenty years before.

Globalization

Perhaps the most important economic change was what became known as the "globalization" of the economy. The great prosperity of the 1950s and 1960s had rested on, among other things, the relative insulation of the United States from the pressures of international competition. As late as 1970, international trade still played a relatively small role in the American economy as a whole, which thrived on the basis of the huge domestic market in North America.

By the end of the 1970s, however, the world had intruded on the American economy in profound ways, and that intrusion increased unabated into the twenty-first century. Exports rose from just under $43 billion in 1970 to over $1 trillion in 2006. But imports rose even more dramatically: from just over $40 billion in 1970 to over $1.8 trillion in 2006. Most American products, in other words, now faced foreign competition inside the United States. The first American trade imbalance in the postwar era occurred in 1971; only twice since then, in 1973 and 1975, has the balance been favorable.

Globalization brought many benefits for the American consumer: new and more varied products, and lower prices for many of them. Most economists, and most national leaders, welcomed the process and worked to encourage it through lowering trade barriers. The North American Free Trade Agreement (NAFTA) and the General Agreement on Trade and Tariffs (GATT) were the boldest of a long series of treaties designed to lower trade barriers stretching back to the 1960s. But globalization had many costs as well. It was particularly hard on industrial workers, who saw their jobs disappear as American companies lost market share to foreign competitors or moved production to low-wage countries.

Costs of Globalization

THE GLOBAL ECONOMY Hundreds of shipping containers, virtually all of them from China, stand waiting for delivery at the Yang Ming container terminal in Los Angeles in February 2001—an illustration of the increasing penetration of the American market by overseas manufacturers and of the growing interconnections between the United States economy and that of the rest of the world. *(Reed Saxon/AP/Wide World Photos)*

SCIENCE AND TECHNOLOGY IN THE NEW ECONOMY

The "new economy" that emerged in the late twentieth and early twenty-first centuries was driven by, and in turn helped to drive, dramatic new scientific and technological discoveries that had profound effects on the way Americans—and peoples throughout the world—lived.

The Digital Revolution

The most visible element of the technological revolution to most Americans was the dramatic growth in the use of computers and other digital electronic devices in almost every area of life.

Among the most significant innovations that contributed to the digital revolution was the development of the microprocessor, first introduced in 1971 by Intel, which represented a notable advance in the technology of integrated circuitry. A microprocessor miniaturized the central processing unit of a computer, making it possible for a small machine to perform calculations that in the past only very large machines could do. Considerable technological innovation was needed before the microprocessor could actually become the basis of what was at first known as a "minicomputer" and then a personal computer. But in 1977, Apple launched its Apple II personal computer, the first such machine to be widely available to the public. Several years later, IBM entered the personal computer market with the first "PC." IBM had engaged a small software development company, Microsoft, to design an operating system for their new computer. Microsoft produced a program known as MS-DOS (DOS for "disk operating system"). No PC could operate without it. The PC, and its software, made its debut in August 1981 and immediately became enormously successful. Three years later, Apple introduced its Macintosh computer, which marked another major innovation in computer technology, among other things because its software—very different from DOS—was much easier to use than that of the PC. But Apple could not match IBM's marketing power, and by the mid-1980s the PC had clearly established its dominance in the booming personal computer market—a dominance enhanced by the introduction of a new software package to replace DOS in 1985: Windows, also developed by Microsoft, which borrowed many concepts (most notably the Graphical User Interface, or GUI) from the Apple operating system.

Development of the PC

The computer revolution created thousands of new, lucrative businesses: computer manufacturers themselves; makers of the tiny silicon chips that ran the computers and allowed smaller and smaller machines to become more and more powerful (most notably Intel); and hardware manufacturers.

The Internet

Out of the computer revolution emerged another dramatic source of information and communication: the Internet. The Internet is, in essence, a vast, geographically far-flung network of computers that allows people connected to the network to communicate with others all over the world. It had its beginning in 1963, in the U.S. government's Advanced Research Projects Agency (ARPA), which funneled federal funds into scientific research projects, many of them defense related. In the early 1960s, J. C. R. Licklider, the head of ARPA's Information Processing Technique Office, was working on a project he called Libraries of the Future, through which he hoped to make vast amounts of information available electronically to people in far-flung areas. In 1963, he launched a program to link together computers over large distances. It was known as the Arpanet. For several years, the Arpanet served mainly as a way for people to make use of what were then relatively scarce computer facilities without having to go to the site of the computer. Gradually, however, both the size and the uses of the network expanded.

Arpanet

This expansion was facilitated in part by two important new technologies. One was a system developed in the early 1960s at the RAND Corporation in the United States and the National Physical Laboratory in England. It was known as "store-and-forward packet switching," and it made possible the transmission of large quantities of data between computers without directly wiring the computers together. The other technological breakthrough was the development of computer software that would allow individual computers to handle the traffic over the network—the Interface Message Processor.

WIRED 6.01 The January 1998 issue of *Wired,* a magazine aimed at young, hip, computer-literate readers, expressed the optimistic, even visionary approach to the possibilities of new electronic technologies that was characteristic of many computer and Internet enthusiasts in the 1990s. *Wired,* which began publication in 1992, was careful to differentiate itself from the slick, commercial computer magazines that were principally interested in trumpeting new products. It tried, instead, to capture the simultaneously skeptical and progressive spirit of a generation to whom technology seemed to define much of the future. *(Designer, John Plunkett; Writer, Louis Rossetto. Copyright © 2002 by the Condé Nast Publications, Inc. All rights reserved.)*

By 1971, twenty-three computers were linked together in the Arpanet, which served mostly research labs and universities. Gradually, interest in the system began to spread, and with it the number of computers connected to it. In the early 1980s, the Defense Department, a major partner in the development of the Arpanet, withdrew from the project for security reasons. The network, soon renamed the Internet, was then free to develop independently. It did so rapidly, especially after the invention of technologies that made possible digital mail (e-mail) and the emergence of the personal computer, which vastly increased the number of potential users of the Internet. As late as 1984, there remained fewer than a thousand host computers connected to the Internet. A decade later, there were over 6 million. And in 2007, over a billion computers were in use around the world, including 250 million in the United States.

As the amount of information on the Internet proliferated, without any central direction, new forms of software emerged to make it possible for individual users to navigate through the vast number of Internet sites. In 1989, World Wide Web Tim Berners-Lee, a British scientist working at a laboratory in Geneva, introduced the World Wide Web, through which individual users could publish information for the Internet, which helped establish an orderly system for both the distribution and retrieval of electronic information.

Access to the Internet, although very widespread, remains unequally distributed. Computers are now commonplace in American homes, but the lower the income level of families, the less likely they are to have computers and Internet access. Similarly, poor schools have much more limited computer and Internet capacity than wealthier ones. This gap in access has come to be known as the "digital divide," a widening gulf between those who have the skills to navigate the new electronic world, skills now essential to all but the least lucrative forms of employment, and those who lack those skills.

Breakthroughs in Genetics

Computer technology helped fuel explosive growth in all areas of scientific research, particularly genetics. Early discoveries in genetics by Gregor Mendel, Thomas Hunt Morgan, and others laid the groundwork for more dramatic breakthroughs—the discovery of DNA by the

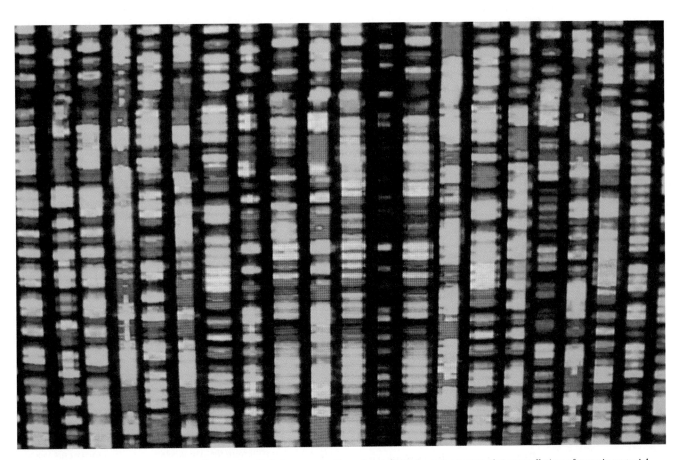

THE HUMAN GENOME This computerized image is a digital representation of part of the human genome, the constellation of genetic material that makes up the human body. The Human Genome Project, one of the most ambitious in the history of science, set out in the late 1990s to chart the human genetic structure. Each color in this image represents one of the four chemical components of DNA, the principal material of genes. *(Mario Tama/Getty Images)*

British scientists Oswald Avery, Colin MacLeod, and Maclyn McCarty in 1944; and in 1953, the dramatic discovery by the American biochemist James Watson and the British biophysicist Francis Crick of its double-helix structure, and thus of the key to identifying genetic codes. From these discoveries emerged the new science—and ultimately the new industry—of genetic engineering, through which new medical treatments and new techniques for hybridization of plants and animals became possible.

Little by little, scientists began to identify specific genes in humans and other living things that determine particular traits, and to learn how to alter or reproduce them. But the identification of genes was painfully slow; and in 1989, the federal government appropriated $3 billion to fund the National Center for the Human Genome,

Human Genome Project

to accelerate the mapping of human genes. The Human Genome Project set out to identify all of the more than 100,000 genes by 2005. But new technologies for research, and competition from other privately funded projects, drove the project forward faster than expected, and it was completed in April 2003.

In the meantime, DNA research had already attracted considerable public attention. The DNA structure of an individual, scientists have discovered, is as unique and as identifiable as a fingerprint. DNA testing, therefore, makes it possible to identify individuals through their blood, semen, skin, or even hair. It played a major role first in the O. J. Simpson trial in 1995 and then in the 1998 investigation into President Clinton's relationship with Monica Lewinsky. Also in 1998, DNA testing appeared to establish with certainty that Thomas Jefferson had fathered a child with his slave Sally Hemings, by finding genetic similarities between descendants of both, thus resolving a political and scholarly dispute stretching back nearly 200 years.

But genetic research is also the source of great controversy. Many people are uneasy about the predictions that the new science might give scientists the ability to alter aspects of life that had previously seemed outside the reach of human control. Some critics fear genetic research on religious grounds, seeing it as an interference with God's plan. Others use moral arguments and express fears that it will allow parents, for example, to choose what kinds of children they will have. And a particularly heated controversy has emerged over the way in which scientists obtained genetic material.

One of the most promising areas of medical research involves the use of stem cells, genetic material obtained in

Moral and Ethical Dilemmas

large part from undeveloped fetuses—mostly fetuses created by couples attempting in vitro fertilization. (In vitro fertilization is the process by which couples unable to conceive a child have a fetus conceived outside the womb using their eggs and sperm and then implanted in the mother.) Anti-abortion advocates denounce stem-cell research, claiming that it exploits (and endangers) unborn children. Supporters of stem-cell research—which shows promising signs of offering cures for Parkinson's disease, Alzheimer's disease, ALS, and other previously uncurable illnesses—argue that the stem cells they use come from fetuses that would otherwise be discarded, since in vitro fertilization always produces many more fetuses than can be used.

The controversy over stem-cell research became an issue in the 2000 campaign. George W. Bush, once he became president, kept his promise to anti-abortion advocates and in the summer of 2001 issued a ruling barring the use of federal funds to support research using any stem cells that scientists were not already using at the time of his decision. Stem-cell research continued, although on a much reduced scale, in institutions whose research was privately funded. Several state governments—among them California and New York—also began to support stem-cell research.

A CHANGING SOCIETY

The American population changed dramatically in the late twentieth and early twenty-first centuries. It grew larger, older, and more racially and ethnically diverse.

A Shifting Population

Decreasing birth rates and growing life spans contributed to one of the most important characteristics of the American population in the early twenty-first century:

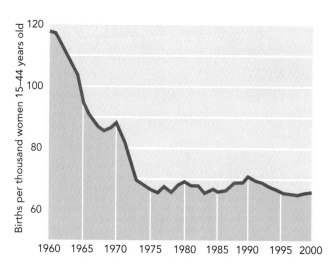

THE AMERICAN BIRTH RATE, 1960–2000 This chart shows the striking change in the pattern of the nation's birth rate from the twenty years after 1940, which produced the great "baby boom." From 1960 onward, the nation's birth rate steadily, and in the 1960s and 1970s dramatically, declined. ◆ *What effect did this declining birth rate have on the age structure of the population?*

its increasing agedness. The enormous "baby boom" generation—people born in the first ten years after World War II—drove the median age steadily upward (from 34 in 1996 to 36 in 2006 to a projected 39 by 2035. This growing population of aging Americans contributed to stresses on the Social Security and Medicare systems. It also had important implications for the work force. In the last twenty years of the twentieth century, the number of people aged 25–54 (known statistically as the prime work force) grew by over 26 million. In the first ten years of the twenty-first century, the number of workers in that age group will not grow at all.

The slowing growth of the native-born population, and the workforce shortages it has helped to create, is one reason for the rapid growth of immigration. In 2006, the number of foreign-born residents of the United States was the highest in American history—more than 35 million people, over 11 percent of the total population. These immigrants came from a wider variety of backgrounds than ever before, as a result of the 1965 Immigration Reform Act, which eliminated national origins as a criterion for admission. The growing presence of the foreign-born contributed to a significant drop in the percentage of white residents in the United States—from 90 percent in 1965 (the year of the Immigration Reform Act) to 78 in 2006. Latinos and Asians were by far the largest groups of immigrants in these years. But others came in significant numbers from Africa, the Middle East, Russia, and eastern Europe.

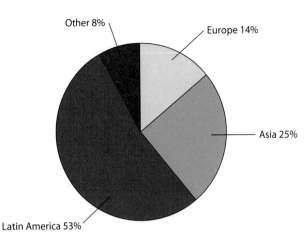

SOURCES OF IMMIGRATION, 1995–2003 The Immigration Reform Act of 1965 lifted the national quotas imposed on immigration policy in 1924 and opened immigration to large areas of the world that had previously been restricted. In 1965, 90 percent of the immigrants to the United States came from Europe. As this chart shows, by 2003 almost the reverse was true. Well over 80 percent of all immigrants came from non-European sources. The most important countries of origin in this period were (in order) Mexico, China, the Philippines, India, Vietnam, and Cuba. ◆ *What impact did this new immigration have on American politics?*

African Americans in the Post–Civil Rights Era

The civil rights movement and the other liberal efforts of the 1960s had two very different effects on African Americans. On the one hand, there were increased opportunities for advancement available to those in a position to take advantage of them. On the other hand, as the industrial economy declined and government services dwindled, there was a growing sense of helplessness and despair among large groups of nonwhites who continued to find themselves barred from upward mobility.

For the black middle class, which by the early twenty-first century constituted over half of the African-American population of America, progress was remarkable in the decades after the high point of the civil rights movement. Disparities between black and white professionals did not vanish, but they diminished substantially. African-American families moved into more affluent urban communities and, in many cases, into suburbs—at times as neighbors of whites, more often into predominantly black communities. The percentage of black high-school graduates going on to college was virtually the same as that of white high-school graduates by the early twenty-first century (although a smaller proportion of blacks than whites managed to complete high school). Just over 17 percent of African Americans over the age of twenty-four held bachelor's degrees or higher in 2005, compared to 29 percent of whites, a significant advance from twenty years earlier. And African Americans were making rapid strides in many professions from which, a

Economic Progress for African Americans

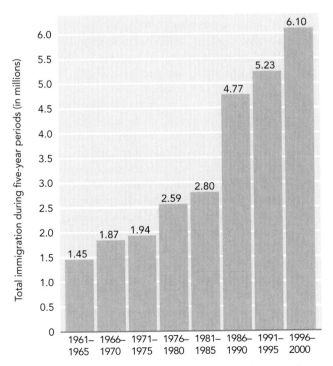

TOTAL IMMIGRATION, 1960–2000 This chart shows the tremendous increase in immigration to the United States in the decades since the Immigration Reform Act of 1965. The immigration of the 1980s and 1990s was the highest since the late nineteenth century. ◆ *What role did the 1965 act have in increasing immigration levels?*

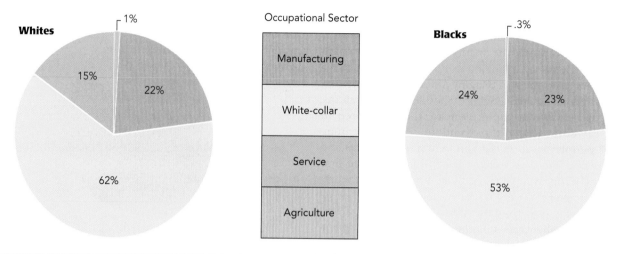

COMPARISON OF BLACK AND WHITE OCCUPATIONAL DISTRIBUTION, 2005 By the early twenty-first century, as this chart makes clear, the African-American middle class had grown dramatically. Over half of all employed black workers in the United States worked in "white-collar" jobs. Perhaps even more striking, given the distribution of the black population a half century earlier, is that almost no African Americans (about one-third of 1 percent) were working in agriculture by the early 2000s. But the gap between black and white workers remained wide in several areas, particularly in the percentage of each group employed in low-wage service jobs. ◆ *What factors contributed to the increase of the black middle class in the years after 1960?*

generation earlier, they had been barred or within which they had been segregated. Over half of all employed blacks in the United States had skilled white-collar jobs in 2005. There were few areas of American life from which blacks were any longer entirely excluded.

But the rise of the black middle class also accentuated (and perhaps even helped cause) the increasingly desperate plight of other African Americans, whom the economic growth and the liberal programs of the 1960s and beyond had never reached. These impoverished people—sometimes described as the "underclass"—made up as much as a third of the nation's black population. Many of them lived in isolated, decaying, and desperately poor inner-city neighborhoods. As more successful blacks moved out of the inner cities, the poor were left virtually alone in their decaying neighborhoods. Less than half of young inner-city blacks finished high school in 2006; more than 60 percent were unemployed. The black family structure suffered as well from the dislocations of urban poverty. There was a radical increase in the number of single-parent, female-headed black households. In 1970, 59 percent of all black children under 18 lived with both their parents (already down from 70 percent a decade earlier). In 2006, only 35 percent of black children lived in such households, while 74 percent of white children did.

Nonwhites were disadvantaged by many factors in the changing social and economic climate of the late twentieth and early twenty-first centuries. Among them was a growing impatience with affirmative action and welfare programs for the poor, as well as a steady decline in the number of unskilled jobs in the economy; the departure

> The "Underclass"

of businesses from their neighborhoods; the absence of adequate transportation to areas where jobs were more plentiful; and failing schools that did not prepare them adequately for employment.

The anger and despair such conditions were creating among inner-city residents became clear in many ways. It was expressed at times artistically, as in some aspects of the most popular new black musical form of the late twentieth century, rap. (See "Patterns of Popular Culture," pp. 908–909.) The anger and frustration became visible even more graphically in the summer of 1992 in Los Angeles. The previous year, a bystander had videotaped several Los Angeles police officers beating an apparently helpless black man, Rodney King, whom they had captured after an auto chase. But an all-white jury in a suburban community just outside Los Angeles acquitted the officers when they were tried for assault. Black residents of South Central Los Angeles, one of the poorest communities in the city, erupted in anger—precipitating the largest single racial disturbance of the twentieth century. There was widespread looting and arson. More than fifty people died.

> Rodney King

What Americans had long called "race relations" grew increasingly sour in these difficult years. Nowhere was this mutual suspicion more evident than in the celebrated trial of the former football star O. J. Simpson, who was accused of murdering his former wife and a young man in Los Angeles in 1994. The long and costly "O. J. trial" was an enormous media sensation for over a year. Throughout the proceedings, opinions about Simpson's guilt broke down strikingly along racial lines. Simpson's acquittal in

> O. J. Simpson Trial

"IGNORANCE = FEAR" The artist Keith Haring (whose work was inspired in large part by urban graffiti) created this striking poster in 1989, the year before he himself died of AIDS, to generate support for the battle against the disease. "ACT UP," the organization that distributed it, was among the most militant groups in demanding more rapid efforts to search for a cure. (*© The Estate of Keith Haring*)

the fall of 1995, after a trial in which the defense tried to portray him as a victim of police racism, caused celebrations in many black communities and a quiet disgust among many whites.

Modern Plagues: Drugs and AIDS

Two new and deadly epidemics ravaged many American communities beginning in the 1980s. One was a dramatic increase in drug use, which penetrated nearly every community in the nation. The enormous demand for drugs, and particularly for "crack" cocaine in the late 1980s and early 1990s, spawned what was in effect a multibillion-dollar industry. Drug use declined significantly among middle-class people beginning in the late 1980s, but the epidemic declined much more slowly in the poor urban neighborhoods where it was doing the most severe damage.

The drug epidemic was related to another scourge of the late twentieth century: the epidemic spread of a new and lethal disease first documented in 1981 and soon named AIDS (acquired immune deficiency syndrome). AIDS Epidemic AIDS is the product of the HIV virus, which is transmitted by the exchange of bodily fluids (blood or semen). The virus gradually destroys the body's immune system and makes its victims highly vulnerable to a number of diseases (particularly to various forms of cancer and pneumonia) to which they would otherwise have a natural resistance. Those infected with the virus (i.e., HIV positive) can live for a long time without developing AIDS, but for many years those who became ill were certain to die. The first American victims of AIDS (and for many years the group among whom cases remained the most numerous) were homosexual men. But by the late 1980s, as the gay community began to take preventive measures, the most rapid increase in the spread of the disease occurred among heterosexuals, many of them intravenous drug users, who spread the virus by sharing contaminated hypodermic needles.

In 2005, there were an estimated 434,000 Americans living with the AIDS virus. But the United States represented only a tiny proportion of the worldwide total of people afflicted with HIV, an estimated 39.5 million people in 2006. Over two-thirds (approximately 25 million) of those cases were concentrated in Africa. Governments and private groups, in the meantime, began promoting AIDS awareness in increasingly visible and graphic ways—urging young people, in particular, to avoid "unsafe sex" through abstinence or the use of latex condoms. The success of that effort in the United States was suggested by the drop in new cases from 70,000 in 1995 to approximately 44,000 in 2005.

RAP

For many generations, much of American popular music has been the product of musical forms created by African Americans: gospel, ragtime, jazz, rhythm and blues, rock, soul, disco, funk, and—in the 1980s and 1990s—rap. Conservative guardians of American culture have repeatedly denounced these new forms of music as subversive, excessively sexual, violent, dangerous. But the music has always survived the attacks.

Rap's musical lineage is a long and complicated one. It has elements of the disco and street funk of the 1970s; of the fast-talking jive of black radio DJs in the 1950s; of the on-stage patter of Cab Calloway and other African-American stars of the first half of the twentieth century. Hence, it contains reminders of tap and break dancing—even of the boxing-ring poetry of Muhammad Ali.

Rap's most important element is its words. It is as much a form of language as a form of music. It bears a distant resemblance to some traditions of African-American pulpit oratory, which also included forms of spoken song. It draws from some of the verbal traditions of urban black street life, including the "dozens"—a ritualized trading of insults particularly popular among young black men.

But rap is also the product of a distinctive place and time: the South Bronx in the 1970s and 1980s and the hip hop culture that was born there and that soon dominated the appearance and public behavior of many young black males. "Hip hop is how you walk, talk, live, see, act, feel," one Bronx hip hopper described it. It created many of the patterns of dress and behavior that became common among inner-city youths: the popularity of athletic clothes, hats, and shoes; the practice of young men giving themselves "street names"; and—in the 1980s at least—graffiti and break dancing. In the 1990s, break dancing lost its popularity, clothes became baggier, hats became larger, and the most popular element of hip hop culture was rap, which had by then been developing for nearly twenty years.

Beginning in the early 1970s, Bronx DJs began setting up their equipment on neighborhood streets and staging block parties, where they not only played records but also put on shows of their own—performances that featured spoken rhymes, jazzy phrases, and pointed comments about the audience, the neighborhood, and themselves. Gradually, the DJs began to bring "rappers" into shows—young men who took the DJ style and developed it into a much more elaborate form of performance, usually accompanied by dancing. As rap grew more popular in the inner city, record promoters began signing some of its new stars. In 1979, the Sugarhill Gang's "Rapper's Delight" became the first rap single to be played on mainstream commercial radio and the first to become a major hit. In the early 1980s, Run-DMC became the first national rap superstars. From there, rap moved quickly to become one of the most popular and commercially successful forms of popular music. In the 1990s and 2000s, rap recordings routinely sold millions of copies.

Rap has taken many forms. There have been white rappers (Eminem, House of Pain), female rappers (Missy Elliot, Queen Latifah), even religious rappers and children's rappers. But it has always been primarily a product of the young male culture of the inner city, and some of the most successful rap has conveyed the frustration and anger that these men have felt about their lives—"a voice for the oppressed people," one rap artist said, "that in many other ways don't have a voice." In 1982, the rap group Grandmaster Flash and the Furious Five released a rap called "The Message,"* a searing description of ghetto culture:

> Got a bum education, double-digit inflation

*Edward Fletcher, M. Glover, and S. Robinson, "The Message," recorded 1982 by Grand Master Flash & The Furious Five. Reprinted by permission of Sugar Hill Music Publishing Ltd.

In the mid-1990s, AIDS researchers, after years of frustration, began discovering effective treatments for the disease. By taking a combination of powerful drugs on a rigorous schedule, among them a group known as protease inhibitors, even people with advanced cases of AIDS experienced dramatic improvement—so much so that in many cases there were no measurable quantities of the virus left in their bloodstreams. The new drugs gave promise for the first time of dramatically extending the lives of people with AIDS, perhaps to normal life spans. The drugs were not a cure for AIDS; people who stopped taking them experienced a rapid return of the disease. And the effectiveness of the drugs varied from person to person. In addition, the drugs were very expensive and difficult to administer; poorer AIDS patients often could not obtain access to them, and the drugs remained very scarce in Africa and other less affluent parts of the world where the epidemic was rampant. The United Nations, many philanthropic organizations, and a number of governments, including the United States, committed significant funds to fight the AIDS crisis in Africa in the 2000s, but progress remained slow.

A CONTESTED CULTURE

Few things created more controversy and anxiety in the 1980s and 1990s than the battles over the character of American culture. That culture had changed dramatically in many ways since World War II. It had seen a profound

RUN DMC The group Run DMC, shown here in concert, was one of rap music's first superstars. They released their first album in 1983 and remained popular fifteen years later, although by then—given the short life span of most groups—they were, by their own admission, senior citizens on the rap circuit. At a concert in New York in 1997, they asked the audience to "put your hands in the air if you love old-school." A critic from *Rolling Stone* wrote that "from the crowd's ecstatic reaction," the answer was clearly yes. *(© Lisa Leone)*

Can't take the train to the job, there's a strike at the station

Don't push me, 'cause I'm close to the edge

I'm tryin' not to lose me head

It's like a jungle sometime it makes me wonder

How I keep from going under.

Similar songs by other artists came to be known as "message rap." In the late 1980s, the Compton and Watts neighborhoods of Los Angeles—two of the most distressed minority communities in the city—produced their own style, known as West Coast rap, with such groups as Ice Cube, Ice T, Tupac Shakur, and Snoop Doggy Dog. Even more than the New York version, West Coast rap often had a harsh, angry character. At its extremes (the so-called gangsta' rap), it could be strikingly violent and highly provocative. Scandals erupted again and again over controversial lyrics—Ice T's "Cop Killer," which some critics believed advocated murdering police; the sexually explicit lyrics of 2 Live Crew and other groups, which critics accused of advocating violence against women.

But it was not just the lyrics that caused the furor. Rap artists were almost all products of tough inner-city neighborhoods, and the rough-edged styles many took with them into the public eye made many people uncomfortable. Some rappers found themselves caught up in highly publicized trouble with the law. Several—including two of rap's biggest stars, Tupac Shakur and Notorious B.I.G.—were murdered. The business of rap, and particularly the confrontational business style of Death Row Records (founded by Dr. Dre, a veteran of the first major West Coast rap group NWA), was a source of public controversy as well.

These controversies at times unfairly dominated the image of rap as a whole in national culture. Some rap is angry and cruel, as are many of the realities of the world from which it comes. But much of it is explicitly positive, some of it deliberately gentle. Chuck D and other successful rappers use their music to exhort young black men to avoid drugs and crime, to take responsibility for their children, to get an education. And the form, if not the content, of the original rappers has spread widely through American culture. Rap has come to dominate the music charts in America, and its styles have made their way onto *Sesame Street* and other children's shows, into television commercials, Hollywood films, and the everyday language of millions of people, young and old, black and white. It has become another of the arresting, innovative African-American musical traditions that have shaped American culture for more than a century.

redefinition of the roles of women. It had produced a mobilization of many minorities and an at least partial inclusion of them into mainstream culture. It had experienced a sexual revolution. It had become much more explicit in its depiction of sex, violence, and dissent. American culture was more diverse, more open, less restrained, and more contentious than it had been in the past. As a result, new controversies and new issues emerged.

Battles over Feminism and Abortion

Among the principal goals of the New Right as it became more powerful and assertive in the late twentieth century, and as it focused on cultural changes it did not like, was to challenge feminism and its achievements. Leaders of the New Right had campaigned successfully against the proposed Equal Rights Amendment to the Constitution. And they played a central role in the most divisive issue of the late 1980s and 1990s: the controversy over abortion rights.

For those who favored allowing women to choose to terminate unwanted pregnancies, the Supreme Court's decision in *Roe* v. *Wade* (1973) had seemed to settle the question. By the 1980s, abortion was the most commonly performed surgical procedure in the country. But at the same time, opposition to abortion was creating a powerful grassroots movement. The right-to-life movement, as it called itself, found its most fervent supporters

"Right-to-Life" Movement

among Catholics; and indeed, the Catholic Church itself lent its institutional authority to the battle against legalized abortion. Religious doctrine also motivated the anti-abortion stance of Mormons, fundamentalist Christians, and other groups. The opposition of some other anti-abortion activists had less to do with religion than with their commitment to traditional notions of family and gender relations. To them, abortion was a particularly offensive part of a much larger assault by feminists on the role of women as wives and mothers. It was also, many foes contended, a form of murder. Fetuses, they claimed, were human beings who had a "right to life" from the moment of conception.

Although the right-to-life movement was persistent in its demand for a reversal of *Roe* v. *Wade* or, barring that, a constitutional amendment banning abortion, it also attacked abortion in more limited ways, at its most vulnerable points. Starting in the 1970s, Congress and many state legislatures began barring the use of public funds to pay for abortions, thus making them almost inaccessible for many poor women. The Reagan and the two Bush administrations imposed further restrictions on federal funding and even on the right of doctors in federally funded clinics to give patients any information on abortion. Extremists in the right-to-life movement began picketing, occupying, and at times bombing abortion clinics. Several anti-abortion activists murdered doctors who performed abortions; other physicians were subject to campaigns of terrorism and harassment. The changing composition of the Supreme Court between 1981 and 2008 (during which time new conservative justices were appointed to the Court) renewed the right-to-life movement's hopes for a reversal of *Roe* v. *Wade*.

The changing judicial climate of the late twentieth and early twenty-first centuries mobilized defenders of abortion as never before. They called themselves the "pro-choice" movement, because they were defending not so much abortion itself as every woman's right to choose whether and when to bear a child. It soon became clear that the pro-choice movement was in many parts of the country at least as strong as, and in some areas much stronger than, the right-to-life movement. With the election of President Clinton in 1992, a supporter of "choice," the immediate threat to *Roe* v. *Wade* seemed to fade. Clinton's reelection in 1996 was, among other things, evidence that the pro-choice movement maintained considerable political strength. But abortion rights remained highly vulnerable. And Clinton's successor, George W. Bush, openly opposed abortion.

> "Pro-Choice" Movement

The Growth of Environmentalism

The environmental movement, which had grown so dramatically in the late 1960s and early 1970s, continued to expand in the 1980s, 1990s, and 2000s. In the decades after the first Earth Day, environmental issues gained increasing attention and support. Although the federal government displayed only intermittent interest in the subject, environmentalists won a series of significant battles, mostly at the local level. They blocked the construction of roads, airports, and other projects that they claimed would be ecologically dangerous, taking advantage of new legislations protecting endangered species and environmentally fragile regions.

> Environmental Activism

In the late 1980s, the environmental movement began to mobilize around a new and ominous challenge, which

MARCH FOR WOMEN'S LIVES This large rally, which began with a march by thousands of women (and some men) down Pennsylvania Avenue in Washington, occurred in April 2004, several months before the presidential election and was meant to demonstrate support for abortion rights in a city whose political institutions were dominated by leaders opposed to abortion. Pro-choice advocates feared that a Bush victory would lead to new appointments to the Supreme Court that would put the 1973 *Roe* v. *Wade*, which legalized abortion, in jeopardy. *(Ron Sachs/Cordis)*

WOMEN'S HISTORY

The rise of women's history in recent decades has produced many debates among historians. But its most important impact has been to challenge scholars to look at the past through a new lens. Historians had long been accustomed to considering the influence of ideas, of economic interests, and of race and ethnicity on the course of history. Women's history challenged them to consider as well the role of gender. Throughout history, many scholars now argue, societies have created distinctive roles for men and women. How those roles have been defined, and the ways in which the roles affect how people and cultures behave, should be central to our understanding of both the past and the present.

Women's history was not new to the 1960s. Just as women had been challenging traditional gender roles long before the 1960s, so too have women (and some men) been writing women's history for many years. In the nineteenth century, such scholarship generally stressed the unrecognized contributions of women to history— for example, Sarah Hale's 1853 *Record of All Distinguished Women from "the Beginning" till A.D. 1850.* Work of the same sort continued into the twentieth century and, indeed, continues today.

But after 1900, people committed to progressive reform movements began to produce a different kind of women's scholarship, in many ways more sociological than historical. It revealed, above all, ways in which women were victimized by a harsh new system of industrialism. In the process, it attempted to raise popular support for reform. Feminist scholars such as Edith Abbott, Margaret Byington, and Katherine Anthony examined the impact of economic change on working-class families, with a special focus on women; and they looked at the often terrible conditions in which women worked in factories, mills, and other people's homes. Their goal was less to celebrate women's contributions than to direct attention to the oppression of women by a harsh capitalist system and arouse sentiment for reform.

Feminism receded from prominence after the victory of the suffrage movement in 1920, and women's history entered a half-century of relative inactivity as well. Women continued to write important histories in many fields, and some—for example, Eleanor Flexner, whose *Century of Struggle* (1959) became a classic history of the suffrage crusade—wrote explicitly about women. Mary Beard, best known for her sweeping historical narratives written in collaboration with her husband, Charles Beard, published a book of her own in 1964, *Women as a Force in History,* in which she argued for the historical importance of ordinary women as shapers of society. But such work at first had little impact on the writing of history as a whole.

As modern feminism began to sweep across society in the 1960s and 1970s, interest in women's history revived as well. Gerda Lerner, one of the pioneers of the new women's history, once wrote of the impact of feminism on historical studies: "The recognition that we had been denied our history came to many of us as a staggering insight, which altered our consciousness irretrievably." For a time, the new women's history repeated the pattern of earlier studies of women. Much of the early work was in the "contributionist" tradition, stressing the way in which women had played more notable roles in major historical events than men had usually acknowledged. Other work stressed ways in which women had been victimized by their subordination to men and by their powerlessness within the industrial economy.

Increasingly, however, women's history began to question the nature of gender itself. Some scholars began to emphasize the artificiality of gender distinctions. The difference between women and men, they argued, was socially constructed. It was also superficial and (in the public world, at least) unimportant. The history of women was, therefore, the history of how men (with the unwitting help of many women) had created and maintained a set of fictions about women's capacities that modern women were now attempting to shatter.

By the early 1980s, some feminists had begun to make a very different argument: that there were basic differences between women and men—not just biological differences, but differences in values, sensibilities, and culture. This, of course, was what most men and many women had believed for decades (indeed centuries) before the feminist revolution. But the feminists of the 1970s and 1980s did not see these differences as evidence of women's incapacities. They saw them, rather, as evidence of an alternative female culture capable of challenging (and improving) the male-dominated world. Some historians of women, therefore, began exploring areas of female experience that revealed the special character of women's culture and values: family, housework, motherhood, women's clubs and organizations, female literature, the social lives of working-class women, women's sexuality, and many other subjects that suggested "difference" more than "contributions" or "victimization." Partly in response, some historians began to make the same argument about men— that understanding "masculinity" and its role in shaping men's lives was as important as understanding notions of "femininity" in explaining the history of women.

The notion of gender as a source of social and cultural difference was responsible for the most powerful challenge women's history has raised to the way in which scholars view the past. It is not enough simply to expand the existing story to make room for women, Joan Scott, one of the most influential theorists of gender studies, has written. Feminist history is, rather, a way of reconceptualizing the past by accepting that notions of gender have been a central force in the lives of societies.

Many historians continue to believe that other categories (race and class in particular) have in fact been more important in shaping the lives of men and women than has gender. But even those who do so are increasingly willing to accept the argument of women's historians: that understanding concepts of gender is an essential part of understanding women's (and men's) lives.

GREENPEACE IN TEXAS Activists from the environmental movement Greenpeace climbed the water tower in Crawford, Texas, the site of President Bush's ranch, and hung this banner attacking his environmental policies in April 2001. At the time, the Bush administration was advocating opening the Arctic National Wildlife Refuge in Alaska to oil drilling and was rejecting the Kyoto Accords, negotiated before the 2000 election, which sought to obligate nations to cooperate in fighting global warming. *(Getty Images)*

became known as "global warming"—a steady rise in the earth's temperature as a result of emissions from the burning of fossil fuels (most notably coal and oil). Although considerable controversy continued for years over the pace, and even the reality, of global warming, by the early twenty-first century a broad consensus was growing around the issue—thanks in part to the efforts of significant public figures such as former vice president Al Gore, who won a Nobel Peace Prize for his efforts, to draw attention to the problem. In 1997, representatives of the major industrial nations met in Kyoto, Japan, and agreed to a broad treaty establishing steps toward reducing carbon emissions and thus slowing or reversing global warming. Opposition to the treaty from Republicans in Congress prevented President Clinton from winning ratification of the treaty. In March 2001, President George W. Bush denounced the treaty for placing too great a burden on the United States and withdrew it from consideration.

The rising popularity of environmental issues reflected an important shift both in the character of the American left and in the tone of American public life generally. Through much of the first half of the twentieth century, American politics had been preoccupied with debates over economic power and disparities of wealth. In the late twentieth and early twenty-first centuries, even though inequality in the distribution of wealth and power was reaching unprecedented levels, such debates had largely ceased. There were, of course, economic implications to environmentalism and other no-growth efforts. But what drove such movements was less a concern about class than a concern about the quality of individual and community life.

Shift away from Class Politics

The Fragmentation of Mass Culture

One of the most powerful cultural trends throughout much of the twentieth century was the growing power and the increasing standardization of mass culture. The institutions of the media—news, entertainment, advertising, and others—grew steadily more powerful. Almost without exception, they also strove to attract the largest possible audience or market. In doing so, they attempted to standardize their products so that they would be familiar and accessible to everyone. This standardization began with mass merchandising in the late nineteenth century; it accelerated in the early twentieth century with the rise of Hollywood movies, national radio networks, and powerful, mass-circulation magazines; it became dramatically more important in the 1950s, with the rise of network television.

Beginning in the 1970s, and accelerating in the 1980s, 1990s, and 2000s, the character of mass culture changed in important ways. There was, of course, continued standardization in many areas. McDonald's, Burger King, and other fast-food chains became the most widely known restaurants in America (and indeed the world). Huge retail chains—Kmart, Wal-Mart, Barnes & Noble, Blockbuster, the Gap, and others—dominated retail sales in many communities. The most popular Hollywood films attracted larger audiences than ever before; and the most powerful media companies produced merchandise that made their film and television characters familiar to almost everyone in the world. But there was also a very different trend at work at the same time: a tendency in both retailing and entertainment to appeal less to mass markets and more to specific segments of the market.

This segmentation was first visible in new ideas about advertising that became powerful in the 1970s, ideas known as "targeting." Instead of finding promotional techniques

Target Marketing

to appeal to everyone, advertisers sought to identify a product with a particular "segment" of the market (men, women, young people, old people, health-conscious people, the rich, people of modest means, children) and create advertisements designed to appeal to it. As if in response, the television networks began to produce programming that focused on particular segments of the audience. Some programs were aimed at women, some at African Americans, some at affluent, urban, middle-class viewers, some at rural and provincial people.

Even more important was the rapid proliferation of media outlets. As late as the 1970s, American television audiences overwhelmingly watched programs on the three major networks: NBC, CBS, and ABC. In the 1980s, that began to change. One reason was the growth of videocassette recorders and, later, digital video discs, which made it easier for viewers to choose their own programming. Another reason was the increasing availability of cable and satellite television, which allowed homes to receive many more channels than ever before. And many people turned away from television and began to explore the powerful new medium of the Internet, with its huge variety of sites tailored to almost every interest and taste.

THE PERILS OF GLOBALIZATION

The celebration of the beginning of a new millennium on January 1, 2000, was a notable moment not just because of the change in the calendar. It was notable above all as a global event—a shared and for the most part joyous experience that united the world in its exuberance. But if the millennium celebrations suggested the bright promise of globalization, other events at the dawn of the new century suggested its dark perils.

Opposing the "New World Order"

In the United States and other industrial nations, opposition to globalization—or to what President George H. W. Bush once called "the new world order"—took several forms. To many Americans on both the left and the right, the nation's increasingly interventionist foreign policy was deeply troubling. Critics on the left charged that the United States was using military action to advance its economic interests, in the 1991 Gulf War and, above all, in the Iraq War that began in 2003. Critics on the right claimed that the nation was allowing itself to be swayed by the interests of other nations—as in the humanitarian interventions in Somalia in 1993 and the Balkans in the late 1990s—and was ceding its sovereignty to international organizations.

> Critics of Intervention

But the most impassioned opposition to globalization in the West came from an array of groups that challenged the claim that the "new world order" was economically beneficial. Labor unions insisted that the rapid expansion of free-trade agreements led to the export of jobs from advanced nations to less developed ones. Other groups attacked working conditions in new manufacturing countries on humanitarian grounds, arguing that the global economy was creating new classes of "slave laborers" working in conditions that few Western nations would tolerate. Environmentalists argued that globalization, in exporting industry to low-wage countries, also exported industrial pollution

PROTESTS IN SEATTLE, 1999 When the World Trade Organization held its annual meeting in Seattle, Washington, in late 1999, thousands of demonstrators crowded into the city to protest the WTO's role in the globalization of the economy and, they believed, the exploitation of working people in the United States and around the world. Their rowdy and at times violent demonstrations postponed the opening of the conference. In this photograph, a protester faces Seattle police in a cloud of tear gas, waiting to be arrested. Similar demonstrations disrupted other meetings of global economic organizations over the next several years, including protests in Washington and Genoa, Italy. *(Reuters NewMedia Inc./Corbis)*

and toxic waste into nations that had no effective laws to control them, and contributed significantly to global warming. And still others opposed global economic arrangements on the grounds that they enriched and empowered large multinational corporations and threatened the freedom and autonomy of individuals and communities.

The varied opponents of globalization were agreed on the targets of their discontent: not just free-trade agreements, but also the multinational institutions that policed and advanced the global economy. Among them were the World Trade Organization, which monitored the enforcement of the GATT treaties of the 1990s; the International Monetary Fund, which controlled international credit and exchange rates; and the World Bank, which made money available for development projects in many countries. In November 1999, when the leaders of the seven leading industrial nations (and the leader of Russia) gathered for their annual meeting in Seattle, Washington, tens of thousands of protesters—most of them peaceful, but some of them violent—clashed with police, smashed store windows, and all but paralyzed the city. A few months later, a smaller but still substantial demonstration disrupted meetings of the IMF and the World Bank in Washington. And in July 2001, at a meeting of the same leaders in Genoa, Italy, an estimated 50,000 demonstrators clashed violently with police in a melee that left one protester dead and several hundred injured. The participants in the meeting responded to the demonstrations by pledging $1.2 billion to fight the AIDS epidemic in developing countries, and also by deciding to hold future meetings in remote locations far from major cities.

Globalization Protested

Defending Orthodoxy

Outside the industrialized West, the impact of globalization created other concerns. Many citizens of nonindustrialized nations resented the way the world economy had left them in poverty and, in their view, exploited and oppressed. In some parts of the nonindustrialized world—particularly in some of the Islamic nations of the Middle East—the increasing reach of globalization created additional grievances, rooted not just in economics but also in religion and culture.

The Iranian Revolution of 1979, in which orthodox Muslims ousted a despotic government whose leaders had embraced many aspects of modern Western culture, was one of the first large and visible manifestations of a phenomenon that would eventually reach across much of the Islamic world and threaten the stability of the globe. In one Islamic nation after another, waves of fundamentalist orthodoxy emerged to defend traditional culture against incursions from the West.

Rise of Islamic Fundamentalism

One product of these resentments was a growing resort to violence as a way to fight the influence of the West. Militants used isolated incidents of violence and mayhem, designed to disrupt societies and governments and to create fear among their peoples. Such tactics are known to the world as terrorism.

The Rise of Terrorism

The term "terrorism" was used first during the French Revolution in the 1790s to describe the actions of the radical Jacobins against the French government. It continued to be used intermittently throughout the nineteenth and early twentieth centuries to describe the use of violence as a form of intimidation against peoples and governments. But the widespread understanding of terrorism as an important fact of modern life is largely a product of the end of the twentieth century and the beginning of the twenty-first.

Origins of Terrorism

Acts of what we have come to call terrorism have occurred in many parts of the world. Irish revolutionaries engaged in terrorism regularly against the English through much of the twentieth century. Jews used it in Palestine against the British before the creation of Israel, and Palestinians have used it frequently against Jews in Israel—particularly in the past several decades. Revolutionary groups in Italy, Germany, Japan, and France have engaged in terrorist acts intermittently over the past several decades.

The United States, too, has experienced terrorism for many years, much of it against American targets abroad. These included the bombing of the Marine barracks in Beirut in 1983, the explosion that brought down an American airliner over Lockerbie, Scotland, in 1988, the bombing of American embassies in 1998, the assault on the U.S. naval vessel *Cole* in 2000, and other events around the world. Terrorist incidents were relatively rare, but not unknown, within the United States itself prior to September 11, 2001. Militants on the American left performed various acts of terror in the 1960s and early 1970s. In February 1993, a bomb exploded in the parking garage of the World Trade Center in New York killing six people and causing serious, but not irreparable, structural damage to the towers. Several men connected with militant Islamic organizations were convicted of the crime. In April 1995, a van containing explosives blew up in front of a federal building in Oklahoma City, killing 168 people. Timothy McVeigh, a former Marine who had become part of a militant antigovernment movement of the American right, was convicted of the crime and eventually executed in 2001.

Most Americans, however, considered terrorism a problem that mainly plagued other nations. One of the many results of the terrible events of September 11, 2001, was to jolt the American people out of complacency and alert them to the presence of continuing danger. That awareness increased in the years following September 11. New security measures changed the way in which Americans traveled. New government regulations altered

SEPTEMBER 11, 2001 One great American symbol, the Statue of Liberty, stands against a sky filled with the thick smoke from the destruction of another American symbol, New York City's World Trade Center towers, a few hours after terrorists crashed two planes into them. *(Daniel Hulshizer/AP/Wide World Photos)*

immigration policies and affected the character of international banking. Warnings of possible new terrorist attacks created widespread tension and uneasiness.

The War on Terrorism

In the aftermath of September 2001, the United States government launched what President Bush called a "war against terrorism." The attacks on the World Trade Center and the Pentagon, government intelligence indicated, had been planned and orchestrated by Middle Eastern agents of a powerful terrorist network known as Al Qaeda. Its leader, Osama Bin Laden—until 2001 little known outside the Arab world—quickly became one of the most notorious figures in the world. Convinced that the militant "Taliban" government of Afghanistan had sheltered and supported Bin Laden and his organization, the United States began a sustained campaign of bombing against the regime and sent in ground troops to help a resistance organization overthrow the Afghan government. Afghanistan's Taliban regime quickly collapsed, and its leaders—along with the

Al Qaeda fighters allied with them—fled the capital, Kabul. American and anti-Taliban Afghan troops pursued them into the mountains, but failed to capture Bin Laden and the other leaders of his organization.

American forces in Afghanistan rounded up several hundred people suspected of connections to the Taliban and Al Qaeda in the aftermath of the fighting and eventually moved these prisoners to a facility at the American base in Guantanamo, Cuba. They were among the first suspected terrorists to be handled under the new and more draconian standards established by the federal government in dealing with terrorism after September 11, 2001. Held for months, and in many cases years, without access to lawyers, without facing formal charges, subjected to intensive interrogation and torture, they became examples to many critics of the dangers to basic civil liberties they believed the war on terror had created. Similar criticisms were directed at the Justice Department and the FBI for their roundup of hundreds of people within the United States, most of them of Middle Eastern descent, on suspicion of terrorism. These suspects too were held for many weeks and months without access to counsel or

Al Qaeda

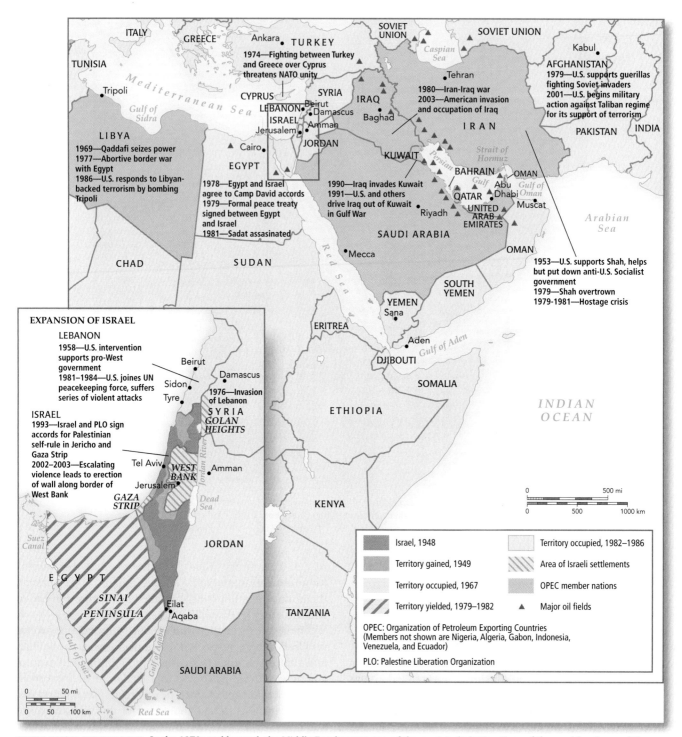

CRISES IN THE MIDDLE EAST In the 1970s and beyond, the Middle East became one of the most turbulent regions of the world and one of the regions most vital to, and difficult for, the United States. The United States intervened in the Middle East frequently during the Cold War and beyond, in ways both large and small, as this map reveals. After the events of September 2001, those interventions increased. ◆ *Why did the United States have so much at stake in the Middle East?*

ability to communicate with their families. Only one such suspect was ever charged with a crime.

Several Supreme Court rulings, including one in 2008, dismissed the Bush administration's argument that detainees in Guantanamo were outside the reach of American law. But the administration was slow to comply.

The Iraq War

In his State of the Union Address to Congress in January 2002, President Bush spoke of an "axis of evil," which included the nations of Iraq, Iran, and North Korea—all nations with anti-American regimes, all nations that either possessed or were thought to be trying to acquire nuclear weapons. Although Bush did not say so at the time, many people around the world interpreted these words to mean that the United States would soon try to topple the government of Saddam Hussein in Iraq.

For over a year after that, the Bush administration slowly built a public case for invading Iraq. Much of that case rested on two claims. One was that Iraq was supporting terrorist groups that were hostile to the United States. The other, and eventually the more important, was that Iraq either had or was developing what came to be known as "weapons of mass destruction," which included nuclear weapons and agents of chemical and biological warfare. Less central to these arguments, at least in the United States, was the charge that the Hussein government was responsible for major violations of human rights. Except for the last, none of these claims turned out to be accurate.

In March 2003, American and British troops, with only scant support from other countries and only partial authorization from the United Nations, invaded Iraq and quickly toppled the Hussein regime. Hussein himself went into hiding but was eventually captured in December 2003. In May 2003, shortly after the American capture of Baghdad, President Bush made a dramatic appearance on an aircraft carrier off the coast of California, where, standing in front of a large sign reading "Mission Accomplished," he declared victory in the Iraq War.

In the months following this event, events in Iraq persuaded many people that the president's claim had been premature. Of the more than 4,000 American soldiers killed in Iraq as of mid-2008, 3,600 of them died after the "Mission Accomplished" speech. And despite significant efforts by the United States and its coalition allies to hand over authority to an Iraqi government and to restore order to the country, insurgents continued to disrupt the recovery with persistent attacks and terrorist actions throughout the fragile nation.

Support for the war in the United States steadily declined in the years after the first claim of victory. The failure of the invaders to find evidence of the "weapons of mass destruction" that the president had so energetically claimed was one blow to the war's credibility. Another blow came from reports of the torture and humiliation of Iraqi prisoners by American soldiers at the Abu Ghraib prison in Baghdad and other sites in Iraq.

The invasion of Iraq was the most visible evidence of a basic change in the structure of American foreign policy

FIGHTING AND REMEMBERING An American B-52 pilot prepares for a night bombing mission in Afghanistan in November 2001, his plane carrying a symbol of the events that precipitated the conflict. *(Department of Defense Visual Information Center/US Air Force Photo by SSgt Larry A. Simmons)*

"MISSION ACCOMPLISHED," 2003   President George W. Bush chose the USS *Abraham Lincoln,* an aircraft carrier moored just off the coast of San Diego, for his first major address after the end of formal hostilities in the Iraq War on May 1, 2003. To strengthen his own identification with the military, he flew in on an S-3 Viking that landed on the carrier's deck and appeared before cameras wearing a flight suit and carrying a helmet. Later, dressed in a conventional business suit, he addressed a crowd of service men and women on the deck, standing beneath a large banner reading "Mission Accomplished." Later, as fighting in Iraq continued with no clear end in sight, and as the war became increasingly unpopular, Bush received much criticism and ridicule for what many Americans considered a premature celebration of victory. *(Reuters/Corbis)*

under the presidency of George W. Bush. Ever since the late 1940s, when the containment policy became the cornerstone of America's role in the world, the United States had worked to maintain stability in the world by containing, but not often directly threatening or attacking, its adversaries. Even after the Cold War ended, the United States continued to demonstrate a reasonable level of constraint, despite its now unchallenged military preeminence. In the administrations of George H. W. Bush and Bill Clinton, for example, American leaders worked closely with the United Nations and NATO to achieve

U.S. international goals and resisted taking unilateral military action.

There had always been those who criticized these constraints. They believed that America should do more than maintain stability, and should move actively to topple undemocratic regimes and destroy potential enemies of the United States. In the administration of George W. Bush, these critics took control of American foreign policy and began to reshape it. The legacy of containment was almost entirely repudiated. Instead, the public stance of the American government was that the United States had the right and the responsibility to spread freedom throughout the world—not just by exhortation and example, but also, when necessary, by military force. In Latvia in May 2005, President Bush spoke of the decision at the end of World War II not to challenge Soviet domination of Eastern Europe, a decision that had rested on the belief that such a challenge would lead the United States into another war. The controversial agreement negotiated at Yalta in 1945 by Roosevelt, Churchill, and Stalin, which failed to end the Soviet occupation of Poland and other Eastern European nations, was, the president said, part of an "unjust tradition" by which powerful governments sacrificed the interests of small nations. "This attempt to sacrifice freedom for the sake of stability," the president continued, "left a continent divided and unstable." The lesson, Bush suggested, was that the United States and other great powers should value stability less and freedom more, and should be willing to take greater risks in the world to end tyranny and oppression.

The Decline of the Bush Presidency

For most of the first three years of his presidency, George W. Bush enjoyed broad popularity. Although his domestic policies never had large public support, Bush was revered by many Americans because of his resolute stance against terrorism. Even the controversial Iraq War helped sustain his popularity for a time in ways that wars almost always draw support to a president during crises.

Bush's domestic policies did little to strengthen him politically. The massive tax cuts of 2001 went disproportionately to very wealthy Americans, reflecting the view of White House economists that the best way to ensure growth was to put money into the hands of people most likely to invest. Other than the tax cuts, Bush's major accomplishment was an education reform bill, known as "No Child Left Behind," which tied federal funding in schools to the success of students in taking standardized tests. Seven years after its passage, there was no significant evidence that the bill had markedly improved student performance. Still other proposals—an effort to privatize some aspects of the Social Security system, for example—never attracted significant support in Congress. Even before the Democrats regained control of the Congress in 2006, Bush found himself unable to make progress on any significant legislation. As a result, the Bush administration began to make much greater use of executive orders—laws and policies that did not require congressional approval—to achieve its goals, especially in the conduct of the "war on terror."

By 2004, when the president faced reelection, his popularity was already in decline, and it seemed by no means certain that he would be reelected. The Democrats rallied behind Senator John Kerry of Massachusetts, a Vietnam veteran with many years of experience in government. Kerry strongly opposed the war in Iraq and based much of his campaign on criticizing the president's policies. But harsh attacks on Kerry, combined with the mobilization of large numbers of conservatives, helped Bush win a narrow victory in an election notable for its very high voter turnout.

The 2004 election was one of the last successful moments in the Bush administration. The war in Iraq continued to go badly, and its unpopularity contributed to the rapidly declining approval ratings of the president himself—ratings that by mid-2008 had reached the lowest level of presidential approval in the history of polling. Perhaps even more damaging to Bush's popularity was the government's response to a disastrous hurricane, Katrina, that devastated a swath of the coastline of the Gulf of Mexico in August 2005 and gravely damaged the city of New Orleans. The federal government's incompetent response to Katrina aroused anger throughout the nation and greatly damaged the reputation of the president and his administration. Scandals in the Justice Department, revelations of illegal violations of civil liberties, revulsion from tactics used against suspected terrorists, and declining economic prospects—culminating in a disastrous financial crisis in early 2008—all reinforced the growing repudiation of the president.

The Election of 2008

The 2008 presidential election was the first since 1952 that did not include an incumbent president or vice president. Both parties began the campaign with large fields of candidates, but by the spring of 2008 the contest had narrowed considerably. Senator John McCain of Arizona, who had lost the Republican nomination to George W. Bush in 2000, emerged from the early primaries with his nomination assured. In the Democratic race, the primaries quickly eliminated all but two candidates. They were Senator Hillary Clinton of New York, the former first lady, and Senator Barack Obama of Illinois, a young, charismatic politician and the son of an African father and a white, Kansas mother. As the first woman and the first African American to have a realistic chance of being elected president, their candidacies aroused high expectations and enormous enthusiasm. The passions driving both campaigns led to a primary contest that lasted much longer than usual. Not until the last primaries in June was it clear that Obama would be the nominee.

McCain and Obama entered the fall campaign with starkly different programs. McCain supported the war in Iraq and pledged continued support for it. Obama proposed a gradual reduction of American troops over a fixed period. McCain opposed national health insurance, Obama supported it. McCain supported additional tax cuts to spur investment, while Obama urged tax increases on the wealthiest Americans. The campaign occurred amid continuing, and indeed escalating, controversy over the policies of the Bush administration and in the face of an economy that continued to weaken.

OBAMANIA Posters of and about Barack Obama were widely visible during the 2008 presidential campaign. In this photograph, a New Yorker walks past one example of the Obama street art that spread through many American cities—and, indeed, through cities around the world. Among the depictions of Obama during the campaign were the work of leading artists, who saw in him a figure of possibly historic significance. *(Photo by Chris McGrath/Getty Images)*

THE 44TH PRESIDENT Barack Obama stands before more than 70,000 people in Chicago's Grant Park on November 4, 2008, moments after his election as president was confirmed. *(AP Photos/Pablo Martinez Monsivais)*

By the time of the party conventions in late August, Barack Obama was leading John McCain in the polls. Shortly before the Democratic convention in Denver, Obama announced his choice of Senator Joseph Biden of Delaware as his running mate, and the day after the Democratic convention adjourned, McCain announced his choice: Sarah Palin, the largely unknown governor of Alaska. Palin's powerful acceptance speech galvanized many Republicans, especially those who shared her very conservative views. For a time, she helped boost McCain's standing in the polls, but her visible inexperience, much ridiculed by comedians, disturbed many voters and, over time, seemed to do serious damage to the Republican campaign.

Far more important to the outcome of the election, however, was the series of financial problems that began in mid-2007, grew slowly worse in the first months of 2008, and reached crisis level over the summer. An important factor in the growth of the financial crisis was a significant downturn in the housing market, which in turn triggered a mortgage crisis. For years, financial institutions had been developing new credit instruments intended to make borrowing easier and cheaper, and which lured millions of

people into taking on large mortgages—often much larger than would traditionally have seemed safe—on very low short-term rates, many of which escalated sharply after the first few years. Unable to pay their mortgages, which were often worth more than the market value of their homes, millions of defaulters abandoned their houses. At first, the defaults affected mostly companies that specialized in home mortgages, but since most mortgages were quickly sold, and often resold several times, the bad debts spread throughout a widening swath of the financial world. Over the summer, some of the nation's most important economic institutions began to fail. Some were rescued (and effectively taken over) by the federal government. Others were bought up at very low prices by larger institutions, and a few—including Lehman Brothers, one of the oldest and most prestigious investment banks in America—collapsed altogether. By mid-September, the financial crisis showed signs of spiraling out of control. Secretary of the Treasury Henry Paulson, supported by other economic leaders, proposed a massive appropriation of federal funds to help the government bail out the banks. Despite considerable opposition to the plan, the administration won congressional approval for a $750 billion package to be used to shore up tottering financial institutions. The bail-out slowed the deterioration of financial institutions, but the credit markets remained constricted, and economic activity by both producers and consumers began to decline.

This extraordinary crisis formed the backdrop against which the two presidential candidates fought out the last two months of their campaign. Neither offered clear or convincing solutions to the crisis, but most voters came to believe that Obama would likely be a better steward of the economy than would McCain. Obama benefited as well from the deep unpopularity of George W. Bush, and from his success at persuading voters that McCain would continue Bush's policies. Despite the often sharp attacks on Obama from the Republicans, he held onto—and indeed increased—his lead through late September and October, helped by a heavily financed and highly disciplined campaign.

On November 4, 2008, Barack Obama won a decisive victory, winning the popular vote 53% to 46% and the electoral vote by an even larger margin. Obama became the first Democratic candidate since Lyndon Johnson to win so large a victory. He succeeded in winning back states that the Republicans had carried in 2000 and 2004—among them Ohio, Florida, Virginia, North Carolina, and Indiana. In both the Senate and the House of Representatives the Democratic Party made substantial gains as well.

By the time of his election, Obama was already a figure of global importance. He was an extraordinary speaker who attracted vast audiences wherever he went. He was young and energetic, with an attractive family. He reminded some voters of John F. Kennedy. And he was the first African American to reach the presidency, an achievement that electrified the nation and much of the world. On the night of his election, millions of people flooded into streets and parks, village squares and public spaces of all kinds, across the United States and in every continent in the world, to celebrate the event. Awaiting Obama were some of the most daunting challenges any president had ever faced. But for a moment, an astonished world stopped to watch an extraordinary moment in history.

CONCLUSION

America in the first years of the twenty-first century was a nation beset with many problems and anxieties. American foreign policy after September 11, 2001, had not only divided the American people but also deeply alienated much of the rest of the world, reinforcing a deep animus toward the United States that had been building slowly for decades. The American economy was struggling to sustain even modest growth in the face of a weakened dollar, rapidly rising public and private debt, and increasing inequality of wealth and incomes. Deep divisions and resentments threatened the unity of the nation and led some Americans to believe that the country was dividing into two fundamentally different cultures.

These and other serious problems do not, however, provide a full picture of the United States in the early twenty-first century. America remains unquestionably the wealthiest and most powerful nation in the world. It remains, as well, among the most idealistic—in the willingness of its people to contribute time, money, and effort to the solution of grave social problems at home and in the world, and in its commitment to principles of freedom and justice that, however contested, remain at the core of the nation's identity. Moving forward into an uncertain future, Americans are not only burdened by difficult challenges, but are also armed with the extraordinary energy and resilience that has allowed the nation—through its long and often turbulent history—to endure, to flourish, and continually to imagine and strive for a better future.

INTERACTIVE LEARNING

The *Primary Source Investigator CD-ROM* offers the following materials related to this chapter:

* Interactive maps: **U.S. Elections** (M7); **Middle East** (M28); and **International Organizations** (M61).
* Documents, images, and maps related to American politics and society in the past fifteen years, including an image from Bill Clinton's inauguration, the text of California's controversial Proposition 187 regarding services for undocumented immigrants, and images and documents related to the September 11, 2001, terrorist attacks.

Online Learning Center (www.mhhe.com/brinkley13e)

For quizzes, Internet resources, references to additional books and films, and more, consult this book's Online Learning Center.

FOR FURTHER REFERENCE

John Lewis Gaddis, *The United States and the End of the Cold War* (1992), *We Now Know: Rethinking Cold War History* (1997), and *Surprise, Security, and the American Experience* (2004) are early examinations of the post–Cold War transformation of the world order. Clinton's own memoir, *My Life* (2004) is a valuable account of his presidency. Theda Skocpol, *Boomerang: Clinton's Health Security Effort and the Turn Against Government in U.S. Politics* (1996) is an account of one of the major setbacks of Clinton's first term. Jeffrey Toobin, *A Vast Conspiracy* (1999) is an account of the scandals that rocked the Clinton presidency. Toobin is also the author of an important account of the disputed 2000 presidential election, *Too Close to Call* (2001). Haynes Johnson, *The Best of Times: America in the Clinton Years* (2001) is an account of the politics and culture of the 1990s. John F. Harris, *The Survivor: President Clinton and His Times* (2005) is a valuable overview of this presidency. David Halberstam, *War in a Time of Peace: Bush, Clinton, and the Generals* (2001) examines the foreign policy and military ventures of the Bush and Clinton years. Samantha Power, *"A Problem from Hell":America and the Age of Genocide* (2003) is a powerful study of a major question in the United States. George Packer, *The Assassin's Gate: America in Iraq* (2006); Jane Mayer, *The Dark Side* (2007); Lawrence Wright, *The Looming Tower: Al-Qaeda and the Road to 9/11* (2006) are among the many important studies of the post-9/11 years and the war in Iraq. *Computer: A History of the Information Machine* (1996), by Martin Campbell-Kelly and William Aspray, is an introduction to the development of one of the critical technologies of the late twentieth century. William Julius Wilson, *The Truly Disadvantaged* (1987) and *When Work Disappears* (1996) are important studies of the inner-city poor from one of America's leading sociologists. David A. Hollinger, *Postethnic America: Beyond Multiculturalism* (1995) is an intelligent and spirited comment on the debates over multiculturalism.

APPENDIXES

The United States

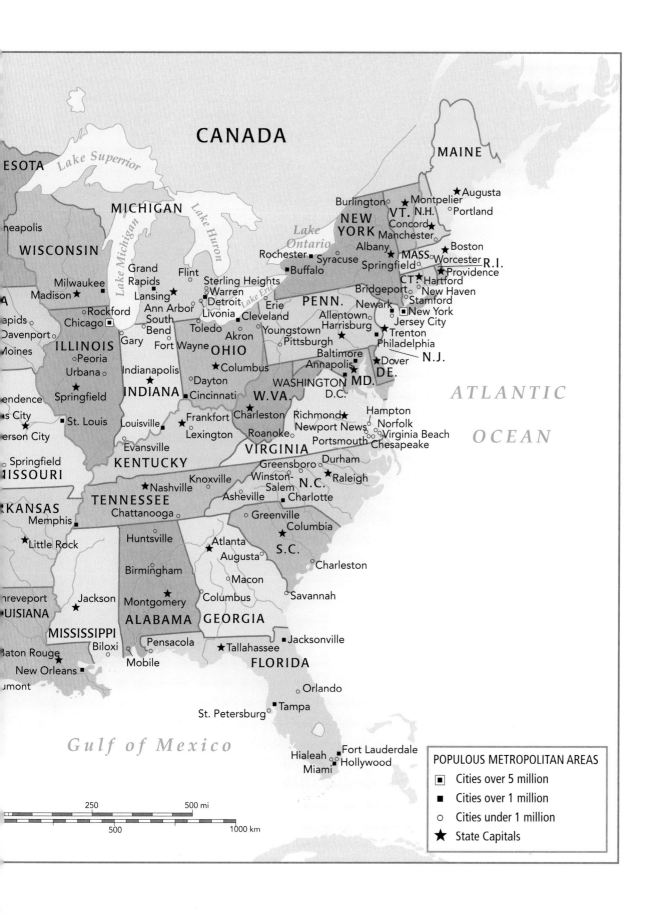

CANADA

MAINE

ESOTA

Lake Superrior

MICHIGAN

Lake Huron

Lake Michigan

Burlington○   ★ Montpelier   ★ Augusta

NEW   VT. N.H.   ○ Portland

YORK   Concord★

Lake   Manchester
Ontario

Albany   ★ Boston

eapolis

WISCONSIN

Rochester ■   Syracuse   ○ Worcester ★

Springfield   MASS.   R.I.

■ Buffalo   CT.★   ○ Providence

Grand   Flint   Bridgeport ○ ★ Hartford

Milwaukee   Rapids   ○   Erie   PENN.   ○ New Haven

Madison ★   Lansing ★ Sterling Heights   Newark   ○ Stamford

○Rockford   ○Warren   Cleveland   Allentown   □ New York

Chicago □   Ann Arbor○ Detroit   ○ Youngstown   Harrisburg ○ Jersey City

apids   South   ○ Livonia   Akron   Pittsburgh   ★ Trenton

Davenport ○   Bend   ○ Toledo   Philadelphia

Moines   Gary   Fort Wayne   OHIO   ○ Dover   N.J.

ILLINOIS   Baltimore ■

○ Peoria   ★ Columbus   Annapolis ★   DE.

Urbana ○   Indianapolis ○   ○ Dayton   WASHINGTON MD.

endence   ★ Springfield   INDIANA   ■ Cincinnati   W. VA.   D.C.

Springfield ★   ★ Charleston   Richmond ★   Hampton ○

s City   ○ Frankfort   Newport News ○ ○ Norfolk

erson City   ○ Louisville   ★   Roanoke ○   Portsmouth ○○ Virginia Beach

■ St. Louis   ○ Lexington   Chesapeake

Evansville ○   VIRGINIA

Springfield ○   KENTUCKY   Greensboro ○ Durham

ISSOURI   Winston-   ○ Raleigh

Knoxville ○   Salem   N.C.

KANSAS   ★ Nashville   Asheville ○ ■ Charlotte

Memphis ■   TENNESSEE   Chattanooga ○   ○ Greenville

★ Little Rock   Huntsville ○   ○ Columbia

Atlanta   Columbia ★

★   S.C.

hreveport ○   Birmingham ○   Augusta ○   ○ Charleston

UISIANA   Jackson ★   ○ Macon

MISSISSIPPI   Montgomery ★   ○ Columbus   ○ Savannah

aton Rouge ★   Biloxi ○   ALABAMA   GEORGIA

New Orleans ■   Pensacola ○   ○ Jacksonville

umont   Mobile ○   ★ Tallahassee

FLORIDA

Gulf of Mexico

○ Orlando

St. Petersburg ○ ■ Tampa

Hialeah ○ ■ Fort Lauderdale
○○ Hollywood
Miami

ATLANTIC

OCEAN

POPULOUS METROPOLITAN AREAS

□ Cities over 5 million

■ Cities over 1 million

○ Cities under 1 million

★ State Capitals

250   500 mi

500   1000 km

Topographical Map of the United States

CANADA

Lake
Nipigon

Lake of
the Woods

Lake Superior

St. Croix R.

Mississippi R.

Minnesota R.

Lake Michigan

Lake Huron

Kankakee R.

Fox R.

Rock R.

Cedar R.

Iowa R.

Des Moines R.

Illinois R.

Lake Erie

Lake Ontario

Mohawk R.

ADIRONDACK
MTS.

Lake
Champlain

Connecticut R.

Hudson R.

St. Lawrence R.

Allegheny R.

Scioto R.

CENTRAL

PLAINS

Missouri R.

Osage R.

Wabash R.

Ohio R.

MTS.

APPALACHIAN MOUNTAINS

SHENANDOAH
VALLEY

ALLEGHENY

James R.

Potomac R.

Chesapeake
Bay

ATLANTIC
OCEAN

OZARK
PLATEAU

White R.

Mississippi R.

Cumberland R.

Tennessee R.

BLUE RIDGE MTS.

Roanoke R.

ATLANTIC COASTAL PLAIN

Arkansas R.

Ouachita R.

Yazoo R.

Saluda R.

Savannah R.

Red R.

Sabine R.

Pearl R.

Alabama R.

Chattahoochee R.

Altamaha R.

Trinity R.

COASTAL PLAIN

Galveston
Bay

Gulf of Mexico

Lake
Okeechobee

0   150   300 miles

0   150   300 kilometers

Land Elevation

Feet	Meters
Over 13,000	Over 3,000
6,560–13,000	2,000–3,000
3,280–6,560	1,000–2,000
660–3,280	2001–1,000
0–660	0–200
Below sea level	Below sea level

ATLANTIC OCEAN

PUERTO
RICO

Caribbean Sea

0   50   100 miles

0   50   100 kilometers

BAHAMAS

CUBA

The World

Abbreviations

ALB.	ALBANIA
AZERB.	AZERBAIJAN
BELG.	BELGIUM
BOS.	BOSNIA-HERZEGOVINA
BULG.	BULGARIA
CRO.	CROATIA
CZECH.	CZECH REPUBLIC
EST.	ESTONIA
HUNG.	HUNGARY
LITH.	LITHUANIA
LUX.	LUXEMBOURG
MACE.	MACEDONIA
MONT.	MONTENEGRO
NETH.	NETHERLANDS
ROM.	ROMANIA
RUSS.	RUSSIA
SERB.	SERBIA
SLOVAK.	SLOVAKIA
SLOVN.	SLOVENIA
SWITZ.	SWITZERLAND
U.A.E.	UNITED ARAB EMIRATES

United States Territorial Expansion, 1783–1898

United States Territorial Expansion, 1783–1898

(1859) Date of statehood

The United States in 1783

Louisiana Purchase, 1803

West Florida annexation, 1810, 1813

Florida: East Florida cession by Spain, 1819

Texas Annexation, 1845

Oregon Country, 1846

Mexican Cession, 1848

Gadsden Purchase, 1853

—— 1819 Treaty with Spain defined border of Oregon and Louisiana

- - - Texas boundary claimed by U.S., 1845–1848

The Declaration of Independence

In Congress, July 4, 1776,

THE UNANIMOUS DECLARATION OF THE THIRTEEN UNITED STATES OF AMERICA

When, in the course of human events, it becomes necessary for one people to dissolve the political bands which have connected them with another, and to assume, among the powers of the earth, the separate and equal station to which the laws of nature and of nature's God entitle them, a decent respect to the opinions of mankind requires that they should declare the causes which impel them to the separation.

We hold these truths to be self-evident, that all men are created equal; that they are endowed by their Creator with certain unalienable rights; that among these, are life, liberty, and the pursuit of happiness. That, to secure these rights, governments are instituted among men, deriving their just powers from the consent of the governed; that, whenever any form of government becomes destructive of these ends, it is the right of the people to alter or to abolish it, and to institute a new government, laying its foundation on such principles, and organizing its powers in such form, as to them shall seem most likely to effect their safety and happiness. Prudence, indeed, will dictate that governments long established, should not be changed for light and transient causes; and, accordingly, all experience hath shown, that mankind are more disposed to suffer, while evils are sufferable, than to right themselves by abolishing the forms to which they are accustomed. But, when a long train of abuses and usurpations, pursuing invariably the same object, evinces a design to reduce them under absolute despotism, it is their right, it is their duty, to throw off such government and to provide new guards for their future security. Such has been the patient sufferance of these colonies, and such is now the necessity which constrains them to alter their former systems of government. The history of the present King of Great Britain is a history of repeated injuries and usurpations, all having, in direct object, the establishment of an absolute tyranny over these States. To prove this, let facts be submitted to a candid world:

He has refused his assent to laws the most wholesome and necessary for the public good.

He has forbidden his governors to pass laws of immediate and pressing importance, unless suspended in their operation till his assent should be obtained; and, when so suspended, he has utterly neglected to attend to them.

He has refused to pass other laws for the accommodation of large districts of people, unless those people would relinquish the right of representation in the legislature; a right inestimable to them, and formidable to tyrants only.

He has called together legislative bodies at places unusual, uncomfortable, and distant from the depository of their public records, for the sole purpose of fatiguing them into compliance with his measures.

He has dissolved representative houses repeatedly for opposing, with manly firmness, his invasions on the rights of the people.

He has refused, for a long time after such dissolutions, to cause others to be elected; whereby the legislative powers, incapable of annihilation, have returned to the people at large for their exercise; the state remaining, in the meantime, exposed to all the danger of invasion from without, and convulsions within.

He has endeavored to prevent the population of these States; for that purpose, obstructing the laws for naturalization of foreigners, refusing to pass others to encourage their migration hither, and raising the conditions of new appropriations of lands.

He has obstructed the administration of justice, by refusing his assent to laws for establishing judiciary powers.

He has made judges dependent on his will alone, for the tenure of their officers, and the amount and payment of their salaries.

He has erected a multitude of new offices, and sent hither swarms of officers to harass our people, and eat out their substance.

He has kept among us, in time of peace, standing armies, without the consent of our legislatures.

He has affected to render the military independent of, and superior to, the civil power.

He has combined, with others, to subject us to a jurisdiction foreign to our Constitution, and unacknowledged by our laws; giving his assent to their acts of pretended legislation:

For quartering large bodies of armed troops among us:

For protecting them by a mock trial, from punishment, for any murders which they should commit on the inhabitants of these States:

For cutting off our trade with all parts of the world:

For imposing taxes on us without our consent:

For depriving us, in many cases, of the benefit of trial by jury:

For transporting us beyond seas to be tried for pretended offences:

For abolishing the free system of English laws in a neighboring province, establishing therein an arbitrary government, and enlarging its boundaries, so as to render it at once an example and fit instrument for introducing the same absolute rule into these colonies:

For taking away our charters, abolishing our most valuable laws, and altering, fundamentally, the powers of our governments:

For suspending our own legislatures, and declaring themselves invested with power to legislate for use in all cases whatsoever.

He has abdicated government here, by declaring us out of his protection, and waging war against us.

He has plundered our seas, ravaged our coasts, burnt our towns, and destroyed the lives of our people.

He is, at this time, transporting large armies of foreign mercenaries to complete the works of death, desolation, and tyranny, already begun, with circumstances of cruelty and perfidy scarcely paralleled in the most barbarous ages, and totally unworthy the head of a civilized nation.

He has constrained our fellow citizens, taken captive on the high seas, to bear arms against their country, to become the executioners of their friends, and brethren, or to fall themselves by their hands.

He has excited domestic insurrections amongst us, and has endeavored to bring on the inhabitants of our frontiers, the merciless Indian savages, whose known rule of warfare is an undistinguished destruction of all ages, sexes, and conditions.

In every stage of these oppressions, we have petitioned for redress, in the most humble terms; our repeated petitions have been answered only by repeated injury. A prince, whose character is thus marked by every act which may define a tyrant, is unfit to be the ruler of a free people.

Nor have we been wanting in attention to our British brethren. We have warned them, from time to time, of attempts made by their legislature to extend an unwarrantable jurisdiction over us. We have reminded them of the circumstances of our emigration and settlement here. We have appealed to their native justice and magnanimity, and we have conjured them, by the ties of our common kindred, to disavow these usurpations, which would inevitably interrupt our connections and correspondence. They, too, have been deaf to the voice of justice and consanguinity. We must, therefore, acquiesce in the necessity, which denounces our separation, and hold them as we hold the rest of mankind, enemies in war, in peace, friends.

We, therefore, the representatives of the United States of America, in general Congress assembled, appealing to the Supreme Judge of the world for the rectitude of our intentions, do, in the name, and by the authority of the good people of these colonies, solemnly publish and declare, that these united colonies are, and of right ought to be, free and independent states: that they are absolved from all allegiance to the British Crown, and that all political connection between them and the state of Great Britain is, and ought to be, totally dissolved; and that, as free and independent states, they have full power to levy war, conclude peace, contract alliances, establish commerce, and to do all other acts and things which independent states may of right do. And, for the support of this declaration, with a firm reliance on the protection of Divine Providence, we mutually pledge to each other our lives, our fortunes, and our sacred honor.

The foregoing Declaration was, by order of Congress, engrossed, and signed by the following members:

JOHN HANCOCK

New Hampshire	**New York**	**Delaware**	**North Carolina**
Josiah Bartlett	William Floyd	Caesar Rodney	William Hooper
William Whipple	Philip Livingston	George Read	Joseph Hewes
Matthew Thornton	Francis Lewis	Thomas McKean	John Penn
	Lewis Morris		

Massachusetts Bay	**New Jersey**	**Maryland**	**South Carolina**
Samuel Adams	Richard Stockton	Samuel Chase	Edward Rutledge
John Adams	John Witherspoon	William Paca	Thomas Heyward, Jr.
Robert Treat Paine	Francis Hopkinson	Thomas Stone	Thomas Lynch, Jr.
Elbridge Gerry	John Hart	Charles Carroll,	Arthur Middleton
	Abraham Clark	of Carrollton	

Rhode Island	**Pennsylvania**	**Virginia**	**Georgia**
Stephen Hopkins	Robert Morris	George Wythe	Button Gwinnett
William Ellery	Benjamin Rush	Richard Henry Lee	Lyman Hall
	Benjamin Franklin	Thomas Jefferson	George Walton
Connecticut	John Morton	Benjamin Harrison	
Robert Sherman	George Clymer	Thomas Nelson, Jr.	
Samuel Huntington	James Smith	Francis Lightfoot Lee	
William Williams	George Taylor	Carter Braxton	
Oliver Wolcott	James Wilson		
	George Ross		

Resolved, That copies of the Declaration be sent to the several assemblies, conventions, and committees, or councils of safety, and to the several commanding officers of the continental troops; that it be proclaimed in each of the United States, at the head of the army.

The Constitution of the United States of America[1]

We the People of the United States, in Order to form a more perfect Union, establish Justice, insure domestic Tranquility, provide for the common defence, promote the general Welfare, and secure the Blessings of Liberty to ourselves and our Posterity, do ordain and establish this CONSTITUTION for the United States of America.

Article I

Section 1.

All legislative Powers herein granted shall be vested in a Congress of the United States, which shall consist of a Senate and House of Representatives.

Section 2.

The House of Representatives shall be composed of Members chosen every second Year by the People of the several States, and the Electors in each State shall have the Qualifications requisite for Electors of the most numerous Branch of the State Legislature.

No Person shall be a Representative who shall not have attained to the Age of twenty-five Years, and been seven Years a Citizen of the United States, and who shall not, when elected, be an Inhabitant of that State in which he shall be chosen.

[Representatives and direct Taxes[2] shall be apportioned among the several States which may be included within this Union, according to their respective Numbers, which shall be determined by adding to the whole Number of free Persons, including those bound to Service for a Term of Years, and excluding Indians not taxed, three fifths of all other Persons.][3] The actual Enumeration shall be made within three Years after the first Meeting of the Congress of the United States, and within every subsequent Term of ten Years, in such Manner as they shall by Law direct. The Number of Representatives shall not exceed one for every thirty Thousand, but each State shall have at Least one Representative; and until such enumeration shall be made, the State of New Hampshire shall be entitled to chuse three, Massachusetts eight, Rhode-Island and Providence Plantations one, Connecticut five, New York six, New Jersey four, Pennsylvania eight, Delaware one, Maryland six, Virginia ten, North Carolina five, South Carolina five, and Georgia three.

When vacancies happen in the Representation from any State, the Executive Authority thereof shall issue Writs of Election to fill such Vacancies.

The House of Representatives shall chuse their Speaker and other Officers; and shall have the sole Power of Impeachment.

Section 3.

The Senate of the United States shall be composed of two Senators from each State, chosen by the Legislature thereof, for six Years; and each Senator shall have one Vote.

Immediately after they shall be assembled in Consequence of the first Election, they shall be divided as equally as may be into three Classes. The Seats of the Senators of the first Class shall be vacated at the Expiration of the second Year, of the second Class at the Expiration of the fourth Year, and of the third Class at the Expiration of the sixth Year, so that one-third may be chosen every second Year; and if Vacancies happen by Resignation, or otherwise, during the Recess of the Legislature of any State, the Executive thereof may make temporary Appointments until the next Meeting of the Legislature, which shall then fill such Vacancies.

No Person shall be a Senator who shall not have attained to the Age of thirty Years, and been nine Years a Citizen of the United States, and who shall not, when elected, be an Inhabitant of that State for which he shall be chosen.

The Vice President of the United States shall be President of the Senate, but shall have no vote, unless they be equally divided.

The Senate shall chuse their other Officers, and also a President pro tempore, in the absence of the Vice President, or when he shall exercise the office of President of the United States.

The Senate shall have the sole Power to try all Impeachments. When sitting for that purpose they shall be on Oath or Affirmation. When the President of the United States is tried, the Chief Justice shall preside: And no person shall be convicted without the Concurrence of two thirds of the Members present.

Judgment in Cases of Impeachment shall not extend further than to removal from Office, and disqualification to hold and enjoy any Office of honor, Trust, or Profit under the United States: but the Party convicted shall nevertheless be liable and subject to Indictment, Trial, Judgment, and Punishment, according to Law.

Section 4.

The Times, Places and Manner of holding Elections for Senators and Representatives, shall be prescribed in each State by the Legislature thereof; but the Congress may at any time by Law make or alter such Regulations, except as to the Places of Chusing Senators.

---

[1]This version, which follows the original Constitution in capitalization and spelling, was published by the United States Department of the Interior, Office of Education, in 1935.

[2]Altered by the Sixteenth Amendment.

[3]Negated by the Fourteenth Amendment.

The Congress shall assemble at least once in every Year, and such Meeting shall be on the first Monday in December, unless they shall by Law appoint a different day.

Section 5.

Each House shall be the Judge of the Elections, Returns and Qualifications of its own Members, and a Majority of each shall constitute a Quorum to do Business; but a smaller number may adjourn from day to day, and may be authorized to compel the Attendance of absent Members, in such Manner, and under such Penalties, as each House may provide.

Each House may determine the Rules of its Proceedings, punish its Members for disorderly Behaviour, and, with the Concurrence of two thirds, expel a Member.

Each House shall keep a Journal of its Proceedings, and from time to time publish the same, excepting such Parts as may in their Judgment require Secrecy; and the Yeas and Nays of the Members of either House on any question shall, at the Desire of one fifth of those Present, be entered on the Journal.

Neither House, during the Session of Congress, shall, without the Consent of the other, adjourn for more than three days, nor to any other Place than that in which the two Houses shall be sitting.

Section 6.

The Senators and Representatives shall receive a Compensation for their Services, to be ascertained by Law, and paid out of the Treasury of the United States. They shall in all Cases, except Treason, Felony, and Breach of the Peace, be privileged from Arrest during their Attendance at the Session of their respective Houses, and in going to and returning from the same; and for any Speech or Debate in either House, they shall not be questioned in any other Place.

No Senator or Representative shall, during the Time for which he was elected, be appointed to any civil Office under the Authority of the United States, which shall have been created, or the Emoluments whereof shall have been increased, during such time; and no Person holding any Office under the United States shall be a Member of either House during his continuance in Office.

Section 7.

All Bills for raising Revenue shall originate in the House of Representatives; but the Senate may propose or concur with Amendments as on other bills.

Every Bill which shall have passed the House of Representatives and the Senate, shall, before it become a Law, be presented to the President of the United States; If he approve he shall sign it, but if not he shall return it, with his Objections, to that House in which it shall have originated, who shall enter the Objections at large on their Journal, and proceed to reconsider it. If after such Reconsideration two thirds of that House shall agree to pass the bill, it shall be sent, together with the objections, to the other House, by which it shall likewise be reconsidered, and if approved by two thirds of that House, it shall become a Law. But in all such Cases the Votes of both Houses shall be determined by Yeas and Nays, and the Names of the Persons voting for and against the Bill shall be entered on the Journal of each House respectively. If any Bill shall not be returned by the President within ten Days (Sundays excepted) after it shall have been presented to him, the Same shall be a Law, in like Manner as if he had signed it, unless the Congress by their Adjournment prevent its Return, in which Case it shall not be a Law.

Every Order, Resolution, or Vote to which the Concurrence of the Senate and House of Representatives may be necessary (except on a question of Adjournment) shall be presented to the President of the United States; and before the Same shall take Effect, shall be approved by him, or being disapproved by him, shall be repassed by two thirds of the Senate and House of Representatives, according to the Rules and Limitations prescribed in the Case of a Bill.

Section 8.

The Congress shall have Power To lay and collect Taxes, Duties, Imposts and Excises, to pay the Debts and provide for the common Defence and general Welfare of the United States; but all Duties, Imposts and Excises shall be uniform throughout the United States;

To borrow money on the credit of the United States;

To regulate Commerce with foreign Nations, and among the several States, and with the Indian Tribes;

To establish an uniform rule of Naturalization, and uniform Laws on the subject of Bankruptcies throughout the United States;

To coin Money, regulate the Value thereof, and of foreign Coin, and fix the Standard of Weights and Measures;

To provide for the Punishment of counterfeiting the Securities and current Coin of the United States;

To establish Post Offices and post Roads;

To promote the Progress of Science and useful Arts, by securing for limited Times to Authors and Inventors the exclusive Right to their respective Writings and Discoveries;

To constitute Tribunals inferior to the Supreme Court;

To define and punish Piracies and Felonies committed on the high Seas, and Offenses against the Law of Nations;

To declare War, grant Letters of Marque and Reprisal, and make Rules concerning Captures on Land and Water;

To raise and support Armies, but no Appropriation of Money to that Use shall be for a longer Term than two Years;

To provide and maintain a Navy;

To make Rules for the Government and Regulation of the land and naval forces;

To provide for calling forth the Militia to execute the Laws of the Union, suppress Insurrections and repel Invasions;

To provide for organizing, arming, and disciplining the Militia, and for governing such Part of them as may be employed in the Service of the United States, reserving to the States respectively, the Appointment of the Officers, and the Authority of training the Militia according to the discipline prescribed by Congress;

To exercise exclusive Legislation in all Cases whatsoever, over such District (not exceeding ten Miles square) as may, by Cession of particular States, and the acceptance of Congress, become the Seat of the Government of the United States, and to exercise like Authority over all Places purchased by the Consent of the Legislature of the State in which the Same shall be, for the Erection of Forts, Magazines, Arsenals, Dockyards, and other needful Buildings;—And

To make all Laws which shall be necessary and proper for carrying into Execution for foregoing Powers, and all other Powers vested by this Constitution in the Government of the United States, or in any Department or Officer thereof.

Section 9.

The Migration or Importation of such Persons as any of the States now existing shall think proper to admit, shall not be prohibited by the Congress prior to the Year one thousand eight hundred and eight, but a tax or duty may be imposed on such Importation, not exceeding ten dollars for each Person.

The privilege of the Writ of Habeas Corpus shall not be suspended, unless when in Cases of Rebellion or Invasion the public Safety may require it.

No bill of Attainder or ex post facto Law shall be passed.

No capitation, or other direct, Tax shall be laid unless in Proportion to the Census or Enumeration herein before directed to be taken.

No Tax or Duty shall be laid on Articles exported from any State.

No Preference shall be given by any Regulation of Commerce or Revenue to the Ports of one State over those of another: nor shall Vessels bound to, or from, one State, be obliged to enter, clear, or pay Duties in another.

No Money shall be drawn from the Treasury, but in Consequence of Appropriations made by Law; and a regular Statement and Account of the Receipts and Expenditures of all public Money shall be published from time to time.

No title of Nobility shall be granted by the United States: And no Person holding any Office of Profit or Trust under them, shall, without the Consent of the Congress, accept of any present, Emolument, Office, or title, of any kind whatever, from any King, Prince, or foreign State.

Section 10.

No State shall enter into any Treaty, Alliance, or Confederation; grant Letters of Marque and Reprisal; coin Money; emit Bills of Credit; make any Thing but gold and silver Coin a Tender in Payment of Debts; pass any Bill of Attainder, ex post facto Law, or Law impairing the Obligation of Contracts, or grant any title of Nobility.

No State shall, without the Consent of the Congress, lay any Imposts or Duties on Imports or Exports, except what may be absolutely necessary for executing its inspection Laws; and the net Produce of all Duties and Imposts, laid by any State on Imports or Exports, shall be for the use of the Treasury of the United States; and all such Laws shall be subject to the Revision and Control of the Congress.

No state shall, without the Consent of Congress, lay any duty of Tonnage, keep Troops, or Ships of War in time of Peace, enter into any Agreement or Compact with another State, or with a foreign Power, or engage in War, unless actually invaded, or in such imminent Danger as will not admit of delay.

Article II

Section 1.

The executive Power shall be vested in a President of the United States of America. He shall hold his Office during the Term of four years, and, together with the Vice President, chosen for the same Term, be elected, as follows:

Each State shall appoint, in such Manner as the Legislature thereof may direct, a Number of Electors, equal to the whole Number of Senators and Representatives to which the State may be entitled in the Congress: but no Senator or Representative, or Person holding an Office of Trust or Profit under the United States, shall be appointed an Elector.

[The Electors shall meet in their respective States, and vote by Ballot for two persons, of whom one at least shall not be an Inhabitant of the same State with themselves. And they shall make a List of all the Persons voted for, and of the Number of Votes for each; which List they shall sign and certify, and transmit sealed to the Seat of the Government of the United States, directed to the President of the Senate. The President of the Senate shall, in the Presence of the Senate and House of Representatives, open all the Certificates, and the Votes shall then be counted. The Person having the greatest Number of Votes shall be the President, if such Number be a Majority of the whole Number of Electors appointed; and if there be more than one who have such Majority, and have an equal Number of Votes, then the House of Representatives shall immediately chuse by Ballot one of them for President; and if no Person have a Majority, then from the five highest on the list the said House shall in like Manner chuse the President. But in chusing the President, the Votes shall be taken by States, the Representation from each State having one Vote; a quorum for this Purpose shall consist of a Member or Members from two-thirds of the States, and a Majority of all the States shall be necessary to a Choice. In every Case, after the Choice of the President, the Person having the greatest Number of Votes of the Electors shall be the Vice President. But if there should remain two or more who have equal votes, the Senate shall chuse from them by Ballot the Vice President.][4]

The Congress may determine the Time of chusing the Electors, and the Day on which they shall give their Votes; which Day shall be the same throughout the United States.

No person except a natural-born Citizen, or a Citizen of the United States, at the time of the Adoption of this Constitution, shall be eligible to the Office of President; neither shall any Person be eligible to that Office who shall not have attained to the Age of thirty-five years, and been fourteen Years a Resident within the United States.

In Case of the Removal of the President from Office, or of his Death, Resignation, or Inability to discharge the Powers and Duties of the said Office, the same shall devolve on the Vice President, and the Congress may by Law provide for the Case of Removal, Death, Resignation, or Inability, both of the President and Vice President, declaring what Officer

_____
[4]Revised by the Twelfth Amendment.

shall then act as President, and such Officer shall act accordingly, until the disability be removed, or a President shall be elected.

The President shall, at stated Times, receive for his Services a Compensation, which shall neither be increased nor diminished during the Period for which he shall have been elected, and he shall not receive within that Period any other Emolument from the United States, or any of them.

Before he enter on the execution of his Office, he shall take the following Oath or Affirmation:—"I do solemnly swear (or affirm) that I will faithfully execute the Office of President of the United States, and will, to the best of my Ability, preserve, protect, and defend the Constitution of the United States."

Section 2.

The President shall be Commander in Chief of the Army and Navy of the United States, and of the Militia of the several States, when called into the actual Service of the United States; he may require the Opinion, in writing, of the principal Officer in each of the executive Departments, upon any subject relating to the Duties of their respective Offices, and he shall have Power to Grant Reprieves and Pardons for Offenses against the United States, except in Cases of Impeachment.

He shall have Power, by and with the Advice and Consent of the Senate, to make Treaties, provided two-thirds of the Senators present concur; and he shall nominate, and by and with the Advice and Consent of the Senate, shall appoint Ambassadors, other public Ministers and Consuls, Judges of the supreme Court, and all other Officers of the United States, whose Appointments are not herein otherwise provided for, and which shall be established by Law: but the Congress may by Law vest the Appointment of such inferior Officers, as they think proper, in the President alone, in the Courts of Law, or in the Heads of Departments.

The President shall have Power to fill up all Vacancies that may happen during the Recess of the Senate, by granting Commissions which shall expire at the End of their next Session.

Section 3.

He shall from time to time give to the Congress Information of the State of the Union, and recommend to their Consideration such Measures as he shall judge necessary and expedient; he may, on extraordinary occasions, convene both Houses, or either of them, and in Case of Disagreement between them, with respect to the Time of Adjournment, he may adjourn them to such Time as he shall think proper; he shall receive Ambassadors and other public Ministers; he shall take care that the Laws be faithfully executed, and shall Commission all the Officers of the United States.

Section 4.

The President, Vice President and all civil Officers of the United States, shall be removed from Office on Impeachment for, and Conviction of, Treason, Bribery, or other high Crimes and Misdemeanors.

Article III

Section 1.

The judicial Power of the United States, shall be vested in one supreme Court, and in such inferior Courts as the Congress may from time to time ordain and establish. The Judges, both of the supreme and inferior Courts, shall hold their Offices during good Behaviour, and shall, at stated Times, receive for their Services, a Compensation, which shall not be diminished during their Continuance in Office.

Section 2.

The judicial Power shall extend to all Cases, in Law and Equity, arising under this Constitution, the Laws of the United States, and Treaties made, or which shall be made, under their Authority;—to all Cases affecting ambassadors, other public ministers and consuls;—to all cases of admiralty and maritime Jurisdiction;—to Controversies to which the United States shall be a Party;—to Controversies between two or more States;—between a State and Citizens of another State;[5]—between Citizens of different States—between Citizens of the same State claiming Lands under Grants of different States, and between a State, or the Citizens thereof, and foreign States, Citizens, or Subjects.

In all Cases affecting Ambassadors, other public Ministers and Consuls, and those in which a State shall be Party, the supreme Court shall have original Jurisdiction. In all the other Cases before mentioned, the supreme Court shall have appellate Jurisdiction, both as to Law and Fact, with such Exceptions, and under such Regulations as the Congress shall make.

The trial of all Crimes, except in Cases of Impeachment, shall be by Jury; and such Trial shall be held in the State where the said Crimes shall have been committed; but when not committed within any State, the Trial shall be at such Place or Places as the Congress may by Law have directed.

Section 3.

Treason against the United States, shall consist only in levying War against them, or in adhering to their Enemies, giving them Aid and Comfort. No Person shall be convicted of Treason unless on the Testimony of two Witnesses to the same overt Act, or on Confession in open Court.

The Congress shall have power to declare the Punishment of Treason, but no Attainder of Treason shall work Corruption of Blood, or Forfeiture except during the Life of the Person attained.

Article IV

Section 1.

Full Faith and Credit shall be given in each State to the public Acts, Records, and judicial Proceedings of every State. And the Congress may by general Laws prescribe the Manner in which such Acts, Records and Proceedings shall be proved, and the Effect thereof.

---

[5]Qualified by the Eleventh Amendment.

Section 2.

The Citizens of each State shall be entitled to all Privileges and Immunities of Citizens in the several States.

A Person charged in any State with Treason, Felony, or other Crime, who shall flee from Justice, and be found in another State, shall on demand of the executive Authority of the State from which he fled, be delivered up, to be removed to the State having Jurisdiction of the crime.

No Person held to Service or Labour in one State, under the Laws thereof, escaping into another, shall, in Consequence of any Law or Regulation therein, be discharged from such Service or Labour, but shall be delivered up on Claim of the Party to whom such Service or Labour may be due.

Section 3.

New States may be admitted by the Congress into this Union; but no new State shall be formed or erected within the Jurisdiction of any other State; nor any State be formed by the Junction of two or more States, or parts of States, without the Consent of the Legislatures of the States concerned as well as of the Congress.

The Congress shall have Power to dispose of and make all needful Rules and Regulations respecting the Territory or other Property belonging to the United States; and nothing in this Constitution shall be so construed as to Prejudice any Claims of the United States, or of any particular State.

Section 4.

The United States shall guarantee to every State in this Union a Republican Form of Government, and shall protect each of them against Invasion; and on Application of the Legislature, or of the Executive (when the Legislature cannot be convened) against domestic violence.

Article V

The Congress, whenever two-thirds of both Houses shall deem it necessary, shall propose Amendments to this Constitution, or, on the Application of the Legislatures of two-thirds of the several States, shall call a Convention for proposing Amendments, which, in either Case, shall be valid to all Intents and Purposes, as part of this Constitution, when ratified by the Legislatures of three-fourths of the several States, or by Conventions in three-fourths thereof, as the one or the other Mode of Ratification may be proposed by the Congress; Provided that no Amendment which may be made prior to the Year One thousand eight hundred and eight shall in any Manner affect the first and fourth Clauses in the Ninth Section of the first Article; and that no State, without its Consent, shall be deprived of its equal Suffrage in the Senate.

Article VI

All Depts contracted and Engagements entered into, before the Adoption of this Constitution, shall be as valid against the United States under this Constitution, as under the Confederation.

This Constitution, and the Laws of the United States which shall be made in Pursuance thereof; and all Treaties made, or which shall be made, under the Authority of the United States, shall be the supreme Law of the Land; and the Judges in every State shall be bound thereby, any Thing in the Constitution or Laws of any State to the Contrary notwithstanding.

The Senators and Representatives before mentioned, and the Members of the several State Legislatures, and all executive and judicial Officers, both of the United States and of the several States, shall be bound by Oath or Affirmation to support this Constitution; but no religious Tests shall ever be required as a qualification to any Office or public Trust under the United States.

Article VII

The Ratification of the Conventions of nine States shall be sufficient for the Establishment of this Constitution between the States so ratifying the same.

Done in convention by the Unanimous Consent of the States present the Seventeenth Day of September in the Year of our Lord one thousand seven hundred and Eighty seven, and of the Independence of the United States of America the Twelfth. In Witness whereof We have hereunto subscribed our Names.[6]

George Washington,
President and deputy from Virginia

New Hampshire
John Langdon
Nicholas Gilman

Massachusetts
Nathaniel Gorham
Rufus King

Connecticut
William Samuel Johnson
Roger Sherman

New York
Alexander Hamilton

Delaware
George Read
Gunning Beford, Jr.
John Dickinson
Richard Bassett
Jacob Broom

New Jersey
William Livingston
David Brearley
William Paterson
Jonathan Dayton

Pennsylvania
Benjamin Franklin
Thomas Mifflin
Robert Morris
George Clymer
Thomas FitzSimons
Jared Ingersoll
James Wilson
Gouverneur Morris

North Carolina
William Blount
Richard Dobbs Spaight
Hugh Williamson

---

[6]These are the full names of the signers, which in some cases are not the signatures on the document.

Maryland

James McHenry

Daniel of St. Thomas Jenifer

Daniel Carroll

Virginia

John Blair

James Madison, Jr.

South Carolina

John Rutledge

Charles Cotesworth
  Pinckney

Charles Pinckney

Pierce Butler

Georgia

William Few

Abraham Baldwin

Articles in Addition to, and Amendment of, the Constitution of the United States of America, Proposed by Congress, and Ratified by the Legislatures of the Several States, Pursuant to the Fifth Article of the Original Constitution[7]

[Article I]

Congress shall make no law respecting an establishment of religion, or prohibiting the free exercise thereof; or abridging the freedom of speech, or of the press; or the right of the people peaceably to assemble, and to petition the Government for a redress of grievances.

[Article II]

A well regulated Militia, being necessary to the security of a free State, the right of the people to keep and bear Arms shall not be infringed.

[Article III]

No Soldier shall, in time of peace, be quartered in any house, without the consent of the Owner, nor in time of war, but in a manner to be prescribed by law.

[Article IV]

The right of the people to be secure in their persons, houses, papers, and effects, against unreasonable searches and seizures, shall not be violated, and no Warrants shall issue, but upon probable cause, supported by Oath or affirmation, and particularly describing the place to be searched, and the persons or things to be seized.

[Article V]

No person shall be held to answer for a capital or otherwise infamous crime, unless on a presentment or indictment of a Grand Jury, except in cases arising in the land or naval forces, or in the Militia, when in actual service in time of War or public danger; nor shall any person be subject for the same offence to be twice put in jeopardy of life or limb; nor shall be compelled in any criminal case to be a witness against himself, nor be deprived of life, liberty, or property, without due process of law; nor shall private property be taken for public use, without just compensation.

[Article VI]

In all criminal prosecutions, the accused shall enjoy the right to a speedy and public trial, by an impartial jury of the State and district wherein the crime shall have been committed, which district shall have been previously ascertained by law, and to be informed of the nature and cause of the accusation; to be confronted with the witnesses against him; to have compulsory process for obtaining witnesses in his favour, and to have the Assistance of Counsel for his defence.

[Article VII]

In suits at common law, where the value in controversy shall exceed twenty dollars, the right of trial by jury shall be preserved, and no fact tried by a jury, shall be otherwise reexamined in any Court of the United States, than according to the rules of the common law.

[Article VIII]

Excessive bail shall not be required, nor excessive fines imposed, nor cruel and unusual punishments inflicted.

[Article IX]

The enumeration in the Constitution, of certain rights, shall not be construed to deny or disparage others retained by the people.

[Article X]

The powers not delegated to the United States by the Constitution, nor prohibited by it to the States, are reserved to the States respectively, or to the people. [Amendments I-X, in force 1791.]

[Article XI][8]

The Judicial power of the United States shall not be construed to extend to any suit in law or equity, commenced or prosecuted against one of the United States by Citizens of another State, or by Citizens or Subjects of any Foreign State.

[Article XII][9]

The Electors shall meet in their respective States and vote by ballot for President and Vice-President, one of whom, at least, shall not be an inhabitant of the same State with themselves; they shall name in their ballots the person

---

[7]This heading appears only in the joint resolution submitting the first ten amendments.

[8]Adopted in 1798.

[9]Adopted in 1804.

voted for as President, and in distinct ballots the person voted for as Vice-President, and they shall make distinct lists of all persons voted for as President, and of all persons voted for as Vice-President, and of the number of votes for each, which lists they shall sign and certify, and transmit sealed to the seal of the government of the United States, directed to the President of the Senate;—The President of the Senate shall, in the presence of the Senate and House of Representatives, open all the certificates and the votes shall then be counted;—The person having the greatest number of votes for President, shall be the President, if such number be a majority of the whole number of Electors appointed; and if no person have such majority, then from the persons having the highest numbers not exceeding three on the list of those voted for as President, the House of Representatives shall choose immediately, by ballot, the President. But in choosing the President, the votes shall be taken by states, the representation from each state having one vote; a quorum for this purpose shall consist of a member or members from two-thirds of the states, and a majority of all the states shall be necessary to a choice. And if the House of Representatives shall not choose a President whenever the right of choice shall devolve upon them, before the fourth day of March next following, then the Vice-President shall act as President, as in the case of the death or other constitutional disability of the President.—The person having the greatest number of votes as Vice-President, shall be the Vice-President, if such number be a majority of the whole number of Electors appointed, and if no person have a majority, then from the two highest numbers on the list, the Senate shall choose the Vice-President; a quorum for the purpose shall consist of two-thirds of the whole number of Senators, and a majority of the whole number shall be necessary to a choice. But no person constitutionally ineligible to the office of President shall be eligible to that of Vice-President of the United States.

[Article XIII][10]

Section 1.
Neither slavery nor involuntary servitude, except as a punishment for crime whereof the party shall have been duly convicted, shall exist within the United States, or any place subject to their jurisdiction.

Section 2.
Congress shall have power to enforce this article by appropriate legislation.

[Article XIV][11]

Section 1.
All persons born or naturalized in the United States, and subject to the jurisdiction thereof, are citizens of the United States and of the State wherein they reside. No State shall make or enforce any law which shall abridge the privileges or immunities of citizens of the United States; nor shall any State deprive any person of life, liberty, or property, without due process of law; nor deny to any person within its jurisdiction the equal protection of the laws.

Section 2.
Representatives shall be apportioned among the several States according to their respective numbers, counting the whole number of persons in each State, excluding Indians not taxed. But when the right to vote at any election for the choice of electors for President and Vice-President of the United States, Representatives in Congress, the Executive and Judicial officers of a State, or the members of the Legislature thereof, is denied to any of the male inhabitants of such State, being twenty-one years of age, and citizens of the United States, or in any way abridged, except for participation in rebellion, or other crime, the basis of representation therein shall be reduced in the proportion which the number of such male citizens shall bear to the whole number of male citizens twenty-one years of age in such State.

Section 3.
No person shall be a Senator or Representative in Congress, or elector of President and Vice-President, or hold any office, civil or military, under the United States, or under any State, who, having previously taken an oath, as a member of Congress, or as an officer of the United States, or as a member of any State legislature, or as an executive or judicial officer of any State, to support the Constitution of the United States, shall have engaged in insurrection or rebellion against the same, or given aid or comfort to the enemies thereof. But Congress may by a vote of two-thirds of each House, remove such disability.

Section 4.
The validity of the public debt of the United States, authorized by law, including debts incurred for payment of pensions and bounties for services in suppressing insurrection or rebellion, shall not be questioned. But neither the United States nor any State shall assume or pay any debts or obligation incurred in aid of insurrection or rebellion against the United States, or any claim for the loss or emancipation of any slave; but all such debts, obligations, and claims shall be held illegal and void.

Section 5.
The Congress shall have the power to enforce, by appropriate legislation, the provisions of this article.

[Article XV][12]

Section 1.
The right of citizens of the United States to vote shall not be denied or abridged by the United States or by any State on account of race, color, or previous condition of servitude—

Section 2.
The Congress shall have power to enforce this article by appropriate legislation.

---

[10]Adopted in 1865.

[11]Adopted in 1868.

[12]Adopted in 1870.

[Article XVI][13]

The Congress shall have power to lay and collect taxes on incomes, from whatever source derived, without apportionment among the several States, and without regard to any census or enumeration.

[Article XVII][14]

The Senate of the United States shall be composed of two Senators from each State, elected by the people thereof, for six years; and each Senator shall have one vote. The electors in each State shall have the qualifications requisite for electors of the most numerous branch of the State legislatures.

When vacancies happen in the representation of any State in the Senate, the executive authority of such State shall issue writs of election to fill such vacancies: *Provided,* That the legislature of any State may empower the executive thereof to make temporary appointments until the people fill the vacancies by election as the legislature may direct.

This amendment shall not be so constructed as to affect the election or term of any Senator chosen before it becomes valid as part of the Constitution.

[Article XVIII][15]

Section 1.
After one year from the ratification of this article the manufacture, sale, or transportation of intoxicating liquors within, the importation thereof into, or the exportation thereof from the United States and all territory subject to the jurisdiction thereof for beverage purposes is hereby prohibited.

Section 2.
The Congress and the several States shall have concurrent power to enforce this article by appropriate legislation.

Section 3.
This article shall be inoperative unless it shall have been ratified as an amendment to the Constitution by the legislatures of the several States, as provided in the Constitution, within seven years from the date of the submission hereof to the States by the Congress.

[Article XIX][16]

The right of citizens of the United States to vote shall not be denied or abridged by the United States or by any State on account of sex.

Congress shall have power to enforce this article by appropriate legislation.

[Article XX][17]

Section 1.
The terms of the President and Vice-President shall end at noon on the 20th day of January, and the terms of Senators and Representatives at noon on the 3d day of January, of the years in which such terms would have ended if this article had not been ratified; and the terms of their successors shall then begin.

Section 2.
The Congress shall assemble at least once in every year, and such meeting shall begin at noon on the 3d day of January, unless they shall by law appoint a different day.

Section 3.
If, at the time fixed for the beginning of the term of the President, the President elect shall have died, the Vice-President elect shall become President. If a President shall not have been chosen before the time fixed for the beginning of his term or if the President elect shall have failed to qualify, then the Vice-President elect shall act as President until a President shall have qualified; and the Congress may by law provide for the case wherein neither a President elect nor a Vice-President elect shall have qualified, declaring who shall then act as President, or the manner in which one who is to act shall be selected, and such person shall act accordingly until a President or Vice-President shall have qualified.

Section 4.
The Congress may by law provide for the case of the death of any of the persons from whom the House of Representatives may choose a President whenever the right of choice shall have developed upon them, and for the case of the death of any of the persons from whom the Senate may choose a Vice-President whenever the right of choice shall have developed upon them.

Section 5.
Sections 1 and 2 shall take effect on the 15th day of October following the ratification of this article.

Section 6.
This article shall be inoperative unless it shall have been ratified as an amendment to the Constitution by the legislatures of three-fourths of the several States within seven years from the date of its submission.

[Article XXI][18]

Section 1.
The eighteenth article of amendment to the Constitution of the United States is hereby repealed.

---

[13]Adopted in 1913.

[14]Adopted in 1913.

[15]Adopted in 1918.

[16]Adopted in 1920.

---

[17]Adopted in 1933.

[18]Adopted in 1933.

Section 2.

The transportation or importation into any State, Territory, or possession of the United States for delivery or use therein of intoxicating liquors, in violation of the laws thereof, is hereby prohibited.

Section 3.

This article shall be inoperative unless it shall have been ratified as an amendment to the Constitution by conventions in the several States, as provided in the Constitution, within seven years from the date of the submission hereof to the States by the Congress.

[Article XXII][19]

No person shall be elected to the office of the President more than twice, and no person who has held the office of President, or acted as President, for more than two years of a term to which some other person was elected President shall be elected to the office of the President more than once.

But this Article shall not apply to any person holding the office of President when this Article was proposed by the Congress, and shall not prevent any person who may be holding the office of President, or acting as President, during the term within which this Article becomes operative from holding the office of President or acting as President during the remainder of such term.

This article shall be inoperative unless it shall have been ratified as an amendment to the Constitution by the legislatures of three-fourths of the several states within seven years from the date of its submission to the states by the Congress.

[Article XXIII][20]

Section 1.

The District constituting the seat of Government of the United States shall appoint in such manner as the Congress may direct:

A number of electors of President and Vice-President equal to the whole number of Senators and Representatives in Congress to which the District would be entitled if it were a State, but in no event more than the least populous State; they shall be in addition to those appointed by the States, but they shall be considered, for the purposes of the election of President and Vice-President, to be electors appointed by a State; and they shall meet in the District and perform such duties as provided by the twelfth article of amendment.

Section 2.

The Congress shall have power to enforce this article by appropriate legislation.

[Article XXIV][21]

Section 1.

The right of citizens of the United States to vote in any primary or other election for President or Vice President, for electors for President or Vice President, or for Senator or Representative in Congress, shall not be denied or abridged by the United States or any state by reason of failure to pay any poll tax or other tax.

Section 2.

The Congress shall have the power to enforce this article by appropriate legislation.

[Article XXV][22]

Section 1.

In case of the removal of the President from office or of his death or resignation, the Vice President shall become President.

Section 2.

Whenever there is a vacancy in the office of the Vice President, the President shall nominate a Vice President who shall take office upon confirmation by a majority vote of both Houses of Congress.

Section 3.

Whenever the President transmits to the President Pro Tempore of the Senate and the Speaker of the House of Representatives his written declaration that he is unable to discharge the powers and duties of his office, and until he transmits to them a written declaration to the contrary, such powers and duties shall be discharged by the Vice President as Acting President.

Section 4.

Whenever the Vice President and a majority of either the principal officers of the executive departments or of such other body as Congress may by law provide, transmit to the President Pro Tempore of the Senate and the Speaker of the House of Representatives their written declaration that the President is unable to discharge the powers and duties of his office, the Vice President shall immediately assume the powers and duties of the office as Acting President.

---

[19]Adopted in 1961.

[20]Adopted in 1961.

[21]Adopted in 1964.

[22]Adopted in 1967.

Thereafter, when the President transmits to the President Pro Tempore of the Senate and the Speaker of the House of Representatives his written declaration that no inability exists, he shall resume the powers and duties of his office unless the Vice President and a majority of either the principal officers of the executive departments or of such other body as Congress may by law provide, transmit within four days to the President Pro Tempore of the Senate and the Speaker of the House of Representatives their written declaration that the President is unable to discharge the powers and duties of his office. Thereupon Congress shall decide the issue, assembling within forty-eight hours for that purpose if not in session. If the Congress, within twenty-one days after receipt of the latter written declaration, or, if Congress is not in session, within twenty-one days after Congress is required to assemble, determines by two-thirds vote of both Houses that the President is unable to discharge the powers and duties of his office, the Vice President shall continue to discharge the same as Acting President; otherwise, the President shall resume the powers and duties of his office.

[Article XXVI][23]

Section 1.
The right of citizens of the United States, who are eighteen years of age or older, to vote shall not be denied or abridged by the United States or by any State on account of age.

Section 2.
The Congress shall have power to enforce this article by appropriate legislation.

[Article XXVII][24]

No law varying the compensation for the services of Senators and Representatives shall take effect until an election of Representatives shall have intervened.

---

[23]Adopted in 1971.

[24]Adopted in 1992.

Presidential Elections

Year	Candidates	Parties	Popular Vote	Percentage of Popular Vote	Electoral Vote	Percentage of Voter Participation
1789	**GEORGE WASHINGTON (Va.)***				69	
	John Adams				34	
	Others				35	
1792	**GEORGE WASHINGTON (Va.)**				132	
	John Adams				77	
	George Clinton				50	
	Others				5	
1796	**JOHN ADAMS (Mass.)**	Federalist			71	
	Thomas Jefferson	Democratic Republican			68	
	Thomas Pinckney	Federalist			59	
	Aaron Burr	Dem.-Rep.			30	
	Others				48	
1800	**THOMAS JEFFERSON (Va.)**	Dem.-Rep.			73	
	Aaron Burr	Dem.-Rep.			73	
	John Adams	Federalist			65	
	C. C. Pinckney	Federalist			64	
	John Jay	Federalist			1	
1804	**THOMAS JEFFERSON (Va.)**	Dem.-Rep.			162	
	C. C. Pinckney	Federalist			14	
1808	**JAMES MADISON (Va.)**	Dem.-Rep.			122	
	C. C. Pinckney	Federalist			47	
	George Clinton	Dem.-Rep.			6	
1812	**JAMES MADISON (Va.)**	Dem.-Rep.			128	
	De Witt Clinton	Federalist			89	
1816	**JAMES MONROE (Va.)**	Dem.-Rep.			183	
	Rufus King	Federalist			34	
1820	**JAMES MONROE (Va.)**	Dem.-Rep.			231	
	John Quincy Adams	Dem.-Rep.			1	
1824	**JOHN Q. ADAMS (Mass.)**	Dem.-Rep.	108,740	30.5	84	26.9
	Andrew Jackson	Dem.-Rep.	153,544	43.1	99	
	William H. Crawford	Dem.-Rep.	46,618	13.1	41	
	Henry Clay	Dem.-Rep.	47,136	13.2	37	
1828	**ANDREW JACKSON (Tenn.)**	Democratic	647,286	56.0	178	57.6
	John Quincy Adams	National Republican	508,064	44.0	83	
1832	**ANDREW JACKSON (Tenn.)**	Democratic	687,502	55.0	219	55.4
	Henry Clay	National Republican	530,189	42.4	49	
	John Floyd	Independent			11	
	William Wirt	Anti-Mason	33,108	2.6	7	
1836	**MARTIN VAN BUREN (N.Y.)**	Democratic	765,483	50.9	170	57.8
	W. H. Harrison	Whig			73	
	Hugh L. White	Whig	739,795	49.1	26	
	Daniel Webster	Whig			14	
	W. P. Magnum	Independent			11	
1840	**WILLIAM H. HARRISON (Ohio)**	Whig	1,274,624	53.1	234	80.2
	Martin Van Buren	Democratic	1,127,781	46.9	60	
	J. G. Birney	Liberty	7,069		—	
1844	**JAMES K. POLK (Tenn.)**	Democratic	1,338,464	49.6	170	78.9
	Henry Clay	Whig	1,300,097	48.1	105	
	J. G. Birney	Liberty	62,300	2.3	—	

*State of residence at time of election.

Year	Candidates	Parties	Popular Vote	Percentage of Popular Vote	Electoral Vote	Percentage of Voter Participation
1848	ZACHARY TAYLOR (La.)	Whig	1,360,967	47.4	163	72.7
	Lewis Cass	Democratic	1,222,342	42.5	127	
	Martin Van Buren	Free-Soil	291,263	10.1	—	
1852	FRANKLIN PIERCE (N.H.)	Democratic	1,601,117	50.9	254	69.6
	Winfield Scott	Whig	1,385,453	44.1	42	
	John P. Hale	Free-Soil	155,825	5.0	—	
1856	JAMES BUCHANAN (Pa.)	Democratic	1,832,955	45.3	741	78.9
	John C. Frémont	Republican	1,339,932	33.1	114	
	Millard Fillmore	American	871,731	21.6	8	
1860	ABRAHAM LINCOLN (Ill.)	Republican	1,865,593	39.8	180	81.2
	Stephen A. Douglas	Democratic	1,382,713	29.5	12	
	John C. Breckinridge	Democratic	848,356	18.1	72	
	John Bell	Union	592,906	12.6	39	
1864	ABRAHAM LINCOLN (Ill.)	Republican	2,213,655	55.0	212	73.8
	George B. McClellan	Democratic	1,805,237	45.0	21	
1868	ULYSSES S. GRANT (Ill.)	Republican	3,012,833	52.7	214	78.1
	Horatio Seymour	Democratic	2,703,249	47.3	80	
1872	ULYSSES S. GRANT (Ill.)	Republican	3,597,132	55.6	286	71.3
	Horace Greeley	Democratic; Liberal Republican	2,834,125	43.9	66	
1876	RUTHERFORD B. HAYES (Ohio)	Republican	4,036,298	48.0	185	81.8
	Samuel J. Tilden	Democratic	4,300,590	51.0	184	
1880	JAMES A. GARFIELD (Ohio)	Republican	4,454,416	48.5	214	79.4
	Winfield S. Hancock	Democratic	4,444,952	48.1	155	
1884	GROVER CLEVELAND (N.Y.)	Democratic	4,874,986	48.5	219	77.5
	James G. Blaine	Republican	4,851,981	48.2	182	
1888	BENJAMIN HARRISON (Ind.)	Republican	5,439,853	47.9	233	79.3
	Grover Cleveland	Democratic	5,540,309	48.6	168	
1892	GROVER CLEVELAND (N.Y.)	Democratic	5,556,918	46.1	277	74.7
	Benjamin Harrison	Republican	5,176,108	43.0	145	
	James B. Weaver	People's	1,041,028	8.5	22	
1896	WILLIAM McKINLEY (Ohio)	Republican	7,104,779	51.1	271	79.3
	William J. Bryan	Democratic-People's	6,502,925	47.7	176	
1900	WILLIAM McKINLEY (Ohio)	Republican	7,207,923	51.7	292	73.2
	William J. Bryan	Dem.-Populist	6,358,133	45.5	155	
1904	THEODORE ROOSEVELT (N.Y.)	Republican	7,623,486	57.9	336	65.2
	Alton B. Parker	Democratic	5,077,911	37.6	140	
	Eugene V. Debs	Socialist	402,283	3.0	—	
1908	WILLIAM H. TAFT (Ohio)	Republican	7,678,098	51.6	321	65.4
	William J. Bryan	Democratic	6,409,104	43.1	162	
	Eugene V. Debs	Socialist	420,793	2.8	—	
1912	WOODROW WILSON (N.J.)	Democratic	6,293,454	41.9	435	58.8
	Theodore Roosevelt	Progressive	4,119,538	27.4	88	
	William H. Taft	Republican	3,484,980	23.2	8	
	Eugene V. Debs	Socialist	900,672	6.0	—	
1916	WOODROW WILSON (N.J.)	Democratic	9,129,606	49.4	277	61.6
	Charles E. Hughes	Republican	8,538,221	46.2	254	
	A. L. Benson	Socialist	585,113	3.2	—	
1920	WARREN G. HARDING (Ohio)	Republican	16,152,200	60.4	404	49.2
	James M. Cox	Democratic	9,147,353	34.2	127	
	Eugene V. Debs	Socialist	919,799	3.4	—	
1924	CALVIN COOLIDGE (Mass.)	Republican	15,725,016	54.0	382	48.9
	John W. Davis	Democratic	8,386,503	28.8	136	
	Robert M. LaFollette	Progressive	4,822,856	16.6	13	
1928	HERBERT HOOVER (Calif.)	Republican	21,391,381	58.2	444	56.9
	Alfred E. Smith	Democratic	15,016,443	40.9	87	
	Norman Thomas	Socialist	267,835	0.7	—	

Year	Candidates	Parties	Popular Vote	Percentage of Popular Vote	Electoral Vote	Percentage of Voter Participation
1932	**FRANKLIN D. ROOSEVELT (N.Y.)**	Democratic	22,821,857	57.4	472	56.9
	Herbert Hoover	Republican	15,761,841	39.7	59	
	Norman Thomas	Socialist	881,951	2.2	—	
1936	**FRANKLIN D. ROOSEVELT (N.Y.)**	Democratic	27,751,597	60.8	523	61.0
	Alfred M. Landon	Republican	16,679,583	36.5	8	
	William Lemke	Union	882,479	1.9	—	
1940	**FRANKLIN D. ROOSEVELT (N.Y.)**	Democratic	27,244,160	54.8	449	62.5
	Wendell L. Willkie	Republican	22,305,198	44.8	82	
1944	**FRANKLIN D. ROOSEVELT (N.Y.)**	Democratic	25,602,504	53.5	432	55.9
	Thomas E. Dewey	Republican	22,006,285	46.0	99	
1948	**HARRY S. TRUMAN (Mo.)**	Democratic	24,105,695	49.5	304	53.0
	Thomas E. Dewey	Republican	21,969,170	45.1	189	
	J. Strom Thurmond	State-Rights Democratic	1,169,021	2.4	38	
	Henry A. Wallace	Progressive	1,156,103	2.4	—	
1952	**DWIGHT D. EISENHOWER (N.Y.)**	Republican	33,936,252	55.1	442	63.3
	Adlai E. Stevenson	Democratic	27,314,992	44.4	89	
1956	**DWIGHT D. EISENHOWER (N.Y.)**	Republican	35,575,420	57.6	457	60.6
	Adlai E. Stevenson	Democratic	26,033,066	42.1	73	
	Other	—	—		1	
1960	**JOHN F. KENNEDY (Mass.)**	Democratic	34,227,096	49.9	303	62.8
	Richard M. Nixon	Republican	34,108,546	49.6	219	
	Other	—	—		15	
1964	**LYNDON B. JOHNSON (Tex.)**	Democratic	43,126,506	61.1	486	61.7
	Barry M. Goldwater	Republican	27,176,799	38.5	52	
1968	**RICHARD M. NIXON (N.Y.)**	Republican	31,770,237	43.4	301	60.6
	Hubert H. Humphrey	Democratic	31,270,533	42.7	191	
	George Wallace	American Indep.	9,906,141	13.5	46	
1972	**RICHARD M. NIXON (N.Y.)**	Republican	47,169,911	60.7	520	55.2
	George S. McGovern	Democratic	29,170,383	37.5	17	
	Other	—	—		1	
1976	**JIMMY CARTER (Ga.)**	Democratic	40,828,587	50.0	297	53.5
	Gerald R. Ford	Republican	39,147,613	47.9	241	
	Other	—	1,575,459	2.1	—	
1980	**RONALD REAGAN (Calif.)**	Republican	43,901,812	50.7	489	52.6
	Jimmy Carter	Democratic	35,483,820	41.0	49	
	John B. Anderson	Independent	5,719,722	6.6	—	
	Ed Clark	Libertarian	921,188	1.1	—	
1984	**RONALD REAGAN (Calif.)**	Republican	54,455,075	59.0	525	53.3
	Walter Mondale	Democratic	37,577,185	41.0	13	
1988	**GEORGE BUSH (Texas)**	Republican	47,946,422	54.0	426	50.2
	Michael S. Dukakis	Democratic	41,016,429	46.0	112	
1992	**WILLIAM J. CLINTON (Ark.)**	Democratic	44,908,233	43.3	370	55.2
	George Bush	Republican	39,102,282	37.7	168	
	Ross Perot	Independent	19,721,433	19.0	—	
1996	**WILLIAM J. CLINTON (Ark.)**	Democratic	47,401,185	49.3	379	
	Robert Dole	Republican	39,197,469	40.7	159	49.0
	Ross Perot	Reform	8,085,294	8.4	—	
2000	**GEORGE W. BUSH (Texas)**	Republican	50,459,211	47.89	271	51.0
	Albert Gore, Jr.	Democratic	51,003,894	48.41	266	
	Ralph Nader	Green	2,834,410	2.69	—	
2004	**GEORGE W. BUSH (Texas)**	Republican	62,028,285	50.73	286	
	John Kerry	Democratic	59,028,109	48.27	251	60.0
	Ralph Nader	Independent	463,647	0.38	—	
2008	**BARACK OBAMA (Ill.)**	Democratic	65,070,489	53	364	61.7
	John McCain	Republican	57,154,810	46	174	

Note: All data from www.fec.gov (federal election commission) www.fec.gov/pubrec/fe2004/2004presgen.shtml

Vice Presidents and Cabinet Members

The Washington Administration (1789–1797)

Vice President	John Adams	1789-1797
Secretary of State	Thomas Jefferson	1789-1793
	Edmund Randolph	1794-1795
	Timothy Pickering	1795-1797
Secretary of Treasury	Alexander Hamilton	1789-1795
	Oliver Wolcott	1795-1797
Secretary of War	Henry Knox	1789-1794
	Timothy Pickering	1795-1796
	James McHenry	1796-1797
Attorney General	Edmund Randolph	1789-1793
	William Bradford	1794-1795
	Charles Lee	1795-1797
Postmaster General	Samuel Osgood	1789-1791
	Timothy Pickering	1791-1794
	Joseph Habersham	1795-1797

The John Adams Administration (1797–1801)

Vice President	Thomas Jefferson	1797-1801
Secretary of State	Timothy Pickering	1797-1800
	John Marshall	1800-1801
Secretary of Treasury	Oliver Wolcott	1797-1800
	Samuel Dexter	1800-1801
Secretary of War	James McHenry	1797-1800
	Samuel Dexter	1800-1801
Attorney General	Charles Lee	1797-1801
Postmaster General	Joseph Habersham	1797-1801
Secretary of Navy	Benjamin Stoddert	1798-1801

The Jefferson Administration (1801–1809)

Vice President	Aaron Burr	1801-1805
	George Clinton	1805-1809
Secretary of State	James Madison	1801-1809
Secretary of Treasury	Samuel Dexter	1801
	Albert Gallatin	1801-1809
Secretary of War	Henry Dearborn	1801-1809
Attorney General	Levi Lincoln	1801-1805
	Robert Smith	1805
	John Breckinridge	1805-1806
	Caesar Rodney	1807-1809
Postmaster General	Joseph Habersham	1801
	Gideon Granger	1801-1809
Secretary of Navy	Robert Smith	1801-1809

The Madison Administration (1809–1817)

Vice President	George Clinton	1809-1813
	Elbridge Gerry	1813-1817
Secretary of State	Robert Smith	1809-1811
	James Monroe	1811-1817
Secretary of Treasury	Albert Gallatin	1809-1813
	George Campbell	1814
	Alexander Dallas	1814-1816
	William Crawford	1816-1817
Secretary of War	William Eustis	1809-1812
	John Armstrong	1813-1814
	James Monroe	1814-1815
	William Crawford	1815-1817
Attorney General	Caesar Rodney	1809-1811
	William Pinkney	1811-1814
	Richard Rush	1814-1817
Postmaster General	Gideon Granger	1809-1814
	Return Meigs	1814-1817
Secretary of Navy	Paul Hamilton	1809-1813
	William Jones	1813-1814
	Benjamin Crowninshield	1814-1817

The Monroe Administration (1817–1825)

Vice President	Daniel Tompkins	1817-1825
Secretary of State	John Quincy Adams	1817-1825
Secretary of Treasury	William Crawford	1817-1825
Secretary of War	George Graham	1817
	John C. Calhoun	1817-1825
Attorney General	Richard Rush	1817
	William Wirt	1817-1825
Postmaster General	Return Meigs	1817-1823
	John McLean	1823-1825

Secretary of Navy	Benjamin Crowninshield	1817-1818
	Smith Thompson	1818-1823
	Samuel Southard	1823-1825

The John Quincy Adams Administration (1825–1829)

Vice President	John C. Calhoun	1825-1829
Secretary of State	Henry Clay	1825-1829
Secretary of Treasury	Richard Rush	1825-1829
Secretary of War	James Barbour	1825-1828
	Peter Porter	1828-1829
Attorney General	William Wirt	1825-1829
Postmaster General	John McLean	1825-1829
Secretary of Navy	Samuel Southard	1825-1829

The Jackson Administration (1829–1837)

Vice President	John C. Calhoun	1829-1833
	Martin Van Buren	1833-1837
Secretary of State	Martin Van Buren	1829-1831
	Edward Livingston	1831-1833
	Louis McLane	1833-1834
	John Forsyth	1834-1837
Secretary of Treasury	Samuel Ingham	1829-1831
	Louis McLane	1831-1833
	William Duane	1833
	Roger B. Taney	1833-1834
	Levi Woodbury	1834-1837
Secretary of War	John H. Eaton	1829-1831
	Lewis Cass	1831-1837
	Benjamin Butler	1837
Attorney General	John M. Berrien	1829-1831
	Roger B. Taney	1831-1833
	Benjamin Butler	1833-1837
Postmaster General	William Barry	1829-1835
	Amos Kendall	1835-1837
Secretary of Navy	John Branch	1829-1831
	Levi Woodbury	1831-1834
	Mahlon Dickerson	1834-1837

The Van Buren Administration (1837–1841)

Vice President	Richard M. Johnson	1837-1841
Secretary of State	John Forsyth	1837-1841
Secretary of Treasury	Levi Woodbury	1837-1841

Secretary of War	Joel Poinsett	1837-1841
Attorney General	Benjamin Butler	1837-1838
	Felix Grundy	1838-1840
	Henry D. Gilpin	1840-1841
Postmaster General	Amos Kendall	1837-1840
	John M. Niles	1840-1841
Secretary of Navy	Mahlon Dickerson	1837-1838
	James Paulding	1838-1841

The William Harrison Administration (1841)

Vice President	John Tyler	1841
Secretary of State	Daniel Webster	1841
Secretary of Treasury	Thomas Ewing	1841
Secretary of War	John Bell	1841
Attorney General	John J. Crittenden	1841
Postmaster General	Francis Granger	1841
Secretary of Navy	George Badger	1841

The Tyler Administration (1841–1845)

Vice President	None	
Secretary of State	Daniel Webster	1841-1843
	Hugh S. Legaré	1843
	Abel P. Upshur	1843-1844
	John C. Calhoun	1844-1845
Secretary of Treasury	Thomas Ewing	1841
	Walter Forward	1841-1843
	John C. Spencer	1843-1844
	George Bibb	1844-1845
Secretary of War	John Bell	1841
	John C. Spencer	1841-1843
	James M. Porter	1843-1844
	William Wilkins	1844-1845
Attorney General	John J. Crittenden	1841
	Hugh S. Legaré	1841-1843
	John Nelson	1843-1845
Postmaster General	Francis Granger	1841
	Charles Wickliffe	1841
Secretary of Navy	George Badger	1841
	Abel P. Upshur	1841
	David Henshaw	1843-1844
	Thomas Gilmer	1844
	John Y. Mason	1844-1845

The Polk Administration (1845–1849)

Vice President	George M. Dallas	1845-1849
Secretary of State	James Buchanan	1845-1849
Secretary of Treasury	Robert J. Walker	1845-1849
Secretary of War	William L. Marcy	1845-1849
Attorney General	John Y. Mason	1845-1846
	Nathan Clifford	1846-1848
	Isaac Toucey	1848-1849
Postmaster General	Cave Johnson	1845-1849
Secretary of Navy	George Bancrocft	1845-1846
	John Y. Mason	1846-1849

The Taylor Administration (1849–1850)

Vice President	Millard Fillmore	1849-1850
Secretary of State	John M. Clayton	1849-1850
Secretary of Treasury	William Meredith	1849-1850
Secretary of War	George Crawford	1849-1850
Attorney General	Reverdy Johnson	1849-1850
Postmaster General	Jacob Collamer	1849-1850
Secretary of Navy	William Preston	1849-1850
Secretary of Interior	Thomas Ewing	1849-1850

The Fillmore Administration (1850–1853)

Vice President	None	
Secretary of State	Daniel Webster	1850-1852
	Edward Everett	1852-1853
Secretary of Treasury	Thomas Corwin	1850-1853
Secretary of War	Charles Conrad	1850-1853
Attorney General	John J. Crittenden	1850-1853
Postmaster General	Nathan Hall	1850-1852
	Sam D. Hubbard	1852-1853
Secretary of Navy	William A. Graham	1850-1852
	John P. Kennedy	1852-1853
Secretary of Interior	Thomas McKennan	1850
	Alexander Stuart	1850-1853

The Pierce Administration (1853–1857)

Vice President	William R. King	1853-1857
Secretary of State	William L. Marcy	1853-1857
Secretary of Treasury	James Guthrie	1853-1857
Secretary of War	Jefferson Davis	1853-1857
Attorney General	Caleb Cushing	1853-1857
Postmaster General	James Campbell	1853-1857
Secretary of Navy	James C. Dobbin	1853-1857
Secretary of Interior	Robert McClelland	1853-1857

The Buchanan Administration (1857–1861)

Vice President	John C. Breckinridge	1857-1861
Secretary of State	Lewis Cass	1857-1860
	Jeremiah S. Black	1860-1861
Secretary of Treasury	Howell Cobb	1857-1860
	Philip Thomas	1860-1861
	John A. Dix	1861
Secretary of War	John B. Floyd	1857-1861
	Joseph Holt	1861
Attorney General	Jeremiah S. Black	1857-1860
	Edwin M. Stanton	1860-1861
Postmaster General	Aaron V. Brown	1857-1859
	Joseph Holt	1859-1861
	Horatio King	1861
Secretary of Navy	Isaac Toucey	1857-1861
Secretary of Interior	Jacob Thompson	1857-1861

The Lincoln Administration (1861–1865)

Vice President	Hannibal Hamlin	1861-1865
	Andrew Johnson	1865
Secretary of State	William H. Seward	1861-1865
Secretary of Treasury	Salmon P. Chase	1861-1864
	William P. Fessenden	1864-1865
	Hugh McCulloch	1865
Secretary of War	Simon Cameron	1861-1862
	Edwin M. Stanton	1862-1865
Attorney General	Edward Bates	1861-1864
	James Speed	1864-1865

Postmaster General	Horatio King	1861
	Montgomery Blair	1861-1864
	William Dennison	1864-1865
Secretary of Navy	Gideon Welles	1861-1865
Secretary of Interior	Caleb B. Smith	1861-1863
	John P. Usher	1863-1865

The Andrew Johnson Administration (1865–1869)

Vice President	None	
Secretary of State	William H. Seward	1865-1869
Secretary of Treasury	Hugh McCulloch	1865-1869
Secretary of War	Edwin M. Stanton	1865-1867
	Ulysses S. Grant	1867-1868
	Lorenzo Thomas	1868
	John M. Schofield	1868-1869
Attorney General	James Speed	1865-1866
	Henry Stanbery	1866-1868
	William M. Evarts	1868-1869
Postmaster General	William Dennison	1865-1866
	Alexander Randall	1866-1869
Secretary of Navy	Gideon Welles	1865-1869
Secretary of Interior	John P. Usher	1865
	James Harlan	1865-1866
	Orville H. Browning	1866-1869

The Grant Administration (1869–1877)

Vice President	Schuyler Colfax	1869-1873
	Henry Wilson	1873-1877
Secretary of State	Elihu B. Washburne	1869
	Hamilton Fish	1869-1877
Secretary of Treasury	George S. Boutwell	1869-1873
	William Richardson	1873-1874
	Benjamin Bristow	1874-1876
	Lot M. Morrill	1876-1877
Secretary of War	John A. Rawlins	1869
	William T. Sherman	1869
	William W. Belknap	1869-1876
	Alphonso Taft	1876
	James D. Cameron	1876-1877
Attorney General	Ebenezer Hoar	1869-1870
	Amos T. Ackerman	1870-1871
	G. H. Williams	1871-1875
	Edwards Pierrepont	1875-1876
	Alphonso Taft	1876-1877

Postmaster General	John A. J. Creswell	1869-1874
	James W. Marshall	1874
	Marshall Jewell	1874-1876
	James N. Tyner	1876-1877
Secretary of Navy	Adolph E. Borie	1869
	George M. Robeson	1869-1877
Secretary of Interior	Jacob D. Cox	1869-1870
	Columbus Delano	1870-1875
	Zachariah Candler	1875-1877

The Hayes Administration (1877–1881)

Vice President	William A. Wheeler	1877-1881
Secretary of State	William M. Evarts	1877-1881
Secretary of Treasury	John Sherman	1877-1881
Secretary of War	George W. McCrary	1877-1879
	Alex Ramsey	1879-1881
Attorney General	Charles Devens	1877-1881
Postmaster General	David M. Key	1877-1880
	Horace Maynard	1880-1881
Secretary of Navy	Richard W. Thompson	1877-1880
	Nathan Goff, Jr.	1881
Secretary of Interior	Carl Schurz	1877-1881

The Garfield Administration (1881)

Vice President	Chester A. Arthur	1881
Secretary of State	James G. Blaine	1881
Secretary of Treasury	William Windom	1881
Secretary of War	Robert T. Lincoln	1881
Attorney General	Wayne MacVeagh	1881
Postmaster General	Thomas L. James	1881
Secretary of Navy	William H. Hunt	1881
Secretary of Interior	Samuel J. Kirkwood	1881

The Arthur Administration (1881–1885)

Vice President	None	
Secretary of State	F. T. Frelinghuysen	1881-1885
Secretary of Treasury	Charles J. Folger	1881-1884
	Walter Q. Gresham	1884
	Hugh McCulloch	1884-1885

Secretary of War	Robert T. Lincoln	1881–1885
Attorney General	Benjamin H. Brewster	1881–1885
Postmaster General	Timothy O. Howe	1881–1883
	Walter Q. Gresham	1883–1884
	Frank Hatton	1884–1885
Secretary of Navy	William H. Hunt	1881–1882
	William E. Chandler	1882–1885
Secretary of Interior	Samuel J. Kirkwood	1881–1882
	Henry M. Teller	1882–1885

The Cleveland Administration (1885–1889)

Vice President	Thomas A. Hendricks	1885–1889
Secretary of State	Thomas F. Bayard	1885–1889
Secretary of Treasury	Daniel Manning	1885–1887
	Charles S. Fairchild	1887–1889
Secretary of War	William C. Endicott	1885–1889
Attorney General	Augustus H. Garland	1885–1889
Postmaster General	William F. Vilas	1885–1888
	Don M. Dickinson	1888–1889
Secretary of Navy	William C. Whitney	1885–1889
Secretary of Interior	Lucius Q.C. Lamar	1885–1888
	William F. Vilas	1888–1889
Secretary of Agriculture	Norman J. Colman	1889

The Benjamin Harrison Administration (1889–1893)

Vice President	Levi P. Morton	1889–1893
Secretary of State	James G. Blaine	1889–1892
	John W. Foster	1892–1893
Secretary of Treasury	William Windom	1889–1891
	Charles Foster	1891–1893
Secretary of War	Redfield Proctor	1889–1891
	Stephen B. Elkins	1891–1893
Attorney General	William H.H. Miller	1889–1891
Postmaster General	John Wanamaker	1889–1893
Secretary of Navy	Benjamin F. Tracy	1889–1893
Secretary of Interior	John W. Noble	1889–1893
Secretary of Agriculture	Jeremiah M. Rusk	1889–1893

The Cleveland Administration (1893–1897)

Vice President	Adlai E. Stevenson	1893–1897
Secretary of State	Walter Q. Gresham	1893–1895
	Richard Olney	1895–1897
Secretary of Treasury	John G. Carlisle	1893–1897
Secretary of War	Daniel S. Lamont	1893–1897
Attorney General	Richard Olney	1893–1895
	James Harmon	1895–1897
Postmaster General	Wilson S. Bissell	1893–1895
	William L. Wilson	1895–1897
Secretary of Navy	Hilary A. Herbert	1893–1897
Secretary of Interior	Hoke Smith	1893–1896
	David R. Francis	1896–1897
Secretary of Agriculture	Julius S. Morton	1893–1897

The McKinley Administration (1897–1901)

Vice President	Garret A. Hobart	1897–1901
	Theodore Roosevelt	1901
Secretary of State	John Sherman	1897–1898
	William R. Day	1898
	John Hay	1898–1901
Secretary of Treasury	Lyman J. Gage	1897–1901
Secretary of War	Russell A. Alger	1897–1899
	Elihu Root	1899–1901
Attorney General	Joseph McKenna	1897–1898
	John W. Griggs	1898–1901
	Philander C. Knox	1901
Postmaster General	James A. Gary	1897–1898
	Charles E. Smith	1898–1901
Secretary of Navy	John D. Long	1897–1901
Secretary of Interior	Cornelius N. Bliss	1897–1899
	Ethan A. Hitchcock	1899–1901
Secretary of Agriculture	James Wilson	1897–1901

The Theodore Roosevelt Administration (1901–1909)

Vice President	Charles Fairbanks	1905–1909
Secretary of State	John Hay	1901–1905
	Elihu Root	1905–1909
	Robert Bacon	1909

Secretary of Treasury	Lyman J. Gage	1901–1902
	Leslie M. Shaw	1902–1907
	George B. Cortelyou	1907–1909
Secretary of War	Elihu Root	1901–1904
	William H. Taft	1904–1908
	Luke E. Wright	1908–1909
Attorney General	Philander C. Knox	1901–1904
	William H. Moody	1904–1906
	Charles J. Bonaparte	1906–1909
Postmaster General	Charles E. Smith	1901–1902
	Henry C. Payne	1902–1904
	Robert J. Wynne	1904–1905
	George B. Cortelyou	1905–1907
	George von L. Meyer	1907–1909
Secretary of Navy	John D. Long	1901–1902
	William H. Moody	1902–1904
	Paul Morton	1904–1905
	Charles J. Bonaparte	1905–1906
	Victor H. Metcalf	1906–1908
	Truman H. Newberry	1908–1909
Secretary of Interior	Ethan A. Hitchcock	1901–1907
	James R. Garfield	1907–1909
Secretary of Agriculture	James Wilson	1901–1909
Secretary of Labor and Commerce	George B. Cortelyou	1903–1904
	Victor H. Metcalf	1904–1906
	Oscar S. Straus	1906–1909
	Charles Nagel	1909

The Taft Administration (1909–1913)

Vice President	James S. Sherman	1909–1913
Secretary of State	Philander C. Knox	1909–1913
Secretary of Treasury	Franklin MacVeagh	1909–1913
Secretary of War	Jacob M. Dickinson	1909–1911
	Henry L. Stimson	1911–1913
Attorney General	George W. Wickersham	1909–1913
Postmaster General	Frank H. Hitchcock	1909–1913
Secretary of Navy	George von L. Meyer	1909–1913
Secretary of Interior	Richard A. Ballinger	1909–1911
	Walter L. Fisher	1911–1913
Secretary of Agriculture	James Wilson	1909–1913
Secretary of Labor and Commerce	Charles Nagel	1909–1913

The Wilson Administration (1913–1921)

Vice President	Thomas R. Marshall	1913–1921
Secretary of State	William J. Bryan	1913–1915
	Robert Lansing	1915–1920
	Bainbridge Colby	1920–1921
Secretary of Treasury	William G. McAdoo	1913–1918
	Carter Glass	1918–1920
	David F. Houston	1920–1921
Secretary of War	Lindley M. Garrison	1913–1916
	Newton D. Baker	1916–1921
Attorney General	James C. McReynolds	1913–1914
	Thomas W. Gregory	1914–1919
	A. Mitchell Palmer	1919–1921
Postmaster General	Albert S. Burleson	1913–1921
Secretary of Navy	Josephus Daniels	1913–1921
Secretary of Interior	Franklin K. Lane	1913–1920
	John B. Payne	1920–1921
Secretary of Agriculture	David F. Houston	1913–1920
	Edwin T. Meredith	1920–1921
Secretary of Commerce	William C. Redfield	1913–1919
	Joshua W. Alexander	1919–1921
Secretary of Labor	William B. Wilson	1913–1921

The Harding Administration (1921–1923)

Vice President	Calvin Coolidge	1921–1923
Secretary of State	Charles E. Hughes	1921–1923
Secretary of Treasury	Andrew Mellon	1921–1923
Secretary of War	John W. Weeks	1921–1923
Attorney General	Harry M. Daugherty	1921–1923
Postmaster General	Will H. Hays	1921–1922
	Hubert Work	1922–1923
	Harry S. New	1923
Secretary of Navy	Edwin Denby	1921–1923
Secretary of Interior	Albert B. Fall	1921–1923
	Hubert Work	1923
Secretary of Agriculture	Henry C. Wallace	1921–1923
Secretary of Commerce	Herbert C. Hoover	1921–1923
Secretary of Labor	James J. Davis	1921–1923

The Coolidge Administration (1923–1929)

Vice President	Charles G. Dawes	1925-1929
Secretary of State	Charles E. Hughes	1923-1925
	Frank B. Kellogg	1925-1929
Secretary of Treasury	Andrew Mellon	1923-1929
Secretary of War	John W. Weeks	1923-1925
	Dwight F. Davis	1925-1929
Attorney General	Harry M. Daugherty	1923-1924
	Harlan F. Stone	1924-1925
	John G. Sargent	1925-1929
Postmaster General	Harry S. New	1923-1929
Secretary of Navy	Edwin Derby	1923-1924
	Curtis D. Wilbur	1924-1929
Secretary of Interior	Hubert Work	1923-1928
	Roy O. West	1928-1929
Secretary of Agriculture	Henry C. Wallace	1923-1924
	Howard M. Gore	1924-1925
	William M. Jardine	1925-1929
Secretary of Commerce	Herbert C. Hoover	1923-1928
	William F. Whiting	1928-1929
Secretary of Labor	James J. Davis	1923-1929

The Hoover Administration (1929–1933)

Vice President	Charles Curtis	1929-1933
Secretary of State	Henry L. Stimson	1929-1933
Secretary of Treasury	Andrew Mellon	1929-1932
	Ogden L. Mills	1932-1933
Secretary of War	James W. Good	1929
	Patrick J. Hurley	1929-1933
Attorney General	William D. Mitchell	1929-1933
Postmaster General	Walter F. Brown	1929-1933
Secretary of Navy	Charles F. Adams	1929-1933
Secretary of Interior	Ray L. Wilbur	1929-1933
Secretary of Agriculture	Arthur M. Hyde	1929-1933
Secretary of Commerce	Robert P. Lamont	1929-1932
	Roy D. Chapin	1932-1933
Secretary of Labor	James J. Davis	1929-1930
	William N. Doak	1930-1933

The Franklin D. Roosevelt Administration (1933–1945)

Vice President	John Nance Garner	1933-1941
	Henry A. Wallace	1941-1945
	Harry S. Truman	1945
Secretary of State	Cordell Hull	1933-1944
	Edward R. Stettinius, Jr.	1944-1945
Secretary of Treasury	William H. Woodin	1933-1934
	Henry Morgenthau, Jr.	1934-1945
Secretary of War	George H. Dern	1933-1936
	Henry A. Woodring	1936-1940
	Henry L. Stimson	1940-1945
Attorney General	Homer S. Cummings	1933-1939
	Frank Murphy	1939-1940
	Robert H. Jackson	1940-1941
	Francis Biddle	1941-1945
Postmaster General	James A. Farley	1933-1940
	Frank C. Walker	1940-1945
Secretary of Navy	Claude A. Swanson	1933-1940
	Charles Edison	1940
	Frank Knox	1940-1944
	James V. Forrestal	1944-1945
Secretary of Interior	Harold L. Ickes	1933-1945
Secretary of Agriculture	Henry A. Wallace	1933-1940
	Claude R. Wickard	1940-1945
Secretary of Commerce	Daniel C. Roper	1933-1939
	Harry L. Hopkins	1939-1940
	Jesse Jones	1940-1945
	Henry A. Wallace	1945
Secretary of Labor	Frances Perkins	1933-1945

The Truman Administration (1945–1953)

Vice President	Alben W. Barkley	1949-1953
Secretary of State	Edward R. Stettinius, Jr.	1945
	James F. Byrnes	1945-1947
	George C. Marshall	1947-1949
	Dean G. Acheson	1949-1953
Secretary of Treasury	Fred M. Vinson	1945-1946
	John W. Snyder	1946-1953
Secretary of War	Robert P. Patterson	1945-1947
	Kenneth C. Royall	1947
Attorney General	Tom C. Clark	1945-1949
	J. Howard McGrath	1949-1952
	James P. McGranery	1952-1953

Postmaster General	Frank C. Walker	1945
	Robert E. Hannegan	1945-1947
	Jesse M. Donaldson	1947-1953
Secretary of Navy	James V. Forrestal	1945-1947
Secretary of Interior	Harold L. Ickes	1945-1946
	Julius A. Krug	1946-1949
	Oscar L. Chapman	1949-1953
Secretary of Agriculture	Clinton P. Anderson	1945-1948
	Charles F. Brannan	1948-1953
Secretary of Commerce	Henry A. Wallace	1945-1946
	W. Averell Harriman	1946-1948
	Charles W. Sawyer	1948-1953
Secretary of Labor	Lewis B. Schwellenbach	1945-1948
	Maurice J. Tobin	1948-1953
Secretary of Defense	James V. Forrestal	1947-1949
	Louis A. Johnson	1949-1950
	George C. Marshall	1950-1951
	Robert A. Lovett	1951-1953

The Eisenhower Administration (1953–1961)

Vice President	Richard M. Nixon	1953-1961
Secretary of State	John Foster Dulles	1953-1959
	Christian A. Herter	1959-1961
Secretary of Treasury	George M. Humphrey	1953-1957
	Robert B. Anderson	1957-1961
Attorney General	Herbert Brownell, Jr.	1953-1958
	William P. Rogers	1958-1961
Postmaster General	Arthur E. Summerfield	1953-1961
Secretary of Interior	Douglas McKay	1953-1956
	Fred A. Seaton	1956-1961
Secretary of Agriculture	Ezra T. Benson	1953-1961
Secretary of Commerce	Sinclair Weeks	1953-1958
	Lewis L. Strauss	1958-1959
	Frederick H. Mueller	1959-1961
Secretary of Labor	Martin P. Durkin	1953
	James P. Mitchell	1953-1961
Secretary of Defense	Charles E. Wilson	1953-1957
	Neil H. McElroy	1957-1959
	Thomas S. Gates Jr.	1959-1961
Secretary of Health, Education, and Welfare	Oveta Culp Hobby	1953-1955
	Marion B. Folsom	1955-1958
	Arthur S. Flemming	1958-1961

The Kennedy Administration (1961–1963)

Vice President	Lyndon B. Johnson	1961-1963
Secretary of State	Dean Rusk	1961-1963
Secretary of Treasury	C. Douglas Dillon	1961-1963
Attorney General	Robert F. Kennedy	1961-1963
Postmaster General	J. Edward Day	1961-1963
	John A. Gronouski	1963
Secretary of Interior	Stewart L. Udall	1961-1963
Secretary of Agriculture	Orville L. Freeman	1961-1963
Secretary of Commerce	Luther H. Hodges	1961-1963
Secretary of Labor	Arthur J. Goldberg	1961-1962
	W. Willard Wirtz	1962-1963
Secretary of Defense	Robert S. McNamara	1961-1963
Secretary of Health, Education, and Welfare	Abraham A. Ribicoff	1961-1962
	Anthony J. Celebrezze	1962-1963

The Lyndon Johnson Administration (1963–1969)

Vice President	Hubert H. Humphrey	1965-1969
Secretary of State	Dean Rusk	1963-1969
Secretary of Treasury	C. Douglas Dillon	1963-1965
	Henry H. Fowler	1965-1969
Attorney General	Robert F. Kennedy	1963-1964
	Nicholas Katzenbach	1965-1966
	Ramsey Clark	1967-1969
Postmaster General	John A. Gronouski	1963-1965
	Lawrence F. O'Brien	1965-1968
	Marvin Watson	1968-1969
Secretary of Interior	Stewart L. Udall	1963-1969
Secretary of Agriculture	Orville L. Freeman	1963-1969
Secretary of Commerce	Luther H. Hodges	1963-1964
	John T. Connor	1964-1967
	Alexander B. Trowbridge	1967-1968
	Cyrus R. Smith	1968-1969
Secretary of Labor	W. Willard Wirtz	1963-1969
Secretary of Defense	Robert F. McNamara	1963-1968
	Clark Clifford	1968-1969

Secretary of Health, Education, and Welfare	Anthony J. Celebrezze	1963-1965
	John W. Gardner	1965-1968
	Wilbur J. Cohen	1968-1969
Secretary of Housing and Urban Development	Robert C. Weaver	1966-1969
	Robert C. Wood	1969
Secretary of Transportation	Alan S. Boyd	1967-1969

The Nixon Administration (1969–1974)

Vice President	Spiro T. Agnew	1969-1973
	Gerald R. Ford	1973-1974
Secretary of State	William P. Rogers	1969-1973
	Henry S. Kissinger	1973-1974
Secretary of Treasury	David M. Kennedy	1969-1970
	John B. Connally	1971-1972
	George P. Shultz	1972-1974
	William E. Simon	1974
Attorney General	John N. Mitchell	1969-1972
	Richard G. Kleindienst	1972-1973
	Elliot L. Richardson	1973
	William B. Saxbe	1973-1974
Postmaster General	Winton M. Blount	1969-1971
Secretary of Interior	Walter J. Hickel	1969-1970
	Rogers Morton	1971-1974
Secretary of Agriculture	Clifford M. Hardin	1969-1971
	Earl L. Butz	1971-1974
Secretary of Commerce	Maurice H. Stans	1969-1972
	Peter G. Peterson	1972-1973
	Frederick B. Dent	1973-1974
Secretary of Labor	George P. Shultz	1969-1970
	James D. Hodgson	1970-1973
	Peter J. Brennan	1973-1974
Secretary of Defense	Melvin R. Laird	1969-1973
	Elliot L. Richardson	1973
	James R. Schlesinger	1973-1974
Secretary of Health, Education, and Welfare	Robert H. Finch	1969-1970
	Elliot L. Richardson	1970-1973
	Caspar W. Weinberger	1973-1974
Secretary of Housing and Urban Development	George Romney	1969-1973
	James T. Lynn	1973-1974
Secretary of Transportation	John A. Volpe	1969-1973
	Claude S. Brinegar	1973-1974

The Ford Administration (1974–1977)

Vice President	Nelson A. Rockefeller	1974-1977
Secretary of State	Henry A. Kissinger	1974-1977
Secretary of Treasury	William E. Simon	1974-1977
Attorney General	William Saxbe	1974-1975
	Edward Levi	1975-1977
Secretary of Interior	Rogers Morton	1974-1975
	Stanley K. Hathaway	1975
	Thomas Kleppe	1975-1977
Secretary of Agriculture	Earl L. Butz	1974-1976
	John A. Knebel	1976-1977
Secretary of Commerce	Frederick B. Dent	1974-1975
	Rogers Morton	1975-1976
	Elliot L. Richardson	1976-1977
Secretary of Labor	Peter J. Brennan	1974-1975
	John T. Dunlop	1975-1976
	W. J. Usery	1976-1977
Secretary of Defense	James R. Schlesinger	1974-1975
	Donald Rumsfeld	1975-1977
Secretary of Health, Education, and Welfare	Caspar Weinberger	1974-1975
	Forrest D. Mathews	1975-1977
Secretary of Housing and Urban Development	James T. Lynn	1974-1975
	Carla A. Hills	1975-1977
Secretary of Transportation	Claude Brinegar	1974-1975
	William T. Coleman	1975-1977

The Carter Administration (1977–1981)

Vice President	Walter F. Mondale	1977-1981
Secretary of State	Cyrus R. Vance	1977-1980
	Edmund Muskie	1980-1981
Secretary of Treasury	W. Michael Blumenthal	1977-1979
	G. William Miller	1979-1981
Attorney General	Griffin Bell	1977-1979
	Benjamin R. Civiletti	1979-1981
Secretary of Interior	Cecil D. Andrus	1977-1981
Secretary of Agriculture	Robert Bergland	1977-1981
Secretary of Commerce	Juanita M. Kreps	1977-1979
	Philip M. Klutznick	1979-1981
Secretary of Labor	F. Ray Marshall	1977-1981

Secretary of Defense	Harold Brown	1977–1981
Secretary of Health, Education and Welfare	Joseph A. Califano Patricia R. Harris	1977–1979 1979
Secretary of Health and Human Services	Patricia R. Harris	1979–1981
Secretary of Education	Shirley M. Hufstedler	1979–1981
Secretary of Housing and Urban Development	Patricia R. Harris Moon Landrieu	1977–1979 1979–1981
Secretary of Transportation	Brock Adams Neil E. Goldschmidt	1977–1979 1979–1981
Secretary of Energy	James R. Schlesinger Charles W. Duncan	1977–1979 1979–1981

The Reagan Administration (1981–1989)

Vice President	George Bush	1981–1989
Secretary of State	Alexander M. Haig George P. Shultz	1981–1982 1982–1989
Secretary of Treasury	Donald Regan James A. Baker III Nicholas F. Brady	1981–1985 1985–1988 1988–1989
Attorney General	William F. Smith Edwin A. Meese III Richard Thornburgh	1981–1985 1985–1988 1988–1989
Secretary of Interior	James Watt William P. Clark, Jr. Donald P. Hodel	1981–1983 1983–1985 1985–1989
Secretary of Agriculture	John Block Richard E. Lyng	1981–1986 1986–1989
Secretary of Commerce	Malcolm Baldrige C. William Verity, Jr.	1981–1987 1987–1989
Secretary of Labor	Raymond Donovan William Brock Ann D. McLaughlin	1981–1985 1985–1987 1987–1989
Secretary of Defense	Caspar Weinberger Frank C. Carlucci	1981–1987 1987–1989
Secretary of Health and Human Services	Richard Schweiker Margaret Heckler Otis R. Bowen	1981–1983 1983–1985 1985–1989
Secretary of Education	Terrel H. Bell William J. Bennett Laura F. Cavazos	1981–1985 1985–1988 1988–1989

Secretary of Housing and Urban Development	Samuel Pierce	1981–1989
Secretary of Transportation	Drew Lewis Elizabeth Dole James H. Burnley	1981–1983 1983–1987 1987–1989
Secretary of Energy	James Edwards Donald P. Hodel John S. Herrington	1981–1982 1982–1985 1984–1989

The George H. W. Bush Administration (1989–1993)

Vice President	J. Danforth Quayle	1989–1993
Secretary of State	James A. Baker III Lawrence S. Eagleburger	1989–1992 1992–1993
Secretary of Treasury	Nicholas F. Brady	1989–1993
Attorney General	Richard Thornburgh William P. Barr	1989–1991 1991–1993
Secretary of Interior	Manuel Lujan	1989–1993
Secretary of Agriculture	Clayton K. Yeutter Edward Madigan	1989–1991 1991–1993
Secretary of Commerce	Robert A. Mosbacher Barbara H. Franklin	1989–1992 1992–1993
Secretary of Labor	Elizabeth Dole Lynn M. Martin	1989–1991 1991–1993
Secretary of Defense	Richard B. Cheney	1989–1993
Secretary of Health and Human Services	Louis W. Sullivan	1989–1993
Secretary of Education	Laura F. Cavazos Lamar Alexander	1989–1991 1991–1993
Secretary of Housing and Urban Development	Jack F. Kemp	1989–1993
Secretary of Transportation	Samuel K. Skinner Andrew H. Card	1989–1992 1992–1993
Secretary of Energy	James D. Watkins	1989–1993
Secretary of Veterans Affairs	Edward J. Derwinski	1989–1993

The Clinton Administration (1993–2001)

Vice President	Albert Gore, Jr.	1993–2001
Secretary of State	Warren M. Christopher Madeleine Albright	1993–1997 1997–2001

Secretary of Treasury	Lloyd Bentsen	1993-1995
	Robert E. Rubin	1995-1999
	Lawrence H. Summers	1999-2001
Attorney General	Janet Reno	1993-2001
Secretary of Interior	Bruce Babbitt	1993-2001
Secretary of Agriculture	Mike Espy	1993-1995
	Daniel R. Glickman	1995-2001
Secretary of Commerce	Ronald H. Brown	1993-1996
	Mickey Kantor	1996-1997
	William M. Daley	1997-2000
	Norman Mineta	2001
Secretary of Labor	Robert B. Reich	1993-1997
	Alexis M. Herman	1997-2001
Secretary of Defense	Les Aspin	1993-1994
	William Perry	1994-1996
	William S. Cohen	1996-2001
Secretary of Health and Human Services	Donna E. Shalala	1993-2001
Secretary of Education	Richard W. Riley	1993-2001
Secretary of Housing and Urban Development	Henry G. Cisneros	1993-1997
	Andrew Cuomo	1997-2001
Secretary of Transportation	Federico Pena	1993-1997
	Rodney E. Slater	1997-2001
Secretary of Energy	Hazel O'Leary	1993-1997
	Federico Pena	1997-1998
	Bill Richardson	1998-2001
Secretary of Veteran Affairs	Jesse Brown	1993-1998
	Togo D. West, Jr.	1998-2000
	Hershel Gober (Acting)	2000-2001

The George W. Bush Administration (2001–09)

Vice President	Richard B. Cheney	2001-
Secretary of State	Colin Powell	2001-2005
	Condoleezza Rice	2005-
Secretary of Treasury	Paul O'Neill	2001-2002
	Kenneth W. Dam (Acting)	2002-2003
	John Snow	2003-2006
	Henry Paulson	2006-
Attorney General	John Ashcroft	2001-2005
	Alberto Gonzales	2005-2007
	Michael Mukasey	2007-
Secretary of Interior	Gale Norton	2001-2006
	Dirk Kempthorne	2006-
Secretary of Agriculture	Ann M. Veneman	2001-2005
	Mike Johanns	2005-2008
	Edward Schafer	2008-
Secretary of Commerce	Don Evans	2001-2005
	Carlos Gutierrez	2005-
Secretary of Labor	Elaine Chao	2001-
Secretary of Defense	Donald Rumsfeld	2001-2006
	Robert Gates	2006-
Secretary of Health and Human Services	Tommy G. Thompson	2001-2005
	Michael O. Leavitt	2005-
Secretary of Education	Roderick Paige	2001-2005
	Margaret Spellings	2005-
Secretary of Housing and Urban Development	Melquiades R. Martinez	2001-2003
	Alphonso Jackson	2003-2008
	Steve Preston	2008-
	Roy Bernardi	2008-
Secretary of Transportation	Norman Mineta	2001-2006
	Mary Peters	2006-
Secretary of Energy	Spencer Abraham	2001-2005
	Samuel W. Bodman	2005-
Secretary of Veteran Affairs	Anthony Principi	2001-2005
	Jim Nicholson	2005-2007
	James Peake	2007-
Secretary of Homeland Security	Tom Ridge	2003-2005
	Michael Chertoff	2005-

Population of the United States, 1790–2006

Year	Population	Percent Increase	Population per Square Mile	Percent Urban/ Rural	Percent White/ Nonwhite	Median Age
1790	3,929,214		4.5	5.1/94.9	80.7/19.3	NA
1800	5,308,483	35.1	6.1	6.1/93.9	81.1/18.9	NA
1810	7,239,881	36.4	4.3	7.3/92.7	81.0/19.0	NA
1820	9,638,453	33.1	5.5	7.2/92.8	81.6/18.4	16.7
1830	12,866,020	33.5	7.4	8.8/91.2	81.9/18.1	17.2
1840	17,069,453	32.7	9.8	10.8/89.2	83.2/16.8	17.8
1850	23,191,876	35.9	7.9	15.3/84.7	84.3/15.7	18.9
1860	31,443,321	35.6	10.6	19.8/80.2	85.6/14.4	19.4
1870	39,818,449	26.6	13.4	25.7/74.3	86.2/13.8	20.2
1880	50,155,783	26.0	16.9	28.2/71.8	86.5/13.5	20.9
1890	62,947,714	25.5	21.2	35.1/64.9	87.5/12.5	22.0
1900	75,994,575	20.7	25.6	39.6/60.4	87.9/12.1	22.9
1910	91,972,266	21.0	31.0	45.6/54.4	88.9/11.1	24.1
1920	105,710,620	14.9	35.6	51.2/48.8	89.7/10.3	25.3
1930	122,775,046	16.1	41.2	56.1/43.9	89.8/10.2	26.4
1940	131,669,275	7.2	44.2	56.5/43.5	89.8/10.2	29.0
1950	150,697,361	14.5	50.7	64.0/36.0	89.5/10.5	30.2
1960	179,323,175	18.5	50.6	69.9/30.1	88.6/11.4	29.5
1970	203,302,031	13.4	57.4	73.5/26.5	87.6/12.4	28.0
1980	226,545,805	11.4	64.0	73.7/26.3	86.0/14.0	30.0
1990	248,718,000	9.8	70.3	77.5/22.5	83.8/16.2	32.9
2000	281,421,906	13.0	79.6	79.0/21.0	83.0/17.0	35.3
2006	299,801,000		84.6	N/A	80.0/20.0	36.4

Employment, 1870–2006

Year	Number of Workers (in millions)	Male/Female Employment Ratio	Percentage of Workers in Unions
1870	12.5	85/15	—
1880	17.4	85/15	—
1890	23.3	83/17	—
1900	29.1	82/18	3
1910	38.2	79/21	6
1920	41.6	79/21	12
1930	48.8	78/22	7
1940	53.0	76/24	27
1950	59.6	72/28	25
1960	69.9	68/32	26
1970	82.1	63/37	25
1980	108.5	58/42	23
1985	108.9	57/43	19
1990	118.8	55/45	16
2000	134.3	53/47	13.5
2006	144.4	54/46	12.0

Production, Trade, and Federal Spending/Debt, 1790–2006

Year	Gross National Product (GNP) (in billions $)	Balance of Trade (in billions $)	Federal Budget (in billions $)	Federal Surplus/Deficit (in billions $)	Federal Debt (in billions $)
1790	—	−3	.004	+0.00015	.076
1800	—	−20	.011	+0.0006	.083
1810	—	−18	.008	+0.0012	.053
1820	—	−4	.018	−0.0004	.091
1830	—	+3	.015	+0.100	.049
1840	—	+25	.024	−0.005	.004
1850	—	−26	.040	+0.004	.064
1860	—	−38	.063	−0.01	.065
1870	7.4	−11	.310	+0.10	2.4
1880	11.2	+92	.268	+0.07	2.1
1890	13.1	+87	.318	+0.09	1.2
1900	18.7	+569	.521	+0.05	1.2
1910	35.3	+273	.694	−0.02	1.1
1920	91.5	+2,880	6.357	+0.3	24.3
1930	90.7	+513	3.320	+0.7	16.3
1940	100.0	−3,403	9.6	−2.7	43.0
1950	286.5	+1,691	43.1	−2.2	257.4
1960	506.5	+4,556	92.2	+0.3	286.3
1970	992.7	+2,511	196.6	+2.8	371.0
1980	2,631.7	+24,088	579.6	−59.5	914.3
1985	4,087.7	−148,480	946.3	−212.3	1,827.5
1990	5,764.9	−101,012	1,251.8	−220.5	4,064.6
2000	9,860.8	−436,104	1,789.6	+237.0	5,674.2
2006	13,252.7	−817,304	2,655.4	−248.0	8,507.0

Note: Page references followed by *i* or *m* refer to figures or maps, respectively.